The Cambridge Guide to the
Museums of Britain and Ireland

THE CAMBRIDGE
GUIDE TO THE
MUSEUMS
OF BRITAIN
AND IRELAND

KENNETH HUDSON

AND

ANN NICHOLLS

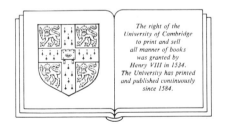

The right of the
University of Cambridge
to print and sell
all manner of books
was granted by
Henry VIII in 1534.
The University has printed
and published continuously
since 1584.

CAMBRIDGE UNIVERSITY PRESS

CAMBRIDGE

NEW YORK   PORT CHESTER

MELBOURNE   SYDNEY

Published by the Press Syndicate of the University of Cambridge
The Pitt Building, Trumpington Street, Cambridge CB2 1RP
40 West 20th Street, New York NY 10011, USA
10 Stamford Road, Oakleigh, Melbourne 3166, Australia

First published 1987
Revised paperback edition published 1989

Printed in Great Britain at the Bath Press, Avon
Maps by Malcolm Barnes

British Library cataloguing in publication data

Hudson, Kenneth.
The Cambridge guide to the museums of
Britain and Ireland.
1. Museums – Great Britain – Guide-books.
I. Title   II. Nicholls, Ann.
069′.0941   AM41

Library of Congress cataloguing in publication data

Hudson, Kenneth.
The Cambridge guide to the museums of
Britain and Ireland.
Includes indexes.
1. Museums – Great Britain – Guide-books.
2. Museums – Ireland – Guide-books.
I. Nicholls, Ann.   II. Title.
AM41.H79   1987   069′.0941   86-34343

ISBN 0 521 32272 3 (First edition)

(Revised paperback edition)
ISBN 0 521 37892 3

Frontispiece: **Toys in the Haggs Castle Museum, Glasgow**

GO

CONTENTS

Acknowledgements

The illustrations in this book are reproduced courtesy of the museums to which they relate. Acknowledgement is also due to the following (references are to page numbers):
Woodmansterne Ltd, Watford, 1, 64, 195, 207, 225, 354, 380 (top); Jeremy Whitaker, Bordon, 6, 215; A. & C. Photography, Belfast, 12; P. J. Gates, 17; English Life Publications Ltd, 24; Fotique, Bath, 30 (btm); Jarrold, Norwich, 50, 271, 392; Neil Bruce, Newbury, 60; Brian Hall, Burnley, 70; National Trust Photo Library/Campbell-Sharp, 77; Pictorial Colour Slides, West Wickham, 80; Photo Precision Ltd, St Ives, Huntingdon, 88; Martin Charles, Isleworth, 116; Pat Sweeney, 127; Irish Tourist Board, 128, 257; Pitkin Colour Slides, 132; John Bethell, 135; John K. Wilkie, Edinburgh, 137; Tom Scott, Edinburgh, 138; Stephen James, Paulton, 160; Trans-Globe, 163; George Young, Inverclyde, 167; Neil Woolford, Worcester, 174; Foster and Skeffington, Hereford, 182; John Brundle, 204; Acanthus, 208; West Park Studios, Leeds, 210; BJP Photography, Hitchin, 214; Rackhams of Lichfield, 216, 217 (top); Colin Randall, Bordon, 219; E. E. Jackson, 220; P. D. Barkshire, 231; Shell Photographic Service, 238; Brian Rybolt, 244; Harvey Photography, Levin, 251; F. C. Scoon, Gloucester, 253; Walton Adam, Reading, 255; Brian Monaghan, Manchester, 263; Nicholas Sargeant, Cheltenham, 284; Edgar Lloyd, Nottingham, 286; Ed Winters, Omagh, 291; R. A. J. Earl, Oxford, 293; Vernon Brooke, Oxford, 294; Ian Fenner, London, 296; John Mills, Liverpool, 306, 323; British Tourist Authority, London, 308; Bowers-Brittain, Saltburn-by-the-Sea, 314; Jeff Bowden, Otterton, 342; Norman Jones, Stoke-on-Trent, 355; Northern Counties Photographers, Stoke-on-Trent, 356; Mike Williams, 368; Charles Woolf, Newquay, 378; R. Bamberough, Horsham, 380 (btm); Royal Commission on Historical Monuments, 387; Ian Watts, 396; S. F. James, 400; Antony Miles, Salisbury, 401; Mike S. Duffy, York, 412 (btm); CEGB Photo Section 422; Eddie Ryle-Hodges, Barnard Castle, 425; Dominic Fontana, Southsea; Martin Trelawney, 428.

INTRODUCTION

Two out of every three museums in this *Guide* did not exist forty years ago. Museums have in fact been one of Britain's few growth industries during the post-war period, and the variety of what is now on offer is remarkable. Art museums, industrial and technical museums, open-air museums, local history museums, toy and doll museums and archaeological museums have all shared in this new passion for preserving and interpreting the past. The movement has been international. Since the mid-Fifties, the total number of museums has gone up by 10 per cent every five years. The phenomenon has, as might have been expected, been most marked in the wealthier countries, but it has also been noticeable among the world's poorer nations. To have a good range of museums is now a matter of national pride and prestige.

But, already, doubts are being expressed and questions asked. Has the process perhaps gone too far? To think only of Britain and Ireland, is it possible for more than 2,000 museums to find a market for their wares, when six or seven hundred were considered sufficient before the great museum boom got under way in the 1950s? Do the potential customers exist in adequate numbers? Will the signs of gradual impoverishment become noticeable? Will the money be there to allow even a majority of our museums to maintain themselves properly and to keep up with current tastes or demands, or will they begin to show their age and lose suitors as a result?

The next ten years should show which way things are going, whether the increase-curve is going to flatten, or perhaps even begin to fall. It could be that this, the first edition of the *Guide*, reflects the museums of Great Britain and Ireland at their peak, numerically at least. Maybe we have been guilty of an obsessive interest in our past and an excessive proportion of our national resources has been devoted to preserving and displaying the remains of what is, after all, a very old civilisation. To devote more time and energy to the present and the future could conceivably be a mark of a healthier and more vigorous society. Perhaps what we need now is not more museums, but better museums, more relevant to the needs of our time. There are certainly some closely concerned with museums who feel that a period of consolidation might be no bad thing.

Already there are indications of changes to come. Casualties have been forecast and some smaller museums, belonging either to private owners or, more usually, to charitable trusts, are now showing distinct signs of financial strain. One of the more remarkable features of the museum scene in this country in recent years has been the spectacular growth of what are generally referred to as 'independent museums'. These museums have not been created by a local authority or by the State and they rely for their continued existence on what visitors pay in the form of entrance fees, on profits from the museum shop or restaurant, together with, if they are lucky, grants from industry, private individuals or public bodies. About a third of all our museums are in this category, a proportion equalled nowhere else in Europe. On the Continent the privately organised and financed museum is still comparatively rare and the idea is viewed in certain countries, notably France and Sweden, with considerable suspicion. It would hardly be an exaggeration to say that in Sweden at least the 'independent museum', like the private school or private clinic, is regarded as abhorrent.

One could fairly claim, however, that in Britain the museum world owes a great deal to the independent museums. A high proportion of the new ideas which have revolutionised the way in which museums are thought about and run have come from this particular source and, with hindsight, it is not difficult to see why. An independent museum is wholly dependent on its ability to attract and please the public. In that sense, its director closely resembles a theatre manager or a concert impresario; if the museum fails to get visitors in sufficient numbers, it must inevitably wither away and die. Local authority museums, like the Science Museum, the National Gallery and the other great State institutions, are not under the same constant, relentless pressure to succeed. For an independent museum, good marketing, good management and, of course, a good product are necessities, not luxuries.

Our best independent museums – Ironbridge, Abbot Hall, the Weald and Downland, the National Motor Museum and others of equal distinction – show how well this lesson has been learnt by those who have been lucky enough or wise enough to find capable, imaginative managers and policy-makers at the time they were launched. Others have been less blessed and have had to find out about the market the hard way. The independent museums have to concern themselves with people even more than with objects. They are in the communications business. And, during the past twenty years, their methods and approach have filtered into the State and local authority museums. The process has been slow and unevenly distributed – a few museums have shown themselves very resistant to change – but, in general, the experiments and rethinking stimulated by commercial need have influenced British museums in a positive and fundamental way, greatly to the benefit of their visitors.

During the past three decades, Britain has been in the vanguard of museum development to such an extent that it would not be unreasonable to claim now, in 1987, that the overall quality of museums here is the highest in the world. One could put this another way by saying that the average visitor can enter a museum, any museum, in this country, with less chance of being seriously disappointed than would be the case anywhere else. That is a real mark of progress and achievement.

Of course, we could hardly have begun to compile a guide to museums without first having made up our minds what a museum is. We saw no reason to be narrow-minded or puritanical here. A museum does not have to call itself a museum in order to be one. So we settled for the definition arrived at by ICOM – the International Council of Museums – nearly twenty years ago: a museum is 'any permanent institution which conserves and displays, for purposes of study, education and enjoyment, collections of objects of cultural or scientific significance'. This appeared at once elastic, liberal and sensible. We rejected the limitations imposed by the American Association of Museums, which declares that, in order to be recognised as such, a museum must be a 'non-profit institution' and employ 'professional staff'. Excellent work is being done in museums by people without any professional qualifications; and surely a museum which contrives to make its income exceed its expenditure should not be regarded as in any way illegitimate.

Our first task, therefore, was to compile a list of all the places which looked as if they might match up to the ICOM criteria. They included 'museums', 'collections', 'centres', 'galleries' and 'historic houses', as well as creations with more exotic titles. Each of them received a simple questionnaire, asking for information which would allow us to prepare an accurate, helpful entry that would do them justice.

With this information at our disposal, and assisted by our personal knowledge of a high proportion of the places concerned, we wrote the entries. A draft was then sent to each museum to ensure its accuracy. With this hurdle cleared, it was possible to print and publish the *Guide*, the first ever to offer a comprehensive catalogue of the museums of Great Britain and Ireland. Though we would not claim to be infallible, we have aimed at absolute completeness and would be pleased to hear of any omissions so that each successive edition of the *Guide* can move closer to our ideal.

It was clear from the beginning that it would be both impossible and unjust to try to indicate the quality of a museum. The only fair way of helping our readers seemed to be to indicate the scope, character and amenities of every museum, leaving it to potential visitors to judge for themselves whether their journey was likely to be worthwhile. We have used enthusiastic adjectives sparingly. When writing to us, a museum may assure us that a particular exhibit or feature is 'unique', 'outstanding', 'world-famous' or 'unforgettable' – its job is to attract customers – but it would be inappropriate for us to echo such words. And this is as true of amenities as of exhibitions. We did not feel able to say, for example, that a particular museum 'has one of the best restaurants in London', although we know from our own pleasant experiences that this is indeed the case.

Usually, but by no means always, the length of an entry provides some guidance as to the interest or importance of a museum. If the size of the annual budget were the sole criterion, we might possibly have allocated ten pages of the *Guide* to the British Museum or the Victoria and Albert, against ten lines to, say, the Tank Museum at Bovington. There are two reasons why we have not done this. The first is that we have been preparing a book for the general public, not for scholars, and for the readership we have in mind the British Museum is not a hundred times more interesting or significant than the Tank Museum. The second reason for our levelling tactics is that a large part of the British Museum's budget is devoted to research activities, with which we are not directly concerned. It functions almost as a university, which the Tank Museum does not. We should hate it to be thought that we are in any way hostile to the great State museums. But we cannot escape the duty – a very agreeable one – of reflecting the museum scene as a whole and of drawing attention to places far distant from Bloomsbury and Exhibition Road, places which in many instances deserve a great many more tourists than they get. Life does look different from Dunfermline or Aberystwyth, and London, Dublin and Edinburgh do not have a monopoly of good things.

Certain information given in the entries should be used with caution, not because it is inaccurate, but because it is, inescapably, generalised. There is simply no room for the fine print. This applies particularly to such practical matters as entrance charges, cafeterias and restaurants, museum shops and the provision made for the disabled. Admission fees vary greatly and increase a little each year in line with inflation, so the details would have been out-of-date almost as soon as they were printed. Cafeterias, restaurants and shops are a rather different matter. The shop may obviously be well-stocked but contain nothing that one particularly wants to buy, the food in the cafeteria may satisfy hungry, undiscriminating children, but be unappealing to adults with a more refined palate. Much the same applies to special facilities for visitors confined to wheelchairs and for the visually-handicapped. Full provision would include lifts, ramps and specially-designed lavatories, and few of the museums listed in the *Guide* in fact include all this. For some it would be out of the question. How, for example, would it be possible to cater adequately for disabled people at a museum which occupies several floors of a working windmill, or which takes its visitors down a coal mine? We have done all we can to give reliable information but a telephone call in advance to check the exact position is always well worthwhile.

Having taken the fundamental decision that there was no essential difference between an historic house and a museum, and that the *Guide* would include both, we found ourselves compelled to work out and observe certain principles. The first was fairly simple. The house must be a complete house, not a ruin, and what it had to offer must not be confined to its architecture and decorations. It must contain objects either interesting in themselves or with interesting historical associations. We could see no reason why a portrait or a piece of furniture or porcelain should become museologically respectable only when it was removed from its original home and placed in a museum of a traditional type. On the contrary, its significance and appeal seemed likely to be much greater if it were left where it was, in a context which enriches it and in which it makes proper sense. The same could be said of industrial machinery. A steam engine in a technical museum does not compare with the same engine at the coal mine or pumping station for which it was designed and where it operated.

In the British Isles one has passed the stage when a museum was synonymous with glass cases, labels and accession registers, but it is taking rather longer to accept that history can often be better served by leaving historical material in the places where it has gradually accumulated over the centuries. In *The Cambridge Guide to the Museums of Britain and Ireland* we are trying to encourage and speed up what amounts to a revolution in museological thinking by including both kinds of museums, those which have come into existence by moving objects into receiving centres and those which leave exhibits in their original surroundings. Each has its special advantages. Would Michael Faraday's laboratory be any more worthy of respect if it had been moved to the Science Museum, instead of being allowed to remain on its original site at the Royal Institution in Albemarle Street? Are the rooms of Charles Rennie Mackintosh's Glasgow home more 'real', more 'professional', in their reconstructed form at the Hunterian Art Gallery then they would have been if the original house had been preserved instead of being demolished? These are questions which, in compiling the present work, we have chosen to disregard because we regard them as outdated and unreal.

Our essential aim has been to produce a volume which can be dipped into with pleasure, one which draws attention to some of the more interesting things on offer in more than 2,000 individual museums throughout the length and breadth of Britain and Ireland. The rest one has to discover for oneself. We should be most grateful if visitors would write to tell us of their experiences.

Kenneth Hudson
Ann Nicholls
18 Lansdown Crescent
Bath BA1 5EX

LOCATION MAPS

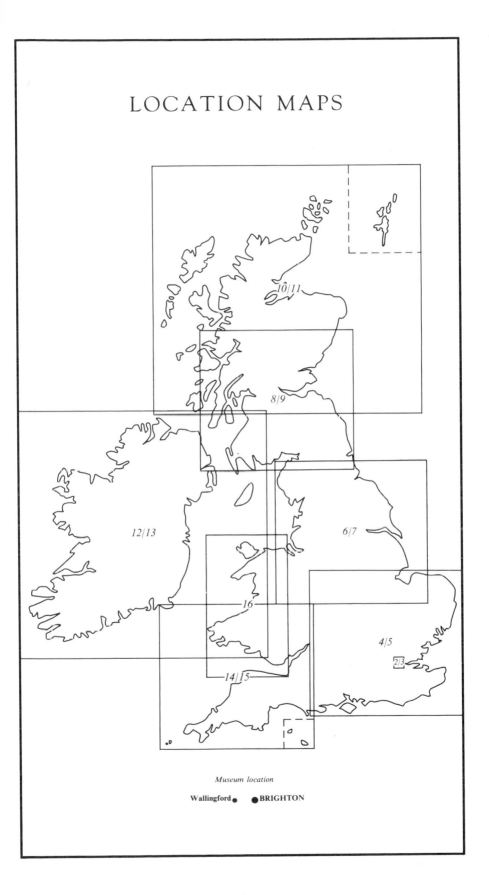

Museum location

Wallingford●   ●**BRIGHTON**

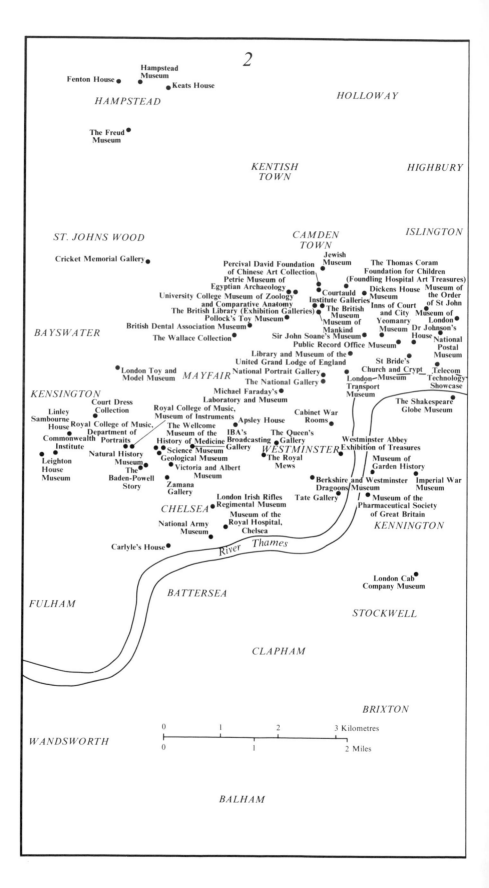

2

HAMPSTEAD

Fenton House

Hampstead Museum

Keats House

HOLLOWAY

The Freud Museum

KENTISH TOWN

HIGHBURY

ST. JOHNS WOOD

CAMDEN TOWN

ISLINGTON

Cricket Memorial Gallery

Jewish Museum

Percival David Foundation of Chinese Art Collection

The Thomas Coram Foundation for Children (Foundling Hospital Art Treasures)

Petrie Museum of Egyptian Archaeology

University College Museum of Zoology and Comparative Anatomy

Courtauld Institute Galleries

Dickens House Museum

Museum of the Order of St John

The British Library (Exhibition Galleries)

The British Museum

Inns of Court and City Yeomanry Museum

Museum of London

Pollock's Toy Museum

BAYSWATER

British Dental Association Museum

Museum of Mankind

Dr Johnson's House

The Wallace Collection

Sir John Soane's Museum

National Postal Museum

Public Record Office Museum

Library and Museum of the United Grand Lodge of England

St Bride's Church and Crypt Museum

Telecom Technology Showcase

London Toy and Model Museum

National Portrait Gallery

The National Gallery

London Transport Museum

KENSINGTON

MAYFAIR

Michael Faraday's Laboratory and Museum

The Shakespeare Globe Museum

Court Dress Collection

Royal College of Music, Museum of Instruments

Apsley House

Cabinet War Rooms

Linley Sambourne House

Royal College of Music, Department of Portraits

The Wellcome Museum of the History of Medicine

IBA's Broadcasting Gallery

The Queen's Gallery

Westminster Abbey Exhibition of Treasures

Commonwealth Institute

Natural History Museum

Science Museum

WESTMINSTER

Leighton House Museum

The Baden-Powell Story

Geological Museum

Victoria and Albert Museum

The Royal Mews

Museum of Garden History

Zamana Gallery

Berkshire and Westminster Dragoons Museum

Imperial War Museum

CHELSEA

London Irish Rifles Regimental Museum

Tate Gallery

Museum of the Pharmaceutical Society of Great Britain

National Army Museum

Museum of the Royal Hospital, Chelsea

KENNINGTON

Carlyle's House

River Thames

London Cab Company Museum

FULHAM

BATTERSEA

STOCKWELL

CLAPHAM

BRIXTON

0   1   2   3 Kilometres

0   1   2 Miles

WANDSWORTH

BALHAM

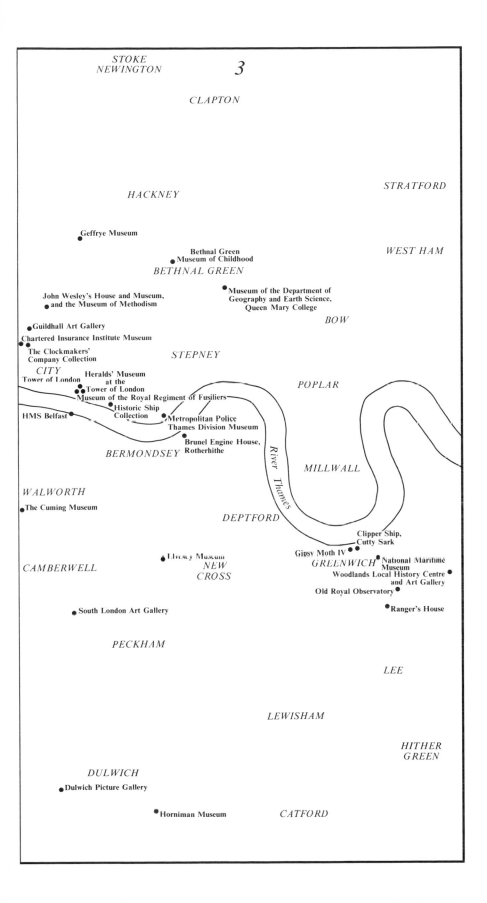

STOKE
NEWINGTON   *3*

CLAPTON

HACKNEY   STRATFORD

●Geffrye Museum

                          Bethnal Green   WEST HAM
                        ●Museum of Childhood
                    BETHNAL GREEN

John Wesley's House and Museum,   ●Museum of the Department of
  ●and the Museum of Methodism   Geography and Earth Science,
                                         Queen Mary College
●Guildhall Art Gallery   BOW
●Chartered Insurance Institute Museum
●The Clockmakers'
  Company Collection   STEPNEY
CITY   Heralds' Museum
Tower of London   at the   POPLAR
        ●●Tower of London
        ●Museum of the Royal Regiment of Fusiliers
          ●Historic Ship
HMS Belfast● Collection   ●Metropolitan Police
                                 Thames Division Museum
                            ●Brunel Engine House,
        BERMONDSEY Rotherhithe
                                              MILLWALL
WALWORTH
●The Cuming Museum

                    DEPTFORD
CAMBERWELL
                                          Clipper Ship,
                                          ●Cutty Sark
                  ●Livesey Museum   Gipsy Moth IV●●
                     NEW   GREENWICH●National Maritime
                     CROSS   Museum
                                     Woodlands Local History Centre●
                                              and Art Gallery
                                     Old Royal Observatory●

        ●South London Art Gallery   ●Ranger's House

        PECKHAM

                                              LEE

                    LEWISHAM

                                              HITHER
                                              GREEN
        DULWICH
        ●Dulwich Picture Gallery

              ●Horniman Museum   CATFORD

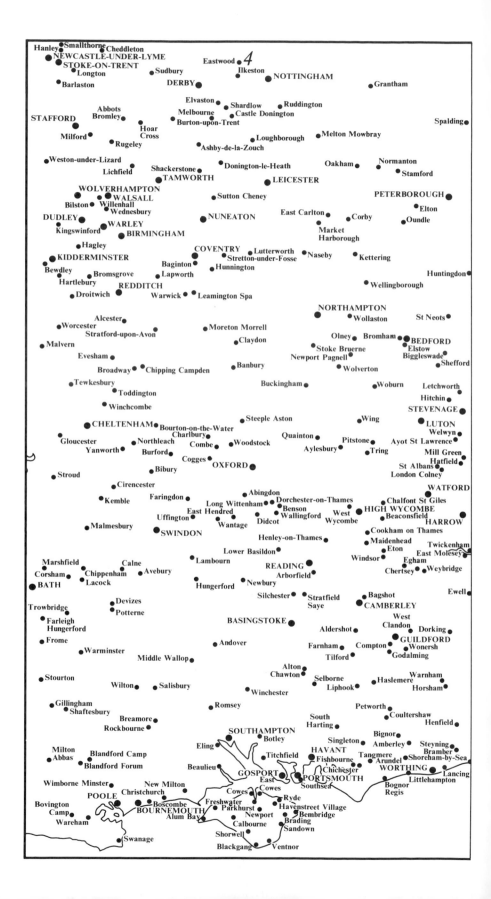

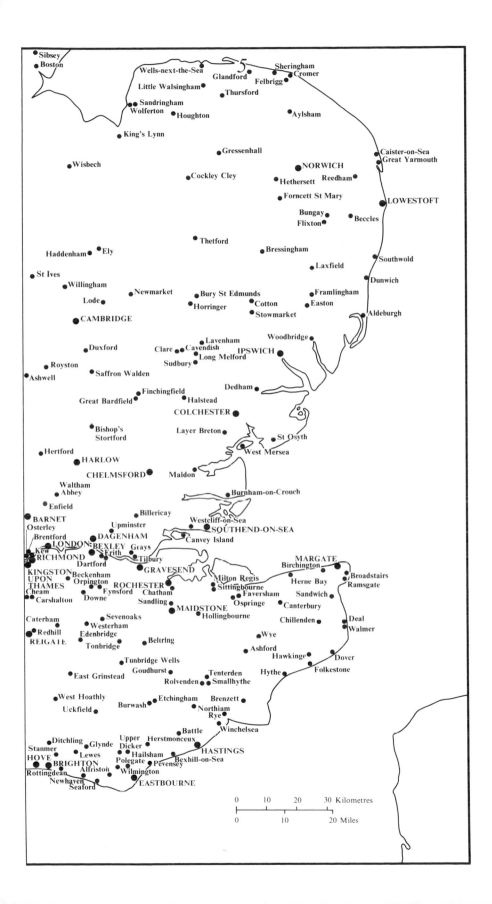

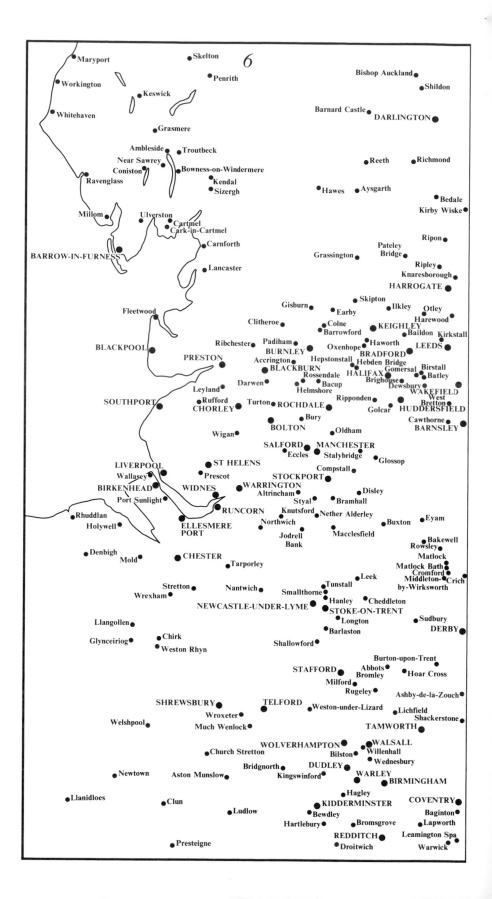

6

Maryport
Skelton
Penrith
Bishop Auckland
Shildon
Workington
Keswick
Barnard Castle
DARLINGTON
Whitehaven
Grasmere
Ambleside
Troutbeck
Reeth
Richmond
Near Sawrey
Coniston
Bowness-on-Windermere
Ravenglass
Kendal
Hawes
Aysgarth
Sizergh
Bedale
Kirby Wiske
Millom
Ulverston
Cartmel
Cark-in-Cartmel
Ripon
Carnforth
Pateley
Bridge
Grassington
BARROW-IN-FURNESS
Ripley
Knaresborough
Lancaster
HARROGATE
Fleetwood
Gisburn
Skipton
Ilkley
Otley
Earby
Harewood
Clitheroe
Colne
KEIGHLEY
Barrowford
Baildon
Kirkstall
BLACKPOOL
Ribchester
Padiham
Haworth
LEEDS
PRESTON
BURNLEY
Oxenhope
BRADFORD
Accrington
Hepstonstall
Hebden Bridge
Birstall
BLACKBURN
Rossendale
HALIFAX
Gomersal
Batley
Darwen
Bacup
Brighouse
Dewsbury
Leyland
Helmshore
Ripponden
WAKEFIELD
SOUTHPORT
Rufford
Turton
ROCHDALE
Golcar
West
Bretton
CHORLEY
Bury
HUDDERSFIELD
Wigan
Oldham
Cawthorne
BOLTON
BARNSLEY
SALFORD
MANCHESTER
LIVERPOOL
ST HELENS
Eccles
Stalybridge
Glossop
Wallasey
Prescot
Compstall
STOCKPORT
BIRKENHEAD
WIDNES
WARRINGTON
Disley
Port Sunlight
Altrincham
Styal
Bramhall
RUNCORN
Knutsford
Nether Alderley
Rhuddlan
Northwich
Buxton
Eyam
Holywell
ELLESMERE
PORT
Jodrell
Bank
Macclesfield
Bakewell
Rowsley
Denbigh
Matlock
Mold
CHESTER
Matlock Bath
Tarporley
Leek
Cromford
Crich
Middleton-
by-Wirksworth
Stretton
Nantwich
Tunstall
Wrexham
Smallthorne
Hanley
Cheddleton
NEWCASTLE-UNDER-LYME
STOKE-ON-TRENT
Llangollen
Longton
Sudbury
Glynceiriog
Chirk
Barlaston
DERBY
Weston Rhyn
Shallowford
Burton-upon-Trent
Abbots
Bromley
Hoar Cross
STAFFORD
Milford
SHREWSBURY
Rugeley
Ashby-de-la-Zouch
Welshpool
TELFORD
Weston-under-Lizard
Lichfield
Wroxeter
Shackerstone
Much Wenlock
TAMWORTH
Newtown
Church Stretton
WOLVERHAMPTON
WALSALL
Bilston
Willenhall
Aston Munslow
Bridgnorth
DUDLEY
Wednesbury
Kingswinford
WARLEY
Llanidloes
Clun
Hagley
BIRMINGHAM
Ludlow
KIDDERMINSTER
COVENTRY
Bewdley
Baginton
Hartlebury
Bromsgrove
Lapworth
Presteigne
REDDITCH
Leamington Spa
Droitwich
Warwick

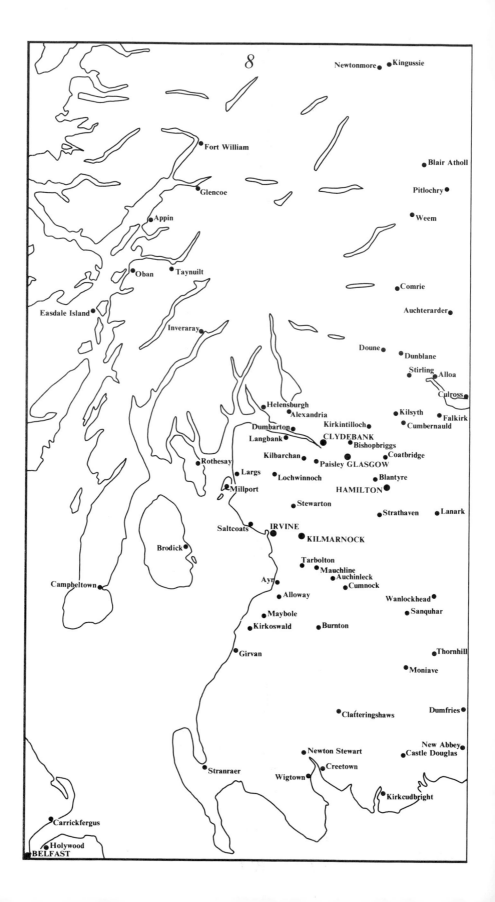

8

Newtonmore • • Kingussie

Fort William •

Blair Atholl •

Glencoe •

Pitlochry •

Appin •

Weem •

Oban • • Taynuilt

Comrie •

Easdale Island •

Auchterarder •

Inveraray •

Doune • • Dunblane

Stirling • Alloa

Culross •

Helensburgh •

Kilsyth •

Alexandria •

Falkirk •

Dumbarton •

Kirkintilloch •

Cumbernauld •

Langbank •

CLYDEBANK

Kilbarchan •

Bishopbriggs •

Rothesay •

Coatbridge •

Paisley GLASGOW

Largs •

Lochwinnoch •

Blantyre •

Millport •

HAMILTON •

Stewarton •

Strathaven •

Lanark •

Saltcoats •

IRVINE •

Brodick •

KILMARNOCK •

Campbeltown •

Tarbolton •

Mauchline •

Ayr •

Auchinleck •

Cumnock •

Alloway •

Wanlockhead •

Maybole •

Sanquhar •

Kirkoswald •

Burnton •

Girvan •

Thornhill •

Moniave •

Dumfries •

Clatteringshaws •

New Abbey •

Newton Stewart •

Castle Douglas •

Creetown •

Stranraer •

Wigtown •

Kirkcudbright •

Carrickfergus •

Holywood •

BELFAST

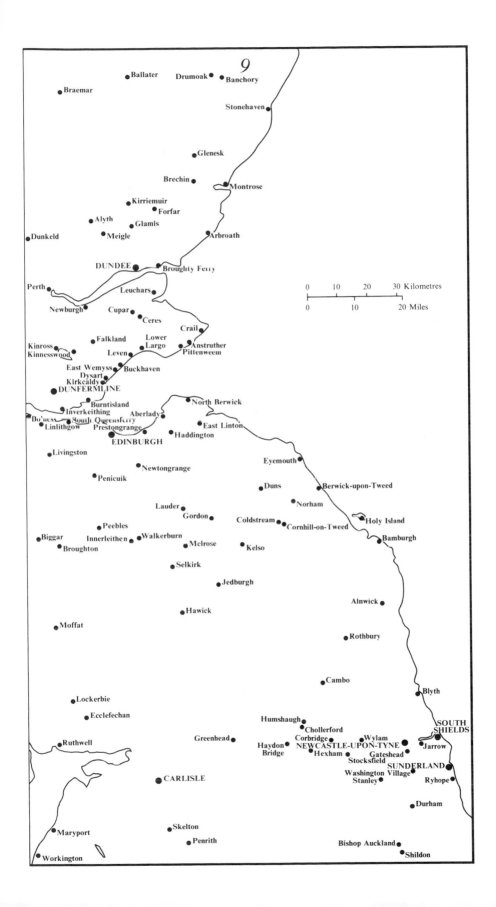

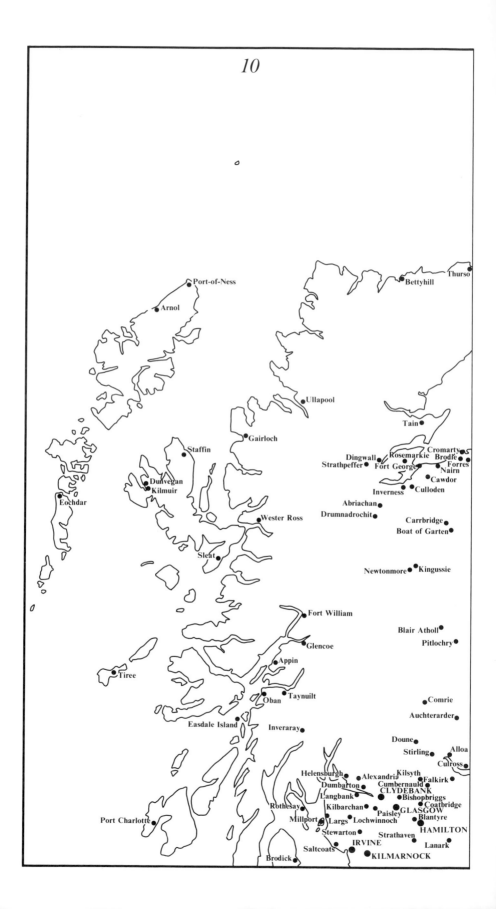

Thurso

Bettyhill

Port-of-Ness

Arnol

Ullapool

Tain

Gairloch

Cromarty

Staffin

Dingwall Rosemarkie Brodie
Strathpeffer Fort George Forres
Nairn
Cawdor

Dunvegan
Kilmuir

Inverness Culloden

Eochdar

Abriachan
Drumnadrochit

Wester Ross

Carrbridge
Boat of Garten

Sleat

Newtonmore Kingussie

Fort William

Blair Atholl

Glencoe

Pitlochry

Tiree

Appin

Taynuilt
Oban

Comrie

Auchterarder

Easdale Island

Inveraray

Doune

Alloa
Stirling
Culross

Helensburgh
Alexandria

Kilsyth
Falkirk
Cumbernauld

Dumbarton
CLYDEBANK

Langbank
Bishopbriggs
Coatbridge

Rothesay
Kilbarchan
GLASGOW

Millport
Paisley
Blantyre

Port Charlotte

Largs Lochwinnoch
HAMILTON

Stewarton
Strathaven

IRVINE
Saltcoats
Lanark

Brodick
KILMARNOCK

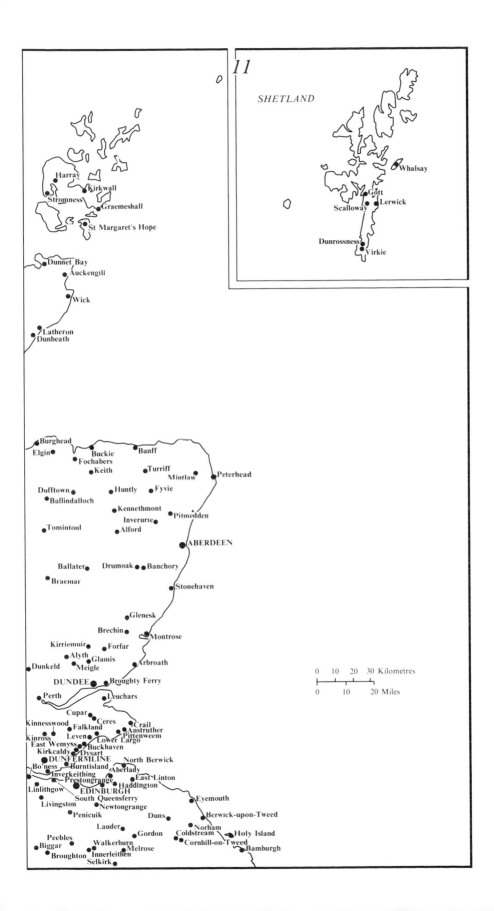

11

SHETLAND

Whalsay

Gott
Lerwick
Scalloway

Dunrossness
Virkie

Harray
Kirkwall
Stromness
Graemeshall
St Margaret's Hope

Dunnet Bay
Auckengill

Wick

Latheron
Dunbeath

Burghead
Elgin
Buckie
Banff
Fochabers
Keith
Turriff
Mintlaw
Peterhead
Dufftown
Huntly
Fyvie
Ballindalloch
Kennethmont
Inverurie
Pitmedden
Tomintoul
Alford

ABERDEEN

Ballater
Drumoak
Banchory
Braemar

Stonehaven

Glenesk

Brechin
Montrose
Kirriemuir
Forfar
Alyth
Glamis
Dunkeld
Meigle
Arbroath

DUNDEE
Broughty Ferry
Perth
Leuchars

Cupar
Ceres
Kinnesswood
Crail
Falkland
Anstruther
Kinross
Leven
Lower Largo
Pittenweem
East Wemyss
Buckhaven
Kirkcaldy
Dysart
DUNFERMLINE
North Berwick
Bo'ness
Burntisland
Aberlady
Inverkeithing
East Linton
Prestongrange
Linlithgow
EDINBURGH
Haddington
South Queensferry
Eyemouth
Livingston
Newtongrange
Penicuik
Duns
Berwick-upon-Tweed
Lauder
Gordon
Norham
Peebles
Coldstream
Holy Island
Biggar
Walkerburn
Cornhill-on-Tweed
Broughton
Innerleithen
Melrose
Bamburgh
Selkirk

0   10   20   30 Kilometres

0   10   20 Miles

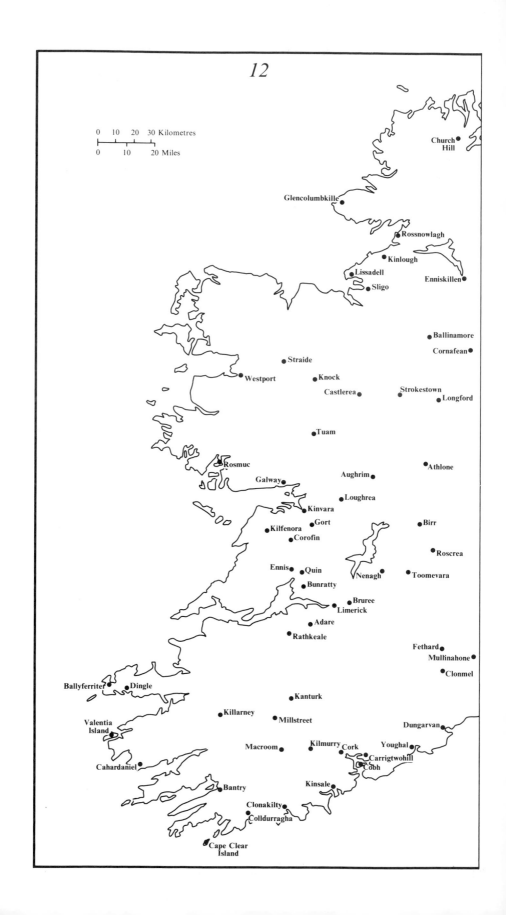

12

0   10   20   30 Kilometres

0   10   20 Miles

Church Hill

Glencolumbkille

Rossnowlagh

Kinlough

Lissadell
Enniskillen
Sligo

Ballinamore
Cornafean

Straide

Knock
Westport
Castlerea
Strokestown
Longford

Tuam

Rosmuc
Athlone

Aughrim
Galway
Loughrea

Kinvara
Gort
Birr
Kilfenora
Corofin
Roscrea

Ennis
Quin
Nenagh
Toomevara
Bunratty

Bruree
Limerick

Adare
Rathkeale
Fethard
Mullinahone
Clonmel

Ballyferriter
Dingle
Kanturk

Killarney
Millstreet
Dungarvan

Valentia
Island
Macroom
Kilmurry
Cork
Youghal
Carrigtwohill
Cobh

Cahardaniel
Kinsale

Bantry
Clonakilty
Colldurragha

Cape Clear
Island

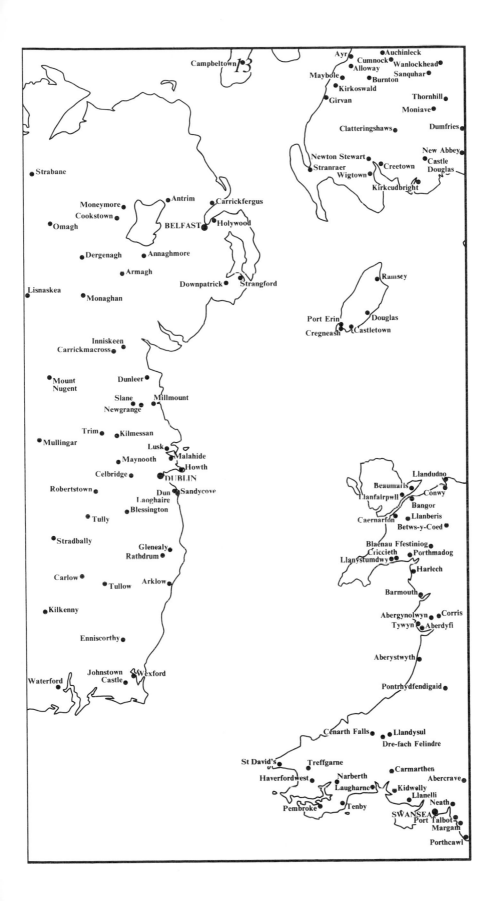

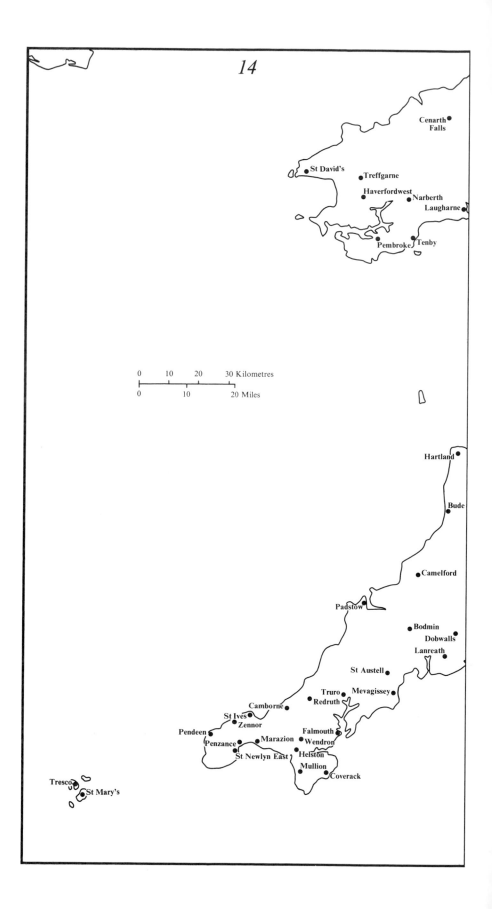

14

Cenarth
Falls

St David's
Treffgarne
Haverfordwest
Narberth
Laugharne
Pembroke
Tenby

0   10   20   30 Kilometres

0   10   20 Miles

Hartland

Bude

Camelford

Padstow

Bodmin
Dobwalls
Lanreath

St Austell

Truro
Mevagissey
Redruth
Camborne
St Ives
Zennor
Pendeen
Falmouth
Marazion
Penzance
Wendron
St Newlyn East
Helston
Mullion
Coverack
Tresco
St Mary's

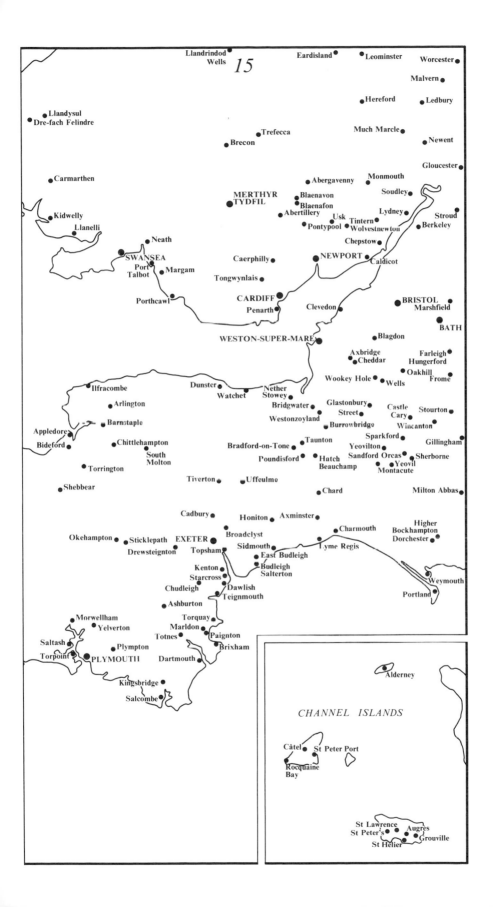

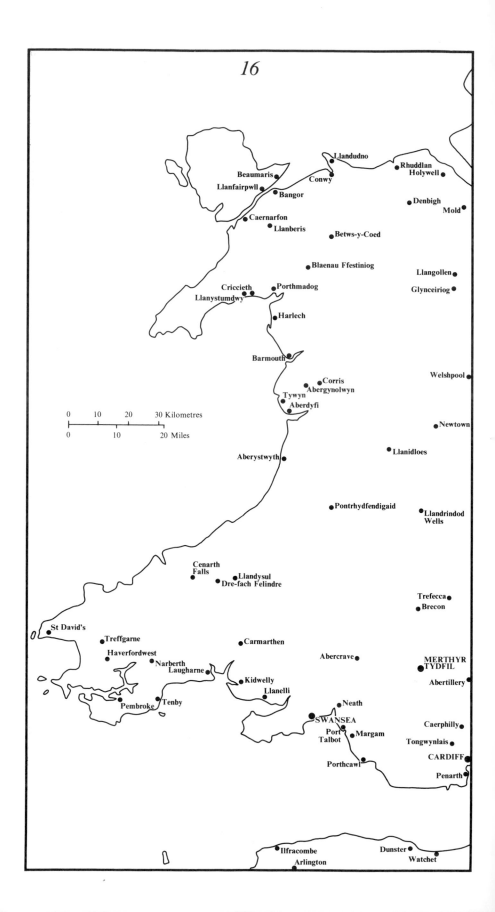

Key to Symbols and Abbreviations

£	Admission charge
F	Free admission
🚗	Visitors' car park
📖	Bookstall
🛍	Shop
☕	Refreshments
⌆	Picnic area
♿	Wheelchair facilities
☐	Temporary exhibitions
🛇	Contact for educational visits
🖝	Guided tours
⊖	Underground station
⇌	British Rail station
NT	National Trust
NTS	National Trust for Scotland
HHA	Historic Houses Association
✜	English Heritage
✤	Cadw: Welsh Historical Monuments
🏛	Scottish Historic Buildings and Monuments

Organisations

The following organisations with museums and historic buildings in their care offer admission free, or on preferential terms, to members and to parties of schoolchildren and students in full-time education.

NT
The National Trust
PO Box 39
Bromley
Kent BR1 1NH
☎ 01 464 1111

NTS
The National Trust for Scotland
5 Charlotte Square
Edinburgh EH2 4DU
☎ 031 226 5922

HHA
Historic Houses Association
38 Ebury Street
London SW1W 0LU
☎ 01 730 9419

✜
English Heritage
Membership Department
Quayside House
429 Oxford Street
London W1R 2HD
☎ 01 355 1303

✤
Heritage in Wales
Cadw: Welsh Historical Monuments
Brunel House
2 Fitzalan Road
Cardiff CF2 1UY
☎ 0222 465511

🏛
Friends of Scottish Monuments
Historic Buildings and Monuments
PO Box 157
Edinburgh EH3 5RA
☎ 031 244 3099

A

Abbots Bromley

The Puppet Theatre Museum

*Edinburgh House, Bagot Street, Abbots Bromley,
Staffordshire WS15 3DA*   ☎ *0283 840348*
*Sun 2–6. Groups at other times by appt (maximum
30).*
🔏 *Douglas S. E. Hayward, Director*
£ 🖉 💺 🚗

The Museum is housed in the building where
the Hayward Marionettes performed regularly
until 1981. The stage and backstage area form
part of the exhibition. At least 200 of the large
collection of puppets are displayed at any given
time. The exhibits also include information on
the history and techniques of the puppet
theatre.

Abercrave

Dan-yr-Ogof Showcaves Museum

*Abercrave (Abercraf), Glyntawe, Upper Swansea
Valley, Swansea, West Glamorgan*
☎ *0639 730284/730693*
Apr–Oct, daily from 10. Winter visits by appt.
🔏 *The Manager*
£ 🎁 💺 🚻 🚗

The Museum is part of the Showcaves complex,
the largest in Western Europe. One of the three
caves, the Bone Cave, gives visitors an insight
into cave archaeology, the animals associated
with caves and the life of man within the cave.
The Dinosaur Park incorporates a short
geological nature trail and includes life-sized
models of dinosaurs.

The complex as a whole aims to show how
caves were formed and discovered and how they
served as animal dens and human habitations.

**Stalagmites and stalactites at the Dan-yr-Ogof
Showcaves, Abercrave.**

Interpretation is provided by dioramas re-
creating historical scenes and by audio systems
relating to the displays.

Aberdeen

Aberdeen Art Gallery

Schoolhill, Aberdeen, Aberdeenshire AB9 1FQ
☎ *0224 646333*
Mon–Wed, Fri, Sat 10–5; Thurs 10–8; Sun 2–5.
🔏 *Ciaran Monaghan, Keeper of Extension
Services*
F 🎁 💺 🚗 ♿

This important Gallery was established in 1884.
The main strength of the collections is in 18th,
19th and 20th-century British art. Many of the
paintings came to the Gallery as gifts from
prominent local people, who also bequeathed
funds for further purchases. Other works have
been donated by the Contemporary Art Society
and the War Artists' Advisory Committee, and
purchased with the help of grants from other
national bodies.

Scottish and local artists are well represented
and the Gallery is especially rich in landscapes
by the French Impressionists. Among the
oustanding works on display are Turner's *Ely
Cathedral*, Sir John Lavery's *Tennis Party*,
Monet's *La Falaise à Fécamp*, Sisley's *La Petite
Place*, and Blake's *Raising of Lazarus*.

Aberdeen Maritime Museum

*Provost Ross's House, Shiprow, Aberdeen,
Aberdeenshire*   ☎ *0224 585788*
Mon–Sat 10–5.
🔏 *The Keeper of Maritime History, Aberdeen Art
Gallery*
F 🎁 🚗

The Museum is housed in the city's oldest
surviving building, the house of an 18th-century
merchant with substantial shipping interests.
The displays are divided into 12 sections. The
first illustrates the development of Aberdeen
Harbour over the past two centuries, a task
which involved two diversions of the River Dee.
Another section tells the story of Aberdeen's
involvement in the Arctic whaling trade, which
lasted from 1752 to the early 1860s. The first
Aberdeen shipyard was opened in 1753 and the
strong local shipbuilding tradition is
documented in a number of exhibits.

Shipowning also receives careful attention, as
does the local fishing industry in its various
branches: small line fishing for haddock, codling
and whiting; herring fishing; trawling, which
made Aberdeen a boom town; and great line
fishing, which used long lines to catch halibut,
turbot, skate, torsk, cod and ling. Other
exhibits present the history of local wrecks and
rescues, and of the London Boats, the
steamships which carried freight and passengers
between Aberdeen and the metropolis and
operated from 1835 until the early 1960s. A
final section deals with the North Sea oil and
gas industry, which brought a new wave of
prosperity to Aberdeen.

Gordon Highlanders Museum

St Luke's, Viewfield Road, Aberdeen,
*   Aberdeenshire AB1 7XH   ☎ 0224 318174*
Wed, Sun 2–5. Closed public holidays.
✠ *The Regimental Secretary*
F ♟ ⚬

The Museum tells the story of the Gordon
Highlanders from 1794, when the Regiment was
raised, to the present day. The exhibits include
uniforms, accoutrements and medals, together
with paintings, prints and photographs relating
to campaigns in which the Gordon Highlanders
have been involved and to Regimental life and
personalities. There is also a display of the
Regimental silver.

Grampian Police Museum

Grampian Police Headquarters, Queen Street,
*   Aberdeen, Aberdeenshire AB9 1BA*
*   ☎ 0224 639111*
By written request only
✠ *The Chairman*
F ⚬

The collection, in the Police Headquarters
building, consists of uniforms, truncheons,
medals, photographs, books and other items
associated with the Police Service.

James Dun's House

61 Schoolhill, Aberdeen, Aberdeenshire AB1 1JT
*   ☎ 0224 646333*
Mon–Sat 10–5. Closed Sun, Dec 25, 26, Jan 1, 2.
✠ *Ciaran Monaghan, Keeper of Extension*
*   Services*
F ⚬ ⚬ ☐

This 18th-century town house has been restored
and converted for use as a museum. The aim has
been to present regional history in a way that is
interesting to children. The displays include
costumes and accessories and a wide range of
bygones, related especially to domestic life and
trades and handicrafts.

Museum of the Department of Natural Philosophy

Department of Natural Philosophy, The University,
*   Aberdeen, Aberdeenshire AB9 2UE*
*   ☎ 0224 40241 extn 5443*
By appt. Display in the entrance hall Mon–Fri 9–5
*   during term.*
✠ *Dr John S. Reid*
F ⚬

The Museum, which is oriented towards an
academic audience, has a good collection of
apparatus used during the past 200 years for
teaching and demonstrating the traditional
branches of physics. Among these are acoustics,
astronomy, electronics, electrostatics,
magnetism, mechanics, optics, wave motion
and X-ray physics.

Museum of the Department of Zoology

Department of Zoology, The University, Aberdeen,
*   Aberdeenshire AB9 2TN   ☎ 0224 40241*
By appt.
✠ *Mrs M. Rebecca*
F ⚬

The Museum contains a comprehensive
collection of the animal kingdom, arranged
mainly for undergraduate teaching. Special
features are important collections of British
birds and eggs.

Provost Skene's House

Guestrow, off Broad Street, Aberdeen,
*   Aberdeenshire AB1 1AR   ☎ 0224 641086*
Mon–Sat 10–5. Closed Sun, Dec 25, 26, Jan 1, 2.
✠ *Ciaran Monaghan, Keeper of Extension*
*   Services*
F ⚬ ⚬ ⚬

The Museum building is an outstanding
example of the 17th-century architecture of the
Scottish burghs. This form developed directly
from the late medieval tower house, with its
extensive fortifications. The title deeds for the
property date from 1545 and the site of the
house on the Guestrow is of great importance in
the history of Aberdeen.

The house has rooms furnished in period style
and there are displays illustrating the history of
Aberdeen and the surrounding area. One of the
most remarkable features is a painted ceiling
dating from about 1630.

University Anthropological Museum

Marischal College, The University, Aberdeen,
*   Aberdeenshire AB9 1AS*
*   ☎ 0224 40241*
Mon–Fri 10–5; Sun 2–5. Closed Sat, Christmas,
*   New Year.*
✠ *Charles Hunt, Curator*
F ⚬ ⚬

The Anthropological Museum was established
in 1907 and is housed in Marischal College, a
Victorian Gothic building of imposing
dimensions and grandeur. The objects in the
Museum's collections have been gathered over a
period of more than two centuries by graduates
of the University. They are particularly strong
in Scottish prehistoric archaeology, Egyptian,
Roman and Greek antiquities, and in
ethnographical material from Africa, America
and the Pacific.

Display on 'The Human Family', University
Anthropological Museum, Aberdeen.

Abergavenny Castle from the Castle Meadows.

Until 1984 the Museum preserved its original appearance and arrangement almost intact, but it has now been reorganized. The first gallery, restored to its Victorian elegance, contains a large number of objects, arranged according to type and explaining their manufacture and use. The second gallery is arranged by themes – including Ghosts and Ancestors; Heroes and Monsters; The Poor; Chiefs and Kings; Priests and Shamans.

Aberdyfi

Outward Bound Sailing Museum

The Wharf, Aberdyfi, Gwynedd   ☎ *0654 72 464*
Easter–Oct. Other times by appt.
Ⓜ *Jon Clift*
Ⓕ ♿

The Museum is accommodated in an old wooden storage building, dating from the days when Aberdyfi was a busy port. The displays illustrate the history of sailing and sailing ships in the area. The emphasis is on the work of the Outward Bound centre, but there are also many pictures and relics of the trading craft which used to operate from Aberdyfi.

Abergavenny

Abergavenny Museum

Castle Street, Abergavenny, Gwent NP7 5EE
    ☎ *0873 4282*
Mar–Oct, Mon–Sat 11–1, 2–5; Sun 2.30–5.
Nov–Feb, Mon–Sat 11–1, 2–4. Closed Dec 25, 26.
Ⓜ *Martin Buckridge, Curator*
Ⓔ ✎ ♿

The Museum is situated in the ruins of the medieval castle, in a house built in 1818–19 by the Marquis of Abergavenny on the site of the original Norman keep.

The displays trace the history of Abergavenny from its origins as the Roman fort of *Gobannium* to the present day. The collections were originally based on material collected during the demolition of medieval streets in the town. These include oak-panelling and fireplaces. Among the other important items now exhibited are the Welsh farmhouse kitchen of *c.* 1900, a 17th-century mural painting of the Adoration of the Magi, discovered in an attic in 1906, and a governess cart built by the local coach-builder, William Probert, at the beginning of the century.

Visitors can also see the craft tools of many trades once carried on in the area – there is a complete saddler's workshop – together with examples of the products of local firms which are in business today. An unusual exhibit is 'Whiskey', a late survivor of the now extinct short-legged, long-bodied turnspit dog.

Abergynolwyn

Abergynolwyn Village Museum

Y Gorlan, 17 Water Street, Abergynolwyn,
    Tywyn, Gwynedd LL36 9YB
Closed weekends
Ⓜ *Mr Lewis Lewis, Treasurer*
Ⓕ ♿

Until recent years, most of the inhabitants of the village of Abergynolwyn were dependent for their living on agriculture and slate quarrying. The little museum concentrates particularly on the life and skills of the quarrymen and their families, with a good collection of the special tools they used to extract and process the slate. There are also a number of photographs of work at the quarry and everyday activities in the village.

Aberlady

Myreton Motor Museum

Aberlady, East Lothian   ☎ *087 57 288*
Easter–Oct, daily 10–6. Nov–Easter, daily 10–1, 2–5. Closed Dec 25.
Ⓕ ✎ ♿

This privately owned museum was opened in 1966 and has since been considerably expanded. Few of the exhibits are of the large, exotic or expensive type. There are some pre-First World War cars, including an Arnold Benz of 1897 and a Wolseley of 1902, but the majority are vehicles seen in large numbers from the early 1920s onwards. All are in running condition and many take part in rallies and are used by television and film companies. A 1925 Morris from the Museum was Dr Cameron's car in the BBC series, *Dr Finlay's Casebook*.

The Museum also has good collections of road signs, posters, petrol cans and gadgets, together with motorcycles from 1903 and cycles from 1866, including a Dursley Pederson of 1908, 'favoured by the clergy', and a 1903 Humber Ladies Model, ridden regularly by its owner until her death in 1974.

Abertillery

Abertillery Museum

County Library, Oak Street, Abertillery,
    Gwent NP3 1TE   ☎ 0633 422729
Tues, Wed 2–4.45; Sat 10–1. Other times by appt
    ex. Mon, public holidays.
🏛 Mrs G. E. M. Andrews, Kings House, Castle
    Street, Caerleon, Gwent NP6 1BR
Ⓕ 🚗

During the 19th century, Abertillery became
the second largest town in Monmouthshire, as a
result of the expansion of its iron and coal
industries, but the subsequent decline in these
industries has produced a steady fall in both the
prosperity and the population of the area. The
Museum, opened in 1972, has to be seen against
this background.

It is concerned primarily with local history
and with social and industrial activities. Its
mining mementoes include a collection of pit-
lamps and samples of coal from all the seams
once worked in the district. Other strong points
of the displays are domestic equipment, tobacco
and snuff boxes, and swords.

Aberystwyth

Aberystwyth Yesterday

The Little Chapel, New Street, Aberystwyth, Dyfed
    ☎ 0970 617119
June–Sept, daily 11–5.
🏛 Mrs Margaret Evans, 6 Laura Place,
    Aberystwyth
Ⓔ 🚗

The Museum is in two parts. The paintings and
photographs are in The Little Chapel, a
converted coach house of c. 1820, and the
clothes, dolls, furniture, jewellery and Welsh
costumes are in the vestry of a Victorian
Wesleyan chapel in Great Darkgate Street. All
the items relate to Aberystwyth and have been
gathered together by the owner, Mrs Margaret
Evans, 'to show her obsessive love for her home
town'.

Mrs Evans also uses empty shop windows
within the town's conservation centre as a
means of extending the museum and of giving
the public a further opportunity to see material
from her large collections.

Ceredigion Museum

Coliseum, Terrace Road, Aberystwyth,
    Dyfed SY23 2AQ   ☎ 0970 617911 extn 252
Mon–Sat 10–5. Closed Good Fri, Christmas–New
    Year.
🏛 The Curator
Ⓕ 🖼 🚗 ♿

The home of the Ceredigion Museum is a former
Edwardian theatre, the stage and balconies of
which have been preserved. The stage is set
with scenery and models, as if a play were in
progress.

The Museum has been planned to reflect the
social and domestic life, work and traditions of
Aberystwyth and its region. There are displays
to illustrate the main occupations of the past –
agriculture; the craft industries, especially
carpentry, clog-making, spinning and weaving;
seafaring; and lead-mining. Associated with the
large agricultural section is a reconstructed and
furnished cottage of c. 1850, with a peat fire and
lath and plaster chimney. There is a chemist's
shop, a dental surgery and exhibits relating to
education, road and rail transport, slate
enamelling, and weights and measures.

The archaeological displays include models of
an Iron Age hill fort and of the castle and walled
town of Aberystwyth.

Mid-Wales Mining Museum

Llywernog Silver-Lead Mine, Ponterwyd,
    Aberystwyth, Dyfed SY23 3AB
        ☎ 0970 85 620
Easter–Aug, daily 10–6. Sept, daily 10–5. Oct,
    daily, 11–4.
🏛 Peter Lloyd Harvey, Museum Director
Ⓔ 🍴 🖼 🛒 🚗

The Museum is at the old Llywernog silver-lead
mine. The exhibitions are housed in a complex
of three mine buildings, the Crusher House
(mid-1860s), the Dressing Shed (1867) and the
Count House (1870), and provide a general
guide to the history and techniques of the local
mining industry, 'the California of Wales', with
a good collection of mining artefacts.

The Miners' Trail through the Museum site is
arranged on a self-guiding principle, with
numbered display panels. It includes a tunnel
and the sites of pumps, waterwheels, a tramway,
a Cornish roll-crusher and the gunpowder store.

Abingdon

Abingdon Museum

The County Hall, Market Place, Abingdon,
    Oxfordshire   ☎ 0235 23703
Daily 2–5. Closed some Bank Holiday Mons.
🏛 The Curator
Ⓔ 🏷 🚗

Abingdon's County Hall, which has housed the
Museum since 1928, was built in 1678 as a
Court House. The displays tell the story of
Abingdon and its district since prehistoric
times. From the Neolithic period onwards,
human settlement is well represented by
archaeological discovery and excavation.
Among the Saxon burial items is a fragment of
the earliest known lyre in Western Europe.
There are carvings, tiles and account rolls from
the medieval Abbey, and early items, including
charters relating to the Borough, which, in
1556, gained control over previously monastic
properties.

Displays for the 17th, 18th and 19th centuries
deal with the Civil War, the industries and
trades of Abingdon, local personalities, the
Abingdon Volunteers, the Wilts and Berks

Canal, the Old Gaol. Two of the Museum's most prized exhibits are the smocks made for the Great Exhibition by a local firm and the 1851 dolls' house which belonged to the six Morland sisters, who contributed items to it throughout their lives.

Abriachan

Abriachan Croft Museum

c/o Old Schoolhouse, Abriachan, Inverness, Inverness-shire IV3 6LB   ☎ 046 386 237
By appt in the summer
⚐ Mrs Katharine Stewart, Curator
F ⌂ ✏

The village of Abriachan declined during the 20th century, with the gradual disappearance of the old crofting system. Nearly all the native families have gone and most of the land is now used for grazing or afforestation. As part of a scheme completed in 1970 for European Conservation Year, pupils from Inverness High School spent two years reconditioning buildings and improving the appearance of the village. Since then the Druim croft house and outbuildings have been restored and furnished in the original style, so that they can function as a museum. There is a comprehensive collection of crofting implements, tools and household equipment, together with many photographs and documents. There is also a Nature Room, which contains geological collections.

Accrington

Haworth Art Gallery

Haworth Park, Manchester Road, Accrington, Lancashire BB5 2JS   ☎ 0254 33782
Daily 2-5 ex Fri. Closed Jan 1, Good Fri, Dec 25, 26.
⚐ Norman T. Potter, Curator
F ⌂ ⟿ ♿

Formerly the home of the Haworth family, who were cotton manufacturers, it was known as Hollins House and was given to the town of Accrington in 1920 to be used as an art gallery and museum. It now contains collections of European paintings, English watercolours, including works by Birkett Foster, Paul Sandby and Samuel Prout, and the largest collection of Tiffany glass in Europe.

The Great Hall at Ragley Hall, Alcester.

Adare

Adare Trinity Museum

Presbytery, Adare, Co. Limerick, Ireland
☎ 061 86177/86208
July–Aug, Mon–Sat 9.30–12.30, 2–6; Sun 2–6
⚐ Fr. J. Browne, P.P.
F

The Museum is on the ground floor of a 13th-century Trinitarian abbey. Some of the displays illustrate social and domestic life in the Adare area during the past 100 years and others show carved stone work and historical items relating to the numerous monasteries and churches which once existed in the district. There are also exhibits of handicrafts and craftsmen's tools.

Alcester

Coughton Court

nr Alcester, Warwickshire B49 5JA
☎ 0789 762435
Mar 29–Apr 3, daily 2–5. Apr 5–27 and Oct, Sat, Sun and Bank Holiday Mon 2–5. May–Sept, Tues–Thurs, Sat, Sun and Bank Holiday Mon 2–6.
⚐ The Custodian
£ ⌂ ☕ ⟿ NT

Coughton Court is two miles north of Alcester, on the A435. Its splendid three-storeyed gatehouse, built c. 1518, is in the centre of 18th-century Gothick wings. The property belonged to the staunchly Catholic Throckmorton family from 1409 to 1946, when the 11th Baronet made it over to the National Trust.

The most famous event in the history of Coughton took place in the gatehouse drawing room on 5th November 1605, when a group, including the wives of the conspirators, waited for news of the Gunpowder Plot.

The contents of the house include fine furniture and porcelain, as well as portraits and memorabilia of the Throckmorton family. The exceptionally comfortable and interesting National Trust tea room has family portraits and Victorian furniture.

Ragley Hall

Alcester, Warwickshire B49 5NJ ☎ 0789 762090
Apr, May, Sept, daily 1.30–5.30 ex. Mon and Fri.
June–Aug, Tues, Wed, Thurs 12–5; Sat, Sun 1.30–5.30; Bank Holiday Mon 12–5.30.
Open by appt throughout year for private tours.
⚐ Lord Hertford
£ ⌂ ☕ ⟿ ♿ HHA

The home of the Marquis and Marchioness of Hertford, Ragley Hall is a country house in the Palladian style, built by Robert Hooke in 1680. The baroque plasterwork covering the walls and ceiling of the entrance hall was designed by James Gibbs in 1750. The circular stable block was constructed to the design of James Wyatt in 1780. It now houses a carriage collection. There

The bedroom occupied by the Prince Regent during visits to Ragley Hall.

is a modern mural, *The Temptation*, covering the South Staircase Hall, painted by Graham Rust between 1969 and 1983. The house contains a fine collection of paintings, furniture and porcelain, mostly 18th century. There are seven family portraits by Sir Joshua Reynolds.

Aldborough

Aldborough Roman Town

Historic Buildings & Monuments Commission, Aldborough Roman Town, nr Boroughbridge, North Yorkshire   ☎ *09012 2768*
Apr–Sept, daily 9.30–1, 2–6.30
▨ *Historic Buildings & Monuments Commission, York*   ☎ *0904 58626*
£ ✪ ✿

The village of Aldborough lies within the boundaries of the former Roman city of *Isurium Brigantum*. It has retained some of the Roman street plan. Part of the Roman town walls have survived, together with two mosaic pavements. An interesting collection of finds discovered during excavations can be seen in the Museum. They consist of iron, bronze, bone and glass items, together with some pottery and tiles. Most of the objects are Roman, but some are Saxon and medieval.

There is a study collection of pottery and glass, not on general display, and a reserve collection of archaeological material, mainly Roman and medieval, which has been given by people living in Aldborough.

Aldeburgh

Aldeburgh Moot Hall Museum

Moot Hall, Aldeburgh, Suffolk
☎ *072885 2158 (Town Clerk)*
May, daily 2.30–5.30. June–Sept, daily 10–1, 2.30–5.30. Open weekends, public holidays in spring.
▨ *The Secretary*
£ *adults only* ✿

Aldeburgh Moot Hall is an important 16th-century listed building. The Museum is concerned mainly with local history, with an emphasis on shipping and trade. There is a good collection of historical records, particularly strong in photographs and other pictorial material.

The principal objects discovered during excavation of the Snape Ship Burial, which pre-dates Sutton Hoo, are preserved in the Museum.

Alderney

The Alderney Society Museum

High Street, Alderney, Channel Islands
☎ *048182 3222*
Mon–Sat 10–12.30. Hydrofoil and Steamer days: Museum open until 3.30 at the discretion of the Custodians. Other times by appt.
▨ *K. Hempel, Curator*
£ ✪

The exhibits in the Museum, which is in the former School House, illustrate the history of Alderney from prehistoric times to the present day. There are displays of archaeology and natural history, medal and stamp collections, and material from wrecks around the Alderney coast. Other exhibits are concerned with the traditional occupations of the island, the domestic and social life and the German occupation of Alderney during the Second World War.

A reference collection of photographs, postcards, prints and documents illustrates the history of the church and of the island's Government.

Aldershot

Airborne Forces Museum

Browning Barracks, Queens Avenue, Aldershot, Hampshire GU11 2DS
☎ *0252 24431 extn Montgomery 619*
Mon–Fri 9–12.30, 2–4.30; Sat 9.30–12.30, 2–4.30; Sun 10–12.30, 2–4.30. Closed Dec 25.
▨ *The Curator*
£ ✪ ↢

The Airborne collection is housed in a specially built museum opened by Field-Marshal Montgomery in 1969. It presents the history of the British Airborne Forces from 1940, when they were first raised, to the present day. In addition to comprehensive displays of uniforms, medals, weapons, airborne vehicles and equipment and aircraft models, there are the original briefing models for the airborne operations of the Second World War, important exhibits of photographic material from 1940 onwards, and dioramas of actions. Visitors can also see sections of gliders, German and American airborne equipment and weapons, a Dakota aircraft in its wartime camouflage and an Argentinian howitzer captured in the Falklands.

Aldershot Military Museum

Queens Avenue, Aldershot,
Hampshire GU11 2LG   ☎ *0252 314598*
Mar–Oct, daily 10–5. Nov–Feb, daily 10–4.30.
Closed Dec 24–26.
◪ *Education Officer, Aldershot Military Historical*
Trust, The Bungalow, Cavans Road,
Aldershot GU11 2LG
£ ▯ ↩ ᵶ

The Museum building is the only surviving
example of Aldershot's original Victorian
bungalow barrack blocks. The Museum has been
established to present the history of Aldershot,
the home of the British Army and the birthplace
of British military aviation, from its beginnings
in 1856 to the present time. There is a
reconstruction of an original Victorian barrack
room, with period uniforms and equipment,
models of successive camps, and a sectional
model of the cavalry barracks, where the horses
were stabled below the men's living quarters, in
order to provide the soldiers with free warmth.

Exhibits of photographs, militaria, plans and
documents illustrate the life of the soldier in
peacetime and show how Aldershot became the
Canadian Army's wartime base in Britain. A
diorama of balloons, airships and early aircraft
recalls the pioneer days of military flying.

Army Physical Training Corps Museum

Army School of Physical Training, Queens
Avenue, Aldershot, Hampshire GU11 2LB
☎ *0252 24431 extn 2131*
Mon–Fri 8–12.30, 2–4.30. Closed Sat, Sun,
Bank Holiday and Aug.
◪ *Major L. Lambert, Hon. Curator*
F ▯ ↩

The Museum was formed in order to present a
picture of the history of the Corps, its
achievements and its personalities. There are
displays of equipment, documents, photographs
and of the militaria of past members of the
Corps. The library section of the Museum
contains a large collection of books and
pamphlets on sport and physical training.

The Gurkha Museum

Queen Elizabeth Barracks, Church Crookham,
Aldershot, Hampshire GU13 0RJ
☎ *0252 613541*
Mon–Fri 9.45–4.30 throughout year. Apr–Oct,
Sat 9.30–4.30. Nov–May, Sat 10–12 by appt.
Check times in advance. The Museum will
shortly be moving to the Peninsula Barracks,
Winchester.
◪ *The Curator*
F ⬭ ↩ ᵶ

The first Gurkha regiments, composed of
soldiers from Nepal, were raised in 1815. The
Gurkha Museum has been formed in order to
commemorate the services of the Gurkhas to the
British Crown from that time onwards. It gives
an impression of the country from which the
Gurkhas have been drawn and provides details
of their activities in many parts of the world.
There is a collection of badges, medals and
militaria of the Gurkha regiments, past and
present.

The Museum will eventually occupy a
permanent home offered by The Royal Green
Jackets in Peninsular Barracks, Winchester.

Queen Alexandra's Royal Army Nursing Corps Museum

Regimental Headquarters, QARANC, Royal
Pavilion, Farnborough Road, Aldershot,
Hampshire GU11 1PZ
☎ *0252 24431 extn 301/315*
Tues, Wed 9–12.30, 2–4.30; Thurs 9–12.30.
Other times by appt.
◪ *Major (Retd) Jill Machray, Curator*
F ▯ ↩

The QARANC Museum illustrates the history
of Army nursing from the Crimean War
onwards. The displays include an interesting
and varied medal collection and personal items
belonging to members of the Corps. The archive
of photographs and documents provides
evidence of the conditions experienced by Army
nurses in war and in peacetime. Among the
many historic exhibits is the carriage used by
Florence Nightingale in the Crimea.

Royal Army Dental Corps Historical Museum

HQ & Central Group RADC, Evelyn Woods
Road, Aldershot, Hampshire GU11 2LS
☎ *0252 24431 extn 3470*
Mon–Fri 10–12, 2–4. Closed Sat, Sun, public
holidays.
◪ *The Curator*
F ▯ ↩

The RADC Museum links dentistry with the
British Army from its earliest days. The
recognition of the necessity to provide dental
treatment for soldiers, leading up to the
formation of a uniformed service, is illustrated
by a series of displays of equipment, documents,
photographs and medals relating both to the
history of the Corps and to developments in
dental techniques.

A reconstructed barrack room of c. 1900 at
Aldershot Military Museum.

Royal Army Medical Corps Historical Museum

Keogh Barracks, Ash Vale, nr Aldershot,
   Hampshire GU11 5RQ
   ☎ *0252 24431 extn Keogh 212*
Mon–Fri 8.30–4. Weekends and evenings by appt.
   Closed public and Bank Holidays.
Ⓜ *Lt. Col. (Retd) R. Eyeions, Curator*
Ⓕ ⬛ ↝ ⬙

The RAMC was formed in 1898, after more than two centuries of fragmented and frequently inefficient administration of the Army's medical services. The Museum covers the whole period of the official medical care of British soldiers, from 1660 onwards, a story which relates to every campaign and battle in which the British Army has been involved.

Royal Army Veterinary Corps Museum

RAVC Laboratory and Stores, Gallwey Road,
   Aldershot, Hampshire GU11 2DQ
   ☎ *0252 24431 extn 2261*
By appt
Ⓜ *Major A. H. Roache, Curator*
Ⓕ ↝

The displays in the RAVC Museum relate to the use of animals by the British Army, both before and since the founding of the Corps. Photographs, documents and equipment illustrate the tasks the Corps has had to face and describe some of its outstanding personalities.

Royal Corps of Transport Regimental Museum

Buller Barracks, Aldershot, Hampshire GU11 2BX
   ☎ *0252 24431 extn 2417*
Mon–Fri 9–12, 2–4.30. Open weekends only for
   group visits by appt.
Ⓜ *The Curator*
Ⓕ ⬛ ↝

The Museum aims to present to its visitors the interesting history of transport in the British Army from the 18th century onwards, beginning with horse-drawn vehicles through to the wide range of mechanised transport in use today. The story is told by means of photographs, models and documents, together with displays of uniforms, badges, swords and regimental militaria.

Alexandria

Tobias Smollett Museum

Castle Cameron, Alexandria, Dunbartonshire
   G83 8QZ   ☎ *0389 56226*
By appt only
Ⓜ *P. Telfer Smollett*
Ⓕ ↝

Castle Cameron is one mile from Balloch on the A82. The Museum contains collections which illustrate the life and work of the novelist and historian, Tobias Smollett (1721–71), including portraits, memorabilia, items of clothing worn by him and first editions of his works. There is also a collection relating to the history of the area.

Alford (Aberdeenshire)

Craigievar Castle

Alford, Aberdeenshire AB3 4RS
   ☎ *033983 635 or 0467 22988*
May–Sept, daily 2–6 (last admission 5.15).
   Pre-booked groups at other times.
   Grounds open all year, 9.30–sunset.
Ⓜ *Mrs F. Scott*
Ⓔ ⬙ ⬙ ↝ [NTS]

Craigievar, an outstanding example of Scottish baronial architecture, is six miles south of Alford, on the A980. The home of the Forbes-Semphill family since the early 17th century, its furnishings, portraits, and personal possessions reflect three centuries of family occupation. The interior is especially remarkable for its splendid Renaissance plasterwork ceilings.

Grampian Transport Museum

Alford, Aberdeenshire AB3 8AD   ☎ 0336 2292
Apr–Sept, daily 10.30–5
Ⓜ *Mike Ward, Curator*
Ⓔ ⬙ ↝ ⬙

This new museum has been planned to illustrate the development of road transport in the North-East of Scotland. All types of vehicle are represented – horse-drawn carriages, bicycles, motorcars, lorries and motorcycles. Perhaps the most remarkable exhibit is the Craigievar Express, a steam tricycle designed and built in 1895 by a local postman, who used it to deliver mail. Wherever possible, vehicles with strong local associations have been selected. There is a reconstruction of a garage workshop of the 1930s and an area showing Aberdeen street scenes.

The Alford Valley Railway Museum, in the restored station at Alford, forms a separate part of the Transport Museum complex. It contains displays illustrating the history of the Great North of Scotland Railway and operates a 2-foot gauge passenger railway between Alford station and Haughton and Murray country parks. The site also has a track circuit for working model steam locomotives.

Alford (Lincolnshire)

The Manor House

Alford and District Civic Trust Ltd, West Street,
   Alford, Lincolnshire
May–Sept, Mon–Fri 10.30–1, 2–4.30. Open
   Spring and August Bank Holiday weekends.
Ⓜ *Mrs S. M. Cooke, The Manor House, West*
   Street, Alford   ☎ 052 12 2278
Ⓔ ⬙

Parts of the thatched, brick-built Manor House date from the 16th century. It is used now as a museum of the traditional occupations and social and domestic life of rural Lincolnshire. A special selection is devoted to agricultural implements and there is a small exhibit of Roman remains found in the area.

Alfriston

Alfriston Clergy House

The Tye, Alfriston, Polegate,
East Sussex BN26 5TL   ☎ 0323 870001
Mar 28–Oct, daily 11–6 or sunset if earlier
⊠ The Administrator
£ ♿ NT

The Clergy House was built c. 1350. An oak-framed Wealden Hall House with wattle and daub walls, the medieval hall has a crownpost roof and much of the original timber framing. By the 19th century, it had been converted into labourers' cottages. The National Trust bought it for £10 in 1896 and carefully restored it. The Clergy House was the first building to be acquired by the Trust.

One of the rooms is used for exhibitions relating to the history of the house and its period.

Alloa

Alloa Museum and Art Gallery

15 Mar Street, Alloa, Clackmannanshire
FK10 1HT   ☎ 0259 722160
Mon, Wed Fri 10.30–6; Tues 10.30–4;
Sat 9.30–12. Closed public holidays.
⊠ The Curator
F ♿ ♿ □

Fifteen Mar Street was built in 1904 as the local Liberal Club. Its displays are devoted to the history of Alloa and the surrounding area. Temporary exhibitions, especially of art and photography, are held in the Museum.

Alloway

Burns Cottage and Museum

Alloway, Ayrshire KA7 4PY   ☎ 0292 41215
Spring, Autumn, Mon–Sat 10–5; Sun 2–5.
June Aug, Mon–Sat 9–7; Sun 10–7.
Winter, Mon–Sat 10–4.
⊠ The Curator
£ ♿ ♿ ♿ ♿

This thatched cottage was the birthplace of Robert Burns. It has been restored to its original appearance, and furnished in the style of the period, with the help of a few items of furniture which belonged to the poet or to his family. A separate museum building has been constructed nearby, to display the large collection of material relating to Burns. These include his duelling pistols, items of furniture, his family Bible, a large number of letters and many of the manuscripts of his songs and poems, including those of Tam O'Shanter and Auld Lang Syne. A recently added section tells the story of Burns's life and achievements, and sets him against the background of his times.

Maclaurin Art Gallery

Rozelle Park, Monument Road, Alloway,
Ayrshire KA7 4NQ   ☎ 0292 43708/45447
Apr–Oct, Mon–Sat 11–5; Sun 2–5. Nov–Mar,
Mon–Sat 11–5. Closed Christmas, New Year.
⊠ Mike Bailey, Curator
F ♿ ♿ ♿ ♿

The Gallery has been established in the converted stables of Rozelle House. Its collection of contemporary art is used as a source of exhibitions which are held both in Rozelle House and in the Gallery. The work of local artists is regularly shown here.

Rozelle House Gallery

Rozelle Park, Monument Road, Alloway,
Ayrshire KA7 4NQ   ☎ 0292 45447/43708
Apr–Oct, Mon–Sat 11–5; Sun 2–5. Closed
Nov–Mar ex. some Sats 2–5.
⊠ Mike Bailey, Curator
F ♿ ♿ ♿ □

Rozelle House dates from 1760, although some additions were made in 1830. It is used for a programme of temporary exhibitions and for longer-term displays based on the collections of Kyle and Carrick District Council. A balance is usually maintained between natural history, local history and historical and contemporary art, in order to provide visitors with a broad range of exhibits at any one time.

On the same premises there is also a military museum, based on the collections of the local regiment, the Ayrshire Yeomanry.

Alnwick

Alnwick Castle Museum

Alnwick Castle, Alnwick, Northumberland
NE66 1NQ   ☎ 0665 602207
May–Sept, daily 1–5 ex. Sat. Open Bank Holiday
Sat.
⊠ The Supervisor, Estates Office
£ ♿ ♿ HHA

The earliest parts of Alnwick Castle date from the 11th century. There were additions in the 14th century – the present owners, the Percy family, acquired the Castle in 1309 – and a major restoration and refurbishment project was carried out by the 4th Duke of Northumberland between 1854 and 1865, when Italian Renaissance-style decorations replaced those created by Robert Adam in the 18th century. The principal apartments of the Castle can be seen by visitors, together with the Armoury, Guard Chamber and Library. The collection of paintings is exceptionally good and includes works by Canaletto, Titian, and Van Dyck.

The Museum in the Postern Tower houses a collection of prehistoric and Roman archaeology, formed by the third and fourth Dukes. There are also displays of Celtic-Irish and Viking material, together with items relating to the history of the Percy family. The most celebrated object on show is the Rudge cup, a Romano-British drinking vessel, with the names of forts along the Roman Wall inscribed around the rim.

Royal Northumberland Fusiliers Regimental Museum

The Abbot's Tower, Alnwick Castle, Alnwick, Northumberland NE66 1NB
☎ *0665 602152 or 0670 818043*
Early May–Sept, daily 1–5 ex. Sat. Other times by appt.
🖾 *T. L. Hewitson, Hon. Curator*
£ ⌀ ⇜

The Museum is in the Abbot's Tower of Alnwick Castle. The Regiment had its origins in the 1670s and the Percy family has been associated with it since 1768. In the ground floor chamber are displayed Colours of battalions in the Regiment and medals awarded to former members, including five Victoria Crosses. The first floor exhibits are devoted to uniforms and equipment in use during the 19th century, with contemporary records, prints and paintings to show how the Regiment was dressed in the 18th century.

The second floor of the Tower takes the history of the Regiment into more modern times. Exhibits illustrate the transition from scarlet uniforms to khaki and include many relics of the First and Second World Wars and subsequent campaigns and the part played by the Regiment. A final display tells the story of St George's Day, 1968, when the Royal Northumberland Fusiliers ceased to exist as such and were embodied in the Royal Regiment of Fusiliers.

Alton

The Allen Gallery

10-12 Church Street, Alton, Hampshire GU34 2BW   ☎ *0420 82802*
Tues–Sat 10–5
🖾 *The Curator*
F ⌀ ⇜

The Allen Gallery consists of a group of 16th and 18th-century buildings which have been considerably altered internally to make them suitable for museum purposes. One gallery contains works by W. H. Allen, a former Principal of Farnham School of Art, including his Studies in Rural Life and Nature. Made in watercolours, pen-and-ink, crayon and pencil, they record various forms of craftsmanship on the land and in the workshop which have been superseded by modern methods.

Six galleries display English ceramics from 1550 to the present day, and silver, including the Tichborne spoons and the Wickham communion set.

Curtis Museum

High Street, Alton, Hampshire GU34 1BA
☎ *0420 82802*
Mon–Sat 10–5
🖾 *The Curator*
F ⌀ ⇜

The Curtis Museum, named after a local doctor, William Curtis, was established in 1854. His

The Royal Northumberland Fusiliers Regimental Museum, Alnwick.

cousin, another William Curtis, was a botanist and a Fellow of the Linnean Society, and a section of the Museum's natural history gallery is devoted to him. Other displays are concerned with archaeology, and with social and industrial history, especially brewing, for which Alton has long been celebrated. The Museum has a considerable collection of the tools used by craftsmen and farm workers, during the days when most jobs were carried out by hand.

Recent modifications to the building have increased the space available for displays. The section devoted to dolls, toys and games has been revived and there is an aquarium designed especially to interest children. The extensions have also provided an opportunity to show recently discovered items, such as material from the Roman cemetery, found in the High Street a few years ago.

Altrincham

Dunham Massey

Altrincham, Cheshire WA14 4SJ ☎ *061 941 1025*
Apr–Oct, daily ex. Fri (including Good Fri).
Garden, restaurant, shop 12–5.30 (Sat, Sun, Bank Holiday Mon 11–5.30). House 1–5 (Sat, Sun, Bank Holiday Mon 12–5). Last admissions 4.30.
🖾 *P. A. F. Veitch, Administrator*
£ ♿ ⬛ ⇜ NT

In the early 18th century, a Georgian house was built around an earlier one at Dunham Massey and additions were made at the beginning of the 20th century. Until 1976 it was the home of the 10th and last Earl of Stamford and now belongs to the National Trust. More than 30 rooms are open to visitors. They contain fine collections of paintings, furniture and Huguenot silver. There is also a good library.

The estate kitchen, laundry and stables are on view, and so is a Jacobean watermill, converted to a sawmill in Victorian times, and in working order. The 250-acre park, which preserves the 18th-century formal design, is celebrated for its herd of fallow deer.

Alum Bay

Museum of Clocks

Alum Bay, Isle of Wight PO39 0JB
☎ *0983 754193*
Good Fri–Sept, daily 10–5 ex. Sat
⊠ *Mr R. Tayler*
£ ♿ ♨

The Museum, formed in 1982 from private collections, contains over 200 working clocks from all parts of the world. Among the more unusual exhibits is a Chinese fire dragon boat clock, a primitive form of alarm clock. The incense stick was lit at one end and as it burned metal balls fell into the boat, making a clatter which woke the sleeper up. There is also a Black Forest trumpeter clock, in which, on the hour, a soldier comes forward through a pair of doors to play a tune; an English 12-tune bracket clock; and an early electric dial clock, which goes for 800 days on a 1½ volt battery. Most of the clocks on show, however, are fine examples of more conventional types.

Alyth

Alyth Folk Museum

Commercial Street, Alyth, Perthshire
May–Sept, Tues–Sat 1 5
⊠ *The Curator, Perth Museum and Art Gallery,*
78 George Street, Perth PH1 5LB
☎ *0738 32488*
£ ♨

The Museum was established in the early 1970s by a group of local people, who ran it until 1977 as an entirely voluntary concern, getting the collections together and carrying out all the everyday tasks on an unpaid basis. Since then, it has been organised as a branch museum of the Museum and Art Gallery in Perth, but carrying

out the same policy of providing a centre which would preserve evidence of life and work in the area during the 19th and early 20th centuries and display it to the public. The collections include domestic equipment, agricultural implements and craftsmen's tools, shown against a background of the history of Alyth. Of special interest is a collection of engineer's tools used by David Lowe, one of the early bicycle makers in the area.

Amberley

Amberley Chalk Pits Museum

Amberley, nr Arundel, West Sussex BN18 9LT
☎ *079 881 370*
Apr–Nov 1, Wed–Sun, Bank Holiday Mon 10–6
⊠ *Howard Stenning, Education Officer*
£ ♿ ⊞ ♨ ♿

This is an open-air museum of regional industry on a 36-acre site. It has been established in the quarry of a former lime-works, which operated from the 1840s to the 1960s. Many of the original quarry buildings have been restored and now form part of the museum. They include the office and kiln blocks, the locomotive sheds and the blacksmith's and bag-mender's shops. Among the buildings which have been brought to the museum site and re-erected are a tanyard and a brickyard drying shed, a toll-house, a stationary engine house and a locomotive shed.

There are special displays relating to water-pumping, road-building, concrete, pottery, radio and printing. A number of one-day events take place each year: a programme is available on request. The transport section is particularly strong in steam and diesel road-rollers, and there is an important industrial narrow-gauge railway collection. The car and coach park was once the goods yard of Amberley railway station.

Ambleside

Rydal Mount

Ambleside, Cumbria LA22 9LU ☎ *09663 3002*
Mar–Oct, daily 10–5. Nov–Feb, daily 10 4
ex. Tues.
⊠ *The Curator*
£ ♿ ♨ [HHA]

William and Mary Wordsworth moved to Rydal Mount in 1813 and remained there until they died, William having been appointed Distributor of Stamps in the County of Westmorland, a position which freed him from financial worries.

The house, which contains Wordsworth family portraits and furniture and some of the poet's personal possessions, is now owned by his great-great-granddaughter, Mary Wordsworth-Henderson, and is maintained as a family home. The four and a half acres of semi-formal garden, which was laid out by William Wordsworth himself, has been described as one of the most interesting small gardens in England.

Road steam-engine, Amberley Chalk Pits Museum.

Andover

Andover Museum

6 Church Close, Andover, Hampshire SP10 1DP
☎ 0264 66283
Tues–Sat 10–5
Ⓚ The Curator
Ⓔ ✎ ♿ ☐

The Museum's Georgian building was formerly Andover Grammar School. There are three galleries on the ground floor. One shows the flora and fauna of the district, with an aquarium containing fish which can be found in the Test Valley, and another is devoted to the history of Taskers of Andover, an engineering firm which specialised in making agricultural machinery and implements. Some of the items in this section are drawn from the historical collection formed by Taskers, which now belongs to the Museum. The third gallery is reserved for recent additions to the Museum's collections.

The second floor has galleries which illustrate the geology and archaeology of the area. The archaeology galleries pay particular attention to the finds from the nearby Danebury hill-fort. This floor also has a large temporary exhibition gallery. The exhibits here are changed monthly, so that regular visitors to the Museum can be sure of having something new to see.

The Museum of the Iron Age

6 Church Close, Andover, Hampshire SP10 1DP
☎ 0264 66283
Tues–Sat 10–5
Ⓚ The Curator
Ⓔ ♿

The Iron Age hillfort of Danebury Ring, west of Stockbridge in Hampshire, has been excavated for 16 years by Professor Barry Cunliffe. Covering an area of two acres and protected by ditches and earth banks, Danebury controlled a large territory. It contained streets of buildings and had facilities for storing great quantities of grain.

A museum to display and explain the finds from the excavations opened in September 1986 as part of the Andover Museum. It is concerned chiefly with Danebury, but also serves to tell the story of southern Britain in the Iron Age.

Annaghmore

Ardress House and Farmyard

64 Ardress Road, Annaghmore, Portadown,
    Co. Armagh, Northern Ireland BT12 1SQ
☎ 0762 851236
Apr–Sept, daily 2–6 ex. Fri. Open Good Fri.
Ⓚ The Administrator
Ⓔ ♿ NT

The farmyard, built in the 19th century, is attached to a much earlier farmhouse. The whole complex belongs to the National Trust. In the yard there is a display of horse-drawn agricultural machinery, all from Armagh and in working order. Farm livestock typical of the area are also exhibited.

The main front and the garden façades of Ardress House were added in the 18th century by the architect, George Ensor, who was also the owner of the house. The plasterwork in the drawing room is of exceptional quality.

The eighteenth-century façade of Ardress House, Annaghmore, was designed by its owner, the architect George Ensor.

Anstruther

The Scottish Fisheries Museum

St Ayles, Harbourhead, Anstruther,
*   Fife KY10 3AB*   ☎ 0333 310628
Apr–Oct, Mon–Sat 10–5.30; Sun 2–5. Nov–Mar,
*   daily 2–5 ex. Tues. Closed Dec 25.*
Ⓜ *The Curator*
Ⓔ ♠ 💺 ⌖

The Museum is housed in a group of 16th to
19th-century buildings grouped around a
cobbled courtyard where, in the past, a
community of fishermen, coopers and brewers
carried on their work. The displays cover nearly
every aspect of the fishing industry, including
whaling and industrial salmon fishing, as well as
the ancillary trades. Among the larger exhibits
are reproductions of the interior of a fisherman's
home as it would have looked c. 1900 and of the
wheelhouse of a fishing boat. There are
excellent collections of model boats,
photographs and equipment, and visitors can
see actual vessels in the courtyard and in the
adjacent harbour. A marine aquarium contains
fish and shellfish found in Scottish waters.

One room is kept as a memorial to fishermen
and lifeboatmen lost at sea and other displays
relate to the superstitions and beliefs of the
Scottish fishing communities, such as never
turning a boat in harbour against the sun, and to
the words, such as pig, rat, minister, and
salmon, which fishermen were forbidden to say.
There is also a section devoted to fisher wedding
customs.

Antrim

Shanes Castle Railway

Shanes Castle, Antrim, Co. Antrim, Northern
*   Ireland BT41 4NE*   ☎ 084941 62216
Apr–May, Sun 12–6. June, Wed, Sat, Sun 12–6.
*   July–Aug, Tues–Thurs, Sat, Sun 12–6.*
*   Sept, Sun 12–6. Bank Holiday 12–6.*
Ⓜ *A. Bell*
Ⓔ ♠ 💺 ⌖

This is perhaps best described as a working
railway museum. It has a specially constructed
one and a half-mile tourist line, using narrow-
gauge industrial rolling stock adapted for the
purpose. The intention is to provide something
of the atmosphere of the old Irish roadside
railways, such as the Clougher Valley and the
Cavan and Leitrim. The line is operated by a
range of steam and diesel engines, which once
served in various forms of industry and which
have been restored and painted in authentic
period liveries. The usual passenger rolling stock
is a set of converted peat wagons and, in
addition, three Belgian tramcars from Charleroi
are used in wet weather and the winter. A
number of Irish narrow-gauge railway items are
also put into service from time to time.

Appin

Appin Wildlife Museum

Appin Home Farm, Appin, Argyll PA38 4BN
*   ☎ 063173 308*
Daily 10–5
Ⓜ *J. Scorgie*
Ⓕ ♠ ⌖

This small museum has unusual and possibly
unique origins. Its founder spent 22 years as a
Glencoe Forest Ranger and during that period
he formed a comprehensive collection of
mounted specimens of local wildlife. This is now
presented as an introduction to the natural
history of the region.

Appledore

North Devon Maritime Museum

Odun House, Odun Road, Appledore,
*   Devon EX39 1PT*   ☎ 02372 74852
Easter–Sept, Tues–Fri 11–1, daily 2–5.30
Ⓜ *Mrs P. M. Wiggett, Hon. Secretary*
Ⓔ 🅰 ⌖

North Devon has a long and interesting
maritime history, of which the Museum
provides a full picture. There are scale models of
ships using North Devon ports from the 17th
century onwards, together with paintings of
ships and maritime scenes, and old photographs
of the district and its people. The former
important trade with Prince Edward Island
receives attention, as does the story of local
lifeboats, wrecks and smuggling. Exhibits deal
with the industries of North Devon, including
shipbuilding, and scale models illustrate the
working of a shipyard, sail-loft and rope-works.
A special display presents the history and
techniques of the different types of fishing
traditionally carried out by boats from the area.

Shanes Castle Railway, Antrim.

Arborfield

The REME Museum

Isaac Newton Road, Arborfield, Reading, Berkshire RG2 9LN
☎ *0734 760421 extn 218*
Mon–Thurs 9.30–12.30, 2–4.30; Fri 9.30–12.30, 2–4. Closed public holidays and weekends, ex. by appt.
The Deputy Curator
F

REME, the Corps of Royal Electrical and Mechanical Engineers, was formed in 1942, with the tasks of maintaining and repairing nearly all military equipment and of advising on its design. In 1958 a Museum was established to preserve what could be rescued to illustrate REME's early history and that of its main ancestor, the engineering branch of the RAOC. The main Museum, now in a new building, tells the story of the development of the Corps by means of a collection of smaller exhibits, photographs, models and documents, while the vehicles, small arms, radar and engineering equipment are kept at the three relevant REME training establishments.

Arbroath

Abbot's House

Arbroath Abbey, Arbroath, Angus DD11 1EG
Apr–Sept, Mon–Sat 9.30–12.30, 1.30–7; Sun 2–7. Oct–Mar, Mon–Sat, 9.30–12.30, 1.30–4; Sun 2–4.
Historic Buildings & Monuments, Edinburgh
☎ *031 5568 400*
£

Arbroath Abbey, a Tironensian monastery, was founded in 1178. The museum is built over an undercroft, which was used as the Abbot's kitchen, and dates from the 12th century. It illustrates the history of both the town and the Abbey of Arbroath. The items on display include effigies carved in wood and stone, and fragments of oak panelling from the Abbot's House itself. Among the wide range of other exhibits are examples of jewellery, Delftware, snuff mills and the traditional Scottish wooden drinking vessels, known as quaichs.

Arbroath Art Gallery

Public Library, Hill Terrace, Arbroath, Angus DD11 1AH ☎ *0241 72248*
Mon–Fri 9.30–6; Sat 9.30–5
District Curator, Montrose Museum and Art Gallery, Panmure Place, Montrose, Angus DD10 8HE ☎ *0674 73232*
F

The Library building, in which the Gallery is situated, is a fine red sandstone building, dating from 1898. It has a sculpted portrait of Queen Victoria set in an alcove above the doorway and, in the grounds, a statue of Robert Burns. The collection consists mainly of watercolours, pastels and oil paintings by local artists, but also includes two paintings, dated 1618, by Pieter Breughel the Younger.

Arbroath Museum

Signal Tower, Ladyloan, Arbroath, Angus DD11 1PU ☎ *0241 75598*
Apr–Oct, Mon–Sat 10.30–1, 2–5. July–Aug also Sun 2–5. Nov–Mar, Mon–Fri 2–5; Sat 10.30–1, 2–5.
See Arbroath Art Gallery
F

The Signal Tower, which houses the Museum, forms part of the Bell Rock Lighthouse complex, and provided living quarters for the lighthouse keepers until the 1950s. The Lighthouse itself was designed by Robert Stephenson and completed in 1813.

The collections are concerned with local archaeology and history and with the wildlife of Arbroath Cliffs. The geology of the district is illustrated by means of exhibits on the quarrying industry. Other industries which have their place in the Museum are lawnmowers, and the production of flax and linen. There are good collections of fishing items, of 19th-century domestic equipment and of material relating to the construction and history of the Bell Rock Lighthouse, whose original fog bell is preserved in the Museum.

St Vigeans Sculptured Stones

St Vigeans, Arbroath, Angus
At all times
Historic Buildings & Monuments, Edinburgh
☎ *031 5568 400*
F

The village of St Vigeans is one and a half miles north of Arbroath. The museum site contains an important collection of 32 early Christian Pictish carved stones.

Sir John Nicholson by J. R. Dickser. Armagh County Museum.

Arklow

Arklow Maritime Museum

St Mary's Road, Arklow, Co. Wicklow, Ireland
June–Sept, daily 10–5
Ⓜ *The Chairman*
Ⓔ *adults only* ♿

The Museum tells the story of Arklow's maritime past. In the days of sail, schooners from Arklow voyaged to every part of Europe and to North and South America. In 1865, at the peak of the trade, there were 168 Arklow-owned ships. The ships are illustrated by paintings and models, and other items on display include sections of the first and second transatlantic cable, laid by the *Great Eastern*, which was under the command of Captain Halpin, born near Arklow.

The firm of John Tyrrell and Sons has been building boats in Arklow for 130 years, and the Museum holds many of its models and drawings.

Arlington

Arlington Court

Arlington, nr Barnstaple, Devon EX31 4LP
    ☎ 027182 296
April or Good Friday–Oct, Sun–Fri & Bank
    Holiday Sat 11–6 (last admission 5.30).
    Gardens & Park, daily 11–6.
Ⓜ *The Administrator*
Ⓔ ♨ 🚍 ♿ & NT

The Chichesters had been at Arlington for four centuries when the present house was built in 1822. It was left to the National Trust by Miss Rosalie Chichester, the last of her line, at her death in 1949, at the age of 84. There are 18th and 19th-century furnishings and paintings, including a watercolour by William Blake, but the essential charm and character of the house is provided by the large and very varied collections accumulated by Miss Chichester during her long life. They include sea shells, exotic birds and butterflies, scale-model sailing ships and yachts, fans, vinaigrettes, snuff boxes, Bilston enamels and a great range of family treasures.

Armagh

Armagh County Museum

The Mall East, Armagh, Co. Armagh, Northern
    Ireland BT61 9BE   ☎ 0861 523070
Mon–Sat 10–1, 2–5. Closed some public holidays.
Ⓜ *The Curator*
Ⓕ ✐ ♿

The collections in the Museum relate to the natural history, archaeology and history of the County of Armagh and the surrounding area. They include prehistoric weapons and implements, historical relics of the City and County, uniforms and equipment of the Irish Volunteer, Yeomanry and Militia regiments, and 18th and 19th-century costumes,

needlework and lace. Among the other more important collections are those of domestic equipment, blacksmith-made tools and fittings, wooden utensils, and straw and rushwork. The natural history gallery has displays dealing with the geology, wildlife and economic history of the region.

The Art Gallery has a number of portraits of local worthies, works by contemporary Irish artists, especially George Russell (AE) of Lurgan and James Sleator of Armagh, as well as pictures of topographical and historical interest.

Royal Irish Fusiliers Museum

Sovereign's House, The Mall, Armagh, Co.
    Armagh, Northern Ireland BT61 9DL
        ☎ 0861 522911
Mon–Fri 10–12.30, 2–4.30. Closed Bank
    Holiday.
Ⓜ *The Curator*
Ⓔ

The collections in the Museum illustrate the history of the Royal Irish Fusiliers, the 87th and 89th Regiment of Foot, and the Armagh, Cavan and Monaghan Militia. The displays include uniforms, badges, documents and equipment, mainly relating to the organisation and activities of the Regiments and the Militia during the 19th century and early 20th century.

Arnol

Blackhouse, Arnol

42 Arnol, Bragar, Isle of Lewis PA86 9DB
Jan 3–Mar & Oct–Dec, Mon–Sat 9.30–4.
    Apr–Sept, Mon Sat 9.30–7.
Ⓜ *Historic Buildings & Monuments, Edinburgh*
        ☎ 031 5568 400
Ⓔ ▮

Blackhouse is in Arnol village. It is a traditional Lewis thatched farmhouse, with its attached barn, byre and stackyard. The house has appropriate furniture and domestic equipment and the outbuildings are equipped as they would have been in their working days.

Arundel

Arundel Museum and Heritage Centre

61 High Street, Arundel, West Sussex
        ☎ 0903 882726
Late May–early Sept, Tues–Sat 10.30–12.30,
    2–5; Sun 2–5. Sept–Oct, Sat 10.30–12.30,
    2–5; Sun 2–5. Open Easter, Bank Holiday.
Ⓜ *The Curator*
Ⓔ ▮ ♿

The Museum is a fine Georgian house near the Castle, in the centre of Arundel. It contains a range of materials relating to the history of the town, castle and former port of Arundel. The collection of old scales and weights and measures is particularly noteworthy.

Arundel Toy Museum

23 High Street, Arundel, West Sussex BN18 9AD
☎ 0903 883101/882908
*Weekends throughout year, 10.30–5. Midwinter
weekends, 2–5. June–Aug, daily 10.30–5.
Open Bank and school holidays. Other times
by appt.*
Mrs Diana Henderson
£ ✎ ☎ □

Housed in a listed cottage, built *c.* 1800, the
Toy Museum is a family collection, assembled
over several generations. The exhibits cover a
wide field, from Noah's arks and animals to
small militaria, and from tin toys to crested
china models. There are toy soldiers, dolls and
dolls'-houses, farm and circus animals, and a
wide range of games. Special exhibitions on
particular subjects are arranged during the spring
and summer.

Ashburton

Ashburton Museum

1 West Street, Ashburton, Devon TQ13 7DT
☎ 0364 53278
Late May–Sept, Tues, Thurs, Fri, Sat 2.30–5
K. J. Watson, Hon. Curator
F ☎

The Museum building, which is within the
town's Conservation Area, had been a draper's
shop and then a barber's until it was acquired for
museum purposes in 1967. During the work of
converting the building to a museum, evidence
was discovered that the attic had been used as
sleeping quarters for apprentices. The emphasis
of the collection is on the history of Ashburton,
and among the exhibits in this section are
examples of locally made pewter, old farm
implements, and 19th-century broadsheets.
There are also geological specimens from the
locality and, as a somewhat unlikely exhibit,
an excellent collection of American Indian
artefacts, given by an American whose father
was born and went to school in Ashburton.

Ashby-de-la-Zouch

Ashby-de-la-Zouch Museum

13–15 Lower Church Street, Ashby-de-la-Zouch,
     Leicestershire   ☎ 0530 415603
*Easter–Sept, Mon–Fri 10–12, 2–4; Sat 10–5,
Sun 2–5*
Mr K. A. Hillier, Greenmantle, Ingles Hill,
     Ashby-de-la-Zouch
£ ✎ ☎ □

Two 18th-century cottages have been converted
for museum purposes. Upstairs, a display
illustrates the history of Ashby and the
reconstruction of a small shop of the 1920s.
Downstairs, together with the Tourist
Information Centre, is a second exhibition area
for temporary exhibitions, six of which are
organised each year on themes of local interest.
A collection of archival material relating to the
area is being developed.

Ashford

Ashford Local History Museum

Ashford Central Library, Church Road, Ashford,
     Kent   ☎ 0233 20649
*Mon, Tues 9.30–6; Wed 9.30–5; Thurs, Fri
9.30–7; Sat 9.30–5. Closed Bank Holiday.*
Miss Mary Winsch, Kent County Museum
     Service, West Malling, Kent ME19 6QE
     ☎ 0732 845845 extn 2129
F ☎

This new museum, opened in 1980, aims to
illustrate the changing history of Ashford and
the surrounding area, with exhibits reflecting
the social and domestic life of the past 150
years, and the occupations carried on in the
district. The collections are being steadily built
up by asking local people to donate items which
relate to three broad topics. These are: life in
the house – cooking, laundering, cleaning,
clothing, toilet articles, children's toys and
games; life at work – local businesses, craft and
trade tools, transport; buildings – building
materials, fittings, signs and notices.

The Intelligence Corps Museum

Templer Barracks, Ashford, Kent TN23 3HH
     ☎ 0233 25251 extn 208
Mon–Fri 10–12, 2–4. Closed public holidays.
The Curator
F ● ☎

British military intelligence is considerably older
than the Intelligence Corps. The Museum tells
the story of both, from the reign of Queen
Elizabeth I to Queen Elizabeth II. The main
emphasis is on the work of the Corps during the
two World Wars and subsequent campaigns, but
earlier periods receive a good deal of attention.
There are, for example, exhibits showing the
work of military intelligence during the Boer
War and the Crimean War. The achievements
of individual intelligence officers are given
prominence in the Museum.

Ashwell

Ashwell Village Museum

Swan Street, Ashwell, Baldock, Hertfordshire
Sun, Bank Holiday 2.30–5
 The Booking Secretary

The building which the Museum has occupied since 1930 is a restored early 16th-century timber-framed house, formerly owned by Westminster Abbey and later by St John's College, Cambridge. Its original purpose was probably the collection of rents and tithes. An extension was built in 1983.

The exhibits consist of everyday objects used in the village and surrounding countryside from pre-Roman times to the present day. What is now a considerable body of historical material has been developed from the collection made by two schoolboys in the 1920s.

Ashwell Village Museum, a two-bay gabled house of the sixteenth century.

Aston Munslow

The White House Museum of Buildings and Country Life

Aston Munslow, nr Craven Arms,
*   Shropshire SY7 9ER*
Easter Sat–Oct, Wed, Sat 11–5. Early July–early
*   Sept, also Thurs 11–5. For Bank Holiday,*
*   check locally.*
 The Resident Director

The homestead on the site of the Saxon manor of *Estune* was the home of the Stedman family from 1332 until 1946 and is still in use as a family dwelling, making it an exceptionally valuable museum of domestic architecture. Rooms have been furnished and equipped for their purpose by continuous habitation, not as a series of period pieces.

Each of the secondary buildings has had its own clearly defined purpose. Visitors can see the 13th-century dovecot; the dairies; the kitchen; the washhouse; the cider house, complete with mill and press; the 16th-century stable block, which began its life as a house; the 17th-century coach house, and the granary, complete with its machinery for milling and dressing corn.

Athlone

Athlone Castle Museum

The Castle, Athlone, Co. Westmeath, Ireland
June–Sept, Mon–Sat 11.30–1, 3–6
 The Curator

There has been a castle at Athlone since 1129, but Athlone Castle as it exists today is largely an 18th to 19th-century reconstruction of a 13th-century building. The Museum is housed in the Keep, with displays consisting mainly of antiquities and material illustrating traditional rural life in the Athlone area. The most notable items are a collection of very fine early Christian grave slabs and memorabilia of the famous tenor, John McCormack, who was born in Athlone.

Auchinleck

The Auchinleck Boswell Museum and Mausoleum

Church Hill, Auchinleck, Ayrshire
  0290 20757/26529
Easter–Oct by appt
 Mr Gordon P. Hoyle (Hon. Curator),
*   131 Main Street, Auchinleck KA18 2AF*

Auchinleck is best known for its associations with James Boswell, the biographer of Dr Johnson, and the Old Church has now been restored by the Boswell Society and converted into a museum of the Boswell family, several members of which are buried in a mausoleum adjoining the Church. The Museum, opened in 1978, contains many items associated with James Boswell and his family. Among them is a set of Canton china with the Boswell crest, brought from China in 1755 by Captain Bruce Boswell, who was employed by the East India Company; silver cutlery, also with the Boswell crest; and a cabinet which was once part of the furnishings of James Boswell's London home. There are Boswell family portraits and a bronze bust of James Boswell, whose burial plaque is also here.

A special section of the Museum is devoted to William Murdoch, the pioneer of lighting and heating by gas, who was baptised in the Old Church. There are also examples of Cumnock pottery, which became famous during the 19th century for the mottos which decorated it and, later, for bearing the name and address of the purchaser.

Miles M14A Magister at Strathallan Aircraft Museum, Auchterarder.

Auchterarder

Strathallan Aircraft Museum

Strathallan Airfield, nr Auchterarder, Perthshire PH3 1LA ☎ *076 46 2545*
Apr–Oct, daily 10–6. Nov–Mar by appt.
R. E. Richardson, Curator

This is a collection of historic, mostly military, aircraft, some of them restored to flying condition. Among those on display are a Lancaster, Swordfish, Fairey Battle, Bolingbroke and Shackleton, and the original Rolls-Royce Flying Bedstead. A de Havilland Comet airliner is open to visitors. The Museum also has a collection of aero engines dating from 1916, an armament exhibit and a number of items of 'nostalgic interest', including a replica of a living-room of the Second World War period.

Auckengill

John Nicholson Museum

Auckengill, Caithness KW1 4XP
June–Aug, Mon–Sat 10–12, 2–4. Other times by appt.
The Curator, Caithness District Council, Bruce Building, Sinclair Terrace, Wick, Caithness KW1 5AB ☎ *0955 3761 extn 274*

The Museum is in the former village school. It reflects the archaeological history of Caithness and the life and work of John Nicholson, a local antiquarian. The displays have three themes – John Nicholson, the man, the general archaeology of Caithness, and Iron Age brochs, of which Caithness has more than any other county. One can be seen half a mile from the Museum. A broch is a circular dry-stone tower, up to 40 feet high when newly built.

Aughrim

St Catherine's National School Museum

Aughrim, Ballinasloe, Co. Galway, Ireland ☎ *0905 73717*
By appt
Martin J. Joyce

Aughrim, a small village off the main road from Ballinasloe to Galway, takes its name from a nearby ridge which, in 1691, was the scene of the battle which decided the Jacobite-Williamite war and considerably influenced the subsequent course of Irish history. The Museum is on the site of the battlefield and displays bullets, cannonballs and other relics of the battle. The collections also include Stone Age and Bronze Age archaeological material, different types of quern, and 19th-century domestic equipment.

Augrès

Sir Francis Cook Gallery

Route de la Trinité, Augrès, Jersey, Channel Islands ☎ *0534 63333*
Open as advertised locally
Education Officer

The Gallery is in a former Methodist chapel and schoolroom, converted by Sir Francis Cook to its present purpose. It has a collection of 1,300 paintings by Sir Francis, of which a small selection is permanently displayed.

Avebury

Alexander Keiller Museum

Avebury, nr Marlborough, Wiltshire SN8 1RF ☎ *06723 250*
Summer, daily 9.30–6.30. Winter, Mon–Sat 9.30–4; Sun 2–4. Closed Jan 1, Dec 24–26.
Historic Buildings & Monuments Commission, Bristol ☎ *0272 734472*
NT

The Museum building is a listed 17th-century coach-house of local stone. It houses Neolithic finds from sites in southern Britain which were mostly excavated by Keiller in the 1920s and 1930s – Avebury, Windmill Hill, West Kennet Long Barrow and Silbury Hill. The displays explain the nature of the sites and illustrate the archaeological material. Special attention is devoted to the history of Avebury and to the excavations carried out there, with photographs, artefacts and reconstructions.

Great Barn Museum of Wiltshire Folk Life

Avebury, nr Marlborough, Wiltshire SN8 1RF
☎ 06723 555
4th week in Mar–Oct, daily 10–5.30. Nov–3rd
week in Mar, weekends only, 1–4.30. Closed
Boxing Day–end of 1st week in Jan. Other
times by appt.
🛪 *The Education Officer*
ⓔ 🕿 ♿ *disabled only*

The thatched Great Barn, 145 feet long and
37 feet wide, was built *c.* 1690. It was used
mainly for storing and threshing corn and during
the summer, when it was almost empty, it may
also have provided covered space for the annual
sheep shearing. In the 1970s it was restored by
the Wiltshire Folk Life Society, to become the
centre of its activities.

The Barn, with its magnificent roof structure,
is the oldest and largest of the Museum exhibits.
The displays inside are devoted to the rural life
and agriculture of Wiltshire during the 19th
century. They include reconstructions of a
blacksmith's forge, wheelwright's shop, saddler's
and cooper's workshops. Other sections deal
with thatching, sheep and shepherding, and
farm implements and equipment. All the
exhibits are open and visitors are allowed to
come into close contact with them.

There is a regular programme of craft
demonstrations and performances of folk
dancing.

Axbridge

King John's Hunting Lodge

The Square, Axbridge, Somerset BS26 2AP
☎ 0934 732012
Mar 28–Sept, daily 2–5
🛪 *The Administrator*
ⓕ 🕿 ♿ ⓝⓣ

Axbridge began as a Saxon market centre and
during the Middle Ages prospered from wool
and cloth. The timber-framed building, now
known as King John's Hunting Lodge, was in
fact a merchant's house built *c.* 1500, nearly 300
years after King John's death. It had shops on
the ground floor, living accommodation above
and bedrooms on the top floor. The National

Trust, its present owners, have put it into good
condition again and restored its medieval
appearance.

The museum collections now installed
illustrate the archaeology and history of
Axbridge. The medieval wool and cloth trade is
strongly featured, together with the domestic
and social life of the period. There are also
many items relating to the government of the
town by its Mayor and Corporation.

Axminster

Axminster Museum

The Old Court House, Church Street, Axminster,
Devon
☎ 0297 24386 *(Tourist Information Centre)*
Easter–Sept, Mon, Tues, Fri 10–4; Sat 10–1
🛪 *Mr William Dobson, Hon. Curator. When the*
Museum is closed, at 43 Brunenburg Way,
Axminster EX13 5RD   ☎ 0297 32844
ⓕ ♿

The Museum is housed on the first floor of an
attractive building constructed in 1864 as a
Magistrates' Court and Police Station, with the
main displays in the former Court Room. The
Victorian police cells are also open for
inspection.

The exhibits are concerned with the history
of the market town of Axminster through the
centuries. They include flint tools and weapons,
Roman tiles, 13th and 16th-century floor tiles
from Newenham Abbey, a Cistercian house,
and relics of the Civil War and Monmouth's
Rebellion. There is a collection of photographs
illustrating the development of trade and
industry in the area during the 19th and 20th
centuries and, for the town's most celebrated
industry, a special display showing the various
processes involved in the manufacture of
Axminster carpets, with examples of early and
recent carpets made in the town. There is also a
growing collection of agricultural implements.

Aylesbury

Buckinghamshire County Museum

Church Street, Aylesbury, Buckinghamshire
HP20 2QP   ☎ 0296 82158/88849
Mon–Fri 10–5; Sat 10–12.30, 1.30–5. Closed
Sun, Jan 1, Good Fri, Dec 25–26.
🛪 *Mr George Lamb, Keeper of Education and*
Extension Services
ⓕ 🕿

A wide range of collections, covering many
aspects of Buckinghamshire, are displayed in an
interesting group of 18th-century buildings in
the centre of Aylesbury. Natural history exhibits
illustrate the different habitats to be found in

**The massive sarsen boulders of the Avebury
Stone Circle, a 4,000 year old temple
excavated by Alexander Keiller in 1934–9.**

the County and the geological collections show the underlying rocks and fossils. Good archaeological collections include a Celtic bronze mirror from Dorton and the finds from the Roman villa at Hambleden. Man's later activities in the area are shown by the Rural Life Gallery, which emphasises the importance of agriculture in the past.

Other notable collections are those of costumes and textiles, modern British studio pottery, and topographical prints and pictures.

Florence Nightingale Museum

Claydon House, Middle Claydon, nr Aylesbury, Buckinghamshire MK18 2EY
    ☎ 029673 349/693
Mar 29–Oct, Sat–Wed 2–6. Bank Holiday Mon 1–6. Closed Thurs, Fri.
🖾 *The Custodian*
£ 🖳 🚗 NT

Claydon House, formerly the home of the Verney family, now belongs to the National Trust. An 18th-century house, it contains splendid state rooms, with elaborate rococo decorations. Florence Nightingale frequently visited Claydon to stay with her sister, Lady Verney, and the bedroom she used can be seen, with its Victorian furnishings and woodwork grained to resemble bamboo. In the Museum Room one case contains objects associated with her and with the Crimean War, during which she became a celebrated public figure. Photographs taken after her return from Scutari show how thin and frail she had become as a result of the strain of organising the hospital there.

Waddesdon Manor

Waddesdon, nr Aylesbury, Buckinghamshire HP18 0JH   ☎ 0296 651211
Mar, Apr, Oct, Wed–Fri 2–5; Sat and Sun 2–6. May–Sept, Wed–Sun 2–6. Good Fri, Bank Holiday Mon 11–6. Closed Wed after Bank Holiday.
🖾 *The Administrator*
£ ♟ 🖳 🚗 NT

Waddesdon, a French Renaissance château in rural Buckinghamshire, was built between 1874 and 1889 for Baron Ferdinand de Rothschild, of the international banking family. Queen Victoria, King Edward VII and King George V were all entertained here. The three members of the family who successively inherited the estate continued the traditions of hospitality, care for the gardens and enlargement of the art collections. When James de Rothschild died in 1957, he left the property and its contents to the National Trust.

Waddesdon is a splendidly preserved monument to a vanished way of life, a museum of social history. But it is also one of Britain's great art museums, with the collection shown in the setting of a home rather than a gallery. French furniture, carpets and porcelain of the 17th and 18th centuries are particularly well represented, but there are also many fine French, Flemish, Italian and Dutch paintings, portraits by Gainsborough, Reynolds and Romney, and a notable collection of arms and armour.

Aylsham

Blickling Hall

Blickling, nr Aylsham, Norfolk NR11 6NF
    ☎ 0263 733084
Mar 29–Oct 26, daily 1–5 ex. Mon and Thurs. Open Bank Holiday Mon. Closed Good Fri.
🖾 *The Administrator*
£ ♟ 🖳 🚗 ♿ NT

Blickling Hall is on the B1354, one mile north-west of Aylsham, which is on the A140 Cromer to Norwich road. It dates from the time of James I and was built for Sir Henry Hobart, his Chief Justice. The rooms are in late 18th-century styles and include a long gallery with an exceptionally good library. The Orangery, probably designed by Humphry Repton in the late 18th century, has an interesting selection of plants and statuary. The gardens, with noble yew hedges, herbaceous borders and a Doric Temple, are in the grand style.

Ayot St Lawrence

Shaw's Corner

Ayot St Lawrence, Welwyn, Hertfordshire AL6 9BX   ☎ 0438 820307
Mar 30–Oct, Mon–Thurs 2–6; Sun, Bank Holiday Mon 12–6.
🖾 *The Custodian*
£ 📷 🚗 NT

George Bernard Shaw built this modest villa for himself and lived in it from 1906 until his death in 1950. The rooms downstairs, including Shaw's study, have been preserved as they were during Shaw's lifetime, with their furniture and personal possessions intact.

Roof finial from the Railway Hotel, Aylesbury, 1898. Buckinghamshire County Museum.

Ayr

Tam O'Shanter Museum

High Street, Ayr, Ayrshire
Apr–May & Sept, Mon–Sat 9.30–5.30.
June–Aug, Mon–Sat, 9.30–5; Sun 2.30–5.
Oct–Mar, Mon–Sat 12–4.
 The Director, Kyle & Carrick District Library
and Museum Service, Carnegie Library,
12 Main Street, Ayr KA8 8ED
☎ *0292 269794*
Ⓔ ◔ ➴

The Tam O'Shanter Museum occupies the only
thatched building remaining in Ayr, retaining
the atmosphere of a Victorian public house. It
contains a wide range of exhibits associated with
the life and work of Robert Burns.

Aysgarth

Yorkshire Carriage Museum

Aysgarth Falls, Aysgarth, Leyburn, North
*   Yorkshire DL8 3SR*   ☎ *09693 652*
Easter–Oct, Mon–Fri 11–5; Sat, Sun, Bank
*   Holiday 10.30–7. Other times by appt.*
Mr Robin Walker, Curator
Ⓔ ♠ ➴ ➴

This is probably the most comprehensive
collection of both everyday and more lavish
horse-drawn vehicles in Britain today, ranging
from smart town coaches to bread vans,
butchers' carts and milk floats. The collection is
housed in Yore Mill, built as a water-powered
cotton mill in 1784, and includes harness, bits,
liveries and many other articles, some of them
rare, from the coaching and driving age. The
displays are changed occasionally, since only
60 vehicles can be shown at any one time.

  Many of the vehicles in the collection are
used for film and television work, and for private
hire, so they are maintained in good condition
and are regularly seen on the road.

B

Bacup

Bacup Natural History Society and Folk Museum

24 Yorkshire Street, Bacup, Lancashire OL13 9AE
Thurs evening from 7.30. Other times by appt.
 Mr A. Hargreaves, 90 New Lane, Bacup
*   OL13 9RN*   ☎ *0706 876488*
Ⓕ ➴

The Museum is an 18th-century building,
originally the Hare and Hounds inn, which
became a doss house early in the 20th century.
In 1947 it was taken over by the Society and
converted into a museum to house the large
collection formed by members since 1878, when
the Society was founded. The items on display
and in store include minerals, fossils, birds,
insects, domestic equipment, craftsmen's tools
and industrial mementoes. An open-air exhibit
is a 19th-century crushing machine, used for
grinding stone into sand.

Pennine Aviation Museum

Moorlands Park, New Line, Bacup, Lancashire
By appt
 D. Stansfield, School House, Sharneyford,
*   Bacup OL13 9UQ*   ☎ *0706 875967*
Ⓕ ➴

The aim of this developing museum is to
preserve items that illustrate the aviation history
of the north-west of England. At present the
Museum has 'substantial remains' of six aircraft.
They are a de Havilland Vampire T.11, built at
Chester; an Avro Anson T.21, built at Leeds; a
Waxo CG-4A Hadrian glider; a Boulton and
Paul Balliol T.2; and an English Electric
Canberra B.2. There are also collections of

Children's goat cart. Aysgarth, Yorkshire Carriage Museum.

engines, wheels and tyres, propeller blades, instruments and radios.

The Museum specialises in the recovery of items from crash sites. Visits to these sites is a popular activity among the Museum's supporters.

Baginton

The Lunt Roman Fort

Coventry Road, Baginton, nr Coventry, West
    Midlands   ☎ 0203 303567
May 24–Sept 28, daily 12–6 ex. Mon, Thurs.
    Open every day Bank Holiday weeks.
    Educational party visits at other times by appt.
Ⓜ The Bookings Secretary (Lunt Fort), Herbert
    Art Gallery and Museum, Jordan Well,
    Coventry, West Midlands CV1 5RW
    ☎ 0203 25555 extn 2315
Ⓔ ⟨⟩ ⌖ ♿

The 1st-century Roman cavalry fort here has been excavated and is being reconstructed in situ. The work so far carried out includes nearly 100 metres of turf and timber rampart, the two-storey Eastern Gateway, the Gyrus – a training ring for cavalry, so far unparalleled in the Roman Empire – and a timber-built granary. The latter now houses a display illustrating life in the fort, with artefacts discovered on the site and full-sized models of a legionary and a cavalryman of the mid-1st century.

The exhibit as a whole provides an excellent introduction to the character and organisation of the Roman army in Britain.

Bagshot

Royal Army Chaplains' Department Museum

RAChD Centre, Bagshot Park, Bagshot,
    Surrey GU19 5PL   ☎ 0276 71717 extn 45
By appt Mon–Fri 10–4. Closed Bank Holiday and
    Aug.
Ⓜ The Curator
Ⓕ ⟨⟩ ⌖

Bagshot Park, the headquarters of the Royal Army Chaplains' Department, was built in 1875–9 on the instructions of Queen Victoria as a residence for her son, Prince Arthur of Connaught, later the Duke of Connaught, on his marriage. Following the death of the Duke, the house was used for military purposes and since 1946 it has been occupied by the Chaplains' Department, which converted the Trophy and Gun Room into a memorial chapel to Chaplains killed during the Second World War. The Museum, opened in 1968, contains the archives and historical relics of the Department and its Chaplains.

The exhibits include a medal collection, Chaplains' uniforms, field communion sets used by Chaplains since 1900 and an interesting range of prisoner-of-war items. The house contains a number of Royal portraits and paintings of military occasions.

Baildon

Bracken Hall Countryside Centre

Glen Road, Baildon, Shipley, West Yorkshire
    BD17 5EA   ☎ 0274 584140
Easter–Oct, Wed–Sun 11–5. Winter, Sun only.
Ⓜ Wendy Emmett
Ⓕ ⌂ ⌖ ♿

The Centre has been created in order to provide visitors with an introduction to the surrounding countryside. There are living exhibits of local wildlife, kept in mini-habitats which are careful reproductions of natural conditions, displays of aspects of local history and exhibits relating to the wider countryside.

Bakewell

Chatsworth

nr Bakewell, Derbyshire DE4 1PN
    ☎ 024688 2204
Mar 23–Oct 26, daily 11.30–4.30 (grounds
    11.30–5). Farmyard: Mar 23–Sept 21, daily
    10.30–4.30.
Ⓜ The Comptroller
Ⓔ ⌂ ⌖ ♿

Chatsworth as it exists today is mainly the result of a rebuilding programme carried out between 1687 and 1707 by William Cavendish, 1st Duke of Devonshire. The north wing was added a century later by the 6th Duke. Visitors are able to see many of the rooms, including the splendid State Apartments. Chatsworth has exceptionally good collections of 18th and 19th-century furniture, which have been augmented by the contents of Devonshire House and Chiswick House in London.

The Old House Museum

Cunningham Place, Bakewell, Derbyshire
Apr 1 or Good Fri if earlier–Oct, daily 2–5.
    Morning or evening group visits by appt.
Ⓜ Dr E. T. Goodwin, 32 Castle Mount
    Crescent, Bakewell DE4 1AT
    ☎ 062981 3647
Ⓔ ⟨⟩

The Museum is in an early Tudor house, with later extensions. In the late 18th century, Sir Richard Arkwright acquired the house and divided it into tenements for people working at his mill. Although it has now been restored, evidence of the Arkwright conversion still remains.

The displays in the Museum are concerned mainly with the social and domestic life and the traditional occupations of the area. There are farm utensils and equipment, and tools connected with lead mining, saddlery, shoemaking, and the crafts of the wheelwright and blacksmith. Other collections include costumes, lacework and children's toys and games. The reproduction of the Victorian kitchen allows many items to be shown in a setting which gives them added meaning.

Ballater

Balmoral Castle

nr Ballater, Aberdeenshire AB3 5TB
    ☎ *03384 334*
May–July, Mon–Sat 10–5
⚑ *The Administrator*
£ ♿ 💼 🅿 &

Balmoral Castle was the Scottish home of Queen Victoria and is still used by the Royal Family. Only the grounds are open to the public, together with an exhibition in the ballroom, where there are displays of paintings, porcelain, silver and other objets d'art, as well as an exhibition outlining the history of the Castle.

Ballinamore

Ballinamore Local Museum

County Library, Ballinamore, Co. Leitrim, Ireland
    ☎ *078 44012*
Mon–Fri 10–1, 2–5
⚑ *The County Librarian*
F 🅿

The village of Ballinamore, halfway between Killeshandra and Drumshanbo, is close to a number of important archaeological sites. Its small museum is concerned, however, not only with archaeology, but also with the traditional life of the district. It has displays of farm equipment and implements, craftsmen's tools and household utensils, dating mostly from the late 19th and early 20th centuries.

Ballindalloch

Glenfarclas Distillery Museum

Glenfarclas Distillery, Ballindalloch, Banffshire
    AB3 9BD   ☎ *08072 257*
Mon–Fri 9–4.30. July–Sept, also Sat 10–4.
    Closed Dec 25, 26, Jan 1, 2.
⚑ *J. & G. Grant (Retail) Ltd*
F ♿ 🅿

The Distillery is 17 miles from Grantown-on-Spey and 18 miles from Elgin. The Museum is constructed around the equipment of an old illicit still and illustrates the processes involved in making whisky by traditional methods.

Ballyferriter

Dingle Peninsula Heritage Centre

Ballyferriter, Co. Kerry, Ireland   ☎ *066 56100*
June–Sept, daily 10.30–6
⚑ *The Manager*
£ 💼 🅿 &

The village of Ballyferriter is eight miles west of Dingle. The Heritage Centre is the old National School building, which has been modified for the purpose. The displays cover the archaeology, history, geology, traditions, language and literature of the Dingle Peninsula.

Bamburgh

Bamburgh Castle

Bamburgh, Northumberland   ☎ *06684 208*
Apr–June & Sept, daily 1–5. July–Aug, daily 1–6.
    Oct, daily 1–4.30.
⚑ *The Secretary*
£ ♿ 💼 🅿

Bamburgh Castle, the 6th-century residence of the Northumbrian kings, was bought by the 1st Lord Armstrong in the late 19th century. It was restored, extended and provided with Victorian domestic amenities in the 1890s, and is the home of the present Lord Armstrong. The museum contains the Castle collections of weapons and armour, together with items lent by the Tower of London and the John George Joicey Museum in Newcastle.

Grace Darling Museum

Bamburgh, Northumberland NE69 7AE
Apr–May, daily 11–6. June–Aug, daily 11–7.
    Sept–mid Oct, daily 11–6.
⚑ *D. W. N. Calderwood, 109 Main Street,*
    Seahouses NE68 7TS   ☎ *0665 720 037*
F ♿

The *Forfarshire*, a paddle-steamer built for the Hull–Dundee run, was wrecked in a storm off the Northumberland coast on September 7, 1838. The crew were saved by William Darling, the keeper of the Longstone Lighthouse, and his 22-year-old daughter, Grace. The exploit has become legendary and is commemorated by the Museum, which is organised by the Royal National Lifeboat Institution. The collections include the original lifeboat, memorabilia and portraits of the Darling family, paintings of the wreck and the rescue, contemporary Press accounts, photographs and replicas of the medals awarded to William and Grace Darling, and relics of the *Forfarshire*.

Banbury

Banbury Museum

8 Horsefair, Banbury, Oxfordshire OX16 8DF
    ☎ *0295 59855*
Apr–Sept, Mon–Sat 10–5. Oct–Mar, Tues–Sat
    10–4.30. Closed Good Fri, Dec 25.
⚑ *The Curator*
F ♿ 💼 🅿 &

The displays reflect the archaeology, history and social culture of the North Oxfordshire area, known locally as 'Banburyshire'.

Sulgrave Manor

Sulgrave, Banbury, Oxfordshire OX17 2SD
    ☎ *029576 205*
Apr–Sept, Thurs–Tues 10.30–1, 2–5.30.
    Oct–Dec & Feb–Mar, Thurs–Tues 10.30–1,
    2–4.
⚑ *The Resident Director*
£ ♿ 🅿

The Oak Parlour, Sulgrave Manor, Banbury.

This mid 16th-century house was built by Lawrence Washington, an ancestor of George Washington, and lived in by members of the family for 120 years. In 1914, when it was in poor condition, it was bought by a body of British subscribers, carefully restored and furnished by joint British and American effort, and opened to the public in 1921.

Two rooms, known as the Porch Room and the Deed Room, are used as a museum. This contains several portraits of George Washington – others can be seen elsewhere in the house – Washington memorabilia, including his saddlebags, his oak wine and spirit chest, a velvet coat belonging to him and a lock of his hair.

Upton House

nr Banbury, Oxfordshire OX15 6HT
☎ 029587 266
Apr–Sept, Mon–Thurs 2–6. Open Bank Holiday Mon and certain weekends during season. Closed Good Fri.
▉ *The Estate Office*
£ ✐ ➔ NT

The house, seven miles north-west of Banbury on the A422, was built in the 1690s by the son of a wealthy London merchant. Some additions were made during the 18th century and in 1927 it was bought by the 2nd Viscount Bearsted, who remodelled it. There are notable Flemish, Dutch, French, Spanish and English paintings, fine English and Continental porcelain, especially Sèvres, 18th-century furniture and Brussels tapestries.

Banchory

Banchory Museum

The Square, Banchory, Kincardineshire
June–Sept, daily 2–5.15 ex. Thurs
▉ *The Museums Curator, Arbuthnot Museum, St Peter Street, Peterhead AB4 6QD*
☎ 0779 77778
F ✐ ➔

The Museum's collections are concerned entirely with the history of the Banchory area. The emphasis is on social and domestic life and on craftsmen's skills. A section of the Museum is devoted to the life and work of the local musician, Scott Skinner, known as 'the Strathspey King'.

Crathes Castle

Banchory, Kincardineshire AB3 3QJ
☎ 033044 525
Easter weekend, then May–Sept, daily 11–6. Garden and grounds open all the year, 9.30–sunset.
▉ *Jeffrey Boughey*
E ✿ ➤ ➔ ⅋ NTS

Crathes Castle, a 16th-century tower house, is three miles east of Banchory, on the A93. The estate was given to the Burnetts by King Robert the Bruce in 1323 and the family lived in the present Castle until 1951, when it was given to the National Trust for Scotland. Among the particularly interesting features are the late 16th-century tempera painted ceilings. There are a number of tapestries and interesting needlework by members of the family. The Horn of Leys, which is on display in the Great Hall, is reputed to have been presented to the Burnetts by Robert the Bruce as a symbol of his gift of the estate to them.

Banff

Banff Museum

High Street, Banff, Banffshire
☎ 0779 77778 (*Arbuthnot Museum*)
June–Sept, daily 2–5.15 ex. Thurs
▉ *See Banchory Museum*
F ✐ ➔

The displays in the Museum illustrate the natural history of the district, together with its social and political history. There are special exhibits relating to two of Banff's most distinguished natives, James Ferguson, the astronomer, and Thomas Edward, the naturalist.

Visitors to the Museum should not miss the stained glass Art Nouveau window on the stairs, a somewhat unexpected feature here.

Bangor

Museum of Welsh Antiquities and Bangor Art Gallery

Old Canonry, Ffordd Gwynedd, Bangor, Gwynedd LL57 1DT
☎ 0248 351151 extn 437 (*Museum*) or 0248 353368 (*Gallery*)
Tues–Sat 12–4.30. Closed Bank Holiday, Christmas and Easter weeks.
▉ *The Curator*
F ✐ ➔ □

The Museum and Gallery are in a mid-Victorian Gothic house. The Art Gallery, on the ground floor, presents a programme of temporary exhibitions, with the aim of showing as wide a range of paintings and sculpture as possible. The Museum is mostly concerned with exhibits from North Wales. It has good collections of 17th to

Dolls in costume at the Museum of Welsh Antiquities, Bangor.

19th-century furniture, both local and imported, and porcelain and pottery. Some of this is shown within the settings of a farmhouse kitchen and a Caernarvonshire country house. There is also a collection of costumes and samplers, mainly from the Victorian period.

Other displays illustrate industries and crafts, especially the production and processing of slate, textiles, fishing and the life of the countryside. There are also exhibits of maps, prints, coins and medals, and of prehistoric, Romano-British and Dark Age antiquities. A collection of agricultural tools in the Old Canonry stables can be seen by appointment.

Penrhyn Castle

Bangor, Gwynedd LL57 4HN
☎ 0248 353084/353356
Apr–Oct 26, daily 12–5 ex. Tues
☒ *The Administrator*
£ ♿ 💻 🚗 NT

Penrhyn Castle was built in the 1820s and 1830s for G. H. Dawkins Pennant, the immensely rich owner of the Penrhyn slate quarries. It was designed by Thomas Hopper, the outstanding architect of the short-lived Norman Revival. Hopper was also responsible for the interior decoration and much of the furniture. The house contains Old Master paintings from the collection formed in the 19th century by the 1st Lord Penrhyn, and a large collection of dolls, established by the National Trust. An important museum of industrial locomotives has been arranged in the huge stables.

School of Animal Biology Museum

Brambell Laboratories, University College of North Wales, Bangor, Gwynedd LL57 2UW
☎ 0248 351151
By appt
☒ *Dr R. W. Arnold*
F 🚗

The main function of this small and attractive museum is undergraduate teaching. Most of the display area in the two-storey purpose-built Museum is given over to a comprehensive range of some 1,500 vertebrate specimens. Invertebrate material is displayed in a separate gallery. In addition to the teaching collections, there is a specialist, primarily entomological collection, mainly of specimens from North Wales.

Bantry

Bantry House

Bantry, Co. Cork, Ireland   ☎ 027 50047
Daily 9–6 (open until 8 in summer).
Closed Dec 25.
☒ *E. R. G. Shelswell-White*
£ ♿ 💻 🚗

This Georgian house, the home of the White family, was built for Richard White, 1st Earl of Bantry. Most of the items in it were collected during the 19th century. They include French and Flemish tapestries, Russian icons, floor tiles from Pompeii, Dutch, German, English and Irish furniture and paintings, and Irish and Spanish chandeliers. There is a permanent outdoor exhibition of modern sculpture.

Barlaston

The Wedgwood Museum

Josiah Wedgwood & Sons Limited, Barlaston,
Stoke-on-Trent, Staffordshire ST12 9ES
  ☎ 078139 4141
Apr–Oct, Mon–Fri & Bank Holiday 9–5,
Sat 10–4. Nov–Mar, Mon–Fri & Bank
Holiday 9–5. Closed 2 weeks at Christmas.
Tours Supervisor

The Museum, opened in 1975 and redesigned in
1985, is located in Wedgwood's modern factory.
The collection contains more than 20,000
pieces, of which about 15,000 are displayed in
the Museum, considerable use being made of
period settings. The 18th-century exhibits
include an extensive range of trial pieces
produced by Josiah Wedgwood (1730–95), in
search of improved ceramic bodies and resulting
in the introduction of Queen's Ware, Black
Basalt and Jasper.

The Museum also includes an art gallery.
Among the artists represented are Reynolds,
Stubbs, Wright of Derby, Romney and Sargent.

Barmouth

Barmouth Lifeboat Museum

RNLI Museum, The Harbour, Barmouth,
Gwynedd LL42 1EH
May–Sept, daily 10–6
The Curator

The Barmouth Lifeboat has a long and
distinguished history, which the Museum
illustrates by means of photographs, documents
and relics, together with memorabilia of
individual members of the crew. To provide a
background to the achievements of the lifeboat
service, there are also displays which tell the
story of ships and seafaring in the Barmouth
area.

Barnard Castle

The Bowes Museum

Barnard Castle, Co. Durham DL12 8NP
  ☎ 0833 37139
Mar, Apr, Oct, Mon–Sat 10–5; Sun 2–5.
May–Sept, Mon–Sat 10–5.30; Sun 2–5.
Nov–Feb, Mon–Sat 10–4; Sun 2–4.
Closed during Christmas week and Jan 1.
The Curator

The Bowes Museum is a French-style museum in
Britain. It was built for John Bowes, a wealthy
coalmine-owner, and his wife, Josephine,
between 1869 and 1876, and opened to the
public, after the Bowes' death, in 1892. Despite
its château-like appearance, the building was
planned as a museum. It was never a family
home.

Reconstructed bottle kiln in the newly
refurbished Wedgwood Museum galleries,
Barlaston.

John Bowes and his wife created a collection
specially for their museum. They bought in bulk
and rarely paid more than £100 for any item.
Most cost less than £10. The El Greco was
bought for £8. Over a period of 15 years they
acquired about 15,000 objects, to which they
added material bought earlier for their homes in
France. The collections of pictures, textiles,
furniture and manuscripts were formed on the
Continent and contained very few English
examples.

After the Bowes' death, the Museum was run
by Trustees, who added considerably to the
collections, especially in the fields of costumes,
dolls, toys and the English decorative arts.
Archaeological finds from the southern half of
Co. Durham are also now included, together
with objects illustrating rural life in Teesdale
during the 17th to 19th centuries.

Since 1956 the Museum has been the
responsibility of Durham County Council.

Barnet

Barnet Museum

31 Wood Street, Barnet, Hertfordshire
  ☎ 01 449 0321 extn 4
Summer, Tues–Thurs 2.30–4.30; Sat 10–12,
2.30–4.30. Winter, Tues and Thurs 2–4;
Sat 10–12, 2–4.
Mr W. S. Taylor, Hon. Curator

This is the Museum of the Barnet and District
Local History Society. Its collections cover a
wide range, from militaria to samplers and from
minerals to old pipes and microscopes. There
are rubbings of brasses in local churches, a
Victorian Room and a number of paintings and
prints of old Barnet. The Museum archive
contains many historical photographs of the
district and written information on houses.

Barnsley

The Cooper Gallery

Church Street, Barnsley, South Yorkshire S70 2AH
  ☎ 0226 242905
Tues 1–5.30; Wed–Sun 10–5.30. Closed Dec 25,
26, Jan 1.
Valerie Millington, Curator

The permanent collection at the Cooper
Gallery consists of 17th to 19th-century
European paintings and British drawings and
watercolours, an important feature of which is
the Sir Michael Sadler collection. There is a
continuous programme of temporary exhibitions
of fine art, craft, photography and design, and
associated activities – workshops, talks and
demonstrations.

Barnstaple

St Anne's Chapel Museum

Church Lane, Barnstaple, Devon
Late Spring Bank Holiday–Sept, Mon–Sat 10–1,
2–5 (Wed 10–1). Enquiries to: North Devon
District Council, Civic Centre, Barnstaple,
EX31 1EA ☎ *0271 72511*
Ⓧ *The Curator*
Ⓔ

The upper part of the Chapel dates from the
early 14th century but the crypt, which was
originally a charnel house, is much older. The
Chapel was used as the local Grammar School
from the 16th century until 1910. Among its
pupils was John Gay, author of *The Beggar's
Opera*. It now displays a variety of objects
relating to the history of Barnstaple. The
material ranges from an old pew end from the
Parish Church to a sky rocket used to celebrate
Queen Victoria's Silver Jubilee, and from a
coaching whip and posthorn used on the
Barnstaple to Lynton coach to a tablecloth
made by refugee Huguenots in 1761 and
presented to the Mayor of Barnstaple to
commemorate his year of office.

Barrowford

Pendle Heritage Centre

Park Hill, Barrowford, nr Nelson, Lancashire
BB9 6JQ ☎ *0282 695366*
Easter–late Nov, Tues, Wed, Thur, Sat, Sun
2–4.30. Other times by appt.
Ⓧ *The Director*
Ⓔ ♦ 🖼 🚗

The Centre, which was established to preserve,
study and promote the region's heritage, is two
miles from Nelson, at the junction of the B6247
and A682. It occupies an attractive group of
buildings at the entrance to Barrowford Park –
Park Hill, a 17th-century manor house, built by
the Bannister family; Lower Park Hill, which
has a 1780 façade, but incorporates part of an
earlier structure; Park Hill Barn, some of which
was built in the mid 17th century; and
Barrowford Toll House, which dates from 1805.

The Museum is in Park Hill. Its permanent
displays illustrate the history of Park Hill and its
estate, and of the Bannister family. There is also
a farming collection, which will eventually be
exhibited in Park Hill Barn.

Barrow-in-Furness

The Furness Museum

Ramsden Square, Barrow-in-Furness,
Cumbria LA14 1LL ☎ *0229 20650*
Mon–Wed, Fri 10–5; Thurs 10–1; Sat 10–4.
Closed public holidays.
Ⓧ *Mr D. J. Hughes*
Ⓕ 🖼 🚗

The Museum's displays show the history and
development of Furness from prehistoric times
up to its 19th and 20th-century growth as a
major shipbuilding centre. The exhibits include
ship models, the first longcase clock made in
Cumbria (1708) and a portrait of Judge Fell, an
important figure in Quaker history.

Barton-on-Humber

Baysgarth Museum

Baysgarth House, Baysgarth Park, Caistor Road,
Barton-on-Humber, South Humberside
DN18 6AH ☎ *0652 32318*
Thurs–Sun 10–4. Open Bank Holiday; closed
Dec 25, 26, Jan 1.
Ⓧ *The Curator*
Ⓕ 🖼 🚗

Baysgarth House was built and modified at
various periods between the 17th and late 19th
centuries. It was given to the Barton-on-
Humber District Council in 1930, together with
its park, for use by the community. The
Museum which it now houses illustrates the
geology, archaeology and history of the district.
A special feature is a fine collection of 18th and
19th-century European and Oriental porcelain.
There is a small section devoted to local military
history.

**Late Saxon burial in a tomb of oolitic limestone
slabs. Baysgarth Museum, Barton-on-Humber.**

Basingstoke

The Vyne

Sherborne St John, Basingstoke, Hampshire
RG26 5DX   ☎ *0256 881337*
Mar 29–Oct 19, Tues–Thurs, Sat, Sun 2–6. Last
admission 5.30. Open Bank Holiday Mon but
closed Tues following. Closed Good Fri.
⚑ *The Administrator*
Ⓔ ♟ ☛ ⇒ ♿ NT

The Vyne is four miles north of Basingstoke,
between Bramley and Sherborne St John on the
A430. It was built in the early 16th century by
William Sandys, the 1st Lord Sandys, who, in
1520, organized the Field of the Cloth of Gold
for Henry VIII. The Sandys, who were
Catholics, encountered difficulties during the
Civil War and the 6th Lord Sandys sold The
Vyne to Chaloner Chute, who became Speaker
of the House of Commons under Richard
Cromwell. The Chutes made important changes
to the house during the 18th century, but Lord
Sandys' splendid chapel, with its fine stalls,
canopy, screen and glass, has been little altered.

The contents of The Vyne are those
accumulated by the Chutes over three centuries.
They include family portraits, 17th and 18th-
century furniture, Soho tapestries, and Meissen
and Bow porcelain figures.

The Willis Museum

Old Town Hall, Market Place, Basingstoke,
Hampshire   ☎ *0256 465902*
Tues–Fri 10–5; Sat 10–4
⚑ *The Curator*
Ⓕ ✎ ⇒

The Museum was formerly Basingstoke Town
Hall, built in 1832. It was refaced and the
ground floor enclosed in 1865. This is primarily
a local museum, with displays illustrating the
archaeology and history of the Basingstoke area
from prehistoric times to the present day. There
are also sections dealing with geology and
natural history, including an aquarium with the
fish found in local rivers.

Recently opened galleries are devoted to the
story of time-keeping, to dolls and toys of the
past 200 years, and to four centuries of
embroidery.

Bath

The American Museum

Claverton Manor, Bath, Avon BA2 7BD
☎ *0225 60503*
Mar 28–Nov 2, Tues–Sun 2–5. Open Bank
Holiday Mon and preceding Sun 11–5.
Groups by appt.
⚑ *Education Officer*
Ⓔ ♟ ☛ ⇒

The Museum occupies a listed early 19th-
century house, which has the added distinction
of being the place where Sir Winston Churchill
made his first speech. Its aim is to show, by
means of a series of completely furnished rooms,

Beckford's Tower, Bath.

how the Americans lived from the 17th to the
19th centuries. The displays include a Puritan
Keeping Room of the 1680s, a tavern kitchen of
the 1770s, a mid 18th-century parlour, an early
19th-century country-style bedroom and a richly
decorated bedroom from New Orleans at the
time of the Civil War.

There are also galleries devoted to the
American Indians, the Shakers, the
Pennsylvania Germans, and the Spanish
colonists of New Mexico. Other exhibits show
the opening of the West, whaling, quilts,
hooked rugs, pewter, glass and silver. In the
grounds there is a replica of a tepee, a Conestoga
wagon, the observation platform of a railway
coach and a gallery which illustrates the forms
and designs of American folk art.

Bath Industrial Heritage Centre

Camden Works, Julian Road, Bath,
Avon BA1 2RH   ☎ *0225 318348*
Feb–Nov, daily 2–5. Dec and Jan, weekends only,
2–5. Groups at other times by appt.
⚑ *Jane Richardson, Curator*
Ⓔ ✎ ☛ ⇒

The Museum building was constructed in 1777
as a Real Tennis court, but only traces of the
original interior remain. It now houses the
Bowler Collection which is presented as a
reconstruction of the works of J. B. Bowler, a
Victorian brass founder, general engineer and
aerated water manufacturer. During 97 years of
trading in Bath, the firm threw practically
nothing away. As a result visitors can see a
remarkable collection of working machinery,
hand-tools, brasswork, patterns, bottles and
documents of all kinds, displayed as realistically
as possible to convey an impression of the

working life of a small provincial family business in Victorian times.

A separate section of the Museum tells the story of Bath stone and looks at all aspects of this important local industry. The 18th-century development of the city, using the characteristic local limestone, gave Bath much of its special architectural quality. The displays include a mine working face in the days before mechanisation, explanations of the tools and skills involved in working the stone, and a look at how it was transported.

Bath Postal Museum

8 Broad Street, Bath, Avon BA1 5LJ
☎ *0225 60333*
Mon–Sat 11–5; Sun 2–5. Closed Dec 24–26.
✗ *Mr Glyn Williams, Education Officer*
£ ♦ ▆ ♠ ⑁

The Museum building, parts of which date back to the 16th century, was Bath's main Post Office in the first half of the 19th century. The first known posting of a Penny Black stamp took place here in May 1840. The Museum displays present a comprehensive history of letter writing and the methods used to carry mail from the earliest clay tablets to the latest electronic transmission of the written word.

There is a special emphasis on Bath's two reformers of the postal service, Ralph Allen and John Palmer. The exhibits include many original letters, quill pens, stamp boxes, a model airship, Post Office antiquities, and a full-scale replica of a 19th-century Post Office.

Beckford's Tower and Museum

Lansdown Road, Bath, Avon BA1 9BH
Apr–Oct, Sat, Sun 2–5, Bank Holiday Mon.
✗ *Hon. Treasurer, Beckford Tower Trust,*
2 Lambridge, Bath BA1 6BJ
£ ⑁

The Tower was built in 1827 for the wealthy traveller, author and eccentric, William Beckford, who had moved to Bath from Fonthill, in Wiltshire. It has since been restored and converted into two flats and a museum. One of the museum rooms relates to Beckford's life at Fonthill, with a large model of his Gothic 'Abbey' there, engravings of its exterior and interior, together with books by and about Beckford.

The second room contains coloured lithographs showing the Tower rooms as they were in 1844, and a collection of editions of Beckford's novel, *Vathek*. The Tower is ascended by a fine staircase cantilevered from the wall, with 154 easy steps to a viewing platform, the 'Belvidere' (Beckford's spelling), which has splendid views over the surrounding countryside.

Geology Museum

18 Queen Square, Bath, Avon BA1 2HP
☎ *0225 28144*
Mon–Fri 9.30–6; Sat 9.30–5. Closed Bank
Holiday and day after Easter Mon, Spring Bank
Holiday, Dec 26.
✗ *The Curator*
F ♠

The Museum is largely based on the work of Charles Moore (1814–81), one of the foremost geologists of the 19th century. His collections, some of which are on display, contain a large number of fossils from the Jurassic rocks of North Somerset. Type specimens and other material not on show can be seen by appointment. The Museum also contains some of the natural history collections of the former Bath Royal Literary and Scientific Society, including a herbarium and a collection of seashells.

Machine shop, Bath Industrial Heritage Centre.

Queen Charlotte by J. J. Zoffany (1733–1810). Bath, Holburne of Menstrie Museum.

Herschel House and Museum

19 New King Street, Bath, Avon BA1 2BL
Mar–Oct, daily 2–5. Nov–Feb, Sun 2–5.
    Groups by appt at any time.
▨ *Hon. Secretary, William Herschel Society*
    at above address ☎ *0225 336228*
£ ✍

Sir William Herschel's house in Bath was built in 1766. From its garden he observed the planet Uranus in 1781. The William Herschel Society restored the house and opened it in 1981 as a museum of Sir William's music and astronomy, with contemporary furniture and instruments. The exhibits are on three floors, in the drawing-room, music room, astronomy room, dining-room and kitchen. Visitors can see Herschel's workshop where he made his powerful telescopes – there is a fine model of his 40-foot telescope – and a display of his astronomical and thermological apparatus.

Holburne of Menstrie Museum

Great Pulteney Street, Bath, Avon BA2 4DB
    ☎ *0225 66669*
Feb–Dec 14, weekdays 11–5; Sun 2.30–6. Open
    on Mon from Easter.
▨ *The Curator*
£ ▪ ▦ ✎ ♿

This 1796–7 building, originally designed to serve as a hotel, was adapted to house the Holburne collection in 1911–15. The exhibits include Flemish, Dutch, Italian and English paintings, especially works by Guardi, Zoffany, Gainsborough and Stubbs; Italian majolica; Renaissance bronzes; miniatures; furniture and glass.

A special section is devoted to 20th-century crafts. Among the items displayed here are woven and printed textiles, pottery by Bernard Leach, furniture and calligraphy. The Crafts Study Centre offers facilities for research in these and allied fields.

Museum of Bookbinding

Manvers Street, Bath, Avon BA1 1JW
    ☎ *0225 66000*
Mon–Fri 9–1, 2.15–5.30. Closed Bank Holiday.
▨ *H. H. Bayntun-Coward*
£ ▪ ♿

Bath is an important centre of craft bookbinding in the English-speaking world. Three internationally famous binding firms, those of Robert Rivière, Cedric Chivers and George Bayntun, have flourished here during the last 150 years. The Museum is in part of the city's old postal sorting office, built in 1870. The remainder of the building is occupied by a workshop for binding and restoring books, and by a bookselling business.

The Museum shows the history and contemporary practice of hand bookbinding, with graphics, displays and reproductions of old illustrations and with actual exhibits illustrating the progress of binding, from wooden boards to modern styles. There is a reconstruction of the first Bayntun shop of 1894, with much of the equipment used at that time. The Bayntun and Rivière toolbooks, portraying more than 10,000 tools, are reproduced on the back wall. There is a section devoted to marbled papers and another to book covers, showing endpapers, bookplates and inside borders. The many treatments of calf, which were in use from the 17th to the 19th century, are also featured in the exhibition.

Museum of Costume

Assembly Rooms, Bennett Street, Bath,
    Avon BA1 2QH ☎ *0225 461111*
Museum: Mar-Oct, Mon–Sat 9.30–6; Sun 10–6.
    Nov–Feb, Mon–Sat 10–5; Sun 11–5.
Fashion Research Centre: Mon–Fri 10–1, 2–5.
    Closed public holidays.
▨ *Bookings Officer*
£ ▪ ♿

In its 18th-century Assembly Rooms, Bath has one of the largest and most comprehensive displays of costume in Britain. The Museum illustrates, with period room settings and dioramas, the history of fashionable dress for men, women and children from the late 16th

Check taffeta dress, 1823. Bath, Museum of Costume.

century to the present day. There are outstanding items of the 16th, 17th and 18th centuries, and extensive 19th and 20th-century collections, including designer clothes, as well as special displays of millinery, jewellery, underwear, dolls and toys. A selection of royal clothes and ceremonial dress is also on view.

A study collection and library on the history of costume and textiles is provided at the Fashion Research Centre, 4 The Circus. The library includes collections of books, periodicals, fashion plates, photographs, patterns and other archival material. Most notable are the Worth and Paquin archives (1902–56) and the *Sunday Times* Fashion Archive (1957–72).

The Assembly Rooms are closed during 1989 for urgent repairs.

No. 1 Royal Crescent

Bath, Avon BA1 2LR ☎ *0225 28126*
Mar–Oct, Tues–Sat 11–5; Sun 2–5. Open Bank
Holiday Mon.
К *The Administrator*
£ **♦** **♿**

No. 1 Royal Crescent was built in 1767–9. Among its distinguished occupants in the early years was the Duke of York, who rented it in 1776. It later fell into disrepair, but in 1967 it became the property of the Bath Preservation Trust and was carefully restored. It is now decorated and furnished as it might have been in 1775.

A Kitchen Museum has been installed in one of the basement rooms. Its fine collection of cooking grates and utensils could have been used in any house in Bath in the 18th century.

Police Museum

Bath Police Station, Manvers Street, Bath,
Avon BA1 1JN ☎ *0225 63451 extn 272*
By appt
К *Inspector K. Jefferies*
F **♿**

The Bath City Police Force was established in 1836. It now forms part of the Avon and Somerset Constabulary. The Museum tells the story of the policing of Bath over a period of 150 years. There are displays of uniforms, weapons of offence and a wide range of other mementoes of the police service, in a force which acquired its first bicycle in 1897, its first policewoman in 1916, and its first motorcar in 1927.

Roman Baths Museum

Pump Room, Stall Street, Bath, Avon BA1 1LZ
☎ *0225 61111*
Mar–June and Sept–Oct, daily 9–6. July–Aug,
daily 9–7. Nov–Feb, daily 9–5; Sun 10–5.
Closed Dec 25–26.
К *Bookings Officer*
£ **♦** **♿**

The Roman bathing establishment, with its magnificent Great Bath, flourished as an important feature of the town of *Aquae Sulis* between the 1st and 5th centuries A.D. It was built around the natural hot spring which rises from the ground at 46.5 °C. The remains of the

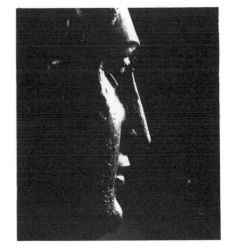

Life-size gilded bronze head of the Roman goddess Sulis Minerva, found beneath Stall Street in 1727. Bath, Roman Baths Museum.

Baths are complete in layout and are amongst the best Roman remains in Britain.

In the Museum one can see mosaics and stone monuments from the Roman town and the surrounding area, along with many votive offerings thrown into the sacred spring. The finest of the exhibits is the gilt-bronze head of the Goddess Minerva. The recently excavated Roman Temple Precinct underneath the Pump Room can also be viewed.

Royal Photographic Society National Centre of Photography

The Octagon, Milsom Street, Bath,
Avon BA1 1DN ☎ *0225 62841*
Mon–Sat: shop 9.30–5.30; galleries 10–5.30 (last
admission 5)
К *Gilly Burnford*
£ **♦** **♿**

The Centre is housed in what was originally an 18th-century chapel. Its collections include rare books, equipment and prints. Among the items on display is the first photograph taken, with the camera used. The four galleries are used for regular exhibitions of both historical and contemporary photographs. The specialist Library and Archive are among the most important in the world.

Victoria Art Gallery

Bridge Street, Bath, Avon BA2 4AT
☎ *0225 461111 extn 418*
Mon–Fri 10–6; Sat 10–5. Closed Sun,
Bank Holiday.
К *Arts Officer*
F **♿** **□**

This purpose-built Gallery was opened in 1900. The decoration features a cast of the Parthenon Frieze below the ceiling. The collection includes European Old Masters and 18th to 20th-century British paintings, drawings and watercolours. Of particular local interest are the works of the

'The Comforts of Bath', a cartoon by Thomas Rowlandson (1756/7–1827). Bath, Victoria Art Gallery.

Barkers of Bath and the famous topographical views by Thomas Malton. The applied arts are well represented by porcelain and pottery, together with the Carr collection of English drinking glasses and the Horstmann collection of English and continental watches of the 18th and 19th centuries. Displays of these items are changed at regular intervals, supplemented by a programme of temporary exhibitions.

With one large gallery and adjacent areas, there is only room to show a small part of the collections at any one time. Many of the best portraits are hung in the Pump Room, the Assembly Rooms and the Guildhall, where they can be easily seen.

Batley

Bagshaw Museum

Wilton Park, Batley, West Yorkshire WF17 0AS
☎ *0924 472514*
Mon–Sat 10–5; Sun 1–5
⚓ *The Curator*
Ⓕ ✎ ✐ ☐

Bagshaw Museum was formerly a private house, built for George Sheard, a local woollen merchant, in 1875. It was bought by Batley Corporation, together with the Wilton Park estate, in 1909 and in 1901–11 Walter Bagshaw, a local JP, arranged three rooms as a museum, with himself as Honorary Curator. When he died, in 1927, the Museum was a flourishing institution, with 12 rooms open to the public.

The Museum is now owned by Kirklees Metropolitan District Council. Its displays cover local history, natural history, ethnography, Egyptian antiquities and Oriental art. Eighty per cent of the large collections is in store, but a wide range of objects is brought out each year and displayed in temporary exhibitions.

Batley Art Gallery

Market Place, Batley, West Yorkshire WF17 5DA
☎ *0924 465151*
Mon–Fri 10–6; Sat 10–4
⚓ *Mr R. Hall, Senior Curator, Huddersfield Art Gallery, Princess Alexandra Walk, Huddersfield, West Yorkshire HD1 2SU*
Ⓕ

This small gallery is in the care of Huddersfield Art Gallery. It has a permanent collection of paintings, drawings and graphics from the mid 19th century up to the present day.

Battle

Battle and District Historical Society Museum

Langton House, Battle, East Sussex BN33 0NG
Apr–Sept, Mon–Sat 10–1, 2–5; Sun 2.30–5.30
⚓ *The Hon. Secretary*
Ⓔ ✎ ✐

The exhibits in the Museum include a diorama which shows the Battle of Hastings at its height and a reproduction of the Bayeux Tapestry. There are also displays of Romano-British material from local excavations and a collection illustrating the history of the Sussex iron industry, including samples of ores and cinders from the furnaces. Other local industries are also represented.

Beaconsfield

Royal Army Educational Corps Museum

Wilton Park, Beaconsfield, Buckinghamshire HP9 2RP   ☎ *04946 6121 extn 286*
By appt
⚓ *The Curator*
Ⓕ

The Museum's collections include the history of education in the British Army, with special reference to the work of the Royal Army Educational Corps and its predecessor, the Corps of Army Schoolmasters, founded in 1846.

Beaulieu

Buckler's Hard Maritime Museum

Buckler's Hard, Beaulieu, Brockenhurst,
Hampshire SO4 7ZN   ☎ 059063 203
Easter–Spring Bank Holiday, daily 10–6. Spring
Bank Holiday–Sept, daily 10–9. Oct-Easter,
daily 10–4.30. Closed Dec 25.
⋈ *Graham Carter, Head of Education and*
Interpretation
£ ♦ 🍴 🚻

Originally intended by the 2nd Duke of
Montagu to be a major port, Buckler's Hard
settled down to life as a shipbuilding village.
Between 1745 and 1822 many wooden ships for
the Navy were built here, including Nelson's
favourite ship, the *Agamemnon*. The Maritime
Museum reflects the shipbuilding history of the
village, with displays on the shipwrights'
techniques, and on Henry Adams, the master
shipbuilder. Displays in the cottages re-create
life at Buckler's Hard in the late 18th century.

Exhibition of Monastic Life

John Montagu Building, Beaulieu, Brockenhurst,
Hampshire SO4 7ZN   ☎ 0590 612345
Easter–Sept, daily 10–6. Oct–Easter, daily 10–5.
Closed Dec 25.
⋈ *See Buckler's Hard Maritime Museum*
£ ♦ 🍴 🚻 &

The Cistercian Abbey at Beaulieu was founded
by King John in 1204. An exhibition explaining
life in the Monastery has been established in the
Frater of the former Lay Brothers' building, the
Domus. The displays illustrate the organisation
of the Monastery, the life of the monks, and
farming methods on the monastic estates.

The National Motor Museum

John Montagu Building, Beaulieu, Brockenhurst,
Hampshire SO4 7ZN   ☎ 0590 612345
Easter–Sept, 10–6. Oct–Easter, 10–5. Closed
Dec 25.
⋈ *See Buckler's Hard Maritime Museum*
£ ♦ 🍴 🚻 &

In 1970, the Montagu Motor Museum, founded
by Lord Montagu in 1952, became the
National Motor Museum, owned and controlled
by a charitable trust, in order to preserve
the collections and the library for the nation.
It is now one of the largest and most
comprehensive automobile museums in the
world, telling the story of motoring from 1894
to the present day.
    To celebrate the centenary of the motorcar, a
permanent feature, 'Wheels – the Legend of the
Motor Car', was opened in 1985. This gives
visitors an automated trip in a moving 'pod',
through a series of dioramas illustrating 100
years of motoring.

Beaumaris

Beaumaris Castle

Beaumaris, Gwynedd   ☎ 0248 810361
Mar 15–Oct 15, daily 9.30–6.30. Oct 16–
Mar 14, Mon–Sat 9.30–4; Sun 2–4.
⋈ *The Custodian*
£ ✎ 🚻 ♿

Built in the 13th and 14th centuries, Beaumaris
Castle was at one time accessible by sea and
there was a dock, but the sea has now receded.
It was the last castle to be built by Edward I
and the Chapel Tower contains an exhibition
on the construction and history of his castles.

Some of the 250 historic cars, commercial vehicles and motorcycles at The National Motor
Museum, Beaulieu.

Beaumaris Gaol

Steeple Lane, Beaumaris, Gwynedd
☏ *0248 810921/723262 extn 269*
Gaol: Mid May–late Sept, daily 11–6. Courthouse: mid May–late Sept, daily 11.30–5.30 (except when court is in session.
⚔ *The Education Officer, Gwynedd Archives Service, Victoria Dock, Caernarfon, Gwynedd*
☏ *0286 4121 extn 2090/2091*
E ⍾

The prison at Beaumaris, built in 1829, has remained unchanged since it was closed in 1878. Visitors can see the cells, including the punishment cell and the condemned cell, and the only treadwheel in Britain to survive on its original site. There is an exhibition of documents illustrating prison life in the 19th century.

The nearby Courthouse, built in 1614 and renovated in the early 19th century, is still in use as a magistrates court and can be visited by the public. Prisoners sentenced here were taken to Beaumaris Gaol.

Museum of Childhood

1 Castle Street, Beaumaris, Gwynedd LL58 8AP
☏ *0248 810448*
Daily 10–6. Closed Dec 25, 26.
⚔ *Robert Brown* ☏ *0248 712498*
E ■ ⍾

The eight rooms of the Museum contain collections illustrating what is described as 'the more pleasurable aspects of family life'. The 2,000 items are arranged according to themes – Audio and Visual Entertainment; Pottery and Glass; Trains, Cars, Clockwork Toys, Ships and Aeroplanes; Children's Toy Savings Boxes; Art Gallery; Educational Toys, Dolls and Games.

Room 1 illustrates home entertainment during the past 150 years. The exhibits include cylinder music boxes, polyphons, phonographs, magic lanterns and early cameras and radios. Demonstrations of a number of them take place every hour.

Victorian Jack-in-the-Box. Beaumaris, Museum of Childhood.

Beccles

Beccles and District Museum

Newgate, Beccles, Suffolk NR34 9QA
☏ *0502 712628*
Apr–Oct, Wed, Sat, Sun, Bank Holiday 2.30–5. Nov–Mar, Sun 2.30–5. Closed Christmas, Jan 1.
⚔ *Walter H. Stock, 39 Kemps Lane, Beccles NR34 9XB.*
F ⍾ ⍾

Opened in 1975, Beccles Museum is staffed and administered entirely by voluntary workers. There is a good display of archaeological material, but most of the exhibits relate to the history of the town. The civic robes and regalia are on view and there are many examples of Victorian dresses, christening robes and dolls. The coinage issued locally in the 17th century is represented by specimens of the 1670 Beccles farthing, together with the dies from which it was struck. There are many examples of the tools used in agriculture and by rural craftsmen, and historical relics of the town's renowned printing industry. The old gaol, demolished in the 1930s, is recalled by chains, handcuffs, yokes and locks.

In the 17th century, Beccles had its own coinage and the Museum has specimens of the 1670 farthing, complete with the original dies from which the coins were struck. These are very rare and, like many of the other items on display here, are on loan from the Town Collection.

Beckenham

Bethlem Royal Hospital Museum

The Bethlem Royal Hospital, Monks Orchard Road, Beckenham, Kent BR3 3BX
☏ *01-777 6611*
Mon–Fri 10–5.30, by appt. Closed public holidays.
⚔ *Patricia Allderidge, Archivist and Curator*
F ⍾ ♿

Bethlem, the original Bedlam, has been caring for the mentally disordered since the 14th century. It moved to Beckenham in 1930 and is now administered jointly with the Maudsley Hospital, with an archives department and a museum which cover the history of both hospitals. Because of shortage of space, most of the Museum's historical material is in store and the exhibition space is devoted entirely to pictures. These include paintings and other works of interest in the fields of psychiatry and psychology, particularly by artists whose work has been influenced in some way by mental disorder. Among the exhibits are the sculptures by C. G. Cibber, known as 'Raving and Melancholy Madness', from the gates of the 17th-century Bedlam.

Bedale

Bedale Hall

Bedale, North Yorkshire DL8 1AA ☎ *0677 23131*
Spring Bank Holiday–Sept, daily 10–4. Oct–May,
 Tues only.
☒ *Museum Co-ordinator*
Ⓕ ⓐ ⓖ

Built in the mid 17th century, extended and
remodelled in the 18th, Bedale Hall was in a
semi-ruinous condition by the 1950s, when
Bedale Rural District Council bought and
restored it, to serve as a new headquarters
building. In 1974, ownership passed to the new
Hambleton District Council.

In 1959 a museum was opened in part of the
Hall. Reorganised and extended in 1985, the
museum houses many examples of local
bygones, photographs and archive material,
such as a 1748 fire engine, household accounts
and craftsmen's tools and indentures from 1648,
plus two original copies of *Hansard* dated 1777.

Bedford

Bedford Museum

Castle Lane, Bedford, Bedfordshire MK40 3XD
 ☎ *0234 53323*
Tues–Sat 11–5, Sun 2–5. Closed Mon (ex. Bank
 Holiday Mon), Good Fri, Christmas.
☒ *The Curator*
Ⓕ ⓠ ⓐ ⓖ

The Museum, opened in 1981, occupies what
was originally Higgins Castle Brewery and
subsequently a clothing factory and a GPO
sorting office. The basis of the collections was
the museum established at Bedford Modern
School, for which the Borough of Bedford took
over responsibility in the late 1950s. The main
displays relate to the human and natural history
of North Bedfordshire. Archaeological material
traces the history of the area from the Ice Age to
the Middle Ages, and includes such important
finds as the Old Warden Iron Age mirror and
the Felmersham bronzes. Later history covers
local industries, such as lacemaking and straw
plaiting, while rural life is illustrated by
reconstructions of a 19th-century kitchen and
dairy, and the all-purpose living room of a
labourer's cottage, as well as by a display of
agricultural tools and implements, and by a
poaching exhibit.

The geology section is based on Bedfordshire
rocks and fossils. The natural history exhibits
contain a number of wildlife habitats, with some
of the birds and mammals of the area.

Cecil Higgins Museum and Art Gallery

Castle Close, Bedford, Bedfordshire MK40 3NY
 ☎ *0234 211222*
Tues–Fri 12.30–5; Sat 11–5; Sun 2–5. Closed
 Good Fri, Dec 25, 26, Mon (ex. Bank Holiday
 Mon).
☒ *Andrea George, Assistant Curator*
Ⓔ *adults only* ⓠ

**English posset pot, about 1690. Bedford,
Cecil Higgins Art Gallery.**

Cecil Higgins, a local brewer, was an
enthusiastic and discriminating collector of
porcelain and glass throughout his life. When
the family business was sold in 1928, he began
to extend his collections, with the aim of
establishing a museum in his home town,
investing money to ensure that further
acquisitions would be made after his death.
The Museum and Gallery combines the original
home of the Higgins family with a new gallery,
added in 1974.

The house displays costumes, toys, lace and
an outstanding collection of furniture, mainly
Victorian. One room is devoted to furniture
designed by the famous Victorian architect,
William Burges. The galleries in the new wing
contain exhibits of ceramics and glass, mainly
of the 17th to 19th centuries. The picture
collection is especially strong in English
watercolours, with nearly every major artist in
this field represented.

Museum of John Bunyan Relics

Bunyan Meeting Free Church, 55 Mill Street,
 Bedford, Bedfordshire ☎ *0234 58075*
May–Sept, Tues–Sat 2–4. Other times by appt.
☒ *The Curator, 71 Curlew Crescent, Bedford*
 MK41 7HY ☎ *0234 58870*
Ⓔ ⓠ

The church which contains the Museum is on
the site of an earlier building where Bunyan was
Pastor from 1672 to 1688. The bronze doors,
presented by the 9th Duke of Bedford in 1876,
have 10 sculpted panels showing scenes from
The Pilgrim's Progress. Among the items on
display are Bunyan's iron anvil and violin, his
vestry chair, the flute he made out of a chairleg
while he was in prison, and the jug used by his
blind daughter, Mary, to take soup to him
during this period. The Church Minute Book
for 1672, in Bunyan's handwriting, is also
shown.

The Museum has the world's largest
collection of translations of *The Pilgrim's
Progress*.

Belfast

Belfast Transport Gallery

*Ulster Folk and Transport Museum, Witham
    Street, Newtownards Road, Belfast, Northern
    Ireland BT4 1HP*   ☎ *0232 51519*
*Mon–Sat 10–5. Closed Dec 25, 26, Jan 1,
    July 12, 13.*
🗶 *The Education Officer, Ulster Folk and
    Transport Museum, Cultra Manor, Holywood,
    Co. Down, Northern Ireland BT18 0EU*
Ⓔ ⬙ ⚲

This Gallery contains part of the Ulster Folk
and Transport Museum's comprehensive
holding of all types of transport. The emphasis
here is on road and rail transport. There are
items from both narrow and standard-gauge
Irish railways, including Maeve, the largest
locomotive ever built in Ireland. The tramway
exhibits contain both horse-hauled and electric
trams, and a 'toastrack' from the Giant's
Causeway Tramway. Horse-drawn road
vehicles, cars and cycles are also well
represented.

Royal Ulster Rifles Regimental Museum

*Regimental Headquarters, The Royal Irish
    Rangers, 5 Waring Street, Belfast, Northern
    Ireland BT1 2EW*   ☎ *0232 232086*
*Mon–Fri 10–12.30, 2–4. Other times by appt.
    Closed public holidays.*
🗶 *Hon. Curator*
Ⓕ ⬙ ⚲

The collection of over 4,000 items has been
largely built up by gifts from various members
and friends of the Regiment. The Museum
holds large collections of uniforms, badges and
medals. The archives include histories of units
of the Regiment, war diaries and many other
documents of interest, including photograph
albums and scrapbooks.

**GSWR Engine No. 800 'Maeve', the largest
ever built in Ireland, 1939. Belfast Transport
Gallery.**

Ulster Museum

*Botanic Gardens, Belfast, Northern Ireland
    BT9 5AB*   ☎ *0232 668251*
*Mon–Fri 10–5; Sat 1–5; Sun 2–5. Closed
    Christmas week, Jan 1, July 12.*
🗶 *Education Officer*
Ⓕ ⬙ ⚲ ⚲

The Ulster Museum is one of Britain's national
museums. Its displays are divided into five
sections. The Department of Antiquities has
important collections of Irish archaeological
material, from the first arrival of man in Ireland,
c. 7000 B.C. until the late 17th century. These
collections include material recovered from the
wrecks of the two Spanish Armada ships,
Girona and *La Trinidad Valencera*. The
Department of Geology contains worldwide
collections of minerals and gemstones, and over
100,000 fossils, mostly Irish. The public displays
for which the Department of Botany and
Zoology is responsible include areas on the
Animals and Plants of Ireland, the Origin,
Structure and Evolution of Life, and the Variety
of Life.

For the past 25 years the Museum has
concentrated on building up its collection of
international modern art, but it also has a small
number of old master paintings, and collections
of Irish art, drawings, watercolours and prints.
The applied art collections include silver, glass,
ceramics, jewellery and furniture, with a bias
towards Irish work.

The Local History Gallery illustrates various
aspects of Ulster history over the past four
centuries, with an emphasis on political and
military events. The collections range from
maps to police and secret society badges, and
from uniforms to the coins and medals of
Ireland. A special section is concerned with the
industrial history and archaeology of Ulster and
especially with the flax and linen industry,
which was formerly of such great importance in
Ulster.

Beltring

Whitbread Hop Farm

*Whitbread and Company plc, Beltring, Paddock
    Wood, Kent TN12 6PY*
    ☎ *0622 872408/872068*
*Easter–late Oct, Tues–Sun 10–5.30. Open Bank
    Holiday Mon.*
🗶 *Mr Peter G. Leslie, Leisure Manager*
Ⓔ ⬙ ⚲ ⚲

This working farm supplies Whitbread's with a
quarter of the hops used in their breweries. A
group of six Victorian oasts has been preserved.
Three of them are now used as museums,
containing exhibits of rural crafts, hop-growing
and processing, agricultural tools and
implements, and horse harness and equipment.
There are regular craft demonstrations.

The Whitbread Shire horses are kept here,
when not working. Their duties include pulling
the coaches of the Lord Mayor of London and
the Speaker of the House of Commons.

Fossil herring 50 million years old, from Wyoming, USA. Belfast, Ulster Museum.

Bembridge

Bembridge Maritime Museum

Sherbourne Street, Bembridge, Isle of Wight
☎ 0983 872223
Apr–Oct 6, daily 10–5.30
🔲 Mr Martin Woodward
🄴 🛆 ↝

The Museum is strong in its collection of objects recovered from shipwrecks. There are also displays relating to early diving equipment, navigation, deep-water sailing ships and paddle steamers, and a number of ship models. A special exhibit tells the story of the Museum's discovery of HM Submarine *Swordfish*.

Ruskin Galleries

Bembridge School, nr Bembridge, Isle of Wight
☎ 0983 872101
By appt
🔲 J. S. Dearden, Curator
🄴 ↝

Bembridge School can be easily reached on a No. 8 bus from Ryde or Sandown. John Howard Whitehouse, the founder of the School, became interested in Ruskin in the 1890s and between then and his death in 1955 built up a large collection of drawings, letters, manuscripts and books by Ruskin, and of drawings by his contemporaries. They are housed in the Ruskin Galleries, which Whitehouse built in 1929. The lower gallery contains the books and the upper gallery the manuscripts and pictures.
Bembridge is the main international centre for Ruskin studies.

Benson

Benson Veteran Cycle Museum

The Bungalow, 61 Brook Street, Benson, Oxfordshire OX9 6LI I ☎ 0491 30414
Easter–Sept, by appt
🔲 Mrs M. F. Passey, Secretary
🄵 ↝

This privately run museum has substantial and interesting collections. It is concerned entirely with cycles and is exceptional in having no motorcycles. The 450 items illustrate the history of cycling and the bicycle and tricycle from its beginnings c. 1818 up to 1930.

Berkeley

Berkeley Castle

Berkeley, Gloucestershire ☎ 0453 810332
Apr & Sept, Tues–Sun 2 5. May Aug, Tues–Sat 11–5; Sun 2–5. Oct, Sun 2–4.30. Bank Holiday Mon 11–5.
🔲 The Custodian
🄴 🛆 ⏻ ↝ [HHA]

Berkeley Castle has been owned and lived in by the Berkeley family since its construction in the 12th century. The rooms shown to visitors during the guided tour include the dining room, Great Hall with minstrels' gallery, kitchens and pantry, drawing room and beer cellars. The furniture is mostly 17th century, but 18th century in the drawing room. There are interesting collections of paintings, family portraits and tapestries.
Edward II is believed to have been murdered here and visitors can see the room, in the Norman keep, where the act is supposed to have taken place.

The Jenner Museum

The Chantry, Church Lane, Berkeley,
Gloucestershire GL13 9BH   ☎ *0453 810631*
Apr–Sept, Tues–Sun & Bank Holiday Mons
11–5.15. Oct, Sun 11–5.15
◪ *The Custodian*
E ⬭ ↝

Edward Jenner, doctor, naturalist and Fellow of
the Royal Society, was born in 1749. He was the
son of the Vicar of Berkeley and spent most of his
life in this small Gloucestershire market town.
He was the discoverer of vaccination against
smallpox and at his home, The Chantry, he
vaccinated the poor free of charge, in a thatched
hut which he called the Temple of Vaccinia. The
Chantry later became the Vicarage, and was
bought in 1980 by the Jenner Appeal, with the
help of a generous gift from a Japanese
philanthropist, and by 1985 had been restored
and converted into a Jenner Museum and
immunology conference centre.
   The Museum displays illustrate the life and
career of Jenner and contains a large collection
of memorabilia and personal possessions. The
Temple of Vaccinia, also restored, can be seen by
visitors.

Berwick-upon-Tweed

Berwick Borough Museum and Art Gallery

Berwick Barracks, Ravensdowne, Berwick-upon-
Tweed, Northumberland TD15 1DG
   ☎ *0289 330933*
Daily 10–6. Closed Christmas, Jan 1.
◪ *Mr R. Doughty, Curator*
E ▮ ↝

The Borough Museum has been installed in one
of Britain's first purpose-built barracks, which
dates from the early 18th century. The Museum
collections illustrate the social and natural
history of Berwick. The Art Gallery has strong
collections of fine and decorative art, including
several hundred objects donated by Sir William
Burrell. These include Impressionist paintings,
Chinese porcelain, Persian tiles, Roman,
Venetian, German and English glass, Delftware,
medieval woodcarvings, Sumerian and Greek
sculpture, Islamic brasses, German pewter and
Chinese bronzes.

The Lady Waterford Hall

Ford Village, Berwick-upon-Tweed,
Northumberland TD15 2QA   ☎ *089082 224*
Daily 10–6.30
◪ *Ford and Etal Estates Office*
E ⬭ ↝

The Lady Waterford Hall was originally the
village school. It is celebrated for the 19th-
century murals painted by Louisa, Marchioness
of Waterford, who used children and their
parents from the Ford Estate as models for Old
and New Testament scenes.

The Lindisfarne Wine and Spirit Museum

Lindisfarne Limited, Palace Green, Berwick-upon-
Tweed, Northumberland TD15 1HR
   ☎ *0289 305153*
Easter–Oct, daily 10–5
◪ *J. Michael Hackett*
F ▮ ↝

The Museum occupies a First World War
barrack block in the grounds of the Governor's
house. It contains a fine collection of the tools
and equipment used in the wine and spirit
trades, including early hydrometers, brass
measures and Customs and Excise instruments.

Museum of the King's Own Scottish Borderers

Ravensdowne Barracks, The Parade, Berwick-
upon-Tweed, Northumberland TD15 1DQ
   ☎ *0289 307426*
Mon–Sat 9.30–4.30; Sun (summer only) 12–5.
◪ *See Ravensdowne Barracks*
E ▮ ↝

The Museum forms part of the complex within
Ravensdowne Barracks (*q.v.*). It illustrates the
history of the Regiment between 1689 and
1889, with good collections of uniforms, medals
and Victorian Regimental silver.

Ravensdowne Barracks

The Parade, Berwick-upon-Tweed,
Northumberland TD15 1DQ ☎ *0289 307881*
Mar 28–Oct, Mon–Sat 9.30–6.30; Sun 2–6.30
◪ *Historic Buildings and Monuments*
Commission, Carlisle   ☎ *0228 31777*
E ▮ ↝ ✜

The Barracks was built in 1717–21 and was one
of the earliest purpose-built barracks in Britain.
   The buildings have recently been restored
and now contain an exhibition on the history of
the British infantry, 1660–1880. The displays
include a reconstructed barrack-room of the
1780s, an Army schoolroom of the 1860s with
period figures, and other tableaux.

**World War I General Service Wagon.
Beverley, Museum of Army Transport.**

Bettyhill

Strathnaver Museum

*Clachan, Bettyhill, via Thurso, Sutherland
    KW14 7SQ*
June–Sept, Mon–Sat 2–5. Other times by appt.
☒ *Mrs P. Rudie, Secretary*   ☎ *06412 330*
£ ⌔ ↩

The village of Bettyhill is on the north coast of
Scotland, on the A836, about 30 miles west of
Thurso. The Museum is in the old parish church
of St Columba, which dates from the early 18th
century. The collections relate to the history
of the life and work of the people of the coast.
A special section deals with the 18th-century
Clearances of Strathnaver, which turned the
crofting areas into great sheep-runs and brought
great distress to the local population. There is
also a Clan Mackay room. The district of
Strathnaver was the Mackay country. It
consisted of the whole north-western corner of
Scotland, 80 by 18 miles, and culminated in
Cape Wrath itself.

Betws-y-Coed

Conwy Valley Railway Museum

*The Old Goods Yard, Betws-y-Coed, Gwynedd
    LL24 0AL*   ☎ *06902 568*
*Easter weekend 10.30–5.30. Then until Spring
    Bank Holiday, Mon–Fri 2–5; Sat, Sun
    10.30–5.30. Spring Bank Holiday–Sept, daily
    10.30–5.30. Oct, Mon–Fri 2–5; Sat, Sun
    10.30 5.*
☒ *The Curator*
£ ▮ � ↩ ఉ

The Museum adjoins the British Rail Betws-y-
Coed station. In addition to a museum train of
historic standard-gauge rolling stock, there is a
working 7¼ inch gauge steam railway, which
runs for three-quarters of a mile through
picturesque surroundings. Two buildings
contain a variety of railway relics and model
locomotives and working layout. Refreshments
are available in a standard-gauge buffet coach
and a former Southern Railway bogie van houses
another model train layout.

Beverley

Beverley Art Gallery and Museum

*Champney Road, Beverley, North Humberside
    HU17 9BQ*   ☎ *0482 882255*
*Mon–Wed, Fri 9.30–12.30, 2–5; Thurs 9.30–12;
    Sat 9.30–4*
☒ *Mrs Woodcock, Beverley Borough Council, The
    Hall, Lairgate, Beverley HU17 8HL*
£ ↩

The main part of the Gallery's collection
consists of works by Fred Elwell, R.A., son of
Fred Elwell, the woodcarver, whose work can be
seen in Beverley Minster. After working for
some years mainly as a portrait painter, he
concentrated on depicting local scenes and

these works form an interesting record of life in
Beverley between the two World Wars. On his
death in 1958 he bequeathed 55 of his pictures
to the town, and the collection has subsequently
been enlarged.

The Gallery has regular exhibitions of works
by local artists and also houses the Beverley
Heritage Centre on a permanent basis. The
Centre, set up in 1984 by the Beverley and
District Civic Society, comprises an extensive
exhibition of models, plans and pictures
illustrating the history of Beverley. There is also
a display relating to the history of the Beverley
Volunteers between 1814 and 1908.

Museum of Army Transport

*Flemingate, Beverley, North Humberside
    HU17 0NG*   ☎ *0482 860445*
Daily 10–5. Closed Dec 25.
☒ *The Director*
£ ▮ ▬ ↩ ఉ

The Museum houses and displays the Royal
Corps of Transport collections of Army road,
rail, sea and air transport, and tells the story of
the development of the Corps, beginning with
the period of the Crimean War. Most of the
exhibits, however, are connected with the
Second World War and post-war years. A
workshop of a Royal Army Service Corps
Company under field conditions shows lorries
under repair and recovery vehicles. There is a
tank rail head, with a tank transporter train,
and the wide range of vehicles on display
includes a 1920 fire engine from Aldershot
and the Rolls-Royce which was Field Marshal
Montgomery's staff car.

A hangar contains a Beaver light aircraft and
a Scout helicopter, and a Blackburn Beverley
aircraft houses a museum of Army Air Supply.

Bewdley

Bewdley Museum

*The Shambles, Load Street, Bewdley, Hereford and
    Worcester DY12 2AE*   ☎ *0299 403573*
Mar–Nov, Mon–Sat 10–5.30; Sun 2–5.30
☒ *Charles Fogg, Curator*
£ ▮ ↩

Located in an 18th-century range of market
buildings, Bewdley Museum's collections
illustrate the traditional crafts and industries of
the Wyre Forest area. These include charcoal-
burning, bark-stripping, tanning, oak basket-
making and brass-founding. A glassblower and a
pewter-maker have workshops within the
Museum. The farming section contains old tools
and implements and dairy equipment. Among
the displays relating to the history of Bewdley is
one on the development of trade on the River
Severn. The lives of notable local people, such
as Stanley Baldwin, are also featured.

Display projects in preparation include the
restoration of a Pickles flat-bed reciprocating
saw from a local sawmill, and a waterwheel-
operated pump.

Bexhill-on-Sea

Bexhill Manor Costume Museum

Manor House Gardens, Old Town, Bexhill-on-Sea, East Sussex TN40 2JA
Apr–Sept, Tues–Fri, Bank Holiday 10.30–1, 2.30–5.30; Sat, Sun 2.30–5.30
 *Mrs C. 1. Portch, 9 The Croft, Sutherland Avenue, Bexhill-on-Sea TN39 3QU*
☎ *0424 215361*
£ ♦ ♠ ♿

The Costume Museum's building was originally the stables and later the library of the Manor House. The displays present a wide range of period costumes, dating from 1740 to 1960. There are also collections of dolls, toys, lace, sewing machines and other domestic items.
    The museum is staffed by voluntary helpers, who give guided tours.

Bexhill Museum

Egerton Park, Bexhill-on-Sea, East Sussex TN39 3HL ☎ *0424 211769*
Tues–Fri, Bank Holiday 10–5; Sat, Sun 2–5
⚑ *The Chairman, Bexhill Museum Association at above address*
£ ♠

The collections and displays of the Museum comprise specimens from abroad as well as local material. They include sections on geology, natural history, marine biology, ornithology and archaeology of the district, as well as local history. An archive of photographs and documents forms part of the Museum.

Bexley

Bexley Museum

Hall Place, Bourne Road, Bexley, Kent DA5 1PQ
☎ *0322 526574*
Mon–Sat 10–5; Sun (summer only) 2–6. Closed Dec 25, 26.
⚑ *The Assistant Curator, Local Studies Section*
F ⬿ ♠ □

Hall Place is a Tudor and Jacobean mansion, set in extensive landscaped gardens. The Great Hall and other rooms are open to the public. The permanent exhibitions in the Museum cover the geology, archaeology and natural history of the Borough, while the temporary exhibitions, of which there are four or five each year, deal mainly with local history. The Museum collections are particularly strong in this field and the system of temporary exhibitions allows more items to be seen than would be possible if coverage was restricted to permanent displays.
    Guided tours can be arranged, if an appointment is made previously.

Bibury

Arlington Mill: Cotswold Country Museum

Bibury, nr Cirencester, Gloucestershire GL7 5NL
☎ *028574 368*
Mar–Oct, daily 10.30–7. Nov–Feb, Sat, Sun 10.30–dusk.
⚑ *Mrs D. Wynne-Jones*
£ ⬿ ♠

The Mill dates from the late 17th century, when it was used both for fulling and for grinding corn. By 1965 it was derelict but, after restoration of the Mill and the adjoining domestic buildings, it was equipped with 18th-century wooden machinery from North Cerney Mill and corn is now being ground again.
    The Museum, in 17 exhibition rooms, has displays of agricultural implements and rural crafts. There is a special exhibition of furniture made to the design of the great Cotswold craftsman, Ernest Gimson. Other exhibits include a collection of Staffordshire figures and a room, complete with furniture, from Keble House, Fairford. Everything in it belonged to John Keble, the noted Victorian hymn writer and author of *The Christian Year*.

Bideford

The Burton Art Gallery

Kingsley Road, Bideford, North Devon
☎ *02372 67611 extn 315*
Mon–Fri 10–1, 2–5; Sat 10–1
⚑ *John Butler, Curator*
F ⬿ ♠

The main collections of this Gallery are paintings and watercolours by English artists, but there are also strong holdings of Napoleonic model ships and English and German pottery and porcelain. Other items on display include pewter, silver, visiting card cases and North Devon slipware.

Arlington Mill, Bibury, from the Mill Pond.

Biggar

Biggar Gasworks Museum

Gasworks Road, Biggar, Ayrshire
    ☎ 0899 21050
Sun (summer only) 11–5. Other times by appt.
🏛 *Department of Public Affairs and Museum*
    Services, Royal Museum of Scotland,
    Chambers Street, Edinburgh EH1 1JF
    ☎ 031 225 7434
F 🖉 🚗 🏛

Biggar, which opened in 1839, is one of only two early gasworks in Britain – the other being at Fakenham – to survive. It ceased operating in 1973 and is now in the care of the Royal Museum of Scotland. The small, compact site illustrates the complete process at a typical hand-fired gasworks in the 19th and early 20th centuries. Modifications were made over the years, and Biggar today looks as it did from 1914 onwards. In addition to the works, visitors are able to see an historical display of gas appliances.

Gladstone Court Museum

Biggar Museum Trust, Moat Park, Biggar,
    Ayrshire ML12 6DT   ☎ 0899 21050
Easter–Oct, daily 10–12.30, 2–5. Closed Spring
    and late Summer Bank Holidays.
🏛 *B. Lambie*
E 🖼

Gladstone Court is a reconstruction of a Victorian shopping street. The shops, with their stock and equipment, include those of a chemist, grocer, bootmaker, dressmaker and watchmaker. Other premises are a bank, photographer's booth, village library and telephone exchange. There is also a generous display of advertisements of the period.

Greenhill Covenanters' House

Biggar Museum Trust, Moat Park, Biggar,
    Ayrshire ML12 6DT   ☎ 0899 21050
Easter–mid Oct, daily 2–5
🏛 *B. Lambie*
E 🚗

The old farmhouse of Greenhill, with its Covenanting associations, originally stood near Wiston, a village 10 miles from Biggar. It became derelict, and in 1975 a start was made on demolishing it and moving it to Biggar, where it was eventually rebuilt and opened as a museum. Some of the rooms have been furnished in 17th and 18th-century style. One of the principal items of furniture is a four-poster bed, made in 1595 for Patrick Levingstone, of Saltcoats Castle, and brought to Biggar in the mid 17th century for Margaret Levingstone, who was fined for her Covenanting activities.

An upstairs room is used as a museum. It contains miniature costume figures depicting the country people of the 1680s, the sort of people who could have been seen at Conventicles, and a copy of the Book of Common Prayer, the service book which caused the riot which started the Covenanting wars.

Biggleswade

The Shuttleworth Collection

Old Warden Aerodrome, nr Biggleswade,
    Bedfordshire SG18 9ER   ☎ 076727 288
Daily 10–4. Nov–Mar 10–3. Closed one week over
    Christmas, and New Year.
🏛 *Mrs Betty Knight*
E 🖼 🎫 🍴 🚗 ♿

The Collection consists of more than 30 historic aircraft in flying condition, ranging from a 1909 Blériot to a 1941 Spitfire. In a former garage and coachhouse there is also a collection of late 19th and early 20th-century motorcars, including a 1898 Panhard Levassor.

World War I Hawker Hind. Biggleswade, The Shuttleworth Collection.

Bignor

Bignor Roman Villa

Bignor, Pulborough, West Sussex RH20 1PH
    ☎ 07987 259
Mar–May, Tues–Sun 10–5.30. June–Oct, daily
    10–5.30
🏛 *The Curator*
E 🍴 🚗 ♿ HHA

The Villa was first discovered and opened to the public in the 1820s. It contains some of the finest mosaics in Britain, with special buildings to protect them. There is a museum which displays material found during the excavations.

Billericay

The Cater Museum

74 High Street, Billericay, Essex CM12 9BS
    ☎ 02774 22023
Mon, Wed, Thurs 2–5; Tues, Fri, Sat 12.30–5.
    Closed Bank Holiday.
🏛 *C. E. Wright, Curator*
F 🖉

The Museum occupies the house, a listed 18th-century building, of the last saddler and harness-maker in Billericay. Principally an exhibition of local bygones, it includes a large collection of late 19th and early 20th-century photographs of the district. Two rooms are furnished as a mid-Victorian sitting room and bedroom. A special feature of the Museum is its large collection of model fire-engines, from very early examples to the 1950s.

Bilston

Bilston Art Gallery and Museum

*Mount Pleasant, Bilston, Wolverhampton,
    West Midlands*   ☎ *0902 49143*
Mon–Sat 10–5. Closed Bank Holiday.
🔌 *The Keeper*
Ⓔ 🐾 🔌 ☐

The Museum is in a converted late Victorian
ironmaster's house. The emphasis of the
collection is on local work, which includes
18th-century painted enamels, 19th-century
japanned ware and Arts and Crafts pottery.
There are also displays of memorabilia of local
personalities.
    The Gallery is also used for temporary
exhibitions on local historical subjects.
Recent themes have included 'Wolverhampton
Motorcycles', 'The Canals of Wolverhampton
and District', and 'Bilston at War'.

Birchington

Powell-Cotton Museum and Quex House

Quex Park, Birchington, Kent CT7 0BH
    ☎ *0843 42168*
*Museum: Sun throughout year 2.15–6. Rooms in
    House and Museum, Apr–Sept, Wed, Thurs,
    Sun, also Bank Holiday and Fri in Aug
    2.15–6. Last admission Apr–Sept 5,
    Oct–Mar 4.30.*
🔌 *Derek R. Howlett, Curator*
Ⓔ 🐾 💺 🔌 ♿ [HHA]

Quex House, the home of the Powell-Cotton
family, is half a mile south of Birchington, on
the B2048. During the summer several rooms
are open to the public. In addition to family
memorabilia, they contain fine collections of
furniture, porcelain, paintings and glass.
    The founder of the Museum, the big-game
hunter, Major P. H. G. Powell-Cotton,

**African diorama with a pair of kudu.
Birchington, The Powell-Cotton Museum.**

inherited Quex House and its estate in 1894. He
devoted his life to the study and collection of
Indian and African fauna and ethnographical
material. Between 1887 and 1939 he made 28
collecting expeditions. The exceptional private
museum which resulted from his efforts contains
animals in superb dioramas, some 65 feet long,
including the first major diorama in the world
(1895). The nine large galleries also contain
important ethnographic collections; guns,
swords and cannon; 17th and 18th-century
Chinese Imperial porcelain; Oriental fine art;
and local archaeology.

Birkenhead

Birkenhead Priory

Priory Street, Birkenhead, Merseyside
*May–Sept, Tues–Sat 9–1.30, 2–4. Oct–Apr,
    Tues–Sat 9–1.*
🔌 *See Williamson Art Gallery*
Ⓕ

The Priory lies in the centre of Birkenhead,
close to the Cammell Laird shipbuilding yard. It
was established in the 12th century on a
headland which is now part of an industrial
area. Parts of the original buildings still survive,
the most substantial remains being those of the
undercroft and the chapter house. The
Victorian church of St Mary's is also on the site.

Williamson Art Gallery and Museum

Slatey Road, Birkenhead, Merseyside L43 4UE
    ☎ *051 652 4177*
Mon–Sat 10–5 (Thurs until 9); Sun 2–5
🔌 *The Curator*
Ⓕ 🐾 🔌 ♿

Victorian oil paintings and 18th and
19th-century British watercolours are well
represented in the Gallery's fine art collections,
which include important works by Philip
Wilson Steer and artists of the Liverpool
School. There is a growing collection of
contemporary works. Prominent in the
decorative arts section is a range of ceramics
produced on Merseyside – Liverpool porcelain,
Seacombe pottery and Della Robbia ware.
    The displays in the Museum reflect the
maritime past of Birkenhead and the Wirral,
and illustrate the history of the region in
general.

Birmingham

Aston Hall

*Aston Park, Trinity Road, Aston, Birmingham,
    West Midlands B6 6JD*   ☎ *021 327 0062*
Easter–Oct, daily 2–5
🔌 *See City Museum and Art Gallery*
Ⓕ ▮ 🔌

Aston Hall was built by Sir Thomas Holte, the
1st Baronet, between 1618 and 1635 and the
family continued to live in the house until 1817.
It was eventually bought by Birmingham

Corporation in 1864. It contains Jacobean decorative plaster and woodwork, together with sculptured fireplaces, all of which are of national importance.

It is now organised as the country house branch museum of Birmingham Museum and Art Gallery. Nearly 30 rooms have been recently redecorated and rearranged in order to give a clearer impression of what it was like to live in them, either in the 1760s or when the house was last substantially altered. Very little furniture remains from the days when the house was lived in, but it now contains many fine paintings, pieces of furniture, textiles, silver and ceramics from the Museum's collections, as well as portraits and heirlooms of the Holte family.

Jacobean fireplace in the Red Room at Aston Hall, Birmingham.

The Barber Institute of Fine Arts

Edgbaston Park Road, Birmingham, West
*   Midlands B15 2TS*   ☎ *021 472 0962*
Mon–Fri 10–5; Sat 10–1. Closed public holidays,
*   Christmas and Easter, and University Closed*
*   Days. Parties by appt only.*
🕅 *Secretary to the Director*
Ⓕ 🗘 🛆

The Institute has a small but important collection of paintings from western Europe up to the early 20th century. There are, in addition, some drawings, sculpture and examples of the decorative arts.

Birmingham Museum of Science and Industry

Newhall Street, Birmingham, West Midlands
*   B3 1RX*   ☎ *021 236 1022*
Mon–Sat 9.30–5; Sun 2–5. Closed Dec 24, 25,
*   Jan 1.*
🕅 *See City Museum and Art Gallery*
Ⓕ 🗘 🖳 🛆 ♿

Founded in 1950, the Museum was established in a group of Victorian factory buildings, with modern additions. It is close to St Paul's Church, which has connections with James Watt, and to the Birmingham jewellery quarter. The Assay Office, set up by Matthew Boulton, is opposite the Museum and there is a towpath walk to Cambrian Wharf, which has access to the national canal system. The James Watt Building, a new extension opened in 1983, is built round the 1779 Boulton and Watt beam engine, which pumped water back to the canal locks at Smethwick. This is by far the oldest working steam engine in the world.

The collections include locomotives, stationary steam engines, gas, oil and hot-air engines, veteran cars – John Cobb's world record-holder is among them – motorcycles and bicycles, and the only surviving Birmingham Tramcar. The aircraft gallery includes a Spitfire and a Hurricane and a number of aircraft engines. There are sections devoted to science, mechanical music, machine tools, clocks, domestic appliances and writing instruments. The arms collection contains exhibits ranging from crossbows to modern firearms.

Regular Steam Days are held on the first and third Wednesday of each month, in addition to Steam Weekends in March and October. There is an annual Traction Engine Rally round the city streets in May and a Stationary Steam Engine Rally in September.

Birmingham Nature Centre

Pershore Road, Edgbaston, Birmingham, West
*   Midlands B5 7RL*   ☎ *021 472 7775*
Easter–Oct, daily 10–2
🕅 *See City Museum and Art Gallery*
Ⓕ 🛆 🖳 🛆

The Centre aims to give city dwellers, especially the younger ones, some understanding of nature and the countryside, and also to provide a pleasant place to stroll. A selection of British and European wildlife is exhibited in naturalistic settings and there are both natural and artificial habitats for plants and for wild species of birds, mammals and insects. The wide range of animals on display is housed in both indoor and outdoor enclosures. The grounds comprise paddocks, waterfowl and fish ponds, streams and rock outcrops.

Birmingham Railway Museum

670 Warwick Road, Tyseley, Birmingham, West
*   Midlands B11 2HL*   ☎ *021 707 4696*
Daily 10–5 or dusk in winter. Closed Dec 25, 26,
*   Jan 1.*
🕅 *Education Officer*
Ⓔ 🛆 🖳 🛆

The Museum occupies part of the site of the Great Western Railway Depot at Tyseley, built in 1908. The collection includes six express locomotives in various stages of restoration. Two, the G.W.R. *Clun Castle* and the L.M.S. *Kolhapur*, have been completely overhauled and are now able to run on the main line. The Museum also possesses historically interesting rolling stock, representing all four pre-nationalisation companies. These include a travelling Post Office van, a G.W.R. Royal Saloon, a G.W.R. Engineers' Saloon and a Pullman Bar Car.

There are plans for the re-erection of the former locomotive roundhouse and for its conversion into an exhibition hall. This will make it possible to display items from the Museum's large collection of railwayana, which is at present in store.

Blakesley Hall

Blakesley Road, Yardley, Birmingham, West Midlands B25 8RN   ☎ *021 783 2193*
Easter–Oct, daily 2–5
Ⅻ *See City Museum and Art Gallery*
F ⬙

Blakesley Road, on which the Hall is situated, runs north off the Stoney Lane section of the outer circle road, near Yardley. Blakesley Hall is a timber-framed yeoman's house, constructed c. 1575. It contains a remarkable first-floor long gallery and, in one of the bedrooms, 16th-century wall paintings. It has been recently restored under the direction of Birmingham City Museum and furnished in accordance with a surviving 16th-century interior.

There are displays on domestic interiors, the development and techniques of timber-framed building, and the history and archaeology of Blakesley Hall. Other cases exhibit the celebrated Temple Balsall collection of post-medieval ceramics. Part of the Barn is used for exhibitions on trades and suburban agriculture.

City Museum and Art Gallery

Chamberlain Square, Birmingham, West Midlands B3 3DH   ☎ *021 235 3890*
Mon–Sat 9.30–5; Sun 2–5
Ⅻ *Schools Liaison Unit*
F ⬙ ⬙ ⬙ ⬙

The Museum and Art Gallery was founded in 1867 and opened in its present building in 1885. Extensions were built in 1912 and 1919 and a Local History Gallery was opened in the former Commercial and Patents Library in 1981. Birmingham has been a rich and powerful city and the collections are now enormous. The Local History section is concerned with the origins and growth of Birmingham and its suburbs from the end of the Middle Ages to the present day. The displays cover social and domestic history, civic life, trades and industries. Natural History has extensive collections of fossils, minerals, plants, marine shells, insects, birds and mammals.

Archaeology is very strongly featured, with material from the Middle and Near East, Greece and Rome, and Central and South America. Most parts of the world are represented in the ethnographical displays, with the Pacific Islands and West Africa as the areas of greatest specialisation and interest. The coin collections cover both the ancient and medieval periods, as well as the past four centuries.

The Fine Arts Galleries show British and European paintings from the 14th to the 20th centuries and are particularly strong in Italian works of the 17th century and in the collection of the English Pre-Raphaelites, the finest in the world. There is also an outstanding collection of English 18th and 19th-century drawings and watercolours.

English furniture and Italian marriage chests of the 19th century are displayed in the Fine Art Galleries and pottery, porcelain, glass, textiles and costumes in the restored Industrial Gallery, a splendid example of Victorian cast-iron architecture. There are also sections devoted to British and European silver, Oriental and Middle Eastern applied art and contemporary British crafts.

Museum of the Department of Geological Sciences

University of Birmingham, PO Box 363, Birmingham, West Midlands B15 2TT   ☎ *021 472 1301*
Mon–Fri 9–5. Closed Bank Holiday and days following.
Ⅻ *The Curator*
F

The displays, which are used for undergraduate teaching purposes, are of mineralogy and stratigraphic palaeontology. Among the collections of fossils, rocks and minerals are a number of particularly fine Silurian (Wenlock) fossils from Dudley, and about 2,000 examples of type and figured specimens.

Blakesley Hall, Birmingham.

National Motorcycle Museum

Coventry Road, Bickenhill, Birmingham,
*   West Midlands B92 0EJ*   ☎ *06755 3311*
Daily 10–6. Closed Dec 25.
W. R. Richards
£ ♦ ⬛ ♙ &

The National Motorcycle Museum is
strategically placed at the junction of the M42
and A45. It has a collection of 600 British
motorcycles – foreign makes are excluded –
dating from 1898 to the present day. There are
rare and famous racing and competition
machines, as well as everyday road models.
All the exhibits have been painstakingly
restored to the original specification, using,
wherever possible, authentic materials. The
aim of the Museum is to provide a social as well
as an engineering history of this once great
British industry.

The Patrick Collection

180 Lifford Lane, Birmingham, West Midlands
*   B30 3NT*   ☎ *021 459 4471/9111*
Apr 10 June, Sept 15–Nov 1, Wed–Mon
*   11.30–5.30. July–Sept 13, daily 11–7.*
Mr H. Webber, General Manager
£ ♦ ⬛ ♙ &

The Museum occupies two purpose-built
exhibition halls on the site of the former King's
Norton Paper Mills. The collection of cars,
dating from 1913, was begun by the Patrick
family, which has been closely associated with
the motor industry since the 1930s. The
Alexick Hall presents cars in their social
context, decade by decade, and the Mansell
Hall presents innovative cars of the 1980s.
At any one time, visitors can see about 50 of
the 160 cars in the Collection, displayed in
settings which reflect the changes in values,
attitudes and aspirations brought about by the
motorcar.

Sarehole Mill

Cole Bank Road, Hall Green, Birmingham,
*   West Midlands B13 0BD*   ☎ *021 777 6612*
Easter–Oct, daily 2–5
See City Museum and Art Gallery
F ♙ ♙

Sarehole Mill, one of the last survivors of more
than 50 watermills in Birmingham, is a good
example of a late 18th-century watermill
building. Most of the present machinery dates
from the 19th century and is in working order.
The Mill was last used commercially in 1919,
and was opened as a museum in 1969, after a
protracted campaign to save it from demolition.
It now contains displays relating to agriculture,
the history of the Mill and the district of Hall
Green, in which Sarehole Mill is located. On
the ground floor there is a reconstructed blade
grinding workshop.
    The Mill has associations with J. R. R.
Tolkien, whose family lived nearby for a
time, and who recalled the area when creating
the Shire in *The Hobbit* and *The Lord of the*
Rings.

A 1949 Norton Dominator. Birmingham,
National Motorcycle Museum.

Weoley Castle Ruins

Alwold Road, Weoley Castle, Birmingham, West
*   Midlands B29 5RX*   ☎ *021 427 1270*
Tues before Easter–Sept, Tues–Fri 2–5, and Bank
*   Holiday Mon*
See City Museum and Art Gallery
£ ♙ ♙

Weoley Castle was a semi-fortified medieval
manor house. Excavations have uncovered rich
finds of tools, coins, domestic pottery, floor
tiles and metalwork, together with some
wooden and leather objects, which have been
preserved as a result of the wet conditions.
    All these objects are displayed in a museum
on the site and illustrate clearly the everyday
lives of the occupants of the manor house.

Birr

Birr Castle Exhibition Gallery

The Estate Office, Birr, Co. Offaly, Ireland
*   ☎ 0509 20056*
May–Sept 7, daily 2.30–5.30
The Administrator
£ *Castle only* ♦ ⬛ ♙

The Gallery is in the early Victorian coach
house and stable block of the Castle. It is
devoted entirely to annual exhibitions and aims
at displaying over a cycle of a decade or so the
principal collections preserved in the Castle,
and in this way at representing the different
aspects of the heritage of the Parsons family,
Earls of Rosse since 1807.
    The first exhibition featured the scientific
achievements of Sir Charles Parsons, the
second, 'Speaking from the Past', presented
extracts from the vast historical archives in the

Muniment Room, the third described the making of the great gardens at Birr and the fourth the pioneering photography of Mary Rosse, wife of the 3rd Earl.

An exhibition in 1986 was based on the collection of dresses, robes and decorations worn by members of the family over the past half-dozen generations, and for 1987 the theme will be the upbringing of the family's children from the 17th century onwards.

Birstall

Oakwell Hall and Country Park

Nutter Lane, Birstall, West Yorkshire WF17 9LG
☎ 0924 474926
Mon–Sat 10–5; Sun 1–5. Parties at other times
  by appt.
◪ The Curator
Ⓕ ✑ ⬤ ⭅

A large timber-framed manor house was built here in the mid 15th century. In the 1580s it was remodelled and encased in stone, and some alterations took place in the first half of the following century. Since then, the structure of the building has changed very little. In 1928 it was bought for public ownership and has been restored and furnished to create an atmosphere of Yorkshire life in the 17th and 18th centuries.

The Oakwell Hall estate is now being developed as a country park, with nature trails, guided walks and an equestrian area. Buildings near the Hall are being used as craftsmen's workshops and as an interpretative centre.

Bishop Auckland

Binchester Roman Fort

Bishop Auckland, Co. Durham
☎ 0388 663089
Apr–Sept, daily 10.30–6 ex. Tues, Wed
◪ The Antiquities Officer, The Bowes Museum,
  Barnard Castle, Co. Durham DL12 8NP
☎ 0833 37139
Ⓔ ✑ ⭅

Vinovia, the Roman fort at Binchester, was one of a chain of forts guarding the road between York and Hadrian's Wall. It was established in A.D. 80 and successive rebuilding and alterations went on until the end of the 4th century. Some parts continued to be used after the Roman withdrawal and there is evidence of Anglo-Saxon and medieval reoccupation. The fort covers about 10 acres and there is a civilian settlement of similar size. Excavation of the area has so far been confined to the house of the commanding officer, with its impressive 4th-century bath suite, which contains the best preserved hypocaust floor of any military site in Britain. The remains of the bath suite have been covered in for protection and the building contains an explanatory display.

The finds from the excavations at Binchester are on show at the Bowes Museum.

Bishopbriggs

Thomas Muir Museum

Huntershill Recreation Centre, Crowhill Road,
  Bishopbriggs, Glasgow, Lanarkshire G66 1RW
By appt
◪ Strathkelvin District Museums, The Cross,
  Kirkintilloch, Glasgow G66 1AB
☎ 041 775 1185
Ⓕ ⭅

The Museum, in part of the Muir family home, contains displays illustrating the life of the 18th-century Scottish radical and reformer, Thomas Muir. The house is now incorporated in the Huntershill Recreation Centre.

Bishop's Stortford

Rhodes Memorial Museum

South Road, Bishop's Stortford, Hertfordshire
  CM23 3JG   ☎ 0279 51746
Mon, Wed–Sat 10–4; Tues 10–12. Closed Bank
  Holiday and first two weeks in Aug.
◪ Mrs A. E. Crooks, Curator
Ⓔ ⭅

The Museum has been arranged in Cecil Rhodes' birthplace. The exhibits illustrate Rhodes' life and achievements against a background of the history of South Africa. There are special displays relating to his connections with the diamond and gold industries and with the Matabele Rebellion and the Boer War.

Blackburn

Blackburn Museum and Art Gallery and Lewis Textile Museum

Museum Street, Blackburn, Lancashire BB1 7AJ
☎ 0254 667130
Mon–Sat 10–5. Closed Good Fri, Dec 25, 26,
  Jan 1 and some Bank Holidays.
◪ The Curator
Ⓕ ✑ ⭅

Medieval illuminated manuscripts, early printed books, Greek, Roman and English coins, and Japanese prints are the most important of the Museum's collections, but there are also good displays of British 19th and 20th-century paintings and watercolours, Oriental and European ceramics and icons, with some sculpture, glass, ivories and metalwork.

The historical collections of the East Lancashire Regiment form a section of the Museum, which also houses the Lewis Textile Museum, illustrating the development of the spinning and weaving industries, especially in Lancashire, with demonstrations of early machines.

The Museum and Library building is interesting in its own right. It is designed in the Gothic style, particular attention being given to architectural detail.

Witton Country Park: Visitor Centre

Preston Old Road, Blackburn, Lancashire
BB2 2TP   ☎ 0254 55423
Thurs–Sat 1–5; Sun 11–5. Open public holidays
ex. Christmas week, Jan 1.
🗴 *The Warden*
Ⓕ 🛆 💺 🚗 ♿ ☐

The Park is one mile west of the town centre, on
the A674 Chorley road. The Visitor Centre, in
the restored coach-houses and stables of the
Witton estate, has displays of carriages, farm
carts, horse-drawn farm machinery, and hand
tools. There is a natural history room, with
displays of stuffed animals and birds, and a
room, formerly a hayloft, for temporary
exhibitions, which are changed monthly.

Blackgang

Blackgang Sawmill and St Catherine's Quay

Blackgang, nr Ventnor, Isle of Wight PO38 2HN
   ☎ 0983 730330
Apr–Sept, daily 10–5
🗴 *S. F. Dabell, Manager*
Ⓔ 🛆 💺 🚗

Blackgang Sawmill tells the story of timber and
its uses. The displays and animated scenes are
set in and around a working replica of a water-
powered sawmill, converted from an early 19th-
century stone barn. The exhibits illustrate
timber-felling, the sawing and transporting of
logs, a range of rural crafts, including those of
the cooper, wheelwright and carpenter, and the
sources of power used, a waterwheel, steam
engine and oil engine.

St Catherine's Quay is a maritime exhibition,
incorporating a reconstruction of a Victorian
quayside scene. There are displays relating to
the RNLI, with the former Flamborough
lifeboat, *The Friendly Forester*, built on the Isle
of Wight in 1953, coastal erosion, travel in the
Solent and shipwrecks. Visitors to the Quay can
also see a reconstruction of an Isle of Wight
beach scene as it might have been in 1890.

**Victorian quayside scene, St Catherine's
Quay, Blackgang.**

Blackpool

Grundy Art Gallery

Queen Street, Blackpool, Lancashire FY1 1PX
   ☎ 0253 23977
Mon–Sat 10–5
🗴 *J. K. Burkitt, Curator*
Ⓕ ✐ 🚗

Over the past 70 years, the Gallery has built up
a representative collection of mainstream
English art of the present century, a selection of
which is normally always on view. Among the
artists represented are Paul Nash, Eric Ravilious
and Augustus John, while earlier painters
include David Roberts, Stanhope Forbes and
Birket Foster, as well as artists who exhibited at
the Royal Academy Summer Shows. At the
moment the Gallery is collecting limited edition
prints by contemporary print makers.

In addition to its paintings, watercolours and
prints, the Grundy Art Gallery has a good
collection of small ivory pieces, in particular
many examples of Japanese netsuke.

Blaenafon

Big Pit Mining Museum

Blaenafon, Gwent NP4 9XP   ☎ 0495 790311
Mar–Nov, daily 10–3.30 (last complete tour)
🗴 *Director*
Ⓔ 🛆 💺 🚗

Big Pit is just off the B4248 between Blaenafon
and Brynmawr. Mining came to an end here in
1980 and Big Pit is the last surviving group of
mining installations in this once important
centre of the coal and iron industries. Visitors
can see the pithead baths, which preserve their
original installations, a photographic exhibition
which shows the history of the pit and the
conditions under which the miners lived and
worked, the winding engine house, and the
blacksmith's forge, and a reconstruction of the
interior of a miner's cottage.

Before going 300 feet underground, visitors
put on a helmet and cap lamp. Once down the
pit, they are given a guided tour by one of a
team of ex-miners. In the course of this they are
able to observe the pit-pony stables, haulage
engines and coal faces, and hear about the
methods of extracting and transporting the coal.

Regrettably, small children cannot be taken
underground, and visitors are reminded to wear
practical shoes and warm clothing for their
underground tour.

Blaenafon Ironworks

Blaenafon, Gwent   ☎ 0495 552036
Apr–Sept, Mon–Sat 10–5; Sun 2–5. By guided
tour only. Last tour 4.30.
🗴 *Torfaen Museum Trust, Blaenafon Ironworks,*
   North Street, Blaenafon
Ⓔ ✐ 🚗

An ironworks was established at Blaenafon in
the 18th century and by 1880 it was one of a

chain of such works which had been established along the northern edge of the South Wales coalfield. Its remains are exceptionally well preserved. They include the original kilns, the water balance tower and the workers' living accommodation, popularly known as 'Stack Square'. There is a site-exhibition on the lives of the ironworkers.

Blaenau Ffestiniog

Gloddfa Ganol Slate Mine

Blaenau Ffestiniog, Gwynedd   ☎ 0766 830 664
Spring Bank Holiday–Sept, weekdays
Mrs V. Davies
£ ● ☕ ⇦ ♿

The Mine is one mile north of Blaenau Ffestiniog, on the A470. Slate was mined on the site in the 1820s, and the scale of operations earned it the reputation of being 'the largest slate mine in the world', until its closure in 1971.

In 1974 one of the abandoned surface levels, called Gloddfa Ganol or Middle Quarry, was opened to the public as the Gloddfa Ganol Slate Mine, with an operating slate mill where the slate is cut, a museum of the slate industry, a natural history museum and a narrow gauge railway museum, as well as Land Rover tours to the higher abandoned workings not normally accessible to the public. In 1976 walk-through tours were extended to the abandoned tunnels and chambers on Floor 5.

Llechwedd Slate Caverns

Blaenau Ffestiniog, Gwynedd LL41 3NB
    ☎ 0766 830306
Apr or Easter–Oct, daily 10–5.15 (4.15 Oct)
Mrs Lis Jones, Marketing Officer
£ *underground tours only* ● ☕ ⇦ ♿

The Caverns are just north of Blaenau Ffestiniog, on the A470. Llechwedd, worked since 1846, is the largest slate mine still operating in Wales. Since 1972 visitors have been able to tour parts of the mine. Two quite different rides are available. On the first, tramway carriages enter the side of the mountain and remain at the same level as the track winds through a succession of chambers which re-create Victorian conditions. Having alighted inside the caverns, passengers are given a demonstration and introductory talk by a miner.

The second ride takes visitors down a 1 in 8 gradient into the Deep Mine. Here they alight at the bottom of the incline for a tour on foot through a network of sound and light tableaux, before returning to the surface again. Above ground, the Slate Heritage Theatre presents a history of slate in pictures, voice and song. Exhibitions on slate mining and mine tramways can also be seen, as well as an old smithy and slate mill.

Slate splitting in the Mill at Llechwedd Slate Caverns, Blaenau Ffestiniog.

Blagdon

Blagdon Beam Engine

Blagdon Pumping Station, Blagdon, Avon
Guided tours by appt. Occasional Open Days.
Mr Chris Klee, Bristol Waterworks Company,
    PO Box 218, Bridgwater Road, Bristol
    BS99 7AV   ☎ 0272 665881
F ⇦ ☞

The Pumping Station and its associated reservoir were built in the 1890s. It originally housed four beam engines. The steam plant consumed eight and a half tons of coal a day. In 1949 two of the beam engines were replaced by electric pumps and the remaining two are now preserved as a museum feature, one of them fitted with an electric motor, to demonstrate its method of operation.

Blair Atholl

Atholl Country Collection

The Old School, Blair Atholl, Perthshire
    ☎ 079 681 232
Easter, late May–Oct, daily 1.30–5.30. July–Aug,
    also 9.30–12.30.
John Cameron
£ ♧ ⇦ ♿

The Museum is in the former village school, built in 1856 and closed in 1972. Its entrance is easily recognised from the statue of a prancing white horse, which for many years stood over the coaching entrance of a local hotel.

The exhibits illustrate life in the village and the glens during the 19th and early 20th centuries. They include items on the school, the church, road, rail and postal services, the vet and the gamekeeper. There are also reconstructions of a smithy and a crofter's living-room.

Blair Castle and Atholl Museum

Blair Atholl, Perthshire PH18 5TH
☎ 079 681 207
Easter week, Sun–Mon in Apr, then daily from
3rd Sun in Apr to 2nd Sun in Oct, Mon–Sat
10–6; Sun 2–6. Last admission 5.
🔲 *Brian H. Nodes, Administrator*
£ ♿ ▬ ♿ HHA

The earliest part of the buildings dates back to
1268. The collections now displayed present a
picture of life in the Castle from the 16th to the
20th century. They include notable furniture,
weapons and armour, as well as porcelain, lace,
embroidery, Jacobite relics, masonic regalia and
children's games.

Clan Donnachaidh Museum

Bruar Falls, Blair Atholl, Perthshire
☎ 079 681 264
Apr–Oct, Mon–Sat 10–1, 2–5.30; Sun 2–5.30
🔲 *The Secretary*
F ⌀ ♿

The Clan Donnachaidh (the name is pronounced
Donnachie) – the children of Duncan – claim
their descent from Donnachadh Reamhair, who
was descended from the Celtic Earls of Atholl
and led his men to fight under King Robert at
Bannockburn in 1314. The Clan's headquarters
is the Museum at Blair Atholl and its traditional
lands stretched from the Moor of Rannoch to the
gates of Perth.

The Museum, opened in 1969, occupies a
purpose-designed building and is planned to
illustrate four interwoven themes – the clan
history, including the principal families; the clan
country, its past, present and future; the work of
the clan society; and the life and achievements of
individual clansmen and clanswomen.

Blandford Camp

Royal Signals Museum

Blandford Camp, Dorset DT11 8RH
☎ 0258 52581 extn 413
Mon–Fri 9–5. Sat by appt.
🔲 *Major A. G. Harfield, Deputy Director*
F ⌀ ♿

Blandford Camp is to the east of Blandford. There
are entrances to it from both the A354 and the
B3082. The Museum contains items relating to
the history of military communications from the
Crimean War to the Falkland Islands campaign,
including the history of the Royal Engineers
(Signal Service) and the Royal Corps of Signals.

Blandford Forum

Blandford Forum Museum

The Old Coach House, Bere's Yard, Market Place,
Blandford Forum, Dorset DT11 7HU
☎ 0258 51115
Easter–Sept, Mon–Sat 10.30–12.30, 2.30–4.30;
Sun 2.30–4.30
🔲 *Mr B. G. Cox, Hon. Curator*
£ *ex. children* ⌀ ♿

The displays, in a converted Georgian coach-
house, illustrate the life and occupations of
people in Blandford and its neighbourhood from
prehistoric times to the present day. There are
good collections of domestic equipment, local
militaria and Victorian and Edwardian
costumes. Among the special features of the
Museum are a Rural Bygones Room and the
Alfred Stevens Art Gallery, in which a number
of special exhibitions are staged each year, by no
means all of them on artistic subjects.

Livingstone's home. David Livingstone
Centre, Blantyre.

Blantyre

The David Livingstone Centre

Station Road, Blantyre, Lanarkshire G72 9BT
☎ 0698 823140
Mon–Sat 10–6; Sun 2–6. Closed Dec 25, 26,
Jan 1, 2.
🔲 *Bill Cunningham, Warden*
£ ♿ ▬ ♿ ♿

David Livingstone, the Scottish missionary and
explorer, was born at Blantyre in 1813, at the
home of his grandparents. The tenement
building which contained his birthplace is now
the David Livingstone Memorial. The single-
room dwelling has been furnished and decorated
to resemble the tenement during Livingstone's
boyhood, and in other rooms of the building,
which once accommodated 24 families, there
are displays to tell the story of the explorer's life.

The Livingstone Gallery contains eight
tableaux, in concrete, which illustrate aspects
of Livingstone's life. An African Pavilion, built
in the shape of a cluster of African huts,
concentrates attention on African life today.
The Social History Gallery, in the former
Works School of the cotton mill, shows the
impact which the Industrial Revolution made
on the people and skills of Scotland.

Blessington

Russborough

Blessington, Co. Wicklow, Ireland   ☎ 045 65239
Easter–Oct, Sun, Bank Holiday 2.30–5.30; June,
   July, Aug daily.
ⓚ The Administrator, Alfred Beit Foundation at
   above address
Ⓔ 🏛 ⬛ ♿

James Leeson, later Earl of Milltown, was the
son of a prosperous Dublin brewer. He began
building his great Palladian mansion at
Russborough in 1741. After several changes
of ownership during the following two centuries,
it was sold in 1952 to Sir Alfred Beit, who
transferred it in 1976 to the Alfred Beit
Foundation, with the object of keeping the
house and art collection intact and open to the
public.

The building is especially noted for its
splendid plasterwork, some of which was carried
out by the Francini brothers. It houses one of
the great privately formed art collections, which
includes paintings by Gainsborough, Goya,
Rubens, Murillo, Vermeer and Velasquez.
There are also magnificent displays of silver,
European porcelain, fine furniture, tapestries,
carpets and Italian bronzes.

The Front Hall at Russborough, Blessington.

Blyth

Blyth Town Museum

18–22 Croft Road, Blyth, Northumberland
   NE24 2JL   ☎ 0670 353218/352116
Apr–Sept, Wed and Sat 10.30–4.30. Other times
   by appt.
ⓚ Miss C. Atkinson, 72 Marine Terrace, Blyth
   NE24 2LR
Ⓔ ♿

The Museum's displays illustrate life in Blyth
and the surrounding area from Victorian times
to the present day. One room is furnished as a
Victorian parlour and another as a Victorian
kitchen.

Boat of Garten

Strathspey Railway Museum

The Station, Boat of Garten, Inverness-shire
   PH24 3BH   ☎ 047983 692
Easter–mid Oct, weekends when railway is
   operating. July–Aug, also Mon–Thurs.
ⓚ The Commercial Manager, Strathspey Railway
   at above address
Ⓕ 🏛 ⬛ ♿

Until the Beeching closures of 1965, Boat of
Garten was an important railway junction, with
lines to Forres, Craigellachie and Aviemore. In
1978, however, the line from Boat of Garten to
Aviemore was reopened as the Strathspey
Railway. The great development of tourism in
the region, especially as a result of the creation
of the Aviemore Centre, has made the line,
which runs through beautiful scenery,

increasingly popular. The trains are steam
hauled and use some carriages of the pre-British
Rail period. The character of the line has been
preserved by carefully restoring any surviving
railway buildings and by moving and re-erecting
others belonging to the old Highland and Great
North of Scotland railway systems.

A Museum has been established in part of the
original Highland Railway station at Boat of
Garten. It contains material relating to British
railways, particularly the Highland and Great
North of Scotland and their successors.

Bodmin

Bodmin Town Museum

Mount Folly Square, Bodmin, Cornwall
   PL31 2DQ   ☎ 0208 5516
Apr–Sept, Tues, Thurs, Sat 10–12, 2–4
ⓚ R. J. Allis, Town Clerk, Bodmin Town
   Council, at above address
Ⓕ ♿

This small museum, run entirely by volunteer
staff, is concerned almost wholly with the
history and natural environment of Bodmin.
There are collections illustrating the geology of
the district and its plants and fauna.

Duke of Cornwall's Light Infantry Museum

The Keep, Victoria Barracks, Bodmin, Cornwall
   PL31 1EG   ☎ 0208 2810
Mon–Fri 8–4.45. Closed Bank Holiday.
ⓚ The Curator
Ⓔ ex children 🏛 ♿

The Barracks are in the outskirts of Bodmin, on
the Lostwithiel road. The Museum building is in
the 1859 Defended Militia Keep, built as part of
the preparations against a threatened invasion
by Napoleon III.

The displays trace the history of the Regiment
from its formation in 1702 until the
amalgamation of 1959. The collection of
military small arms is exceptionally fine. It
includes examples of every principal musket and
machine gun used by the infantry of the line
since the mid 18th century, together with a
large number of foreign weapons.

Lanhydrock

Bodmin, Cornwall PL30 5AD   ☎ 0208 3320
Apr–Oct, daily including Good Fri, Bank Holiday,
11–6. Nov–Mar, garden only, daily during
daylight hours.
⚔ *The Administrator*
🇪 🏠 💻 🚗 ♿ NT

The manor of Lanhydrock belonged to the
Robartes family from 1620 until it was given to
the National Trust in 1953. Most of the house,
completed in 1640, was destroyed by fire in
1881. The north wing, including the Long
Gallery, survived. The house was rebuilt to the
original plan after the fire and, as visitors now
see it, vividly recalls the splendour of the late
Victorian period. The kitchen quarters are
complete, with all their fittings, and there is
good 18th-century furniture and Brussels and
Mortlake tapestries. The family portraits include
works by Kneller and Romney.

Pencarrow House

Bodmin, Cornwall PL30 3AG   ☎ 020884 369
Easter–Oct 15, Sun–Thurs 1.30–5. June–Sept 10
and Bank Holiday, 11–5.
⚔ *The Administrator*
🇪 *guided tours only* 💻 🚗 ♿

Pencarrow is four miles north-west of Bodmin.
Built in the 18th century, it continues to be
owned by the Molesworth-St Aubyn family and
there is an interesting series of family portraits,
including a self-portrait by Catherine St Aubyn
and works by Reynolds, Northcote and Devis.
Among the other paintings is one by Samuel
Scott, showing the tenements on Old London
Bridge in the early 18th century. The
furnishings are mainly 18th and early 19th
century.

**Nineteenth-century uniforms. Bodmin, The
Duke of Cornwall's Light Infantry Museum.**

Bognor Regis

Bognor Regis Local History Museum

Hotham Park Lodge, High Street, Bognor Regis,
West Sussex PO21 1HW
May 24–Sept 7, Wed, Sat, Sun 1–5. Open Easter
Sat, Sun, Mon 1–5.
⚔ *The Museum Co-ordinator*
🇫 🌀 🚗 ♿

The Museum building was constructed *c.* 1900
as the lodge to what was then known as Aldwick
Manor, built by Sir Richard Hotham, a wealthy
Southwark hatter, in the 1790s. Bognor Regis is
a creation of the 19th and early 20th centuries,
and the main exhibition illustrates the history
and development of the town, and of the seaside
which forms part of it. Other displays, changing
throughout the year, cover such themes as
notable visitors, tradesmen, sea bathing and
transport developments. The kitchen area of the
house contains a collection of household
equipment.

Bolton

Bolton Museum and Art Gallery

Le Mans Crescent, Bolton, Greater Manchester
BL1 1SE   ☎ 0204 22311 extn 379
Mon, Tues, Thurs, Fri 9.30–5.30; Sat 10–5.
Closed Sun, Wed, Bank Holiday.
⚔ *Senior Keeper of Educational Services*
🇫 🏠 💻 🚗 ♿

The collections in Bolton Museum are wide-
ranging. They include Egyptian antiquities,
geology, botany and zoology, early textile
machines and English and European paintings
and sculpture. There are also displays of pottery,
porcelain and glass, and English watercolours
and drawings.
    An aquarium in the basement contains fish
and other marine life of the waters around the
British coasts.

Bolton Steam Museum

Northern Mill Engine Society, The Engine House,
Atlas No. 3 Mill, Chorley Old Road, Bolton,
Greater Manchester BL1 4LB
Every Sun: static viewing only. Steam Days: Easter
Mon, Spring and Summer Bank Holiday.
For other days, please check locally.
⚔ *Mr E. Hanson, Curator, 57 Sheriff Street,*
Rochdale, Greater Manchester OL12 6QR
🇪 🚗

Atlas No. 3 Mill is a mile and a half north-west
of the centre of Bolton. The Museum displays
the Society's collection of stationary steam
engines, mainly from textile mills in the North-
West, which have been rescued from
destruction and fully restored to run in
steam again. They include an 1840 beam
engine; an 1893 non-dead-centre vertical
engine; a 1902 tandem-coupled horizontal
engine; and an 1860 'A-frame' vertical engine.

Hall i' th' Wood

Green Way, off Crompton Way, Bolton, Greater
*   Manchester BL1 8UA   ☎ 0204 51159*
Apr–Sept, Mon–Sat 10–6; Sun 2–6. Oct–Mar,
*   Mon–Sat 10–5. Closed Dec 25, 26, Jan 1,*
*   Good Fri.*
£ ⊘ ♿

Hall i' th' Wood is two miles north-east of
Bolton town centre, off the Crompton Way
road. The first part of the house was built in
1485 and there were additions in 1591 and
1648. It was refurnished and presented to
Bolton by the 1st Lord Leverhulme. As visitors
see it today, it is furnished in 18th-century style.
    The house was the home of Samuel
Crompton, the inventor of the spinning mule,
and material connected with him is displayed
here, together with other items of local and
industrial history.

Local History Museum

Little Bolton Town Hall, St George's Street,
*   Bolton, Greater Manchester BL1 2EN*
*   ☎ 0204 22311 extn 6193*
Mon–Sat 10–5. Closed Bank Holiday.
◪ *The Custodian*
F ⊘ ♿

This was Bolton's first Town Hall. It was also
used as a magistrate's court, and visitors can still
see the dock and the stairway to the cells. The
collections illustrate the archaeology, social
history, crafts and trades of Bolton. Among the
exhibits is a horse-drawn fire engine and a
reconstruction of a skip basketmaker's
workshop.

Smithhills Hall Museum

Smithhills Dean Road, Bolton, Greater Manchester
*   BL1 7NP   ☎ 0204 41265*
Apr–Sept, Mon–Sat 10–6; Sun 2–6. Oct–Mar,
*   Mon–Sat 10–5. Closed Dec 25, 26, Jan 1,*
*   Good Fri.*
◪ *The Custodian*
£ ⊘ ♥ ♿

The earliest part of the Hall dates from the 14th
century. Additions were made in the 16th
century. Outstanding features of the building
are the open roof construction in the Great Hall
and the linenfold panelling in the withdrawing-
room. The rooms have 17th-century oak
furniture.

Tonge Moor Textile Museum

Tonge Moor Library, Tonge Moor Road, Bolton,
*   Greater Manchester BL2 2LE ☎ 0204 21394*
Mon, Thurs 2–7.30; Tues, Fri 9.30–5.30; Sat
*   9.30–12.30. Closed Wed, Sun, Bank Holiday.*
◪ *See Bolton Museum and Art Gallery*
F ⊘

The Museum is two miles north of the town
centre, on the Burnley road. It is devoted
entirely to the conservation and display of early
textile machinery, including Crompton's mule,
Hargreaves' spinning jenny and Arkwright's
water-frame.

Bo'ness

Bo'ness Heritage Area

Bo'ness Heritage Trust, Bo'ness Station, Bo'ness,
*   West Lothian EH51 0AD   ☎ 0506 825855*
Steam railway & other facilities Easter–Sept,
*   Sat, Sun 11–5. Birkhill Mines Aug–Sept.*
◪ *Bill Breakell, Director*
£ ♦ ♥

The Heritage Area is being developed by the
Bo'ness Heritage Trust to improve and explain
features of historic interest in the Forth Valley.
The sites include Birkhill clay mine, an
important centre of the fireclay industry,
Kinneil Colliery and Bo'ness harbour and docks.
By the side of the Forth, a Scottish township is
being reconstructed, using buildings rescued
from demolition in Central Scotland and
providing space for workshops, exhibitions and
living accommodation.
    The buildings acquired so far range from two
First World War aircraft hangars to a locally
produced 1930s telephone kiosk. Shops and
public buildings are to be added.

Bo'ness Steam Railway

Scottish Railway Preservation Society, Union
*   Street, Bo'ness, West Lothian EH51 0AD*
*   ☎ 0506 822298*
Easter–Sept, Sat, Sun 12–5
◪ *The Secretary*
£ *Train trip only* ♦ ♥ ♿

On rehabilitated land by the side of the River
Forth, a number of old railway buildings and
items of equipment have been re-erected to
recall how passenger and freight traffic used to
be handled by Scotland's railways. From the
terminus station at Bo'ness, steam trains
operate over several miles of track, and will
eventually form a link between a number of
industrial museum sites to be developed by the
Bo'ness Heritage Trust. Items from the Society's
large collection of Scottish railway vehicles
are either used on the line or are on public
display.

Kinneil Museum

Duchess Anne Cottages, Kinneil Estate, Bo'ness,
*   West Lothian   ☎ 0506 824318*
Apr–Sept, Mon–Fri 10–12.30, 1.30–5; Sat 10–5.
*   Closed public holidays.*
◪ *The Curator, Falkirk Museums, Hope Street,*
*   Falkirk, Stirlingshire FK1 5AU*
*   ☎ 0324 24911 extn 2202*
F ⊘ ♿ ▣

The Kinneil Estate lies on the western side of
Bo'ness and is signposted from the A993. The
Museum is housed in a converted 17th-century
stable block at Kinneil House. The lower floor is
devoted to a display on the history of Bo'ness
and the upper floor to exhibits relating to the
estate, special attention being given to Kinneil
House, James Watt's workshop, Kinneil
Church and village, the Roman fortlet on the
Antonine Wall, and the natural history of the
area.

Underground, in the levels, at the Poldark
Mining Museum, Helston.

Gold Anglo-Saxon disc-brooch inlaid with garnets from Kingston, Kent. 7th century AD. Liverpool, Merseyside County Museums.

Japanese netsuke figure of a man on a fish. Hastings Museum and Art Gallery.

Pocket watch by William Ilbery, London, about 1800. Lincoln, The Usher Gallery.

Flowers by the jeweller Peter Carl Fabergé
(1846-1920). London, The Queen's Gallery.

Ceremonial Marriage Rings, Italian, early 17th
and 18th century. London, The Jewish Museum.

The cargoboat 'Raven', 1871. Windermere Steam-boat Museum.

Finds from the 'Mary Rose', Henry VIII's flagship. which sank in the Solent on 19 July 1545. Portsmouth, The Mary Rose Trust.

'Cat' by Louis Wain. Beckenham, The Bethlem
Royal Hospital Museum.

Detail of 'Work' by Ford Madox Brown (1821-93). Manchester City Art Gallery.

Late 19th century pen and wash drawing of the dye plant turmeric. Bradford, The Colour Museum.

Opposite:

Captain Robert Falcon Scott and his companions, Dr Edward Wilson, Lieutenant B.H.R. Bowers, Captain L.E.G. Oates, and Petty Officer Evans at the South Pole, 17 January 1912. Historic photograph in the Scott Polar Research Institute, Cambridge.

'When the Gloaming comes' by Archibald Thorburn. Liskeard, The Thorburn Museum and Art Gallery.

Enamel snuffbox. Bilston Museum and Art Gallery.

'Animals of the Plains', an African diorama at the Powell-Cotton Museum, Birchington.

Opposite:

Kingfishers. Dublin, The National Museum of Ireland.

Queen Victoria and the Prince and Princess of Wales in the Royal Waiting Room. Windsor, Madame Tussaud's Royalty and Railways Exhibition.

The 'Craigevar Express', a steam tricycle built by a local postman in 1895 for use in delivering mail, pictured here in the grounds of Craigevar Castle. Alford, Grampian Transport Museum.

Rothe House, Kilkenny.

Opposite:

Byre dwelling from Magheragallon, Co. Donegal. Holywood, Ulster Folk and Transport Museum.

Alton Mill, an 18th century water-mill transferred from its original site near Ipswich to the Museum of East Anglian Life, Stowmarket.

An early Logie Baird television. Hastings, Old Town Hall Museum.

Ray Cotterell, Master Cooper, at work in his Shop at the Museum of Cider, Hereford.

Life-size Sri Lankan mask used in healing rituals. London, Museum of Mankind.

Vehicles from the Museum of British Road Transport, Coventry.

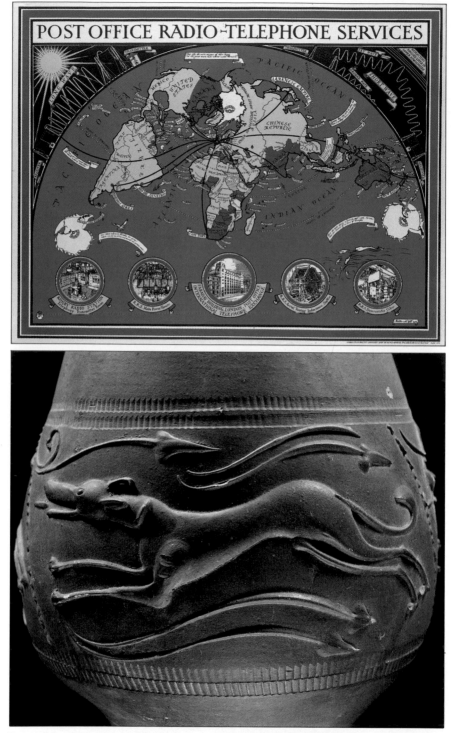

Poster of the 1930's. Telecom Technology Showcase, London.

Roman drinking beaker with slip-trailed decoration of a hunting-dog, 3rd century AD. Corbridge Roman Site.

Historic packaging and advertising material in The Robert Opie Collection, Gloucester.

Part of the Red Baron display at Torbay Aircraft Museum.

The Museum Shop at the Bethnal Green Museum of Childhood, London.

'Conversation with Magic Stones' by Barbara Hepworth (1903-75). St Ives, The Barbara Hepworth Museum.

Boroughbridge

Aldborough Roman Museum

Boroughbridge, North Yorkshire   ☎ *09012 2768*
Mar 29–Oct 14, Mon–Sat 9.30–6.30; Sun
2–6.30. Oct 15–Mar 28, Mon–Sat 9.30–4;
Sun 2–4. Closed Dec 24–26, Jan 1.
🏛 *Historic Buildings & Monuments Commission,*
York   ☎ *0904 58626*
Ⓔ 🌳 ✿

Aldborough, three-quarters of a mile south of
Boroughbridge, on a minor road off the B6265,
is on the site of the Roman town which was the
capital of the Brigantes, the largest tribe in
Roman Britain. The museum contains Roman
finds from the excavations, including pottery,
coins and metalwork.

Boscombe

Museum of Childhood

39 Ashley Road, Boscombe, Bournemouth, Dorset
☎ *0202 33173*
May–Sept, Sun–Fri 10–5. Oct–Apr, Mon–Fri
10–5.
🏛 *The Curator*
Ⓔ 🌳 ☛

The Museum has displays of dolls, comics,
Meccano sets, Hornby trains, model ships and
boats, jigsaws, games, toys and books. There is
also a reconstruction of a Victorian nursery,
with toys, games and a doll's house.

Boston

Guildhall Museum

South Street, Boston, Lincolnshire   ☎ *0205 65954*
Apr–Oct, Mon–Fri, 9.30–4; Sat 9.30–4.
Oct–Apr, Mon–Sat 9.30–5.
🏛 *The Curator*
Ⓔ 🌳

The Guildhall, at one time the centre of
Boston's municipal activities, is a considerably
modified 15th-century building, recently
refurbished and restored. It has associations with
the Pilgrim Fathers, some of whom are reputed
to have been held in two cells preserved on the
ground floor. The Museum contains displays
relating to local history and archaeology.
Among the exhibits are firemarks, agricultural
implements, civic items, topographical prints
and pictures and a number of portraits of local
worthies.

Botley

Hampshire Farm Museum

Upper Hamble Country Park, Brook Lane, Botley,
Hampshire SO3 2ER   ☎ *04892 87055*
Daily 10–6 (last admission 5)
🏛 *The Curator*
Ⓔ 🍴 ☛ ♿

The Museum is signposted from Exit 8 on the
M27. It has been set up to show, explain and
demonstrate agricultural change in Hampshire
between 1850 and 1950. The buildings at
Manor Farm, the centre of the Museum's
activities, have been modified and have
changed their function over the years, to meet
new requirements. Three other buildings, a
forge, wheelwright's workshop and staddle barn,
have been rescued from demolition elsewhere
and re-erected at Manor Farm. They form part
of the historical survey.

The displays make use of a wide range of
tools, implements and machinery. The livestock
kept on the farm also illustrates the changes
which have taken place in farming during the
past century. The Dairy Shorthorn cow, for
instance, and the Wessex Saddleback pig, were
once common in the area, but are rarely seen
there today.

The house at Manor Farm contains a
medieval open hall, and there is also a 13th-
century church on the site.

Bournemouth

The Casa Magni Shelley Museum

Bournemouth and Poole College of Art and Design,
Boscombe Manor, Beechwood Avenue,
Boscombe, Bournemouth, Dorset BH5 1NB
☎ *0202 303571*
June–Sept, Mon–Sat 10.30–5.30. Oct–May,
Thurs–Sat, 10.30–5.30. Closed Dec 25,
Jan 1, Good Fri.
🏛 *See Russell-Cotes Art Gallery and Museum*
Ⓔ 🌳 ☛

The Museum consists of collections illustrating
the life and work of the poet, Percy Bysshe
Shelley, housed in the building which was for
half a century the home of the poet's son, Sir
Percy Florence Shelley. The collections were
originally at Casa Magni, Lerici, Italy, the
poet's last home.

Museum of the Bournemouth Natural Science Society

39 Christchurch Road, Bournemouth, Dorset
BH1 3NS   ☎ *0202 23525*
By appt only
🏛 *The Hon. Secretary*
Ⓕ ☛

The Society and the Museum were formed in
1883 and re-formed in 1903. The Museum has
occupied its present building, a listed Victorian
house, since 1919. It holds a number of
collections, many not displayed, but all
accessible for research purposes. The principal
sections include archaeology, where there is
material of national importance, especially in
Egyptology and in finds from local excavations;
botany, based on a herbarium of local plants;
geology, with important collections of fossils
and minerals; zoology, where the emphasis
is on butterflies, insects, birds and eggs,
and on a diorama display of New Forest
mammals.

Russell-Cotes Art Gallery and Museum

East Cliff, Bournemouth, Dorset BH1 3AA
☎ *0202 21009*
Mon–Sat 10–5.30. Closed Dec 25, 26, Good Fri.
▨ *The Curator*
Ⓔ ✎ ▬ ☎ ▢

Sir Merton Russell-Cotes was the owner of the fashionable Royal Bath Hotel in Bournemouth. In 1894 he built East Cliff Hall as his home and presented it to the town in 1908, to become its municipal Art Gallery and Museum, on condition that he and his wife could continue to live in it during their lifetime. The Art Gallery was added to the original house between 1919 and 1926. The collections remain much the same as they were at his death in 1921, with some additions from bequests and donations.

The house contains fine examples of 17th to 19th-century English and French furniture, and English and Continental pottery, porcelain and paintings. One room is devoted to memorabilia of Sir Henry Irving and others to the art and antiquities of Japan and Burma.

The Art Gallery is used during certain months of the year to display pictures and sculpture from Bournemouth Museums' permanent collection, and at other times for temporary exhibitions.

Transport Museum

Mallard Road, Bournemouth, Dorset BH8 9PN
Daily ex. Sun 10–5.30
▨ *See Russell-Cotes Art Gallery and Museum*
Ⓔ ✎ ☎

Bournemouth Transport Museum is a joint venture between Bournemouth Museums and the Bournemouth Passenger Transport Association. It is at present in temporary accommodation at Mallard Road Bus Depot. The collection of vehicles, formerly belonging to Bournemouth Corporation, includes buses, trams and trolleybuses, as well as an 1882 horse-tram. Two Mobile Museums, in a double-decker and a single-decker bus, are also based at Mallard Road.

Bourton-on-the-Water

Cotswold Motor Museum

The Old Mill, Bourton-on-the-Water,
Gloucestershire GL5 2BY   ☎ *0451 21555*
Feb–Nov, daily 10–6
▨ *Michael Cavanagh*
Ⓔ ■ ☎

The Motor Museum contains cars and motorcycles from the vintage years up to the 1940s and 1950s, including sporting and racing machines. The atmosphere of motoring in the past is re-created by means of more than 600 old advertising signs and by an extensive collection of wheeled toys. A local motorcycle workshop and garage of the 1920s has been reconstructed in the Museum, and near it are two touring caravans of the same date, furnished and equipped in the style of the period.

'Venus Verticordia' by Dante Gabriel Rossetti (1828–82).

Village Life Exhibition

The Old Mill, Bourton-on-the-Water,
Gloucestershire GL5 2BY   ☎ *0451 21555*
Feb–Nov, daily 10–6
▨ *Michael Cavanagh*
Ⓔ ■ ☎

Parts of the Mill building date back to the 18th century. Milling finally came to an end here in 1949. The first floor now houses an exhibition of village life. The exhibits include a reconstruction of an Edwardian village shop, with a bedroom above, and of a blacksmith's forge and a kitchen. There is also a model of the Mill as it was in its operating days, and a collection of sewing machines, toys and other everyday objects.

Bovington

The Tank Museum

Bovington Camp, Wareham, Dorset BH20 6JG
☎ *0929 462721 extn 463/329*
Daily 10–5. Closed for Christmas and New Year.
▨ *Mr E. Bartholomew*
Ⓔ ■ ▬ ☎ ♿

Founded in 1923 as the Royal Tank Corps Museum, the present Tank Museum illustrates the history of all Regiments of the Royal Armoured Corps, past and present. Its collection of more than 150 armoured fighting vehicles is one of the largest in the world. They originate from the United Kingdom and 12 other countries – Australia, Argentina, Brazil, Canada, France, Germany, Italy, Japan, South Africa, Sweden, the United States and the USSR. The earliest exhibit, a Hornsby Chain Track Tractor, dates from 1909 and the earliest tank from 1915.

There are separate exhibitions of armaments, engines, uniforms, medals, equipment, memorabilia and campaign relics. The explanatory material includes video displays, working models, simulators and a section of a Centurion tank. The Museum maintains a large library and photographic archive.

Bowness-on-Windermere

Windermere Steamboat Museum

Rayrigg Road, Bowness-on-Windermere, Cumbria
LA23 1BN   ☎ 09662 5565
Apr–Oct, daily 10–5
🖾 Education Officer
Ⓔ 🛉 ⬛ ↔ ♿

The Museum lies a quarter of a mile north of
Bowness, on the A592 Ambleside road. Its
lakeshore site includes a large wet-dock area.
The collection comprises 35 steam, sail and
motorboats, nearly all in working order and
many afloat. It includes *Dolly*, one of the two
oldest working steamboats in the country, built
before 1850 and salvaged from the lake bed.
Other steamers include the Furness Railway
Company's cargo boat, *Raven* (1871), the
Clyde-built TSSY *Esperance* (Captain Flint's
houseboat in Arthur Ransome's *Swallows and
Amazons*); and the elegant and luxurious
Branksome, with her sumptuous upholstery and
décor, built as a private launch for a wealthy
lakeshore resident.

Bradford

Bolling Hall Museum

Bowling Hall Road, Bradford, West Yorkshire
BD4 7LP   ☎ 0274 723057
Apr–Sept, Tues–Sun 10–5. Oct–Mar, Tues–Sun
10–6. Open Bank Holiday Mon. Closed
Dec 25, 26, Good Fri.
🖾 Teacher/Research Assistant, Museum Loans
Service, Rosemount, Clifton Villas,
Manningham, Bradford 9
☎ 0274 492276
Ⓕ ✎ ↔

Bolling Hall is one mile from the city centre,
on the A650 Bradford–Wakefield road. The
earliest parts of the house date from the 15th
century and additions and modifications were
made during the 16th, 17th and 18th centuries.
Presented to the City of Bradford in 1912, it was
opened three years later as a period house and
museum of local history.

It contains an outstanding collection of 17th-
century oak furniture, displayed in the rooms
belonging to that period. The Georgian wing
has fine Chippendale furniture, including a very
grand couch bed originally made for Harewood
House. Other displays include children's toys
and furniture and a room devoted to the story of
the 'Bradford Pals' Battalion in the First World
War. Local topographical illustrations and other
historical material relating to the district are
at Bolling Hall but, owing to great pressure on
space, only a small selection can be displayed.
The remainder, however, can be seen by
appointment.

Bradford Industrial Museum

Moorside Mills, Moorside Road, Bradford, West
Yorkshire BD2 3HP   ☎ 0274 631756
Tues–Sun 10–5. Open Bank Holiday Mon. Closed
Dec 25, 26, Good Fri.
🖾 Keeper of Education
Ⓕ ✎ ⬛ ↔ ♿

The original Moorside Mill was built for worsted
spinning in 1875. A second mill was added in
1916 and production continued until 1970, after
which the premises were converted into
Bradford's Industrial Museum, which opened in
1974.

The Museum specialises in the history of the
wool manufacturing industry, and has an
important collection of worsted textile
machinery, with many working exhibits. There
are, in addition, a motive power gallery, with
live steam demonstrations every Wednesday
afternoon and on the first Saturday in each
month, and a transport collection, which
includes a range of Bradford-built Jowett cars
and the only surviving Bradford tram. Moorside
House, the former mill-owner's residence, has
been furnished in Victorian style, with partial
gas lighting, to reflect the income and taste of a
comfortably-off member of the middle class.

Cartwright Hall Art Gallery

Lister Park, Bradford, West Yorkshire BD9 4NS
☎ 0274 493313
Apr–Sept, Tues–Sun and Bank Holiday Mon
10–6. Oct–Mar, Tues–Sun 10–5.
Closed Good Fri, Dec 25, 26.
🖾 The Curator
Ⓕ ⬛ ↔ �𝌆

The Gallery was built in 1904 in honour of
Edmund Cartwright (1743–1823), inventor of
an early power loom. The display area, on three
floors, is devoted to temporary exhibitions, and
to 19th and 20th-century paintings, prints and
sculpture from the permanent collection,
including works by Reynolds, D. G. Rossetti
and Guido Reni.

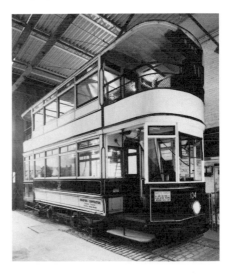

No. 104, the last tram to run in Bradford,
1950. Bradford Industrial Museum.

Colour Museum

*Perkin House, 82 Grattan Road, Bradford, West
    Yorkshire BD1 2JB*   ☎ *0274 725138*
*Tues–Fri 2–5; Sat 10–4. Open Tues–Fri mornings
    for groups by appt.*
🅜 *Jonathan Platt, Curator*
Ⓕ 🕮 🍴 ♿

The Museum is situated in a former wool
warehouse. One gallery houses a variety of
interactive displays explaining the science of
colour. This contains exhibits illustrating the
importance of colour in everyday life, the
spectrum, the basis of colour vision, colour
blindness, the effect of mixing colours and how
colours arise in materials. A second gallery
concentrates on the industrial history of the
coloration industries. The displays here cover
the development of textile printing, natural
and synthetic dyes, the dyeing industry and
instruments for measuring colour.

National Museum of Photography, Film and Television

Prince's View, Bradford, West Yorkshire BD5 0TR
    ☎ *0274 727488*
*Tues–Sun 11–6 (special exhibitions, box office,
    shop and coffee bar open until 7.30). Closed
    Jan 1, Good Fri, May Day, Dec 25, 26.*
🅜 *Adrian Budge or Dave Richards*
    ☎ *0274 725347*
Ⓒ 🍴 🖵 🍴 ♿

During the post-war redevelopment of Bradford,
a new theatre was constructed in the city centre.
It was, however, never used for its original
purpose and now houses the Museum, which
presents and explores the past, present and
future of photography, film and television. The
galleries show the part played by photography in
the lives of everyone. Working models, original
equipment, dramatic reconstructions and the
pictures themselves allow visitors to experience
the full range of photographic possibilities, from
the camera obscura to satellites, from galaxy to
microbe and from photojournalism to
portraiture. Special galleries illustrate the
history and techniques of television, and the
Kodak collections, recently transferred to the
Museum, cover the development of amateur
photography.
    The Museum possesses Britain's only IMAX
theatre. Its 64-foot by 52-foot cinema screen is
the largest in the country.

West Yorkshire Transport Museum

*Ludlam Street Depot, Mill Lane, off Manchester
    Road, Bradford, West Yorkshire BD5 0HG*
    ☎ *0274 736006*
One Sun in the month. Telephone for exact dates.
🅜 *The Project Co-ordinator*
Ⓕ 🕮 🍴

Ludlam Street bus depot, a building in the
Egyptian style, was opened in 1931. It now
serves the West Yorkshire Transport Museum
as a permanent workshop and store, and as
an exhibition centre while the new Transport
Museum is being developed on a 30-acre site at
Low Moor. The collection at present contains
over 100 vehicles and includes buses, lorries,
trams, electric trains, fire engines and
equipment used for highway maintenance.
    A five-mile stretch of railway through
the Spen Valley to Heckmondwike is being
electrified to serve as an operational tramway.
Many of the vintage buses are in a fully
roadworthy condition and are kept licensed, so
that they can be used for group hire at any time.

Bradford-on-Tone

Sheppy's Museum

*R. J. Sheppy & Son, Three Bridges, Bradford-on-
    Tone, Taunton, Somerset TA4 1ER*
    ☎ *082346 233*
*Apr–May, Sept, Mon–Sat 8.30–7. June–Aug,
    Mon–Sat 8.30–8. Oct–Mar, Mon–Sat
    8.30–6. Easter–Christmas, Sun 12–2.*
🅜 *Mr Richard Sheppy*
Ⓕ 🍴 🍴

The Sheppy family have been cidermakers since
the early 19th century. The Museum, adjoining
the firm's orchards and modern cider-plant,
contains old cidermaking equipment,
agricultural implements and coopers' and other
craftsmen's tools.

Brading

Brading Roman Villa

Brading, Isle of Wight   ☎ 0983 406223
*Apr–Sept, Mon–Sat 10–5.30; Sun 10.30–5.30.
    Other times by appt.*
🅜 *Messrs Neates, Staple Chambers, Staple
    Gardens, Winchester SO23 8SR*
Ⓒ 🕮 🍴

The site of the Villa is signposted from the
A3055 Sandown to Ryde road. It was excavated
between 1880 and 1895. In 1900 a timber and
corrugated-iron building was erected over the
site, which was opened to the public at an
entrance fee of 3d. The main attraction is
the early 3rd-century floors, which are in
exceptionally good condition and contain
designs and representations not found elsewhere
in Britain. A wide range of objects was
discovered in the course of the excavations and
they are all displayed in the Museum.

Lilliput Museum of Antique Dolls and Toys
High Street, Brading, Isle of Wight PO36 ODJ
☎ *0983 407231*
Mar 16–Sept, daily 9.30–10 pm. Oct–Dec 23,
daily 10–5.
🛠 *Mrs M. D. Munday-Whitaker*
£ 🏠 ⇨

The Museum was established in Brading in
1974. It was formed from the Munday family's
private collection, one of the most important in
Britain. The exhibits are remarkable, in that
nearly every item has its personal history
displayed with it. This has been made possible
by the fact that every doll or toy has been
acquired from its original owner, or from a
descendant.

The dolls on show include a Queen Anne
wooden doll, of *c.* 1725, a Princess Caroline
doll, of *c.* 1790, two wax dolls of *c.* 1860 by the
celebrated maker, Madame Augusta Montanari
of London, and others by equally famous French
and German makers, such as Jules Steiner,
Armand Marseille, Kammer and Reinhardt,
Käthe Kruse and Simon and Halbig. This is very
much a connoisseurs' museum, with exhibits of
exceptional quality. The services of a dolls'
hospital are available.

Braemar

Braemar Castle
Braemar, Aberdeenshire   ☎ *03383 219*
May–1st Mon in Oct, daily 10–6
🛠 *The Custodian*
£ 🏠 ⇨ HHA

The Castle is half a mile north of Braemar, on
the A93. Built in the 17th century, it was
restored in the mid 18th and converted from a
fortress into a family home in the early 19th.
The furniture is mainly 18th century mahogany.
Six rooms are open to visitors, in addition to the
guard room, the original kitchen and an
underground prison. Other exhibition rooms on
the ground floor contain items relating to the
history of the family, the Castle and the estate,
a special feature being a Victorian kitchen
display.

1958 AEC Reliance coach. Bradford,
West Yorkshire Transport Museum.

Bramber

House of Pipes
Bramber, Steyning, West Sussex BN4 3WE
☎ *0903 812122*
Daily 9–7. Closed Dec 25.
🛠 *Anthony Irving*
£ 🏠 🚻 ⇨ ♿

The collection of 38,000 items from 180
countries has been formed to show the part that
smoking has played in the lives of people
throughout the world. The exhibits are arranged
in the form of a Victorian shopping arcade.
They include pipes, cigarette holders, matches,
lighters, packaging, advertisements, display
material, shopfittings, snuff, snuff boxes, trade
tokens, tobacco cutters and tobacco jars – the
full range of what the Museum's creator calls
'smokiana'.

Kammer & Reinhardt character dolls, *c.* 1912.
Brading, The Lilliput Museum of Antique
Dolls and Toys.

Bramhall

Bramall Hall
Bramhall Park, Bramhall, Stockport, Cheshire
SK7 3NX   ☎ *061 485 3708*
Apr–Sept, Tues–Sun, Bank Holiday Mon 12–5.
Oct–Dec & Feb–Mar, Tues–Sun 12–4.
🛠 *The Manager*
£ 🏠 🚻 ⇨

Bramhall can be reached by taking the A5102
off the A6, or from Manchester going south on
the A34. The Hall, a magnificent half-timbered
house, was built mainly in the 15th and 16th
centuries. It was the home of the Davenport
family for five centuries. During the 19th
century, wealth from hatting, sugar and cotton
was used to maintain and improve Bramall as a
family home. Together with its 60-acre park, it
is now in the possession of the Borough of
Stockport.

The furnishings and decorations of the house
reflect the long period of domestic occupation.
There is early stained glass in both the Great

Hall and the Domestic Chapel. The wall-paintings in the Chapel tell the story of the Reformation and those in the Ballroom use contemporary sources to represent a picture of life in the 16th and 17th centuries. The 16th-century heraldic tapestry, 20 feet long, is one of the finest in the country, and other notable exhibits include Victorian furniture by A. W. Pugin, a series of Davenport family portraits dating from 1616 to 1850, and a collection of paintings by the 19th-century romantic artist, Herbert Schmalz.

A new display, 'Images of Bramall', contains paintings and photographs of the Hall.

Breamore

Breamore Countryside Museum

Breamore, nr Fordingbridge, Hampshire SP6 2DF
☎ 0725 22270
Apr–Sept, Tues, Wed, Thurs, Sat, Sun, public holidays, 2–5.30
🖾 John Forshaw
Ⓔ ▮ � 🖾 & [HHA]

The village of Breamore lies off the A338, nine miles south of Salisbury. The Museum, in the grounds and outbuildings of Breamore House, illustrates the changes in village life over the past 150 years. There are re-creations of a farmworker's cottage, dairy, wheelwright's shop, blacksmith's forge, farm brewery and cider barn, and of a saddler's and cobbler's workshop. The stables, built c. 1700, are used to display vehicles of the horse era, including the 'Red Rover' London to Southampton stagecoach.

The house, which dates from 1583, has fine collections of the furniture and paintings accumulated by 10 generations of the Hulse family.

Brechin

Brechin Museum

Public Library, St Ninian's Square, Brechin, Angus DD9 7AA   ☎ 03562 2687
Mon, Tues, Fri 9.30–6; Wed 9.30–7; Sat 9.30–5
🖾 See Montrose Museum and Art Gallery
Ⓕ ⧉

The displays in the Museum feature the Burgh regalia, church plate, local archaeology, handicrafts, craftsmen's tools and domestic equipment. A number of works by the etcher and watercolourist, David Waterson, are also on show.

Brecon

Brecknock Museum

Captain's Walk, Brecon, Powys LD3 7DW
☎ 0874 4121
Mon–Sat 10–5, including Bank Holiday. Closed Good Fri, Dec 25, 26.
🖾 The Curator
Ⓕ ▮ ⧉ &

The building which now houses the Museum was built in 1842 as the Shire Hall and Court of Assize. The Museum's collections illustrate the life and history of the Brecknock District of Powys. The exhibits include examples of agricultural implements used in the area, a traditional Welsh kitchen, a reconstructed blacksmith's shop, and a fine collection of Welsh lovespoons. The natural history section contains examples of wildlife from four typical local habitats and the archaeology gallery traces the story of Brecknock back to the Stone Age, including material from the nearby Roman site, Brecon Gaer.

A reconstruction of the 1843 Assize Court can be seen in the original Court Room at the Museum.

South Wales Borderers and Monmouthshire Regiment Museum

The Barracks, Brecon, Powys LD3 7EB
☎ 0874 3111 extn 310
Apr–Sept, daily 9–1, 2–5. Oct–Mar, Mon–Fri 9–1, 2–5.
🖾 Major R. P. Smith, Curator
Ⓔ ⧉ ⧉ &

The Museum is situated on the A40 alongside the Barracks, on the eastern boundary of the town. Constructed in 1805, it is the oldest building in the Barracks. The displays illustrate the history of the 24th Regiment (The South Wales Borderers), with the associated Militia and Volunteer Units, from its inception in 1689 to its amalgamation with the 41st Regiment (The Welch Regiment) in 1969. The new Regiment is known as The Royal Regiment of Wales.

The 24th Regiment is remembered particularly for its service in the Zulu War of 1879, when the 1st Battalion was almost annihilated at Isandhlwana, and for the epic defensive battle fought at Rourke's Drift.

The collections of uniforms, equipment, weapons, paintings and trophies tell the story of the Regiment's 280 years of service.

Brentford

British Motor Industry Heritage Trust Museum

Syon Park, Brentford, Middlesex   ☎ 01 560 1378
Daily 10–5.30. Closed Dec 25, 26.
🖾 Mr D. Bishop
Ⓔ ▮ ⧉ ⧉ & &

The collection was originally formed as Leyland Historic Vehicles in 1975, in order to bring together the extensive collections of historic vehicles and archives which had been preserved over the years by many of the constituent companies in British Leyland. About 100 of the total of 300 vehicles are displayed at Syon Park at any given time. The individual makes include Albion, Alvis, Austin, Daimler, Jaguar, Lanchester, Land Rover, Range Rover, M.G., Morris, Riley, Rover, Standard, Trojan, Triumph and Wolseley.

Kew Bridge Engines Trust and Water Supply Museum

Green Dragon Lane, Brentford, Middlesex
TW8 0EF   ☎ *01 568 4757*
Sat, Sun, Bank Holiday Mon 11–5 throughout
year, except weekend preceding Christmas Day.
🄺 Mr A. A. Cundick, General Manager
🄴 🅟 🖉 🖳 🚶

The Museum is housed in a restored Victorian pumping station, which once supplied water to the whole of West London. The original four Cornish beam engines have been preserved, and three of them are in operating condition. The collection also includes steam engines from other parts of the country, all restored to working order, diesel engines, and miscellaneous exhibits associated with the history of steam power and water supply.

The Musical Museum

368 High Street, Brentford, Middlesex TW8 0BD
    ☎ *01 560 8108*
Apr–Oct, Sat, Sun 2–5. One-hour conducted
tours. No children under 5.
🄺 *The Director*
🄴 🅟 🖉 🖵

The Museum is at present housed in a late Victorian church. The largest object in its collection is the Mighty Wurlitzer, which was shipped to England from Chicago in 1931 and installed in the Regal Theatre, Kingston-upon-Thames. It has been at the Musical Museum since 1972. Other items in the Museum include orchestrions, reproducing pianos, a busker's street barrel organ, musical boxes and phonographs. Also on show is the 1908 Fotoplayer, the only surviving example in Europe. It provided music and sound effects to accompany the old silent films.

Syon House

Syon Park, Brentford, Middlesex TW8 8JF
    ☎ *01 560 0881*
Good Fri or Apr 1–last Sun in Sept, Sun–Thurs
12–5. Oct, Sun 12–5.
🄺 *The Administration Manager*
🄴 🅟 🖉 🖳 🚶 HHA

The connection of the Earls of Northumberland with Syon House began in 1594, when the 9th Earl was granted a lease by the Queen. The 13th Earl, who became the 1st Duke, commissioned Robert Adam to remodel, redesign and refurnish the house, and 'Capability' Brown to lay out the gardens. The Conservatory and Riding School were built by the 3rd Duke, but otherwise Syon House remains much as Robert Adam left it, and it is still the home of the present Duke and Duchess.

The collection of Royal and family portraits is among the finest in Britain. They are painted on wood, copper and canvas and the subjects include Charles I and Charles II, Elizabeth, Queen of Bohemia, and Lady Jane Grey. Among the artists represented are Van Dyck, Reynolds, Lely and Gainsborough. The house also contains much notable 18th-century furniture, a remarkable 1635 map, showing the Manor of Syon, and the huge Sèvres Vase, presented to the 3rd Duke of Northumberland by Charles X of France. The domed Great Conservatory includes an aviary and an aquarium and there is a six-acre rose garden.

Brenzett

Brenzett Museum

Ivychurch Road, Brenzett, Romney Marsh,
    Kent TN29 0EE
Easter–Sept, Sun 11–5. July–Aug, also
    Tues–Thurs 2–5. Bank Holiday 11–5.
    Other times by appt.
🄺 *John Elgar-Whinney, Curator, 37 Ness Road,*
    Romney Marsh TN29 9EL   ☎ *0679 20606*
🄴 *ex. school parties* 🅟 🖉 🚶 ♿

During the Second World War, the present Museum building served as a Women's Land Army hostel. A door bearing W.L.A. graffiti forms an exhibit in the Museum. Many of the wartime aerial battles took place over the area and a nearby field was used by the R.A.F. as an advanced airfield during the flying bomb attacks of 1944.

The collections include a wide range of engines and other relics from British and American wartime aircraft. Most of the items have been recovered from crash sites. There is also an example of the 4½ ton dam-buster bomb, designed by Sir Barnes Wallis in 1943.

An open-air section, to display local artefacts, is at present being assembled in the grounds of the Museum.

German Weber 'Brabo', 1920s. Coin-operated, the instrument contains a piano, with mandolin attachment, violin pipes and xylophone. Brentford, The Musical Museum.

Bressingham

Bressingham Steam Museum

Bressingham, Diss, Norfolk IP22 2AB
☎ 037988 386
Easter Sun, Mon, then 1st Sun in May to last Sun
  in Sept, 11.30–6. Thurs from end of May to
  2nd in Sept, 11.30–5.30. Aug, also Wed
  11.30–5.20. Open Late Summer Bank
  Holiday.
◪ The Curator
Ⓔ ✎ ◧ ⚓ ♿

Bressingham is two and a half miles west of Diss,
on the A1066 road to Thetford. The Live Steam
Museum which adjoins the celebrated
Bressingham Gardens has one of the most
comprehensive collections of steam engines in
the world. The main-line locomotives include
Oliver Cromwell, Royal Scot and Duchess of
Sutherland, and there is a wide range of road and
industrial engines, all carefully restored,
together with a steam-operated Victorian
roundabout. The Exhibition Hall contains
displays of smaller exhibits, illustrating the
working of railways in the days of steam.
    There are rides on three steam-hauled narrow
gauge railways, running on five miles of track,
and footplate travel on main-line locomotives.

Bridgnorth

Midland Motor Museum

Stourbridge Road, Bridgnorth, Shropshire
  WV15 6DT   ☎ 07462 61761
Mar–May, Mon–Sat 10–5; Sun, Bank Holiday
  10–6. June–Aug, daily 10–6. Sept–Oct,
  Mon–Sat 10–5; Sun, Bank Holiday 10–6.
  Nov–Feb, daily 10–5. Closed Dec 25.
◪ Mrs G. Barker
Ⓔ ♨ ◧ ♨ ⚓ ♿ ☐

The Museum, situated on the A458, two miles
from Bridgnorth, specialises in sports and racing
cars and motorcycles. The 100 vehicles on
display date from the 1920s to the 1980s. They
include examples of cars which raced on the pre-

**1938 Frazer Nash BMW 328, a successful
sports car of the 1930s. Bridgnorth, Midland
Motor Museum.**

Second World War circuit at Brooklands, and
others of the 1930s Grande Classe. There are
frequent changes in the exhibits, especially in
the case of vehicles on loan.

Northgate Museum

High Street, Bridgnorth, Shropshire
Apr–Sept, Sat, Bank Holiday 2–4. Also mid July–
  early Sept, Mon–Wed 2–4.
◪ Mr and Mrs J. Ritter, 38 Bernards Hill,
  Bridgnorth WV15 5AS   ☎ 07462 5056
Ⓕ ✎

Northgate is part of the town walls of
Bridgnorth. It has been rebuilt several times,
the last occasion being 1740. It was refaced with
stone in 1911. The collections cover 3,000 years
of local history. The earliest items are Bronze
Age tools, found at Eardington. There is also
Roman and medieval material. The weapons on
display date from the Civil War and include a
wheellock pistol found hidden in the Governor's
house.
    The 18th-century turret clock is in working
order. Agriculture and the countryside are
represented by smocks, tools, animal and man-
traps, and veterinary instruments. Among the
other exhibits is a model of a steam engine for
mine pumping, made by the Hazeldine
Company in Bridgnorth to the design of Richard
Trevithick and Andrew Vivian, and a coracle
used by fishermen on the River Severn.
    The Museum has a large and varied collection
of prints and paintings showing the
development of Bridgnorth from medieval times
to the present day. There are also photographic
copies of the Town Charters from the time of
Charles II onwards. Most of the pre-1642
Charters were destroyed when St Leonard's
Church was destroyed during the Civil War.

Bridgwater

Admiral Blake Museum

Blake Street, Bridgwater, Somerset TA6 3AR
  ☎ 0278 456127
Mon–Tues, Thurs–Sat 11–5; Wed 11–8; Sun 2–5
◪ R. L. Nicholson, Administrator
Ⓕ ✎ ⚓

Admiral Blake (1599–1657) was born in the
house now occupied by the Museum. The Blake
Room contains a diorama of the Battle of Santa
Cruz, Blake's greatest victory over the
Spaniards, a number of his personal belongings,
including his sea-chest, and original letters
to the Admiralty written by him. In the
archaeological section there is Neolithic,
Bronze Age, Iron Age, Romano-British and
medieval material from sites in and around
Bridgwater. Among the exhibits relating to the
later history of Bridgwater, there is a diorama of
the Battle of Sedgemoor, together with relics of
the Battle, models of Bridgwater Docks and of
ships using the Docks, and displays illustrating
the local brick and tile industry, which include
the celebrated, but misnamed, Bath Bricks,
made from the mud of the River Parrett.

Bridlington

Bayle Museum

Bayle Gate, Old Town, Bridlington, North
    Humberside
June–Sept, Tues–Thurs 2–4.30; Tues, Thurs
    7–9.30. Other times by appt.
🔲 Secretary to the Trustees, Mr J. S. Walker,
    58 Viking Road, Bridlington YO16 5TW
🔲 🔲 🔲

The Museum occupies a monastic gatehouse,
built in 1388, which contains the former
manorial court room. The displays reflect life in
and around Bridlington from the Middle Ages to
the present day. There are reconstructions of a
cobbler's shop and Victorian kitchen and special
displays devoted to local agriculture and
maritime history and to the Bridlington Green
Howards.

Brighouse

Smith Art Gallery

Halifax Road, Brighouse, West Yorkshire
    HD6 2AF   ☎ 0484 719222
Apr–Sept, Mon–Sat 10 5; Sun 2.30–5.
    Oct–Mar, Mon–Sat 10–5.
🔲 Leisure Services Department, Wellesley Park,
    Halifax, West Yorkshire
🔲 🔲 🔲

Between 1870 and 1905, Alderman William
Smith formed a collection of works of art which
he considered to be morally elevating. They
included 17th-century Dutch and Flemish
paintings and 19th-century paintings and
watercolours. Among the more notable of these
works with moral messages are Thomas Faed's
The Mitherless Bairn, and Marcus Stone's Silent
Pleading. There are also a number of Victorian
landscapes.

Brighton

Art Gallery and Museum

Church Street, Brighton, East Sussex BN1 1UE
    ☎ 0273 603005
Tues–Sat 10–5.45; Sun 2–5. Closed Good Fri,
    Dec 25, 26, Jan 1.
🔲 Education Services Officer
🔲 🔲 🔲 🔲

The Museum building was remodelled from
stabling and coach-houses which formed part of
the Royal Stables built by the Prince of Wales in
the early 1870s. There are sections devoted to
Art Nouveau and Art Deco, Sussex archaeology
and folk life, ceramics, ethnography and
Brighton history. There are some Old Master
paintings and watercolours, and an
unconventional costume gallery, deliberately
planned to provoke thought about the wearing
of clothes.

Barlow Collection

Library Building, University of Sussex, Falmer,
    Brighton, East Sussex BN1 9QL
    ☎ 0273 678678
Tues, Thurs during term-time 11.30–2.30. Other
    times by appt.
🔲 Charles Dudley, Commercial Manager,
    Refectory Building
🔲 🔲 🔲

The University of Sussex is on the A27, midway
between Brighton and Lewes. The Collection is
considered to be the most important of its kind
in Europe. It reflects 3,000 years of Chinese
civilisation, with exhibits of ceramics, bronzes
and figurines. The figurines in particular are of
high quality.

**Publicity poster by Henry Gawthorn, 1920s.
Brighton Art Gallery and Museum.**

Booth Museum of Natural History

194 Dyke Road, Brighton, East Sussex BN1 5AA
    ☎ 0273 552586
Mon–Wed, Fri, Sat 10–5; Sun 2–5. Closed Good
    Fri, Dec 25, 26, Jan 1.
🔲 Dr Philip L. Armitage, Principal Keeper of
    Natural Sciences
🔲 🔲 🔲 🔲

This is a purpose-built museum, erected in 1874
by Edward Booth to house his collection of
British birds. In addition to a comprehensive
display of birds mounted in settings which re-
create their natural habitats, there are galleries
of vertebrate evolution, butterflies of the world,
and Sussex geology, including the fossil bones of
Iguanodon, the local dinosaur.
    There are reference collections of insects,
osteology, palaeontology, eggs, and bird and
mammal skins, together with herbaria.

Brighton Aquarium and Dolphinarium

Marine Parade, Madeira Drive, Brighton, East
    Sussex BN2 1TB   ☎ 0273 604234
Daily 10–5. Closed Dec 25.
🔲 Party Booking Organiser
🔲 🔲 🔲 🔲

Brighton's elegant Aquarium was opened in
1872. Nowadays it presents a wide range of
aquatic creatures, in conditions similar to their
native habitats. These include local sea and

fresh-water fish, tropical species, reptiles, molluscs and amphibia. The collections illustrate evolutionary development, types of locomotion, protective colouring and feeding habits.

The Sea Pool Arena has Dolphin Shows at specific times throughout the day and the Aquarium's breeding group of California sea-lions are given opportunities to demonstrate their learning abilities and co-ordination, both on land and in the water.

HMS Cavalier

Brighton Marina, Brighton, East Sussex BN2 5UF
    ☎ *0273 699919*
Daily from 10.30. Closed Dec 24, 25.
🗷 *The Secretary, HMS Cavalier Trust, Brighton Marina*
£ ▮ ↩

HMS *Cavalier*, launched in 1944, is the only surviving destroyer to have seen active service in the Second World War, and the last representative of the long line of destroyers which originated with HMS *Havock* in 1893. The ship was laid up in 1972 and now belongs to the HMS *Cavalier* Trust, which has preserved it as a museum. Visitors are able to tour the ship and inspect her accommodation and equipment.

Preston Manor (The Thomas-Stanford Museum)

Preston Park, Brighton, East Sussex BN1 6SD
    ☎ *0273 63005 extn 59*
Wed–Sat 10–5; Tues, Sun 10–1, 2–5. Open Bank Holiday Mon. Closed Good Fri, Dec 25, 26.
🗷 *Education Services Officer*
£ ✑ ⬛ ↩

Preston Manor is two miles from Brighton town centre, on the A23 London road. Built *c.* 1739 and extended and remodelled in 1905, the house incorporates 13th-century features in the basement. The home of the Stanford family for nearly 200 years, it was presented to Brighton Corporation by Sir Charles and Lady Thomas-Stanford in 1932, together with its collections of furniture, pictures, porcelain and silver.

It is furnished and decorated to show the way of life of a rich family in the years before the First World War. The rooms contain a wide-ranging collection of both English and Continental furniture, as well as notable 18th and 19th-century silver and plated ware. The entrance hall displays walnut furniture from the 1680s to the 1730s. The paintings and watercolours are mainly by 19th-century English artists.

In 1939 the widow of the celebrated furniture historian, Percy Macquoid, presented her late husband's outstanding collection of English and Continental furniture and decorative art to the Museum, which also has a good collection of 18th-century English drinking glasses.

The Royal Pavilion

Brighton, East Sussex BN1 1UE ☎ *0273 603005*
June–Sept, daily 10–6. Oct–May, daily 10–5.
    Closed Dec 25, 26.
🗷 *Public Relations Officer*
£ ▮ ✑ ⬛

The Royal Pavilion was designed by John Nash and built between 1815 and 1822 for George, Prince of Wales, later George IV. The picturesque exterior recalls Moghul India, whilst the so-called Chinese taste prevails in the sumptuous furnished interiors, which include the recently restored Music Room, severely damaged by fire in 1975. The displays include much of the original furniture lent by H.M. The Queen, and a magnificent collection of Regency silver and silver-gilt. The fully-equipped kitchens are a notable feature of the exhibits in the Royal Pavilion.

Stanmer Village Rural Museum

Stanmer Park, Brighton, East Sussex
Easter–Oct, Thurs, Sun, Bank Holiday, 2.30–5
🗷 *The Secretary, Stanmer Preservation Society, 91 Vale Avenue, Brighton BN1 8UB*
    ☎ *0273 509640*
F ✑ ↩

Stanmer is three miles north of Brighton on the A27 Lewes road. The Museum, organised by the Stanmer Preservation Society, is in the yard of Stanmer House, built in 1722 for the Pelhams, Earls of Chichester. The house itself is not open to the public.

The Society has built up a collection of agricultural implements, blacksmiths' and wheelwrights' tools, domestic equipment and photographs, illustrating the history of Stanmer. A donkey wheel and a horse-gin have also been preserved.

The Entrance Hall, Preston Manor, Brighton.

Bristol

Blaise Castle House Museum

Henbury, Bristol, Avon BS10 7QS
☎ *0272 506789*
Sat–Wed 10–1, 2–5. Closed Thurs, Fri, Good Fri,
Dec 25–27, Jan 1.
🅺 *See City of Bristol Museum and Art Gallery*
Ⓕ ✎ 🚗

Blaise Castle, four miles from the city centre on
the B4055, is set in 300 acres of wooded
parkland, landscaped by Humphry Repton. It
contains the social history collections belonging
to the City of Bristol Museum and Art Gallery.
The displays contain furnishings, kitchen
equipment, costumes, toys and games. There
are also exhibits devoted to the local history of
Blaise and Henbury.

Bristol Industrial Museum

Prince's Wharf, Prince Street, Bristol, Avon
BS1 4RN   ☎ 0272 299771 extn 290/257
Sat–Wed 10–1, 2–5. Closed Thurs, Fri, Good Fri,
Dec 25–27, Jan 1.
🅺 *See City of Bristol Museum and Art Gallery*
Ⓕ 🍴 🚗

The Museum is in a dockside transit shed of the
1950s, with cranes of the same period preserved
outside with a surviving section of the docks
railway network, now used for the Museum's
steam train operation.

  The collections cover the manufacturing and
transport history of Bristol and its region. Local
railway material is strongly represented,
including gauge 0 and 1 models, especially a
working layout of gauge 1 historic models. The
Museum has the world's earliest purpose-built
motor caravan, the *Wanderer*, 1885, and the
first steam-driven motorcar, the 1875 Grenville
Steam Carriage. The definitive collection of
Bristol-built Rolls-Royce aero-engines is here,
and the aeronautical section also includes the
mock-up of a nose section of Concorde used in
its development, and a replica of the 1910
Bristol Boxkite.

  The important maritime collection illustrates
the history of the Port of Bristol, and many
other local industries, especially tobacco, glass,
and wagon and carriage building, are
represented by comprehensive collections.

City of Bristol Museum and Art Gallery

Queen's Road, Bristol, Avon BS8 1RL
☎ *0272 299771*
Mon–Sat 10–5. Closed Good Fri, May Day, Late
Spring Bank Holiday Mon, Tues, Dec 25–27,
Jan 1.
🅺 *Schools Organiser*
Ⓕ 🍴 🖼 🚗 ♿

The listed 1905 Museum building, with an
extension added in 1928, is of considerable
architectural importance. The collections cover
a wide field: paintings – the works by artists of
the Bristol School are particularly important –
drawings, watercolours, prints; sculpture;
ceramics, especially of local manufacture;

exceptional 18th to 19th-century glass,
including many important Bristol pieces;
Oriental fine and applied art, with the largest
collection of Chinese glass outside China;
costumes and textiles. There are galleries of
British and foreign natural history, special
attention being paid to the plants, insects, birds
and animals of South-West England, and good
collections of rocks, minerals and fossils.
The Museum has both local and worldwide
collections of archaeology and ethnography,
with a new gallery devoted to Egyptian
antiquities and a fine display of ancient glass.

The Georgian House

7 Great George Street, Bristol, Avon BS1 5RR
☎ *0272 299771 extn 237*
Mon–Sat 10–1, 2–5. Closed Good Fri, May Day,
Late Spring Bank Holiday Mon, Tues,
Dec 25–27, Jan 1.
🅺 *See City of Bristol Museum and Art Gallery*
Ⓕ

This typical Georgian town house was built
c. 1790 for a wealthy sugar merchant. Three
floors are open to the public, and the rooms are
furnished much as they would have been in the
1790s, with locally made furniture, ceramics
and glass. The kitchen and laundry area
contains contemporary equipment and there
is an unusual cold-water plunge bath in the
basement

S.S. Great Britain

Great Western Dock, Gas Ferry Road, Bristol,
Avon BS1 5TY   ☎ 0272 20680
Daily 10–6 (10–5 in winter). Closed Dec 24, 25.
🅺 *S.S. Great Britain Trading Ltd at above address*
Ⓔ 🍴 🖼 🚗

The *Great Britain* was built in Bristol and
launched in 1843. Designed by Isambard
Kingdom Brunel, she was the world's first
ocean-going, propeller-driven iron ship. For
43 years she served both as a passenger liner and
a cargo vessel. After her early voyages to
America, she carried emigrants to Australia and
was used as a troop ship in the Crimean War and
during the Indian Mutiny. She was abandoned
in the Falkland Islands in 1886 and used as a
storage hulk. In 1970 she was towed back to
Bristol and laid up in the dock where she was
built. Work on restoring her 1843 appearance
is well advanced.

The S.S. *Great Britain* at sea, 1845.

Harveys Wine Museum

12 Denmark Street, Bristol, Avon BS1 5DQ
☎ *0272 277661*
Mon–Fri by appt. Closed Bank Holiday.
𝕏 *Public Relations Department*
Ⓔ 🛆 ✐ ✍

The Museum is in part of a range of 13th-century cellars originally used as store rooms by the Hospital of the Gaunts. It explains how wine is made and stored, and displays the articles used in its production, serving and drinking. There are important exhibits of bottles, corkscrews, decanters, silver decanter labels, tastevins and 18th-century English drinking glasses. A section of the Museum contains items which illustrate the history of Harveys during the Victorian and Edwardian periods.

The Jack Harvey Memorial Library, of books and manuscripts relating to the wine trade, is available for use by students.

John Wesley's Chapel: the New Room

36 The Horsefair, Bristol, Avon BS1 3JE
☎ *0272 24740*
Mon, Tues, Thurs–Sat 10–4. Closed Sun, Wed, Bank Holiday.
𝕏 *The Warden*
Ⓕ ✐ ✍

This is the oldest Methodist building in the world. The foundation stone was laid by John Wesley in 1739 and the Chapel was extended in 1748. Above it are rooms where both John and Charles Wesley lived at certain periods. There are a number of items associated with the Wesleys and with the early days of the New Room. They include furniture, a 1761 organ, letters and membership lists in John Wesley's handwriting. An equestrian statue of John Wesley and a statue of Charles Wesley stand in the courtyards in front of the Chapel.

Wesley's Chapel with its double pulpit. John Wesley's New Room, Bristol.

Kings Weston Roman Villa

Long Cross, Lawrence Weston, Bristol, Avon
☎ *0272 299771*
Sat–Wed 10–4. Key from Blaise Castle House Museum, Henbury.
𝕏 *See City of Bristol Museum and Art Gallery*
Ⓕ ✍

The Roman country house on this site was in use c. 268–368 A.D. Visitors can see the mosaics, the foundations of the bath complex and other parts of the excavated remains.

Maritime Heritage Centre

Gas Ferry Road, Bristol, Avon BS1 5TY
Daily 10–6 (10–5 in winter). Closed Dec 24, 25.
𝕏 *See City of Bristol Museum and Art Gallery*
Ⓕ 🍴 ✍ ♿

The Centre adjoins the dock where the S.S. *Great Britain* is under restoration. It introduces the theme of shipbuilding in Bristol over a period of 200 years, as illustrated by the important collection of models, paintings and archive material assembled by the Bristol shipbuilders, Charles Hill and Sons, and their predecessor, James Hilhouse. A reconstruction, with some original parts, of an early Bristol-built iron vessel designed by Isambard Kingdom Brunel to dredge the harbour, forms a central exhibit, and there are further displays which relate to the *Great Britain* within the Great Western dry dock.

National Lifeboat Museum

Prince's Wharf, Wapping Road, Bristol, Avon BS1 4RN ☎ *0272 213389*
Daily 10.30–4.30. Winter times may vary.
𝕏 *C. E. Reeves, Curator*
Ⓔ 🛆 ✐ ✍ ♿

The Museum building is on the site of Patterson's Dock, where Brunel's *Great Western* was launched. It houses the only collection of historic lifeboats in the British Isles. The earliest of the nine boats is the *Thomas Lingham*, of 1904, and the most recent, the *North Foreland*, built in 1951. A great deal of restoration is necessary and visitors to the Museum are able to watch the work in progress. The collection also includes launching carriages and other lifeboat equipment.

The Red Lodge

Park Row, Bristol, Avon BS1 5LJ
☎ *0272 299771 extn 236*
Mon–Sat 10–1, 2–5. Closed Good Fri, May Day, Late Spring Bank Holiday Mon, Tues, Dec 25–27, Jan 1.
𝕏 *See City of Bristol Museum and Art Gallery*
Ⓕ ✍

The Red Lodge was built c. 1590 and three of the first-floor rooms still have oak panelling, plasterwork and carved stone chimneypieces of this period. The rest of the house was altered in the first quarter of the 18th century and is now furnished in the style of both periods.

St Nicholas' Church Museum

St Nicholas Street, Bristol, Avon BS1 1UE
    ☎ *0272 299771 extn 243*
Mon–Sat 10–5. Brass Rubbing Centre 10–12,
    1–4. Closed Good Fri, May Day, Late Spring
    Bank Holiday Mon, Tues, Dec 25–27, Jan 1.
▨ *See City of Bristol Museum and Art Gallery*
F ▮ ⊶

This 18th-century parish church, with a 14th-century lower church, has been converted to museum use, with a Brass Rubbing Centre as part of the complex. A curfew bell is still rung each evening at nine o'clock.

The Museum displays include antiquities which illustrate the development of medieval Bristol, 18th to 19th-century watercolours of the Bristol area, and examples of local church art, especially church plate. A prominent feature of the Museum is the huge altarpiece painted by William Hogarth for St Mary Redcliffe.

Thomas Chatterton's House

Redcliffe Way, Bristol, Avon BS1 6NL
    ☎ *0272 299771*
▨ *See City of Bristol Museum and Art Gallery*
F ⊶

The poet, Thomas Chatterton, was born in Bristol in 1752. His father was a schoolmaster, and the family house, Chatterton's birthplace, has been preserved. Attached to it is the original front of Redcliffe School, which he attended and which was immediately to the south of the house, but it was demolished when the new road, Redcliffe Way, was built. The house commemorates Thomas Chatterton and his family.

Brixham

British Fisheries Museum

Old Market House, The Quay, Brixham, South
    Devon TQ5 8AW   ☎ *08045 2861*
June–Sept, Mon–Sat 9–1, 2–6; Sun 10–1, 2–5.
    Oct–May, Mon 2–5; Tues–Fri 9–1, 2–5;
    Sat 9–1
▨ *Information Assistant at above address*
£ *ex. children* ♤ **⊶ ♿**

The Museum shares Brixton's original Market House with the Tourist Information Centre. It illustrates the history of the fishing industry from the Middle Ages to the present day. There are exhibits devoted to early fishing methods, the Icelandic and Newfoundland cod fisheries, the evolution of the fishing smack and its replacement by the steam drifter. Other sections of the Museum are concerned with Common Market policy and with the reorganisation of deep-sea fishing since 1945.

Brixham Museum

Bolton Cross, Brixham, South Devon TQ5 8LZ
    ☎ *08045 3203*
Easter–Oct, Mon–Sat 10–5.30; Sun 11–1,
    2.30–5.30. Other times by appt.
    ☎ *08045 2455*
▨ *The Secretary, Brixham Museum and History*
    Society
£ ♤

Brixham Police Station and Sergeant's House has been converted into Brixham Museum, which is devoted almost entirely to the history, trade and industry of the town. Fishing and shipbuilding play a prominent part in the displays, with exhibits of shipbuilding tools, navigational instruments and models of famous Brixham trawlers. Models are used to illustrate the story of all the Brixham lifeboats from 1867 onwards and the Museum also houses the HM Coastguard National Museum, which has a range of life-saving apparatus used during the 19th and early 20th centuries.

Among the episodes which receive special attention is the landing of William of Orange at Brixham in 1688, the part played by the town in the British defence system during the Napoleonic Wars and the building in a local yard of the ship, *Mayflower II*, which made the repeat voyage of the Pilgrim Fathers in 1957.

Broadclyst

Killerton

Broadclyst, nr Exeter, Devon EX5 3LE
    ☎ *0392 881345*
Apr–Oct daily including Good Fri, 11–6.
    Garden open daylight hours throughout year.
▨ *The Administrator*
£ ▮ ⬛ ⊶ ♿ NT

Killerton is seven miles north-east of Exeter, on the Cullompton road. The home of the Aclands since the Civil War, it was rebuilt for the 7th Baronet in 1778 and given to the National Trust in 1944. It now houses the Paulise de Bush Collection of costumes, which is displayed in a series of rooms furnished in different periods, from the 18th century to the present day.

The splendid gardens contain an ice house and the former stables have been converted to accommodate a shop and an exhibition explaining the history and character of the Killerton estate. Visitors can also see the 19th-century chapel close to the house.

Fishing smack BM161 Valerian, part of the photographic collection at Brixham Museum.

Broadstairs

Crampton Tower Museum

High Street, Broadstairs, Kent   ☎ *0843 64446*
1st Sun in May–2nd Sun in Sept, Sun–Tues, Fri
2.30–5
🏛 *Miss N. Leggatt, Hon. Secretary, 46 Dumpton*
Park Drive, Broadstairs CT10 1RJ
F ⬙ ⬈

The flint-built tower next to the Post Office
originally formed part of Broadstairs' first public
water supply system. A listed building, it now
contains a museum to commemorate the
achievements of Thomas Russell Crampton
(1816–87), the celebrated Victorian engineer,
who was a native of Broadstairs. Crampton is
chiefly remembered as a designer of railways and
locomotives, but he was also much concerned
with gas and waterworks and with the
underwater telegraph cable. He was the first to
lay an effective cable under the English
Channel running between Dover and Calais.
His other inventions included a rotary dust-fuel
furnace, used at Woolwich Arsenal, brickmaking machinery and an automatic tunnel-
boring machine. He planned and built
Broadstairs Gasworks, personally subscribing
much of the capital.

The Museum contains models, Crampton
working drawings and patents, and various items
concerned with railways in the Broadstairs area.
There are, in addition, relics of the Thanet
Electric Tramways. A large building, which
was also part of the local waterworks, designed
by Crampton in 1859, contains various
transport exhibits including the Broadstairs
Stage Coach.

Broadway

Snowshill Manor

nr Broadway, Gloucestershire WR12 7JU
☎ *0386 852410*
Apr and Oct, Sat, Sun 11–1, 2–5. May–Sept,
Wed–Sun, Bank Holiday Mon 11–1, 2–6.
🏛 *The Administrator*
£ ⬈ NT

Snowshill Manor is three miles south-west
of Broadway. Although there is evidence of
the older medieval building, which had once
belonged to Catherine Parr, the wife of Henry
VIII, the present house dates from the 16th,
17th and early 18th centuries. In 1919 it was
bought by a wealthy scholar, architect and
artist-craftsman, Charles Wade (1883–1956),
who restored it and spent much of his life filling
it with an extraordinarily wide and eclectic
collection of craftsmanship, which he presented
to the National Trust, together with the house,
in 1951.

The items in the collection range from
Samurai armour to camel trappings, and from
Persian lamps to early bicycles. Charles
Wade's stimulating style of arrangement
remains.

Brodick

Brodick Castle

Brodick, Isle of Arran, Bute KA27 8HY
☎ *0770 2202*
Easter weekend 1–5. Apr, Mon, Wed, Sat 1–5.
May–Sept, daily 1–5.
🏛 *The Administrator*
£ ⬩ ⬙ ⬈ ⬧ NTS

Brodick Castle, which was owned by the Dukes
of Hamilton until 1895, was subsequently the
home of the Duke and Duchess of Montrose.
Since 1958 it has belonged to the National
Trust for Scotland, which has paid particular
attention to looking after the magnificent
gardens. Part of a 13th-century round tower was
incorporated into the 16th-century building and
other additions were made in Victorian times.

The 10th Duke of Hamilton married the
daughter of William Beckford, and part of
Beckford's great art and furniture collections are
at Brodick Castle. To this the Victorian Dukes
added their own acquisitions of sporting pictures
and trophies. There are also many family
portraits and portrait busts and an exceptionally
fine collection of silver.

The kitchen has been restored to the state in
which it functioned during the 19th century, in
order to meet the needs of a large household.
In the oldest part of the Castle, a stone-walled
chamber has been reconstructed as a prison, one
of the many uses to which the room was put
during its 700-year life.

Isle of Arran Heritage Museum

Rosaburn, Brodick, Isle of Arran, Bute KA27 8DP
☎ *0770 2636*
May–Sept, Mon–Fri 10–1, 2–5
🏛 *The Secretary*
£ ⬙ ⬩ ⬈ ⬈

The Museum consists of a group of buildings
which were originally an 18th-century farm and
smithy. The cottage is furnished in the style of
the late 19th and early 20th centuries, and a
stable block contains displays of local geology,
archaeology – including a Bronze Age cist – and
social history. There is a collection of farm
implements used on the Island.

Brodie

Brodie Castle

Brodie, nr Forres, Moray   ☎ *03094 371*
Easter–Sept, Mon–Sat 11–6; Sun 2–6.
Grounds open all year, 9.30–sunset.
🏛 *NTS Representative*
£ ⬩ ⬈ ⬈ NTS

The Castle of the Brodies was burned during the
Montrose campaigns of 1645 and largely rebuilt.
Additions were made in the 19th century. It now
belongs to the National Trust for Scotland. The
house contains French furniture, English,
Continental and Chinese porcelain and an
important collection of 17th-century Dutch and
18th-century English paintings.

John Buchan and his family in the 1920s.
Historic photograph at the John Buchan
Centre, Broughton

Bromham

Bromham Water Mill

Bromham, Bedfordshire   ☎ 02302 4330
Apr–Oct, Wed, Thurs, Sat, Sun, Bank Holiday
  Mon 2–6
◪ Director of Leisure Services, County Hall,
  Bedford MK42 9AP   ☎ 0234 63222
Ⓔ ⬤ ⬤ ⬤

The Mill adjoins the A428 Bedford to
Northampton road, at the west end of Bromham
Bridge. A listed building, this restored working
water mill now contains a museum of milling
history and an interpretative centre of the
surrounding countryside.

Bromsgrove

Avoncroft Museum of Buildings

Stoke Heath, Bromsgrove, Hereford and Worcester
  B60 4JR   ☎ 0527 31886
March and Nov, Tues–Thurs, Sat, Sun, Bank
  Holiday, 11–4.30. Apr–May and Sept–Oct,
  Tues–Sun, Bank Holiday 11–5.30. June–Aug,
  daily 11–5.30.
◪ Mrs Jennifer A. Costigan, Deputy Director
Ⓔ ⬤ ⬤ ⬤ ⬤

The Museum is three miles south of
Bromsgrove, off the A38 Bromsgrove bypass and
400 yards north of its junction with the B4091.
Its primary aim is to rescue historic buildings
from destruction, rather than to illustrate the
social history of a community.

   Among the 18 buildings already on the site
are a 15th-century merchant's house from
Bromsgrove, a thatched barn from Cholstrey in
Herefordshire, and an 18th-century forge
cottage. A Warwickshire windmill grinds corn
for flour and a Bromsgrove nailshop is now used
by the Museum's blacksmith. Among the rarer
attractions are the Counting House from
Bromsgrove cattle market, an ice house from
Tong in Shropshire, and a three-seater earth
closet from Herefordshire.

The Bromsgrove Museum

26 Birmingham Road, Bromsgrove, Hereford and
  Worcester B61 0DD   ☎ 0527 77934
Mon–Sat 10–4; Sun 2–5
◪ The Director
Ⓔ ⬤ ⬤ ⬤

Formerly known as the Norton Collection
Museum, the Bromsgrove Museum is developing
in stages. The first phase includes displays
relating to the social and industrial history of
the area, with exhibits covering glass, button,
nail and salt-making, and the work of the
Bromsgrove Guild, which made the gates of
Buckingham Palace and the Liver Birds on the
Liverpool Assurance Company in Liverpool.
The second phase will be concerned with the
social history of the 19th and early 20th
centuries, with displays in appropriate shop
fronts.

Broughton

John Buchan Centre

Broughton, Tweeddale
Easter–mid Oct, daily 2–5
◪ Biggar Museum Trust, Moat Park, Biggar,
  Lanarkshire ML12 6DT   ☎ 0899 21050
Ⓔ ⬤ ⬤

John Buchan, later Lord Tweedsmuir, and best
known for his thriller, The Thirty-Nine Steps,
had family links with Broughton, a village 29
miles south of Edinburgh on the A701. The
former church building, where his relatives
regularly worshipped, and where he himself
often attended services, now contains a museum
illustrating his career and achievements, as a
novelist, lawyer, politician, soldier, historian,
biographer and Governor-General of Canada.
The collections include photographs, books and
a number of the personal possessions of John
Buchan and his family.

Broughty Ferry

Broughty Castle Museum

Broughty Ferry, nr Dundee, Angus
  ☎ 0382 76121/23141
Mon–Thurs, Sat 10–1, 2–5. Sun (July–Sept only)
  2–5. Closed Christmas and the New Year.
◪ McManus Galleries, Albert Square, Dundee,
  Angus DD1 1DA
Ⓕ ⬤ ⬤ ⬤

Broughty Ferry is five miles east of Dundee,
on the coast road. The Castle is, in fact, a
reconstructed fort, overlooking the mouth of
the Tay. The emphasis of the Museum is on
local history, with special displays on fishing,
the lifeboat and tourism. Other sections are
devoted to the wildlife of the Tay estuary,
weapons and armour, military history and
Dundee's former whaling industry.

Bruree

De Valera Cottage

Knockmore, Bruree, Co. Limerick, Ireland
On request to Mrs Nora O'Gorman who lives
*   100 yards north of the Cottage*
◪ *Mrs Nora O'Gorman*
Ⓕ ⌂ ⚲

In 1885 the two-year-old Éamon de Valera was
brought here from the United States to be
placed in the care of his maternal grandmother.
The cottage, 20 miles south of Limerick, in
which he was reared, had just been completed
by the Kilmallock Board of Guardians. A neat,
well-built stone house, it contains a kitchen-
cum-living room and two small bedrooms
downstairs, and another bedroom upstairs in the
loft. Now a National Monument, it has been
restored to its original appearance, and
furnished with period items or, in some
instances, replicas of originals.

De Valera Museum

Bruree, Co. Limerick, Ireland
Sun, Thurs 2.30–5.30. Other times by appt.
◪ *Mainchín Seoighe, Curator, Tankardstown,*
*   Kilmallock*   ☎ *Kilmallock 97*
Ⓕ ⌂ ⚲

Bruree, one mile east of the main Cork to
Limerick road, was the home of Éamon de
Valera, later President of Ireland. He attended
school there in the building which is now the
Museum. It contains the largest collection of de
Valera memorabilia on display in Ireland. The
exhibits include school books; a lock of his hair,
cut off by his grandmother when he was a little
boy; letters; photographs; a jacket, hat and
walking stick; prayer books; rosaries; and his
1916 Rising and Irish War of Independence
service medals.

The Museum also has some important
archaeological material, including stone and
bronze axes, and a good collection of items
illustrating rural life in the area, especially
farm implements, craftsmen's tools and
domestic equipment.

Buckhaven

Buckhaven Museum

above Buckhaven Library, College Street,
*   Buckhaven, Fife*
Mon, Tues, Thurs, Fri 2–5
◪ *Museum Secretary, Museum and Art Gallery,*
*   War Memorial Gardens, Kirkcaldy, Fife*
*   KY1 1YG*   ☎ *0592 260732*
Ⓕ

The Museum has been formed in order to tell
the story of Buckhaven, which has been
described as 'a full-flavoured fishertown'. There
are displays illustrating the history and
techniques of the local fishing industry and the
life of the families who earned a living from it.
A feature of the Museum are the re-creations of
the interiors of the homes of past generations of
Buckhaven people.

Buckie

Buckie Maritime Museum and Peter Anson Gallery

Townhouse West, Cluny Place, Buckie,
*   Banffshire AB5 1HB*
*   ☎ 0309 73701 (Falconer Museum)*
Mon–Fri 10–8; Sat 10–12. Closed public holidays.
◪ *District Curator, Falconer Museum, Tolbooth*
*   Street, Forres, Moray IV36 0PH*
Ⓕ ⌂ ⌂ ☐

The Museum's collections illustrate the history
of the town of Buckie, with special reference to
the fishing industry. There are displays showing
the boats and techniques employed, coopering,
navigation, and the achievements of the local
lifeboat.

The Art Gallery presents changing
exhibitions drawn from its collection of more
than 400 watercolours by Peter F. Anson,
mostly of Scottish fishing scenes.

Buckingham

Buckingham Movie Museum

Printers Mews, Market Hill, Buckingham,
*   Buckinghamshire MK18 1JX ☎ 0280 816758*
Wed–Sun, Bank Holiday Mon 10–5. Closed
*   Dec 25, 26.*
◪ *The Director*
Ⓔ ⌂ ⌂

Based on the John Burgoyne-Johnson
collection, the Museum presents a
comprehensive survey of amateur film-making,
from 1912, when Charles Pathé first made home
movies safe, to the present day. The collection
of equipment includes over 200 projectors and
100 cine-cameras and accessories. There are
frequent shows of old films and demonstrations
of equipment.

Buckhaven Museum.

Bude

Bude Historical and Folk Exhibition

The Wharf, Bude, Cornwall EX23 8LG
    ☎ 0288 3576
Easter–Oct 10–4 (later if weather permits)
⊠ *The Clerk, Bude-Stratton Town Council,*
    The Castle, Bude EX23 8LG
£ ⌀ ⬛ ↩ ᴋ

Bude tub-boat canal, the longest in the country, was a remarkable example of early 19th-century civil engineering, providing a navigable link with the Tamar and the English Channel, and access to the Bristol Channel, by means of a sea-lock. The Museum, in part of the canal buildings, which also served as the forge, illustrates the history and working of the canal, by means of early photographs, models, drawings, plans and maps. Other exhibits deal with the development of Bude, with shipwrecks and the history of the local lifeboat.

Budleigh Salterton

Fairlynch Arts Centre and Museum

27 Fore Street, Budleigh Salterton,
    Devon EX9 6NG   ☎ 03954 2666
Easter Sat–Oct, daily 2.30–5. July–Aug, also
    10.30–12.30. Dec 26 Jan 15, daily
    2.30–4.30.
⊠ *The Secretary*
£ ⌀ ↩

The Museum, a listed building, is a marine *cottage orné*, built c 1810, with a thatched roof, lookout tower and chapel windows. Indoors is a pretty double-wing staircase. The displays illustrate the mainly 19th-century development of the town and the character of the surrounding area, with its prehistoric habitation sites and continuous recorded history from Domesday onwards, and a particularly interesting natural environment of coast, river valley and upland commons and two unique geological features, the Bunter pebble beds and radio-active nodular formations.

One of the Museum's strongest points is its very fine collection of 19th-century costumes and Honiton lace.

Otterton Mill Museum and Gallery

Otterton Mill, nr Budleigh Salterton, Devon
    EX9 7HG   ☎ 0395 68521/68031
Easter–Oct, daily 10.30–5.30. Nov–Easter, Sat,
    Sun 2–5. Closed Dec 25, Jan 1.
⊠ *Mrs Desna Greenhow, Director*
£ ♦ ⬛ ↩

A mill on this site, off the A376 Budleigh Salterton to Newton Poppleford road, has been grinding corn since the 10th century. The present mill was rebuilt in the 1840s, on its original foundations, and has been restored with as few changes as possible to function as it did at the turn of the century, when its fortunes began to decline. A pair of stones, powered by the River Otter, is now producing wholemeal flour.

The building also contains a museum, to illustrate the use of water to drive mill machinery and the various processes which are involved in the production of flour. Other displays are devoted to Honiton lace-making, and there are regular displays of crafts and fine art and exhibitions on historical themes.

Bungay

Bungay Museum

Waveney District Council Offices, Broad Street,
    Bungay, Suffolk
Mon–Fri during office hours
⊠ *Dr L. H. Cane, Curator, 6 Woodland Drive,*
    Bungay NR35 1PE   ☎ 0986 2548
£ ↩

This small Museum shows the history of Bungay and the surrounding district, mainly by means of photographs and prints. There are displays of fossils, flint arrowheads and coins.

Bunratty

Bunratty Castle and Folk Park

Bunratty, Co. Clare, Ireland   ☎ 061 61511
Daily 9.30–5.30 (later in summer months).
    Closed Good Fri, Christmas.
⊠ *Mr T. Sheedy, Manager*
£ ♦ ⬛ ⌀ ↩ ᴋ *except in Castle*

The first Castle at Bunratty was built c. 1250. Between then and the mid 15th century it was destroyed and rebuilt several times. The present Castle dates from 1467. In the 1950s it was restored to its medieval condition by its owner, Lord Gort, who furnished it and presented it to a Trust formed for the purpose. Its 15th to 17th-century furniture, tapestries and paintings are of Irish, English and European origin.

In the adjoining Folk Park are replicas of rural and town houses and workshops from many parts of Ireland, furnished and equipped as they appeared in the 19th century. There are regular demonstrations of thatching and milling.

Bunratty Castle in its present form dates from 1467, though there was already a castle on the site two hundred years before.

Burford

Tolsey Museum

High Street, Burford, Oxfordshire
Early Apr–last Sun in Oct, daily 2.30–5.30
⚑ *Mrs D. Wise, Secretary, Wakefield, Pound*
Lane, Clanfield, Oxfordshire
☎ *036781 294*
£ ✎ ⊸

Housed, together with the Council Chambers, in a 15th-century building, the Tolsey Museum is devoted to the history of Burford, in its political, social and industrial aspects. There are exhibits of local handicrafts and craftsmen's tools, and visitors can also see displays of 14th to 16th-century charters and the town maces.

Burghead

Burghead Museum

16–18 Grant Street, Burghead, Forres
Tues 1.30–5; Thurs 5–8.30; Sat 10–12
⚑ *District Curator, Falconer Museum, Tolbooth*
Street, Forres IV36 0PH **☎** *0309 73701*
F ☐

The displays at Burghead Museum relate to local geology, archaeology and history. There are sections on Burghead Fort and the Pictish 'bull' symbol stones associated with it, the Lairds of Duffus, the harbour and fishing industry, and the unique 'Burning of the Clavie' fire ceremony. The exhibits are drawn from the collections of Moray District Council's museum service and regular changes are made in the displays.

Burnham-on-Crouch

The Burnham Museum

4 Providence, Burnham-on-Crouch, Essex
Wed, Sat 11–4; Sun 2–4.30. Closed Jan–Feb.
⚑ *Mrs B. Perren, Hon. Secretary, 72 High Street,*
Burnham-on-Crouch, Essex CM0 8AA
☎ *0621 782670*
£ ▮ ⊸

The Museum is in a converted 19th-century warehouse. Its collections all come from within the Dengie Hundred of Essex and illustrate the traditional life of the area. The emphasis is on agricultural and maritime history.

Burnley

Queen Street Mill

Harle Syke, Burnley, Lancashire BB10 2HX
☎ *0282 59996*
Mar 20–Sept 28, daily 10.30–4.30 ex. Tues, Wed
⚑ *Visitor Services Officer*
£ ▮ ⬛ ⊸ ♿

Harle Syke is three miles from the centre of Burnley, on the Briercliffe Road. Queen Street Mill, built in 1894, is a fully operational steam-powered cotton-weaving mill, the last of its kind and now preserved as a museum by Pennine Heritage Ltd. Visitors can experience the traditionally noisy working atmosphere of hundreds of Lancashire looms crammed tightly together and driven by the steam-engine, *Peace*.

Cloth is woven at the Mill, just as it was 100 years ago. The traditional skills are being preserved by employing experienced mill workers. In addition to opportunities for watching the production of cloth, there are displays illustrating the history of the textile industry, especially in Lancashire, and the lives of the workers and their families.

Towneley Hall Art Gallery and Museums

Towneley Hall, Burnley, Lancashire BB11 3RQ
☎ *0282 24213*
Mon–Fri 10–5.30 (until 5.15 in winter);
Sun 12–5. Closed Christmas week.
⚑ *The Curator*
F ✎ ⬛ ⊸ ♿

Towneley Hall is on the A671 Burnley to Todmorden road. Parts of the house date from the 14th century, but most of it is Tudor and 17th century, with 18th-century modifications. Now a museum, it contains a number of period rooms, including an Elizabethan Long Gallery and an entrance hall with plasterwork by Vassali, completed in 1729. The collections include 18th to 19th-century English watercolours, notably Zoffany's portrait of Charles Towneley, 18th and 19th-century glass, ivories, and Chinese pottery and porcelain. Some of the historical collections of the East Lancashire Regiment are also here.

There is a natural history centre, with associated nature trails.

Weavers' Triangle Visitor Centre

85A Manchester Road, Burnley, Lancashire
BB11 1JZ
Apr–Sept, Tues, Wed, Sun 2–4. Parties at other
times by appt.
⚑ *Janet Hill, Education Officer*
☎ *0282 57367*
F ✎ ⊸

The building dates from c. 1800 and originally served as a toll house for barges using the Leeds and Liverpool Canal. The museum has been established in its two rooms and is concerned mainly with Burnley's traditions and archaeology as a leading cotton-weaving town. By means of photographs, drawings, maps, models and objects, the displays explain the techniques of cotton-manufacturing and introduce the Weavers' Triangle, a well-preserved Victorian area on both sides of the Leeds and Liverpool Canal. The Triangle contains a complete cross-section of 19th-century buildings dating from the days when Burnley could claim to be the cotton-weaving capital of the world – weaving sheds, spinning mills, warehouses, foundries, domestic buildings and a school.

The Weavers' Triangle Visitor Centre, Burnley.

Burntisland

Burntisland Museum

above Burntisland Library, High Street,
Burntisland, Fife
Mon Sat 10–12.30, 1.30–5
🏛 *Museum Secretary, Museum and Art Gallery,*
War Memorial Gardens, Kirkcaldy, Fife
KY1 1YG ☎ 0592 260732
F ♿

The Museum has displays relating to the history of Burntisland and its important maritime connections. There is a special exhibit on Burntisland Shipbuilders.

Burrowbridge

Allermoor Pumping Station

Burrowbridge, Bridgwater, Somerset TA7 0RB
☎ 082369 324
Mon–Sat by appt
🏛 *Mr L. W. Musgrave, Resident Attendant, or*
Wessex Water Authority, King's Square,
Bridgwater, Somerset
F ♿

The Pumping Station is 100 yards down the riverside road from its junction with the A361, opposite the King Alfred Hotel. It is equipped with the original 1869 Easton, Amos and Anderson engine, with its boiler, which worked until 1955. Two other Easton engines, dated 1864 and 1869, are also preserved here, having been brought in from other sites. All three engines are coupled to Appold pumps.

A dray and shire horses outside the Bass Museum of Brewing History, Burton-upon-Trent

Burton Agnes

Burton Agnes Hall

Estate Office, Burton Agnes, Driffield, East
Yorkshire YO25 0ND ☎ 026289 324
Apr–Oct, daily 11–5
🏛 *Estate Office*
£ 🛍 🍴 ♿ ♿

Burton Agnes Hall, a Grade I listed house, is midway between Driffield and Bridlington, on the A166. It was built between 1598 and 1610 and contains fine wood, stone, plaster and alabaster overmantels. There are good collections of English and French Impressionist and Post-Impressionist paintings, and Chinese porcelain, displayed in room settings.

Burton-upon-Trent

Bass Museum of Brewing History

Horninglow Street, Burton-upon-Trent,
Staffordshire ☎ 0283 45301
Mon–Fri 10.30–5; Sat, Sun 11–5
🏛 *Mrs B. Hyde, Education Officer*
£ 🛍 🍴 ♿ ♿

The former brewery carpenters' workshop, which houses the Museum, was built in 1866. The displays illustrate the history and development of brewing in Britain from the 18th century to the present day, with an emphasis on the Bass Company and on brewing in Burton-upon-Trent. Among the special themes are the influence of the pub on social life, and Bass advertising. There are interesting collections of ale glassware and brewery transport, a model of Burton-upon-Trent in 1921, and a reconstruction of an Edwardian taproom.

The brewery Shire horses can be seen in the stable area, and brewery tours are available, by appointment only.

Hoar Cross Hall

Hoar Cross, nr Burton-upon-Trent, Staffordshire
DE13 8QS   ☎ *028375 224*
Spring Bank Holiday–early Sept, Sun, Bank
Holiday 2–5. Enquire locally for summer
weekday opening times.
🏛 *Mr D. Gareth Evans*
£ 🖊 💺 🚻 ♿

Hoar Cross is seven miles west of Burton-upon-
Trent and 10 miles north of Lichfield. The Hall
is a 70-roomed Elizabethan-style mansion. It
was built for Hugo Meynell Ingram to replace
the Elizabethan house which still stands nearby,
and was modelled on part of Temple Newsam,
the Meynells' Elizabethan mansion in Leeds. It
has fine oak panelling and moulded ceilings and
William Morris wall-coverings, the original
printing blocks for which have been preserved.
The furniture and paintings are mostly
Victorian and there are other rich collections of
Victoriana, including teapots, tapestry, sewing
machines, beadwork embroidery, needlework
and costumes.

Burwash

Bateman's

Burwash, Etchingham, East Sussex TN19 7DS
☎ *0435 882302*
Apr–Oct, Sat–Wed 11–6
🏛 *The Administrator*
£ 🍴 💺 🚻 NT

Bateman's was built in 1634 as a Sussex
ironmaster's home. Now the property of the
National Trust, it was the home of Rudyard
Kipling from 1902 until his death in 1936. He
wrote many of his best-known books here and
his study and other rooms have been kept as
they were in his lifetime. A restored 1750
watermill grinds corn for flour and alongside
can be seen a working water-driven turbine,
installed by Kipling to generate electricity.

Bury

Bury Art Gallery and Museum

Moss Street, Bury, Lancashire   ☎ *061 761 4021*
Mon–Fri 10–6; Sat 10–5. Closed public holidays.
🏛 *Senior Curator*
F 🖊 🚻

Hoar Cross Hall, Burton-upon-Trent.

The Art Gallery contains mainly 19th-century
English paintings and watercolours, including
works by Turner and Constable. The local
history displays illustrate the social and
industrial history of Bury.

As a quite separate feature, the Museum
houses two fine models of British-made
warships, the Japanese battleship, *Hatsuse*
(1901), and the Argentine cruiser, *25 de Mayo*
(1891). Both ships were built at Armstrong's
Elswick yard on the Tyne. The *Hatsuse* had a
short life. She was torpedoed and sunk during
the Russo-Japanese War, four years after being
commissioned.

Bury Transport Museum

Castlecroft Road, off Bolton Street, Bury,
Lancashire BL9 0LN   ☎ *061 674 7790*
Sat, Sun, Bank Holiday Mon 11–5. Locomotive in
steam last Sun of month and Bank Holiday
Mon.
🏛 *Publicity Officer*
£ 🍴 💺 🚻

The collection comprises both road and rail
vehicles. The road vehicles include buses,
lorries, motorcycles, fire engines and a steam
roller. The railways are represented by main line
steam and diesel locomotives, and shunting and
industrial locomotives. There is also a collection
of railway passenger rolling stock, rail-mounted
cranes and freight vehicles.

It is hoped to use the railway vehicles on the
Bury to Rawtenstall Railway, which is to be
preserved.

Lancashire Fusiliers Regimental Museum

Wellington Barracks, Bolton Road, Bury,
Lancashire BL8 2PL   ☎ *061 764 2208*
Mon–Wed, Fri, Sat 9.30–5
🏛 *Regimental Secretary, Royal Regiment of*
Fusiliers
£ 🖊 🚻

The Museum's displays illustrate the history of
the Regiment from 1688 to the present day.
They include weapons, uniforms, trophies,
paintings and Regimental colours. There are
memorabilia of Wolfe, Napoleon and
Wellington, and relics of the Battle of Minden
and Gallipoli. The collection in the Medal
Room covers all the wars and campaigns in
which the Regiment took part.

**Bateman's, Burwash, built by a local
ironmaster in 1634, and from 1902 the home
of Rudyard Kipling.**

Bury St Edmunds

The Gershom-Parkington Memorial Collection of Time Measurement Instruments

Angel Corner, 8 Angel Hill, Bury St Edmunds,
Suffolk IP33 1UZ   ☎ *0284 63233 extn 227*
Apr–Oct, daily 10–1, 2–5. Nov–Feb, daily 10–1,
2–4.
🅇 *The Borough Curator*
🅕 ⛬

The Museum occupies a fine Queen Anne house, built in 1702. The collection of clocks and other instruments for measuring time contains items dating from the 16th century onwards and is considered to be one of the finest of its kind in the world.

Moyse's Hall Museum

Cornhill, Bury St Edmunds, Suffolk IP33 1DX
☎ *0284 53233 extn 236*
Mar–Oct, Mon–Sat 10–1, 2–5. Nov–Feb,
Mon–Sat, 10–1, 2–4. Closed Good Fri,
Easter Sat, May Day, Bank Holiday in winter.
🅇 *The Curator*
🅔 ⌕ ⛬

Moyse's Hall was built *c.* 1180, probably as a merchant's house. It has its original vaulted ceiling and Norman windows. The 15th-century modifications and enlargements include a fine timber roof and arches constructed of very early bricks. The contents mainly relate to Suffolk. There is a comprehensive display of birds and collections of firearms made by local gunsmiths, snuffboxes, miniatures, armorial china, 17th and 18th-century embroidery, and toys.

The archaeological section includes some fine flint tools, the largest Bronze Age hoard of swords, ornaments and objects yet found in Western Europe; a group of Iron Age drinking vessels, probably concealed during Boudicca's revolt against the Romans; grave goods from three Anglo-Saxon cemeteries and domestic items excavated at the site of the Anglo-Saxon village at West Stow; and Norman carvings from the Abbey.

The most popular items, however, are a gibbet cage and relics of William Corder, who was executed in 1828 for the murder of Maria Marten in the Red Barn. The Museum has his pistols, death mask and scalp, and the account of the trial bound in his own skin.

The Suffolk Regiment Museum

The Keep, Gibraltar Barracks, Bury St Edmunds,
Suffolk IP33 3RN   ☎ *0284 2394*
Mon–Fri 10–12, 2–4. Closed Bank Holiday.
🅇 *Mr J. Easlea, Museum Attendant*
🅕 ⌕ ⛬

The Regiment was raised in 1685 by Henry Howard, 7th Duke of Norfolk, as part of the army formed by James II to counter the Monmouth Rebellion. Since then its titles have been the Duke of Norfolk's Regiment, the 12th Foot and the 12th (East Suffolk) Regiment. In 1959 it was amalgamated with the Royal Norfolk Regiment to become the 1st East Anglian Regiment (Royal Norfolk and Suffolk) and in 1964, as a result of further reorganisation of the infantry, it became the 1st Battalion of the Royal Anglian Regiment.

The Museum contains items connected with the history of regular battalions of the Regiment, as well as the Militia, Volunteer, Territorial and wartime battalions. The weapons range from the wheel-lock musket of 1680 to the automatic weapons of the Second World War. The earliest uniform is an officer's mess jacket of 1830. The medals on display have all been awarded to members of the Regiment and date from 1690 to 1959. Drums hidden in Belgium in 1940 are also exhibited.

Woolpit Bygones Museum

The Institute, Woolpit, Bury St Edmunds, Suffolk
Easter–last weekend in Sept, Sat, Sun 2–5
🅇 *Mr John Wiley, Walnut Tree Cottage,*
Green Road, Woolpit IP30 9RF
☎ *0359 40822*
🅔 ⛬ 🅟 ▢

Woolpit is midway between Bury St Edmunds and Stowmarket, close to the A45. The Museum contains a varied collection of items from the village and its immediate surroundings, recalling events, characters, crafts and livelihoods of the past. The displays are changed annually. A special exhibit is devoted to the 400-year history of the Woolpit brickmaking industry, with photographs, brickmaking equipment and examples of locally made bricks.

At a nearby farm, the Museum has its 'Farming in a Suffolk Village' section, containing implements and equipment from the days of horse power up to the introduction of the tractor. These items are in working condition.

Buxton

Buxton Micrarium

The Crescent, Buxton, Derbyshire SK17 6BQ
☎ *0298 78662*
End of Mar–early Nov, daily 10–5
🅇 *Mrs Janet Carter*
🅔 ⛬ ⛬

Buxton Micrarium is a pioneering venture, created to introduce the public to the vast world of natural objects and creatures. Specially designed microscopes project on to television-size screens and are operated by push-button controls. The equipment allows visitors of all ages to explore the world revealed by the microscope. Hundreds of specimens are available for this purpose. They include rocks, minerals, microscopic plants and animals, sections of animal and plant tissues and organs, feathers and human ear-bones.

Among the special displays are a unique collection of preserved snowflakes, a demonstration of growing microcrystals under polarised light and a living ant colony, offering greatly magnified views of ant development and behaviour within the nest.

Buxton Museum and Art Gallery

Terrace Road, Buxton, Derbyshire SK17 6DJ
☎ 0298 4658   ·
*Tues–Fri 9.30–5.30; Sat 9.30–5. Closed Good
Fri.*
⌘ *Education Officer*
Ⓕ ▉ ✿ ⅋ ☐

The Museum building, dating from the late 19th
century, was one of Buxton's 'Hydropathic
Hotels'. It retains some good stained glass. The
displays cover the geology, prehistory, Roman
and medieval archaeology of the Peak District;
the rise of tourism, and of antiquarian and
geological studies in the area during the 18th
and 19th centuries. There is a special emphasis
on the local Blue John and Ashford Marble
industries, and on the decorative arts associated
with them. The collections also include 19th
and 20th-century oil paintings, watercolours
and prints, which are usually on display during
the winter months. Temporary art exhibitions,
mainly of work by local artists, are shown
throughout the year.

Cadbury

Fursdon House

Cadbury, nr Exeter, Devon EX5 5JS
☎ 0392 860860
*Easter Sun and Mon, then May–Sept, Thurs, Sun,
Bank Holiday, 2–5.30. July–Aug, also open
Wed 2–5.30.*
⌘ *Mr E. D. Fursdon*
Ⓔ ▉ ▅ ✿ [HHA]

The Fursdons came to Fursdon in the reign of
Henry III and have been here ever since. They
have survived by concentrating on the running
of their estate and by being very careful to avoid
the high offices of State. The present house was
built in the early 17th century and some
alterations were made in 1732.

Fursdon House has an interesting collection
of family possessions which have accumulated
over the centuries. These include, in addition to
furniture and portraits, many everyday items
from the past, such as a slipper bath, toy soldiers
and scrapbooks. There is also a display of family
costumes, which is changed annually. A court
dress dating from 1753 is permanently on
display.

Visitors can also see a collection of Iron Age
and Roman material, including coins and
jewellery found during excavations at South
Cadbury, an Iron Age hillfort on the estate, a
number of old estate maps and letters, including
two signed by Charles I.

Caerleon

**Caerleon Roman Fortress: Amphitheatre,
Barracks and Fortress Baths**

Caerleon Amphitheatre, Caerleon, Gwent
☎ 0633 421656
*Mar 15–Oct 15, daily 9.30–6.30. Oct 16–
Mar 14, Mon–Sat 9.30–4, Sun 2–4.*
⌘ *The Custodian*
Ⓔ ▉ ✿

The Fortress at Caerleon, the Roman *Isca*, was
the headquarters of the Second Augustan
Legion, which was permanently based in Britain
and consisted of 5,000–6,000 men. The
excavated remains include a large and well-
preserved amphitheatre and the sites of a
barracks, baths and town wall. The new Visitor
Centre at the Roman Baths contains an
interpretative exhibition for the whole site,
designed by the National Museum of Wales.

Caernarfon

Caernarfon Castle

Caernarfon, Gwynedd LL57 2AY   ☎ 0286 3094
*Mar 15–Oct 15, daily 9.30–6.30. Oct 16–
Mar 14, Mon–Sat 9.30–4; Sun 2–4.*
⌘ *The Custodian*
Ⓔ ▉ ✿ ✤

The Castle, which is very largely intact, was
built 1283–1330, incorporating part of an 11th-
century Norman motte and bailey. The son of
Edward I, later Prince of Wales and Edward II,
was born here in 1284 and in 1969 Caernarfon
Castle was the site of the investiture of HRH
Prince Charles as Prince of Wales. Exhibitions
in the Eagle Tower illustrate the history of the
Castle and of the Princes of Wales who have
been associated with it.

Royal Welch Fusiliers Regimental Museum

*Caernarfon Castle, Caernarfon, Gwynedd
LL57 2AY*   ☎ 0286 3362
*Mid Mar–mid Oct, daily 9.30–6.30. Rest of year
Mon–Sat 9.30–4; Sun 2–4. Closed
Dec 24–26, Jan 1.*
⌘ *Captain B. H. Finchett-Maddock*
Ⓔ ✍ ✿

The Museum is in the Queen's Tower of
Caernarfon Castle, built between 1283 and
1323. The exhibits cover the history of the
Regiment from 1689, when it was raised by Lord
Herbert of Cherbury, to the present day. It is
the oldest infantry regiment in Wales and the
displays of uniforms, weapons, equipment,
pictures, medals and documents in the Museum
illustrate the many campaigns and battles in
which its members have played a prominent
part. These include the Battle of the Boyne,
the American War of Independence, the
Napoleonic Wars, the Crimean War, the Indian
Mutiny, and the Boer War.

Careful attention has been paid to the special
customs of the Regiment, which include the
eating of the leek on St David's Day.

Roman auxiliary infantryman, about AD 100.
Caernarfon, Segontium Roman Fort Museum.

Segontium Roman Fort Museum

Beddgelert Road, Caernarfon, Gwynedd
   ☎ 0286 5625
Mar–Apr, Oct, Mon–Sat 9.30–5.30; Sun 2–5.
   May–Sept, Mon–Sat 9.30–6; Sun 2 6.
   Nov–Feb, Mon–Sat 9.30–4; Sun 2–4.
   Closed Good Fri, May Day, Dec 24–26,
   Jan 1.
🏛 *The Custodian*
F ✐ ✎

The Roman auxiliary fort of *Segontium*,
overlooking the town of Caernarfon, is one of
the most famous in Britain. The Museum,
which is on the site of the fort, tells the story of
the conquest and occupation of Wales by the
Romans and describes the military organisation
of the day, the garrisons of *Segontium*, and the
history of the fort as illustrated by its remains.
It also displays finds from the excavations at
Segontium which throw light on daily life in
this remote Roman outpost. A model of a fully
equipped Roman auxiliary infantryman of the
early 2nd century A.D. forms the centrepiece
of the exhibition.

Seiont II Maritime Museum

Victoria Dock, Caernarfon, Gwynedd
   ☎ 0248 600835
May–Sept, daily 1–5 or dusk. Pre-booked parties
   during winter months.
🏛 *Mr F. R. Jones, Secretary, Seiont II Maritime*
   Trust, Foelas, Tregarth, Bangor, Gwynedd
   LL57 4AW
F ✐ ✎

Part of the Museum building was at one time
the Caernarfon town mortuary, located at the
Victoria Dock because of the number of
casualties which occurred when the dock was

first opened in 1868. The displays concentrate
on the history of Caernarfon as a harbour and
port since Roman times. Special attention is
paid to the slate trade, maritime education –
the Mrs Ellen Edward School of Navigation and
Seamanship achieved a great reputation – and
passenger traffic, particularly emigration.
   The centrepieces of the Museum are the coal-
fired steam grab-dredger and buoy tender, *Seiont
II*, restored to full working order, and the motor
ferry, *Nantlys*, the last and most modern
survivor of the long series of ferries which
crossed the Menai Strait from the 13th century.
Nantlys, with a traditional timber hull, was built
in 1920, on the shore of the Strait. She operated
until 1976. Her engine was overhauled in the
workshops of the Welsh Slate Museum at
Llanberis.

Caerphilly

Caerphilly Castle

Caerphilly, Mid Glamorgan   ☎ 0222 883143
Mar 15–Oct 15, daily 9.30–6.30. Oct 16–
   Mar 14, Mon–Sat 9.30–4; Sun 2–4.
🏛 *The Custodian*
E ✐ ✎ ✤

Built in the 13th century, Caerphilly Castle is
the second largest castle area in Britain. From
the late 18th century to 1950 it belonged to the
Marquesses of Bute, who repaired and improved
it. Now in State ownership, the Great Hall has
been re-roofed and the lakes and moats, drained
by Cromwell's soldiers, have been refilled.
   An interpretative exhibition on the first floor
of the Gatehouse presents the story of the Castle,
with the help of models, maps and plans.

Caherdaniel

Derrynane House

Caherdaniel, Co. Kerry, Ireland   ☎ 0667 5113
May–Oct 1, Mon–Sat 9–6; Sun 11–7.
   Oct 2–Apr, daily 1–5 ex. Mon.
🏛 *Mr Michael Maher*
E ✐ ✎

Derrynane is one mile from Caherdaniel, just off
the main Waterville to Sneem road. The house
was the ancestral home of Daniel O'Connell,
one of the greatest figures in Irish history.
Born in 1775, O'Connell inherited Derrynane
in 1825. After his death, it remained the home
of his descendants until 1958. It now belongs to
the Irish nation and is managed by the National
Parks and Monuments branch of the Office of
Public Works, which has restored the house.
There are many O'Connell family portraits and
items of furniture, notably in the dining-room
and drawing-room. The study and library serve
mainly to house a collection of memorabilia and
personal possessions of Daniel O'Connell.

Caister-on-Sea

Caister Castle Motor Museum

Caister-on-Sea, nr Great Yarmouth, Norfolk
    ☎ *057284 251*
Mid May–last Fri in Sept, Sun–Fri 10.30–5
Ⓧ *Dr Hill*
Ⓔ Ⓓ ▣ ⌖

Caister Castle, a fortified manor house, was the home of Sir John Falstaff, whose family lived here for several generations. The present owner has a wide-ranging collection of steam cars and motorcars, including a Panhard-Levassor of 1893 and the first production model of the Ford Fiesta.

Calbourne

Calbourne Water Mill and Rural Museum

Calbourne, Isle of Wight PO30 4JN
    ☎ *098378 277*
Easter–Oct, daily 10–6
Ⓧ *Mr A. R. Weeks*
Ⓔ ▯ ▣ ⌖

A mill at Calbourne is mentioned in the Domesday Book, and one was producing flour on the same site until 1955. In 1894 a roller plant was added, necessitating extensions to the building. A steam engine was installed to provide extra power, both for stone grinding and for the roller mill. It supplements the 20-foot overshot waterwheel, which is still operational.

In addition to the milling machinery, the Museum preserves a wide range of agricultural bygones, including a wheat cleaner, an oat crusher, a maize and bean kibbler, a rare hand mill operated by two people, a cheese-press, and various items of early dairy equipment. There is also a collection of fossils found on the Isle of Wight.

Caldicot

Caldicot Castle Museum

The Castle, Caldicot, Gwent NP6 4HU
    ☎ *0291 420241*
Mar–Oct, Mon–Fri 11–12.30, 1.30–5; Sat 10–1,
    1.30–5; Sun 1.30–5
Ⓧ *Miss June Rowles, Castle Keeper*
Ⓔ *ex. educ. groups* Ⓓ ⌖

Caldicot is an almost complete castle, with 12th and 14th-century towers and curtain walls, and a 14th-century gatehouse. Considerable restoration work was carried out during the Victorian period. The Castle itself is the principal exhibit. The displays within it include costumes and period furniture, with a special feature on Nelson's flagship, the *Foudroyant*, which the restorer of Caldicot once owned.

Caldicot Castle. In front of the 14th-century Woodstock Tower is a cannon from Nelson's flagship, HMS *Foudroyant*.

Calne

Bowood House

Calne, Wiltshire SN11 0LZ   ☎ *0249 812102*
Apr–Sept, daily 11–6
Ⓧ *Miss Sally Crossland, House Manager*
Ⓔ ▯ ▣ ⌖ ♿ HHA

The entrance to Bowood is in Derry Hill village, midway between Calne and Chippenham, just off the A4. The house, largely designed by Henry Keene and Robert Adam in the late 18th century, has been the home of members of the Lansdowne family ever since. The rooms open to the public include the library, the laboratory in which Dr Joseph Priestley, the 1st Lord Lansdowne's librarian and tutor to his sons, discovered oxygen in 1774, and the orangery, now converted into a picture and sculpture gallery.

A series of exhibition rooms is devoted to the history of the family, from Georgian times to the present day. Among the contents are costumes worn by the 1st Marquess and his wives, Lord Byron's Albanian costume, and a collection of Victoriana, including Queen Victoria's wedding chair. There is also an important collection of Indian material formed by the 5th Lord Lansdowne during his term as Viceroy of India and, in the Upper Tower, a display of watercolours, miniatures and family jewellery.

Bowood has one of the most beautiful parks in England. Landscaped by 'Capability' Brown in 1762–8, it contains an exceptionally fine, well-labelled and catalogued collection of trees, shrubs and plants.

Camberley

National Army Museum (Sandhurst Depts)

Royal Military Academy Sandhurst, Camberley,
    Surrey GU15 4PQ   ☎ *0276 63344 extn 457*
Mon–Fri, by appt only. Applications in writing,
    a week in advance.
Ⓧ *Assistant Director, Sandhurst Departments*
Ⓕ ⌖

The Indian Army Memorial Room and the Hastings Room are in Old College and commemorate the Indian Army and that of the East India Company. Famous Indian regiments such as Skinner's Horse, Probyn's Horse and the Gurkhas are represented by uniforms, weapons and regimental plate. The portraits include those of Field Marshals Auchinleck, Slim and Wavell. There is a display of specimen medals illustrating the numerous awards made over a period of 150 years to men who served with the Indian Army.

Royal Army Ordnance Corps Museum

RAOC Training Centre, Blackdown Barracks, Deepcut, Camberley, Surrey GU16 6RW
☎ *0252 24431 extn 515/516*
Mon–Thurs 8.30–12.30, 1.30–4.30; Fri 8.30–12.30, 1.30–4. Closed Sat, Sun, public holidays.
◪ *The Curator*
Ⓕ ♿

The Royal Army Ordnance Corps was formed in 1918. It had been preceded since 1414 by the Office and Board of Ordnance, the Military Store Department, the Military Store Staff Corps, the Ordnance Store Corps and the Army Ordnance Corps. The Museum illustrates the origins, antecedents and achievements of the Corps. There are exhibits of uniforms, medals and sporting trophies, in addition to the RAOC archives, which contain orders, reports, letters and other historical documents.

Staff College Museum

Staff College, Camberley, Surrey GU15 4NP
☎ *0276 63344 extn 650*
By written appt. Closed Bank Holiday.
◪ *Hon. Curator*
Ⓕ ♿

The Museum is housed in the 1857 building of the original Army Staff College. The displays illustrate the history of the Staff College and of the Army Staff Officers connected with it.

Cambo

Wallington

Cambo, Morpeth, Northumberland NE61 4AR
☎ *067074 283*
Mar 28–Apr 6, daily 2–6. Apr 7–30, Wed, Sat, Sun 2–6. May–Sept, daily 2–6 ex. Tues. Oct, Wed, Sat, Sun 2–6.
◪ *C. R. A. Olliver, Administrator*
Ⓔ ♨ 🍴 ♿ ♿ NT

This National Trust house was built in 1688 on the site of a medieval castle. It was altered in the 1740s. The rooms open to visitors range from the mid Georgian salon to the late Victorian nursery, and contain remarkable plasterwork and fine furniture, porcelain, needlework and paintings. The central hall was added in the mid 19th century and is decorated with paintings by John Ruskin, William Bell Scott and others.

There is a good collection of dolls' houses, a museum containing articles connected with the house and the surrounding area, and a display of coaches.

Camborne

Camborne Museum

The Cross, Camborne, Cornwall TR14 8HA
Mon–Wed, Fri 3–5; Sat 10–12
◪ *Mr M. K. Matthews, Helston Folk Museum, Church Street, Helston, Cornwall TR13 8SZ*
Ⓕ

The Museum contains general collections relating to Camborne and the surrounding region, with minerals as a strong feature. A section is devoted to Roman influence in the area and there is a special exhibit relating to the Cornish inventor, Richard Trevithick.

Cornish Engines

East Pool, Camborne, Cornwall
Apr–Oct, daily including Good Fri 11–6 or sunset if earlier
◪ *National Trust, Bodmin*　　☎ *0208 4281*
Ⓔ ♨ NT

The Cornish beam-engine, built by such famous local firms as Harvey's of Hayle, was renowned throughout the world for its economy, reliability and long life. During the 1930s, these engines began to disappear from their native county and the Cornish Engines Preservation Society was formed in order to save a representative selection of them. In 1967 the Society gave the engines to the National Trust. Two of them are at East Pool and others can be seen at the South Crofty Mine, near Camborne and the Levant Mine, near St Just. The fifth, the Restowrack engine, is at present not on public display. The five add up to an engineering museum of international importance.

The landscape of Cornwall is a museum commemorating the Cornish engine. The ruined engine houses to be seen everywhere, with their machinery long since removed, are given meaning by the five complete engines.

Cambridge

Cambridge and County Folk Museum

Castle Street, Cambridge CB3 0AQ
☎ 0223 355159
Tues–Sat 10.30–5; Sun 2.30–4.30
⚔ Educational Assistant (booking essential for
    groups of more than 10)
Ⓔ ⬛ ☐

The former White Horse Inn, which houses
the Museum, was built in the 16th and 17th
centuries. The collections cover the everyday
life of people in the city of Cambridge and the
county of Cambridgeshire from c. 1650 to the
present day. Ten exhibition rooms are devoted
to: trades and occupations – this room includes
the original bar of the White Horse, which was
used as such until 1934; cooking and lighting;
the kitchen; domestic crafts; the city and
university; dolls' houses, miniature furniture,
dolls, toys and games; the farm; the Fens and
folklore; and costume and dress.

Fitzwilliam Museum

Trumpington Street, Cambridge CB2 1RB
☎ 0223 337733/332900
Tues–Sat 10–5; Sun 2.15–5. Open Easter Mon,
    Spring and Summer Bank Holidays. Closed
    Mon, Dec 24–Jan 1, Good Fri, May Day.
⚔ Keeper of Administration
Ⓕ ⬛ ✎ ▆ ☛ ♿

The original Museum buildings, designed by
George Basevi, were opened in 1848. Major
extensions were carried out between 1924 and
1975. The Fitzwilliam contains the Fine Art
collections of the University, most of which
have been acquired through private
benefactions, and which comprise Egyptian,
Greek, Near Eastern and Roman antiquities;
coins and medals; medieval manuscripts;
paintings and drawings; prints; Oriental and
Occidental pottery and porcelain; textiles; arms
and armour; and medieval and Renaissance
objects of art. There is also a notable library.

Kettle's Yard

Castle Street, Cambridge CB3 0AQ
☎ 0223 352124
House: daily 2–4. Gallery: Tues, Wed, Fri, Sat
    12.30–5.30; Thurs 12.30–7; Sun 2–5.30.
⚔ Education Officer
Ⓕ ✎ ☐

Kettle's Yard has been created from a conversion
of four 17th-century buildings, with a modern
extension. It has been conceived as a home,
rather than a museum, and every attempt is
made to preserve an intimate atmosphere. It
houses a substantial collection of British art of
the early 20th century, collected by Jim Ede and
placed together in a domestic setting, with
books, furniture and other objects.
    There is also a gallery for temporary
exhibitions with changing displays of
20th-century art. Works in all media are
shown. There is an extensive education
programme.

Museum of Classical Archaeology

Sidgwick Avenue, Cambridge CB3 9DA
☎ 0223 62253 extn 29
During term-time, daily 9–5.30; otherwise 9–1,
    2.15–5. Closed Christmas, Easter.
⚔ Mr R. A. Papworth, Museum Supervisor
Ⓕ ☛

The Museum, funded and administered by the
University of Cambridge, houses and displays
most attractively one of the largest, and perhaps
the finest, collection of plaster casts of Greek
and Roman sculpture in the world.

Statuary in the Museum of Classical
Archaeology, Cambridge.

Museum of the Scott Polar Research Institute

Lensfield Road, Cambridge CB2 1ER
☎ 0223 66499
Mon–Sat 2.30–4. Closed some public and
    University holidays.
⚔ The Curator
Ⓕ ✎

The collections include material relating to the
Arctic and the Antarctic. There are relics from
several expeditions to both Polar regions,
notably those of Robert Falcon Scott; a
selection of Eskimo carvings and other artefacts;
a display of scrimshaw; physical and
glaciological information about the Poles;
Antarctic ornithology. Several sledges, types
of ski, and other equipment are also on view.
    The Institute also has a comprehensive Polar
library and archive.

Sedgwick Museum

Downing Street, Cambridge CB2 3EQ
☎ 0223 355463
During term-time, Mon–Fri 9–5; Sat 9–12.30
⚔ The Curator
Ⓕ ✎ ♿

The ornate staircase leading to the Museum
from the car park has a carved bison at its foot,
and the building has carvings of dinosaurs and
other animals on its Downing Street frontage.
The Museum possesses more than half a million
catalogued fossils, with large numbers on
display. Arranged according to their age, with
geographical and taxonomic subgroupings, they
are widely used in University teaching of Earth
Sciences and in international research on fossil
groups.

University Museum of Archaeology and Anthropology

Downing Street, Cambridge CB2 3DZ
☎ *0223 337733*
Mon–Fri 2–4; Sat 10–12.30. Closed Dec 24–
Jan 1 and one week at Easter.
▯ *The Curator*
▯ ▱

The Museum is a purpose-built Edwardian building, which incorporates the Inigo Jones screen from Winchester Cathedral. The collections illustrate the prehistory of all parts of the world, from the origin of mankind to the rise of literate civilisation, as well as the traditional and changing culture of more recent peoples in all continents. A large part of the collections is the result of pioneering archaeological and anthropological research by Cambridge-based scholars. The Museum also acts as the local archaeological museum for the Cambridge region. Its prime function is as a teaching and research institution for Cambridge University, but a great effort is also made to produce enjoyable and useful displays for a less specialist public. The galleries are being completely refurbished and the new Gallery of World Prehistory and Local Archaeology is now open.

University Museum of Zoology

Downing Street, Cambridge CB2 3EJ
☎ *0223 358717*
Mon–Fri 2.15–4.45. Closed Sat, Sun, Bank
Holiday, including one week at Christmas and
Easter
▯ *The Director*
▯

The Museum consists of collections of zoological specimens used for teaching and research, housed in a modern building. There are spectacular displays of marine invertebrates, exotic birds and mammal skeletons, included within a survey of the animal kingdom.

Whipple Museum of the History of Science

Free School Lane, Cambridge CB2 3RH
☎ *0223 358381 extn 340*
Mon–Fri 2–4. Occasionally closed during vacations.
▯ *The Curator*
▯ ▱

The main gallery of the Museum was once the Free School, founded by Stephen Perse in the early 17th century. The collections comprise scientific instruments and apparatus dating from the 16th to the 20th century. Many of the exhibits illustrate the University's own contribution to the history of science. Particular strengths are traditional mathematical instruments, such as sundials, quadrants and astrolabes, surveying instruments and microscopes. Navigation, astronomy and physics are also well represented.

Camelford

North Cornwall Museum and Gallery

The Clease, Camelford, Cornwall PL32 9PL
☎ *0840 212954*
Apr–Sept, Mon–Sat 10–5
▯ *Sally Holden*
▯ ▱ ▱ ▯

Opened in 1974, the Museum occupies a building that was originally used for making coaches and wagons. The collections cover many aspects of life in North Cornwall from 50 to 100 years ago, including farming, the dairy, cider-making and wagon-building. There are sections displaying the tools of the carpenter, cooper, blacksmith, saddler, cobbler, tailor, printer, doctor and quarryman. On the domestic side is a wide range of exhibits, ranging from lace bonnets to early vacuum cleaners, together with a good collection of Cornish and Devonshire pottery. A special feature is the reconstruction of a moorland cottage at the turn of the century.

The Gallery has changing exhibitions of paintings and crafts throughout the season.

Campbeltown

Campbeltown Museum

Public Library, Hall Street, Campbeltown,
Argyll PA28 6BJ   ☎ *0586 52366 extn 218*
Mon, Tues, Thurs, Fri 10–1, 2–5; Wed, Sat
10–1, 2–5. Closed public holidays.
▯ *Branch Librarian*
▯

The Museum is concerned mainly with the geology, natural history and history of Kintyre. There are special displays relating to fishing and the sea and to Scottish weapons and craftsmen's tools. There is also a collection of paintings.

Model totem pole from Queen Charlotte Island, Canada. Cambridge, University Museum of Archaeology and Anthropology.

Canterbury

Canterbury Heritage

Poor Priests' Hospital, Stour Street, Canterbury, Kent
Mon–Sat 10.30–4.30. Closed Good Fri, Dec 25–26, Jan 1.
ぺ *See Royal Museum and Art Gallery*
£ ✏ ♿

The Hospital was founded c. 1200 to house poor priests. The present building, dating from 1373, has recently been restored by Canterbury City Council. Canterbury Heritage takes the form of a time-walk through the story of Canterbury, with objects from the city's historical collections to support the displays and models.

The Queen's Regiment Museum

Howe Barracks, Canterbury, Kent CT1 1JU
☎ *0227 457411*
Mon–Fri 10–12.30, 2–4. Closed Sat, Sun, Bank Holiday.
ぺ *See Royal Museum and Art Gallery*
F ✏ ♿

The Museum's display of uniforms, weapons, medals, pictures, documents and equipment covers 400 years of military history and illustrates the story of The Queen's Regiment and the six Regiments from which it was formed in 1966.

Royal Museum and Art Gallery

High Street, Canterbury, Kent CT1 2JE
☎ *0227 452747*
Mon–Sat 10–5. Closed Good Fri, Dec 25, 26, Jan 1.
ぺ *The Curator*
F ✏ ♿

The Museum occupies part of the interesting late Victorian building of Dr Beaney's Institute. There are displays of natural history, local archaeology and pottery and porcelain. The art collections include paintings, engravings and topographical prints. The historical collections of The Buffs, the Royal East Kent Regiment, also form part of the Museum.

Anglo-Saxon disc brooch with garnet inlay. Canterbury, Royal Museum.

The Roman Mosaic

Butchery Lane, Canterbury, Kent
Apr–Sept, Mon–Sat 10–1, 2–5. Oct–Mar, Mon–Sat 2–4. Closed Good Fri, Dec 25, 26, Jan 1.
ぺ *See Royal Museum and Art Gallery*
☎ *0227 452747*
£ ✏ ♿

Canterbury's underground museum preserves in the Roman levels the foundations of a town house, with two mosaic floors and the remains of its heating system. There are also displays illustrating everyday life during the period of the Roman occupation. These include objects discovered in the course of excavations in the city.

The West Gate

St Peter's Street, Canterbury, Kent
Apr–Sept, Mon–Sat 10–1, 2–5. Oct–Mar, Mon–Sat 2–4. Closed Good Fri, Dec 25, 26, Jan 1.
ぺ *See Royal Museum and Art Gallery*
£ ✏ ♿

This is the rebuilding, carried out c. 1380, of an earlier gate. Its twin drum towers were originally fitted with gates, portcullis and drawbridge. There is a display of arms and armour in the former Guard Chamber.

Canvey Island

Castle Point Transport Museum

Point Road, Canvey Island, Essex
☎ *0268 684272*
Sun 11–3, by appt only. Open Day: 2nd Sun in Oct.
ぺ *The Curator*
F ♿ ⬛

The Museum, run entirely by volunteers, contains buses and coaches built between 1935 and 1965. Most of the exhibits were formerly owned by the Eastern National Omnibus Company or by companies which it absorbed. Other items have been acquired from Southend Corporation. Coaches owned by members of the Museum Society are also on display.

Dutch Cottage Museum

Long Road, Canvey Island, Essex
Spring Bank Holiday Mon–Sept, Wed, Sun 2.30–5. Bank Holiday 10.30–1, 2.30–5.
ぺ *Mr G. J. Johnson, Secretary, 3 Oakfield Road, Benfleet, Essex SS7 5NS*   **☎** *03745 4005*
F ✏ ♿

The cottage housing part of the Museum dates from 1618. It was probably used by one of the Dutch workmen brought over by Cornelius Vermuyden to reclaim land from the sea and to unite the five islands of Canvey into a single unit. A new exhibition room has been constructed to display the many exhibits which could no longer find a place in the cottage.

The displays include 18th and 19th-century furniture and domestic equipment, farm implements, eel spears formerly used in the area, models of types of sailing ships which passed Canvey at various periods in its history, corn dollies, and embanking tools once used to maintain the local sea-walls and ditches. There is also a collection of archaeological finds made in recent years which help to reconstruct a picture of life on Canvey in prehistoric times and during the Romano-British and medieval periods.

Cape Clear Island

Iarsmalann Chléire

Lios Ó Móine, Cape Clear Island, Skibbereen, Co. Cork, Ireland   ☎ *021 293638*
June–Aug, daily 3.30–5.30
🏛 *Éamon Lankford, Fán, Bóthar Theas na Dubhghlaise, Corcaigh*
£ ✎ ♿

The Irish-speaking island of Cape Clear (Oileán Cléire) lies about eight miles off Baltimore. Traditional customs have persisted longer here than on the mainland and the Museum contains a large collection of objects relating to the history of the Island which have been presented by members of the local community. These cover fishing, farming, handicrafts and domestic life, together with the archaeological evidence of the prehistoric inhabitants of Cape Clear Island.

Cardiff

National Museum of Wales

Cathays Park, Cardiff, South Glamorgan CF1 3NP   ☎ *0222 39/951*
Tues–Sat 10–5; Sun 2.30–5. Closed Good Fri, May Day, Dec 24–26, Jan 1.
🏛 *Senior Officer, Museum Schools Service*
F ♦ ♿ ♿

The Museum was designed as an integral part of Cardiff's civic centre in Cathays Park. The emphasis of the permanent collections is on the story of Wales from the earliest times. The galleries illustrate Welsh geology, plants and animals, as well as the story of man, his work and his art. The art collection is of international standing and is particularly strong on works by French Impressionist and Post-Impressionist painters, including Monet, Renoir, Cézanne and Pissarro.

The industrial section has original objects and machines relating to the older industries, together with dioramas and models. There is a mining gallery and other displays tell the story of iron, steel and tinplate manufacture in Wales. The modern industries featured include electricity and oil-refining.

The National Museum of Wales, Cardiff, from Cathays Park.

The Welch Regiment Museum of the Royal Regiment of Wales

Black and Barbican Towers, Cardiff Castle, Cardiff, South Glamorgan CF1 2RB
☎ *0222 29367*
Daily 10–6 (10–4 in winter). Closed Dec 25, 26, Jan 1.
🏛 *The Curator*
£ ✎ ♦ ♿

The Regimental Museum is housed in the Black and Barbican Towers of Cardiff Castle and in the Portcullis Chamber which links them. It illustrates the history of the Welch Regiment (41st/69th Foot) from its formation in 1719 until 1969, and its close association with the Principality through the Militia, Volunteers, Territorials and other Auxiliary units of South Wales. Among the items of particular interest is the Colour of the 4th Regiment of American Infantry taken at Fort Detroit in 1812. There is also a fine collection of Welsh military insignia. The Museum buidings include a working portcullis.

Welsh Folk Museum

St Fagans, Cardiff, South Glamorgan CF5 6XB
☎ *0222 569441*
Mon–Sat 10–5; Sun 2.30–5. Closed Good Fri, May Day, Dec 24–26, Jan 1.
🏛 *Education Officer*
£ ♦ ♿ ♿ ♿ ♿

The Museum, which illustrates the traditional life and culture of Wales, is four miles west of Cardiff, near Junction 33 on the M4 motorway. The open-air section, covering a site of about 100 acres, contains a number of buildings moved from other parts of Wales. These include farmhouses, cottages, a tannery, forge, tollhouse, cockpit, chapel and working woollen and flour mills. Among the craftsmen who give demonstrations on Saturday mornings throughout the summer months are a cooper and a woodturner.

In St Fagans, an Elizabethan mansion with formal gardens within the curtain wall of a Norman castle, are the Galleries of Material Culture, which have displays of costumes, transport, agricultural implements, furniture and domestic equipment.

Welsh Industrial and Maritime Museum

Bute Street, Cardiff, South Glamorgan CF1 5AN
    ☎ *0222 481919*
*Tues–Sat 10–5; Sun 2.30–5. Open Bank Holiday
    Mon. Closed Good Fri, May Day, Dec 24–26,
    Jan 1.*
⋈ *The Curator*
Ⓕ 🏛 🚗 ♿

Situated in the dock area of Cardiff, the
Museum, which is still in the course of
development, has been set up in order to
interpret the industrial and maritime heritage of
Wales. There are at present two galleries which
trace the history of motive power in Wales and
an open-air section which displays a wide range
of machines, vehicles and ships. A railway
exhibition is housed nearby at Bute Railway
Station.

Cark-in-Cartmel

Craft and Countryside Museum

*Holker Hall, Cark-in-Cartmel, nr Grange-over-
    Sands, Cumbria LA11 7PL   ☎ 044853 328*
*Easter–last Sun in Oct, Sun–Fri 10.30–6 (last
    admission to hall and grounds 4.30)*
⋈ *Mrs C. Johnson, Administrator*
Ⓔ 🖼 🚗 ♿ [HHA]

The new wing of Holker Hall is Victorian,
completed in 1884. The displays at the Craft
and Countryside Museum illustrate the natural
history and traditional crafts of the area,
including horn-making, bobbin-making, slate-
working and the history and techniques of the
Flookburgh fishermen.

Lakeland Motor Museum

*Holker Hall, Cark-in-Cartmel, nr Grange-over-
    Sands, Cumbria LA11 7PL   ☎ 044853 509*
*Easter–last Sun in Oct, Sun–Fri 10.30–6 (last
    admission to hall and grounds 4.30)*
⋈ *The Manageress, Holker Hall*
Ⓔ 🏛 🖼 🚗 ♿

The Museum is in the converted stables of
Holker Hall. The collection of vintage, veteran
and unusual cars, motorcycles, cycles and
miscellaneous motoring items date from the
1880s to the 1960s. A re-creation of a 1920s
garage contains signs and equipment of the
period and there is a splendid collection of petrol
pumps, advertisements and equipment relating
to the Esso Petroleum Company and its
precedessors.

Carlisle

Carlisle Museum and Art Gallery

*Tullie House, Castle Street, Carlisle, Cumbria
    CA3 8TP   ☎ 0228 34781*
*Apr–Sept, Mon–Fri 9–6.45; Sat 9–5, Sun
    (June–Aug only) 2.30–5. Oct–Mar, Mon–Sat
    9–5.*
⋈ *The Curator*
Ⓕ 🍽 🚗

The Museum building, a Jacobean house with
Victorian extensions, is named after the Tullie
family, who occupied it from the early 17th
century until 1817. There are important
collections relating to the prehistoric and Roman
periods in Cumbria. The Roman items come
mainly from excavations in the Cumbrian
section of Hadrian's Wall and the Roman city of
Carlisle, *Luguvalium*. The natural history and
geological collections are mainly local in origin
and are particularly strong in birds and minerals.
The art collections emphasise 19th and 20th-
century British paintings and 18th and 19th-
century English porcelain, with excellent
examples from all the major factories. Toys and
dolls, costumes and musical instruments are also
well represented.
    The social history collections include a wide
range of objects from 1600 to the present day.
There are displays on farming, weaving, firearms,
the fire service, law and order, photography,
pharmacy and the State-managed public houses.

Guildhall Museum

Greenmarket, Carlisle, Cumbria
Mid May–mid Sept, Tues–Sat 12–4
⋈ *See Carlisle Museum and Art Gallery*
Ⓕ 🍽 🖼 🚗

The Guildhall is an early 15th-century timber-
framed building, originally a house, but used as a
Guild meeting place for over 350 years. It now
contains displays on the history of the medieval
Guilds and on the building itself. Major exhibits
include the city's medieval iron-bound
muniment chest and town bell, both dating from
c. 1400; Guild and city silver – two 1599 silver
bells are reputed to be the earliest surviving
horse-racing prizes in the country; medieval
measures and pottery; civic regalia; the pillory
and stocks.

**Making roofing slates at the Craft and
Countryside Museum, Cark-in-Cartmel.**

Museum of the Border Regiment and the King's Own Border Regiment

*Queen Mary's Tower, The Castle, Carlisle,
Cumbria CA3 8UR* ☎ *0228 32774*
*Mar 15–Oct 15, daily 9.30–6.30. Oct 16–
Mar 14, Mon–Sat 9.30–4; Sun 2–4. Closed
Dec 24–26, Jan 1.*
⚑ *The Curator*
£ ♠ ✍

The Museum building was the 16th-century
Great Hall of the former Palace. The Museum is
arranged chronologically, telling the history of
the Regiment from 1680 to the present day.
There are displays of uniforms, pictures,
documents, medals and silver. The collection of
trophies is particularly important, with items
from China, India, Russia, the Middle East and
Africa. The history of the local Cumbria units
from 1800 onwards is well represented.

Visitors can also see video programmes
explaining battles in which the Regiment fought
between 1811 and 1944, and also recent
ceremonial parades.

Citizen Soldier Showcase. Carlisle, Museum of
the Border Regiment and King's Own Border
Regiment.

The Prior's Tower Museum

*Carlisle Cathedral, Carlisle, Cumbria CA3 8TZ
End of May–mid Sept, Mon–Fri 10–9 (rest of year
11–5). Sun by appt for parish parties.
Closed Dec 25–26, Easter Day.*
⚑ *Mrs S. Holmes, 19 Castle Street, Carlisle
CA3 8TZ* ☎ *0228 25195*
F ♠ ■ ✍

The Priory of Augustinian canons served
Carlisle Cathedral from the 11th century until
the Dissolution in the 16th century. The
Museum is housed in the Prior's bedroom on the
second floor of the early 13th-century Pele
Tower attached to the Deanery. The Prior's
Room on the first floor has a splendid panelled
ceiling of 45 panels, dating from 1510.

The Museum collection consists of articles
connected with the site from Roman times to
the present day. There are portraits of Deans,
17th and 18th-century Cathedral plate, 15th-
century copes, and the cope, mitre and pastoral
staff used during the 1920s by Bishop Williams.

Fragments of stone, tiles and pottery are
reminders that there were Roman and Saxon,
as well as medieval buildings on the site.

Charters of the Cathedral are on show from
time to time, together with early 17th-century
books from the Cathedral Library. In one corner
of the Prior's bedroom, the garderobe, or
lavatory, still remains, with its shaft going down
the corner turret to the ground.

Carlow

Carlow County Museum

Town Hall, Carlow, Co. Carlow, Ireland
☎ *0503 42666*
*June–Sept, daily 2.30–5.30. Oct–May, Sun
2.30–5.30.*
⚑ *Mr Sean O'Leary, Hon. Secretary, Old Carlow
Society, Montgomery Street, Carlow*
☎ *0503 43492*
£ ✎ ✍

Carlow County Museum is concerned mainly
with life in the region during the 19th and early
20th centuries. The range of exhibits is very
wide. It includes a blacksmith's forge, an old-
time kitchen and bar, a huckster's shop, a dairy,
and collections of agricultural implements and
craftsmen's tools. There are also displays of
ecclesiastical vestments and altar requisites;
natural history; archaeology; locally made lace;
pewter; glass; military uniforms dating from the
Crimean and First and Second World Wars.

The Picture Gallery contains portraits of
people connected with the political, industrial,
ecclesiastical and sporting activities of the area.

Carmarthen

Carmarthen Museum

Abergwili, Carmarthen, Dyfed SA31 2JG
☎ *0267 231691*
*Mon–Sat 10–4.30. Closed Good Fri, Christmas
week.*
⚑ *C. J. Delaney, Curator*
£ ♠ ✍ &

The Museum is in the former Palace of the
Bishops of St David's, a much adapted and
altered medieval building. After various 19th-
century changes and improvements, all but the
west wing was gutted by fire in 1903. Rebuilding
was completed in 1907 and the building has
remained substantially the same since then. In
1974 the Bishop of St David's moved to a new
palace.

The displays in the Museum cover all aspects
of the history and culture of the area, the former
County of Carmarthenshire. There are sections
on archaeology; social history; ceramics,
including examples from the Museum's
collection of Swansea, Llanelly and Glamorgan
pottery; costumes and accessories; dairying;
local crafts; prints and drawings. In addition,
there are collections of geology, natural history,
and uniforms, weapons, medals and honours of
the various Militia and Volunteer units
associated with the area.

Carnforth

Carmarthen Fire Brigade, about 1896.
Historic photograph in Carmarthen Museum.

Leighton Hall

Carnforth, Lancashire LA5 9ST ☎ 0524 734474
May–Sept, Tues–Fri, Sun 2–5
⚔ Mrs R. G. Reynolds
☐ ♿ 🅿 🚻 HHA

Parts of Leighton Hall date from Tudor and
Jacobean times, but most of the building is 18th
century, with a south wing added in 1871.
There is an exceptionally fine collection of 18th
and 19th-century furniture made by Gillows of
Lancaster, resulting from family links with the
firm.

Steamtown Railway Museum

Warton Road, Carnforth, Lancashire LA5 9HX
☎ 0524 734220
Daily ex. Christmas Day, summer 9–5, winter
10–4
⚔ Miss S. A. Cooke, Secretary
☐ ♿ 🅿 🚻

The Museum is a short distance from Carnforth
railway station. Carnforth Motive Power Depot
was one of the last in the country to retain steam
locomotives. In 1968 a private company leased
the Depot and built up an important collection
of locomotives and coaches. Steamtown covers
26 acres and is complete with offices,
workshops, working coaling plant, turntable,
water columns and signal box. Some of the
locomotives occasionally haul special trains on
the British Rail system.

On Sundays from Easter to October, daily in
July and August, and all Bank Holidays, a
passenger service is operated on a mile of
standard-gauge track, and during the same
period there is another service on a 15-inch
gauge line.

Carrbridge

Landmark Visitor Centre

Carrbridge, Inverness-shire PH23 3AJ
☎ 047984 613
Apr–May and Sept–Oct, daily 9.30–6. June–Aug,
daily 9.30–9.30. Nov–Mar, daily 9.30–5.
⚔ Mr D. Fullerton, Manager
☐ ♿ 🅿 🚻

The Centre aims to provide an introduction to
the history, natural environment and wildlife of
the Highlands. There are nature trails, a separate
Nature Centre, and the Highland Sculpture
Park, which contains what is probably Scotland's
largest display of contemporary sculpture.

Carrickfergus

Combined Irish Cavalry Regiments Museum

Carrickfergus Castle, Carrickfergus, Co. Antrim,
    Northern Ireland   ☎ 02383 62273
Apr–Sept, daily 10–6. Oct–Mar, daily 10–4.
    Closed Easter Mon, Dec 25, 26.
⚔ The Keeper
☐ ♿ 🚻

Carrickfergus Castle, the home of the Museum,
dates from the 12th century. The collections of
uniforms and equipment, medals, weapons,
documents and pictures illustrate the history of
seven regiments: the 5th Dragoon Guards, 6th
Inniskilling Dragoons, 5th Royal Inniskilling
Dragoon Guards, 4th Queen's Own Hussars, 8th
King's Own Hussars, Queen's Royal Irish
Hussars and North Irish Horse.

Carrickmacross

'Celebration of Irish' Museum

Carrickmacross, Co. Monaghan, Ireland
☎ 042 61398
Fri 1.30–3.30. Other times by appt.
✠ Peadar O'Casaide, Curator
Ⓕ ◄

The Museum occupies a former secondary school, built in the early years of the present century. Its collections illustrate the history of the area and include farm and household equipment, 18th and 19th-century estate surveys and maps, and old photographs of local interest.

Carrigtwohill

Fota House

Fota Island, Carrigtwohill, Co. Cork, Ireland
☎ 021 812555
First Sat in Apr–Sept, Mon–Sat 11–6; Sun 2–6. Rest of year Sun, Bank Holiday 2–6. Groups by appt.
✠ Christina Neylon, Curator
Ⓔ ✎ ⬛ ◄ ♿

Fota Island is nine miles east of Cork, on the Cobh road. Fota House was built in the 1820s for the Smith-Barry family, once Earls of Barrymore, by Sir Richard Morrison, who created here some of the finest neo-classical interiors in Ireland. It has been restored to display a collection of Irish landscape paintings, dating from the mid 18th to the mid 19th century. The works are arranged in chronological order, illustrating the history of Irish painting during the period. Background material is provided by some English and a small collection of 17th-century Flemish paintings.

The rooms are furnished with fine examples of Irish craftsmanship. Period wallpapers and curtains have been incorporated where possible. The estate includes Fota Wildlife Park, created by the Royal Zoological Society of Ireland with the primary aim of breeding groups of animals that are endangered in the wild, and Fota Arboretum, which is one of the most notable in Ireland.

Carshalton

Little Holland House

40 Beeches Avenue, Carshalton, Surrey SM5 3LR
☎ 01 647 5168
Mar–Oct, 1st Sun of month and Bank Holiday Sun, and Mon 12–6
✠ The Borough Heritage Officer, Central Library, St Nicholas Way, Sutton, Surrey
Ⓕ ✎

Frank R. Dickinson (1874–1961) was a painter who seldom exhibited, a poet who never published, a woodcarver, furniture-maker and metalsmith who hardly earned a penny at his craft. He and his wife built, decorated and furnished Little Holland House with their own hands. Unaltered, it is now maintained as a museum by the Borough of Sutton. It represents the ideas and beliefs of one man, who was a follower of William Morris and John Ruskin and totally immersed in the Arts and Crafts style.

Cartmel

The 1658 Art Gallery of Wood Carvings

Cartmel, nr Grange-over-Sands, Cumbria LA11 6QF   ☎ 044854 392
Daily 10–5. Other times on request.
✠ Mrs E. Margaret Gibbon, Curator
Ⓔ ◄ ♿

The Gallery is in a 1658 cruck barn. The attached house dates from the 15th century. The exhibits consist of large sculptures by Michael Gibbon. New works by the artist continue to be added to the collection.

Blind persons are especially welcome, and are guided through the Gallery by touch.

Castle Cary

Castle Cary Museum

The Market House, Castle Cary, Somerset BA7 7AL   ☎ 0963 50277
Apr–Oct, daily 10.30–12.30, 2.30–4.30
✠ Roger Otton, Radio House, Castle Cary BA7 7BS
Ⓕ ✎ ◄

Castle Cary is of Saxon origin and was initially a fortified settlement. It developed as a market town and by the 17th century there was a flourishing woollen industry, later succeeded by the manufacture of rope, twine, webbing and woven horsehair fabric, which is still a speciality of the town.

The Museum, in the 1856 Market House, has collections illustrating the history of Castle Cary, with an emphasis on the 19th and 20th centuries. The collections include domestic equipment, details of former trades and industries, old photographs and documents, and information concerning the social life of previous generations.

Castle Donington

The Donington Collection

Donington Hall, Castle Donington, Derbyshire DE7 2RP   ☎ 0332 810048
Daily 9–5. Closed Dec 25, 26.
✠ The Curator
Ⓔ ♦ ⬛ ◄ ♿

The Museum forms part of Donington Park motor racing circuit, eight miles south of Derby. The Donington Collection is the world's largest collection of Grand Prix single-seater racing cars.

Castle Douglas

Castle Douglas Art Gallery
Market Street, Castle Douglas, Kirkcudbrightshire
DG7 1BE   ☎ 0557 30291 extn 321
On application during office hours to District
Council Sub-Office, St Andrew Street
⌦ Director of Administration, Stewartry District
Council, Kirkcudbright DG6 4JG
🄵 ✒ ☐

The District Council's Art Gallery houses a
permanent collection of paintings by Ethel
Bristowe and has a programme of temporary
exhibitions, mostly of works by local artists.

Castleford

Castleford Museum Room
Castleford Library, Carlton Street, Castleford,
West Yorkshire   ☎ 0977 559552
Mon–Fri 2–5. Closed public holidays.
⌦ Mrs G. Spencer, Wakefield Art Gallery,
Wentworth Terrace, Wakefield, West
Yorkshire   ☎ 0927 370211 extn 7190
🄵 ✒

Housed in Castleford Library, the Museum
Room displays a small but good collection of
Castleford pottery and glass, together with finds
from Roman Castleford (Lagentium).

Castlerea

Clonalis House
Castlerea, Co. Roscommon, Ireland
     ☎ 0907 20014
May–June, Sat, Sun 2–5.30. July–Aug, Mon–Sat
11–5.30; Sun 2–5.30. Other times by appt.
⌦ Mrs Marguerite O'Conor Nash
🄴 ♟ 🖴 ✒

Clonalis House is on the Ballyhaunis road, west
of the town. The mansion, built in 1878, is the
ancestral home of the O'Conors, once the High
Kings of Ireland and Kings of Connaught.
Clonalis contains collections illustrating the

The Nautical Museum, Castletown.

history and traditions of the O'Conors,
including manuscripts and documents, the
Coronation Stone of the Kings of Connaught,
and the 18th-century harp of O'Carolan, last
of the Gaelic bards.

Castletown

The Nautical Museum
Bridge Street, Castletown, Isle of Man
May 5–Sept 27, Mon–Sat 10–1, 2–5; Sun 2–5.
⌦ The Secretary, Manx Museum, Crellin's Hill,
Douglas, Isle of Man   ☎ 0624 75522
🄴 ✒ ✒

The Nautical Museum presents a picture of the
maritime life of the Isle of Man in the days of
sail. The displays centre on the armed schooner-
rigged yacht, Peggy, built in Castletown in 1791
and still in her original boat-cellar. The exhibit
also contains papers and personal possessions of
the Quayle family, who built the yachts. The
collections also include a wide range of nautical
equipment and relics, ship models, and
photographs of Manx sailing vessels. There
is a reconstruction of a sailmaker's loft.

Part of the original building is designed to
resemble a cabin of the Nelson period.

Câtel

Guernsey Folk Museum
Saumarez Park, Câtel, Guernsey, Channel Islands
     ☎ 0481 55384
Mid Mar–mid Oct, daily 10–5.30
⌦ Derrick Eury, Curator
🄴 ♟ 🖴 ✒

The Museum, which has a strong Franco-
Norman flavour, is administered by the
National Trust of Guernsey and occupies a
group of 18th-century cottages in the grounds of
the home of the 19th-century admiral, Lord
James de Saumarez. The collections cover a
wide range of rural activities, from cider-making
and ploughing with 'la grande Tchérue' (the
great plough) to granite quarrying. There are
reconstructions of a late 19th-century kitchen,
bedroom and wash-house.

Caterham

East Surrey Museum
1 Stafford Road, Caterham, Surrey CR3 6JG
     ☎ 0883 40275
Wed, Sat 10–5; Sun 2–5. Closed Dec 25.
⌦ The Curator
🄴 ✒ 🖴 ✒

The Museum is close to Caterham station.
It contains displays illustrating the geology,
archaeology, natural history and history of the
area. There are also exhibits of paintings and
handicrafts.

Cavendish

Nether Hall

Cavendish Manor Vineyards, Cavendish, Sudbury,
    Suffolk CO10 8BX   ☎ 0787 280221
Daily 11–4
⚉ Mr B. T. Ambrose
⬚ ⬚ ⬚ ⬚ ⬚

Nether Hall, a 15th-century house, is on the
A1902, three miles west of Long Melford. The
art gallery in the house contains 17th to 19th-
century paintings, and in the barn there are
displays of old agricultural implements and
equipment and of other items illustrating life
and work in the countryside before the coming
of mechanisation.

The Sue Ryder Foundation Museum

Sue Ryder Foundation, Cavendish, Sudbury,
    Suffolk CO10 8AY   ☎ 0787 280252
Mon–Sat 10–5.30; Sun 10–11, 12.15–5.30.
    Closed Dec 25.
⚉ Lady Ryder of Warsaw
⬚ ⬚ ⬚ ⬚ ⬚

The Foundation's Museum is in the grounds of
the Sue Ryder Home for the Sick and Disabled
in Cavendish, on the A1092, between Long
Melford and Clare. It reflects the life of Sue
Ryder, especially during the Second World War
and her work and that of the Foundation in
Britain and overseas.

Cawthorne

Cannon Hall Museum

Cawthorne, Barnsley, South Yorkshire S75 4AT
    ☎ 0226 790270
Mon–Sat 10.30–5; Sun 2.30–5. Closed Good Fri,
    Dec 25–27.
⚉ Brian Murray, Curator
⬚ ⬚ ⬚

Cannon Hall, a late 17th-century house
remodelled in the mid 18th century, is on the
A635 road, five miles west of Barnsley. It has a
collection of furniture from the 17th to the early
20th century, arranged in period rooms. The
paintings include works by John Constable,
George Morland, Peter Lely and David Roberts.

**1920 Royal Enfield motorcycle and sidecar.
Celbridge Motor Museum.**

A display of glassware illustrates various aspects
of glassmaking techniques from the 18th to the
mid 20th century. Pottery is also well
represented, with 19th and 20th-century art
pottery and representative items from a number
of the more important English factories, such as
Minton, Royal Doulton and Wedgwood.

Cawthorne Victoria Jubilee Museum

Taylor Hill, Cawthorne, Barnsley, South
    Yorkshire S75 4HH   ☎ 0226 791273
Apr–Oct, Thurs, Sat, Sun 2–5.30
⚉ Douglas N. Stables, 9 Maltkin Row,
    Cawthorne, Barnsley S75 4HH
⬚ ⬚

The Museum building is of cruck frame and post
and truss construction. It contains displays of
ethnography, birds and eggs, local history,
domestic equipment, craftsmen's tools and
handicrafts.

Celbridge

Castletown House

Celbridge, Co. Kildare, Ireland   ☎ 01 288252
Apr–Sept, Wed, Sat, Sun 2–6. Oct–Mar,
    Sun 2–5. Groups by appt.
⚉ The Curator
⬚ ⬚ ⬚ ⬚

The Palladian mansion of Castletown is
Ireland's largest house. It was built in the early
18th century for the Speaker of the Irish
Parliament, William Conolly, and remained in
the possession of the Conolly family until 1965.
Visitors are able to see some of the most
splendid reception rooms in the country, with
Irish-made furniture, and, downstairs, the dairy,
still room, harness room, nursery, servants'
rooms and servants' dining hall, all of which still
contain their furnishings and working
equipment. Castletown at one time employed
103 servants and there are displays describing
their life and duties. The Victorian kitchen,
which had to produce meals for all the servants,
as well as the Conolly family and their guests, is
also on view.

Exhibits in the dining-room describe 18th
and 19th-century social life, menus and table
manners. The drawing-rooms, which have
remained unchanged since the 18th century, are
similarly illustrated, and brought to life with
descriptions of the colourful personalities who
have lived at Castletown.

Celbridge Motor Museum

Temple Mills House, Celbridge, Co. Kildare,
    Ireland   ☎ 01 288297
By appt
⚉ J. Ellis
⬚ ⬚

The Museum lies half a mile up the Ardclogh
road from the bridge at Celbridge. It contains a
collection of vintage and veteran cars and
motorcycles, mostly used in Ireland.

Cenarth Falls

The Fishing Museum

Salmon Leap, Cenarth Falls, Dyfed
☎ *0239 710894*
Easter–Oct, daily 10–5
Ⓜ *Mrs C. Smith*
Ⓔ ♠ ⌇

Cenarth, famous for its Teifi coracles, lies on the A484 between Cardigan and Newcastle Emlyn, beside the River Teifi.

More than 400 exhibits illustrate the history of rod and line fishing. There are beavers, sturgeon and river wild life. Guided tours and coracle demonstrations can be arranged. The Salmon Leap Art Gallery within the Museum exhibits watercolours by Welsh artists.

Ceres

Fife Folk Museum

Old High Street, Ceres, Fife
Apr–Oct, Mon, Wed–Sat 2–5; Sun 2.30–5.30
Ⓜ *The Hon. Curator*   ☎ *033 482 380*
Ⓔ ⌇

The Museum, owned and administered by the Central and North Fife Preservation Society, is in the town's 17th-century Tolbooth-Weigh House, to which an extension built of traditional materials has been added. The collections and displays illustrate the social and economic history of rural Fife.

Chalfont St Giles

Chiltern Open Air Museum

Newland Park, Gorelands Lane, Chalfont St Giles, Buckinghamshire HP8 4AD ☎ *02407 71117*
Easter Sun–Sept, Wed, Sun, Bank Holiday 2–6.
Parties at other times by appt.
Ⓜ *Martin Bluhm, Education Officer*
Ⓔ ♠ 🖵 ⌇

The Museum consists of traditional buildings from the Chilterns and the surrounding area, which have been moved to the site. The 14 buildings so far re-erected or in the process of re-erection include a blacksmith's forge, a furniture workshop and a number of farm buildings of different types. A further 14 buildings, including a late 13th-century tithe barn, are stored, awaiting attention. Some of the buildings house exhibits of machinery, domestic equipment and other relevant items.

A wide range of materials has been used in the construction of the buildings. There are brick, flint and boarded walls and thatched, tiled and slated roofs. Timber-framing, including cruck-framing, is also represented. There is a reconstruction of an Iron Age hut.

The Museum is managed, and much of the work of reconstruction and restoration carried out, by volunteers.

Milton's Cottage

21 Deanway, Chalfont St Giles, Buckinghamshire
HP8 4JH   ☎ *02407 2313*
Feb–Oct, Tues–Sat 10–1, 2–6; Sun 2–6. Open
Spring, Summer Bank Holiday 10–1, 2–6.
Ⓜ *Lt. Col. W. D. Clark, Curator*
Ⓔ ⌀ ⌇

The cottage, a 16th-century building, contains collections illustrating the life and times of the poet, John Milton, and of the history of the cottage, the village and the surrounding area. There are portraits of Milton and first editions of *Paradise Lost* and *Paradise Regained*.

Chard

Chard and District Museum

Godworthy House, 15 High Street, Chard,
Somerset
Mid May–mid Sept, Mon–Sat 10.30–4.30. Closed
Bank Holiday.
Ⓜ *Mrs M. E. Edwards, 13 Helliers Road, Chard*
TA20 1LL
Ⓔ ⌀

The Museum buildings were formed out of a group of 16th-century cottages and the adjoining 15th-century New Inn, with its skittle alley. The displays are concerned with the history, industries and personalities of the Borough from 1235 onwards. There are special displays relating to cider-making; laundry-work; artificial limbs, which were invented in Chard; and John Stringfellow, the pioneer of powered flight. Other collections are of Donyatt pottery, Chard clay pipes, farm vehicles and tools, local geology and 19th-century Chard posters.

Hornsbury Mill, Chard, across the Mill Pond.

Wine trade display. Chepstow Museum.

Forde Abbey

Chard, Somerset TA20 4LU   ☎ *0460 20231*
May–Sept, Wed, Sun 2–6. Open Easter Sun,
Bank Holiday Mon 2–6. Gardens only
Apr–Oct, Mon–Fri 11–4 30
🖾 *The Administraton*
[F] 🛊 📖 🖝 [HHA]

Forde Abbey is four miles south-east of Chard,
off the A30. It was originally a Cistercian
monastery and much of the monastic building,
including the cloister, survives. In 1649 the
property was bought by Edward Prideaux,
Attorney-General to Oliver Cromwell, who
transformed it into a palazzo in the Italian style.

The Great Hall contains a refectory table
made from an oak grown in the park of the
Abbey. Other noteworthy features include fine
plasterwork in many of the rooms and Mortlake
tapestries which were woven especially for the
Salon c. 1659 and were made after cartoons by
Raphael, now preserved in the Victoria and
Albert Museum.

Hornsbury Mill

Chard, Somerset TA20 3AQ   ☎ *04606 3317*
Apr–Sept, Mon–Sat 10.30–6; Sun 12–6.
Oct–Mar, Wed–Sat 10.30–6; Sun 12–6.
🖾 *Mr J. T. Wightman*
[E] 🛊 📖 🖝

The Mill is one and a half miles from Chard on
the A358 Taunton road. There has been a mill
on the site since the 14th century. The present
overshot waterwheel dates from 1870 and the
complete milling machinery and equipment is
still intact. The displays within the Mill include
agricultural implements, craftsmen's tools,
domestic equipment and clothing.

Charlbury

Charlbury Museum

Corner House Community Centre, Market Street,
Charlbury, Oxfordshire
Business hours of nearby chemist shop
🖾 *Mr P. G. Hilton, Bell Yard Cottage,*
Charlbury, Oxfordshire OX7 3PP
[E] *for loan of key* 🖝

The exhibits in the Museum relate to the history
of Charlbury and the surrounding area. They
include agricultural and craftsmen's tools,
household equipment and handicrafts, together
with archaeological and geological material
from the district.

Chatham

Royal Engineers Museum

Ravelin Building, Brompton Barracks, Chatham,
Kent ME4 4UG   ☎ *0634 44555 extn 312*
Tues–Fri 10–5; Sun 11.30–5. Check locally for
Bank Holiday opening times.
🖾 *The Curator*
[E] 🛊 🖝

The Royal Engineers Museum illustrates the
history of early military engineering and
describes the development and work of the Corps
from its medieval origins to date. In addition to
its purely military collections, the Museum also
holds much material of ethnographical and
general interest, which reflects the nearly
worldwide involvement of the Corps in civil
engineering projects, such as mapping and road-
building. Particularly prized is a collection of
items relating to the life and work of General
Charles Gordon, killed at Khartoum in 1885.
This includes a large collection of Chinese
ceremonial dress awarded to Gordon for his
services to the Emperor in 1864.

Chawton

Jane Austen's House

Chawton, Hampshire GU34 1SD   ☎ *0420 83262*
Apr–Oct, daily 11–4.30. Nov–Dec and Mar,
Wed–Sun 11–4.30. Jan–Feb, Sat, Sun
11–4.30. Closed Dec 25, 26.
🖾 *Miss Jean K. Bowden, Curator*
[E] 🖊 🖝

The house was built c. 1645 as a posting inn.
It was altered in 1809, when Mrs Austen came
to live here with her daughters, and looks
substantially the same now as in the Austens'
time. There are many items associated with Jane
Austen and her family, including the topaz
crosses given to Jane and Cassandra by their
brother, Charles, the patchwork quilt made by
Jane and her mother and sister, and a large
number of letters and documents. The table on
which Jane Austen wrote *Mansfield Park*, *Emma*
and *Persuasion* is in the dining-parlour, as is part
of the Wedgwood dinner service bought by her
brother, Edward.

Cheam

Whitehall, Cheam.

Whitehall

1 Malden Road, Cheam, Sutton, Surrey SM3 8QD
☎ *01 643 1236*
Apr–Sept 2–5.30; Sat, Sun 10–5.30. Bank
Holiday Mon 2–5.30. Oct–Mar, Wed, Thurs,
Sun 2–5.30; Sat 10–5.30. Closed Dec 24–
Jan 1.
𝕏 *The Curator*
£ ◊ ⬛ ✎ □

Whitehall is a 16th-century timber-framed
building, with later additions. It is now
maintained by the London Borough of Sutton as
an arts, crafts and local history centre. There
are permanent displays of material from the
excavations at Nonsuch Palace, Cheam Pottery
and Cheam School, the origins of which are
closely associated with Whitehall. Temporary
exhibitions are arranged of art and craft work
and on themes of historical and general interest.

Cheddar

Cheddar Caves Museum

Cheddar, Somerset BS27 3QF   ☎ *0934 742343*
Easter–early Oct, daily 10–6
𝕏 *The Manager*
£ ◊ ⬛ ✎

The displays and exhibits in the Museum
include the celebrated 10,000-year-old skeleton
of Cheddar Man, a reconstructed cave setting
illustrating the daily life of Palaeolithic man,
and several dioramas showing settlement in the
Mendip area from Stone Age times to the
present day.

Cheddleton

Cheddleton Flint Mill

Cheddleton, nr Leek, Staffordshire
☎ *0782 502907*
Sat, Sun 2–5. Other times by appt.
𝕏 *Mr E. E. Royle*
F ◊ ✎

There has been a watermill at Cheddleton on
the River Churnet, four miles from Leek on the
A520 Stone road, since the 13th century. What
is now called the South Mill was originally used
to grind corn, but during the 18th century the
growing ceramics industry in the Stoke-on-
Trent area created a demand for powdered flint,
which is used to improve the texture of
earthenware and tiles. The South Mill was
therefore converted to grind flint and in
c. 1800 the North Mill was built for the same
purpose. The Caldon Canal links the Mill to the
Potteries.
　The Mill complex has been preserved by the
Cheddleton Flint Mill Industrial Heritage Trust.
There are displays to explain each exhibit and
how the Mill works.

Chelmsford

Chelmsford and Essex Museum incorporating The Essex Regiment Museum

Oaklands Park, Moulsham Street, Chelmsford,
Essex CM2 9AQ   ☎ *0245 353066/260614*
Mon–Sat 10–5; Sun 2–5. Closed Good Fri,
Dec 25, 26. Open most public holidays.
𝕏 *The Curator*
F ◊ ✎ □

The Museum occupies an Italianate residence,
built for a local brewer in 1865. During the past
50 years the emphasis has been increasingly on
Chelmsford and the county of Essex, and most
of the foreign material has been disposed of to
other museums. There are permanent
collections of natural history, including geology;
archaeology; Victoriana; local industrial
material; ceramics; coins and medals; paintings;
costumes; glass; domestic and farm equipment;
craftsmen's tools. The Museum of the Essex
Regiment is also housed here.
　Temporary exhibitions, each lasting from four
to six weeks, are an important part of the
Museum's programme. Two are usually in
progress at any one time.

Cheltenham

Cheltenham Art Gallery and Museum

Clarence Street, Cheltenham, Gloucestershire
GL50 3JT   ☎ 0242 237431
Mon–Sat 10–5.30. Closed Bank Holiday.
▨ Education Officer, 40 Clarence Street,
Cheltenham GL50 3NX
🅕 ✐ ♿

The Arts and Crafts collections at Cheltenham
are of national importance, with furniture by
Gimson, the Barnsleys, Voysey, Ashbee and
Gordon Russell. The Hull Grundy gift to the
Gallery comprises Arts and Crafts metalwork
and jewellery.
   There are also collections of 17th-century
Dutch paintings, 17th to 20th-century British
paintings, English furniture, ceramics, glass
and pewter.
   The displays in the Museum are of local
geology, archaeology and history, and the
traditional rural life of the area. A special
section is devoted to Edward Wilson, the
Antarctic explorer.

Gustav Holst, 1923.

Gustav Holst Birthplace Museum

4 Clarence Road, Cheltenham, Gloucestershire
GL52 2AY   ☎ 0242 524846
Tues–Fri 12–5.30; Sat 11–5.30. Closed Bank
Holiday.
▨ See Cheltenham Art Gallery and Museum
🅕 ✐

The composer, Gustav Holst, was born
at 4 Clarence Road, a typical Cheltenham
Regency house, in 1874. The Museum
illustrates Holst's working life and his music and
reflects domestic life in the 19th century. The
displays include Holst's grand piano, made
c. 1850, a selection of his published music
which illustrates his development as a
composer, and a chronological survey of his
career, with photographs, pictures, concert
programmes and other documents.

The remainder of the Museum consists of
period rooms: a late Regency sitting room and
Victorian bedroom on the first floor, and a
working Victorian kitchen, scullery, laundry
and servants' rooms in the basement.

Pittville Pump Room Museum: Gallery of Fashion

Pittville, Cheltenham, Gloucestershire GL52 3JE
            ☎ 0242 512740
Apr–Sept, Tues–Sun 10.30–5. Oct–Mar,
Tues–Sat 10.30–5. Open Easter, Spring and
August Bank Holiday Mon.
▨ See Cheltenham Art Gallery and Museum
🅔 ✐ ♿

The Pump Room, opened in 1830, is a Regency
building at the head of Pittville Park. The
Museum is on the upper floors. It contains
displays of costumes, textiles and accessories
from the 1760s to the present day, shown
within the context of the history of
Cheltenham. The collections include the Hull
Grundy gift of jewellery dating from the late
18th to the early 20th century.

Chepstow

Chepstow Museum

Gwy House, Bridge Street, Chepstow, Gwent
NP6 5EZ   ☎ 02912 5891
Mar–Oct, Mon–Sat 11–1, 2–5; Sun 2–5. Open
Bank Holiday Mon.
▨ The Curator
🅔 ex. educ. parties ✐ ♿ & □

Gwy House was built c. 1790 and still retains
most of its original layout and decorative
features. The Museum displays concentrate on
the history and development of Chepstow and
the surrounding area. 'Chepstow at Work' looks
at the trades, industries and commercial activity
of Chepstow, past and present, with exhibits on
the port, shipbuilding and engineering works,
salmon-fishing, the commercial life of this once
busy market town, and today's industries,
including brush-making and tourism. 'Chepstow
at Play' presents a picture of the sports and
entertainments enjoyed by local inhabitants.
There is a display of domestic equipment and
changing exhibitions, including the Museum's
fine collection of 18th to 20th-century local
topographical prints.

Chertsey

Chertsey Museum

The Cedars, 33 Windsor Street, Chertsey, Surrey
KT16 8AT   ☎ 09328 65764
Tues, Thurs 2–5; Wed, Fri, Sat 10–1, 2–5.
Closed Bank Holiday.
🅕 ✐

The Cedars is a late Georgian listed building.
The local history collections tell the story of the
present Borough of Runnymede, with exhibits
ranging from prehistoric weapons, including a

Bronze Age shield, to objects from a local iron foundry. Of particular interest are a fine Viking sword and a collection of material relating to the Benedictine Abbey at Chertsey.

Other displays are of furniture, glass, clocks, toys and 18th-century Meissen porcelain figures. The Olive Matthews collection of costumes and fashion accessories covers the period from 1700–1960, although most of the items belong to the years 1740–1850.

Chester

Cheshire Military Museum

The Castle, Chester, Cheshire CH1 2DN
☎ *0244 27617*
Daily 9–5. Closed Good Fri, Dec 23–Jan 3.
🚺 *The Curator*
£ ✎ 🚪

The Cheshire Military Museum displays the Colours and Standards, uniforms, badges, equipment, weapons, medals, silver, pictures and various other militaria of four famous Regiments, whose historic home is Chester and the County of Cheshire – the 5th Royal Inniskilling Dragoon Guards, the 3rd Carabiniers, the Cheshire Yeomanry, and the Cheshire Regiment. The displays cover the 300 years of the Regiments' history, with exhibits ranging from the remains of a standard carried at the Battle of the Boyne to present-day weapons and uniforms. Almost all the parts of the world in which the British Army has been engaged in one way or another are represented, including the Antarctic, where Captain Lawrence Oates, the polar explorer, lost his life. His unique Polar Medal is displayed in the Museum.

Grosvenor Museum

27 Grosvenor Street, Chester, Cheshire CH1 2DD
☎ *0244 21616/313858/316944*
Mon–Sat 10.30–5; Sun 2–5.30. Closed Good Fri, Dec 24–26.
🚺 *Education Officer*
F 🕯

Founded in 1886, the Museum contains displays of international importance illustrating the organisation of the Roman Army and a large collection of Roman tombstones and inscriptions. Other collections cover the natural history, local history and archaeology of Chester and Cheshire. The Museum is noted for its local paintings and watercolours and for its silver, much of which was made and assayed in Chester. The Mayor's Parlour from the King's Arms Kitchen is a reconstruction of the 19th-century room where the Honourable Incorporation, a debating and wagering club, staged a satire on the City Council, electing its own Mayor, Sheriffs and other officials.

The Castle Street Georgian house, the former town house of the Swettenham and the Comberbach families, dating from c. 1680, is part of the Grosvenor Museum. It contains a fine late 17th-century staircase, 17th and 18th-century panelled rooms, Stuart, mid Georgian and 18th-century period rooms, with many examples of local furniture, and reconstructions of a Victorian kitchen and laundry, together with a gallery of 19th and 20th-century costume.

Chesterfield

Hardwick Hall

Doe Lea, Chesterfield, Derbyshire S44 5QJ
☎ *0246 850430*
Apr–Oct, Wed, Thurs, Sat, Sun, Bank Holiday Mon, 1–5.30 or sunset if earlier. Closed Good Fri. Garden daily 12–5.30.
🚺 *The Administrator*
£ 🕯 🚾 🚪 NT

Hardwick Hall is nine and a half miles south-east of Chesterfield on the A617. Built between 1591 and 1597 by the redoubtable Bess of Hardwick – Elizabeth, Dowager Countess of Shrewsbury – it still contains a number of items of furniture which she valued. Now a National Trust property, Hardwick is particularly celebrated for its remarkable 16th and 17th-century tapestries and its 16th-century embroideries, some of which may well have been made by Bess herself. The entrance hall contains patchwork appliqué hangings representing allegorical subjects. They were probably made out of copes and altar frontals taken from monasteries at the Dissolution.

Many of the embroideries were table-carpets, made at a time when carpets were more likely to be draped over tables than spread on the floor. There are also embroidered cushions, pillow cases, and bed-hangings, all of remarkable quality.

The impressive house has good gardens, orchards and a herb garden and is surrounded by a park containing Whiteface Woodland sheep and a herd of Longhorn cattle.

Victorian farm kitchen with black-leaded range. Chester, Grosvenor Museum.

The Peacock Heritage Centre

Low Pavement, Chesterfield, Derbyshire S40 1PB
☎ 0246 207777
*Mon–Sat 12–5. Closed Easter Mon, May Day,
Dec 25, 26, Jan 1.*
◪ *Mrs B. Wainwright, Tourism Officer*
🅵 ♟ ✎ ☐

The early 16th-century timber-framed building
is thought to have served originally as a
guildhall. It was later used as dwellings, a shop
and a public house. During the late 1970s it was
carefully restored and is now the regional
Tourist Information and Heritage Centre.

Visitors are able to see the high quality of
workmanship of the timber structure, especially
in the first-floor hall and the open-truss roof.
Temporary exhibitions on subjects of local and
regional interest are regularly arranged.

Chichester

Chichester District Museum

*29 Little London, Chichester, West Sussex
PO19 1PB*   ☎ 0243 784683
*Tues–Sat 10–5.30. Closed Good Fri, Dec 25,
Jan 1.*
◪ *The Curator*
🅵 ⵯ ✎

The Museum is a converted 18th-century corn
store. Its displays provide an introduction to the
geology, archaeology and history of the district.
There are particularly strong collections relating
to Roman and Saxon Chichester, to the
Church, and to the Civil War. Among the most
popular exhibits are the full-size figure of a
Roman legionary in full armour, and the mobile
city stocks and whipping post, used to pull
offenders round the Market cross, to be pelted
with rotten fruit and eggs by onlookers.

The entrance portico of Goodwood House,
Chichester, by James Wyatt (1746–1813).

Goodwood House

Goodwood, Chichester, West Sussex PO18 0PX
☎ 0243 774107
*May 4–Oct 6, Sun, Mon, plus Tues–Thurs in
Aug 2–5. For groups: lunch or dinner tours at
all times. Closed event days.*
◪ *C. P. Nicoll, West Sussex Countryside Studies
Trust, Goodwood House*
🅴 ♟ 🚊 ✎ ♿ 〔HHA〕

Goodwood is four miles to the north-east of
Chichester, signposted from the A27 at the east
end of the Chichester bypass. The house is the
seat of the Dukes of Richmond and Gordon and
it is still lived in by the family. As one sees it
today, it is largely the result of the initiative of
the 3rd Duke. In about 1760, the Duke
employed Sir William Chambers to rebuild the
house around its Jacobean core and towards the
end of the century he commissioned James
Wyatt to add a remarkable octagon with a tower
at each corner. Only three sides of this octagon
were, in fact, completed.

What can be seen in Goodwood House today
are the accumulated collections of nine Dukes
of Richmond. They include Canaletto's first
London pictures, painted from the windows of
Richmond House; a notable series of family
portraits; French and English furniture of the
finest quality; Sèvres porcelain, Gobelins
tapestries and mementos of many royal visitors.
The artists represented include Van Dyck, Lely,
Kneller, Reynolds, Stubbs, who stayed at
Goodwood for nine months, Romney and
Lawrence, as well as Gianoni, Salvator Rosa
and the Smith brothers of Chichester.

Every room has notes on the principal objects
to be found in it and there are carefully trained
guide-hostesses, who make a point of knowing
the answers to difficult questions.

Guildhall Museum

*Priory Park, Priory Road, Chichester, West Sussex
June–Sept, Tues–Sat 1–5*
◪ *See Chichester District Museum*
☎ 0243 784683
🅵 ⵯ ✎

The Guildhall was built in the late 13th century
as the church of the Franciscan Friary. Later,
between 1541 and 1731, it was the city's
Guildhall and then, until the 1850s, its
Courthouse. It continued to be used for
important civic events until 1888. It now houses
a branch of the District Museum and has
displays of archaeological material, chiefly from
excavations in Chichester. These include
tombstones, inscriptions and an altar dating
from the Roman period. The 18th-century bell
from the Market Cross is also here.

Mechanical Music and Doll Collection

Church Road, Portfield, Chichester, West Sussex
☎ 0243 785421
*Easter–Sept, daily 10–6. Easter, Sat, Sun 10–5.
Open any evening by appt. Closed Dec 25, 26.*
◪ *The Curator*
🅴 ⵯ ✎

The former Victorian church housing the
collection is one mile east of Chichester, just off
the A27. Most of the exhibits illustrate the
craftsmanship and inventiveness of the
Victorian period. The mechanical musical
instruments – musical boxes, phonographs,
barrel-organs, mechanical pianos, fair and
dance organs – have all been carefully restored
and are in full working order. They are

explained and demonstrated to visitors throughout the day.

Other objects of the period include stereoscopic viewers, magic lanterns and Victorian natural history exhibits. The doll collections contain both wax and bisque-headed Victorian dolls, together with felt and velvet dolls dating from the 1920s.

Bisque-headed Victorian dolls. Chichester, Mechanical Music and Doll Collection.

Roman Palace and Museum

*Salthill Road, Fishbourne, Chichester, West Sussex
    PO19 3QR*   ☎ *0243 785859
Mar–Apr and Oct, daily 11–5. May–Sept, daily
    10–6. Nov, daily 10–4. Dec–Feb, Sun 10–4.*
✯ *Education Officer*
Ⓔ ♟ 💺 ➔ ♿

The Museum presents the remains of the North wing of a 1st-century palace of Italianate style, protected by a modern cover-building. Visitors can see Britain's largest group of 1st-century mosaics, as well as several floors of the 2nd and 3rd centuries. Parts of the underfloor heating systems have also survived.

The most important finds from the excavations are shown in a separate part of the Museum, supported by photographs, plans and models. A reconstruction of a dining-room suggests what one room in the Palace may have looked like c. 100 A.D. A project devoted to Roman farming indicates the types of crops and animals which would have been seen on a Romano-British farm (open late spring to early autumn).

The northern half of the formal garden attached to the Palace has been restored to its original plan.

Museum of the Royal Corps of Military Police

*Roussillon Barracks, Chichester, West Sussex
    PO19 4BN   ☎ 0243 786311 extn 237/238
May–Sept, Tues–Sun 10–12.30, 1.30–4.15.
    Oct–Apr, Tues–Sat 10.30–12.30, 1.30–4.15.*
✯ *Lt. Col. (Retd) R. A. Costain*
Ⓔ ♟ ➔

The Museum occupies the Keep of the original barracks built by French prisoners of war in 1803–4. The displays illustrate the history of the Corps from its Tudor origins until the present day. There are special exhibits comparing life in the Corps in National Service days and in 1980, on the Military Policeman's life and duties in the modern garrison-town of Rheindahlen, and on the methods by which the modern soldier-detective fights crime.

Other sections of the Museum deal with the activities of the Corps in the Second World War and with the duties involved in protecting senior officials and diplomats in such difficult locations as Northern Ireland and Beirut. The Ceremonial Section contains an historical display of uniforms and an exhibit of medals earned by members of the Corps.

Pallant House Gallery

*9 North Pallant, Chichester, West Sussex
    PO19 1TJ   ☎ 0243 774557
Tues–Sat 10–5.30. Closed Bank Holiday.*
✯ *The Curator*
Ⓔ ✐ ➔

Pallant House dates from 1713. It contains the collection of modern art formed by the late Dean Walter Hussey and given by him to the city of Chichester. It includes works by Moore, Sutherland, Ceri Richards, John Piper and Geoffrey Clarke. The restored rooms display Georgian furniture and pictures, Bow porcelain, 18th-century drinking glasses and other examples of fine and applied art from the period c. 1700–1900.

Chillenden

Chillenden Windmill

*Chillenden, Next Wingham, nr Canterbury, Kent
Apr–Sept, Sun, Bank Holiday 2–4.30. Group
    visits at other times by appt.*
✯ *Mrs Nicolas Ellen, Secretary of the Friends
    of Chillenden Windmill   ☎ 0227 720464*
Ⓕ ✐ 💺 ➔

The Mill stands on the left of the road from Canterbury and Wingham before reaching Chillenden. Built in 1868, it is a late example of a trestle post mill. Now owned by Kent County Council, it is run as a museum by the Friends of Chillenden Windmill, who are using it as a repository for historical material connected with the Mill. Most of the machinery and equipment still remains, although the Mill is no longer in working order.

Visitors can also see a collection of old photographs of Kentish windmills, most of which have been demolished.

Chippenham

Dyrham Park

nr Chippenham, Wiltshire SN14 8ER
   ☎ 027582 2501
Apr–May and Oct, Sat–Wed 2–6 or dusk if earlier.
   June–Sept, Sat–Thurs 2–6. Park 12–6.
🕅 *The Administrator*
Ⓔ 🕭 ⬛ ⬆ NT

Dyrham Park, now a National Trust property,
is eight miles north of Bath on the A46. It
was built between 1691 and 1702 for William
Blathwayt, Secretary at War and Secretary
of State to William III. The rooms are
substantially as they were in Blathwayt's time.
Some are panelled in cedar and Virginian
walnut and one has its original leather wall
hangings.

Yelde Hall Museum

Market Place, Chippenham, Wiltshire SN15 3HL
   ☎ 0249 651488
Mid Mar–Oct, Mon–Sat 10–12.30, 2–4.30.
   Closed Bank Holiday.
🕅 *Hon. Curator, c/o Chippenham Town Council,*
   12 The Causeway, Chippenham SN15 3BT
Ⓕ

Yelde Hall was built *c.* 1500. The Museum
collections relate entirely to the history of
Chippenham, which is also illustrated by means
of photographic displays.

Chipping Campden

Woolstaplers Hall Museum

High Street, Chipping Campden, Gloucestershire
   GL55 6HB   ☎ 0386 840289
Apr–Oct, daily 11–6
🕅 *The Curator*
Ⓔ 🖉 🚗

Woolstaplers Hall is believed to have been built
c. 1340 by the Calf family of woolstaplers, a
well-known local family in the 13th and 14th
centuries. The Hall, in which the wool
merchants did their buying, has an
exceptionally fine timber roof. The Museum
displays include a wide range of domestic
equipment, 19th-century woodworkers' tools
and the entire contents of a local cobbler's shop,
closed in 1980. One room is devoted to relics of
a cinema of the 1920s, with the original Kalee
silent projectors, later converted for sound, tip-
up plush seats, and the cinema's excise licence.

Chirk

Chirk Castle

Chirk, Clwyd LL14 5AF   ☎ 0691 777701
Mar 30–Sept 28, Sun, Tues–Thurs, Bank Holiday
   12–5. Oct 4–26, Sat, Sun 12–5.
🕅 *The Administrator*
Ⓔ 🕭 ⬛ ⬆ NT

Chirk Castle, built in 1310, is a good example of
a Marcher fortress. It was remodelled internally
in the 18th century and now contains elegant
staterooms with elaborate plasterwork,
tapestries, and fine Adam style furniture. The
entrance gates were made by the Davies brothers
in 1721.

Chittlehampton

Cobbaton Combat Vehicles Museum

Chittlehampton, Umberleigh, North Devon
   EX37 9SD
Apr–Oct, daily 10–6
🕅 *Preston Isaac*
Ⓔ 🖉 🚗

Woolstaplers Hall, Chipping Camden.

The Museum's main collection consists of more than 30 Second World War British and Canadian tanks, trucks, guns and armoured cars, which have been restored to running order. Other displays have been formed to illustrate the theme 'Britain at War'.

Chorley

Astley Hall Museum and Art Gallery

Astley Park, Chorley, Lancashire ☎ 02572 62166
Apr–Sept, daily 12–6. Oct–Mar, Mon–Fri 12–4; Sat 10–4; Sun 11–4.
▨ The Amenities Officer, Public Baths, Union Street, Chorley
🅔 ⬿ ⬿

The ceilings in the Great Hall and drawing-room of this late 16th-century house are ornately worked in plaster, leather and lead and are of exceptional historical importance. There is a fine collection of furniture, paintings and pottery. The Leeds pottery is particularly noteworthy. Other interesting items on display include the shovel-board table in the Long Gallery and the celebrated Sirloin Chair, from which the joint of beef was knighted.

An Elizabethan four-poster bed at Astley Hall, Chorley.

Christchurch

Christchurch Tricycle Museum

Quay Road, Christchurch, Dorset BH23 1BY ☎ 04252 3240
Easter–Oct, daily 10–5.30
▨ Roger T. C. Street, Brook Cottage, 57 Smugglers Lane North, Highcliffe, Christchurch BH23 4NQ
🅔 ⬿ ⬿

The Museum is housed in a stone building dating from c. 1325, which originally formed part of the medieval Priory of Christchurch Twynham, dissolved by Henry VIII in 1539. It was re-roofed and fully restored in 1985 for use as a museum. This is believed to be the only museum in the world devoted solely to the multi-wheeled cycle, with more than 30 adult and children's tricycles from Victorian times to the present day.

Visitors can also see jointed models in period costume ('the family'), a Victorian street scene with a tricycle shop mural, and a large number of early photographs and pictures.

The Red House Museum and Art Gallery

Quay Road, Christchurch, Dorset BH23 1BU ☎ 0202 482860
Tues–Sat 10–5; Sun 2–5
▨ The Curator
🅔 ex. educ. parties ⬿ ⬿ ☐

The Museum is an 18th-century parish workhouse. Its collections illustrate the natural history and history of Christchurch and its surrounding area. There is a gallery of fashionable dress from 1865 to 1915, an aquarium, a formal herb garden and a garden containing a collection of old varieties of roses, paeonies and other plants.

A number of exhibitions on local themes are arranged each year.

St Michael's Loft Museum

Christchurch Priory, Christchurch, Dorset BH23 1BU   ☎ 0202 485804
Spring Bank Holiday weekend, then mid June–mid Sept, 10.30–12.30, 2.30–4.30. Closed Sun mornings and other services. Other times by appt.
▨ Head Verger
🅔 ex. children ⬤ ⬿

The Museum is in a room above the Lady Chapel of the Priory, reached by a spiral staircase of 75 steps. It was formerly used by the monks as a place to teach the novices. From 1662 to 1869, it was the Grammar School of Christchurch, then a private academy, run by the Vicar. Since 1980 it has contained the Museum, which aims to show something of the life of the Priory and of the people who lived nearby. The exhibits include examples of stonework and carving from Saxon to Tudor times, mostly from the Priory, and items connected with the school. There is also the Christchurch Tithe Map, and many paintings, drawings and photographs of the Priory and the town in earlier times. A display of bibles and prayer books includes a copy of the Breeches Bible.

A small part of the Museum's collection is located in aumbrys in the church itself.

Chudleigh

Ugbrooke House

Chudleigh, Devon TQ13 0AD   ☎ 0626 852179
Sat, Sun & Bank Holidays in May, then June–Sept, Sat, Sun
▨ The Secretary
🅔 ex. guided tours ⬛ ⬿ ⬥ ⬿

The Tudor family house at Ugbrooke was incorporated in Robert Adam's new building of 1760. The Cliffords have been Catholics since 1672 and the chapel here was designed by Adam. The sitting-room has a celebrated

Chippendale bookcase and the portraits by Lely in the drawing-room include one of the 1st Lord Clifford, which is among his best works. Other exhibits include Hepplewhite chairs, needlework, tapestries, vestments, uniforms and a silver-gilt ewer and dish, given to the family by Charles II. There is also a Chinese armorial dinner service made in 1740 for the 4th Lord Clifford.

Church Hill

The Glebe Gallery (The Derek Hill Collection)

Church Hill, Letterkenny, Co. Donegal, Ireland
    ☎ *Church Hill 71*
Apr–Sept, Mon–Sat 10–6; Sun 1–6
🏛 *Mrs Frances Bailey*
£ ✉ ♿ ☐

The Gallery is to be found at the northern end of Lough Gartan, 11 miles north-west of Letterkenny and one mile beyond the village of Church Hill. The outbuildings of St Columb's, the old Glebe House (1828), have been converted to house the Gallery. The house has been the home of the portrait and landscape painter, Derek Hill (b. 1916), since 1953 and will be open to the public.

Derek Hill's house and surrounding gardens and his very personal art collection has been given to the Irish nation. It includes paintings by Annigoni, Bratby, Bonnard, Braque, Picasso, Sutherland and Landseer, as well as works by leading Irish artists. There are also ceramics from Islamic countries and textiles by William Morris.

Church Stretton

Acton Scott Working Farm Museum

Wenlock Lodge, Acton Scott, nr Church Stretton,
    Shropshire SY6 6QN   ☎ 06946 306/307
Apr–Oct, Mon–Sat 10–5; Sun, Bank Holiday
    10–6
🏛 *The Keeper*
£ ♿ ▮ ✉ ♿

The Museum occupies a range of late 18th-century farm buildings, formerly part of the Home Farm of Acton Scott, together with a four-bay cart shed and a horse-gin house which have been brought to the site and re-erected. Acton Scott Hall, close to the Museum, dates from 1580–5 and is one of the earliest brick buildings in the area.

The Working Farm Museum demonstrates life on a Shropshire upland farm before the coming of the petrol engine. Its 22 acres are worked with Shire horses, allowing visitors to watch 19th-century arable techniques in action. The farm is stocked with horses, cows, pigs and poultry of breeds rarely seen today.

Wemyss ware jug, early 20th century. Church Hill, The Glebe Gallery.

Cirencester

Corinium Museum

Park Street, Cirencester, Gloucestershire GL7 2BX
    ☎ 0285 5611
Apr–Oct, Mon–Sat 10–5.30, Sun 2–5.30.
    Nov–Mar, Tues–Sat 10–5; Sun 2–5. Open
    Bank Holidays
🏛 *Chief Receptionist*
£ ▮ ✉ ♿

The Museum takes its name from *Corinium*, the Roman name for Cirencester, which was the second largest town of Roman Britain. The displays are arranged in chronological order, beginning with a newly-designed Cotswold prehistoric gallery and progressing through the Roman period to Saxon and medieval times. The exhibits include mosaics of high quality, full-scale reproductions of a Roman kitchen, dining-room and stonemason's workshop, personal possessions, jewellery, pottery and coins. A small Anglo-Saxon display is supplemented by notable finds from recent cemetery excavations, and the medieval section illustrates religious and secular life.

One of the great medieval abbeys was at Cirencester, and its story is told in the Museum. Other exhibits relate to the Cotswold wool trade, and to the history of Cirencester from Tudor times onwards.

Ploughing before the age of the tractor. Acton Scott Working Farm Museum, Church Stretton.

The 13th-century Manor House at Donington-le-Heath, Coalville.

Clare

Ancient House Museum

High Street, Clare, Sudbury, Suffolk CO10 8NY
☎ 0787 277865
Easter–mid Oct, Wed–Sat 2.30–4.30; Sun
11–12.30, 2.30–4.30. Open Bank Holiday
2.30–4.30. Parties at other times by appt.
⧊ The Curator
🄴 ✑ ⇄

The timber-framed house, dated 1473 on the west gable, was, according to tradition, the priest's house. It is now held in trust by the Clare Parish Council. The collections displayed in it have nearly all come from people in the town and mostly belong to the 19th and early 20th centuries. They include prehistoric, Roman, Norman and medieval archaeological material, agricultural implements, saddlers' tools, domestic and shop equipment, clothes and educational items.

Clatteringshaws

Galloway Deer Museum

Clatteringshaws, New Galloway,
    Kirkcudbrightshire DG7 3SQ   ☎ 06442 285
Easter–mid Oct, daily 10–5
⧊ The Forester
🄵 ✑ ⇄ ♿

Clatteringshaws is five miles west of Galloway on the A712. The displays in the Museum relate to the red deer, roe deer and wild goats found in the area. There are also exhibits of other local wildlife, and of the geology of the district.

Claydon

Granary Museum

Butlin Farm, Claydon, Banbury, Oxfordshire
    OX17 1EP   ☎ 0295 89258
Mon–Sat 9.30–dusk; Sun 10.30–6.30
⧊ Andrew F. Fox
🄵 ⌂ 🖾 ⇄

The Museum collections are displayed in a former granary, a disused cowshed, part of which still has its 1942 fittings, and a new covered yard built for the purpose. There are exhibits of domestic equipment, agricultural implements, and tools once used by rural craftsmen.

Clevedon

Clevedon Court

Clevedon, Avon BS21 6QU   ☎ 0272 872257
Apr–Sept, Wed, Thurs, Sun, Bank Holiday Mon,
    2.30–5.30
⧊ The Administrator
🄴 🖾 ⇄ NT

Clevedon Court, which was given to the National Trust in 1961, is one and a half miles east of Clevedon, on the B3130. It was built in 1320, although there is an earlier 13th-century tower, and is one of the few houses of the period to have survived. It was bought in 1709 by Abraham Elton, a wealthy Bristol merchant, and his descendants continue to live there. The house contains an interesting series of family portraits and in the 13th-century kitchen there is a representative collection of the curious Elton ware, which was created by a member of the Elton family in the 1880s and came to enjoy an international reputation.

Clitheroe

Clitheroe Castle Museum

Castle House, Clitheroe, Lancashire BB7 1BA
        ☎ 0200 24635
Easter–Oct, daily 2–4.30
⧊ Chief Executive and Town Clerk's Dept, Ribble
    Valley Borough Council, Church Walk,
    Clitheroe   ☎ 0200 25111
🄴 ✑

Castle House, which is now the Museum, was built in the late 18th century as a residence for the Steward of the Honor. The exhibits relate to local archaeology, with finds from the Ribble Valley; the history of the ancient Borough of Clitheroe, illustrated by objects, photographs, plans and documents; the trades and crafts of the area, with a variety of tools and equipment and reconstructed clogger's and printer's workshops; and domestic life, with household objects arranged in a hearthside section.

Clonakilty

West Cork Regional Museum

Western Road, Clonakilty, Co. Cork, Ireland
June–Sept, daily 10.30–5.30. Oct–May, as
    advertised.
⧊ Michael C. O'Connell, Hon. Secretary
🄴 ✑ ⇄

The Museum building was the former Methodist National School, dating from 1889, and lies on the main road to Skibbereen. The exhibits illustrate the history and traditional culture of the West Cork region. Among the trades covered are coopering, shoemaking, brewing, lace-making, boatbuilding and butter-making.

Clonmel

Tipperary (South Riding) County Museum

County Hall, Clonmel, Co. Tipperary, Ireland
☎ *052 21399 extn 349*
Tues–Sat 10–1, 2–5. Closed public holidays.
 The Curator

The Museum's displays and collections are concerned with the archaeology and history of the South Riding of Tipperary. The recently renovated gallery contains a series of exhibits dating from prehistoric to modern times, as well as a selection from the Museum's collection of works by modern Irish artists.

Clun

Clun Town Trust Museum

Town Hall, Clun, nr Craven Arms, Shropshire
☎ *05884 247*
Tues, Sat 2–5. Open Bank Holiday Sat, Mon,
Tues 11–1, 2–5. Other times by appt.
 Mrs F. Hudson, Florida Villa, Clun

The Town Hall, which houses the Museum, was built of the stone from the old Castle Courthouse. The archaeological section contains maps of earthworks and a good collection of flint tools and weapons. There are other exhibits of smocks, samplers, domestic equipment, agricultural tools and implements, and local rocks and minerals.

Clydebank

Clydebank District Museum

Old Town Hall, Dumbarton Road, Clydebank,
Dunbartonshire
Mon, Wed 2–5; Sat 10–5
 Chief Librarian, Central Library, Dumbarton
Road, Clydebank

The Old Town Hall, in which the Museum is located, was opened in 1902. The emphasis is on local industry and social history, with special collections of ship models and sewing machines.

Coalville

The Manor House

Donington-le-Heath, nr Coalville, Leicestershire
☎ *0530 31259*
Wed before Easter–last Sun in Sept, Wed–Sun
2–6. Open summer Bank Holiday Mon, Tues.
 The Administrator

Donington-le-Heath is reached by taking the unclassified road which joins the B585 at Hugglescote. The Manor House dates from *c.* 1280 and is the oldest domestic building in Leicestershire. It has been little altered, except for the insertion of mullion windows *c.* 1600 and the loss of the outside staircase. It is now furnished with 16th and 17th-century oak furniture and the kitchen has a rush-strewn floor and hanging game and herbs. One bedroom is decorated with coloured stencilled designs on the walls and is equipped with a pole for hanging clothes. The peregrine falcon belonging to the master of the house is also here. Another bedroom contains what is known as 'King Richard's bedstead', the king in question being Richard II.

Coatbridge

Summerlee Heritage Trust

West Canal Street, Coatbridge, Lanarkshire
 ML5 1QB ☎ *0236 31261*
Easter–Sept, daily 10–5
 The Curator

Summerlee preserves and interprets items illustrating the social and industrial history of Scotland's iron and steel and heavy engineering industries. The 130,000 square foot machine exhibition hall has been converted from a crane factory. It contains working collections of machinery and equipment, driven by line shafting. Other exhibits include a steam winding engine, formerly at Cardowan Colliery, railway locomotives and two steam cranes.

Cobh

Cobh Museum

High Road, Cobh, Co. Cork, Ireland
May–Sept, Wed, Sun 3–6. Oct–Apr, Sun 3–6.
 Mrs M. O'Brien, Hon. Secretary, West End
Terrace, Cobh ☎ *021 811562*

The Museum is in a former Presbyterian church, built in 1854. Its collections are concerned mainly with the history of Cobh as a former naval base and transatlantic port. As well as ship models and charts, visitors can see items from the liner *Lusitania*, which foundered off the Old Head of Kinsale after being struck by a German torpedo during the First World War.

Cockley Cley

Iceni Village and Museums

Cockley Cley, nr Swaffham, Norfolk PE37 8AG
☎ *0760 21339*
Easter Sat–Sept, daily 2–5.30
 Mr L. A. Ferguson, Estate Office

Cockley Cley is three miles south-west of Swaffham, off the A1065. The museum complex contains four units – a reconstruction of an Icenean village of *c.* 60 A.D., a carriage museum, an agricultural museum and a museum of East Anglian life.

The Icenean village is believed to be on the original site, with its spring of fresh water, and includes a moat, stockade, drawbridge, roundhouse of the chief, long house, chariot house with chariots, snake pit, smoke house, grain store, iron smelter and lookout tree. The Carriage Museum displays horse-drawn vehicles dating back to the 19th century, including a landau, phaeton, brougham, governess carts, traps and children's carriages.

In the Agricultural Museum there is a range of farm implements and equipment covering a time-span of 200 years. Among the exhibits are seed-dressers, alarm guns, traps and a horse-drawn single-cylinder threshing engine, with its accompanying machinery. The East Anglian Museum, in an Elizabethan forge, contains paintings and displays illustrating life in the Norfolk Brecklands since prehistoric times.

Cogges

Cogges Farm Museum

Cogges, nr Witney, Oxfordshire OX8 6LA
☎ 0993 72602
Apr 29–Oct 26, Tues–Sun 10.30–5.30 (until 4.30 in Oct). Open Bank Holiday Mon.
▯ The Curator
▯ ▯ ▯ ▯ ▯

The Museum site contains the moated area of the first manor house built in the 12th century. The existing manor house dates from the 13th century, with many subsequent modifications and additions. The farm buildings have been constructed at various times during the 17th to 20th centuries.

The aim of the Museum is to show a working Oxfordshire farm as it was in the early 20th century. There are displays of machinery and tools in a farmyard setting, together with livestock of the period. Horses are worked and machinery used and, on days announced in advance, there are demonstrations of hurdle-making, thatching, shoeing horses, steam threshing, butter-making and cooking on the vast cast-iron ranges of the farmhouse kitchen.

The furnishings and equipment of the manor house, with a working kitchen and dairy, reflect the same period, and the walled garden next to the house is planted with flowers and vegetables typical of the Edwardian period.

Colchester

Colchester and Essex Museum

The Castle, Colchester, Essex CO1 1TJ
☎ 0206 712481/2
Apr–Sept, Mon–Sat 10–5; Sun 2.30–5.
Oct–Mar, Mon–Fri 10–5; Sat 10–4.
Closed Good Fri, Dec 25–27.
▯ The Curator, c/o Museum Resource Centre, 14 Ryegate Road, Colchester CO1 1YG
▯ ▯

Colchester Castle, c. 1076, is one of the earliest stone castles in Britain and is built directly on top of the foundations of the Roman Temple of Claudius. It contains archaeological material from sites in Essex. The collections from Roman Colchester are of exceptional quality and interest.

Hollytrees Museum

High Street, Colchester, Essex CO1 1UG
☎ 0206 712481/2
Apr–Sept, Mon–Sat 10–1, 2–5. Oct–Mar, Mon–Fri 10–1, 2–5; Sat 10–1, 2–4.
Closed Good Fri, Dec 25–27.
▯ See Colchester and Essex Museum
▯ ▯

'The Hollytrees' was built in 1718 and extended in 1785. Its displays illustrate the social history of Essex in the 18th and 19th centuries, with collections of costumes, toys and domestic equipment.

The Minories

74 High Street, Colchester, Essex CO1 1UE
☎ 0206 577067
Tues–Sat 11–5; Sun 2–6. Closed Good Fri, Dec 25, 26.
▯ The Administrator
▯ ex. Tues ▯ ▯ ▯

The Gallery, accommodated in a distinguished Georgian house, has concentrated on building up a permanent collection of works by 20th-century artists who have had some connection with the region. It is also responsible for putting on exhibitions, courses, seminars and workshops which are intended to play a significant part in the artistic life of East Anglia. The important research library includes the personal collections of Paul and John Nash. The exhibitions are often shown elsewhere after the original showings in Colchester. Recent subjects have included 'Mark Gertler', 'Six British Blacksmiths', 'Quilting, Patchwork and Appliqué, 1700–1982' and 'Paul Nash Book Design'.

The Sir Alfred Munnings Art Museum, Colchester.

Natural History Museum

All Saints' Church, High Street, Colchester, Essex
  ☎ 0206 712481/2
Apr–Sept, Mon–Sat 10–1, 2–5. Oct–Mar,
  Mon–Fri 10–1, 2–5, Sat 10–1, 2–4.
  Closed Good Fri, Dec 25–27.
Ⓜ *See Colchester and Essex Museum*
Ⓕ ✏

The former All Saints' Church, which houses
the Museum, has a 15th-century tower. Its
displays relate to the natural history of Essex,
with a special emphasis on the impact which
man has had on the environment. Many of the
exhibits are presented in the form of dioramas.

Sir Alfred Munnings Art Museum

Castle House, Dedham, Colchester, Essex
  CO7 6AZ   ☎ 0206 322127
Early May–early Oct, Sun, Wed, Bank Holiday
  Mon 2–5. Aug also Thurs, Sat 2–5.
Ⓜ *Secretary to the Trustees*
Ⓔ ✏ ✎ □

Castle House, part Tudor, part Georgian, was
the home of Sir Alfred Munnings from 1919
until his death in 1959. It now contains a large
collection of his paintings, sketches, and other
work, in the setting of the house in which he
lived and had his studios. There are many
studies of racehorses and of racing, equestrian
portraits and hunting scenes. Several large early
canvases are in the Courtyard Gallery and
examples of his early poster work in the Studios.
The exhibitions are changed from time to time
and augmented by paintings by Munnings
borrowed from private sources.

Social History Museum

Holy Trinity Church, Trinity Street, Colchester,
  Essex   ☎ 0206 712481/2
Apr–Sept, Mon–Sat 10 1, 2–5. Oct–Mar,
  Mon–Fri 10–1, 2–5; Sat 10 1, 2–4.
  Closed Good Fri, Dec 25–27.
Ⓜ *See Colchester and Essex Museum*
Ⓕ ✏

The tower of Holy Trinity Church dates from
c. 1000, the church itself from the 14th century.
The displays illustrate the traditional rural life
and handicrafts of Essex.

Adjusting the Combe Mill clock.

Coldstream

Coldstream Museum

Market Square, Coldstream, Berwickshire
  TD12 4BJ   ☎ 0890 2630
Mid May–June & early Sept–late Oct, Tues–Sun
  2–5. July–Aug, daily 2–5.
Ⓜ *Miss I. J. Ross, Leet Villa, Coldstream*
Ⓔ ✎

In the courtyard of this building, General
Monck raised the Coldstream Guards. A display
in the Museum tells the story of the Guards.
There are also exhibits illustrating the social and
domestic history of the Coldstream area.

The Hirsel Homestead Museum and Craft Centre

Coldstream, Berwickshire TD12 4LP
  ☎ 0890 2834
'All reasonable hours' every day of the year
Ⓜ *Hon. Caroline Douglas-Home, Estate Office,*
  The Hirsel, Coldstream TD12 4LP
Ⓔ ♿ ✎ &

The Museum, at the west end of Coldstream, on
the A697, is in an early 19th-century complex
of farm and stable buildings. The displays show
the characteristics of the estate and how it has
been organised and worked over the centuries,
together with the history of the Home family,
who have lived at Hirsel since the early 17th
century, and of Hirsel House. The themes and
exhibits cover archaeology, farming, forestry,
the estate workshops, the laundry, the gardens,
the dovecote, and natural history.

Colne

British in India Museum

Sun Street, Colne, Lancashire BB8 0JJ
  ☎ 0282 63129
May–Sept, 1st Sat, Sun in each month, 2–5
Ⓜ *Henry Nelson*
Ⓔ ✎ ✎

The Museum is designed to illustrate the life
and achievements of the British in India. The
collections include paintings, photographs,
uniforms, coins, medals, postage stamps and
model soldiers, as well as a wide range of
documents. There is a working model of the
Kala–Simla Railway.

Combe

Combe Mill

Blenheim Estates Sawmill, Combe, Oxfordshire
3rd Sun in May, late summer Bank Holiday Sun,
  Mon, 3rd Sun in Oct, 10–5
Ⓜ *Mrs P. A. Simmons, Combe Mill Society,*
  10 Market Street, Chipping Norton,
  Oxon OX7 5NQ   ☎ 0608 3377
Ⓔ ✎ ✎

Combe Mill and the village of Combe are near
Long Hanborough on the A4095 Woodstock to

Witney road, within the area of the Blenheim Estate. The Domesday Survey refers to a mill here. In the 19th century the Blenheim Estate workshops, which were on the site, became increasingly busy and in 1852 a steam engine was installed to supplement the existing waterwheel which was used to drive the workshop machinery. After lying idle for many years, the old beam-engine with its Cornish boiler has been put back into working order by the Combe Mill Society and is steamed occasionally during the summer. The waterwheel system has also been restored.

Compstall

Athenaeum

Andrew Street, Compstall, Cheshire SK6 5HN
    ☎ 061 427 2041
Mon, Wed 2–5, Tues, Fri 2–5, 6–8. Closed public holidays.
🏛 *Mrs H. Hamer, Librarian*
Ⓕ ⚓

The Athenaeum building houses a library and a small museum. The museum section is devoted to displays of geology, butterflies, and to items connected with the history of the area.

Compton

The Watts Gallery

Down Lane, Compton, nr Guildford, Surrey GU3 1DQ   ☎ 0483 810235
Apr–Sept, Sun–Tues, Fri 2–6; Wed, Sat 11–1, 2–6. Oct–Mar, Gallery closes at 4. Closed Thurs, Good Fri, Dec 24, 25.
🏛 *The Curator*
Ⓕ ✎ ⚓

The Gallery contains a representative collection of the work of George Frederic Watts, O.M., R.A. (1817–1904). The exhibits consist mostly of paintings by Watts, but there are some drawings and sculpture, and a few paintings by other Victorian artists.

The nearby Watts Memorial Chapel, built by Mrs Watts, is a remarkable edifice.

Comrie

Scottish Tartans Museum

Davidson House, Drummond Street, Comrie, Perthshire PH6 2DW   ☎ 0764 70779
Apr–Sept, Mon–Sat 10–5; Sun 2–4. Oct–Mar, 4 days a week 2–5; Sat 10–1.
🏛 *The Museum Keeper*
Ⓕ ⚓

The Museum houses a comprehensive collection of objects and pictures illustrating the origins and development of tartans and Highland dress. There is a dye garden, containing plants which have been used for the dyeing of tartan cloth, and a weaver's cottage, where handloom weaving is demonstrated.

Coniston

Brantwood

Coniston, Cumbria LA21 8AD   ☎ 0966 41396
Mid Mar–mid Nov, daily 11–5.30. Mid Nov–mid Mar, Wed–Sun 11–4.
🏛 *Bruce Hanson, Manager*
Ⓔ ⚓ 🍴 ⚓ ♿

Brantwood, the home of John Ruskin from 1872 until his death in 1900, lies on the eastern shore of Coniston Water, two and a half miles from Coniston village. The original Lakeland cottage was extended by Ruskin into a rambling 30-room mansion with many interesting architectural features. It contains a large collection of Ruskin's paintings and drawings, together with works by some of his friends, including T. M. Rooke, Sir Edward Burne-Jones and William Holman Hunt. Some of his furniture and a number of his personal possessions are also on display, and his coach and his boat, *Jumping Jenny*, are to be seen in the coach house.

The windows have been arranged to take advantage of the remarkable views. Some of the finest are from the turret in what was Ruskin's bedroom and from the seven lancet windows in the dining-room.

Brantwood, Coniston.

Ruskin Museum

Yewdale Road, Coniston, Cumbria
Mid Mar–Oct, daily 9.30–dusk
🏛 *Mr J. Dawson, Hon. Curator, Park Side, Haws Bank, Coniston, Cumbria LA21 8AR*
    ☎ 096 41387
Ⓔ ⚓

The Museum was opened in 1901, and it looks today very much as it did then, a splendid period piece and a good example of what a modern museum was like at the beginning of the century. It presents a comprehensive picture of the life and work of the artist and philosopher. There is a collection of paintings and drawings by Ruskin and by members of his circle, many personal relics including a number of letters, and part of his collection of geological specimens. The Museum also contains more general material of local interest, especially pictures of Lake District scenes, dating from the 18th century onwards.

Conwy

Aberconwy House

Castle Street, Conwy, Gwynedd ☎ *049263 2246*
Mar 28–Sept 29, Wed–Mon 11–5. Oct 4–26, Sat,
Sun 11–5.
📠 *The Curator*
£ 🏛 🚻 NT

This National Trust property dates from the
14th century. It now houses the Conwy
Exhibition, which presents a survey of life in the
Borough from Roman times to the present day.

Conwy Castle

Conwy, Gwynedd ☎ *049263 2358*
Mar 15–Oct 15, daily 9.30–6.30. Oct 16–
Mar 14, Mon–Sat 9.30–4; Sun 2–4.
📠 *The Custodian*
£ 🏛 🚻 ⚘

Construction of the Castle was begun in 1283
by Edward I and completed in 1292. It is an
outstanding example of European military
architecture. The Chapel Tower contains a
recently installed exhibition on the design
and history of the castles of Edward I.

Plas Mawr

The Royal Cambrian Academy of Art, High Street,
Conwy, Gwynedd LL32 8DE.
☎ *049263 3413*
Feb–Mar, Nov, Wed–Sun 10–4. Apr–Oct, daily
10–6. Closed Dec, Jan.
📠 *Mr L. H. S. Mercer, Secretary/Curator*
£ 🖊 🚻

Plas Mawr is an Elizabethan mansion, built
1577–80, in virtually its original condition. The
first owner was Robert Wynne, whose initials
are to be seen in the celebrated plasterwork.
The house came into the possession of the
Mostyn family, and in 1877 the then Lord
Mostyn allowed the recently founded Royal
Cambrian Academy to lease Plas Mawr as its
headquarters and his son has continued the
practice.

**The Elizabethan Banqueting Hall at Plas
Mawr, Conwy.**

Ten of the 14 rooms are open to the public.
They contain furniture dating from the Middle
Ages to the early 19th century. The Academy
stages art exhibitions in the house from March
to November each year.

Cookham on Thames

Stanley Spencer Gallery

Kings Hall, Cookham on Thames, nr Maidenhead,
Berkshire ☎ *06285 26557/20043*
Easter–Oct, daily 10.30–6. Nov–Easter, Sat, Sun,
public holidays, 11–5.
📠 *The Hon. Secretary*
£ ✐ 🚻 ♿

The Gallery is in the former Wesleyan Chapel,
which Spencer attended as a child. It contains a
permanent collection of the artist's works,
together with letters, documents and
memorabilia. Each summer, in a special
exhibition, it also displays important works by
Spencer which are on loan from private and
public collections.

Cookstown

Wellbrook Beetling Mill

20 Wellbrook Road, Corkhill, Cookstown,
Co. Tyrone, Northern Ireland BT80 9RY
Apr–Sept, Sat–Thurs & Bank Holiday 2–6.
Open Good Fri. Other times by appt.
📠 *The Administrator, Springhill, Moneymore,*
Co. Londonderry, Northern Ireland
BT45 7NQ ☎ *06487 48210*
£ 🏛 🚻 NT

The Mill, now in the care of the National Trust,
is four miles west of Cookstown, half a mile off
the Cookstown to Omagh road. The water-
powered hammer mill was used for the final
process in linen manufacture. The original
machinery is in working order.

Cooldurragha

Ceim-Hill Museum

Cooldurragha, Union Hall, Co. Cork, Ireland
Daily 9.30–7
📠 *Miss Thérèse O'Mahony, Curator*
£ 🚻

Cooldurragha is seven miles west of
Rosscarbery. The Museum is in a traditional
type of farmhouse. Its collections, which either
belonged to the O'Mahony family or were found
on the family hill farm, illustrate the story of the
district from prehistoric times onwards. Special
attention is paid to lace and frieze-making, the
use of natural dyes and the practice of folk
medicine.

Corbridge

Corbridge Roman Site

Corbridge, Northumberland NE45 5NT
☎ *043471 2349*
Mar 28–Oct, Mon–Sat 9.30–5.30; Sun 2–6.30.
Nov–Mar 27, Mon–Sat 9.30–1, 2–4; Sun
2–4. Closed Dec 24–26, Jan 1.
◪ *Historic Buildings & Monuments Commission,*
Carlisle ☎ *0328 31777*
◨ ⬙ ⬗ ⬖ ⬗

The Museum, a modern, purpose-built
structure, illustrates the history of Roman
Corbridge. The displays are centred on the wide
range of objects found during the excavations at
Corbridge and cover both Roman military and
domestic life in the area.

Cork

Cork Public Museum

Fitzgerald Park, Mardyke, Cork, Co. Cork,
Ireland ☎ *021 270679*
Mon–Fri 11–1, 2.15–5 (until 6 pm June–Aug);
Sun 3–5. Closed public holidays and Bank
Holiday weekends.
◪ *The Curator*
◨ *ex. Sun* ⬙ ⬛ ⬗

Housed in a Georgian mansion, the Museum
deals mainly with the history of the city of Cork
from earliest times. The archaeology section
includes material from the Stone Age to the early
Christian period. The Garryduff Gold Bird and
the Cork Helmet Horns are among the objects on
display. There are also items found during the
excavation of medieval sites in the city.

Several rooms are devoted to the municipal
history of Cork, with exhibits of banners,
guildhall furniture, glass and lace. The section
devoted to the 1916–21 period concentrates on
the patriot Lord Mayors, Terence MacSwiney
and Tomás MacCurtain.

Special attention is paid to the Cork Butter
Market, which exported to many parts of the
world between 1770 and 1800. The Museum's
outstanding exhibits include the Glass Grace
Cup of Cork Corporation, the silver collar
presented by Queen Elizabeth I to Maurice
Roche, Mayor of Cork in 1571, the Municipal
silver oar of c. 1690, and a number of silver
Freedom Boxes.

Crochet collar, 1883. Cork Public Museum.

Relief of the sun-god Jupiter Dolichenus.
Corbridge Roman Site.

Crawford Municipal Art Gallery

Emmet Place, Cork, Co. Cork, Ireland
☎ *021 965033*
Mon–Fri 10–5; Sat 10–1. Closed Bank Holidays
& several days at Christmas.
◪ *The Curator*
◨ ⬙ ⬗

The northern wing of the Gallery is the original
Cork Customs House, built in 1724. The
remainder of the building dates from 1884. There
are excellent collections of Irish 20th-century
paintings and of works by artists of the Newlyn
School. The print collection is mainly of 20th-
century woodcuts. The Harry Clarke Room
includes three stained glass windows and the
designs for his Eve of St Agnes window.

The nucleus of the sculpture on display in the
Gallery is the collection of classical statues made
by Canova in 1819, but there are also works by
modern Irish and British artists.

Cornafean

Pighouse Collection

Corr House, Cornafean, Co. Cavan, Ireland
☎ *049 37248*
By appt, or when owner is present. Usually closed
Dec, Jan.
◪ *Mrs M. P. Faris*
◨ ⬛ ⬗

Cornafean is 10 miles west of the town of Cavan,
a mile north of the Cavan-Arragh road. The
Museum, in the former piggery of Corr House,
consists of everyday acquisitions made by
members of the Faris family over a period of more
than 150 years. The 2,700 items range from
Victorian dresses to old bills and from household
equipment to embroidery.

Cornhill-on-Tweed

Heatherslaw Mill

Ford Forge, Cornhill-on-Tweed, Northumberland
TD12 4TJ ☎ 089082 338
Apr (or Easter if earlier)–Sept, daily 11–6. Oct,
Sat, Sun 10–5. Pre-booked parties during
winter months.
🔌 Heatherslaw Mill Charitable Trust, Ford and
Etal Estates, Estate Office, Ford, Berwick-
upon-Tweed, Northumberland.
£ 🚻 💷 🅿

Signposted off the A697 Morpeth to Cornhill
road, the Mill, a listed building and England's
most northerly water-driven cornmill, lies
between Ford and Etal on the B6354, on the
banks of the Till, a tributary of the Tweed.
There has been a mill on the site since the 13th
century. The present building, a double mill,
dates from the mid 19th century. One set of
machinery has been restored to working
condition and produces wholemeal flour and
pearl barley, the other is 'exploded', to show
its construction.

Corofin

Clare Heritage Centre

Church Street, Corofin, Ennis, Co Clare, Ireland
☎ 065 27955
Daily 10–6. Closed weekends Nov–Mar. Other
times by appt.
🔌 Mr Naoise Cleary
£ 🅿

The Centre occupies a former church (Church
of Ireland), which dates back to c. 1717. During
the work of restoration and conversion, it was
discovered that the building had originally been
a barn. An extension, the Dr George
Macnamara Gallery, was added in 1980. The
exhibits in the main building are concerned
with conditions in Co. Clare in the 19th
century and with the emigration which resulted
from them. The new Gallery houses a
comprehensive genealogical research service for
persons with Clare ancestry.

Corris

Corris Railway Museum

Station Yard, Corris, Machynlleth, Powys
SY20 9SS ☎ 065 473 343
Easter weekend, May 24–30, Jul 14–Aug 30,
Mon–Fri, Bank Holiday weekends 10.30–5.
Apr 1–4, May–Jul 11, Sept 1–12, Mon–Fri
2–5.
🔌 The Curator
£ 🖋 🅿

The Corris, built in 1859, was the first narrow-
gauge line in mid-Wales. Passengers were
carried from 1883 to 1930, when the line came
under Great Western control. Slate trains
continued to run until 1948. The locomotives,
brake van and a number of wagons were bought

by the Talyllyn Railway and can now be seen in
use there. Part of the track is now being
reinstated by the Corris Railway Society, which
has established a museum in the railway's former
stable block. The displays relate to the history of
the railway and the quarries it served, the major
items being wagons and the remains of a former
Corris Railway bogie coach, built c. 1898.

Corsham

Bath Stone Quarry Museum

Pickwick Quarry, Bradford Road, Corsham,
Wiltshire SN13 9LG ☎ 0249 716288
By appt, parties only
🔌 The Curator
£

The aim of the Museum, which visitors can see
in the course of development, is to present the
story of Bath stone from its extraction at the
quarry to the finished product, ready to be used
in building work. Tours begin with a walk down
the 160 steps of the mine's slope shaft into a
labyrinth of underground workings to see how
the quarrymen picked and sawed out the huge
blocks by hand. The gravity-propelled trolleys,
which brought the stone up from the mine, are
on display, together with the stacking ground,
where the 'green' blocks were seasoned, and a
mason's yard, where the traditional craft still
used by today's mason is demonstrated.
The Museum also contains displays
illustrating the geology, history and technology
of the Bath stone industry and the natural
history of the underground areas.

Corsham Court

Corsham, Wiltshire ☎ 0249 712214
Jan 15–Dec 15, Sat–Tues 2–4. June–Sept,
Bank Holiday Mon 2–6.
🔌 Lord Methuen
£ 🖋 🅿 ♿ HHA

The first part of the house dates from the 16th
century. Remodelling was carried out in the
18th century, mainly to house the picture
collection, and additions were made in the 19th
century. The State Rooms include the three-
cube picture gallery, with 18th-century
mahogany furniture, possibly by Chippendale,
and Adam mirrors. The pictures include the
original 17th-century collection of Italian,
French and Flemish paintings. There are also
many Methuen family portraits, especially by
Reynolds.

Cotton

Mechanical Music Museum

Blacksmith Road, Cotton, nr Stowmarket, Suffolk
☎ 0449 781354
June–Sept, Sun 2.30–5.30
🔌 Mon–Fri evenings: Mr R. Finbow, Station
Road, Bacton, nr Stowmarket IP14 4NH
£ 🖋 💷 🅿

A 92-key Mortier organ at the Mechanical
Music Museum, Cotton.

The Museum's collections cover a wide range of
mechanical instruments. There are street
pianos, pianolas, musical boxes, polyphones,
organettes, a musical Christmas tree and a
musical chair. The organs include examples of
fairground organs, reed organs, barrel organs,
player organs, a theatre organ – the Mighty
Wurlitzer – and a very large café organ.

The Museum holds nostalgic concerts several
times a year, when the museum building is
transformed into a 1930s-style cinema. The
vintage projectors come to life and the Mighty
Wurlitzer rises from its pit, ready for a
thunderous recital.

Coultershaw

Coultershaw Beam Pump

Coultershaw, Petworth, West Sussex
Apr–Sept, 1st & 3rd Sun in month, 11–4
✠ *Mr R. M. Palmer, Sussex Industrial*
  Archaeology Society, 11 Arlington Close,
  Goring-by-Sea, West Sussex BN12 4ST
£ *ex. children* ✐ ⚘

Coultershaw is two miles south of Petworth on
the A285. The Beam Pump, a scheduled
monument, was installed in 1790 to pump water
from the River Rother to Petworth. It has been
restored to working order and now pumps water
to a fountain. The Museum building, an old
barn which has been re-erected on this
attractive site, has exhibits illustrating the
history and development of pumps and the
water supply, and also the natural history of the
Rother Valley.

Coventry

Coventry Toy Museum

Whitefriars Gate, Much Park Street, Coventry,
  West Midlands CV1 2LT ☎ *0203 27560*
Apr–Oct, Mon–Sat 10–6; Sun 2–6. Nov–Mar,
  by appt.
✠ *Ron Morgan*
£ ✐ 🏭 ⚘

Whitefriars Gate, which houses the Museum,
was built in 1352 as the main gateway of the
Friary. It now contains a collection of dolls, toys
and games dating from 1750 to 1960. There is
also a display of amusement machines.

Coventry Whitefriars

London Road, Coventry, West Midlands
Thurs–Sat 10.30–5. Closed Dec 25, 26, public
  holidays.
✠ *See Herbert Art Gallery and Museum*
F ⚘

The Whitefriars was a Carmelite friary founded
in 1342. The remaining cloister wing was
converted into a dwelling house after the
Dissolution and later became the city's
workhouse. The displays in the Museum on the
site include material discovered during
excavations, together with medieval, post-
medieval and 19th-century sculpture. There is
an interpretative guide to the site.

Herbert Art Gallery and Museum

Jordan Well, Coventry, West Midlands CV1 5RW
  ☎ *0203 25555 extn 2315*
Mon–Sat 10–5.30; Sun 2–5.30. Closed Good Fri,
  Dec 25, 26, Jan 1.
✠ *City Arts and Museum Officer*
F ♿ ⚘ &

The collections in the Art Gallery concentrate
on works by British artists. They include
watercolours, paintings and sculpture and 20th-
century figure drawings, together with local
topography and portraits, and paintings on the
theme of Lady Godiva. Graham Sutherland's
studies for the tapestry in Coventry Cathedral
are on display and the Gallery has the Poke
Collection of English furniture, silver and
paintings on long-term loan.

The principal Museum displays are Phoenix,
the story of Coventry, and Animal Movement.
There is also a Vivarium.

Museum of British Road Transport

St Agnes Lane, Hales Street, Coventry, West
  Midlands CV1 1PN
Apr–Sept, Mon–Fri 10–4; Sat, Sun 10–5.30.
  Oct–Mar, Fri 9.30–4; Sat, Sun 10–5.
✠ *The Manager*
£ ♿ ⚘ &

The Museum was established to illustrate the
notable contribution that the West Midlands,
and especially Coventry, has made to the
development of the British road transport
industry from the mid 19th century to the
present day. The collections include 200
bicycles, 75 motorcycles, more than 150 motor
vehicles and a wide range of equipment and
accessories.

Coverack

Poldowrian Museum of Prehistory

Poldowrian, Coverack, Helston, Cornwall
☎ 0326 280468
*Open some days during summer months, otherwise
by appt*
⚔ *Peter Hadley*
£ *donations welcome* ⚓

The Museum is at Poldowrian Farm, the turning
to which is two miles beyond Goonhilly Earth
Station on the St Keverne road from Helston. It
is believed to be the only museum in the United
Kingdom devoted entirely to prehistory. It
provides an outline of prehistory in simple
terms and against this background displays some
of the many stone tools, worked flints and
pottery found on the farm, which is situated on
Britain's most southerly coast. These include
finds from sites excavated in 1978 and 1980,
with radiocarbon datings ranging from
1500–4500 B.C. The nearby sites, among which
is a Bronze Age round house, may also be
visited.

Cowes

Cowes Maritime Museum

Beckford Road, Cowes, Isle of Wight PO31 7SG
☎ 0983 293341
*Mon–Fri 9.30–6; Sat 9.30–4.30. Closed Bank
Holiday and preceding Sat.*
⚔ *Mrs K. W. Harrison*
£ ⚓

The Museum display consists mainly of models,
paintings and prints of ships and other items of
local maritime interest, together with a large
library of books and periodicals relating to
shipbuilding, sailing, shipping and navigation
in general. There are also special collections of
photographs of sailing and steam yachts and of
photographs illustrating the history of the
shipbuilding firm of J. Samuel White.

**The ferry *Audrey*, built by J. Samuel White &
Co. Ltd. of Cowes, under full steam in 1927.
Historic photograph in the Cowes Maritime
Museum.**

Sir Max Aitken Museum

The Prospect, 83 High Street, Cowes, Isle of Wight
☎ 0983 295144
Mon–Fri 10–12. Other times by appt.
⚔ *Mrs E. Gale, 2 Tudor House, Bath Road,
Cowes, Isle of Wight*   ☎ 0983 297049
£

The Museum is in the former Ratsey and
Lapthorn sail-loft. It contains the collection of
nautical items belonging to Sir Max Aitken,
who was a keen yachtsman. There are many
paintings of maritime subjects, half models and
full models of ships, including a number of Sir
Max Aitken's own yachts, and souvenirs of
former royal yachts. Among the more unusual
exhibits are Queen Victoria's croquet set from
Osborne House and a 'Wave Subduer' oil sack,
which was hung over the bow in order to allow a
controlled flow of oil on to rough seas.

Coxwold

Shandy Hall

Coxwold, nr York, North Yorkshire YO6 4AD
☎ 03476 465
*June–Sept, Wed 2–4.30, Sun 2.30–4.30. Other
times by appt.*
⚔ *Mrs J. Monkman*
© ♟ ⚓

Shandy Hall was built during the medieval
period as a priest's house. It later became the
parsonage and, in 1760, the Rev. Laurence
Sterne took up residence and carried out
'elegant improvements'. He wrote *Tristram
Shandy* and *A Sentimental Journey* here. It has
been restored by the Laurence Sterne Trust and
now looks substantially as it did in the 1760s,
with an 18th-century library which includes
many rare and first editions of Sterne's works,
with illustrations to the novels. The building
also contains wall-paintings of *c.* 1450. It is still
a lived-in house, surrounded by a cottage
garden.

Crail

Crail Museum and Heritage Centre

Marketgate, Crail, Fife   ☎ 0333 50869
*Easter and May–Sept 21, Mon–Sat 10–12.30,
2–5, Sun 2–5*
⚔ *The Curator*
£ ⚓

Crail Museum was established by Crail
Preservation Society in 1979. The displays
cover many aspects of the history of the Royal
Burgh of Crail and of life in the town, past and
present. Among the themes which receive
particular attention are the harbour, the
Church, golf, Crail as a trading port in the 17th
and 18th centuries, schools, the guilds, modern
crafts, local architecture, and the wartime Royal
Naval Air Station, HMS *Jackdaw*.

Creetown

Gem-Rock Museum

Chain Road, Creetown, Kirkcudbrightshire
    DG8 7HJ   ☎ 067182 357
Easter–Oct, daily 9.30–6. Nov–Easter, daily
    9.30–5. Closed Christmas and New Year.
𝕄 Mr T. Stephenson
🄴 🅵 🖅 🄰 ♿

The former granite-built Area School has been
converted to museum use. The aim of the
Museum is to show the variety of mineral forms
created by nature. There are special displays of
fluorescent minerals and Scottish beach agate,
and many examples of cut stones and gemstone
carvings. The Museum also contains a lapidary
workshop, which is responsible for the cutting
and polishing of many of the exhibits which
visitors can see in the Museum.

Cregneash

Cregneash Folk Museum

Cregneash, Isle of Man
May 5–Sept 27, Mon–Sat 10–1, 2–5; Sun 2–5.
𝕄 The Secretary, Manx Museum, Crellin's Hill,
    Douglas, Isle of Man   ☎ 0624 75522
🄴 🖉 🖅 🄰

Cregneash village is near Port St Mary and Port
Erin. The Museum illustrates life in a typical
Manx crofting and fishing community at the
turn of the century. Most of the buildings are
thatched, and include a crofter-fisherman's
cottage; a weaver's shed, with its handloom; a
turner's shed, with a treadle lathe; a farmstead;
and a smithy.
    Spinning demonstrations are given on
Wednesdays and Thursdays and a blacksmith
works in the smithy on two days each week,
carrying out tasks which illustrate various
aspects of the craft.

Criccieth

Criccieth Castle

Criccieth, Gwynedd   ☎ 076671 2227
Mar 15–Oct 15, daily 9.30–6.30. Oct 16–
    Mar 14, Sat 9.30–4; Sun 2–4. Mon–Fri open
    any reasonable time.
𝕄 The Custodian
🄴 🅵 🄰 ♿

Built in the early 13th century by Llewellyn the
Great, Prince of North Wales, Criccieth Castle
was strengthened by Edward I and extended by
Edward II. A former cottage just outside the
Castle contains an exhibition, 'Castles of the
Welsh Princes', which includes models and
carved stone fragments and illustrates the
design, materials and construction of nine
medieval castles in Wales.

Crofts at the Folk Museum, Cregneash.

Crich

National Tramway Museum

Crich, Matlock, Derbyshire DE4 5DP
    ☎ 077385 2565
Good Fri–Apr 6, daily 10.30–6.30. Apr 12–Oct,
    Sat, Sun, Bank Holiday 10.30–6.30. Also
    May 5–Sept, Mon–Thurs 10.30–5.30, plus
    Fri May 30, July 25 and during Aug.
𝕄 The Manager/Publicity Officer
🄴 🅵 🖅 🍴 🄰 ♿

The Tramway Museum was established in order
to preserve an important collection of tramcars,
built between 1873 and 1953, from Britain and
abroad. As a setting for the trams a Victorian
street scene has been created, with items
brought from a number of cities. The façade of
Derby Assembly Room (1765) has been re-
erected at Crich. The upper floors of the
building behind it now house the Museum's
library and archive, and the ground floor has the
Transport for the Masses exhibition, which
shows the social effects of the electric tram in
the late 19th and early 20th centuries.
    There is a regular tram service on the scenic,
mile-long track, much of which is built on the
site of a narrow-gauge mineral line originally
developed by George Stephenson.

Cromarty

Hugh Miller's Cottage

Church Street, Cromarty, Ross and Cromarty
    IV11 8XA   ☎ 03817 245
Easter–Sept, Mon–Sat 10–12, 1–5. From June 1
    also Sun 2–5.
𝕄 Mary Fyfe, Lydia Cottage, Cromarty
🄴 🖉 🅽🆃🆂

The birthplace of the stonemason turned
geologist, writer, newspaper editor and
churchman, is the last surviving thatched
cottage in Cromarty. Built in 1711 by Hugh
Miller's great-grandfather, it still has the
chimney used for smoking fish brought from the
harbour a few hundred yards away. The house is
furnished with early 19th-century items. It also
contains memorabilia and personal possessions,
reproduction copies of the evangelical paper
Hugh Miller edited, The Witness, and a
selection of fossils from his remarkable
collection.

Cromer

Cromer Museum

East Cottages, Tucker Street, Cromer, Norfolk
NR11 7PD   ☎ *0263 513543*
Mon–Sat 10–5 (closed Mon 1–2); Sun 2–5.
Closed Good Fri, Dec 25, 26, Jan 1.
⚑ *The Curator*
£ ⚏

The row of Victorian fishermen's cottages in which the Museum is situated was acquired and renovated by Cromer Town Council. The displays illustrate the natural environment and history of Cromer and the surrounding area. There are exhibits relating to coastal erosion, to the rocks, fossils, jet and amber to be found on the beaches, and to the prehistoric remains in the Forest Bed. A section of the Museum is devoted to the variety of natural habitats to be found in the coastal region and to the wildlife to be observed there. Other exhibits are concerned with local archaeology, the longshore fishing industry, especially crabbing, the Cromer lifeboat, the coastal shipping trade which flourished before the coming of the railway, and the history of Cromer as a watering place.

Making crab pots. Cromer Museum.

Wharf to Leawood Pumphouse, are available on Saturdays, Sundays and Bank Holidays from the beginning of April to the end of September.

Cromford

Arkwright's Mill

Lea Road, Cromford, Derbyshire DE4 3RR
   ☎ *062982 4297*
Wed, Thurs, Fri 10–4.30; Sun & Bank Holiday
   11–5. Also Sat (Easter–Oct only) 11–5.
⚑ *Interpretive Supervisor*
£ ⚏ ♿

In 1771 Richard Arkwright established the world's first successful water-powered cotton-spinning mill at Cromford. After 200 years of industrial use, the Cromford Mills were bought by the Arkwright Society, for restoration and preservation.

The Museum is housed in a mill building (c. 1790), adjacent to Arkwright's 1771 cotton mill. It contains two exhibitions. The first relates to the life of Sir Richard Arkwright and to the development of the British cotton industry, and the second, 'Cromford Village', to the social implications of Arkwright's vision of the Factory Settlement.

Cromford Wharf Steam Museum

Old Wharf, Mill Lane, Cromford, Derbyshire
   DE4 3RQ   ☎ *062982 3727*
Apr–Sept: enquire locally for times
⚑ *General Manager*
£ ⚏ ♿

The Steam Museum is part of a range of exhibits provided by the Cromford Canal Society and renovated by the Society. They include Leawood Pumphouse, which contains an 1894 steam-powered beam pumping engine, restored to working condition by members of the Society. Two-hour boat trips in the horse-drawn narrow boat, *John Gray*, from Cromford

Cromwell

The Vina Cooke Museum of Dolls and Bygone Childhood

The Old Rectory, Cromwell, Newark,
   Nottinghamshire NG23 6JE   ☎ *0636 821364*
Open all year (times vary, so check locally)
⚑ *Vina Cooke*
£ ⚏ ♿

Cromwell is five miles north of Newark, just off the A1. The Museum is in a late 17th-century house, with a fine staircase. The collection includes dolls' houses, 19th and 20th-century dolls made of wood, wax, porcelain and cloth, and fabric dolls representing present-day celebrities.

Culloden

Culloden Visitor Centre

Culloden, nr Inverness, Inverness-shire
   ☎ *0463 790607*
Easter–May, Oct 1–24, daily 9.30–5.30.
   June–Sept, daily 9–7.30.
⚑ *Mrs Rhona Mori*
£ ♿ ♿ **NTS**

The 1745 Jacobite Rising ended when Prince Charles Edward's army was defeated at Culloden on April 16, 1746. The National Trust for Scotland now owns the Graves of the Clans, the Well of the Dead, the Memorial Cairn, the Cumberland Stone, Old Leanach farmhouse and a large part of the battlefield.

The Visitor Centre at the site includes an historical display and an audio-visual programme which interprets the Battle of Culloden and its background.

Culross

Culross Palace

Culross, nr Dunfermline, Fife   ☎ *0383 880608*
Easter Sat and Sun, Apr–Sept, Mon–Sat 9.30–7;
  Sun 2–7. Oct–Mar, Mon–Sat 9.30–12.30,
  1.30–4; Sun 2–4.
🔾 *Mrs Gillon*
Ⓔ ▮ ➔ [NTS] ▦

The Palace, or Place, of Culross was built
between 1597 and 1611 by George, later Sir
George, Bruce of Culross, a prosperous
merchant, whose wealth had been acquired in
commerce, collieries and the local saltpans. He
expanded his house from one small block to its
present extent and it has remained unaltered
since its completion, a fine example of a town
mansion of the period. There are painted
wooden walls, ceilings and roof beams inside the
house that give it an additional importance.
Most of the paintings represent Biblical
subjects.

Town House

Sandhaven, Culross, Fife KY12 8HT
  ☎ *0383 880359*
Easter weekend, May–Sept, Daily 11–1, 2–5.
🔾 *Mr A. Forbes*
Ⓔ 🗘 ➔ [NTS]

The restored village of Culross provides an
interesting introduction to Scottish domestic
life in the 16th and 17th centuries, when
Culross was a thriving community with a
flourishing sea-going trade, mainly in coal and
salt. During the past 50 years the buildings have
been restored by the National Trust for
Scotland, with the dual aim of providing
modern living standards and preserving
characteristic architecture. The Town House is
maintained as a museum and can be visited by
the public. It contains an audio-visual
presentation, available in foreign languages,
which explains the history of Culross and its
buildings and the restoration work that has been
carried out on them.
   A visit to the Town House is intended to
serve as an introduction to Culross and to make
a tour of the locality more interesting and more
fruitful.

Cumbernauld

Cumbernauld Museum

Ardenlea House, The Wynd, Cumbernauld,
  Dunbartonshire G67 2ST   ☎ *0236 735077*
Offices open daily 10–5; Museum, Thurs 2–8
🔾 *The Curator*
Ⓕ 🗘 ➔ □

The Museum is in Cumbernauld Village, not
Cumbernauld New Town. Its displays illustrate
the history of the Cumbernauld area from
prehistoric times until the early 20th century.
Temporary exhibitions organised by the
Museum are held in Cumbernauld Central
Library.

Cumnock

Baird Institute Museum

Lugar Street, Cumnock, Ayrshire
  ☎ *0290 22024*
Tues, Fri 1.30–4; Sat 11–1. Closed public
  holidays.
🔾 *Cumnock District Library Headquarters,*
  Bank Glen, Cumnock KA18 1PQ
Ⓕ 🗘 ➔ □

The Baird Institute building is an excellent
example of Victorian architecture. The Museum
collections concentrate on the history of the
Cumnock area. There are special displays of
local pottery and wooden ware and a regular
programme of temporary exhibitions.

Cupar

Hill of Tarvit

Cupar, Fife KY15 5PB   ☎ *0334 53127*
Easter, Apr–Oct, Sat, Sun 2–6. May–Sept, daily
  2–6 (last admission 5.30). Gardens and
  grounds open all year, 10–dusk.
🔾 *Mrs Isobell S. Hanlin*
Ⓔ 🗘 ▬ ♿ ➔ [NTS]

Hill of Tarvit, now the property of the National
Trust for Scotland, lies off the A916, two and a
half miles south of Cupar. The Edwardian
mansion was built for Frederick Sharp, a
Dundee financier and jute manufacturer. It
was designed by Sir Rober Lorimer and the
workmanship is of a very high standard. The
rooms contain Frederick Sharp's notable
collections of French, Chippendale and
vernacular furniture, paintings by Dutch and
Scottish artists, Flemish tapestries and Chinese
porcelain and bronzes.

Cusworth

Cusworth Hall Museum

Cusworth, Doncaster, South Yorkshire DN5 7TU
  ☎ *0302 782342*
Apr–Oct, Mon–Thurs, Sat 11–5; Sun 1–5.
  Nov–Mar, Mon–Thurs, Sat 11–4; Sun 1–4.
🔾 *Mr R. M. Ward, Head of Study Centre*
Ⓕ 🗘 ➔

Cusworth Hall lies north of Doncaster. The
road to it is signposted, just before the junction
of the A638 and A635. The 18th-century house
received certain internal modifications early in
the present century. It is now a museum which
illustrates life in South Yorkshire during the past
200 years. The displays include furniture,
domestic equipment, costumes, toys,
educational material, transport, agriculture and
trades and crafts. Other sections illustrate the
life of the mining communities and recreational
pursuits.
   The Study Centre for schoolchildren provides
facilities for a wide range of activities based on
the Museum's collections.

D

Dagenham

Valence House Museum

Becontree Avenue, Dagenham, Essex RM8 3HT
    ☎ *01 592 2211*
Mon–Fri 9.30–1, 2–4.30.
🖾 *The Curator*
Ⓕ ✐ ➴

Valence House dates mainly from the 17th century. There are two panelled rooms of this period. The Museum contains archaeological material from the locality, including Stone and Bronze Age implements, Roman pottery, and Anglo-Saxon ornaments and weapons. There are a number of topographical and historical paintings, including some of Barking by Thomas Wakeman (1812–78), together with maps, prints and charts. The Fanshawe family portraits, from the 16th century onwards, were given to the Borough in 1963 by Captain Aubrey Fanshawe, R.N. They include works by Gheeraedts, William Dobson, Lely and Kneller. The Fanshawes held manors in Dagenham and Barking for 350 years.

Dalmellington

Scottish Industrial Railway Centre

Minnivey Colliery, Burnton, Dalmellington, Ayrshire
May–Sept, last Sun in each month, 11–4.
    Steam Weekend July 12–13 and other dates as advertised.
🖾 *Mr John Ackroyd, 52 Caprington Avenue, Kilmarnock, Ayrshire*
Ⓔ ✐ ➴

Burnton lies off the A713 Dalmellington to Ayr road. A growing collection of industrial railway locomotives is being brought together here, and it is open on specific days to give visitors the opportunity of seeing steam locomotives at work hauling demonstration trains of appropriate wagons and vans. During 1986, passenger trips were introduced on the same short stretch of track.

Darlington

Darlington Art Gallery

Crown Street, Darlington, Co. Durham DL1 1ND
    ☎ *0325 462034*
Mon–Fri 10–8; Sat 10–5.30. Closed Bank Holiday and preceding Sat.
🖾 *Divisional Librarian*
Ⓕ ➴ ☐

The Gallery's permanent collection consists of over 350 pictures, mainly of local and regional interest, and including several important contemporary works.

Darlington Railway Centre and Museum

North Road Station, Darlington, Co. Durham DL3 6ST   ☎ *0325 460532*
Mon–Sat 10–4; Sun 2–4. Closed Dec 24–26, Jan 1.
🖾 *Mr S. G. Dyke, Administrative Officer*
Ⓔ ✐ ➴ ♿

North Road Station was built in 1842 for the Stockton and Darlington Railway. The Museum collection includes locomotives, rolling stock, models, photographs, documents and other items relating to railways in the North-East, with particular reference to the Stockton and Darlington Railway. The principal large exhibits are the Stockton and Darlington locomotives No. 1, *Locomotion* (1825) and No. 25, *Derwent* (1845).

Raby Castle

Staindrop, Darlington, Co. Durham DL2 3AH
    ☎ *0833 60202*
Apr–June, Wed, Sun 2–5. July–Sept, Sun–Fri 2–5. Last admission 4.30. Park and gardens 1–5.30.
🖾 *The Curator*
Ⓔ ▮ ➴ ➴

Raby is a fully furnished home, illustrating the transition from a medieval fortress to a comfortable country house. The 14th century Great Kitchen and Servants Hall are still to be seen, together with a Minstrels' Gallery. The 12th-century stained glass in the Chapel came originally from the Abbey of Saint-Denis. The house contains collections of paintings, Meissen china, and English and French furniture.

Dartford

Dartford Borough Museum

Market Street, Dartford, Kent DA1 1EU
    ☎ *0322 343555*
Mon, Tues, Thurs, Fri 12.30–5.30; Sat 9–1, 2–5
🖾 *The Curator*
Ⓕ ✐ ➴

The Museum's collections cover local geology, archaeology, natural and social history. The archaeological section contains important prehistoric, Roman and Saxon material from such celebrated sites as Swanscombe, Lullingstone, Darenth and Riseley.

Dartmouth

Dartmouth Town Museum and Newcomen Engine House

The Butterwalk, Dartmouth, Devon TQ6 9PZ
    ☎ *08043 2923*
May–Oct, Mon–Sat 11–5. Nov–Apr, Mon–Sat 2.15–4.
🖾 *The Curator*
Ⓔ ➴

The Museum is in a former merchant's house of 1640, which has its original panelling and plasterwork. The displays relate to the history of

Dartmouth and its maritime associations, and include paintings, prints, photographs and more than 140 ship models.

The adjacent Newcomen Engine House contains an atmospheric pressure steam engine, built by Thomas Newcomen c. 1725, and in working order.

Darwen

Sunnyhurst Wood Centre

off Earnsdale Road, Darwen, Lancashire
☎ 0254 71545
Tues, Thurs, Sat, Sun, Bank Holiday, 2–4.30.
Closed Dec 25, 26, Jan 1.
Ⅺ Museums Manager, Blackburn Museum,
Museum Street, Blackburn, Lancashire
BB1 7AJ
Ｆ Ⅻ ⌂

The Centre occupies a 19th-century woodkeeper's cottage. Its displays illustrate the history and natural history of Darwen and the surrounding area.

Dawlish

Dawlish Museum

The Knowle, Barton Terrace, Dawlish, Devon
May–Sept, Mon–Sat 10–12.30, 2–5; Sun 2–5
Ⅺ Mrs G. Wright, Hon. Secretary, Brunswick
House, Brunswick Place, Dawlish
Ｅ ⌂

The Museum's collections illustrate the growth of Dawlish from an agricultural village to a select resort. Exhibits of furniture, domestic equipment and everyday articles are displayed in room settings. These include a parlour, nursery and kitchen. Other sections of the Museum relate to local trade and industry, military and railway history, and costumes. There are also collections of toys, rocks and shells.

Deal

Deal Archaeological Collection

Deal Library, Broad Street, Deal, Kent
☎ 0304 374726
Mon, Tues, Thurs 9.30–6; Wed 9.30–1; Fri, Sat
9.30–5. Closed public holidays.
Ⅺ Miss J. Vale, Curator, Kent County Museum
Service, West Malling Air Station,
West Malling, Kent ME19 6QE
☎ 0732 845845 extn 2137
Ｆ ⌂

The Museum displays some of the more interesting archaeological finds that have been made in the Deal area. These include prehistoric, Roman and Saxon material and objects from the deserted medieval port of Stonar.

Maritime and Local History Museum

22 St George's Road, Deal, Kent CT14 6BA
☎ 0304 362896
May–Sept, daily ex. Fri 10–4
Ⅺ The Director
Ｅ Ⅻ ⌂

The permanent displays in the Museum are concerned with the town's maritime history. The local history exhibits are changed annually.

The Museum

Town Hall, High Street, Deal, Kent
By appt
Ⅺ Mrs M. Porter, Administrative Assistant,
5–11 King Street, Deal   ☎ 0304 351161
Ｆ ⌂

The Town Hall was built in 1803, in 18th-century style. The Museum contains mainly civic collections, with paintings, photographs and memorabilia of Mayors and Councillors. There is a good portrait of Elizabeth Carter, a friend of Dr Johnson, who lived in Deal until her death in 1806. Roman coins and pottery and robes of Barons of the Cinque Ports are also on display.

Time-Ball Tower

Victoria Parade, Deal, Kent CT14 7BP
☎ 0304 360897
Easter–Sept, Tues–Sun 12–5. Oct–Easter, parties
by appt.
Ⅺ The Curator, Dover Museum, Ladywell,
Dover, Kent CT16 1DQ
Ｅ Ⅻ

The Tower was built in 1821 as one of a chain of 17 semaphore towers. In 1854 it was equipped with a time-ball, which drops daily at 1 pm down a 15-foot mast on the roof. The displays, funded jointly by Dover District Council and British Telecom International, illustrate the history of maritime communications, from shutter telegraphs, semaphores and time-balls to satellites. There is also a collection of watercolours by J. L. Roget, a Victorian artist, who painted many views of the area.

Saddler at work. Elvaston Castle Working Estate Museum, Derby.

Denbigh

Denbigh Castle Museum

Denbigh, Clwyd   ☎ 074571 3979
Mar 15–Oct 15, daily 9.30–6.30. Oct 16–
Mar 14, Sat 9.30–4; Sun 2–4.
⊠ *Cadw, Cardiff* ☎ 0222 465511
£ ⟳ ⇆ ✿

Denbigh Castle was built between 1282 and
1311. During subsequent centuries it gradually
fell into ruin and is now preserved by the Welsh
Historical Monuments Commission, Cadw. The
Museum is within the Castle grounds and
contains displays illustrating the history of
Denbigh, its Castle and other monuments in the
town. Other exhibits relate to methods of castle
warfare, the campaigns and castles of Edward I
in North Wales, Richard Dudley, Earl of
Leicester, who owned the Castle at one time,
and Sir Henry Morton Stanley, the explorer,
who was born in a cottage just below the Castle
walls.

Derby

Derby Industrial Museum

The Silk Mill, off Full Street, Derby, Derbyshire
DE1 3AR   ☎ 0332 31111 extn 740
Tues–Fri 10–5; Sat 10–4.45. Closed Bank
Holiday Mon, Tues.
⊠ *Sue Christian, extn 793*
£ ⟳ ⇆ ઼

The Silk Mill, in which the Museum is located,
was built between 1717 and 1721. It was the
prototype for the modern factory and a model
for subsequent factory development. After a fire
in 1910, it had to be substantially rebuilt. The
Museum is still being developed. Its displays
provide an introduction to the industrial history
of Derby and Derbyshire. There are sections on
mining and quarrying, general and railway
engineering, and the manufacture of bricks and
stoneware. The Museum also has a famous and
growing collection of Rolls-Royce aero engines,
ranging from an Eagle of 1915 to an RB211 from
the first TriStar airliner.

Derby Museum and Art Gallery

The Strand, Derby, Derbyshire DE1 1BS
    ☎ 0332 31111
Tues–Sat 10–5. Closed Bank Holiday.
⊠ *Education Officer*
£ ● ⇆ ▢

Most of the displays in the Museum are closely
related to the region. They include exhibits on
local prehistory, life in Derby during the period
of the Roman occupation, and medieval Derby.
Sections are devoted to the geology and wildlife
of the district, and to objects made from Blue
John and Ashford Black Marble. Outstanding
exhibitions include works by the late 18th-
century painter, Joseph Wright of Derby, and
Derby porcelain from 1750 to the present day.

Elvaston Castle Working Estate Museum

Borrowash Lane, Elvaston, nr Derby, Derbyshire
DE7 3EP   ☎ 0332 71342
Easter–Oct and some weekends in winter,
Wed–Sat 1–5, Sun and Bank Holiday 10–6.
Last admission 30 mins before closing.
⊠ *The Curator*
£ ● ▬ ⇆ ઼

The buildings which comprise the Museum are
the original estate workshops, contemporary
with Elvaston Castle, which is an early 19th-
century rebuild of an early castle. The Elvaston
estate was a close-knit, self-sufficient
community, with its own craftsmen, tradesmen,
labourers and their families. The workshops
have been restored and illustrate the work of the
sawyer, blacksmith, wheelwright, carpenter,
plumber, saddler and cobbler, while old breeds
of livestock and vintage implements and
machinery reflect the agricultural basis of the
estate economy. Aspects of domestic life are
shown in the cottage, wash-house and dairy,
and visitors have the opportunity of involving
themselves, in the company of staff in period
costume, with life and work as it was at Elvaston
in 1910.

**Medieval wood carving from St Alkmund's.
Derby Museum and Art Gallery.**

Indian Museum

Kedleston Hall, Derby, Derbyshire DE6 4JN
    ☎ 0332 842191
Easter Sun, Mon, Tues, then Sun from Apr 27–
Aug, 1–5.30. Also Bank Holiday Mon,
Tues (ex. Tues following May Day). 1–5.30.
Park and gardens, 12–6.
⊠ *E. H. Payne*
£ ⟳ ▬ ⇆ [HHA]

Kedleston Hall was designed by Robert Adam
and is one of the finest examples of his work to
be seen in Britain. The Indian Museum contains
a wide range of material, including weapons and
ivories, collected by Lord Curzon when he was
Viceroy of India, 1898–1905.

Royal Crown Derby Museum

194 Osmaston Road, Derby, Derbyshire DE3 8JZ
☎ *0332 47051*
Mon–Fri 9–12.30, 1.30–4. Closed Good Fri,
Easter Mon, one week at May Bank Holiday,
Christmas.
Ⓧ *Miss S. Morecroft*
Ⓕ ♣ ♠

The building – a large dome – in which the
Museum is housed is on the site of the original
Derby workhouse. The displays illustrate the
history of Derby china, from *c.* 1750 to the
present day, and cover the Nottingham Road,
King Street and Osmaston Road manufactories.
The exhibits include some of the early patch
mark figures, topographical pieces and a
selection of rare blue and white ware. There is
also a fine biscuit group, dated 1775 and, for the
period 1811–48, finely gilded vases, teapots and
figures and some of the earliest of the Japanese
patterns for which Derby is celebrated.

For the Osmaston Road factory there is
outstanding work by Désiré Leroy, with
elaborately gilded and jewelled patterns.
Among the more modern products, there are
commemorative items and pieces made for
Royalty.

**Porcelain figure of Jupiter brandishing a
thunderbolt, 1769–86. Derby, Royal Crown
Derby Museum.**

Dergenagh

President Grant's Ancestral Home

Dergenagh, Ballygawley, Co. Tyrone, Northern
Ireland   ☎ *066252 7133*
Easter–Sept, daily 10–6. Oct–Easter, Mon–Thurs,
11–3. Closed Dec 25, 26, Jan 1.
Ⓧ *Assistant Recreation Officer, Dungannon*
District Council, Dungannon, Co. Tyrone
Ⓔ ♣ ✐ ♠

The farm of Ulysses S. Grant's mother's
ancestors, the Simpsons, is about 11 miles from
Dungannon on the A4 road to Ballygawley. The
buildings have been restored to the appearance
of a typical Irish mid 19th-century smallholding,
with livestock, crops, implements, furnishings,
and domestic equipment of the period. The
Simpsons were subsistence farmers and their
holding was under 10 acres.

Devizes

Devizes Museum

Wiltshire Archaeological and Natural History
Society, Long Street, Devizes, Wiltshire
SN10 1NS   ☎ *0380 77369*
Mon–Sat 10–1, 2–5 (closes at 4 in winter)
Ⓧ *The Education Officer*
Ⓔ ♣ ♠

The Museum is the headquarters of the
Wiltshire Archaeological and Natural History
Society, formed in 1853. The prehistoric
collections are of international standing and
include weapons, exotic ornaments and items of
personal finery. There is a Henge Monument
Room and galleries devoted to the archaeology
of the Roman, Saxon and Medieval periods.
The exhibits in the Natural History Gallery
have recently been completely reorganised and
redisplayed. The Picture Gallery has a window
by John Piper.

Devizes Wharf Canal Exhibition Centre

The Wharf, Devizes, Wiltshire SN10 1EB
☎ *0380 71279*
Easter–Oct, 10–5.30. Other times by appt.
Ⓧ *The General Secretary, Kennet and Avon*
Canal Trust, The Wharf, Devizes
Ⓔ ♣ ✐ ♿

The Centre occupies a former canal granary,
built in 1810. By means of objects, original
documents and pictures, the Canal Exhibition
re-creates the history of the Kennet and Avon
Canal, with particular emphasis on the people
who constructed it and worked on it.

Dewsbury

Dewsbury Museum

Crow Nest Park, Dewsbury, West Yorkshire
WF13 2SA   ☎ *0924 468171*
Mon–Sat 10–5; Sun 1–5. Closed Dec 24–26,
Jan 1.
Ⓧ *Senior Curator, Oakwell Hall Country Park,*
Nutter Lane, Birstall, Batley, West Yorkshire
Ⓕ ✑ ▮ ♠ ▢

Crow Nest Park is three-quarters of a mile from
the town centre, on the Heckmondwike road,
just off the A644 from Dewsbury to
Huddersfield. Most of the house dates from the
early 19th century, although parts probably
belong to the late 16th or 17th centuries. The
main galleries are devoted to the theme of
'Childhood', particular attention being given
to the story of 'Children at Work' during the
Industrial Revolution and to 'Children at Play'
in the 19th and 20th centuries. There is also a
1940s classroom available for use by school
parties, and a section on children's books.

Didcot

Didcot Railway Centre

Great Western Society, Didcot, Oxfordshire
OX11 7NJ   ☎ *0235 817200*
Mar–Oct, Sat, Sun, Bank Holiday 11–5. Late
July–Aug, also Mon–Fri 11–5. Group visits at
other times by appt.
◩ *Jeanette Howse, Marketing Executive*
£ ♦ ⬛ ⟲

Didcot Railway Centre covers 16 acres and sets
out to re-create the Golden Age of the Great
Western Railway. The buildings include the
1932 steam engine shed; a signal box moved to
the site from Radstock; the goods transfer shed;
a ticket office from Welford Park Station. A
comprehensive collection of GWR steam
locomotives and rolling stock has been
established, together with a museum of smaller
relics.

On Steaming Days, which are normally the
first and last Sunday of each month, Bank
Holidays, and all Wednesdays and Sundays in
August, visitors can ride on steam trains along
two demonstration lines. There is also a
signalling display and a working exhibit of
Brunel's broad gauge railway system.

Dingle

The Dingle Collection

Branch Library, Dingle, Co. Kerry, Ireland
          ☎ *066 51499*
Tues, Thurs, Fri 11 1.30, 2.30 6, 7 8.30;
Wed 11–1.30, 2.30–6; Sat 11–1.30,
2.30–5.30
◩ *Branch Librarian*
F ⟲

The Collection concentrates on the social and
political history of the area. Special features are
a display of objects relating to the local patriot,
Thomas Ashe, and a Gaelic reference library.

Dingwall

Dingwall Museum

Town House, High Street, Dingwall, Ross-shire
IV15 9RY
May–Sept, daily 10–12, 2–4. Evening visits
by arrangement.
◩ *Mr J. R. Macleod, 'Lindholme', Bridaig*
Avenue, Dingwall IV15 9NG
£ ⟲ ⟲

The Museum tells the story of the Royal Burgh
of Dingwall from 1226 to the present day.
There are also displays relating to the County
Regiment, the Seaforth Highlanders, and to
General Sir Hector Macdonald.

Disley

Lyme Park

Disley, Stockport, Cheshire SK12 2NX
          ☎ *06632 2023*
Mar 28–Sept 28, Sun, Good Fri, Bank Holiday
Mon 1–5.30; Tues–Sat 2–4.30. Oct 1–26,
Sat and Sun 1–3.30.
◩ *The Education Officer*
£ ♦ ⬛ ⟲ ⬥ NT

The Lyme estate belonged to the Legh family
from 1346 until 1946, when it was given to the
National Trust. The present house was built
c. 1550 and given a Palladian exterior by
Giacomo Leoni in the 1720s. The contents of
the house reflects its long history and its
association with the Leghs. There are early
Mortlake tapestries and the furniture includes
early Chippendale chairs covered with the fabric
of the cloak that Charles I wore to his execution.
Other notable features are the family portraits
and limewood carvings by Grinling Gibbons.

**Celebrating the 150th anniversary of the
foundation of the Great Western Railway at
Didcot Railway Centre, 1985.**

Ditchling

Ditchling Museum

Church Lane, Ditchling, Hassocks, West Sussex
*   BN6 8TB*   ☎ *07918 4744*
Apr–Oct, Mon–Sat 10.30–5; Sun 2–5.
*   Nov–Mar, Sat 10.30–5; Sun 2–5.*
🏛 *The Curator*
£ ♿ 💷 🅿 🚻 ▢

The Museum, housed in the former village
school (1838), presents the history of the area in
diorama form, together with exhibits of
agricultural and craftsmen's tools, household
equipment, costumes, games and pastimes. A
special section is devoted to the celebrated
Ditchling Craftsmen, who lived here in the
1920s, especially the alphabet designer, Edward
Johnston. The exhibits in the Museum are
changed frequently.

Dobwalls

Thorburn Museum and Gallery

Dobwalls, Cornwall   ☎ *0579 20325/21129*
Easter–Oct, daily 10–6. Nov–Easter, daily 11–5.
*   Closed Dec 25, 26, Jan 1.*
🏛 *John Southern*
£ ♿ 💷 🅿 🚻

The exhibitions in the Museum portray the life
and times of the celebrated wildlife painter,
Archibald Thorburn (1860–1935). The 200
paintings on view represent the largest display of
his work which can be seen by the public. There
are also exhibits of sketches, books, letters,
photographs, proofs, prints and memorabilia,
together with reconstructions of his house and
studio, and environmental scenes.

Doddington

Doddington Hall

Doddington, Lincoln, Lincolnshire LN6 4RU
*   ☎ 0522 694308*
May–Sept, Sun, Wed, Bank Holiday Mon, Easter
*   Mon 2–6. Parties at other times by appt.*
🏛 *Mr and Mrs Antony Jarvis*
£ ♿ 💷 🅿 HHA

Doddington, one of the great Elizabethan
houses, was completed in 1600 by Robert
Smythson. Most of the present woodwork and
plasterwork dates from 1760–5. The house
contains a good series of family portraits and
some interesting furniture, including
Cromwellian bobbin-turned chairs and two
16th-century Venetian chests. There is a display
of 17th and 18th-century porcelain in the Long
Gallery and 17th-century Flemish tapestries in
the Holly Room.

Doncaster

Doncaster Museum and Art Gallery

Chequer Road, Doncaster, South Yorkshire
*   DN1 2AE*   ☎ *0302 4287*
Mon–Thurs, Sat 10–5; Sun 2–5. Closed
*   Christmas period.*
🏛 *The Curator*
F ⌨ 🅿 🚻

The Museum has good collections of English
glassware and ceramics, with a special emphasis
on the work of the Yorkshire potteries. The Art
Gallery contains both British and Continental
works, including a number of outstanding Dutch
paintings. A special section is devoted to
paintings and mementoes of horse-racing. There
are large and attractive displays of birds and
minerals.

Doncaster Museum now houses the historical
collections of the King's Own Yorkshire Light
Infantry, which has been transferred from their
former premises at Pontefract.

Dorchester

Dinosaur Museum

Icen Way, Dorchester, Dorset DT1 1EW
*   ☎ 0305 69880*
Daily 10–5.30. Closed Dec 25, Jan 1.
🏛 *Mrs J. D. Ridley*
£ ♿ 💷 🅿 🚻

The Museum occupies an 1896 building in the
Arts and Crafts style, with both exterior and
interior terracotta ornamentation of high
quality. The displays illustrate the world of the
dinosaur, with computerised, mechanical and
electronic displays supplementing fossil
skeletons, footprints and life-size
reconstructions. Many items in the fossil
collection can be touched and handled by
visitors, who are encouraged to answer questions
for themselves by interacting with the exhibits.
The displays are placed at different levels, to
meet the needs of all age-groups and of people in
wheelchairs.

**The Victorian Gallery of 1880 at the Dorset
County Museum, Dorchester.**

Dorset County Museum

High Street West, Dorchester, Dorset DT1 1XA
  ☎ 0305 62735
Mon–Sat 10–5. Closed Good Fri, Dec 25, 26,
  Jan 1.
◪ *Schools Organiser*
Ⓔ ✎ ⚓ ☐

The 1884 Museum building is an important
feature of the turreted and spired centre of the
town. Its interior is notable for its fine ironwork
gallery and for its original colour scheme. The
collections, which have been built up
continuously by the Dorset Natural History
and Archaeological Society since 1846, cover
anything to do with Dorset, below, on or above
the ground. The natural history gallery
concentrates on the conservation of the variety
of Dorset habitats. The geological gallery
illustrates the rock types and fossils which can
be found in the county, and the archaeology
gallery stresses the need to preserve sites in
the region.
    A special section is devoted to the rural and
industrial past of Dorset, and the large
collections of photographs, drawings, paintings
and costume may be seen if a prior booking is
made. The reconstruction of Thomas Hardy's
study from his home at Max Gate forms the
heart of the Museum's large and important
Hardy collection. Other famous Dorset people
and local history in general are also well
represented.

Dorset Military Museum

The Keep, Bridport Road, Dorchester, Dorset
  DT1 1RN   ☎ 0305 64066
Mon–Fri 9–1, 2–5, throughout year. Sat 9–1
  (Oct–June) and 9–1, 2–5 (July–Sept).
◪ *The Curator*
Ⓔ ✎ ⚓

The Keep, which contains the Museum, was
built in 1879 as the gateway to the Dorsetshire
Regiment Depot. The displays tell the story over
the past 300 years of the Dorset Regiment, the
Militia, the Volunteers of the County, the
Queen's Own Dorset Yeomanry, and the
Devonshire and Dorset Regiment. There are
also exhibits of uniforms, medals, silver
and paintings. Thirty-seven colours of the
Dorset Regiments are laid up in Sherborne
Abbey.

Dorchester-on-Thames

Dorchester Abbey Museum

Abbey Guest House, Dorchester-on-Thames,
  Oxfordshire OX9 8HH
  ☎ 0865 340056
Easter weekend, then May–Sept, Tues–Sat, Bank
  Holiday 10.30–12.30, Sun 2–6. Closed Mon
  except Bank Holiday Mon.
◪ *Canon R. Nichols, The Rectory, 10 Manor*
  Farm Road, Dorchester-on-Thames
  OX9 8HZ   ☎ 0865 340007
Ⓕ ▮ ⬛ ⌇ ⚓

The medieval front of the Abbey Guest House,
now the Museum of Dorchester-on-Thames.

The 14th to 15th-century Guest House is all
that remains of the former Augustinian Abbey.
Additions were made in 1652, when it became
the Grammar School. The Museum, in the
room formerly used by the Grammar School, has
displays illustrating the archaeology and history
of Dorchester-on-Thames. These include aerial
photographs of prehistoric sites, Roman, Saxon
and medieval material, and items from the
Grammar School.

Dorking

Polesden Lacey

Polesden Lacey, Dorking, Surrey RH5 6BD
  ☎ 0372 52048
Mar and Nov, Sat, Sun 2–5. Apr–Oct,
  Wed–Sun 2–6. Garden daily 11 dusk.
  Bank Holiday Sun, Mon 11–6.
◪ *The Administrator*
Ⓔ ▮ ⬛ ⚓ ♿ Ⓝⓣ

Polesden Lacey lies off the A246 Leatherhead to
Guildford road. The turning is signposted at
Great Bookham. Originally a Regency villa,
built c. 1824, it was extended in the early 1900s
by the celebrated hostess, the Hon. Mrs Ronald
Greville, who often entertained Royalty here.
The house, now a National Trust property,
contains 17th and 18th-century silver, majolica,
Chinese porcelain, French furniture and Dutch
paintings. Among the portraits are works by
Lawrence and Raeburn.

Douglas

The Manx Museum

Crellin's Hill, Douglas, Isle of Man
  ☎ 0624 75522
Mon–Sat 10–5. Closed Good Fri, morning of
  Tynwald Day (usually July 5), Dec 25, 26.
◪ *The Secretary*
Ⓕ ▮ ⚓

This is the National Museum of the Island.
It contains a reconstructed 19th-century
farmhouse, barn and dairy and collections of

Manx archaeology, social history and natural history. There are paintings of Manx subjects and works by Manx artists, and a memorial room to T. E. Brown, the Manx poet.

Doune

Doune Motor Museum

Carse of Cambus, Doune, Perthshire
☎ *0786 841203*
Apr–Oct, daily 10–5
🗓 *The Curator*
Ⓔ 🛏 💺 ↩

The Museum's collection is of vintage and veteran cars of the more distinguished and expensive kind. Among the makes represented are Aston Martin, Bentley, Jaguar, Lagonda and Rolls-Royce, including what is claimed to be the second oldest Rolls-Royce in the world.

Dover

Connaught Pumping Station

*Dover Transport Museum Society, Connaught
    Road, Dover, Kent   ☎ 0304 204612
Easter–Sept, Sun, Bank Holiday 11–5*
🗓 *Colin Smith, 33 Alfred Road, Dover
    CT16 2AD*
Ⓔ ↺ 💺 ↩

The Pumping Station is in the care of Dover Transport Museum Society. The displays of local transport history are illustrated by models, relics and full-sized exhibits. Also on show are an inverted triple expansion engine (1939) by Worthington Simpson, an 1878 Fox-Walker locomotive and an 1890 Folkestone cliff lift.

Dover Museum

Ladywell, Dover, Kent CT16 1DQ
☎ *0304 201066*
*Mon, Tues, Thurs–Sat 10–4.45. Closed
    Christmas week.*
🗓 *The Curator*
Ⓕ ↺ ↩ ☐

The Museum occupies part of Dover Town Hall, built in 1203. The collections concentrate on the natural and local history of Dover, especially its development as a cross-Channel port. There are regular temporary exhibitions.

The Grand Shaft

Snargate Street, Dover, Kent
☎ *0304 201066 (Dover Museum)*
May 24–Sept 13, Sat 2–5. Other times by appt.
🗓 *See Dover Museum*
Ⓔ ↩

The Shaft is now in the care of Dover Museum. Built in 1809, as part of the defences against a possible Napoleonic invasion, it consists of a 140-foot triple spiral staircase, designed to facilitate the rapid movement of British troops from the town of Dover to the fortifications on the Western Heights.

Roman Dover Tourist Centre

Painted House, New Street, Dover, Kent
☎ *0304 203279*
Apr–Oct, Tues–Sun 10–5
🗓 *Mr B. J. Philp*
Ⓔ ↺ ↩

Discovered during excavations in 1971, the Roman House was built c. 200 A.D. It was partly demolished and buried by the Roman army c. 270. Large areas of wall paintings have survived intact and the walls exist to a height of six feet in three rooms. Complete underfloor heating systems are in place below the pink mortar floors. Across the west side of the Roman House are the defensive wall and bastion of the Roman fort, built c. A.D. 270, the construction of which destroyed parts of three rooms.

Drawings, photographs and plans explain the discovery and preservation of the Painted House and illustrate other aspects of Roman Dover. Some of the outstanding objects found during the 1970–5 excavations are also on display, and the site is being developed as a Roman Tourist Centre.

Downe

Down House Darwin Museum

*Down House, Luxted Road, Downe, Orpington,
    Kent BR6 7JT   ☎ 0689 59119
Mar–Jan, Tues–Thurs, Sat, Sun 1–6. Open Bank
    Holiday Mon. Closed Dec 24–26. Groups
    by appt.*
🗓 *Philip Titheradge, Custodian*
Ⓔ 🛏 ↩ ♿

Down House was the home of Charles Darwin. Visitors can see his study, where he wrote *The Origin of Species*, and the drawing-room, with its original furnishings. There is an exhibition explaining the principles of Darwin's theory of evolution and the researches which provided the evidence on which it was based.

**Napoleonic ship model made of bone.
Dover Museum.**

Downpatrick

Down Museum

The Mall, Downpatrick, Co. Down, Northern
Ireland　☎ 0396 5218
Tues–Fri 11–5; Sat 3–5. Also open Sun afternoons
in July, Aug. Closed public holidays in winter.
✗ *The Assistant Curator*
F ⊘ ⇔

The Museum, which is under development, is in
the 18th-century county gaol complex, which
adjoins Down Cathedral and the traditional
burial place of St Patrick, patron saint of
Ireland. Stage One of the Museum, which is
now open, is in the gatehouses of the gaol
and contains a display on the life of Patrick
and his association with Down, based on what
is actually known, as distinct from later
embroidery. Stage Two, in the former
Governor's house, is due to open in 1987 and
will be devoted to the history of County Down,
including its arts and crafts. Stage Three will
enable visitors to see the well-preserved
interior of an 18th-century Irish gaol.

Charles Darwin, whose home was at Down
House in Kent from 1842 until his death
forty years later.

Dre-fach Felindre

Museum of the Welsh Woollen Industry

Dre-fach Felindre, Llandysul, Dyfed SA44 5UP
☎ 0559 370929
Apr–Sept, Mon–Sat 10–5. Oct–Mar, Mon–Fri
10–5. Evening visits for pre-booked parties.
Closed Good Fri, May Day, Dec 24–26,
Jan 1.
✗ *Dr Dyfed Elis-Gruffydd, Officer in Charge*
F ⬛ ⬛ ⌂ ⇔ ♿

The Museum is situated three and a half miles
east of Newcastle Emlyn and half a mile south of
the A484 Carmarthen to Newcastle Emlyn
road. It occupies the former Cambrian Mills,
the largest of the 23 mills and 19 weaving shops
which were in production in the area at the turn
of the century. Melin Teifi, a working mill,
occupies part of the Museum buildings and
forms part of the exhibition.

The interpretive exhibition traces the
manufacture of woollen cloth from fleece to
fabric and shows the development of Wales'
most important rural industry from its domestic
beginnings to the 19th and early 20th-century
factory units. There are large collections of
textile machinery and tools, a working
waterwheel and a number of gas, oil and steam
machines. There are regular demonstrations of
manufacturing processes and a display of the
products of contemporary woollen mills in
Wales.

Drewsteignton

Castle Drogo

Drewsteignton, Devon EX6 6PB　☎ 06473 3306
Mar 28–Oct, daily 11–6
✗ *The Administrator*
£ ⬛ ⬛ ⌂ ♿ NT

Castle Drogo is two miles north-east of
Chagford and one mile south of the A30.
Designed by Sir Edwin Lutyens, it was built
between 1910 and 1930 for Julius Drewe,
founder of the Home and Colonial Stores, who
made his fortune and retired at the age of 33.
It is now a National Trust property. The
furnishings, including some fine tapestries, are
simple and appropriate to the bare granite walls
and unpainted woodwork. The gunroom
contains an exhibition of plans and photographs
showing the house under construction.

Droitwich

Hanbury Hall

Droitwich, Hereford and Worcester WR9 7EA
☎ 052784 214
Apr–Oct, Sat, Sun & Easter Mon 2–5. May–Sept,
Wed–Sun & Bank Holiday Mon 2–6. Evening
visits for pre-booked parties on 3rd Wed of each
month during season, 7.30–9.30.
✗ *The Administrator*
£ ⬛ ⬛ ⌂ ♿ NT

Hanbury Hall is two and a half miles east of
Droitwich and one mile north of the B4090.
Now a National Trust property, it was built in
1701 for Thomas Vernon, a barrister and MP for
Worcester, and has been little altered since.
Noteworthy features of the interior are its
splendid staircase ceiling and murals by James
Thornhill, who painted the Great Hall at
Greenwich, and good 18th-century furniture,
mainly mahogany. The Long Room contains
the Watney collection of flower paintings and
porcelain.

Drumnadrochit

Loch Ness Monster Exhibition

Loch Ness Centre, Drumnadrochit, Inverness-
shire   ☎ *04562 573*
Apr–Sept, daily 9–9.30. Oct–Mar, daily 10–4.
Closed Dec 25, Jan 1.
🕅 *Miss C. Boyle*
Ⓔ ♠ 🖤 🖪

The Exhibition presents the full story of the search for the Loch Ness Monster, from 565 A.D. to the present day. There is also a section on the natural history of the Loch, with an emphasis on its deep water fauna.

Drumoak

Drum Castle

Drumoak, by Banchory, Kincardineshire AB3 3EY
☎ *03308 204 or 0467 22988*
May–Sept, daily 2–6 (last admission 5.15).
Grounds open all year, 9.30–sunset.
🕅 *Mrs Krista Chisholm*
Ⓔ 🖪 ⊕ ♠ ⑂ [NTS]

Drum Castle is off the A93, three miles west of Peterculter. The 13th-century tower house, with 17th and 19th-century additions, was bequeathed to the National Trust for Scotland in 1975. The large square tower was the work of Richard Cementarius, the King's Master Mason. In 1323 King Robert the Bruce gave a charter of the Royal Forest of Drum to his armour-bearer and clerk-register, William de Irwin, and the family connection remained unbroken until 1975. The Castle contains good Georgian furniture, needlework, family portraits and porcelain. The Victorian kitchen is a special feature of the house.

Dublin

Archbishop Marsh's Library

St Patrick's Close, Dublin 8, Ireland
☎ *01 753917*
Mon 2–4; Wed–Fri 10.30–12.30, 2–4; Sat
10.30–12.30. Closed Bank Holiday.
🕅 *The Librarian*
Ⓔ *Donations* ⊘

This is a 17th-century chained stall library. Visitors can see the cages in which books were locked away from readers and the remains of the chaining system used to secure the folio volumes. The 25,000 books were collected by five different people, with wide-ranging interests. Jonathan Swift was a governor of the Library and James Joyce studied here. There is a special collection of 17th-century French Huguenot books.

Chester Beatty Library and Gallery of Oriental Art

20 Shrewsbury Road, Dublin 4, Ireland
☎ *01 692386/695187*
Tues–Fri 10–5; Sat 2–5. Closed Bank Holiday
Tues.
🕅 *The Director*
Ⓕ ♠ 🖤

Sir Alfred Chester Beatty (1875–1968) was one of the world's greatest collectors of Islamic and Oriental art. He settled in Ireland in 1950 and left his collections to the Irish nation. There are major collections of Biblical papyri, 13th to 19th-century manuscripts and miniature paintings from Persia, India, Turkey and the Arab world, 16th and 17th-century Moghul Court art, and paintings representing the 18th and 19th-century Rajput schools, together with material of Thai, Burmese, Tibetan and Indonesian origin.

The Japanese print collection is one of the most comprehensive in the world. There are also collections of netsuke and other decorative art forms. The Library has the world's largest collection of Chinese jade books and rhinoceros horn cups. There are, in addition, Chinese snuff-bottles, painted scrolls, albums, seals, textiles and furniture.

The Western collections include manuscripts, wood-cuts and engravings by major European artists, and 18th and 19th-century books with coloured plates and fine bindings.

Classical Museum

University College Dublin, Belfield, Dublin 4,
Ireland   ☎ *01 693244 extn 8218*
By appt
🕅 *Mr V. Connerty, Curator*
Ⓕ 🖪 🖤

The Classical Museum at University College was founded early in the present century through the efforts of the Rev. Henry Browne, the Professor of Greek. The displays include Greek vases, Roman pottery and glass, Greek and Roman coins, and inscriptions. There are also papyrus fragments, lamps, terracottas, miscellaneous metal items and a sarcophagus.

Archaic stone head of a woman, probably Sicilian. Classical Museum, University College, Dublin.

Dublin Civic Museum

South William Street, Dublin 2, Ireland
Tues–Sat 10–6; Sun 11–2
⚑ *The Curator*
Ⓕ ☐

The Museum, in the former City Assembly House, is the headquarters of the Old Dublin Society. The displays tell the story of the City and County of Dublin from medieval times to the present century. The exhibits include early maps and prints and a wide variety of historic objects, ranging from Viking artefacts to wooden watermains and from a model of Jacob's biscuit factory to the head of the statue of Lord Nelson, which stood in O'Connell Street until 1965.

There are frequent temporary exhibitions of material drawn from the Museum's collections and archives.

Dunsink Observatory

Castleknock, Dublin 15, Ireland
☎ *01 387911/387959*
Public Open Nights, Sept–Mar, normally 1st and
3rd Sat in month
⚑ *Professor P. A. Wayman, Director*
Ⓕ ↩

The Observatory lies two miles north of Phoenix Park. It was founded in 1785 as the astronomical and meteorological observatory of the University of Dublin, Trinity College. The Meridian Room, rebuilt after a fire in 1977, contains an exhibition of old instruments and other items, including the two original Regulator Clocks by John Arnold, c. 1787.

Other buildings at Dunsink include the elegant dome housing the Grubb refractor of 1868 with a Cauchoix 12-inch lens of 1829. This instrument is no longer suitable for scientific work, but is kept in use for occasional visitors and for the Public Nights. Admission is free, but by ticket only. Tickets may be obtained by applying in writing to the Observatory, enclosing a stamped addressed envelope.

Garda Museum

Garda Headquarters, Phoenix Park, Dublin 8,
Ireland ☎ *01 771156/773626*
During office hours, by appt
⚑ *The Commissioner*
Ⓕ ↩

The former Constabulary of Ireland Depot, construction of which began in 1839, is now being restored. The Museum is in the residence of the Force Surgeon, in use between 1842 and 1922. The collections illustrate the history and traditions of the Constabulary of Ireland (1822–1922), the Dublin Metropolitan Police (1836–1925) and the Garda Síochána, from 1922 onwards. The displays include uniforms, insignia, documents, photographs, books and memorabilia of members of the three Forces.

Geological Museum

Trinity College, Dublin 2, Ireland
☎ *01 772941 extn 1477*
Mon–Fri 9–5 by appt. Closed Bank Holiday.
⚑ *Dr John R. Nudds, Curator*
Ⓕ ✏ ↩

The design of the Geological Museum at Trinity College, built 1853–7, was inspired by the Byzantine architecture of Venice. It contains rich floral carvings and ornamental stonework of Connemara, Cork and Kilkenny marble. The collections are mainly palaeontological and mostly Irish – with the addition of the John Joly mineral collection which covers a wider geographical field – and includes more than a thousand type specimens.

Guinness Museum

The Hop Store, Arthur Guinness Son & Company,
St James's Gate, Dublin 8, Ireland
☎ *01 756701 extn 5358*
Mon–Fri 10–4.30
⚑ *The Manager*
Ⓕ ☕ ▥ ↩

The new Guinness Museum, opened in 1986, is in the former Hop Store of the St James's Gate Brewery. The displays relate to brewing, distribution and sale of the Company's products over a period of more than two centuries, and to the Guinness involvement in the life and economy of Dublin since 1759. The sections devoted to coopering and to advertising are particularly interesting.

Heraldic Museum

Genealogical Office, Dublin Castle, Dublin,
Ireland
By appt, Mon–Fri 10–1, 2.15–4.45
⚑ *The Curator*
Ⓕ ♿

The Heraldic Museum is attached to the Genealogical Office at Dublin Castle, although both are due to be transferred to the former Kildare Street Club in the near future. The collection includes china, glass, wooden and other objects bearing heraldic devices. Among the special exhibits are ceremonial robes and tabards and a Dutch etched glass beaker with the arms of James II.

A Crown Sergeant in the Dublin Metropolitan Police, about 1880. Historic photograph in the Garda Museum, Dublin.

The Hugh Lane Municipal Gallery of Modern Art

Charlemont House, Parnell Square, Dublin 1, Ireland   ☎ *01 741903*
Tues–Sat 9.30–6; Sun 11–5
🖩 *Ethna Waldron, Curator*
Ⓕ 🗇 🖳

The house in Parnell Square dates from 1763. The Museum extension was built in 1933. The important collection of 19th and 20th-century works of art includes paintings by Corot, Constable, Augustus John, Monet and Degas. There are also a number of examples of European stained glass made during the period, as well as modern Irish paintings and sculpture.

Museum of Childhood

20 Palmerston Park, Rathmines, Dublin 6, Ireland
☎ *01 973223*
Sept, Nov–June, Sun 2–5.30. July–Aug, daily 2–5.30. Closed Oct.
🖩 *Mme Joanne Mollereau*
Ⓔ 🗇 🚌

The displays in the Museum are of a wide range of nursery mementoes, including dolls, toys and teddy bears. The collection of dolls' houses covers the period 1730–1930 and has, as one of its principal features, the travelling dolls' house which used to belong to 'Sissi', the Empress Elizabeth of Austria.

National Gallery of Ireland

Merrion Square West, Dublin 2, Ireland
☎ *01 608533*
Mon–Sat 10–6; Sun 2–5. Open until 9 on Thurs.
🖩 *Education Officer*
Ⓕ 🍴 🖳 🚌 ♿

The Gallery's collection of over 2,500 oil paintings spans European art from the early Renaissance to the beginning of the 20th century. There are also extensive holdings of drawings, watercolours and engravings, together with a considerable sculpture collection. The early Italian and 19th-century French works are particularly noteworthy and the Gallery possesses one of the finest and most extensive Dutch collections outside the Netherlands. Irish art is well represented. The Gallery holds an annual exhibition of its collection of over 30 Turners during the month of January.

The National Portrait Collection is also kept here.

National Museum of Ireland

Kildare Street and 7–9 Merrion Row, Dublin 2, Ireland   ☎ *01 765521*
Tues–Sat 10–5; Sun 2–5. Closed Good Fri, Dec 25.
🖩 *Felicity Devlin, Education Officer*
Ⓕ 🗇

The collections of the Museum cover archaeology, history and art. The archaeological section is particularly noteworthy for its extensive collections of prehistoric gold ornaments and early Christian metalwork, and for the special exhibition of Viking material.

The displays of art include both Irish and foreign silver, glass, ceramics and textiles, with the decorative art of Japan and China as an important feature.

The historical section of the Museum illustrates the political history of Ireland from 1700 until the achievement of independence.

National Transport Museum

Howth Castle, Dublin 13, Ireland
☎ *01 480831/475623*
Sun 2–6. Other times by appt.
🖩 *W. Kelly, 39 Dunree Park, Coolock, Dublin 5*
Ⓔ 🚌

The Museum is in newly opened premises in the grounds of Howth Castle. The collections include trams, buses and lorries, as well as steam-driven and horse-drawn vehicles. Nearly all the items have an Irish connection. Among the more noteworthy exhibits are an 1889 Merryweather fire engine and Howth Tram No. 9 (1902).

National Wax Museum

Granby Row, Parnell Square, Dublin 1, Ireland
☎ *01 746416*
Daily 10–5.30. Closed Good Fri, Dec 24–26.
🖩 *Kay Murray*
Ⓔ 🍴 🖳 🚌

The Museum contains over 100 figures, representing two centuries of Irish history. The celebrities shown range from Wolfe Tone, Parnell and the 1916 leaders to distinguished actors, and from all the Presidents and Taoiseachs of the Republic to James Joyce and his contemporaries in the literary field.

Noted world personalities, such as the Pope and the President of the United States, are also represented. The Popemobile, the special vehicle used by Pope John Paul during his visit to Ireland, is also on display.

Model of a pot still, about 1887.
Dublin, National Museum of Ireland.

Natural History Museum

National Museum of Ireland, 7–9 Merrion Row,
Dublin 2, Ireland ☎ *01 765521*
Tues–Sat 10–5; Sun 2–5. Closed Good Fri,
Dec 25.
🕱 *See National Museum of Ireland*
F ✎

The Museum was founded by the Royal Dublin
Society. The nucleus of its collections was
formed when the Society bought the famous
Leskean Collection of minerals and insects in
1792. The present Museum was built in 1857
and transferred to State ownership in 1877. It
contains worldwide collections of zoological
specimens, ranging from protozoa to mammals.

The displays include an Irish and world
collection, extinct and nearly extinct
mammals and birds, molluscs, butterflies, big
game heads and the fine Blashka glass models of
marine life.

Pearse Museum

St Enda's Park, Rathfarnham, Dublin 16, Ireland
☎ *01 934 208*
Daily 10–12.30, 2–6 (closes at 4 in winter)
🕱 *The Curator*
F ✎ ↩

The Museum, five miles from the centre of
Dublin, occupies an 18th-century house set in
25 acres of grounds, which are adorned with
pseudo-Celtic follies. Through its collections of
documents, photographs and memorabilia, the
Museum provides a comprehensive view of the
life of Patrick Pearse, a key figure in the Irish
republican tradition, and in the events leading
to the 1916 Rising. It also illustrates the ideals
which inspired his school, St Enda's.

Plunket Museum of Irish Education

Church of Ireland College of Education, Upper
Rathmines Road, Dublin 6, Ireland
☎ *01 970033*
Mon–Fri afternoons during term-time, by appt
🕱 *The Keeper*
F ↩

The Museum's displays illustrate various periods
and significant developments in Irish
educational history by means of reconstructions,
photographs, books and equipment. The
collections include early 19th-century
textbooks, Lancastrian-style tablets and early
educational aids.

R.T.E. Broadcasting Museum

29 Lower Rathmines Road, Portobello, Dublin 6,
Ireland ☎ *01 932798*
By appt, normally Mon–Fri mornings. Groups
limited to 20. Closed Christmas, Easter, public
holidays.
🕱 *Paddy Clarke, Curator*
F ↩

The Museum is temporarily located in the
basement of a radio studio four miles from the
broadcasting centre at Donnybrook. The studio/
museum building was formerly a church and
the museum collection is in the old crypt. The
displays, which cover both radio and television,
illustrate the history of Radio Telefís Éireann,
the Irish National Broadcasting Service, from
1926 onwards, recalling major occasions in the
development of the service and the people
associated with it. There is an extensive
collection of radio and television receivers and
exhibits on the early Marconi stations in Ireland
and on the story of transatlantic cable
telegraphy from Valentia Island, Co. Kerry.

Weingreen Museum of Biblical Antiquities

Trinity College, Dublin 2, Ireland
☎ *01 772491 extn 1409*
🕱 *Rev. J. R. Bartlett, Curator*
F ♙ 🖼 ↩ ♿

The Museum is in the Arts and Social Sciences
Building of Trinity College. The collection
comprises about 2,000 objects, representing the
cultures of ancient Palestine, Egypt and
Mesopotamia. Most of the items on display
come from excavations at Lachish, Jericho and
Jerusalem, with further material from Buseirah
and Tawilan in Jordan. There is a representative
selection of Palestinian pottery, including a
sequence of lamps, together with other objects
of stone, bone, metal, glass, faience and wood,
ranging from Neolithic to medieval times. The
Museum also contains an Assyrian relief from
Nimrud, an anthropomorphic clay coffin lid
from Lachish, and a collection of casts of Near
Eastern inscriptions.

Early wireless display. Dublin,
Radio Telefís Éireann Broadcasting Museum.

Dudley

The Black Country Museum

Tipton Road, Dudley, West Midlands DY1 4SQ
☎ 021 557 9643
Daily 10–5 (earlier closing in winter).
Closed Dec 25.
🏛 *The Visits Organiser*
🄴 🛆 🖵 ↝ ♿

All the historic buildings which form part of the
Museum have been moved from elsewhere in
the district and carefully reconstructed on the
26-acre site. The Museum illustrates the social
and industrial history of the Black Country,
through open-air exhibits, working
demonstrations, transport systems and
interpretive displays. Special features include
ironworking displays, an electrical tramway, a
replica coal-pit and early fairground items.
    The Museum adjoins the Dudley Canal
Tunnel and a group of former lime-kilns.
There are regular boat trips into the man-made
limestone caves.

Dudley Museum and Art Gallery

St James's Road, Dudley, West Midlands
DY1 1HU   ☎ 0384 55433 extn 5530
Mon–Sat 10–5. Closed Dec 24, 25, Jan 1 and
Bank Holiday.
🏛 *The Curator*
🄵 ↝ ☐

The permanent displays in the Museum include
a Geological Gallery, with large collections of
minerals and local limestone and coal measure
fossils, and the Brooke Robinson Collection of
17th to 19th-century European paintings,
Japanese netsuke and inro, English enamels and
furniture, and oriental and European ceramics.
There are regular temporary exhibitions of
material drawn from the Museum's other
collections of paintings, drawings and
watercolours, which include many items
illustrating the history of the area.

Dufftown

Dufftown Museum

The Tower, The Square, Dufftown, Moray
AB5 4AD   ☎ 0309 73701
Mid May–June, Sept, Mon–Sat 9.30–5.30.
July–Aug, Mon–Sat 9.30–6.30; Sun 2–6.30.
🏛 *District Curator, Falconer Museum, Tolbooth*
Street, Forres, Moray IV36 0PH
🄵 ⌀ ↝

The clock tower which contains the Museum
dates from the 1820s, although the clock itself,
known as 'the clock which hanged Macpherson',
is older. It comes from Banff, and takes its name
from the legend that a criminal due to hang was
pardoned at the last moment, but did hang even
so, because the clock had been advanced.
    The Museum is devoted to local history and
focuses on specific topics, such as Belvenie
Castle, Mortlach Kirk, Lord Mountstephen,
and local businesses.

The Glenfiddich Distillery Museum

The Glenfiddich Distillery, Dufftown, Moray
AB5 4DH   ☎ 0340 20373
Jan 6–May 9 and Oct 13–Dec 19, Mon–Fri
9.30–4.30. May 10–Oct 12, Mon–Sat
9.30–4.30. Closed Dec 24–Jan 1.
🏛 *Mr Mike R. Don, Public Relations Manager*
🄵 🛆 ↝ ♿

The Glenfiddich Distillery, half a mile north of
Dufftown on the A941 road, is itself a living
museum, with regular guided tours for visitors.
The Malt Barn, which forms part of the tour,
contains items relating to the history of the
Distillery and to the Grant family which
founded it. These include late 19th-century
furniture, which belonged to William Grant,
many of the distillery ledgers, coopers' tools,
and distillery equipment used in the past.

Dumbarton

Denny Ship Model Experiment Tank

Denny Ship Model Experiment Tank Building,
Glasgow Road, Dumbarton G82 1QS
☎ 0389 63444
🏛 *The Supervisor*
🄵

The Tank, which is in a Grade A listed
building, now forms part of the Scottish
Maritime Trust. It was built in 1883 to the
design of the pioneer researcher, William
Froude, and, as the world's first commercial ship
model test facility, it gave Denny Brothers the
opportunity for scientific testing which allowed
them to become Scotland's leading constructors
of fast and comfortable ships.
    The Tank also tested the hulls and propellers
for a variety of vessels, such as *Shamrock*, First
World War fast petrol craft and the aircraft
carriers *Ark Royal* and *Bulwark*. The Museum
has preserved intact the workshops, record
stores and 100m long tank.

Dumfries

Burns House

Burns Street, Dumfries, Dumfriesshire DG1 2PS
☎ 0387 55297
Apr–Sept, Mon–Sat 10–1, 2–5; Sun 2–5.
Oct–Mar, Tues–Sat 10–1, 2–5.
🏛 *See Dumfries Museum*
🄴 ⌀ ↝

Burns House was the home of Robert Burns for
the three years before his death in 1796. One
room contains an exhibition devoted to Burns
and his works, and the remainder are furnished
in the local late 18th-century style.

Dumfries Museum

The Observatory, Dumfries, Dumfriesshire
DG2 7SW   ☎ 0387 53374
Apr–Sept, Mon–Sat 10–1, 2–5; Sun 2–5.
Oct–Mar, Tues–Sat 10–1, 2–5.
🏛 *Mr D Lockwood, Curator*
🄵 *ex. Camera Obscura* 🛆 ↝

Dumfries Museum.

Dumfries Museum was established in 1835 in a converted windmill. The geological and zoological collections reflect the history of the area, and there are exhibitions of local history and archaeology which contain items ranging from neolithic stone axes and medieval tripod pots to 19th-century medical equipment. Most aspects of crafts and trades are covered. These displays include wood and leather-working tools.

Paintings of local scenes and portraits of local celebrities are hung around the gallery walls and there is a display of early maps. The Museum has a good costume collection, spanning the period from the late 18th century to the present day. One large gallery is devoted to the history of Dumfries and the surrounding area since medieval times.

Dumfries Priory Christian Heritage Museum

Maxwell Street, Dumfries, Dumfriesshire
    DG2 7AW   ☎ 0387 62323
Easter–Sept, Mon–Sat 10–1, 2–5; Sun 2–5.
    Oct–Nov, by appt only.
� Mother M. Simon
Ⓔ ▮ ▆ ◆ ♿

The Museum is in the former school wing of the Benedictine Priory. Its displays tell the story of monastic life in the south-west of Scotland from the time of St Ninian until the present day. Special features include embroidered vestments, a section illustrating the daily life of the nuns and the Abbey, and a miniature son et lumière, where models of the principal abbeys are illuminated as their story is told.

Ellisland Farm

Holywood Road, Dumfries, Dumfriesshire
    DG2 0RP   ☎ 0387 74426
All year round 'at all reasonable times'
� Mrs M. Gordon
Ⓕ ◆

The Farm lies six miles north-east of Dumfries, on the A76 Dumfries to Kilmarnock Road. It was at one time rented by Robert Burns, but he failed to make a living from it and in 1789 took up a post as Exciseman. The farmhouse contains exhibits connected with the poet and his family, and the granary beside the cottage has been converted into a museum of farming life, with displays mounted by the Country Life section of the National Museum in Edinburgh.

Old Bridge House Museum

Mill Road, Dumfries, Dumfriesshire DG2 7BE
    ☎ 0387 56904
Apr–Sept, Mon–Sat 10–1, 2–5; Sun 2–5
� See Dumfries Museum
Ⓕ ◿ ◆

Old Bridge House is a 17th-century building, which stands at one end of the 15th-century bridge over the River Nith. Now a museum, it contains six period rooms, with displays related to the history of the area.

Robert Burns Centre

Mill Road, Dumfries, Dumfriesshire DG2 7BE
    ☎ 0387 64808
Apr–Sept, Mon–Sat 10–1, 2–5; Sun 2–5.
    Oct–Mar, Tues–Sat 10–1, 2–5.
� See Dumfries Museum
Ⓕ ex. Auditorium ▮ ▆ ◆

The Centre is in a converted 18th-century mill, on the banks of the River Nith. It contains exhibitions, including an audio-visual presentation on Robert Burns and his life in Dumfries, and on the growth of interest in his life and poetry.

Dunbeath

Laidhay Croft Museum

Dunbeath, Caithness KW6 6EH
Apr–Sept, Sun–Sat 10–5
� Mrs E. Cameron
Ⓔ ◿ ◆

The croft is furnished and equipped as it would have appeared in the early years of the present century, with its byre, kitchen, living-room and box-beds. The cruck barn at the rear of the croft contains many examples of early agricultural machinery.

Dunblane

Dunblane Cathedral Museum

The Dean's House, The Cross, Dunblane,
    Perthshire
June–Sept, Mon–Sat 10.30–12.30, 2.30–4.30
� Mrs M. Carson, Hon. Curator, 32 Montrose
    Way, Dunblane FK15 9JL
Ⓕ ◿ ◆

The former Dean's House, built in 1624, has recently been restored and now contains two dwelling houses, as well as the Cathedral Museum. The Museum's collections are mainly concerned with the history of the town and cathedral of Dunblane, but some exhibits refer to the wider history of Scotland and to the Presbyterian Church. Among the more interesting displays are an exceptionally fine collection of Communion tokens, a collection of beggars' badges and several items relating to the 17th-century Bishop Leighton. The pictures include one by Turner.

Dundee

Barrack Street Museum

*Barrack Street, Ward Road, Dundee, Angus
    DD1 1PG*
    ☎ *0382 23141 (McManus Galleries)*
Mon–Sat 10–5. Closed Christmas and New Year.
🏛 *See McManus Galleries*
F ♿ ➹

This is Dundee's natural history museum. There
are displays illustrating the wildlife of the
Dundee area, on the geology and wildlife of the
coast and of the Lowlands and Highlands of
Scotland. The exhibits include an observation
beehive and the skeleton of the Great Tay
whale.

The Frigate *Unicorn*

Victoria Dock, Dundee, Angus DD1 3JA
    ☎ *0382 21558*
Apr–mid Oct, Wed–Mon 11–5
🏛 *Development Manager*
E ♿ ➹

The *Unicorn*, a 46-gun frigate, was launched in
1824. It is the oldest British-built warship afloat
and is now being restored to her original
condition. Naval guns and other artefacts of the
period help to tell the story of how 19th-century
sailors lived, ate, slept and fought on board.
    The *Unicorn* was a Royal Naval Reserve drill
ship at Dundee for nearly a century. There is a
special RNR exhibition to commemorate this.

McManus Galleries

Albert Square, Dundee, Angus DD1 1DA
    ☎ *0382 23141*
Mon–Sat 10–5. Closed Christmas and New Year.
🏛 *Extension Services*
F ● ➹ ♿

The Galleries occupy a recently restored
Victorian Gothic building, designed by Gilbert
Scott. The local history section has displays
relating to the social and civic history of
Dundee, to the trade and industry of the area,
and to archaeology. The art galleries contain
collections of 19th and 20th-century paintings,
mainly by Scottish artists, as well as sculpture
and ceramics.

The Mills Observatory

*Balgay Park, Glamis Road, Dundee, Angus
    DD2 2UB*   ☎ *0382 67183/23141*
*Apr–Sept, Mon–Fri 10–5; Sat 2–5. Oct–Mar,
    Mon–Fri 3–10; Sat 2–5. Closed Christmas
    and New Year.*
🏛 *The Astronomer (parties must book)*
F ♿ ☎ ➹

Balgay Park is one mile west of the city centre.
It was endowed to John Mills, a Dundee twine
manufacturer and amateur astronomer, who
died in 1889. The Mills Observatory, built in
1935, is Britain's only full-time public
observatory, in which visitors can use the
telescopes, including one of 1871, with its
original clockwork motor, to observe the sun,
moon, stars and planets. The 22-foot dome is

made of papier mâché on a steel frame. It can be
rotated by hand, to allow viewing in any
direction.
    The display area contains models, diagrams
and photographs illustrating many aspects of
astronomy and space exploration. A number of
exhibits relate to the history of astronomy in the
Dundee area.

Dunfermline

Andrew Carnegie Birthplace Museum

Moodie Street, Dunfermline, Fife KY12 7PL
    ☎ *0383 724302*
*Apr–Oct, Mon–Sat 11–5 (Wed until 8); Sun 2–5.
    Nov–Mar, daily 2–4.*
🏛 *The Custodian*
F ♿ ➹ ♿

The Museum consists of two linked buildings,
the original weaver's cottage in which the
industrialist and philanthropist Andrew
Carnegie was born in 1835, in an upstairs room
above his father's loom shop, and the Memorial
Hall, where the displays tell the story of
Carnegie's life and achievements. The cottage is
furnished to show it as it was during Andrew
Carnegie's boyhood. Among the exhibits in the
Memorial Hall is a re-creation of Carnegie's
study and the original draft for $1½ million
given by Carnegie to build the Peace Palace at
The Hague, together with a silver model of the
building.

Dunfermline District Museum

Viewfield Terrace, Dunfermline, Fife KY12 7HY
    ☎ *0383 721814*
*Mon–Sat 11–5. Closed Dec 25, 26, Jan 1, 2 and
    local public holidays.*
🏛 *The Curator*
F ● ➹

Dunfermline was at one time the world's largest
producer of damask table linen, of which the
Museum possesses an important collection. The
displays include an 1835 handloom, complete
with jacquard harness and pattern cards, and a
collection of the specialised tools of the trade.
    Among the other exhibits are long-case
clocks, a rare astronomical clock, and paintings
by Noël Paton and William Gillies.

Pittencrieff House Museum

Pittencrieff Park, Dunfermline, Fife
    ☎ *0383 722935*
May 3–Sept 7, daily 11–5 ex. Tues
🏛 *See Dunfermline District Museum*
F ● ➹

Pittencrieff House dates from c. 1610. The stone
for its construction probably came from the nearby
monastic ruins. The top storey was added later,
in 1731. The house and estate had many owners,
the last being Andrew Carnegie, who bought it
in 1902 and gave it to the Burgh of Dunfermline
in the following year. The Museum within
Pittencrieff House has exhibits illustrating the
history of Dunfermline and a display of costumes
from the District's large collection.

Dungarvan

Dungarvan Museum

*Old Market House, Lower Main Street,
Dungarvan, Co. Waterford, Ireland*
☎ 058 41231
*Mon–Wed, Fri 11.30–8.30; Thurs 11.30–6.
Closed public and church holidays.*
🖾 *Hon. Secretary, Dungarvan Museum Society,
at above address*
F 🗘 ⚲

The market town and small seaport of
Dungarvan, the administrative centre of Co.
Waterford, grew up in the shelter of an Anglo-
Norman castle. The new Museum, which is
being created by members of the Museum
Society, occupies the upper floor of the 17th-
century Market House. It aims to reflect the
social, archaeological and economic history of
the town.

Dunkeld

Dunkeld Cathedral Chapter House Museum

Cathedral Street, Dunkeld, Perthshire PH8 0AW
☎ 03202 249
*Easter–Oct, daily 9.30–7. Nov–Easter, daily
10–4. Guided tours for pre-booked parties.*
🖾 *The Rev. T. Dick, Cathedral Manse, Dunkeld*
F ⚲ □ ☛

Dunkeld Cathedral was built between 1312 and
1501. The Chapter House, which contains the
Museum, dates from 1469. The items on display
include a wide range of ecclesiastical artefacts,
two of the most notable being an Ionic cross slab
from the 9th-century monastery which formerly
occupied the site of the Cathedral and, also
from the 9th century, the Pictish Apostles
Stone, showing the Feeding of the Five
Thousand. In addition, the Museum has
temporary displays reflecting different aspects of
social history.

The Scottish Horse Museum

*The Cross, Dunkeld, Perthshire
Easter, then Whitsun–Sept, daily 10.30–12.30,
2–5*
🖾 *The Curator*
E ⚲

The displays in the Museum illustrate the
history of the Regiment. The exhibits include
uniforms, medals and campaign relics.

Dun Laoghaire

National Maritime Museum of Ireland

*Haigh Terrace, Dun Laoghaire, Co. Dublin,
Ireland* ☎ 01 800969
May–Sept, Tues–Sun, 2.30–5.30
🖾 *The Hon. Administrator*
E 🗘 ⚲

The Museum is in the former Mariners' Church,
which served the local Church of Ireland

congregation, including Royal Navy guardships
in the harbour. The Church includes two
prisoners' docks in the gallery, from which
prisoners under escort could participate in
Sunday services. The Museum has retained the
excellent Victorian stained glass, which
includes windows modelled on the Five Sisters
windows in York Cathedral.

The Museum's collections cover most aspects
of Irish maritime history. Of particular interest
is the Bantry Longboat, a French ship's boat of
1796, believed to be the oldest of its kind in the
world. The lighthouse display contains the
optic from the Baily lighthouse at Howth and
many other exhibits illustrate the history of
lighthouse engineering. The history of Irish
lifeboats and Ireland's indigenous small craft
have separate display areas. A wide range of
material relating to the *S.S. Great Eastern* is on
view, bequeathed by the family of her Captain,
Robert Charles Halpin. The Museum also
houses a fine collection of maps, charts, nautical
instruments and marine paintings and prints.
There is also a library of books and pamphlets
relating to the maritime history of Ireland.

**Lighthouse reflector at the National Maritime
Museum of Ireland, Dun Laoghaire.**

Dunleer

Rathgory Transport Museum

Rathgory, Dunleer, Co. Louth, Ireland
☎ 041 38648 51389
Sun 2–6 and by appt
🖾 *Jim or Paddy Byrne, 1 Fire Station, Scarlet
Street, Drogheda, Co. Louth, Ireland*
E ⚲ ♿

The Museum's collections include 35 vintage cars, the earliest of which dates from 1906, and three fire engines from the 1930s. There are also a number of motorcycles, a worldwide collection of number plates, models, accessories and other items of motoring interest. A separate section is devoted to stationary engines.

Dunnet Bay

Dunnet Pavilion

Dunnet Bay Caravan Site, Dunnet Bay, Caithness
*   KW14 8XD   ☎ 084782 319*
Apr–Sept, Tues, Wed, Fri, Sat, Sun 10–5
❧ *The Ranger, Upper Gills, Canis Bay,*
*   Caithness*
F ❧ ☛

The Pavilion is on the A836 at the north end of Dunnet Bay, two miles north of Castletown. It contains displays relating to the natural history of Caithness, especially Dunnet Bay. A microscope and books are available to visitors for the purpose of identifying natural history items found in the Dunnet area. The Ranger will provide guided walks around Dunnet to view the plant and animal life.

Duns

Biscuit Tin Museum

Manderston, Duns, Berwickshire TD11 3PP
*   ☎ 0361 83450*
Mid May–Sept, Thurs, Sun & Bank Holiday Mon
*   in May & Aug, 2–5.30. Other times by appt.*
❧ *Mr A. B. N. Palmer*
E ❧ ⬛ ❧

Manderston is two miles west of Duns, on the A6105. The late 18th-century mansion was rebuilt in 1903–5 by Sir James Miller, who inherited a large fortune from his father, Sir William, who traded with Russia in hemp and herrings and was honorary British Consul at St Petersburg for 16 years. The house is now occupied by Sir William's great-great-grandson, Adrian Palmer.

The Museum displays over 200 biscuit tins made for Huntley and Palmer between 1873 and the present day.

Early fire engines at the Rathgory Transport Museum, Dunleer.

Jim Clark Memorial Trophy Room

44 Newtown Street, Duns, Berwickshire
*   TD11 3AU   ☎ 0316 82600 extn 36*
Easter–Oct, Mon–Sat 10–6; Sun 2–6
❧ *Mr F. Waddell or Mr R. Spence*
E ❧

The Scottish racing motorist, Jim Clark (1936–68), was an Honorary Burgess of the Burgh of Duns. The large collection of trophies won by him in the course of his successful international career was presented to the town by his parents. The earliest trophy is dated 1956 and the last 1968. Among the awards are 25 for Grand Prix victories.

Dunster

Dunster Castle

Dunster, nr Minehead, Somerset TA24 6SL
*   ☎ 0643 821314*
Apr–Sept, Sat–Wed 11–5. Oct–Nov, Sat–Wed
*   2–4.*
❧ *The Administrator*
E ● ❧ NT

The earliest surviving part of the Castle is the 13th-century gateway. The home of the Luttrell family for 600 years, it was given to the National Trust in 1976. New buildings were erected in the 16th, 17th, 18th and 19th centuries. The 18th-century morning room contains paintings showing the Castle and estate as they were in the 18th century. On the first floor, in what was formerly the banqueting hall, there is a fine set of 17th-century leather hangings depicting the story of Antony and Cleopatra. An 18th-century water mill in the grounds was restored to working order in 1979.

Dunvegan

Dunvegan Castle

Dunvegan, Isle of Skye   ☎ 0667 53493
Apr–May 16 & Oct, Mon–Sat 2–5. May 17–
*   Sept, Mon–Sat 10.30–5.*
❧ *John MacLeod of MacLeod*
E ● ⬛ ❧ ⬧ HHA

The Castle is on the north-west of the Isle of Skye, reached via the A863 from Sligachan. It is claimed to be the oldest house in Scotland continuously occupied by the same family, the Chiefs of Macleod. There was probably a castle here in the 9th century, but the present main buildings were constructed between the 13th and 16th centuries. The house contains memorabilia of the celebrated Dame Flora MacLeod and earlier members of the family, together with Jacobite relics and trophies brought back from India by General MacLeod. There is 16th and 17th-century furniture and Reynolds' portrait of Dr Johnson.

The Piping Centre

Borreraig, Dunvegan, Isle of Skye IV55 8ZY
☎ 047081 213
Easter–mid Oct, Mon–Sat 10–6. July–Aug, also Sun 2–6.
☒ *The Curator*
£ ⬙ ▪ ↩

By the 17th century the MacCrimmons had become celebrated as composers, performers and teachers of Piobaireachd. From 1500 to 1800 they were hereditary pipers to the Macleod Chiefs and until 1772 they maintained a famous piping college, first at Galtrigall and then at Borreraig. The Centre faces the ruins of the College and contains exhibits illustrating the history of the Highland Bagpipe and its music, together with memorabilia of the MacCrimmons and other noted piping families.

Dunwich

Dunwich Museum

St James' Street, Dunwich, nr Saxmundham, Suffolk IP17 3EA
Mar–Apr, Sat, Sun 2–4.30. May–July, Sept, Tues, Thurs, Sat, Sun 2–4.30. Aug, daily 2–4.30. Oct, Sat, Sun 2–4.30. Other times by appt.
☒ *Hon. Curator* ☎ 072873 358
£ *ex. pre-booked groups* ⬙ ↩

One section of the Museum illustrates the history of Dunwich from the Roman occupation to the present day, including extensive coverage of the Saxon and medieval towns now lost to the sea and the notorious 'rotten borough'. The second group of displays is concerned with the natural history of the local habitats – seashore, sandy heathland, salt marshes, woods and farmland. Dunwich Common (National Trust) and the Minsmere Bird Reserve (Royal Society for the Protection of Birds) are within walking distance of the Museum.

Durham

The Dormitory Museum

The Cathedral, West Cloister, Durham, Co. Durham DH1 3EH ☎ 0385 62489
Apr–Sept, daily 10.30–3.30
☒ *The Librarian, The Dean and Chapter Library, The College, Durham DH1 3EH*
£ ▴ ⬙ ▪ □

The monks' dormitory at Durham was rebuilt in 1398–1404. Its most notable feature is its open timber roof. The principal beams are made from the trunks of 21 oak trees and are over 40 feet long. In 1850–5 the dormitory was restored for use as a library, and until the opening of the Treasury in 1978 it also housed the Cathedral's main museum. It is now used for temporary exhibitions of items drawn from the Cathedral's resources of material relating to the Church, City and County. There is also a large

permanent exhibition of Anglo-Saxon sculptured stones from Durham County and the surrounding area.

Durham Castle

Durham, Co. Durham ☎ 0385 65481
July–Sept, daily 10–4.30. Oct–June, Mon, Wed, Sat 2–4.
☒ *The Bursar, University College, Palace Green, Durham*
£ *guided tours only* ⬙

The earliest parts of the Castle date from the late 12th century. Additions were made in the 13th and 14th centuries, and much rebuilding was carried out in the 1840s, in order to provide accommodation for students at the University. The Great Hall contains a good collection of portraits and a number of items of Cromwellian armour.

Durham Cathedral Treasury

The College, Durham, Co. Durham DH1 3EH
☎ 0385 62489
Mon–Sat 10.30–4.30; Sun 2–4
☒ *See The Dormitory Museum*
£ ▴ ⬙ ▪

The Treasury is situated in the undercroft of the 14th-century Cathedral Dormitory. The relics from the coffin of St Cuthbert (d. 687) – the cross, the small altar, the embroidery and the incised wood fragments of the 7th-century coffin itself – are at the hub of the exhibition. There are also 8th to 15th-century illuminated manuscripts from the Saxon monastic houses in Northumbria and from the Benedictine monastery at Durham. Other displays include archival seals, 17th and 18th-century gilt altar plate, 16th and 17th-century copes, manuscript music books and the grotesque, lively 12th-century Sanctuary knocker from the North door of the Cathedral.

The bronze sanctuary ring of Durham Cathedral, about 1175, now displayed in the Cathedral Treasury.

Durham Heritage Centre

St Mary-le-Bow, North Bailey, Durham,
   Co. Durham DH1 3ET
Last weekend in May–last weekend in Sept, daily
   2–4.30. Closed Durham Miners' Gala Day
   (3rd Sat in July).
✉ *The Supervisor*
£ ✐ ⚲

The medieval church of St Mary-le-Bow was
rebuilt in the late 17th century. Its fine 17th
and 18th-century woodwork includes the
judicial bench of the Chancery Court of the
County Palatine of Durham and Sadberge. The
Centre is organised around an interpretative
exhibition on the conservation of the heritage
of Durham and the surrounding area, and on the
developments which have taken place in recent
times. The exhibits include life-size figures
in period costume. There are audio-visual
presentations on the history and environment
of Durham.

Durham Light Infantry Museum and Arts Centre

Aykley Heads, Durham, Co. Durham DH1 5TU
   ☎ *0385 42214*
Tues–Sat 10–5; Sun 2–5. Closed Mon ex. Bank
   Holiday.
✉ *Nerys A. Johnson, Keeper-in-Charge, or*
   Stephen Shannon, Military Assistant
£ ✐ ▬ ⚲ ♿

The much-praised modern building containing
the Museum and the Arts Centre was opened in
1968. There are displays on two floors covering
the history of the Durham Light Infantry
Regiment from 1758 to 1968, with exhibits of
models, weapons, uniforms, photographs and
large-scale equipment, including a Desert Jeep
and Bren Carrier, presented in a way which is
intended to interest the non-specialist, as well
as the military historian.

The Arts Centre organises about 16
exhibitions a year, of paintings, sculpture, prints
and photographs, as well as on themes of local
historical interest.

Durham University Oriental Museum

Elvet Hill, Durham, Co. Durham DH1 3TH
   ☎ *0385 66711*
Mar–Oct, Mon–Sat 9.30 1, 2 5; Sun 2–5.
   Nov-Feb, Mon–Fri 9.30–1, 2–5.
✉ *Mr John Ruffle, Keeper*
£ ✐ ⚲

The Museum's collections cover the whole of
the Orient and range from Ancient Egypt to
modern Japan. They are particularly strong in
the arts and crafts of Egypt and China, but Japan
and the Indian sub-continent are also well
represented.

The Museum of Archaeology, Old Fulling Mill

The Banks, Durham, Co. Durham DH1 3EB
   ☎ *0385 64466 extn 581*
Apr–Sept, Mon–Fri 10–4; Sat, Sun 2–4.
   Oct–Mar, daily 2–4.
✉ *The Hon. Curator*
F ● ⚲

The Museum, organised by the University of
Durham, occupies an 18th-century fulling mill,
which incorporates a late medieval structure.
The displays cover the archaeology of Durham,
and in particular Durham City, from prehistoric
to late medieval times. The Roman material
includes Samian ware and there are also late
Saxon wood and leather objects from Durham
City and an extensive medieval collection from
the city and the surrounding region, notably the
material from recent excavations at Bearpark,
the Manor of the Prior of Durham.

Duxford

Imperial War Museum, Duxford Airfield

Duxford Airfield, Duxford, Cambridge,
   Cambridgeshire CB2 4QR
   ☎ *0223 835000/833963*
Mid Mar–early Nov, daily 10.30–5.30.
   Last admissions 4.45 or dusk if earlier.
   Closed Good Fri, May Day Bank Holiday.
✉ *Schools Officer*
£ ● ▬ ⚲ ♿

Duxford is south of Cambridge, on the A505
Royston to Newmarket road. Duxford Airfield
preserves all the main features of a Battle of
Britain fighter station and incorporates hangars
which date from the First World War. The
impressive series of civil aircraft, including
Concorde, is maintained by members of the
Duxford Aviation Society. Duxford was an
American base from 1943 to 1945 and the
Museum has a collection of American military
aircraft which is unique in Europe.

Duxford is the home not only of the finest
collection of military and civil aircraft in
Britain, but also of a wide variety of other
military exhibits, ranging from tanks, trucks and
artillery to radar equipment, missiles and midget
submarines.

**A military vehicle rally at the
Durham Light Infantry Museum.**

Most of the 100 or so aircraft on show belong to the Museum's own collection, permanently preserved and displayed at Duxford, together with the civil airliners collected and cared for by the Duxford Aviation Society. There are also a number of privately owned aircraft, many of them in flying condition, which are on loan to the Museum. A full programme of air displays and other special events is mounted each year.

A giant superhangar, built with both government and private funding, was opened in 1986. Other developments planned to take place in the near future include the renovation of the former station cinema and of the original Battle of Britain Operations Room, which is to be restored to its 1940 appearance.

Dysart

McDouall Stuart Museum

Rectory Lane, Dysart, Fife
June–Aug, daily 2–5
☒ *Museum Secretary, Museum and Art Gallery,*
*   War Memorial Gardens, Kirkcaldy*
*   Fife KY1 1YG*   ☎ *0592 260732*
Ⓕ ⊘ ☛

Dysart was the birthplace of John McDouall Stuart, the Australian explorer, who was the first man to cross Australia, from the south to the north coast. The displays tell the story of his life and achievements and devote particular attention to his pioneering journey of 1861–2.

Other exhibits in the Museum illustrate the history of Dysart and the surrounding district.

E

Earby

Lead Mines Museum

The Old Grammar School, School Lane, Earby,
*   Colne, Lancashire*   ☎ *0282 843210*
1st Sun in Apr–last Sun in Oct, 2–6.
*   Also Thurs 6–9 pm.*
☒ *Mr Peter Dawson, 41 Stoney Bank Road,*
*   Earby, Colne BB8 6RU*
Ⓔ ⊘ ☛

The former Grammar School, which houses the Museum of the Earby Mines Research Group, was built in the 17th century. It contains a comprehensive collection of Yorkshire Dales mining relics, including mine tubs, smaller implements, mining machinery, miners' personal belongings, models, photographs, mine plans and minerals.

The Group has the expertise and equipment to re-open collapsed workings if permission can be obtained, and in this way unusual exhibits can sometimes be obtained for the Museum. Lead mining was once an important industry in the Yorkshire Dales and the numerous sites where it was carried on have been systematically recorded. A member of the Group is always available to advise on sites to visit.

Eardisland

Burton Court

Eardisland, nr Leominster, Hereford and Worcester
*   ☎ 05447 231*
Spring Bank Holiday–mid Sept, Wed, Thurs, Sat,
*   Sun 2.30–6*
☒ *Mrs R. M. Simpson*
Ⓔ ☛ ☛ ♿ HHA

Eardisland is four and a half miles west of Leominster. There was a timber-framed house on the site of the present Burton Court as early as the 14th century. Part of it survives as today's Great Hall. The remainder of the front of the house was built in Regency times. In 1865 the estate was bought by John Clowes and the house was Victorianised, by installing large-pane windows and adding a conservatory. In 1912 Clough Williams-Ellis was commissioned to make alterations to the façade.

Burton Court, still a family home, now contains collections of 18th to 19th-century English costumes, Chinese costumes and embroidery, a working model fairground, ship models, natural history specimens and sporting trophies.

Aircraft on display at the Imperial War Museum's out-station at Duxford Airfield.

Easdale Island

Easdale Island Folk Museum

Easdale Island, By Oban, Argyll
☏ 08523 382
*Apr–Oct, Mon–Sat 10.30–5.30; Sun 10.30–5.
Other times by appt.*
✂ *Jean Adams, 5 Easdale Island, By Oban*
©

Easdale Island is 16 miles south of Oban. During the 17th, 18th and 19th centuries the island had an important roofing slate industry. The slate was accessible and easily transported by sea, and large quantities were shipped overseas, especially to Canada, Australia and America. In 1881 the island was hit by a freak storm. The quarries were flooded to the brim and the industry never recovered.

The Museum illustrates the industrial and domestic life of the Slate Islands during the 19th century. There are also collections of documents relating to the Friendly Societies and to the 1st Argyll and Bute Artillery Volunteers.

Eastbourne

Eastbourne Lifeboat Museum

Grand Parade, Eastbourne, East Sussex
☏ 0323 30717
Mid Mar–Dec, daily 10–dusk
✂ *G. J. E. Howard, The Curator, Redwood,
Upperton Road, Eastbourne*
☏ 0323 33291
© ✎ ♿

The Museum building was originally the Lifeboat House. It contains displays illustrating the work of the Royal National Lifeboat Institution and the history of the Eastbourne Lifeboat.

The Royal Sussex Regiment Museum

*Sussex Combined Services Museum, Redoubt
Fortress, Royal Parade, Eastbourne, East
Sussex BN21 4BP*   ☏ 0323 33952
Easter–Oct, daily 10–5.30. Open Bank Holiday.
✂ *The Manager*
© ⚑ ✎ ♿ ♿

The Museum's collections of uniforms, medals, weapons, equipment and campaign medals illustrate the history of the former Royal Sussex Regiment from 1701 to 1966. Photographs, books and documentary material relating to the Regiment are held at the West Sussex Record Office in Chichester.

Sussex Combined Services Museum

*Redoubt Fortress, Royal Parade, Eastbourne,
East Sussex BN21 4BP*   ☏ 0323 33952
Easter–Oct, daily 10–5.30. Open Bank Holiday.
✂ *The Manager*
© ⚑ ♿ ♿

The Redoubt, which has been restored to house the Museum, is a circular casemated fortress built in 1804–8 to defend the coast against a French invasion. The displays present the military history of Sussex since Roman times, with exhibits of armour, uniforms, weapons and equipment. A series of detention cells has also been preserved.

Tower 73: The Wish Tower Invasion Museum

King Edward's Parade, Eastbourne, East Sussex
☏ 0323 35809
Easter–Oct, daily 9.30–5.30. Open Bank Holiday.
✂ *See Sussex Combined Services Museum*
© ⚑ ♿ ♿

Tower 73 is a restored Martello Tower, built in 1801 for coastal defence during the Napoleonic Wars. The displays show the historical background, disposition, building and manning of these forts, together with documents relating to Tower 73 and examples of equipment, weapons and uniforms.

Towner Art Gallery and Eastbourne Local History Museum

*High Street/Manor Gardens, Old Town,
Eastbourne, East Sussex BN20 8BB*
☏ 0323 21635/25112
Mon–Sat 10–5; Sun 2–5. Closed Mon in winter.
✂ *The Curator*
© ✎ □

The Gallery and Museum occupy an 18th-century mansion, formerly Eastbourne Manor House. The Gallery collections comprise more than 3,000 items, mostly 19th and 20th-century paintings, watercolours and prints. Especially noteworthy are a group of Georgian caricatures, by George Cruikshank; an important collection of watercolours of Sussex scenes; and the largest collection of works by the Eastbourne artist, Eric Ravilious (1903–42). Over 20 temporary art exhibitions are held each year.

The Officers' Mess at the Sussex Combined Services Museum, Eastbourne.

The Local History Museum traces the history of human occupation in the Eastbourne area from Neolithic times to the present day. The exhibits include artefacts, models and photographs. The Bell collection of butterflies is also displayed at the Museum.

East Budleigh

James Countryside Collection

Bicton Park, East Budleigh, Devon EX7 7DP
   ☎ *0395 68465*
Apr–Oct, daily 10–6
◪ *Sandra George, Curator*
£ ♿ ▣ ♨ ⛫

Bicton House, the seat of the Rolle/Clinton family, was sold to Devon County Council in 1957 to be used as an agricultural and horticultural training college, but the gardens and pinetum were retained. The gardens had been neglected since 1935, but in 1961 it was decided to restore them and to open them to the public. In 1968 a Countryside Museum was added, largely planned and organised by N. D. G. James, Agent to the Clinton Devon Estates.

The aim has been to illustrate the changes in farming and rural life caused by the replacement of the horse by the tractor and the motorcar. There are collections of farm implements, carts, wagons and tractors. Special sections are devoted to cidermaking, estate work, forestry and barn equipment and to the work of the thatcher, ploughman, saddler and blacksmith.

East Carlton

Industrial Heritage Centre

East Carlton Countryside Park, East Carlton, Market Harborough, Leicestershire LE16 8YD
   ☎ *0536 770977*
Apr–Oct, daily 10–6. Nov–Mar, daily 11–4.
   Closed for 5 days during Christmas period.
◪ *The Warden*
🄵 ⌖ ▣ ♨ ➔ ♿

The Museum is in the stable block of East Carlton Hall, rebuilt in 1768. Its displays show the origins and development of the Northamptonshire iron industry. The exhibits include fossils found in the iron ore quarries and archaeological material showing evidence of ironworking in the Corby area by the Romans, Celts and Saxons, and up to Elizabethan times. Most of the items in the collections, however, relate to the arrival of Lloyds in the 1880s, the construction of 'The Works' in 1934 and the subsequent development of Corby New Town.

Large exhibits, together with reconstructions, models, drawings, photographs and video presentations, are used to explain processes ranging from quarrying ore to steelmaking and tube forming. The change from a rural area to an industry-based New Town is featured in the displays, with details of the lives of the people involved.

East Cowes

Osborne House

East Cowes, Isle of Wight   ☎ *0983 200022*
1st Mon in Apr–2nd Sun in Oct, daily 10–5
◪ *Mr R. Underwood, State Apartments*
   Supervisor
£ ♿ ▣ ♨ ➔ ⛫

Osborne House, one mile south-east of East Cowes, was built at Queen Victoria's own expense in 1845 as her seaside home, and designed under the supervision of the Prince Consort, by Thomas Cubitt. Visitors are able to see the Queen's private rooms, virtually unchanged since the death of the Queen in 1901, the State Apartments and the Privy Council Chamber. Swiss Cottage, the small house used by the royal children, is also on show. The collection of Indian gifts presented to Queen Victoria in 1897 is displayed in the Durbar Room.

East Grinstead

Standen

East Grinstead, West Sussex RH19 4NE
   ☎ *0342 23029*
Apr–Oct, Wed, Thurs, Sat, Sun 2–6.
   Closed Good Fri & Bank Holiday.
◪ *The Administrator*
£ ♿ ▣ NT

Standen was built in 1894 as a country house for James Beale, a solicitor who specialised in work for the railway companies, and was designed by Philip Webb. The Beales' youngest daughter, Helen, continued to live in the house after her parents' death and preserved it as she had known it when she was a child. Given to the National Trust in 1972, it is the only Philip Webb house to survive without alteration.

Philip Webb was a co-founder of the Society for the Protection of Ancient Buildings and a life-long friend of William Morris, and many of the furnishings at Standen were made by Morris & Company, the firm founded by Morris, Burne-Jones, Rossetti and Webb in 1861.

Town Museum

East Court, College Lane, East Grinstead, West Sussex RH19 3LT
Wed 2–4; Sat 2–5 and some Bank Holiday afternoons. Closes at 4 Nov–Mar. Closed Dec 25.
◪ *Mr M. J. Leppard, Hon. Curator, 20 St George's Court, East Grinstead RH19 1QP*
   ☎ *0342 22511 evenings only*
🄵 ⌖ ➔

East Court, which now contains the Museum, was originally a private house, built in 1769, extended and adapted in 1908 and converted to municipal use in 1946. The displays tell the story of East Grinstead and the way of life of its people in the past. There is a good collection of local handicrafts, 19th and 20th-century pottery being particularly strongly represented.

East Hendred

Champs Chapel Museum

Rosewall, Chapel Square, East Hendred, Wantage,
  Oxfordshire OX12 8JN   ☎ 0235 833761
Apr–Sept, Sun 2.30–4.30. Nov–Mar, Sun
  2.30–3.30.
🗚 Clerk to the Parish Council
Ⓕ ◿ ✍ ☐

The Museum occupies part of a 15th-century
wayside chapel, built by the Carthusian monks
of Sheen, Surrey. It was restored in 1973–4 and
now serves as a Library, Museum and meeting
place for the Parish Council. The displays
present material of local interest. A special
exhibition is staged each summer.

East Kilbride

Hunter House

75 Maxwelton Road, East Kilbride, Lanarkshire
  G74 3LW   ☎ 03552 23993
By appt
🗚 East Kilbride District Council, Civic Centre,
  East Kilbride G74 1AB   ☎ 03552 28777
Ⓔ ✍

Hunter House, a farmhouse built c. 1700, is at
Long Calderwood, two miles south-east of the
town centre of the New Town of East Kilbride.
It was the birthplace of John and William
Hunter, the celebrated 18th-century physicians
and surgeons, and has been preserved as a
memorial to them, with displays illustrating
their life and work.

East Linton

Preston Mill and Phantassie Doocot

East Linton, East Lothian   ☎ 0620 860426
Apr–Sept, Mon–Sat 10–12.30, 2–5.30; Sun
  2–5.30. Oct, Mon–Sat 10–12.30, 2–4.30;
  Sun 2–4.30. Nov–Mar, Sat 10–12.30,
  2–4.30; Sun 2–4.30.
🗚 Nigel Buchan-Watt
Ⓔ ◿ ✍ [NTS]

Parts of Preston Mill date from the 17th
century, but considerable rebuilding and
modernisation was carried out during the 18th
century. The iron waterwheel, 13 feet in
diameter and just over three feet wide, was cast
in 1760, probably at the Carron Foundry,
Falkirk. The Mill was restored and put into
working order in the 1960s and 1970s, and
visitors can watch all the processes required to
turn grain into oatmeal.

Phantassie Doocot, the Mill's near
neighbour, is one of the biggest and most
remarkable dovecotes in the British Isles, with
nesting places for more than 500 birds. The
walls project upwards in the form of a horseshoe-
shaped hood, to enclose a sloping tiled roof.
This faces south, giving the birds the maximum
benefit of sunshine and shelter.

East Molesey

Hampton Court Palace

East Molesey, Surrey KT8 9AU   ☎ 01 977 8441
Apr–Sept, Mon–Sat 9.30–6; Sun 11–6.
  Oct–Mar, Mon–Sat 9.30–5; Sun 2–5.
  Closed Dec 24–26, Jan 1.
🗚 Office of the Palace Superintendent
Ⓔ ♿ ☕ ✍ ♿

The building of the Royal Palace of Hampton
Court, on the north side of the River Thames,
by Hampton Court Bridge, was begun by
Cardinal Wolsey in 1514. Additions were made
for Henry VIII and later by Christopher Wren
for William III. The State Rooms contain
notable collections of furniture, tapestries and
paintings.

The east side of the Clock Court was
remodelled in 1732 by William Kent for George
II, who was the last sovereign to live at
Hampton Court. The Palace has been open to
the public since 1838.

The famous maze dates from the reign of
William III.

Mounted Branch Museum

Metropolitan Police Mounted Branch, Imber
  Court, East Molesey, Surrey KT8 0BT
  ☎ 01 541 1212/2784/2794
By appt, but open during Metropolitan Police Show
  & Dog Show or when adjoining Police Sports
  Club is open to the public
🗚 Chief Superintendent
Ⓕ ☕ ✍

The Museum illustrates the origins and
development of the Metropolitan Police
Mounted Branch from the time of the Bow
Street Patrol to the present day. The items on
display include uniforms and equipment,
saddles, harness, paintings and photographs.
There are also relics of Billie, the White Horse
of Wembley, three Dickin medals presented to
police horses during the Second World War,
and a life-size model of a horse wearing
ceremonial kit.

Easton

Easton Farm Park

Easton, nr Woodbridge, Suffolk IP13 0EQ
  ☎ 0728 746475
Easter–Sept, daily 10.30–6
🗚 The Manager
Ⓔ ♿ ☕ 🍴 ✍ ♿

The Farm Park provides a museum within the
context of a working farm. The Victorian
buildings house historical collections of
agricultural machinery and equipment and
tractors. There is an octagonal Victorian dairy
and a blacksmith's shop, in which visitors can
sometimes see horses being shod. By contrast,
special walkways and a viewing gallery above
the modern milking parlour give a good view of
today's large-scale milk production.

East Retford

The Bassetlaw Museum

Amcott House, 40 Grove Street, East Retford,
Nottinghamshire DN22 6JU
☎ *0777 706741 extn 257*
Mon–Fri 10–1, 2–5. Closed Bank Holiday.
☒ *Mr Malcolm J. Dolby, Curator*
☐ ⌀ ✎

The Museum, which is under development,
occupies a late 18th-century house, built for the
town's M.P., Sir Wharton Amcotts. There is
good decorative plasterwork in the principal
rooms. The collections relate mostly to the
history and archaeology of the Bassetlaw
District, the most northerly third of the County
of Nottinghamshire, and include the nine
Retford Borough Charters, which begin in
1313. The Museum also holds the Wyse Bequest
of pottery, porcelain and glass.

East Wemyss

Wemyss Environmental Education Centre

East Wemyss Primary School, School Wynd,
East Wemyss, Kirkcaldy, Fife KY1 4RN
☎ *0592 714479*
Mon–Fri 9–4.30. Mar–Nov, also 2nd Sun in
month, 2–6. Closed Dec 23–Jan 4.
☒ *Mrs A. Watters, The Markinch Centre,*
Bowling Green Road, Markinch,
Fife KY7 6BD
☐ ⌀ ☕ ✎

Wemyss includes the three villages of East
Wemyss, West Wemyss and Coaltown of
Wemyss. The Centre has built up a collection of
interpretive material about the history,
people, industries, geology, botany and wildlife
of the Wemyss villages, as a means of
stimulating interest in the local environment.

Hampton Court Palace, East Molesey. The
Clock Court and George II's Gateway, 1732.

Eastwood

D. H. Lawrence Birthplace Museum

8a Victoria Street, Eastwood, Nottingham,
Nottinghamshire ☎ *0773 763312*
Daily 10–5. Closed Dec 24–Jan 1.
☒ *The Curator*
☐ ⌀ ✎

Eastwood is seven miles from Nottingham and
three miles from Junction 26 of the M1. The
house at 8a Victoria Street has been restored
and furnished to the style of a miner's home of
1885, when the Lawrence family lived there. A
video presentation in the Exhibition Room tells
the story of Lawrence's early years in the district.

Ecclefechan

Carlyle's Birthplace

The Arched House, Ecclefechan, Lockerbie,
Dumfriesshire DG11 3DG
☎ *05763 666*
Easter weekend, then May–Sept, Mon–Sat 10–12,
1–5. June–Sept, also Sun 2–5.
☒ *Mrs Nancy Walter*
☐ ⌀ [NTS]

In 1795 Thomas Carlyle, the 19th-century
historian, essayist, social reformer and prophet,
was born in the first floor bedroom of the north
wing of the Arched House, which was built by
his father and uncle, who were both master
masons. The bedroom has been re-created as it
would have been in Carlyle's time, and
restoration has also been carried out in other
parts of the house. The furnishings, many of
which belong to the Carlyle family, personal
relics, documents and early photographs
illustrate Carlyle's wide range of activities.

'Alice Leck', a wax doll and case of 1861. Eccles, Monks Hall Museum.

Eccles

Monks Hall Museum

42 Wellington Road, Eccles, Lancashire M30 0NP
☎ *061 789 4372*
Mon–Fri 10–12.30, 1.30–5; Sun 2–5.
Closed Good Fri, Dec 24–26, Jan 1.
🗷 *Principal Museums Officer*
F 🖉 🚗

Monks Hall, part of which is timber-framed and dates from the 16th century, is the earliest secular building in Eccles. Now a museum, it contains a collection of toys and games built up over many years by Salford Museums and Art Galleries. Among the items displayed are a fine late Victorian dolls' house and a range of dolls dating from the late 18th century onwards. Another area of the Museum is concerned with local material of social and industrial interest, including a Nasmyth steam hammer and a Gardner gas engine.

Edenbridge

Chiddingstone Castle

nr Edenbridge, Kent   ☎ *0892 870347*
End of Mar–Sept, Wed–Sat 2–5.30. Mid June–
mid Sept, also Tues. Sun, Bank Holidays
11.30–5.30. Oct, weekends only. Parties
at other times by appt.
🗷 *Miss M. H. Eldridge, Hon. Secretary*
£ 🚻 🍴 🚗 ♿

The Castle is an alteration of an older building, in the castle style, carried out c. 1805 by W. Atkinson, the architect of Scone Palace and Abbotsford. It has good furniture, Stuart and Jacobite relics, pictures and manuscripts, Japanese swords, and one of the finest private collections of Japanese lacquerware in the world. There are also displays of Egyptian antiquities, Buddhist images and relics, and two noteworthy Georgian barrel organs.

Hever Castle

Edenbridge, Kent TN8 7NG   ☎ *0732 865224*
Easter–Oct, daily 12–6
🗷 *Estate Office*
£ 🚻 🍴 🚗 HHA

The earliest parts of Hever Castle date back to c. 1270 and in the late 15th century the Bullen, or Boleyn, family built a dwelling-house inside the walls. In the early 1900s William Waldorf Astor restored the Castle and created the Tudor village behind it. Anne Boleyn spent much of her early life at the Castle and a number of her personal possessions and memorabilia are to be seen here. The Astor legacy includes the great garden, the lake, the maze and a large collection of furniture, pictures and objets d'art from the Tudor and later periods. A room at the Castle contains an exhibition commemorating the contribution made by four generations of Astors to the restoration and refurbishment of the Castle and the estate.

Kent and Sharpshooters Yeomanry Museum

Hever Castle, Edenbridge, Kent TN8 7NG
☎ *0732 865224*
Easter–Oct, daily 12–6
🗷 *Estate Office*
£ 🚻 🍴 🚗

The Museum tells the story of the East Kent Yeomanry, West Kent Yeomanry and 3rd/4th County of London Yeomanry (Sharpshooters), by means of paintings, photographs, uniforms, badges, medals, weapons and models.

Edinburgh

Braidwood and Rushbrook Fire Museum

McDonald Road, Edinburgh EH3 9DE
☎ *031 228 2401*
Daily 9–4, 7–9 subject to a fire engine being on
station. Otherwise by appt.
🗷 *The Firemaster, Lothian & Borders Fire*
Brigade, Brigade Headquarters, Lauriston
Place, Edinburgh EH3 9DE
F 🚗

The Museum, in an old fire station, contains fire engines and fire-fighting equipment dating from the early 19th century to the present day. There is also an international collection of badges, medals, photographs and records relating to fire-fighting.

Canongate Tolbooth

163 Canongate, Edinburgh EH8 8DN
☎ *031 225 2424 extn 6638*
June–Sept, Mon–Sat 10–6. Oct–May, Mon–Sat
10–5. During Edinburgh Festival, also
Sun 2–5. Closed Christmas and New Year.
🗷 *See Huntly House Museum*
F 🖉 □

The Tolbooth, in the Royal Mile, was the courthouse, prison and centre of municipal affairs of the once independent burgh of the Canongate. Temporary exhibitions are often staged here and it also contains the J. Telfer

Dunbar tartan collection. Visitors to the Scottish Stone and Brass Rubbing Centre at the Tolbooth can make rubbings of replicas of medieval brasses and Pictish inscribed stones.

City Art Centre

1–4 Market Street, Edinburgh EH1 1DE
    ☎ *031 225 2424 extn 6650*
June–Sept, Mon–Sat 10–6. Oct–May, Mon–Sat 10–5. During Edinburgh Festival, also Sun 2–5. Closed Christmas and New Year.
⚑ *Keeper of Fine Art Collections*
F ⌘ 🖴 ♿ □

This late 19th-century listed building was erected as a warehouse for *The Scotsman* and was later used as a market. It now houses the City's large permanent collection of paintings, drawings, prints and sculpture, mostly by Scottish artists. The works range in date from the 17th century to the present day and include topographical views of Edinburgh and portraits of eminent citizens. Late 19th and early 20th-century artists are well represented and the number of more recent works continues to grow.

The Centre has studios for working artists and craftsmen and stages a wide programme of temporary exhibitions drawn both from the United Kingdom and from abroad.

Cockburn Museum of Geology

University of Edinburgh, Grant Institute of Geology, West Mains Road, Edinburgh EH9 3JW   ☎ 031 667 1081 extn 3577
Mon–Fri 9–5. Closed Christmas and New Year.
⚑ *Peter Aspen, Curator*
F ⌘ ⚓

The collections in the Museum are mainly designed to be used in the teaching of undergraduates and for research purposes, but many of the displays of rocks, fossils and minerals are of more general interest.

The Fruitmarket Gallery

29 Market Street, Edinburgh EH1 1DF
    ☎ *031 225 2383*
Tues–Sat 10–5.30
⚑ *Ms Moira Innes*
F ♦ 🖴 ⚓ □

The Gallery, with its extensive programme of video shows and lectures, is one of the most important art centres in Scotland. It is · concerned with international contemporary art and organises a series of exhibitions throughout the year, each lasting for an average of six weeks.

The Georgian House

7 Charlotte Square, Edinburgh EH2 4DU
    ☎ *031 225 2160*
Apr–Oct, Mon–Sat 10–4.30; Sun 2–4.30. Nov, Sat 10–4; Sun 2–4.
⚑ *Mrs Shelagh Kennedy*
E ♦ NTS

The north side of Charlotte Square, which includes No. 7 'The Georgian House', now a National Trust for Scotland property, is one of

Robert Adam's greatest achievements in the field of urban architecture. The Georgian rooms have been restored to their original 18th-century colour schemes and are furnished in the style of the time. The basement kitchen contains period equipment and is presented to show the conditions under which 18th-century domestic servants worked. There is an audio-visual programme to illustrate the life of the family which once lived in the house.

Gladstone's Land

447B Lawnmarket, Royal Mile, Edinburgh
    ☎ *031 226 5856*
Easter Oct, Mon–Sat 10–5; Sun 2–5. Nov, Sat 10–4.30, Sun 2–4.30. Last admission 30 mins before closing.
⚑ *Miss Sheila Bassett*
E ♦ NTS

The exterior of Gladstone's Land, built in 1620, is itself a museum of the 'tall lands' of 17th-century Edinburgh. At that time the town was becoming so overcrowded that the only way to increase the accommodation was to build upwards. Gladstone's Land is the most important remaining example of this type of 17th-century building in Edinburgh. It contains fine painted ceilings and is arranged and furnished as it would have been when it was the home of a prosperous Edinburgh merchant.

Holyrood Park Visitor Centre

Holyrood Lodge, Holyrood Road, Edinburgh EH8 8AX   ☎ 031 556 7561
Easter–mid Sept, daily 10–5.30. Mid Sept–Dec 24, Sat, Sun 10–4,
⚑ *Michael M. Scott, 24 Gardner's Crescent, Edinburgh EH3 8DE*
F ♦ ⚓

The Centre, managed by the Scottish Wildlife Trust and the Historic Buildings and Monuments division of the Scottish Development Department, is in the 1857 lodge building of Holyrood Park. It contains pictorial displays on the history, archaeology, geology and natural history of Holyrood Park. Binoculars are provided to view the bird life of Salisbury Crags.

The Newliston Bed at the Georgian House, Edinburgh.

Huntly House Museum

142 Canongate, Edinburgh EH8 8DD
☎ *031 225 2424 extn 6689*
June–Sept, Mon–Sat 10–6. Oct–May, Mon–Sat,
*   10–5. During Edinburgh Festival, also*
*   Sun 2–5. Closed Christmas and New Year.*
The Curator

The Museum building, dating from the 16th
century, is one of the finest early houses in the
Royal Mile. Huntly House is Edinburgh's main
museum of local history. It includes period
rooms and reconstructions relating to traditional
industries and aspects of the city's history. It also
has important collections of Edinburgh silver
and glass, Scottish pottery, shop signs, and
memorabilia and personal possessions of Field
Marshal Earl Haig, Commander-in-Chief of the
British forces during the later stages of the First
World War.

The small rooms of Huntly House have been
preserved, giving the museum an intimate
atmosphere and allowing natural transitions
from one theme to another.

John Knox House Museum

45 High Street, Royal Mile, Edinburgh EH1 1SR
☎ *031 556 6961*
Mon–Sat 10–4.30
H. G. Lindley, Curator

The house which now contains the Museum was
built at some time before 1490 and restored
during the 1980s. It was owned by the Arres
family up to 1568 and possibly used by John
Knox as a manse between 1568 and 1572, when
he was resident in Edinburgh. It has always had
shops of varying trades on the ground floor and
in the basement. The house contains 16th-
century panelling and a painted ceiling, and is
furnished in a manner which gives an
impression of how it may have looked in Knox's
lifetime.

Lady Stair's House

Lady Stair's Close, Lawnmarket, Edinburgh
*   EH1 2PA   ☎ 031 225 2424 extn 6593*
June–Sept, Mon–Sat 10–6. Oct–May, Mon–Sat
*   10–5. Closed Dec 25, 26, Jan 1–3.*
Keeper of Social History, Huntly House
*   Museum*

Built in 1622, Lady Stair's House was
remodelled between 1893 and 1897 for the Earl
of Roseberry, to be used as his town house. Now
a museum, it contains displays relating to the
life and work of Scotland's three great literary
figures of the late 18th and 19th centuries,
Robert Burns, Sir Walter Scott and Robert
Louis Stevenson. A number of Scottish
museums pay tribute to one or other of these
writers, but Lady Stair's House is the only place
where they are commemorated together.

Lauriston Castle

Cramond Road South, Edinburgh EH4 5QD
☎ *031 336 2060*
Apr–Oct, Sat–Thurs 11–1, 2–5 (last tour 4.20).
*   Nov–Mar, Sat, Sun 2–4 (last tour 3.20).*
*   All visits by guided tour only.*
The Custodian

This is a late 16th-century tower house, greatly
extended in the 1820s in the Jacobean style.
The last occupants were Mr and Mrs William
Reid, who bought the property in 1902 and used
it as a domestic setting for their collections of
furniture, Derbyshire Blue John ornaments,
Crossley wool mosaics, engravings and minor
objets d'art. The Reids left Lauriston to the
Scottish nation, a condition of the bequest
being that it should be maintained much as it
was in their lifetime. Visitors therefore see
rooms which show the leisured lifestyle of the
well-to-do middle classes during the years just
before the First World War.

The Maltings

Cramond Village, Edinburgh EH4 6NU
June–Sept, Sat, Sun 2–5
Cramond Heritage Trust Secretary,
*   13 Inveralmond Drive, Edinburgh EH4 6JX*

The Museum occupies the former maltings of
the 18th-century village of Cramond. Its
display, 'The Story of Cramond', illustrates life
in the district from pre-Roman times to the 20th
century. Sections are devoted to the heyday of
the Presbyterian Church in its role as educator,
spiritual guide and arbiter of moral issues; the
work of the 18th-century improving landlords;
the brief 19th-century industrial period and the
development of the suburban village of today.

**Mid 19th-century Scottish 'saut bucket',
the figures based on Burns' poem 'Souter
Johnnie'. Edinburgh, Huntly House Museum.**

Museum of Childhood

42 High Street, Royal Mile, Edinburgh EH1 1TG
  ☎ *031 225 2424 extn 6645*
June–Sept, Mon–Sat 10–6. Oct–May, Mon–Sat
  10–5. During Edinburgh Festival, also
  Sun 2–5. Closed Christmas and New Year.
The Keeper
Ⓕ ✑

This recently extended museum was the first in
the world to be devoted solely to the history of
childhood. There are displays relating to the
health, upbringing, education and dress of
children, and important historical collections of
toys, games, books and hobbies.

Museum of Communication

James Clerk Maxwell Building, University of
  Edinburgh, Mayfield Road, Edinburgh
  EH9 3JL   ☎ *031 667 1081*
Mon–Fri 9–9; Sat, Sun 9–7. Closed Dec 23–Jan 6.
Ⓜ *C. H. C. Matthews, Curator, 22 Kinglass*
  Avenue, Bo'ness, West Lothian EH51 9QA
  ☎ *0506 824507*
Ⓕ ✎ ♿

The aim of the Museum is to outline and
illustrate the development of communication by
electrical means and to use the collections in the
teaching of science. The exhibits include radio
transmitting and receiving equipment, thermionic
valves, radiosonde, audio equipment, recorders,
hearing aids, radar, telephones and a wide range
of components. Special features include the radar
equipment used on the TSR2 aircraft and the
handmade equipment used in the course of the
research which led to the development of
wartime radar.

Museum of Lighting

59 St Stephen Street, Edinburgh EH3 5AH
  ☎ *031 556 4503*
Sat 12–6 Not suitable for group visits.
Ⓜ *Mr W. M. Purves, Curator*
Ⓕ ♦ ✎

The Museum is in a restored Georgian shop,
within Edinburgh's New Town conservation
area. The collection illustrates the progress made
in domestic, transport and industrial lighting
from the 18th century to the early 20th century.
Records relating to the manufacture of gas
mantles and oil lamp chimneys show the scale
and diversity of the Victorian lighting industry.
The Museum workshop, which restores all types
of lighting equipment, contains hand-operated
machines from the 19th-century lampmakers,
Bocock, of Mott Street, Birmingham, whose
Seahorse brand was familiar to generations of
sailors.

Museum of the Royal College of Surgeons of Edinburgh

Nicolson Street, Edinburgh EH8 9DW
  ☎ *031 556 6206*
Mon–Fri 9–5. Closed during examinations; please
  check dates locally.
Ⓜ *Mr I. S. Kirkland, Conservator*
Ⓕ

Installed in a building designed by William
Playfair in 1832, the Museum illustrates the
history of surgery in Edinburgh from 1505 to
1900. The main part of the collection consists
of surgical pathological specimens, only a third
of which are on display. The Museum also has
the Menzies Campbell Collection, the most
comprehensive dental collection in Europe.

National Gallery of Scotland

The Mound, Edinburgh EH2 2EL
  ☎ *031 556 8921*
Mon–Sat 10–5; Sun 2–5. Extended opening hours
  during Edinburgh Festival. Closed May Day,
  Dec 25, 26, Jan 1, 2.
Ⓜ *Mrs Pat Fitzgerald, Education Officer*
Ⓕ ♦ ✎ ♿

The Gallery occupies an early 19th-century neo-
classical building designed by William Playfair.
Its collection of paintings contains works dating
from the 14th century to 1900. Among the
British and European artists represented are
Gainsborough, Constable, Van Dyck, Gauguin,
El Greco, Monet, Rembrandt, Titian,
Velasquez, Degas and Cézanne. Scottish
painters are also much in evidence.

There are important collections of prints,
drawings and watercolours, including the
Vaughan bequest of Turner watercolours and
works by Dürer, Goya and Rembrandt.

Nelson Monument

Calton Hill, Edinburgh EH7 5AA
  ☎ *031 556 2716*
Apr–Sept, Mon 12.30–6; Tues–Sat 10–6.
  Oct–Mar, Mon–Sat 10–3.
Ⓜ *See Huntly House Museum*
Ⓔ ✑ ✎

The Monument, erected in 1815, and now in
the care of Edinburgh City Museums, was one of
the earliest to be completed in memory of
Nelson. It provides splendid views of Edinburgh
and its surroundings. An interesting feature is
the time-ball mechanism at the top of the
telescope-shaped tower. The ball drops daily at
1 pm, except on Sundays.

An Aeriola I valve receiver of 1922.
Edinburgh, Museum of Communication.

Palace of Holyroodhouse

Royal Mile, Edinburgh EH8 8DX
☎ 031 556 7371
Guided tours throughout the year ex. for 2 weeks
in late May and 3 weeks in late June.
Closed Dec 25, 26, Jan 1–4.
🖾 The Superintendent
Ⓔ ♿ 🏛

Work began on the Royal Palace in 1500, but it
was radically reconstructed in 1671. It is the
official residence of Her Majesty The Queen in
Scotland.
    Visitors can see the Throne Room and private
dining room, as well as the State Apartments of
Charles II and Mary, Queen of Scots. There are
portraits, tapestries and furniture of several
periods, together with needlework, some of
which was executed by members of the Royal
Family.

Royal Museum of Scotland (1)

Chambers Street, Edinburgh EH1 1JF
☎ 031 225 7534
Mon–Sat 10–5; Sun 2–5. Closed Dec 25, 26, 31,
Jan 1, 2, May 5.
🖾 Education Department
Ⓕ ♿ 🖼 ↺ ♿

Formerly known as the Royal Scottish Museum,
this is one of the most comprehensive museums
in Europe. Its building, an outstanding example
of Victorian architecture, has been described as
a 'huge elegant bird-cage of glass and iron'. The
principal displays cover the decorative arts of
the world, geology, natural history and science
and technology.
    This comprehensive collection, which is
housed in one building, includes European and
Oriental ceramics and metalwork, Egyptian art
and archaeology, arms and armour and primitive
art.
    The collections of natural history and of
fossils and minerals are of international
importance. The technology displays include
'Wylam Dilly', one of the oldest locomotives in
existence, and there is an excellent collection of
scientific instruments.

Royal Museum of Scotland (2)

Queen Street, Edinburgh EH2 1JD
☎ 031 557 3550
Mon–Sat 10–5; Sun 2–5. Closed Dec 25, 26, 31,
Jan 1, 2, May 5.
🖾 See Royal Museum of Scotland (1)
Ⓕ ♿ ↺ ♿

Until 1985 this section of the Royal Museum of
Scotland was called the National Museum of
Antiquities of Scotland. Designed by the late
Victorian architect, R. Rowand Anderson, its
building has been labelled a Venetian Gothic
Palace. Its collections include prehistoric and
Roman archaeology, coins and medals, carved
stones, as well as Stuart relics, Highland
weapons, domestic equipment, costumes and
textiles.
    The Museum shares premises with the
National Portrait Gallery.

Royal Observatory Visitor Centre

Royal Observatory, Blackford Hill, Edinburgh
    EH9 3HJ   ☎ 031 667 3321
Mon–Fri 10–4; Sat, Sun 12–5. Also open on clear
    evenings, Oct–Mar. Closed Dec 25, 26, Jan 1.
🖾 Visitor Centre
Ⓔ ♿ ♿

Blackford Hill is three miles south of the centre
of Edinburgh. The large Victorian Observatory
commands one of the finest views of the city.
    The exhibition illustrates the work of the
Observatory and explains many aspects of
modern astronomy. The displays include some
of the oldest and largest telescopes in Britain.

The Royal Scots Regimental Museum

The Castle, Edinburgh EH1 2YT
    ☎ 031 336 1761 extn 4267
Apr–Sept, Mon–Sat 9.30–4.30; Sun 11–4.30.
    Oct–Mar, Mon–Fri 9.30–4.30.
🖾 Lt. Col. J. L. Wilson Smith, Director
Ⓕ ♿ ♿

The Royal Scots is the oldest Regular Regiment
in the British Army. The Museum shows
uniforms and regimental insignia from 1633 to
the present day. There are large displays of
campaign relics, medals and decorations,
colours, pipe banners, silver, weapons,
paintings, drawings and photographs.

Russell Collection of Harpsichords and Clavichords

St Cecilia's Hall, Niddry Street, Cowgate,
    Edinburgh EH1 1LJ
    ☎ 031 667 1011 extn 4415
Wed, Sat 2–5. (Mon–Sat 10.30–12.30 during
    Edinburgh Festival.) Closed Bank Holiday and
    Edinburgh long weekends.
🖾 Fiona Donaldson, University of Edinburgh,
    Faculty of Music, Alison House, 12 Nicolson
    Square, Edinburgh EH8 9DF
Ⓔ ♿ ♿

St Cecilia's Hall was built in 1864 for the
Edinburgh Musical Society. It is the oldest
concert hall in Scotland and is still regularly
used for concerts, sometimes using instruments
from the Russell Collection, which is one of the
most important collections of early keyboard
instruments in the country. It includes
harpsichords, virginals, spinets, clavichords,
chamber organs and early pianos.

Scottish Agricultural Museum

Ingliston, Edinburgh, Lothian
    ☎ 031 333 2674 or 031 556 8921
May–Sept, Mon–Fri 10–4; Sun 2–5
🖾 Education Officer
Ⓕ ♿ ♿

The Museum occupies a purpose-designed
building on the Royal Highland Society's
showground on the A8 road to Edinburgh
airport. Its displays are based on the large
collection of the Royal Museum of Scotland and
illustrate the history of farming and rural life
throughout Scotland. In arranging the exhibits,
particular care has been taken to explain the

way in which tools and equipment were used, so that visitors can learn about processes and techniques, as well as artefacts.

Displays illustrate the changes brought about in the pattern of rural life by the Clearances and by the Crofters Act.

Scottish National Gallery of Modern Art

Belford Road, Edinburgh EH4 3DR
☎ *031 556 8921*
Mon–Sat 10–5; Sun 2–5. Extended opening during Edinburgh Festival. Closed Dec 25, 26, 31, Jan 1, 2, May Day.
◪ *See National Gallery of Scotland*
Ⓕ ♿ 🖼 🚗 🚻

The Gallery occupies the building of the former John Watson's School, designed by William Burn in the neo-classical style in 1828. It contains the national collection of 20th-century paintings, sculpture and graphic art, including works by Derain, Matisse, Braque, Giacometti, Picasso, Hockney and Hepworth. Artists of the Scottish School are also well represented.

Scottish National Portrait Gallery

1 Queen Street, Edinburgh EH2 1JD
☎ *031 556 8921*
Mon–Sat 10–5; Sun 2–5. Extended opening during Edinburgh Festival. Closed Dec 25, 26, 31, Jan 1, 2, May Day.
◪ *See National Gallery of Scotland*
Ⓕ ♿ 🚻

The striking red sandstone building in which the Gallery is housed was completed in 1889. It is decorated internally with a painted frieze and murals by William Hole. The collection consists of portraits of people who have been influential in Scottish life from the 16th century to the present day, including Prince Charles Edward Stuart, Flora MacDonald, David Hume, Robert Burns, Sir Walter Scott, Ramsay MacDonald and Hugh MacDiarmid. Among the artists whose work is represented are Epstein, Gainsborough, Kokoschka, Lely, Raeburn, Ramsay and Reynolds.

The Gallery also has an important print collection and holds Scotland's national collection of photography, which includes 5,000 photographs by Hill and Adamson.

Scottish National War Memorial

The Castle, Edinburgh EH1 2YT
☎ *031 226 7393*
Apr–Sept, Mon–Sat 9.30–6; Sun 11–5.
Oct–Mar, Mon–Sat 9.30–5; Sun 11–5.
Closed Dec 25, 26, Jan 1–3.
◪ *Area Superintendent, Crown Square, The Castle (for visits to the castle)*
Ⓔ *Castle only* ♿ 🚗

Designed by one of the foremost architects of the day, Sir Robert Lorimer, and opened in 1927, the Memorial was established in order to pay tribute to the Scottish men and women who died in the First World War. It has subsequently been adapted to perform a similar function in respect of the Second World War. The reason

for including it here is that 200 of the country's leading artists and craftsmen were engaged to work on the Memorial, so that it can fairly be described as a highly important gallery of fine, decorative and applied art. The work includes sculptures in stone and bronze, woodcarving, stained glass, heraldry and ironwork.

Scottish Telecommunications Museum

Morningside Old Telephone Exchange, 4 Newbattle Terrace, Edinburgh EH10 4RT
By appt
◪ *Mr A. G. Carmichael, British Telecom Caledonian House, Canning Street, Edinburgh EH3 8TA* ☎ *031 222 2383*
Ⓕ 🚗

The Museum building, dating from 1925, was designed to house one of Edinburgh's first automatic telephone exchanges. The collections contain items from all over Scotland which illustrate the development of the telephone service from 1878 to the present day. The material on display includes manual and automatic exchanges – among them is a switchboard from Portree in the Isle of Skye, which was the last manual exchange in the United Kingdom – apparatus supplied to customers, overhead and underground line plant, transmission, telegraph and power equipment, tools and testers. Many of the exhibits have been restored to working order. The Museum's storage space, on the ground floor and in the basement, includes a garage, with two restored Morris Minor vans, formerly used by the telephone service.

Scottish United Services Museum

The Castle, Edinburgh EH1 2NG
☎ *031 226 6907*
Apr–Sept, Mon–Sat 9.30–6; Sun 11–5.
Oct–Mar, Mon–Sat 9.30–5; Sun 11–5.
Closed Dec 25, 26, Jan 1–3
◪ *The Keeper*
Ⓔ *Castle only* ♿ 🚗

This is Scotland's National Military Museum. Its displays relate to the Army, Navy and Air Force for all periods of their history. There is a remarkably complete series of Scottish military uniforms and fine collections of paintings, prints, weapons and equipment.

Scott Monument

East Princes Street Gardens, Edinburgh EH2 2EJ
☎ *031 225 2424 extn 6596*
Apr–Sept, Mon–Sat 9–6. Oct–Mar, Mon–Sat 9–3.
◪ *See Huntly House Museum*
Ⓔ ✏

The monument to Sir Walter Scott, built in 1846, is a prominent feature of Princes Street and those who are able to face the climb to the top are rewarded with wonderful views of Edinburgh. There is, in addition, an interesting display at the base which describes the Monument and the materials and problems involved in its construction.

Exhibition of paintings by Jack Bush at the
Talbot Rice Art Centre, Edinburgh, 1980.

Talbot Rice Art Centre

Old College, South Bridge, Edinburgh EH8 9YL
☎ *031 667 1011 extn 4308*
Mon–Fri 10–5 *(also open Sat during exhibitions).*
Closed public holidays and 8 working days
following Dec 25.
Dr Duncan Macmillan, Curator
F ☺ ☎ ♿

The Centre is housed in the Old College of the
University of Edinburgh, one of Robert Adam's
most important public buildings, completed
after Adam's death by William Playfair. The
permanent display room is devoted to the
collection of bronzes and paintings, especially
Dutch, formed by Sir James Erskine of Torrie in
the early 19th century. The large second gallery
shows mainly contemporary Scottish art, but
from time to time exhibitions are arranged
which present works from earlier periods.

University of Edinburgh Collection of Historic Musical Instruments

*Reid Concert Hall, Bristo Square, Edinburgh
EH8 9AG* ☎ *031 667 1011 extn 2573*
*Wed 3–5; Sat 10–1. During Edinburgh Festival
also open Mon–Fri 2–5.*
The Curator
F ☺ ☎

The Reid Concert Hall was built in 1860.
It contains a fine organ by Ahrends. The
collection of instruments displayed here covers
the period from the Renaissance to the present
day, and is complementary to that of the Russell
Collection of harpsichords and clavichords,
also administered by the University.

The collections are large and cover the full
range of instruments. More than 1,000 items are
on display. They include stringed instruments,
woodwind, bagpipes and brass, together with a
variety of ethnic material. The exhibits

document the history and development of the
orchestra, the wind band, and dance and brass
bands. Attention is also given to popular and
parlour music and to music in the theatre.

University of Edinburgh, Department of Archaeology Teaching Collection

*Department of Archaeology, University of
Edinburgh, 16–20 George Square, Edinburgh
EH8 9JZ* ☎ *031 667 1011 extn 2436*
By appt only, normally Mon–Fri 9.30–5.30
Mrs A. E. W. Gunson, Curator/Librarian
F ☎

The Museum is in the basements of the
department. The range of the collection is
extensive and worldwide. It includes
Palaeolithic and Mesolithic flints from Europe,
the Americas, Africa and Asia. There is a large
Near Eastern and Aegean section, covering the
Palaeolithic to Late Classical periods, with
special emphasis on the Cypriote material. The
European material illustrates all the main
prehistoric cultural periods and the British
extends from Lower Palaeolithic to Late
Medieval.

In addition, there is a considerable bone
reference collection, including both large and
small, wild and domestic animals and the only
fish bone reference collection to be found
in Scotland.

Egham

Egham Museum

*Literary Institute, High Street, Egham, Surrey
TW20 9EW*
Thurs 2–4.30; Sat 10.30–12.30, 2.30–4.30
J. E. Mills, Hon. Curator, 35 Trotsworth
Avenue, Virginia Water, Surrey
F ☺ ☎

The collections in the Museum illustrate the
archaeology and history of Egham, Thorpe and
Virginia Water. It has displays relating to
Magna Carta, which was sealed nearby at
Runnymede, and to Thomas Holloway, who
built Royal Holloway College and Holloway
Sanitorium.

The Picture Gallery

*Royal Holloway and Bedford New College, Egham
Hill, Egham, Surrey TW20 0EX*
☎ *0784 34455*
By appt only
Conference Manager
E ☺ ☎

The collection in the Gallery consists of
paintings, mostly Victorian, which were
assembled by the millionaire, Thomas
Holloway, and given to the Royal Holloway
College on its foundation.

Elgin

Elgin Museum

1 High Street, Elgin, Moray IV30 1EQ
☎ 0363 3675
Apr–mid Sept, Mon–Fri 10–4; Sat 10–12.
   Mid Sept–Mar, Sat 10–12.
🖾 Hon. Curator
🄴 ⬙ ⬤

This, the Museum of the Moray Society, is one
of the few remaining museums in Scotland
which is still run by its own founding society. It
was established in 1836 and has interesting local
collections of natural history, social history and
archaeology, including Pictish stones. Other
material on display includes ethnographical
items brought back from abroad by local people
during the 19th century, a famous collection of
fossil fish, and the Elgin Reptiles.

Eling

Eling Tide Mill

The Tollbridge, Eling, Totton, Southampton,
   Hampshire SO4 4HF   ☎ 0703 869575
Easter–Sept, Wed–Sun 10–4.
🖾 The Mill Manager
🄴 ⬙ ⬤

This is the only known productive tide mill in
Western Europe. There are two complete sets of
milling machinery, installed by Armfields of
Ringwood at the turn of the century. One set
has been restored to operating condition and
regularly produces stone-ground flour. The
unrestored machinery forms the setting of a
display illustrating the miller's life and work
at the beginning of the present century. There
are also exhibits of millwrighting, millstone
production and dressing and grain transport by
road and water.

Ellesmere Port

The Boat Museum

Dockyard Road, Ellesmere Port, South Wirral
   L65 4EF   ☎ 051 355 5017
Daily 10–5. Closed Dec 24–26 and Fri,
   Nov–Mar.
🖾 Mrs Hazel Moody, Education Officer
🄴 🍴 🖪 ♿ ⬤ ♿

Ellesmere Port is at the northern end of the
Shropshire Union Canal, at its junction with
the Manchester Ship Canal. The whole
Museum area was once a major transhipment
port, enabling cargoes to be transferred between
ocean-going craft and the smaller boats of the
British canal system.
   The Museum buildings are the old warehouses
and workshops of the Shropshire Union
transhipment dock. The core of the Museum's
collection is over 50 canal and river craft,
ranging from both narrow and wide canal boats
to tugs and ice-breakers. Restoration work takes

place at the Museum and visitors are often able
to see the traditional boat-building techniques
in progress. There are exhibitions tracing the
development of the Port of Manchester and of
Ellesmere Port as an industrial town and telling
the story of canal building, carrying on the
canals and the life of the boat people. The Pump
House contains engines which worked the
hydraulic lifting gear in the docks. These have
been restored and are regularly in steam. A row
of cottages built in 1833 have been furnished to
show how dock workers lived, from Victorian
times until the 1950s. The Energy Exhibition
follows the development and uses of energy over
the last 300 years.

Elstow

Elstow Moot Hall

Elstow, Bedfordshire   ☎ 0234 66889
Easter (or Apr 1)–Oct, Tues–Sat, Bank Holiday
   Mon 2–5; Sun 2–5.30.
🖾 Director of Leisure Services, County Hall,
   Bedford MK42 9AP   ☎ 0234 63222
🄴 ⬙ ⬤

Elstow Moot Hall is in Elstow village, just off
the old A6 road. The medieval building has
been fully restored and now contains exhibits
relating to the life and times of John Bunyan.
The timber-framed Moot Hall was originally
used to store the stalls and other equipment used
in fairs and markets on the Village Green, and
to settle disputes that came up in the course of
these activities.

Elton

Elton Hall

Elton, Peterborough, Cambridgeshire PE8 6SH
   ☎ 08324 468
Easter–Aug, Sun, Mon 2–5. May–Aug, also Wed.
   Open all Bank Holiday.
🖾 House Manager, Estate Office
🄴 🖪 ⬤ HHA

Elton Hall is eight miles west of Peterborough,
on the A605. The earliest part of the building
dates from 1475 and it has been enlarged and
remodelled several times during the following
centuries. Since 1660 it has been the home of
the Proby family. The contents represent the
tastes of successive generations of the family and
include a fine collection of European and
English paintings, ranging from works by early
Dutch and German artists to Millais and Alma
Tadema. Constable and Gainsborough are also
represented and there are a number of paintings
by Sir Joshua Reynolds, who was a friend of the
family. The French, English and Dutch
furniture is also notable.
   Elton Hall has a large and exceptionally good
library, with an important liturgical collection,
which includes Henry VIII's Prayer Book, with
handwritten inscriptions by the King himself
and by two of his wives.

Ely

The Stained Glass Museum

North Triforium, Ely Cathedral, Ely,
  Cambridgeshire
  ☎ 0353 5103/60148
Mar–Oct, Mon–Fri 10.30–4.30; Sat, Bank
  Holiday 10.30–4.30; Sun 12–3.
🖾 *The Curator*
Ⓔ ♦ 💻 ♿

The Museum is the only one in the country
which is devoted to stained glass. It was
established in 1972, with the object of rescuing
fine glass from redundant churches, and opened
to the public in 1975 in the magnificent setting
of the nave gallery, which offers spectacular
views of the Cathedral from a level not
otherwise accessible to visitors. Access is by
spiral staircase.

The exhibits include more than 60 windows
from medieval to modern times, a photographic
display of the styles and techniques of medieval
glass, and models of a modern stained glass
workshop. The collection is strongest in 19th-
century glass, with examples of work from all
the leading studios and designers. Also displayed
are selected entries from an annual competition
organised by the British Society of Master Glass-
Painters.

Enfield

Forty Hall Museum

Forty Hill, Enfield, Middlesex EN2 9HA
  ☎ 01 363 8196
Easter–Sept, Tues–Sun 10–6. Oct–Easter,
  Tues–Sun 10–5.
🖾 *Museums Officer, c/o Display Section,*
  Southgate Old Town Hall, Palmers Green,
  London N13   ☎ 01 882 8841 extn 144
Ⓕ ⊘ 💻 ♿

Forty Hall was built in 1629 and altered in the
18th century. It has interesting plasterwork of
both periods. In addition to the period
furnishings, it now contains collections of 17th
and 18th-century watercolours and drawings, as
well as rooms devoted to local history displays.

Ennis

De Valera Library and Museum

Harmony Row, Ennis, Co. Clare, Ireland
☎ 065 21616
Mon–Wed, Fri 11–9; Thurs 11–5.30. Closed
  public holidays.
🖾 *County Librarian, Clare County Library,*
  Ennis
Ⓕ ♿ ☐

The Museum occupies part of a former
Presbyterian church (1856). It contains local
history displays and a collection of paintings
donated by St Flannan's College. There is a
regular programme of temporary exhibitions.

The Annunciation, c. 1340.
Ely, The Stained Glass Museum.

Enniscorthy

County Museum

The Castle, Enniscorthy, Co. Wexford, Ireland
June–Sept, Mon–Sat 10–6; Sun 2–5.30.
  Feb–May, Oct–Nov, daily 2–5.30.
🖾 *Fintan Murphy, Hon. Secretary and Curator*
Ⓔ ⊘ ♿

The Museum is housed in an early 13th-century
castle, restored and enlarged 1900–3. The
collections illustrate the ecclesiastical,
agricultural, military, maritime and industrial
history of the town and county of Wexford.
Among the items of special interest are an
Ogham stone, and a collection of old types of
lighting equipment, including stone lamps,
rushlight holders, and hob lamps. The Maritime
Room has a number of figureheads from ships
lost off the Wexford coast.

Enniskillen

Fermanagh County Museum

Castle Barracks, Enniskillen, Co. Fermanagh,
  Northern Ireland   ☎ 0365 25050 extn 244
May–Sept, Mon–Fri 10–12.30, 2–5; Sat 2–5.
  July–Sept, Sun 2–5. Oct–Apr, Mon–Fri
  10–12.30, 2–5.
🖾 *The Curator*
Ⓕ ⊘ ♿

The 15th-century castle which houses the
Museum was built by the Maguires, the ruling
Gaelic chieftains of the locality. Later, after
the defeat of the Maguires, the castle was
refurbished for use by the English settlers. The
collections reflect the prehistory and history of
County Fermanagh, and include geology and
natural history, Iron Age material, early
Christian and medieval stone carvings, and
Belleek pottery.

Florence Court

Enniskillen, Co. Fermanagh, Northern Ireland
  ☎ 036582 249
Daily 12–6 ex. Tues
🖾 *The Administrator*
Ⓔ ♦ 💻 ♿ Ⓝ Ⓣ

Florence Court was built for the Cole family at various periods during the second half of the 18th century. It was given to the National Trust in 1953. A fire in 1955 destroyed much of the interior, but it has since been carefully restored to its 18th-century appearance. Visitors are now able to obtain an impression of the house as it was during the lifetime of William Willoughby Cole (1756–1803), who was created the 1st Earl of Enniskillen in 1789, with the drawing-room, dining-room, library and a bedroom all furnished in period style and with an excellent model of 'downstairs' as it would have been at the time.

The house is presented as the centrepiece of a self-contained rural community, with its blacksmith's forge, sawmill and ice-house all preserved.

Royal Inniskilling Fusiliers Regimental Museum

The Castle, Enniskillen, Co. Fermanagh, Northern Ireland ☎ *0365 23142*
Mon–Fri 9.30–12.30, 2–4.30. Closed Bank Holiday.
🖾 *The Curator*
Ⓔ 🖉 🖝

The Museum occupies the Old Magazine of the Castle Keep. The displays cover the history of the Regiment from 1689 to 1968, with collections of medals, weapons, uniforms, colours, badges, maps, pictures, documents and general militaria. There is a comprehensive library of books and pamphlets relating to the Regiment and to the British Army.

Eochdar

Eochdar Croft Museum

Bualadubh, Eochdar, South Uist PA81 5RQ
May–Sept, Mon–Sat 10–5 on request
🖾 *The Curator*
Ⓔ 🖝

The Museum occupies a thatched cottage typical of the Outer Hebrides. It has been appropriately furnished and contains, in addition to domestic equipment, a loom and crofting tools.

Erith

Erith Museum

Erith Library, Walnut Tree Road, Erith, Kent ☎ *0322 36582*
Mon, Wed, Sat 2–5. Closed public holidays.
🖾 *Assistant Curator, Local Studies Section, Hall Place, Bourne Road, Bexley, Kent DA5 1PQ*
Ⓕ 🖉

Erith Museum shares its collections with Bexley Museum, but its displays are devoted to the history of the town of Erith. They cover the archaeology and social history of Erith, with a reproduction of an Edwardian kitchen and a special section on local industries.

Etchingham

Haremere Hall

Etchingham, East Sussex TN19 7QJ ☎ *058081 245*
House: Bank Holiday Sun and Mon only, 2–5.30, otherwise open to pre-booked parties of 20 or more. Gardens: Easter–Sept, daily.
🖾 *House Manager*
Ⓔ ♿ ⬛ HHA

Haremere Hall is on the A265 between the villages of Etchingham and Hurst Green. It is an early 17th-century manor house and is particularly notable for its woodwork and for its collection of 18th and 19th-century furniture, and of rugs, pottery and ornaments from the Middle and Far East.

The farm, worked by Shire horses, arranges demonstrations daily at 11 and 3 between Easter and the end of September.

Eton

Eton College Natural History Museum

Eton College, Eton, Windsor, Berkshire SL4 6DB ☎ *0753 860669*
Tues, Thurs, Sun 2–5 during term-time
🖾 *Mr R. Fisher, Hon. Curator*
Ⓕ

The Museum contains modest collections of fossils and mounted birds and animals which have been built up over a considerable period of time. Its associations are essentially with the College, but it has a number of attractions for members of the general public.

The Museum of Eton Life

Eton College, Eton, Windsor, Berkshire SL4 6DB ☎ *0753 863593*
Mar 28–Oct 5, daily 10.30–5 during term time
🖾 *The Custodian*
Ⓔ 🖉

Eton College was founded by Henry VI in 1440. The Museum, in the vaulted College Hall Undercroft, tells the story of the College. There are memorabilia of former masters and Head Masters, and displays devoted to daily life and duties, food and living conditions, punishments, uniforms, and school books and equipment. Other sections include the history of rowing at the College and the Officer Training Corps.

A reconstruction of a typical study and an audio-visual presentation supplement the other items in the Museum.

Myers Museum

Eton College, Eton, Windsor, Berkshire SL4 6DB ☎ *0753 866230*
Sun 2.30–4.30 during term-time. Other times by appt.
🖾 *The Curator*
Ⓕ 🖝

The Museum is in an early 16th-century gatehouse. Its basis is the collection of Egyptian archaeology made by Major W. J. Myers between 1883 and his death in 1899, which includes a wide range of objects, dating from Predynastic times to the Coptic period. It is particularly strong in glazed ware of all periods. Of more general interest are wooden models from tombs and a well-preserved panel portrait from a mummy of the 2nd century A.D.

There are, in addition, a number of Greek vases and a large collection of prehistoric flint implements.

Evesham

Almonry Museum

Abbey Gate, Evesham, Hereford and Worcester
    WR11 4BG   ☎ 0386 6944
Good Fri–Sept, Tues, Thurs–Sat, Bank Holiday
    10–5; Sun 2–5.
ℵ Mr C. W. T. Huddy
£ ex. children ♥ ♿

The Museum is owned by Evesham Town Council and managed by the Vale of Evesham Historical Society. It occupies a half-timbered building, which forms part of the Almonry of the Benedictine Abbey at Evesham, and contains a varied collection of exhibits reflecting the history of the Vale of Evesham from prehistoric times to the present day. The exhibits include Romano-British, Anglo-Saxon and medieval items, together with material illustrating the history of the monastery. There is also a collection of agricultural implements.

The Almonry Museum, Evesham.

Ewell

Bourne Hall Museum

Spring Street, Ewell, Epsom, Surrey KT17 1UF
    ☎ 01 393 9573
Mon, Wed, Thurs 10–5; Tues, Fri 10–8;
    Sat 9.30–5
ℵ Museum Officer
F ▮ ♿ ♿

Bourne Hall Museum is basically a local history museum, but some of its collections range over a wider field. There is a celebrated collection of some of the earliest wallpapers ever made (c. 1690) and the Ann Hull Grundy Collection of costume jewellery. Other items featured in the displays include prehistoric material found in the vicinity, Victorian and more modern costumes and accessories, and early cameras and radio sets.

Exeter

The Devonshire Regiment Museum

Wyvern Barracks, Topsham Road, Exeter, Devon
    EX2 6AE   ☎ 0392 218178
Mon–Fri 9–4.30. Closed public holidays.
ℵ The Curator
F ♥ ♿

The Museum's displays illustrate the history of the Regiment. They contain uniforms, weapons, medals, photographs and documents, as well as portraits and the Regimental Colours.

Exeter Maritime Museum

The Quay, Exeter, Devon EX2 4AN
    ☎ 0392 58075
June–Sept, daily 10–6. Oct–May, daily 10–5.
    Closed Dec 25, 26.
ℵ The Director
£ ▮ ▮ ♿

The indoor displays of the Maritime Museum are in and around early 19th-century warehouses by the side of the Exeter Canal Basin. The floating exhibits are moored at the Canal Wharf. The boats on display are drawn from every continent and include British, American, Arab, Chinese and Indian craft. Amongst them is what is claimed to be the world's oldest working steamboat, the dredger designed by Isambard Kingdom Brunel for use in Bridgwater docks.

Guildhall

High Street, Exeter, Devon
    ☎ 0392 77888 (Exeter City Council)
Mon–Sat 10–5.30, except when in use for civic
    functions
ℵ See Royal Albert Memorial Museum
F ♿

The Guildhall, a 12th-century hall with a Tudor portico, is probably the oldest civic building still in use, as a Court and for meetings of the City Council. There are displays of the City's regalia and silver, and of miscellaneous items of historical significance, including the sword presented by the City to Lord Nelson and the Battle Ensign of HMS *Exeter*, sunk during the Second World War. Among the portraits are those of Princess Henrietta Maria, General Monck, and George II as Prince of Wales.

Royal Albert Memorial Museum

Queen Street, Exeter, Devon EX4 3RX
    ☎ 0392 265858
Tues–Sat 10–5.30. Closed Bank Holiday.
Ⓧ *Education Officer*
Ⓕ ⍩

The building, which dates from 1864, has been described as the best Victorian building in the city. The architect, J. Hayward, used a variety of materials in the construction, including Chudleigh limestone, Aberdeen granite, Pocombe stone, Bath stone and Bishop's Lidiard stone, producing what is in effect a museum of stone. The Museum has large and important collections of natural history, archaeology and ethnography, and there are interesting exhibits of Exeter silver, clocks and watches, lace, costumes and Devon pottery. The Fine Art galleries specialise in works by Devon artists.

St Nicholas Priory

Mint Lane, off Fore Street, Exeter, Devon
    ☎ 0392 265858
Ⓧ *See Royal Albert Memorial Museum*
Ⓔ ⍩ ⍩

The Museum consists of the 15th-century Guest Hall of the former Priory, built over a Norman undercroft. It contains period furnishings.

Eyam

Eyam Private Museum

'Le Roc', Lydgate, Eyam, Derbyshire S30 1QU
    ☎ 0433 31010
Mon Sat, by appt
Ⓧ *Clarence Daniel, Curator*
Ⓕ *donations welcome* ⍩ ⍩

Clarence Daniel's museum is concerned with the history and industries of Eyam. The collections include local fossils and minerals; prehistoric tools and weapons; lead-mining tools, with pictures and documents showing the old workings and processes; samples of silk woven in Eyam, with shuttles and tools; specimens of the rare inlaid Ashford marble; crest china relating to Derbyshire; flints, pottery and other archaeological material. A special section is devoted to the story of the plague in Eyam, 1665–6.

Visitors can also see the celebrated Hopper Ring, given by Richard III to his mistress, Anne Hopper. The ring has a central ornament which was said to be a piece of the true Cross and which sick people touched in the hope of a miracle cure, a practice which gave rise to the superstition of 'touching wood'.

Eyemouth

Eyemouth Museum

*Auld Kirk, Market Place, Eyemouth, Berwickshire
    TD14 5HE*   ☎ 0390 50678
Easter–Oct, Mon–Sat 10–6; Sun 2–6
Ⓧ *The Curator*
Ⓔ ⍩ ⍩ ⍩

The Museum was opened in 1981 as a memorial to the 189 local fishermen who lost their lives in a great storm a century earlier, in October 1881. It is housed in the Auld Kirk, built in 1812, and presents the history of the Eyemouth area and its people, with a special emphasis on the fishing industry, farming and the traditional trades and handicrafts.

The Eyemouth Tapestry is also on display. Fifteen feet long, it was made by local people between 1980 and 1982 to commemorate the Great Disaster of 1881.

Eynsford

Lullingstone Roman Villa

Eynsford, Dartford, Kent DA4 0JA
    ☎ 032286 3467
Sun 9.30–12.30
Ⓧ *Historic Buildings & Monuments Commission,
    London*   ☎ 01 211 8828
Ⓔ ⍩ ⍩

Lullingstone lies half a mile south-west of Eynsford, off the A225 road. The Museum displays and interprets a large country village, lived in during much of the period of Roman occupation. The site contains splendid mosaics.

The villa is to be re-displayed during the next few years, with a museum exhibition and re-created room settings.

Mosaic floor showing the abduction of Europa by Jupiter in the guise of a bull. Fourth century A.D. Eynsford, Lullingstone Roman Villa.

Falkirk

Falkirk Museum

15 Orchard Street, Falkirk, Stirlingshire
FK1 1RE   ☎ 0324 24911 extn 2472
Mon–Fri 10–12.30, 1.30–5; Sat 10–5.
Closed public holidays.
◙ The Curator, Museum Administration, Public
Library, Hope Street, Falkirk FK1 5AU
Ⓕ ♠ ♿

The emphasis of the Museum is on the history
of Falkirk. There is a natural history section
and displays of Dunmore pottery and local
ironfounding products.

Falkland

The Royal Palace of Falkland

Falkland, Fife   ☎ 033757 397
Easter–Sept, Mon–Sat 10–6; Sun 2–6. Oct, Sat,
Sun 2–6. (Last admission 5.15.)
◙ NTS Representative
Ⓔ ♠ ♿ [NTS]

The earliest part of the Palace, the North
Range, was burned down by Cromwell's troops,
probably by accident. The surviving East and
South Ranges were built by James IV and
James V in the late 15th and early 16th
centuries. After the failure of the 1715 Rising,
the Palace, which was Crown property,
gradually fell into disrepair, but in 1887 John
Crichton Stuart, 3rd Marquess of Bute, acquired
the Keepership and began a programme of
restoration, refurbishment and furnishing which
was continued by his son and grandson. In 1952
the National Trust for Scotland was appointed
as Deputy Keeper.

Visitors to the Palace can now obtain a good
impression of its former grandeur. In the Old
Library there is a collection of books, papers,
family photographs and miscellaneous family
possessions which has been assembled as a
memorial to the three generations of Crichton
Stuarts whose work has saved the Palace for
posterity.

The Royal Tennis Court at Falkland Palace,
built in 1539 for James V, is unique. It is the
only surviving example of the jeu carré court,
which has penthouses on only two sides, instead
of three, and four window-like apertures in the
wall at the service end. There is an active
playing group associated with the court.

Falmouth

Falmouth Art Gallery

Municipal Buildings, The Moor, Falmouth,
Cornwall TR11 2RT   ☎ 0326 313863
Mon–Fri 10–1, 2–4.30. Closed Dec 24–Jan 1.
◙ Kate Dinn, Curator
Ⓕ ♠ ☐

The permanent collection includes paintings by
Waterhouse, Munnings, Laura Knight, and
Falmouth's best-known painter, Henry Scott
Tuke (1858–1929), as well as a fine collection
of 18th and 19th-century maritime paintings
and prints. Due to a lack of exhibition space,
the permanent collection is only shown
periodically, and the programme of regularly
changed exhibitions throughout the year
comprises one-man shows by contemporary
artists, travelling exhibitions and subjects of
local interest, in addition to one exhibition of
major artistic importance each year.

Falmouth Maritime Museum

2 Bell's Court, Falmouth, Cornwall
☎ 0326 318107
Museum: daily 10–4 except Sun in winter.
Tug: Easter–Sept, Sun–Fri 10–4.
◙ Lt. Cdr. John W. Beck, Hon. Secretary,
Higher Penpol House, Mawnan Smith,
Falmouth   ☎ 0326 250507
Ⓔ ✎ ♠

The Museum was founded in 1981 to specialise
in the maritime history of Cornwall and of
South-West Cornwall in particular, using the
collection provided on permanent loan by the
Royal Cornwall Polytechnic Society as a
nucleus for the displays. The Museum is in two
parts, at 2 Bell's Court, where the Riot Act was
read to mutinous Packet Men in 1810, and on
the steam tug St Denys, which has interesting
engineering features and which worked in
Falmouth between 1929 and 1980. The displays
cover the themes of ship and boatbuilding,
trade, ports, communications – especially the
Falmouth Packet Service – safety and rescue,
wrecks and war.

**The Golden Bed of Brahan, Falkland Palace, in
which James V of Scotland died in 1542.**

Faringdon

Buscot Park

nr Faringdon, Oxfordshire SN7 8BU
    ☎ *0367 20786 (Mon–Fri)*
*Good Fri–Sept, Wed–Fri, 2nd and 4th weekends
    each month, 2–6. (Last admission 5.30.)*
▨ *Estate Office*
Ⓔ 🏭 🚻 NT

Buscot Park, a late Georgian house, now the
property of the National Trust, is noteworthy
for its furniture and its paintings. The pictures
include works by, among others, Reynolds,
Angelica Kauffmann, Gainsborough, Murillo
and Rembrandt. Sir Alexander Henderson, the
first Lord Faringdon, the Scottish industrialist
and founder of Golders Green Crematorium,
also collected paintings by the artists of his day –
Rossetti, Ford Madox Brown, Watts, Millais
and Landseer – and they are here at Buscot
Park. The drawing room has a series of wall-
paintings, *The Legend of the Briar Rose*,
by Burne-Jones, which are accompanied by late
Victorian furniture, and in the dining room
there are 1953 rococo murals, with Sheraton
period chairs from Clumber Park.

Farleigh Hungerford

Farleigh Castle

Farleigh Hungerford, Somerset   ☎ *02214 4026*
*Mar 29–Oct 14, daily 9.30–6.30.
    Oct 15–Mar 28, Mon–Sat 9.30–4, Sun 2–4.
    Closed Dec 24–26, Jan 1.*
▨ *Historic Buildings & Monuments Commission,
    Bristol*   ☎ *0272 734472*
Ⓔ 🚻 ✚

The Castle was built between 1369 and 1383.
The Outer Bailey and a Barbican to the Inner
Gatehouse were added *c.* 1425. Most of what
remains consists of ruins, but in a surviving
section there is an exhibition of arms and
armour, mainly of the Civil War period, and
fragments of medieval stained glass.

Farnham

Farnham Museum

38 West Street, Farnham, Surrey GU9 7DX
    ☎ *0252 715094*
*Tues–Sat 11–1, 2–5. Bank Holiday Mon 2–5.
    Closed Dec 25, 26.*
▨ *The Keeper*
Ⓕ 🌿 🚻

Wilmer House, the home of the Museum, was
built in 1718. It has good panelling and carving
and one of the finest cut, moulded and rubbed
brick façades in the country. The Museum tells
the story of Farnham's development from its
geological origins to the 20th century. There are
special exhibits on hop-growing and drying, on
William Cobbett, who was born in Farnham,
and on the timber roof-structure of Westminster
Hall, which was prefabricated in Farnham in
1394–5. Other interesting items in the
collection include a Georgian dolls' house and a
number of models of industrial and commercial
buildings in the district.
    One of the Museum's most treasured
possessions is the John Henry Knight archive, a
fine collection of photographs of farming and
country life in the late 19th century.

**A hand-pulled baker's van at the Old Kiln
Agricultural Museum, Tilford, near Farnham.**

Faversham

Fleur de Lis Heritage Centre

13 Preston Street, Faversham, Kent ME13 8NS
☎ 0795 534542
Easter–Oct, Mon–Wed, Fri, Sat 9.30–1, 2–4.30.
    Nov–Easter, Mon–Wed, Fri, Sat 10–1, 2–4.
    Open to parties at other times by appt.
◪ House Manager
£ ▮ ᴀ

The Centre occupies a 15th-century building,
once an inn, with interesting panelling. In 1551
a successful plot to murder Thomas Arden, a
former Mayor, was hatched here. The crime was
given dramatic form in the play Arden of
Faversham (1592). The Centre's displays trace
the development of social life, industry and
architecture in one of Britain's best-preserved
historic towns. There is a re-creation of an
Edwardian barber's shop, exhibits on the local
brick and explosives industries, and a village
automatic telephone exchange of the 1950s.
Other themes featured in the displays are hop-
picking, breweries, shipbuilding, transport, fire
services, schools, hospitals, churches, cinemas,
pubs, farmhouses and oasthouses.
    The Museum is staffed by members of the
Faversham Society and all profits are devoted to
the improvement of the town's Conservation
Area. Brochures describing the particularly
interesting parts of Faversham are available in
French, German and Dutch.

An early example of domestic labour-saving
technology – a box mangle of c. 1850 at the
Fleur de Lis Heritage Centre, Faversham.

Felbrigg

Felbrigg Hall

Felbrigg, Norwich, Norfolk NR11 8PR
☎ 026375 444
Mar 29–Oct 26, Mon, Wed, Thurs, Sat, Sun 2–6;
    Bank Holiday 1.30–5.30. Gardens from 11.
◪ The Administrator
£ ▮ ▣ ♺ ᴀ ⅙ [NT]

The Hall is near Felbrigg village, two miles
south-west of Cromer, off the A148. Built in
1620, and now a National Trust property, it is
one of the finest 17th-century houses in Norfolk
and its exterior remains substantially unaltered.
The magnificent rooms retain their original
18th-century furniture, paintings and portraits,
together with the library. The grounds contain a
restored dovecot and a walled garden.

Fethard

Fethard Folk Farm and Transport Museum

Cashel Road, Fethard, Co. Tipperary, Ireland
☎ 052 31516
May–Oct, Mon–Sat 10–6; Sun 1.30–6
◪ Margaret Mullins
£ ♺ ▣ ᴀ ⅙

The main building of the Museum was formerly
a railway goods store, dating from 1882. The
horse-drawn vehicles include carriages, hearses,
jaunting cars, traps and delivery cars. There is
also a wide range of horse-drawn agricultural
machines, together with collections of bicycles,
perambulators and wheelchairs. Among the
crafts and trades represented by tools and
equipment are those of the cobbler, cooper,
miller, coachbuilder and blacksmith.
    The Museum has an old farm kitchen, dairy
and laundry sections, pub fittings and a large
collection of domestic equipment.

Finchingfield

Finchingfield Guildhall Museum

Church Hill, Finchingfield, nr Braintree, Essex
Sat, Sun 2–5
◪ T. J. Bigmore, Curator, 'Hilltop', Bardfield
    Road, Finchingfield, nr Braintree, Essex
    CL7 4LX   ☎ 0371 810456
[F]

The Museum is in part of the town's 15th-
century Guildhall. The collections are mainly
illustrative of various aspects of local history,
with some Roman material from sites in the
area.

Fleetwood

Fleetwood Museum

Dock Street, Fleetwood, Lancashire FY7 6AQ
☎ 03917 6621
Easter–Oct, Thurs–Tues 2–5
◪ Lancashire Museum Service, Stanley Street,
    Preston PR1 4YP   ☎ 0772 264075
£ ♺ ᴀ

The Museum tells the story of Fleetwood and of
the Lancashire fishing industry. The local
history exhibits deal with the development of
the town of Fleetwood from its beginnings in
1836 to the present day. The section devoted to
the fishing industry contains models of distant
water and inshore vessels, together with original

fishing gear. A replica trawler bridge has been constructed and part of an Icelandic trawler shows the very large scale of the equipment used for deep water fishing. A large map indicates the routes to the northern fishing grounds and the types of fish caught.

The tools used for gathering and processing shellfish are on display, together with photographs of fishermen using them. There are also exhibits relating to commercial salmon fishing and to longshore fishing with set nets.

Flixton

Norfolk and Suffolk Aviation Museum

Flixton, nr Bungay, Suffolk
Apr–May and Sept–Oct, Sun, Bank Holiday,
10–5. June, Tues–Thurs 7 9pm; Sat 10 5;
Sun and Bank Holiday 10–9. July–Aug,
Tues 7–9pm; Wed, Thurs 10–5, 7–9; Sun,
Bank Holiday, 10–9.
🕴 *The Secretary*
F 🛈 ♿

The Norfolk and Suffolk Aviation Museum's collection spans over 70 years of powered flight, with an emphasis on East Anglia. In addition to 16 aircraft displayed in the open air, there is an exhibition hall, with displays devoted to general aviation history and to three special themes, 'The Great War', 'Post-War Aviation' and 'The Eighth Air Force in East Anglia'. Among the exhibits are engines and other items recovered from crash sites, uniforms and a wide range of aviation relics and mementoes.

The Museum has a large library and photographic archive.

Fochabers

Fochabers Folk Museum

Pringle Church, High Street, Fochabers, Moray
IV32 7PF ☎ *0343 820345*
May–Oct, daily 9–1, 2–6. Nov–Apr, daily 9–2,
2–5. Closed Dec 25, 26, Jan 1–3.
🕴 *Mr Gordon Christie, The Nurseries, Fochabers*
£ ♿

The Folk Museum is in a former church, built in 1900. Its displays illustrate the history of the village of Fochabers since the late 18th century and include a collection of horse gigs and carts.

Tugnet Ice House

Tugnet, Spey Bay, Fochabers, Moray IV32 7PJ
June–Sept, daily 10–4 'and at all reasonable times
outside these hours'
🕴 *Curator, Falconer Museum, Tolbooth Street,*
Forres, Moray IV36 0PH ☎ *0309 73701*
F ⊘ ♿ ♿

To reach the Museum, leave the A96 just west of Fochabers and follow the road marked 'Spey Bay' through Tugnet village almost to the River Spey, from where the Ice House is signposted.

The displays illustrate the techniques and history of commercial salmon fishing on the Spey, with models, photographs and examples

of the equipment used. The geography, wildlife, history and industries of the Lower Spey region are also featured, with a special exhibit relating to the building of wooden ships at Kingston, directly across the Spey from Tugnet.

Folkestone

Cherry Garden Upper Works

Folkestone & District Water Company, Cherry
Garden Lane, Folkestone, Kent CT19 4QB
☎ *0303 76951*
By appt
🕴 *General Manager*
F

The waterworks building at Cherry Garden contains a large collection of steam plant, including a portable loco-type boiler, an 1889 duplex non-rotative triple expansion horizontal pumping engine by James Simpson and a single cylinder steeple engine, built c. 1865. The original workshop is also on view.

Folkestone Museum and Art Gallery

Grace Hill, Folkestone, Kent CT20 1HD
☎ *0303 57583*
Mon, Tues, Thurs, Fri 9–5.30; Wed 9–1;
Sat 9–5. Closed public holidays.
🕴 *Miss M. Winsch, Kent County Museum*
Service, West Malling, Kent ME19 6QE
☎ *0732 845845 extn 2129*
F ♿

The Museum dates back to the formation of the Folkestone Natural History Society in 1868. The Society's collection of fossils was given temporary accommodation in the Sessions House and in 1888 the present building, designed to house both a museum and a library, was opened. The present collections contain local chalk fossils; natural history, including geology, birds, plants, shells and insects, especially butterflies; Iron Age, Roman and Saxon finds from the area, especially from Dover Hill Saxon cemetery and from Folkestone Roman Villa; objects illustrating the history of the town and its harbour; paintings, drawings, prints, china and coins.

Forfar

Forfar Museum and Art Gallery

Meffan Institute, Forfar, Angus DD8 1BB
☎ *0307 63468*
Mon–Wed, Fri 9.30–7; Thur, Sat 9–5
🕴 *District Curator, Montrose Museum and Art*
Gallery, Panmure Place, Montrose
DD10 8HE ☎ *0674 73232*
F ♿

Among the exhibits of interest in this district museum are the Burgh regalia, local archaeological items and material relating to the flax industry, which was important here in the 19th century. The Art Gallery displays paintings by J. W. Herald and other local artists.

1873 Hick Hargreaves Engine. Industrial Steam Museum, Forncett St Mary.

Forncett St Mary

Forncett Industrial Steam Museum

Low Road, Forncett St Mary, Norwich, Norfolk
NR16 1JJ   ☎ 050841 8277
May–Oct, Sun 2–6. Spring and Late Summer
Bank Holidays 2–6. Other times by appt.
Steam Day: 1st Sun in month, every Sun in
Aug and Bank Holiday.
⚑ Dr R. N. Francis
Ⓔ ⬜ ⬛ ⇜

Forncett St Mary lies off the B1135
Wymondham to Bungay road. The village is
signposted at Hapton. The Museum has a
collection of 18 stationary steam engines,
rescued from locations where they could no
longer be kept. It includes one of the engines
which used to open Tower Bridge and an 85-ton
triple expansion inverted vertical engine from
Dover Waterworks. Nine of the engines can be
seen running on Steam Days, the oldest being
an 1873 single cylinder Corliss valve gear
engine, built by Hick Hargreaves.

Forres

Falconer Museum

Tolbooth Street, Forres, Moray IV36 0PH
☎ 0309 73701
Mid May–June and Sept, Mon–Sat 9.30–5.30.
July–Aug, Mon–Sat 9.30–6.30; Sun 2–6.30.
Oct–mid May, Mon–Fri 10–4.30.
Closed public holidays.
⚑ District Curator
Ⓕ ⬤ ⇜

The Museum is named after two brothers who
were born in the town and who were co-
founders of the Museum, Alexander Falconer, a
Calcutta merchant, and Hugh Falconer, one of
the leading geologists and botanists of his time,
whose researches led to the establishment of tea-

growing in India. The Museum building,
completed in 1871, is an important element in
the Forres landscape. It has sculptured heads of
famous scientists, together with that of Sir
Walter Scott, above the windows and door
outside.

The displays feature aspects of the local and
natural history of the Forres area, with changing
thematic exhibitions. There are collections of
local birds and mammals, an important group of
local fish fossils, archaeological items from the
Culbin Sands, and a display on Hugh Falconer.

Fort George

Regimental Museum of the Queen's Own Highlanders

Fort George, Ardersier, By Inverness,
Inverness-shire IV1 2TD
Apr–Sept, Mon–Fri 10–6; Sun 2–6. Oct–Mar,
Mon–Fri 10–4. Closed Good Fri–Easter Mon,
Dec 24–26, Jan 1.
⚑ Regimental Headquarters, Queen's Own
Highlanders, Cameron Barracks, Inverness
IV2 3XD   ☎ 0463 224380
Ⓔ ⇜

Fort George lies off the A96, about 13 miles east
of Inverness. The Museum is in what was
formerly the Lieutenant Governor's house of the
historic 18th-century fort. Its collections of
uniforms, medals, colours, pipe banners,
paintings, documents and photographs cover
the period from 1778 to the present day.

Fort William

West Highland Museum

Cameron Square, Fort William, Inverness-shire
PH33 6AJ   ☎ 0397 2169
June and Sept, Mon–Sat 9.30–5.30. July–Aug,
Mon–Sat 9.30–9. Oct–May, Mon–Sat 10–1,
2–5. Closed Dec 25, 26, Jan 1, 2.
⚑ The Curator
Ⓔ ⇜

The Museum occupies one of the oldest
buildings in Fort William, formerly a branch of
the British Linen Bank. The exhibits illustrate
many aspects of the district and its history,
including geology, wildlife, Fort William as a
garrison town, and the Ben Nevis weather
observatory. There is a reconstruction of the
interior of a crofter's house, together with
displays of tartans and maps and a collection of
items connected with the 1745 Jacobite rising,
including the anamorphic painting of Prince
Charles Edward Stuart, known as the Secret
Portrait. When first seen it appears to be a
meaningless blur of paint, but the panel reveals
a perfect likeness when reflected in a polished
cylinder.

Framlingham

Lanman Museum

Framlingham Castle, Framlingham, Suffolk
IP13 8BP   ☎ *0728 723330*
Easter–Sept, Mon–Thurs, Sat 10–12.30, 2–4.30;
Sun 2–4.30
⚅ *Mr S. G. Gray, Hon. Curator, 16 Market*
Hill, Framlingham, Suffolk IP13 9AN
Ⓔ ⬗ ☛ ☐

The Museum occupies one large room in
Framlingham Castle. The collection consists of
objects of historical, educational or artistic
interest connected with the town of
Framlingham and the surrounding villages.
The Museum is organised on a basis of
changing exhibitions.

390th Bomb Group Memorial Air Museum

Parham Airfield, nr Framlingham, Woodbridge,
Suffolk
Last Sun in March–Oct, Sun and Bank Holiday
1–6
⚅ *Mr I. L. Hawkins (Secretary/Treasurer),*
29 Birch Avenue, Bacton, Stowmarket, Suffolk
IP14 4NT   ☎ *0449 781561*
Ⓕ ⬗ ☛

The Museum is reached by turning east off the
A12 opposite Glenham Hall. Located in a
former Second World War airfield control
tower built in 1942, it is a memorial to the
members of the 390th Bombardment Group of
the U.S. 8th Army Air Force, based at
Framlingham from 1943 to 1945, and to other
Allied airmen operating from bases in East
Anglia during the Second World War.
  The collections include engines and other
components of crashed U.S. and Allied aircraft,
and many photographs and mementoes of the
wartime life of both airmen and civilians. There
are reconstructions of a radio hut and of a
wartime office.

Freshwater

Medina Camera Museum

Golden Hill Fort, Freshwater, Isle of Wight
  ☎ *0983 753380*
Late Mar–Oct, daily 10–6. Open during Christmas
period, 10–4. Check locally for spring opening
date.
⚅ *Mr Ken Robson, Director, Golden Hill Fort*
Enterprises Ltd, 3 Mengham Road, Hayling
Island, Hampshire PO11 9BG
Ⓔ ⬗ ☛ ☛ ⬥

The Museum is in the former powder magazine
of the Golden Hill Fort complex, built during
the 1860s. It is based on a collection of more
than 60 cameras, taking both still and moving
pictures, dating from the 1880s. It includes
many rare examples.
  The Museum is dedicated to one of the
pioneers of photography, Julia Margaret
Cameron, who established her home at
Freshwater Bay in 1860.

Frome

Frome Museum

1 North Parade, Frome, Somerset BA11 1AT
Mon–Sat 10–5
⚅ *Hon. Curator*
Ⓔ ⬗ ☛ ☛

The building occupied by the Museum was built
in 1868 as Frome Scientific and Literary
Institute. The displays are in the course of
development. Those now on view provide an
outline of life in the area since prehistoric times.
At present there is an emphasis on the history of
local industries, including cloth-making, metal-
casting, printing and quarrying. There is a good
local geological section, and a library and
archive of books and documents relating to the
district.

Fyvie

Fyvie Castle

Fyvie, Banff and Buchan AB5 8JS   ☎ *06516 266*
May–Sept, daily 11–6 (last admission 5.15).
  Grounds: all year round, daily 9.30–sunset.
⚅ *Mrs Jean Gowans*
Ⓔ ☛ ☛ ⬥ [NTS]

The oldest part of Fyvie, now a National Trust
for Scotland property, dates from the 13th
century and is a magnificent example of Scottish
baronial architecture. The special attractions
include the great wheel staircase and the 17th-
century morning room, with its contemporary
plasterwork and panelling and a lush Edwardian
interior created by the first Lord Leith. The
portraits include works by Raeburn, Ramsay,
Gainsborough, Opie and Hoppner and there are
also 16th-century tapestries and a collection
of weapons and armour.

'General William Gordon' by Batoni, 1766.
Fyvie Castle.

G

Gainsborough

Gainsborough Old Hall

Parnell Street, Gainsborough, Lincolnshire
DN21 2NB   ☎ *0427 2669*
Mon–Sat 10–5; Sun (Easter–Oct only) 2–5.
   Evening parties by appt. Closed Good Fri,
   Dec 25, Jan 1.
🖾 *Mrs Jenny Vernon*
🅴 ⬗ 🖻 ↩

Gainsborough Old Hall is a 15th-century timbered manor house. Richard III and Henry VIII stayed here, the latter in 1520 when his future wife, Catherine Parr, was also a visitor. After it ceased to be a private residence in 1720, it became tenements, a public house, a linen factory, a theatre, a church and a corn exchange. The modern restoration began in 1949 and in 1979 Lincolnshire County Council assumed responsibility for the building. The rooms are now being reinstated to illustrate daily life at various periods during the Old Hall's varied history. There are permanent displays on Richard III and on the medieval wool trade, and a collection of 17th-century portraits of members of the Hickman family.

Richmond Park Exhibition Centre

Richmond Park House, Morton Terrace,
   Gainsborough, Lincolnshire
Daily during daylight. Closed Good Fri,
   Dec 25, 26, Jan 1.
🖾 *See Gainsborough Old Hall*
🅵 ☐

Richmond Park House was built in the mid-Victorian period. It is used mainly for temporary exhibitions, but there is a small collection of local social history material and one room is furnished and displayed as a Victorian parlour.

Gairloch

Gairloch Heritage Museum

Achtercairn, Gairloch, Ross-shire ☎ *044583 243*
Easter–Sept, Mon–Sat 10–5
🖾 *W. R. M. Murdoch, Aird House, Badachro,*
   Gairloch IV21 2AB
🅴 ⬗ 🖻 ↩

The Museum, which occupies a former farmstead, has been created in order to illustrate and interpret life in the parish of Gairloch since prehistoric times and to conserve items of interest from within the area. The displays, which are accompanied by leaflets on special subjects, cover archaeology, wildlife, agriculture, dairying, wood processing and the domestic arts. Among the exhibits of particular interest are a Pictish carved stone and the interior of a croft house, a schoolroom and a

shop. Outside the Museum building are two restored fishing boats, both built locally early in the present century.

Galway

Galway City Museum

Spanish Arch, Galway, Co. Galway, Ireland
Whit Sat–Sept, Mon–Sat 10–1, 2.30–5.30;
   Sun 2.30–5.30
🖾 *Hon. Curator*
🅴 ⬗ ↩

Galway became a flourishing Anglo-Norman colony in the 14th century and has subsequently been renowned both as a trading and as an educational centre. The Museum, in a building adjoining the Spanish Arch on the old town wall, was the former home of the sculptress, Clare Sheridan, and contains items relating to the history of the town and to its notabilities.

The James Mitchell Museum

Department of Geology, University College,
   Galway, Co. Galway, Ireland
      ☎ *091 24411 extn 126/351*
Mon–Fri 9–5 during term-time. Other times
   by appt.
🖾 *Dr D. A. T. Harper*
🅵 ↩ ☐

The Museum is contemporary with the opening of the College in 1849 and much of its original Victorian character has been preserved. The core of the collection is William King's type and figured material of the Permian fossils of England, which was in the Museum from the beginning and which he supplemented throughout the tenure of his Chair (1849–83). There are now some 2,500 fossil invertebrate, vertebrate and plant specimens, and 2,000 mineral and rock specimens from locations throughout the world.

Gateshead

Bowes Railway Heritage Museum

Springwell Village, Gateshead, Tyne and Wear
   NE9 7QJ   ☎ *091416 1847*
Operating days: please check locally for dates.
   Static: Easter–Oct, daily 9.30–3.30.
🖾 *Bill and Georgina Craddock, 112 Donvale*
   Road, District 2, Washington NE37 1DN
🅴 *train rides only* 🅸 ⬗ 🖻 ↩

The Bowes Railway, called the Pontop and Jarrow Railway until 1932, was one of a number of colliery railways developed in North-East England to carry coal to the rivers for shipment. Its oldest section was designed by George Stephenson in 1826. It had seven rope-worked and three locomotive sections and for a time it ran its own passenger service. In 1976 Tyne and Wear District Council bought the one-and-a-quarter miles between Blackfell Bank Head and Springwell Bank Head, together with the link to the Pelaw Main Railway, the engine houses, line-side cabins and well over 40 of the Railway's historic wagons. It later acquired the 19th-century engineering and wagon shops, together with much of their machinery. Now a scheduled monument, the Bowes Railway, the world's only standard-gauge rope-hauled railway, is being restored to its original condition.

A number of diesel and steam locomotives and a range of rolling stock is on display. On operating days passenger trains and the rope haulage system are in use.

Shipley Art Gallery

Prince Consort Road, Gateshead, Tyne and Wear NE8 4JB ☎ *091 4771495*
Mon–Fri 10–5.30; Sat 10–4.30; Sun 2–5.
Closed Good Fri, Dec 25, 26, Jan 1.
Ⓜ *Gwen Massey* ☎ *0632 327734*
Ⓕ ⬙ ⬛ ⬛ ▢

The Gallery, in its typical turn-of-the-century classical building, has collections of 16th and 17th-century North European and Italian paintings and 19th-century British paintings, shown by means of changing displays. Its collection of contemporary crafts is the largest in the North of England and there are about 10 exhibitions of traditional and contemporary crafts each year. The Gallery organises year-round training courses in craft skills and is the specialist centre for teaching the art of Durham quilting.

Gillingham

Gillingham Local History Museum

Church Walk, Gillingham, Dorset
Apr–Sept, Fri; Sat 3–5. Other times by appt.
Ⓜ *Mr P. J. Crocker, Clay Pitts, School Road, Gillingham SP8 4QR* ☎ *07476 2173*
Ⓕ ⬛

A pair of 200-year-old cottages has been converted to form the Museum building. The displays are of objects which have been used or manufactured locally or which illustrate themes of local interest, ranging from fossils to life during the Second World War. Special attention is given to the history of the local silk industry.

Girvan

McKechnie Institute

Dalrymple Street, Girvan, Ayrshire KA26 9AE
☎ *0465 3643*
Tues–Sat 10–4. July–Aug, also Mon 11–4.
Ⓜ *Hon. Curator*
Ⓕ ⬙ ⬛

The Museum is housed in the former subscription library, constructed in 1888 in the Scottish Baronial style. The art section includes late Victorian Scottish landscapes and contemporary works by local artists. Among the exhibits in the Museum are relics recovered in

1977 by the Girvan Sub-Aqua Club from the S.S. *Wallachia*, a cargo ship sunk off Argyll in 1895. There is also a display of railway equipment and winkies, glessies and early nets recall the days of ringnet fishing, once important in the area.

Penkill Castle

Girvan, Ayrshire KA26 9TQ ☎ *046587 261*
By appt
Ⓜ *The Secretary*
Ⓔ *includes tour and lunch* ⬙ ⬛

This imposing 15th-century castle was modified and extended during succeeding centuries. It had close associations with the Pre-Raphaelite movement. Dante Gabriel Rossetti and his sister, Christina, both wrote poems here. The Castle contains noteworthy tapestries and paintings, together with 17th and 18th-century furniture.

Gisburn

Tom Varley's Museum of Steam

Todber Caravan Park, Gisburn, nr Clitheroe, Lancashire ☎ *02005 332*
Daily 10–5. Closed Dec 25, 26, Jan 1.
Ⓜ *Tom Varley*
Ⓔ ⬙ ⬛

The Museum concentrates on Burrell and Aveling fairground steam engines, but the collection covers a wider range and includes an 1862 Aveling and an 1872 Howard, which are among the oldest traction engines in existence. There is a 115-key Verbeeck Centenary steam organ and the only known Foster steam wagon, now under restoration.

Glamis

Angus Folk Museum

Kirkwynd, Glamis, Angus DD8 1RT
☎ *030784 288*
Easter weekend, then May–Sept, daily 12–5
Ⓜ *Mrs I. MacKnight, Lochmill House, Glengate, Kirriemuir, Angus* ☎ *0575 72292*
Ⓔ ⬙ ⬛ [NTS]

The Angus Folk Collection, one of the finest in Scotland, is housed in Kirkwynd Cottages, a row of six early 19th-century cottages with stone-slabbed roofs, restored and adapted to museum purposes by the National Trust for Scotland. The collection illustrates many aspects of country life in the past and includes a Victorian parlour and a cottar house kitchen with box beds. The old local craft of linen weaving is represented by a hand-loom and spinning-wheel, and their accessories, and by many examples of the cloth produced.

The displays also include a wide range of domestic equipment, collected from all parts of the County of Angus and a good collection of local maps, from the 17th century onwards.

Glamis Castle

Glamis, Angus DD8 1RJ   ☎ *030784 242*
Easter weekend, then May–Sept, Sun–Fri 1–5.30
⋈ *The Secretary*
Ⓔ ⛫ 🅿 ♿ Ⓗ ⬚HHA⬚

The property of the Earl of Strathmore and the
family home of Queen Elizabeth the Queen
Mother, the Castle is a mile from Glamis, off
the A94 south of Forfar. It is mostly 17th
century, with some rebuilding after a fire in
1800. There are tapestries, paintings and
armour and numerous memorabilia of the
Queen Mother.

The Italian Garden, laid out in the present
century, is open to the public.

Glandford

Shell Museum

Glandford, Holt, Norfolk NR25 7JR
        ☎ *0263 740081*
Mon–Thurs 10–12.30, 2–4.30; Fri, Sat 2–4.30
⋈ *Mrs Sheila Pufahl, Church House, Glandford*
Ⓔ ⬚ ♿

Glandford is on the B1156 Holt to Blakeney
road. The Museum, in the centre of the village
near the church, was built in 1915 by Sir Alfred
Jodrell of Bayfield Hall, to house the collection
of shells which he had formed over a period of
60 years and which came from all over the
world. The collection has been constantly
added to since Sir Alfred's death.

The displays also include jewels, pottery and
specimens of agate ware.

**Milanese armour, about 1455.
Glasgow, Art Gallery and Museum.**

Glasgow

Art Gallery and Museum

Kelvingrove, Glasgow G3 8AG
        ☎ *041 357 3929*
Mon–Sat 10–5; Sun 2–5. Closed Dec 25, Jan 1.
⋈ *Education Officer* ☎ *041 334 1131*
Ⓕ ⛫ 🅿 ♿ &

The Museum, the headquarters of the City of
Glasgow's Museums and Art Galleries
Department, was opened in 1902. The
geological gallery contains a stratigraphic
treatment of fossils, with an emphasis on the
eras of greatest significance in Scotland, as well
as a selection of minerals and rocks. An entire
room is devoted to birds, some of them, such as
the Moa, Huia, Quetzal and Great Auk, now
very rare or extinct. The habitats which make
up typical Scottish scenes are illustrated by
plants and animals in naturalistic settings.

In the archaeological gallery the main theme
is Scottish prehistory, together with selections
from the Egyptian and Cypriot collection. An
adjacent gallery displays firearms, Scottish
weapons and militaria and the internationally
important collection of European arms and
armour. The ethnography gallery shows a
selection from the Museum's large collection
illustrating non-European cultures. The North
American Indian, South Pacific and Japanese
exhibits are particularly noteworthy.

The department of decorative art has silver,
metalwork, jewellery, ceramics, glass, furniture,
costumes and textiles, mostly of Western
European origin and covering the period from
the Renaissance to the present day. Kelvingrove
has the finest civic collection of European
paintings in Britain, the main strengths being in
Dutch 17th-century and French 19th to early
20th-century paintings, and in Scottish art in all
media from the 17th century to the present day.

The Burrell Collection

Pollok Country Park, 2060 Pollokshaws Road,
        Glasgow G43 1AT
        ☎ *041 649 7151*
Mon–Sat 10–5; Sun 2–5. Closed Dec 25, Jan 1.
⋈ *See Art Gallery and Museum*
Ⓕ ⛫ 🅿 ♿ &

The Burrell Collection was presented to the
City of Glasgow in 1944 by Sir William and
Lady Burrell. Sir William was a wealthy
shipowner with a longstanding passion for art
collecting. The collection he formed contains
more than 8,000 items and covers a remarkable
range. It includes antiquities from Iraq, Egypt,
Greece and Italy, Oriental ceramics, jades and
bronzes, and 18th and 19th-century Japanese
prints. There is a fine collection of carpets, rugs,
ceramics and metalwork from the Near East.

Sir William amassed a comprehensive
collection of North European decorative arts,
particularly of the 14th to 17th centuries. The
tapestries and stained glass are world-famous.
The European paintings range from the 15th
century to the early 20th, French 19th-century
artists being particularly well represented.

The distinguished new building which houses the Collection incorporates medieval architectural stonework in the structure.

Camphill House Museum of Costume

*Queen's Park, Pollokshaws Road, Glasgow
G41 2EW* ☎ *041 632 1350*
By appt
◪ *Assistant Keeper in Charge*
Ⓕ ↩

Although the collection and reference library are already accessible to students and researchers by appointment, Camphill House is not yet open to the public.

The Museum houses one of the largest costume collections in Scotland. The emphasis is on clothing made and worn in the West of Scotland, but there are significant holdings of high fashion items from elsewhere, included mainly for purposes of comparison.

Collins Gallery

*University of Strathclyde, 22 Richmond Street,
Glasgow G1 1XQ* ☎ *041 552 4400 extn 2416*
Mon–Fri 10–5; Sat 12–4. Closed Bank Holiday.
◪ *Tessa Jackson, Curator*
Ⓕ ◿ ☐

The Gallery's collections mostly illustrate the history of the University of Strathclyde, which was founded in 1796. There is, in addition, a collection of paintings, prints, watercolours and drawings by contemporary British artists. An important historical collection of scientific instruments, including mining equipment and photographic apparatus, is housed by the Gallery and is also displayed around the campus of the University.

Glasgow School of Art

167 Renfrew Street, Glasgow G3 6RQ
☎ *041 332 9797*
*Mon–Fri 10–12, 2–5. Closed Easter week,
Christmas week & Bank Holiday. Parties must
book in advance.*
◪ *The Director*
Ⓔ ▮

The School of Art is the most important building designed by the celebrated Glasgow architect, Charles Rennie Mackintosh. It contains a substantial collection of furniture, watercolours and architectural designs and drawings by Mackintosh. All the principal rooms are open to the public.

Haggs Castle Museum

100 St Andrew's Drive, Glasgow G41 4RB
☎ *041 427 2725*
Mon–Sat 10–5; Sun 2–5. Closed Dec 25, Jan 1.
◪ *Assistant Keeper in Charge*
Ⓕ ◿ ↩

Haggs Castle, built in 1585, was the residence of the Maxwell family until 1732, when it was abandoned and fell into ruins. Restored in the 19th century, it became a museum in 1976. The displays are designed to make history more interesting to children. They include a reconstructed 16th-century kitchen, a Victorian nursery and a Mary, Queen of Scots exhibition room. The Museum has a fine collection of dolls and toys.

The main emphasis of the Museum is on learning-by-doing and activity sessions, ranging from making butter and cheese to weaving and sewing rag dolls, which form an important part of group visits. An 18th-century cottage next to the Castle has been converted into workshops for these sessions.

Hunterian Art Gallery

*University of Glasgow, 82 Hillhead Street,
Glasgow* ☎ *041 330 5431*
*Main Gallery: Mon–Fri 9.30–5; Sat 9.30–1.
Mackintosh House: Mon–Fri 9.30–12.30,
1.30–5; Sat 9.30–1. Closed public holidays.
No charge except for admission to Mackintosh
House on weekday afternoons and Sat.*
◪ *The Secretary*
Ⓔ ◿ ↩

This purpose-built Gallery, opened in 1980, has the largest permanent exhibition anywhere of the works of J. M. Whistler, including paintings, prints and drawings. There is also a collection of furniture, silver and porcelain which belonged to him. The Gallery's paintings include works by Rembrandt, Chardin, Reynolds and Pissarro, with a strong representation of 19th and 20th century Scottish artists. The print collection, the largest in Scotland, contains over 15,000 items, by artists ranging from Dürer to Hockney. Contemporary sculpture is shown in the Sculpture Courtyard.

A separate section of the Gallery displays furniture and designs by Charles Rennie Mackintosh and includes the Mackintosh House, a reconstruction of the principal rooms from the architect's Glasgow home, now demolished, at 78 Southpark Avenue, containing his furniture and decorative schemes.

**Athenian tetradrachm.
Glasgow, Hunterian Museum.**

Hunterian Museum

University of Glasgow, University Avenue,
*   Glasgow G12 8QQ*
   ☎ *041 339 8855 extn 4221*
Mon–Fri 9.30–5; Sat 9.30–1. Closed some public
*   holidays.*
Ⓚ *Anne Tynan Extn 4213*
Ⓕ 🏛 💺 🚗

The Museum is housed within the University's
1870 neo-Gothic buildings, designed by Sir
George Gilbert Scott. It was opened to the
public to display the extensive collections of the
celebrated physician and anatomist, Dr William
Hunter, which had been bequeathed to the
University. The present sections relate to
geology – rocks, minerals and fossils, including
the 'Bearsden shark'; archaeology – early
civilisations in Scotland, up to the Roman
occupation; ethnography – material brought
back from Captain Cook's voyages; Greek,
Roman and Scottish coins.

Lillie Art Gallery

Station Road, Milngavie, Glasgow G62 8AQ
   ☎ *041 956 2351 extn 226*
Tues–Fri 11–5, 7–9; Sat, Sun 2–5.
*   Closed Dec 25, 26, Jan 1, 2.*
Ⓚ *Mrs E. M. Dent, Curator*
Ⓕ 🖼 🚗 ♿ □

The Gallery is seven miles north of Glasgow, off
the A81. The permanent collections consist of
20th-century Scottish paintings and crafts.
There are, in addition, temporary exhibitions of
both historical and contemporary art, and
occasionally of archaeology and natural history.

Museum of Transport

Kelvin Hall, 1 Bunhouse Road, Glasgow G3 8DP
   ☎ *041 357 3929*
Mon–Sat 10–5; Sun 2–5. Closed Dec 25, Jan 1.
Ⓚ *See Art Gallery and Museum*
Ⓕ 🏛 💺 🚗 ♿

The Museum occupies part of the premises of
what was the largest indoor exhibition centre
outside London, converted in 1983. A wide
range of horse-drawn vehicles can be seen and
the story of the Glasgow trams is illustrated by
exhibits ranging from a horse-drawn tram to the
Cunarder. Scottish locomotives are well
represented, with King George VI's royal saloon
on loan from the National Railway Museum.
The development of shipbuilding on the Clyde
is illustrated with models of sailing ships,
merchantmen, warships and liners. A notable
feature is a reconstruction of a 1938 Glasgow
street.

People's Palace Museum

Glasgow Green, Glasgow G40 1AT
   ☎ *041 554 0223*
Mon–Sat 10–5; Sun 2–5. Closed Dec 25, Jan 1.
Ⓚ *See Art Gallery and Museum*
Ⓕ 🏛 💺 🚗

The Museum is housed in an impressive red
sandstone building in the French Renaissance
style, with large cast iron and glass winter
gardens attached. The People's Palace was
designed and built as part of a Victorian plan
to provide pleasant educational and leisure
facilities for working-class people. The displays
cover the history of Glasgow from 1175 to the
present day. The collections are arranged by
theme and include the history of the tobacco
trade, social and domestic life in Glasgow,
politics and religion, the trade unions, the
suffragettes and the women's movement. Other
themes are the rise of socialism, temperance and
drunkenness, the history of photography, life in
two World Wars, the peace movement, and
entertainments, including music hall, cinema,
football and boxing.
   The emphasis is on people as well as places,
and the Museum has portraits of famous
Glaswegians, from St Mungo to Billy Connolly.
There are special collections of Glasgow stained
glass and ceramic tiles.

Pollok House

2060 Pollokshaws Road, Glasgow G43 1AT
   ☎ *041 632 0274*
Mon–Sat 10–5; Sun 2–5. Closed Dec 25, Jan 1.
Ⓚ *See Art Gallery and Museum*
Ⓕ 🏛 💺 🚗

Pollok House, the ancestral home of the
Maxwells, is Glasgow's major surviving piece of
18th-century domestic architecture. It dates
from c. 1750, with Edwardian additions, and
was given to the City in 1966. Most of the
furniture dates from the mid 18th century to
1820. It is complemented by displays of silver
and ceramics from the collections of the
Maxwell family and the Glasgow Museums.
Pollok House has one of the finest groups of
Spanish paintings in Britain. Acquired by Sir
William Stirling Maxwell, the 9th Baronet, at a
time when Spanish art was neglected and
underrated, the collection covers the whole
field of Spanish painting from the late 16th
century onwards and includes works by El
Greco, Murillo and Goya.

Reading caravan, 1919.
Glasgow, Museum of Transport.

Provand's Lordship

3 Castle Street, Glasgow G4 0RB
☎ *041 552 8819*
Mon–Sat 10–5; Sun 2–5. Closed Dec 25, Jan 1.
☒ *See Art Gallery and Museum*
F ☗ ⌀

Provand's Lordship, the only remaining part of the medieval cathedral precinct, was built in 1471 as a manse serving the Cathedral and St Nicholas Hospital. It is the oldest house in Glasgow and, after the Cathedral, the oldest building. It now contains period displays, ranging from a reconstruction of a priest's chamber of *c.* 1500 to a sweet shop of 1900, which illustrate the different uses to which the house has been put during its long life. Mary, Queen of Scots is reputed to have stayed here, and there is a small collection of royal portraits and 17th-century Scottish furniture.

Regimental Museum of the Royal Highland Fusiliers

Regimental Headquarters, The Royal Highland
Fusiliers, 518 Sauchiehall Street, Glasgow
G2 3LW ☎ *041 332 0961*
Mon–Thurs 9–4.30; Fri 9–4. Closed Dec 25, 26,
Jan 1, public holidays.
☒ *Major D. I. A. Mack*
F ⌀ ⌀

The Royal Highland Fusiliers is the Glasgow and Ayrshire infantry regiment, taking its present title in 1959, when the Royal Scots Fusiliers and the Highland Light Infantry were amalgamated. The Museum's displays of uniforms, weapons, pictures, medals, mementoes, models and other militaria illustrate the history of the Regiment from 1678 to the present day.

Rutherglen Museum

King Street, Rutherglen, Glasgow G73 1DQ
☎ *041 647 0837*
Mon–Sat 10–5; Sun 2–5. Closed Dec 25, Jan 1.
☒ *Alistair R. Gordon, Assistant Keeper in Charge*
F ⌀ ⌀ ☐

The Museum is concerned with local history. Its collections illustrate the civic, ecclesiastical, industrial and social history of the former Royal Burgh of Rutherglen from its foundation in the 12th century to the present day. Of particular interest are a late 14th-century statue of St Eligius, the patron saint of jewellers; examples of the products of the Caledonian Pottery, mainly from its years at Rutherglen; models of ships built at the Rutherglen yard of T. B. Seath and Co.; and paintings and photographs of the Burgh from 1860 onwards.

The displays are changed periodically, to give visitors full opportunity to appreciate the range and variety of the collections.

Springburn Museum and Exhibition Centre

179 Ayr Street, Glasgow G21 4BW
☎ *041 557 1405*
Mon–Fri 10.30–5; Sat 10–1, Sun & public
holidays 2–5. Closed Dec 24–26, Jan 1–2.
☒ *Mark O'Neill, Curator*
F ⌀ ⌀ ☐

The Museum and Exhibition Centre arranges changing exhibitions to present the social history of the area and to reflect community life at the present time. In what was once the most important place in Europe for the manufacture of railway locomotives, the lives of railway workers and their families are a central theme of the displays. Other industries, home life and housing, religion, the co-operative movement, trade unions and friendly societies are also covered.

The Tenement House

145 Buccleuch Street, Garnethill, Glasgow
G3 6QN ☎ *041 333 0183*
Easter–Oct, daily 2–5. Nov–Easter, Sat, Sun 2–4.
Weekday morning visits by groups by appt.
☒ *Lorna Hepburn*
Ⓔ [NTS]

Now the property of the National Trust for Scotland, the Tenement House was built in 1892, when Garnethill was a superior residential district in Glasgow's West End. In 1911 the first-floor flat became the home of Agnes Reid Toward, a shorthand-typist with a local shipping firm, who lived here for 54 years, part of the time with her widowed mother. The flat, consisting of a kitchen, parlour, bedroom, hall and bathroom, has changed very little since the 1890s, and visitors are able to see not only the furniture and fittings of this late Victorian home, but also many of Miss Toward's personal papers – letters, postcards, calendars, recipes, receipted bills and photographs – which give a remarkably complete picture of her life and of the period.

Provand's Lordship, the oldest house in Glasgow, built in 1471.

Glastonbury

The Gatehouse Museum

Abbey Gatehouse, Magdalen Street, Glastonbury,
     Somerset BA6 9EL   ☎ 0458 32267
June–Aug, daily 9–7.30. Sept–May, 9.30–dusk.
     Closed Dec 25.
⚑ The Custodian
£ ♿ ⊷

The Museum is in the Gatehouse of
Glastonbury Abbey. It contains a collection of
tiles, carved stonework and miscellaneous
artefacts from the site of the ruined Abbey,
together with a model showing how the Abbey
may have looked in 1539, before the
Dissolution.

Glastonbury Lake Village Museum

The Tribunal, High Street, Glastonbury, Somerset
     BA6 9DP   ☎ 0458 32949
Mar 15–Oct 15, Mon–Sat 9.30–1, 2–6.30; Sun
     2–6.30. Oct 16–Mar 14, Mon–Sat 9.30–1,
     2–4; Sun 2–4. Closed Dec 24–26, Jan 1.
⚑ Historic Buildings & Monuments Commission,
     Bristol   ☎ 0272 734472
£ ⊘ ⊷

The Tribunal, which contains the Museum, was
built in 1385 as a courthouse for the Abbots of
Glastonbury. The displays show a wide range of
objects discovered during the excavations at the
site of the Lake Village, which was occupied
between c. 250 B.C. and 50 A.D.
     There is also an exhibition of photographs of
the trackways which were constructed across the
lake area c. 8000–400 B.C. and have recently
been excavated.

Somerset Rural Life Museum

Abbey Farm, Chilkwell Street, Glastonbury,
     Somerset BA6 8DB   ☎ 0458 32903
Easter–Oct, Mon–Fri 10–5; Sat, Sun 2–6.
     Nov–Easter, Mon–Fri 10–5; Sat, Sun 2.30–5.
     Closed Good Fri, Dec 25.
⚑ The Secretary
£ ♿ ⊑

The principal buildings of the Museum are the
farmhouse, built in 1896, and the magnificent
14th-century barn of Glastonbury Abbey, which
has recently been restored. The displays in the
barn and the farm buildings surrounding the
courtyard illustrate the tools and techniques of
farming in Victorian Somerset. Other exhibits
relate to such local specialities as willow-
growing, mud-horse fishing, peat-digging and
cider-making.
     The Abbey Farmhouse is devoted to the
social and domestic life of Victorian Somerset.
A special feature is a carefully researched and
documented exhibition which tells the story of a
local farmworker, John Hodges, from the cradle
to the grave. In the cellar there is a
reconstruction of a traditional farmhouse
cheese room.

Glencoe

Glencoe and North Lorn Folk Museum

Glencoe, Argyll
May 15–Sept, Mon–Sat 10–5.30
⚑ Miss B. Fairweather, Invercoe House, Glencoe
£ ⊘ ⊷

The buildings of the Museum consist of two
croft cottages, heather-thatched as they were in
the past, each with its own byre, and adjacent
outbuildings. The cottages have been made into
a single building, with displays of costumes and
accessories, weapons, Jacobite and Clan relics,
toys and old domestic equipment. One byre
contains exhibits relating to dairying and the
other to the history of the Ballachulish slate
quarries. Laundry equipment and blacksmith's
tools are shown in a modern building, and there
are also exhibits of agricultural implements and
tools and natural history items.

Glencolumbkille

Glencolumbkille Folk Museum

Glencolumbkille, Co. Donegal, Ireland
     ☎ Glencolumbkille 17
Mon–Sat 10–5; Sun 12–6
⚑ The Curator
£ ⊘ ⊑ ⊷ ♿

The Museum takes the form of a group of four
thatched cottages, each furnished to illustrate a
distinct period during the past 200 years. They
present a picture of the domestic and social life
of a village in this very rural part of Ireland at a
time when the traditional pattern of society was
being weakened by emigration and by influences
from the town.

**The medieval tithe barn of Glastonbury
Abbey, now part of the Somerset Rural Life
Museum.**

Glenealy

Robert Sheane's Agricultural Museum

Ballydowling, Glenealy, Co. Wicklow, Ireland
☎ 0404 5608
During normal working hours, or by appt
🕱 *Robert Sheane*
£ ↩

The Museum is one mile west of Glenealy village and six miles west of Wicklow. It occupies a building constructed 80 years ago as a cart shed and now converted to museum purposes. Robert Sheane runs a local agricultural machinery and equipment business and the Museum's large collections of implements, tractors and farm equipment have been built up as a hobby over the years.

Among the earlier items are an 1865 chaff cutter, a 1918 Austin tractor, in daily use until 1958, an 1870 forge-made potato fork, a pair of beam scales, used from 1850 until 1930 for weighing hay, an 1898 corn drill and an 1880 sausage maker. The collection as a whole illustrates the extreme thriftiness of the Irish farming community and the unwillingness to throw anything away until it is manifestly worn out and beyond repair.

Glenesk

Glenesk Folk Museum

The Retreat, Glenesk, Angus DD9 7YT
☎ 03567 236/254
Easter weekend, then Sun 2–6 until May 31.
June–Sept, daily 2–6.
🕱 *The Curator*
£ ▮ � ↩ □

Glenesk lies off the A966 Brechin to Fettercairn road, six miles from Brechin. The Folk Museum's collections cover all aspects of rural life in the Glenesk area, most of the items having been given or lent by local people. The Museum's policy is to change the exhibits every year whenever possible.

Glossop

Dinting Railway Centre

Dinting Lane, Glossop, Derbyshire ☎ 04574 5596
Daily 10–5. Closed Dec 25, 26.
🕱 *Mr K. J. Tait, Secretary, 73 Derby Road,*
   Heaton Moor, Stockport, Cheshire SK4 4NG
£ ▮ ▮ ♨ ↩

The Centre is a mile from Glossop, just off the A57 and adjacent to Dinting railway station. It is based on a Great Central Railway locomotive shed, which has been greatly expanded and improved, and preserves 12 steam locomotives, ranging from express passenger types to smaller industrial engines.

One locomotive is operational and gives free brake van rides on Sundays from March to October, and on Bank Holiday weekends. A variety of special events is organised.

Gloucester

City Museum and Art Gallery

Brunswick Road, Gloucester, Gloucestershire
   GL1 1HP   ☎ 0452 24131
Mon–Sat 10–5
🕱 *The Curator*
F ✐ ↩

The Museum occupies a Cotswold stone hall in Elizabethan Renaissance style, built in 1895, extended in 1898 and horizontally divided in 1957. The Art Gallery was added in 1965.

The collections are divided into three main parts. The natural history section shows the rocks, minerals and fossils of Gloucestershire, together with the birds, mammals, fish, moths, butterflies and beetles of the region, displayed with the help of many dioramas and a freshwater aquarium. Archaeology is represented by prehistoric, Roman and medieval finds from Gloucester and Gloucestershire, by Celtic metalwork, including the famous Birdlip mirror, by Anglo-Saxon sculptured cross-shafts and wooden bowls, and by a unique Norman backgammon set.

The Art Gallery has paintings by English and Continental artists, including Brueghel, Gainsborough, Lawrence, Turner, Sickert and Wilson Steer. There are also collections of 18th-century walnut furniture, barometers, long-case clocks, domestic silver, Staffordshire porcelain and Bristol blue glass.

Gloucester Folk Museum

99–103 Westgate Street, Gloucester,
   Gloucestershire GL1 2PG   ☎ 0452 26467
Mon–Sat 10–5
🕱 *Mr C. I. Morris, Deputy Curator and Keeper of*
   Local History
F ✐ ↩

The Museum is in three adjoining timber-framed buildings. 99/101 Westgate Street is a late 15th-century merchant's house and 103 is early 17th century. An annealing forge, used in making brass pins by hand, can still be seen on the second floor of 99/101.

The exhibits illustrate the social history, crafts, industries, customs and traditions of the City and County of Gloucester. On the ground floor there are displays on the horn industry, Bishop Hooper, laundry equipment, a kitchen range and equipment, glass, ceramics, pewter, toys, games, and some working models. A cow byre, Double Gloucester dairy, ironmonger's shop and wheelwright and carpenter workshops may also be seen.

The first floor offers weights, measures and balances, fishing on the River Severn, the Port of Gloucester from 1580 onwards, the Civil War in Gloucester, and the customs and traditions of the County. The top floor features the manufacture of brass pins in Gloucester, a basket-making display, a cobbler's workshop and Victorian agriculture in Gloucestershire.

Gloucestershire Regiment Museum

Custom House, 31 Commercial Road, Gloucester,
*   Gloucestershire GL1 2HE*   ☎ *0452 22682*
Mon–Fri 10–5. Open some public holidays.
🔾 *The Curator*
£ 🔾

The former Custom House, which contains the
Museum, was built in 1845 to allow Customs
and Excise control of foreign trade through
Gloucester Docks. The displays present nearly
300 years of the history of the Gloucestershire
Regiment, with collections of uniforms,
weapons, medals, models, pictures and archival
material. There is particularly comprehensive
coverage of the activities of the Regiment
during the Korean War.

The Robert Opie Collection

Albert Warehouse, Gloucester Docks, Gloucester,
*   Gloucestershire GL1 2EH*   ☎ *0452 302309*
Tues–Sun, Bank Holiday 10–6.
*   Closed Dec 25, 26. Evening visits by appt.*
🔾 *Mrs Linda Hale*
£ 🍴 🍺 🔾 ♿

The Albert Warehouse was built in 1851 to
cater for the growth in the corn trade through
Gloucester Docks. The Robert Opie Collection
comprises nearly 300,000 packaging and
promotional items from the 19th and 20th
centuries – tins, cartons, packets, display cards,
posters, boxes and bottles – and the Museum's
displays present a selection of them, reflecting
profound changes in taste, style, fashion and
social habits.

Early 20th-century packaging.
Gloucester, The Robert Opie Collection.

Transport Museum

The Old Fire Station, Bearland, Gloucester,
*   Gloucestershire*
By appt only. Transport items may be viewed from
*   the street at all times through glass doors.*
🔾 *See Gloucester Folk Museum*
F

The collection features vehicles made or used in
Gloucestershire and includes a horse-drawn

manual fire-engine of c. 1895, a horse-drawn
tram of 1880, a Gloucestershire type of farm
wagon, and three Dursley-built Pedersen cycles.

Glynceiriog

Ceiriog Memorial Institute

High Street, Glynceiriog, nr Llangollen, Clwyd
*   ☎ 069172 8811*
Apr–Sept, daily 1–6
🔾 *Miss E. M. Jones, Rhydlafar, Glynceiriog,*
*   nr Llangollen LL20 7EY*   ☎ *069172 383*
F 🔾

The Institute building has stained-glass windows
depicting eminent Welshmen. The Museum
collections also have a strongly Welsh flavour,
with portraits and busts of celebrities, a framed
copy of the American Declaration of
Independence, shown here as the work of a
Welshman, Thomas Jefferson, and a Zionist
tribute to Lloyd George, who had supported the
Jewish claim to a National Home in Palestine.
Among the other exhibits are archaeological
finds from the area and relics of the Glyn Valley
Tramway.

Glynde

Glynde Place

Glynde, Lewes, East Sussex BN8 6SS
*   ☎ 079159 248*
June–Sept, Wed, Thurs 2.15–5.30.
*   Open Easter Sun, Mon, Bank Holiday.*
🔾 *Lord Hampden*
£ 🍺 🔾

Glynde Place lies off the A27 between Lewes
and Eastbourne. Built of Sussex flint, it is a good
example of an Elizabethan manor house. The
stable block and clock tower were added during
the 18th century. The home of Viscount and
Viscountess Hampden, it has remained in the
occupation of the same family ever since it was
built. Among the more interesting contents of
the house are portraits by Hoppner, Lely and
Zoffany, bronzes by Francesco Bertos and a
collection of 18th-century needlework.

Godalming

Godalming Museum

109A High Street, Godalming, Surrey
*   GU7 1HR*
*   ☎ 0483 426510*
Tues–Sat 10–5
🔾 *Arts and Museums Division, Waverley Borough*
*   Council, The Burys, Godalming GU7 1HR*
F 🔾 🔾

The Museum has moved from its cramped
accommodation in The Pepperpot to a building
across the road which dates in part from 1400.
The collections in the Museum illustrate the

history of the town and its immediate area. There are displays of local geology and of prehistoric and Romano-British archaeology. Other exhibits deal with law and order, town government, local trades and industries and local personalities, including Sir Edwin Lutyens, Gertrude Jekyll, and James Oglethorpe, the founder of Georgia.

Golcar

Colne Valley Museum

Cliffe Ash, Golcar, Huddersfield, West Yorkshire HD7 4PY   ☎ *0484 659762*
Sat, Sun, Bank Holiday 2–5. Closed Christmas week.
⚐ *Sheila Osborn*   ☎ *0484 653331*
Ⓔ 🗇 💻 🐾 ▢

The Colne Valley Museum Trust was set up in 1970 to preserve the group of three weavers' cottages formerly known as Spring Rock. Visitors to the Museum, which is run entirely by its members on a voluntary basis, can see a loom-chamber, with working hand-looms and a spinning jenny, a weaver's living room of c. 1850, a gas-lit clogger's workshop, and two kitchen-living rooms.

Gomersal

Red House Museum

Oxford Road, Gomersal, West Yorkshire BD19 4JP   ☎ *0274 872165*
Mon–Sat 10–5; Sun 1–5
⚐ *The Curator*
Ⓕ 🗇 🐾

Red House was built in 1660 and was once used as the Gomersal Bank. Charlotte Brontë spent many weekends here and in her novel, *Shirley*, she features both the house and the family, the Taylors, who were mill-owners and who owned the house until 1920. It is now furnished in the style of the residence of a wealthy family of the 1820s, and there are displays on local history and on the way of life Red House represents. There is also a library of works relating to the Brontë family, which may be consulted.

A number of special events are held each year in the Museum grounds. They include a craft fair, brass band concerts, and an historic vehicles rally.

Goole

Goole Museum and Art Gallery

Goole Library, Market Square, Carlisle Street, Goole, North Humberside DN14 5AA   ☎ *0405 2187*
Mon–Fri 10–5; Sat 9.30–12.30, 2–4. Closed Bank Holiday.
⚐ *County Heritage Officer, Central Library, Albion Street, Kingston-upon-Hull, North Humberside HU1 3TF*   ☎ *0482 224040*
Ⓕ 🐾

The displays in Goole Museum are concerned with the growth and development of the town and port, and with the early history of the surrounding area. Special exhibits deal with inland waterways, shipping, railways and various aspects of trade and commerce. The main feature of the Art Gallery is a series of maritime paintings by the Goole artist, Reuben Chappell (1870–1940).

Gordon (Aberdeenshire)

Haddo House

Gordon, Aberdeenshire AB4 0ER   ☎ *06515 440*
May–Sept, daily 2–6. Closed 3rd weekend in May.
⚐ *Isobel Nicolson*
Ⓔ 🍴 💻 🐾 ♿ [NTS]

This elegant house, now the property of the National Trust for Scotland, dates from the early 18th century and was designed by William Adam. The Palladian-style entrance on the first floor is especially interesting. The decoration and furnishing is mainly late 19th century. Among the exhibits is a set of hand-painted porcelain, presented to the Countess of Aberdeen in 1898 by members of the Senate and the House of Commons in Canada.

Gordon (Berwickshire)

Mellerstain House

Mellerstain, Gordon, Berwickshire TD3 6LG   ☎ *057381 225*
May–Sept, Mon–Fri, Sun 12.30–5
⚐ *The Curator*
Ⓔ 🍴 💻 🐾 [HHA]

Mellerstain, designed by Robert Adam, has plasterwork ceilings and decoration of exceptionally high quality. The Library is considered to be one of Adam's finest achievements. The house contains period furniture, many good pieces of needlepoint and embroidery, and a notable art collection.

The library of Mellerstain House, Gordon.

Gort

Thoor Ballylee

Gort, Co. Galway, Ireland   ☎ 091 31436
May–Sept, daily 10–6
⊠ Miss M. Frances MacNally, Curator
£ ⬛ ⬛

Thoor Ballylee is four miles north-east of Gort,
off the Gort to Loughrea road and off the Gort
to Galway road. A 16th-century tower house,
with cottage attached, it was at one time the
property of the poet, W. B. Yeats, who lived
here during the 1920s. It was restored and
converted into a Yeats museum in 1965 and
contains some of Yeats' furniture, china and
other memorabilia, together with first and other
early editions of his work.

Gosport

Gosport Museum

Walpole Road, Gosport, Hampshire PO12 1NS
    ☎ 0705 588035
May–Sept, Tues–Sat 9.30–5.30, Sun 1–5;
    Oct–April, Tues–Sat 9.30–5.30.
⊠ Denise Cutts, Curator
F ⬤ ⬛

The Museum is an interesting turn-of-the-
century building in the Art Nouveau style.
Across the front is a stone frieze, which shows
the supposed story behind the naming of
Gosport. The panels on the east and west sides
portray other legends about the district.

Gosport Museum tells the story of Gosport
from prehistoric times to the present day. Many
aspects of its life are covered, from the local
photographic societies to crafts and industries.
There are displays illustrating the interesting
geology of the area, and the fossil exhibits
include dinosaur bones and sharks' teeth.

Royal Navy Submarine Museum and HMS Alliance

HMS Dolphin, Gosport, Hampshire PO12 2AB
    ☎ 0705 529217
Apr–Oct, daily 10 to last tour 4.30.
    Nov–Mar, daily 10 to last tour 3.30.
    Closed Dec 24, 25.
⊠ Mrs J. R. Corcoran, Museum Liaison Officer
£ ⬛ ⬛ ⬛

The Museum tells the story of submarines from
the earliest experiments to the present nuclear-
powered vessels. A special display explains how
a nuclear power-plant functions. HMS Alliance
is an interesting blend of old and new, with her
living spaces still providing reminders of
wartime austerity, but with more modern
torpedo fire-control, sensors and navigational
equipment. An introductory audio-visual
presentation explains how a submarine works
and visitors then tour the ship with retired
submariner guides.

Alliance provides a strong contrast to Britain's
first submarine, Holland 1, which was salvaged in
1982 and is now on view at the Museum.

Gott

Tingwall Agricultural Museum

2 Veensgarth, Gott, Shetland ZE2 9SB
    ☎ 059584 344
Tues, Thurs, Sat 10–1, 2–5; Wed 10–1; Sun 2–5
⊠ Jeanie Sandison
£ ⬛ ⬛

The Museum is off the A971, five miles west of
Lerwick on the main Hillswick road. It contains
exhibits illustrating the traditional life of
Shetland, with an emphasis on crofting, fishing
and domestic life. Shetland folklore evenings
are held at the Museum during the summer
months.

Tingwall is a museum on a working croft. The
buildings, which were constructed to serve a
sheep farm, date from the middle of the 19th
century. Every tour is personally guided by the
Curator.

Goudhurst

Finchcocks, Living Museum of Music

Goudhurst, Kent TN17 1HH   ☎ 0580 211702
Easter–July and Sept, Sun 2–6. Aug, Wed–Sun
    2–6. Open Bank Holiday Mon. Other times
    between Apr and Oct by appt.
⊠ Mrs Katrina Burnett
£ ⬛ ⬛ ⬛

Finchcocks, a Grade I listed building, is a
Georgian baroque house, built in 1725 and
distinguished for its brickwork. It now contains
the historical collection of keyboard instruments
formed by the pianist, Richard Burnett. Of the
70 instruments, over 30 have been restored to
full playing condition. The main body of the
collection consists of a comprehensive range of
early pianos, and there are also harpsichords,
virginals, chamber organs and barrel organs.
There is also a collection of paintings and of
furniture associated with musical performances.

Finchcocks is a musical centre of
international repute and many activities take
place here, including an annual Festival. There
are demonstration tours of the collection and
informal recitals by professional musicians
whenever the house is open to the public.

Graemeshall

Norwood Museum

Graemeshall, Holm, Orkney KW17 2RX
    ☎ 085678 217
May–Sept, Tues, Wed, Thurs, Sun 2–5, 6–8
⊠ Mrs C. Wood
£ ⬛ ⬛

The Museum, which is near the Churchill
Barriers, houses furniture from the district and
from further afield, together with objets d'art
and artefacts of historical significance. A special
feature of the Museum is the large collection of
Golden Copper lustre ware.

Grangemouth

Grangemouth Museum

Grangemouth Library, Bo'ness Road,
*   Grangemouth, Stirlingshire FK3 8AG*
Mon–Sat 2–5
🏛 *The Curator, Falkirk Museum, Hope Street,*
*   Falkirk FK1 5AU*   ☎ *0324 24911 extn 2472*
🅵 ♿

The exhibits in the Museum illustrate the
development of Sealock into the town and port
of Grangemouth. There are special displays
relating to the Forth and Clyde Canal,
including model locks, and to shipbuilding, and
the exhibits include a model of the world's first
practical steamship, the *Charlotte Dundas*.

Grantham

Belton House

Grantham, Lincolnshire NG32 2LG
☎ *0476 66116*
Apr–Oct, Wed–Sun & Bank Holiday Mon
*   1–5.30. Closed Good Fri.*
🏛 *The Administrator*
🅴 ♿ 🍴 ♿ NT

Belton House is two and a half miles north of
Grantham, on the A207. It was built between
1685 and 1689 and has been the home of the
Brownlow family ever since. The 18th-century
furniture includes work by Kent and there are
Grinling Gibbons carvings in the chapel gallery.
Among the artists represented by the paintings
in the house are Lely, Reynolds, Romney and
Rembrandt.

The library contains mementoes of Edward
VIII, to whom Lord Brownlow was Lord-in-
Waiting, and his abdication.

Belvoir Castle

nr Grantham, Lincolnshire NG32 1PD
☎ *0476 870262*
Mid March–Sept, Tues–Thurs, Sat 12–6;
*   Sun 12–7. Oct, Sun 2–6. Good Fri, 12–6.*
*   Bank Holiday Mon, 11–7.*
🏛 *Jean Clarke, Estates Office*
🅴 ♿ 🍴 ♿ HHA

Belvoir Castle, the home of the Duke of
Rutland, is seven miles from Grantham, off the
A607 Grantham to Melton Mowbray road. The
original castle was destroyed by warfare and by a
disastrous fire in 1816, and in its present form
owes much to the inspiration of Elizabeth, the
5th Duchess. The decoration, much of it by
Matthew Wyatt, and furnishings are on a
magnificent scale. The portraits include works
by Hoppner, Reynolds, Holbein – the full-
length portrait of Henry VIII – Closterman and
Dame Laura Knight, with a number of portrait
busts by Nollekens. Other artists represented in
the collection are Van Dyck, Poussin,
Gainsborough and Jan Steen.

The Castle also houses the Regimental
Museum of the 17th/21st Lancers, 'the Death or
Glory Boys'.

Grantham Museum

St Peter's Hill, Grantham, Lincolnshire
*   NG31 6PY*   ☎ *0476 68783*
May–Sept, Mon–Sat 10–5; Sun 2–5.
*   Oct–April, Tues–Sat 10–12.30, 1.30–5.*
🏛 *A. Wood*
🅴 ♿ ♿

The Museum, administered by Lincolnshire
County Council, contains displays of local
prehistoric, Roman and Saxon archaeology and
of material illustrating the history, trades and
industries of Grantham. The exhibits include
Victorian domestic equipment, craftsmen's tools
and costumes.

A special section is devoted to Sir Isaac
Newton, who attended the Grammar School in
Grantham.

Grasmere

Dove Cottage and The Grasmere and Wordsworth Museum

Town End, Grasmere, Ambleside, Cumbria
*   LA22 9SG*   ☎ *09665 544*
Apr–Sept, Mon–Sat 9.30–5.30; Sun 11–5.30.
*   Oct–Mar, Mon–Sat 10–4.30; Sun 11–4.30.*
*   Closed Nov, Jan 1, Grasmere Sports Day.*
🏛 *Information Officer*
🅴 ♿ ♿ □

Dove Cottage, a 17th-century tavern, was the
home of William Wordsworth and his sister,
Dorothy, from 1799 to 1808. After the
Wordsworths left, Thomas De Quincey and his
family lived there for more than 20 years. The
cottage has been restored, but little changed,
and is furnished with Wordsworth's possessions.
It has been open to the public since 1891.

The nearby Grasmere and Wordsworth
Museum is housed in a mid 19th-century
coachhouse and barn. It has been arranged to
illustrate Wordsworth's life and the
development of his poetry, and to place
Wordsworth within the context of the scenery
and people of the Lake District. The exhibits
include manuscripts, books, paintings,
drawings, photographs and a number of the
poet's personal possessions.

Wordsworth's home at Dove Cottage, Grasmere.

Grassington

Upper Wharfdale Folk Museum

6 The Square, Grassington, Skipton, North
   Yorkshire BD23 5HA   ☎ 0756 752800
Apr–Oct, daily 2–4.30. Nov–Mar, Sat, Sun
   2–4.30.
▨ Mr R. D. Crosthwaite, 23 Raines Meadows,
   Grassington, Skipton BD23 5NB
▣ ⌖ ▟ ▰

Housed in two cottages built for lead miners, the
collections illustrate the history of the Dales,
with a special emphasis on farming, lead mining
and domestic life.

Gravesend

Gravesham Museum

High Street, Gravesend, Kent   ☎ 0474 323159
Mon, Tues, Thurs, Fri 2–5; Sat 10–1.
   Closed public holidays.
▨ Miss J. Vale, Kent County Museum Service,
   West Malling, Kent ME19 6QE
   ☎ 0732 845845 extn 2137
▣

The Museum occupies part of Gravesend's
former Police Station. It collects and preserves
material relating to the archaeology and history
of the town of Gravesend and the Borough of
Gravesham. The displays feature some of the
finds made by members of Gravesend Historical
Society during their excavations of the
important Roman site at Springhead, as well as
a wide range of objects illustrating the everyday
life of people in Gravesend during the past 200
years.

Grays

Thurrock Local History Museum

Central Complex, Orsett Road, Grays, Essex
   RM17 5DX   ☎ 0375 33325
Mon–Fri 10–8; Sat 10–5. Closed Bank Holiday.
▨ Mr Randal Bingley, Curator
▣ ⌖ ▰ ♿

The Museum's collections relate to the
prehistoric, Romano-British and pagan Saxon
archaeology of the district and to its social,
agricultural and industrial history.

Great Ayton

Captain Cook's School Room

101 High Street, Great Ayton, Middlesbrough,
   Cleveland
Easter–Sept, daily 2–4.30. Oct, Sat, Sun 2–4.30.
   Other times by written request.
▨ Hon. Secretary   ☎ 0642 722327
▣ ⌖ ▰

Captain Cook spent his boyhood in Great
Ayton. The Museum commemorating him is in
two sections. The first, the Cook Room, is

devoted to his life and to his three voyages of
discovery. It contains some of his personal
effects, maps, charts, pictures, South Sea
islander weapons, and a collection of Mrs
Cook's crockery, including half a dinner service,
the other half of which is in the Museum of
Victoria, British Columbia.

The second section, the Ayton Room,
describes life in the village in Cook's time. It has
a model of his parents' cottage, which was taken
to Australia in 1934 and re-erected there.

Great Bardfield

Bardfield Cottage Museum

Cage Cottage, Great Bardfield, Braintree, Essex
   CM7 4ST
Easter Sat–last Sun in Sept, Sat, Sun, Bank
   Holiday Mon 2–6
▨ Mr K. F. James, Hon. Curator
   ☎ 0371 29476
▣ ⌖ ▰

The 16th-century thatched cottage which now
houses the Museum was originally built as an
almshouse by William Bendlowes, Serjeant-at-
Law (1516–84). The collections consist of
agricultural and craftsmen's tools, old domestic
equipment and local historical relics given over
the past 20 years by people living in the area.

The former local lock-up – The Cage – a
quarter of a mile away, is in the care of the
Museum and open at the same times. It is fitted
out as it was in the 19th century, with a prisoner
inside. An audio-visual system explains its
history and use.

Great Grimsby

Welholme Galleries

Welholme Road, Great Grimsby, South
   Humberside DN32 9LP
   ☎ 0472 59161 extn 402
Tues–Sat 10–5. Closed public holidays.
▨ The Curator
▣ ⌖ ▰ ♿

The building which houses the Welholme
Galleries was built in 1907 as a Congregational
church, in a style described by Pevsner as
'eccentric'. It contains some pleasant stained
glass, a mixture of Edwardian and 19th century,
salvaged from an earlier chapel. It was
converted to a museum between 1977 and 1979.

The displays reflect the history of Grimsby
and the surrounding area. There is a good
collection of ship models – steam trawlers, small
fishing craft, warships, merchant ships, and
bone models made by French prisoners of war
between 1790 and 1815. Other items in the
collections include paintings of ships at sea, a
very large archive of photographs and drawings
relating to Grimsby and Lincolnshire in the
19th and early 20th centuries, agricultural
implements, Georgian and early Victorian
police truncheons, craftsmen's tools, costumes
and domestic equipment.

Great Yarmouth

Elizabethan House Museum

4 South Quay, Great Yarmouth, Norfolk
NR30 2QH   ☎ *0493 855746*
June–Sept, Sun–Fri 10–1, 2–5.30. Oct–May,
Mon–Fri 10–1, 2–5.30. Closed Bank Holidays
Oct–May.
🔲 *The Museums Teacher*
Ⓔ ✐ 🖬 ✿

Number 4 South Quay was built in 1596. Its fine plaster ceiling, fireplaces and panelling have been preserved. The collections mainly illustrate the social and domestic history of the area. The house contains period furniture, together with paintings and glass. There are also displays of toys and games, lighting, cooking, cleaning and washing equipment. Silver from the Borough regalia is also on show.

Maritime Museum for East Anglia

Marine Parade, Great Yarmouth, Norfolk
NR30 2EN   ☎ *0493 842267*
June–Sept, Sun–Fri 10–5.30. Oct–May, Mon–Fri
10–1, 2–5.30. Closed public holidays between
Oct and May.
🔲 *See Elizabethan House Museum*
Ⓔ ✐ 🖬

The Museum building, dating from 1860, was formerly a home for shipwrecked sailors. The displays illustrate the maritime history of Norfolk and the surrounding area, including the Broads, and cover shipbuilding, merchant and naval shipping, sailors' crafts, life-saving, Lord Nelson, and inland waterways. There is a good collection of small marine engines. The local vessels preserved at the Museum include the unique Broadland racing lateener, *Maria*, built in 1827.

Old Merchant House

South Quay, Great Yarmouth, Norfolk
NR30 2QH   ☎ *0493 857900*
Apr–Sept, Mon–Fri 9.30–6, tour only
🔲 *Historic Buildings and Monuments*
  Commission, Cambridge   ☎ *0223 358911*
Ⓔ 🖬 ✿

This early 17th-century house is now arranged as a museum of decorative ironwork from the 17th to the 19th century. The collection includes fireplaces and door and wall fittings.

Tolhouse Museum

Tolhouse Street, Great Yarmouth, Norfolk
NR30 2SQ   ☎ *0493 858900*
June–Sept, Sun–Fri 10–5.30. Oct–May, Mon–Fri
10–1, 2–5.30. Closed public holidays between
Oct and May.
🔲 *See Elizabethan House Museum*
Ⓕ ✐ 🖬

The mid 13th-century Tolhouse is one of England's oldest municipal buildings. It was used as a courthouse and a gaol until the late 19th century. Four of the cells can be viewed and there are displays relating to the gaol. Other exhibits illustrate the history of the area during the Roman and medieval periods, Yarmouth's holiday industry, Zeppelin raids during the First World War and life on the home front in the Second World War. There is also a display of early bicycles and bicycling equipment.

Greenhead

Roman Army Museum

Carvoran, Greenhead, Via Carlisle, Cumbria
CA6 7JB   ☎ *06972 485*
Mar–Oct daily (check locally for opening times).
  Nov and Feb, Sat, Sun. Closed Dec–Jan.
🔲 *Mrs Patricia Birley, Curator*
Ⓔ ♟ 🖬 🍴 🖬 ♿

The Museum is close to Hadrian's Wall, adjoining the Roman fort of *Magnis*, the modern Carvoran, which once housed a cohort of Syrian archers, who formed part of the auxiliary garrison of the Wall. It contains exhibitions on the life and conditions of service of the Roman soldier, within the context of the growth and influence of the Roman Empire. Visitors can see a large-scale model of the Fort and life-sized figures displaying the armour, weapons and uniforms of both legionary and auxiliary soldiers.

Greenock

McLean Museum and Art Gallery

9 Union Street, Greenock, Renfrewshire
PA16 8JH   ☎ *0475 23741*
Mon–Sat 10–12, 1–5. Closed public holidays.
🔲 *Valerie Boa, Curator*
Ⓕ ✐

The Museum was built in 1876 by James McLean, a local timber merchant. The collections cover the fields of natural history and geology, archaeology, Egyptology, ethnography, the fine and decorative arts and local history. There are exhibits of ship and engine models and of items connected with the engineer, James Watt (1736–1819), who was born in Greenock.

Pumping engine. Greenock, McLean Museum.

Gressenhall

Norfolk Rural Life Museum

*Beech House, Gressenhall, Dereham, Norfolk
    NR20 4DR*   ☎ 0362 860563
*Early Apr–Sept, Tues–Sat 10–5; Sun 2–5.30.
    Open Bank Holiday Mon 10–5.*
◪ *The Curator*
Ⓔ ◩ ◂ ♿

The Museum is in the former House of Industry,
or workhouse, of the Mitford and Launditch
Union, a large and handsome brick building,
completed in 1777. The displays cover rural life
in Norfolk over the last 200 years, with an
emphasis on agriculture. The collection of farm
tools and implements, many of them made
locally, is one of the best in the country. There
are reconstructions of a saddler's, baker's,
wheelwright's and blacksmith's shop, and of an
old-fashioned general store and seed merchant's
shop. There is also a typical farmworker's
cottage of about 1910–20.

  Other displays feature dairying, ironfounding,
education, shoemaking, tailoring, the building
trades and other rural crafts and industries. An
engine room contains steam and oil engines,
together with items of machinery.

**Victorian seed-merchant's shop.
Gressenhall, Norfolk Rural Life Museum.**

Grouville

La Hougue Bie Museum

Grouville, Jersey, Channel Islands ☎ 0534 53823
Mar 18–Nov 2, Tues–Sun 10–5
◪ *Education Officer*
Ⓔ ◖ ◂

The Museum site is about three miles from St
Helier. Its central feature is the great mound of a
Neolithic tomb, which has two medieval
chapels on top of it, one built in the late 12th or
early 13th century, the other *c.* 1520. Within
the grounds, there are also museums devoted to
the geology and archaeology of Jersey, to the
story of the German occupation of the island, to
agricultural history, and to the Jersey Eastern
and Western Railways, the first of which closed
in 1929 and the second in 1936.

Guildford

Guildford House Gallery

155 High Street, Guildford, Surrey GU1 3AJ
        ☎ 0483 503406
Mon–Sat 10.30–4.50. Closed public holidays.
◪ *Exhibitions Officer*
Ⓕ ◖ ◂ ☐

Guildford House was built in 1660. In the 19th
century it was converted into a shop and served

in this capacity until 1956, when it was bought by the Corporation, to be used as a centre for exhibitions and educational activities.

The permanent collection is shown periodically. It contains a series of portraits by the Guildford artist, John Russell, R.A. (1745–1806), as well as craftwork and topographic and contemporary paintings. The annual temporary exhibition programme includes major touring or historical exhibitions, paintings in many media, and craftwork.

Guildford Museum

Castle Arch, Quarry Street, Guildford, Surrey
GU1 3SX　　　　　☎ 0483 503497
Mon–Sat 11–5. Closed Good Fri, Dec 25, 26.
🏛 *The Curator*
Ⓕ ✎

Displayed in a Jacobean house, with chalk fireplaces, the Museum's collections cover archaeology, local history and needlework. The archaeology gallery shows what life was like in Surrey from 400,000 B.C. to 1500 A.D. The local history exhibits include a reconstruction of a West Surrey cottage room, the ironwork collections of the famous gardener, Gertrude Jekyll, Wealden glass and iron, and a Victorian childhood room. The Museum also has a large collection of photographs and drawings of the Guildford area.

The needlework collection is of special interest, with fine examples of samplers, baby linen and Surrey smocks.

Loseley Park

Guildford, Surrey GU3 1HN　　☎ 0483 571881
Late May Sept, Wed Sat 2 5. Open May and
　　August Bank Holiday Mon 2–5.
🏛 *The Leisure Warden, Estate Office*
Ⓔ ♨ 💺 ↩ [HHA]

Loseley Park lies to the west of the A3100 Guildford to Godalming road. It was built in 1562 by Sir William More, an ancestor of the present owner and occupier, from stone brought from the ruins of Waverley Abbey. The internal features include panelling from Henry VIII's Nonesuch Palace, and fine ceilings and chimneypieces. The collections of paintings, tapestries and 17th and 18th-century furniture are also noteworthy.

The Sutton Place Heritage Trust

Sutton Place, nr Guildford, Surrey GU4 7QV
　　☎ 0483 504455
Tues–Sun, guided tours of house and gardens
　　at 10, 11, 12, 2, 3, 4 by arrangement.
　　Closed Bank Holiday.
🏛 *Bookings Manager*
Ⓔ ✎ 💺 ↩ ▢ 🐄

A Grade I listed building, Sutton Place was built for Sir Richard Weston c. 1523 and remained in the possession of the family until 1920. It now belongs to a Trust which was set up with the aim of preserving the house, with its gardens and estate, as well as its extensive collection of works of art, and of encouraging the performing and visual arts.

There are some pieces of original Tudor furniture made for the house, and other items in the collection include early English ceramics, pre-Columbian terracotta figurines, and an outstanding collection of Impressionist and contemporary paintings, including one of Ben Nicholson's last works.

There is a programme of temporary exhibitions, showing works borrowed from outside and from the permanent collections.

Women's Royal Army Corps Museum

Queen Elizabeth Park, Guildford, Surrey
GU2 6QH
　　☎ 0252 24431 extn Guildford 265
Mon–Fri 9–4. Sun by appt only. Closed Bank
　　Holiday.
🏛 *The Curator*
Ⓕ ♨ ↩

Queen Elizabeth Park lies two miles west of Guildford, off the A322. The Museum is in the course of reconstruction. The displays of uniforms, photographs, documents and other items cover the period during which women have served in the British Army, from 1917 to the present day. Among the exhibits are the uniforms worn by HM The Queen as a 2/Subaltern ATS in 1945 and subsequently as an Hon. Brigadier WRAC before her accession. The Museum also has the ATS and WRAC uniforms, including brocade Mess Dress, worn by the late Princess Royal as Controller Commander ATS and WRAC.

Haddenham

The Farmland Museum

50 High Street, Haddenham, nr Ely,
　　Cambridgeshire CB6 3XB　　☎ 0353 740381
1st Sun of each month, 2–dusk. Easter–Sept,
　　Wed 10–5.
🏛 *Hon. Curator*
Ⓔ ✎ ↩

The Museum has been developed since 1969 as a family enterprise. The exhibits, indoors and outdoors, now cover the large garden of No. 50 in the High Street. The original museum building, formerly the garden shed, is now used for natural history, geology and archaeology, specially arranged to attract children. Other sections are devoted to the production, processing and retailing of milk; domestic equipment; agricultural tools and implements – the Museum has the largest collection of Fen farming equipment to be found anywhere; rural crafts and local history. There are regular demonstrations in the blacksmith's forge and wheelwright's shop.

Haddington

Jane Welsh Carlyle Museum

Lodge Street, Haddington, East Lothian EH41 3EE
☎ 062082 3738
Apr–Sept, Wed–Sat 2–5
⊠ Mrs Pamela C. Roberts, Lamp of Lothian
    Trust, Haddington House, Sidegate,
    Haddington
£ ⌀

The house, which dates from c. 1800, was the
family home of Jane Welsh Carlyle (1801–66),
the wife of Thomas Carlyle, who described the
drawing-room, the background to his courtship,
as 'the finest apartment I ever stood or sat in,
bearing the stamp of its late owner's solid
temper'. The room is furnished to reflect the
personality and tastes of Jane's father, a local
doctor, and his wife. In the dressing-room,
where Carlyle slept on his visits, are portraits of
the famous people Thomas and Jane Carlyle
attracted to themselves, and of the luminaries of
the literary world who gathered round them
when they moved to Chelsea.

Lennoxlove House

Haddington, East Lothian   ☎ 062082 3720
Apr–Sept, Wed, Sat, Sun 2–5. Guided tours only.
⊠ The Secretary
£ ⬛ ↩ HHA

Lennoxlove, the home of the Dukes of
Hamilton, is one and a half miles south of
Haddington on the B6369. Most of the
furniture, including some French items, was
brought from Hamilton Palace in Lanarkshire,
demolished after 1920. An escritoire, a cabinet
and a worktable were presents from Charles II to
the Duchess of Lennox. Among the portraits are
two by Raeburn. There are collections of
armorial and crested china and two exhibits of
particular interest, the death mask of Mary,
Queen of Scots and a silver casket given to her
by her first husband, Francis II of France.

Hagley

Hagley Hall

Hagley, nr Stourbridge, West Midlands DY9 9LG
☎ 0562 882408
July–Aug, Sun–Fri 2–5
⊠ The Secretary
£ ⬛ ⬛ ↩ HHA

Hagley is on the A456 Birmingham to
Kidderminster road. The Palladian Hall was
built between 1756 and 1760 for George, 1st
Lord Lyttelton, and has remained in the family
ever since. It is now the home of Viscount and
Viscountess Cobham, the 8th Lord and Lady
Lyttelton. The house contains 18th-century
Italian plasterwork of very high quality, 18th-
century furniture and a large collection of family
portraits, including works by Van Dyck,
Reynolds, Lely, Benjamin West and Allan
Ramsay.

The Drawing Room contains exceptionally
well-preserved tapestries, with brilliantly
coloured pheasants, parrots and eagles among
garlands of flowers and fruit, woven at the Soho
factory in 1725. The Gallery, which extends the
whole length of the east front of the house, was
intended for the display of paintings and
sculpture, and has now been restored to its
former magnificence after being used for family
cricket practice in the 19th century.

Hailsham

Hailsham Museum

South View, Western Road, Hailsham, East Sussex
    BN27 3DN
June–Aug, Wed 10.30–1
⊠ Mrs M. Alder, 12 Hawthylands Crescent,
    Hailsham, East Sussex   ☎ 0323 840947
F ↩

The Museum's displays relate to the history of
the Hailsham area. They include agricultural
and domestic equipment, and there is a
collection of 19th and 20th-century photographs
illustrating Hailsham as it used to be.

Halifax

Bankfield Museum

Akroyd Road, Halifax, West Yorkshire HX3 6HG
    ☎ 0422 54823/52334
Mon–Sat 10–5; Sun 2.30–5. Closed Dec 25, 26,
Jan 1.
⊠ Leisure Services Department, Calderdale
    Borough Council, Wellesley Park, Halifax
    ☎ 0422 59454
F ⌀ ↩

Bankfield is a mile from the centre of Halifax,
on the A629 Queensbury road. Built during the
1850s and 1860s, it was formerly the home of a
local textile manufacturer, Sir Edward Akroyd.
The internal decorations were carried out by
Italian craftsmen and include fine wall and
ceiling paintings.
    The collections include late 18th to mid-20th
century topographical paintings of local subjects
and works by artists born in the district. Among
those represented are Copley Fielding and
Matthew Smith. Nineteenth-century
watercolours include works by Roger Fry, John
Nash and Sickert. There are also displays of
English costume and textiles from India, Burma,
China, Africa and the Balkans. Further sections
are devoted to natural history, especially in the
North of England, toys, and 16th and 17th-
century Halifax yeomen's houses.

Calderdale Industrial Museum

Winding Road, Halifax, West Yorkshire HX1 1PR
    ☎ 0422 59031
Tues–Sat 10–5; Sun 2–5. Open Bank Holiday
    Mon.
⊠ See Bankfield Museum
£ ⌀ ↩ ⓑ

Horse-drawn baker's van. Historic photograph in the National Museum of the Working Horse, Halifax.

The Museum occupies a 19th-century mill, adjoining the historic Piece Hall. It reflects the wide range of local industries, from toffee to reflecting road studs, and from carpets to washing machines and the Halifax Building Society, and concentrates particularly on the textile and engineering trades, with good collections of original machinery, much of it, including steam engines, operational. There is also a reconstruction of a corner of Victorian Halifax, where the exhibits include a pawnbroker's shop and a privy.

Throughout the Museum care has been taken to present the different industries within their social context and to avoid the creation of purely technological displays. The same policy has been followed in the adjoining Piece Hall Pre-Industrial Museum.

An audio-visual presentation provides a general introduction to the character and history of Calderdale's industries and throughout the Museum an effort has been made to capture not only the sights, but also the sounds and smells of Halifax at work.

Horses at Work: National Museum of the Working Horse

Dobbin's Yard, South Parade, Halifax, West
Yorkshire HX1 2LY ☎ *0422 46835*
Mar–Dec, daily 10–5. Closed Dec 25.
⊠ *Mrs L. A. Killick*
Ⓚ ▤ ▦ ◕ ⅎ

The Museum occupies a former goods transhipment shed, which included a granary, of the Lancashire and Yorkshire Railway. The buildings have been restored to house a photographic exhibition illustrating the history of horse-drawn transport. Different types of horses, from the heavy cartage and dray horses to the lighter cobs and delivery horses, are stabled on the site and used to demonstrate grooming, harnessing and working methods, with examples of vehicles from many areas of Britain.

Museum of the Duke of Wellington's Regiment

Bankfield Museum, Akroyd Road, Halifax,
West Yorkshire HX3 6HG
☎ *0422 51823/52331*
Mon–Sat 10–5; Sun 2.30–5. Closed Dec 25, 26,
Jan 1.
⊠ *See Bankfield Museum*
Ⓕ ◔ ◕

This section of Bankfield Museum tells the story of the Duke of Wellington's Regiment, with displays containing uniforms, weapons and equipment, pictures, medals and documents. There are also personal possessions and memorabilia of the 1st Duke of Wellington.

Piece Hall Pre-Industrial Museum

Piece Hall, Halifax, West Yorkshire HX1 1PR
☎ *0422 59031*
Apr–Sept, Mon–Sat 10–6; Sun 10–5. Oct–Mar,
daily 10–5.
⊠ *See Bankfield Museum*
Ⓕ ◔ ◕

Piece Hall was built by private subscription in 1779 for the sale of lengths of cloth 'pieces', manufactured on hand looms in the valleys and on the moors around Halifax. The Museum illustrates the production of cloth from fleece to piece before the Industrial Revolution. There is a spinner's cottage and a weaver's loom chamber, as well as workshops for preparing the wool and finishing the cloth. A merchant can be seen selling his wares in an original Piece Hall room setting.

An art gallery which specialises in works by contemporary artists adjoins the Museum.

Shibden Hall, Folk Museum of West Yorkshire

Halifax, West Yorkshire HX3 6XG
☎ *0422 52246*
Apr–Sept, Mon–Sat 10–6; Sun 2–5. Mar,
    Oct–Nov, Mon–Sat 10–5; Sun 2–5. Feb,
    Sun 2–5. Closed Dec–Jan.
■ *See Bankfield Museum*
E ⚷ 🗨 ❖

This fine half-timbered house, a Grade I listed
building, dates from *c.* 1520, with some later
additions. It contains furnishings, mainly of the
17th and 18th centuries, displayed in period
room settings in order to give the house the
appearance of being lived in.

In a 17th-century Pennine barn there are
collections of horse-drawn vehicles, harness and
other accessories, and of agricultural tools and
implements, as well as a brewhouse and a dairy.
Around an open courtyard are reconstructions
of the workshops of 19th-century craftsmen,
including those of a clogger, cooper and
wheelwright, as well as a public house and an
estate worker's cottage, all arranged to produce
the impression that the occupant has just gone
to lunch.

Halstead

The Brewery Chapel Museum

Adams Court, off Colne Valley Close, Halstead,
    Essex CO9 1JQ
Apr–Oct, Sat 10–5; Sun 2–5
■ *Graham S. Slimming, Hon. Curator,*
    'Rivendell', Toppesfield Road, Great Yeldham,
    Halstead CO9 4HD
F ❖ ♿ □

The building, which dates from 1883, is a
particularly fine example of Victorian brickwork.
It is unusual in that it was built as a Chapel and
reading room for a brewery, T. F. Adams and
Sons. The Museum is run by Halstead and
District Local History Society, in conjunction
with its Archive and Study Centre. The
collection which the Society holds is largely of
19th and 20th-century material relating to the
district. The permanent display devoted to
Halstead and the surrounding villages emphasises
the connection with Courtaulds Silk Mill. There
is a regular programme of temporary exhibitions,
drawing on the Society's collection and
illustrating local historical themes.

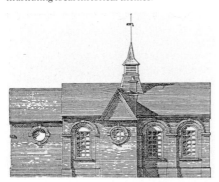

The Brewery Chapel Museum, Halstead.

Hamilton

Hamilton District Museum

129 Muir Street, Hamilton, Lanarkshire ML3 6BJ
☎ *0698 283981*
Mon–Sat 10–5. Closed Sun, every Sat preceding
    Bank Holiday, May Day holiday Monday,
    Dec 25, 26, Jan 1–3.
■ *Joyce J. R. Brown, Museum Education Officer*
F ● ❖

No. 129 Muir Street was built as a coaching inn
in 1696. The 18th-century stable is now a
display area, as is the Fives Court and Assembly
Room, which has its original plasterwork and a
musicians' gallery dating from 1784. The
displays illustrate a wide range of subjects
relating to the history and character of
Hamilton, including its natural history,
agriculture, archaeology and industry. Among
the special features are a reconstructed
Victorian kitchen and an extensive transport
section, with a four-in-hand coach, Victorian
fire-engine and hearse, and many other horse-
drawn and motor vehicles.

The Museum also has a large Harry Lauder
collection, which includes stage costumes,
photographs, records and other memorabilia of
the Scottish music-hall artist.

Regimental Museum of the Cameronians
(Scottish Rifles)

Mote Hill, off Muir Street, Hamilton, Lanarkshire
    ML3 6BJ ☎ *0698 428688*
Mon, Tues, Thurs–Sat 10–12, 1–5; Wed 10–12.
    Closed public holidays.
■ *The Curator*
F ⚷ ❖

The Museum building was originally the riding
school of Hamilton Palace. The displays tell the
story of the history of the Regiment from 1689
to 1968 and include banners, medals, uniforms
and campaign relics.

Hanley

Stoke-on-Trent City Museum and Art Gallery

Bethesda Street, Hanley, Stoke-on-Trent,
    Staffordshire ST1 3DE ☎ *0782 273173*
Mon–Sat 10.30–5; Sun 2–5. Closed Good Fri
    and Dec 25–Jan 1.
■ *The Director*
F ● 🗨 ❖ ♿

The Museum, in a modern building designed for
the purpose, has departments of fine art,
decorative arts, natural history, archaeology and
social history, and its collections of ceramics are
among the finest in the world, with a strong
emphasis on pottery and porcelain made in
Staffordshire. The art gallery is concerned
almost entirely with British art of the 18th, 19th
and 20th centuries.

Reconstructed Victorian kitchen,
Hamilton District Museum.

Harewood

Harewood House

Harewood, Leeds, West Yorkshire LS17 9LQ
☎ 0532 886225
Apr–Oct, daily 10–5.30. Nov, Feb–Mar, Sun
10–5.30.
K Mr C. Williams
C **â** **L** **ø** **&** **HHA**

Harewood House was built between 1759 and
1771 and has been lived in by the Lascelles
family ever since. The young Robert Adam
designed the ceilings, walls, chimneypieces and
other fittings, and Harewood provides an
exceptionally good opportunity to see his work
at its best. Thomas Chippendale made a great
deal of furniture for the house and much of it
survives. The Long Gallery contains Chinese
porcelain and an important collection of 18th-
century English portraits, and elsewhere in the
house there are Italian portraits, including two
by Bellini, 18th-century landscapes of
Harewood by Turner, Girtin and others,
paintings by Angelica Kauffmann, Antonio
Zucchi and El Greco, and a collection of
Sèvres porcelain.

Harlech

Harlech Castle

Harlech, Gwynedd LL46 2YH   ☎ 0766 780552
Mar 15–Oct 15, daily 9.30–6.30. Oct 16–
Mar 14, Mon–Sat 9.30–4; Sun 2–4.
K The Custodian
C **â** **ø** **✿**

Harlech Castle, much photographed against the
background of the mountains of Snowdonia,
was built in 1283–9 in order to establish the
military position of Edward I in the area. Its
defences were strengthened at various times
during the 14th century. It was besieged and
badly damaged by the Parliamentarians during
the Civil War, but repairs were eventually
carried out during the 19th and 20th centuries.
A recently installed exhibition in the gatehouse
tells the story of Harlech and deals also with the
design and history of the castles of Edward I.

Harlow

Harlow Museum

Passmores House, Third Avenue, Harlow, Essex
CM18 6YL   ☎ 0279 446422
Fri–Mon, Wed 10–5; Tues, Thurs 10–9.
Closed Dec 25, 26.
K Museum Assistant
F **ø** **æ**

Passmores House contains a brick-clad Tudor-
framed building with a Georgian façade, added
c. 1727. The Museum presents the archaeology
and history of the Harlow area from prehistoric
times to the building of the New Town. There is
an interesting collection of Iron Age coins and
Roman material from the Temple of Minerva
and the civil settlement at Harlow, including
the head of the cult statue, and a large quantity
of material from local post-medieval slipware
kilns. Other exhibits relate to geology, both
local and national, natural history, agriculture
and rural life.

Mark Hall Cycle Museum

Muskham Road, Harlow, Essex CM20 1LJ
            ☎ 0279 39680
Daily 10–5. Closed Dec 25, 26.
K Mr John S. Collins
F **â** **æ** **&**

The Museum is in Mark Hall's 19th-century
stable block. It was created in order to display
the collection of cycles and accessories which
was begun by John Collins in 1948, when he
joined the family cycle business in Harlow, and
which illustrates the history of the bicycle from
1818 to the 1980s. Introductory displays tell the
story of Mark Hall and of the Collins family.

Two of the three walled gardens behind the
Museum have been laid out as a 17th-century
herb garden and an ornamental fruit garden.
The third is divided into sections, showing four
types of garden as they would have been in the
past – a rose garden, a herbaceous garden, a
vegetable garden and a typical cottage garden.

Harray

Corrigall Farm Museum

Harray, Orkney Islands   ☎ 085677 411
Apr–Sept, Mon–Sat 10.30–1, 2–5; Sun 2–7
K Mr B. S. Wilson, Tankerness House Museum,
      Broad Street, Kirkwall, Orkney KW15 1DH
      ☎ 0586 3191
F **ø** **æ** **&**

The Museum building is in a restored 19th-
century farmhouse and steading, with stone
roofs and floor and a circular grain drying kiln
attached to the barn. The furnishings and
implements are of the 19th century or earlier.
Of special interest are Orkney straw chairs and
utensils, a single-stilted wooden plough, an ox-
wagon with solid wooden wheels, and a parish
hand-loom. The livestock includes locally
favoured breeds of poultry and the native North
Ronaldsay sheep.

Harrogate

Harrogate Art Gallery

Public Library, Victoria Avenue, Harrogate,
*   North Yorkshire*   ☎ *0423 503340*
Mon–Fri 10–5; Sat 10–4
🏛 *Harrogate Museums & Art Gallery Service,*
*   Knapping Mount, West Grove Road,*
*   Harrogate HG2 2AE*
🄵 ☐

The Gallery's permanent collections are of
English paintings and watercolours. A selection
from the collections is always on show. A
number of temporary exhibitions from other
sources are arranged throughout the year.

Royal Pump Room Museum

Royal Parade, Harrogate, North Yorkshire
☎ *0423 503340*
Mon–Sat 10.30–5; Sun 2–5. Closed Dec 25, 26,
*   Jan 1.*
🏛 *See Harrogate Art Gallery*
🄴 🐾

The Museum is in Harrogate's historic Pump
Room which includes the old Sulphur Well in
the basement, where the water can be tasted,
the octagonal Pump Room, built in 1842, and
the larger annexe, which dates from 1913. It
contains displays relating to the history of
Harrogate and the surrounding district,
including exhibits of pottery, costumes and
Victoriana.

Harrow

Uxbridge and Middlesex Yeomanry and Signals Trust

Elmgrove Road Territorial Army Centre, Harrow,
*   Middlesex*   ☎ *01 427 6890*
By appt
🏛 *Captain D. W. Manders, 76 Hertingfordbury*
*   Road, Hertford SG14 1LB*   ☎ *0992 57018*
🄵 🐾

The Museum is in the 1937 Territorial Army
Centre, designed for the use of the Royal
Engineers Searchlight team. The displays of
uniforms, saddlery, weapons, documents,
signals equipment and general militaria relate to
a number of regiments, the County Cavalry
Regiment, 1797–1920; the Divisional Cavalry
Mounted Signals Regiment, 1920–40; the
Armoured Signals Regiment, 1940–47; the
Airborne Signals Regiment, 1947–60; and the
Army Signals, 1960–85.

Hartland

Hartland Quay Museum

Hartland, nr Bideford, North Devon
☎ *02373 693*
Easter week, then Whitsun–Sept, daily 11–5
🏛 *Mr M. Nix, Bucks Cliff House, Bucks Mills,*
*   nr Bideford EX39 2DZ*
🄴 🍴 💺 🐾

The Museum is in a group of 18th-century
cottages and cellars and is devoted to the natural
environment and history of the North-West
Devon coastal region. The rocky coast has been
the scene of many shipwrecks and the Wreck
Room gives details of them from the 17th
century to the most recent casualty, the
Johanna, which in 1983 was looted by people
from all over the South-West. Special exhibits
are concerned with the coastal trade, lime-
burning and sand landing. The geological and
natural history displays, together with a marine
aquarium, provide an introduction to the local
environment. A smuggling exhibit is in
preparation.

Hartlebury

Hereford and Worcester County Museum

Hartlebury Castle, Hartlebury, nr Kidderminster,
*   Hereford and Worcester DY11 7XZ*
☎ *0299 250416*
Mar–Oct, Mon–Fri 2–5; Sun 2–6
🏛 *Mr G. L. Shearer, County Museum Officer*
🄴 🍴 💺 ♿ 🐾 ☐

The Museum is housed in the North Wing of
Hartlebury Castle, the residence of the Bishop
of Worcester. The collections illustrate life in
Herefordshire and Worcestershire since
prehistoric times and the displays, which are
changed frequently, cover agriculture, social
and domestic life, and crafts and industries.
Among the exhibits are reconstructions of a
kitchen, with an 18th-century spit, and butter,
cheese and marzipan moulds, a tailor's shop
from Upton-on-Severn, and a Victorian
drawing room. A Georgian Room contains 18th
and 19th-century furniture, costumes, porcelain
and glass and along the walls of one staircase
there is an exhibition of the work of the
Bromsgrove Guild, the internationally famous
art and craft society which was founded in
Bromsgrove by Walter Gilbert in 1894 and
continued until 1966. There are also collections
of gypsy caravans and other horse-drawn
vehicles, toys, dolls, weights and measures, and
clocks and other time-measuring instruments.

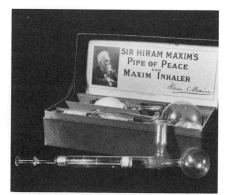

Sir Hiram Maxim's Pipe of Peace. Hartlebury,
Hereford and Worcester County Museum.

Hartlepool

Gray Art Gallery and Museum

Clarence Road, Hartlepool, Cleveland TS24 8BT
☎ *0429 266522 extn 259*
Mon–Sat 10–5.30; Sun 3–5. Closed Good Fri,
Dec 25, 26, Jan 1.
◪ *The Curator*
🅕 ⌀ ⇌ &

The Museum building was formerly 'The
Willows', a mid-Victorian mansion given to the
town in 1921 by Sir William Cresswell Gray,
Hartlepool's leading shipbuilder. An extension,
housing the Art Gallery, was added in 1973.
The Museum has displays of local history,
emphasising Hartlepool's 19th-century
expansion, archaeology and natural history,
especially birds and marine life. The art
collection is particularly strong in 19th and
20th-century oil paintings and watercolours.
There are interesting collections of Japanese
arms and armour, netsuke, Tibetan images of
Buddha and Chinese *famille rose* porcelain.
    The Museum grounds are being developed
with reconstructed buildings. These include a
smithy, the 1900 electric tramway office, and a
brine pumping engine.

Hartlepool Maritime Museum

Northgate, Hartlepool, Cleveland TS24 0LT
☎ *0429 272814*
Mon–Sat 10–5. Closed Good Fri, Dec 25, 26,
Jan 1.
◪ *The Curator*
🅕 ⌀ ⇌

An important port in the Middle Ages,
Hartlepool declined during the following
centuries into a mere fishing village. The
opening of the East Durham coalfield and the
construction of a railway from the collieries to
Hartlepool in the 1830s transformed the
situation. By the 1890s Hartlepool, together
with the Victorian new town of West
Hartlepool, had become the third busiest
English port and a major shipbuilding centre.
    The Museum illustrates the Hartlepool
industries of shipbuilding, marine engineering,
shipping and fishing. The exhibits include an
important collection of ship models, a simulated
ship's bridge, one of the earliest gas-lit
lighthouse lanterns and a reconstruction of a
fisherman's cottage. The Fish Quay and working
port can be viewed from the Museum windows.

Haslemere

Haslemere Educational Museum

High Street, Haslemere, Surrey GU27 2LA
☎ *0428 2112*
Apr–Oct, Tues–Sat 10–5; Sun 2–5. Nov–Mar,
Tues–Sat 10–4. Closed Dec 25, 26, Jan 1.
◪ *The Curator*
🅔 ▮ ⇌

Haslemere Museum has fine collections of
British birds and mammals, together with
exhibits of plants and geology, and an
explanation of the relationship between the
geology, scenery and land use of the area. It was
probably the first museum in Britain to include
living specimens among the objects exhibited
and this tradition has continued until the
present time.
    The History Gallery shows the progress of
mankind since prehistoric times and displays
local archaeological material within this more
general context. For later times there are
exhibits illustrating the history of transport,
agriculture and domestic life. There are
reconstructions of a local cottage kitchen of
c. 1800 and of a local blacksmith's forge, and
displays relating to glass-making and ironworking which were once important industries
in the area, and to the peasant crafts of
Northern Europe.

Hastings

Fishermen's Museum

Rock-a-nore Road, Hastings, East Sussex
Spring Bank Holiday–Sept 30, Sun–Fri 10.30–12,
2.30–5.30
◪ *John Burton, 11 Harold Road, Hastings*
    TN35 5NT   ☎ *0424 424787*
🅕 ⌀ ⇌

The Museum, which is devoted to the history of
the fishing and boatbuilding industries of the
town, and to the life of the men who worked in
them, is in the former Fishermen's Church of St
Nicholas, built in 1854 and in use for its original
purpose until 1935. The central feature of the
Museum is the *Enterprise*, the last of the
Hastings clinker-built sailing luggers. There are
exhibits describing the techniques and
equipment used by local fishermen, with
models, paintings and photographs of fishing
boats and other vessels.

Hastings Museum and Art Gallery

John's Place, Cambridge Road, Hastings, East
    Sussex TN34 1ET   ☎ *0424 435952*
Mon–Sat 10–1, 2–5; Sun 3–5. Closed Good Fri,
Dec 25, 26.
◪ *Miss Victoria Williams, Curator*
🅕 ⌀ ⇌

The Museum is housed in a 1923 neo-Tudor
mansion. Its displays cover local geology,
zoology, archaeology and history. There are
important collections of Sussex and Wealden
pottery and ironworking, the examples of cast-
iron firebacks being especially interesting.
Other sections show British and European
ceramics, and the arts and crafts of the Pacific
and American Indians. The Durbar Hall, an
Indian palace carved from wood, was built for
the 1886 Colonial Exhibition and subsequently
bought by Earl Brassey. It contains exhibits
illustrating the life and travels of Lord and Lady
Brassey, with ethnographical material from the
Pacific Islands.

Old Town Hall Museum of Local History

High Street, Hastings, East Sussex TN34 3EW
☎ 0424 425855
*Easter–Sept, Mon–Sat 10–1, 2–5. Oct–Easter,
Sun 3–5.*
☒ *See Hastings Museum and Art Gallery*
£ ⬭

The former Town Hall was built in 1823. The
downstairs arches originally formed an open
market area, but were later enclosed to form
Hasting's first police station. The section
dealing with the history of Hastings includes
exhibits on the growth of tourism and on famous
people who have lived in the area, including
Logie Baird, Grey Owl, Titus Oates, Teilhard
de Chardin and Robert Tressell. Special displays
are devoted to the Battle of Hastings, the
Cinque Ports, and maritime history –
smuggling, shipwrecks, fishing.

**The Old Town Hall Museum of Local History,
Hastings.**

Hatch Beauchamp

Hatch Court

Hatch Beauchamp, Somerset TA3 6AA
☎ 0823 480208
*July–Sept 16 & Aug Bank Holiday Mon,
2.30–5.30. May–Sept 16, pre-booked parties
daily except Thurs.*
£ 🖼 📷 HHA

Hatch Court is six miles from Taunton, on the
A358. A Palladian-style mansion, it dates from
1755, with additions and much of the interior
decoration carried out c. 1800. It contains 17th
and 18th-century furniture, as well as a good
collection of pictures and porcelain displayed in
a specially designed semi-circular room. There is
also a museum of Canadian militaria.

Hatfield

Hatfield House

Hatfield Park, Hatfield, Hertfordshire AL9 5NQ
☎ 07072 62823
*Mar 25–2nd Sun in Oct, Tues–Sat 12–5; Sun
2–5.30. Open Bank Holiday Mon 11–5.*
☒ *The Curator*
£ 🚹 🖼 📷 ♿

Hatfield House was built 1607–11 by Robert
Cecil, 1st Earl of Salisbury. It has been the
family home of the Cecils ever since. The
surviving wing of the Royal Palace of Hatfield,
where Elizabeth I spent much of her girlhood,
stands in the grounds. The Queen held her first
Council of State here in 1558. There are
memorabilia of her, including the Rainbow
Portrait, to be seen in Hatfield House, together
with notable collections of paintings, furniture,
tapestries and armour. The Chapel has its
original stained glass.

The recently created Knot Garden contains
plants known in England in the 15th to 17th
centuries, including those introduced to this
country by John Tradescant.

Havant

Havant Museum and Art Gallery

East Street, Havant, Hampshire PO9 1BS
☎ 0705 451155
Tues–Sat 10–5
☒ *The Curator*
F ⬭ 📷

The Museum building, which dates from the
1870s, was formerly a private house. There are
displays illustrating the archaeology and history
of the Havant area, and the Museum also
exhibits in three rooms the notable collection of
sporting firearms formed by C. G. Vokes.

One room shows these weapons in the
manner in which they would have been found in
an old house, another deals with the wild
fowling which was popular in the district in
Victorian times, and the third covers the
historical development of the mechanism of
firearms.

A special section of the Museum is devoted to
local industries, especially glove-making.

Havenstreet Village

Isle of Wight Steam Railway and Isle of Wight
Railway Heritage Museum

*The Railway Station, Havenstreet Village, nr Ryde,
Isle of Wight PO33 4DS*   ☎ 0983 882204
*Station and Museum open daily June–Aug. Trains
operate Sun (Mar 30–Sept); Thurs (July–Aug)
and Bank Holiday; daily week before late
Summer Bank Holiday. Special chartered
openings for large parties out of season
by arrangement.*
☒ *The Commercial Manager*
£ 🚹 🖼 📷 ♿

Havenstreet lies halfway between Ryde and
Newport. The last publicly operated steam
passenger train between Havenstreet and
Wootton, on the Newport–Ryde section, has
been bought by a group of interested local
people, who have formed the Isle of Wight
Railway Co. Ltd., in order to continue
operations. Visitors are able to ride on faithfully
restored Edwardian steam trains and visit the
workshops, signal box and displays of railway
equipment.

Haverfordwest

Castle Museum and Art Gallery

*The Castle, Haverfordwest, Pembrokeshire, Dyfed
    SA61 2EF*   ☎ *0437 3708*
*June–Sept, Mon–Sat & Bank Holiday 10–5.30.
    Oct–May, Tues–Sat & Bank Holiday, 11–4.
    Closed Good Fri, Dec 25, 26, Jan 1.*
▨ *See Scolton Manor Museum*
£ ▮ ⇨ □

Construction of the Castle began in 1128, but
most of the buildings date from the 13th
century. The Museum occupies the former
County Gaol, built in 1820 in the Outer Ward
of the Castle. The displays relate to the town
and former County of Haverfordwest and to the
collections of militaria formed by the Pembroke
Yeomanry Trust and by the Museum itself. The
latter are arranged to illustrate two themes – the
Norman Conquest of Wales and the associated
building of castles, and the origin and
development of uniform from armour and
heraldry. There are also exhibits of coins
and medals and of recently discovered
archaeological material.
    Selections from the fine and applied art
collections are shown in temporary exhibitions,
arranged to illustrate themes.
    The Art Gallery maintains an up-to-date
Register of Pembrokeshire Artists, available to
researchers and those interested in buying works.

Graham Sutherland Gallery

*Picton Castle, The Rhos, Haverfordwest, Dyfed
    SA62 4AS*   ☎ *043786 296*
*Apr–Sept, Tues–Sun 10.30–12.30, 1.30–5. Open
    Bank Holiday Apr–Sept. Other times by appt.*
▨ *Hon. Secretary, Picton Castle Trust*
£ ⬙ ⇨ ⅋ □

The Gallery possesses the largest public
collection of works by Graham Sutherland,
many of them inspired by the surrounding
countryside. The exhibits are changed from
time to time and there is also a programme of
temporary exhibitions by other well-known
artists.

Penrhôs Cottage

*Llanycefn, Maenclochog, Haverfordwest,
    Pembrokeshire, Dyfed SA62 5QL*
    ☎ *0437 82328*
*Easter, then May–Sept, Tues–Sat 10–12.30,
    2.30–6; Sun 2.30–6*
▨ *See Scolton Manor Museum*
£ ⬙ ⇨

Penrhôs Common is now almost completely
enclosed, but it was formerly a bleak and
exposed area on a high north–south ridge, to the
east of the B4313. The original cottage, now
restored and appropriately furnished, would
have been constructed and roofed in one night,
with a fire going by sunrise. Once this was
achieved, the squatter could then lay claim to as
much land as lay within a stone's throw of the
door. Such homes produced many famous
Welshmen and Welsh women.

Scolton Manor Museum

*Spittal, Haverfordwest, Pembrokeshire, Dyfed
    SA62 5QL*   ☎ *043782 328*
*June–Sept, Tues–Sun & Aug Bank Holiday
    10.30–6. School & coach parties all year round
    by appt only.*
▨ *The Curator*
£ ▮ ⬛ ⇨ ⅋

The Museum is on the B4329 Cardigan
road, five and a half miles north-east of
Haverfordwest. Scolton Manor was built in
1840. Its grounds are managed as a country park
and the attractive stables and carriage house are
also open to the public. The developing displays
illustrate the history and natural environment of
Pembrokeshire, with a well-equipped local
history research centre. Among the major
exhibits is the 0-6-0 ST Fox Walker
Locomotive, *Margaret*, supplied in 1878 to the
Maenclochog and Rosebush Railway.

Hawes

Upper Dales Folk Museum

*Station Yard, Hawes, Wensleydale, North
    Yorkshire DL8 3NT*   ☎ *09697 494*
*Easter or Apr 1–Sept, Mon–Sat 11–5; Sun 2–5.
    Oct, Tues, Sat, Sun 2–5. Half-term holiday,
    open all week*
▨ *The Curator*
£ ⬙ ⇨ ⅋

The Museum occupies what was the goods
warehouse at Hawes Station, built in 1883 in
the Victorian Gothic style. The collections,
formed by Marie Hartley and Joan Ingilby in the
course of their researches, illustrate the
traditional rural life of Wensleydale and
Swaledale. The exhibits cover domestic
equipment and the household crafts and a wide
range of rural skills and occupations, including
hand-knitting and the making of Wensleydale
cheese.

Hawick

Hawick Museum and The Scott Gallery

*Wilton Lodge Park, Hawick, Roxburghshire
    TD9 7JL*   ☎ *0450 73457*
*Apr–Sept, Mon–Sat 10–12, 1–5; Sun 2–5.
    Oct–Mar, Mon–Fri 1–4; Sun 2–4.*
▨ *District Museums Curator*
£ ⬙ ⇨ □

The Museum's exhibits are devoted to the
history and natural environment of Hawick and
the Border Region. There are good geological,
archaeological and natural history displays, and
social history collections which concentrate
mainly on domestic life in and around Hawick
in the 19th and early 20th centuries. The
knitwear and hosiery industry, which made
Hawick internationally important, is well
represented in the Museum, by exhibits of
machinery, photographs and other material.

Hawkinge

Kent Battle of Britain Museum

Aerodrome Road, Hawkinge, nr Folkestone, Kent
☎ 030389 2779
Easter–Sept, Sun and Bank Holiday 11–5.30.
July–Aug, also Mon–Fri 2–5.
◪ *Mr L. Green, 'Wings', 27 Canterbury Road,*
Hawkinge, nr Folkestone
£ ⬧ ♿ ♿

The RAF airfield at Hawkinge lies west of the
A240, north of its junction with the M20.
Housed in RAF buildings, some dating from the
1920s, the collection aims to re-create the
history and atmosphere of the Battle of Britain,
in which Hawkinge played an important rôle.
The Museum contains relics, memorabilia and
documentation relating to the Battle of Britain
period, as well as earlier aviation material.
A special display on the history of Hawkinge
Airfield from 1912 to 1961 is mounted in the
aircraft control building, which was the centre
of all the air operations out of Hawkinge in
1940. The Lord Dowding Hangar is now open.

Haworth

Brontë Parsonage Museum

Haworth, Keighley, West Yorkshire BD22 8DR
☎ 0535 42323
Apr–Sept, daily 11–5.30. Oct–Jan and Feb 22–
Mar, daily 11–4.30. Closed Dec 24–26,
Feb 1–21.
◪ *The Custodian*
£ ⬧ ♿ ☐

The Parsonage, once the home of the Rev.
Brontë and his family, and now the property of
the Brontë Society, has its main rooms
decorated in early 19th-century style and
arranged as they were in the Brontës' day, with
original furnishings and paintings. A large
number of books, manuscripts, drawings and
personal possessions relating to the family are
also on display, together with a permanent
exhibition, 'The Brontës: a family history', and
special temporary exhibitions.

Haydon Bridge

Housesteads Roman Fort Museum

Haydon Bridge, Hexham, Northumberland
NE47 4NN ☎ 04984 363
Mar 15–Oct 15, Mon–Sat 9.30–6.30; Sun
2–6.30. Oct 16–Mar 14, Mon–Sat 9.30–4;
Sun 2–4. Closed Dec 24–26, Jan 1.
◪ *Historic Buildings & Monuments Commission,*
Carlisle ☎ 0228 31777
£ ⬧ ♿ ✿

This site-museum outlines the history of the
Fort and illustrates it with finds from the long
series of excavations of both the Fort and the
surrounding settlement. Models include a life-
sized replica of a Roman auxiliary soldier,
complete with his equipment.

Hebden Bridge

Automobilia

Billy Lane, Old Town, Hebden Bridge, West
Yorkshire HX7 8RY ☎ 0422 844775
Apr–Sept, Tues–Sun 12–6. Oct–Mar, Sat, Sun
12–6. Open Bank Holiday.
◪ *The Curator*
£ ⬧ ♿ ♿ ♿

Accommodated in an 1897 warehouse, the
Museum's collections consist of pre-1939 cars,
motorcycles and bicycles, Austin Sevens and
Morrises being particularly featured.

Helensburgh

The Hill House

Upper Colquhoun Street, Helensburgh,
Dunbartonshire ☎ 0436 3900
Daily 1–5 (last admission 4.30). Closed
Dec 24–26, Jan 1.
◪ *Bob Sawyer*
£ ⬧ ♿ [NTS]

The Glasgow publisher, Walter W. Blackie,
commissioned The Hill House from Charles
Rennie Mackintosh in 1902. It is considered to
be the finest example of Mackintosh's domestic
architecture. Now in the care of the National
Trust for Scotland, it contains Mackintosh
furniture and the gardens are being restored to
the original design.
Visitors to the house can see an audio-visual
programme on the life of Mackintosh.

Helmshore

Helmshore Textile Museums

Higher Mill, Holcombe Road, Helmshore,
Rossendale, Lancashire BB4 4NP
☎ 0706 226459/218838
Mar, Mon–Fri 2–5. Apr–June, Mon–Fri,
Sun 2–5. July–Aug, Mon–Fri 10–5; Sat,
Sun 2–5. Sept, Mon–Fri 10–5; Sun 2–5.
Oct, Mon–Fri, Sun 2–5. Open Bank Holiday
weekends, and throughout winter for school
parties and guided tours.
◪ *Mr D. Chadwick, Museum Teacher*
£ ⬧ ♿ ♿ ♿

Housed in two former textile mills, Helmshore
Textile Museums aim to give a picture of the
development of Lancashire's textile industry.
The earlier mill, a water-powered fulling mill,
was built in 1789. The restored 18-foot diameter
waterwheel and fulling stocks are demonstrated
daily. This mill also houses an internationally
important collection of early textile machines,
including some original ones from Arkwright's
mill at Cromford. This collection can be seen
only by parties which book in advance.
The other part of the Museum Complex
consists of a three-storey mill, originally
constructed in the early 19th century and largely
rebuilt in 1859–60, after a fire. This contains a

complete set of condenser cotton preparation and spinning machinery. The main spinning room remains in its original condition, with much of the machinery restored to running order and demonstrated regularly. There is also an exhibition gallery telling the story of Lancashire's textile industry.

Helmsley

Rievaulx Abbey

Rievaulx, Helmsley, North Yorkshire
☎ *04396 228*
Mar 29–Oct 14, daily 9.30–6.30.
Oct 15–Mar 28, Mon–Sat 9.30–4; Sun 2–4.
Closed Dec 24–26, Jan 1.
Ⓜ *Historic Buildings & Monuments Commission, York* ☎ *0904 58626*
Ⓔ ✐ 🅰 ✿

Rievaulx is two and a half miles west of Helmsley, on a minor road off the B1257. The site museum contains a display of stone carvings, floor tiles and other items from the ruins of the Cistercian abbey of Rievaulx, set in the context of the history of the Abbey.

Rievaulx Terrace and Temples

Rievaulx, Helmsley, North Yorkshire
☎ *04396 340*
Apr–Oct, daily 10.30–6 (Ionic Temple closed 1–2). Closed Good Fri.
Ⓜ *National Trust, York* ☎ *0704 702021*
Ⓔ 🏛 🅰 [NT]

The grass terrace and classical temples, one in the Doric, the other in the Ionic style, overlooking the ruins of Rievaulx Abbey, were constructed *c.* 1758 by Thomas Duncombe whose house, Duncombe Park, was a mile away. Now the property of the National Trust, they are among the finest achievements of the 18th-century landscape architects. The elegant room in the Ionic temple, with elaborate plasterwork and a painted ceiling by Giovanni Borgnis, contains 18th-century furniture and a Worcester dinner service. In the basement there is an exhibition on English landscape design in the 18th century, and of the Victorian albums of Duncombe family, owners of the temples and the terrace for 200 years.

Helston

Cornwall Aero Park and Flambards Victorian Village

Culdrose Manor, Helston, Cornwall TR13 0GA
☎ *0326 57340/574549*
Easter–Oct, daily 10–5
Ⓜ *Mr J. K. Hale, Chief Executive*
Ⓔ 🏛 ▦ ♿ 🅰 ♿

The Aero Park, together with Flambards Victorian Village and Britain in the Blitz, are on the Helston side of Culdrose Air Station, off the A3083. The collection of military aircraft is arranged in a parkland setting and specialises in allowing visitors access to the flight decks of the aeroplanes, helicopters and hovercraft. The Battle of Britain Gallery illustrates the achievements of the men who took part in it.

Flambards Victorian Village is a full-scale reconstruction of a turn-of-the-century street, with shops, carriages and fashions, and Britain in the Blitz re-creates a city street during the Second World War, with exhibits that include a Morrison table-shelter and a pub crowded with uniformed men and women of the Allied forces.

Helston Folk Museum

The Old Butter Market, Church Street, Helston, Cornwall TR13 8SZ
Mon, Tues, Thurs–Sat 10.30–1, 2–4.30; Wed 10.30–12
Ⓜ *Mr M. K. Matthews, Museum Officer*
Ⓕ ✐

The Museum is in Helston's former Market House, built in 1837–8. The emphasis of the displays is on the crafts and industries which flourished in and around Helston during the 19th and early 20th centuries, including mining, quarrying and fishing. Among the vehicles on display are a butcher's cart, a wagonette used by a member of the local gentry, and a parish bier.

Brunswick Square at Flambards Victorian Village, Helston.

Henfield

Henfield Parish Museum

New Village Hall, Henfield, West Sussex BN5 9DB
Tues, Thurs, Sat 10–12; Wed 2.30–4.30
Ⓜ *Mrs Dorothy R. Chalmers, 'Highdene', Henfield BN5 9DA*
☎ *0273 492988*
Ⓕ ✐ 🅰 ♿

The entire contents of the Museum, which belongs to the Parish, have been presented by local people over the past 55 years, creating their own record of the history of the village. The exhibits range from a redundant post-box to an eel-spear, and from a shepherd's crook to a woodpecker's nest cut from a silver birch tree on Henfield Common. There is a comprehensive display of farm tools, dresses and uniforms.

Henley-on-Thames

Fawley Court

D.M. College and Museum, Henley-on-Thames,
    Oxfordshire RG9 3AE   ☎ 0491 574917
Jan 2–May, Wed, Sun 2–5. July–Aug, Wed,
    Thurs, Sun 2–5.30. Sept–Dec 20, Wed,
    Sun 2–5. Open Aug Bank Holiday. Closed
    for one week at Christmas, Easter and
    Whitsun.
◼ The Curator
£ ⊘ ⋒ ♿ HHA

Fawley Court is half a mile from Henley, in the
direction of Marlow. It was rebuilt to a design by
Wren in 1684 and in 1690 the drawing-room
was given a Grinling Gibbons ceiling. In the
1770s James Wyatt was responsible for the
redecoration and remodelling of a number of
the rooms, and in 1771 Capability Brown was
commissioned to landscape the park. The house
was enlarged and refaced with red brick during
the second half of the 19th century. In 1953 the
Polish Congregation of Marian Fathers bought
and restored Fawley Court, which was by then
in poor condition, and established a school and
a Polish Museum and Library.

Stonor Park

nr Henley-on-Thames, Oxfordshire RG9 6HF
    ☎ 049163 587
Apr–Sept, Wed, Thurs, Sun 2–5.30. Aug,
    2–5.30. Bank Holiday Mon 11–5.30.
◼ The Administrator
£ ▮ ⬛ ⋒ HHA

Stonor Park dates from the 12th century, with
considerable alterations and extensions of
c. 1540 and mid 18th century. The Stonors,
who have always lived here, have been an
influential Catholic family. In 1968 the house
acquired a bequest of mainly Italian pictures,
sculpture and objets d'art, including works by
the Tiepolos, Tintoretto, Riccio and Algardi. A
collection of furniture, paintings and tapestries
has been lent from Sawston Hall by Mrs
Huddleston, and five 18th-century Flemish
tapestries by a friend. The dining-room
wallpaper (1812), by Joseph Dufour, shows the
important buildings of Paris side by side along
the Seine.

Hepstonstall

Heptonstall Old Grammar School

Heptonstall, Hebden Bridge, West Yorkshire
    HX7 7LY   ☎ 0422 843738
Apr and Sept, Sat, Sun 2–6. May–Aug, Mon,
    Wed, Thurs, Fri 11–4; Sat, Sun 12–5.
    Oct–Mar, Sat, Sun 1–5.
◼ Leisure Services Department, Calderdale
    Borough Council, Wellesley Park, Halifax
    ☎ 0422 59454
£ ⊘ ⋒

The 18th-century Grammar School has been
preserved as a museum, together with 18th and
19th-century furniture and equipment. The
displays illustrate the history of this Pennine
handloom weaving village, with exhibits
relating to agriculture, crafts, domestic life and
leisure activities. There is a reconstruction of
the cottage of a fustian cutter and, among the
Museum's more remarkable features, dies and
other equipment used by the notorious 18th-
century coin clippers and counterfeiters, the
Cragg Coiners.

Hereford

Bulmer Railway Centre

Whitecross Road, Hereford, Hereford and
    Worcester
Easter or Apr–Sept, Sat, Sun 2–5. Steam Days
    as advertised, 11–5.
◼ The Publicity Officer, 6000 Locomotive
    Association, 8 Little Birch Croft, Whitchurch,
    Bristol BS14 0JB
£ ⊘ ⬛ Steam Days only ⋒

The Centre provides a base for three working
examples of express passenger steam
locomotives, ex-GWR 6000 'King George V',
ex-LMS 6201 'Princess Elizabeth', and ex-SR
35028 'Clan Line'. Special steam days are
arranged from time to time and the Centre is also
a working depot for main-line steam operations
in the area. On occasions, other locomotives
visit the Centre and take part in its activities.

Churchill Gardens Museum

Venns Lane, Hereford, Hereford and Worcester
    ☎ 0432 268121 extn 207/334 (City
    Museum)
Tues–Sat 2–5. During summer, also Sun 2–5.
    Closed Good Fri, Dec 25, 26.
    Open Bank Holiday Mon.
◼ See City Museum
£ ⊘ ⋒

The Museum is in a Regency country house,
with Victorian additions, and in the attached
coach-house. It contains displays of costumes,
furniture and paintings, mainly of the 18th and
19th centuries. The period rooms include a

**Figure of a standing lady. Chinese, Late Han
dynasty (25–221 A.D.). Hereford, City
Museum and Art Gallery.**

Victorian nursery, a butler's pantry and parlour, an 18th-century Chinoiscric room and an early 19th-century room. The Museum exhibits the Sandford Collection of straw and corn dollies, formerly at Eye Manor, and has a new costume display collection.

The Brian Hatton Gallery contains paintings by the Hereford-born artist, Brian Hatton (1887–1916), who was killed during the First World War.

City Museum and Art Gallery

Broad Street, Hereford, Hereford and Worcester
*   HR4 9AU   ☎ 0432 268121 extn 207/334*
Apr–Sept, Tues, Wed, Fri 10–6; Thurs 10–5;
*   Sat 10–5. Oct–Mar, Tues, Wed, Fri 10–6;*
*   Thurs 10–5; Sat 10–4. Closed Good Fri,*
*   Dec 25, 26. Open Bank Holiday Mon.*
Museums Curator
F 🛈 🚃 ♿

The Victorian Gothic building which now houses the Museum dates from 1872. The exterior contains much ornamental carving.

The Museum displays illustrate the natural history, early history and traditional culture of Hereford and the area surrounding it. The natural history collections include an observation hive and beekeeping displays, and among the archaeology exhibits are finds from Iron Age hillforts and from the Roman town of *Magnus* (Kenchester).

The Art Gallery, which changes exhibitions each month, has an important collection of early English watercolours. The works of modern artists and local painters are also well represented.

Herefordshire Light Infantry Regimental Museum

TA Centre, Harold Street, Hereford, Hereford
*   and Worcester   ☎ 0432 272914*
Mon–Fri 9.30–4
Captain Marsh
£ 🚃

The Museum's collections illustrate the history and achievements of the Regiment. The displays include uniforms, weapons, medals, Colours and documents.

Herefordshire Waterworks Museum

Broomy Hill Road, Hereford, Hereford and
*   Worcester   ☎ 0432 274104*
Apr–May, 1st Sun in each month, 2–5. June–July,
*   Sun 2–5. Aug, daily 2–5. Open Bank Holiday*
*   weekends in steam. Other times by appt.*
The Secretary, 87 Ledbury Road, Hereford
*   HR1 1RQ*
£ ⟁ 🚃 ♿

Situated in listed buildings, the Herefordshire Waterworks Museum shows, in conjunction with the adjoining modern operating works, the complete story of water supply from river to tap, with pumps and gauges that can be operated by the visitor. The larger items of plant are on their original sites and provide a useful comparison with more modern electric equipment. The most impressive exhibit is the vertical, inverted, triple-expansion condensing engine built in 1895 by Worth, Mackenzie and Co. of Stockton-on-Tees, which is the oldest survivor of this type of engine in Britain. It is steamed on Bank Holiday weekends, together with a smaller Duplex engine by the same maker, installed 10 years later. Steam is provided by a Lancashire boiler of 1895.

Museum of Cider and King Offa Distillery

The Cider Mills, Pomona Place, Whitecross Road,
*   Hereford, Hereford and Worcester HR4 0LW*
*   ☎ 0432 54207*
Apr–Oct, daily 10–5.30. Nov–Mar, pre-booked
*   parties only.*
Museum Assistant
£ 🛈 🚃 🚃

The Museum of Cider tells the story of cider-making from the traditional farmhouse methods to the coming of mechanical production. The exhibits include a farm cider house, with all its equipment, together with a complete set of travelling cidermaker's equipment, which used to be taken from farm to farm. The original champagne cider cellars, where the champagne

Sampling the exhibits at the Hereford Museum of Cider.

method was first applied to cider-making, have been restored and can be seen with their tiers of bottles. Another cellar display illustrates cider production in the late 1920s, with the hydraulic presses and machinery for washing, filling, bottling and corking. Visitors can also see the resident cooper at work, using tools and methods identical to those employed four centuries ago.

The King Offa Distillery produces cider brandy, using copper stills brought from Normandy. Cider brandy was common in England in the 16th and 17th centuries, but was gradually taxed out of existence. The Museum has a licence to distil and is the first producer for over 200 years of cider brandy, which is sold in the museum shop.

Old House Museum

High Town, Hereford, Hereford and Worcester
   ☎ *0432 268121 extn 207/334 (City
   Museum)*
*Mon 10–1; Tues–Fri 10–1, 2–5.30; Sat 10–1,
   2–5.30 (10–1 in winter). Closed Good Fri,
   Dec 25, 26. Open Bank Holiday Mon.*
⌘ *See City Museum*
Ⓔ *ex. Mon* ⌀ ⇜

The Old House, built in 1621, was originally
part of Butchers' Row. The porch has the Coat
of Arms of the Butchers' Guild of London over
the doorway. The house contains 17th-century
furniture on three floors, including four-poster
beds in the bedrooms. There are also model
displays of Hereford during the Civil War,
together with armour of the period.
   During the 19th and early 20th centuries, this
magnificent timber-framed house was used as a
saddler's, a hardware shop, a fish shop and
a bank. There are wall-paintings, panelling and
plasterwork, and other architectural items,
notably fireplaces, brought from elsewhere.

St John and Coningsby Medieval Museum

*Widemarsh Street, Hereford, Hereford and
   Worcester HR4 9HN   ☎ 0432 272837*
Easter–Sept, Tues–Thurs, Sat, Sun 2–5
⌘ *The Curator*
Ⓔ ⌀ ⇜

The 13th-century building, on the site of a
former hostelry of the Knights Hospitalier of St
John of Jerusalem, has been restored to its 17th-
century condition. In the adjacent gardens are
the ruins of Blackfriars Monastery and the ruins
of the only remaining Preaching Cross in the
country. The displays illustrate the history of
the Order of St John and the wars during the
300 years of the Crusades, in exhibits including
armour and emblazons. There are also models,
in period dress and bandages, of the Coningsby
pensioners who used the hospital on the site and
an exhibit commemorating Nell Gwyn, one
of Hereford's most celebrated natives.

Herne Bay

Herne Bay Museum

High Street, Herne Bay, Kent   ☎ 0227 360151
*Mon, Tues, Fri 9.30–7; Wed 9.30–1; Sat
   9.30–5. Closed public holidays.*
⌘ *Miss M. Winsch, Kent County Museum
   Service, West Malling, Kent ME19 6QE
   ☎ 0732 845845 extn 2129*
Ⓕ ⇜

The exhibits in the Museum are mainly related
to the growth and development of the town and
district, a story which is illustrated by paintings,
prints and photographs of local scenes, and by
maps. There are also exhibits of fossils found in
the area, prehistoric archaeology and Roman
material from Reculver.

**The Kitchen of the Old House Museum,
Hereford.**

Herstmonceux

Royal Greenwich Observatory

*Herstmonceux Castle, Hailsham, East Sussex
   BN27 1RP   ☎ 0323 833171*
*Easter–Sept, daily 10.30–5.30 (last admission
   4.30)*
⌘ *Exhibition Manager*
Ⓔ ⌑ ⬛ ⇜ ♿

Herstmonceux Castle was built in 1441. The
interior was demolished in 1776, to provide
materials for building nearby Herstmonceux
Place. Rebuilding and restoration was carried
out during the earlier part of the present
century, and in 1946 the house and estate were
sold to the Government to be the future home
of the Royal Greenwich Observatory. The
Castle now houses a Conference Centre and a
Craft Centre, which displays and demonstrates
traditional Sussex crafts.
   The exhibitions, in two rooms on the ground
floor of the Castle, cover the history of the
Castle and the Observatory and also the local
flora and fauna. There is also a display showing
the work of astronomers and their present-day
picture of the universe. During weekday
afternoons an astronomer is usually available to
answer visitors' questions.

Hertford

Hertford Museum

*18 Bull Plain, Hertford, Hertfordshire SG14 1DT
   ☎ 0992 52686*
*Tues–Fri 10–5; Sat 10–1, 2–5. Closed public
   holidays.*
⌘ *The Curator*
Ⓕ ⌀ ⇜

The theme of the Museum is the story of East
Hertfordshire. The earliest exhibits, rocks found
900 feet below the surface, are over 400 million
years old. From more recent periods, there are
also Palaeolithic axes, found on the banks of the
River Lea, and the fossil remains of animals,
including the hippopotamus.
   The Museum has sections on natural history,
archaeology, agriculture and rural life, and
aspects of town life. It also includes the Museum
of the Hertfordshire Regiment, with collections
illustrating its history up to and including the
Second World War.

Hessle

Hessle Whiting Mill

Hessle Foreshore, Hessle, Humberside
☎ *0482 882255*
May–Sept, Sun 2–4.30
🗽 *Mrs Woodcock, Beverley Borough Council, The
Hall, Lairgate, Beverley, Humberside*
£ ⃠ ↩

The Mill, which dates from c. 1810, was built to
crush whiting for use in whitewash and as a mild
abrasive. It was fitted with five single-sided
roller sails and air brakes, an advanced feature at
the time. In addition to driving the crushing
rollers, the windmill also powered two pumps,
one for lifting water from a well on the site and
the other for pumping the chalk slurry to
settling tanks.

The tower, with most of its internal
machinery, has survived. A collection of
photographs of the mill and the chalk quarry,
together with diagrams showing how the mill
operated, are on display inside the tower.

Hethersett

Fire Service Museum

*Fire Service Headquarters, Norwich Road,
Hethersett, Norfolk HR9 3DM*
☎ *0603 810351*
🗽 *R. G. Vertigan, Divisional Officer*
£ ⃠ ↩

The collections at the Museum consist of
firefighting appliances and other equipment and
mementoes relating to the history of the Norfolk
Fire Service. The Museum has an extensive
specialist library and access is also available to
major appliances stored elsewhere in the
county.

Hexham

Chesterholm Museum

*The Vindolanda Trust, Bardon Mill, Hexham,
Northumberland NE47 7JN   ☎ 04984 277
Jan 2–Feb and Nov, daily 10–4. Mar, Oct, daily
10–5. Apr, Sept, daily 10–5.30. May–June,
daily 10–6. July–Aug, daily 10–6.30.
Closed Christmas period.*
🗽 *The Education Officer*
£ ⃠ ⬛ ↩ ↩

Vindolanda, just to the south of Hadrian's Wall,
was the base for 500 Roman auxiliary soldiers.
Excavations have uncovered part of the 4th-
century fort and the centre of the civilian
settlement, which lay outside the walls of the
fort. A wide range of finds from the excavations
is displayed at Chesterholm, a country house

adjacent to *Vindolanda*. The collection is
especially important for its examples of Roman
leather and textiles, but there are also many
items of jewellery, pottery, metal and wood.
The exhibits include a full-scale reconstruction
of a civilian kitchen found at *Vindolanda*.

Middle March Centre for Border History

*Manor Office, Hallgate, Hexham, Northumberland
NE46 3NH   ☎ 0434 604011 extn 259
Easter Mon–Oct, Mon–Fri 10–4.30. Aug, also
Sat, Sun 2–5.*
🗽 *Mrs F. Fairbairn, Museum Technician*
£ ⃠ ↩

Hexham's old gaol, which was built of re-used
Roman stone in 1330–2, has the distinction of
being the first purpose-built prison in England.
The building retains most of its original features,
the only substantial alteration being the
construction of a new staircase in the 1860s.

The Museum, which provides audio-visual
displays and coin-operated commentaries, as
well as static exhibitions, gives an insight into
the activities of the Border Marches during the
16th century, a time when protracted warfare
between England and Scotland had left the
Borders devastated, with growing rivalry
between the leading families and with survival
depending on sheep-stealing and cattle-rustling.

Higher Bockhampton

Hardy's Cottage

*Higher Bockhampton, nr Dorchester, Dorset
DT2 8QJ   ☎ 0305 62366
Garden: Apr–Oct, daily ex. Tues morning, 11–6
or sunset if earlier. House by appt.*
🗽 *The Tenant*
£ *House only* ⃠ ↩ [NT]

The thatched cottage, built by Thomas Hardy's
great grandfather in 1800, lies three miles
north-east of Dorchester, half a mile south of
the A35. It contains the room where Hardy was
born in 1840 and the room where, in the 1870s,
he wrote *Under the Greenwood Tree* and *Far
from the Madding Crowd*, after giving up his
career as an architect in order to write. It has
been very little altered, and is now owned by the
National Trust.

**Roman bronze dog from the well of the
water-goddess Conventina. Humshaugh,
Chesters Roman Fort Museum.**

High Wycombe

Disraeli Museum

Hughenden Manor, High Wycombe,
    Buckinghamshire HP14 4LA   ☎ 0494 32580
Mar, Sat, Sun 2–6. Mar 31–Oct, Wed–Sat 2–6,
    Sun, Bank Holiday Mon 12–6.
Ⓝ The Administrator
Ⓔ ♠ ⬅ & [NT]

Hughenden Manor is a mile and a half north of
High Wycombe on the A4128 road to Great
Missenden. Benjamin Disraeli bought it in
1848, clothed the stucco in brick and
completely remodelled the house, giving it its
present Victorian Tudor appearance. He and his
wife are buried in the churchyard in the park.
    Hughenden, now a National Trust property,
contains much of Disraeli's furniture, portraits
of his family, friends and political associates,
and much of his library. The Disraeli Room, the
Politician's Room and the Berlin Congress
Room provide clues to different aspects of his
character. In his study, visitors can see portraits
of his father and mother, the black-edged
notepaper that he always used after his wife's
death, his school books, some of the novels he
wrote in this room, and his wife's diaries.

Wycombe Chair Museum

Castle Hill House, Priory Avenue, High Wycombe,
    Buckinghamshire HP13 6PX   ☎ 0494 23879
Mon, Tues, Thurs, Fri, Sat 10–1, 2–5.
    Closed Bank Holiday.
Ⓝ The Curator
Ⓕ ⬅

Castle Hill House, set in the grounds of a
medieval motte and bailey, is a late 17th-
century building, with 18th-century additions.
High Wycombe is a traditional centre of chair-
making and the Museum specialises in its history
and techniques, especially relating to the
Windsor chair. There are also displays
illustrating cane and rush seating and lace-
making, which was once important in the area,
as well as the general history of furniture and of
the High Wycombe furniture industry.

Hitchin

Hitchin Museum and Art Gallery

Paynes Park, Hitchin, Hertfordshire SG5 1EQ
    ☎ 0462 34476
Mon–Sat 10–5. Closed public holidays.
Ⓝ Schools Service Officer, Old Ambulance
    Station, Paynes Park, Hitchin, Hertfordshire
    ☎ 0462 52666
Ⓕ ⬅

The Museum concentrates on the history of the
Hitchin area, with a special emphasis on the
development of local industries. The important
costume collections have recently been
redisplayed. Other sections of the Museum are
devoted to natural history, the story of the
Hertfordshire Yeomanry Regiment,
archaeology and art.

Hollingbourne

Eyhorne Manor

Hollingbourne, nr Maidstone, Kent ME17 1UU
    ☎ 062780 514
May–Aug, Sat, Sun, Bank Holiday Mon, 2–6.
    Aug, also Tues, Wed, Thurs, 2–6.
Ⓝ Mr and Mrs Derek Simmons
Ⓔ ♠ ⬅

This is a fully restored early 15th-century manor
house, with 17th-century additions. There are
models showing the original construction and
evolution of the house up to the present day.
One of the 14 rooms which can be visited
contains a large collection of historic laundry
equipment.

Holy Island

Lindisfarne Priory Museum

Holy Island, Northumberland   ☎ 028989 200
Mar 29–Oct 14, daily 9.30–6.30. Oct 15–
    Mar 28, Mon–Sat 9.30–4; Sun 2–4.
    Closed Dec 24–26, Jan 1.
Ⓝ Historic Buildings & Monuments Commission,
    Carlisle   ☎ 0228 31777
Ⓔ ⬅ ⬅

Holy Island, off the Northumberland coast, can
be reached across a causeway at low tide. Tide
tables are posted at each end of the causeway.
The Museum displays Anglo-Saxon sculpture
and medieval pottery found at Lindisfarne
Priory, established in the 7th century.

Holywell

Grange Cavern Military Museum

Grange Lane, Holway, Holywell, Clwyd
    ☎ 0352 713455
Easter–Oct, daily 9.30–6. Feb–Mar, Sat, Sun
    10–5. Group visits throughout year by appt.
Ⓝ Mr J. Povey
Ⓔ ♠ ⬅ ⬅ &

The two-and-a-half acre Grange Cavern was
excavated in the early 19th century, the
carboniferous limestone being used in the
construction of Liverpool South Docks. The
underground workings provided a secure bomb
store during the Second World War when
11,000 tons of bombs were kept here.
    The collections now housed in the Cavern
include over 70 military vehicles of all types,
mostly dating from the Second World War,
as well as heavy guns and military motorcycles.
A separate museum, the Inner Museum,
contains a collection of badges, buttons and
medals, some dating back to the 18th century,
together with helmets and uniforms of different
nations. Among the special features are a
replica of a First World War field trench, an
Anderson air-raid shelter, and a Falklands War
display.

Holywood

Ulster Folk and Transport Museum

*Cultra Manor, Holywood, Co. Down, Northern
    Ireland BT18 0EU   ☎ 02317 5411
May–Sept, Mon–Sat 11–6; Sun 2–6. Oct–Apr,
    Mon–Sat 11–5; Sun 2–5. Closed Christmas
    period.*
🏾 *Education Secretary*
£ ♣ 🖼 🅰 ♿

The Museum is on the A2 Belfast to Bangor
road, seven miles from Belfast. With both
indoor and open-air sections, it illustrates the
way of life, past and present, and the customs of
the people of Northern Ireland. Examples of
vernacular buildings, including houses,
workshops, a church and a school, have been
brought from all over Ulster and erected in
settings which re-create the original
environment. Both in the old buildings and in
specially designed galleries, there are displays of
furnishings and of domestic and craftsmen's
equipment, presented in a way which allows
visitors to understand its use and purpose.

    The extensive transport collections illustrate
the history of land, water and sea transport in
Ireland, and its influence on the social life of the
community.

**Hill farm from Coskib, Co. Antrim,
reconstructed at the Ulster Folk and
Transport Museum, Holywood.**

Honiton

Allhallows Museum

*High Street, Honiton, Devon EX14 8PE
Mid May–Oct, Mon–Sat 10–5*
🏾 *The Curator*
£ ✏️ 🅰

The main gallery of the Museum is the town's
oldest building and was formerly the chancel of
the medieval Chapel of Allhallows. The
exhibits are related to the history of Honiton,
but particularly to Honiton lace, of which the
Museum has large and important holdings.

Hornsea

Hornsea Museum of Village Life

*11 Newbegin, Hornsea, North Humberside
    HU18 1AB   ☎ 04012 3430/3443
Easter–July 19 and Sept 11–Oct, daily 2–5.
    July 20–Sept 10, Mon–Sat 11–5; Sun 2–5.*
🏾 *Mrs C. F. Walker, Hon. Curator*
£ ♣ 🅰 □

Housed in an 18th-century farmhouse, with its
associated outbuildings, the Museum's
collections reflect the village life and local
history of North Holderness. There are accurate
representations of the dairy, kitchen, parlour
and bedroom of a century ago, and the tools of
local craftsmen are displayed in their settings.
There is also a photograph room, with changing
exhibitions of material drawn from the
Museum's collection of photographs and
postcards of local scenes, and a local industry
display, in which special attention has been paid
to the Hornsea Brick and Tile Works (c
1868–96), and the Hull and Hornsea Railway
(1864–1964). Local personalities
commemorated in the Museum include the vast
and enormously strong Rose Carr, who ran a
stable and carrier's business, and could carry two
16-stone sacks of corn.

Horringer

Ickworth

*The Rotunda, Horringer, Bury St Edmunds,
    Suffolk IP29 5QE   ☎ 028488 270
Mar 29–Apr and Oct, Sat, Sun 1.30–5.30.
    May–Sept, Tues, Wed, Fri, Sat, Sun
    1.30–5.30. Open Bank Holiday Mon.*
🏾 *The Administrator*
£ ♣ 🖼 🅰 ♿ [NT]

The village of Horringer is three miles south-
west of Bury St Edmunds on the west side of the
A143. The house, Ickworth, begun in 1794 and
completed c. 1830, is an architectural curiosity.
It consists of an elliptical rotunda connected by
two curved corridors to flanking wings. The
contents include late Regency and 18th-century
French furniture, an outstanding collection of
domestic and ambassadorial silver, sculpture and
family portraits of the Earls of Bristol. There is a
fine orangery and interesting gardens.

Horsham

Horsham Museum

*9 The Causeway, Horsham, West Sussex
        ☎ 0403 54959
Oct–Mar, Tues–Fri, 1–5; Sat 10–5.
    Apr–Sept, Tues–Sat 10–5.*
🏾 *Elizabeth E. Kelly, Curator*
F ✏️ 🅰

The Museum occupies a 15th-century timber-
framed house, modified and extended at various
later dates up to the 18th century. It has good
collections within the fields of local history,

agriculture and the rural and domestic crafts. Other displays are of archaeology, geology and the decorative arts.

The Museum area includes a reconstructed 18th-century timber-framed barn and a walled garden containing a variety of rare herbs, shrubs and flowers.

Houghton

Houghton Hall Soldier Museum

Houghton Hall, Houghton, King's Lynn, Norfolk
PE31 6UE   ☎ 048522 569
Easter Sun–last Sun in Sept, Thurs, Sun, Bank
Holiday, 12–5
◙ *The Administrator, Estate Office*
Ⓔ *House only* 🍴 🚆 🅰 🚗 ♿

Houghton Hall is 14 miles from King's Lynn, on the A148 Fakenham road. The 18th-century Palladian mansion was built for Sir Robert Walpole and contains many of the original furnishings, including some by William Kent. The stables contain heavy horses and Shetland ponies, as well as an exhibition of carriages and harness.

There is an important collection of 20,000 model soldiers, some of which are arranged in battle scenes. In addition, there are a number of items of militaria and an exhibition of paintings, watercolours and prints on military subjects. These mostly date from the late 19th century and include works by the leading military artists of the time.

Hove

The British Engineerium

off Nevill Road, Hove, East Sussex BN3 7QA
☎ 0273 559583
Daily 10–5. Closed one week before Christmas.
◙ *Mrs Daphne Munro, Secretary to the Director*
Ⓔ 🔖 🚗

The Engineerium is in Brighton's 1866 water pumping station, with its 100-foot chimney, classic panchromatic brickwork and 1876 Eastons & Anderson beam engine, now restored. The original coal store is now the Museum's display area. It contains, on the ground floor, the Corliss engine which won first prize when shown at the Paris International Exhibition of 1889, together with traction engines, steam fire engines, a hot air engine bay, and a display illustrating the history of the electric motor.

Both the beam engine and the Corliss engine operate in steam on Sundays and Bank Holidays throughout the year. The Engineerium also has what is believed to be the finest collection of steam models in Europe, including the original model locomotive made by George Stephenson and the original design model of Timothy Hackworth's 'Sans Pareil', which came second to the 'Rocket' in the 1829 Trials.

Hove Museum and Art Gallery

19 New Church Road, Hove, East Sussex
BN3 4AB   ☎ 0273 779410
Tues–Fri 10–5; Sat 10–4.30
◙ *The Curator*
Ⓕ 🔖 🚗

The Museum has outstanding collections of 18th and early 19th-century British pottery and porcelain, 20th-century British drawings and paintings, and historic dolls. Other sections contain toys, 18th-century paintings, furniture, glass, silver, watches, and coins and medals.

There are also military exhibits and displays illustrating the history of Hove and of Sussex.

Howth

National Transport Museum Project

Howth Castle, Howth, Co. Dublin, Ireland
Easter–Oct, daily 2–6. Other times by appt for
parties.
◙ *Mr Liam Kelly, 39 Dunree Park, Coolock,*
Dublin 5   ☎ 01 480831
Ⓔ 🔖 🚗

As the owner of Howth Castle phases out his farming activities, the agricultural buildings are becoming available for the expansion of the Museum project, which is at present organised on a voluntary basis. The Museum Society has a collection of over 100 vehicles, including horse-drawn vehicles, electric trams, steam-powered vehicles, petrol and diesel buses and commercial vehicles, fire appliances and military transport.

Eighteenth-century wooden doll dressed in silk. Huddersfield Art Gallery.

Huddersfield

Huddersfield Art Gallery

*Princess Alexandra Walk, Huddersfield, West
Yorkshire HD1 2SU*
☎ *0484 513808 extn 216*
Mon–Fri 10–6; Sat 10–4. Closed Bank Holiday.
🕴 *Robert Hall, Senior Curator*
Ⓕ 🚗 ⅃ ☐

As a whole, the Gallery's collections reflect
national developments in 20th-century British
paintings, sculpture and graphics, as well as the
variety of work produced by artists of the
Kirklees area. Of particular importance are
works by members of the Camden Town Group.
British art of the 1940s and 1950s is also well
represented, with important works by Francis
Bacon, L. S. Lowry, Augustus John, Edward
Burra, David Bomberg and Henry Moore.
  The permanent collection is shown in
conjunction with a varied programme of
temporary exhibitions, demonstrations,
workshops and gallery talks.

Tolson Museum

*Ravensknowle Park, Wakefield Road,
Huddersfield, West Yorkshire HD5 8DJ*
☎ *0484 530591/541455*
*Mon–Sat 10–5; Sun 1–5. Closed Christmas
and New Year.*
🕴 *The Curator*
Ⓕ 🗘 🚗

The Museum building, in the Italianate style,
was completed in 1862 as the mansion of John
Beaumont. The archaeological displays contain
prehistoric, Roman, Saxon and medieval
material from sites in the area, and the
geological and natural history exhibits are also
closely related to Huddersfield and West
Yorkshire. The past and present industries of
Huddersfield are well represented and the large
transport section includes both mechanical and
horse-drawn vehicles, the emphasis being on
items with local connections. Domestic
equipment figures strongly in the social history
displays.

Humshaugh

Chesters Roman Fort Museum (Clayton Memorial Museum)

Humshaugh, nr Hexham, Northumberland
☎ *043481 379*
Mar 15–Oct 15, daily 9.30–6.30.
  Oct 16–Mar 14, Mon–Sat 9.30–4; Sun 2–4.
🕴 *Historic Buildings & Monuments Commission,
  Carlisle*   ☎ *0228 31777*
Ⓔ 🗘 🖭 🚗 ⅃ ✠

The Museum, built c. 1895, was designed by the
noted Victorian architect, Richard Norman
Shaw. It is a fine example of a period museum,
with many of its original fittings still intact. The
collection comprises almost entirely Roman
material recovered from excavations carried out
along the line of Hadrian's Wall by John
Clayton (1792–1890), a former owner of the
Chesters Estate and a noted local antiquary. It is
particularly rich in sculpture and inscriptions,
but also includes a wide variety of objects from
everyday Romano-British life.

Hungerford

Littlecote House

Hungerford, Berkshire   ☎ *0488 82170*
*Open daily 10–6. Last admission 30 mins
  before closing.*
🕴 *Estate Office*
Ⓔ 🏠 🖭 🚗 ⎡HHA⎤

The house dates from the 15th century and has
been owned successively by the Darrell, Popham
and Wills families. There is a large collection of
weapons, armour and buff uniform coats of the
Cromwellian period and, in the Parlour, a
number of wall paintings reputed to have been
the work of Dutch prisoners-of-war in the
1660s. The Chinese Room contains a fine suite
of Chippendale furniture and in the Long
Gallery there are portraits and items of furniture
of different periods.

Hunnington

Blue Bird Museum

*Blue Bird Confectionery Limited, Hunnington,
  Halesowen, West Midlands B62 0EN*
☎ *021 550 8011*
*Mon–Fri 9–1, 2–5; Sat 9–12.30, 2–5; Sun 2–5.
  Closed Christmas period.*
🕴 *Miss Deana Towers*
Ⓔ 🏠 🚗

The Museum contains tins, photographs,
publicity literature and other historical material
dating back to 1895, when the company was
founded, and before the move to Hunnington.
From the brand name 'Harvino' to the present
Blue Bird symbol, the displays illustrate the

**'Pendent' by Edward Wadsworth, 1942.
Huddersfield Art Gallery.**

Sweet tins in the Blue Bird Museum, Hunnington.

developments which have taken place within this confectionery company as fashion and public preferences change. Photographs show the company's former Lion Toffee Mills in Birmingham, the building of the present Hunnington factory during 1926–7, and the improvements in production methods and working conditions.

Huntingdon

Cromwell Museum

*Grammar School Walk, Huntingdon,
    Cambridgeshire*   ☎ *0480 52861*
*Apr–Oct, Tues–Fri 11–1, 2–5; Sat, Sun 11–1,
    2–4. Nov–Mar, Tues–Fri 2–5; Sat 11–1,
    2–4; Sun 2–4. Open Good Fri.*
🏛 *The Museums Assistant, County Library,
    Princes Street, Huntingdon PE18 6NS*
        ☎ *0480 52181*
Ⓔ ✐ ➤

The building which houses the Museum is the remaining part of the Hospital of St John the Baptist, founded in the reign of Henry II. In 1547, at the Dissolution, it was converted into a free school, of which both Oliver Cromwell and Samuel Pepys were subsequently pupils. The surviving remnant, the western end of the hall, has been restored several times.

The Museum illustrates the history and activities of the Parliamentary–Commonwealth side of the Puritan Revolution 1640–60 but, in the case of material relating to the Cromwell family, the period begins earlier and ends later. The collection includes many portraits, including miniatures; personal possessions of Oliver Cromwell and members of his family; letters, documents, pamphlets and diaries; swords and armour.

There are seven portraits of Oliver Cromwell himself, and 13 of his family. Other subjects include Charles I, George Monck, Duke of Albemarle, Thomas Fairfax and Sir Harry Vane. Among the memorabilia of Oliver Cromwell are his apothecary's chest, a death mask, some of his swords, riding boots and spurs and his despatch box, as well as a large number of autograph letters, pamphlets and ordinances illustrating his career and period of rule.

Huntly

Brander Museum

The Square, Huntly, Aberdeenshire
        ☎ *0779 77778 (Arbuthnot Museum)*
Tues–Sat 10–12, 2–4
🏛 *See Arbuthnot Museum, Peterhead*
Ⓕ ✐ ➤

The Museum collections are concerned with the social history, crafts and occupations of the Huntly area of Aberdeenshire.

Hutton le Hole

Ryedale Folk Museum

Hutton le Hole, North Yorkshire YO6 6UA
        ☎ *07515 367*
Last Sun in Mar–Oct, daily 11–6
🏛 *Douglas Smith, Curator*
Ⓔ ✐ ➤

The Museum, in the North York Moors National Park, is housed in a group of 18th-century farm buildings, with an open-air section in the grounds behind the Museum. The displays illustrate the daily life of the people who inhabited the Ryedale area from prehistoric times to the present day. There are exhibits of material related to rural and agricultural crafts, including a complete iron foundry and an Elizabethan glass furnace. The open-air section contains a medieval longhouse, a 16th-century manor house, an 18th-century crofter's cottage, an operational blacksmith's forge, and an important collection of farm wagons, implements and machinery.

Hythe

Hythe Local History Room

Oaklands, Stade Street, Hythe, Kent CT21 6BG
        ☎ *0303 66152*   •
*Mon 9.30–1, 2–6; Tues 9.30–1, 2–5; Wed,
    Thurs 9.30–1, 2–5; Fri 9.30–1, 2–7;
    Sat 9.30–1, 2–4. Closed public holidays.*
🏛 *Miss M. Winsch, Kent County Museum
    Service, West Malling, Kent ME19 6QE*
        ☎ *0732 845845 extn 2129*
Ⓕ

The displays here cover local archaeology and material relating to the history of Hythe and the Cinque Ports. There are collections of costumes, 17th-century maps, fire insurance plates, paintings and 17th-century oak furniture.

Ilfracombe

Chambercombe Manor

Chambercombe Lane, Ilfracombe, Devon
EX34 9RJ   ☎ 0271 62624
Easter–Sept, Mon–Fri 10.30–12.30, 2–4.30;
    Sun 2–4.30
▨ Mrs Penny Gravell
£ 🔾 💻 🚗

There was probably a manor here in the 11th
century, but the present building dates from the
14th and 15th centuries. Eight rooms are open
to the public. They contain furniture dating
from the early 15th century to the mid 19th
century.

Ilfracombe Museum

Wilder Road, Ilfracombe, Devon EX34 8AF
    ☎ 0271 63541
Easter–Oct, daily 10–5.30. Nov–Easter, Mon–Sat
    10–12.30 Closed Dec 25, 26.
▨ The Curator
£ ex. pre-booked educ. groups 🔾 🚗 ♿

The Museum's main building dates from 1885.
It was formerly the laundry of the now
demolished Ilfracombe Hotel. The Museum was
founded in 1931 by Mervyn G. Palmer, a one-
time explorer and freelance collector for the
British Museum. Its collections cover a wide
field and include natural history, archaeology
and local history. Victorian material is
particularly abundant and includes an ornate
1846 press, used to print the local newspaper.
Other exhibits show woodworkers' and cobblers'
tools and equipment from the end of the 18th
century onwards, laundry and other domestic
equipment, and railway relics. The Museum
now has a Brass Rubbing Centre.

Ilkeston

Erewash Museum

High Street, Ilkeston, Derbyshire DE7 5JA
    ☎ 0602 303361 extn 331
Thurs, Fri, Sat 10–4. Closed Good Fri and
    Christmas week.
▨ The Curator
F 🔾 🚗

The main part of the house which is now
Erewash Museum dates from the late 18th
century. It was extensively restyled and added to
c. 1860. Period room displays include a
Victorian drawing-room with costume figures,
a reconstructed terraced-house scullery and a
larger kitchen display.
    Other rooms display civic regalia and other
material reflecting the past social and economic
life of the area.

Ilkley

Manor House Art Gallery and Museum

Castle Yard, Ilkley, West Yorkshire LS29 9DT
    ☎ 0943 600066
Tues–Sun 10–5. Open Bank Holiday Mon.
    Closed Good Fri, Dec 25, 26.
▨ Assistant Keeper
F 🔾 🚗 □

The Manor House is an Elizabethan building,
constructed on part of the site of the Roman fort
of Verbeia, near an exposed section of Roman
wall. The ground floor gallery contains Roman
material from local excavations and a section
illustrating the history of Ilkley as a flourishing
spa resort. Part of the house has recently been
re-displayed with 17th and 18th-century
furniture, in the style of a farmhouse parlour-
kitchen.
    Exhibitions change approximately every six
weeks, emphasising the work of artists living in
the region.

White Wells, Ilkley.

White Wells

Wells Road, Ilkley, West Yorkshire LS29 9LH
Easter–Oct 15, Sat, Sun, Bank Holiday 2–6
▨ Mr and Mrs D. Dawson, Wardens
F 🔾 💻 🚗

In the late 18th and early 19th centuries the
springs at Ilkley were used for the newly
fashionable cold water bath cure. The former
bath house cottage buildings, with one of the
plunge baths still preserved, now accommodates
a museum and forms a focal point in this stretch
of moorland, which has been much favoured by
many generations of artists. There are displays of
the flora, fauna, rocks and minerals to be found
on the moor and in the surrounding area.

Immingham

Immingham Museum and Gallery

Bluestone Corner, Immingham, South Humberside
    DN40 2DX   ☎ 0469 75777
Apr–Sept, Wed–Sun 2–4. Oct–Mar, Sat, Sun
    2–4.
▨ Mr B. Mummery, Curator, 5 Alderney Way,
    Immingham DN40 1RB
F 🚗 □

The Museum is housed in a former Methodist chapel, built in 1883. Its displays concentrate on the history of Immingham and the surrounding area and show the development of the town from Roman times up to the building of the docks in 1912. A feature of the Museum is the reconstruction of a local chemist's shop as it looked during the period 1912–40.

Temporary exhibitions around special areas of interest, such as wildlife, toys and games, and agriculture are arranged from time to time and visitors can also see the Museum's large collection of photographs showing life in Immingham from c. 1900 onwards.

Innerleithen

Traquair

Innerleithen, Peeblesshire EH44 6PW
☎ *0896 830323*
Easter–mid Oct, daily 1.30–5.30. July–Sept 15,
daily 10.30–5.30. Other times by appt.
 Mr P. Maxwell Stuart
£ ● ▆ ◄ HHA

Originally a Royal hunting lodge, Traquair has a claim to being the oldest continuously inhabited house in Scotland. Twenty generations of the same family have lived here and 27 Scottish and English monarchs are said to have visited it. The emphasis of the contents is on family possessions, rather than fine furniture. The 18th-century library is almost intact.

The 200-year-old brewhouse at Traquair makes and sells exceptionally strong ale.

Inniskeen

Inniskeen Folk Museum

Inniskeen, Co. Monaghan, Ireland
May–Aug, Sun 3–5.30
 Mrs M. Quinn, 'Lisrolagh', Inniskeen
☎ *042 78109*
£ ◄

The Museum is in a former Church of Ireland church, built in 1853. The collections illustrate the history of the district and its traditional life and customs. There is a section devoted to the poet, Patrick Kavanagh (1904–67), who was born at Mucker, near Inniskeen. It includes his death mask.

Inveraray

Auchindrain Open Air Museum of Country Life

Inveraray, Argyll PA32 8XN   ☎ *0499 5235*
Easter–May & Sept, Sun–Fri 11–4.
June–Aug, daily 10–5.
 The Curator
£ ● ▆ ◄

The Museum is five and a half miles south-west of Inveraray, on the A83. It consists of the original buildings of a West Highland township,

formerly under a communal tenancy for many centuries. The dwelling houses and other buildings illustrate, together with their contents, the traditional life of the West Highlanders, their methods of farming and the ways in which they provided themselves with the necessities for survival.

Inveraray Bell Tower

All Saints' Episcopal Church, The Avenue,
Inveraray, Argyll
Late May–Sept, Mon–Sat 10–1, 2–5; Sun 3–6.
Pre-booked parties at other times.
 Norman Chaddock, Blencathra, Tighcladich,
St. Catherine's, via Cairndow, Argyll
PA25 8AZ   ☎ *0499 2433*
£ ◔ ◄

The Tower, very popular with visiting ringers, contains the third heaviest ring of 10 bells in the world. Exhibited in it are church brasses and vestments, and displays relating to the techniques of change-ringing and to the history of the bells at Inveraray.

Inveraray Castle

Cherry Park, Inveraray, Argyll   ☎ *0499 2203*
1st Sat Apr–June & Sept–2nd Sun Oct,
Mon–Thurs, Sat 10–1, 2–6; Sun 1–6.
July–Aug, Mon–Sat 10–6, Sun 1–6.
 The Factor
£ ● ▆ ◄ HHA

The present Castle is half a mile north of Inveraray, on the A83. It was built in the mid 18th century and is the residence of the Dukes of Argyll and the headquarters of the Clan Campbell, and has been fully restored after a serious fire in 1975. The family tree occupies the whole of one wall in the Clan Room and the armoury hall, extending the full height of the house, is decorated with armour from top to bottom. Among the other family treasures on view are the Beauvais tapestries in the drawing room, the portraits in the saloon and the Crown Derby and Meissen porcelain in the circular china closet.

Inverkeithing

Inverkeithing Museum

Queen's Street, Inverkeithing, Fife KY11 1LS
☎ *0383 413344*
Wed, Sun 11–5. Closed Dec 25, 26, Jan 1, 2,
local public holidays.
 Dunfermline District Museum, Viewfield
Terrace, Dunfermline KY12 7HY
☎ *0383 721814*
F ◄

The Museum is in part of the buildings of a 14th-century Friary, its displays illustrating the history of this ancient Burgh. There is a special section relating to the life and achievements of Admiral Sir Samuel Greig, who was born close to the Museum. Greig was seconded to the Imperial Russian Navy, which he reorganised, during the reign of Catherine the Great.

Inverness

Inverness Museum and Art Gallery

Castle Wynd, Inverness, Inverness-shire IV2 3ED
☎ *0463 237114*
Mon–Sat 9–5. Closed public holidays in winter.
▣ *The Curator*
Ⓕ ▪ ▬ ↩

The Museum illustrates the social and natural history, archaeology and geology of the Highlands. Dioramas form an important part of the displays and there are reconstructions of a taxidermist's shop and an Inverness cottage as it looked in the 1930s. There is an important collection of Highland silver. Other features of the Museum are a display on the Clans and a number of paintings by Scottish artists.

Inverurie

Carnegie Museum

The Square, Inverurie, Aberdeenshire
Mon–Fri 2–5; Sat 10–12
▣ *See Arbuthnot Museum, Peterhead*
Ⓕ ⬙ ↩

The Carnegie Museum contains displays relating to the prehistoric archaeology, geology and natural history of the area. There are exhibits of domestic equipment, craftsmen's tools and coins, and a special section devoted to the Great North of Scotland Railway.

Castle Fraser

Sauchen, Inverurie, Aberdeenshire AB3 7LD
☎ *03303 463 or 0467 22988*
May–Sept, daily 2–6 (last admissions 5.25).
Gardens open all year, 9.30–sunset.
▣ *Mrs P. Miller*
Ⓔ ▬ ⬗ ↩ [NTS]

Castle Fraser is three miles south of Kemnay, off the B993. One of the Castles of Mar, it was built c. 1575 by the 6th Laird, Michael Fraser, incorporating an earlier building. Two great families of master masons, Bel and Leiper, took part in the work, which was completed in 1636. The contents include early oak furniture and 17th to 19th-century Fraser family portraits.

Ipswich

Christchurch Mansion

Christchurch Park, Soane Street, Ipswich,
Suffolk IP4 2BE
☎ *0473 213761/2 (Ipswich Museum)*
Mon–Sat 10–5; Sun 2.30–4.30. Closes at dusk in
winter. Closed Good Fri, Dec 25, Jan 1.
▣ *See Ipswich Museum*
Ⓕ ⬙ ↩

The house which is now the Museum was built in 1548. Additions and modifications were made to it at various times up to the 1920s. The large collections of furniture and the decorative arts include 18th-century Chinoiserie

lacquerwork, 16th-century tapestries, lantern and longcase clocks. pottery, porcelain, glass – especially 18th-century wine-glasses – and pewter. There are also interesting 17th to 19th-century portraits. The Servants' Wing contains the kitchen, with its copper pans, moulds and roasting spits, and the servants' hall, with the table being laid for a meal. The 18th-century State Rooms on the first floor provide a striking contrast to conditions below stairs. Some rooms still contain the original wallpaper of the 1730s.

In the Wolsey Gallery Suffolk artists are well represented, with paintings by Gainsborough, Constable, John Moore, the Smyths, Alfred Munnings and Wilson Steer. There are also displays of 20th-century prints and sculpture, of costumes and of material illustrating the history of Ipswich and the surrounding area.

Ipswich Museum

High Street, Ipswich, Suffolk IP1 3QH
☎ *0473 213761/2*
Mon–Sat 10–5. Closed Bank Holiday.
▣ *J. G. Fairclough, Educational Liaison Officer*
Ⓕ ⬙ ↩

The façade of the Museum building is distinguished by excellent late Victorian terracotta mouldings. The displays feature ethnological material from Africa, Asia, the Pacific and the Americas, and worldwide natural history exhibitions, especially tropical insects and shells and British birds.

The archaeological galleries cover the archaeology of Suffolk from prehistoric times to the medieval period and include replicas of the Mildenhall and Sutton Hoo treasures and the Ipswich torcs. The recently reorganised Roman gallery includes reconstructions of a Roman bakery and a domestic interior.

Irvine

Scottish Maritime Museum

Laird Forge, Gottries Road, Irvine, Ayrshire
KA12 8QE ☎ *0294 78283*
May–Sept, Mon–Fri 10–4; Sat, Sun 2–5.
Oct–Apr, Mon–Fri 10–4.
▣ *Education Officer*
Ⓔ ▪ ↩

This new and expanding museum, housed in the Laird Forge, famous as makers of block pulleys for the Royal Navy, is devoted to the maritime history of Scotland. It possesses a number of sea-going craft, which visitors can board in the harbour, ranging from an early 19th-century barge to an experimental wind turbine boat and including a tug, yachts, lifeboats, fishing vessels and the last surviving Kirkintilloch-built puffer. On summer weekends there are trips on the *Seamew*, the tender for Sir Thomas Lipton's yacht, *Shamrock*.

There is a large collection of 19th and 20th-century machinery and tools, displayed in a former shipyard building; boatbuilders, welders, riggers, painters and fitters can be seen at work on restoration and reproduction projects.

Jarrow

Bede Gallery

*Springwell Park, Butchersbridge Road, Jarrow,
    Tyne and Wear NE32 5QA* ☎ *091 4891807*
*Tues–Fri 10–5; Sun 2–5. Closed 2 weeks during
    Christmas period.*
◪ *Vincent Rea, Director*
Ⓕ ◷ ⬤ ⌨

The Gallery occupies a former Second World
War civil defence headquarters. One section
contains exhibits reflecting the social and
industrial history of Jarrow, and the remainder
of the space is devoted to exhibitions of
contemporary art by nationally and internationally
known artists, sculptors and photographers, as
well as by professional artists from the north of
England.

Bede Monastery Museum

*Jarrow Hall, Church Bank, Jarrow, Tyne and
    Wear NE32 3DY*   ☎ *091 4892106*
*Apr–Oct, Tues–Sat 10–5.30; Sun 2.30–5.30.
Nov–Mar, Tues–Sat 11–4.30; Sun
2.30–5.30. Open Bank Holiday Mon.
Closed Christmas and New Year.*
◪ *Senior Education Assistant*
Ⓔ ⌷ ⬤ ⌨

Jarrow Hall is an 18th-century house, a feature
of which is the Oval Room. It contains an
interpretive display of archaeological material
from the excavations at St Paul's Monastery, a
short distance from the Museum. The exhibits
include a model of the Monastery during its years
of activity and a conjectural re-assembly of a
window made up of fragments of coloured Saxon
glass found on the site. There is also an
introductory audio-visual presentation
explaining the building of the Monastery and the
life of the monks, a pictorial history of the Hall,
and a herb garden where visitors can see many of
the culinary and medicinal plants grown by the
monks.

Jedburgh

Jedburgh Castle Jail

Castle Gate, Jedburgh, Roxburghshire TD8 6QD
    ☎ *0835 63254*
Easter–Sept, Mon–Sat 10–12, 1–5; Sun 2–5
◪ *See Hawick Museum*
Ⓔ

This is the only remaining Scottish example
of a 19th-century Howard Reform Prison. The
outstanding features of the Jail are the cells and
the prison blocks, which remain much as they
were in 1823. The interpretive displays include
reconstructed rooms illustrating prison life and
associated activities and the development of the
town of Jedburgh as a Royal Burgh.

Mary, Queen of Scots House

Queen Street, Jedburgh, Roxburghshire
    ☎ *0835 63301*
*Easter–Oct, Mon–Sat 10–12, 1–5; Sun 2 5.
    June–Aug, also Sun 10–12.*
◪ *See Hawick Museum*
Ⓔ ◷ ⌨

The building is a 16th-century house, in which
Mary Stuart is said to have stayed in 1566. The
interior has been restored and furnished as
nearly as possible to its mid 16th-century
appearance and the garden contains some
famous ancient pear trees. There are also
displays illustrating the life of Mary, Queen
of Scots and her visit to Jedburgh.

Jodrell Bank

Jodrell Bank Visitor Centre

Jodrell Bank, nr Macclesfield, Cheshire SK11 9DL
    ☎ *0477 71339*
*Mar 12–Oct, daily 10.30–5.30. Nov–Mar 11,
    Sat, Sun 2–5. Winter weekday visits by appt.*
◪ *Dr Anne Cohen*
Ⓔ ⌷ ⬤ ⊕ ⌨ ♿

The University of Manchester's 250-foot radio
telescope at Jodrell Bank is one of the largest
fully steerable instruments in the world. The
Visitor Centre offers displays on the techniques
of radio astronomy, with working models, and
on the planets, stars and galaxies. The
exhibition of astronomy, optics and space
includes weather maps from Meteostat and a
demonstration of satellite television. The
planetarium gives regular presentations showing
the stars visible at night.

Johnstown Castle

Irish Agricultural Museum

*Castle Farmyard, Johnstown Castle, Wexford,
    Co. Wexford, Ireland* ☎ *053 42888*
*May–June and Sept–Nov 5, Mon–Fri 9–5;
    1.30–5; Sun 2–5. July–Aug, Mon–Fri 9–5;
    Sat, Sun 2–5. Nov 6–Apr, Mon–Fri 9–12.30,
    1.30–5.*
◪ *Dr A. M. O'Sullivan, Curator*
Ⓔ ⌷ ⬤ ⊕ ⌨ ♿

The Museum is in early 19th-century restored
farm buildings in the grounds of Johnstown
Castle, four miles south-west of Wexford on the
road to Murrintown. The main sections of the
farmyard, including the harness room, stables
and cow-byre, have been retained and
converted to museum use.
    The exhibits illustrate the history of Irish
agriculture and rural life. There are displays on
rural transport and the activities of the
farmyard and the rural household, together with
a large dairying section and a major collection of
Irish country furniture. Reconstructions of the
workshops of rural craftsmen are in the process of
development.

Kanturk

St Peter's Church Museum

Kanturk, Co. Cork, Ireland
Open summer Sun (check locally)
⚑ *Mr P. O. Sullivan, 27 Percival Street,*
*   Kanturk, Co. Cork*   ☎ 029 50598
£ ◇ ♿

The emphasis of the collection is on domestic
equipment and agricultural implements. There
are also a good set of cooper's tools and of
workhouse, First World War, and railway relics.
The history of the area is further illustrated by
maps, photographs, newspapers and diaries,
including one of exceptional interest for the
years 1840–60. One of the Museum's more
unusual possessions consists of the clippers
used on the 1938 Grand National winner,
Workman, which was bred locally.

Keighley

Cliffe Castle Art Gallery and Museum

Keighley, West Yorkshire BD20 6LH
*   ☎ 0535 664184*
Apr–Sept, Tues–Sun 10–6. Oct–Mar, Tues–Sun
*   10–5. Closed Good Fri, Dec 25, 26.*
⚑ *Graham Wilkinson, Assistant Keeper*
F ♟ ♿

This is the general museum for the Bradford
area. It occupies a mansion built c. 1880. It has
been much altered, but the decorated ceilings in
the suite of reception rooms and the hammer-
beam roof of the concert room still survive. The
reception rooms are furnished in period style
and contain a set of fine French cut-glass
chandeliers of c. 1840.
    There are displays which illustrate the
geology and natural resources of the area,
together with local and British wildlife. Other
galleries contain exhibits of the decorative arts,
including local pottery, social history, toys and
dolls. The local crafts featured in the Museum,
some with reconstructed workshops, include
clog-iron and nail-making.

East Riddlesden Hall

Bradford Road, Keighley, West Yorkshire
*   BD20 5EL*   ☎ 0535 607075
Apr–May & Sept–Oct, Wed–Sun 2–6. June–Aug,
*   Bank Holiday Mon 11–6. Last admission 5.30.*
*   Closed Good Fri.*
⚑ *The Administrator*
£ ♟ ♿ NT

The oldest part of the house is the Banqueting
Hall, which dates from 1602. A new wing was
added in 1636 and a further West Wing in 1692,
although only the façade of this remains. The
property was taken over by the National Trust

in 1934 and has since been extensively restored.
The kitchen, dining-room, drawing-room,
banqueting-room and a bedroom and powder
room are all on view, each with appropriate
furniture and equipment. There is fine panelling
and plasterwork, and collections of pewter,
domestic utensils, stump-work pictures and four-
poster beds. The large medieval tithe barn in
the grounds is now used to display old farm
wagons.

Keith

Keith Art Gallery

Church Road, Keith, Banffshire AB5 3BR
Late May, June and Sept 1–15, Mon–Sat
*   10–5.30. July–Aug, Mon–Sat 10–6; Sun 2–6.*
⚑ *District Curator, Falconer Museum, Tolbooth*
*   Street, Forres IV36 0PH*   ☎ 0309 73701
F ◇

The former Art Gallery is in the process of
transformation into a museum of local history.
At present the collection consists mainly of
photographs of Keith and the surrounding
district, and copies of documents relating to the
town, but its character will change as more
three-dimensional objects are added to the
displays.

Kelso

Floors Castle

Kelso, Roxburghshire TD5 7SF   ☎ 0573 23333
Easter weekend, then Apr 27–Sept, Sun–Thurs
*   11–5.30. July–Aug, Sun–Fri 11–5.30*
⚑ *The Factor, Roxburghe Estate Office*
£ ♟ ♨ ♿ HHA

The Castle, the residence of the Dukes of
Roxburghe, is a mile from Kelso, on the A6089.
Designed by William Adam, it dates from 1721
and additions, by W. H. Playfair, were made in
the 1840s. Once described as 'the largest
inhabited house in Britain', it has fine
collections of English and French furniture,
tapestries, paintings and porcelain. There is
a display of family heirlooms in one of the
domestic wings.

Kelso Museum

Turret House, Abbey Court, Roxburghshire
*   TD5 7JA*   ☎ 0573 25470
May 9–Oct, Mon–Sat 11–12.30, 1.30–6;
*   Sun 2–6*
⚑ *District Museums Curator, Hawick Museum,*
*   Wilton Lodge Park, Hawick, Roxburghshire*
*   TD9 7JL*   ☎ 0450 73457
£ NTS

Kelso Museum is in an 18th-century house, now
owned by the National Trust for Scotland. The
displays illustrate the growth of Kelso and its
importance as a market town. There is a special
exhibit on the history of the local skinning
industry.

Kendal

Abbot Hall Art Gallery

Kirkland, Kendal, Cumbria LA9 5AL
    ☎ 0539 22464
*Mon–Fri 10.30–5.30; Sat, Sun 2–5. Closed Good
    Fri and 2 weeks at Christmas.*
▨ *Mrs C. Trelogan, Museum Assistant*
£ ▯ ⇦ ⴲ

Abbot Hall was built in 1759, reputedly to the
design of Carr of York, the leading Northern
architect of the period. The ground-floor rooms
have been restored to their original splendour.
The collection contains items of local
significance and national importance, including
a number of portraits by George Romney,
among them his masterpiece, *The Gower Family*.
There are also portraits by Romney's one-time
pupil, Daniel Gardner. The Gallery has a fine
collection of watercolours, those by John Ruskin
being particularly noteworthy.

Period cabinets display 18th-century
porcelain, silver and glass. The famous
furniture-makers, Gillows of Lancaster, are well
represented in the Gallery.

The collection of contemporary art, shown
from time to time, includes work by Kurt
Schwitters, Ben Nicholson, William Johnstone,
John Piper, Norman Adams, Keith Vaughan,
Barbara Hepworth, Hans Arp, Elizabeth Frink
and Lucie Rie.

Kendal Museum

Station Road, Kendal, Cumbria LA9 6BT
    ☎ 0539 21374
*Mon–Fri 10.30–5; Sat 2–5. Closed Good Fri and
    2 weeks at Christmas.*
▨ *The Curator*
£ ⃠ ⇦ ⴲ

The Museum, recently entirely reorganised,
displays and interprets the natural history and
human story of the Lake District. It is housed in
a former wool warehouse, built *c.* 1850. The
Natural History Gallery shows how the rocks
have been formed and the landscape shaped and
a series of reconstructions of typical Lake
District habitats, closely based on actual

localities, provide a realistic setting for the
specimens of plants and animals. The World
Wildlife Gallery originally housed the trophies
of a local big-game hunter, Colonel Edgar
Harrison, and his friends, together with a wide
range of cased animals from all over the world.
These have now been restored and presented in
a completely different way.

The Kendal and Westmorland Gallery tells
the story of Kendal and the surrounding area
back to prehistoric times, the emphasis
throughout being on people, not objects. There
are special displays on Adam Sedgwick, the
great 19th-century geologist, who was born near
Kendal, and on some of the famous scientists –
Dalton, John Gough and his son, Thomas –
who lived and worked in Kendal and whose
names are closely bound up with the history of
Kendal Museum.

Museum of Lakeland Life and Industry

Kirkland, Kendal, Cumbria LA9 5AL
    ☎ 0539 22464
*Mon–Fri 10.30–5; Sat, Sun 2–5. Closed Good Fri
    and 2 weeks at Christmas.*
▨ *See Abbot Hall Art Gallery*
£ ▯ ⇦

The Museum building was converted from
Abbot Hall's stable block. Its displays are
concerned with the social and economic history
of the area. A photographic display showing
man's impact on the natural landscape from
prehistoric times onwards provides an
introduction to the district. A wide range of
trades and occupations are represented in the
exhibits, including farming and the Kendal
woollen industry, and there are reconstructions
of a smithy, a wheelwright's shop and a printer's
workshop, together with a 17th-century parlour
and bedroom.

A recent addition to the Museum is a
reconstruction of a Victorian street scene, with
a chemist's shop, tailor's, penny bazaar and
pawnbroker's.

Kennethmont

Leith Hall

*Kennethmont, By Huntly, Aberdeenshire
    AB5 4NQ* ☎ 04643 216
May–Sept, daily 2–6 (last guided tour 5.15)
▨ *NTS Representative*
£ ⃠ ▣ ⇦ ⴲ NTS

Leith Hall, now a property of the National Trust
for Scotland, is seven miles from Huntly on the
A97. Built in 1650 and extended three times, in
1756, 1868 and 1912, it was always the home of
the Leith and Leith-Hay family until it was
given to the Trust in 1945. It contains a large
collection of 18th and 19th-century furniture,
porcelain and pictures, together with many
portraits and personal possessions of the family.

The Breakfast Parlour, Abbot Hall, Kendal.

The Painter's Shop. Kendal, Museum of Lakeland Life and Industry.

Kenton

Powderham Castle

Kenton, nr Exeter, Devon EX6 8JQ
☎ 0626 890243
Sun of Late Spring Bank Holiday–2nd Thurs in Sept, 2–5.30. Closed Fri–Sat.
⚇ *Castle Administrator*
[£] [♿] [📷] [☕] [HHA]

Powderham Castle, the home of the Earl and Countess of Devon, is on the A379 Exeter to Dawlish road. The oldest part of the Castle dates from the 14th century and it has been considerably extended and remodelled subsequently. The Great Hall has Victorian linenfold panelling and numerous family portraits, and elsewhere there is gilt furniture and ivory silk upholstery.

Keswick

Keswick Museum and Art Gallery

Fitz Park, Keswick, Cumbria CA12 4NF
☎ 0596 73263
Apr–Oct, Mon–Sat 10–12.30, 2–5.30.
⚇ *The Curator*
[£] [♿]

The late Victorian building was designed to house the Museum, which could perhaps be described as a general Victorian museum with literary and geological leanings. The collections are very broad and range from butterflies and moths to dolls, fossils, and stone axes. The Museum's main strength, however, lies in geology and in its world-famous collection of the manuscripts of the English Romantic poets, especially Wordsworth and Southey. It also possesses manuscripts by Sir Hugh Walpole, including those of the Rogue Herries novels.

One of the Museum's special attractions is Flintoft's 1867 model of the Lake District, made at three inches to the mile and accurate both horizontally and vertically. It is much used by visitors planning walking tours and other excursions.

The Pencil Museum

The Cumberland Pencil Company, Greta Bridge, Keswick, Cumbria CA12 5NG
☎ 0596 73626/72116
Mar–Oct, Mon–Fri 9.30–4.30; Sat, Sun 2–5
⚇ *The Supervisor*
[£] [♿] [☕] [&]

The first graphite pencils ever produced came from Keswick in the mid 16th century, using Borrowdale plumbago, which was ideally suited to the purpose. The Cumberland Pencil Company was set up in the early 1800s. Its museum, which includes carefully restored equipment and machinery, traces the development of the pencil from its cottage industry origins to the writing instrument we know today. The exhibits include many examples of early pencils, together with some interesting curios, such as the wartime pencil which contained a hidden map and compass, and a giant pencil, 7 feet long and in the same proportions as its more usual 7-inch equivalent.

Kettering

Alfred East Art Gallery

Sheep Street, Kettering, Northamptonshire
Mon–Wed, Fri, Sat 10–5
⚇ *Kettering Borough Council, Bowling Green Road, Kettering NN15 7QX* ☎ 0536 85211
[F] [☕]

The Gallery displays a collection of oil paintings, watercolours and etchings by Sir Alfred East R.A. (1849–1913), presented to his native town by the artist. The Gallery, which also contains a general collection of paintings, watercolours and prints, was built to house Sir Alfred's gift.

Boughton House

nr Kettering, Northamptonshire NN14 1BJ
☎ 0536 82248
Aug, daily 2–5. Grounds: 12–6.
⚇ *The Administrator*
[£] [♿] [📷] [☕] [&] [HHA]

Boughton House is three miles north of Kettering, off the A43. The original buildings were bought by Sir Edward Montagu in 1528 from St Edmundsbury Abbey. The north front was added in the 1690s by the 1st Duke of Montagu, but since then there have been few external changes. The original hammer-beam roof of the Great Hall still survives, together with panelling from oaks felled on the estate. The Hall also has silver candle sconces with the cipher of Charles II, Mortlake tapestries – there are others elsewhere in the house – and portraits, including one of Elizabeth I by Marcus Gheeraester.

There are late 17th to early 18th century ceiling paintings by Chéron and a remarkable collection of other paintings, including works by El Greco, Tenier, Murillo and Van Dyck. The furnishings are also notable. Among them are porcelain, rugs, chinoiserie cabinets, and chests with inset Sèvres plaques.

Westfield Museum

West Street, Kettering, Northamptonshire
Mar–Oct, Wed–Fri 12–5; Sat, Sun 2–5.
⚑ *See Alfred East Art Gallery*
F

Westfield Museum, which occupies an 1870 Victorian villa, built in the Gothic style, tells the story of the Kettering area from the earliest times to the present day. One room is devoted to the geology of this part of Northamptonshire and contains fossils and specimens of rocks, minerals and metal ores. The Archaeology Room displays prehistoric, Romano-British, Anglo-Saxon and medieval material discovered locally, including a good collection of Samian ware and gilt Saxon brooches.

The Local History Room is concerned with the history of Kettering during the past 250 years. Two further rooms are used to present the history of Kettering's shoe-making industry. The first is given over to shoe-making machines and the second to footwear, with an exhibition showing how a boot is made by hand.

Kew

Kew Palace

Royal Botanic Gardens, Kew, Richmond, Surrey
TW9 3AB **☎** *01 940 1171*
Apr–Sept, daily 11–5.30.
⚑ *The Administrator*
£ ≜ ≞ ⌕ ⅋

Kew Palace, also known as the Dutch House, was built in 1631 by a Dutch merchant, Sir Hugh Portman. It was bought in 1781 by Queen Charlotte and afterwards became a residence of George III. The building now contains period furniture and memorabilia of George III.

Museums of the Royal Botanic Gardens

Royal Botanic Gardens, Kew, Richmond, Surrey
TW9 3AB **☎** *01 940 1171*
Daily 10–8 in summer, 10–4 in winter. Check
closing times locally. Closed Dec 25, Jan 1.
Refreshments available Mar–Nov only.
Mar–Nov, Tea Bar only, 10–3.
⚑ *The Administrator*
£ ≜ ≞ ⌕ ⅋

Of the Museum's buildings at Kew, Museum 1, by Decimus Burton, is listed as Grade II, as is the Orangery, by William Chambers. There are a number of listed buildings at Kew, including the 18th-century Pagoda (Chambers) and Palm House (Burton), both of which are Grade I. The large collections in the Museums are concerned with the plants used by man and as food for farm and domestic animals. They include an important collection of timber specimens.

A new Museum is at present under construction.

Kidderminster

Kidderminster Art Gallery and Museum

Market Street, Kidderminster, Hereford and
Worcester DY10 1AB **☎** *0562 66610*
Mon, Tues, Thurs–Sat 11–4.
Closed Bank Holiday.
⚑ *The Curator*
F ⌕ ⅋ □

The Art Gallery specialises in paintings, drawings and prints of the Kidderminster area, with changing monthly exhibitions of items drawn from the collections. Because of the condition of the building, no museum displays are on view at the moment.

Kidwelly

Kidwelly Industrial Museum

Kidwelly, Dyfed SA17 4LW **☎** *0554 891078*
Easter–Sept, Mon–Fri 10–5; Sat, Sun 2–5
(last admission at 4)
⚑ *Ms S. Thomas, Curator*
£ ⌕ ≞ ⌕ ⅋ ✿

The Museum is in the surviving part of Kidwelly Tinplate Works, where tinplate was made by hand. Visitors can see the hot and cold rolling mills with their original machinery. The assorting and boxing rooms are now used as display galleries to tell the story of the Kidwelly area and the development of the tinplate industry, which began on the site in 1737.

There is also a section relating to the local coal industry, centred on the pithead gear and steam winding engine from Morlais colliery, where the exhibition explains the geology of the area and illustrates the history of the local coal industry.

The Pagoda erected for Princess Augusta at the Royal Botanic Gardens, Kew, to designs by Sir William Chambers, 1761–2.

Kilbarchan

Weaver's Cottage

The Cross, Kilbarchan, Renfrewshire PA10 2JG
☎ 05057 5588
*Easter–May and Sept–Oct, Tues, Thurs, Sat, Sun,
2–5. June–Aug, daily 2–5.*
Ⓚ *Mrs Margaret Currie, 9 Clochoderick Avenue,
Kilbarchan* ☎ 05057 5234
Ⓔ ♨ ⬛ [NTS]

Built in 1723 and still used for weaving until
the 1940s, this is a typical cottage of an 18th-
century handloom weaver, and an interesting
example of the cruck method of construction, in
which the weight of the roof is carried not by
the walls, but by a framework of trusses formed
of split, curved tree trunks, anticipating the
technique of modern steel-framed buildings.

The kitchen and two bedrooms have been
restored and furnished in the style of the 19th
century. A former store, now converted into a
tea room, has showcases containing tools of the
weaver's trade, and throughout the cottage
there are portraits of some of the former weavers
of Kilbarchan, including Willie Meikle. The
basement weaving shop has been restored and
now has Willie Meikle's handloom, in full
working order, together with its accessories, and
a number of his personal possessions. A second
loom is available for training purposes.

The Weaver's Cottage, Kilbarchan.

Kilfenora

Burren Display Centre

Kilfenora, Co. Clare, Ireland ☎ 065 88030
*Mar 17–Apr, daily 10–1, 2–5. May, daily 10–6.
June–Aug, daily 10–7. Sept–Oct, daily
10–5.30.*
Ⓚ *The Manager*
Ⓔ ♦ ⬛ ♨ ♿

The Burren is an exceptionally interesting area,
both geologically and archaeologically. The
Display Centre, opened in 1975, provides an
introduction to its natural environment and
history. A scale landscape model explains the
geology and settlement patterns of the Burren
and other exhibits deal with the farming system
and bird, animal and plant life. There are also
examples of fossils found locally.

Kilkenny

Kilkenny Castle

Kilkenny, Co. Kilkenny, Ireland ☎ 056 21450
*Oct–Easter, Tues–Sun 10.30–1, 2–5. Easter–
June 1, daily 10–5. June 2–Sept, daily 10–7.*
Ⓚ *The Curator*
Ⓔ ♨ ⬛ ♨ ▢

The Castle dates from the 13th century. It was
extensively rebuilt in the 1830s. From the 14th
century it was the principal seat of the Butlers,
the Earls and Dukes of Ormonde. It now houses
the Butler collection of paintings and tapestries,
together with other possessions and memorabilia
of the family. Also on display is a large
permanent collection of modern – especially
Irish – art.

Rothe House

Parliament Street, Kilkenny, Co. Kilkenny, Ireland
☎ 056 22893
*Apr–Oct, Mon–Sat 10.30–12.30, 2.30–5;
Sun 3–5. Nov–Mar, Sat, Sun 3–5.*
Ⓚ *The Administrator*
Ⓔ ♨ ♨

Built in the 16th century, the house is named
after its original owner, the merchant, John
Rothe. In 1962 it was bought by the Kilkenny
Archaeological Society and, after restoration,
opened to the public in 1966 as a museum
illustrating the history of the city and county of
Kilkenny. The collections contain geological,
archaeological, historical and ethnographical
material.

Killarney

Muckross House

National Park, Killarney, Co. Kerry, Ireland
☎ 064 31440
*Easter–June and Oct, daily 10–7. July–Aug, daily
9–9. Nov–Mar 16, Tues–Sun 11–5.
Closed Dec 24, 25*
Ⓚ *The Manager*
Ⓔ ♦ ⬛ ♨

Muckross House was built in 1843 for Henry
Arthur Herbert. It remained in the possession of
the Herbert family until the end of the century
and in 1929 became the property of the Irish
nation. Stripped of its furnishings, it remained
empty until 1964, when it was opened as a
museum of the life and social history of the
people of County Kerry. A number of rooms
have been appropriately furnished, to give an
impression of the house as it was in its days as a
private residence on the grand scale.

The displays illustrate life in Kerry between
c. 1800 and 1950, with sections devoted to
dairying, housing, fuel, lighting and crafts. The
collections range from household equipment to
farm implements and craftsmen's tools. An
important feature of the Museum is its
programme of craft demonstrations. A weaver,
blacksmith, basketmaker, potter and
bookbinder are regularly to be seen at work.

Transport Museum of Ireland

East Avenue, Killarney, Co. Kerry, Ireland
☎ 064 31060
Daily 10–8
⚔ Denis Lucey
£ ⇜

The Museum's collection comprises cars dating from 1901 to 1922, all in excellent mechanical condition. There is also a comprehensive range of 19th-century bicycles and tricycles, together with motoring and cycling accessories, components and advertising material.

Kilmarnock

Dean Castle

Dean Road, Kilmarnock, Ayrshire
May 12–Sept 22, Mon–Fri 2–5; Sat, Sun 12–5.
    Other times by appt for pre-booked parties.
⚔ See Dick Institute
£ ⬤ ⬛

The Keep of Dean Castle dates from the 14th century, the palace from the 15th century. The collections consist of European weapons and armour – the displays of swords and decorative armour are especially noteworthy – tapestries, mainly of the 15th and 16th centuries, and 16th and 17th-century musical instruments, especially lutes, guitars, spinets and organs.

Dick Institute

Elmbank Avenue, Kilmarnock, Ayrshire KA1 3BU
    ☎ 0563 26401
Apr–Sept, Mon, Tues, Thurs, Fri 10–8; Wed,
    Sat 10–5. Oct–Mar, Mon–Sat 10–5.
⚔ The Curator
F ⇜ ♿

The Institute contains both an Art Gallery and a Museum. The Art Gallery has frequently changing exhibitions of works drawn from the permanent collection, which includes paintings by Constable, Corot, Millais, Alma Tadema, Lord Leighton and artists of the Glasgow School. The displays in the Museum, which is at present undergoing modernisation, cover natural history, especially Scottish birds, geology, fossil corals and archaeology, Iron Age artefacts from crannogs being a strong feature. There are also sections devoted to local social and industrial history, to lace and to Ayrshire embroidery.

Kilmessan

Kilmessan Museum

The Library, Kilmessan, Co. Meath, Ireland
Wed, Fri 2–5; Tues 7–9
⚔ The Curator
F ⇜

The Museum and Library are in a former Church of Ireland parish church, built in the early 19th century. The exhibits illustrate the archaeology and history of the area.

Kilmuir

Skye Museum of Island Life

Kilmuir, Isle of Skye   ☎ 047052 279
Apr–Oct, Mon–Sat 9–6
⚔ Mrs A. Mackenzie, 8 Hungladder, Kilmuir
£ ⬤ ⇜ ♿

The Museum occupies a group of thatched cottages, typical of the croft houses of Skye a century ago, and the displays illustrate the way of life of the community at that time. Each building concentrates on a particular theme, such as the work of the blacksmith and weaver and the domestic life and equipment of the islanders.

Kilmurry

MacSwiney Memorial Museum

Kilmurry, Lissarda, Co. Cork, Ireland
    ☎ 021 336252
Sun 3–6. Other times by appt.
⚔ Mrs Mary O'Sullivan, Hon. Curator
£ ⇜

Terence MacSwiney, Lord Mayor of Cork, died in British captivity in 1920 after a hunger strike lasting 74 days. The Museum, established in his memory by local people and run by volunteers, is in a village 18 miles from Cork City, off the Cork to Macroom road. The collections illustrate the archaeology, history and traditional rural life of the area.

Kilsyth

Kilsyth Museum

Colzium House, Colzium Lennox Estate, Kilsyth,
    Glasgow G65 0RZ
Apr–Sept, Wed 2–8. Oct–Mar, Wed 2–5.
⚔ The Curator, Cumbernauld and Kilsyth District
    Museums, Ardenlea House, The Wynd,
    Cumbernauld, Glasgow G67 2ST
    ☎ 0236 735077
F ⇜ ☐

The Museum is on the eastern outskirts of Kilsyth, on the A803. It occupies an early 19th-century mansion, now a listed building, which adjoins the site of Colzium Castle. The displays are devoted mainly to the history of the Kilsyth area, with an emphasis on the medieval period. Temporary exhibitions, organised by the Museum, are held in Kilsyth Library.

Kingsbridge

The Cookworthy Museum

The Old Grammar School, 108 Fore Street,
    Kingsbridge, Devon TQ7 1AW
Easter–Sept, Mon–Sat 10–5. Oct, Mon–Fri
    10–4.30.
⚔ The Curator
£ ⬤ ☐

The Museum is in the town's former Grammar School, a building dating from 1671. It is named after William Cookworthy, born in Kingsbridge in 1705, who discovered china clay in Cornwall and became the first Englishman to make true porcelain. The displays illustrate the history of rural life in Devon. There are a costume room and a farming gallery and reconstructions of a 19th-century farmhouse kitchen, scullery and dairy. Other parts of the Museum are devoted to toys and dolls, craftsmen's tools, and a complete Edwardian pharmacy.

There are demonstrations of rural crafts on the second and fourth Fridays in July and August.

King's Lynn

The Lynn Museum

Market Street, King's Lynn, Norfolk PE30 1NL
   ☎ 0553 775001
*Mon–Sat 10–5. Closed Good Fri and public
   holidays.*
 Deputy Curator
£ ◇ &

The Museum building was formerly a non-conformist chapel, constructed in 1859 in the High Victorian Gothic style of the 'church outside, chapel inside', type. The exhibits are concerned with the natural history, archaeology and history of West Norfolk. Special attention is given to the port of Lynn, which dates from c. 1100. The Museum has the only large collection of pilgrims' badges outside London, and a few exhibits relate to the 18th-century Greenland whale-fishing, to which Lynn sent ships, and to the town's 19th-century agricultural engineering industry, of which the best-known figure was Frederick Savage, who also had a great reputation as a designer and manufacturer of fairground rides.

Among the more remarkable items on display is a tiger shot in India in 1876 by Edward, Prince of Wales. It stood in Sandringham House until 1928, when it was presented to the Museum.

Museum of Social History

27 King Street, King's Lynn, Norfolk PE30 1HA
   ☎ 0553 775004
*Tues–Sat 10–5. Closed Good Fri and public
   holidays.*
 See The Lynn Museum
£ ◇

The Georgian fronted house at 27 King Street was completely remodelled in the late 17th and early 18th centuries. It now contains displays illustrating the social history of West Norfolk, with a special emphasis on domestic life. There is a parlour furnished in Victorian style, with some earlier items, and a kitchen, in which most of the equipment is 19th century. Other rooms are devoted to exhibitions of toys and costumes and to a display of 18th and 19th-century glass.

A brass rubbing centre is also accommodated in the Museum.

King's Mills

The Guernsey Tomato Centre

*Pres du Douit, King's Mills, Guernsey, Channel
   Islands*   ☎ 0481 54389
Easter–Sept, daily 10–5
 The Curator
£ ● ■ ✈ &

The Centre has been planned to show the changes which have taken place in tomato-growing in Guernsey since the first commercial crop was grown in the 1880s. The displays are housed in a group of glasshouses, built at various dates between the 1890s and the 1970s. Four of these are growing crops, mainly tomatoes, but with some grapes and flowers, to illustrate the history of the local glasshouse industry, and others contain a museum of old tomato-growing equipment, a conservatory-type cafeteria and a display of the main local vegetables.

Kingston-upon-Hull

Burton Constable Hall

Sproatley, Kingston-upon-Hull, North Humberside
   ☎ 0401 62400
*Easter Sat–last Sun in Sept, Sat, Sun 1–5.
   Garden: daily 12–5.*
 The Controller
£ ● ■ ✈

Burton Constable is seven and a half miles north-east of Hull. The original house is Tudor, but it was extended and remodelled in the 18th and 19th centuries. An exhibition in the Muniment Room explains the origins of the house and subsequent modifications. The rococo decorations are impressive and there is much good furniture, including 85 pieces by Chippendale. The house is set in a Capability Brown landscape.

**'The Artist's Mother, 1924' by Mark Gertler.
Kingston-upon-Hull, The University of Hull
Art Collection.**

Corn Exchange Museum

36 High Street, Kingston-upon-Hull, North
Humberside
Mon–Sat 10–5; Sun 1.30–4.30. Closed Good Fri,
Dec 24–26, Jan 1.
School Services Officer
F

The Museum occupies the former Victorian
Corn Exchange. The archaeological section
features the prehistory and early history of
Humberside. The exhibits include mosaics
found at the Roman villa at Horkstow, South
Humberside and material from Iron Age chariot
burials on the Wolds.

The transport displays include 18th and 19th-
century horse-drawn vehicles, horse-brasses and
horseshoes, a Kitson steam tram, bicycles,
motorcycles and motorcars, especially of the
period 1890–1910, and a small amount of
railway material.

Ferens Art Gallery

Queen Victoria Square, Kingston-upon-Hull,
North Humberside HU1 3RA
Mon–Sat 10–5; Sun 1.30–4.30. Closed Good Fri,
Dec 25, 26.
See Town Docks Museum
F

The Gallery contains 16th and 17th-century
European paintings, especially of the Dutch and
Italian schools, Humberside marine paintings,
and 20th-century English paintings and
sculpture.

Posterngate Gallery

6 Posterngate, Kingston-upon-Hull, North
Humberside
Mon–Sat 10–5; Sun 1.30–4.30. Closed Good Fri,
Dec 25, 26.
See Town Docks Museum
F

The exhibitions in the Gallery are devoted to
paintings, drawings, prints and crafts by
contemporary artists, most of them English.

Springhead Waterworks Museum

Yorkshire Water, Springhead Pumping Station,
Springhead Avenue, Willerby Road, Kingston-
upon-Hull, North Humberside HU5 5HZ
Sat, Sun, Bank Holiday 10–5
Area Manager, Yorkshire Water, Essex House,
Manor Street, Kingston-upon-Hull HU1 1YW
☎ *0482 28591*
F

The Museum is housed in the Springhead
Pumping Station, built in the 1860s. A single-
acting Cornish beam engine, erected in 1876,
has become the centrepiece around which a
Waterworks Museum has been formed. Among
the items on show are 17th and 18th-century
wooden pipes discovered under the streets of
Hull, together with the tools used for making
this kind of pipe.

Town Docks Museum

Queen Victoria Square, Kingston-upon-Hull,
North Humberside HU1 3DX
☎ *0482 222737*
Mon–Sat 10–5; Sun 1.30–4.30.
School Services Officer
F

The Museum is in the former Dock Office, built
c. 1870. The Court Room of the Docks Board
and other parts of the fine Victorian interior
have been preserved. There are displays relating
to whales and whaling, to the local fishing and
trawling industries, to shipbuilding and to ships
which used the Port of Hull.

The University of Hull Art Collection

The Middleton Hall, University of Hull,
Cottingham Road, Kingston-upon-Hull, North
Humberside HU6 7RX ☎ *0482 46311*
During term-time, Mon, Tues, Thurs, Fri 2–4;
Wed 12.30–4
John G. Bernasconi, Hon. Curator
F

The University Art Collection specialises in
British art of the period 1890–1940 and covers
paintings, sculpture, drawings and prints. It
includes works by Beardsley, Sickert, Steer,
Lucien Pissarro, Augustus John, Stanley Spencer,
Wyndham Lewis and Ben Nicholson. Artists of
the Camden Town Group and the Bloomsbury
Circle are particularly well represented.

Also featured is a display of Chinese ceramics
on long-term loan from the Thompson Collection,
Hong Kong, which concentrates on the Transitional Period of Chinese history, c. 1620–80, and
is outstanding for its Fujian white ceramics and
Jingdechen blue and white porcelain.

Wilberforce House and Georgian Houses

23–25 High Street, Kingston-upon-Hull, North
Humberside
Mon–Sat 10–5; Sun 1.30–4.30. Closed Good Fri,
Dec 25, 26.
See Town Docks Museum
F

Of this group of 17th and 18th-century merchants'
houses, No. 25 was the birthplace of William
Wilberforce, the slave emancipator. The Museum
contains displays relating to Wilberforce and to
slavery and there are also period rooms, an early
20th-century chemist's shop and exhibits of dolls,
costumes, militaria and Hull silver.

Kingston upon Thames

Kingston upon Thames Museum and Heritage Centre

Fairfield West, Kingston upon Thames, Surrey
KT1 2PS ☎ *01 546 5386*
Mon–Sat 10–5. Closed public holidays.
Heritage Officer
F

The Museum's collections cover local archaeology, especially of the Bronze Age and the Anglo-Saxon period, history and natural history. There is also an exhibition on the life and work of Eadweard Muybridge (1830–1904), the photographer of movement and pioneer of the motion picture. The items on display include Muybridge's zoopraxiscope.

Kingswinford

Broadfield House Glass Museum

Barnett Lane, Kingswinford, West Midlands
DY6 9QA ☎ *0384 273011*
Tues–Fri 2–5, Sat 10–1, 2–5; Sun 2–5.
Closed Dec 25, 26, Jan 1.
🅺 *The Curator*
🅵 ▪ ↝

Glass-making in the Stourbridge area dates back to the early 17th century, when glass-makers from Normandy and Lorraine settled in the district. To begin with, window glass and bottles were the main products, but in the 18th century the glass-houses began producing the tableware and ornamental glass for which the district became renowned.

The Museum is in a listed late Georgian building, with attractive plasterwork and a fine staircase. Its displays illustrate the history of glass making from the Roman period to the present day, with an emphasis on the range of coloured glass and crystal produced by the Stourbridge industry during the 19th century. There are exhibits of old glass-making equipment and, at the rear of the Museum, studios for designing and making glass.

Kingussie

Highland Folk Museum

Duke Street, Kingussie, Inverness-shire PH21 1JG
☎ *05402 307*
Apr–Oct, Mon–Sat 10–6; Sun 2–6. Nov–Mar,
Mon–Fri 10–3. Closed Dec 25, 26, Jan 1
and public holidays Nov–Mar.
🅺 *The Curator*
🅴 ↺ ↝ ♿

Opened in 1935, this is probably the oldest folk museum in Britain. The reception building is an 18th-century shooting lodge. The indoor displays, most of which are interpretive in nature, deal with the clans, costume, handicrafts and social life of the Scottish Highlands. There are important collections of vernacular furniture and textiles.

Kinlough

Kinlough Folk Museum

Kinlough, Co. Leitrim, Ireland
Key from Mrs Muriel Kerr, who lives opposite
🅺 *Patrick Gallagher, Curator, Askill, Via*
Ballyshannon, Co. Leitrim ☎ *072 51586*
🅵

Part of the building which contains the Museum was originally a public house. Its original appearance has been retained. The collections illustrate the history of the area, with domestic equipment, agricultural implements, craftsmen's tools and weapons, election posters and a poteen still, and a reconstruction of a traditional farmhouse kitchen. There is an archive of photographs of local interest.

Kinnesswood

Michael Bruce Cottage Museum

The Cobbles, Kinnesswood, Kinross, Perthshire
KY13 7HL
Apr–Sept, daily 9–5 (keys at garage)
🅺 *Mr David M. Munro, Rose Cottage,*
Kinnesswood, Kinross KY13 7HL
🅵 ↺

Kinnesswood is four miles east of Kinross on the A911 road to Leslie. The Museum is housed in an 18th-century weaver's cottage, the birthplace of the poet, Michael Bruce (1746–67). The exhibits include the published works of Michael Bruce, a display of vellum-maker's tools, and a wide range of items representative of life in Kinnesswood during the past 200 years.

Kinross

Kinross Museum

High Street, Kinross, Kinross-shire
May–Sept, Tues–Sat 1–5
🅺 *See Perth Museum and Art Gallery*
🅵

The basis of the Museum is the collection formed by David Marshall, who died in 1902. In 1903 a building was erected to house a Library and the Marshall Collection. The displays are mainly of local interest and cover archaeology, social history, weights and measures, and material relating to the early textile industry of the area.

Kinsale

Kinsale Regional Museum

Kinsale, Co. Cork, Ireland
Daily 2–5.30
🅺 *Hon. Curator* ☎ *021 772044*
🅴 ↝

The Museum is in an 18th-century tholsel, joined to the 17th-century market house. Its collections illustrate the history of the town and include the Charters of the old Kinsale Corporation; relics of the Siege and Battle of 1601–2 and the Siege of 1690; a model of HMS *Kinsale*, launched in 1700; local coinage; examples of local lace; the slipper of the Kinsale giant, Patrick Cotter O'Brien; and a harpoon gun from Scott's Antarctic expedition. There is also a shipsmith's forge and a collection of craftsmen's tools.

Dunguaire Castle, Kinvara.

Kinvara

Dunguaire Castle

Kinvara, Co. Galway, Ireland
Apr–Sept, daily 9.30–5.30
**Manager, Bunratty Castle and Folk Park*
☎ 061 61511

The Castle is a restored 16th-century tower house, with its enclosing wall intact, on a promontory overlooking Galway Bay. An interpretive exhibition describes the history of the site since early Christian times and explains the features of the Castle and its literary associations through a previous owner, Oliver St John Gogarty. There is also information about other important houses in the district.

Kirby Wiske

Sion Hill Hall

Kirby Wiske, nr Thirsk, North Yorkshire YO7 4EU
☎ 0845 587206
Last Sun in May–Sept, 2–5. Other times by appt.
**The Curator*

Sion Hill Hall was built in 1912. In 1961 it was bought by H. W. Mawer specifically to house his collection, which by then was becoming too large to accommodate at Great Ayton Hall, where he was living. Since his death in 1982, both the Hall and the collection have been owned by a charitable trust.

The collection contains Georgian, Regency and Victorian furniture, together with porcelain and pottery from Dresden, Sèvres, Derby, Chelsea and other celebrated factories. There is also a large collection of paintings and clocks.

Kirkcaldy

Kirkcaldy Museum and Art Gallery

War Memorial Gardens, Kirkcaldy, Fife KY1 1YG
☎ 0592 260732
Mon–Sat 11–5; Sun 2–5. Closed public holidays.
**Museum Secretary*

The Museum is concerned with the natural history, geology, prehistory and history of Fife. There is a section devoted to local industries, especially the manufacture of linoleum. There are temporary exhibitions and archival film, video and events throughout the year.

The important collection of 19th and 20th-century English and Scottish art is particularly noted for its holdings of William McTaggart and S. J. Peploe, but also includes modern works. Among the decorative arts the products of local potteries, especially Wemyss ware, are well represented.

Kirkcudbright

E. A. Hornel Art Gallery and Library

Broughton House, High Street, Kirkcudbright,
*   Kirkcudbrightshire DG6 4JX   ☎ 0557 30457*
Easter–Oct, Mon–Sat 11–1, 2–5. Nov–Easter,
*   Tues, Thurs 2–5.*
**Hon. Librarian*

Built in the early 18th century and considerably altered and extended subsequently, Broughton House was the home of Edward Atkinson Hornel who, on his death in 1933, left the house, together with its furnishings, library and works of art to the Stewartry of Kirkcudbright, for use as an art gallery and reference library. Several of the rooms are open to the public, with many of their original contents and with memorabilia of Hornel and of other artists of the Glasgow School and of Kirkcudbright.

Hornel's studio contains a number of his paintings, some unfinished. The Sampler Room has a notable display of samplers dating from the reign of George III to Victorian times, which were collected by Hornel's sisters. The Library comprises about 15,000 books and manuscripts. Among its more important contents are letters relating to the Border Ballads and from Sir Walter Scott and Thomas and Jane Carlyle; a large collection of the early editions of the works of Robert Burns; and the Galloway Collection, which contains nearly everything that has ever been published in or about Galloway.

The Stewartry Museum

St Mary Street, Kirkcudbright, Kirkcudbrightshire
*   ☎ 0557 30797*
Apr–June and Sept–Oct, Mon–Sat 11–1, 2–4.
*   July–Aug, Mon–Sat 11–5.*
**Hon. Curator*

The collections in the Museum relate entirely to Galloway. There are displays of shells and marine life, birds and birds' eggs, butterflies and moths, and collections illustrating prehistoric and Viking settlement in the region. Other exhibits relate to domestic life, lace and embroidery, spinning, poaching, rural craftsmen, the Galloway Regiments and the prison system.

Special attention is paid to the career of John Paul Jones (1747–92), one of the founders of the American Navy, who was born at Arbigland, in the Stewartry of Kirkcudbright, and a section of the Museum is devoted to the history of the shipping, ports and harbours of Galloway.

Kirkintilloch

The Auld Kirk Museum

Cowgate, Kirkintilloch, Dunbartonshire G66 1PW
☎ 041 775 1185
Tues, Thurs, Fri 2–5; Sat 10–1, 2–5
🏶 The Curator
Ⓕ ✒ ☐

The Auld Kirk, a Grade A listed building, dates from 1644 and served as a parish church until 1914. It was opened for museum purposes in 1961 and is now used for changing exhibitions on a wide range of subjects of local interest, including natural history, local history, art and photography.

The Barony Chambers Museum

The Cross, Kirkintilloch, Dunbartonshire
G66 1PW   ☎ 041 775 1185
Tues, Thurs, Fri 2–5; Sat 10–1, 2–5.
Closed Dec 25, 26, Jan 1, 2.
🏶 The Curator
Ⓕ ✍ ✒

The Museum building was erected in 1814-15, as a replacement for the Old Tolbooth. It functioned as Town Hall, Council Chambers and Court Room, and also housed the town jail and a school. For some years during the present century it served as offices for a firm of solicitors and in 1982 it was opened as a museum of local life, illustrating the social and industrial history of Kirkintilloch and the surrounding area over the last two centuries.

A 'single-end' tenement flat and wash house have been reconstructed to show the living conditions of working-class families in the early part of the 20th century. The story of the local weaving, mining, boatbuilding and iron-founding industries is told by means of displays of tools, equipment and photographs and other exhibits explain how the Forth and Clyde Canal and the Monkland and Kirkintilloch and the Edinburgh and Glasgow railways influenced the social and industrial life of the area.

Kirkleatham

Kirkleatham 'Old Hall' Museum

Kirkleatham, Redcar, Cleveland TS10 5NW
☎ 0642 479500
Apr–Sept, Tues–Sun 9–5. Oct–Mar, Tues–Sun 10–4.
🏶 Mr D. H. Warren, Administrator
Ⓕ 🛢 🏭 ✒

Sir William Turner, who died in 1693, was born in Kirkleatham. He made a fortune as a London clothier and, as Lord Mayor after the Great Fire, played a leading part in the rebuilding of the city. He founded and endowed almshouses and an orphanage in his native village and at his death left money to build and endow a free grammar school. This functioned successfully until 1738, when the building became, first, a public museum and lending library, one of the first in the country, and afterwards a dwelling house. During the 1970s it was restored to its original appearance and in 1981 it reopened as a museum.

Its displays illustrate the social and industrial history of the towns and villages of the Borough of Langbaurgh. There is also an exhibit devoted to the Turner family, who built the Hall. Kirkleatham village, with its fine 17th and 18th-century buildings, is now a conservation area.

Kirkoswald

Souter Johnnie's Cottage

Kirkoswald, Ayr, Ayrshire KA19 8HY
☎ 06556 603
Apr–Oct, daily 12–5
🏶 Elizabeth M. Mackie, 37 Merkland Place, Kirkoswald, Ayr
Ⓔ Ⓝ Ⓣ Ⓢ

This thatched cottage was the home of John Davidson, on whom Robert Burns modelled Souter (Cobbler) Johnnie, in his narrative poem 'Tam O'Shanter'. The cottage, now a property of the National Trust for Scotland, displays Burns relics, a collection of cobblers' tools and, in a reconstructed alehouse, life-size stone figures of the Souter, Tam, the innkeeper, and his wife.

Kirkstall

Abbey House Museum

Abbey Road, Kirkstall, Leeds, West Yorkshire
LS5 3EH   ☎ 0532 755821
Apr–Sept, Mon–Sat 10–6; Sun 2–6. Oct–Mar, Mon–Sat 10–5; Sun 2–5. Closed Dec 25.
🏶 The Curator
Ⓔ 🛢 🏭 ✒ ♿

The Museum building was formerly the Great Gate House of Kirkstall Abbey, which dates from 1152–82. After the Dissolution of the Monasteries, the last Abbot, John Ripley, lived in the Gatehouse until his death in 1568 and was responsible for its conversion into a dwelling house. It was bought by Leeds Corporation in 1925 and is now the City's museum of social history. The displays include 18th to 20th-century costumes, toys and dolls and a large collection of domestic appliances and tableware, much of it shown in room settings. There are reconstructions of three street scenes of late 18th and 19th-century cottages, workshops and shops, using equipment, fittings and stock brought from buildings in Leeds which were scheduled for demolition. Among the trades represented are those of a chemist, potter, haberdasher, gentlemen's hairdresser, grocer, ironmonger, clay-pipe maker, saddler, blacksmith, handloom weaver, tintack maker, wheelwright and joiner, tobacconist, musical instrument maker, clock and watchmaker, and printer and stationer.

Kirkwall

Tankerness House Museum

Broad Street, Kirkwall, Orkney KW15 1DH
☎ 0856 3191
Mon–Sat 10.30–12.30, 1.30–5. Closed Dec 25, 26, Jan 1, 2.
Museums Officer
F ⬙ ↪

The Museum building, with its arched gateway and forecourt, is a fine example of a 16th-century Scottish town house. The displays tell the story of life in Orkney over 5,000 years and include archaeological material of the Neolithic, Bronze Age, Iron Age, Pictish and Viking periods. Among the exhibits is the Westray Stone, the finest example of Neolithic spiral carving to have been found in the United Kingdom. Other items in the collection relate to local crafts and trades, especially the straw-plait industry, and to domestic life. There are also examples of local weights and measures.

Kirriemuir

Barrie's Birthplace

9 Brechin Road, Kirriemuir, Angus DD8 4BX
☎ 0575 72646
May–Sept, Mon–Sat 11–5.30; Sun 2–5.30
Mrs Elizabeth M. Drainer, 19 Strathmore Avenue, Kirriemuir DD8 4DJ ☎ 0575 72538
£ ⬙ ↪ NTS

This two-storeyed house, now a property of the National Trust for Scotland, was the birthplace, in May 1860, of the author and playwright, Sir James Barrie. The Museum contains many of Barrie's personal possessions, including his desk, together with original manuscripts of his works. There are also two original Peter Pan costumes. The outside wash house, said to have been his first theatre and his inspiration for the Wendy House in *Peter Pan*, houses a Peter Pan exhibition.

Kirton in Lindsey

Lincolnshire and Humberside Railway Museum

Mount Pleasant Windmill, Kirton in Lindsey, Gainsborough, Lincolnshire DN21 4NH
☎ 0652 648251
Easter–Sept, Wed–Sun, Bank Holiday 11–4.30. Oct–Dec 22, Sun 11–4.30.
Mr and Mrs A. Turner
£ 🚻 ♿ ↪

The Museum, next door to the Mount Pleasant Windmill, is just north of Kirton in Lindsey on the B1398 Lincoln to Scunthorpe road. The windmill is a typical Lincolnshire tower mill, built in 1875, and with its machinery nearly complete, it still grinds corn occasionally although, since restoration of the sails still has to be undertaken, power is provided by a vintage portable steam engine.

The Museum covers most aspects of the old railways of the area, from tickets and buttons to signals and a locomotive, from a working signal box to a complete Halt and from documents to models. A working narrow gauge railway is under construction and will give visitors an opportunity to sample an unusual and exciting ride.

Neolithic carved stone from Westray, Orkney. Kirkwall, Tankerness House Museum.

Knaresborough

Old Courthouse Museum

Castle Grounds, Knaresborough, North Yorkshire
Apr–Sept, daily 10–5. Oct–Mar, Sun 1.30–4.
Closed Dec 25, 26, Jan 1.
Ⓜ *See Harrogate Art Gallery*   ☎ 0423 503340
Ⓔ ✏ ♿

Parts of the Museum building date from the 14th century. The original Court room has been preserved, complete with its furniture. It contains a scene reconstructing a legal transaction which took place here in 1602. Other displays illustrate various aspects of the history of Knaresborough.

Knock

Knock Folk Museum

Knock, Co. Mayo, Ireland   ☎ 094 88100
Daily 10–6.30
Ⓜ *The Curator*
Ⓔ 🖃 ♿ ♿

The Museum has been created mainly for the benefit of the large number of pilgrims visiting the celebrated Marian shrine at Knock. Its collections illustrate the traditional life and customs of the West of Ireland. The exhibits, arranged in approximations to their original settings, give a picture of farming, crafts and domestic life at the end of the 19th century. There are also displays relating to the religious life of the people and to the history of Knock Shrine, since its beginnings in 1879.

Knutsford

Tatton Park

Knutsford, Cheshire WA16 6QN ☎ 0565 54822
Apr–May 18 and Sept 2–Oct, Mon–Sat 1–4;
Sun, public holidays 1 5. May 19–Sept 1,
Mon–Sat 1–5; Sun, public holidays 12–5.
Nov and Mar, Sun 1–4.
Ⓜ *Schools Officer*
Ⓔ 🏛 🖃 ♿ ♿ NT

The present house at Tatton Park was built by Samuel and Lewis Wyatt for the Egerton family during the first decade of the 19th century. It was bequeathed to the National Trust in 1958 by the 4th and last Lord Egerton, a noted traveller and big-game hunter, who had also been a pioneer motorist, aviator and wireless enthusiast, and is now managed and financed by Cheshire County Council.

The Egerton family museum, in the former Tenants' Hall, displays a large collection of the 4th Lord Egerton's hunting trophies, together with many of his personal possessions and a number of horse-drawn vehicles. The house contains interesting porcelain, glass, silver, paintings and furniture, mainly by Gillow of Lancaster. On the estate is an arboretum, large deer park and a farm worked as in the 1930s.

L

Lacock

Fox Talbot Museum of Photography

Lacock, nr Chippenham, Wiltshire SN15 2LG
☎ 024973 459
Mar–Oct, daily 11–6 or dusk if earlier.
Closed Good Fri.
Ⓜ *Mr R. E. Lassam, Curator*
Ⓔ ✏ ♿ ♿ □ NT

A National Trust enterprise, the Museum is in a converted 16th-century barn, at the gates of Lacock Abbey. It contains collections commemorating the pioneering photographic achievements of William Henry Fox Talbot (1800–77), whose home was at the Abbey. The exhibits include cameras and other apparatus used by Fox Talbot and examples of his pictures (Calotypes). The Museum also organises temporary exhibitions related to the history of photography and to the work of contemporary photographers.

The Museum forms part of the National Trust complex of Lacock Abbey, which has been inhabited continuously since the 13th century and is still lived in by the Talbot family, and the village of Lacock, where the carefully preserved 13th to 19th-century houses present a remarkable panorama of English domestic architecture.

Lackham Agricultural Museum

Lackham College of Agriculture, Lacock,
nr Chippenham, Wiltshire SN15 2NY
☎ 0249 656111
June–Oct, Mon–Fri 10 5
Ⓜ *Senior Warden*
Ⓔ ✏ ♿

Partly housed in reconstructed farm buildings, which are included in the exhibits, the Museum illustrates the history of agriculture and rural crafts, with collections of tools and machinery. Among the themes of the displays are trapping and poaching, woodland crafts, the blacksmith, the wheelwright, ditching, drainage and the farm dairy.

Lanark

New Lanark Conservation Village

The Counting House, New Lanark, Lanark
M11 9DG   ☎ 0555 61345
Visitor Centre: Mon–Fri 9–5; Sat, Sun 2–5.
Village open at all times.
Ⓜ *Pamela A. Mill, Lanark Conservation Trust*
Ⓕ ✏ 🖃 ♿ 🖼

New Lanark is south of Lanark, close to the River Clyde. The Conservation Village contains the restored buildings of the late 18th and early 19th-century cotton-spinning village, of which Robert Owen became manager in 1800 and where he put into practice his ideas for improving the conditions of industrial workers.

The old Dyeworks has been taken over by the Scottish Wildlife Trust to tell the story of the Falls of Clyde and the natural heritage of the area. There are four Falls Days during the summer, when the hydro-electric power station is closed for maintenance, allowing an increased flow through the Gorge.

Lancaster

Cottage Museum

15 Castle Hill, Lancaster, Lancashire
☎ *0524 64637*
Mar 22–Apr 6, May 5–Sept 21, daily
𝕏 *See Lancaster City Museum*
£

The Cottage forms half of a larger house, built in 1739, which was divided into two dwellings *c.* 1820. In its present arrangement as a museum, it reconstructs the internal layout and furnishings of a better-off working class home of the period when the house was divided. There is also a display of original documents illustrating the history of the property.

Judges' Lodgings

Church Street, Lancaster, Lancashire LA1 1YS
☎ *0524 32808*
Good Fri–Apr and Oct, Mon–Fri 2–5. May–June, Mon–Sat 2–5. July–Sept, Mon–Fri 10–1, 2–5; Sat 2–5.
𝕏 *Assistant Keeper*
£ 🏛 🎖 📷

The Judges' Lodgings, a distinguished and impressively sited town house, contains two distinct museums, the Gillow and Town House Museum and the Museum of Childhood. The first has exhibits illustrating the history and products of the famous Lancaster cabinet-making firm of Gillows, together with period room settings containing furniture by Gillows and other local makers. These include a parlour of *c.* 1750, a dining-room and servants' hall of *c.* 1820 and a bedroom of *c.* 1850.

In the Museum of Childhood visitors can see displays of dolls from the Barry Elder Collection, showing the variety and types of dolls produced over the last three centuries, together with toys and games and reconstructions of a Victorian Schoolroom, and Edwardian day and night nurseries.

King's Own Regimental Museum

Lancaster City Museum, Market Square, Lancaster, Lancashire LA1 1HT
☎ *0524 64637*
Mon–Fri 10–5; Sat 10–3. Closed Dec 25–Jan 1.
𝕏 *See Lancaster City Museum*
F 📷

This was the first such museum to be brought under the care of a local authority. Its displays illustrate the history of the King's Own Royal

Lancaster Regiment from the late 17th century to 1959. Among the exhibits are medals, uniforms, including early examples, and items concerning local militia units. There is an important archive of books, photographs and documents relating to the Regiment and a large index of information concerning former members.

Lancaster City Museum

Market Square, Lancaster, Lancashire LA1 1HT
☎ *0524 64637*
Mon–Fri 10–5; Sat 10–3. Closed Dec 25–Jan 1.
𝕏 *Museum Education Officer*
F 📷 📷

Lancaster City Museum occupies the old Town Hall, built in 1783. The collections illustrate the archaeology and history of the Lancaster area, which includes Morecambe and Heysham. Among the subjects which receive particular attention are the archaeological finds from the area, the town's importance as a cabinet-making centre and its wide range of other industries, including textiles, linoleum, pottery, clog-making, hand-knitting and oatcake-making.

There are good collections of the fine and decorative arts, which include many local topographical paintings and photographs. Among the Museum's more noteworthy exhibits are an 18th-century fire engine and a 7th-century log coffin burial excavated at Quernmore.

Lancaster Maritime Museum

Custom House, St George's Quay, Lancaster, Lancashire LA1 1RB   ☎ *0524 64637*
Apr–Oct, daily 11–5. Nov–Mar, daily 2–5. Closed Dec 25–Jan 1.
𝕏 *See Lancaster City Museum*
F 📷 📷 ♿

The Museum is in Lancaster's former Custom House, built in 1764 by Richard Gillow, during the Golden Age of the town's overseas trade. The collections illustrate this trade during the 18th and early 19th centuries, especially with the West Indies, together with the development of shipbuilding and allied activities which were associated with it. Other displays show the former importance of the fishing and shellfish-gathering economy in Morecambe Bay and the Lune estuary. The exhibits include fishing equipment, the 'Hannah', an 18-foot boat used for salmon fishing on the Lune, and a reconstruction of an early 20th-century fisherman's cottage.

Further sections of the Museum contain ship models, examples of raw materials transported via the smaller ports and the Lancaster Canal, and a reconstruction of the room used by the Collector of Customs, as it looked in about 1880. The reminiscences of Morecambe fishing families are featured in the Museum's audio-visual presentations of fishing and boatbuilding. The 35-foot pleasure boat, *Coronation Rose*, is also preserved in the Museum.

The Elizabethan Great Hall at Packwood House, Lapworth.

Lancing

Lancing College Museum

Lancing College, Lancing, West Sussex
*   BN15 0RW*   ☎ *07917 2213*
During term-time, 'at reasonable times'
🆇 *Rev. J. W. Hunwicke*
🅵 🔺

The Museum's collections comprise partly
archaeological material discovered in the course
of excavations carried out within the College
area, and partly gifts made by former pupils. The
second group of exhibits covers the field of
Greek, Roman and Egyptian studies, and of
ethnology.

Langbank

Finlaystone Doll Collection

Langbank, Renfrew, Renfrewshire PA14 6TJ
☎ *047554 285*
Apr–Aug, Sun 2.30–4.30. Other times by appt.
🆇 *Mrs George MacMillan*
🅴 ✍ 🔺 ♿

Finlaystone House, the home of the
Cunninghams, Earls of Glencairn, for five
centuries, lies off the A8, west of Langbank. It is
now a centre for the Clan MacMillan, being the
home of its Chief. The international collection
of more than 600 dolls, half of which are on
show at any particular time, was begun by the
present Mrs MacMillan's mother and is now
displayed in the former Billiard Room. The
exhibits range from a pre-Inca doll to papier-
mâché Bulgarian dolls of *c.* 1920, and the
materials from plaster to fine bisque.

Langton Matravers

Coach House Museum

St George's Close, Langton Matravers, Swanage,
*   Dorset*   ☎ *0929 423168*
Daily ex. Sun 10.30–12.30, 2–4.
*   Closed Dec 25, 26.*
🆇 *The Curator, Barton, The Hyde, Langton*
*   Matravers, Swanage, Dorset*
🅴 🔺

The Museum's collection illustrates the history
of the local stone industry from Roman times to
the present day. The displays include quarrying
equipment, stone-masons' tools, a full-scale
model of a section of underground working and
examples of the test pieces produced by
apprentices. There are also photographs
illustrating the quarrymen's work and the
ceremonies of the Ancient Order of Purbeck
Marblers and Stonecutters.

Lanreath

Lanreath Farm and Folk Museum

Churchtown, Lanreath, Looe, Cornwall
*   PL13 2NX*   ☎ *0503 20321/20349*
Easter–June, daily 11–1, 2–5. July–Sept, daily
*   10–6. Oct, daily 11–1, 2–5.*
🆇 *Mr L. Facey*
🅴 🍴 🔺

The buildings housing the Museum include a
barn which was the collecting centre for tithes
from the parish until 1886. The collections,
which illustrate the social, domestic and
agricultural history of the area, have been
formed by the Facey family. They include
craftsmen's tools, farm implements and
machinery and a wide range of household
equipment. Among the more unusual items on
display are an 1865 lawnmower, an early ice-
cooled refrigerator, a whimble, used for
making straw rope, and the Lanreath tug-o-war
rope, which has been regularly in service since
1912.

Lapworth

Packwood House

Lapworth, Warwickshire B94 6AT
☎ *05643 2024*
Apr–Sept, Wed–Sun, Bank Holiday Mon 2–6.
*   Oct, Sat, Sun 2–5. Closed Good Fri.*
🆇 *The Custodian*
🅴 ✍ 🔺 🄽🅃

Packwood began life as a Tudor farmhouse.
Additions were made in the 17th century, the
original timbering was stuccoed in the 19th
century and extensive alterations made to the
interior early in the 20th century. The house
and estate, now the property of the National
Trust, are exactly as they were in the time of
Mr Baron Ash, after the First World War.
There are collections of 17th and 18th-century

furniture, with some earlier pieces, French and Flemish tapestries, and Italian and other embroideries, together with stained and painted glass. The whole of the interior is of great significance, reflecting as it does the taste of a wealthy and knowledgeable connoisseur in the period between the Wars.

Largs

Kirkgate House

Manse Court, Largs, Ayrshire KA30 8AW
    ☎ *0475 687081*
June–Sept, Mon–Sat 2–5. Other times by appt.
Mrs J. D. Mensing, 12 Scott Crescent,
    Largs KA30 9PE   ☎ *0475 673731*
F ✐

Kirkgate House is a former weaver's cottage, one of the oldest buildings still in use in Largs. The collections illustrate the history of the town and include Mauchline ware, early photographs and archival and photographic material relating to Sir Thomas Brisbane (1773–1860), and Largs' connections with Australia. The Museum also contains a complete record of graves in the nearby churchyard.

Latheron

Clan Gunn Museum

Old Latheron Church, Latheron, Caithness
May–Sept, Mon–Sat 11–5
Mr M. Gunn, Kirkhill, Wick, Caithness
    ☎ *0955 4771*
£ ♟ ♨

Housed in the former village church, the Museum, opened in 1985, presents the history of the Clan Gunn. There is a comprehensive library on the Clan and on Caithness.

Lauder

Border Country Life Museum

Thirlestane Castle, Lauder, Berwickshire
    TD2 6RU   ☎ *05782 430*
May 12–June and Sept, Wed, Sun 2–5.
    July–Aug, Sat–Thurs 2–5.
Catriona Dodd, Administrator
£ ♟ ♨ ♨

The Museum occupies the south wing of Thirlestane Castle, home of the Maitland famiy since the 16th century. This wing is made up of the rooms and work areas once used by the servants. The displays provide an imaginative interpretation of the history of rural life in the Border region. They include the Finds Room, with its prehistoric grave, the Riverbank Room, showing wildlife and fishing along the River Tweed, and the Chapter House, which depicts monastic life. There are also reconstructions of a country tailor's shop, a joiner's shop and a dairy, and a veterinary section.

Nineteenth-century Jumeau dolls.
Laugharne, Little Treasures Doll Museum.

Laugharne

Little Treasures Doll Museum

Ravenhall, Duncan Street, Laugharne, Dyfed
    SA33 4RY
Easter–Sept, daily 11–5. Other times by appt.
Polly Edge   ☎ *099421 554*
£ ♟ ♨

The Museum is in a converted 18th-century barn. Its collection is mainly of dolls, dating from 1800 to 1940, but it also includes dolls' houses, dolls' and babies' prams, teddy bears, baby clothes and accessories, and children's china and furniture. A turn-of-the-century nursery has its rocking-horses and figures of small occupants.

The emphasis is on German character dolls, but there are also French, English and American examples.

Lavenham

The Priory

Water Street, Lavenham, Suffolk CO10 9RW
    ☎ *0787 247417*
Mar 28–Apr 6, Mon–Sat 2–5.30. May 3–Sept,
    Mon–Sat 2–5.30. Also open Sun during Aug
    and Bank Holiday.
A. Casey
£ ♟ ♨ HHA

The Priory at Lavenham originally belonged to a Benedictine order and subsequently became the home of medieval wool merchants, an Elizabethan rector and finally, in 1979, after it had been uninhabited and derelict for many years, of the Casey family, who have restored it. The complex timber structure is made up of five separate frames, with the original medieval hall-house at the centre. The Great Hall has a huge inglenook fireplace and a Jacobean staircase. Elizabethan wall-paintings have been discovered during the restoration work.

There is a display of photographs showing the restoration in progress and a collection of

objects found in the building. Throughout the
Priory, which is a Grade I listed building, are
paintings, drawings and a stained-glass window
by the Hungarian artist, Ervin Bossanyi
(1881–1975), best known for his windows in
Canterbury Cathedral and in Washington
Cathedral in the United States.

Laxfield

Jacobs Farm Children's Museum

St Jacobs Hall, Laxfield, Woodbridge, Suffolk
  ☎ 098683 657
*Apr–Oct, Tues–Thurs, Sun 10–5. Open daily
during school holidays throughout year.
Groups (minimum 10 persons) by appt.*
◪ *Mrs C. E. Reynolds*
£ ✎ ✐ ♿

Jacobs Hall, now being restored, is a moated
house, built by the Jacobs family in the 16th
century and altered in the 18th. It is one mile
north of Laxfield, on the B1117 between
Halesworth and Framlingham. The Museum
contains a large collection of toys, dating from
the mid 18th century to the 20th century. There
is a working model railway layout and an
Edwardian schoolroom, in which children can
dress up in period clothes and use the classroom
equipment.

All the farm buildings are open to visitors and
contain old tools, implements and equipment
which are still in use on the farm.

Layer Breton

Shalom Hall

Layer Breton, nr Colchester, Essex
Aug, Mon–Fri 10–1, 2.30–5.30
◪ *Lady Phoebe Hillingdon*
F

Shalom Hall is seven miles south-west of
Colchester and two miles from the A12. Built in
the 19th century, it has a collection of 17th and
18th-century French furniture and porcelain,
together with portraits by celebrated English
artists, including Gainsborough and Sir Joshua
Reynolds. The house is still occupied as a family
home.

Leamington Spa

Warwick District Council Art Gallery and Museum

Avenue Road, Leamington Spa, Warwickshire
CV31 3PP   ☎ 0926 26559
*Mon–Sat 10–1, 2–5. Closed Good Fri, Christmas,
New Year holiday.*
◪ *Mrs Margaret A. Slater, Curator*
F ✎ ✐ ♿ □

The Gallery's permanent collection includes
Dutch and Flemish Old Master paintings, 20th-
century paintings and watercolours, 16th and
19th-century pottery and porcelain, 18th-

century drinking glasses and 20th-century
English glass. There is also a good collection of
paintings by the Leamington artist, Thomas
Baker.

Each year there are a number of temporary
exhibitions of works by artists resident in the area.

**Armour in the Hall of Eastnor Castle,
Ledbury.**

Ledbury

Eastnor Castle

Ledbury, Hereford and Worcester HR8 1RN
  ☎ 0531 2304
*Easter–Sept, parties by appt. Mid May–Sept, Sun,
Bank Holiday Mon 2.30–5.30. July–Aug,
also Wed, Thurs 2.30–5.30.*
◪ *Hon. Mrs Hervey-Bathurst*
£ ✎ ✐ HHA

Eastnor Castle is two miles east of Ledbury on
the A438. Built in 1812 for Earl Somers, in the
neo-Gothic style, and with interior decorations
by A. W. Pugin, G. E. Fox and Robert Smirke,
it has continued in the possession of the Somers
and Somers Cocks families and, through
marriage, of the present occupants, Major
and Mrs Hervey-Bathurst. There are large
collections of armour, mostly Italian and
German, and of swords and other weapons. The
18th and 19th-century family portraits include
works by Romney and Angelica Kauffmann, and
among the other artists represented in the house
are Van Dyck, Kneller, Lely, Reynolds, G. F.
Watts, J. P. Hackert and Sir Thomas Lawrence.
There are fine Brussels and Flemish tapestries,
and English and Italian embroideries.

A small room adjoining the Library contains
family and other photographs by the celebrated
Victorian photographer, Julia Margaret
Cameron, who was a sister of Virginia,
Countess Somerset.

Leeds

City Art Gallery

Calverley Street, Leeds, West Yorkshire LS1 3AA
☎ 0532 462495
Mon, Tues, Thurs, Fri 10–6; Wed 10–9;
    Sat 10–4; Sun 2–5
⚑ Principal Keeper
🅵 🏛 🗪 ♿

The Gallery's collections are held in common
with those of Temple Newsam House and
Lotherton Hall. The Art Gallery houses the
prints and drawings, including a fine collection
of British Romantic watercolours, most of the
paintings after 1800 and the modern sculpture.
There are important collections of 20th-century
British paintings, particularly work by members
of the Camden Town Group, and late 19th and
early 20th-century French painters, including
Courbet, Sisley, Signac and Derain, are also
well represented. The sculpture collection is
strong in works by Epstein and Henry Moore.

Leeds Industrial Museum

Armley Mills, Canal Road, Leeds, West Yorkshire
    LS12 2QF   ☎ 0532 637861
Apr–Sept, Tues–Sat 10–6; Sun 2–6 (last
    admission 5). Oct–Mar, Tues–Sat 10–5;
    Sun 2–5 (last admission 4). Open Bank
    Holiday Mon. Closed Dec 25.
⚑ Mr R. Bex
🅴 🏛 🗫 🗪 ♿

Armley Mills, which dates from 1806, was at
one time the world's largest woollen mill. The
four-storeyed stone building, with its unique
fireproof construction, is one of Britain's most
impressive industrial monuments. Originally
water-powered, it was converted to steam in the
late 19th century. Its galleries show the
development of the principal Leeds industries,

'Maternity' by Henry Moore (1898–1976).
Leeds, City Art Gallery.

including textiles, clothing, optics and heavy
engineering. The textile exhibits cover the
complete production of woollen cloth, using
both static displays and working machinery.
    The local tailoring and garment-making
industry is realistically illustrated by
reconstructions of early sweatshops and fully
equipped workrooms and showrooms.
Engineering is represented by machine tools and
workshops. As Leeds was a major world centre
of locomotive construction, a collection of
engines made by local companies has been
established. Restored narrow gauge locomotives
are driven around the museum site on open
days. The Armley Palace Picture Hall, a
reconstructed cinema of the 1920s, shows early
films on original projectors of the period,
commemorating the important part played by
Leeds in the optical and cinematographic
industries.

Lotherton Hall

Aberford, Leeds, West Yorkshire LS25 3EB
    ☎ 0532 813259
Tues–Sun, Bank Holiday Mon 10.30–6.15 or
    dusk. Closed Dec 25, 26.
⚑ The Keeper
🅴 🏛 🗫 🗪

The Hall was built by Colonel Frederick
Richard Trench Gascoigne between 1896 and
1907 around a small 18th-century house. In
1968 it was given to the City of Leeds, together
with its park and gardens, by his son, Sir Alvary
Gascoigne, and is now used as a museum of the
decorative arts.
    It displays the Gascoigne family collection of
furniture, porcelain, silver and paintings,
including Pompei Batoni's celebrated portrait of
Sir Thomas Gascoigne (1745–1810). Other
items from the Gascoigne collection include
18th and 19th-century silver-gilt race-cups. The
exhibits also include early Oriental ceramics and
an important collection of 19th and 20th-
century arts and crafts, including furniture,
ceramics, textiles and 18th to 20th-century
fashion.

Museum of the History of Education

Parkinson Court, University of Leeds, West
    Yorkshire LS2 9JT ☎ 0532 431751 extn 6159
By appt only
⚑ The Curator
🅵 🗪

The Museum was established in the 1950s
primarily for the use of students and members of
staff. It has a substantial collection of textbooks
and children's exercise books, from the 17th
century onwards, which are arranged as far as
possible according to the main subjects of the
curriculum. There is also an extensive display of
objects used by teachers and pupils – desks,
slates, pens, ink, chalk, canes and a punishment
book – together with examples of science-
teaching apparatus and of practical work. The
Museum also maintains a collection of samples
of work by trainee teachers and of the detailed
records of their progress.

Temple Newsam House

Leeds, West Yorkshire LS15 0AE
☎ *0532 647321*
*Tues–Sun, Bank Holiday Mon 10.30–6.15 or
dusk in winter. May–Sept, open until 8.30
on Wed.*
▨ *Education Officer*
Ⓔ ▮ ▦ ▰

This Tudor-Jacobean mansion has splendid
18th-century Regency and Victorian interiors.
The 917-acre Park was landscaped by Lancelot
'Capability' Brown in the 1760s and contains
seven specialist gardens. The Home Farm has
rare breeds of livestock.

The magnificent country-house collections of
furniture, silver, ceramics and other items is the
finest publicly owned collection of the
decorative arts outside London, and the
pictures, too, are noteworthy. The Ingram
(Viscounts Irwin) family pictures form the basis
of the paintings collection, just as the furniture
they commissioned for the Long Gallery in 1745
forms the core of the furniture collection, which
includes, besides, the Chippendale library
writing table, made for Harewood House, c. 1770.

Leek

The Brindley Mill and James Brindley Museum

Mill Street, Leek, Staffordshire ☎ *0538 381446*
*Easter–June, Oct, Sat, Sun, Bank Holiday Mon
2–5. July–Aug, daily (ex. Wed) and Bank
Holiday Mon 2–5.*
▨ *Kenneth N. Crawford, Hon. Secretary,
5 Daintry Street, Leek ST13 5PG*
Ⓔ ⌀ ▰

The great 18th-century millwright and engineer,
James Brindley, spent part of his childhood at
Leek and set up his millwright's business in the
town in 1742. The water-powered cornmill
which he designed in 1752 is fully operational.
After being abandoned in 1940, it has been fully
restored and illustrates the evolution of milling
practice over a period of 225 years.

The Museum set up within the Mill is a
centre of information on the life and work of
James Brindley (1716–72). The exhibits include
two of his personal possessions, a surveyor's level
and a notebook containing accounts of visits.

Leek Nicholson Institute Museum

Stockwell Street, Leek, Staffordshire ST13 6HQ
☎ *0538 382721*
Mar–Oct, daily 1–5 ex. Mon, Thurs, Sun
▨ *Mr G. N. Hyde, Assistant Secretary,
Staffordshire Moorlands District Council,
New Stockwell House, Leek ST13 6HQ*
Ⓕ ▰

This handsome late Victorian Institute, with
its high copper-domed tower, was built to house
a library, art gallery and museum. The
collections are concerned mainly with the
history, topography and personalities of the
area.

Leicester

Belgrave Hall

*Church Road, off Thurcaston Road, Belgrave,
Leicester, Leicestershire* ☎ *0533 666590*
*Mon–Thurs, Sat 10–5.30; Sun 2–5.30.
Closed Dec 25, 26.*
▨ *See Leicestershire Museum*
Ⓕ ⌀ ▰

Belgrave Hall is one and a half miles from the
centre of Leicester, just off the A6 Leicester to
Loughborough road. It was built in 1709–13 and
stands in fine grounds, which include period and
botanic gardens. The rooms are furnished in a
series of styles, ranging from the late 17th
century to the Victorian period, with an
emphasis on the 18th century. The drawing-
room contains some of the best furniture. The
'lion mask' suite of 12 chairs and a setting,
which date from the late 1720s, are of
particularly high quality. The dining-room and
principal bedroom have late 18th-century
furniture. There is also a music room and a
19th-century bedroom and nursery.

The Kitchen of Belgrave Hall, Leicester.

East Midlands Gas Museum

*Emgas Service Centre, Aylestone Road, Leicester,
Leicestershire LE2 7HQ*
☎ *0533 549414 extn 2192*
*Tues–Fri 12.30–4.30. Closed Bank Holiday Tues,
Good Fri.*
▨ *Museum Assistant*
Ⓕ ⌀ ▰

The Museum occupies a fine example of a
Victorian gas works gate house, built in 1878. It
has a four-dial clock tower, containing the
original mechanism and bells. The displays
cover a wide range of objects and archive
material illustrating the history of the
production and distribution of gas in the East
Midlands area. There is a particularly
interesting collection of items relating to

domestic lighting, cooking and heating. These include a number of unusual exhibits, such as hairdryers, magic lanterns and a gas-driven radio.

The Guildhall

Guildhall Lane, Leicester, Leicestershire
Mon–Thurs, Sat 10–5.30; Sun 2–5.30.
    Closed Dec 25, 26.
▓ See Leicestershire Museum
Ⓕ ⟳ ↩

The building is the late medieval hall of the Corpus Christi Guild of Leicester, later used as the Town Hall of Leicester until 1875. The Great Hall is timber-framed, the late 14th-century eastern end having trusses of cruck construction, with king-posts on the collar beams. The western end is 15th century. The building also contains the late 15th-century Mayor's Parlour, with a fireplace of 1637 and the Mayor's Chair of the same date and style, the 16th-century Recorder's bedroom and the Town Library of 1632.

Across the courtyard is the town's original police station with its cells.

Jewry Wall Museum and Site

St Nicholas Circle, Leicester, Leicestershire
Mon–Thurs, Sat 10–5.30; Sun 2–5.30.
    Closed Dec 25, 26.
▓ See Leicestershire Museum
Ⓕ ⟳

The Jewry Wall, 9 metres high and 45 metres long, is one of the largest sections of Roman masonry still standing in Britain. The site adjacent to it is that of the 2nd-century baths of Roman Leicester.

The Museum's collections and displays are concerned with the history of human settlement in Leicester from the earliest times to the present day. Among the more important exhibits are the Bronze Age Welby hoard, a Roman milestone, Roman wall-plaster, Romano-British mosaics and an Anglo-Saxon burial. There is also late medieval painted glass formerly in Wygston's House.

Leicestershire Museum and Art Gallery

New Walk, Leicester, Leicestershire LE1 6TD
    ☎ 0533 554100
Mon–Thurs, Sat 10–5.30; Sun 2–5.30.
    Closed Dec 25, 26.
▓ Keeper of Education
Ⓕ ▪ ↩

The Museum contains sections devoted to British and foreign natural history, minerals and palaeontology, including an articulated dinosaur display. There is also an Egyptology gallery. The Art Gallery has an internationally celebrated collection of German Expressionist paintings and graphics, and a collection of English and European art from the 16th century to the present day. The French paintings include The Choirboy by Georges de la Tour. The displays and collections of decorative art feature English ceramics from the 17th century onwards,

Oriental, Middle Eastern and Continental ceramics, English drinking glasses, French cut glass and English silver of the 16th to 20th centuries.

Leicestershire Museum of Technology

Abbey Pumping Station, Corporation Road,
    off Abbey Lane, Leicester, Leicestershire
    ☎ 0533 661330
Mon–Thurs, Sat 10–5.30; Sun 2–5.30.
    Closed Dec 25, 26.
▓ See Leicestershire Museum
Ⓕ ▪ ▆ Steam Days only ↩

The Museum is in the late Victorian pumping station for the sewerage system of Leicester. It contains the original four beam-engines, together with other steam engines and a 1935 84-ton Ruston Bucyrus steam shovel. Among the other exhibits are a printing shop, a collection of horse-drawn and mechanical transport, and a display illustrating the history of machine knitting. The Museum holds Steam Days five times a year. On these occasions, the beam engines and other steam engines run under steam and the knitting machinery can also be seen working.

Museum of the Royal Leicestershire Regiment

The Magazine, Oxford Street, Leicester,
    Leicestershire
Mon–Thurs, Sat 10–5.30; Sun 2–5.30.
    Closed Dec 25, 26.
▓ See Leicestershire Museum
Ⓕ ⟳

The Museum is housed in the early 16th-century gateway to the Newarke, at that time a walled area outside the town of Leicester. The displays include uniforms and equipment, medals, weapons, documents, photographs, battle trophies and other relics relating to the Royal Leicestershire Regiment (17th Foot).

Newarke Houses Museum

The Newarke, Leicester, Leicestershire
Mon–Thurs, Sat 10–5.30; Sun 2–5.30.
    Closed Dec 25, 26.
▓ See Leicestershire Museum
Ⓕ ▪

The buildings comprise a 16th-century Chantry house and a 17th-century dwelling house, with some 19th-century additions. The Museum's collections and displays concentrate on the history of Leicestershire from c. 1500 onwards. The displays include a panelled room, with 17th-century furniture, a 19th-century street scene, showing local domestic industries, a clockmaker's workshop and an early 20th-century village shop. Among the other exhibits are locally made clocks, toys and games, furniture by Ernest Gimson and the Cotswold group of craftsmen, and clothes and furniture which belonged to Daniel Lambert (1770–1809), claimed to be England's heaviest man.

There is a pleasant garden behind the Museum.

Wygston's House, Museum of Costume

12 Applegate, St Nicholas Circle, Leicester,
Leicestershire
Mon–Thurs, Sat 10–5.30; Sun 2–5.30.
Closed Dec 25, 26.
🗿 *See Leicestershire Museum*
[F] [🕮] [🚻]

Wygston's House is a late 15th or early 16th-
century timber-framed building, with the front,
in brick, dating from 1796. The main part of the
collection and displays consists of costumes and
accessories from the 18th century to the present
day. There are also exhibits of textiles and
reconstructions of a draper's and a shoe shop of
the 1920s.

Leominster

Croft Castle

nr Leominster, Hereford and Worcester HR6 9PW
☎ *056885 246*
Apr and Oct, Sat, Sun and Easter Mon 2–5.
May–Sept, Wed–Sun and Bank Holiday Mon
2–6.
🗿 *The Administrator*
[£] [🚻] [NT]

The Castle is five miles north-west of
Leominster. It was the home of the Croft family
from the 11th century until 1750, when their
declining fortunes compelled them to sell the
property, and again since 1923. Lord Croft now
lives in the Castle, which today belongs to the
National Trust
   The walls and towers of the present Castle
probably date from the 14th or 15th century.
In the 18th century the building was given sash
windows and remodelled internally in the
Gothick style, which provides a particularly
suitable setting for Lord Croft's fine collection
of Gothick furniture. The house also contains a
series of pastel portraits of members of the Croft
family.
   The Croft estate has some of the finest oaks
in Britain, with girths of 40 feet, and a 350-
year-old avenue of sweet chestnuts half a mile
long.

Leominster Folk Museum

Etnam Street, Leominster, Hereford and
*   Worcester HR6 8AN*   ☎ *0568 5186*
Apr–Oct, Mon–Sat 10–1, 2–5
🗿 *The Director*
[£] [🖼] [🚻]

The Museum, staffed and run entirely by
volunteers, is housed in a former Mission
Hall, built in 1855 to serve labourers on the
railway. Most of what is on show has been
given or lent by local people and the aim of
the Museum is to present a picture of life in
the district as it was in the past. The displays
include material from Iron Age forts and
Roman settlements in the area; costumes;
items illustrating local trades and
occupations; and displays relating to the
Turnpike Trusts.

Lerwick

Böd of Gremista

Lerwick, Shetland Islands
Open Spring 1987
🗿 *Mr T. M. Y. Manson, 93 Gilbertson Road,*
*   Lerwick, Shetland*   ☎ *0595 4632*
[£]

The 'böd' or booth, is the only one so far
restored of the many in Shetland which were
connected with the deep-water fishing industry
of the 18th and 19th centuries. The factor and
his family lived on the upper floors and
negotiations with the fishermen took place on
the ground floor.
   Arthur Anderson, co-founder of the
Peninsular and Oriental Steam Navigation
Company, was born in this building in 1792. He
was the son of Robert Anderson, the fish factor
in charge at the time. In later life, Arthur
Anderson was a generous benefactor to his
native islands, and the house contains an
exhibition illustrating his life and
achievements.

Shetland Museum

Lower Hillhead, Lerwick, Shetland Islands
*   ZE1 0EL*   ☎ *0595 5057*
Mon, Wed, Fri 10–7; Tues, Thurs, Sat 10–5.
*   Closed public holidays.*
🗿 *Mr A. Williamson, Curator*
[F] [🖼] [🚻] [♿]

This is a regional museum, created to illustrate
the theme, 'Life in Shetland through the Ages'.
The collections include archaeology, farming
and rural crafts, seafaring and fishing, and
Shetland textiles. There are growing study
collections of Shetland natural history,
including a registered herbarium.
   The collections of textiles, items
salvaged from wreck sites, ship models and
natural history are of international
importance.

The Shetland Croft House Museum

Voe, Dunrossness. Enquiries to Shetland Museum,
*   Lerwick.*
Tues–Sun 10–5. Closed public holidays.
🗿 *Mr A. Williamson, Curator*
[£] [🚻]

The house, steading and water-mill which
comprise the Shetland Croft House Museum are
fairly typical of mid 19th-century Shetland croft
buildings. The basis of the household economy
was the sea, not the land. The crofter was a
fisherman, seaman or whaler and most of the
work on the land was done, in his absence, by
his wife and family. The Croft has been
furnished with equipment to show how such
a family, consisting of grandparents, parents
and children, lived. The initiative to create
it as a museum came from a group of
Shetland expatriates, the Hamefarirs, who
visited their homelands in 1960. Their
financial support helped make the venture
possible.

Letchworth

First Garden City Heritage Museum

296 Norton Way South, Letchworth, Hertfordshire
*   SG6 1SU*   ☎ *0462 683149*
Mon–Fri 2–4.30; Sat 10–1, 2–4
🏛 *Mr R. Lancaster, Curator*
F 🔖 ♿

296 Norton Way South was built in 1907 as
offices for the architects of Letchworth Garden
City, Parker and Unwin, and was later lived in
by Barry Parker. It is in a typical Parker style,
with a thatched roof. The Museum's displays
illustrate the birth and development of the
Garden City movement and the personalities
involved. Additional material relates to the
social and economic history of Letchworth.
There are extensive collections of architectural
drawings and photographs, referring specially to
the work of Barry Parker.

Letchworth Museum and Art Gallery

Broadway, Letchworth, Hertfordshire SG6 3PF
*   ☎ 0462 685647*
Mon–Sat 10–5. Closed public holidays.
🏛 *Schools Service Officer, Old Ambulance*
*   Station, Paynes Park, Hitchin, Hertfordshire*
*   SG5 1EQ*   ☎ *0462 52666*
F 🔖 ♿ ☐

The Museum occupies listed buildings, designed
by Barry Parker, the architect of Letchworth
Garden City. The emphasis of the displays is on
local archaeology. Of particular importance is
the material from the burial of an Iron Age
chieftain at Baldock, and there are also finds
from recent excavations at Iron Age and Roman
sites in the same area. The natural history
section concentrates on local wildlife. The Art
Gallery is mainly used for housing temporary
exhibitions.

Leuchars

Earlshall Castle

Leuchars, St Andrews, Fife KY16 0DP
*   ☎ 033483 205*
Easter, Sat, Sun & Mon, then Thurs–Sun until
*   last Sun in Sept, 2–6 (last admission 5.15)*
🏛 *The Administrator*
£ ♟ 🍴 ♿

The Castle, built in 1546 by Sir William Bruce,
is still under the occupation of the same family.
It was restored at the end of the 19th century by
Sir Robert Lorimer. Earlshall is shown to the
public as a family home, containing notable
collections of Scottish broadswords, Jacobite
glass and relics, and examples of the work of
Robert Lorimer in stained glass, metalwork and
woodcarving. There are some very fine painted
ceilings.

First Garden City Heritage Museum,
Letchworth.

Leven

Leven Museum

Leven Library, South Street, Leven, Fife KY8 4PF
Mon–Sat 10–12.30, 2–5
🏛 *See Kirkcaldy Museum and Art Gallery*
F ♿

The Museum presents the history of the town
and its buildings and people, as shown in old
photographs, paintings and drawings.

Lewes

Anne of Cleves House Museum

Southover High Street, Lewes, East Sussex
*   N7 1JA*   ☎ *0273 474610*
Mid Feb–mid Nov, Mon–Sat 10–5.30. Apr–Oct,
*   also Sun 2–5.30.*
🏛 *The Custodian*
£ 🔖

The Museum occupies a complex of five
buildings, the earliest a timber-framed house
c. 1500, surrounding a courtyard garden. Its
displays include furniture, domestic equipment
and a wide range of material illustrating the
everyday life of local people during the 19th and
early 20th centuries. Special attention is given
to the Wealden iron industry and to the history
of the town of Lewes.

Firle Place

nr Lewes, East Sussex BN8 6LP
*   ☎ 079159 335*
June–Sept, Wed, Thurs, Sun 2.15–5.
*   Also Bank Holiday Sun & Mon at Easter,*
*   May, Spring Bank Holiday & Aug.*
*   Other times by appt.*
🏛 *Mrs Quentin Gage, Showing Secretary*
£ ♟ 🍴 ♿ HHA

Firle Place is near Lewes, close to the A27 and
approximately halfway between Brighton and
Eastbourne. It has been the home of the Gage
family since the 15th century. The original
Tudor manor house was considerably altered in

The Drawing Room of Firle Place, Lewes.

the mid 18th century. The pictures and furniture belonging to the house received notable additions from the Cowper collections at Panshanger in Hertfordshire, inherited by Imogen, wife of the 6th Viscount Gage, through her mother, Lady Desborough. Firle Place now contains one of the most important country house collections of the south of England.

There is a good series of family portraits – the artists represented include Gainsborough, Reynolds, Zoffany, Lawrence and Hoppner – and there are fine English and European paintings, mostly from the Cowper collection. The 18th and 19th-century English and French furniture is of exceptional quality, as is the Sèvres and English porcelain.

Military Heritage Museum

West Street, Lewes, East Sussex BN7 2NJ
☎ 0273 473139
Mon–Fri 10–1, 2–5. Occasional weekend & holiday opening, enquire locally.
Ⓜ *Paul Cole-King, Curator*
Ⓔ ▲ ⌂ ☐

The Museum was opened on its present site in 1984. It occupies part of the first floor of the premises of a firm of auctioneers specialising in arms, armour and militaria. The Edwardian building was formerly used as a grocer's and haberdasher's shop. The displays cover the history of the British Army from 1660 to 1914, with exhibits that include uniforms, equipment and a wide range of weapons.

Temporary exhibitions in the foyer are devoted to special themes, such as 'British Infantry Swords', 'Scottish Regiments' and 'Weapons Used Against The British Soldier'.

Museum of Sussex Archaeology

Barbican House, High Street, Lewes, East Sussex BN7 1YE   ☎ 0273 474379
Apr–Oct, Mon–Sat 10–5.30; Sun 11–5.30. Nov–Mar, Mon–Sat 10–5.30.
Ⓜ *John Houghton, General Administrator*
Ⓔ

The Museum occupies a 16th-century timber-framed building, remodelled, with a brick façade and fine oak staircase, for an 18th-century wool merchant. The displays tell the story of human settlement in Sussex from the time of the

earliest stone implement-using hunters up to the medieval period. The six galleries contain material from many of the country's most important archaeological sites, with interpretive models and dioramas. Full-scale replicas of an axe-polishing stone, a vertical loom and Roman querns allow visitors to experiment with ancient handicrafts.

Leyland

British Commercial Vehicle Museum

King Street, Leyland, Preston, Lancashire PR5 1LE
☎ 0772 451011
Easter–Sept 28, Tues–Sun 10–5. Oct–Nov, Sat, Sun 10–5.
Ⓜ *The Manager*
Ⓔ ▲ ⌂ ⅍

The Museum's collection illustrates the history of British commercial vehicles, from the horse-drawn period to the present day. The 40 exhibits include steam wagons, buses, lorries, vans and fire-engines, all of which have been carefully restored and are in a roadworthy condition.

South Ribble Museum and Exhibition Centre

The Old Grammar School, Church Road, Leyland, Preston, Lancashire   ☎ 0772 422041
Tues, Fri 10–4; Thurs 1–4; Sat 10–1. Closed public holidays.
Ⓜ *The Custodian*
Ⓕ ⌂

The timber-framed building which now houses the Museum dates from the second half of the 16th century and was formerly Leyland's Free Grammar School. The displays include archaeological material from excavations at the Roman site at Walton-le-Dale, and a wide range of smaller items relating to the history of the town and the area.

Lichfield

Hanch Hall

Lichfield, Staffordshire WS13 8HH
☎ 0543 490308
Apr–May, Sun & Bank Holiday 2–6. June–Sept, Tues–Thurs, Sat, Sun, daily 2–6.
Ⓜ *The Secretary*
Ⓔ ▲ ▬ ⌂

Hanch Hall is on the B5014, four miles north-west of Lichfield. There has been a house on the site since the 13th century, but the present building contains architectural features ranging from the 15th century to the Victorian period. By the 1970s it had fallen into disrepair, but is now being progressively restored. It is lived in by the present owners and visitors receive a guided tour through the residential part of the house. Other rooms contain displays of needlework, costumes, dolls, teapots and postal history. There is also local history material transferred from the old Lichfield City Museum.

Heritage Exhibition and Treasury

St Mary's Centre, Market Square, Lichfield,
* Staffordshire*   ☎ *0534 256611*
Daily 10–4.30. Closed Spring Bank Holiday Mon,
* Dec 25, 26, Jan 1.*
⚑ *Mrs K. Coghill, Administrator*
Ⓔ ♠ ▭ ↪ ♿

Facing redundancy, St Mary's Church was
converted to meet a number of community
needs, including a Heritage Exhibition. The
Chancel and Dyott Chapel have been retained
for regular worship. The Heritage displays cover
various aspects of the history of Lichfield during
the past 2,000 years.

There is an audio-visual presentation of the
1643 siege of Lichfield Cathedral during the
Civil War. The Treasury houses civic and local
parish silver.

Letocetum Roman Site and Museum

Wall, nr Lichfield, Staffordshire WS14 0AM
    ☎ *0543 480768*
Mar 14–Oct 16, Mon–Sat 9.30–6.30; Sun
  2–6.30. Oct 17–Mar 13, Wed–Sat
  9.30–4.30; Sun 2–4.30. Alternate Tues
  closed Oct 17–Mar 13.
⚑ *Historic Buildings & Monuments Commission,*
  Wolverhampton   ☎ *0902 765105*
Ⓔ ↪ ♿ ✿

The Museum is two and a half miles from
Lichfield, off the A5 between Muckley Corner
Island and Shenstone Wall Island. It contains
coins, pottery and other items discovered in the
course of the excavations at *Letocetum*. Visitors
can also see the remains of the cold, warm and
hot baths, which were in use during the Roman
occupation.

Museum of The Staffordshire Regiment (The Prince of Wales's)

Regimental Headquarters, Whittington Barracks,
  Lichfield, Staffordshire WS14 9PY
    ☎ *0543 433333 extn 229*
Mon–Fri 9–4.30. Closed Dec 25–Jan 1 & Bank
  Holidays. Parties at other times by appt.
⚑ *The Curator*
Ⓕ ⚲ ↪ ♿

The Museum is just outside Whittington
Barracks on the A51 Lichfield to Tamworth
road, three miles from Lichfield. The displays
cover the former South and North Staffordshire
Regiments, amalgamated in 1959, their
predecessors, the 38th, 64th, 80th and 98th
Regiments, the King's Own Stafford Militia,
and the Staffordshire Rifle Volunteers.

The Museum exhibits a good range of
uniforms, badges, medals, weapons and war
trophies, spanning the history of the Regiment
from its origins in 1705 to the present day.
There is relics from the Sikh Wars, the
Crimea, Indian Mutiny, Zulu War, Egypt,
Sudan, South Africa and both World Wars.
The medals display includes seven of the
13 Victoria Crosses awarded to men of the
Regiment. The Museum Library contains,
among other books and documents relating to
the Regiment, a good collection of war diaries.

Samuel Johnson Birthplace Museum

Breadmarket Street, Lichfield, Staffordshire
  WS13 6LG   ☎ *0543 264972*
May–Sept, Mon–Sat 10–5; Sun 2.30–5.
  Oct–Apr, Mon–Sat 10–4. Closed Good Fri,
  Spring Bank Holiday, Dec 25, 26, Jan 1.
⚑ *The Curator*
Ⓔ ♠ ↪

The house where Samuel Johnson was born in
September 1709 had been completed in the
previous year. The collections now displayed in
it illustrate Johnson's life, work and personality,
and set him against the background of his
friends and contemporaries. The wide range of
exhibits shown to visitors include books,
manuscripts, furniture, pictures and personal
possessions.

Sandfields Pumping Station

Chesterfield Road, Sandfields, Lichfield,
  Staffordshire WS14 0AA
By appt. Occasional Open Days.
⚑ *Operations Manager, South Staffordshire*
  Waterworks Company, Green Lane, Walsall,
  Staffordshire WS2 7PD   ☎ *0992 38282*
Ⓕ ↪

A Cornish beam-engine, built by J. Davies of
Tipton, has been preserved here in its original
engine-house. The engine was installed in 1873
as part of the local water supply system. Its
bearings are supported in the best High
Victorian fashion, on a Tuscan arcade, with
three arches and fluted columns.

The Treasury at St Mary's Heritage Exhibition
Centre, Lichfield.

The Parlour at the Samuel Johnson Birthplace Museum, Lichfield.

Limerick

The Hunt Museum

National Institute of Higher Education,
Plassey Technological Park, Limerick,
Co. Limerick, Ireland   ☎ 061 333644
Apr–Sept, daily 9.30–5. Other times on written
application.
🏛 *The Curator*
£ ⬛ 📷 🚻

The Hunt Museum is two miles from Limerick City on the Dublin side. It contains an exhibition of Irish antiquities and European art collected by the late John Hunt and his wife, Gertrude, and reflects their personal interests. Apart from a large number of flint and polished stone artefacts, most of the material in the antiquities section belongs to the Bronze Age, chiefly Irish, although there are a number of British items, including crosses and liturgical vessels, together with some ceremonial and domestic silver, medieval crucifix figures, ivories and bronzes, and Limoges enamels.

Limerick City Gallery of Art

Pery Square, Limerick, Co. Limerick, Ireland
☎ 061 310633
Mon–Fri 10–1, 2–6 (2–7 on Thurs); Sat 10–1.
Closed Bank Holiday and public holidays.
🏛 *Paul M. O'Reilly, Director*
F ⬛ 📷 🚻

The interesting neo-Romanesque building which now contains the Gallery dates from 1903. It was built as the City Library, an art gallery section being added in 1948. The Library has been recently relocated and the Gallery now occupies the whole of the premises. Most of the paintings in the permanent collection are by Irish artists or by artists with Irish connections. They range in date from the 18th to the 20th century and include good examples of the work of Jervas, Carver, Barrett, Mulcahy, Hone, Osbourne, Yeats, Orpen, Keating and Henry.

The house overlooking the Market Square, Lichfield, in which Dr Johnson was born on 18 September 1709.

Limerick Museum

1 John's Square North, Limerick, Co. Limerick,
Ireland   ☎ 061 47826
Tues–Sat 10–1, 2.15–5. Closed public holidays.
🏛 *Mr L. Walsh, Curator*
F 📷 🚻

The Museum occupies the ground floors and basements of two inter-connecting houses in a renovated mid 18th-century square. The main part of its collection consists of objects illustrating the history of the City of Limerick and the surrounding area. These include archaeological material ranging in date from the Stone Age to the medieval period, the City insignia, Limerick silver, lace and furniture, and 19th-century trade guild regalia.

Among other exhibits are coins, dating from the Viking period to the present time, including local tokens, 17th to 19th-century local private banknotes, 16th to 19th-century maps of Limerick, topographical paintings, prints and photographs, and Limerick-printed books and newspapers. There are also natural history and ethnographical collections. The ethnographical material illustrates the native cultures of Australia, the Pacific Islands and the American Indians.

Linby

Newstead Abbey

Linby, Nottinghamshire NG15 8GE
☎ 0623 793557
Good Fri–Sept, daily 1.45–5
🏛 *The Curator*
£ ⬛ 📷 🚻

Newstead Abbey is 12 miles north of Nottingham on the A60. An Augustinian house, it was founded in 1170 by Henry II as the Priory of St Mary. In 1540, after the Dissolution of the Monasteries, it was bought, together with 750 acres of land, by Sir John Byron and remained in the family until 1817 when Lord Byron, the poet, sold it to help meet his debts. In 1931 it became the property of the City of Nottingham.

It now houses a series of collections, in period

settings. The Byron Museum displays an important collection of the poet's manuscripts and letters, first editions of his works, portraits, his dog's inscribed brass collar, personal possessions, including shoe lasts made to correct his deformed right foot, a lock of his hair and much of his furniture. There is a collection of Crimean war relics, formed by General Gerald Goodlake, brother-in-law of William Frederick Webb, who owned Newstead from 1859 to 1899. General Goodlake was one of the first people to be awarded a Victoria Cross, in 1854.

The Abbey's outstanding English and Continental furniture includes a set of early 18th-century Dutch walnut chairs and a suite of Flemish furniture of the same period. One room contains hand-painted Japanese wall panels, some dating back to the 17th century. There are pictures and plans illustrating the evolution of Newstead's architecture since the 17th century and displays of 14th and 15th-century manuscripts and relics of the medieval Priory.

Lincoln

City and County Museum

Broadgate, Lincoln, Lincolnshire LN2 1EZ
    ☎ 0522 26866
Mon–Sat 10–5.30; Sun 2.30–5
🗓 *Ms M. Solly, Assistant Keeper of Archaeology*
🇪 🖊 🖼

The Museum building was formerly part of a Franciscan friary. The archaeological displays illustrate the history of human settlement in Lincolnshire from prehistoric times to 1750.

There is also a natural history and geology section. This includes freshwater aquaria and the fossilised skeleton of a plesiosaur.

Lincoln Cathedral Treasury

The Cathedral, Lincoln, Lincolnshire LN2 1PX
    ☎ 0522 30320
May–mid Sept, daily 2.30–4.30
🗓 *Chapter Clerk*
🇫 🖊 🖼 🖼 ☐

The Treasury contains gold and silver plate from churches in the Diocese of Lincoln. Some of them are on permanent display, but most are shown in temporary exhibitions, renewed each year. Among the more important permanent exhibits are the medieval chalices and patens taken from the graves of Bishops Grosseteste, Sutton and Gravesend. The collection also includes the bronze Anglo-Saxon hanging bowl, made *c.* 700, which was discovered in 1978 on the site of the church of St Paul-in-the-Bail, Lincoln.

Cathedral treasuries have existed for a long time on the Continent, but Lincoln was the pioneer in England. Until recent times, what is now the Treasury was known as the Medicine Chapel and used as the vergers' mess room.

'Lincoln Cathedral and Brayford Pool'
by John Wilson Carmichael, 1858.
Lincoln, The Usher Gallery.

Lincoln Transport Museum

Lincolnshire Vintage Vehicle Society, Whisby Road,
    Doddington Road, Lincoln, Lincolnshire
May–Sept, Sun 2–5. Open day usually 3rd Sun
    in May.
🗓 *The Secretary*
🇪 🖊 🖼

The Museum's collection consists of cars, commercial and public service vehicles, and motorcycles, a high proportion of which have connections with Lincoln or Lincolnshire. The cars date from *c.* 1900 to the late 1940s and early 1950s, and include a good range of Austins, mostly locally registered. The public service vehicles cover the period from 1927 to the late 1960s. Among the commercials are one of the few petrol-engined AEC lorries still surviving, and a 1927 Dennis 4-tonner.

Museum of Lincolnshire Life

Burton Road, Lincoln, Lincolnshire LN1 3LY
    ☎ 0522 28448
Mon–Sat 10–5.30; Sun 2–5.30. Evening parties
    by appt.
🗓 *Mr Rodney Cousins, Keeper of Social History*
🇪 🖼 🖼 ♿

The Museum is housed in buildings known as the Old Barracks, erected in 1856 as the headquarters of the Royal North Lincoln Militia and now listed as an historic building by the Department of the Environment. When the Museum was established, the aim was to present a picture of the agricultural, industrial and social history of Lincolnshire from Elizabeth I to Elizabeth II, but at the present time the emphasis is on the 19th and early 20th centuries.

There is a large collection of locally made agricultural and industrial machinery, together with horse-drawn vehicles and displays devoted to domestic, community and commercial life within the County, and to crafts and trades. The historical collections of the Royal Lincolnshire Regiment are now housed in the Museum. They include uniforms, weapons, medals, Regimental silver, documents, photographs and paintings.

Usher Gallery

Lindum Road, Lincoln, Lincolnshire LN2 1NN
  ☎ *0522 27980*
*Mon–Sat 10–5.30; Sun 2.30–5. Closed Good Fri,
  Dec 25, 26.*
🗓 *Keeper of Art*
£ ♨ ♿

The Gallery was opened in 1927. Its
construction was financed from a bequest to the
City Council by the Lincoln jeweller, James
Ward Usher, who made a large fortune from the
sale of replicas of the Lincoln Imp. The Gallery
was designed to house his collection of clocks
and watches, miniatures, porcelain, silver and
enamels. The Curtois exhibition gallery was
built in 1959 and a coin gallery was added in
1972 to display the Sir Francis Hill collection of
Anglo-Saxon and Norman coins from
Lincolnshire mints. Further exhibitions present
a comprehensive history of English coins and
tokens from pre-Roman times to the present,
with a special emphasis on items connected with
Lincolnshire.

The paintings in the collection include works
of the Italian, Dutch and Flemish schools, and
since the 1930s a large number of English 20th-
century paintings have been presented by the
Contemporary Art Society. The Usher Gallery
has the largest public collection of oils and
watercolours by the Staffordshire-born artist,
Peter de Wint (1784–1849), who married the
sister of the Lincoln-born artist, William
Hilton, and came to live in Lincoln. A number
of other Lincolnshire artists are represented in
the Gallery, which also possesses a large
collection of oils, watercolours and drawings
of Lincolnshire scenes.

A section of the Gallery is devoted to
portraits and personal effects of Alfred Lord
Tennyson, the Poet Laureate, who was born at
Somersby Rectory in Lincolnshire.

Linlithgow

Linlithgow Union Canal Museum

*Canal Basin, Manse Road, Linlithgow, West
  Lothian EH48 6AJ*
Easter–Sept, Sat, Sun 2–5 or by appt
🗓 *Mrs Lyn Alps, Bookings Secretary, 2 St
  Ninian's Avenue, Linlithgow*
  ☎ *0506 844916*
F ♨ ♿

The Museum, in a former stable for canal
horses, is concerned mainly with the Glasgow
and Edinburgh Union Canal. The displays
include documents and other objects relating to
the inception, construction and use of the Canal.
The *Victoria*, a replica of a Victorian canal boat,
operates from the wharf outside the Museum.

Liphook

Hollycombe Steam Collection

*Hollycombe Steam and Woodland Garden Society,
  Iron Hill, Liphook, Hampshire GU30 7UP*
  ☎ *0428 724900*
*Easter weekend–Oct 12, Sun, Bank Holiday 1–6.
  Schools Weeks: July 7–11, Aug 17–31, daily
  1–6. Rides from 2.*
🗓 *The Secretary*
£ 🍴 🚽 ♿

Hollycombe is one and a half miles south-east of
Liphook on the Midhurst road. The collection
includes a steam sawmill, a Marenghi fairground
organ and steam-powered agricultural
machinery. There are operating steam railways
and special events.

**Burrell Gold Medal traction engine
'Sunset No. 2'. Liphook, Hollycombe Steam
Collection.**

Lisnaskea

Rural Life Museum

The Library, Lisnaskea, Co. Fermanagh, Northern
Ireland
Mon, Tues, Fri 9.15–5; Wed 9.15–7.30;
Sat 9.15–12.30
⚑ The Curator, Fermanagh County Museum,
Castle Barracks, Enniskillen, Co. Fermanagh
☎ 0365 25050 extn 244
F

Lisnaskea is 12 miles from Enniskillen and its
Museum forms part of the Fermanagh County
Museum. Its displays cover the traditional rural
life of Co. Fermanagh, with special sections
devoted to farm livestock, scythe-stone making,
straw and rush-work and shoemaking.

Lissadell

Lissadell House

Lissadell, nr Raghly, Co. Sligo, Ireland
☎ 091 63150
May–Sept, Mon–Sat 2–5.15 (last tour 4.30)
⚑ Miss Aideen Gore-Booth
£ ♦ ⬛ ↩

Lissadell, four and a half miles east-north-east of
Raghly, was built c. 1830 by Sir Robert Gore-
Booth, the 4th Baronet. It was the home of the
Arctic explorer, Sir Henry Gore-Booth
(1843–1900) and of his two daughters, Eva, the
poetess, and Constance, who became Countess
Markievicz and who was condemned to death
for her part in the 1916 Easter Rising, but was
eventually reprieved. The house, which is still
the Gore-Booth family home, contains much
good china, silver and glass, as well as a large
collection of Italian paintings in carved
Florentine frames collected during the Grand
Tour, and works by Irish artists, including
George Russell and Countess Markievicz and
her husband. There are also many mementoes of
the family's travels, including sporting trophies
and the 4th Baronet's travelling library of 48
miniature leather-bound volumes.

Lady Sefton's Bedroom at Croxteth Hall,
Liverpool.

Littlehampton

Littlehampton Museum

12A River Road, Littlehampton, West Sussex
BN17 5BN   ☎ 0903 715149
Apr–Oct, Tues–Sat 10.30–1, 2–4. Nov–Mar,
Thurs–Sat 10.30–1, 2–4.
⚑ Museum Services Officer, Arun District
Council, Littlehampton, West Sussex
BN17 5EP   ☎ 0903 716133
F ⬩ ↩ □

The Museum building was formerly the home of
a Littlehampton sea-captain and shipowner.
The Museum is noted for its marine paintings
and watercolours and also has an extensive map
collection and engravings of local scenes and
landscapes of the Sussex area. The
archaeological section displays Roman material
from local excavations and a Bronze Age hoard
found at Flansham, near Littlehampton.

Little Walsingham

The Shirehall Museum

Common Place, Little Walsingham, Norfolk
NR22 6BP   ☎ 032872 510
Maundy Thurs–Sept, daily 11–1, 2–4. Oct, Sat,
Sun 11–1, 2–4.
⚑ The Curator, c/o The Cromer Museum, East
Cottages, Tucker Street, Cromer, Norfolk
NR11 7PD   ☎ 0263 514343
£ ⬩ ↩

The Museum occupies a Georgian courthouse
with its original fittings and prisoners' lockup,
which was constructed within the shell of a
medieval building with a 15th-century roof. At
its peak, Walsingham was second only to
Canterbury as a place of pilgrimage. An
exhibition in the Museum tells the story of the
medieval pilgrimage and the Shrine of Our
Lady, which was suppressed by Henry VIII, but
revived in the present century.

Liverpool

Croxteth Hall and Country Park

Croxteth Hall Lane, Liverpool, Merseyside
L12 0HB   ☎ 051 338 5311
Good Fri–Oct 25, Hall, Farm, Walled Garden &
Cafeteria 11–5. Oct 26–Good Fri, Heritage
Exhibition only, daily 11–4. Farm 11–4 on
Craft Fair Suns, 1–4 other days.
Refreshments summer only.
⚑ The Curator
£ ♦ ⬛ ↩

Croxteth, given to the City of Liverpool in
1974, was formerly the home of the Earls of
Sefton. The original building dates from 1602
and further wings were built in 1702 and 1902.
An audio-visual show tells the story of this

historic sporting estate and, throughout the house, life at Croxteth as it was in 1905 is re-created by means of costume groups and rooms furnished in the style of the period. There are Sefton family portraits, equestrian portraits, mainly by Towne, and two of the more sumptuous kind of Edwardian bathroom.

The walled kitchen garden and glasshouses have been carefully maintained and the Home Farm has been developed as a centre for uncommon breeds of farm animals. There is also a carriage collection and craftsmen's workshop.

Lark Lane Motor Museum

1 Hesketh Street, Liverpool, Merseyside L17 8XJ
☎ *051 727 7757/2617*
Sun & most Bank Holidays 10–5. Parties by appt.
The Curator
£

The Museum is housed in a garage built in 1921 for the Crossville Bus Company. More recently it served as a repair garage for a removal firm and has been restored by the present owners, making use of cast-ironwork from historic buildings recently demolished on Merseyside.

The collection consists of cars, motorcycles and a wide range of mechanical devices. The Museum is exceptional in having the facilities to carry out restoration projects for other museums and individuals and in being in a position to manufacture one-off items required for restoration work or as replicas. Most of the vehicles on display are in roadworthy condition.

Liverpool Museum

William Brown Street, Liverpool, Merseyside L3 8EN ☎ *051 207 0001*
Mon–Sat 10–5; Sun 2–5. Closed Good Fri, Dec 24–26, Jan 1.
Keeper of Educational Services
F

In 1851 the 13th Earl of Derby bequeathed his extensive natural history collections to the City of Liverpool. To house the collections, the Liverpool businessman, William Brown, financed an impressive building, which was opened in 1861, and in 1867 the basis of the Museum was extended by the gift of a large collection of antiquities, historical relics and pottery from the wealthy Liverpool goldsmith, Joseph Mayer.

Since then the collections have expanded enormously to more than a million items, covering most aspects of natural and human history. The displays include a vivarium and aquarium, and sections devoted to land transport, natural history, the social, industrial and maritime history of Merseyside, archaeology, ethnology, the decorative arts, the physical sciences, and time-keeping. There is also a Space Gallery and a Planetarium.

Liverpool Scottish Regimental Museum

Forbes House, Score Lane, Childwall, Liverpool, Merseyside L16 2NG ☎ *051 772 7711*
Tues evenings, 8–10. Other times by appt.
Mr Dennis Reeves, Hon. Curator
F

The collection of uniforms, weapons, equipment, photographs and documents illustrates the history of the Regiment from 1900 to the present day.

Merseyside Maritime Museum

Pier Head, Liverpool, Merseyside L3 1DN
☎ *051 709 155*
Open daily 10.30–4.30
Visitor Services Officer
£

The buildings of this dockside museum include the former headquarters (1883) of the Liverpool pilotage service, the 1765 dry docks, with the original cast-iron dock furniture, the Albert Dock warehouse – an 1846 Grade I listed building – and the 1852 Piermaster's house. There is a growing collection of full-size craft, including the pilot boat, *Edmund Gardner* (1953) and important collections of models, paintings and marine equipment. Special exhibits illustrate the history of cargo-handling in the Port of Liverpool and the development and operation of the enclosed dock system.

A new section of the Museum tells the story of the seven million emigrants who passed through Liverpool between 1830 and 1930.

The wharf at the Canning Half-tide Dock, Liverpool, with the Merseyside Maritime Museum in the background.

Museum of Labour History

Islington, Liverpool, Merseyside L3 8EE
☎ *051 2070001*
Mon–Sat 10–5; Sun 2–5. Closed Good Fri, Dec 24–26, Jan 1.
Education Officer
F

Opened in March 1986, in the former County Sessions House erected in 1884, the Museum tells the story of working-class life on Merseyside from 1840 to the present day. There is an introductory audio-visual programme, *Merseyside – the People's Story*, and displays on employment, housing – including a reconstructed street and scullery – education, with a part-reconstruction of an Edwardian classroom, leisure and trade unionism. A display of trade union banners can be seen in the main Court Room.

Museum of the School of Dental Surgery

University of Liverpool, Pembroke Place, Liverpool, Merseyside L69 3BX
☎ *051 709 0141*
By appt
The Curator
F

The Museum, which is over a hundred years old, is primarily intended for members of the dental and allied professions and for medical historians, but members of the general public are welcome, provided previous notice has been given. There are exhibits of dental pathology and a large number of artefacts relating to dentistry, including fine collections of early dentures and extracting instruments.

Speke Hall

The Walk, Liverpool, Merseyside L24 1XD
☎ *051 427 7231*
Apr–Sept, Mon–Sat 10–5; Sun 2–7. Oct–Mar, Mon–Sat 10–5; Sun 2–5. Last admission one hour before closing. Closed Good Fri, Dec 24–26, Jan 1.
The Curator
£ ♿ NT

Speke Hall, now a National Trust property, is eight miles south-east of Liverpool city centre, one mile off the A561 and near Liverpool Airport. One of England's finest timber-framed manor houses, it was built piecemeal between the late 15th and early 17th centuries by members of the Norris family. In 1795 after a period of neglect, the house and estate were bought by Richard Watt, a Liverpool merchant, and remained in the same family until the death of Miss Adelaide Watt. After a period in the hands of Trustees, the house and grounds were accepted by the National Trust in 1943. They are now administered by Merseyside County Council on behalf of the Trust.

Visitors can see eight of the rooms, together with the remarkable Great Hall. The principal features of the interior are the panelling and the plasterwork. The 'Elizabethan' and 'Gothic' furnishings reflect the taste of the Watt family in the 19th century. They include a fine collection of clocks and Mortlake and Flemish tapestries. The Kitchen and Servants' Hall are complete with the appropriate equipment.

A spyhole in the Blue Bedroom and hiding places alongside the chimneys in the Green and Tapestry Bedrooms are reminders of the days when Catholic priests used the house as a refuge.

Sudley Art Gallery

Mossley Hill Road, Liverpool, Merseyside L18 8BX
☎ *051 724 3245*
Mon–Sat 10–5; Sun 2–5. Closed Good Fri, Dec 24–26, Jan 1.
See Walker Art Gallery
F

Sudley is an early 19th-century neo-classical building, with additions made in the 1880s by the Liverpool shipowner, George Holt, when he bought the property. It contains Holt's collection of paintings, composed chiefly of 18th and 19th-century works by British artists, including Gainsborough, Romney, Turner, Bonington and the Pre-Raphaelites. The most important items are Gainsborough's *Viscountess Folkestone*, a sympathetic study of old age, and Turner's *Rosenau*, the German home of the Prince Consort.

The Gallery also has displays of late 19th-century 'New Sculpture' from the Walker Art Gallery and ship models and children's toys from Merseyside Museums.

University of Liverpool Art Gallery

3 Abercromby Square, PO Box 147, Liverpool, Merseyside L69 3BX
☎ *051 709 6022 extn 3170*
Mon, Tues, Thurs 12–2; Wed, Fri 12–4. Closed Bank Holiday and Aug.
The Curator, Art Collections
F

The building is a typical early 19th-century Liverpool merchant's terrace house in a square of such houses. An effort has been made to retain its character while adapting it as an art gallery. The Gallery displays sculpture, paintings, drawings, prints, furniture, ceramics, silver and glass selected from the University's collections. The early English watercolours are outstanding, including works by Turner, Girtin, Cozens and Cotman, among others. The early English porcelain is also of good quality, with examples from nearly all the main factories, including Chelsea, Worcester, Derby and Bow.

There are oil paintings by Turner, Audubon, Joseph Wright of Derby and Augustus John. Contemporary work includes sculpture by Elizabeth Frink, paintings by Lucien Freud and Bridget Reilly, and prints by Howard Hodgkin and David Hockney.

Speke Hall, Liverpool, one of Britain's most elaborate half-timbered houses.

Walker Art Gallery

William Brown Street, Liverpool, Merseyside
L3 8EL ☎ *051 227 5234 extn 2064*
Mon–Sat 10–5; Sun 2–5. Closed Good Fri,
Dec 24–26, Jan 1.
Refreshments weekends only.
🚻 *Education Officer*
F ✏ ■

The Gallery's collections are of European
painting and sculpture from the 14th to the 20th
century and are particularly noteworthy for the
early Italian and Flemish paintings, some
collected in the early 19th century by the
Liverpool solicitor and philanthropist, William
Roscoe, and by the Liverpool Royal Institution.
Later European paintings include works by
Rubens, Rembrandt and Poussin, with the
French Impressionists strongly featured. The
gallery has Degas' *Woman Ironing*. British
paintings range from the portrait of Henry VIII
after Holbein to Gainsborough's *Countess of
Sefton*. Among the other 18th-century English
painters represented are Stubbs, Wilson and
Wright of Derby.

The 19th-century paintings are dominated by
Turner, Millais, Watts and the Pre-Raphaelites,
with many narrative paintings, including the
celebrated *And when did you last see your father?*
by W. F. Yeames. The 20th-century exhibits
range from Sickert and Gilman to Hockney,
with many works from recent John Moore
exhibitions. The Gallery's sculpture collection
is notable for the works by Gibson and the 'New
Sculpture' of the 1890s.

Livingston

Livingston Mill Farm

Millfield, Kirkton, Livingston, West Lothian
E1154 1AR ☎ *0506 414957*
Easter–Oct, daily 10–5. Oct–Easter, 1st Sat,
Sun of each month 1–4.
🚻 *The Secretary*
E 🍴 ■ 🚗 ♿

The Museum is in two parts. The 16-foot
waterwheel, which provides the power to drive a
threshing mill and machinery for grinding and
dressing corn, is the focus of a display which
traces the history of cereals and pulses as food
crops and of the farming methods and
machinery used. The parallel themes narrow the
perspective to farming in West Lothian,
showing the changes in farming practices and
land usage, the effects of industrialisation, the
post-war development leading to the growth of
Livingston New Town and present land use.

The setting for the Museum is a small
demonstration farm, scaled for educational
purposes, where tools and implements are
shown both in action and as static displays. The
buildings date from the 18th century but, as part
of a working farm until the 1960s, they have
been subject to continuous change. They have

been restored and equipped to give an
impression of the farm as it was in the 19th
century.

Llanberis

Amguedda Gogledd Cymru (Welsh Environmental Gallery)

Llanberis, Gwynedd LL55 4UR ☎ *0286 870636*
June–Sept, Mon–Sat 10–5; Sun 1.30–5.
🚻 *The Principal Officer*
F 🍴 🚗 ♿

This building on the shores of the Padarn Lake
has been provided by the Central Electricity
Generating Board to house the National
Museum of Wales's project in North Wales. The
aim of the displays in this purpose-built centre is
to interpret the natural environment of
Snowdonia and to illustrate the social,
historical, economic and cultural development
of the region.

The Welsh Slate Museum

Gilfach Ddu, Llanberis, Gwynedd LL55 4TY
  ☎ *0286 870630*
Easter Sat–Apr, daily 9.30–5.30. May–Sept,
  daily 9.30–6.30. Closed May Bank Holiday.
  Oct–Easter, weekdays by appt.
🚻 *The Curator*
L ✏ ■ 🚗

The Museum is located within what were, until
the closure of the great Dinorwic slate quarry in
1969, the quarry's main repair and maintenance
workshops and the place where the rough blocks
were converted into roofing slates. The
buildings were reputedly designed on the pattern
of a British army fort in India. The machinery
in the workshops was powered by a waterwheel
50 feet in diameter, which is now restored and
working again.

Most of the tools and machines have been
kept in their original location and condition,
and many are still demonstrated by members of
the Museum staff. The fitting and blacksmiths'
shops, foundry, Pelton wheel, timber sawing
sheds and pattern lofts can all be seen. There are
comprehensive interpretive displays of the
Welsh slate industry and the quarryman's craft.

**The blacksmith's shop at The Welsh Slate
Museum, Llanberis.**

Llandrindod Wells

Llandrindod Wells Museum

Temple Street, Llandrindod Wells, Powys
　LD1 5DL　　　　　　　　☎ 0597 4513
Apr–Sept, Mon–Sat 10–12.30, 2–5. Oct–Mar,
　Mon–Fri 10–12.30, 2–5; Sat 10–12.30.
　Closed Easter, Dec 25, 26 and Bank Holiday.
◪ The Curator
£ ⊘ ⌷

The Museum was founded in 1911 to house
material from the excavations at the nearby
Roman fort of Castell Collen. The archaeology
gallery today contains chiefly prehistoric and
Roman finds and includes a complete dug-out
boat, discovered in the River Itmon and in
remarkably good condition.

The main gallery is devoted to the history and
development of the Spa. The collection
illustrates life in Llandrindod Wells in its
heyday, between the arrival of the railway in
1865 and the outbreak of the First World War.

Tom Norton's Collection of Old Cycles and Tricycles

The Automobile Palace, Llandrindod Wells,
　Powys LD1 5HL　　　　　　☎ 0597 2214
Mon–Sat 8–5. Closed Bank Holiday.
◪ T. Norton
F ⊘ ⌷

Tom Norton (1870–1955) started his cycle and
sports equipment business in Llandrindod Wells
in 1898. In 1913 he built the Automobile
Palace to accommodate his expanding motoring
interests, which included the operation of bus
and coach services. The collection now
displayed at the Automobile Palace covers the
whole history of the bicycle. The earliest model
dates from 1867 and the most recent, a Moulton
M2 de Luxe, from 1965. There are two Penny
Farthings, three Velocipedes, popularly known
as Boneshakers, and three tricycles, one, of
1879, a tandem, which was rescued from a scrap
merchant and painstakingly rebuilt.

Tom Norton himself patented and registered
the design of more than 30 items. In the main,
they were concerned with motorcar accessories,
but four were directly connected with cycles and
bicycles. He maintained a keen interest in
cycling throughout his long life and at the age of
81 he was elected President of the Fellowship of
Old Time Cyclists.

Llandudno

Llandudno Doll Museum and Model Railway

Masonic Street, Llandudno, Gwynedd LL30 2DU
Good Fri–Sept, Mon–Sat 10–1, 2–5.30; Sun
　2–5.30
◪ Mr and Mrs Bellamy, Fantaisie,
　Nant-Y-Gamar Road, Llandudno LL30 1BW
　☎ 0492 76312
£ ⊘ ⌷

The Museum building, dating from 1850, is one
of the oldest in Llandudno. The ground floor
was once used as a stable for delivery horses and
more recently as a bakery. The doll collection
contains over a thousand items, ranging in date
from the 16th century to the present day. There
are also displays of toys, fashions and fashion
accessories, lace and lace bobbins, and
needlework. One room is set aside for a scale
model working railway.

Llandudno Museum

Chardon House, 17–19 Gloddaeth Street,
　Llandudno, Gwynedd LL30 2DD
　☎ 0492 76517
Opening 1987. Please check times locally.
◪ Mrs D. Maywood, Curator
£ ⌷ ⅃ □

Exhibits in the Museum cover the archaeology,
history and early industry of the area, with a
special section on early 20th-century tourism
and entertainment.

The Chardon bequest of fine and decorative
arts is displayed in period rooms – a Victorian
parlour and Edwardian dressing room – and in
temporary exhibitions.

Llandysul

Maesllyn Woollen Mill Museum

Maesllyn, Llandysul, Dyfed SA44 5LO
　☎ 023975 251
Easter–Oct, Mon–Sat 10–6; Sun 2–6.
　Nov–Easter, Mon–Sat 10–5. Closed Dec 25.
　Other times by appt.
◪ The Curator
£ █ ▆ ⌷ ⅃

The Mill, built in 1881 to carry out all the
processes of woollen manufacture, lies between
Croeslanon on the A486 and Penrhiwpal on the
B4571. It was never a commercial success, but
the quality of its buildings and machinery were
such that it has functioned to this day with very
little modification.

It is now a privately run museum, which
preserves the atmosphere of a Victorian mill and
where the changes from hand spinning and
weaving to powered machinery are explained
and demonstrated. Some of the machinery is
driven from the restored waterwheels.

There is a secondary collection of artefacts

**One of the early bicycles at Tom Norton's
Automobile Palace, Llandrindod Wells.**

not directly concerned with wool, but with the period of the Mill's history. A Nature Trail follows the course of the waterway.

Llanelli

Bwlch Farm Stable Museum

Bwlch Farm, Bynea, Llanelli, Dyfed SA14 9ST
☎ 0554 772036
Open at any reasonable time
✗ *Mrs E. M. Hughes*
F ▣ ⇻

The farm is near the small village of Bynea on the Swansea to Llanelli road. The stable, which contains the Museum, forms part of the original long Welsh farmhouse which, according to tradition, was established in the 15th century by two brothers, Albert and Robert Bonville, who arrived from France by rowing boat. The Bonville family continued to live here until 1953.

The collection in the Museum includes Roman archaeological material found in the area, farm implements and tools, and relics of the Second World War.

Parc Howard Museum

Parc Howard, Llanelli, Dyfed
Apr–Sept, daily 9–6. Oct–Mar, daily 9.30–5.
✗ *Mr D. F. Griffiths, Borough Librarian,*
Borough of Llanelli Public Library, Vaughan
Street, Llanelli SA15 3AS ☎ 0554 773538
F ⬦

The displays here are mainly concerned with the industrial and social history of Llanelli. The Museum possesses the largest collection of Llanelli pottery, and also has a number of paintings by Welsh artists.

Llanfairpwll

Plas Newydd

Llanfairpwll, Anglesey, Gwynedd LL61 6EQ
☎ 0248 714/795
Mar 28–Sept, Sun–Fri 12–5 (last admission 4.30).
Oct, Fri and Sun only.
✗ *The Administrator*
£ ▪ ▣ ⇻ NT

Between 1783 and 1809 the old manor house at Plas Newydd was converted into a mansion in the Gothic and neo-Classical styles, the architects being James Wyatt and Joseph Potter. The Gothic Hall has a gallery and elaborate plasterwork fan vaulting. The dining room contains Rex Whistler's largest mural painting.

Now a National Trust property, with appropriate furniture and paintings, Plas Newydd contains a military museum, with relics of the Battle of Waterloo, where the 1st Marquess of Anglesey lost a leg.

Llangollen

Canal Museum

The Wharf, Llangollen, Clwyd LL20 8TA
☎ 0978 860702
Easter weekend, Whitsun–Sept, daily 10–5.30.
✗ *6 Skips Lane, Christleton, Chester, Cheshire*
CH3 7BE
£ ▪

The Museum, in a restored canal warehouse built by Thomas Telford, contains displays explaining the history, design, construction and operation of British canals. There are exhibits relating to freight and the way it was handled, to the living conditions of the people who operated the canals and lived on the boats, to the wildlife to be found along the canals and to the present-day recreational use of the canal system.

Valle Crucis Abbey

Llangollen, Clwyd ☎ 0978 860326
Mar 15–Oct 15, daily 9.30 6.30. Oct 16–
Mar 14, Mon–Sat 9.30–4; Sun 2–4.
✗ *The Custodian*
£ ⬦ ⇻ ✿

The 13th and 14th-century Cistercian Abbey is now mostly in a ruinous condition. There is a display of sculptures and inscribed stones from the Abbey buildings in the former monks' dormitory and, in a small adjoining room, an exhibition on Valle Crucis and on the history and organisation of the Cistercian Order.

Llanidloes

Llanidloes Museum of Local History and Industry

Old Market Hall, Shortbridge Street, Llanidloes,
Powys SY18 6AD
Easter week & Spring Bank Holiday Sept, daily
ex. Sun 11–1, 2–5.
✗ *The Curator, Powysland Museum, Salop Road,*
Welshpool, Powys SY21 7EG ☎ 0938 4759
F ⬦ ⇻

The Museum building was formerly the town's market hall. Dating from c. 1600, it is the only example of a black and white timber-framed market hall in Wales. The collections illustrate the social and industrial history of Llanidloes and the surrounding countryside. There are

The Octagon Room at Plas Newydd, Llanfairpwll.

mementoes of the activities of the Chartists in the town in 1839 and among the other exhibits are a reconstructed Welsh kitchen, and a model of pithead winding gear.

Llanystumdwy

Lloyd George Memorial Museum

Llanystumdwy, Criccieth, Gwynedd
LL52 0SH   ☎ *076671 2654*
May–June and Sept, Mon–Fri 10–5.
July–Aug, Mon–Fri 10–5; Sat, Sun 2–4.
◪ *The Curator*
£ ⬭ ➴

The Museum's collection illustrates the life and career of Earl Lloyd George of Dwyfor. The exhibits include caskets, deeds of freedom, scrolls and other mementoes of the Liberal leader and Prime Minister.

Lochwinnoch

Lochwinnoch Community Museum

High Street, Lochwinnoch, Renfrewshire
PA12 4AB   ☎ *0505 842615*
Mon, Wed, Fri 10–1, 2–5, 6–8; Tues, Sat
10–1, 2–5
◪ *Field Officer*
F ➴ □

Lochwinnoch is 9 miles south-west of Paisley on the Largs road. The Community Museum, which is in a purpose-built extension of the old village school, features a series of changing exhibitions reflecting the history of local agriculture, industry and rural life.

Lockerbie

Rammerscales

Lockerbie, Dumfriesshire DG11 1LD
☎ *038781 361*
July–Aug, early Sept, Tues–Thurs & alternate
Sun 2–5
◪ *Mrs Baye*
£ ♜ HHA

This 18th-century house has furniture of the period and a collection of mainly 20th-century paintings and sculpture, with works by Scottish artists and by Pasmore, Hepworth and Piper. The dining table is made from timber from HMS *Bellerophon*, upon which Napoleon surrendered.

Lode

Anglesey Abbey

Lode, Cambridge, Cambridgeshire CB5 9EJ
☎ *0223 811200*
Mar 29–Apr 27, Sat, Sun, Bank Holiday 1.30–
5.30. Apr 30–Oct 12, Wed–Sun 1.30–5.30.
◪ *The Administrator*
£ ♜ ➰ ➴ NT

The village of Lode is six miles north-east of Cambridge on the B1102. Anglesey Priory, founded in 1135, was an Augustinian monastery. The present house on the site dates from *c.* 1600 and contains fragments of the monastery. In 1926 the property, which now belongs to the National Trust, was bought by Huttleston Broughton, later to become Lord Fairhaven, who, over a period of 40 years, established the very attractive gardens, which cover 100 acres and contain a splendid collection of statuary. The house is sumptuously furnished and the works of art displayed in it include crucifixes, silver gilt, Italian mosaics, tapestries, Oriental hardstones and figure sculpture.

In 1934 Lord Fairhaven bought Lode watermill, on the edge of his estate. Most of the machinery is intact and in working order. Special displays in the Visitor Centre explain how the gardens were created and how the National Trust cares for the statuary.

London

Apsley House

149 Piccadilly, London W1V 9FA
☎ *01 499 5676*
Tues–Thurs, Sat 10–6; Sun 2.30–6
⊖ *Hyde Park Corner*
◪ *Mrs M. Scott, Administrator*
£ ⬭ ➴

Apsley House, at Hyde Park Corner, was built between 1771 and 1778 for the 2nd Earl Bathurst, from designs by Robert Adam. It was bought in 1807 by Lord Wellesley, who employed James Wyatt to carry out alterations and improvements, and he in turn sold it to his brother, the Duke of Wellington, who made certain changes, including having the house encased in Bath stone.

In 1947 the 7th Duke offered the house to the nation, together with its magnificent collections of furniture, paintings, plate, porcelain, batons, orders, decorations and personal relics. It was opened to the public as the Wellington Museum in 1952 and since then extensive alterations and redecorations have taken place, in order to restore the interiors to their appearance at the time of the 1st Duke.

The Baden-Powell Story

The Scout Association, Baden-Powell House,
Queen's Gate, London SW7 5JS
☎ *01 584 7030*
Daily 9–6. Closed Dec 25, 26.
⊖ *Gloucester Road*
◪ *The Manager*
F ⬭ ➲ ⬭

Baden-Powell House, opened in 1961, is an international Scout hostel. It contains a small museum, The Baden-Powell Story, which illustrates the life and achievements of Lord Baden-Powell, the founder of the Scout movement.

Bakelite Museum

The 'Bakelite' Museum Society, 12 Mundania
Court, Forest Hill Road, East Dulwich,
London SE22 0NQ   ☎ *01 691 2240*
Normally Tues 12–9 but check times locally.
Parties limited to 8.
⊖ *Honor Oak Park*
⚿ *The Curator*
Ⓕ *Donations welcome* 📖 ➘

The Bakelite Museum is a collection of about 7,000 objects made from plastics, especially for domestic purposes, from the time of their first appearance in the mid 19th century until the present day. Examples of most plastics are included, from Parkestine and Celluloid to Bakelite, Beetle, Polystyrene and Acrylic. The emphasis is on the interwar years, the heyday of Bakelite. Most of the kitchen appliances and household gadgetry in the collection belong to the same period.

The Museum also maintains a reference archive of publications relating to plastics.

Berkshire and Westminster Dragoons Museum

1 Elverton Street, Victoria, London SW1P 2QJ
☎ *01 856 7995 or 01 928 7786*
Mon–Fri 9–5. Closed Bank Holiday.
⊖ *St James's Park*
⚿ *Captain J. W. Annett, Curator*
Ⓕ

The Museum's collections present the history of the Westminster Dragoons and the Berkshire and Westminster Dragoons, both Territorial Army Regiments in the Royal Armoured Corps. There are also exhibits relating to the early Volunteer Militia of Westminster through to the Imperial Yeomanry days and to the Armoured Car Company of the 1920s.

Bethnal Green Museum of Childhood

Cambridge Heath Road, London E2 9PA
☎ *01 980 3204/4315*
Mon–Thurs, Sat 10–6; Sun 2.30–6. Closed Bank
Holiday, Dec 24–26, Jan 1.
⊖ *Bethnal Green*
⚿ *See Victoria and Albert Museum*
Ⓕ 🍴 ➚ ♿

The Bethnal Green Museum of Childhood is a branch of the Victoria and Albert Museum. The iron framework of its building was originally part of the predecessor of the Victoria and Albert, known, from its industrial appearance, as the Brompton Boilers. It was reconstructed, with an outer skin of brick, in Bethnal Green in 1872.

The Museum's collection of toys and dolls is one of the largest in the world. There is a fine collection of dolls' houses. The oldest was made in Nuremberg in 1673, but most of the others are English and give an interesting picture of domestic life over several centuries. Other sections of the Museum are devoted to puppets, children's dress and furniture, and to a wide range of games and toy soldiers.

Among the other attractions are rattles and feeding bottles, paintings of children by Victorian artists, and children's books.

The Tate Baby House, about 1760. London, Bethnal Green Museum of Childhood.

British Dental Association Museum

64 Wimpole Street, London W1M 8AL
☎ *01 935 0875*
By appt only
⊖ *Regent's Park*
⚿ *The Curator*
Ⓕ

The collections in the Museum consist of instruments, equipment, appliances, pictures and other material which illustrate the history of the art and science of dental surgery, especially in Great Britain.

The British Library (Exhibition Galleries)

Great Russell Street, London WC1B 3DG
☎ *01 636 1544*
Mon–Sat 10–5; Sun 2.30–6. Closed Good Fri,
1st Mon in May, Dec 24–26, Jan 1.
⊖ *Tottenham Court Road*
⚿ *Education and Exhibitions Officer*
Ⓕ 🍴 ➚ ♿

The Galleries, in the British Museum building, contain permanent displays of items from the Library's collections. In the Grenville Library are Western illuminated manuscripts, including the 14th-century Luttrell Psalter and the Harley Golden Gospels of c. 800. The Manuscript Saloon is devoted to manuscripts of historical and literary interest. Here, two of the four copies of King John's Magna Carta and the Lindisfarne Gospels are on display, and almost every major literary figure is represented in a section devoted to English literature.

In the King's Library are illuminated manuscripts in Oriental languages, book-bindings from the 16th century onwards and many famous items reflecting the history of printing, including the world's earliest dated example, the Diamond Sutra from China of 868 and Caxton's first work. There are also documents and books on Shakespeare and items from the Library's philatelic collection.

The British Museum

Great Russell Street, London WC1B 3DG
☎ *01 636 1555*
   Recorded information: ☎ *01 580 1788*
Mon–Sat 10–5; Sun 2–6.30. Closed Good Fri,
   1st Mon in May, Dec 24–26, Jan 1.
⊖ *Tottenham Court Road*
⊠ *Education Service (extn 510/511)*
Ⓕ *ex. special exhibitions* ▮ ▣ ⧗ □

The present Museum buildings were designed by
Robert Smirke and completed by his younger
brother, Sydney. Work began in 1824 and took
over 30 years. Extensions were added in 1884,
1914, 1938 and 1978. The celebrated domed
Reading Room was built in 1857.

   The British Museum, which is a major
research institution, houses the national
collections of archaeology and art, representing
human achievement from prehistoric times to
the 20th century. The collections and displays
in the Galleries are in the care of nine
Departments – Egyptian, Greek and Roman,
Western Asiatic, Prehistoric and Romano-
British, Medieval and Later, Coins and Medals,

Oriental, Prints and Drawings, and Ethnography.
The ethnographical collections are displayed at
the Museum of Mankind, Burlington Gardens.

Bruce Castle Museum

Lordship Lane, Tottenham, London N17 8NU
☎ *01 808 8772*
Daily 1–5. Open Bank Holiday. Closed Good Fri,
   Dec 25, 26, Jan 1.
⊖ *Wood Green*
⊠ *Miss C. F. Tarjan, Curator*
Ⓕ ✐ ☛

Bruce Castle was the Manor House of
Tottenham. It is a Grade I listed building, mainly
17th and 18th century, with a 16th-century brick
tower, the purpose of which is unknown. The
Museum contains the local history material for
the Borough of Haringey, including archives,
photographs and paintings. The Museum also
houses the Morton Collection of British Postal
History, a section of which is on display.

   The Museum of the Middlesex Regiment is at
Bruce Castle.

Brunel Engine House, Rotherhithe

Tunnel Road, off Rotherhithe Street, London SE16
May–Sept, Sun 11–4. Oct–Apr, 1st Sun in each
   month, 11–4.
⊖ *Rotherhithe*
⊠ *Rotherhithe Community Workshop, Hope*
   (Sufferance) Wharf, Rotherhithe Street,
   London SE16
Ⓕ ✐

The engine house at Rotherhithe was built by
Sir Marc Isambard Brunel to contain the steam
engines which drained the celebrated Thames
Tunnel, the first major underwater thoroughfare
in the world. Constructed between 1825 and
1843, under very difficult conditions, it was
opened as a pedestrian route, but was bought for
railway purposes in 1865. It now carries a section
of the London Underground.

   The Engine House was restored in 1975–9 and
now contains an exhibition describing the
building of the Thames Tunnel and the
contribution made by Brunel to the development
of tunnelling techniques.

Cabinet War Rooms

Clive Steps, King Charles Street, London
   SW1A 2AQ   ☎ *01 930 6961*
Tues–Sun 10–5.50. Last admission 5.15.
   Open Easter Mon, Spring and Summer Bank
   Holiday. Closed Good Fri, May Bank Holiday,
   Dec 24–26, Jan 1. May be closed at short
   notice on State occasions.
⊖ *Westminster*
⊠ *The Curator*
Ⓔ ▮ ⧗

**Sardonyx cameo of the Emperor Augustus
(63BC–AD14). London, British Museum.**

**Gold and garnet jewel from the Anglo-Saxon
ship-burial at Sutton Hoo, Suffolk. About
AD625. London, British Museum.**

The War Rooms are the most important surviving part of the underground emergency accommodation which was constructed to protect the Prime Minister, the War Cabinet and the Chiefs of Staff against air attacks during the Second World War. The suite of 19 rooms includes the Cabinet Room, the Transatlantic Telephone Room, from which Churchill could speak directly to President Roosevelt in the White House, the Map Room, where information about operations on all fronts was collected, and the Prime Minister's Room, which served as Churchill's emergency office and bedroom throughout the War.

Carlyle's House

24 Cheyne Row, Chelsea, London SW3
☎ *01 352 7087*
Mar 29–Oct, Wed–Sun, Bank Holiday Mon 11–5
  (last admission 4.30). Closed Good Fri.
⊖ *Sloane Square*
👤 *The Administrator*
£ NT

Thomas Carlyle and his wife lived in this early 18th-century terrace house from 1834 until their respective deaths in 1866 and 1881. In 1881 it was bought by public subscription, and furniture and personal possessions were returned to the house. In 1936 it passed to the National Trust.

Visitors now see it much as it was in Carlyle's day. Apart from the furnishings and the trivia of everyday life, the house contains portraits, manuscripts, prints, books and relics of many eminent 19th-century figures, including Goethe and Mazzini.

Chartered Insurance Institute Museum

20 Aldermanbury, London EC2V 7HY
☎ *01 606 3835*
Mon–Fri 9.30–4.30. Closed Bank Holiday.
⊖ *Moorgate*
👤 *M. J. B. Lovegrove*
F ⬀

The Museum contains objects and documents relating to the history of fire insurance. There is an extensive collection of fire marks.

Chiswick House

Burlington Lane, London W4 2RS
☎ *01 995 0508*
Mar 15–Oct 15, daily 9.30–6.30. Oct'16–
  Mar 14, Wed–Sun 9.30–4.
⊖ *Hammersmith*
👤 *Historic Buildings & Monuments Commission,*
  London   ☎ *01 211 8828*
£ ⬀ ■

Richard Boyle, 3rd Earl of Burlington (1695–1753), was the greatest patron of learning and the arts of his day. He designed his Palladian villa at Chiswick c. 1725 and co-operated with William Kent on a number of features of the interior. After Lord Burlington's death, the house passed into the possession of the Dukes of Devonshire, who entertained Royalty here. In 1892 the 8th Duke removed the art treasures to Chatsworth and other family

seats, and the house and grounds were occupied as a private lunatic asylum. In 1928 it was bought by Middlesex County Council. It is now in the care of English Heritage.

Its importance and interest lies in its architectural features and in its decoration. There is a display of architectural drawings on the ground floor relating to the construction of the house.

Winston Churchill with Captain Richard Pim RNVR in the Map Room of the 'No. 10 Annexe'. London, The Cabinet War Rooms.

Church Farm House Museum

Greyhound Hill, Hendon, London NW4 4JR
☎ *01 203 0130*
Mon, Wed–Sat 10–1, 2–5.30; Tues 10–1; Sun
  2–5.30. Closed Good Fri, Dec 25, 26, Jan 1.
⊖ *Hendon Central*
👤 *Mr Gerrard Roots, Curator*
F ⬀ ⬀ □

The Museum building is a former farm house, built c. 1660. The attics, which show how the roof tiles are laid on top of thatch, may be seen on request. The collections are mainly within the areas of domestic life and social history, special attention being paid to the development of north-west London. There are two period rooms, the kitchen, which is in the style of c. 1820, and the dining-room, which is of the 1850s.

Temporary exhibitions on local and social history and the decorative arts are an important part of the Museum's programme.

Clipper Ship, Cutty Sark

King William Walk, Greenwich, London
  SE10 9HT   ☎ 01 858 3445 or 01 853 3589
Apr–Sept, Mon–Sat 10–6; Sun 12–6. Oct–Mar,
  Mon–Sat 10–5; Sun 12–5. Closed Dec 24–26,
  Jan 1.
⊖ *Surrey Docks*
👤 *The Master*
£ ■ ⬀

The *Cutty Sark* is the last and most famous of the 19th-century ships that raced home from China with the new season's tea. Visitors can tour every part of the ship and go down into the dry dock to see the ship's splendid lines from below. There is a fine collection of ships' figureheads.

The Clockmakers' Company Collection

The Clock Room, Guildhall Library,
  Aldermanbury, London EC2P 2EJ
  ☎ *01 606 3030 extn 2865/2866*
Mon–Fri 9.30–5. Closed Bank Holiday.
⊖ *Bank*
⋈ *Cedric Jagger, Keeper*
Ⓕ ⬗

This private collection, originally formed *c.* 1814 for the instruction of apprentices, was made accessible to the public in 1873, at the invitation of the Corporation of London, which still provides suitable premises and display facilities. Its particular strength is the work of the more eminent London makers, but there are good examples of clocks made by Continental craftsmen, among exhibits illustrating the development of clockmaking from the 15th to the early 20th century. Prominent among the items on show is the fifth marine chronometer made by John Harrison, the great 18th-century pioneer of exceptionally accurate clocks for navigational purposes.

Commonwealth Institute

Kensington High Street, London W8 6NQ
  ☎ *01 603 4535*
Mon–Sat 10–5.30; Sun 2–5. Closed Good Fri,
  May Bank Holiday, Dec 24–26, Jan 1.
⊖ *High Street Kensington*
⋈ *Education Department*
Ⓕ *ex. special exhibitions* ▮ ⬛ ⬗ ⬥ ☐

The Institute aims to spread knowledge and understanding of many aspects of the Commonwealth. It has over 40 self-contained exhibitions, each devoted to an individual Commonwealth country and illustrating the history, scenery, wildlife, economy and arts and crafts of that country. There is also a programme of changing art exhibitions by Commonwealth artists, thematic displays on current issues, educational events and a library and resource centre.

Courtauld Institute Galleries

Woburn Square, London WC1H 0AA
  ☎ *01 580 1015*
Mon–Sat 10–5; Sun 2–5. Closed public holidays.
⊖ *Russell Square*
⋈ *Miss R. Featherstone, 41 Gordon Square,*
  London WC1H 0PA   ☎ *01 387 0370*
Ⓔ ⬗ ⬗

The Galleries, which form part of the University of London, are best known for their collection of Impressionist and Post-Impressionist paintings, but also contain Old Master collections of very high quality, with works from the early 14th century onwards.

Court Dress Collection

Kensington Palace, London W8 4PX
  ☎ *01 937 9561*
Mon–Sat 9–5; Sun 1–5 (last admission 4.15).
  Closed Good Fri, Dec 24–26, Jan 1.
⊖ *Queensbury*
⋈ *The Office Manager, State Apartments*
Ⓔ ⬗ ⬗

Kensington Palace, originally built in 1607, was altered for William III by Sir Christopher Wren and decorated for George I by William Kent. The collection of Court Dress and uniform is of items worn at the British Courts from *c.* 1750 onwards, displayed in the context of rooms restored to their original 19th-century apppearance.

Cricket Memorial Gallery

Lord's Cricket Ground, St John's Wood Road,
  London NW8 8QN   ☎ *01 289 1611*
Cricket match days: Mon–Sat 10.30–5.
  Other times by appt.
⊖ *St John's Wood*
⋈ *The Curator*
Ⓔ ⬗ ⬛ ⬗

The M.C.C. began forming a collection of cricket bygones in 1865. Until 1953 it was housed in the Members' Pavilion, but in that year a public museum and gallery, in a converted racquets court, was opened as an international memorial to cricketers killed in the two World Wars. This now houses about half of the M.C.C.'s collection of paintings and cricketana, and exhibits are exchanged from time to time between the Gallery and the Pavilion. The displays in the Gallery include paintings, ceramics, objets d'art, trophies and personalia illustrating the history of cricket. The most famous exhibit is probably The Ashes.

The Cuming Museum

155–157 Walworth Road, London SE17 1RS
  ☎ *01 703 3324/5529*
Mon–Wed, Fri 10–5.30; Thurs 10–7; Sat 10–5.
  Closed Bank Holiday.
⊖ *Elephant and Castle*
⋈ *The Keeper*
Ⓕ

The Museum has developed from the collection built up by Richard Cuming and his son from 1782 onwards. The displays illustrate the history

**Mid-Victorian Court Dress.
London, Court Dress Collection.**

of the local community and its environment from a desolate prehistoric riverside, through a small market town at the foot of London Bridge to the present industrial sprawl.

The exhibits include Roman boat timbers, sculpture from a medieval priory, now Southwark Cathedral, equipment and products of the local Delftware pottery industry, personal possessions of Michael Faraday, the water-pump from the Marshalsea debtors' prison, and a penny-in-the-slot machine which dispensed milk when the dairy was closed. There are also milk delivery handcarts, a model for a proposed Shakespeare memorial by George Tinworth, a leading designer for Doultons, implements used in the hop trade, formerly very important in Southwark, and a sandwich, dated 1915, containing hair of a child with whooping cough, to be given to a dog to transfer the illness to the animal by magic.

Dickens House Museum

48 Doughty Street, London WC1N 2LF
    ☎ *01 405 2127*
Mon–Sat 10–5. Closed Bank Holiday.
⊖ *Russell Square*
𝕏 *Dr David Parker, Curator*
£ ▮ ♿

Charles Dickens lived at 48 Doughty Street between April 1837 and December 1839. It was here that he consolidated his reputation, completing *Pickwick Papers*, writing all of *Nicholas Nickleby* and most of *Oliver Twist*, and beginning *Barnaby Rudge*. The Museum collects and displays books, letters, manuscripts, pictures, furniture and personalia relating to Dickens. Some of the rooms have been reconstructed to present the appearance they are judged to have had during Dickens' residence in the house.

Dr Johnson's House

17 Gough Square, London EC4A 3DE
    ☎ *01 353 3745*
May–Sept, Mon–Sat 11–5.30. Oct–Apr,
    Mon–Sat 11–5. Closed Good Fri, Dec 24
    and public holidays.
⊖ *Blackfriars*
𝕏 *The Curator*
£ ♢

Of the many houses in London in which Dr Johnson lived, 17 Gough Square is the only one that survives. Built *c.* 1700, it has seven rooms. It has been preserved and restored as a memorial to the compiler of the first definitive English dictionary and the subject of the most celebrated biography.

There is a good collection of portrait-prints of Johnson and the members of his circle. Of particular interest among the original portraits are those of Elizabeth Carter, the noted classical scholar, by Catherine Read, and of Anna Williams, Johnson's blind adopted sister, by Frances Reynolds, Sir Joshua's sister. The other exhibits include holograph letters from Johnson and Boswell, a number of personal relics and the Probate copy of Johnson's will.

Dulwich College Picture Gallery

College Road, London SE21 7AD ☎ *01 693 5254*
Tues–Sat 10–1, 2–5; Sun 2–5. Closed Good Fri,
    Dec 25, 26, Jan 1 and Bank Holiday.
⇌ *West Dulwich*
𝕏 *Mrs Gillian Wolfe*
£ *ex. children* ♢ ♿

This pioneering building, the first in England to be designed specifically to house an art gallery, dates from 1811, ten years before the establishment of the National Gallery. The architect was Sir John Soane. With its 13 rooms and about 300 pictures on view, the Gallery is on a pleasantly small scale and can easily be seen in half a day.

The collections include both familiar works and interesting lesser known paintings, mostly 17th century – Poussin, Claude, Rubens, Van Dyck, Teniers, Murillo, Rembrandt, Ruysdael, Hobbema and many other Dutch artists. The 18th century is represented by English portraitists, including Hogarth, Reynolds, Gainsborough and Lawrence, and works by Watteau, Tiepolo and Canaletto.

The interior of Dr Johnson's House in Gough Square, London, where he lived when he was producing *The Rambler* and his celebrated *Dictionary*.

Epping Forest Museum and Queen Elizabeth's Hunting Lodge

Rangers Road, Chingford, London E4 7QH
    ☎ *01 529 6681*
Wed–Sun 2–6 or dusk if earlier. Open Bank
    Holiday, ex. Dec 25, 26.
⇌ *Chingford*
𝕏 *The Curator*
£ ♢ ♿

The Museum, situated in Epping Forest, occupies a three-storeyed, timber-framed hunting-grandstand, built in 1543 for Henry VIII. Some of the displays illustrate the present-day natural history of the Forest, and others show how the environment has been changed over the centuries by man's activities. The exhibits include hunting weapons, animal traps and man-traps, as well as mounted and preserved specimens of wildlife and plants.

Fenton House

Hampstead Grove, Hampstead, London
NW3 6RT   ☎ 01 435 3471
Easter Mon–Oct, Sat–Wed 11–6. Open Bank
    Holiday Mon.
⊖ Hampstead
🕅 The Administrator
Ⓔ 〔NT〕

Fenton House, a National Trust property, dates
from the late 17th century. It is used to display,
in an appropriate setting, the Binning collection
of furniture and porcelain, and the Benton-
Fletcher collection of early musical instruments.

The Freud Museum

20 Maresfield Gardens, Hampstead, London
NW3 5SX   ☎ 01 435 2002
Mon–Sat 10–5; Sun 1–5
⊖ Finchley Road
🕅 The Curator
Ⓔ ⌂

The Freud Museum contains the household
and personal possessions of Sigmund Freud,
founder of psychoanalysis, and his daughter,
Anna Freud, a leading authority on child
psychoanalysis.
    Freud left Vienna in 1938 as a refugee from
the Nazis and settled at 20 Maresfield Gardens.
He was permitted to bring with him to London
his household furnishings, extensive library and
a collection of about 1,800 Classical, Egyptian
and Oriental antiquities. These remained in the
house after Sigmund Freud's death in 1939. On
the death of Anna Freud in 1982 the house and
its contents were developed as a museum.

Geffrye Museum

Kingsland Road, London E2 8EA
    ☎ 01 739 8368/9893
Tues–Sat 10–5; Sun 2–5. Bank Holiday 10–5.
    Closed Mon (unless a Bank Holiday),
    Good Fri, Dec 24–26, Jan 1.
⊖ Liverpool Street
🕅 Head of Education Services
Ⓕ ▰ ♿

The Museum occupies the former almshouses of
the Ironmongers' Company, built in 1713. The
exhibits, illustrating the development of
domestic design, are arranged in a series of
room settings covering the period 1600–1939.
Other features include a reconstruction of an
18th-century woodworker's shop, an open-
hearth kitchen and John Evelyn's Closet of
Curiosities. The paintings have been chosen
principally to illustrate costume and social life.
A separate gallery displays costumes and
accessories from the Museum's collection.

Geological Museum

Exhibition Road, South Kensington, London
SW7 2DE   ☎ 01 589 3444
Mon–Sat 10–6; Sun 2.30–6. Closed Good Fri,
    May Bank Holiday, Dec 24–26, Jan 1.
⊖ South Kensington
🕅 Education Department
Ⓔ ▰ ♿

Now part of the Natural History Museum, the
Geological Museum is one of the world's leading
earth science museums. The exhibitions
illustrate the general principles of geological
science and include 'Story of the Earth', 'Britain
before Man', 'British Fossils', and 'Treasures of
the Earth'. There are extensive collections of
gemstones, British fossils, rocks and minerals.

Gipsy Moth IV

King William Walk, Greenwich, London
SE10 9HT   ☎ 01 858 3445
Apr–Sept, Mon–Sat 10.30–6; Sun 12–6.
    Oct, Mon–Sat 10.30–5; Sun 12–5.
⊖ Surrey Docks
🕅 The Master, C. S. Cutty Sark, King William
    Walk, Greenwich, London SE10 9HT
Ⓔ ▰ ➸

This is the yacht in which Sir Francis
Chichester made his single-handed voyage
around the world in 1966–7. There are
exhibits illustrating the voyage and the
conditions under which Sir Francis lived.

Grange Museum of Local History

Neasden Lane, London NW10 1QB
    ☎ 01 908 7432
Mon, Tues, Thurs, Fri 12–5; Wed 12–8;
    Sat 10–5. Closed Bank Holiday & official
    Council holidays at Easter & Christmas.
⊖ Neasden
🕅 Education Officer
Ⓕ ⌂ ➸

The Museum, which houses the local history
collections of the London Borough of Brent,
stands on a large traffic island 10 minutes' walk
from Neasden station (Jubilee Line). Access is
by means of two footbridges. The building was
originally the stabling of a substantial farm, built
in 1709 and converted c. 1810 into a Gothick
cottage.
    Commonplace objects, many comparatively
recent, have been collected to illustrate
everyday life in the area. The permanent
displays are arranged in topics – work, leisure,
the home, childhood, transport, war. Two
period rooms, a Victorian parlour and a 1930s
lounge, represent the main periods of building
development in the area. An Edwardian draper's
shop from Willesden has been reconstructed in
the Museum, and there is a display of British
Empire Exhibition souvenirs.

'The First Leap' by Sir Edwin Landseer
(1802–73). London, Guildhall Art Gallery.

**Stanhope iron printing press of 1804.
London, Gunnersbury Park Museum.**

Greenwich Borough Museum

232 Plumstead High Street, London SE18 1JL
☎ *01 855 3240*
Mon 2–8; Thurs–Sat 10–1, 2–5. Closed Dec 25
   and Bank Holiday.
≥ *Woolwich Arsenal*
⚔ *The Curator*
Ⓕ 🖉

The Museum collects and interprets material
which illustrates the local and natural history of
the large area covered by the London Borough
of Greenwich. The collections cover geology,
including many local fossils, and the birds,
animals and insects found in the district. Local
archaeology forms a major part of the history
collections. The more recent past is reflected in
exhibits of household and personal objects, tools,
coins and building fittings of the last 300 years.

Guildhall Art Gallery

Aldermanbury, London EC2P 2EJ
☎ *01 606 3030*
Permanent Collection: by appt only.
   Temporary Exhibitions: Mon–Sat 10–5.
⊖ *Bank*
⚔ *Miss Vivien Knight, Curator*
Ⓕ 🖉 □

The Corporation of London has a permanent
collection of approximately 3,000 paintings and
items of sculpture. The building was destroyed
during wartime bombing raids and because
attempts to build a new Gallery failed, the
collection has had to be displayed at outside
exhibitions or in public buildings within the
City. It is strong in Victorian and 18th-century
works, and among the artists represented are
Rossetti, Holman Hunt, Constable, Dyce and
Millais. There are more than a thousand works
by Sir Matthew Smith.

Gunnersbury Park Museum

Gunnersbury Park, London W3 8LQ
   ☎ *01 992 1612*
Mar–Oct, Mon–Fri 1–5; Sat, Sun, Bank Holiday
   2–6. Nov–Feb, Mon Fri 1–4; Sat, Sun, Bank
   Holiday 2–4. Closed Good Fri, Dec 24–26.
⊖ *Acton Town*
⚔ *The Curator*
Ⓕ 🖉 🖙

The Museum occupies an early 19th-century
mansion, enlarged and improved by Sydney
Smirke for Nathan Mayer Rothschild and his
son, Lionel. The estate remained a Rothschild
property until 1925 and is now a museum of
local history for the London Boroughs of Ealing
and Hounslow. The collections include flint
implements and prehistoric metalwork; local
maps and views, including watercolours of the
former 17th-century Gunnersbury House, once
the home of Princess Amelia, the daughter of
George II; industries, among them the Acton
laundries and the 20th-century factories along
the Great West Road; domestic life, with some
equipment shown in the Rothschilds' 19th-
century kitchens; crafts and tools; costumes and
textiles; toys, dolls and games. Two of the
Rothschild carriages are also on display.

Hampstead Museum

*Burgh House, New End Square, London
   NW3 1LT*   ☎ *01 431 0144*
Wed–Sun 12–5. Bank Holiday 2–5.
   Closed Good Fri & Christmas.
⊖ *Hampstead*
⚔ *The Curator*
Ⓕ 🖉 💺 □

Burgh House was built in 1703 and was enlarged
in the 1720s by the spa physician of Hampstead
Wells. After the Second World War it was
bought by Hampstead Borough Council and
restored. A second restoration and refurbishment
took place in 1977–9. The collections now
displayed illustrate the history of Hampstead,
and are particularly rich in paintings, old
photographs and postcards. The exhibits are
changed frequently.

Heralds' Museum at the Tower of London

*Tower of London, Tower Hill, London
   EC3N 4AB*   ☎ *01 584 0930*
Apr–Sept, Mon–Sat 9.30–5.45; Sun 2–5.30.
   Closed Good Fri & May Bank Holiday.
⊖ *Tower Hill*
⚔ *Miss Sybil Burnaby, College of Arms, Queen
   Victoria Street, London EC4* ☎ *01 236 9857*
Ⓔ 🍴 💺 □

The Museum contains important items from the
historical collections of the College of Arms,
illustrating the development and applications of
heraldry from the Middle Ages to the present
day. The exhibits include heraldic manuscripts
and heraldry used on glass, precious metals,
porcelain and textiles. There are also the
crowns and crests of past Knights of the Garter,
and shields painted with the arms of former
heralds.

Historic Ship Collection

East Basin, St Katharine's Dock, London E1 9AF
☎ 01 481 0043
Daily 10–5
⊖ *Tower Hill*
🏛 *The Superintendent of Ships, 52 St Katharine's*
   Way, London E1 9LB
Ⓔ 🗝 🖼 🚶

Designed by Thomas Telford and mostly built in
the 1820s, St Katharine's Dock was one of the
finest 19th-century complexes of dock buildings
in Europe. The Dock was closed in 1968 and has
since been converted to make it suitable for
today's needs, by a blend of conservation and
new buildings. The Historic Ship Collection,
formed by the Maritime Trust, is now kept in
part of the Dock. It includes the sailing barge,
Cambria (1906), the coaster *Robin* (1890), the
herring drifter *Lydia Eva* (1930), the *Nore Light
Vessel* (1931), and the steam tugs *Challenge*
(1931) and *Portwey* (1937).

   The topsail schooner, *Kathleen & May*,
berthed here until 1985, now has her own
purpose-built dock at St Mary Overy, Southwark.

HMS *Belfast*

Symons Wharf, Vine Lane, Tooley Street, London
   SE1 2JH   ☎ 01 407 6434
Mar 20–Oct, daily 11–5.50. Nov–Mar 19, daily
   11–4.30. Closed Good Fri, 1st Mon in May,
   Dec 24–26, Jan 1.
⊖ *London Bridge*
🏛 *Schools Officer*
Ⓔ 🚻 🖼

The cruiser, HMS *Belfast*, launched in 1938, is
the last of the Royal Navy's big ships whose
main armament was guns. She is now
permanently moored in the Thames, opposite
the Tower of London, as a floating naval
museum. Visitors may tour many parts of the
ship, which has been preserved as far as possible
in her original condition.

   Among the areas open to visitors are the
operations room, messdecks, which are fitted
out both in the traditional and in a more
modern style, sick bay, boiler room, engine
room, Captain's and Admiral's bridges, galley,
punishment cells and two of the four 6-inch gun
turrets. There are also special displays on mines,
the development of the battleship, and D-Day.

Hogarth's House

Hogarth Lane, Great West Road, London
   W4 2QN   ☎ 01 994 6757
Apr–Sept, Mon, Wed–Sat 11–6; Sun 2–6.
   Oct–Mar, Mon, Wed–Sat 11–4; Sun 2–4.
   Closed first 2 weeks in Sept and last 3 weeks
   in Dec.
⊖ *Hammersmith*
🏛 *The Custodian*
Ⓕ 🗝 🚶

This Georgian house, close to the River
Thames, was Hogarth's country home for 15
years. It contains memorabilia of the artist,
copies of his paintings and many of his most
famous engravings.

HMS *Belfast* in the Pool of London.

Horniman Museum

London Road, Forest Hill, London SE23 3PQ
   ☎ 01 699 1872/2339/4911
Mon–Sat 10.30–6; Sun 2–6. Closed Dec 24–26.
≋ *Forest Hill*
🏛 *Mrs M. Mellors, Education Centre*
Ⓕ 🚻 🖼 🚶

The main buildings of the Museum date from
1901. They are in the Art Nouveau style and
were designed to house the collections of
Frederick John Horniman, M.P., the tea
magnate. A decorative mosaic panel occupies
the whole length of the main façade, the figures
being larger than life-size. It depicts, in
allegorical form, the course of human life.

   The Museum contains ethnographical
collections from all parts of the world,
illustrating man's beliefs and progress in the arts
and crafts since prehistoric times. Musical
instruments, among them the celebrated
Dolmetsch Collection, form an important
section. There are also large natural history
collections.

IBA's Broadcasting Gallery

Independent Broadcasting Authority, 70 Brompton
   Road, London SW3 1EY   ☎ 01 584 7011
Mon–Fri, guided tours at 10, 11, 2 and 3.
   Prior booking essential. Minimum age 16.
   Maximum 30 people. Closed Bank Holiday.
⊖ *Knightsbridge*
🏛 *Enquiries to IBA at above address*
Ⓕ 🚻

The Broadcasting Gallery of the Independent
Broadcasting Authority re-creates the history of
radio and television, and of their predecessors in
the field of home entertainment. The exhibits
range from early Victorian parlour games to the
technology of satellite and cable. There is a
replica of the studio at Alexandra Palace, where
broadcast television began in 1936. A sound-
and-light display shows the different stages of a
typical television drama production.

   There are two multi-screen audio-visual
presentations. The first explains how a major
news item is covered on Independent Television
News and the second considers the ways in
which television and radio may develop in the
21st century.

Imperial War Museum

Lambeth Road, London SE1 6HZ
    ☎ *01 735 8922*
Mon–Sat 10–5.50; Sun 2–5.50. Closed Good Fri,
    May Day Bank Holiday, Dec 24–26, Jan 1.
● *Lambeth North*
🅺 *Schools Officer*
Ⓕ ▲

The Museum building was originally the
Bethlem Royal Hospital or Bedlam, completed
in 1815. In 1846 a dome designed by Sydney
Smirke was added. The collections are devoted
to all aspects of the armed conflicts which have
involved Britain and the Commonwealth as
well as to military affairs. Among the exhibits
are uniforms, photographs, documents, medals
and posters. The Museum's collection of British
20th-century art is outstanding and can be seen
by appointment.

Inns of Court and City Yeomanry Museum

10 Stone Buildings, Lincoln's Inn, London
    WC2A 3TG   ☎ *01 405 8112*
By appt
● *Chancery Lane*
🅺 *The Curator*
Ⓕ

The Museum occupies the former Writ Clerks'
office, a building dating from 1777. The
collection illustrates the history of the Inns of
Court and City Yeomanry and its predecessor
regiments since 1798. The exhibits cover a wide
range of material relating to the Regiment's
activities and include uniforms, weapons,
medals and documents.

The Iveagh Bequest, Kenwood

Hampstead Lane, London NW3 7JR
    ☎ *01 348 1286*
Feb–Mar and Oct, daily 10–5. Apr–Sept, daily
    10–7. Nov–Jan, daily 10–4. Closed Good Fri,
    Dec 24, 25.
● *Archway*
🅺 *Miss Gene Adams, ILEA Museums Adviser*
Ⓕ *ex. special exhibitions* ▲ 🖃 ◢ ♿ ▢ ♨

Robert Adam remodelled Kenwood for Lord
Mansfield in the neo-classical style in the 1760s
and was also responsible for much of the interior
decoration and design of the furnishings. The
18th-century furniture in the house includes
some of the original Kenwood pieces. There are
also displays of 18th-century shoe buckles and
jewellery. Edward Guinness, 1st Earl of Iveagh,
saved Kenwood from demolition in 1925 and
bequeathed his collection of paintings. There
are works by Gainsborough, Reynolds, Romney
and Turner. Vermeer, Van Dyck, Rembrandt,
Frans Hals and Cuyp are also represented.
    Special exhibitions are organised each year on
some aspect of the 18th century, and during the
spring and autumn music and poetry recitals are
held on Sunday evenings in the Orangery. In the
summer months, there are concerts by the lake.

**'Careless Talk Costs Lives', a poster from the
Second World War in the Imperial War
Museum.**

Jewish Museum

Woburn House, Upper Woburn Place, London
    WC1H 0EP   ☎ *01 388 4525*
Tues–Thurs 10–4; Sun, Fri 10–12.45 (summer
    only: Fri until 4). Closed Mon, Sat, public
    & Jewish holidays.
● *Russell Square*
🅺 *The Secretary*
Ⓕ 🕮 ◢ ♿

The aim of the Museum is to illustrate Jewish
life, history and religion, particularly in Britain,
by objects of historical interest and artistic
merit. The collection includes ritual objects
from early City of London synagogues, 1st and
2nd-century coins, 18th and 19th-century
ceramic figures of Jewish pedlars, and Sabbath
lamps and candlesticks. There are also
decorated scroll-cases and, as the centrepiece of
the Museum, a large 16th-century Ark, in
which the Scrolls of the Law were kept in the
synagogue.

John Wesley's House and Museum, and the Museum of Methodism

47–49 City Road, London EC1Y 1AU
    ☎ *01 253 2262*
Mon–Sat 10–4; Sun after 11 am service.
    Other times by appt. Closed Dec 25, 26.
● *Old Street*
🅺 *The Curator*
Ⓢ ▲

John Wesley laid the foundation stone of the
New Chapel, in what is now City Road, in
1778. He himself lived in a house, 47 City

**The South Front at Kenwood designed by
Robert Adam.**

Road, beside the front courtyard of the Chapel. The Museum of Methodism is in the crypt of the Chapel, which has been recently restored. Its collections tell the story of Methodism from its 18th-century beginnings to the present day. John Wesley's house contains items of his furniture, in addition to books, letters and other possessions, including his hat, cravat, travelling cloak, shoes and buckles. There is also the celebrated electrical machine which he designed for the treatment of melancholia.

Keats House

Wentworth Place, Keats Grove, Hampstead, London NW3 2RR ☎ *01 435 2062*
Mon–Sat 10–1, 2–6; Sun & Bank Holiday 2–5. Closed Good Fri, Easter Sat, May Day Bank Holiday, Dec 25, 26, Jan 1.
⊖ *Belsize Park*
🏛 *Mrs C. M. Gee, Curator*
Ⓕ ⌕ ⚲

Once a pair of semi-detached villas, built in 1815–16 and later made into a single house, Keats House has been restored and redecorated in the style of the period of the poet's residence, 1818–20. Care has been taken to give it the atmosphere of a house, rather than a museum, and the rooms are furnished accordingly. They contain relics, books, letters and portraits of John Keats, who spent the most creative years of his life here. The exhibits range from his student medical notebook to the engagement ring he gave to Fanny Brawne. There are also many items associated with the poet's circle of friends, such as Leigh Hunt and Joseph Severn, the artist.

Leighton House Museum

12 Holland Park Road, London W14 8LZ ☎ *01 602 3316*
Mon–Sat 11–5 (closes at 6 during exhibitions). Closed Bank Holiday.
⊖ *High Street Kensington*
🏛 *Stephen Jones, Curator*
Ⓕ ⌕ □

12 Holland Park Road was designed and built for Lord Leighton, who lived here from 1866 until his death in 1896. The Museum includes period rooms, paintings, drawings and sculpture by Lord Leighton, his friends and contemporaries, and an Arab Hall.

Library and Museum of the United Grand Lodge of England

Freemasons' Hall, Great Queen Street, London WC2B 5AZ ☎ *01 831 9811*
Mon–Fri 10–5. Sat by appt. Closed public holidays and preceding Sat.
⊖ *Covent Garden*
🏛 *Librarian & Curator*
Ⓕ ⌕

The Museum is concerned with the history of Freemasonry, mainly in England and Wales. A large part of its holding consists of mid 18th to 20th-century regalia and medals, but there are also good collections of glass, porcelain –

including rare Masonic Čhien Lung – silverware, enamels and snuffboxes. The portraits include several of Royal Freemasons.

Linley Sambourne House

18 Stafford Terrace, Kensington, London W8 7BH
Mar–Oct, Wed 10–4; Sun 2–5. Parties of 15+ on other days by appt.
⊖ *High Street Kensington*
🏛 *Mrs A. Wilson, Administrator, at above address or at The Victorian Society, 1 Priory Gardens, London W4 1TT* ☎ *01 994 1019*
£ ■ ⚲

Stafford Terrace was built between 1868 and 1874. Edward Linley Sambourne, a successful *Punch* cartoonist, moved into No. 18, a standard London terraced house on five floors, in 1871. The Greater London Council bought it from Sambourne's granddaughter, Anne, Countess of Rosse, in 1980. The interior has remained virtually unchanged since Linley Sambourne lived in the house. It has retained its original furnishings, decorations and pictures during the three generations of occupancy by the same family. The William Morris wallpapers are still intact and there are many pictures by Linley Sambourne and his friends, together with a large collection of photographs taken by him as aids for drawing his cartoons.

Livesey Museum

682 Old Kent Road, London SE15 1JF ☎ *01 639 5604*
Mon–Sat 10–5 during exhibitions
⊖ *Elephant and Castle*
🏛 *Janet Vitmayer or Isabel Hughes*
Ⓕ ⌕ ⚲ □

What is now the Livesey Museum was erected in 1890 as 'Camberwell Public Library No. 1', the gift of Sir George Livesey, former Chairman of the South Metropolitan Gas Company and a noted philanthropist. The rear of the building was badly damaged by wartime bombing, but the

A school group visiting the Music Hall Exhibition at the Livesey Museum.

attractive front part was reopened in 1974 as a gallery for changing exhibitions, many of which deal with the history of Southwark.

The damaged rear area has been transformed into a courtyard, where visitors can see large permanent exhibits of local interest such as the old Newington Tollgate and the mosaics from the demolished Old Kent Road Library.

London Cab Company Museum

1–3 Brixton Road, London SW9 6DJ
   ☎ *01 735 7777*
Mon–Fri 9–5, Sat 9–2. Closed Bank Holiday.
 ⊖ *Oval*
 ⍟ *Mr G. W. Trotter*
 Ⓕ

The Museum contains examples of London taxi-cabs, from 1907 to the present day. The UNIC, of which the Museum has a 1907 model, was manufactured from 1904 to 1921 and worked on the London streets until 1931. It is still operational and is much in demand for film, television and special functions. The collection also includes the first London taxi to have front-wheel brakes, the first to be fitted with a driver's door, the first to carry an illuminated roof sign, and the first to have an adjustable driver's seat and a fully enclosed driving cabin.

London Irish Rifles Regimental Museum

Duke of York Headquarters, King's Road, Chelsea, London SW3 4RX
Open 3 days a year, on the nearest Sunday to Mar 17, Sept 25 and Nov 11.
 ⊖ *Sloane Square*
 ⍟ *The Curator*
 Ⓕ

The collections cover the general history of the Regiment from 1859 to 1967, when it was reduced from battalion to company strength, with an emphasis on 1859–1900, the South African War, and the two World Wars.

London Toy and Model Museum

23 Craven Hill, London W2 3EN
   ☎ *01 262 7905/9450*
Tues–Sat 10–5.30, Sun & Bank Holiday Mon 11–5.30. Closed Dec 25.
 ⊖ *Bayswater*
 ⍟ *Assistant Curator*
 Ⓔ ♿ ⌷ ♨

The Museum, which opened in 1982, is in two adjacent listed Victorian houses. It holds one of the most notable collections of commercially-made toys and models on public display in Europe, with items by all the major manufacturers. Special sections are devoted to Paddington Bear, British and Continental dolls from 1750 onwards, the Tiatsa collection of over 25,000 model cars, and toy animals. The range of teddy bears is particularly good, incorporating the late Peter Bull's collection, and tin toys by the great Victorian and Edwardian makers are also well represented.

The comprehensive train collection traces the history of the toy and model train from the mid 19th century onwards. A display featuring the Flying Scotsman illustrates the development of British locomotive design. Model trains can be watched working on the outdoor tracks and children can enjoy a journey on a ride-on steam railway.

The annual Teddy Bears' Picnic at the London Toy and Model Museum.

London Transport Museum

Covent Garden Piazza, London WC2E 7BB
   ☎ *01 379 6344*
Daily 10–6 (last admission 5.15).
   Closed Dec 24–26.
 ⊖ *Covent Garden*
 ⍟ *The Keeper*
 Ⓔ ♿ ⌷ ♨ ♿

The Museum building in Covent Garden formerly housed London's main flower-market and dates from 1871–2. The collection includes horse and motorbuses, trams, trolleybuses and Underground rolling stock, and illustrates the development of London's public transport system and the influence it had on life in the capital.

The story is told with the help of contemporary illustrations, photographs, tickets, uniforms, signs, video programmes showing transport in action, and working models. Posters from London Transport's celebrated collection are on display.

Metropolitan Police Thames Division Museum

Wapping Police Station, 98 Wapping High Street, London E1 9NE   ☎ *01 488 5391*
By appt in writing
 ⊖ *Wapping*
 ⍟ *The Superintendent*
 Ⓕ

The Museum is housed in the former carpenter's workshop (1872). The exhibits date from 1798, when the Marine Police was established, and include portraits of the founders, written and printed documents, models of river-craft, uniforms and a wide range of equipment. There are also relics of the Wapping and Shadwell murders, and paintings, prints and photographs of the Thames Police since its beginnings.

Michael Faraday's Laboratory and Museum

The Royal Institution, 21 Albemarle Street, London
*   W1X 4BS*   ☎ *01 409 2992*
Tues, Thurs 1–4
⊖ *Green Park*
⊠ *The Librarian*
Ⓔ ✍

The Royal Institution, which houses the Museum, is an historic building in its own right. Founded in 1799, the premises are a conversion of two early 18th-century houses, with considerable alterations, including the addition of the present imposing façade, undertaken during the 19th century.

Michael Faraday's Laboratory, where many of his most important discoveries were made, was restored in 1972 to the form it was known to have had in 1845. The recently created Museum adjoining the laboratory contains a collection of original apparatus which shows the more important aspects of Faraday's immense contribution to the advancement of science during his 50 years at the Institution.

Museum of Artillery

The Rotunda, Repository Road, Woolwich, London
*   SE18 4JJ*   ☎ *01 856 5533 extn 385*
Apr–Oct, Mon–Fri 12–5; Sat, Sun 1–5.
*   Nov–Mar, Mon–Fri 12–4; Sat, Sun 1–4.*
*   Closed Good Fri, Dec 24–26, Jan 1.*
⇌ *Woolwich Dockyard*
⊠ *The Curator*
Ⓕ ✍ ⌂

The Museum building was designed by John Nash in 1819. Its collections trace the development of ordnance from the 14th century to the present day. There are also displays of fuses, ammunition, artillery instruments, rockets and edge weapons.

Museum of Garden History

St Mary at Lambeth, Lambeth Palace Road,
*   London SE1 7JU*   ☎ *01 261 1891*
Mon–Fri 11–3; Sun 10.30–5. Closed from 2nd
*   Sun in Dec to 1st Sun in Mar.*
⊖ *Westminster*
⊠ *The Chairman, The Tradescant Trust,*
*   74 Coleherne Court, London SW5 0EF*
Ⓕ ✍ ⚏ ⅋

The Church of St Mary-at-Lambeth adjoins Lambeth Palace, the London residence of the Archbishop of Canterbury. Closed in 1972, it was rescued from dereliction, re-roofed and restored by The Tradescant Trust, which is establishing the first Museum of Garden History on the premises. The displays illustrate the lives and achievements of the two John Tradescants, father and son, whose tomb is in the churchyard of St Mary-at-Lambeth. The Tradescants were gardeners successively to the first Lord Salisbury, the Duke of Buckingham, Charles I and Henrietta Maria. They brought back from their travels in Europe and America many of the flowers, shrubs and trees we take for granted in our gardens today, and propagated them in their celebrated garden at Lambeth. Their museum of 'all things strange and rare' formed the basis of the Ashmolean Museum, Oxford.

Other exhibits in the Museum of Garden History relate to famous plant-hunters and to yesterday's gardening tools.

Museum of London

London Wall, London EC2Y 5HN
*   ☎ 01 600 3699*
Tues–Sat 10–6; Sun 2–6. Closed Mon, including
*   Bank Holiday Mon, and Dec 24–26.*
⊖ *Barbican/Moorgate*
⊠ *Chief Education Officer*
Ⓕ ⛨ ⚏ ⌂ ⅋

The Museum of London illustrates the history of London and its people from prehistoric times to the present day. The galleries are arranged in chronological order and all the exhibits are set in their social context. The items on display include everyday domestic equipment, shop fronts, bank and pub interiors, vehicles, costumes, photographs, the fine and decorative arts, industrial relics and archaeological finds.

Especially popular features are the Lord Mayor's coach, 'The Great Fire Experience' – an audio-visual display – the model of a Roman waterfront, and the full-size reconstruction of a 17th-century room from Poyle Park.

Museum of Mankind

Ethnography Department of The British Museum,
*   Burlington Gardens, London W1X 2EX*
*   ☎ 01 437 2224*
Mon–Sat 10–5; Sun 2.30–6. Closed Good Fri,
*   May Day Bank Holiday & Christmas.*
⊖ *Piccadilly Circus*
⊠ *Education Service*
Ⓕ ⛨ ⌂ ⅋

The Museum's building was designed by James Pennethorne, the adopted son and pupil of John Nash, and opened in 1869. Its façade is notable

The 17th-century knot-garden at the Museum of Garden History.

for the series of statues of men eminent in philosophy and science. The first occupant of the building was the University of London, which used it as its administrative headquarters, and between 1902 and 1970 it passed into the hands of the Civil Service Commission.

The Museum's vast collections come from the indigenous peoples of Africa, the Pacific, the Americas and parts of Europe and Asia. They include both outstanding works of non-Western art and everyday objects, and range in size from tiny ivory carvings to canoes, from dolls to totem poles. Recent and contemporary cultures are represented, as well as those known only from the archaeological record. The Museum is noted for the large and elaborate reconstructions used in its displays, which allow visitors to experience something of the life and environment of other societies.

Museum of the Department of Geography and Earth Science, Queen Mary College

Queen Mary College, Mile End Road, London
E1 4NS   ☎ *01 980 4811 extn 3633*
Daily 9–5. Closed Bank Holiday, Easter and
Christmas.
⊖ *Stepney Green*
▨ *The Curator*
Ⓕ 🔊 ♿

The Museum's comprehensive collections of rocks, minerals and fossils are used in conjunction with teaching and research in earth sciences in the Department, especially in connection with the knowledge and use of geological materials in civil engineering.

Museum of the Order of St John

St John's Gate, St John's Lane, Clerkenwell,
London EC1M 4DA ☎ *01 253 6644 extn 35*
Tues, Fri 10–6; Sat 10–4, with guided tours at
11 & 2.30. Closed Bank Holiday, Easter &
Christmas.
⊖ *Farringdon*
▨ *Museum & Library Secretary*
Ⓔ ♿ 🔊

Founded at the beginning of the 12th century in Jerusalem, the Order of St John was a religious order, with a dual function of caring for the sick and defending the Holy Lands. In England, the Order was dissolved by Henry VIII in 1540. The British Order of St John was established as a charitable organisation in the 19th century in the tradition of the medieval Knights Hospitaller and went on to found the St John Ambulance. In 1888 the Order received a charter, making it a Royal Order of Chivalry with the monarch as its sovereign head.

The Museum is situated in an early 16th-century Gatehouse, once the main entrance to the Priory of the Knights of St John in Clerkenwell, now the headquarters of the modern British Order of St John. The 15th-century Grand Priory Church and Norman crypt also survive from the Priory. The collections, which include paintings, silver and furniture, relate to the history of the Order of St John and of St John Ambulance.

Museum of the Pharmaceutical Society of Great Britain

1 Lambeth High Street, London SE1 7JN
    ☎ *01 735 9141*
By appt only, Mon–Fri 9–5. Closed public &
    Bank Holidays.
⊖ *Lambeth North*
▨ *Museum Officer*
Ⓕ

The collection covers a wide range of material relating to the history and development of pharmacy. A representative selection is displayed throughout the Society's headquarters in Lambeth High Street and includes English pharmaceutical Delftware, with some 17th and 18th-century dated examples, 18th and 19th-century Leedsware and other items of creamware, stoneware and earthenware. Pharmaceutical glass, silver, pewter and treen used for storage, dispensing and display are well represented, together with microscopes, medicine chests, weights, scales and measures.

Leedsware leech jar, about 1780. Museum of the Pharmaceutical Society of Great Britain.

Museum of the Royal Hospital, Chelsea

The Royal Hospital, Chelsea, London SW3 4SL
    ☎ *01 730 0161*
Apr–Sept, Mon–Sat 10–12, 2–4; Sun 2–4.
    Oct–Mar, Mon–Sat 10–12, 2–4.
    Closed Bank Holiday.
⊖ *Sloane Square*
▨ *The Adjutant*
Ⓕ

The part of the Royal Hospital containing the Museum was designed by Sir John Soane and dates from 1819. The displays illustrate the history of the Hospital, the home of the Chelsea Pensioners. The large collection of medals comes from Pensioners who bequeathed them to the Royal Hospital. Other parts of the Hospital include buildings designed by Sir Christopher Wren. They contain a number of late 17th and early 18th-century paintings, and a statue of Charles II by Grinling Gibbons.

Museum of the Royal Regiment of Fusiliers

*The Tower of London, Tower Hill, London
EC3N 4AB*   ☎ *01 480 6082 or 01 709 0765*
*Apr–Sept, Mon–Sat 9.30 5.15; Sun 2–5.30.
Oct–Mar, Mon–Sat 9.30–4.30. Closed Good
Fri & Dec 25.*
⊖ *Tower Hill*
⚑ *Chief Clerk*
£ ⚲

The Regiment was raised in the Tower in 1865.
The Museum illustrates its history, with
collections of uniforms, weapons, documents,
paintings and medals. Among the exhibits of
special interest are a silver vase presented to the
Regiment by William IV, the original Victoria
Cross struck for the approval of Queen Victoria,
and nine other Victoria Crosses, including one
of the first two to be won in the First World
War.

National Army Museum

Royal Hospital Road, Chelsea, London SW3 4HT
☎ *01 730 0717*
*Mon–Sat 10–5.30; Sun 2–5.30. Closed Good Fri,
May Day Bank Holiday, Dec 24–26, Jan 1.*
⊖ *Sloane Square*
⚑ *Keeper of Education*
F ⚲ ⚑ ⚲ ♿

The Museum was established in 1960, to
collect, preserve and exhibit objects and records
relating to the regular and auxiliary forces of the
British Army and to encourage research into
their history and traditions. It is the only
museum in Great Britain dealing with the Army
as a whole during the five centuries of its
existence and includes the story of the colonial
forces and of the Indian Army up to
Independence in 1947.

**Nelson as a young Captain, aged 22, by
J. Rigaud, 1781. National Maritime Museum.**

Two galleries are devoted to a chronological
survey of the development, organisation and
achievements of the Army from 1485–1982.
The Uniform Gallery contains a selection of the
20,000 items in the collection, and there are
also displays of weapons, badges, medals and
insignia, including the decorations of H.R.H.
the Duke of Windsor and the batons of five
Field Marshals. The Art Gallery contains the
best of the Museum's collection of 17th, 18th
and 19th-century portraits and paintings of
military subjects.
    The Weapon Gallery traces the development
of hand-held weapons used by British soldiers
from medieval times to the present.

The National Gallery

Trafalgar Square, London WC2N 5DN
☎ *01 839 3321*
*Mon–Sat 10–6; Sun 2–6. Closed Good Fri,
May Day Bank Holiday, Dec 24, 25, Jan 1.*
⊖ *Trafalgar Square*
⚑ *Education Department*
F ⚲ ⚑ ⚲ ♿

The Gallery building, designed by William
Wilkins, was completed in 1838. There are
more than 2,000 pictures in the collection,
which covers the major European schools up to
1900 and has the reputation of being the most
representative and best-balanced collection in
the world. Among the artists represented are
Leonardo, Raphael, Titian, Rembrandt,
Vermeer, Rubens, Poussin, Velasquez, Hogarth,
Constable, Turner, Cézanne and Renoir.

National Maritime Museum

Romney Road, Greenwich, London SE10 9NF
☎ *01 858 4422*
*Mar 30–Oct 26, Mon–Sat 10–6; Sun 2–6.
Oct 27–Mar 29, Mon–Sat 10–5; Sun 2–5.*
⊖ *Surrey Docks*
⇄ *Maze Hill*
⚑ *Schools Liaison Officer*
£ ⚲ ⚑ ⚲ ♿

The central feature of the main Museum
buildings is Inigo Jones's Queen's House. The
Museum's displays illustrate the role the sea has
played in British history. Ship design plays an
important part in the exhibits, with many actual
boats and hundreds of detailed models. There
are large collections of compasses, telescopes,
sextants, maps and charts and interesting
examples of ships' logs. Among the weapons
exhibited are ships' guns, muskets, pistols,
swords and cutlasses. Visitors can also see ships'
furniture and fittings, uniforms and many
personal items associated with famous figures in
Britain's maritime history, such as the bullet-
holed coat in which Nelson died.
    The Museum has extensive collections of
historic paintings, prints, drawings and
photographs relating to maritime scenes and
personalities.

Queen Elizabeth I in her coronation robes, 1558. National Portrait Gallery.

National Portrait Gallery

St Martin's Place, London WC2H 0HE
☎ 01 930 1552
Mon–Fri 10–5; Sat 10–6; Sun 2–6.
Closed Good Fri, May Day Bank Holiday,
Dec 24–26, Jan 1.
☉ *Trafalgar Square*
⚑ *John Cooper, Head of Education*
Ⓔ *ex. special exhibitions* ▮ ♻ ⚑ □

The present Gallery, in the style of an Italian palazzo, opened in 1896. Round the exterior is a frieze of busts of Hogarth, Lawrence and other celebrated British portrait artists. The aim of the Gallery is to collect likenesses of famous British men and women, in media which include paintings, drawings, sculpture, photographs and videos. The criteria for admission are the importance of the subject and the authenticity of the portrait, which must be taken from life.

The 9,000 portraits date from Tudor times to the present day and include kings and queens, scholars, statesmen, soldiers, poets, sportsmen and scientists.

National Postal Museum

London Chief Post Office, King Edward Street,
London EC1A 1LP ☎ 01 432 3851
Mon–Thurs 10–4.30; Fri 10–4.
Closed Bank Holiday.
☉ *St Pauls*
⚑ *The Director*
Ⓕ ♻ ⚑ ♿ □

The Museum possesses worldwide collections of postage stamps, particular strengths being the Victorian stamps donated by R. M. Phillips, the Berne world collection and the Frank Staff collection of stamps with maritime subjects and of transatlantic covers. There are frequent special exhibitions.

Natural History Museum

Cromwell Road, South Kensington, London
SW7 5BD ☎ 01 938 9123
Mon–Sat 10–6; Sun 2.30–6. Closed Good Fri,
May Bank Holiday, Dec 24–26, Jan 1.
☉ *South Kensington*
⚑ *Visitor Resources Department*
Ⓔ ▮ ⚍ ⚑ □

The Natural History Museum, designed by Alfred Waterhouse, is among the greatest of Victorian buildings. Internally, it is richly decorated with terracotta mouldings of plants and animals. It holds one of the most extensive collections in the world of natural history specimens of all kinds – living and fossil plants and animals, minerals, rocks and meteorites. Most of the display galleries have been completely modernised in recent years and a number of theme exhibitions introduced. These include Human Biology, Man's Place in Evolution, Origin of Species, Introducing Ecology, Dinosaurs and their Living Relatives, and Discovering Mammals.

North Woolwich Old Station Museum

Pier Road, North Woolwich, London E16 2JJ
☎ 01 474 7244
Mon–Sat 10–5; Sun & Bank Holiday 2–5
⇌ *North Woolwich*
⚑ *Assistant Curator, Extension Services*
Ⓕ ▮ ♿

North Woolwich Old Station, built in the early 1850s, owes its size and grandeur to the profitable river trade which developed from the adjoining pier and from the garden and dance parties held in North Woolwich Gardens, now the Royal Victoria Gardens. It has been restored to its pre-First World War condition. Three exhibition galleries tell the story of the Great Eastern Railway, which became part of the L.N.E.R. in the regrouping in 1923. The ticket office is set out as it would have been during the period 1914–39, much of the equipment coming from the ticket offices at Bethnal Green.

Old Royal Observatory

National Maritime Museum, Romney Road,
Greenwich, London SE10 9NF
☎ 01 858 1167
Mar 30–Oct 26, Mon–Sat 10–6; Sun 2–6.
Oct 27–Mar 29, Mon–Sat 10–5; Sun 2–5.
☉ *Surrey Docks*
⇌ *Maze Hill*
⚑ *See National Maritime Museum*
Ⓔ ▮ ⚑

The Observatory was set up on the orders of Charles II primarily to enable longitude to be calculated accurately. The buildings, including Flamsteed House, which was designed by Wren, form part of the National Maritime Museum and house important exhibits of astronomical and navigational instruments, including some of the Observatory's original telescopes. The brass line passing through the Courtyard marks longitude zero.

Passmore Edwards Museum

Romford Road, Stratford, London E15 4LZ
☎ 01 534 4545 extn 5670
Mon–Fri, 10–6; Sat 10–5; Sun and Bank
  Holiday 2–5. Parties by appt.
⇌ Stratford East
▣ Principal Assistant
F ▪

Opened in 1900, the Museum occupies a
building designed for the purpose and now
listed Grade II. It is concerned with the
biology, geology, archaeology and local
history of the County of Essex. The 9-acre
churchyard of St Mary Magdalene, East Ham, is
cared for by the Museum as its natural history
reserve. An additional exhibit is the Thames
sailing barge, Dawn, built in 1897 at Maldon,
Essex, and preserved in a seaworthy condition.

Percival David Foundation of Chinese Art Collection

53 Gordon Square, London WC1H 0PD
☎ 01 387 3909
Mon 2–5; Tues–Fri 10.30–5; Sat 10.30–1.
  Closed Bank Holiday and preceding Sats,
  and during Aug.
⊖ Russell Square
▣ Ms R. Scott, Curator
F ⬚

The collection of Chinese ceramics, belonging
mainly to the 10th to 18th centuries, formed by
Sir Percival David was given to the University
of London in 1950. It reflects Chinese court
taste of the 18th century. A number of pieces
were previously in the possession of Chinese
emperors and some bear imperial inscriptions. A
separate collection of monochrome porcelain,
given by the Hon. Mountstuart Elphinstone in
1952, is also on display.

Petrie Museum of Egyptian Archaeology

University College London, Gower Street, London
  WC1E 6BT   ☎ 01 387 7050 extn 6178
Mon–Fri 10–12, 1.15–5. Closed Bank Holiday,
  1 week at Christmas and Easter, and for
  4 weeks in summer (check locally).
  Parties by appt.
⊖ Euston Square
▣ Assistant Curator
F ⬚

The Museum building was once a stable for
brewery dray horses. The collection of material
from archaeological sites ranges from the
prehistoric to the Roman periods of Egyptian
history. The Petrie Museum is not primarily
concerned with art, but contains exhibits of
considerable artistic interest, including the
Koptos lions and Amarna sculpture.

Pollock's Toy Museum

1 Scala Street, London W1P 1LT ☎ 01 636 3452
Mon–Sat 10–5. Closed Good Fri, Easter Mon,
  Dec 25, 26.
⊖ Goodge Street
▣ Hon. Secretary
£ ▪

The Museum is in two small 18th-century
houses. The small rooms and narrow winding
staircases give it a certain dolls' house quality. It
adjoins Pollock's Theatrical Print Warehouse,
where Pollock's Toy Theatres and their
associated plays are sold, preserving the
tradition of the Victorian Juvenile Drama. The
collections include dolls of china, wood, fabric,
celluloid, wax and composition; dolls' houses;
rocking horses; tin and lead toys; teddy bears;
folk toys from many countries; puppets; toy
theatres; board games; and optical, mechanical
and constructional toys.

Sandstone relief of the Princess Sitamun,
daughter of Amenophis III (1386–1349 BC),
Petrie Museum of Egyptian Archaeology.

Public Record Office Museum

Chancery Lane, London WC2A 1LR
☎ 01 405 0741
Mon–Fri 10–4.30. Closed Bank Holiday.
⊖ Chancery Lane
▣ Assistant Keeper
F ⬚ □

The Museum is in the Grade II listed building of
the Public Record Office, on the site of the
13th-century Rolls Chapel. It has a small
permanent exhibition of manuscripts and
archives of national importance, illustrating
many well-known episodes in British, colonial
and international history.

The Queen's Gallery

Buckingham Palace, London SW1 1AY
☎ 01 930 4832
Tues–Sat 11–5; Sun 2–5. Closed Mon ex. Bank
  Holidays.
⊖ Victoria
▣ The Registrar, Lord Chamberlain's Office,
  St James's Palace, London SW1
£ ▪

The Gallery was constructed in 1962 on the site
of the Buckingham Palace Private Chapel,
which was destroyed in an air raid in 1940. It
presents regular exhibitions of items drawn from
the extensive Royal Collections of paintings,
drawings, furniture, tapestries, sculpture,
porcelain and other works of art. Among the
subjects of past exhibitions have been Sèvres
porcelain, Holbein drawings, Canaletto
paintings, Royal Children, Britain's Kings and
Queens, Fabergé, and animal paintings.

Ranger's House

Chesterfield Walk, Blackheath, London SE10 8QX
        ☎ 01 853 0035
Feb–Oct, daily 10–5. Nov–Jan, daily 10–4.
        Closed Good Fri, Dec 24, 25.
⊖ *Blackheath*
▨ *Miss Gene Adams, ILEA Museums Adviser*
        ☎ 01 348 1286
♧ ♠ &

What is now known as Ranger's House was built
in 1682 on the edge of Greenwich Park. Its
earlier occupants included the 4th Earl of
Chesterfield and the Duchess of Brunswick,
mother of Queen Caroline, wife of George IV.
In 1815 it became the official residence of the
Ranger of Greenwich Park. The Greater
London Council converted it to an art gallery in
1974. Its principal contents are now the
paintings included in the Suffolk Collection,
which formerly belonged to the Earls of Suffolk
and Berkshire. Among these is a series of full-
length Jacobean portraits by William Lely and a
group of Royal portraits by Lely.
    The 17th and 18th-century furnishings are
appropriate to the house and the paintings, and
on the first floor there is the Dolmetsch
Collection of musical instruments.

Royal Air Force Museums

Grahame Park Way, Hendon, London NW9 5LL
        ☎ 01 205 2266
Mon–Sat 10–6; Sun 2–6. Closed Good Fri, May
        Day Bank Holiday, Dec 24–26, Jan 1.
⊖ *Colindale*
▨ *Mr Michael C. Nutt*
£ ▮ ▆ ♠ &

The Museum buildings, situated on 10 acres of
the historic former airfield at Hendon,
incorporate two hangars constructed in 1915.
The displays cover the history of the Royal Air
Force and its predecessors and of aviation
generally. The collections include over 150
aircraft, of which 40 are on display. Among the
other exhibits are aero-engines, propellers,
instruments, navigation aids, armament,
uniforms, decorations, trophies and paintings.
    Within the Museum complex are two special
exhibitions, the Battle of Britain Museum, with
British and German aircraft and other relics of
the air attack of 1940, and the Bomber
Command Museum, which presents aircraft and
a wide range of mementoes of the Allied
bombing offensive.
    All three sections of the Museum contain
realistic reconstructions of historic settings
connected with R.A.F. history, from a Royal
Flying Corps workshop of the First World War
to a Battle of Britain Operations Room.

Royal Artillery Regimental Museum

Royal Artillery Institution, Old Royal Military
        Academy, Woolwich, London SE18 4DN
        ☎ 01 856 5533 extn 2505
Mon–Fri 10–12.30, 2–4. Closed Bank Holiday.
⇌ *Woolwich Arsenal*
▨ *The Director*
F ♧ ♠

The Museum occupies part of the Royal Military
Academy, built in 1805. It outlines the history
of the Royal Regiment of Artillery from its
formation in 1716 to the present day. The
displays include uniforms, weapons, paintings,
and trophies associated with the Regiment.

Royal College of Music, Department of Portraits

Royal College of Music, Prince Consort Road,
        London SW7 2BS   ☎ 01 589 3643
By appt only, Mon–Fri. Closed for 10 days at
        Easter & Christmas.
⊖ *South Kensington*
▨ *Keeper of Portraits*
F ▆

The College possesses a comprehensive
collection of portraits of musicians, comprising
200 original portraits and many thousands of
prints and photographs. Among the particularly
noteworthy items are *Gluck* by Houdon, *Haydn*
by Thomas Hardy, *Farinelli* by Nazari,
Paderewski by Burne-Jones, and *Sir George Grove*
by Gilbert. The Department also has a large
collection of concert programmes, with items
dating from the 18th century to the present day.

Royal College of Music, Museum of Instruments

Royal College of Music, Prince Consort Road,
        London SW7 2BS   ☎ 01 589 3613
Mon, Wed 11–4.30 during term-time. Parties &
        special visits by appt.
⊖ *South Kensington*
▨ *Mrs Elizabeth Wells, Curator*
£ ▆

The College's internationally renowned
collection of historic musical instruments has
been formed from gifts made since the
foundation of the College in 1883. There are
now some 500 keyboard, wind and stringed
instruments, dating from the 16th to the 20th

**Venetian Harpsichord, 1531. Royal College of
Music, Museum of Instruments.**

centuries. Among the exhibits are the South German clavicytherium, made c. 1480 and believed to be the earliest surviving stringed keyboard instrument, the Trasuntino harpsichord, made in Venice in 1531, Handel's spinet, and Haydn's clavichord. A small ethnological section includes instruments from Asia and Africa.

The Royal Mews

Buckingham Palace, London SW1W 0QH
    ☎ *01 930 4832 extn 634*
*Wed, Thurs 2–4. Closed if a Royal carriage
    procession or a Bank Holiday falls on an
    open day.*
⊖ *Victoria*
Ⓜ *The Office Keeper*
Ⓔ ⌖ ♿

The stables and coach houses at Buckingham Palace were redesigned by John Nash for George IV in 1824 and they became the Royal Mews in 1825. They now contain the Gold State Coach, the other important ceremonial coaches, including the Coronation Coach, built in 1762, and most of the State carriage horses.

In the Old Barracks at Hampton Court Palace, there is a summer exhibition of vehicles, liveries, ceremonial saddles, harness and photographs.

St Bride's Church and Crypt Museum

Fleet Street, London EC4Y 8AU   ☎ *01 353 1301*
Daily 8.30–5.30
⊖ *Blackfriars*
Ⓜ *Mr Mark Upton, Lay Assistant*
Ⓕ ⌖ ♨

The present St Bride's is the eighth church to have stood on the site. It is a reconstruction, based on the original plans and drawings, of the church built by Sir Christopher Wren after the Great Fire in 1666 and largely destroyed in an air raid in 1940. The Museum presents the history of the eight churches from the 6th century onwards. The Crypt also contains

The early 17th-century Globe Theatre in Southwark. Model in The Shakespeare Globe Museum.

archaeological material, including a Roman pavement, from most of the buildings which have occupied the site. There are also social history displays, relating especially to the development of printing and the newspaper industry. The exhibits include costumes and a coffin proof against body-snatchers.

Science Museum

*Exhibition Road, South Kensington, London
    SW7 2DD*   ☎ *01 938 8000*
*Mon–Sat 10–6; Sun 2.30–6. Closed Good Fri,
    May Day Bank Holiday, Dec 24–26, Jan 1.*
⊖ *South Kensington*
Ⓜ *Education Department*
Ⓔ ⌖ ⬛ ♿

The Science Museum had its origin in the scientific and educational collections of the South Kensington Museum, opened in 1857. The construction of the present buildings took place by stages from 1913 onwards. The collections cover a wide range of subjects from the pure sciences to engineering, and from transport to space technology, illustrating the ways in which science and industry have influenced our lives. The exhibits include working models and historic machinery, instruments and equipment.

Two floors devoted to the Wellcome Museum of the History of Medicine tell the story of medicine from Neolithic times to the present day.

The Shakespeare Globe Museum

Bear Gardens, Bankside, London SE1 9EB
          ☎ *01 928 6342*
Tues–Sat 10–5.30; Sun 2–6.
⊖ *Cannon Street*
Ⓜ *Museum Manager*
Ⓔ ⌖

The Museum is housed in a former 18th-century coffee warehouse, a short distance from the site of Shakespeare's Globe Theatre. Its displays trace the history of the English theatre from 1576, when the first purpose-built theatre opened in London, to 1642, when the theatres were closed during the Civil War. The exhibits include a full-size replica of the 1616 Cockpit stage, which is used both for public performances and for workshops.

Silver Studio Collection

*Middlesex Polytechnic, Bounds Green Road,
    London N11 2NQ*   ☎ *01 368 1299 extn 399*
*Mon–Fri 10–4. Closed Dec 25, 26 & Bank
    Holiday.*
⊖ *Bounds Green*
Ⓜ *The Keeper*
Ⓕ ⌖ ⬛ ♨ ♿

The Museum includes the complete contents of what was in its day Britain's largest commercial design studio. Founded by Arthur Silver in 1880, it functioned until 1963. It also has one of the most important collections of late 19th and early 20th-century wallpapers and textiles in Europe.

Wallpaper design, about 1890, in the Silver Studio Collection.

Sir John Soane's Museum

13 Lincoln's Inn Fields, London WC2A 3BP
☎ 01 405 2107
Tues–Sat 10–5. Closed Bank Holiday & Dec 24.
↔ *Holborn*
🚻 *Peter Thornton, Curator*
Ⓕ ✏

12, 13 and 14 Lincoln's Inn Fields were designed by Sir John Soane, and built 1812–14. 12 and 13, together with the back part of 14, now form the Museum. The interior of 13, Soane's own house and museum, is one of his finest architectural achievements. The present Museum contains his wide-ranging collection of Greek and Roman antiquities and architectural fragments; Renaissance sculpture and casts; and 18th-century paintings, drawings, engravings and sculpture. Among the particular treasures are two series of paintings by Hogarth, *The Rake's Progress* and *The Election*; paintings by Turner, Canaletto, Watteau, Piranesi and Sir Thomas Lawrence; the Egyptian sarcophagus of Seti I; and a fragment from the frieze of the Erectheum in Athens.

South London Art Gallery

Peckham Road, London SE5 8UH
☎ 01 703 6120
Tues–Sat 10–6; Sun 3–6. Closed Bank Holiday and between exhibitions.
↔ *Oval*
🚻 *Kenneth Sharpe, Keeper*
Ⓕ ✏ ⌨ □

The Gallery originally formed part of the South London Working Men's College, which was established in 1868. With the support of leading figures in the art world, notably Lord Leighton, the present purpose-built gallery was opened to the public in 1891. The most important collection is of paintings of the Victorian period, including works by Ford Madox Brown,

Lord Leighton and G. F. Watts. In 1960 the Gallery began to acquire 20th-century original prints and aims to collect the best prints produced each year by British artists. There is also a comprehensive collection of topographical drawings and drawings of Southwark.

Temporary exhibitions are arranged each year, covering a wide field – sculpture, paintings, drawings, jewellery, embroidery, photography, pottery, woodcarving, and local and social history.

Southside House

3 Woodhayes Road, Wimbledon, London
   SW19 4RJ   ☎ 01 946 7643
Oct–Mar, Tues, Thurs, Fri, guided tours hourly, 2–5. Other times (ex. Sun) by appt.
↔ *Wimbledon*
🚻 *The Administrator*
Ⓔ ☞

Southside House was built in 1687 by the Pennington-Mellor family, who still live here. Badly damaged during Second World War air raids, it has since been restored and is one of the oldest houses in Greater London which continues to be used as a private residence. It contains 17th to 19th-century furniture and paintings.

Among the many celebrities associated with the house and its owners are King Charles II, Marie Antoinette, Frederick, Prince of Wales – the son of George II – Admiral Lord Nelson, Lady Hamilton and Axel Munthe.

Tate Gallery

Millbank, London SW1P 4RG   ☎ 01 821 1313
   Recorded information: ☎ 01 821 7128
Mon–Sat 10–5.50; Sun 2–5.50. Closed Good Fri, May Day Bank Holiday, Dec 24–26, Jan 1.
↔ *Pimlico*
🚻 *Education Department*
Ⓕ *ex. special exhibitions* 🍴 🖥 ♿ □

The Gallery opened in 1897, the building being paid for by Sir Henry Tate – of Tate and Lyle,

'Whaam!' by Roy Lichtenstein, 1963. Tate Gallery.

the sugar refiners – whose gift of 70 recent British paintings and sculptures formed the nucleus of the collection. Extensions were built in 1899–1906, also at Sir Henry's expense, and in 1910, 1926, 1937 and 1979. The Clore Gallery, to house the Turner collection, opened in the Spring of 1987.

The Tate Gallery houses two national collections. The British Collection covers the period c. 1500–1900 and consists of watercolours, drawings, engravings, sculpture and paintings. Hogarth, Blake, Stubbs, Constable and the Pre-Raphaelites are particularly strongly represented. The Modern Collection includes paintings and sculpture by British artists born after 1860 and by foreign artists from the Impressionists onwards. There is also a large collection of prints, dating from the mid 1960s to the present day.

The Gallery mounts a continuous programme of temporary exhibitions.

Telecom Technology Showcase

Baynard House, 135 Queen Victoria Street,
*   London EC4V 54AT*   ☎ *01 248 7444*
Mon–Fri 10–5. Closed Bank Holiday.
⊖ *Blackfriars*
𝕂 *Bookings Clerk*
F 🛆 ♿ ⬜

This is Britain's major museum of tele-communications. It presents the history of telecommunications over a period of nearly 200 years, from the semaphore apparatus of 1794 to today's electronic equipment. Displays show the development of the railway and public telegraph service, submarine cables and cable-laying, early experiments with the telephone and the beginning of the radio telephone.

There are many working exhibits, some of which visitors can activate themselves. A complete working telephone exchange allows a call to be made and its progress observed through the system. Among the many individual exhibits are telephone instruments used by Royalty, early telephone directories and historic telephone kiosks. The Showcase is brought up to date with explanations of Prestel and optical fibre, and there are changing exhibitions which present the latest telecommunication equipment.

Thames Barrier Visitors Centre

Unity Way, Woolwich, London SE18 5NJ
    ☎ *01 854 1373*
Mon–Fri 10.30–5; Sat–Sun 10.30–5.30.
    Closed Dec 25, 26, Jan 1.
⇌ *Charlton*
𝕂 *General Office*
F 🛆 ⬛ ♿ ♿

The Thames Barrier, constructed to prevent London from disastrous flooding, was opened in 1984. A remarkable civil engineering achievement, it is the world's largest movable flood barrier. The exhibition and audio-visual presentation in the Visitors Centre show why the Barrier was needed and explain its operation. There is also a working model of the Barrier and a film telling the story of its construction.

The Thomas Coram Foundation for Children (Foundling Hospital Art Treasures)

40 Brunswick Square, London WC1N 1AZ
    ☎ *01 278 2424*
Mon–Fri 10–4. Closed public holidays & when the
    rooms are in use (please check locally).
⊖ *Russell Square*
𝕂 *The Director & Secretary*
£ ✎ ♿

The Foundation, formerly known as the Foundling Hospital, was established in 1739 by Captain Thomas Coram. William Hogarth was one of the first Governors and his portrait of Coram is the outstanding item in the collection of about 120 paintings, sculptures and other historic material, which includes two further paintings by Hogarth, together with works by Gainsborough, Reynolds, Wilson, Hudson, Millais, Roubiliac and Rysbrack. George Frederick Handel, the composer, became a Governor in 1750, and his annual performance of *Messiah* in the Hospital Chapel raised large sums for the Charity. At his death in 1759 he bequeathed a fair copy of *Messiah*, now known as the Foundling Hospital Version, to the Hospital in his will. This, together with the conducting score of his *Foundling Hospital Anthem* and the keyboard of the organ he presented to the Chapel, are on display at the Museum.

Tower of London

Tower Hill, London EC3N 4AB ☎ *01 709 0765*
Mar–Oct, Mon–Sat 9.30–5; Sun 2–5.
    Nov–Feb, Mon–Sat 9.30–4.
    Closed Good Fri, Dec 24–26, Jan 1.
    Jewel House usually closed Feb.
⊖ *Tower Hill*
𝕂 *The Administrator*
£ 🛆 ⬛

Construction of Her Majesty's Royal Palace and Fortress of the Tower of London began in 1078.

The 'New Court Speaking Set No. 2', designed for the Rothschild family of New Court about 1900. Telecom Technology Showcase.

It has been a state prison since Norman times, and the scene of many celebrated executions, and in the course of its history it has provided accommodation for the public records, the Royal Menagerie, the Royal Mint, the first Royal Observatory and the Courts of Justice.

The White Tower contains the National Collection of Arms and Armour, together with a number of historical relics, including the cloak in which General Wolfe died at Quebec in 1759 and the daggers of Colonel Blood, who attempted to steal the Crown Jewels in 1671. The Crown Jewels and Regalia are displayed in the Wakefield Tower, built c. 1220.

University College Museum of Zoology and Comparative Anatomy

University College, Gower Street, London
WC1E 6BT   ☎ *01 387 7050 extn 416*
Mon–Fri 9–5. Open to the general public by appt only. Closed for 1 week at Easter & Christmas.
⊖ *Euston Square*
🏛 *The Curator*
🅕

The Museum was started in 1828 by Robert Edmund Grant, the first professor of zoology in England, and still contains some of his specimens. Primarily intended for teaching purposes, the collections cover the whole range of the animal kingdom and include many rare specimens.

Vestry House Museum

Vestry Road, Walthamstow, London E17 9NH
☎ *01 527 5511 extn 4391*
Mon–Fri 10–1, 2–5.30; Sat 10–1, 2–5.
Closed public & Bank Holidays.
⊖ *Walthamstow Central*
🏛 *The Keeper*
🅕 ✎ □

The Museum occupies a building dating from 1730, which was originally Walthamstow Parish Workhouse. Its displays illustrate life in the Waltham Forest area from the Stone Age to the present day, with exhibits on local archaeology, costume, crafts, trades and industries, trade vehicles, and Victorian and Edwardian domestic life. The most notable item on show is the Bremer Car, built locally c. 1892 and reputedly the finest British motorcar.

There is also a large collection of photographs, covering all aspects of life in the district from 1860 onwards.

The old workhouse building was afterwards used as a police station and one of the mid 19th-century cells has been preserved.

Victoria and Albert Museum

Cromwell Road, South Kensington, London
SW7 2RL   ☎ *01 938 8500*
Mon–Thurs, Sat 10–5.50; Sun 2.30–5.50.
Closed May Day Bank Holiday, Dec 24–26, Jan 1.
⊖ *South Kensington*
🏛 *Education Department*
🅕 *Donations expected* ♿ 🚻 ㊑ □

Created during the second half of the 19th century, the Victoria and Albert Museum contains the world's greatest collection of the decorative arts, brought together from five continents. In several miles of galleries, there are displays of paintings, jewellery, sculpture, costume, furniture, ceramics, and armour. Individual galleries exhibit objects from the Far East and India, and prints, drawings, photographs and paintings are to be seen in a new sixth floor wing, named after Sir Henry Cole, the Museum's first Director.

Among the special attractions are the Victorian Cast Courts, the Fakes Gallery and the Constable Collection. The Museum also has a continuous programme of temporary exhibitions and houses the National Art Library.

The Wallace Collection

Hertford House, Manchester Square, London
W1M 6BN   ☎ *01 935 0687*
Mon–Sat 10–5; Sun 2–5. Closed Good Fri, May Day Bank Holiday, Dec 24–26, Jan 1.
⊖ *Bond Street*
🏛 *Miss S. Gaynor*
🅕 ✎ ㊑

Hertford House was built in the late 1770s for the 4th Duke of Manchester, as the family's town house. It was bought by the 2nd Marquess of Hertford in 1797. In the early 1870s Sir Richard Wallace, the illegitimate son of the 4th Marquess, made alterations to the building and arranged the Hertford family art collection in furnished rooms and in purpose-built galleries. His widow, Lady Wallace, bequeathed the house and the collection to the nation in 1897. Today it is displayed in 25 galleries on the ground and first floors of Hertford House.

The paintings, of the Italian, Dutch, Flemish, Spanish, French and English Schools, include Rembrandt's *Titus*, *The Laughing Cavalier* by Frans Hals, and *Lady with a Fan* by Velasquez. There is French 18th-century furniture of high quality, and Sèvres porcelain, together with 16th-century Italian maiolica, Venetian glass, Limoges enamels, silver and silver-gilt and other medieval and Renaissance works of art. Among other important parts of the Museum's collection are English and Continental miniatures and the paintings of Richard Parkes Bonington.

Early 19th-century hand-painted tea service illustrating local houses in Walthamstow. Vestry House Museum.

The Wellcome Museum of the History of Medicine

*Science Museum, Exhibition Road, South
Kensington, London SW7 2DD*
☎ *01 938 8000*
*Mon–Sat 10–6; Sun 2.30–6. Closed Good Fri,
May Day Bank Holiday, Dec 25, 26, Jan 1.*
⊖ *South Kensington*
⚑ *Education Department*
£ ⌂ ☕ ♿

The Wellcome Museum is the world's largest
collection of items illustrating the history of
medicine. The Introductory Gallery contains 43
dioramas and reconstructions concerned with
practical aspects of medicine – a Roman field
hospital, Naval surgery in 1800, and a visit to
the dentist in 1980. The main gallery presents
objects in chronological displays and by
specialisms – medicine in tribal societies, 19th-
century hospital medicine, the influences of war
and exploration on medicine, 20th-century
medical research.

Westminster Abbey Exhibition of Treasures

Westminster Abbey, London SW1P 3PA
☎ *01 222 5152 extn 57*
*Daily 10.30–4.30 (last admission 4). Closed
Good Fri & Dec 25 and when special
services are in progress.*
⊖ *St James's Park*
⚑ *The Receiver General*
£ ✐

The Exhibition, which has recently been
completely redesigned, is in the Norman
Undercroft of the Abbey, probably used by the
monks as a Common Room. The displays are
related to the history and architecture of
Westminster Abbey. There is a remarkable
collection of realistic wooden and wax funeral
effigies, dating from the 14th to the early 19th
centuries, the earliest being that of Edward III
(d. 1377). Other exhibits include coronation
regalia and furniture, and copes and plate from
the Abbey and St Margaret's, Westminster.

William Morris Gallery

*Water House, Lloyd Park, Forest Road,
Walthamstow, London E17 4PP*
☎ *01 527 5544 extn 4390*
*Tues–Sat 10–1, 2–5. Also 1st Sun of each month,
10–12, 2–5. Closed public holidays.*
⊖ *Walthamstow Central*
⚑ *Education Officer*
F ✐ ↩

William Morris was born in Walthamstow in
1834. From 1848 to 1856 the Morris family
home was the Water House, an 18th-century
building. Since 1950 it has housed the William
Morris Gallery, with a collection illustrating the
achievements of the designer, craftsman, poet
and socialist, whose work revolutionised the
taste of the 19th century.

The Gallery's displays include wallpapers,
printed and woven textiles, embroideries,
rugs and carpets, furniture, stained glass and
ceramics designed by Morris and his
associates.

Wimbledon Lawn Tennis Museum

*The All England Club, Church Road, Wimbledon,
London SW19 5AE*   ☎ *01 946 6131*
*Tues–Sat 11–5; Sun 2–5. Closed public & Bank
Holidays & Fri–Sun preceding Championships.*
⊖ *Southfields*
⚑ *The Curator*
£ ⌂ ↩

In a building adjoining the Centre Court, the
Museum illustrates the history of lawn tennis,
introduced in 1870, and the games which
preceded it. Among the exhibits are trophies,
clothing, an early tennis racquet workshop, a
Victorian parlour furnished with tennis items,
and an 1877 dressing room.

Wimbledon Society Local History Museum

*Village Club and Lecture Hall, Lingfield Road,
Wimbledon, London SW19*   ☎ *01 946 9529*
Sat 2.30–5. Closed Dec 25–26.
⊖ *Wimbledon*
⚑ *Norman Plastow, Far House, Hillside,
Wimbledon, London SW19*   ☎ *01 947 2825*
F ✐ ↩ □

The Museum's collections, which illustrate the
history and natural environment of Wimbledon,
are arranged in 10 sections – watercolours and
prints, photographs, maps, artefacts, books,
manuscripts, ephemera, archaeology, natural
history and press-cuttings – each with a
specialist curator. In addition to the permanent
displays, there are always four temporary
exhibitions, each illustrating a particular theme.

Wimbledon Windmill Museum

*Windmill Road, Wimbledon Common, London
SW19 5NR*
*Easter–Oct, Sat, Sun & public holidays 2–5.
Open at other times by appt for school &
group visits.*
⊖ *Putney Bridge*
⚑ *The Clerk & Ranger, Manor Cottage,
Wimbledon Common*   ☎ *01 788 7655*
£ *ex. school parties* ✐ ☕ ↩

The Museum is housed in a windmill built in
1817, which retains many of its original

**'The Annunciation', a cartoon for stained glass
at St Michael's Church, Brighton, by William
Morris, 1862. William Morris Gallery.**

features, but has not been a working mill for more than 160 years. The displays, on the first floor of the mill, show the history of windmills and milling, with detailed models, pictures and the machinery and tools of the trade, including over 150 woodworking tools donated by a former millwright. Many of the exhibits may be handled by children, including a hand-quern, which can be be used to make flour.

Woodlands Local History Centre and Art Gallery

90 Mycenae Road, Blackheath, London SE3 7SE
☎ *01 858 4631*
Local History Centre: Mon, Tues, Thurs 9–8;
Sat 9–5. Art Gallery: Mon, Tues, Thurs, Fri
10–7.30; Sat 10–6; Sun 2–6.
≉ *Westcombe Park*
🅺 *Local History Librarian (Local History Centre)*
or Exhibitions Organiser (Art Gallery)
Ⓕ 🔾 ✏ ☐

Woodlands was built in 1774 as a country villa for John Julius Angerstein, a marine insurance underwriter, known as the 'Father of Lloyds'. His collection of paintings formed the nucleus of the National Gallery. The Local History Centre contains material relating to the history of the London Borough of Greenwich. Particularly noteworthy are the historic watercolours and drawings, and the large collection of photographs of Victorian street life.

The Art Gallery has no permanent collections, but organises monthly exhibitions.

Zamana Gallery

Ismaili Centre, 1 Cromwell Gardens, London
SW7 2SL ☎ *01 584 6612*
Mon–Thurs, Sat 10–5.30; Sun 1–5.30.
Guided tour 2.30 each day.
⊖ *South Kensington*
🅺 *Jane De'Athe, Acting Director*
Ⓕ ☎ 🚆

Wimbledon Windmill, Britain's only example of a Dutch 'wip mill', built in 1817.

The Gallery, in the much-discussed Ismaili Centre opposite the Victoria and Albert Museum, is devoted to increasing public awareness of the arts and architecture of the Third World, with an emphasis on Islamic cultures. Three or four exhibitions are arranged each year and care is taken to ensure that the exhibits are of high quality and presented in a way which will attract and interest a wide range of visitors.

London Colney

Mosquito Aircraft Museum

P.O. Box 107, Salisbury Hall, London Colney,
St Albans, Hertfordshire ☎ *0727 22051*
Easter–June & Oct, Sun & Bank Holiday Mon
10.30–5.30. July–Sept, Thurs 2–5.30; Sun &
Bank Holiday Mon 10.30–5.30. Other times
by appt for groups.
🅺 *The Curator*
⒠ ♠ 🚆 ⌕

The Museum, established in 1958 to preserve the prototype Mosquito, is Britain's oldest aircraft museum. It adjoins the London Colney roundabout on the A6 between Barnet and St Albans. It is in the grounds of Salisbury Hall, a 17th-century manor house, and on the site where the de Havilland Mosquito was designed and first built. The collection includes 17 de Havilland types, the earliest being the 1917 B.E.2e. Among them are three Mosquitoes.

Longford

St Mel's Diocesan Museum

The Presbytery, Longford, Co. Longford, Ireland
☎ *043 46465*
Apr–Sept, Mon, Wed 11–1; Sat 1–3; Sun 4–6.
Other times by appt.
🅺 *The Rev. Administrator*
Ⓕ 🚆

The foundation stone of the Cathedral at Longford was laid in 1840 and building work was completed in 1893. The Museum contains a wide variety of religious, archaeological and folk life material. Among the exhibits are the 10th-century Crozier of St Mel and a 13th-century French crozier from Limoges. There are also extensive collections of Penal Day Crosses and chalices and other items of church plate, as well as medals, coins and ornaments. The folk life material consists mainly of domestic equipment.

Long Melford

Melford Hall

Long Melford, Sudbury, Suffolk
Mar 29–Sept 28, Wed, Thurs, Sun & Bank
Holiday Mon 2–6
🅺 *The Administrator*
⒠ 🔾 🚆 NT

Built in the mid 16th century, Melford Hall has been little changed externally since Queen Elizabeth was entertained here in 1578. It became the property of the Parker family in 1786 and the 12th Baronet still lives in the house, which is now the property of the National Trust. The contents include 18th and 19th-century furniture, Parker family portraits, including two by Romney, and a number of maritime paintings acquired by the Parkers, who had strong naval connections over a long period. There are also a number of pieces of Chinese porcelain taken in 1762 by Admiral Sir Hyde Parker from the captured Spanish galleon, *Santissima Trinidad*, which was carrying gifts from the Emperor of China.

Beatrix Potter was a frequent visitor to Melford Hall, which has memorabilia relating to her.

Longton

Gladstone Pottery Museum

Uttoxeter Road, Longton, Stoke-on-Trent, Staffordshire ST3 1PQ   ☎ 0782 319232
Mon–Sat 10.30–5.30; Sun & Bank Holiday 2–6. Closed Dec 25.
🎭 *Mrs Edna Bailes*
£ 🍴 💺 🅿

The Museum is set in a Victorian potbank or pottery factory. The buildings consist of four bottle ovens surrounded by workshops and an engine house. The central courtyard is cobbled. The bottle ovens are among the very few still remaining of what was once a characteristic feature of the Potteries.

Gladstone tells the story of the British pottery industry, by means of both displays and workshop demonstrations. Specialised galleries illustrate the history of the industry in Staffordshire, social history, tiles and tile-making, sanitary ware, colour and decoration, and clay as a building material.

Long Wittenham

Pendon Museum of Miniature Landscape and Transport

Long Wittenham, Abingdon, Oxfordshire OX14 4QD   ☎ 086730 7365
Sat, Sun 2–6. Bank Holiday 11–6. Closed Christmas period.
🎭 *Special Showings Organiser*
£ 🍴 💺 🅿

Pendon Museum was established on its present site in 1954. It aims to reproduce, in miniature, aspects of the English countryside as it was in the early 1930s. All the models are made to a high standard of historical accuracy. The imaginary Madder Valley Railway runs through a series of places recalling parts of Hampshire, Dorset, Oxfordshire and Wales. The Dartmoor scene illustrates the railway traffic of 1923–37 on a branch line of the Great Western Railway.

The latest part of the Museum is the Vale Scene, based on the Vale of the White Horse, with model buildings illustrating a cross-section of local building styles and materials over the years.

Loughborough

Great Central Museum

Great Central Station, Loughborough, Leicestershire LE11 1RW   ☎ 0509 230726
Tues–Thurs 10–12, 2–4 (non-Steam Days). Sat, Sun 10–4 (Steam Days). Refreshments Steam Days only.
🎭 *The Curator*
£ 🚲 💺 🅿

The Museum is housed in Loughborough's Great Central Station. It contains a collection of railway relics, with the Great Central and London and North Eastern Railways strongly featured. The display includes the photographs taken by S. W. A. Newton showing the construction of the Great Central Railway in the 1890s and is the most complete photographic record of its kind.

The Museum forms part of an overall project to preserve and operate a main line steam railway.

Old Rectory Museum

Rectory Place, Loughborough, Leicestershire LE11 1UW
Apr–Oct, Sat 10–4
🎭 *Leisure Services Dept, Borough of Charnwood, Macaulay House, 5 Cattle Market, Loughborough LE11 3DH   ☎ 0509 263151*
£ 🅿

The Old Rectory ceased to be used for its original purpose in 1958. At that time it included medieval, 16th and 17th-century elements and had been modified and partly rebuilt in the late 18th and early 19th centuries. During the 1960s everything but the medieval core of the building was demolished and restoration work was carried out on what remained.

A display shows how the Rectory was enlarged and changed over the centuries. There are also exhibits of other archaeological material from the area.

War Memorial and Carillon

Queen's Park, Loughborough, Leicestershire
Good Fri–Sept, daily 2–5.30
🎭 *See Old Rectory Museum*
£ 🚲 💺 🅿

The Museum is housed within the War Memorial building, which contains a carillon of 47 bells. The collection comprises mementoes, both civilian and military, of the First and Second World Wars. The exhibits include weapons, medals, postcards, photographs, and a wide range of military equipment.

Loughrea

Loughrea Cathedral Museum

St Brendan's, Loughrea, Co. Galway, Ireland
☎ 091 41212
Apr–Sept, daily 2–8. Oct–Mar, daily 2–5.
🅺 The Rev. Administrator
Ⓕ 🖉 🚶

The Museum is in the grounds of St Brendan's
Cathedral, which also contains a 15th-century
tower, the gateway to the medieval town. In it
are 13th, 15th and 17th-century Irish carved
wooden figures, 15th to 18th-century
vestments, an impressive series of 15th to 19th-
century chalices. The Cathedral itself is a
good example of the Celtic Revival.

Louth

Louth Museum

4 Broadbank, Louth, Lincolnshire LN11 0EQ
Wed 1–4; Sat 1.30–4; Sun 2.30–4.
    July–Sept 15, also Mon, Tues, Thurs 2–4.
🅺 Mr C. Simpson, Hon. Curator
☎ 0507 603026
Ⓔ ex. children 🚶

The Museum's collections include fossils,
butterflies and moths, household equipment,
craftsmen's tools and 19th-century Louth-made
carpets. There is also a comprehensive display of
paintings by the Louth artist, Bennet Hubbard.

Lower Basildon

Basildon Park

Lower Basildon, Reading, Berkshire RG8 9NR
☎ 07357 3040
Mar 29–Oct, Wed–Sat 2 6, Sun & Bank Holiday
    Mon 12–6. Last admission 5.30.
    Closed Good Fri.
🅺 The Administrator
Ⓔ 🖘 ▆ 🚶 [NT]

Designed by John Carr of York and completed in
1783, Basildon lay in a derelict condition at the
end of the Second World War but was
subsequently restored under the aegis of Lord
and Lady Iliffe. There is an important collection
of 17th and 18th-century paintings. The
furniture is mainly English of the mid 18th
century, with some Continental pieces.

Lower Broadheath

Elgar Birthplace Museum

Crown East Lane, Lower Broadheath, Worcester,
    Hereford and Worcester WR2 6RH
    ☎ 090566 224
Feb 16–Apr & Oct–Jan 15, Thurs–Tues
    1.30–4.30. May–Sept, Thurs–Tues 10.30–6.
🅺 The Curator
Ⓔ 🖘 🚶

The early 19th-century cottage in which Edward
Elgar was born in 1857 now contains a
collection of material illustrating the life and
work of the composer, including manuscripts,
scores, concert programmes, ceremonial robes
and press-cuttings. The photographs range from
family snapshot albums to records of formal and
ceremonial occasions. Elgar's desk has been
arranged by his daughter in the way her mother
prepared it when her father was composing.

Lower Largo

Alexander Selkirk Museum

Cardy House, Lower Largo, Fife KY8 6BJ
    ☎ 0333 320753
June–Aug, Fri–Sun 2–4. Other times by appt.
🅺 Mrs I. Jardine
Ⓕ 🖉 🚶

The Museum represents an attempt by the
descendants of Alexander Selkirk to
acknowledge the contribution that the name of
Alexander Selkirk, better known as Robinson
Crusoe, has made to English literature. The
displays illustrate Selkirk's life and the story of
his exile on Juan Fernandez Island.

Lowestoft

Lowestoft and East Suffolk Maritime Museum

Sparrows Nest Park, Whapload Road, Lowestoft,
    Suffolk NR32 1XG   ☎ 0502 61963
May–Sept, daily 10–5
🅺 A. Hadfield, Hon. Secretary
Ⓔ 🖘 🚶 ♿

The Museum is housed in a former fisherman's
cottage. Its collections of models, paintings and
old photographs illustrate the history of the
local fishing industry. The Cox Collection of
model lifeboats, from the days of sail to the
present time, is also displayed at the Museum.

Lower Largo, the Alexander Selkirk Museum.

Lowestoft Museum

Broad House, Nicholas Everitt Park, Oulton
Broad, Lowestoft, Suffolk NR33 9JR
☎ *0502 511457*
Mar 29–Apr 13 & May 26–Sept 27, Mon–Sat
10.30–1, 2–5; Sun 2–5. Apr 19–May 25,
Sat 2–5; Sun 2–4. Oct, Sat, Sun 2–4.
Ⓜ *Mrs A. M. Turner, Secretary, 11 Cotmer*
Road, Lowestoft NR33 9PN ☎ *0502 65371*
Ⓔ Ⓓ ⬤

The Museum, which is concerned with the
history of the Lowestoft area, occupies a late
17th-century house, with Victorian additions,
set in parkland adjoining Oulton Broad. It
contains a large collection of Lowestoft
porcelain. Other exhibits include fossils, flint
implements, Roman and medieval archaeology
from sites in the district, domestic utensils,
shoes, paintings, prints and photographs of local
scenes and personalities.

Broad House, the home of Lowestoft Museum.

Ludlow

Ludlow Museum

The Buttercross, Ludlow, Shropshire
☎ *0584 3857*
Apr–Sept, Mon–Sat 10.30–1, 2–5.
June–Aug, also Sun 10.30–1, 2–5.
Ⓜ *John Norton, Curator*
Ⓔ *ex. children* ⬤ ⬤ ☐

The Butter Cross, which contains the Museum,
was built between 1743 and 1746. The displays
illustrate the history of the town since its
foundation in the 11th century, together with
its geographical setting. There are exhibits
relating to Ludlow's commercial growth during
Tudor and early Stuart times, to its
development as a fashionable resort during the
18th century, and to its subsequent function as a
small market town. Two period rooms, one a
parlour and the other the Museum Curator's
study as it was c. 1900, reflect life in Ludlow in
the Victorian period. Other Victorian displays
include a model of the Railway Station, built in
1852, demolished in 1968 and replaced by the
present much smaller and meaner platforms and

shelters, and a collection of printed ephemera
about local celebrations for Queen Victoria's
Coronation and Jubilee.

Lusk

The Willie Monks Museum

The Square, Lusk, Co. Dublin, Ireland
☎ *01 437276*
Easter–Sept, Sun & Bank Holiday 2.30–6
Ⓜ *Mr Tom Seaver, 'Moylough', The Commons,*
Lusk ☎ *01 437645*
Ⓔ ⬤

Lusk is 13 miles north of Dublin, just off the
Belfast road. The Museum, which opened in
1982, is in a former Church of Ireland church
and is named after a noted local antiquarian.
Among its exhibits are agricultural tools and
implements, dairying equipment, and a replica
of a thatched cottage, which contains furniture
and household objects which would have been
seen in the district 50 and 100 years ago. Other
displays feature local trades and industries,
handicrafts, bulb-growing, paintings and
historical events which have taken place in the
area.

Luton

Luton Museum and Art Gallery

Wardown Park, Luton, Bedfordshire LU2 7HA
☎ *0582 36941*
Apr–Sept, Mon–Sat 10.30–5; Sun 1.30–6.
Oct–Nov & Feb–Mar, Mon–Sat 10.30–5;
Sun 1.30–5. Dec–Jan, Mon–Sat 10.30–5.
Ⓜ *The Curator*
Ⓕ Ⓓ ⬤

Luton Museum occupies a Victorian mansion in
an extensive park. The displays illustrate the
natural history, archaeology and social history of
the area and include good collections of
costumes and accessories, needlework, lace, toys
and dolls. Luton's celebrated straw hat industry
is specially featured.
There are reconstructions of a lacemaker's
cottage and kitchen, and of a street scene. The
medieval guild registers of both Luton and
Dunstable are preserved at the Museum, which
also has a local history archive and a herbarium
of plants which can be found in Bedfordshire.

The Wernher Collection

Luton Hoo, Luton, Bedfordshire LU1 3TQ
☎ *0582 22955*
Mar 22–Oct 12, Mon, Wed, Thurs, Sat
11–5.45; Sun 2–5.45
Ⓜ *Mrs J. R. Hills, Administrator*
Ⓔ Ⓓ ▆ ⬤ ⬤ ⟦HHA⟧

The Luton Hoo estate is on the southern
outskirt of Luton. Construction of the house,
designed by Robert Adam for the 3rd Earl of
Bute, was begun in 1767, but the building has
since been considerably altered. The house now
displays the Wernher Collection, which was

begun by Sir Julius Wernher in the late
Victorian period and which includes paintings
by Rembrandt, Titian and other celebrated
artists, tapestries, furniture, medieval ivories,
16th-century jewellery, bronzes, maiolica and
English porcelain. There are also portraits and
memorabilia of the Russian Imperial family,
together with jewelled objects by Carl Fabergé,
brought to England by Lady Zia Wernher, who
was herself a member of the Imperial family.

A special exhibition explains the
involvement of the Wernhers with Luton Hoo
and with horse-racing, and tells the story of the
house and the estate.

Lutterworth

Stanford Hall Motorcycle Museum

*Stanford Hall, Lutterworth, Leicestershire
LE17 6DH*   ☎ 0788 860250
*Easter–Sept, Thurs, Sat, Sun 2.30–6. Bank
Holiday Mon & Tues following, 12–6.*
◪ *The Administrator*
Ⓔ ⬚ ⬛ ⬚ ⬚ ⬚ HHA

Stanford Hall is one and a half miles from
Swinford, which is on the B5414, seven and a
half miles north-east of Rugby. Stanford has
been the home of the Cave family, represented
today by Lady Braye, since 1430. The present
Hall was built in the 1690s, when the old Manor
House was pulled down. Open to the public, it
contains fine paintings, antique furniture and
family costumes.

The Museum is in the 1730 stable block. The
collection of motorcycles ranges in date from
1903 to the late 1970s. All the machines are in
running order and many are used for rallies.
There are frequent changes of exhibits, so that
even regular visitors can expect to find
something new.

Lydney

Norchard Steam Centre

*Dean Forest Railway, New Mills, Lydney,
Gloucestershire GL15 4ET*   ☎ 0594 43423
*Museum: Wed, Sat, Sun 11–5 and weekdays
during school summer holidays.
Steam Centre open daily for static viewing.
Enquire locally for Steam Days (usually
May–Sept, Sun; Aug, Wed).*
◪ *The Administrative Director*
Ⓔ *Steam Days only* ⬛ ⬛ ⬚ ⬚ ⬚

The Dean Forest Railway Society was formed in
1970 to buy the four-mile Lydney–Parkend
branch line from British Rail and to operate it as
a steam railway. By 1975 a Steam Centre had
been established at Norchard, adjacent to the
line, and the track is now being developed to
passenger-carrying standard. The station is an
original 1875 Severn and Wye structure from
Drybrook Road, a junction in the Forest of
Dean. The ticket office was formerly at Yatton
on the Bristol to Weston-super-Mare line and
most of the other buildings were at railway

locations in the Gloucester area.

The exhibits include locomotives, freight and
passenger rolling stock, a 45-ton steam crane
and many smaller railway relics, such as signs
and lamps.

Lyme Regis

Dinosaurland

Coombe Street, Lyme Regis, Dorset DT7 3PR
    ☎ 02974 3541
Mar–Sept, daily 10–9. Oct–Feb, Sat, Sun 10–5.
◪ *Peter & Cindy Langham*
Ⓔ ⬛ ⬛

The cliffs and beaches of Lyme Regis are among
the richest sources of fossil remains in Europe.
This new museum, in a former United Reformed
Church, contains a wide range of locally
discovered fossils, from ammonites to
ichthyosaurs, together with specially made
models of prehistoric animals. There is also a
display on the religious history of the building.

The Lyme Regis (Philpot) Museum

Bridge Street, Lyme Regis, Dorset DT7 3QA
    ☎ 02974 3370
*Apr–Oct, Mon–Sat 10.30–1, 2.30–5;
Sun 2.30–5*
◪ *Hon. Secretary*
Ⓔ ⬚ ⬚

Approximately half the Museum collections
relate to geology – the famous local Jurassic
fossils – and half to local history. There is a good
lace collection, an early 18th-century fire
engine, and displays concerning famous visitors
to Lyme, such as James McNeil Whistler. There
are also exhibits relating to the Monmouth
Rebellion, the Siege of 1644 and other
important events in the history of Lyme.

**GWR 5541 tops the bank on the approach
to the Norchard Steam Centre, Lydney.**

M

Macclesfield

Capesthorne Hall

Macclesfield, Cheshire SK11 9JY
☎ *0625 861221/861439*
Apr, Sun 2–5. May and Sept, Wed, Sat, Sun 2–5. Jun–Aug, Tues–Thurs, Sat, Sun 2–5. Open Good Fri & Bank Holiday during season. Gardens open 12–6.
The Administrator
£ HHA

The present house, which replaced an earlier one on the site, was built in 1722 and altered in 1837 and 1867. It is today the home of the Bromley-Davenport family who, together with their ancestors, the Capesthornes and the Wards, have lived here since Domesday. The house contains an important collection of paintings, furniture, sculpture, Greek vases and silver, as well as family archives dating back to the 12th century.

Gawsworth Hall

Gawsworth, nr Macclesfield, Cheshire
☎ *02603 456*
Mar 23–Oct 27, daily 2–6. Christmas week 2–4.30. Open-air theatre June–July.
The Administrator
£

Gawsworth is four miles south-west of Macclesfield, on the A536. The half-timbered Tudor house was at one time the home of Mary Fitton, a maid of honour at the court of Queen Elizabeth I. It is visited as a family home, of exceptional architectural interest, especially for its timber structure, and with a good collection of pictures, including one by Turner.

Paradise Mill, Working Silk Museum

Paradise Mill, Old Park Lane, Macclesfield, Cheshire SK11 6TJ ☎ *0625 618228*
Tues–Sun 2–5. Open Bank Holiday. Closed Good Fri, Dec 25, 26, Jan 1. Parties mornings & evenings by appt.
Education Officer
£

Silk handloom weaving began in Macclesfield in the 1750s. Paradise Mill, a typical Victorian silk mill, houses the last handloom business in the town. It closed in 1981. Twenty-six of the Jacquard looms remain in their original setting and have been restored to allow the skills of a dying craft to be demonstrated. There are supporting exhibitions illustrating working conditions and telling the story of the family firm, Cartwright & Sheldon, which ran the mill. Yarn preparation machinery and a design and card-cutting room have been assembled, and the Manager's Office has been reconstructed as it was in the 1930s.

The Victorian School Room at The Silk Museum, Macclesfield, Christmas 1984.

Trained guide demonstrators are available and special guides conduct parties on the Silk Trail and Town Trails of Macclesfield.

The Silk Museum

Macclesfield Sunday School Heritage Centre, Roe Street, Macclesfield, Cheshire SK11 6XD
☎ *0625 613210*
Tues–Sat 10–5; Sun 2–4. Open Bank Holiday. Closed Good Fri, Dec 25, 26, Jan 1.
See Paradise Mill
F

The Heritage Centre occupies the former Macclesfield Sunday School, built in 1813 by public subscription to bring together many separate Sunday Schools in the town. At the peak of its activity it registered 2,500 pupils.

The Centre now contains two exhibitions. The first is devoted to the history of the building and of the Macclesfield Sunday School. It traces the national development of the Sunday School Movement and explains the part played by the Macclesfield Sunday School in the religious, educational and social life of the town. The second exhibition is concerned with the history of Macclesfield from Norman times to the present day and, in particular, describes the rise and fall of the once important local silk industry within the context of social and industrial change.

West Park Museum

Prestbury Road, Macclesfield, Cheshire
Easter Sat–Sept, Tues–Sun 2–4.30. Oct–Easter, Sat, Sun 2–4.30.
Mrs M. Warhurst, Cheshire Museums, 162 London Road, Northwich, Cheshire CW9 8AB ☎ *0606 41331*
F

West Park is a purpose-built museum, opened in 1898. The interior is modelled on a gallery at the Whitworth Art Gallery, Manchester, and includes a frieze of plaster casts of the Elgin Marbles. The Museum was founded by the Brocklehurst family, 'for the education and refinement and pleasure of the people for all time to come'. Marianne Brocklehurst, one of the Museum's principal founders, went on several tours of Egypt and many of the objects she brought back are exhibited in the Museum.

Members of the family were involved in many aspects of Macclesfield life and the collections they gave to the Museum reflect this – objects relating to the silk industry and works by local artists, including C. F. Tunnicliffe. More recent gifts have strengthened the displays of local history and topography.

Macroom

Macroom Museum

Castle Street, Macroom, Co. Cork, Ireland
☎ 026 41272
Mon–Fri 11–1, 2–5
🅺 *The Curator*
🄴 🖎 ☛

The Museum's collections illustrate life in the Macroom area during approximately the past 150 years. The exhibits include domestic equipment, craftsmen's tools, farm implements, documents and old photographs.

Maidenhead

Courage Shire Horse Centre

Cherry Garden Lane, Maidenhead Thicket, Maidenhead, Berkshire SL6 3QD
☎ 062882 3917
Mar–Oct, daily 11–4.
🅺 *Mr B. S. Bush, Manager*
🄴 🍴 🚋 ♿ ☛ ⬤

The Centre is just off the A4, west of its junction with the A423. It houses the renowned Shire horses belonging to Courage's, the brewing firm, together with a collection of harness. There is a display of the rosettes and trophies won by Courage horses over the years. On two or three days each week visitors are also able to watch a farrier shoeing the horses.

Brewer's dray at the Courage Shire Horse Centre, Maidenhead.

Henry Reitlinger Bequest

Oldfield, Guards Club Road, Maidenhead, Berkshire SL6 8DN ☎ 0628 21818
Apr–Sept, Tues–Thurs 10–12.30, 2.15–4.30.
Also 1st Sun in each month, 2.30–4.30.
🅺 *Mrs M. Cocke, Resident Trustee*
🄵 ☛

Oldfield, a riverside house built in 1906, is south of Maidenhead Bridge. The art collections it contains were formed by Captain H. S. Reitlinger. They include Chinese porcelain, Dresden ware, Chelsea figures, Islamic pottery, netsuke and German and Dutch glass paintings. There are displays of maiolica and a collection of paintings, prints and engravings, including works by Goltzius, whose work influenced Rembrandt, Turner and Constable.

One room in the house is devoted to exhibits of local archaeology and history, provided and arranged by the Maidenhead Archaeological and Historical Society.

Maidstone

The Dog Collar Museum

Leeds Castle, Maidstone, Kent ME17 1PL
☎ 0622 65400
Apr–Oct, daily 11–5. Nov–Mar, Sat, Sun 12–4.
🅺 *Sales and Reservations Officer*
🄴 🖎 ☛ ♿

The Museum is housed in part of the Edward I gatehouse of Leeds Castle. Its collection of dog collars, spanning four centuries, is the finest in the world. The collars are mainly European and some of the more recent ones have remarkable histories. There are examples of iron, brass, silver and leather collars, many of them being splendidly decorated. The spiked collars designed for dogs involved in hunting, bull-baiting and bear-baiting are of particularly formidable appearance.

Replicas have been made of some of the collars, with Braille inscriptions, in order that they can be handled and appreciated by blind people.

Maidstone Museum and Art Gallery

St Faith's Street, Maidstone, Kent ME14 1LH
☎ 0622 54497/56405
Mon–Sat 10–5.30. Closed Bank Holiday.
🅺 *Education Officer*
🄵 🖎

The central part of what is now the Museum building dates from 1562, with an early 16th-century long gallery behind. The Great Hall and the withdrawing room above are panelled, the former retaining its screen, the latter having a fine contemporary fireplace and screen.

The collections cover the archaeology, natural history and social history of Kent, the fine and applied arts, both European and

Oriental, costume, weapons and armour, ethnography, photography and musical instruments. Of particular interest are jewellery and glass from pagan Anglo-Saxon cemeteries, ethnographical material from the Pacific, especially Melanesia, North-West America and Alaska, and the extensive collections of Japanese prints, pottery, armour, swords, furniture and lacquer.

There is a large collection of watercolours by William Alexander, mainly of Chinese subjects, and miniatures by William Hazlitt. A large gallery is devoted to a comprehensive collection of the birds of Kent. The costume collection specialises in the 20th century and includes the extensive wardrobe of Doreen Lady Brabourne, dating from 1930 to 1970.

Museum of the Queen's Own Royal West Kent Regiment

Maidstone Museum and Art Gallery, St Faith's Street, Maidstone, Kent ME14 1LH
☎ *0622 54497/56405*
Mon–Sat 10–5.30. Closed Bank Holiday.
🕱 *Education Officer*
Ⓕ ⬭

The Museum now forms part of Maidstone Museum. Its collections illustrate the history of the 50th and 97th Regiments of Foot and of the West Kent Militia. There are displays of uniforms, weapons, medals, pictures and campaign relics relating to the Regiment.

The Tyrwhitt-Drake Museum of Carriages

Mill Street, Maidstone, Kent ME15 6YE
Apr–Sept, Mon–Sat 10–1, 2–5; Sun 2–5;
Bank Holiday 11–5
🕱 *See Maidstone Museum*
Ⓔ ⬭ ⬤

The collection, formed by Sir Garrard Tyrwhitt-Drake, 12 times Mayor of Maidstone, is housed in the old stables of the Archbishop's Palace. The stables are 50 yards long and were built c. 1390 to provide accommodation for the numerous carts, horses and retainers required by the Archbishops of Canterbury on their journeys between Canterbury and Lambeth.

The 50 vehicles in the Collection date from 1675, but most of them were made during the 19th century. All are in their original, unrestored condition. There are also sedan chairs, sleighs and handcarts. Exhibits of particular interest include a Dress Landau built by Hooper for Queen Victoria c. 1870, George III's travelling chariot of c. 1780, and a hansom cab owned by Sir H. M. Stanley. The Museum also has the carriage made in 1840 for the Earl of Moray to use on his honeymoon. The marriage did not take place and the carriage is consequently in mint condition.

Sir Garrard Tyrwhitt-Drake was a horse enthusiast and drove his own gig for local transport until 1926. Brought up in the days when British carriages, horses and general equipment were the finest in the world, he was afraid that the younger generation would grow up knowing nothing of this form of transport. 'In a very few years,' he said, 'the only examples in existence will be in a museum such as this.'

Malahide

Malahide Castle

Malahide, Co. Dublin, Ireland
☎ *01 452655/542371*
Apr–Oct, Mon–Fri 10–5; Sat 11–6, Sun &
Bank Holiday 2–6. Nov–Mar, Mon–Fri 10–5;
Sat, Sun & Bank Holiday 2–5. Closed Dec 25.
🕱 *The Administrator*
Ⓔ ⬤ ⬛ ⬤

The Talbot family lived at Malahide Castle for 791 years, from 1185 to 1976. The oldest part of the present building dates from the 14th century. When the last Lord Talbot de Malahide died, the property was bought by Dublin County Council. It now contains 16th to 19th-century Irish furniture, early 18th-century painted leather wall hangings and a collection of portraits, on loan from the National Gallery in Dublin. These include 31 portraits of members of the Talbot family. To the portraits the National Gallery has added battle, sporting and other pictures, to create a panorama of Irish life over the last few centuries.

Maldon

Maldon Museum

71 High Street, Maldon, Essex
Sat 10.30–1, 2–5.30
🕱 *Mrs C. Backus, Chairman, 18 Market Hill,*
Maldon　　　　☎ *0621 52493*
Ⓕ ⬭ ⬤ ☐

Maldon Museum is chiefly concerned with the natural and local history of the district. The displays take the form of temporary exhibitions, of which there are, on average, five a year.

'Whistler' mask used by the North American Kwakuitl Indians. Maidstone Museum and Art Gallery.

Malmesbury

Athelstan Museum

Town Hall, Cross Hayes, Malmesbury, Wiltshire
☎ 06662 2143
Apr–Sept, Tues–Sat 10.30–12.30, 1–3.
    Oct–Mar, Wed, Fri, Sat 1–3.
Ⓧ *The Curator*
Ⓕ ✑ ✎

Malmesbury is the oldest borough in England.
Its Museum, named after the Saxon king whose
remains are buried near the Abbey, is in the
Town Hall. The collection illustrates the
archaeology and history of the area. There are
special displays relating to Malmesbury lace, the
Malmesbury branch railway, costumes, and a
local engineering company. Other exhibits
include the town's 18th-century hand-drawn
fire-engine, early bicycles, a William II penny,
minted in the town, and an 18th-century
drawing by Thomas Girtin of the Malmesbury
Cross.

Malton

Castle Howard Costume Galleries

Castle Howard, Malton, York, North Yorkshire
    YO6 7DA   ☎ 065384 333
Mar 25–Oct, daily 11–5 (last admission 4.30).
    Grounds & gardens, 10–6.30.
Ⓧ *The Curator*
Ⓔ ♦ ▣ ✎ ♿ ☐

Castle Howard is 6 miles south-west of Malton,
off the A64. It has the unusual distinction of
having been open to the public since it was
built. The later Stable Court, by John Carr of
York, contains the largest private collection of
period costume in Britain. Each year a different
selection is displayed, in settings which reflect
the atmosphere of the period. The collection
contains domestic, occupational, ceremonial,
ecclesiastical, theatrical and children's items.

Malton Museum

Town Hall, Market Place, Malton, North
    Yorkshire YO17 0LT   ☎ 0653 5136
May–Sept, Mon–Sat 10–4; Sun 2–4. Oct–Apr,
    Sat 1–3. Closed Dec. Parties by appt.
Ⓧ *Mrs P. Wiggle*   ☎ 0653 2610
Ⓔ ✑ ✎

The Museum is in Malton's 18th-century Butter
Market and original Town Hall. It has
archaeological collections from Malton, Norton
and the surrounding Ryedale area, spanning the
period from the earliest settlers, c. 8000 B.C. to
medieval times. The Roman material is the
most comprehensive, but prehistoric cultures
are also well represented. The displays, set in
chronological order, aim at telling the story of
man's activities in the area in an imaginative
way, with objects shown alongside photographs
and models.

Malvern

Malvern Museum

Abbey Gateway, Abbey Road, Malvern, Hereford
    and Worcester   ☎ 06845 67811
Easter–Oct, Mon–Sat 10.30–5; Sun 2–4.
    Check locally.
Ⓧ *Mrs Baynham, Administrative Curator*
Ⓔ ✑

The Museum is housed in one of the two
surviving buildings of Malvern's Benedictine
monastery, founded in 1085, the other being
the Priory Church. Parts of the Gatehouse date
from the late 15th century, since when it has
been enlarged and restored several times.
    The collections reflect the history of the town
from medieval times to the present day. Of
particular interest are exhibits relating to the
monastery, the Malvern water cure, the
Malvern Festival, and the development of radar
at the Royal Signals and Radar Establishment.

Manchester

Athenaeum Gallery

81 Princess Street, Manchester M1 4HR
    ☎ 061 236 9422
Mon–Sat 10–6; Sun 2–6 during exhibitions.
    Closed for short periods between exhibitions
    and Good Fri, Dec 25, 26, Jan 1.
Ⓧ *Education Service*
Ⓕ ✑ ✎ ☐

The Gallery, which has recently been enlarged
and modernised, accommodates temporary
exhibitions, both from Manchester City Art
Gallery's permanent collection and from outside
sources. The emphasis is on works by
contemporary artists.

Fletcher Moss Art Gallery

Stenner Lane, Didsbury, Manchester, Greater
    Manchester M20 8AU   ☎ 061 445 1109
Apr–Sept, Wed–Mon 10–6; Sun 2–6
Ⓧ *See Athenaeum Gallery*
Ⓕ ✑ ✎

The building now occupied by the Art Gallery
was formerly known as the Old Parsonage. Most
of it dates from c. 1800, but parts are much
earlier. It was renamed in honour of Alderman

Malahide Castle, Co. Dublin

Fletcher Moss, a keen antiquarian and local historian, who bequeathed it, together with the gardens and surrounding parkland, to the City of Manchester in 1919. It now contains 17th to 19th-century paintings, drawings, prints, maps and views relating to Manchester and the surrounding region. Among the artists represented are Thomas Stringer of Knutsford, Arthur Devis, Joseph Parry, Henry Liverseege, Adolphe Valette and L. S. Lowry. There is also a good collection of locally made ceramics, glass and furniture.

Fletcher Moss wanted the house and its contents to remain intact as far as possible to show 'what a comfortable house of the olden times was like', but it became difficult to maintain and many features, such as the fireplaces and stained glass, were removed. Attempts are now being made to restore something of its original character, while keeping it as a museum.

Gallery of English Costume

Platt Hall, Platt Fields, Rusholme, Manchester
*   M14 5LL   ☎ 061 224 5217*
Mon, Wed–Sat 10–6; Sun 2–6. Nov–Feb closes 4.
🅺 *The Keeper*
Ⓕ ✐ ♿

Platt Hall is two miles south of Manchester. It was built in 1762–4 as the home of a textile manufacturer and is surrounded by a large park. The Gallery was opened in 1947, to house the collection formed by Dr C. Willett Cunnington, and has since been developed into one of the largest costume museums in Britain, reflecting dress of the 17th to 20th centuries. From the beginning, the aim has been to include items which illustrate the clothing of society as a whole. Millworkers' shawls are considered as important as the most expensive ballgowns. There is a large collection of accessories and more than 150 dolls, selected for the information they provide about the way in which costume was worn at different periods.

The Gallery offers excellent research facilities. Its library of some 180,000 items contains not only modern costume books, but also rare works from the 18th and 19th centuries, such as magazines and etiquette books, as well as a large number of fashion plates and photographs.

Greater Manchester Museum of Science and Industry

Liverpool Road Station, Liverpool Road,
*   Castlefield, Manchester M3 4JP*
*   ☎ 061 832 2244*
Daily 10–5 (last admission 4.30).
*   Closed Dec 23–25.*
🅺 *Graham Breeds, Education Service*
Ⓕ 🍴 🖤 ✐ ♿

The Museum occupies five historic buildings – the world's oldest passenger railway station, listed Grade I; the oldest railway warehouse in the world, listed Grade II; a railway freight shed of the 1850s; a fireproof warehouse of c. 1880; and an iron-framed Victorian market-hall. The aim of the Museum is to portray the role played by Greater Manchester in the development of science and industry and to present the story of Greater Manchester itself, the world's first industrial conurbation. The collections reflect these themes.

A strong emphasis is placed on restoring exhibits to fully operating condition and on regularly demonstrating them. The Power Hall contains an extensive display of mill engines, all demonstrated with steam every afternoon. Internal combustion engines, road vehicles and railway locomotives also illustrate the importance of Manchester in the production of power plant. The Warehouse Exhibition presents exhibits of textile machinery, printing, papermaking and computers, in all of which Manchester has been a pioneer.

The Electricity Gallery tells the story of the generation, distribution and use of electricity from its beginnings to the present day. There is also a special display, 'Microscopes in Manchester', and an exhibition and audio-visual presentation on the Liverpool and Manchester Railway. The Air and Space Gallery shows the history of manned flight and space exploration, and contains historic aircraft.

Visitors can watch restoration work in progress in the large Museum workshop.

Greater Manchester Police Museum

Newton Street, Manchester M1 1ES
*   ☎ 061 855 3290*
Mon–Fri, by appt only. Closed public holidays.
🅺 *The Curator*
Ⓕ ✐

The Museum building is in a former police station, built in 1879. Visitors can see the original Charge Office and cells. The displays of uniforms, equipment and photographs show the development of policing in Manchester from 1819 to the present day. There are also special exhibits on forging and counterfeiting.

Design commissioned by the Manchester Cotton Board from the House of Lachasse, 1953. Manchester, Gallery of English Costume.

Heaton Hall

Heaton Park, Manchester M25 5SW
☎ 061 773 1231
Apr–Sept, Mon, Wed–Sat 10–6; Sun 2–6
⚑ *See Athenaeum Gallery*
Ⓕ 🌳 🍴 🚶

Heaton Hall was rebuilt during the 1770s for Sir
Thomas Egerton, who later became the Earl of
Wilton. The architects were James and Samuel
Wyatt. The family sold the property to
Manchester Corporation, together with its 600
acres of parkland. It has recently been restored.
Particularly attractive features include the
Music Room, which has an 18th-century organ
by Samuel Green, and the Cupola Room, with
painted decorations by Biagio Rebecca.
The house contains fine 18th-century
furniture and 17th to 19th-century paintings,
including works by Richard Wilson, Romney,
Reynolds, Joseph Wright of Derby, Thomas
Barker of Bath, and Sir Henry Raeburn.

Holden Gallery

Faculty of Art and Design, Manchester Polytechnic,
Grosvenor Building, All Saints, Manchester
M15 6BR ☎ 061 228 6171 extn 2277
Mon–Fri 10–4 during term-time
⚑ *Mr M. Mason*
Ⓕ 🚶

The Gallery's main collections are of ceramics,
metalwork and glass, with a particular emphasis
on the Arts and Crafts Movement. Among the
particularly notable exhibits are items of Tiffany
glass, Royal Lancastrian pottery, examples of
tiles by De Morgan and copperware by Benson.

Manchester City Art Gallery

Mosley Street, Manchester, Greater Manchester
M2 3JL ☎ 061 236 9422
Mon–Sat 10–6; Sun 2–6. Closed Good Fri,
Dec 25, 26, Jan 1.
⚑ *See Athenaeum Gallery*
Ⓕ 🍴 🚶

The Gallery, designed by Charles Barry, was
opened in 1823. It has recently been
redecorated and stencilled in neo-classical and
Victorian styles. The entrance hall contains
casts of the Parthenon frieze. The important
collections of British and European paintings,
drawings and prints include works by Stubbs,
Gainsborough, Turner, Duccio and Canaletto.
The Gallery has a celebrated collection of Pre-
Raphaelite and High Victorian paintings. The
decorative arts are represented by collections of
ceramics, glass, silver and furniture.

Manchester Jewish Museum

190 Cheetham Hill Road, Manchester M8 8LW
☎ 061 834 9879
Mon–Thurs 10.30–4; Sun 10.30–5.
Closed Dec 25, 26, Jan 1 & Jewish Holidays.
⚑ *Mrs Sandra Lord, Education Officer*
Ⓔ 🍴 🚶 ☐

The Museum is in a former Spanish and
Portuguese synagogue, built in 1873–4. The
central part of the synagogue has been retained

intact, to provide an introduction to Jewish
religious customs. The former succah provides
a location for temporary exhibitions, which
change at approximately three-monthly
intervals.
The exhibition in the former Ladies Gallery
shows the evolution of Manchester Jewry
against the background of major developments
in Anglo-Jewish history. It re-creates the
experience of the Jewish community by means
of objects, photographs and tape-recorded
interviews. The display is enhanced by detailed
reconstructions of the home life, work, worship
and leisure of Jews drawn to Manchester from
every part of the world.

The Manchester Museum

The University, Oxford Road, Manchester,
M13 9PL ☎ 061 275 2634
Mon–Sat 10–5. Closed Good Fri, May Day Bank
Holiday, Dec 25, 26, Jan 1.
⚑ *Education Department* ☎ 061 273 2892
Ⓕ 🍴 🍴 🚶

The Museum is part of the University of
Manchester. Most of the building it occupies
was designed by Alfred J. Waterhouse and dates
from 1888. There are important collections
within the fields of archaeology, Egyptology,
botany, entomology, ethnology, geology,
numismatics, zoology and archery. The large
gallery of British fossils includes dinosaur
remains.
There are spectacular displays of Egyptian
mummies and Egyptian antiquities, excavated
by Sir William Flinders Petrie. The Japanese
exhibits and the material relating to archery are
noteworthy features of the Museum.

The Cupola Room at Heaton Hall,
Manchester, the work of Biagio Rebecca
(1735–1808).

Museum of Transport, Greater Manchester

Boyle Street, Cheetham, Manchester M8 8UL
☎ 061 205 2122
Apr–Oct, Wed, Sat, Sun & Bank Holiday 10–5
▓ Education Officer
☐ ♠ ⚓ ⛫ □

The Museum, in one of Manchester's original
bus garages, is one mile north of the city centre,
close to the junction of the A665 and A6010. It
houses one of the largest collections of buses and
coaches in Britain. In addition to over 60
vehicles formerly in service in the Greater
Manchester area, there are displays of tickets
and ticket-issuing machines, uniforms, engines,
gearboxes, maps, plans and photographs. The
aim is to maintain the vehicles in a roadworthy
condition and visitors are able to watch
restoration work in progress.

The displays are changed regularly and
sometimes include material from outside the
Museum's collections.

Whitworth Art Gallery

The University, Oxford Road, Manchester
M15 6ER   ☎ 061 273 4865
Mon–Wed, Fri, Sat 10–5; Sat 10–5; Thurs 10–9.
Closed Christmas.
▓ Gallery Services Officer
☐ ♠ ⛫ ⚓ ⛫

The Gallery, opened in 1890, resulted from a
legacy by the Manchester engineer and
machine-tool manufacturer, Sir Joseph
Whitworth. It now contains one of the world's
greatest collections of English watercolours,
as well as the finest collection of European
drawings, prints and engravings in the North of
England. There are important sections devoted
to British, European and Oriental textiles,
historic wallpapers, Pre-Raphaelite drawings
and 20th-century British art.

Wythenshawe Hall

Wythenshawe Park, Northenden, Manchester
M23 0AB   ☎ 061 998 2331
Check locally for opening times
▓ See Athenaeum Gallery
☐ ⚲ ⛫ ♠

The Hall was built c. 1540 by Robert Tatton,
to replace an earlier building on the site. It was
extended and improved by the Tatton family
during the 17th and 18th centuries and again
during the 19th. In 1926 it was given to the City
of Manchester, which carried out an extensive
programme of restoration and reconstruction.
Visitors now see it as a country house, furnished
to reflect the tastes of the Tatton family, who
lived at the Hall for more than 350 years. The
central portion, arranged as a museum, contains
collections of paintings, especially of the 17th
century, Royal Lancastrian pottery, weapons
and armour. There are also exhibitions
illustrating the history of the area.

Print by Ikkaisai Yoshitoshi. Manchester,
Whitworth Art Gallery.

Mansfield

Mansfield Museum and Art Gallery

Leeming Street, Mansfield, Nottinghamshire
NG18 1NB   ☎ 0623 646604
Mon–Fri 10–5; Sat 10–1, 2–5.
Closed Bank Holiday.
▓ Miss A. Griffin, Administrative Assistant
☐ ⚲ ♠ ⛫ □

The principal displays in the Museum are of fine
and applied art, natural history and local
history. The Buxton Gallery contains
watercolours of old Mansfield, and porcelain
and pottery with local connections. The
Whitaker Gallery is devoted to the history and
ecology of Mansfield and the surrounding area,
including Sherwood Forest and the Dukeries.
Temporary exhibitions occupy two further
galleries.

Marazion

St Michael's Mount

Marazion, nr Penzance, Cornwall TR17 0HT
☎ 0736 710507
Mar 28–May, Mon, Tues, Wed, Fri (including
Good Fri) 10.30–5.45. Last admission 4.45.
June–Oct, Mon–Fri 10.30–5.45. No guided
tours. Nov–Mar 26, Mon, Wed, Fri by guided
tour only, leaving at 11, 12, 2 & 3, weather
& tide permitting.
▓ Mr O. Bartle, Manor Office, Marazion
☐ ♠ ⛫ [NT]

St Michael's Mount is approached on foot over
the causeway at low tide or, during the summer
months only, by ferry at high tide. Edward the

Confessor established a monastery here, dependent on the Benedictine Abbey of Mont-Saint-Michel in Normandy. After 1425, it became a garrisoned fortress and eventually, in 1660, it passed into the possession of the St Aubyn family, who gave it to the National Trust in 1954 and still live in it.

Considerable additions and alterations have been made over the centuries, especially in the Victorian period. There are Gothic Chippendale chairs in the Drawing Room, watercolours of Mont-Saint-Michel in the Library and a collection of sporting weapons in the Armoury.

Margam

Margam Abbey and Stones Museum

Margam, Port Talbot, West Glamorgan SA13 2AP   ☎ *0656 742618*
Easter–Sept, Mon–Sat 10.30–5.30. Other times by appt.
◨ *The Vicar, Margam Vicarage, Bertha Road, Margam, Port Talbot SA13 2AP*
☎ *0639 891067*
Ⓔ *Museum only* ● 💺 ✈ ♿

The ruins of the Cistercian Abbey, the nave of which now serves as the parish church, and the 19th-century castle are the central features of a 1,000-acre Country Park, run by West Glamorgan County Council. An exhibition in the Castle's former squash court portrays the long history of the estate from Iron Age times onwards, and just outside the church, which has windows by William Morris, is the Stones Museum. The Stones are Roman and Early Christian monuments. They have been brought together from several sites in the district and range in date from the 4th to the 11th centuries. There are also a number of medieval grave-slabs.

Margate

Tudor House Museum

King Street, Margate, Kent CT9 1XZ
Mid May–mid Sept, Mon–Sat 10–12.30, 2–4.30
◨ *Mr C. Wilson, Thanet District Council, PO Box 9, Margate CT9 1XZ*
☎ *0843 225511 extn 317*
Ⓔ 🖉 ✈

The timber-framed Tudor House, which dates from the early 16th century, is the oldest domestic building in Margate. Constructed apparently as a yeoman's house, it was converted into three cottages *c.* 1815. During the 1950s it was restored as nearly as possible to its original condition and opened as a museum of local and domestic history. The heavily moulded beams, panelling, decorated plasterwork and elaborate projecting windows make it a most unlikely building to have existed in the little 16th-century fishing hamlet of Margate, and its history remains a puzzle.

Market Harborough

Langton Hall

West Langton, nr Market Harborough, Leicestershire   ☎ *084884 240*
Good Fri–Sept, Thurs, Sat, Sun & Bank Holiday Mon & Tues 2–5
◨ *Mr G. R. Spencer*
Ⓔ ● 💺 ✈ [HHA]

The Hall contains some Tudor work, but the main part of the house was built in the 18th and early 19th centuries, with extensions added during the Edwardian period. It contains an important collection of classical Chinese furniture, acquired in China by Charles Chandler, great-grandfather of the present owner, together with Biedermeier pieces commissioned by Mr Spencer's grandmother in the 1920s. There is also French furniture in the ballroom and in one of the bedrooms. The dining room walls are covered with Venetian lace.

The Harborough Museum

Council Offices, Adam and Eve Street, Market Harborough, Leicestershire LE16 7AG
☎ *0858 32468*
Mon–Sat 10–4.30; Sun 2–5.
Closed Good Fri, Dec 25, 26.
◨ *Keeper of Education, Leicestershire Museums, 96 New Walk, Leicester LE1 6TD*
☎ *0533 554100*
Ⓕ ● ✈

The collection and displays relate to Market Harborough itself and to the surrounding area within a 10-mile radius, which includes over 50 parishes. The permanent exhibition illustrates particular themes – the market town; shops and shopkeepers; canals and railways; the industrialised town. The largest section relates to the history and products of R. and W. H. Symington, in whose former factory the Museum is housed, and includes a changing section on the foundation garments made by this important local manufacturer. Elsewhere, there are displays on agriculture, the Battle of Naseby, the Roman town of Meabourne, and other themes.

Rockingham Castle

Market Harborough, Leicestershire LE16 8TH
☎ *0536 770240*
Easter Sun–Sept, Thurs, Sun, Bank Holiday Mon & Tues following 2–6. Aug, also Tues 2–6. Other times by appt.
◨ *The Secretary*
Ⓔ ● 💺 ✈ ♿

The Castle was built by William the Conqueror, on the site of an earlier fortification, and was used as a royal fortress until 1530, when Henry VIII granted it to Edward Watson, whose descendants still live here. There is a collection of 17th-century armour in the Tudor Great Hall, and 17th to 20th-century pictures in the Long Gallery, where Charles Dickens produced and acted in plays. Special exhibitions arranged in recent years have included a naval exhibition containing the memorabilia and trophies of many generations of sailors who had connections with Rockingham, and 'Rockingham Castle and the Civil War', tracing the role played by Rockingham and neighbouring houses during this period.

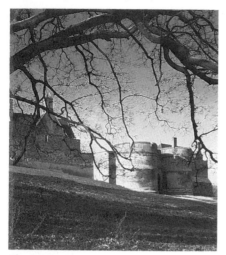

The massive Norman gatehouse of Rockingham Castle, Market Harborough.

Marldon

Compton Castle
Marldon, Paignton, Devon TQ3 1TA
☎ 08047 2112
Mar–Oct, Mon, Wed, Thurs 10–12.15, 2–5.
   Other times by appt.
❦ Mr and Mrs G. E. Gilbert, Administrators
£ ↩ NT

Compton Castle is one mile north of Marldon and four miles west of Torquay. It dates mainly from the 14th to 16th centuries and, with a 19th-century interruption, has been the home of the Gilbert family for 600 years. In the 16th century, the Gilbert brothers, John, Humphrey and Adrian, were closely associated with Elizabethan naval defence, exploration and colonial settlement in America.

By 1800 the Castle was in a ruinous condition. The Gilberts sold it and bought it back in 1930 in order to restore and rebuild it. It was given to the National Trust in 1951, but the Gilberts continued to live here. There is an exhibition in the Great Hall relating to the Gilbert family. The 16th-century kitchens can also be visited.

Marshfield

Castle Farm Museum
Marshfield, nr Chippenham, Wiltshire SN14 8BU
Mid June–mid Sept, Wed, Sat, Sun 2–6
❦ Mr R. W. Knight
£ ↩ ☕ ↩

Castle Farm is a working farm. The present farmhouse and outbuildings date from the late 18th century, but there is an earlier farmhouse, or longhouse, a rare and exceptionally complete example of its type, surviving from the second half of the 16th century. A number of the buildings at Castle Farm – the Nag Stable, the Shepherd's House, the Coach House, the Back Kitchen, with the Granary over it, and the Dairy – are open to the public. They contain a wide range of tools, implements and equipment used in the many crafts associated with agriculture and dairying. In the kitchen, visitors can see the original stone rubbing sink, bread oven, beer copper and wash boiler.

The Shepherd's House was in use until 1920 and in it are the Shepherd's stove, smocks and tools.

Maryport

Maritime Museum
1 Senhouse Street, Shipping Brow, Maryport,
   Cumbria CA15 6AB   ☎ 0900 813738
May–Oct, Mon–Sat 10–1, 2–5; Sun 2–5.
   Nov–Apr, Mon, Tues, Thurs–Sat 10–12,
   2–4.
❦ Miss Janet Baker, Curator, Helena Thompson
   Museum, Park End Road, Workington,
   Cumbria CA14 4DE   ☎ 0900 62598
F ↩

The Museum is in the former Queen's Head inn, which houses collections illustrating the maritime history of Maryport. Among the Museum's special features are exhibits devoted to Fletcher Christian and to Thomas Henry Ismay, founder of the White Star Line.

Matlock

Caudwell's Mill
Rowsley, Matlock, Derbyshire DE4 2EB
   ☎ 0629 734374
July–Aug, Sun 10–5. Also open other summer Sun
   & Bank Holiday Mon – check locally.
❦ The Manager
£ ♦ ☕ ↩

The Mill is on the A6, between Matlock and Bakewell. It is a roller flour-mill driven by a water-turbine, with machinery dating mainly from the early years of the present century. A separate animal-feed mill is driven by another turbine. The mill, preserved as it was when commercial operation ceased in 1978, represents the era when science took over from the craft tradition based on waterwheels and stones. Caudwell's Mill is a rare survival of its period, because it is in a village, whereas most roller mills were at the ports and were too large for preservation.

Milling still takes place here from time to time and wholemeal flour is sold to local bakers, as well as directly to the public.

Matlock Bath

Matlock Bath Model Railway Museum

*Royal Bank Buildings, Temple Road, Matlock
Bath, Matlock, Derbyshire DE4 3PG*
☎ 0629 3993
Open one day each month: please check locally
Mrs J. T. Statham, Slater's Plastikard Ltd,
*Royal Bank Buildings, Temple Road, Matlock
Bath*
£ ▪ ⇔ &

The Museum is on the A6 Derby to Buxton
road, one mile from Matlock. It contains one of
the most remarkable O-gauge layouts in the
country, showing by means of a diorama 54 feet
long the former station and quarry sidings at
Millers Dale in the heart of the Derbyshire Peak
District. The model locomotives, which run
through the station in automatic sequence,
represent LMS designs of the early part of the
present century.

The Station at the Matlock Bath Model
Railway Museum.

Peak District Mining Museum

*The Pavilion, Matlock Bath, Matlock, Derbyshire
DE4 3PS* ☎ 0629 3834
*Mid Feb–mid Nov, daily 11–4. Mid Nov–mid Feb,
Sat, Sun 11–4. Opening hours may be extended
during the summer months: please check locally.*
The Manager
£ ▪ ⇔

Matlock Bath, one mile south of Matlock on the
A6, is a former spa. The Museum is in the Pump
Room, built in 1907, where visitors used to take
the waters. Its displays illustrate the history of
the extensive lead-mining industry of the Peak
District, which was carried on from Roman
times until the present century. Among the
exhibits are geological specimens, minerals,
tools, the unique laws which governed the
organisation of the industry, and models,
replicas, photographs and diagrams explaining
the developing technology. Richard
Trevithick's giant water pressure engine is the
centrepiece of the Museum.

Visitors are encouraged to handle the
exhibits, to pump water with the rag-and-chain
hand-pump, and to try for themselves the
reconstructions of climbing-shafts and tunnels,
in order to gain a first-hand impression of the
miners' working conditions.

Mauchline

Burns House Museum

4 Castle Street, Mauchline, Ayrshire
☎ 0290 50045
*Easter–Sept, Mon–Sat 11–12.30, 1.30–5.30.
Other times by appt.*
The Secretary
£ ⊘ ⇔

Externally, 4 Castle Street is a typical 18th-
century Scottish village house. Internally, it has
been redesigned with an open two-storey
gallery. There is a display of Burns memorabilia
connected with his stay in the house and with
his four years in Mauchline. There is also a large
exhibit of Mauchline boxware and a room
devoted to the sport of curling. The curling
stones are made in the village, one of only two
production centres in the world.

Maybole

Culzean Castle

Maybole, Ayrshire KA19 8LE ☎ 06556 274
*Easter–Sept, daily 10–6. Oct, daily 12–5.
Country Park: all year round, 9–sunset.*
Michael Tebbutt, Administrator
£ ▪ ⊟ ⇔ & NTS

Culzean Castle, completed in 1792, is Robert
Adam's finest country house. It has recently
been restored by the National Trust for Scotland
and contains Chippendale and Sheraton
furniture. The Visitor Centre, in converted
18th-century farm buildings, has displays on the
development of the estate and on the earlier
agricultural and social history of the area. There
is also a three-dimensional exhibit on the
geology and scenery of the area and a
reproduction of Adam's London studio in the
Adelphi.

Maynooth

The College Museum

*St Patrick's College, Maynooth, Co. Kildare,
Ireland* ☎ 01 285222
Sun 3–6 (summer only). Weekdays by appt.
The Rev. Dr Casey, Curator
F ⊘ ⇔

The Museum has two main collections,
ecclesiastical and scientific. The ecclesiastical
section contains liturgical vestments, books,
ornaments and documents. There are also
triptychs, penal crosses, medals, rosaries,
missals and breviaries. The exhibits in the
scientific section include early 19th-century

instruments made by the Rev. Dr Nicholas Callan (d. 1864), including his induction coils, batteries, electric motors and Repeater. Among the other items displayed are part of the 1898 Marconi wireless apparatus, microscopes, sextants, spectrometers, early galvanometers, theodolites, telephones, morse apparatus, static electricity machines and sirens.

Meigle

Meigle Museum

Dundee Road, Meigle, Perthshire PH12 8RN
☎ 08284 307
Mar 24–Sept, Mon–Sat 9.30–7. Oct–Mar 23, Mon–Sat 9.30–4. Closed Dec 25, 26, Jan 1, 2.
🏛 *Historic Buildings & Monuments, Edinburgh*
☎ 031 5568 400
£ ✏ ➡ 🏛

The Museum is in the former village school. It contains a notable collection of 25 sculptured monuments of the Celtic/Pictish period, one of the most important groups of Dark Age sculpture in Western Europe.

Melbourne

Melbourne Hall

Melbourne, nr Derby, Derbyshire DE7 1EN
☎ 03316 2052
June–1st Wed in Oct, Wed 2–6. Gardens open Apr–Sept, Wed, Sat, Sun, Bank Holiday Mon 2–6. Parties by appt.
🏛 *Miss M. E. G. Dorehill, Co-ordinator*
£ ♦ 🚻 ➡

The original 12th-century building at Melbourne was the property of the Bishops of Carlisle. It was restored by Charles I's Secretary of State and enlarged by Queen Anne's Vice-Chamberlain. It has many historical associations. In the mid 17th century, the Puritan divine, Richard Baxter, wrote *The Saints' Everlasting Rest* here. In the 19th century it was the home of the Prime Minister, Lord Melbourne, and his wife, Lady Caroline Lamb, the friend of Lord Byron, and it was later inherited by Lady Palmerston.

Melbourne Hall is now the home of the 12th Marquis of Lothian, It contains important collections of furniture, paintings, porcelain and silver, and a feature of the celebrated garden is the carefully restored wrought-iron pergola, made by Robert Bakewell in the 18th century.

Melrose

Abbotsford House

Melrose, Roxburghshire TD6 9BQ   ☎ 0896 2043
Apr–Oct, Mon–Sat 10–5, Sun 2–5
🏛 *Mrs P. Maxwell-Scott*
£ ✏ 🚻 ➡ &

Abbotsford, three miles from Melrose on the B6360, was Sir Walter Scott's home from 1812 to his death in 1832. It is still lived in by his descendants. Visitors can see his study, library, drawing room and entrance hall and the dining room in which he died, together with his collection of historic relics, especially armour and weapons. The exhibits include Rob Roy's gun, a lock of Prince Charlie's hair, and what are claimed to be the keys of Lochleven Castle, thrown into the loch after Queen Mary's escape. An item of special interest is the toadstone amulet, set in silver, which belonged to Sir Walter's mother. Toadstone was supposed to be a sovereign charm against fairies and, on this account, mothers used to hang pieces of it around the necks of their new-born babies.

Many interesting people came to stay at Abbotsford as guests of Sir Walter. Among them were Maria Edgeworth, William Wordsworth, Thomas Moore and Washington Irving.

Melton Mowbray

Melton Carnegie Museum

Thorpe End, Melton Mowbray, Leicestershire
☎ 0664 69946
Easter–Sept, Mon–Sat 10–5; Sun 2–5. Oct–Easter, Mon–Fri 10–4.30; Sat 10.30–4. Closed Good Fri, Dec 25, 26.
🏛 *Keeper of Education*
F ♦ ➡

The Museum's displays illustrate aspects of life in six different areas of the Borough of Moulton in north-west Leicestershire. The exhibits include documents from the Melton Town Estate, reconstructions of a 19th-century drawing room in Melton and a wheelwright's shop. Visitors can also see a wide range of craftsmen's tools and birds, animals and fossils from the area. One gallery in the Museum is devoted to paintings and prints on sporting subjects.

Merthyr Tydfil

Cyfarthfa Castle Museum and Art Gallery

Cyfarthfa Park, Merthyr Tydfil, Mid Glamorgan CF47 8RE   ☎ 0685 723201
Apr–Sept, Mon–Thurs, Sat 10–1, 2–6; Fri 10–1, 2–5; Sun 2–5. Oct–Mar, Mon–Thurs, Sat 10–1, 2–5; Fri 10–1, 2–4; Sun 2–5. Closed Good Fri, May Day Bank Holiday, Dec 25, 26, Jan 1.
🏛 *The Curator*
£ *ex. children* ✏ ➡

The Museum is in part of a 19th-century mock-Gothic ironmaster's 'castle'. It has displays illustrating the history of Merthyr Tydfil and the natural history of the town. Other exhibits include Egyptian and Oriental antiquities, paintings, drawings, watercolours, ceramics, silver, coins and medals. A feature of the Museum is a reconstruction of a Welsh kitchen.

Joseph Parry's Birthplace

4 Chapel Row, Merthyr Tydfil, Mid Glamorgan
DF48 1BN   ☎ 0685 83704
Mon, Wed, Fri 1.30–5. Closed Bank Holiday.
Parties by appt.
Ⓜ *Mr Richard Hayman, 1 The Triangle, Cefn*
Coed, Merthyr Tydfil
Ⓕ ✐ ➷

Four Chapel Row, the birthplace of the
composer and conductor, Dr Joseph Parry
(1841–1903), is a typical early 19th-century
ironworker's house. Now a museum, it contains
displays illustrating Parry's life and
achievements and telling the story of the
industrial development of Merthyr Tydfil during
the 18th and 19th centuries.

Mevagissey

Mevagissey Folk Museum

Frazier House, East Quay, Mevagissey, Cornwall
☎ 0726 843568
Easter–Sept, Mon–Fri 11–6; Sat, Sun 2–4.
Ⓜ *Mrs M. Hooper, Four Winds, Chapel Point*
Lane, Portmellon, Mevagissey PL26 6PP
Ⓔ ✐ ➷

The Museum is housed in a former boatbuilder's
workshop and yard, dating from 1745. Its
collections illustrate the traditional life and
occupations of the district and include a granite
apple-crusher and cider-press, a 19th-century
horse-driven barley thresher, and one of the
doors of the local lock-up. There is a
reconstruction of a Cornish kitchen and a
number of items connected with domestic and
social life during the past hundred years. The
crafts involved in boatbuilding, farming, china-
clay working, fishing and copper-mining are also
represented.

Middlesbrough

Captain Cook Birthplace Museum

Stewart Park, Marton, Middlesbrough, Cleveland
☎ 0642 311211
Daily 10–6 (summer); 10–4 (winter).
Last admission 45 mins before closing.
Closed Dec 25, 26, Jan 1.
Ⓜ *H. Wade, Curator*
Ⓔ ♦ ▆ ➷ ♿

The Museum is a modern building in the
grounds of Stewart Park, close to the granite
vase which marks the site of the cottage where
James Cook was born in 1728. The open-plan
displays follow the life of Cook from the time of
his birth at Marton to the streets of Staithes,
where he worked as a shop apprentice and to the
quayside at Whitby. There is a reconstruction of
the below-deck accommodation in his famous
ship, the *Endeavour*, and galleries illustrating
each place he visited until his death in Hawaii
in 1779. The exhibits include ethnographical
material from the countries he explored during
his voyages.

Cleveland Gallery

Victoria Road, Middlesbrough, Cleveland TS1 3QS
☎ 0642 248155 extn 3375
Tues–Sat 12–7. Closed public holidays.
Ⓜ *Mike Hill*
Ⓕ ✐ ➷ ☐

The Gallery's permanent collections include old
maps of the North-East, the decorative arts of
the 16th to 20th centuries and contemporary
drawings, acquired as a result of the Cleveland
Drawing Biennale. The displays take the form of
temporary exhibitions from the collections and
are changed every four to six weeks.

Dorman Memorial Museum

Linthorpe Road, Middlesbrough, Cleveland
TS5 6LA   ☎ 0642 813781
Mon–Fri 10–6, Sat 10–5
Ⓜ *H. Wade, Curator*
Ⓕ ✐

The Museum was opened in 1904 as a memorial
to Lt G. L. Dorman, who was killed in the Boer
War. It houses extensive natural history
collections, including molluscs, birds and birds'
eggs, insects and mammals, together with
geological specimens, mostly from the locality.
Other sections of the Museum cover the
development of Middlesbrough and the
industrial and social history of the area.

Middlesbrough Art Gallery

320 Linthorpe Road, Middlesbrough, Cleveland
TS1 4AW   ☎ 0642 247445
Mon–Sat & Bank Holiday 10–6. Closed Good
Fri, Dec 25, Jan 1. Closed between exhibitions.
Ⓜ *Fine Arts Officer*
Ⓕ ✐ ➷ ♿ ☐

Since its creation in 1958, the Gallery has
concentrated on building up a comprehensive
collection of 20th-century British art. The
policy has been to have no permanent display
and to present constantly changing exhibitions
of works from the collection. Items not on view
at any particular time may be seen on
application to the Fine Arts Officer.

Newham Grange Leisure Farm Museum

Coulby Newham, Middlesbrough, Cleveland
☎ 0642 316762
Apr–Oct, daily 10–6 (last admission 4.30).
Nov–Mar, Sun 10–dusk.
Ⓜ *Bookings Clerk*   ☎ 0642 245432 extn 3836
Ⓔ ♦ ✐ ➷

The Museum is housed in buildings of a working
farm. The exhibits, which cover all aspects of
the history of farming in Cleveland, include
reconstructions of a farmhouse kitchen, a
veterinary surgeon's room and a saddler's shop.
There are collections of farm tools, implements
and equipment.
   Visitors can see examples of rare breeds of
livestock and can become acquainted with
farming practice through a series of farm
trails.

Middleton-by-Wirksworth

Middleton Top Engine House and High Peak Junction Workshops

Middleton Top Engine House, Middleton-by-Wirksworth, Derbyshire
☎ 062982 3204/2831
Engine House: Easter–Oct, Sun 10.30–5, also
1st Sat in month (when engine is working)
10.30–5. Visitor Centre: Jan–Easter,
Nov–Dec, Sat, Sun 10–4. Easter–Oct, Sat,
Sun 10–6. Also open midweek during some
summer months (check locally). Workshops:
Easter week, then Apr–Oct, Sat, Sun
10.30–12, 12.45–5. Also open May Day
Bank Holiday & daily, May 27–Aug.
🖾 Ken Harwood, High Peak Junction
Workshops, nr Cromford, Derbyshire
£ ♢

The Cromford and High Peak Railway, opened
in 1831, was built to connect the Cromford and
Peak Forest Canals. The High Peak Junction
Workshops date from the first stages of the
railway, being constructed between 1826 and
1831, and many of the tools and items of
equipment – some of them are very rare
survivals – date from this period.

The Middleton beam-engine, built by the
Butterley Company in 1829 and designed to
haul wagons up the 1 in 8¾ Middleton Incline,
worked for 136 years until it was finally retired
in 1967. It has been fully restored by
volunteers and can be seen in operation on the
first Saturday in each month.

The Visitor Centre at Middleton Top tells
the story of the Cromford and High Peak
Railway. The 17½-mile-long route of the
former railway, from High Peak Junction to
Dowlow near Buxton, has been developed for
walking, cycling and riding as the High Peak
Trail.

Middle Wallop

Museum of Army Flying

Army Air Corps Centre, Middle Wallop,
nr Stockbridge, Hampshire SO20 8DY
☎ 0264 62121 extn 421/428
Daily 10–4.30. Closed during Christmas
(check locally).
🖾 The Curator
£ ♟ 🍴 ♿ ⅄

The Museum is on an operational airfield, five
miles from Andover on the A343. It is in a
specially designed building, opened in 1984.
The exhibits illustrate over 100 years of the
British Army's flying history, from balloons in
Bechuanaland to helicopters in the Falklands
campaign of 1982. In addition to a range of
Army fixed-wing aircraft, there is a display of
Hafner rotorcraft, which includes the first
British helicopter. The collection also includes
two Argentine Pucara fighter ground attack
aircraft and a captured Huey helicopter, used by
the Argentine Air Force.

A glimpse into the possible future of Army
flying is provided by a display of remotely
piloted helicopters. Aircraft engineering in the
Army is illustrated by means of tableaux and
dioramas.

Milford

Shugborough

Milford, nr Stafford, Staffordshire ST17 0XB
☎ 0889 881388
Mid Mar–mid Oct, Tues–Fri & Bank Holiday
Mon 10.30–5.30; Sat, Sun 2–5.30.
Open Good Fri. Mid Oct–mid Mar, Tues–Fri,
10.30–4.30; 1st & 3rd Sun of each month
2–4.30.
🖾 The Director
£ ♟ 🍴 ♿ ⅄ [NT]

Shugborough has been the home of the Anson
family since 1624. The central block of the
present house was built in 1693 and extensions
and remodelling were carried out in 1745–58
and between 1790 and 1806. Most of the
original contents were sold in 1842 to meet the
debts of the 1st Earl of Lichfield. The house was
given by the Treasury to the National Trust in
1960 in lieu of death duties and has since been
maintained and administered by Staffordshire
County Council, with the present
representatives of the family continuing to
occupy one wing.

Shugborough contains a fine collection of
18th-century English and French furniture,
ceramics, paintings and silver, much of which
was acquired during the 19th century by the 2nd
Earl. Among the special features are items of
furniture by Gillow of Lancaster, a series of
studies of animals by Sir Edwin Landseer, who
was a friend of the Ansons, watercolours of the
house and park, a large collection of paintings of
horses and foxhounds, and many family
portraits.

The Anson Room contains a large number of
relics and mementoes of Admiral Lord Anson
(1697–1762), the circumnavigator, together
with prints of ships and naval engagements
associated with his long career.

MUSEUM OF ARMY FLYING   MIDDLE WALLOP

Shugborough Park Farm Museum

Shugborough Estate, Milford, nr Stafford,
Staffordshire ST17 0XB   ☎ *0889 881388*
Mid Mar–mid Oct, Tues–Fri & Bank Holiday
Mon 10.30–5.30; Sat, Sun 2–5.30.
Open Good Fri. Mid Oct–mid Mar, Tues–Fri
10.30–4.30; 1st & 3rd Sun of each month
2–4.30.
❑ *The Director*
Ⓚ ■ ▧ 👁 ♿

The farm complex was planned by Samuel
Wyatt and completed in 1805. It was originally
designed as the home farm of the estate, but·has
been tenanted since the mid 19th century. In
1975 it was taken over by the Staffordshire
Museum Service as the home of its agricultural
collection and its developing herds of local farm
livestock.

The displays illustrate the agricultural
history of Staffordshire and the Shugborough
Estate, with special features on the story of
ploughing and cultivation, barn machinery, the
transition from horses to tractors, and food
production by cottagers. The restored Mill
Block has been developed as a working corn
mill, driven by a waterwheel, and also contains
displays on milling and agriculture. The
farmhouse is being restored as a 19th-century
farm steward's house. The living conditions of
the cottagers and tenant farmers of the 18th and
19th centuries are also illustrated.

Staffordshire County Museum

Shugborough Estate, Milford, nr Stafford,
Staffordshire ST17 0XB   ☎ *0889 881388*
Mid Mar–mid Oct, Tues–Fri & Bank Holiday
Mon 10.30–5.30; Sat, Sun 2–5.30.
Open Good Fri. Mid Oct–mid Mar, Tues–Fri
10.30–4.30; 1st & 3rd Sun of each month
2–4.30.
❑ *The Director*
Ⓚ ■ ▧

Shugborough is six miles east of Stafford, car
access being through the lodge gates at Milford,
on the A513 Stafford to Lichfield road. The
Museum, in the 18th-century service block of
the Hall, has displays covering the social and
agricultural history of rural Staffordshire. The
stables, laundry, ironing room, brewhouse and
coachhouse have been restored almost to their
original condition, with their original
equipment. The collection of horse-drawn
vehicles ranges from family coaches and
carriages to farm carts. The smithy and living-
room of a Mayfield blacksmith, Charles
Woodward, who died in 1974, have been
reconstructed in two rooms of the stable yard.
There are also reconstructions of a tailor's shop
and a village general stores.

There is a costume gallery, where the items
are frequently changed and date from the late
18th to the mid 19th centuries. A reconstructed
schoolroom uses furniture and fittings from a
number of Staffordshire schools to re-create the
atmosphere of a classroom early this century.
The Toy Gallery displays 18th to early 20th-
century children's toys, games and amusements.

The West Midlands Art Craft Collection shows
current work of some of the best craftsmen in
the area.

Mill Green

Old Mill House Museum and Mill Green Watermill

Mill Green, Hatfield, Hertfordshire AL9 5PD
   ☎ *07072 71362*
Tues–Fri 10–5; Sun & Bank Holiday 2–5
❑ *Dr Christine Johnstone, Curator*
Ⓜ ▧ 👁 □

The village of Mill Green is at the junction of
the A1000 and A414, between Hatfield and
Welwyn Garden City. The Museum consists of
an 18th-century brick-built, three-storey
watermill, with early 19th-century wood and
iron machinery, now fully restored. The 18th-
century miller's house adjoining the Mill
contains two permanent galleries, with displays
illustrating the social history of the
Welwyn-Hatfield area. Different sections deal
with domestic life, industry, building, war,
leisure and archaeology. A third gallery houses
seven temporary exhibitions each year.

Millmount

Millmount Museum

Millmount, Drogheda, Co. Louth, Ireland
June–Sept, Tues–Sun 11–1, 3–6
❑ *Mrs M. Corcoran, 5 Crushrod Avenue,*
   Drogheda, Co. Louth   ☎ *041 36391*
Ⓚ 👁 ♿

The collection consists of material illustrating
the traditional culture of the district. There are
exhibits of domestic equipment, handicrafts and
craftsmen's tools. An outstanding feature is the
display of late 18th and early 19th-century guild
and trade banners. Also on show is a Boyne
coracle made in 1944, the last of a long line of
such boats made in the locality from the same
materials and by the same methods for more
than 4,000 years.

Millom

Millom Folk Museum

St George's Road, Millom, Cumbria LA18 4DD
   ☎ *0675 2555*
Easter week, Spring Bank Holiday week, then
   Whitsun–mid Sept, Mon–Sat 10–5; Sun 2–5
❑ *The Secretary*
Ⓚ Ⓜ 👁

The Museum, in a former school, is devoted to
the traditional life and occupations of the area,
and is administered by Millom Folk Museum
Society. All the items in the collection were
given by local people. There are displays
relating to the Hodbarrow iron ore mines,
including a full-scale reproduction of a drift at
the mine, complete with the actual cage used at

the Moorbank Shaft. Other trades and industries represented in the Museum include agriculture, weaving and blacksmithing, with a replica of a forge. Further sections are devoted to natural history, religion, costumes and domestic life. A reconstruction of a miner's cottage contains household items of the early 20th century.

Millport

Museum of the Cumbraes

Garrison House, Millport, Isle of Cumbrae
     KA28 0DG   ☎ 0475 530741
June–Sept, Tues–Sat 10–4.30. Hours variable
     remainder of year: enquire locally.
🔾 Curatorial Assistant
🅕 ⮌

This local museum illustrates the history of the Great and Little Cumbraes. The collections date mostly from the 19th and early 20th centuries and include household items, postcards, documents, photographs and maps. There is also a range of equipment from a domestic wash-house of c. 1878 – a brick-built, coal-fired clothes boiler, wooden sinks and a mangle.

Robertson Museum and Aquarium

University Marine Biological Station, Millport,
     Isle of Cumbrae KA28 0EG
     ☎ 0475 530581/2
🔾 The Secretary
🅔 ⬦

The Marine Station, the oldest in Scotland, is on the east of the island, at Keppel Pier. The Museum is dedicated to the Victorian naturalist, Dr David Robertson. It has a scale model of the underwater topography of the Clyde area and presents the story of the sea and its inhabitants, showing how they live, how they are adapted to their environment and how they interact with each other. It also provides visitors with information about the biology of the local invertebrates and fish in the Aquarium. These include conger eels, lobsters and octopuses.

Millstreet

Millstreet Local Museum

Carnegie Hall, Millstreet, Co. Cork, Ireland
     ☎ 029 70343
Sun 3–5. Other times by appt.
🔾 Millstreet Museum Society
🅕 ⬦ ⮌

The collections of the Museum, which opened in 1980, are mainly of local interest. They include the 1910 William Lawrence collection of photographs, the Liscahane Ogham stone and a wide range of objects reflecting the social, economic and military history of the Millstreet area.

Milton Abbas

Park Farm Museum

Park Farm, Milton Abbas, Blandford, Dorset
     DT11 0AX   ☎ 0258 880216
Daily 10–6
🔾 Mr & Mrs C. H. R. Fookes
🅔 ♨ ⬛ 🕓 ⮌

The Museum is in a range of thatched buildings, formerly used as stables. Its collections relate to the history and agriculture of the district, and include farm implements, wagons, tractors, a blacksmith's forge – open on Mondays and occasionally on other days – and equipment from Milton Abbas brewery. There are farm animals for children to touch and feed.

Milton Regis

The Court Hall

High Street, Milton Regis, Sittingbourne, Kent
Apr–Oct, 2nd & 4th Sat in month, 2.30–5.30.
     July–Aug, all Sats 2.30–5.30.
🔾 Dr R. Baxter, Tudor Cottage, Cellar Hill,
     Lynsted, nr Sittingbourne
🅕 ⬦ ⮌

The Court Hall, a timber-framed building with a crown post roof, dates from c. 1450. It contains two lock-ups. The displays illustrate the archaeology and history of the district.

Mintlaw

North East of Scotland Agricultural Heritage Centre

Aden Country Park, Mintlaw, by Peterhead,
     Aberdeenshire AB4 8LD   ☎ 0771 22807
Apr & Oct, Sat, Sun 12–5. May–Sept, daily
     11–5. Parties by appt.
🔾 Andrew F. Hill, Curator
🅕 ♨ ⬛ ⮌ ♿

The Centre is off the A92 Ellon-Fraserburgh road, and is housed within the restored buildings of an early 19th-century estate home farm, constructed on a semi-circular plan. Nearby are the consolidated ruins of the estate mansion, laundry, gas works, ice-house and walled garden. The displays show everyday life on the former Aden estate during the 1920s and an exhibition on farming in north-eastern Scotland.

Moffat

Moffat Museum

The Neuk, Church Gate, Moffat, Dumfriesshire
     DG10 9EG   ☎ 0683 20868
Easter–June & Sept, Mon, Tues, Thurs–Sat
     10.30–1, 2.30–5; Sun 2.30–5.
July–Aug, Mon–Sat 10.30–1; 2.30–5;
     Sun 2.30–5.
🔾 The Secretary, Moffat Museum Trust
🅔 ⬦

The Museum's displays are concerned with the archaeology and history of Moffat and the surrounding area. Among the themes covered are farming, the rise of the Spa, religion, education, leisure pursuits and local celebrities.

Mold

Daniel Owen Museum

Daniel Owen Centre Library, Earl Road, Mold, Clwyd CH7 1AP   ☎ *0352 4791*
Mon–Fri 9.30–7; Sat 9.30–12.30. Library also open Sat 2–4.
 *The Librarian*
F 🖉 ♨ ♿

The Museum commemorates the writer and Methodist preacher, Daniel Owen (1836–95), who was born in the town and spent much of his life there. The displays illustrating his life and work include original manuscripts, the tools he used in his trade as a tailor, and a number of his personal possessions.

Monaghan

Monaghan County Museum

The Hill, Monaghan, Co. Monaghan, Ireland
☎ *047 82928*
Tues–Sat, 11–1, 2–6. June–Aug, also Sun 2–6. Closed public holidays.
🖾 *The Curator*
F 🖉 ♨ ♿

From its restricted space in Monaghan Courthouse, the Museum moved in 1986 to its present home, refurbished and extended with assistance from the European Economic Community's Regional Fund. The displays deal with the prehistory, history, traditional life and natural history of County Monaghan. The prehistory displays include the Lisdrumturk cauldron and a new exhibit on the Museum's own excavation at the Black Pig's Dyke. Within the historic period, after the coming of Christianity to Ireland c. 450 A.D., there is a wide range of objects of everyday use excavated at the sites of the crannogs (lake-dwellings), and interesting examples of Christian metalwork, including the celebrated 14th-century Cross of Clogher.

Other sections of the Museum are devoted to the 19th-century lace industry at Carrickmacross and Clones, and to the local flora and fauna. Smaller displays deal with canals, railways, forestry, costumes and coins.

The new Art Gallery extension houses a collection of paintings and textiles which the museum has been unable to display up to now.

Moneymore

Springhill

Moneymore, Magherafelt, Co. Londonderry, Northern Ireland BT45 7NQ ☎ *06487 48210*
Easter, Apr–May, Sept, Sat, Sun, Bank Holiday 2–6. June–Aug, daily ex. Tues 2–6. (July–Aug, Sun 2–7.)
🖾 *The Administrator*
E 🛎 ♨ ♿ NT

Springhill is one mile from Moneymore on the B18 road to Coagh. Built in the 17th century, it was extended in the 18th and 19th centuries, and was the home of the same family for 10 generations. The house, now a National Trust property, contains mid 18th-century hand-blocked wallpaper, family furniture, paintings, ornaments and other items, including the Duke of Marlborough's medicine chest.

The outbuildings house a large costume collection, ranging in date from the 18th century to the present day. The displays are changed each year.

Moniaive

Maxwelton House Museum

Maxwelton House, Maxwelton, Moniaive, By Thornhill, Dumfriesshire DG3 4DX
☎ *08482 385*
July–Aug, Mon–Thurs 2–5. Parties by appt all year round.
🖾 *Mr Paul Stenhouse*
E

Maxwelton House, reputedly the birthplace of Annie Laurie, is three miles from Moniaive and thirteen from Dumfries, on the B729. The Museum, which occupies part of the 15th-century building, has a collection of 18th to 19th-century farm tools and implements and household equipment. The displays also include items used in dairying and in gardening.

The Cross of Clogher, probably 14th century. Monaghan County Museum.

Monmouth

Monmouth Museum

Priory Street, Monmouth, Gwent NP5 3XA
    ☎ 0600 3519
*July–Aug, Mon–Sat 10–1, 1.30–6; Sun
    2.30–5.30. Sept–June, Mon–Sat 10.30–1,
    2–5; Sun 2–5. Open Bank Holidays.
    Closed Dec 25, 26, Jan 1.*
⚑ *The Curator*
£ ⊘ ♿

The Museum is divided into two parts – the
Nelson Collection and the Local History
Centre. The Nelson Collection comprises items
relating to Lord Nelson and his career, and
includes commemorative glass, china, silver,
books, prints, pictures, medals, models and
naval equipment. Among the exhibits is
Nelson's fighting sword. A special display is
devoted to exposing fake Nelson relics.

The Local History Centre traces the
development of the town of Monmouth, using
objects, documents, photographs, paintings and
prints. A section of the Centre illustrates the
career of Charles Stewart Rolls, the co-founder
of Rolls Royce, who lived in the district.

Montacute

Montacute House

Montacute, Somerset TA15 6XP
    ☎ 0935 823289
*Mar 28–Oct, Wed–Mon 12.30–6. Last admission
    5.30. Other times by written appt.*
⚑ *The Administrator*
£ ♟ 🖿 ♿ [NT]

Montacute is four miles west of Yeovil, on the
A3088. The house was built by Sir Edward
Phelips, later Master of the Rolls, in the 1580s
and 1590s and modified in 1786. It contains
pleasant rustic plasterwork, telling the story of
the punishment meted out to an idle husband,
and 16th-century panelling. The Long Gallery
and adjoining rooms now contain an important
exhibition of Tudor and Jacobean portraits on
loan from the National Portrait Gallery.
Elsewhere in the house, now owned by the
National Trust, there is 17th and 18th-century
furniture, and Flemish and French tapestries.
Formal gardens, with topiary and splendid yew
hedges, surround the house on three sides.

Montrose

Montrose Museum and Art Gallery

Panmure Place, Montrose, Angus DD10 8HE
    ☎ 0674 73232
*Apr–June & Sept–Oct, Mon–Sat 10.30–1, 2–5.
    July–Aug, Mon–Sat 10.30–1; 2–5; Sun 2–5.
    Nov–Mar, Mon–Fri 2–5; Sat 10.30–1, 2–5.*
⚑ *Norman K. Atkinson, District Curator*
F ⊘ ♿

The building, specially designed for the purpose,
dates from 1842. The Museum has extensive
local collections, which include three Pictish
sculptured stones, the Marquis of Montrose's
sword, and Montrose pottery and silver. The
Maritime Gallery contains items relating to the
whaling industry and a small collection of
Napoleonic material, including a cast of
Napoleon's death mask.

The Art Gallery features local artists and
local views, and includes sculpture by William
Lamb and paintings by George Paul Chalmers,
James Morrison and Edward Baird. The Natural
History Gallery presents the wildlife of Angus in
habitat settings and also has collections of agates
and fossils.

Sunnyside Museum

*Sunnyside Royal Hospital, Montrose, Angus
    DD10 9JP*   ☎ 067483 361
Easter–Nov, Wed 2–3.30
⚑ *The Curator*
F 🖿 ♿

To reach the Museum, leave Montrose on the
Aberdeen road and then, a little way beyond the
town, take the Laurencekirk road to Hillside.
The Hospital, which dates from 1781, was the
first asylum to be established in Scotland. The
Museum illustrates the history of psychiatry in
Scotland, especially at Sunnyside Royal
Hospital. Among the exhibits are
administrative records from 1797, clinical
records from 1815, photographs taken in
Victorian and Edwardian times, medical
instruments, a straitjacket, firefighting
uniforms, replicas of nursing uniforms and
examples of patients' craftwork.

**Arbroath fisherwoman in traditional costume.
Montrose Museum and Art Gallery.**

William Lamb Memorial Studio

24 Market Street, Montrose, Angus DD10 8NB
July–Aug, Sun 2–5. Other times by appt.
See Montrose Museum and Art Gallery
F

This memorial gallery to William Lamb (1893–1951) shows his sculpture studio, workshop and living-room, set out with a selection of his works – sculpture, woodcarvings, etchings, drawings and watercolours – together with his modelling and woodcarving tools and his original hand-made furniture.

Moreton Morrell

Warwickshire Museum of Rural Life

Warwickshire College of Agriculture, Moreton Morrell, nr Warwick, Warwickshire
☎ *0926 493431 extn 2021*
Department of Countryside Interpretation
☎ *0926 651367*
F

Moreton Morrell is seven miles south of Warwick. The Museum is at present in a 1941 cookhouse, with pseudo-Georgian windows and rustic additions. It represents an attempt to show part of the Warwickshire Museum's rural life collections after 40 years in store. The displays present implements and equipment associated with the more important farming activities such as ploughing, sowing, harvesting and dairying. Among the exhibits are some fine locally made ploughs.

Morwellham

Morwellham Quay

Morwellham, Tavistock, Devon PL19 8JL
☎ *0822 832766*
Daily 10–6 (dusk in winter). Closed Dec 25.
The Director
£

Morwellham is off the A390 between Tavistock and Gunnislake. During the 19th century, Morwellham Quay was a busy port on the River Tamar, serving the important copper-mining industry near Tavistock. By the end of the century, it had fallen into disrepair and is now being restored by the Morwellham Trust as an open-air museum. There are displays illustrating the history of Morwellham and of the copper industry, and recalling life in the area in Victorian times.

Other exhibits include the workshops of a blacksmith, cooper, assayer and chandler, a 19th-century cottage, the remains of railway inclined planes, and working waterwheels. Different aspects of the area are explained by means of riverside and woodland trails and by a 19th-century farm, with appropriate animals and implements. Visitors can take a train into the George and Charlotte Mine, and can ride in a carriage on the Duke's Drive.

Mount Nugent

Crover Folk Museum

Lough Sheelin, Mount Nugent, Kells, Co. Cavan, Ireland ☎ 049 40206
Mar–Sept, daily 2–6
Mrs Anita Matthews
F

The Museum is in former farm buildings, near the ruins of Crover Castle. The collections illustrate the history and character of agriculture and rural life in the area from the 18th century onwards. There are reconstructions of a cottage kitchen and a dairy and the exhibits include farm implements and blacksmiths' tools.

Much Marcle

Hellen's

Much Marcle, Ledbury, Hereford and Worcester HR8 2LY ☎ 053184 668
Good Fri–Sept, Wed, Sat, Sun & Bank Holiday Mon 2–6
Mr D. Sales, Custodian
£

Hellen's is on the Ledbury to Ross-on-Wye road, four miles from Ledbury. Dating from 1292, the house is one of the oldest private residences in England. It has passed, through marriage, from the Audley family to the Walwyns, Kemeys, Vaughan-Mellors and finally to the Munthes, descendants of the Swedish doctor and philanthropist, Axel Munthe. The archives include the original Plantagenet Court Rolls, describing the sessions of the Courts Baron held in the Audley Castle which preceded Hellen's on the site, and which was the boyhood home of the friend of the Black Prince and hero of Poitiers, Sir James Audley, who was created the First Knight of the Garter in 1344. The house also has associations with the 14th-century Queen Isabella of England, and with Henry VIII's daughter, Mary.

Few houses contain as long or as comprehensive a series of family portraits as Hellen's, or a more interesting collection of furnishings and historic relics.

The Victorian chandler's shop at Morwellham Quay.

Much Wenlock

Much Wenlock Museum

High Street, Much Wenlock, Shropshire
TF13 6HR   ☎ *0952 727773*
Apr–May & Sept, Mon–Sat 10.30–1, 2–5.
June–Aug, daily 10.30–1, 2–5.
◪ *Yvette Staelens, Curator*
ⓔ *ex. children* ▮ ◢ ⴺ

The Museum building, which dates from 1879, was originally the Butter Market. In 1919–20 it was converted into the town's War Memorial Hall and for many years it was used for whist drives and dances and as a cinema. The museum displays concentrate on the history and character of Much Wenlock and the surrounding area. The geology and natural history of Wenlock Edge are specially featured and other exhibits are concerned with Much Wenlock Priory, local trades and crafts and the town in medieval times. Other displays deal with Yarchester Roman villa, and with the Wenlock Olympics Society, which celebrated its hundredth games in 1986. There is also a reconstruction of a pre-1914 shop, which contains decorated tins and boxes and other forms of early packaging.

Mullinahone

Threshing Museum

Carrick Road, Mullinahone, Co. Tipperary,
Ireland   ☎ *052 53144*
By appt
◪ *David O'Brien*
ⓕ ◢ ⴺ

The threshing items in the collection include a Garvie threshing mill dating from the 1920s, a 1930s winnowing machine and elevator, and a Jones baler, made in the early 1940s. Among other farming implements on display is a 1918 McCormack reaper and binder and a 1945 Fordson tractor.

Mullingar

Cathedral Museum

The Cathedral, Mullingar, Co. Westmeath, Ireland
Mon–Sat 10–1. Closed Bank Holiday.
◪ *The Curator*
ⓕ ◢

The Museum houses mainly ecclesiastical exhibits from the Diocese, especially crucifixes, vestments and chalices, dating from c. 1600. Of particular interest are a number of items associated with St Oliver Plunkett.

Mullingar Military Museum

Columb Barracks, Mullingar, Co. Westmeath,
Ireland   ☎ *044 48391*
Mon–Fri 9–12.30, 2–4.30 or by appt
◪ *The Curator*
ⓕ ◢ ⴺ

The Museum is in the 18th-century headquarters building of the 4th Field Artillery Regiment. The collection contains items of military and historical interest brought back by the Regiment from different parts of the world. These range from dug-out canoes to fragments of Israeli jets from the Sinai Desert, and include old battalion flags and pennants and pre-1939 Irish Army full-dress uniform.

Mullingar Town Museum

Old Market House, Mullingar, Co. Westmeath,
Ireland
Daily 11–1, 2.30–5
◪ *Hon. Secretary*
ⓕ ◢

The collections, formed by the Mullingar Archaeological and Historical Society, are of items relating to the history of the area and include farm implements, domestic equipment, Stone and Bronze Age tools and weapons. There is also a set of 15th and 17th-century Irish coins and trade tokens.

Mullion

Victoriana Plus

The Old School, Nancemellon Road, Mullion,
Cornwall   ☎ *0326 241108*
Easter–Oct, Mon–Sat 10–6; Sun 9.30–5.
Pre-booked parties during winter months.
◪ *Mrs Jackie Winter-Hill*
ⓔ ⌀ ◢

The Museum is housed in an early 20th-century granite-built school. All the proceeds from the exhibition are devoted to the Seal Sanctuary at Gweek. There is a large display of lamps, dating from c. 1000 B.C. to c. 1920 and other exhibits include Victorian and Edwardian costumes and accessories, fire-fighting equipment and firemen's uniforms, toys, bicycles and domestic equipment. Among the other attractions are a large working model of a South Wales coalmine, completed in the 1890s, and a model of a fairground in 1910.

Murton

Yorkshire Museum of Farming

Murton, York, North Yorkshire YO1 3UF
                 ☎ *0904 489966*
Mar 2–Oct 25, daily 10.30–5.30 (last admission
4.30). Other times by appt.
◪ *The Administrative Director*
ⓔ ▮ ⬛ ◢ ⴺ

The Museum is three miles east of York, at the intersection of the A166 York to Bridlington and the A64 Leeds to Scarborough roads. It adjoins York's new Livestock Market and owes much to the close connections which have been established with the farming community. The aim has been to illustrate the changes which have taken place in the English countryside and in farming practice, especially during the past 150 years.

The Visitors' Centre houses special exhibitions, together with the library, shop and restaurant. The Four Seasons Gallery has displays showing how life on land is related to the seasonal tasks. The Livestock Building contains live pigs, cattle and sheep, together with the tools of husbandry, a vet's surgery of the 1930s, and a blacksmith's forge. Other full-scale reconstructions include a small chapel where the annual Harvest Festival is held, an ironmonger's shop and an agricultural show tent.

Nairn

Cawdor Castle

Cawdor, Nairn IV12 5RD   ☎ 06677 615
May–Sept, daily 10–5.30 (last admission 5)
🖾 The Earl of Cawdor
£ 🍴 💺 🎨 🚶 ♿ HHA

The Castle is on the B9090, between Inverness and Nairn. It has been the home of the Thanes of Cawdor since it was built in 1370, and displays the Cawdor collections of portraits, paintings, English, Flemish and French tapestries, books, furniture, porcelain and silver, formed over many generations. The present Cawdors are keen collectors of contemporary art and the house contains many examples of their acquisitions of paintings and sculpture.

The wide range of historic items includes the present Lord Cawdor's Aikido black belt, guns from a French force which attempted to invade Fishguard in 1797 and which surrendered to the 1st Lord Cawdor, as well as 2nd and 3rd Folio Shakespeares, and a nameplate from an engine of the Great Western Railway, of which the 3rd Lord Cawdor was Chairman. He had a rule that if any train was more than two minutes late, an explanation had to be in his office by 9 o'clock the following morning.

Nairn Fishertown Museum

Laing Hall, Union Street, Nairn, Inverness-shire
IV12 4PP   ☎ 0667 52064
Mon, Wed, Fri 6.30–8.30; Tues, Thurs, Sat 2–4
🖾 B. N. Mein, 37 Park Street, Nairn
£ 🖼 🚶

The Museum's displays tell the story of the local fishing industry, with its traditional emphasis on herring fishing and packing. The collections include fishing equipment and other relics from the late 19th century onwards, as well as old photographs of the boats and of the fishermen and their families.

Nantwich

Nantwich Museum

Pillory Street, Nantwich, Cheshire CW5 5BQ
☎ 0270 627104
Mon, Tues, Thurs–Sat 10.30–4.30.
Closed Good Fri, Dec 25, 26.
🖾 Mrs S. Pritchard, Curator
F 🖼 🚶

The Museum's displays illustrate the history of Nantwich and the local community. There is a good collection of old photographs and material relating to the industries and trades of the area. Special attention is given to the history and techniques of Cheshire farmhouse cheesemaking.

Narberth

Blackpool Mill

Canaston Bridge, Narberth, Dyfed SA67 8BL
☎ 09914 233
Thurs before Easter–Sept 30, daily 11–6
🖾 Mrs Hawce, Manageress
£ 🍴 💺

The Mill was built in 1813 on the site of an iron forge which had ceased operating a few years earlier. In 1968 Lady Victoria Dashwood began the restoration of the Mill and its machinery, and in 1982 the basement was altered to provide a series of caves, in which visitors could see full-size models of brown bears, hyaenas and other extinct wild animals from this part of Wales. Bones and teeth of these prehistoric animals have been found in a number of local caves, especially near Tenby. The last museum cave has a huge replica of the legendary Welsh dragon. The Museum also contains collections of butterflies, birds' eggs, local animals and models of steam engines, together with the bench and tools of a wheelwright who worked in the district.

Naseby

Naseby Battle and Farm Museum

Purlieu Farm, Naseby, Northamptonshire
NN6 7DD   ☎ 0604 740241
Easter–Sept, Sun & Bank Holidays 10–5.
Parties at other times by appt.
🖾 Mrs R. Westaway, Ivydene, Naseby
NN6 7DD
£ 🖼 🎨

In 1645 the Battle of Naseby decided the outcome of the Civil War. The Museum recaptures the event by means of relics from the battlefield and a relief map of the site on which 800 model figures represent the 21,000 who fought in the battle. There are also exhibits illustrating the social history and occupations of the area, with reconstructions of 19th-century cottage rooms, domestic and farm equipment and craftsmen's tools.

There is also, as a separate venture, a collection of British and American vintage tractors.

Near Sawrey

Hill Top

Near Sawrey, Hawkshead, Cumbria LA22 0LF
☎ 09666 269
Mar 26–Nov 2, Mon–Thurs, Sat 10–5.30;
Sun 2–5.30 (last admission 5 or dusk if earlier).
Owing to the size of the house, admission may
be restricted.
◻ The Custodian
£ ♠ ☂ ₰ NT

Hill Top, which belongs to the National Trust,
is a 17th-century farmhouse where Beatrix
Potter lived before her marriage in 1913 and in
which she wrote many of her Peter Rabbit
books. The house remained a family possession
and contains its original furniture and china.
A number of her books are illustrated with
drawings of Hill Top and its furnishings.

Neath

Cefn Coed Museum

Blaenant Colliery, nr Crynant, Neath, West
Glamorgan SA10 8SN   ☎ 0639 750556
Mar–Oct, daily 11–6 (last admission 5.15).
Parties during winter by appt.
◻ The Manager
£ ♠ ☂ ₰ ♿

The Museum, north of Neath, is housed in the
surface buildings of the former Cefn Coed
colliery, which closed in 1968. The mine
equipment which has been preserved includes
the main winding engine, together with
stationary engines and the boilers which feed
the steam engines.
    An exhibition has been created, which
outlines the history of the coal industry in
the locality from the 17th century to the
present, with particular reference to the Cefn
Coed pit.

Nenagh

Nenagh District Heritage Centre

Nenagh, Co. Tipperary, Ireland   ☎ 067 32633
May 15–Oct, Mon–Fri 10.30–5; Sat, Sun 2.30–5
◻ The Administrator
£ ⬚ □

The Centre's displays are in two buildings of
the former County Gaol, the Governor's House
and the Gatehouse, which includes the
condemned cells and the execution room.
There are models in the cells and a tableau can
be seen through a peephole in the execution
room door. Other exhibitions have the general
theme, 'Lifestyles in North West Tipperary' and
are changed from time to time. The area's
principal natural resource, Lough Derg on the
River Shannon, receives considerable attention
in the displays, which are complemented by
audio-visual presentations.

Nether Alderley

Nether Alderley Mill

Nether Alderley, nr Macclesfield, Cheshire
☎ 0625 523012
Mar 30–June & Oct, Wed, Sun & Bank Holiday
Mon 2–5.30 or dusk. July–Sept, Tues– Sun
& Bank Holiday Mon 2–5.30.
◻ Mr J. R. Allen, 7 Oak Cottages, Styal,
Wilmslow, Cheshire SK9 4JQ
£ ⬚ ₰ NT

The Mill is one and a half miles south of
Alderley Edge, on the east side of the A34. The
stone-built mill, with a stone-tiled roof, dates
from the 15th century, but the wooden internal
framing, secured with wooden pins, is
Elizabethan. The wooden machinery and
overshot waterwheels have been restored to
working condition. Wheat is ground for
demonstration purposes and the flour produced
is available for sale. Access to all the floors of
the Mill makes it possible for visitors to get a
clear impression of the processes involved.

Nether Stowey

Coleridge Cottage

35 Lime Street, Nether Stowey, Bridgwater,
Somerset TA5 1NQ   ☎ 0278 732662
Apr–Sept, Tues–Thurs, Sun 2–5. Other times
by appt.
◻ Mrs Rosemary M. Cawthray, Custodian
£ ⬚ ₰ NT

Coleridge and his wife, with their infant son,
Hartley, moved to the cottage in December
1796 and stayed for three years. During part of
this time, Wordsworth and his sister, Dorothy,
were living nearby at Alfoxden and the two
families saw one another nearly every day. The
building was much altered during the 19th
century. It passed into the possession of the
National Trust in 1909, as one of the Trust's
first properties, and great efforts have been made
to reproduce something of the atmosphere of the
cottage as it was during the Coleridges' tenancy.

New Abbey

Shambellie House Museum of Costume

New Abbey, nr Dumfries, Dumfriesshire
☎ 038785 375
May 10–Sept 15, Thurs–Sat, Mon 10–5.30;
Sun 12–5.30
◻ John Robertson
F ⬚ ₰

Shambellie House (1856), a small country
house, was designed by the noted Scottish
architect, David Bryce. The Museum collection
consists of late 18th to early 20th-century
European fashionable dress, mainly women's
clothes and accessories. In 1977 the 2,000-item
collection was given by Charles Stewart of
Shambellie to what was then the Royal Scottish
Museum. Each year there is a new display of

items from the collection, supplemented by material from the Royal Museum of Scotland's own very large costume collection.

Newark

Millgate Folk Museum

Millgate, Newark, Nottinghamshire NG24 4TS
☎ 0636 79403
Apr–Sept, Mon–Fri 10–12, 1–5; Sat, Sun 2–6.
Oct–Nov, Mon–Fri 10–12, 1–5.
Bank Holiday Mon 1–5.
Closed Dec 25, 26, Jan 1.
N *The Manager*
£ ✐ ➳

The Museum, by the side of the River Trent, was formerly a warehouse owned by the Trent Navigation Company. The exhibits illustrate the social life, trades and occupations of Newark from Victorian times until the outbreak of the Second World War. Domestic life is presented in a series of reconstructed rooms and there is a street of 19th-century shops, containing goods of the period. There are displays of tools and equipment used in malting, blacksmithing and farming, and a workshop in which printing is carried on in the traditional way. The toy room contains a wide range of children's books and model cars, trains and aeroplanes.

Newark Air Museum

The Airfield, Winthorpe, Newark, Nottinghamshire
NG24 2NY   ☎ 0636 707170
Apr–Oct, Mon–Fri 10–5; Sat 1–5; Sun 10–6.
Nov–Mar, Sun 10–dusk.
N *Public Relations Officer*
£ ♨ ➳ ⓗ

The Museum is two miles east of Newark, off the A46. It contains over 30 aircraft, mainly post Second World War fighters and trainers. There are also collections of aero-engines, ground equipment and other aviation items.
   Some of the aircraft were flown directly to the Museum, making use of the airfield's original wartime runway. One of the most impressive aeroplanes on show is an Avro Vulcan B.2 XM594. Its cockpit is opened to visitors during the weekends.

Newark Museum

Appletongate, Newark, Nottinghamshire
NG24 1JY   ☎ 0636 702358
Mon–Wed, Fri 10–1, 2–5; Thurs 10–1.
Apr–Sept, also Sun 2–5.
N *The Curator*
F ✐ ➳

The Museum is housed in the former Magnus Grammar School, a mainly early 19th-century building, with part dating from 1530. The collections illustrate the natural history, archaeology and history of Newark and its immediate area.

Lace-trimmed satin teagown, about 1888. New Abbey, Shambellie House Museum of Costume.

Newark Town Hall

Market Place, Newark, Nottinghamshire
NG24 1DU   ☎ 0636 700200
Mon–Fri 10–12, 2–4. Other times by appt.
Closed Christmas & Bank Holiday.
N *Mr M. J. Wilson, Town Clerk*
F ➳

The Town Hall, designed by John Carr, dates from 1774–6 and is considered to be one of the finest in Britain. It displays the municipal collection of silver and silver gilt plate, mostly made in the 17th and 18th centuries, and the silver coins, known as the Newark Siege Pieces, struck during the 1645–6 siege of Newark during the Civil War. Other exhibits include Newark's early records and a number of paintings, among them several by Joseph Paul.

St Mary Magdalene Treasury

Parish Church, Newark, Nottinghamshire
☎ 0636 706473
Mon–Sat 9–11.45, 1.15–4.45
N *The Curator, Mr G. P. Bennett, 20 London*
Road, Newark NG24 1TW
£ ✐ ➳

St Mary Magdalene, Newark, is the first parish church in the country to have its own Treasury. The display, in the 12th-century crypt, includes St Mary's own fine collection of plate, together with items from Southwell Minster and from churches in other towns and villages in Nottinghamshire.
   Among the exhibits, dating from the 16th to the 19th centuries, are chalices, flagons, candlesticks and patens. Some of the silver belongs to the Civil War period, when Newark played an important part in the Royalist cause.

Newburgh

Laing Memorial Museum

High Street, Newburgh, Fife KY14 6DX
Summer: Mon–Fri 11–6; Sat, Sun 2–5.
Winter: Wed 2–7; Thurs–Sun 2–5.
⬚ *The Curator, North East Fife District Council,*
   Cupar, Fife KY15 4TA   ☎ *0334 53722*
Ⓕ ᴧ

The Museum dates from 1896 and houses the personal collection of Alexander Laing, a Victorian banker, who was also the local historian and antiquarian. The collection contains archaeology, social history, ethnography, geology and natural history specimens, as well as furniture, paintings and decorative art from his home. There is also part of the geological collection of Laing's uncle, the Rev. John Anderson, the discoverer of the fossil fish deposits at Dura Den, Fife.

The Laing collection is particularly interesting, since it has been left practically undisturbed since Victorian times and provides an excellent opportunity to study the taste and methods of the period.

A new display illustrates four aspects of Victorian Scotland – emigration, the self-help ethic, antiquarianism and the debate about whether living organisms were created in their present form or evolved over a period of time.

Newbury

Newbury District Museum

The Wharf, Newbury, Berkshire RG14 5AS
   ☎ *0635 30511*
Apr–Sept, Mon, Tues, Thurs–Sat 10–6; Sun &
   Bank Holiday 2–6. Oct–Mar, Mon, Tues,
   Thurs–Sat 10–4.
⬚ *The Curator*
Ⓕ ⬛ ᴧ

Part of the Museum is in the remaining wing of a cloth mill built in 1627, part in an early 18th-century granary, used as a store for the wharf of the Kennet Navigation and the Kennet and Avon Canal. The new display galleries, opened in 1985, illustrate the traditional trades and industries of West Berkshire; the history of Newbury Wharf, the Kennet Navigation (1723) and the Kennet and Avon Canal (1810); ballooning, both modern and historic, especially the local invention of a hot-air burner. The story of the Civil War, including the 1643 and 1644 Battles of Newbury is told by means of an audio-visual presentation and relics of the battles.

The older displays cover local archaeology, history, geology and natural history; early technology, particularly metalworking; the decorative arts, including pewter, ceramics, and the splendid late 19th-century harness from the Earl of Carnarvon's state coach. There is also the George Park History of Photography Collection of 65 cameras and a wide range of photographic accessories.

Newcastle-under-Lyme

Borough Museum and Art Gallery

The Brampton, Newcastle-under-Lyme,
   Staffordshire ST5 0QP   ☎ *0782 619705*
Mon–Sat 9.30–1, 2–6. May–Sept, also Sun
   2–5.30.
⬚ *The Curator*
Ⓕ ⬚ ᴧ ᴧ

The Museum and Art Gallery contain ceramics, glass, paintings and watercolours, mainly of the 18th and 19th centuries. Other displays cover the social and civic history of Newcastle-under-Lyme and the archaeology of the area. A reconstruction of a Victorian street scene has a number of shops, stocked with the appropriate goods of the period.

A children's toy gallery is being organised and arranged and should be opened during 1987.

Newcastle upon Tyne

Blackfriars

Blackfriars Tourist Centre, Monk Street,
   Newcastle upon Tyne NE1 4XW
   ☎ *0632 615367*
Apr–Sept, daily 10–5. Oct–Mar, Tues–Sat
   10–4.30. Closed Good Fri, Dec 25, Jan 1.
⬚ *The Manager*
Ⓔ ⬛ ᴧ

The Museum building represents the most complete survival of a medieval friary in Britain. The first and third rooms are devoted to slide-tape presentations showing the development of Newcastle and the growth of its trade and industries. The middle room contains a series of model buildings, illustrating different architectural styles and featuring examples which can still be seen in the city today. Throughout, wall panels provide additional information about the Tyne, street names and the changing street pattern.

Greek Museum

Department of Classics, The University,
   Newcastle upon Tyne NE1 7RU
   ☎ *0632 328511 extn 3966*
Mon–Fri 10–4.30. Other times by appt.
   Closed Bank Holiday.
⬚ *Dr A. J. S. Spawforth*
Ⓕ ᴧ ᴧ

The Museum, created within the last 30 years, houses mainly Greek and Etruscan antiquities, together with some items of Near Eastern, Celtic and Roman manufacture. Among the particular strengths of the collection are Athenian pottery, with some fine pieces of red-figure and over a hundred examples of undecorated or black-glaze ware; Etruscan Bucchero pottery; and a series of architectural terracottas from Sicily and Magna Graecia. Metalwork is also well represented, with an interesting range of Greek weapons and armour, bronze figurines and ornamental fittings from metal vessels.

Hancock Museum

Barras Bridge, Newcastle-upon-Tyne NE2 4PT
☎ 091 2322359
Mon–Sat 10–5; Sun 2–5. Closed Good Fri,
    Dec 25, 26, Jan 1.
The Curator
ⓔ ♠ ⚲ ♿

Now part of the University of Newcastle, the
Hancock Museum began as a private collection
in the 18th century. It is named after two
Victorian natural history enthusiasts closely
associated with the Museum and what was then
the Natural History Society of Northumbria,
John and Albany Hancock. The collection now
contains over 171,000 specimens of animals,
plants, fossils, minerals and rocks, together with
160,000 insects. During the past 10 years all the
main displays have been completely overhauled.
These include the Bird Room, Zoology Room,
Geology Gallery and, most recently, Abel's
Ark, for young visitors, and the Thomas Bewick
Room.

Hatton Gallery

The University, Newcastle-upon-Tyne,
    NE1 7RU   ☎ 0632 328511 extn 2057
Mon–Fri 10.30–5.30; Sat 10.30–4.30
ⓧ *Sara Selwood, Exhibitions Officer*
ⓕ ☐

The Gallery has a continuous programme of
temporary exhibitions of contemporary and
historical art. Wherever possible, it uses
material from its permanent collection as
exhibits. Certain items are always on show.
They include Kurt Schwitters' last large relief,
the *Elterwater Merzbarn*, and the Fred and
Diana Uhlman collection of African sculpture.

John George Joicey Museum

City Road, Newcastle-upon-Tyne
    ☎ 091 2324562
Mon–Fri 10–5.30; Sat 10–4.30
ⓧ *See Laing Art Gallery*
ⓕ ⚲ ♠

The Museum occupies a three-storeyed
building, dating from 1681. Originally an
almshouse, it was later known as the Holy Jesus
Hospital. At the east end of the building, and
forming part of the Museum, is the 16th-century
Austin Tower. There are period rooms
illustrating living styles from the early Stuart to
the late Victorian periods and displays of local
history and of European weapons and armour.
Among the special features are an exhibition of
sporting guns and gunmakers' tools, an
armourer's workshop moved from Alnwick
Castle, historic weights and measures of the
City of Newcastle, and a group of swords made
at Shotley Bridge, Durham.
    The Museum also contains the Regimental
Museum of the 1st/19th The King's Royal

Hussars and the now disbanded Northumberland Hussars.

Laing Art Gallery

Higham Place, Newcastle-upon-Tyne NE1 8AG
    ☎ 0632 327734
Mon–Fri 10–5.30; Sat 10–4.30; Sun 2.30–5.30.
    Closed Good Fri, Dec 25, 26, Jan 1.
ⓧ *Gwen Massey, Group Education Officer*
ⓕ ⚲ ♠ ⚲ ☐

One of the special features of the Gallery is its
collection of paintings by the early 19th-century
Northumberland artist, John Martin. There are
also displays of British and Tyneside silver,
pottery and glass, including 18th-century
enamelled glass by William Beilby of Newcastle,
and changing exhibitions of items from the large
collection of costumes and accessories and of
British watercolours. Two stained glass windows
by Edward Burne-Jones are also on show.
    The four first floor galleries devoted to British
paintings and sculpture include works by
Reynolds, Landseer and Burne-Jones and, from
the present century, Stanley Spencer and Henry
Moore.

Museum of Antiquities

The Quadrangle, The University, Newcastle-upon-
    Tyne NE1 7RU
    ☎ 091 2328511 extn 3844/3849
Mon–Sat 10–5. Closed Good Fri, Dec 24–26,
    Jan 1.
ⓧ *The Keeper*
ⓕ ♠ ♠

This is the principal museum for Hadrian's
Wall. It contains scale models, life-size figures of
Roman soldiers and a reconstruction of a
Temple of Mithras. The collections of
archaeological finds from sites in the region
cover the prehistoric, Roman, Anglo-Saxon
and medieval periods, from about 6000 B.C. to
A.D. 1600.

**Terracotta antefix in the shape of a Gorgon's
head, c. 500 B.C. Newcastle-upon-Tyne,
Greek Museum.**

Museum of Mining

The University, Queen Victoria Road, Newcastle-
upon-Tyne NE1 7RU
☎ 0632 328511 extn 3118
Mon–Fri 9–5. Closed Bank Holiday.
Ⓜ Professor J. F. Tunnicliffe
Ⓕ ⌐

The Museum, which forms part of the
University's Department of Mining
Engineering, contains an extensive collection of
miners' lamps and of other tools and items of
equipment illustrating the history of the mining
industry.

Museum of Science and Engineering

Blandford House, West Blandford Street,
Newcastle-upon-Tyne NE1 4JA
☎ 0632 326789
Mon–Fri 10–5.30; Sat 10–4.30. Closed Good
Fri, Dec 25, Jan 1.
Ⓜ Mr Norman Tomlin, Group Education Officer
Ⓕ ⌨ ⌐ ⌐ ⌐

The magnificent early 19th-century building
which houses the Museum was formerly the
headquarters of the Co-operative Wholesale
Society. The displays relate to mechanical and
electrical engineering, mining, shipbuilding,
science and a wide range of manufacturing
industries, with special reference to the North-
East. There is also a maritime collection and a
large gallery with exhibits illustrating the history
and development of motive power. The recently
opened section, Pioneers of Tyneside Industry,
presents the achievements of Parsons,
Stephenson, Swan and other notable figures of
the 19th and early 20th centuries.

Some of the Museum's larger exhibits are kept
at the workshop and store at Middle Engine
Lane, Wallsend. These include George
Stephensons's Killingworth locomotive of 1826,
a Robert Stephenson long-boiler locomotive of
1883 and two early electric locomotives, built
c. 1900. This depot is not normally open to the
public, but Open Days are held during the
summer months, the dates being announced in
the local press and obtained on application to
the Museum of Science and Engineering.

National Bagpipe Museum

The Black Gate, St Nicholas Street, Newcastle-
upon-Tyne NE1 1RQ   ☎ 091 615390
Mon–Sat 9.30–5.30; Sun 10.30–5. Closed some
Bank Holidays. Check locally.
Ⓜ The Warden
Ⓔ ⌨ ⌐

The Museum is in the 13th-century gateway to
the Castle Garth of Newcastle-upon-Tyne
Keep. Over a hundred sets of pipes are on
display. The emphasis is on the Northumbrian
small pipes and on Lowland pipes, but there are
also good examples of Scottish, Irish and
Continental European bagpipes.

Newent

The Falconry Centre

Newent, Gloucestershire GL18 1JJ
☎ 0531 820286
Mar–Oct, Wed–Mon 10.30–5.30
Ⓜ Mrs Bateson
Ⓔ ⌨ ⌐ ⌐ ⌐

The Museum provides a survey of the history
of the art of falconry. There is a comprehensive
archive of photographs, and special attention is
drawn to the role of the falconer in conservation
projects. The collection of stuffed birds
illustrates both falcons and their prey.

Newgrange

Newgrange Information Centre

Newgrange, Co. Meath, Ireland   ☎ 041 24274
May, Sept, daily 10–6. June–Aug, daily 10–7.
Ⓜ Tourism Officer, Louth & Meath, Tourist
Information Centre, Market Square, Dundalk,
Co. Louth   ☎ 042 35484
Ⓕ ⌨ ⌐

The great Neolithic burial mound of Newgrange
is on the N51 Drogheda to Slane road. The
displays in the Centre are built around replicas
of objects discovered during archaeological
excavations at the site. There are also
photographs of the layout of the various historic
sites in this part of the Boyne Valley.

Newhaven

Newhaven Local and Maritime Museum

West Foreshore, Newhaven, East Sussex
Good Fri–Oct, Sat, Sun, Bank Holiday 2.30–6
Ⓜ Mr Peter Bailey, 51 Hillcrest Road,
Newhaven BN9 9EE   ☎ 0273 514760
Ⓔ ex. children ⌨ ⌐

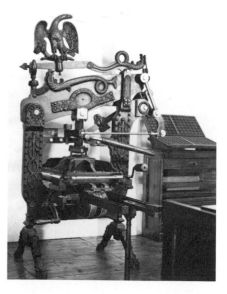

**Cast-iron printing press in
the Museum of Science and Engineering,
Newcastle-upon-Tyne.**

The Newhaven Historical Society is responsible for the Museum. The collections illustrate the history of the town and especially its maritime associations. There is a large photographic collection, covering Newhaven scenes, activities and personalities from Victorian times onwards.

Newhaven Military Museum

The Fort, Newhaven, East Sussex BN9 9DL
☎ 0273 513600
Apr–Sept, daily 11–4. Oct–Mar, Sat, Sun 11–3.30.
▨ *The Curator*
£ ▮ ▦ ⌂ &

Constructed in 1862, the Fort, set deep in the headland, commands a wide field of fire over Seaford Bay and the approaches to Newhaven Harbour. It comprises a complex of magazines, barrack rooms, underground passageways, tunnels and galleries around a central parade ground. Since 1981, it has been restored to its 1870 condition. Graphic display panels and an audio-visual presentation, in part of the former officers' quarters, tell the story of the Fort from the time of its construction to the present day, and the Museum, in the former underground magazine for the Eastern Battery, illustrates the rôle of Newhaven Fort in coastal defence, with special reference to the 1942 Dieppe raid and to both military and civilian life in two World Wars.

Newmarket

National Horseracing Museum

99 High Street, Newmarket, Suffolk CB8 8JL
☎ 0638 667333
Easter–Dec 8, Tues–Sat 10–5; Sun 2–5. Closed Mon, ex. Aug, Mon and Bank Holiday Mon.
▨ *The Curator*
£ ▮ ▦ ⌂ &

The Museum, established in 1983 in Newmarket's elegant early 19th-century Subscription Rooms, illustrates the history of racing in Britain since the time of Charles II. The displays cover racehorse breeding, outstanding horses, great jockeys and famous owners and trainers, with a special section devoted to bookmakers and betting. Other parts of the collection include trophies, saddles, whips, racing colours, and sporting paintings and prints. Changes are made to the exhibits each year.

New Milton

Sammy Miller Museum

Gore Road, New Milton, Hampshire BH25 6TF
☎ 0425 619696
Apr–Sept, daily 10.30–4.30. Oct–Mar, Sat, Sun 10.30–4.30.
▨ *S. H. Miller*
£ ▮ ▦ ⌂

The Museum has one of the largest collections of historic, racing and trials motorcycles in the world. All fully restored, they include the oldest known Norton (1905), reputed to have been the personal motorcycle of James Lansdown Norton, and a 1908 Triumph which was found in new condition. Among the racing machines is the only surviving example of the 1939 495cc AJS Four, the first to lap a Grand Prix course at 100 mph and the 1939 250cc DKW, claimed to be 'indisputably the loudest racing motorcycle ever made, with an engine that can be heard eight miles away'.

The exhibits include special engines and a wide range of accessories and components.

Newport (Gwent)

Newport Museum and Art Gallery

John Frost Square, Newport, Gwent NP9 1HZ
☎ 0633 840064
Mon–Thurs 9.30–5; Fri 9.30–4.30; Sat 9.30–4. Closed Bank Holiday.
▨ *Schools Officer*
F ▮ ⌂

The displays in the Museum relate to the archaeology, local history and natural history of Newport and Gwent. The archaeological material includes the finds excavated at the Roman town of *Venta Silurum* (Caerwent). The local history section illustrates the story of Newport from its medieval beginnings to its development as a major industrial town in the 19th and 20th centuries. Among the themes featured are the port, mining, ironworking, local crafts and manufacturing industries, social and domestic life and the 1839 Chartist riots.

The Natural History Gallery concentrates on the plant and animal life of Gwent and has displays of mammals, birds, insects, rocks and fossils, some of which are shown in habitat settings. The Art Gallery contains 18th and 19th-century English watercolours, local prints and drawings, Staffordshire pottery figures and a growing collection of Welsh paintings, studio ceramics and modern prints. A Brass Rubbing Centre is also on the premises.

Tredegar House

Coedkernew, Newport, Gwent NP9 9YW
☎ 0633 62275
Good Fri–last Sun in Sept, Wed–Sun & Bank Holiday 12.30–4.30
▨ *The Commercial Manager*
£ ▮ ▦ ⌂

The signposted turning to Tredegar House is two miles west of Newport town centre, on the A48. Tredegar was the home of the Morgan family for over 500 years, from the early 15th century until 1951. It was extended and remodelled between *c.* 1664 and 1672 and further modifications took place during the 19th century.

In 1974 it was bought by Newport Borough Council, which began a programme of restoration, decorating and furnishing the different rooms in a way which would re-create the characteristic styles of the 17th, 18th, 19th and 20th centuries, and provide an insight into the life of a noble residence from both the master's and the servants' point of view. Among the 'downstairs' accommodation which can be visited is the Bells Passage, the Butler's Pantry, the Plate Scullery, the Steward's Room, the Cellars, the Game Larder, the Great Kitchen, the Meat Larder, the Pastry Room, the Still Rooms, and the Housekeeper's Room. Many of the estate buildings have been restored and put to new uses, including the provision of pottery, weaving, toymaking, glass engraving and woodcarving workshops.

Newport (Isle of Wight)

Carisbrooke Castle Museum

Carisbrooke Castle, Newport, Isle of Wight
PO30 1XY   ☎ *0983 523112*
Mid Mar–mid Oct, daily 9.30–6.30. Apr–Sept,
Sun 11–6.30. Mid Oct–mid Mar, Mon–Sat
9.30–4; Sun 2–4. Closed Dec 24–26, Jan 1.
⚑ *Museum Schools Officer*
£ ♞ ✈ ↩

The Museum is in the Castle's former Governor's Lodge, the home of Queen Victoria's youngest daughter, Beatrice, until her death in 1944. The main displays relate to various aspects of the history of the Isle of Wight and to the history of the Castle. There is also an interesting collection of views of the Island by the 19th-century watercolourist, John Nixon. The upper gallery contains a fine 1602 chamber organ and a collection of Stuart relics, especially material connected with Charles I, who was imprisoned here in 1647–8, before his execution. Another section of the Museum is devoted to memorabilia of Alfred, Lord Tennyson, including items used by him when he lived on the Isle of Wight.

A favourite exhibit in the Castle is a well-preserved donkey-wheel, used for raising water from the Castle's 700-year-old well.

Newport Pagnell

Chicheley Hall

Newport Pagnell, Buckinghamshire MK14 9JJ
   ☎ *023065 252*
Sun & Bank Holiday, 2.30–6
⚑ *Mr Robertson*
£ ♞ ✈ ↩ [HHA]

Chicheley Hall is one and a half miles from Newport Pagnell, on the Bedford road. The early 18th-century house contains a good collection of paintings and watercolours on naval subjects, together with an interesting range of memorabilia and personal possessions of Admiral Lord Beatty.

Newtongrange

Scottish Mining Museum – Newtongrange

Lady Victoria Colliery, Newtongrange, Midlothian
EH22 7QN   ☎ *031 663 7519*
Tues–Fri 10–4.30; Sat–Sun 12–5
⚑ *Education Officer*
£ ♞ ✈ ↩ ♿

The Museum is at the end of the Coal Heritage Trail, which begins at Prestongrange, the Scottish Mining Museum's other site. Along the Trail are information boards, which tell the story of 800 years of coalmining in Scotland.

At Newtongrange, the Museum is housed in a Victorian colliery building, where a series of tableaux re-create the atmosphere of the village and describe the construction and operation of the Lady Victoria Colliery. At the pithead visitors can see the Grant Ritchie steam winding engine, erected in 1895.

Newtonmore

Clan Macpherson House and Museum

Clan Macpherson House, Newtonmore,
Inverness-shire   ☎ *05403 332*
May–Sept, Mon–Sat 10–5.30; Sun 2.30–5.30
⚑ *Mr Andrew McPherson, Curator*
F ✍ ↩

The House displays historical relics of the Clan Macpherson and its relations with neighbouring clans. These include mementoes of the 'Forty-five' and other Highland battles, the Black Chanter which is reputed to have fallen from Heaven at the battle of North Inch of Perth, and the Green Banner, which ensured that the Clan never lost a battle when it was present on the battlefield. Among other interesting exhibits is the fiddle on which James Macpherson played the Rant before he was illegally hanged at Banff, and the silver epergne, which commemorates one of Cluny Macpherson's escapes after Culloden.

The Badge of the Clan Macpherson.
Newtonmore, Clan Macpherson House.

Newton Stewart

The Museum

York Road, Newton Stewart, Wigtownshire
Apr–June, Mon–Sat 2–5.30. July–Sept, Mon–Sat
2–5.30; Sun 2–5.
◩ Miss H. Drew, Corsbie Cottage, Newton
Stewart DG8 6JB   ☎ 0667 2106
Ⓔ ⬙ ⬤

The Museum occupies a former Free
Presbyterian church, a listed building in a
conservation area. The displays illustrate
Scottish social and domestic life and the
development of agriculture. The exhibits
include reconstructions of a blacksmith's shop,
dairy, nursery, farm kitchen, costumes room,
craftsmen's tools, household equipment, lace
and embroidery, together with documents and
photographs relating to the history of the area.

Newtown

Newtown Textile Museum

5–7 Commercial Street, Newtown, Powys
SY16 2BL
Apr–Oct, Tues–Sat 2–4.30. Other times by appt.
◩ Peter Lewis, Milford Hall, Newtown, Powys
SY16 3HG   ☎ 0686 26243
Ⓕ ⬤

At the end of the 18th century Newtown began
to develop as an important centre of the woollen
industry, producing high-quality flannel on
handlooms. After a period of decline in the
previous two decades, the introduction of
steam-driven machinery brought about a
temporary revival in the 1860s, but the local
manufacturers failed to meet the competition of
other areas of Britain, especially Yorkshire, and
the mills gradually shut down, the last in 1935.
    In 1967 a museum illustrating the story of the
local woollen industry was opened in the top
floors of an 18th-century building which, in the
days of the handloom weavers, was half
dwelling-house, half workshop. There are also
exhibits relating to the history of the local
railways and canal.

Robert Owen Memorial Museum

The Cross, Broad Street, Newtown, Powys
SY16 2BB   ☎ 0686 26345
Mon–Fri 9.45–11.45, 2–3.30; Sat 10–11.30.
Open some summer Bank Holidays.
◩ John Davidson, Hon. Secretary
Ⓕ ⬙ ⬤

The former Newtown Free Library, now the
home of the Museum, was built in 1903. The
displays are devoted to the life and ideas of the
social reformer, Robert Owen (1771–1858),
who was born and died in Newtown. The
emphasis is on the period 1800–24, when Owen
managed the cotton mills and workers' village at
New Lanark, wrote A New View of Society, and
campaigned for factory reform and for
communal villages for the unemployed. The
Museum has an important collection of

portraits, documents, publications and personal
possessions relating to Owen and his times and
these form the basis of the exhibition, which
opened in its present premises in 1983.

The W. H. Smith Museum

W. H. Smith & Son Limited, 24 High Street,
Newtown, Powys SY16 2NP   ☎ 0686 26280
Mon, Thurs, Sat 9–5; Tues, Wed, Fri 9–5.30.
Closed Bank Holiday.
◩ Mrs H. Hyde, Curator
Ⓕ ⬤

The Museum is on the first floor of the
Newtown branch of W. H. Smith. The shop has
been completely restored to its 1927
appearance, when the branch first opened. It
has the original oak shop front, tiling and
mirrors, plaster relief decoration and other
details. The displays, which include models,
photographs and a variety of historical
mementoes, illustrate the history of W. H.
Smith from its beginning in 1792 until the
present day. Among the special themes covered
are newspaper and magazine distribution,
railway bookstalls, and W. H. Smith's
circulating library.

Norham

Norham Station

Station Road, Norham, Berwick-on-Tweed,
Northumberland TD15 2LW   ☎ 0289 82217
Mon, Thurs & Bank Holiday 2–5. Other times
by appt.
◩ Mrs K. M. Short, Station House, Norham
Ⓕ ⬙ ⬤ ⬥

The Station is eight miles west of Berwick-
upon-Tweed. Built in 1847 and closed in 1964,
it stands on the oldest branch line in
Northumbria.
    The signal box, stationmaster's office, porters'
room, lamp room and booking office remain as
they were in 1964. The station complex also
contains a goods warehouse, and coal and lime
storage bunkers. The signal box is still equipped
with its original telegraph system, incorporating
bells and block instruments.

Normanby

Normanby Hall

Normanby, Scunthorpe, South Humberside
DN15 9HU   ☎ 0724 720215
Apr–Oct, Mon, Wed–Sun. Nov–Mar, Mon–Fri,
Sun. Closed Good Fri, Dec 25, 26, Jan 1.
Check locally for times.
◩ The Curator, Borough Museum and Art
Gallery, Oswald Road, Scunthorpe DN15 7BD
☎ 0724 843533
Ⓔ ⬙ ⬛ ⬤

The Hall is four miles north of Scunthorpe, on
the B1431. The mansion, designed by Sir
Robert Smirke, dates from 1830. It has been
redecorated and refurnished in period style by

Scunthorpe Museum and Art Gallery, with collections of furniture, some by Gillow of Lancaster, textiles, paintings, ceramics, silver, costumes and uniforms. The Stable Complex includes a Craft Centre and a Countryside Interpretation Centre, which provides information about the Park and the surrounding countryside.

Normanton

Normanton Church Water Museum

Rutland Water, Normanton, Oakham,
*   Leicestershire LE15 8PX*   ☎ 078086 321
Apr–Oct, daily 11–4, weekends and Bank Holiday
*   11–5. Nov–Mar, Sun only 11–4.*
🔊 *Reservoirs Manager, Old Hall, Whitwell,*
*   Oakham, Leicestershire*
£ ✐ ▆ ⚶

Normanton Church is close to the A606, five miles west of Stamford and five miles east of Oakham. The Church, which formerly adjoined the Normanton estate, is now surrounded by Rutland Water, Europe's largest man-made lake, constructed during the 1970s. The building, floodlit at night, has been protected against water damage by sealing the outside walls and raising the floor inside several feet.

The Museum in the Church contains displays on the history of the public water supply since Roman times and on the history of Rutland and Normanton. The collections include Victorian craftsmen's tools and agricultural implements.

Northampton

Abington Museum

Abington Park, Northampton NN1 5LW
*   ☎ 0604 31454*
Mon–Sat 10–12.30, 2–6. Apr–Sept, also Sun
*   2.30–5. Closed Good Fri, Dec 24–26.*
🔊 *See Central Museum and Art Gallery*
F ✐ ▆

The earliest part of the former Manor House, which now houses the Museum, probably dates from the 15th century. Rebuilding and modifications were carried out during the 16th, 17th and 18th centuries. Further changes were made when the house and the park became the property of Northampton Corporation in the 1890s.

The displays are changed from time to time and, apart from a number of items connected with the history of the house and exhibits of 17th to 19th-century furniture, the collections are mainly concerned with social history. They include agricultural implements, craftsmen's tools, domestic equipment, costumes, lace – mainly Bedfordshire Maltese and Buckinghamshire Point – musical instruments and sewing machines. There are also natural history collections, formed in the Victorian and Edwardian periods.

Althorp

near Northampton NN7 4HG
Daily 1.30–5.30. Bank Holiday 11–6.
*   Connoisseurs' Day, Wed 1.30–5.30.*
🔊 *The Countess Spencer*
£ ✐ ▆ ⚶

Althorp, the home of Earl and Countess Spencer, is five miles north-west of Northampton, on the A428. The original house was built by Sir John Spencer, *c.* 1508. Modifications were made in the 17th and 18th centuries and in 1786–7 the house was entirely remodelled and refaced. The present gardens date from the 1860s.

There are fine collections of English and French furniture, European and Chinese porcelain and of European paintings, including many portraits by Reynolds, Gainsborough and Van Dyck, and among the other artists represented by works at Althorp are Rubens, Salvator Rosa, Sir William Orpen, Sargent and Sir William Nicholson. There are also, in the entrance hall, a group of large paintings by John Wootton showing Lord Spencer and his friends riding with the Althorp and Pytchley Hunt.

The celebrated Spencer Library, which comprised 40,000 early printed books, including 58 Caxtons, was sold complete in 1892 and is now the John Rylands Library at the University of Manchester.

Castle Ashby House

Castle Ashby, Northampton NN7 1LQ
*   ☎ 060129 234*
Parties by appt
🔊 *Mr B. Stuart-Barker*
£ ✐ ▆ ⚶ HHA

Castle Ashby is six miles north-east of Northampton. The house, a Grade I listed building, was mostly built between *c.* 1570 and

St Matthew's Church, Normanton, now marooned in Rutland Water. The portico and tower date from 1764, the nave and chancel from 1911.

c. 1630, with interior decorations dating from the late 17th century to the late 19th. The grounds were landscaped by Capability Brown, and the formal gardens, with the Orangery and Archway, were designed by Matthew Digby Wyatt. The terracotta terraces, designed c. 1860 by Blashfield, are of exceptional quality.

Sir William Compton bought the manor in 1512 and it has been owned by the family, afterwards the Earls and Marquesses of Northampton, ever since. The rooms of the house reflect changing tastes over 400 years. There is late 17th and 18th-century English furniture and collections of porcelain, 19th-century sculpture and Old Master paintings, mostly acquired during the 19th century. There is a fine series of family portraits, including works by Dobson, Philips, Reynolds, Raeburn, Buckner and Landseer.

The Compton family archives are kept at Castle Ashby and may be consulted by approved researchers.

Central Museum and Art Gallery

Guildhall Road, Northampton NN1 1DP
☎ 0604 34881 extn 391
Mon–Sat 10–6. Closed Good Fri, Dec 24–26.
Keeper of Education & Extension Services
F ▲

The Museum is particularly distinguished by possessing the largest historical collection of boots and shoes and shoe-making machinery in the world, with items ranging from Cromwellian boots to Queen Victoria's wedding shoes. There are also displays of shoemakers' tools and a reconstruction of a mid 19th-century cobbler's shop. The Northamptonshire Room displays selections from the Museum's collections of glass and pottery and archaeological material from sites in the county, including a bust thought to be of the Roman emperor, Lucius Verus, found during ironstone quarrying at Duston, and Saxon jewellery from cemeteries at Brixworth and Holdenby.

The Art Gallery contains 15th to 19th-century European paintings, the Italian schools being particularly well represented, and a considerable collection of works by 18th to 20th-century British artists, including Crome, Morland, Sickert and John Nash.

Museum of Leathercraft

60 Bridge Street, Northampton NN1 1PA
☎ 0604 34881 extn 391
Mon–Sat 10–1, 2–5.15. Closed Good Fri, Dec 25, 26.
See Central Museum and Art Gallery
F ⊘ ✎

The former Blue Coat School, which houses the Museum, was built in 1812. In the front wall are statues representing pupils in their Blue Coat uniform. The displays are of leather goods from early historical times to the present day. Special sections are devoted to gloves, costume, saddlery and leather wall paintings. The exhibits include the domestic and the industrial, the artistic and the strictly functional. Among

the more notable items are a coracle, an Egyptian loincloth 3,500 years old, a collection of leather bottles, and the casket given by the Holy Roman Emperor, Charles I, to Isabella of Portugal as a betrothal gift.

Museum of the Royal Pioneer Corps

Simpson Barracks, Wootton, Northampton
NN4 0HX   ☎ 0604 62742 extn 34
Mon–Fri 9–4.30. Other times by appt.
Major (Retd) E. R. Elliott, Curator
F ⊘ ✎

The displays include uniforms, weapons, awards, campaign medals, pictures, trophies and relics associated with the Corps. Among the exhibits are many German items and there is a good collection of hand guns.

Museums of the Northamptonshire Regiment and the Northamptonshire Yeomanry

Abington Park Museum, Abington Park, Northampton NN1 5LW   ☎ 0604 31454
Mon–Sat 10–12.30, 2–6. April–Sept, also Sun 2.30–5.
Closed Good Fri, Dec 24–26.
See Central Museum and Art Gallery
F ⬛

Abington is a 15th-century manor house, largely rebuilt in the mid 18th century. The building houses part of the Northampton Borough Museum as well as the Museums of the Northamptonshire Regiment and the Northamptonshire Yeomanry. The displays illustrate the history of the Regiments since 1741, with exhibits of uniforms, weapons, campaign relics, paintings and photographs, together with part of the collections of Regimental silver.

North Berwick

Museum of Flight

East Fortune Airfield, North Berwick, East Lothian EH39 5LF   ☎ 062088 308
July–Aug, daily 10–5; Sun 11–5. Open at other times, usually public holidays in spring & autumn: check locally. Other visits by appt.
Department of Public Affairs & Museum Services, Royal Museum of Scotland, Chambers Street, Edinburgh EH1 1JF
☎ 031 225 7534
F ✎ ⬤

The Museum of Flight is one of the National Museums of Scotland outstations. The airfield dates from the First World War and the collection is housed in two Second World War hangars. There is a wide range of aircraft, aero-engines and rockets, including a 1930 Puss Moth, a 1934 Weir autogiro, a Spitfire, a Lightning, the last Comet airliner to fly in commercial colours, a Vulcan bomber which saw action in the Falkland War, an Olympus jet engine and a Blue Streak rocket. A special display features the R34 airship, which took off from East Fortune in 1919 to make the first two-way flight across the Atlantic.

North Berwick Museum

School Road, North Berwick, East Lothian
EH39 4JU   ☎ 0620 3470
July–Sept, Mon–Sat 10–1, 2–5; Sun 2–5
◩ District Librarian, Library Headquarters,
Lodge Street, Haddington, East Lothian
EH41 3DX   ☎ 062082 4161
Ⓕ ✐ ☞

The Museum's collections are concerned with
the natural history, archaeology and history of
the area, with a special emphasis on domestic
life in the past. The displays are to be rearranged
and redesigned in the near future.

Northiam

Perigoe Workshop Museum

Northiam, Rye, East Sussex TN31 6PP
☎ 07974 3203
Apr–Sept, Wed, by appt
◩ Mrs P. Rigby, Friars Cote Farm, Dixter Lane,
Northiam, Rye, East Sussex
Ⓔ ☞

The Museum illustrates the history of an old-
established family business of builders and
undertakers, with the workshops shown as they
were when in use and containing the tools used
by four generations of Perigoes. The collections
also include the Northiam parish hearse, which
could be drawn either by hand or by a pony, and
which was bought in 1897 to commemorate
Queen Victoria's Diamond Jubilee.

William Perigoe, the founder of the business,
was apprenticed here in 1875 as a carpenter.

Northleach

Cotswold Countryside Collection

Northleach, Cheltenham, Gloucestershire
GL54 3JH   ☎ 0451 60715
Apr–Oct, Mon–Sat 10–5.30; Sun 2–5.30
◩ Assistant Curator
Ⓔ ♿ ☞ ☞ ♿

The Museum is in buildings of the 1791 House
of Correction, one of a series of country prisons
which led the field in prison reform. The former
prison atmosphere is re-created in the surviving
cell block and court room.

The Countryside Collection illustrates the
social and agricultural history of the
Gloucestershire countryside in the days of
horses. There is an exceptionally good
collection of farm wagons, together with horse-
drawn implements and hand-tools. Panel
displays illustrate and explain the farming
seasons and the processes involved in farm
work. The tasks of the carter, shepherd and
wheelwright are shown, together with the
domestic skills of the laundry and dairymaid.

**Original cell, as now presented in Sir George
Onesiphorus Paul's original House of
Correction. Northleach, Cotswold
Countryside Collection.**

Northwich

The Salt Museum

162 London Road, Northwich, Cheshire
CW9 8AB   ☎ 0606 41331
Easter–June & Sept, Tues–Sun & Bank Holiday
Mon 2–5. July–Aug, Tues–Sat 10–5;
Sun 2–5. Oct–Easter, Tues–Sat 2–5.
Closed Good Fri, Dec 24–26.
◩ Visits Organiser
Ⓔ ✐ ☞

The Salt Museum is housed in the district's
former workhouse, a listed building which dates
from 1837. The displays tell the story of salt-
making in Cheshire from Roman times to the
present day. Models, photographs, maps,
diagrams and objects are used to show where salt
is found and how it is extracted, transported and
used. There are explanations of the vacuum
process of salt production as well as Cheshire's
traditional open-pan method, which evaporates
brine. The displays provide information on the
working environment in the saltworks, living
conditions in the salt towns, Trade Unions,
Friendly Societies, and the leading 19th-century
saltworks proprietors.

Norwich

**Bridewell Museum of Norwich Trades and
Industries**

Bridewell Alley, St Andrew's Street, Norwich
NR2 1AQ   ☎ 0603 611277 extn 298
Mon–Sat 10–5. Closed Good Fri, Dec 23–26.
◩ See Castle Museum
Ⓔ ✐ ☞

The Museum building was formerly a prison. Its
knapped flint side wall is said to be the best in
the country. The last room on the visitor's route
through the Museum features Norfolk-made
clocks and other displays illustrate local
markets, the food industries, ironfounding and
engineering, brewing and printing. Sections are
devoted to the once-important Norwich textile
industry and to shoe manufacturing. There is a
well-stocked period pharmacist's shop.

Conical lumps of salt, The Salt Museum.

Castle Museum

Norwich NR1 3JU   ☎ 0603 611277
Mon Sat 10-5; Sun 2-5. Closed Good Fri,
Christmas, Jan 1.
🕅 *Education Officer*
🄴 🛈 🛢 🤝 ♿

The Castle Keep, constructed between 1100
and 1130, is the oldest part of the Museum
building. It contains displays of medieval
objects, armour, three Norwich Snapdragons,
Egyptian mummies and an exhibition
illustrating the links between Norfolk and
Europe, which have existed since prehistoric
times. The themes covered in the exhibition
range from trade and commerce to tourism,
agriculture and horticulture.

The exhibits elsewhere in the Museum cover
the ecology and natural history of Norfolk,
archaeology and social history. There are also
collections of paintings and watercolours,
especially by artists of the Norwich School,
Norwich silver and ceramics. The Museum has
the finest public collection of Lowestoft
porcelain in the world.

John Jarrold Printing Museum

Jarrold Printing Company, Whitefriars, Norwich
NR3 1SH   ☎ 0603 660211
By appt
🕅 *The Secretary*
🄴 🤝

The Museum of this old-fashioned printing
company occupies three rooms at the works, one
of which is listed Grade II, as being of special
architectural and historical importance. The
displays include a range of letterpress type, both
founder's metal and wood letter, a
representative collection of platen presses,
mainly in working order and in use, hand presses
dating from 1840, and both hand and
mechanical binding equipment.

**The steel space structure of Norman Foster's
Sainsbury Centre for the Visual Arts,
Norwich**

Museum of the Royal Norfolk Regiment Association

The Royal Anglian Regiment (Norfolk),
Britannia Barracks, Norwich NR1 4HJ
☎ 0603 628455
Mon–Fri 9–12.30, 2–4.30. Closed public holidays.
🕅 *Regimental Secretary*
🄵 🤝

The Museum illustrates the history of the
Regiment from 1685 to 1985. The collections
relate to the Royal Norfolk Regiment and to its
predecessors, the 9th Foot, East Norfolk
Regiment and successors, the 1st East Anglian
Regiment and the 1st Royal Anglian Regiment.
The exhibits include uniforms, paintings,
sketches, Regimental silver, campaign medals
and decorations, including the six Victoria
Crosses awarded to soldiers of the Regiment.

The Mustard Shop Museum

3 Bridewell Alley, Norwich NR2 1AQ
☎ 0603 627889
Mon, Wed, Fri, Sat 9–5.30; Tues 9.30–5.30
🕅 *Mr Don Hoffman, Manager*
🄵 🛈

The Museum, at the back of the Mustard Shop,
is entirely devoted to the history of mustard, and
illustrates the growing, processing and the
involvement of the Colman family. It traces the
history of Colmans from the beginning of the
firm in 1814 to the present day. The displays
include archival material, particularly
advertisements and posters, together with a
celebrated collection of mustard pots.

Sainsbury Centre for Visual Arts

University of East Anglia, Norwich NR4 7TJ
☎ 0603 56060/56161 extn 2470
Daily 12–5, ex. Mon
🕅 *Miss Sue Flaxman*
🄴 🛈 🛢 ♿ □

The Sainsbury Centre was opened in 1978, and
houses the Robert and Lisa Sainsbury Collection
and the University of East Anglia Art History
Sector. The Collection comprises objects and
paintings from many cultures, with strong

holdings of Oceanic, African, native North American and Pre-Columbian Art, as well as works by 20th-century artists. Moore, Epstein, Giacometti and John Davies are each represented by a number of pieces.

The building, designed by Foster Associates, is of considerable technical interest.

St Peter Hungate Church Museum

Elm Hill, Norwich NR3 1MN
    ☎ *0603 611277 extn 296*
Mon–Sat 10–5. Closed Good Fri, Christmas, Jan 1.
🏛 *See Castle Museum*
🄵 ✑ ♿

The 15th-century church is noted for its hammer-beam roof and the Norwich painted glass in the east and west windows. The Museum's displays illustrate the theme of art and craftsmanship in the service of Christianity. The exhibits date from the 9th to the 20th century and include medieval illuminated books, monumental brasses and musical instruments. Many of the objects on show are from local churches and chapels.

There is a Brass Rubbing Centre at the Museum.

Strangers Hall Museum

Charing Cross, Norwich, Norfolk NR2 4AL
    ☎ *0603 611277 extn 275*
Mon–Sat 10–5. Closed Good Fri, Dec 23–26, Jan 1.
🏛 *See Castle Museum*
🄴 ✑ ♿

Strangers Hall is a medieval merchant's house, with a 14th-century vaulted undercroft and a 16th-century Great Hall, with a minstrel's gallery. It now houses a museum of urban life, containing rooms furnished in the style of various periods from the 16th century onwards. Among the exhibits are a set of 15th-century tapestries, a chandelier of 18th-century Irish glass, Norwich shop signs, costumes and toys. The Lord Mayor's coach is also kept here.

Nottingham

Brewhouse Yard Museum

Castle Boulevard, Nottingham NG7 1FB
    ☎ *0602 483504*
Daily 10–12, 1–5. Closed Dec 25.
🏛 *C. Hogg*
🄵 ♿ ♿

The Museum occupies five houses, built in 1670, and a series of caves or cellars cut into the Castle Rock behind the houses. The displays illustrate aspects of daily life in Nottingham during the 17th to 20th centuries, with a series of period rooms. There are also reconstructions of a cooper's shop and of a toyshop and a schoolroom of the 1930s. Other exhibits are devoted to local working conditions, transport, sickness and health, popular Nottingham pastimes of yesterday and today, such as the

Goosefair, cockfighting, bingo and pub games. A recently opened section presents local shops and services in the city from 1919–39.

Displays in the caves show some of the uses to which local caves have been put during the 19th and 20th centuries. These include ale cellarage, wash houses, and Second World War air-raid shelters. The open land around the Museum buildings contains native British trees, culinary and medicinal herbs, and plants traditionally grown in cottage gardens, as well as plants of special local significance.

Canal Museum

Canal Street, Nottingham NG1 7ET
    ☎ *0602 598835*
Apr–Sept, Wed–Sat 10–12, 1–5.45; Sun 1–5.45. Oct–Mar, Wed, Thurs, Sat 10–12, 1–5; Sun 1–5.
🏛 *Mr T. Cockcroft, Curator*   ☎ *0602 284602*
🄵 ✑ ♿

The Museum is in a canal warehouse, built in the 1890s. Inside the building is the former canal basin. The displays show the history of the River Trent and its local tributaries and the associated canal system. Among the themes illustrated are the natural environment, archaeological evidence, transport on the waterways, bridges, ferries and floods. Two narrow boats are maintained in working condition.

Castle Museum

Nottingham NG1 6EL   ☎ *0602 483504*
Apr–Sept, daily 10–5.45. Oct–Mar, daily 10–4.45. Closed Dec 25.
🏛 *Education Officer*
🄵 *ex. Sun and Bank Holiday* ♿ ♿ ♿ ♿ ☐

The Castle is a 17th-century mansion built for the Dukes of Newcastle on the site of a medieval

Gatehouse into the Outer Bailey of Nottingham Castle; *c.* 1250, the upper parts restored in the last century.

royal castle. Fragments of the old castle survive in the grounds, the most important being the outer bailey gatehouse, dating from 1251–5. There are collections of ceramics, silver, glass and medieval Nottingham alabaster carvings. The paintings in the art gallery include works by the Nottingham-born artists, R. P. Bonington and Thomas and Paul Sandby.

The History of Nottingham Gallery shows a selection of the Museum's extensive collections of archaeological and historical material relating to the area. There are also exhibits of Greek and Roman art and archaeology, Oriental art and ethnography. The Regimental Museum of the Sherwood Foresters is housed in the Museum and contains collections of uniforms, weapons, medals and campaign relics.

The temporary exhibitions organised by the Museum place a particular emphasis on modern art.

Green's Mill and Science Centre

Belvoir Hill, Sneinton, Nottingham
☎ *0602 503635*
Wed–Sun 10–12, 1–5. Closed Dec 25.
◪ *Education Officer, Green's Mill*
Ⓕ ◷ ⇰ ♿

This 19th-century windmill once belonged to George Green (1793–1841), miller and mathematician. It has been restored to full working order. Displays in buildings around the mill yard illustrate the history of windmills and milling techniques, together with the life of George Green and his contribution to physics.

The Lace Centre

Severns Buildings, Castle Road, Nottingham NG1 6AA   ☎ *0602 413539*
Daily 10–5. Closed Dec 25, 26.
◪ *Mr J. E. Richards, Chairman*
Ⓕ ● ⇰

The Severns is a timber-framed 17th-century house, opposite the Robin Hood statue. The Lace Centre occupies the ground floor of the building. Set up by Jack Richards, who spent a lifetime in the lace industry before retiring from the family firm, it contains displays giving the history of Nottingham lace and lacemaking, together with a wide range of modern lace. Bobbin lacemaking is demonstrated on Thursday afternoons during the summer months.

Museum of Costume and Textiles

43–51 Castle Gate, Nottingham NG1 6AF
☎ *0602 483504*
Daily 10–5. Closed Dec 25.
◪ *Keeper of Costume*
Ⓕ ◷ ⇰

The Museum is in a row of elegant terrace houses, built in 1788. It contains the Lord Middleton collection of 17th-century costume, the 1632 Eyre map tapestries of Nottingham-

shire, and period rooms displaying costume from the mid 18th century to 1960. The very fine lace collections trace the development of local lace from the earliest hand-made pieces to the important rôle played by Nottingham in the history of machine-made lace. There are also collections of printed, woven and knitted textiles.

Nottingham Industrial Museum

Courtyard Buildings, Wollaton Hall, Nottingham NG8 2AE   ☎ *0602 284602*
Apr–Sept, Mon–Sat 10–6; Sun 2–6. Oct–Mar, Thurs, Sat, 10–4.30; Sun 1.30–4.30. Closed Dec 25.
◪ *The Curator*
Ⓕ *ex. Sun and Bank Holiday* ● ⇰ ♿

The Museum is in the 18th-century stables, carriage house and service buildings of the Wollaton estate. It presents the history of Nottingham's industries, including machine lace, hosiery, pharmaceuticals, printing, engineering, tobacco and bicycles. A series of reconstructed craftsmen's workshops shows tools and equipment in the settings in which they were used. There is a beam pumping engine and a collection of other prime movers. One of the most popular exhibits is a pair of working steam ploughing-engines.

The transport collection includes horse-drawn carriages, motorcycles and cars.

Nottingham Natural History Museum

Wollaton Hall, Nottingham NG8 2AE
☎ *0602 281333/281130*
Apr–Sept, Mon–Sat 10–7; Sun 2–5. Oct–Mar, Mon–Sat 10–dusk; Sun 1.30–4.30. Closed Dec 25.
◪ *Education Officer*
Ⓕ *ex. Sun and Bank Holiday* ◷ ⇰ ♿

Wollaton Hall, completed in 1588, is three miles west of Nottingham, between the A609 and A52. The architect, Robert Smythson, created what was, in effect, a sham medieval castle. The interior was remodelled in the 18th

Jack Richards inside The Lace Centre, Nottingham

century. The early 19th-century camellia house has been recently restored.

The Natural History Museum has extensive and worldwide natural history collections. The ground floor galleries concentrate on mammals and birds, many set in dioramas. Upstairs, the displays are of insects, invertebrates, fossils and minerals. A new gallery is devoted to the natural history of Nottinghamshire, illustrating its geology and natural areas and drawing attention to recent conservation problems.

Thrumpton Hall

Nottingham NG11 0AX   ☎ *0602 830333*
By appt for parties of 20 or more
⚑ *The Hon. Mrs George Seymour*
E ⚑ ☛

This early 17th-century house is occupied by its owners, who personally conduct visitors on tours of the rooms. It is noted for its staircase, which is of exceptional quality, and also contains fine 17th and 18th-century furniture and paintings.

University Art Gallery

Department of Fine Art, University of Nottingham,
    University Park, Nottingham NG7 2RD
    ☎ *0602 506101 extn 2269*
During University terms only, Mon–Fri 10–7;
    Sat 11–5
⚑ *Mrs Joanne Wright, Curator*
F ✎ ⚑ ⚑ ♿ □

The University is on the outskirts of Nottingham, near the suburb of Beeston. The Gallery organises temporary exhibitions during term-time. There are six or seven of these a year, on subjects ranging from *Drawing in the Italian Renaissance Workshop* and *F. M. Dostoevsky*, organised through a cultural exchange programme with the USSR, to the work of contemporary artists and sculptors.

Nuneaton

Nuneaton Museum and Art Gallery

Riversley Park, Nuneaton, Warwickshire
    CV11 5TU   ☎ *0203 326211 extn 473*
Apr–Sept, Mon–Fri 12–7; Sat, Sun 10–7.
    Oct–Mar, Mon–Fri 12–5; Sat, Sun 10–5.
    Closed Good Fri, Dec 25, 26.
⚑ *The Curator*
F ✎ ⚑ □

In the lower galleries of the Museum there are permanent displays of geology, later Roman and medieval archaeology, ethnography and fine and applied art. The upper galleries house changing art exhibitions, mainly of works by local artists.

The Museum has an important collection of material associated with George Eliot, who was born in the area. Other exhibits include the Canon Turner Collection of Baffinland Eskimo items, a collection of portrait miniatures by Lady Stott (May B. Lee), and *Before the Deluge*, a painting by the 16th-century artist, Roelandt Savery.

Nunnington

Nunnington Hall: The Carlisle Collection of Miniature Rooms

Nunnington Hall, Nunnington, Helmsley, North
    Yorkshire YO6 5UY   ☎ *04395 283*
Easter–June & Sept–Oct, Tues–Thurs, Sat, Sun
    2–6. July–Aug, Tues–Thurs, Sat, Sun 12–6.
    Bank Holiday Mon 11–6. Last admission 5.30.
⚑ *The Administrator*
E ⚑ ⚑ ⚑ NT

Nunnington Hall, a private home since the Dissolution of the Monasteries, is in Rydale, four and a half miles south-east of Helmsley. The south side was remodelled in the late 18th century, and the Hall, family bedrooms, nursery and visiting maids' rooms are all open to the public.

There are 15th-century French and 17th-century Flemish tapestries, together with the collection of furniture, porcelain and paintings formed by Mrs Roland Fife, who left the house to the National Trust in 1952. The Trust has since brought to Nunnington Mrs F. M. Carlisle's collection of miniature rooms, previously on show at her home, Pyt House, Ashampstead. These are usually one-eighth natural size, and range from a Chippendale library to a Regency games room. Nearly every room contains Mrs Carlisle's own contribution of stitched petit point for carpets and upholstery.

Oakham

Oakham Castle

Oakham, Rutland, Leicestershire   ☎ *0572 3654*
Apr–Oct, Tues–Sat & Bank Holiday Mon 10–1,
    2–5.30; Sun 2–5.30. Grounds: daily
    10–5.30. Nov–Mar, Tues–Sat & Bank
    Holiday Mon 10–1, 2–4; Sun 2–4. Grounds:
    daily 10–4. Closed Good Fri, Dec 25, 26.
⚑ *The Director, Leicestershire Museums and*
    Art Galleries, 96 New Walk, Leicester
    LE1 6TD   ☎ *0533 554100*
F ✎ ⚑

Oakham Castle is, in fact, the Great Hall of the former Norman Castle and dates from the 12th century. The two stone arcades have elaborately carved capitals, similar to those in Canterbury Cathedral. Its walls are covered, on the inside of the building, by a collection of horseshoes of different sizes. The custom, still preserved, demands that a peer of the realm passing through Oakham for the first time must forfeit a horseshoe to the Lord of the Manor. There are now more than 200 shoes, dating from the 15th century to the present day.

Rutland County Museum

Catmos Street, Oakham, Rutland, Leicestershire
*   LE15 6HW*   ☎ *0572 3654*
Apr–Oct, Tues–Sat & Bank Holiday Mon 10–1,
*   2–5; Sun 2–5. Nov–Mar, Tues–Sat & Bank*
*   Holiday Mon 10–1, 2–5. Closed Good Fri,*
*   Dec 25, 26.*
⚑ *See Oakham Castle*
F 🏛 ♿

The 18th century building now occupied by the
Museum was originally the riding school of the
Rutland Fencible Cavalry. Its collections are
mainly concerned with the history of Rutland,
particular attention being paid to the rural life
of the area as it was before the coming of the
automobile. The displays include agricultural
implements, tools and equipment used by
craftsmen and archaeological material
discovered in the course of excavation of local
sites.

Oban

McCaig Museum

Corran Halls, Oban, Argyll PA34 5AB
Mon, Wed, Thurs, Fri 10–1, 2–8; Sat 10–1,
*   2–5.30. Closed public holidays.*
⚑ *Branch Librarian, Oban Library*
*   ☎ 0631 6421*
F ♿

The Museum collections relate to the history
and natural environment of Oban. They include
archaeological finds, coins, old photographs and
specimens of local wildlife.

The Great Hall of Oakham Castle.

Okehampton

Okehampton and District Museum of Dartmoor Life

3 West Street, Okehampton, Devon EX20 1HQ
*   ☎ 0837 3020*
Apr–Oct, Mon–Sat 10.30–4.30
⚑ *Alan Endacott, Curator*
£ 🏛 ☕ ♿

Okehampton Museum is in a three-storey mill
and warehouse, built in 1811, in a cobbled
courtyard surrounded by old cottages. Its
exhibits illustrate man's relationships with
Dartmoor since prehistoric times and relate to
the geology, archaeology and later history of the
area. Farming, handicrafts, mining and
quarrying, peat-cutting and china-clay working
feature in the displays, together with a 'cradle
to grave' exhibition on the life of ordinary
people in the 19th century, and a reconstructed
Victorian cottage interior.

Oldham

Local Interest Centre

Greaves Street, Oldham, Lancashire OL1 1QN
*   ☎ 061 678 4657*
Mon, Wed, Thurs, Fri 10–5; Tues 10–1; Sat
*   10–4. Closed Good Fri–Easter Mon, 1st*
*   weekend in Sept, Dec 25, 26, Jan 1.*
⚑ *Keeper (Industrial and Social History)*
F ♿

The Centre's collections illustrate the geology,
archaeology and urban social history of the area.
There is also a research collection of
entomological specimens.

**'My kitchen' by Harold Harvey.
Oldham Art Gallery.**

Oldham Art Gallery

Union Street, Oldham, Lancashire OL1 1DN
☎ 061 678 4653
*Mon, Wed, Thurs, Fri 10–5; Tues 10–1; Sat
   10–4. Closed Good Fri–Easter Mon,
   1st weekend Sept, Dec 25, 26, Jan 1.*
⚑ *Keeper (Fine and Decorative Art)*
F ⚓ □

The Gallery organises exhibitions of
contemporary paintings, sculpture and
photographs. There are also regular thematic
exhibitions, based on the permanent
collections, which concentrate especially on
Victorian and 20th-century British paintings,
and 18th and 19th-century British watercolours.

Saddleworth Museum and Art Gallery

*High Street, Uppermill, Oldham, Lancashire
   OL3 6HS*   ☎ 04577 4093
Mon–Fri 10–5; Sat, Sun 2–5
⚑ *The Curator*
F ⚱ ⚓

The Saddleworth Museum is in a former cotton
mill, by the side of the Huddersfield Canal. The
collections illustrate the geology and natural
environment of the area, together with its
history and traditional life. There are displays
of archaeology and local customs and
reconstructions of period rooms and a weaver's
cottage.

Old Whittington

Revolution House

*Old Whittington, Chesterfield, Derbyshire
   S40 9LA*   ☎ 0246 32088
*May Day–2nd Sun in Sept, Wed–Sun & Bank
   Holiday 11–12.30, 1.30–3.30*
⚑ *Mr G. Cass, Chesterfield Borough Council,
   Queen's Park, Chesterfield S40 2LD*
F ⚓

In 1688 the Earl of Devonshire, the Earl of
Danby and John Holderness, heir of the Earl of
Holderness, met in Old Whittington at the
Cock and Pynot Inn to draw up plans which led
to the dethronement of James II and the
accession of William III. The inn was
subsequently incorporated into a dwelling
house, known locally as Revolution House. It
fell into disrepair, but was restored during the
1930s and is now a listed building. It contains
17th-century furniture and fittings, a display of
Whittington glass, and the Handford Collection
of local history documents. The chair in which
the Earl of Devonshire is supposed to have sat
during the fateful meeting is now in Hardwick
Hall, but a copy, presented by the Dowager
Duchess of Devonshire, can be seen in
Revolution House.

The collection of glassware made in
Whittington during the period 1704 to 1850 is
unique. The pieces shown are believed to be the
only items known to survive from this once
thriving local industry.

Olney

Cowper and Newton Museum

*Orchard Side, Market Place, Olney,
   Buckinghamshire MK46 4AJ* ☎ 0234 711516
*Easter–May & Oct, Tues–Sat 10–12, 2–5.
   June–Sept, Tues–Sat 10–12, 2–5; Sun
   2.30–5. Nov–Easter, Tues–Sat 2–4.
   Open Bank Holiday Mon.*
⚑ *Mrs S. T. Bull*
E ⚱ ⚓

Orchard Side is the house in which William
Cowper, the poet and hymnwriter, lived and
entertained his friends between 1768 and 1786,
in order to be near his friend, the Rev. John
Newton, author of *Amazing Grace* and other
well-known hymns. The Museum contains
memorabilia of both Cowper and Newton,
together with a specialist Cowper library and
manuscript collection. There is also a local
collection, the contents of which range from
geological specimens to material relating to the
trades of the town. Lace-making, once an
important cottage industry here, is particularly
featured.

**'Orchard Side', Olney, as it appeared in
Cowper's day.**

Omagh

Ulster-American Folk Park

Mellon Road, Camphill, Omagh, Co. Tyrone,
*   Northern Ireland BT78 5QY*
*   ☎ 0662 3292/3/4*
Easter–early Sept, Mon–Sat 11–6.30, Sun &
*   public holidays 11.30–7. Mid Sept–Easter,*
*   Mon–Fri ex. public holidays 10.30–5.*
▣ Education Officer
F ▮ ◼ ♠ 占

The Folk Park is situated four miles north of
Omagh, on the A5 to Newtownstewart and
Londonderry. It is an outdoor museum of
traditional buildings, displaying examples of
Ulster and American vernacular buildings. It is
laid out in an Old World Area and a New World
Area, illustrating the history of 18th and 19th-
century emigration from Ulster to North
America. Each area contains examples of the
dwelling houses, farm buildings and workshops
that the emigrants would have been familiar
with on both sides of the Atlantic.

The Folk Park's collections of furniture,
kitchen equipment, farm implements and
craftsmen's tools are displayed in the exhibit
buildings. A new emigration complex contains a
street of shops and a quay section of an Ulster
port with a full-scale replica of an early 19th-
century emigrant ship. Traditional crafts are
demonstrated regularly and special displays of
seasonal festivals and customs, such as
Halloween, Harvest Home and Christmas
Mumming are also organised.

Wheel hooping at the blacksmith's forge.
Omagh, Ulster-American Folk Park.

Orpington

London Borough of Bromley Museum

The Priory, Church Hill, Orpington, Kent
*   BR6 0HH   ☎ 0689 31551*
Mon–Wed, Fri 9–6; Sat 9–5. Closed public
*   holidays.*
▣ The Curator
F ♠

The nucleus of the present Museum comes from
the large archaeological and ethnological

collections formed by the first Lord Avebury,
formerly Sir John Lubbock (1834–1913), a
friend of Charles Darwin.

The Museum occupies a medieval building,
with Tudor and later additions. The exhibits
cover the prehistory and history of man, from
the Stone Age onwards, with an emphasis on
the Roman, Saxon, Victorian and Edwardian
periods. There are also collections of geology
and ethnography.

Ospringe

Maison Dieu

London Road, Ospringe, Faversham, Kent
*   ☎ 0795 762604*
Mar 15–Oct 15, Sat, Sun 9.30–6.30
▣ Historic Buildings & Monuments
*   Commission, Tunbridge Wells*
*   ☎ 0892 24376*
E ⬗ ✿

The Maison Dieu is an early 16th-century
timber-framed building, which incorporates
fragments of a 13th-century hospital and shelter
for pilgrims. The upper floor contains a display
of Roman burial objects – pottery, glass and
jewellery – found in the surrounding area.

Osterley

Osterley Park House

Osterley Park, Osterley, Isleworth, Middlesex
*   ☎ 01 560 3918*
Tues–Sun 11–5. Closed Dec 24–26, Jan 1.
▣ The Administrator
E ⬗ ◼ ♠ 占 NT

Osterley was built by Sir Thomas Gresham in
the 1570s and it was completely remodelled
between 1761 and 1782 by Robert Adam, with
decorations and furniture designed by him. The
house and grounds were given to the National
Trust by the 9th Earl of Jersey in 1949. They
were subsequently leased to the Department of
the Environment, which now maintains the
property. The furniture, mainly 18th century,
was bought by the Nation and placed in the
custody of the Victoria and Albert Museum,
which administers the house itself.

Ten of the magnificently decorated and
furnished rooms are open to the public. They
include the Eating Room, Library, Breakfast
Room, Drawing Room, Tapestry Room, State
Bedroom and Etruscan Dressing Room.

Otley

Otley Museum

Civic Centre, Cross Green, Otley, West Yorkshire
*   ☎ 0943 461052*
Mon, Tues, Fri 10–12.30. Other times by appt.
▣ Mr Paul Wood, Hon. Keeper
F ⬗ ♠

The Museum is in the former Otley Mechanics Institute, built in 1871. Its displays reflect the archaeology and history of Otley and the surrounding district, over a span of 12,000 years. The collections range from flint tools to bus tickets and include craftsmen's tools, household equipment and other items belonging to daily life.

Oundle

Southwick Hall

nr Oundle, Peterborough, Northamptonshire
PE8 5BL   ☎ 0832 74013/74064
May 28–Aug 20, Wed 2.30–5. June 29–July 27,
Sun 2.30–5. Open Bank Holiday weekends.
◆ The Secretary
£ ■ ♿ HHA

The earliest parts of Southwick Hall date from c. 1300. The house was substantially rebuilt in the 16th century and additions were made during the 18th century. It has been continuously occupied as a home by three families, the Knyvetts, Lynnes and Caprons. Its special attractions include exhibitions of Victoriana and Edwardiana, agricultural and carpentry tools, and bricks bearing the makers' names. There is also a display of fossils and archaeological finds.

Oxenhope

Keighley and Worth Valley Railway Museum

Oxenhope Station, Oxenhope, nr Haworth,
    West Yorkshire   ☎ 0535 45214
Sat, Sun & Bank Holidays 10–5. July–Aug, also
    Wed 10–5.
◆ The Curator, Haworth Station, Haworth, West
    Yorkshire BD22 8NJ
£ ♿ ■ ♿

The Museum adjoins Oxenhope Station, on the privately run Keighley and Worth Valley Railway. It includes standard gauge steam locomotives, including those used in the filming of The Railway Children, vintage railway carriages, a Pullman car, signals, station name-signs and other railway relics.

Oxford

Ashmolean Museum of Art and Archaeology

Beaumont Street, Oxford OX1 2PH
    ☎ 0865 512651
Tues–Sat 10–4; Sun 2–4; most Bank Holiday Mon
    2–5. Closed Good Fri–Easter Sun, St Giles'
    Fair (Mon/Tues following 1st Sun in Sept),
    & Christmas/New Year.
◆ Education Service
F ♿ ♿

The Ashmolean, including the Taylor Institute, was designed by C. R. Cockerell and completed in 1845. The southern front is one of the finest neo-Grecian buildings in Britain. It is the private museum of the University of Oxford, but has been open to the public since 1683. The surviving nucleus of the Founding (Tradescant) Collection is at the heart of the four present Departments. Antiquities contains prehistoric, Greek and Roman objects, Cretan and Cypriot finds, the Arundel classical marbles and the Alfred Jewel. The Department of Western Art has works of the 15th to 18th-century Italian School, from Uccello to Tiepolo; paintings by Claude Poussin and the French Impressionists, especially Pissarro; English 18th and 19th-century paintings, particularly by Samuel Palmer and the Pre-Raphaelites; and an important collection of drawings, notably by Raphael, Michelangelo and Rembrandt, together with bronzes, silver, ceramics and musical instruments.

The Heberden Coin Room is second in Britain only to that of the British Museum. The Department of Eastern Art has major collections of Chinese and Japanese porcelain, sculpture and lacquerwork, Chinese bronzes, Tibetan art, Indian sculpture and paintings, and Islamic pottery and metalwork.

The Bate Collection of Historical Instruments

Faculty of Music, University of Oxford,
    St Aldate's, Oxford OX1 1DB
    ☎ 0865 247069
Mon–Fri 2–5. Closed Dec 25 & part of University
    vacations: check locally.
◆ The Curator
F donations welcome ♿ ♿ □

The Museum contains the most comprehensive collection in England of European woodwind, brass and percussion instruments and the finest Javanese Gamelan in Britain, recently presented by the Indonesian Minister of Forestry. There is also the William C. Retford Memorial Collection of bows and bow-making equipment and instruments from the Roger Warner and Taphouse keyboard collections. The Museum has six of the instruments shown in Zoffany's painting of The Sharp Family's Musical Boating Party.

A special exhibition is arranged each academic term. It continues throughout the following vacation.

**'Head of a Youth' by G. B. Piazzetta
(1682–1754). Oxford, Ashmolean Museum.**

Manual switchboards and an early telephone kiosk in the British Telecom Museum, Oxford.

British Telecom Museum

35 Speedwell Street, Oxford OX1 1RH
    ☎ 0865 246601
By appt only, Mon–Fri 10–12, 2–4. Closed Bank Holiday.
⚑ *The Curator*
Ⓕ

The British Telecom Museum at Oxford's Telephone Exchange was founded in 1962. Its exhibits comprise a selection of telephone and telegraph equipment illustrating the history and evolution of telecommunications. Over 150 telephones are displayed, ranging from Alexander Graham Bell's 'Gallows' telephone of 1875 to modern instruments. Among other exhibits are telephone kiosks and early manual switchboards.

Some of the equipment is in working order and calls can be made through early automatic exchanges and switchboards, using telephones of the period. Several of the exhibits in the telegraph section pre-date the invention of the telephone.

Christ Church Picture Gallery

Christ Church, Oxford OX1 1DP
    ☎ 0865 276172
Easter–Sept, Mon–Sat 10.30–1, 2–5.30; Sun 2–5.30. Oct–Easter, Mon–Sat 10.30–1, 2–4.30; Sun 2–4.30. Closed week following Easter Mon & Christmas week.
⚑ *Assistant Curator*
Ⓔ ✍

The Gallery building, inside Canterbury Quadrangle, was designed by Powell and Moya and was opened in 1968. The collection consists of paintings and drawings of the late 14th to mid 18th centuries. Mostly Italian works are involved, but there are some by notable artists from Northern Europe, including Hugo van der Goes, Frans Hals and Van Dyck. Italian paintings include Annibale Caracci's *Butcher's Shop*, and among the drawings are works by Leonardo, Michelangelo and Raphael. The Gallery also houses an important collection of 18th-century English glass.

The Frank Cooper Collection

Frank Cooper Ltd, 84 High Street, Oxford OX1 4BG   ☎ 0865 245125
Mon–Sat 10–6. Closed Bank Holiday.
⚑ *Miss Lynn Chamberlain*
Ⓕ ▲ ⇌

The Frank Cooper shop and memorabilia collection is on the site of the original Frank Cooper grocery shop, established in 1874, where the marmalade was once sold. The Angel Inn, claimed to be the first coffee-house in England, had previously occupied the site.

The Museum tells the story of how Sarah Cooper's marmalade, sold over the counter in her husband's shop, achieved its worldwide popularity, necessitating the building of a factory within 25 years. There is an interesting collection of Seville orange cutters and stone jars, and a tin of marmalade which was taken on Scott's expedition to the Antarctic in 1910.

Museum of the History of Science

The Old Ashmolean Building, Broad Street, Oxford OX1 3AZ   ☎ 0865 277280
Mon–Fri 10.30–1, 2.30–4. Closed Easter & Christmas weeks & Bank Holiday.
⚑ *The Secretary*
Ⓕ ✍

The Museum is one of the finest examples of 17th-century architecture in Oxford, originally built to house the University's School of Natural History, a chemical laboratory, and the first public museum in the country – the Ashmolean. It has an unrivalled collection of early astronomical, surveying, navigational and mathematical instruments and the largest collection of astrolabes in the world. The optical collections include early telescopes, spectrometers, microscopes and photographic apparatus and there is a fine collection of watches and of the mechanisms of Oxfordshire clocks.

In the former chemical laboratory in the basement there is an exhibition of air pumps, frictional electrical machines and other early physics apparatus, an important collection of early 19th-century chemical glassware, and a small collection of surgical and dental instruments. Several exhibits, such as the penicillin display and H. G. J. Moseley's X-ray spectrometers, are of special interest for the history of science in Oxford.

Museum of Modern Art

30 Pembroke Street, Oxford OX1 1BP
    ☎ 0865 722733
Tues–Sat 10–5; Sun 2–5. Closed Good Fri, Dec 25 & Bank Holiday.
⚑ *Toby Jackson, Education Officer*
Ⓕ *ex. special exhibitions* ▲ 💻 ⇌ ☐

The Museum was founded in 1966, in a converted brewery, by a group of enthusiasts who felt that contemporary art was not adequately represented in the cultural life of Oxford. The original intention was to build up a

'The Siege of Oxford, 1645' by Jan de Wyck. Museum of Oxford.

permanent collection of 20th-century art, but almost immediately the policy moved towards exhibitions, including historical and group surveys, retrospective exhibitions by established artists and displays of work by younger contemporary artists. The approach is strongly international.

Six groups of exhibitions are held each year, usually with three or four exhibitions taking place at the same time.

Museum of Oxford

St Aldate's, Oxford OX1 1DZ   ☎ 0865 815559
Tues–Sat 10–5. Closed Good Fri, Dec 25, 26.
Ⓝ The Curator
Ⓕ ⬤

The Museum is housed on two floors of the south-west corner of Oxford's 1893 Town Hall. It tells the story of the growth of Oxford from the earliest times to the present day. The exhibits are complemented by a series of reconstructed furnished period rooms, including an Elizabethan inn parlour, an 18th-century student's room, a 19th-century working-class kitchen and a corner of Cape's Cash Drapery.

Individual exhibits of note include the complete base of a Roman pottery kiln, the oldest surviving English town seal (1191), Jan de Wyck's remarkable painting of the Siege of Oxford in 1645, and an 18th-century fire-engine. An electrically operated car-engine and working fairground models add movement to the displays.

Oxford Cathedral Treasury

Christ Church, Oxford OX1 1DP
    ☎ 0865 724620
Easter–Sept, daily 9–6. Oct–Easter, daily 9–4.30.
    Closed Dec 25, and Sun before 1.
Ⓝ Edward Evans, Dean's Verger
Ⓔ ⬤

The 13th-century Cathedral Chapter House, which houses the Museum, displays the College and Cathedral plate and an interesting loan exhibition of church plate from parishes in the Diocese of Oxford.

Oxford City Council Plate Room

Town Hall, St Aldate's, Oxford OX1 1DX
    ☎ 0865 249811
By appt
Ⓝ Director of Planning Estates & Architecture
Ⓕ

The exhibition contains a collection of City plate and other treasured civic possessions dating back to the 14th century.

Oxford University Museum

Parks Road, Oxford OX1 3PW   ☎ 0865 57529
Mon–Sat 12–5. Closed Maundy Thurs, Good Fri
    & Sat, Dec 24–Jan 1.
Ⓝ Head Porter
Ⓕ ⌫

The Museum building is in the 19th-century Gothic revival style, with carved decoration and ornamental ironwork. It houses the University's extensive scientific collections in zoology, entomology, geology and mineralogy, which are second in importance only to those in the Natural History Museum in London.

The zoology section contains a comprehensive collection of preserved specimens from all over the world, including more than 1,000 type specimens and those assembled by the early African explorer, Burchell. The Hope entomological collection has more than 15,000 specimens.

The geological collection is also rich in type specimens and includes the collections of the eminent 19th-century geologists, William Buckland, Charles Lyell and John Phillips.

Pitt-Rivers Museum

South Parks Road, Oxford OX1 3PP
☎ *0865 512541*
Mon–Sat 2–4. Closed Easter & Christmas weeks.
🖪 *Curator's Secretary*
F 🖉

The Museum, which forms part of a University teaching department, possesses one of the six most important ethnographic collections in the world, a major collection of prehistoric archaeology, and a fine British and European folk life section. The musical instrument collection, which represents many cultures throughout the world, is one of the three largest in existence.

In accordance with the deed of gift, the displays are arranged typologically, to illustrate technical and evolutionary principles. In a building nearly a century old, this has resulted in gross overcrowding. A new building, opened in 1986, has exhibitions of pre-agricultural archaeology and of musical instruments, supplemented, in the case of the latter, by sophisticated audio-visual equipment, which makes it possible to appreciate the instruments in a realistic context.

Regimental Museum of the Oxfordshire and Buckinghamshire Light Infantry

Territorial Army Centre, Slade Park, Headington,
Oxford OX3 7JJ   ☎ *0865 778479*
Mon–Fri 10–12.30, 2–4
🖪 *The Curator*
F 🖚 ♿

The Museum contains exhibits of the militaria of the County Regiment, now incorporated in The Royal Green Jackets. The displays include a fine medal collection, uniforms, badges, pictures and silver of the Regular, Territorial and former Militia Battalions of the Regiment, together with some items relating to the Queen's Own Oxfordshire Hussars.

Rotunda Museum of Antique Dolls' Houses

Grove House, 44 Iffley Turn, Oxford OX4 4DU
1st Sun in May–mid Sept, Sun 2–5. Parties of
12 or more at other times by appt.
🖪 *Mrs Graham Greene*
F 🖚

The Museum, opened in 1962, was built to harmonise with the adjoining 1780 house, which was the home of the mother and sisters of Cardinal Newman. The exhibits have been collected personally by the owner, Mrs Greene, the author of *English Dolls' Houses* (1955) and *Family Dolls' Houses* (1972), who has inspected and measured at least 1,500 old dolls' houses. The Museum is claimed to be the only one in the world showing solely dolls' houses and their contemporary furniture.

When Mrs Greene began collecting in 1944, there was little interest in early toys and dolls. Collectors became interested in the 1950s.

Part of the collection of ceramics in the Museum of Modern Art, Oxford.

P

Padiham

Gawthorpe Hall: The Rachel Kay Shuttleworth Textile Collections

Gawthorpe Hall, Padiham, nr Burnley,
Lancashire BB12 8UA   ☎ *0282 78511*
Easter–June & Sept, Wed, Sat, Sun 2–6.
July–Aug, Tues also 2–6.
🖪 *The Curator*
F 🖩 🖚

Gawthorpe Hall, on the Burnley to Preston road, was built in 1602. It now contains the textile collections formed by Rachel Kay Shuttleworth, who collected textiles and embroideries of high quality from all over the world and used them when teaching craft techniques. The 12,000 items now at Gawthorpe include embroidery, lace, costume, weaving, printing and needlework tools. There is an important specialist library for use by students, together with pattern books for weaving, whitework and other embroidery.

Padstow

Butterfly World

Padstow Bird Gardens, Fentonluna Lane,
Padstow, Cornwall PL28 8BB
☎ *0841 532262*
Daily 10.30–8 (10.30–5 in winter)
🖪 *J. H. Brown*
F 🖩 🖵 🖚

Butterfly World is part of the Tropical Bird and Butterfly Gardens at Padstow. It contains a comprehensive collection of butterflies and moths from all over the world. Many are shown in their natural environment. The displays mix scientific accuracy and educational requirements with the decorative colour and splendour of the butterflies. Live tropical and native species can be observed in breeding flights throughout the summer months. There are also exhibits showing the history of butterfly collecting.

Padstow Museum

The Institute, Padstow, Cornwall ☎ *0841 532574*
Easter–Sept, Mon–Fri 10–12.30, 2–5;
    Sat 10–12.30
🗷 *Mrs J. Lowe, 8 Cross Street, Padstow*
    PL28 8AT
£ 🚶

The Museum displays illustrate the history of
Padstow and its maritime associations. There
are finds from a Celtic burial ground and special
features on the Padstow lifeboat, shipwrecks,
shipbuilding, and the 'Obby Oss' May Day
celebrations.

World War II Hawker Hurricane.
Paignton, Torbay Aircraft Museum.

Paignton

Kirkham House

Kirkham Street, off Cecil Road, Paignton, Devon
    ☎ *0803 522775*
Mar 29–Oct 14, Mon–Sat 9.30–6.30; Sun
    2–6.30
🗷 *Historic Buildings & Monuments Commission,*
    Bristol   ☎ *0272 734472*
£ ⌀ ♿

This well-preserved 15th-century stone house
was probably the home of a prosperous merchant
or an official of the Bishop's Palace. It now
contains a collection of modern furniture made
by British craftsmen.

Torbay Aircraft Museum

Higher Blagdon, Paignton, Devon TQ3 3YG
    ☎ *0803 553540*
Apr–Oct, daily 10–6
🗷 *Mrs Pam Fraser, Secretary*
£ 🍴 ♿ 🅿 🚶 🚻

The turning to the Museum is signposted from
the A385 Totnes to Paignton road. The
complex housing the collections was originally
built as the home of the South Devon Hunt,
including stables, kennels, paddock, horse-
boxes and a polo field. The Museum's policy in

the extensive indoor galleries has been to mount
exhibitions which would appeal to people of all
ages and especially to those who are not
particularly aviation-minded. With this in
mind, technical details are kept to a minimum
and the emphasis is always on people. Outside,
about 20 helicopters and jet and propeller
aircraft are on display.

The Torbay Model Railway, the Kenneth
More Gardens and the Devonshire Collection of
Period Costumes are associated with the
Museum and are included in the admission
charge.

Paisley

Paisley Museum and Art Gallery

High Street, Paisley, Renfrewshire PA1 2BA
    ☎ *041 889 3151*
Mon–Sat 10–5. Closed public and local holidays.
🗷 *Chief Curator, Renfrew District Museums*
    and Art Galleries Service
F 🍴 🚶

Paisley shawls are a major feature of the
Museum. The collection includes over 700
shawls of different types and styles, and
examples are always on show. The displays in
this purpose-built gallery trace the history of the
Paisley patterns and illustrate the development
of weaving techniques and the social aspects of
the industry. The Local History Gallery presents
the social and economic history of Paisley, with
exhibits relating both to work and to leisure.
The Natural History Gallery, in addition to its
general displays, shows the geology and wildlife
of the area.

There are approximately 1,500 sculptures,
drawings, prints and paintings in the fine arts
collection, the emphasis being on works by
Scottish and French artists. Within the
decorative art section, the ceramics are
particularly notable. The studio pottery
collection is considered to be the best in
Scotland.

Parkhurst

Roman Villa

Cyprus Road, Newport, Isle of Wight
Easter–Sept, Sun–Fri 10–4.30. Oct–Easter,
    by appt.
🗷 *Mr F. Basford, Curator, County*
    Archaeological Centre, 61 Clatterford Road,
    Carisbrooke, Isle of Wight PO30 1NZ
    ☎ *0983 529963*
£ 🚶

Situated in a residential area of Newport,
2 miles from Parkhurst, the Museum is a cover
building for an excavated Roman villa and for
material discovered in the course of the
excavations. There is a fine bath suite and
hypocaust system, and some of the raised floor
still in situ, as well as three complete tesselated
floors and portions of two others.

One room has been reconstructed as a Roman kitchen, with dressed models and a supporting audio-visual display.

Pateley Bridge

Nidderdale Museum

Council Offices, King Street, Pateley Bridge, Harrogate, North Yorkshire HG3 5LE
Spring Bank Holiday–Sept, daily 2–5. Oct–Easter, Sun 2–5. Easter–Spring Bank Holiday, Sat, Sun 2–5. Parties at other times by appt.
Ⓚ Mrs E. Burgess, Greystones, Pateley Bridge, Harrogate HG3 5AY   ☎ 0423 711225
Ⓔ ◌ ◄

The Museum building was originally the local workhouse, erected in 1863. The nine rooms used for displays illustrate all aspects of life in the Dales as it used to be in the past. The exhibits include domestic, farming and industrial material, costumes, a cobbler's shop, solicitor's office and general store and a Victorian parlour.
Background information is provided by an excellent collection of old photographs.

Peebles

Tweeddale Museum

Chambers Institute, High Street, Peebles EH45 8AG   ☎ 0721 20123
Mon–Fri 10–5. Closed local holidays.
Ⓚ District Curator
Ⓕ ◄ ▢

The Museum occupies part of a building given to the town in the 1850s by the Chambers publishing family, 'as a place of enlightenment'. The collections of natural history, ethnography and archaeology are typical of a well-stocked museum of that period. Displays of material drawn from them are changed about four times a year. The large temporary exhibition gallery is used mainly for displays of arts and crafts.

Pembroke

National Museum of Gypsy Caravans, Romany Crafts and Lore

Commons Road, Pembroke, Dyfed
       ☎ 0646 681308
Easter–Sept, Sun–Fri 10–5
Ⓚ Alastair Campbell
Ⓔ ◌ ◄

The Museum aims to provide a representation of traditional gypsy life, with the aid of an outstanding collection of caravans, together with carts, tools and many other types of artefact relevant to the gypsy way of life. Visitors can also see displays of Romany crafts.
The Museum is also actively concerned with the building, decoration and restoration of gypsy wagons and carts, as a means of keeping the tradition alive.

Penarth

Turner House Gallery

Plymouth Road, Penarth, South Glamorgan CF6 2DM   ☎ 0222 708870
Tues–Sat 11–12.45, 2–5; Sun 2–5. Closed Good Fri, May Day Bank Holiday, Dec 25, 26. Open other Bank Holidays.
Ⓚ Mrs E. Brace, Custodian
Ⓕ ◌ ▢

The Gallery is a branch of the National Museum of Wales. It arranges exhibitions of 16th to 20th-century art, mostly paintings, drawn from the collections of the National Museum. These are changed every one or two months.

Pendeen

Geevor Tin Mining Museum

Geevor Tin Mines plc, Pendeen, Penzance, Cornwall TR19 7EW   ☎ 0736 788662
Apr–Oct, daily 10–5.30
Ⓚ Mrs M. S. Pettet
Ⓔ ◌ ▣ ◄

The Museum contains mineral collections from around the world, as well as specimens found at Geevor, models, reconstructions and photographs of earlier forms of mining in and around West Cornwall, including part of the man-engine used at Levant Mine up to 1919; tools and old miners' lamps; old surveying instruments, and a collection of tin marks. The Locke Stamps are also on display as a separate exhibit.

Penicuik

Scottish Infantry Divisional Museum

The Scottish Division Depot, Glencorse Barracks, Milton Bridge, Penicuik, Midlothian EH26 0NP   ☎ 0968 72651 extn 239
By appt, Mon–Fri 8.30–12.30, 1.30–3.30
Ⓚ Officer Commanding, HQ Company
Ⓔ ◄

The Museum collection concentrates on the history of infantry weapons. Their presentation in the Museum is linked to the development of the Scottish Division.

Penrith

Dalemain

Penrith, Cumbria CA11 0HB   ☎ 08536 450
Easter–mid Oct, Sun–Thurs 11.15–5
Ⓚ Mrs Dixon, Dalemain Estate Office
Ⓔ ◌ ▣ ◄ ♿ HHA

Dalemain comprises a 12th-century pele tower, with medieval and Tudor additions. The house was given a Georgian front in 1745. Within the mansion is a fine range of furniture and pictures collected by members of the Hasell family, which has owned Dalemain since 1679. The

16th-century Great Barn houses an agricultural collection and a fell pony museum, and visitors can also see the Regimental memorabilia of the Westmorland and Cumberland Yeomanry.

Penrith Museum

Robinson's School, Middlegate, Penrith, Cumbria CA11 7PT   ☎ *0768 64671*
Apr–May & Oct, Mon–Sat 10–5. June–Sept, Mon–Sat 10–7; Sun 1–6. Nov–Mar, Mon, Tues, Thurs 10–5. Closed Dec 25, 26, Jan 1.
🏛 *Miss C. A. Goss, Curator*
Ⓕ 🖉 🕭

The Museum building dates from 1670. It was originally a charity school, established with money left by William Robinson, who lived in Penrith but made his fortune as a grocer in London. It remained a school until 1970. The collections cover local archaeology, history and geology, with the general theme, 'The Story of the Eden Valley'. The exhibits include Stone Age artefacts from local sites and finds from excavations at a Roman fort in the neighbourhood. Other displays show the growth of Penrith as a market town. Among the items on display are the 'multure' dishes which were used to measure corn in the markets.

Penrith Steam Museum

24 Castlegate, Penrith, Cumbria CA11 7JB
☎ *0768 62154*
Good Fri–Easter Mon, then Spring Bank Holiday–Sept, Mon–Fri 10–5. Closed Sat except Bank Holiday. Pre-booked parties by appt.
🏛 *Mr D. Cuttriss*
Ⓔ 🖉 🕭 ♿

From 1859 to 1959 the buildings occupied by the Museum belonged to a firm of agricultural engineers, run by three generations of the Stalker family. The displays illustrate the history of the business and include steam engines, the foundry, machine shop, pattern shop, blacksmith's shop, engine house and office and one of the workmen's cottages.

Penzance

Penlee House Museum

Penlee Park, Penzance, Cornwall TR18 4HF
☎ *0736 63625*
Mon–Fri 10.30–4.30; Sat 10.30–12.30
🏛 *Town Clerk, Penzance Town Council, St John's Hall, Penzance TR18 2QR*
Ⓕ *ex. special exhibitions* 🖉 🕭

Penlee House was built in 1865. The Museum's archaeological collections trace the history of man in the Cornish peninsula since Neolithic times. Other displays illustrate the natural environment of the area and the wide range of birds, animals, plants and insects they support. Further exhibits relate to local industries, particularly mining and fishing, and domestic and social life in the past.

Roman cremation urn. Penrith Museum.

Perth

The Black Watch Museum

Balhousie Castle, Hay Street, Perth PH1 5HR
☎ *0738 21281 extn 30*
Easter–Sept, Mon–Fri 10–4.30; Sun & public holidays 2–4.30. Oct–Easter, Mon–Fri 10–3.30. Other times by appt.
🏛 *Regimental Secretary*
Ⓕ 🖉 🕭

The Museum is in a 12th-century Tower House, with Victorian wings added. The collections illustrate the history of the 42nd/73rd Highland Regiments over a period of 250 years and include uniforms, colours, paintings and Regimental silver.

Perth Museum and Art Gallery

George Street, Perth PH1 5LB   ☎ *0738 32488*
Mon–Sat 10–1, 2–5. Closed public holidays in winter.
🏛 *Education Officer*
Ⓕ 🖉 🕭

The Marshall Monument, which dates from 1824, was extended in 1935 to house the collections of earlier museums of antiquities and the natural sciences, and to include an art gallery. Most of the paintings and drawings in the Gallery are Scottish, the main strength being in 19th- and 20th-century works with a Perthshire connection. The emphasis in the print collection is on French and British examples of the 'etching revival' period, including works by Legros, Whistler and Sir D. Y. Cameron. The sculpture collection comprises portrait busts and small bronzes by Sir Alfred Gilbert. There are also good collections of long-case clocks, Perth art glass and silver.

The Human History section of the Museum holds collections of archaeology, local and social history, costumes, historic photographs, maps and documents, costumes, ethnography, weapons and armour. The items in the large natural history collection were mostly collected by naturalists in the old county of Perthshire, which corresponds roughly with the present Perth and Kinross District.

Scone Palace

Perth, Perthshire PH2 6BD ☎ *0738 52300*
Good Fri–mid Oct, Mon–Sat 10–5.30;
Sun 12–5.30 (July–Aug, 11–5.30)
◪ *The Administrator*
Ⓔ 🚶 💺 ✍ ♿

Scone Palace, the home of the Earls of
Mansfield, is two miles from Perth, on the A93
Blairgowrie road. Scone became the capital of
Scotland and the crowning place of its kings, in
A.D. 800, when Kenneth MacAlpine defeated
King Drostan of the Picts and brought the Stone
of Scone here. The Gothic modelling and
redecoration carried out by William Atkinson in
1802 effectively disguised the old palace. There
are remarkable collections – French furniture,
European carved ivory, clocks, silk wall
hangings and bed-hangings made by Mary,
Queen of Scots. A complete room is devoted to
Chelsea, Sèvres, Meissen and other porcelain,
and there is a fine collection of Vernis Martin
objets d'art. Visitors can also see a photographic
family record and an exhibition illustrating
estate management.

Peterborough

Peterborough Museum and Art Gallery

Priestgate, Peterborough, Cambridgeshire PE1 1LF
  ☎ *0733 43329*
May–Sept, Tues–Sat 10–5. Oct–Apr, Tues–Sat
12–5. Closed Dec 25, Jan 1.
◪ *The Curator*
Ⓕ ✏ ✍

Established in 1880, the Museum houses
collections of a mainly local nature. There are
sections devoted to geology, archaeology and
natural history, and among the special features
of the displays is a collection of objects made by
Napoleonic prisoners-of-war, who were interned
at Norman Cross from 1796 to 1816.

Porcelain and glass are well represented in the
Art Gallery. The Fine Art collection comprises
mainly portraits and landscapes, including a
portrait by Sickert and two Turner watercolours.

Peterhead

Arbuthnot Museum

St Peter Street, Peterhead, Aberdeenshire
  AB4 6QD ☎ *0779 77778*
Mon–Sat 10–2, 2–5. Closed public & local
holidays.
◪ *The Curator*
Ⓕ ✏ ✍

The Museum, which is also the headquarters of
the North-East of Scotland Museums Service,
concentrates on collections and displays which
illustrate the history of the area. Among the
subjects specially represented are the fishing,
whaling and granite industries. There is a good
coin collection and an interesting photographic
archive.

Petworth

Petworth House

Petworth, West Sussex GU28 0AE
  ☎ *0798 42207*
Apr or Easter–Oct, Tues–Thurs, Sat, Sun 2–6
(last admission 5.30). Extra rooms shown
Tues. Open Bank Holiday Mon but closed
Tues following. Closed Good Fri.
◪ *The Administrator*
Ⓔ 🚶 💺 ✍ ♿ Ⓝ🅣

There has been a house on the site of Petworth
since the early 14th century, but what one sees
today is substantially the result of a rebuilding
undertaken by the 6th Duke of Somerset in
1688. Modifications were made in the late 18th
century and in 1827–46 and 1869–72. In 1750
the estate passed to the Wyndham family and in
the following year Charles Wyndham, 2nd Earl
of Egremont, engaged 'Capability' Brown to
landscape the park. The 3rd Earl augmented
Petworth's great collections of paintings and
sculpture with works by contemporary British
artists, many of whom were his friends. He was
succeeded by his natural son, who later became
Lord Leconfield, and in 1974 the 3rd Lord
Leconfield gave the house and park to the
National Trust.

Petworth is renowned for its paintings and
among more than 200 exhibited in the public
rooms are works by Van Dyck, Lely, Claude,
Reynolds and Turner. The woodcarving in the
house is notable, with examples, in the Carved
Room, of the work of Grinling Gibbons and
John Seldon. An exceptional collection of
classical and neo-classical sculpture is displayed
in the North Gallery. Particularly celebrated are
the *Leconfield Aphrodite*, attributed to Praxiteles,
and Flaxman's masterpiece, *St Michael slaying*
Satan.

The Carved Room, one of the State rooms
at Petworth.

Pevensey

Pevensey Court House and Museum

High Street, Pevensey, East Sussex BN24 5LF
June–Sept, daily 10.30–1, 2.30–5
Mr C. S. Murrell, Curator   ☎ 0323 767573

Pevensey Court House was built *c*. 1595. The
Court Room has an area of only 14 by 18 feet.
By the Municipal Corporation Act of 1882,
Pevensey ceased to be a Borough and no more
cases were tried after that. The present Court
furnishings are Victorian. The Borough Weights
and Measures are displayed in the former Robing
Room and visitors can also inspect the two cells,
where prisoners were kept, and the small yard
allowed to them for exercise. In 1940, the
wooden bunks in the cells were covered with
zinc, so that the cells could be used as a
mortuary, should air-raids have produced fatal
casualties in the town.

Other exhibits in the Museum include a
collection of photographs and postcards
illustrating the more recent history of Pevensey,
mementoes of the 1908 Pevensey Pageant, a
wide range of Victoriana, and ironware and
blacksmith's tools from the forge at Stone Cross,
which closed in the late 1970s after being a
feature of the district for generations.

Pickering

Beck Isle Museum of Rural Life

Bridge Street, Pickering, North Yorkshire
*   YO18 8DU*   ☎ 0751 73653
Apr–Oct, daily 10.30–12.30, 2–5
Mr T. Rosney

The Museum building, a house standing on a
prominent site beside Pickering Beck, dates from

c. 1750. In 1818 it was adapted by William
Marshall, the celebrated agriculturalist, to
provide suitable accommodation for an
agricultural college. The establishment founded
by Marshall was the first agricultural college in
Britain.

Beck Isle Museum is staffed and operated
entirely by volunteers. Its aim is to reflect local
life and customs, and to illustrate social and
domestic life in the area during approximately
the last 200 years. The exhibits include
reconstructions of workshops and shops, models
of carts and gypsy caravans, washing and sewing
machines, early 20th-century photographic
items, costumes and toys. The Museum also has
extensive collections of farm tools, machinery
and equipment. Other displays relate to the
wildlife of the area and to the whaling industry
formerly carried on from Whitby. For many years
this made an important contribution to the
economy of the town.

Pitlochry

Pass of Killiecrankie

nr Pitlochry, Perthshire   ☎ 0796 3233
Apr–June & Sept–Oct, daily 10–6.
*   July–Aug, daily 9.30–6.*
The Warden
£ *ex. children*   [NTS]

The wooded gorge of Killiecrankie, now owned
by the National Trust for Scotland, is three miles
north of Pitlochry. In 1689 it was the site of the
Battle of Killiecrankie, when King William's
troops were routed by the Jacobite army of
'Bonnie Dundee'. The exhibition centre at the
site contains models of the Pass and the battle
and a display illustrating the course of the battle.

Mowing gang, 1910.
Pitstone Green Farm Museum.

Pitmedden

Museum of Farming Life

Pitmedden House, Pitmedden, Ellon,
Aberdeenshire AB4 0PD   ☎ 06513 2352
May–Sept, daily 11–6 (last admission 5.15)
▨ *Mrs Veronica Woodman*
Ⓔ ⬗ ⬛ ⬕ ⬕ [NTS]

Pitmedden, now the property of the National
Trust for Scotland, is best known for its Great
Garden, a remarkable late 17th-century formal
garden in the French style, now fully restored and
carefully maintained. The Museum is based on a
group of 18th and 19th-century farm buildings. It
displays the large collection of farm tools and
domestic equipment given to the Trust in 1978
by William Cook, who farmed at Little Meldrum,
near Pitmedden. These items, augmented by
other gifts, are shown in a furnished farmhouse
and bothy, and in the restored outbuildings, with
interpretive panels telling the history of Scottish
farming. There is, in addition, an exhibition on
the history of gardening in Scotland and a
collection of rare and interesting sheep.

The hayloft over the stable is used for spinning
and weaving demonstrations and for art
exhibitions.

Pitstone

Pitstone Green Farm Museum

Pitstone, Leighton Buzzard, Bedfordshire LU7 9EY
    ☎ 0296 668223
Open Days: 2nd Sun in June, July & Sept, 11–5.
Parties at other times by appt.
▨ *Mrs R. Comben, 23 High Street, Ivinghoe,*
    nr Leighton Buzzard
Ⓔ ⬗ ⬕

The Museum is in the centre of Pitstone village,
just off the B488 and B489 roads, between Tring
and Dunstable. It is the focus of the activities of
the Pitstone Local History Society, which is
actively engaged in restoration and
archaeological work in the area.

The early 19th-century buildings housing the
collections form part of a working farm. The
displays include farming and domestic items,
mostly from within a 25-mile radius of the
Museum. The crafts of the blacksmith,
wheelwright and shoe-repairer are shown in
particular detail and the farming exhibits range
from large horse-drawn implements to small
hand-tools. There are also many old photographs
and documents illustrating life in the district and
archaeological finds from local excavations.

Pittenweem

Kellie Castle

Pittenweem, Fife KY10 2RF   ☎ 03338 271
Easter and May–Sept, 2–6. April and Oct, Sat,
Sun 2–6.
▨ *NTS Representative*
Ⓔ ⬗ ⬛ ⬕ [NTS]

The Castle, which since 1970 has belonged to
the National Trust for Scotland, is a fine
example of late 16th and early 17th-century
Scottish domestic architecture, with interesting
decorated plaster ceilings in five of the principal
rooms. In 1948 it was bought from the Earl of
Mar and Kellie by the Lorimer family, who had
occupied it as tenants since 1878. One of the
Lorimers, John, was a painter and another,
Robert, a successful architect.

The late 17th to early 20th-century
furnishings include needlework pictures,
tapestry, and a Stodart forte-piano of 1826. The
late 17th-century withdrawing room, now a
dining room, is decorated with 64 painted
panels, depicting the romantic landscapes
popular at the time. A room is devoted to the
work of Robert Lorimer, including items of
furniture designed by him.

Lochty Private Railway

Lochty Farm, Carnbee, Pittenweem, Fife
    Y10 2SA
Mid June–Sept 7, Sun 2–5 (steam trains).
    Lochty Station is open most Suns in year
▨ *The Secretary, Fife Railway Preservation*
    Group, 48 Hendry Road, Kirkcaldy, Fife
    KY2 5JN   ☎ 0592 2264587
Ⓔ ⬕ ⬕

Lochty Station is on the B940 Cupar-Crail road,
seven miles from Crail. Visitors can travel on
steam-hauled trains, on a preserved stretch of
track. The rolling stock collection includes
industrial locomotives from five manufacturers
and is representative of the types used in and
around Fife. The passenger coaches are mostly
standard British Rail Mark I of 1956–60,
together with an observation car from the
Coronation Express, dating from 1937. The
freight wagons are types used by industries in
Fife between 1900 and 1975. There is also a
representative collection of semaphore signals
and associated equipment.

Plymouth

City Museum and Art Gallery

Drake Circus, Plymouth, Devon PL4 8AJ
    ☎ 0752 668000 extn 4878
Mon–Fri 10–5.30; Sat 10–5
▨ *The Secretary*
Ⓕ ⬗ ⬕ ⬕

The Museum's natural history collections
specialise in local material and include an
important collection of minerals from the
South-West. There are also worldwide plant
and insect collections. The ethnographical
section has tribal artefacts from Oceania,
Africa, America and Asia, and the
archaeological collection also includes
worldwide material, although it specialises in
prehistoric and later finds from Dartmoor and
the Plymouth area. There are also displays
reflecting the social history of the South-West.

Fine art is represented mainly by 18th and
19th-century paintings, special attention being

given to artists, such as Reynolds and Prout, with Plymouth associations. The decorative art collections include ceramics, glass, silver and costumes, Plymouth and Oriental porcelain being a feature of the displays. The Museum also holds collections of Old Master drawings and early printed books.

Elizabethan House

32 New Street, Plymouth, Devon PL1 2NA
Easter–Sept, Mon–Fri 10–1, 2.15–5.30;
　　Sat 10–1, 2.15–5; Sun 3–5. Oct–Easter,
　　Mon–Sat 10–1, 2.15–4.30.
⚑ *See City Museum and Art Gallery*
£ *ex. pre-booked parties* ⚲ ⚑

The Elizabethan House is a 16th-century house, of stone and timber-framed construction, in the historic quarter of Plymouth. It has been furnished in period style, in order to give visitors an impression of living conditions in Tudor and Jacobean times.

Merchant's House Museum

33 St Andrew's Street, Plymouth, Devon
Mon–Fri 10–1, 2–5.30; Sat 10–1, 2–5.
　　Easter–Sept, also Sun 3–5.
⚑ *See City Museum and Art Gallery*
£ *ex. pre-booked parties* ⚲ ⚑

This is a 16th-century house, with 17th-century additions. It contains displays illustrating the social, economic and maritime history of Plymouth up to 1670.

Plympton

Saltram House

Plympton, Plymouth, Devon PL7 3UH
　☎ *0752 336546*
Sun–Thurs & Bank Holiday 12.30–6.
　　Kitchen & Art Gallery in Chapel, 11–6.
　　Last admission 5.30. Garden open daily 11–6,
　　during daylight hours Nov–Mar.
⚑ *The Administrator*
£ ⚑ **⚐** ⚑ ⚒ [NT]

Saltram House, a National Trust property, situated in a landscaped park, is three and a half miles east of Plymouth city centre, between the A38 and the A379. Built for the Parker family in the reign of George II on the site of an earlier Tudor house, it has its original contents. There is magnificent plasterwork and decoration, including two important rooms designed by Robert Adam, and fine period furniture, woven Axminster carpets, china and pictures, including a number of portraits by Sir Joshua Reynolds, who was a friend of the family. The lemon and orange trees from the orangery are taken out of doors each summer.

The stable block contains a small collection of railway material and an exhibition on 'Mr Parker's Horses', while the chapel has an exhibition of the work of local artists.

Pocklington

Penny Arcadia

Ritz Cinema, Market Place, Pocklington,
　　North Yorkshire YO4 2AR　　**☎** *07592 3420*
May & Sept, daily 2–5. June–Aug, daily 10–5.
　　Other times by appt.
⚑ *The Curator*
£ ⚲ ⚑ ⚑ ⚑

The Museum is housed in what is still a cinema, built in the garden of reputedly the finest house in Pocklington (c. 1720), through which the public enters the new building. It contains a comprehensive collection of coin-operated amusement machines, which illustrate technical developments and trends in popular art and entertainment over the past 100 years. Many machines demonstrate the ways in which the anti-gambling laws were circumvented.

As the exhibits show, many popular entertainments, such as the cinema, the record industry and photography, have their roots in amusement machines. The historical significance of the collection is explained by means of an audio-visual presentation, a stage show and a guided tour, during which the exhibits are demonstrated.

Stewart's Gardens and Museum

Burnby Hall, Pocklington, York, North
　　Yorkshire YO4 2AQ　　　　**☎** *07592 2068*
May–Sept, daily 10–7
⚑ *The Administrator*　　　　**☎** *07592 3403*
£ ⚐ ⚑ ⚑

This purpose-built Museum, displaying sporting trophies and ethnographical material collected during his world travels, was left to the people of Pocklington by the late Major P. M. Stewart on his death in 1962. The Major took a keen

Enamel-decorated coffee pot of Plymouth porcelain, about 1769. Plymouth, City Museum and Art Gallery.

interest in the arts, religions, everyday life and weapons of the countries he visited. The exhibits in the Museum range from African musical instruments and Burmese religious objects to domestic utensils from India.

The hunting and fishing trophies include Major Stewart's largest salmon from Norway (1902), tarpon from Mexico, sharks from Florida and Australia, trout, deer, birds and giant eels from New Zealand, and moose and caribou from Canada.

Polegate

Polegate Windmill and Milling Museum

Park Croft, Polegate, East Sussex
Easter–Sept, Sun 2–5. Aug, also Bank Holiday
  & Wed.
🏠 *Mr C. Waite, 48a Wannock Lane, Lower*
  Willingdon, East Sussex BN20 9SD
£ ⬓

Built in 1817, this tower mill ceased to be driven by wind during the Second World War. As the result of a campaign by the Eastbourne and District Preservation Society, the Mill was saved from demolition and restored to working order in 1967, with all its internal machinery intact. The adjoining storeroom has been converted into a milling museum, and houses a collection of models and objects associated with milling. The exhibits include photographs and documents relating to Sussex wind and watermills.

Pontefract

Pontefract Museum

Salter Row, Pontefract, West Yorkshire WF8 1BA
  ☎ *0977 797289*
Mon–Sat 10.30–12.30, 1.30–5. Closed public &
  local government holidays.
🏠 *Mr R. van Riel, Keeper*
F ⬓ ⬓ ☐

The Museum is in an Art Nouveau building, designed as a Carnegie Free Library and opened in 1904. There are permanent displays on the archaeology and history of the town and its castle. These include finds from Pontefract Castle and from excavations at St John's Priory and a painting by Alexander Kierinx showing Pontefract as it was in 1635, before the Civil War. The displays on more recent history include sections on the local liquorice and coal industries.

There is a regular programme of temporary exhibitions, with material sometimes drawn from the collections of Wakefield Art Gallery and Museums, and sometimes brought in from outside. These cover a wide range of topics, from painting, photography and cartoons to exhibitions of community history, set up in association with local societies.

The tiled and mosaic-floored entrance to Pontefract Museum.

Pontrhydfendigaid

Strata Florida Abbey

Pontrhydfendigaid, Ystrad Meurig, Dyfed
  SY25 6ES   ☎ *09745 261*
Mar 15–Oct 15, Mon–Sat 9.30–6.30; Sun
  2–6.30. Oct 16–Mar 14 by appt.
🏠 *The Custodian*
£ ⬓

Strata Florida Abbey, a Cistercian house, was founded in 1164. The Church was consecrated in 1201 and by 1235 the monastery buildings were virtually complete. The Abbey subsequently became an important centre of Welsh culture and influence. In 1951 a memorial slab to the 14th-century lyric poet, Dafydd ap Gwilym, was placed in the Abbey Church to commemorate his burial here.

The entrance building contains an exhibition presenting the history of the Abbey. Welsh poems can be listened to on handsets.

Pontypool

Junction Cottage, Pontymoel

Lower Mill, Pontymoel, Pontypool, Gwent
Apr–Sept, daily 2–5
🏠 *See The Valley Inheritance*
£ ⬓

Junction Cottage, located at the point where the Monmouthshire and the Brecon and Abergavenny Canals meet, was built in 1814 as a canal tollkeeper's cottage. Now the property of the British Waterways Board, it contains an exhibition on the history and operation of the local canal system, managed by the Torfaen Museum Trust.

The Valley Inheritance

Park Buildings, Pontypool, Gwent NP4 6JH
  ☎ *04955 52036*
Mon–Sat 10–5; Sun 2–5. Closed Dec 25.
🏠 *Visitor Services Unit*
£ ⬓ ⬓ ⬓

The Valley Inheritance occupies the former stables of Pontypool Park House, the mansion of the Hanbury family who, from the late 17th

century onwards, did much to develop Torfaen as an industrial centre. Built during the 1930s, the stables, which included a carriage house, remained in use until 1915, when the last squire of Pontypool, John Hanbury, died. In 1979, after being used for a great variety of purposes, they were taken over by the Torfaen Museum Trust, which continued a programme of restoration begun in 1975 by the Torfaen Borough Council.

The displays in the Museum tell the story of the eastern valley of Gwent from the earliest times to the present day. They include sections on the iron, steel, coal and tinplate industries and on social conditions in the Valley during the past two centuries.

Poole

Guildhall Museum

Market Street, Poole, Dorset BH15 1NP
☎ *0202 675151*
Mon–Sat 10–2; Sun 2–5
⚔ *Mrs M. Ellis*
£ *✐* *▢*

The Guildhall was built in 1761 together with a new house and was used for all meetings of the Corporation until 1932. The former Council Chamber and Court Room now contains exhibitions illustrating the development of Poole from the 12th century to the present day, based on historic documents, maps, paintings and civic regalia.

On the ground or market floor visitors can see an audio-visual presentation of life in 19th and 20th-century Poole, illustrated by contemporary photographs. The Temporary Exhibition Gallery is used to explore in greater detail aspects of life in the town's past, present and future.

The Poole Study Collection, which can be seen by appointment, has collections of photographs, drawings, prints, paintings, maps and ephemera. It also contains the Museum's library and sound archives.

Maritime Museum

Paradise Street, The Quay, Poole, Dorset
☎ *0202 675151*
Mon–Sat 10–2; Sun 2–5
⚔ *Mrs M. Ellis*
£ *✐* *↩*

The Museum is housed in part of a 15th-century quayside woolhouse, known as the Town Cellars, and in the adjoining Oakleys Mill, an 18th to 19th-century grain and feed mill. The displays trace the history of Poole's maritime community – the merchants and seamen, the fishermen, the shipwrights and allied craftsmen, and the tradesmen of the port. The exhibits include boats, ship-models, shipbuilding tools, navigation instruments and objects associated with naval celebrities.

Statue at the entrance to the Royal National Lifeboat Institution Museum, Poole.

The Old Lifeboat House

East Quay, Poole, Dorset   ☎ *0202 671133*
Easter–Sept, daily 10.15–12.30, 2.15–5
⚔ *David R. Green*
F *↩*

Poole's 19th-century lifeboat house no longer accommodates the town's modern lifeboat, which is kept afloat, but is run as a museum by and for the support of the Poole branch of the Royal National Lifeboat Institution. The main exhibit is the former Poole lifeboat, *Thomas Kirk Wright*, which was built in 1938 and was kept in and launched from the lifeboat house until she went out of service in 1962. She was one of 18 lifeboats which took part in the Dunkirk evacuation of 1940, from which she was towed home badly damaged.

Royal National Lifeboat Institution Museum

West Quay Road, Poole, Dorset BH15 1HZ
☎ *0202 671133*
Mon–Fri 9.30–4.30. Closed Bank Holiday.
⚔ *David R. Green*
F *✐* *↩* *⅋*

Situated within the headquarters of the RNLI, which provides the back-up service for 200 lifeboat stations throughout the country, the Museum traces the Institution's 160-year-old history by means of models, paintings, photographs, medals, memorabilia and commemorative items. Among the celebrities featured are Sir William Hillary, founder of the RNLI, and Henry Blogg of Cromer, the most decorated of all lifeboatmen. A 'D' class lifeboat, bought over 10 years ago as a result of a BBC *Blue Peter* appeal, is on display at the Museum.

Scaplen's Court

High Street, Poole, Dorset   ☎ *0202 675151*
Mon–Sat 10–2; Sun 2–5
⚔ *Mrs M. Ellis*
£ *🏛*

Scaplen's Court was built in the 15th century as a merchant's house. By the late 18th century the entire south front was refaced with nine inches of brickwork and fitted with windows of the period. Further deterioration took place during the 19th and in the early 20th centuries. The rear part of the building was extensively restored during the 1950s and a new frontage built in 1985–6.

The old kitchen buttery and pantry of the medieval merchant's home has exhibits of household cleaning and laundry equipment and cooking and food preparation utensils dating from the post-medieval period to the early 20th century. In the Solar and first floor bedrooms exhibitions trace the domestic life of Poole over the centuries.

Port Charlotte

Museum of Islay Life

Port Charlotte, Isle of Islay, Argyll PA48 7UA
☎ 049 685 358
Apr–Sept, Mon–Fri 10–5; Sat, Sun 2 5.
Oct–Mar, Mon–Fri 10–4.30.
◪ Mrs Carol-Ann Jackson, Keeper & Secretary
Ⓔ *ex. children* ⬥ ⬥

The Museum is in a redundant church, overlooking Port Charlotte Bay. The church was built by men and women of the parish, by their own labour, when the Free Church broke away from the Church of Scotland in 1843. The building was converted to the Museum of Islay Life in 1977. A Lapidarium was added in 1984.

The exhibits are mainly of archaeological and historical material relating to the Island. One section is devoted to domestic items, mainly from the Victorian period, displayed in two room settings, a bedroom and a kitchen. There is also a 'blackhouse', showing the stages in thatching and the general layout of the house; a series of displays on wrecks which occurred off the coast of Islay; spinning and weaving equipment; exhibits showing the methods of whisky-making, including an illicit still; and collections of wheelwrights', coopers', leatherworkers' and farm tools.

Port Erin

Aquarium

Department of Marine Biology, University of Liverpool, Port Erin, Isle of Man
☎ 062483 2027
◪ Professor T. A. Norton
Ⓕ ⬥

The Aquarium contains live specimens of fish, shellfish and other invertebrates to be found in the Irish Sea. There are displays to help with the identification of marine creatures, to illustrate the history and current activities of the Department and to present aspects of marine biology of interest to the general public.

Porthcawl

Porthcawl Museum

Old Police Station, John Street, Porthcawl,
Mid Glamorgan CF36 3BD
Mon–Fri 2.30–4.30; Sat 10–12, 2.30–4.30.
Closed Christmas Day.
◪ Hon. Secretary
Ⓔ ⬥ ⬥ ◻

The Museum is in part of Porthcawl's mid 19th-century Police Station. The collection has been formed since 1972 by the town's Museum Society and includes material relating to the geology, natural history, archaeology, history and costume of Porthcawl and its environs. The displays are changed regularly, in order to provide variety over the year and to allow as much of the collection as possible to be seen by the public.

Porthmadog

Ffestiniog Railway Museum

Harbour Station, Porthmadog, Gwynedd
LL49 9NF ☎ 0766 2340/2384
Open during train service hours
◪ Ffestiniog Railway Company
Ⓕ *Donations welcome* ⬥ ⬥ ⬥

The Museum occupies the former railway goods shed, built 1878–9. The displays tell the story of the pioneering 2-foot gauge Ffestiniog Railway, and among the exhibits are signals and early rail sections; a wooden slate wagon of 1857; an iron horse dandy of 1861; 'Princess', the line's first steam locomotive (1863); an open four-wheel carriage built for the start of passenger services in 1865; a hearse van; and a slate wagon with its two-ton load of slate. A notable item in the Museum's collection is 'Taliesin', the Fairlie patent double engine of 1886.

There is a remarkably complete archive, documenting the history, from 1832 onwards, of the railway which inspired the development of narrow-gauge railways worldwide.

Porthmadog Maritime Museum

Oakley No. 1 Wharf, The Harbour, Porthmadog,
Gwynedd LL49 9NF ☎ 0766 3736
Last weekend in May–Sept, daily 10–6. Pre-booked
parties at other times by appt.
◪ Mr E. Davies, 'Gowerian', Borth y Gest,
Porthmadog LL49 9UA ☎ 0766 2864
Ⓔ ⬥ ⬥

The Maritime Museum is housed in a quayside shed, formerly used for storing slates. Its collections illustrate the shipbuilding industry which developed at Porthmadog during the 18th and 19th centuries, and the voyages of the wooden sailing ships which took cargoes all over the world, especially roofing slates produced in quarries around Blaenau Ffestiniog. The story is told by means of models, paintings, prints, photographs, tools, equipment, documents and newspaper cuttings.

Portland

Portland Museum

217 Wakeham, Portland, Dorset ☎ *0305 821804*
May–Sept, Mon–Sat 10–5.30; Sun 11–5.
Oct–Apr, Tues–Sat 10–1, 2–5.
Closed Good Fri, Dec 25, 26, Jan 1.
⚑ *The Curator*
📧 🖉 ♿

The Museum, housed partly in two old cottages
and partly in a new extension, tells the story of
Portland since prehistoric times. The exhibits
include two great rarities, a pair of iron ingots,
dating from *c.* 400 B.C., and the Rosette Gem,
a limestone slab containing topaz-coloured
crystals. There is also a roof slate from Portland
prison, engraved with a delicate lace pattern by
a man imprisoned for forgery. There are special
displays devoted to old domestic equipment and
to Dr Marie Stopes, the birth control pioneer,
who did much to establish the original Portland
museum. One room contains exhibits relating to
the shipwrecks which have occurred off Portland
and the adjoining coast.

Port-of-Ness

Ness Historical Society Museum

The Old School, Lionel, Port-of-Ness, Isle of Lewis
PA86 0TG ☎ *085181 576*
Mon–Fri 9–5
⚑ *The Secretary, Comunn Eachdraidh Nis,*
23 South Dell, Ness, Isle of Lewis
📧 🖉 ♿

The Museum is 26 miles from Stornoway, at the
furthermost northerly point of the Isle of Lewis.
Its collections are devoted to the history and
occupations of the Ness area of Lewis. There is a
large collection of photographic, printed and
written material and the exhibits include fishing
equipment, domestic utensils and implements
used in crofting.

Portsmouth

Charles Dickens' Birthplace Museum

393 Old Commercial Road, Portsmouth,
Hampshire PO1 2JS
Mar–Oct, daily 10.30–5.30
⚑ *See City Museum and Art Gallery*
📧 🖉 ♿

Charles Dickens was born at 393 Old
Commercial Road in 1812. The house was
restored in 1970 and furnished to illustrate the
kind of home which John and Elizabeth Dickens
would have created for themselves. An exhibition
room shows items which once belonged to the
novelist. They include a set of his waistcoat
buttons, a signed cheque, a lock of his hair and
the couch on which he died in 1870.

City Museum and Art Gallery

Museum Road, Portsmouth, Hampshire
PO1 2LJ ☎ *0705 827261*
Daily 10.30–5.30. Closed Dec 24–26.
⚑ *Visitor Services Organiser*
📧 🍴 🖂 ♿

The Museum is in a Victorian barrack block,
built in the style of a French château. Its
collections include English furniture, pottery,
clocks, glass, and paintings and prints of subjects
in Portsmouth and the surrounding area. There
are also displays of domestic equipment covering
the 17th to 20th centuries.

Eastney Pumping Station

Henderson Road, Eastney, Portsmouth, Hampshire
PO4 9JF
Apr–Sept, daily 1.30–5.30. Steam Weekends:
as advertised, 1.30–5.30. Oct–Mar, Steam
Weekends only 1st Sun of each month,
1.30–5.30.
⚑ *See City Museum and Art Gallery*
📧 🖉 ♿

The Pumping Station, designed to pump
sewage, is a 19th-century building, housing a
pair of Boulton and Watt steam engines, which
are among the largest still working in the British
Isles, together with several smaller steam
engines. All the engines have been carefully
maintained and are in operating condition.
The building adjoining the steam engine
house contains Crossley gas engines and four
Tangye pumps dating from 1904.

Fort Widley

Portsdown Hill Road, Portsmouth, Hampshire
PO6 3LS
Apr–Sept, Sat, Sun & Bank Holiday 1.30–5.30
⚑ *See City Museum and Art Gallery*
📧 🖉 ♿

Fort Widley is a Palmerston Fort, built in
1861–5 on the orders of Lord Palmerston to
defend Portsmouth from the north. Now
maintained as a museum, it contains a labyrinth
of underground passages, magazines and gun
emplacements.

'The Garden of the Hesperides'
by Lord Leighton, 1892. Port Sunlight,
Lady Lever Art Gallery.

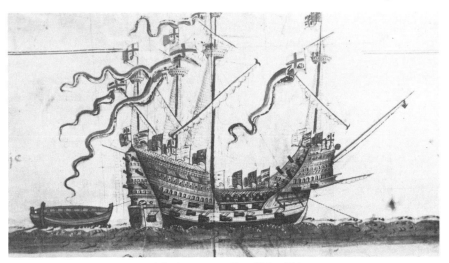

The only contemporary picture of the *Mary Rose*, in the margin of an inventory of the King's ships known as the Anthony Roll, 1546.

HMS *Victory*

HM Naval Base, Portsmouth, Hampshire
PO1 3PZ   ☎ *0705 826682*
Mar–Oct, Mon–Sat 10.30–5.30; Sun 1–5.
Nov–Feb, Mon–Sat 10.30–4.30; Sun 1–4.30.
Closed Dec 25.
🗷 *The Commanding Officer*
£ 🛈 💺 🖼

The keel of HMS *Victory* was laid at Chatham in 1759. She was the flagship of Admiral Lord Nelson at the Battle of Trafalgar in 1805 and she still serves as the flagship of the Commander in Chief Naval Home Command. She is preserved in dry dock and is manned by serving officers of the Royal Navy and Royal Marines, who conduct visitors on tours between decks.

The *Mary Rose* Ship Hall and Exhibition

HM Naval Base, Portsmouth, Hampshire
PO1 3LR   ☎ *0705 750521*
Mar–Oct, daily 10.30–5.30. Nov–Feb, daily 10.30–5. Closed Dec 25.
🗷 *The Mary Rose Trust, 48 Warblington Street, Portsmouth PO1 2ET*
£ 🛈 💺 🖼 ♿

The Ship Hall is based on an old dry dock, itself an Historic Monument, while the Exhibition is housed in an early 19th-century timber building, which was originally a masthouse. In the Ship Hall is displayed what remains of Henry VIII's warship, the *Mary Rose*, which sank off Portsmouth in 1545 and was raised in 1982. Visitors can see the reconstruction and conservation of the surviving starboard hull structure.

The Exhibition shows more than a thousand of the 14,000 objects recovered by divers from the wreck. These include weapons – especially longbows – personal possessions and clothing of the crew, cooking and eating utensils, and fittings from the ship.

Royal Naval Museum

HM Naval Base, Portsmouth, Hampshire
PO1 3LR   ☎ *0705 733060*
Daily 10.30–5, with some seasonal variations.
Closed Dec 25–Jan 2 inclusive.
🗷 *The Archivist*
£ 🛈 💺 🖼 ♿

Part of the Museum is housed in three Georgian storehouses, which form part of the original 18th-century Royal Dockyard. The displays illustrate the history of the Royal Navy from Tudor times to the South Atlantic campaign of 1982, with special emphasis on the social development of the Navy and on the Nelson and Victorian periods. Among the exhibits are personal items relating to Lord Nelson and his officers and men, ships' figureheads, ship models, naval campaign medals and a fine collection of paintings.

Port Sunlight

Lady Lever Art Gallery

Port Sunlight, Wirral, Merseyside L62 5EQ
    ☎ *051 645 3623*
Mon–Sat 10–5; Sun 2–5. Closed Good Fri,
Dec 24–26, Jan 1.
🗷 *Assistant Keeper*
£ 🖉 🖼

The Beaux-Arts classical building dates from 1914–22. The collections, mainly of British art, were formed by the Gallery's founder, William Lever, Viscount Leverhulme (1851–1925), who also established the soap firm, Lever Brothers, and the model village of Port Sunlight. The principal collections are of British 18th to 19th-century paintings; 19th-century British watercolours; British and Continental sculpture, especially of the late 19th century; 16th to 18th-century furniture, mainly English and including an outstanding collection of late 18th-century marquetry commodes; 17th to 19th-century tapestry and needlework; Wedgwood pottery; Chinese ceramics, jades and hardstones; and antique sculpture and Greek vases.

Miners underground on the Return Roadway.
Welsh Miners' Museum, Port Talbot.

Port Talbot

The Welsh Miners' Museum

Afan Argoed Country Park, Cynonville, Port
   Talbot, West Glamorgan
Apr–Sept, daily 10.30–6. Oct–Mar, Sat, Sun
   10.30–5.
🄭 Mr G. Thomas, Director/Secretary, 16 Percy
   Road, Cynonville, Port Talbot
☎ 0639 850875
Ⓔ ♠ 🖱 ⚓

The Museum is six miles from Port Talbot on
the A4107 Afan Valley road. It was created as a
community enterprise, in order to tell the story
of the Welsh miner from the earliest days of
mining in the Welsh Coalfield. The exhibits
include a replica of a coal mine, equipment,
clothing and personal possessions of miners, and
photographs and documents illustrating
different aspects of coalmining and the society
of which it formed a part.

Potterne

Wiltshire Fire Defence Collection

Wiltshire Fire Brigade Headquarters, Manor
   House, Potterne, Devizes, Wiltshire SN10 5PP
☎ 0380 3601
By appt only. Closed Bank Holiday.
🄭 Chief Fire Officer
Ⓕ ⚲ ⚓

The stable block and coachman's rooms in
which the Museum is housed form part of an
18th-century manor house. The main part of
the stable building has been arranged to
represent the engine house in the days when the
equipment was pulled by horses. This section of
the Museum also contains two Merryweather
hand-pumps, a range of ladders and fire-buckets,
and historic photographs. In other rooms there
is a comprehensive collection of 18th to 20th-
century fire-fighting equipment.

Poundisford

Poundisford Park

Poundisford, Taunton, Somerset TA3 7AF
☎ 082342 244
Apr–June & Sept 1–18, Wed, Thurs & Bank
   Holiday 11–5. July–Aug, Wed–Fri & Bank
   Holiday 11–5.
🄭 R. W. Vivian-Neal
Ⓔ ⚲ 🖱 ⚓ [HHA]

Poundisford Park is three and a half miles south
of Taunton, on a road signposted from the
B1370 north of Corfe. It is a Grade I listed
building dating from the mid 16th century, with
18th-century additions. Elizabethan moulded
plaster ceilings are one of the more important
architectural features. Poundisford contains
collections of portraits, porcelain, glass,
furniture and costume, but it is laid out and
presented to the public as a family home, a
living museum, changing and developing as
time goes on. There are plans to adapt the 18th-
century barn to the display of exhibits
illustrating the traditional life and crafts of the
surrounding countryside.

Prescot

Prescot Museum of Clock and Watchmaking

34 Church Street, Prescot, Merseyside L34 3LA
☎ 051 430 7787
Tues–Sat & Bank Holiday Mon 10–5; Sun 2–5.
   Closed Good Fri, Dec 24–26, Jan 1.
🄭 The Curator
Ⓕ ♠ ⚓

Prescot is on the A57 Liverpool to Warrington
road, 10 miles from Liverpool. The Museum
occupies a late 18th-century house on a corner
site in the Town Centre Conservation Area.
The displays tell the story of the South-West
Lancashire watch and watch toolmaking trades,
which existed from c. 1600 to the 1960s. An
introductory section is devoted to the history of
time measurement and other exhibits illustrate
the products of the industry, the watch and tool-
makers and the tool merchants, against the
social and industrial background of the area.
   There is a reconstruction of a traditional
workshop, equipped with a range of hand tools
and machinery. This is contrasted with a
reconstruction of part of the Lancashire Watch
Company's steam-powered factory, established
in 1899 to make complete watches under one
roof. An accompanying display gives the history
of the factory and the reasons for its closure in
1910.
   The Museum also presents modern
developments in watch and clockmaking,
including the application of electronics to
horology, and contrasts hand and steam-
powered manufacturing methods with those in
use today.
   The town of Prescot is one of the earliest
settlements on Merseyside. Much of its centre is
now a conservation area and provides a Town
Trail to guide visitors around the landmarks.

Horse-drawn fire engines at the Wiltshire
Fire Defence Collection, Potterne.

Presteigne

Presteigne and District Museum

Shire Hall, Presteigne, Powys
Whitsun–June & Sept–mid Oct, Tues, Sat
    10.30–1, 2.30–5. July–Aug, Tues, Thurs, Sat
    10.30–1, 2.30–5. Parties by appt.
🕵 Mr C. E. V. Fullaway, Hafod, Broad Street,
    Presteigne   ☎ 0544 26744
🅴 ⊘ ➤

The Museum, staffed by volunteers, is in part of
the 1829 Shire Hall, which was used as the
administrative centre of Radnorshire until 1889
and as the judicial centre for the County until
1970. The collections illustrate social life in the
area during the 18th, 19th and 20th centuries,
and include domestic equipment, craftsmen's
tools, clothing, documents and photographs, as
well as a wide range of everyday objects.

Preston

Harris Museum and Art Gallery

Market Square, Preston, Lancashire PR1 2PP
    ☎ 0772 58248
Mon–Sat 10–5. Closed Bank Holiday.
🕵 Education Officer
🅵 ⊘ ➤

The Museum's displays are devoted to the social
history of the area and to archaeological
material from regional sites. The Art Gallery
has extensive collections of costumes, paintings,
drawings, prints and watercolours, including
works by 18th, 19th and 20th-century British
artists, especially members of the Devis family.
The decorative arts section has new permanent
displays of ceramics and glass.

Lancashire County and Regimental Museum

Old Sessions House, Stanley Street, Preston,
    Lancashire PR1 4YP   ☎ 0772 264075
Mon–Wed, Fri, Sat 10–5. Closed Bank Holidays.
🕵 Fergus Read, Assistant Keeper
🅵 ⊘ ➤

The Old Sessions House in Preston, dating from
1825 and now a Grade II listed building, was
used for court purposes until 1900. It now
houses under one roof displays illustrating the
history of the County of Lancashire and of a
number of the regiments associated with it.

    The story of the County begins in the 12th
century, when the name 'Lancashire' first
appears in the written records and continues
through to the present day. In the modern
section, visitors can sit at the teacher's desk in a
Victorian classroom, read the oath from an
authentic witness box and lie on the bed of a
prisoner's cell.

    There is a gallery devoted to the Duke of
Lancaster's Own Yeomanry, the oldest active
yeomanry regiment in Britain. It shows the
development of the Regiment since its
beginnings during the Revolutionary and
Napoleonic Wars.

The Loyal Regiment (North Lancashire) Museum

RHQ QLR, Fulwood Barracks, Preston,
    Lancashire PR2 4AA
    ☎ 0772 716543 extn 2362
Tues, Thur 9–12, 2.15–4. Closed public holidays.
🕵 Major (Retd) N. J. Perkins,
🅵 ⊘

The Museum at Fulwood Barracks houses the
regimental collections of the 47th and 81st The
Loyal Regiment (North Lancashire), now
absorbed into The Queen's Lancashire
Regiment.

    Uniforms, medals and weapons can now be
seen at the Lancashire County and Regimental
Museum, while the exhibits at Fulwood
Barracks include memorabilia of General Wolfe,
of General Sir Richard Farren, who commanded
the 47th at the Battle of Inkerman, and of
Major G. Forster Sadleir, who in 1819 became
the first European to cross the Arabian desert on
foot. Among the special exhibits is the much-
travelled silver mounted Maida Tortoise, relic of
an emergency meal eaten by General Sir James
Kempt after a victory against Napoleon in 1806.

Prestongrange

Scottish Mining Museum, Prestongrange

Prestongrange, Prestonpans, East Lothian
    ☎ 031 665 9904
Tues–Fri, 10–4.30; Sat–Sun 12–5
🕵 The Director, Scottish Mining Museum,
    Newtongrange   ☎ 031 663 7519
🅵 ➤ ♿

The Museum at Prestongrange is the starting
point of the Coal Heritage Trail, which takes
visitors by way of Tranent and Fa'side to the

Lady Victoria Colliery, the Scottish Mining Museum's second site at Newtongrange.

At Prestongrange, there is a Visitor Centre; substantial remains of a Hoffmann brick kiln; an exhibition hall containing relics of the mining industry; and, dominating the site, the Cornish Beam Pumping Engine built by Harveys of Hale in 1874.

Quainton

Buckinghamshire Railway Centre

Quainton Road Station, Quainton, Aylesbury,
*   Buckinghamshire HP22 4BY   ☎ 029675 450*
Easter–Oct, Sun & Bank Holiday 10–5
◙ *Chris Tayler, 161 Carterhatch Road, Enfield,*
*   Middlesex EN3 5LZ*
£ ▉ ▆ ☛

The Centre is at Quainton Road Station on the former Great Central/Metropolitan line, now used for freight only, six miles north-west of Aylesbury. It is a standard gauge working railway museum, run entirely by volunteers and formed in 1969 to preserve steam locomotives and other rolling stock and equipment of all kinds such as we used on the railways before modernisation in the 1950s. Many of the steam engines have been restored to full working order.

An Irish crannog or lake dwelling of the Iron Age, reconstructed at Quin as part of the Craggaunowen Project.

Quin

The Craggaunowen Project

Craggaunowen, Quin, Co. Clare, Ireland
*   ☎ 061 72178*
Apr–May & Sept, daily 10–6. June–Aug, daily
*   10–6.30.*
◙ *Mr T. Sheedy, Manager, Bunratty Castle and*
*   Folk Park, Bunratty, Co. Clare*
*   ☎ 061 61511*
£ ▉ ☛

The Project is situated in wooded country two miles east of Quin. The site consists of a medieval tower house, which contains a display of furniture and objets d'art, including some rare Irish pieces. There are also reconstructions of Iron Age settlements, a lake dwelling and a ring fort, and the leather boat, *Brendan*, sailed by Tim Severin from Ireland to Newfoundland, re-enacting a voyage believed to have been made by St Brendan the Navigator in the 6th century.

Knappogue Castle

Quin, Ennis, Co. Clare, Ireland   ☎ 061 71103
Apr–Oct, daily 9.30–5.30 (last admission 5).
*   Medieval banquets are held twice nightly.*
◙ *Mr F. Gleeson, Manager*
£ ▉ ▆ ☛

Knappogue Castle is one of 42 castles built by the McNamara tribe, which ruled over the territory of Clancullen from the 5th to the 15th century. The Castle, constructed in the 15th century and extended in the 19th, was extensively restored during the late 1960s and early 1970s, and furnished in a way which would reflect its varied history. There are reconstructions of a smithy and other craftsmen's workshops.

R

Ramsey

'The Grove' Rural Life Museum

Andreas Road, Ramsey, Isle of Man
May 5–Sept 26, Mon–Fri 10–5; Sun 2–5
🏛 *The Secretary, Manx Museum, Crellin's Hill,*
Douglas, Isle of Man ☎ *0624 75522*
£ ⬦ 🖼 🐾

This early Victorian house, with its outbuildings, illustrates the living style of a comfortably-off family of the time. There is a series of Victorian period rooms, a display of 19th-century costumes, and collections of dolls, toys and Victorian greetings cards. The outbuildings contain early beekeeping equipment, agricultural implements and horse-drawn vehicles, together with a horse-driven threshing mill.

The garden, paddock and surrounding fields form an attractive setting for the Museum.

Ramsgate

Ramsgate Motor Museum

Westcliff Hall, Ramsgate, Kent CT11 9JX
☎ *0843 581948*
Easter–Oct, daily 10.30–6
🏛 *The Curator*
£ ⬦

The exhibition hall of the Museum was originally a theatre and is cut into the cliff face, with its roof forming the end of the main seafront promenade. It contains 140 motorcars, motorcycles and pedal cycles made between 1860 and 1960, together with motoring accessories, equipment and advertisements.

Ramsgate Museum

Ramsgate Library, Guildford Lawn, Ramsgate,
Kent CT11 9AY ☎ *0843 593532*
Mon–Wed 9.30–6; Thurs, Sat 9.30–5;
Fri 9.30–8. Closed Bank Holiday.
🏛 *Miss M. Winsch, Kent County Museum*
Service, West Malling, Kent ME19 6QE
☎ *0732 845845 extn 2129*
F 🐾

The Museum contains objects, pictures and documents illustrating the history of Ramsgate as a fishing port and tourist centre. There is a special collection of painted pot lids.

Rathdrum

Parnell Museum

Avondale House, Rathdrum, Co. Wicklow, Ireland
May–Sept, daily 2–6
🏛 *The Curator*
F 🐾

Avondale was the birthplace and family home of the Irish patriot and political leader, Charles Stewart Parnell (1846–91). The house has been restored as a memorial to Parnell, with furnishings of the period and many of his papers and personal possessions. Three rooms are at present on view, including the Blue Room, which has excellent plasterwork.

Rathkeale

Castle Matrix

Rathkeale, Co. Limerick, Ireland ☎ *069 64284*
May 15–Sept 15, Sat–Tues 1–5. Other times
by appt.
🏛 *The Curator*
£ 🐾 ☐

Castle Matrix, built in 1440, is the headquarters of the Irish International Arts Centre and the Heraldry Society of Ireland. It contains collections of tapestries, period furniture, objets d'art and documents related to the history of the area and the Castle.

There is a regular programme of temporary exhibitions of original prints by well-known graphic artists. The large library is divided into three principal areas of study – heraldry, military architecture from the 15th century to modern times, and the graphic arts. The print collection includes examples of original prints by all the master printmakers, from Dürer and Rembrandt to modernists.

Ravenglass

Muncaster Castle

Ravenglass, Cumbria ☎ *06577 614/203*
Good Fri–Sept, Tues–Sun & Bank Holiday Mon
1.30–4.30. Garden 12–5.
🏛 *The Administrator*
£ 🛏 🖼 🐾 [HHA]

The present Castle was built in 1862–6, incorporating some earlier work, but the Pennington family has lived here since the 13th century. The contents include a good collection of 17th-century furniture and many family portraits by, among others, Lely, Kneller, Gainsborough, Reynolds and de Lazlo. The dining room has embossed leather hangings above the panelling, and there are also collections of tapestries and porcelain.

Muncaster Mill

Ravenglass, Cumbria CA18 1ST ☎ *06577 232*
Apr–May & Sept, Sun–Fri 11–5. June–Aug,
Sun–Fri 10–6. Other times by appt.
🏛 *The Miller*
£ 🛏 🐾

This water-driven corn mill has been renovated by the Ravenglass and Eskdale Railway Company for the Eskdale (Cumbria) Trust. The original 19th-century machinery is in regular use, producing a range of traditional stone-ground flours.

Railway Museum

The Ravenglass and Eskdale Railway Company
*   Limited, Ravenglass, Cumbria CA18 1SW*
    ☎ 06577 226
Mar–Oct, daily when trains are running and
*   Sat–Sun in winter. On request at other times.*
*   Closed Dec 20–25.*
🕅 *The General Manager*
Ⓔ 🎫 💻 🅿 ♿

The Museum is housed in a former station of the
Furness Railway. Its collections illustrate the
history of the narrow-gauge Ravenglass and
Eskdale Railway, which dates from 1876 as a
passenger railway and had its origins as a railway
built to haul iron-ore from the local mines and
quarries. The exhibits include relics,
photographs and models, and there is an audio-
visual programme.

Visitors can travel 7 miles inland on the
Ravenglass and Eskdale Railway, from the coast
to Eskdale, on steam-hauled trains. There is a
choice of open or closed carriages.

Ravenshead

The Gordon Brown Collection

Longdale Rural Craft Centre, Longdale Lane,
*   Ravenshead, Nottinghamshire NG15 9AH*
    ☎ 0623 794858/796952
Daily 9–6. Closed Dec 25–26.
🕅 *Ms Hilary Scarlett, Administrator*
Ⓔ 🎫 💻 🅿 ♿

The Centre, the headquarters of the
Nottinghamshire Craftsmen's Guild, occupies
the buildings of a former poultry and mushroom
farm, to which extensions have been added.
There are displays of craftsmen's tools and
equipment, including items from one of the
country's largest private collections of hand
tools. Demonstrations of a wide range of crafts
can be seen in the Centre's workshops.

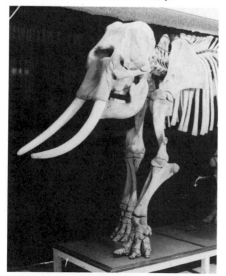

Skeleton of a young elephant.
Reading, Cole Museum of Zoology.

Reading

Blake's Lock Museum

Gas Works Road, off Kenavon Drive, Reading
*   RG1 3DH*   ☎ 0734 590630
Wed–Fri 10–5; Sat, Sun 2–5.
*   Closed Bank Holiday.*
🕅 *See Museum and Art Gallery*
Ⓕ 📷 🅿 🍴

The Museum occupies a brick-built Victorian
pumping station by the side of the River
Kennet, close to its junction with the Thames.
The displays, based mainly on 19th and early
20th-century material, concentrate on the
trades and industries of Reading, other than the
traditional Three Bs – biscuits, beer and bulbs.
There are reconstructions, using original
material, of a printer's workshop, a bakery, and
a barber's, and more general displays include
brickmaking, ironfounding, pharmacies, tailors,
sweetmakers, toy shops, dairying, Cock's sauce,
shoes and mineral water manufacture.

The waterways section includes the wharves,
the Kennet and Avon Canal, bridges, mills and
the natural history of the rivers and the canal.
Boatbuilding, once an important local industry,
is represented and so is the recreational use of
the Thames, fishing and the Reading Regatta
being especially featured.

Cole Museum of Zoology

Department of Pure and Applied Zoology,
*   The University, Whiteknights, Reading*
*   RG6 2AJ*   ☎ 0734 875123 extn 7655
Mon–Fri 9–5.30. Closed Easter & Christmas.
🕅 *Head of Department*
Ⓕ 💻 🅿 ♿

The Museum is in the University, on the south
side of Reading, and is displayed in the Foyer of
the Department of Pure and Applied Zoology. It
was created by Professor F. J. Cole between
1906 and 1939. The exhibits were contributed
by friends, colleagues and former students
throughout the world and, together, they
constitute one of the finest teaching museums in
Britain.

Among the Museum's particular treasures are
a number of delicate preparations of corals,
medusae and sea-pens with polyps expanded,
from the Marine Biological Laboratory at
Naples, prepared specially for the Museum by
Cavaliere Salvatore Lo Bianco and probably the
last specimens preserved by a man regarded as
the greatest of all preparators of marine
material.

Museum and Art Gallery

Blagrave Street, Reading RG1 1QH
    ☎ 0734 55911
Mon–Fri 10–5.30; Sat 10–5. Closed Bank
*   Holiday.*
🕅 *The Director*
Ⓕ 📷 🍴 □

The Museum, a Grade II listed building, forms
part of the Town Hall complex (1875–97),
designed by Alfred Waterhouse, Thomas

Reconstruction of a kitchen at Silchester, the Roman *Calleva Atrebatum*. Reading, Museum and Art Gallery.

Lainson and W. R. Howell. The collections illustrate the history and natural history of the Reading area. The Roman antiquities from Silchester are the outstanding archaeological collection, but the visitor can also see Palaeolithic material from Berkshire and Romanesque carved stones from Reading Abbey. More recent exhibits relate to the social and industrial history of Reading and include a collection of Huntley and Palmer biscuit tins. The natural history displays are complemented by an aquarium and an observation beehive.

The Art Gallery concentrates on 20th-century British art, but, for the 19th century, there is a comprehensive collection of Baxter prints and topographical drawings. Frequent temporary exhibitions are held.

Museum of English Rural Life

The University, Whiteknights, Reading RG6 2AG
    ☎ *0734 857123 extn 475*
Tues–Sat 10–1, 2–4.30. Closed public holidays.
🗷 *The Keeper*
🇪 *ex. children* 🖉 📠

The Museum is two miles south-east of Reading on the A327 Aldershot road. It is, in its own words, 'a national resource and information centre for the history of the countryside'. The exhibitions illustrate agricultural tools and implements, rural industries and domestic equipment of the last 200 years. They include a systematic collection of farm wagons and ploughs and emphasise the contrast between the products of country workshops and the factory-made goods which became available after 1840.

The archival collections of the Institute of Agricultural History may be consulted by appointment. They consist of a comprehensive library, a million photographic prints, and the records of farms, agricultural machinery manufacturers and country organisations.

The Ure Museum of Greek Archaeology

Department of Classics, The University, Whiteknights, Reading RG6 2AA
    ☎ *0734 875123 extn 269/358*
Mon–Fri 9–5. Closed Bank Holiday.
🗷 *The Curator*
🇫 📠 ♿

The Museum was established in the early 1920s by Professor P. N. Ure and his wife, A. D. Ure, who acted as Curator until 1976. Their aim was to build up a collection of Greek pottery that should be representative of as many as possible of the areas of manufacture, and also a collection of objects used by the Greeks, both in daily life and as offerings to the dead. The Museum also contains a collection of Egyptian antiquities, mainly from Thebes, Memphis, Meydum and Abydos, including material from the excavations by Flinders Petrie and Garstang.

Redcar

Royal National Lifeboat Institution Zetland Lifeboat Museum

Old Lifeboat House, King Street, Redcar, Cleveland TS10 3AG
May–Sept, daily 11–4
🗷 *Mrs S. Dunford, Hon. Secretary, 208 Laburnum Road, Redcar TS10 3AG*
    ☎ *0642 47960*
🇫 🖉 📠

The *Zetland*, built by Henry Greathead at South Shields in 1800, is the oldest surviving lifeboat in the world. Built of oak, she had 78 years of service and saved more than 500 lives. She is housed in a late 19th-century boathouse. An upstairs gallery has displays of paintings, postcards and photographs illustrating the history of Redcar as a fishing village and tourist town. There is also a collection of model ships and a reconstruction of the interior of a local fisherman's cottage.

Redditch

National Needle Museum

Forge Mill, Needle Mill Lane, Redditch, Hereford and Worcester B97 6RR   ☎ *0527 62509*
Apr–Oct, Mon–Fri 11–4.30; Sat 1–5; Sun 11.30–5
🗷 *The Curator*
🇪 🍴 🛍 📠

Forge Mill is the world's only surviving water-powered needle mill. The 18th-century building contains a working waterwheel and original needle-making machinery. There is also a series of displays illustrating the technology of the industry and the social conditions of the workers in Redditch during the period when the town was the world centre of the needle industry.

The surrounding parkland contains the ruins of Bordesley Abbey.

Redhill

Royal Earlswood Hospital Museum

Redhill, Surrey RH1 6JL   ☎ 0737 639591
By appt only
☒ The Administrator
£ ↩

The Museum's collections consist of objects
and documents illustrating the history and
achievements of the Hospital in its work with
mentally handicapped people. The exhibits
include band instruments, invitations to charity
events, paintings, china, photographs and
documents. There is a special display of the
work of J. H. Pullen, the Genius of Earlswood,
who was classed as an Idiot Savant.

Redruth

Camborne School of Mines Geological Museum

Trevenson, Pool, Redruth, Cornwall TR15 3SE
☎ 0209 714866
Mon–Fri 9–4.30. Closed Bank Holiday.
☒ Dr R. L. Atkinson, Curator
F ⟐ ↩

The Museum is on the campus of Cornwall
College of Further and Higher Education,
halfway between Camborne and Redruth on the
A3047. It houses a collection of rocks and
minerals which has accumulated since the
School was established in the 1880s. Some of
the material was donated as complete
collections, but much was brought back by
students from mines in many different countries.
The displays include fossils, gemstones, local
minerals, structures and radioactive materials.

There are specialised sections showing
different aspects of geology and mineralisation.
Many of the exhibits are irreplaceable, having
been collected in the days before mechanisation
in the mines destroyed the fine specimens once
obtainable.

Reedham

Berney Arms Windmill

nr Reedham, Norfolk   ☎ 0493 700605
Mar 28–Sept, Mon–Sat 9.30–6.30; Sun 2–6.30
☒ Historic Buildings & Monuments Commission,
    Cambridge   ☎ 0223 358911
£ ↩ ⌗

Three and a half miles north-east of Reedham,
on the north bank of the River Yare and
accessible only by boat or by train to Berney
Arms Station (necessitating a quarter of a mile
walk), this is one of the best and largest of the
marsh mills remaining in Norfolk. It has seven
floors, making it a landmark for miles around,
and is in working order. A site exhibition tells
the story of the mill.

Reeth

Swaledale Folk Museum

Reeth, nr Richmond, North Yorkshire D11 4RT
☎ 0748 84373
Good Fri–Oct, daily 10.30–6. Pre-booked parties
    at other times.
☒ Donald J. Law, Curator
£ ⟐ ↩

The main Museum building was constructed
c. 1830 as a Methodist Sunday School. Other
parts of the collection are housed in an 18th-
century cottage. The displays reflect the
traditional life and occupations of Swaledale
and Arkengarthdale. Among the subjects which
receive special attention are leadmining, sheep
and cattle farming, domestic and family life,
games and toys, religion, local architecture and
building techniques, and village customs.

Reigate

Museum of the Holmesdale Natural History Club

14 Croydon Road, Reigate, Surrey RH2 0PG
Open to non-members for the week preceding the
    Spring Bank Holiday
☒ Hon. Secretary, 105 Blackborough Road,
    Reigate RH2 7BY   ☎ 07372 46574
F ⟐ ↩

The Museum includes fossils, local
archaeological finds and a good collection of
British birds, together with a herbarium. There
is also a collection of photographs and postcards
illustrating changes in the area during the
present century.

The view from the Royal Box at the
Georgian Theatre, Richmond.

Retford

National Mining Museum

Lound Hall, Haughton, Retford, Nottinghamshire
DM22 8DF   ☎ 0623 860728
Tues–Sat 10.30–5.30; Sun 2.30–5.30. Closed
    Bank Holiday.
▓ Professor A. R. Griffin, Hon. Curator
£ ⃠ ▆ ┻ ♿

The Museum contains colliery plant and
equipment from many parts of Britain. The
exhibits include steam winding and pumping
engines, saddle-tank locomotives, coalface
machinery, miners' lamps, tools, surveying
instruments and safety equipment. There are
also simulations of underground mining
activities.

Rhuddlan

Rhuddlan Castle

Rhuddlan, Clwyd   ☎ 0745 590777
Mar 15–Oct 15, daily 9.30–6.30.
    Oct 16–Mar 14, Sat 9.30–4; Sun 2–4,
    Mon–Fri at any reasonable time.
▓ The Custodian
£ ⃠ ┻ ♿ ✿

The construction of Rhuddlan Castle was begun
in 1277 and completed five years later. It was
one of the Iron Ring of castles built by Edward I
as part of his campaign to subdue the Welsh.
During the Civil War, the Castle was besieged
and left in a ruinous condition by the
Parliamentarians. Taken into the care of the
State in 1944, it now contains an exhibition on
the design and history of Edward I's castles.

Ribchester

Ribchester Roman Museum

Riverside, Ribchester, nr Preston, Lancashire
PR3 3XS   ☎ 025484 261
Mar–May & Sept–Oct, daily 2–5. June–Aug,
    daily 11 30–5. Nov–Feb, Sun 2–4.
▓ The Curator
£ ⃠ ┻

The Museum contains material from the Roman
fort of Bremetenacum, including coins, pottery
and jewellery. There is also the tombstone of a
Roman cavalry soldier and a replica of the
famous parade helmet discovered on the site.
The excavated area adjoining the Museum
reveals part of the granary and gateway.

Richmond (Surrey)

Ham House

Richmond, Surrey TW10 7RS   ☎ 01 940 1950
Tues–Sun 11–5. Closed Good Fri, May Day Bank
    Holiday, Dec 24–26.
▓ The Administrator
£ ⃠ ▆ ┻ ♿ NT

Ham House was built in 1610, modified in
1637–9 and enlarged and given its present
appearance during the 1670s by the Duke and
Duchess of Lauderdale, who furnished the house
in an exceptionally luxurious manner. Much of
the furniture seen at Ham House today dates
from this last period, although some was added
in the 1720s. The house is now a National Trust
property, administered by the Victoria and
Albert Museum.
    The large collection of paintings and family
portraits includes works by Hoppner, Reynolds,
Kneller, Constable and Lely. A small room has
been set aside for a collection of miniatures,
many of which were on open display in the
house in the 17th century. A former bedroom
has been converted into a special Museum
Room, to allow examples from the rich
collection of rare textiles to be displayed with
adequate protection from light, dirt and wear-
and-tear. It also contains a remarkably well-
preserved toilet seat of 1729 and the inventories
of the house drawn up in 1677, 1679 and 1683.

Richmond (Yorkshire)

The Georgian Theatre Royal and Theatre Museum

Victoria Road, Richmond, North Yorkshire
DL10 4DW   ☎ 0748 3021
May–Sept, Mon–Fri, Sun 2.30–5; Sat & Bank
    Holiday, 10.30–1. Other times by appt.
▓ Bryan Rochford, Theatre Manager
£ ⃠ ┻

The Theatre, seating 200 people, was built by
the actor-manager, Samuel Butler, in 1788. It
continued as a theatre until 1848 and then, over
a century, served as wine vaults, an auction
room, a corn-chandler's and a salvage depot.
Restoration work began in 1960 and the
building reopened as a theatre in 1963.
    The Theatre Museum contains a collection of
original playbills from 1792 to the 1840s and the
oldest and largest complete set of painted
scenery in Britain, dating from 1836. There are
also displays of model theatres, star photographs
and photographs of visits paid to the Theatre
Royal since its reopening by members of the
Royal Family.

The Green Howards Museum

Trinity Church Square, Richmond, North
    Yorkshire DL10 4QN   ☎ 0748 2133
Feb, Mon–Fri 10–4.30. Mar & Nov, Mon–Sat
    10–4.30. Apr–Oct, Mon–Sat 9.30–4.30;
    Sun 2–4.30.
▓ The Curator
£ ▆ ┻

The Museum is housed in the former Trinity
Church, a Grade I listed building, parts of
which date from the 12th century. The displays
tell the story of the Regiment, which was
formed in 1688 to fight for William of Orange
against James II. There are more than 80
uniforms in the collection, the earliest dating
from 1780, together with headdresses, buttons,

badges and other items of equipment. The 3,000 medals on show include Victoria Crosses won by members of the Regiment.

Among the many personal and campaign relics are drums captured from the Russians in the Crimea, the Regimental Colours carried at the Battle of the Alma, a 1688 musket and a pair of blood-stained pistol holsters belonging to the Grand Old Duke of York. The picture collection includes war photographs taken in the Crimea and later in India and on the North-West Frontier.

Richmondshire Museum

Ryder's Wynd, Richmond, North Yorkshire DL10 4JA
Easter–Oct, daily 2–5. Bank Holiday & school holidays, also Mon–Fri 10.30–12.30.
🏛 *Hon. Curator*
£ ⬿

The main gallery of the Museum is a former carpenter's workshop. The roof of the new gallery contains timbers rescued from a demolished cruck house. The Museum, run by volunteers, illustrates the development of the Richmond area since 1071, with some earlier archaeological material. The exhibits include Anglo-Saxon carved stones, farming and craftsmen's tools and equipment, and lead-mining relics. There are also costumes, examples of needlework, reconstructions of a carpenter's and a blacksmith's shop, a large-scale model of Richmond railway station, and a collection of old photographs and prints depicting life and buildings in the district.

A popular exhibit is the set of James Herriot's veterinary surgery which was used in the BBC television series, *All Creatures Great and Small*.

Ripley

Ripley Castle

Ripley, nr Harrogate, North Yorkshire HG3 3AY
☎ *0423 770152*
Apr–May, Sat, Sun 11.30–4.30. June–
2nd weekend in Oct, Tues–Thurs, Sat, Sun,
11.30–4.30.
🏛 *The Estate Office*
£ ⬤ ⬛ ⬛ HHA

The Ingilby family has been at Ripley since the 14th century and the Castle is still their home. Parts of the present building date from the 15th and 16th centuries – there is a wagon-roof ceiling of 1555 – the remainder from 1784.

The collections in the house reflect the long Ingilby occupation of Ripley Castle. There is excellent 18th and 19th-century furniture, a long series of family portraits, and 16th to 19th-century paintings. Among the more interesting of the other items are maiolica plates and pharmacy jars, Civil War armour and weapons, an Armada chest, a cock-fighting chair, and a priest's secret hiding place.

Rochdale Pioneers Memorial Museum, the home of the Co-operative Movement.

Ripon

Newby Hall

Ripon, North Yorkshire HG4 5AE
☎ *09012 2583*
Apr–Sept, Tues–Sun 1–5. Garden: 11–5.30.
Open Bank Holiday Mon.
🏛 *Katherine Arnold, The Estate Office*
F ⬤ ⬛ ⬤ ⬛ HHA

Newby Hall is three miles south of Ripon, off the B6265. The main block of the house was built in the 1690s and changes and additions were made during the second half of the 18th century, much of the interior design being by Robert Adam. A further wing was added in Victorian times. The same family has occupied the house since 1748.

Newby Hall is well known for its Chippendale furniture, Gobelins tapestries and large collection of classical sculpture, acquired in Italy in 1765 by William Weddell, one of the great English dilettanti collectors of the mid 18th century. The Chamber Pot Room contains examples from all over Europe and from the Far East. Many of the pots are extremely rare. They range from rough 16th-century peasant ware to fine examples of 18th and 19th-century china.

The magnificent formal gardens cover 25 acres and were created by the present owner's father between 1921 and 1977.

Norton Conyers

Ripon, North Yorkshire HG4 5EH
☎ *076584 333*
June–Sept 7, Sun 2–5.30. Also open Bank Holiday Sun & Mon. Closed Dec 24–26, Jan 1. Parties at other times by appt.
🏛 *Beatrice, Lady Graham*
£ ⬿ ⬛ HHA

Norton Conyers is three and a half miles north-east of Ripon, on the road to Wath. The essential structure of the present house dates from 1490. Considerable remodelling took place in Jacobean times and in the later 18th century. In 1624 it was bought by Richard Graham,

Gentleman of the Horse to the Duke of Buckingham, and has remained in the occupation of the family ever since. Norton Conyers contains 16th to 19th-century furniture, English, Continental and Chinese porcelain and many family portraits, including two by Romney. Among the other pictures is one of the Quorn Hunt, painted by John Ferneley in 1822. There are also watercolours and lithographs of Victorian celebrities, together with Graham family wedding dresses.

James II paid a visit to Norton Conyers in 1679 and Charlotte Brontë in 1839. A Graham family legend of a mad woman confined in the attic of a house is reputed to have been the inspiration for the mad Mrs Rochester in *Jane Eyre.*

Ripon Prison and Police Museum

St Marysgate, Ripon, North Yorkshire HG4 1LX
May–Sept, Tues–Sun 1.30–4.30
Dr J. K. Whitehead, Curator, Trinity Cottages,
    4 Kirkby Road, Ripon HG4 2ET
    ☎ 0765 3706

The prison complex includes a House of Correction, built in 1686 and now a private house, and the Liberty Prison, which dates from 1815 and which still has its original iron doors and windows. The old gaol building was used as a prison for felons between 1816 and 1887, then until 1956 as Ripon Police Station. The ground floor has displays of police mementoes and equipment from the 17th century to the present day. In the nine cells on the first floor are exhibits illustrating 17th to 19th-century methods of confinement and punishment.

Wakeman's House Museum

Market Place, Ripon, North Yorkshire
May–Sept, Mon–Sat 10–5; Sun 1–5
Harrogate Museums and Art Gallery Service,
    West Grove Road, Harrogate, North
    Yorkshire HG1 2AE   ☎ 0423 503340

Wakeman's House was once the home of Hugh Ripley, the last Wakeman and first Mayor of Ripon, and is reputed to be haunted by his ghost. Apart from the ghost, it now contains displays illustrating the history of Ripon.

Ripponden

Ryburn Farm Museum

Ripponden, West Yorkshire HX4 4DF
Mar–Oct, Sat, Sun & public holidays 2–5
Leisure Services Department, Wellesley Park,
    Halifax, West Yorkshire   ☎ 0422 59454

The Museum is housed in a late 18th-century farm building in Ripponden's conservation area. The displays illustrate the working of a typical Pennine farm of the pre-industrial area, with exhibits reflecting the dual economy of agriculture and textile manufacturing.

Robertstown

Robertstown House and Falconry

Robertstown, Co. Kildare, Ireland
Daily 11–5
The Administrator

The Falconry of Ireland, which has been set up for educational and research purposes, is situated behind a recently restored 18th-century hotel, on the banks of the Grand Canal. Visitors can inspect the birds at close quarters and see them in flight during demonstrations. There is a collection of items illustrating the history and techniques of falconry.

Rochdale

Rochdale Art Gallery

Esplanade, Rochdale, Greater Manchester
    OL16 1AQ   ☎ 0706 47474 extn 764
Mon–Fri 10–5; Wed 10–1; Sat 10–4
Arts and Exhibitions Officer

The Gallery has an historically varied collection, based on the collecting policies of 19th-century local industrialists, the 20th-century local bureaucracy and, since 1945, a professional art historian and curator. There are interesting exhibits of Victorian narrative painting, mid 20th-century British figurative art and contemporary issue-based work.

Changing exhibitions are a central feature of the Gallery's approach today. About 20 are arranged each year, with the aim of encouraging a critical attitude to the art of the present day and the art of the past.

Rochdale Museum

Sparrow Hill, Rochdale, Greater Manchester
    OL16 1QT   ☎ 0706 47474 extn 769
Mon–Fri 12–5; Sat 10–1, 2–5. Closed public
    holidays & Dec.
The Curator

The Museum occupies an 18th-century vicarage. Its collections illustrate the history of the Rochdale area and include archaeological and folk-life material, as well as exhibits of the natural history of Rochdale and its surroundings. Special emphasis is placed on local celebrities, especially John Bright, M.P., and Gracie Fields.

Rochdale Pioneers Memorial Museum

31 Toad Lane, Rochdale, Greater Manchester
Tues–Sat 10–12, 2–4
The Librarian, Co-operative Union Ltd,
    Holyoake House, Hanover Street, Manchester
    M60 0AS   ☎ 061 832 4300

31 Toad Lane is regarded as the home of the worldwide Co-operative Movement, because it contains the room in which the Rochdale

Equitable Pioneers Society opened their grocery store in 1844. The building has been restored and the front room furnished, arranged and stocked as it was in the 1840s. The Museum has displays of documents and mementoes which tell the story of the Rochdale Pioneers Society from 1844 up to the 1944 centenary celebrations.

Rochester

Guildhall Museum

High Street, Rochester, Kent ME1 1QU
    ☎ 0634 48717
Daily 10–12.30, 2–5.30. Closed Good Fri, Dec 25, 26, Jan 1.
🏛 *The Curator*
🄴 ✎ ⇄

The Guildhall dates from 1687. The main staircase and the principal chamber have fine decorated plasterwork ceilings, presented to Rochester by Admiral Sir Cloudesley Shovell, who was Member of Parliament for the city at the time. His portrait, together with those of other notable local M.P.s, hangs in the Council Chamber. Adjoining the original building are more recent additions, which now contain most of the Museum galleries.

The collections include local archaeology and history, weapons and armour, dolls, Victoriana, models of sailing barges and fishing vessels and of Short's flying boats. The Museum also has a magnificent late 18th-century carpenter's tool chest, the most important to survive from this period. The original inventory and price list of the tools at the time of their purchase in 1796 is still preserved.

Rockbourne

Rockbourne Roman Villa

Rockbourne, nr Fordingbridge, Hampshire SP6 3PG   ☎ 07253 445
Apr–June, & Sept–Oct, Mon–Fri 2–6; Sat, Sun 10.30–6. July–Aug, daily 10.30–6.
🏛 *The Curator*
🄴 ✎ ⇄

The Villa is about three miles north of Fordingbridge. It was discovered towards the end of the Second World War and excavated during the 1950s and 1960s. In 1974 a museum was constructed next to the site and today contains most of the materials recovered from the excavations and an interpretation of the evidence provided by the archaeological work. The exhibits include a wide range of ironwork, jewellery, native and imported pottery and examples of the building materials used in the construction of the Villa.

In addition, there are displays of other archaeological material from the Rockbourne and Fordingbridge area, from the Stone Age to the 18th century.

Rocquaine Bay

Fort Grey Maritime Museum

Rocquaine Bay, Guernsey, Channel Islands
    ☎ 0481 65036
Apr 14–Oct 12, daily 10.30–12.30, 1.30–5.30. Open public holidays.
🏛 *See Guernsey Museum and Art Gallery*
🄴 ✎ ⇄

Fort Grey, a Martello Tower built in 1804, is on a small island in Rocquaine Bay, connected to the shore by a stone causeway. The Museum's displays concentrate on the shipwrecks which have occurred off Guernsey's west coast between 1770 and 1974. There are special exhibits on navigation and underwater archaeology.

Rolvenden

The C. M. Booth Collection of Historic Vehicles

Falstaff Antiques, 63–67 High Street, Rolvenden, nr Cranbrook, Kent TN17 4LP
    ☎ 0580 241234
Mon–Sat 10–6. Closed some Wed afternoons.
🏛 *Mr C. M. Booth*
🄴 ♦ ⇄

The main feature of the Collection is the series of Morgan three-wheel cars, dating from 1913 to 1935. Ten of these are usually on display. Other exhibits include the only known example of a Humber Tri-Car, made in 1904, together with a 1929 Morris van, a 1936 Bampton caravan and a wide range of motorcycles, bicycles and tricycles. All the items on show are in working order and many are used on the road each year.

There are also displays of toy and model cars, road signs, accessories and other automobilia.

1927 Morgan 'Aero' with a 1078cc British Anzani engine. Rolvenden, The C. M. Booth Collection of Historic Vehicles.

The William and Mary Stable Building containing the Mountbatten exhibition at Broadlands, Romsey.

Romsey

Broadlands

Romsey, Hampshire SO51 9ZD ☎ *0794 516878*
Apr–Sept, Tues–Sun 10–5. Aug–Sept, Bank
Holiday, also Mon 10–5.
◾ *Tim King, Marketing Manager*
Ⓔ ▮ 🖳 ↝ ⎣HHA⎦

Broadlands, once owned by Lord Palmerston, was the home of the Earl and Countess Mountbatten of Burma and is now occupied by their grandson, Lord Romsey. The house, with its remarkable collection of furniture and paintings, is open to the public.

An exhibition in the stable block tells the story of the life of Lord and Lady Mountbatten. Among the notable items on display are the personal Samurai sword of the Commander of the Japanese Forces in South-East Asia during the Second World War, a large collection of polo trophies and the ensign of HMS *Kelly*, the leader of the 5th Destroyer Flotilla, which Lord Mountbatten commanded. The exhibits also include Lady Mountbatten's wedding train and Lord Mountbatten's robes and medals. Outside can be seen a Japanese gun captured in Burma and Lord Mountbatten's Rolls Royce.

Roscrea

Roscrea Heritage Centre

Castle Complex, Roscrea, Co. Tipperary, Ireland
☎ *505 21850*
May–Oct, Mon–Fri 10–5; Sat, Sun 2–5.
Other times by appt.
◾ *The Administrator*
Ⓔ ▮ 🖳 ↝

The Centre occupies a distinguished 18th-century house, Damer House, and its annexe, which are within the courtyard of the 13th-century Roscrea Castle, an irregular polygonal structure with gatetower and corner turrets linked by a curtain wall. The collections include late 19th-century household items of a traditional type and 16th to 19th-century archival material relating to the area. Fine copy examples of the Irish Gospel books, such as

Dimma, Mac Regol and the Stowe Missal, form the scriptorium of a changing display on the Monastic Midlands of Ireland.

Rosemarkie

Groam House Museum

High Street, Rosemarkie, Ross-shire
June–Sept 20, Mon–Sat 10.30–12.30,
2.30–4.30; Sun 2.30–4.30
◾ *Mrs Elizabeth Marshall, 17 Mackenzie Terrace,*
Rosemarkie IV10 8UH   ☎ *0381 20924*
Ⓔ 🗫 ↝

The Museum displays illustrate Pictish culture, the history of the parish of Rosemarkie, and the life and prophecies of Coinneach Odhar, the 17th-century folk hero of Ross-shire, who is said to have been convicted of witchcraft and burned in a spiked tar barrel.

Outstanding among the Museum's exhibits is a collection of 8th to 9th-century sculpted stones, with Pictish, Celtic and Christian symbols.

Rosmuc

Patrick Pearse's Cottage

Rosmuc, Co, Galway, Ireland
Apr–Sept, daily 10.30–12.30, 2.30–6.30.
Other times by appt.
◾ *Office of Works, Athenry, Co. Galway*
Ⓕ ↝

This is a restoration of the cottage used by Patrick Pearse (1879–1916), leader of the 1916 Rising, as a refuge. The interior, though burned by the Black and Tans, has been reconstructed and contains a number of mementoes of Pearse.

Rossendale

Rossendale Museum

Whitaker Park, Haslingden Road, Rawtenstall,
Rossendale, Lancashire BB4 6RE
☎ *0706 217777*
Apr–Sept, Mon–Fri 1–5; Wed also 6–8;
Sat 10–12, 1–5; Sun 2–4. Oct, Mon–Fri 1–5;
Sat 10–12, 1–5; Sun 2–4. Nov–Mar,
Mon–Fri 1–5; Sat 10–12, 1–5. Bank Holiday
2–5. Closed Dec 24–26, Jan 1.
◾ *The Curator*
Ⓕ ▮ 🖳 ↝

The Museum is in a former millowner's mansion, built in 1840. Its collections illustrate the social and industrial history of Rossendale, with sections devoted to natural history, furniture, costumes, coins and medals and the fine arts. Among the particular features are portraits of Rossendale textile and footwear manufacturers; 19th to 20th-century pocket watches; souvenir pottery; headed notepaper used by local brass bands; prints and photographs of the Rossendale Hunt; and a number of toll-boards from local turnpikes.

Rossnowlagh

Donegal Historical Society Museum

Franciscan Friary, Rossnowlagh, Co. Donegal, Ireland   ☎ *072 51342*
◙ *Lucius J. Emerson, Hon. Curator*
    ☎ *072 51267*
Ⓕ ▮ ✍

The Museum, five miles north of Ballyshannon, is run entirely by volunteers. Its collections illustrate the development of Donegal from prehistoric times to the present day. Each summer the Museum organises an exhibition of paintings and sculpture by artists from the North of Ireland.

Rothbury

Cragside

Rothbury, Morpeth, Northumberland NE65 7PX
    ☎ *0669 20333*
Apr & Oct, Wed, Sat, Sun 2–5.
    May–Sept, Tues–Sun 2–6.
◙ *The Administrator*
Ⓔ ▮ ⬛ ✍ ♿ NT

Cragside, now a National Trust property, is one and a half miles north-east of Rothbury, off the B6431 Rothbury to Alnwick Road. The mansion, designed mainly by Norman Shaw, and the 900-acre park were created from 1864 onwards by the 1st Lord Armstrong, the inventor, engineer, industrialist and armament king. Cragside was the first house in the world to be lit by electricity generated by water-power.

The Visitor Centre describes the building of the house and the development of its environment. Thirty rooms of the house are open to visitors. They contain original furniture, some made by Gillow of Lancaster, William Morris wallpaper, Pre-Raphaelite paintings from the Evelyn de Morgan collection and other pictures collected by Lord Armstrong himself. The famous hydraulic lift and spit are also on show. There are a number of mementoes and photographs of Lord and Lady Armstrong and scientific apparatus and early electrical equipment illustrating Lord Armstrong's interests can be seen in the study and the gun room.

Rotherham

Art Gallery

Walker Place, Rotherham, South Yorkshire S65 1JH   ☎ *0709 382121*
Mon, Wed–Fri 10–6; Sat 10–5. Closed Bank Holiday.
◙ *See Clifton Park Museum*
Ⓔ ▮ ⬛ ✍ ♿

The Art Gallery houses Rotherham's permanent collections of ceramics and pictures. There is a collection of Rockingham pottery and porcelain numbering over 1,000 pieces, together with items from other Yorkshire potteries, and a selection of 18th and 19th-century English and Continental pottery and porcelain.

The Fine Art collection includes paintings, watercolours and sculpture, and a large number of prints and drawings, mostly topographical. Many of the works in the collection have local associations and most are by 19th-century British artists.

Clifton Park Museum

Clifton Lane, Rotherham, South Yorkshire S65 2AA   ☎ *0709 382121*
Apr–Sept, Mon–Thurs, Sat 10–5; Sun 2.30–5.
    Oct–Mar, Mon–Thurs, Sat 10–5; Sun 2.30–4.30.
◙ *Mr M. Densley*
Ⓕ ✍ ✍

The Museum is in a late Georgian building, reputedly designed by John Carr of York and formerly the home of Joshua Walker of Rotherham, son of Samuel Walker, the ironfounder. The collections, displays and educational programme reflect the activities, history and environment of the area. There are sections devoted to archaeology, social and natural history and fine and applied art.

The archaeology collections contain material from excavations at the nearby Roman forts at Templebrough and there are new galleries featuring local prehistory and natural history and the story of glassmaking in the district. The former importance of the ceramics industry is illustrated in a local pottery and porcelain gallery and by the main displays of Rockingham ware in the restored period rooms.

Model of a glassblower at work. Rotherham, Clifton Park Museum.

York and Lancaster Regimental Museum

Central Library and Arts Centre, Walker Place,
Rotherham, South Yorkshire S65 1JH
☎ 0709 382121
Mon, Wed–Fri 10–6; Sat 10–5. Closed Bank
Holiday.
ℵ *See Clifton Park Museum*
Ⓕ ♿ ▣ ♠

With its recruiting area based on Barnsley,
Rotherham and Sheffield, the York and
Lancaster Regiment, disbanded in 1968, had
very strong connections with South Yorkshire.
Considerably augmented by material from other
museums and by private donations since the
transfer of the collections from Sheffield, the
modern displays illustrate the history of the
Regiment both at home and during its overseas
postings and campaigns, since its establishment
in 1758.

The exhibits, which also reflect the history
of the associated militia, volunteer and
territorial units, include weapons, uniforms,
campaign relics, the band, sport, as well as
Regimental Colours and silver. Among the
special features are a First World War trench
scene, a section devoted to Field Marshal
Plumer, a prominent member of the Regiment,
and a revolving display of nearly 1,000
medals. These include seven awards of the
Victoria Cross made to soldiers serving in the
Regiment.

Rothesay

Bute Museum

Stuart Street, Rothesay, Isle of Bute
Apr–Sept, Mon–Sat, 10.30–12.30, 2.30–4.30.
Also Sun, mid Jun–mid Sept, 2.30–4.30.
Oct–Mar, Tues–Sat 2.30–4.30.
Closed Dec 25, 26, Jan 1, 2.
ℵ *Hon. Secretary, Buteshire Natural History*
Society ☎ 0700 3380
Ⓔ ♿ ♠ ☐

The Museum is run by the Buteshire Natural
History Society. The exhibits tell the story of
the Island's geology, prehistory and early way of
life, as well as showing the birds and mammals
and the marine life of the foreshores. The
Neolithic material includes pottery from a
domestic site and a group of pots from the
Glenvodean burial cairn. There is a great
variety of finds discovered during excavations at
the site of the Iron Age fort at Dunagoil.

The comprehensive collection of birds
features especially sea birds and duck, and there
is a display of birds' pellets. One of the seashore
exhibits illustrates the natural history of the
different tidal zones. A popular feature of the
natural history section of the Museum is a
Touch Table for children with a wide range of
objects which visitors are encouraged to handle.
These include a variety of skulls and horns, a
shark vertebra and examples of wool and nuts.

A section of the Museum is devoted to the
history of the River Clyde steamers, with 40
models of ships, from the *Comet* onwards. The

exhibition of objects reflecting everyday life in
Bute is frequently changed, to provide variety
for visitors.

Rottingdean

The Grange Art Gallery and Museum

The Green, Rottingdean, East Sussex BN2 7HA
☎ 0273 31004
Mon, Thurs, Sat 10–5; Tues, Fri 10–1, 2–5;
Sun 2–5. Closed Good Fri, Dec 25, 26, Jan 1.
ℵ *Education Officer, Art Gallery and Museum,*
Church Street, Brighton BN1 1UE
☎ 0273 603005
Ⓕ ♿ ♠

Rottingdean Grange was built as the Vicarage in
the second quarter of the 18th century.
Alterations and additions were made c. 1800
and the house was remodelled by Sir Edwin
Lutyens in 1919. The painter, William
Nicholson, lived at The Grange from 1912 to
1914 and in 1954 the house was sold to Brighton
Corporation. During the 19th and early 20th
centuries Rottingdean was a place much
frequented by artists and writers. The former
homes of Edward Burne-Jones and Rudyard
Kipling are nearby.

The Museum contains a display of
photographs, paintings and documents
illustrating the history of Rottingdean, and a
collection of letters, books and paintings
relating to Kipling. Two rooms are devoted
to toys, dating from the mid 19th century to the
1930s. The exhibition includes an Edwardian
nursery, in which there is an exceptionally large
rocking horse, designed to seat three or more
children. Rocking-horses of this size and
carrying capacity are very rare.

The Entrance Front. Rottingdean,
The Grange Art Gallery and Museum.

Royston

Royston and District Museum

Lower King Street, Royston, Hertfordshire
*   SG8 7AL*   ☎ *0763 42587*
Wed, Sat 10–5. Other times by appt.
🔾 *John Roles, Curator*
Ⓕ 🔾 🚗

Royston Museum is in a converted
Congregational Church Sunday School, built in
1879 and retaining most of its original features.
The displays illustrate the development of
Royston and its area from prehistoric to modern
times. There are good collections of
photographs and topographical views of the
district; paintings and etchings by E. H.
Whydale; a local stamp and letter collection
with items dating from the 17th century; and an
exhibition of 20th-century ceramics and glass,
including examples of the work of Bernard
Leach, Hans Coper, Lucie Rie and David Pease.

The Museum also has a slate commemorative
plaque by David Kindersley and a wrought iron
screen by Giuseppe Lund, both specially
commissioned.

Wimpole Hall

Arrington, nr Royston, Hertfordshire SG8 0BW
*   ☎ 0223 207257*
Tues–Thurs, Sat, Sun 1–5.30.
*   Home Farm: 10.30–5.*
🔾 *The Administrator*
Ⓔ 🏛 💺 🚗 ♿ Ⓝ🅣

Wimpole Hall, the largest house in
Cambridgeshire, is close to the point at which
the A603 from Cambridge meets the A14 from
Royston. It was left to the National Trust in
1976. The earliest part of the house dates from
the mid 17th century. Substantial additions and
alterations were made during the 18th century
and the first half of the 19th. The whole estate
of 3,000 acres has been kept intact and includes,
in addition to the Hall itself, the Model Home
Farm, designed by Sir John Soane. The Park is
an excellent example of Capability Brown and
Humphry Repton landscapes.

The Hall contains fine 18th and 19th-century
carving and plasterwork decoration, together
with furniture of the same periods. The large
collection of paintings, prints and watercolours
includes works by John Wootton, David Cox,
R. P. Bonington, Ramsay and Romney. The
Home Farm has a museum of agricultural
implements and also exhibits a number of
uncommon breeds of farm livestock.

Ruddington

Ruddington Framework Knitters' Museum

Chapel Street, Ruddington, Nottinghamshire
*   NG11 6HE*   ☎ *0602 846914*
By appt
🔾 *Mrs J. B. Coates, 34 Musters Road,*
*   Ruddington NG11 6HW*   ☎ *0602 211858*
Ⓔ 🔾 🚗

The Museum, off the A60, four miles south of
Nottingham, illustrates the living and working
conditions of 19th-century framework knitters,
in a group of purpose-built houses and
workshops, which have been restored by a Trust
and equipped with original machinery, much of
it now in working condition. There is an audio-
visual description of the industry in the East
Midlands and two exhibitions, one showing the
general development of framework knitting and
the other telling the story of handframe knitting
in Ruddington.

The Museum contains a workshop of
restoration and framesmithing and, with an
apprentice learning frame-knitting from the
Technical Director, the Trust is now working
for the preservation of the craft itself.

Two of the houses have now been furnished.
One was formerly occupied by a framework
knitter, the other by a hosier.

Ruddington Village Museum

The Hermitage, Wilford Road, Ruddington,
*   Nottinghamshire*
Tues 10.30–12; Fri 7.30–9pm. Closed Easter
*   Sun, Dec 25, 26 & Bank Holiday.*
*   Open summer weekends as advertised.*
🔾 *Mrs D. M. Shrimpton, 36 Brook View Drive,*
*   Keyworth, Nottinghamshire NG12 5JN*
*   ☎ 06077 2795*
Ⓔ 🔾 🚗

The Museum is in the oldest house in
Ruddington, with indications of an original
medieval manor still visible. The
collections reflect the history of Ruddington
since medieval times, and include
archaeological material from local excavations
and a wide range of photographs, documents
and records. One room is used for special
exhibitions of topical interest, each of which
remains on view for approximately a year.

A large collection of local source material and
a growing library are available for research
purposes.

**David Kindersley's slate plaque on the front of
Royston Museum.**

Rufford

Rufford Old Hall

Rufford, nr Ormskirk, Lancashire LA40 1SG
☎ 0704 821254
Apr–Oct, Sat–Thurs 2–6 *(last admission 5.30)*.
   Closed Good Fri. Garden 11–6.
☒ *The Administrator*
£ ▪ ☲ ☌ NT

Rufford Old Hall, the home of the Hesketh
family, is five miles north of Ormskirk, on the
A59. It has a late 15th-century Great Hall, with
a fine hammerbeam roof, and extensions built in
the 17th and 19th centuries. When it was
transferred to the National Trust in 1936, Lord
Hesketh included in the gift collections of 17th-
century oak furniture and 16th-century
tapestries, weapons and armour.
   The hall now houses the Philip Ashcroft Folk
Museum, which illustrates the traditional life
and occupations of this part of Lancashire
during the centuries since the Hall was built.

Rugeley

Brindley Bank Pumping Station and Museum

Wolseley Road, Rugeley, Staffordshire WS15 2EU
Occasional Open Days, otherwise by appt.
☒ *Operations Manager, South Staffordshire*
   Waterworks Company, Green Lane, Walsall,
   Staffordshire WS2 7PD   ☎ 0922 38282
F ☌

The Museum is on the Stafford road out of
Rugeley. Its principal exhibit is a Hawthorn
Davey tandem compound horizontal steam
engine, which was brought into service, driving
two bucket pumps, in 1907. The display also
includes flowmeters, pumps, maps, documents
and other items illustrating the history of the
Waterworks and the public water supply in the
area.

Runcorn

Norton Priory Museum

Warrington Road, Runcorn, Cheshire WA7 1RE
☎ 09285 69895
Mar–Oct, Mon–Fri 12–5; Sat, Sun 12–6.
   Nov–Feb, daily 12–4. Closed Dec 24–26.
☒ *Educational Visits Organiser*
£ ⌀ ☲ ☌ &

Norton Priory, an Augustinian house, was
established in the 12th century. In 1545 the
buildings and lands were bought by the Brooke
family, who made Norton their residence. They
built a Tudor mansion there, later replaced by a
Georgian country house, which was demolished
in 1928. The site then became an abandoned
and overgrown wilderness. The extensive site of
the Priory was excavated during the 1970s and
the large and wide-ranging finds discovered
then are displayed now in a modern museum.
   The exhibition tells the story of the Priory
and of monastic life and of the medieval crafts

employed here, such as tile-making, bell-
founding and stonemasonry. There are fine
collections of carved stonework and medieval
floor-tiles. The foundations of the Priory
buildings can now be clearly followed and
visitors can also see the Undercroft building, of
c. 1200, with its fine Norman doorway, the only
substantial part of the Priory to survive.

**Statue of St Christopher of *c.* 1400,
preserved in the slype at Norton Priory
Museum, Runcorn.**

Ruthwell

Duncan Savings Bank Museum

Ruthwell, Dumfriesshire DG1 4NN
☎ 038787 640
Apr–Sept, daily 10–6. Oct–Mar, daily 10–4.
   Evening visits by appt.
☒ *Mrs Mary H. Martin, Custodian*
F ⌀ ☌

The Museum building is a typical example of
18th-century Scottish cottage architecture. The
displays trace the growth of the Savings Bank
movement from its beginnings in the Ruthwell
Parish Bank, started by the Rev. Henry Duncan
in 1810, to the nationwide Trustee Savings
Bank of today. The exhibits include documents,
records and letters relating to the early savers,
and there are other items providing information
about their daily lives.
   There is a collection of home savings boxes,
coins and banknotes from many parts of the
world, and other sections illustrate the influence
of the Friendly Societies on village life and the
part played by the Rev. Duncan in rescuing and
restoring the 8th-century Ruthwell Cross.

Ryde

Cothey Bottom Heritage Centre

Brading Road, Ryde, Isle of Wight PO33 1QG
☎ 0983 68431
Easter–Oct, daily 10–6
⚥ Mrs Anne Morton
£ ⌾ ⬛ ⚓ ♿

The Centre is on the A3055, one mile from
Ryde. Its Museum contains the Norman Ball
Transport Collection of cars and motorcycles,
steam-driven vehicles and fire-engines, which
ranges from 1902 to the late 1960s, together
with displays illustrating the social and domestic
history of the Isle of Wight.

Rye

Cherries Folk Museum

Cherries, Playden, Rye, East Sussex TN31 7NR
☎ 0797 223224
By appt
⚥ The Curator
F ⚓

The Museum illustrates life in the area before
1946. There are sections devoted to the church;
the farmer and his wife; ploughing, trapping,
hedging and ditching; kitchen, dairy and
poultry; the housewife. Other exhibits present a
picture of rural crafts and trades as they used to
be before the coming of motor-driven transport.
The occupations covered include those of the
blacksmith, wheelwright, saddler, apothecary,
baker and innkeeper.

Lamb House

West Street, Rye, East Sussex TN31 7ES
Mar 29–Oct, Wed, Sat 2–6 (last admission 5.30)
⚥ The Custodian
£ NT

Lamb House was built in 1723 by James Lamb,
13 times Mayor of Rye, an office held by his son
for 20 terms. In 1899 it was bought by Henry
James, who spent much of the last 18 years of his

1934 Lagonda tourer.
Ryde, Cothey Bottom Heritage Centre.

life here. The house was visited by most of
James's distinguished literary contemporaries. It
was presented to the National Trust in 1950 and
is now tenanted, with three rooms on the ground
floor open to the public and containing some of
the novelist's furniture and part of his library,
together with a number of portraits of him.

Ypres Tower Museum

Gun Garden, Rye, East Sussex TN31 7HE
☎ 0797 223254
Easter–mid Oct, Mon–Sat 10.30–1, 2.15–5.30;
   Sun 11.30–1, 2.15–5.30. Last admission
   30 mins before closing.
⚥ Hon. Curator
£ ⌾ □

This local history museum is housed in a 13th-
century tower. The collections consist of objects
which have belonged to people living in Rye or
the immediate area, or which have been made
in the town or stocked in its shops. They relate
to maritime Rye, the Cinque Ports, the Barons
of the Cinque Ports, 13th, 14th, 19th and 20th-
century pottery, domestic equipment, toys and
dolls, agriculture and political printing.
   There are different displays of material each
year from the permanent collections.

Ryhope

Ryhope Engines Museum

Ryhope Pumping Station, Ryhope, Sunderland,
   Tyne and Wear SR2 0ND   ☎ 0783 210235
Easter–Dec, Sat, Sun 2–5. Steaming Days include
   Bank Holiday weekends and two other days as
   advertised.
⚥ The Secretary, Ryhope Engines Trust,
   3 Broxbourne Terrace, Sunderland
£ ⌾ ⬛ ⚓

The Museum is on the A1018, about three miles
south of Sunderland. Ryhope Pumping Station,
a listed building, was constructed by the
Sunderland and South Shields Water Company.

Its two steam-powered beam engines, built by R. and W. Hawthorn of Newcastle-upon-Tyne, were in use from 1869 until 1967. Since then, a Trust was formed to preserve the Pumping Station as nearly as possible in its 1869 condition. They are kept in working order and periodically steamed. There is also an exhibition of items associated with the supply and use of water.

Saffron Walden

Audley End

Saffron Walden, Essex   ☎ *0799 22399*
Easter–Oct, Tues–Sun & Bank Holiday Mon 1–6.
  Open Good Fri. Grounds open 12–6.30.
  Last admission to house and grounds 5.
◪ *The Administrator*
£ ⬙ ▆ ⬟ ✿

Audley End, once the largest house in England, was built between 1605 and 1614 for Thomas Howard, 1st Earl of Suffolk. Sir John Vanbrugh demolished the front wings in 1721 and the interior of the ground floor of the south wing was considerably remodelled by Robert Adam in the 1760s. The contents of the house, now administered by English Heritage, are almost all original. They include 17th to 19th-century furniture, tapestries, pottery and porcelain, paintings and Howard family portraits. The lower gallery contains a collection of stuffed animals and birds.

The park was landscaped by Capability Brown in the 1760s.

Saffron Walden Museum

Museum Street, Saffron Walden, Essex CB10 1JL
  ☎ *0799 22494*
Apr–Sept, Mon–Sat 11–5. Oct–Mar, Mon–Sat
  11–4. Sun & Bank Holiday throughout year
  2.30–5. Closed Good Fri, Dec 24, 25.
◪ *Maureen Evans*
F ⬙ ⬗ ⬠

Occupying an 1834 building, the Museum has collections of local archaeology and history, natural history, ethnography and ceramics. There are also displays of furniture and woodwork, with a very rare early Tudor bed as a special feature.

A new 'Costume in Context' gallery was opened in 1984, showing 18th and 19th-century clothes and accessories, together with 19th-century dolls and toys and items connected with the local Militia.

St Albans

City Museum

Hatfield Road, St Albans, Hertfordshire AL1 3RR
  ☎ *0727 56679*
Mon–Sat 10–5. Closed Dec 25, 26, Jan 1.
◪ *Mrs F. Hebditch*
F ⬙ ⬗

The building, which dates from the end of the 19th century, was designed for museum purposes and retains some of the original internal features. The collections and exhibits relate to the natural and social history of the area. Many of the natural history exhibits are presented in the form of habitat dioramas and an interesting feature of the historical displays is a series of miniature period rooms.

The Salaman Collection of craftsmen's tools is shown in reconstructed workshops, with a recorded commentary made by Sir Bernard Miles.

St Albans Organ Museum

320 Camp Road, St Albans, Hertfordshire
  AL1 5PB
Sun 2.15–4.30. Other times by appt.
  Closed Dec 25
◪ *Bill Walker* ☎ *0727 51557 or Ralph*
  Seabrook ☎ *0727 68979*
£ ⬤ ⬗ ⬠ ♿

The Museum is administered by the St Albans Musical Museum Society, a Trust formed in 1978 to care for and display the collection of mechanical musical instruments formerly owned by Charles Hart, a long-standing resident of St Albans until his death in 1983. The exhibits, which are regularly demonstrated, include four large organs, by Mortier, De Cap and Bursens, two duo-art pianos by Steinway and Webber, a Mills Violano-Virtuoso (automatic violin and piano), and various disc music-boxes and other small instruments.

Among the instruments under restoration are two theatre organs, a 3 manual, 10 rank Wurlitzer, formerly at the Grand Cinema, Edmonton, and a 3 manual, 6 rank Rutt, from the Regal at Hyams Park.

'Four Columns' (97-key) Mortier organ, still in regular use at the St Albans Organ Museum.

Verulamium Museum

St Michael's, St Albans, Hertfordshire AL3 4SW
☎ 0727 66100 extn 2419
Apr–Oct, Mon–Sat 10–5.30; Sun 2–5.30.
Nov–Mar, Mon–Sat 10–4; Sun 2–4.
Closed Dec 25, 26, Jan 1.
▨ Keeper of Education
£ ▮ ♿

The Museum is in St Michael's village,
signposted from the A414 to Hemel Hempstead.
It is on the site of the important Roman city of
Verulamium and displays material discovered
during the excavations there, forming one of the
best late Iron Age and Roman collections outside
London. The exhibits include fine mosaics,
reconstructions of painted wall-plasters and the
celebrated Verulamium Venus statuette.

St Austell

Wheal Martyn Museum

Carthew, nr St Austell, Cornwall
☎ 0726 850362
Apr–Oct, daily 10–6. Open Bank Holiday.
Other months by appt.
▨ The Manager
£ ▮ ▰ ♿

Wheal Martyn, which is partly an indoor and
partly an outdoor museum, tells the story of the
Cornish china-clay industry. The Museum
includes two old clay works and illustrates china-
clay extracting and processing as they were
carried out up to the Second World War, together
with the social and domestic life of the workers in
the industry.

Equipment has been moved to Wheal Martyn
from elsewhere in the china-clay area, but
buildings and machinery which are not
transportable are presented as satellite sites,
administered by the Museum.

St David's

Bishop's Palace

St David's, Dyfed   ☎ 0437 720517
Mar 15–Oct 15, daily 9.30–6.30. Oct 16–
Mar 14, Mon–Sat 9.30–4; Sun 2–4.
▨ The Custodian
£ ⌀ ♿

In the late 13th and 14th centuries, the Palace,
hitherto a building of modest size, was greatly
enlarged and embellished. After the Reformation,
the Palace was neglected and by the end of the
17th century it had become uninhabitable. In
1932 the representative body of the Church in
Wales placed it in the care of the State.

An exhibition on the site provides visitors
with information about Bishop Henry Gower,
who was responsible for the large-scale
rebuilding in 1327–47, and about the
preservation work carried out in recent years.
A reconstruction of the buildings as they were
before 1536 gives an impression of the Palace at
the peak of its importance.

Mosaic of the sea-god Oceanus from a house
at Verulamium, 2nd century A.D.
St Albans, Verulamium Museum

St Helens

Pilkington Glass Museum

Prescot Road, St Helens, Merseyside WA10 3TT
☎ 0744 692499/692104
Mon, Tues, Thurs, Fri, 10–5; Sat, Sun & Bank
Holiday 2–4.30. Mar–Oct only, Wed 10–9.
Closed Dec 25–Jan 1.
▨ Ian Burgoyne, Curator
F ⌀ ♿ &

The Museum occupies part of the headquarters
building of Britain's largest glass-making
concern. It was created to illustrate the history
of glass-making techniques and glass products,
from prehistoric times to the present day. The
development of the Pilkington Company itself
also forms part of the displays.

St Helens Museum and Art Gallery

College Street, St Helens, Merseyside WA10 1TW
☎ 0744 24061 extn 2959
Mon–Fri 10–5; Sat 10–1. Closed public holidays.
▨ The Curator
F ⌀ ♿ & □

The displays in the Museum illustrate the
geology, natural history, archaeology and
industries of the area, including mining and the
manufacture of clay pipes, earthenware, bottles
and Beecham's Pills. The natural history section
is mainly devoted to the flora and fauna of the
Sankey Valley Linear Park.

In the Art Gallery, the selection on view
from the permanent collections includes works
by local artists and some of more general interest
from the private collections of Sir Joseph
Beecham and the Pilkington family. The Guy
and Margery Pilkington watercolour bequest
includes studies by David Cox, Samuel Prout,
Copley Fielding, Peter de Wint and Myles
Birket Foster.

St Helier

The Jersey Museum

9 Pier Road, St Helier, Jersey, Channel Islands
☎ 0534 75940
Mon–Sat 10–5. Closed Good Fri, Dec 25, 26,
Jan 1.
🖾 Education Officer
Ⓔ ✑ ♿

Since 1893, the Jersey Museum has occupied
what was formerly a private house, built in
1817. An extension was added in 1977. The
Museum, which is at present being enlarged, has
collections covering many aspects of the island's
history and natural environment. These include
a wide range of domestic equipment,
furnishings, natural history, shipping and
shipbuilding, commerce, postal services, coins
and banknotes. There are several period rooms
and a reconstruction of a pharmacy of the
1880s.

Special sections of the Museum are devoted
to photographic equipment, silver, pewter and
musical instruments, and to the celebrated
Victorian beauty, Lillie Langtry, born in Jersey
in 1853. The Barreau Art Gallery, which forms
part of the Museum, contains works on Jersey
subjects and by artists who have had close
connections with the island.

St Ives (Cambridgeshire)

The Norris Museum

The Broadway, St Ives, Huntingdon,
Cambridgeshire PE17 4BX   ☎ 0480 65101
May–Sept, Tues–Fri 10–1, 2–5; Sat 10–12, 2–5;
Sun 2–5. Oct–Apr, Tues–Fri 10–1, 2–4;
Sat 10–12. Closed Bank Holiday.
🖾 The Curator
Ⓔ ✑ ♿

**Upper room of the Barbara Hepworth
Museum, St. Ives**

The Museum building incorporates re-used
medieval stonework from St Ives Priory. The
Norris Museum is the museum of
Huntingdonshire and tells the story of the
county – technically abolished in 1974 – from
earliest times to the present day. Its displays
include fossils of dinosaurs, fish and sharks and
the remains of mammoths, found locally. There
are tools of the Stone Age, tools and pottery of
the Beaker People and the Bronze Age, pottery
and metalwork of the Iron Age, and extensive
Roman collections. Further exhibits cover the
Saxon and medieval periods, and special
attention is paid to the Huntingdonshire witch
trials of the 16th and 17th centuries and to local
involvement in the English Civil War.

There is an interesting display of objects made
by French prisoners-of-war held in the camp at
Norman Cross during the Napoleonic Wars.
The local craft of making pillow lace is
described, and there is a good collection of
Fenland ice skates.

St Ives (Cornwall)

Barbara Hepworth Museum and Sculpture Garden

Trewyn Studio, Barnoon Hill, St Ives, Cornwall
TR26 1AD   ☎ 0736 796226
Apr–June, Sept, Mon–Sat 10–5.30. July–Aug,
Mon–Sat 10–6.30; Sun 2–6. Oct–Mar,
Mon–Sat 10–4.30. Closed Good Fri,
Dec 25, 26.
🖾 The Curator
Ⓔ ✑

The early 19th-century granite house was the
home of the sculptor, Dame Barbara Hepworth,
from 1949 to 1975. The studio was damaged in
the fire that caused the artist's death, and
although no works of art were destroyed, much
of the furniture and many books cannot be
exhibited. Instead, an attempt has been made to
reconstruct something of the feeling the Trewyn
Studio had in the 1950s, when Barbara
Hepworth was working there.

There are 40 sculptures and 8 paintings, ranging in date from 1928 to 1974. Photographs, writings and other memorabilia illustrate the artist's private and professional life. Many of the larger pieces of sculpture have been placed in the adjoining garden, with its exotic sub-tropical plants and trees. Also to be seen are the plaster and stone-carving studios, left almost untouched since Barbara Hepworth's death, with half-finished works and the tools she used on view.

The St Ives Museum

Wheal Dream, St Ives, Cornwall
☎ 0736 796005
Mid May–Sept, daily 10–5
Ⓚ *Hon. Secretary*   ☎ 0736 795575
Ⓔ 🐾 🛇

The building housing the Museum was constructed on the site of an unsuccessful copper mine. It was built originally to provide a place for curing and packing pilchards for export to Italy and subsequently served as a Bible Christian Chapel, a laundry, a cinema and a British Sailors Society Museum.

The exhibits in the Museum illustrate many aspects of the history of the St Ives area. There are models of ships and other mementoes of the Hain Steamship Company, the clockwork mechanism from Pendeen lighthouse, which never failed during its 77 years of service, the flags of a number of maritime organisations, and a collection of Gibson photographs of wrecks on the Cornish coast. Other items on show include a reconstruction of a Cornish kitchen, a working model of Levant mine, a trap which caught three mice at a time, and what is claimed to be the last steam-powered saw in the world, made by Holman Bros. of Camborne.

The audio-visual display re-creates St Ives as it was before the coming of the tourist trade.

St Lawrence

German Underground Hospital

Meadowbank, St Lawrence, Jersey, Channel Islands   ☎ 0534 63442
First Sun in Mar–1st Sun in Nov, daily 9.30–5.30. Nov–Dec, Feb, Thurs 12–5; Sun 2–5. Check winter opening times locally.
Ⓚ *The Curator*
Ⓔ 🛏 🐾

The Underground Hospital is the largest single remaining German installation in Jersey and originally formed part of the Atlantic Wall defence system of the Third Reich. By means of both static and audio-visual displays, the exhibition tells the story of the German occupation and the construction of the Underground Hospital. There is an extensive collection of contemporary equipment, documents, photographs and letters. Among the exhibits is one of the small boats used by wartime escapees from Jersey.

St Margaret's Hope

Orkney Wireless Museum

Church Road, St Margaret's Hope, Orkney Isles KW17 2SR   ☎ 085683 462
Apr 30–Sept, daily 10–8
Ⓚ *Mrs MacDonald*
Ⓔ 🐾 🛇 ♿

This collection of radio equipment covers the period from the crystal set to the transistor. It includes wireless sets of the 1930s and displays illustrating communications at the naval base at Scapa Flow. There are also photographs of the WAAF and WREN operators, and maps, charts and photographs showing the Navy's boom defence and the Army's 80 heavy anti-aircraft gunsites.

St Mary's

Isles of Scilly Museum

Church Street, St Mary's, Isles of Scilly, Cornwall TR21 0JT   ☎ 0720 22337
Mid Mar–Oct, Mon–Sat 10–12, 1.30–4.30. Whitsun–mid Sept also open 7.30–9 pm. Nov–mid Mar, Wed 2–4 or by appt. Closed Good Fri, Dec 25.
Ⓚ *The Secretary*
Ⓔ 🐾

The Museum contains displays relating to the geology, archaeology, history, flora and fauna of the Isles of Scilly. Special sections are devoted to prehistoric and Roman archaeology, to shipwrecks which have taken place around the islands, and to social and domestic life during the 19th century.

St Neots

Longsands Museum

Longsands Community College, Longsands Road, St Neots, Huntingdon PE19 1LQ   ☎ 0480 72229 extn 48
School terms, Mon–Fri 1.30–4.30
Ⓚ *Hon. Curator*
Ⓕ 🐾

Inside the Orkney Wireless Museum, St Margaret's Hope.

The Museum's displays illustrate life in the district since Roman times. They include domestic equipment, craftsmen's tools, costumes, transport items and pastimes. A section is devoted to local geology. The most important collections are of agricultural hand tools and of archaeological material, which is mainly Roman and includes what is believed to be the largest collection of fragments of Roman votive figurines from any site in Britain.

St Newlyn East

Trerice

St Newlyn East, nr Newquay, Cornwall TR8 5JJ
0637 875404
Apr–Oct, daily 11 6 (last admission 5.30)
⚐ The Administrator
£ ♠ ☕ ♿ NT

Trerice was built in 1573 by Sir John Arundell, on the site of an earlier house, and is notable for its exceptionally fine plasterwork and fireplaces. It was bought empty by the National Trust and now contains 17th and 18th-century English oak, mahogany and walnut furniture, with some English porcelain.

In the barn visitors can see an exhibition illustrating the history of the lawnmower.

St Osyth

St Osyth's Priory

St Osyth, Essex   **☎** 0255 820492
Easter weekend, then May–Sept, east wing of house daily 10.30–12.30, 2.30–4.30. Gardens and monuments 10–5.
⚐ Mr Somerset de Chair
£ ♠

St Osyth is four miles west of Clacton, on the B1027. The Augustinian Priory was established c. 1127. Visitors can see the gatehouse tower, the undercroft, now converted into a chapel, and other remains of the monastic buildings. The east wing of the private residence contains paintings by Van Dyck and Stubbs.

St Peter Port

Castle Cornet

St Peter Port, Guernsey, Channel Islands
☎ 0481 21657
Apr–Oct, daily 10.30–5.30. Open public holidays.
⚐ See Guernsey Museum and Art Gallery
£ ex. school parties **♠ ☕ ☕ ♠**

Castle Cornet, on the seaward side of St Peter Port harbour, is basically a medieval building, with Elizabethan outer battlements and important Georgian, Victorian and Second World War (German) additions.

The Museums are in barrack buildings dating from the mid 18th century. The collections consist chiefly of maritime and military material. There are ship paintings and models, a

medal and trophy room, a section devoted to the Royal Guernsey Militia and an art gallery which displays paintings of local scenes.

Guernsey Museum and Art Gallery

Candie Gardens, St Peter Port, Guernsey, Channel Islands   **☎** 0481 26518
Apr–Oct, daily 10.30–5.30. Nov–Mar, daily 10.30–4.30. Open public holidays. Closed 5 days at Christmas.
⚐ Museum Education Officer   **☎** 0481 28671
£ ex. school parties **☕ ☕ ♠ ♿ □**

This new purpose-built Museum was opened in 1979. Its octagonal galleries repeat the shape of an original Victorian bandstand, which is incorporated in the building and used as the museum tea room. The collections are based on those formed by the Lukis family during the 19th century, which consisted mainly of local archaeology. The displays present a portrait and pedigree of Guernsey, through exhibitions on natural history and geology, archaeology and history.

The Art Gallery contains paintings, mainly watercolours, of local scenes. It also displays china made specially for Guernsey families and Oriental porcelain.

Hauteville House

38 rue de Hauteville, St Peter Port, Guernsey, Channel Islands   **☎** 0481 21911
Apr–Sept, Mon–Sat 10–11.30, 2–4.30.
Oct and Dec–Mar, Mon–Sat 10.30–11.30, 2.30–4.30.
⚐ The Administrator
£ ♠ ☕

Hauteville House was Victor Hugo's home during his far from uncomfortable period of exile from France (1856–70). The rooms were decorated by Hugo himself in a very idiosyncratic manner and contain good collections of furniture, tapestries and china, as well as memorabilia of the poet.

St Peter's

Jersey Motor Museum

St Peter's Village, Jersey, Channel Islands
☎ 0534 82966
Mid Mar–Oct, daily 10–5
⚐ F. M. Wilcock
£ ♠ ☕ ☕

The Museum occupies a former wine-bottling factory. The collection covers a wide range of vehicles. There are veteran and vintage cars, motorcycles, Allied and German military vehicles of the Second World War, aero-engines, and an 1875 Jersey steam railway coach, together with displays of accessories and photographs.

Among the exhibits are a motorcar used by Sir Winston Churchill, the Rolls-Royce allocated to General Montgomery in 1944 while planning the D-Day operations, and a Sunbeam motorcycle, presented to him in 1948.

St Peter's Bunker Museum

St Peter's Village, Jersey, Channel Islands
    ☎ 0534 81048
Mar–Nov, daily 10–5
Ⓜ *The Curator*
Ⓔ ▌ ▟ ↩

The underground bunker at St Peter's was built
in 1942 by the German Todt Organisation,
using Russian and other slave labour. The six
rooms in the bunker contain original fittings and
equipment, together with large collections of
weapons, uniforms, instruments and other
material belonging to the occupying forces.
There are also displays illustrating the life of
Jersey people under the occupation.

Salcombe

Overbeck's Museum

Sharpitor, Salcombe, Devon TQ8 8LW
    ☎ 054884 2893
Apr–Oct, daily 11–1, 2–6
Ⓜ *The Administrator*
Ⓔ ▌ ↩ Ⓝ Ⓣ

Sharpitor is one and a half miles south-west of
Salcombe. Built in 1913, it replaced an earlier
house of the same name. In 1928 it was sold to
Otto Christoph Joseph Gerardt Ludwig
Overbeck, a research chemist of Dutch descent.
He built up large collections of curiosities,
family heirlooms, books and natural history. On
his death in 1937 he left Sharpitor to the
National Trust, for use 'as a public park and
museum and a Hostel for Youth'.

The Museum displays Mr Overbeck's
collections, which range from mantraps to ship
models and from Victorian domestic equipment
to handcuffs and snuff boxes. A section is
devoted to the career, inventions and
enthusiasms of Otto Overbeck, including his
non-alcoholic beer and electric rejuvenator. His
collections of commemorative china, Victorian
and Edwardian dolls, shells, natural curiosities
and stuffed birds are also displayed here.

Under the stairs, the National Trust has made
a secret room for children. It contains dolls and
toys, room settings from dolls' houses, and
miniature furniture and tea services.

Salford

Ordsall Hall Museum

*Taylorson Street, Salford, Greater Manchester
    M5 3EX   ☎ 061 872 0251*
*Mon–Fri 10–12.30, 1.30–5; Sun 2–5.
    Closed Good Fri, Dec 25, 26, Jan 1.*
Ⓜ *Keeper, Social History*
Ⓕ ⌀ ↩

This is a Grade I listed building. It comprises an
early 16th-century timber-framed Great Hall,
part of a 14th-century cross wing and an early
17th-century wing. Major restoration work was
carried out in 1896–7 and 1960–72.

The Great Hall and Star Chamber have
appropriate furniture and fittings, and the
kitchen is furnished as it might have been in the
19th century, when the Hall was tenanted by
farmers. The displays in two upstairs rooms draw
on the collections of Salford Museums and Art
Galleries to illustrate the history of the area and
the daily lives of local people.

Salford Museum and Art Gallery

*Peel Park, The Crescent, Salford, Greater
    Manchester M5 4WU   ☎ 061 736 2649*
*Mon–Fri 10–5; Sun 2–5. Closed Good Fri,
    Dec 25, 26, Jan 1.*
Ⓜ *Principal Museums Officer*
Ⓕ ⌀ ↩ □

The Museum has a large collection of social
history material, much of which is displayed in
Lark Hill Place, a reconstruction of a 19th-
century street, which includes items rescued
from now-demolished houses and shops in the
Salford area. Among the exhibits here are a
pawnbroker's, a clogmaker's, a public house, a
chemist's and a typical corner shop. There is
also a series of period rooms, illustrating living
styles from the 17th century to Victorian times.

One room in the Art Gallery contains
Victorian paintings, sculpture and decorative
arts, and another is devoted to paintings and
drawings by L. S. Lowry, together with
memorabilia of the artist.

Salford Museum of Mining

*Buile Hill Park, Eccles Old Road, Salford,
    Greater Manchester M6 8GL
        ☎ 061 736 1832*
*Mon–Fri 10–12.30, 1.30–5; Sun 2–5.
    Closed Good Fri, Dec 25, 26, Jan 1.*
Ⓜ *The Keeper of Industrial Archaeology*
Ⓕ ⌀ ↩

Buile Hill was built between 1825 and 1827 to
the design of Sir Charles Barry. It is his only
known attempt at the Greek neo-classical style.
The top floor and porte-cochère were added in
the 1860s. Since the Second World War, the
house and its basement have been developed as
a realistic mining museum. Buile Hill No. 1 has
a series of underground scenes showing coalmining techniques at different periods. Buile
Hill No. 1 Drift re-creates the atmosphere of a
working drift mine in the 1930s. The other
underground and surface displays include a
coalface, a pityard, a lamp-room, pithead baths
and a blacksmith's shop.

Salisbury

**The Duke of Edinburgh's Royal Regiment
Museum**

*58 The Close, Salisbury, Wiltshire SP1 2EX
        ☎ 0722 336222 extn 2683*
*Apr–June & Sept, Sun–Fri 10–5. July–Aug,
    daily 10–5. Oct–Mar, Mon–Fri 10–5.
    Last admission 4.30. Closed Dec 23–Jan 2.*
Ⓜ *The Curator*
Ⓔ ⌀ ↩

The Museum is in The Wardrobe, a Grade I listed building. Part of the house dates from the 15th century. The exhibits, shown in four rooms on the ground floor, illustrate the history of the Regiment over a period of more than 200 years and include uniforms, weapons, equipment, campaign relics and a display of medals and Regimental silver.

Mompesson House

The Close, Salisbury, Wiltshire SP1 2EL
☎ *0722 335659*
Mar 29–Oct, Sat–Wed 12.30–6 or sunset if earlier. Nov 22–Dec 21, Sat, Sun 2–4 by appt only.
 The Administrator
£ NT

The house, one of the finest in the Cathedral Close and distinguished by its fine plasterwork ceilings and overmantels, was built by Charles Mompesson in 1701. It was restored by Denis Martineau who gave it to the National Trust in 1952. The Trust acquired it without contents but has since installed fine period furniture and the important Turnbull collection of 18th-century English drinking glasses.

Salisbury and South Wiltshire Museum

The King's House, 65 The Close, Salisbury, Wiltshire SP1 2EN   ☎ *0722 332151*
Apr–June & Sept, Mon–Sat 10–5. July–Aug, Mon–Sat 10–5; Sun 2–5. Oct–Mar, Mon–Sat 10–4. Closed Dec 25, 26, Jan 1.
 The Curator
£   □

The Museum building, known since the early 17th century as the King's House, was originally the Salisbury residence of the Abbots of Sherborne and was called Sherborne Place. Between 1851 and 1978 it was the Diocesan Training College. On the closure of the College, the lease was bought by the Museum, established elsewhere in Salisbury in 1860, and the Museum opened in its new premises in 1981.

It contains very important archaeological collections, illustrating Man's activities in Wiltshire from Palaeolithic times to the Saxon period. Special exhibits are devoted to Stonehenge and to the pioneering work of Lieut. Gen. Pitt-Rivers, which established archaeology as a scientific discipline. The Hugh Shortt Galleries tell the story of the City of Salisbury, with an emphasis on life during the medieval period and including the Drainage Collection, a large group of everyday objects discovered in the drainage channels which once flowed through the streets of Salisbury. Dr Neighbour's Surgery is an authentic reconstruction of an Amesbury doctor's surgery, presented in the style of the 1940s.

The Museum has an important post-medieval ceramics collection, displayed in its own gallery, and the Print Room houses regularly changing exhibitions of the Museum's extensive collection of paintings, prints, drawings and photographs of Salisbury and the historic sites of South Wiltshire.

Saltash

Cotehele Quay Museum

St Dominick, nr Saltash, Cornwall PL12 6TA
☎ *0579 50830*
Apr–Oct, daily 11–6
 The Curator
F *Donations welcome* NT

Cotehele Quay is the main West Country outstation of the National Maritime Museum, whose Museum there tells the story of the Tamar sailing barge, *Shamrock*, and of the local shipping, shipbuilding and related industries. *Shamrock*, built in 1899 at Stonehouse, Plymouth, is the principal exhibit in the Museum. She worked until 1970 and then, beached and in a semi-derelict condition, she was rescued from breaking up and between 1974 and 1979 restored to her 1921 condition by means of a project organised by the National Trust, which has also restored Cotehele Quay to its 19th-century appearance. The *Shamrock* is now owned jointly by the Trust and by the National Maritime Museum.

Saltcoats

North Ayrshire Museum

Manse Street, Kirkgate, Saltcoats, Ayrshire KA25 5AA   ☎ *0294 64174*
Apr–Sept, Mon–Sat 10–4.30. Oct–Mar, Thurs–Sat 10–4. Other times by appt.
 Susan Allison
F

The Museum is in the former Ardrossan Parish Church, built in 1744 and said to have been visited by Robert Burns. Its displays feature local industries, including coal-mining, fishing, salt-making, the Ayrshire lace-works, weaving and spinning. There are also collections of historic photographs of the area and of paintings by local artists, from 1850 onwards.

The entrance to the Pitt-Rivers Collection at the Salisbury and South Wiltshire Museum, Salisbury.

Sandford Orcas

Sandford Orcas Manor House

Sandford Orcas, Sherborne, Dorset DT9 4SB
☎ *096322 206*
Easter Mon 10–6, then May–Sept, Sun 2–6;
  Mon 10–6. Pre-booked parties of 10 or
  more at other times.
⚑ *Mr M. T. Medlycott*
£ **⚑** **HHA**

The Manor House was built c. 1550, on the
foundations of a medieval house. It has been
little altered during the following centuries.
Only three families have owned it since the
1380s. The present family, the Medlycotts,
have been here for 250 years. The Great Hall
has a fine Jacobean screen, while the Parlour,
Great Chamber and Gatehouse Chamber are
wainscoted and the stone-mullioned windows
contain heraldic glass. There are collections of
Jacobean, Queen Anne and Chippendale
furniture, family portraits, porcelain, 14th to
17th-century stained glass windows, rugs,
tapestries and needlework. The paintings are
particularly strong on 17th-century Dutch and
18th-century English works, and include four by
Gainsborough.

Sandling

Museum of Kent Rural Life

Lock Lane, Sandling, Maidstone, Kent
  ME14 3AU   ☎ *0622 63936*
Easter–mid Oct, Mon, Tues, Thurs–Sat 10–4.30;
  Sun 2–4.30
⚑ *Anita Hood, Keeper*
£ **⚑** **⚑** **⚑** **⚑** **&**

The Museum, a long-term project, is being set
up on 27 acres of land, next to Allington Lock.
Its aim is to interpret the Kent countryside and
its farming history by means of buildings,
displays and live exhibits. Displays of
agricultural implements, harness and dairy
equipment have been set up in the cowshed and
in the oast house are introductory exhibitions
about farming in Kent, together with some of
the larger items, including wagons, from the

Museum's collections. Planting has been
completed in the orchard, hop garden and
market garden, and an arable rotation, hay
meadow, herb garden and sheep flock
established.

Sandown

Museum of Isle of Wight Geology

High Street, Sandown, Isle of Wight PO36 8AF
  ☎ *0983 404344*
Mon–Fri, 9.30–5.30; Sat 9.30–4.30.
  Closed Bank Holiday.
⚑ *The Curator*
£ **⚑**

The Museum, which contains more than 20,000
specimens, was opened in its present form in
1985. The displays show how the rocks, and the
fossils they contain, can be used to interpret the
geological history of the Isle of Wight, and to
show how the Island is divided into two areas,
the Cretaceous and the more recent Palaeogene.
The geological evidence is also used to
demonstrate that the Isle of Wight, like other
parts of Britain, has suffered several periods of
extremely cold climate, interspersed with
warmer phases. Two dioramas contrast the
fauna present on the Island during the last warm
and cold periods. A final exhibit attempts to
forecast what the area may look like in 100,000
years' time as a result of similar changes in the
future.

Sandringham

Sandringham House Museum

Sandringham, nr King's Lynn, Norfolk PE35 6EN
  ☎ *0553 772675*
Mar 30–Sept 25, House: Mon–Thurs 11–4.45;
  Sun 12–4.45. Grounds: Mon–Thurs 10.30–5;
  Sun 11.30–5. House closed July 21–Aug 9;
  grounds July 25–Aug 6; also at other times
  when H.M. The Queen or any member of the
  Royal Family is in residence.
⚑ *Mr R. S. French, Estate Office*
£ *House only* **⚑** **⚑** **⚑** **⚑**

Sandringham is eight miles from King's Lynn,
on the A149. A late 18th-century house, it was
bought for the Prince of Wales in 1862 and
completely rebuilt in 1870. Extensive repairs
were carried out after a serious fire in 1891. It is
still in the possession of the Royal Family and
part of the Queen's thoroughbred stud are
housed here and at nearby Wolferton.
   The Ranger's Room contains an interpretive
display of birds, trees and animals which can be
seen in the Country Park, and a Museum houses
vintage Royal motorcars, big game trophies, and
gifts presented to the Royal Family. There are
also collections of dolls and of archaeological
finds from the area.

**The oast house at the Museum of Kent Rural
Life, Sandling.**

Sandtoft

Sandtoft Transport Centre

*Belton Road, Sandtoft, nr Doncaster, South
    Yorkshire
Easter–Sept, Sat, Sun 12–6. Also open Bank
    Holiday Sun & Mon.*
🕮 *Mr P. Goddard, 7 Norwood Avenue, Auckley,
    Doncaster DN9 3JA*   ☎ *0302 771520*
Ⓔ ♟ 🚍 🚃

The Centre is being established on four acres of
a former RAF wartime airfield. Its aim is
primarily to preserve and operate trolleybuses,
but the collection also includes motor-buses and
other items of transport interest, including an
1892 steam-tram shelter from Huddersfield.
There are now more than 60 vehicles from all
parts of Britain and from the Continent, many
kept and maintained under cover.
    The traction poles and overhead fittings on
the operating track come from Bradford,
Walsall, Bournemouth, Cardiff, Huddersfield,
Reading and Teesside.

Sandwich

Richborough Castle

Sandwich, Kent   ☎ *0304 612013*
*Mar 15–Oct 15, daily 9.30–6.30.
    Oct 16–Mar 14, Mon–Sat 9.30–4; Sun 2–4.
    Closed Dec 24–26, Jan 1.*
🕮 *Historic Buildings & Monuments Commission,
    Tunbridge Wells*   ☎ *0892 48166*
Ⓔ 🖉 🚗 ♨

Richborough Castle is one and a half miles
north of Sandwich, off the A257. It was built at
the point where the Roman army landed in
A.D. 43. The Museum displays Roman pottery,
coins and other objects discovered during
excavations of the site.

Sandwich Town Museum

The Guildhall, Sandwich, Kent   ☎ *0304 617197*
*Mon, Thurs, tours at 10.45, 11.45, 2.15 & 3.15.
    Other times by appt.*
🕮 *Town Clerk's Office, 1 Potter Street,
    Sandwich*
Ⓔ 🚗 ♿ 🚻

The present Guildhall, the town's third, was
built in 1579 and enlarged in 1912 and 1973. It
contains a variety of exhibits illustrating the
municipal history of Sandwich. These include
portraits of mayors and other notabilities,
charters, the Mayor's chair of 1561, the Moot
Horn, the Hog Mace, the Beadle Staff and a
selection of seals. The Water Bailiff's baton,
with a crown and a silver oar, gave the bearer
the King's authority to board and search any
vessel in the harbour. The Mayor's robes are
completely black, as a sign of mourning for John
Drury, Mayor of Sandwich, who was killed in
1457 by a raiding party from Honfleur. Visitors
can also see the Mayor's blackthorn wand,
which is carried on ceremonial occasions to
repel witches and other malevolent forces.

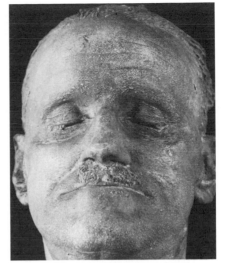

**Bronze death-mask of James Joyce, 1941.
Sandycove, Joyce Museum.**

Sandycove

James Joyce Museum

Joyce Tower, Sandycove, Co. Dublin, Ireland
    ☎ *01 809265*
*May–Sept, Mon–Sat 10–1, 2–5; Sun 2.30–6.
    Other times by appt.*   ☎ *01 808571*
🕮 *The Curator*
Ⓔ 🖉 🚗

The Museum, in a Martello Tower, is on the
seafront, a mile east of Dun Laoghaire. The
Tower, which still has many of its original
fittings, was the setting for the first chapter of
Ulysses. The exhibits relate to Joyce's life and
career and include personal possessions, such as
his guitar, waistcoat, travelling trunk and piano;
letters and autographs; rare and signed editions
of his works; photographs of Joyce, his family,
friends and residences; paintings and drawings;
a bust of Joyce by Milton Hebald, and one of the
two original death-masks made in 1941. There
are also items relating to the Dublin of *Ulysses*
and to the history of the Tower and Joyce's
connection with it.

Sanquhar

Royal Burgh of Sanquhar Museum

*The Tolbooth, High Street, Sanquhar,
    Dumfriesshire DG4 6BL*   ☎ *06592 303*
Apr–Oct, Mon–Sat 2–4. Other times by appt.
🕮 *Mr Tom Johnston, Hon. Curator*
Ⓕ 🚗

This is a local history museum, housed in the
old Tolbooth, built in the 1750s by William
Adam from stone taken from Sanquhar Castle.
The collections include stone axe-heads and
othe prehistoric material, and a variety of local
antiquities. There is also a display relating to the
Admirable Crichton, born at Sanquhar in 1560.

Scalloway

Scalloway Museum

Main Street, Scalloway, Shetland
May–Sept, Tues–Thurs, Sat, Sun 2–4.
 Other times by appt.
❚ *Mrs Jemima Walterson, Greystones, Berry*
 Road, Scalloway
F ✐ ✍

The Museum building served for a long time as a
draper's shop and was subsequently a restaurant.
There is a comprehensive collection of objects
relating to Scalloway and the nearby islands,
dating from Neolithic times to the present day.
There is also a large photographic archive. A
special feature of the Museum is the section
dealing with Scalloway's rôle in the Second
World War. After Norway fell to the Germans,
thousands of people headed westwards. A few
hundred of them stayed in Scalloway, forming
themselves into an efficient fighting unit, which
sailed to Norway to land agents and saboteurs
and returned with more refugees. Their
operations became known as the Shetland Bus.

Scarborough

Art Gallery

The Crescent, Scarborough, North Yorkshire
 YO11 2PW   ☎ *0723 374753*
Tues–Sat 10–1, 2–5. June–Sept, also Sun 2–5.
❚ *Director of Tourism and Amenities,*
 Londesborough Lodge, The Crescent,
 Scarborough
F ✐

The Gallery occupies a classical stone villa,
built in the 1820s. The nucleus of the collection
is a series of local scenes painted during the last
200 years. On permanent display is a group of
paintings given by Tom Laughton, once
Scarborough's leading hotelier and brother of
the actor, Charles Laughton. These range from
17th-century portraits to 20th-century works by
Matthew Smith and Gaudier Brzeska. The
exhibits include paintings by Atkinson
Grimshaw, who spent some years in
Scarborough, and Lord Leighton, who was born
a short distance from the Gallery.

The Rotunda

Vernon Road, Scarborough, North Yorkshire
☎ *0723 374839*
Tues–Sat 10–1, 2–5. June–Sept, also Sun 2–5.
 Closed public holidays.
❚ *See Art Gallery*
F ✐ ✍

The Rotunda is an outstanding example of a
purpose-built Georgian museum, with many
original showcases and fittings. There are
extensive collections of archaeological material

from regional sites and exhibits illustrating local
social history, especially the development of the
world's first seaside spa resort.

Wood End, Museum of Natural History

The Crescent, Scarborough, North Yorkshire
 YO11 2PW   ☎ *0723 367326*
Tues–Sat 10–1, 2–5. Spring Bank Holiday–Sept,
 also Sun 2–5. Closed Good Fri, Dec 25, 26,
 Jan 1.
❚ *See Art Gallery*
F ✐ ✍ ☐

The Museum has changing displays of the flora
and fauna of the Scarborough district, including
a section on the geology of the area. A
conservatory, built in the 1870s, contains
tropical plants and there is a large aquarium,
with freshwater and tropical species. The
Sitwell Wing has books, paintings and other
exhibits relating to the literary activities of the
Sitwell family, who lived in the house from
1870 until the 1930s.

Scunthorpe

Scunthorpe Museum and Art Gallery

Oswald Road, Scunthorpe, South Humberside
 DN15 7BD   ☎ *0724 843533*
Mon–Sat 10–5; Sun 2–5. Closed Dec 25, 26.
❚ *The Secretary*
F ✐ ✍ ☐

The core of the Museum building is the
Victorian vicarage of the Church of St
Lawrence, Frodingham. The displays include a
Countryside Gallery, showing the geology and
natural history of the area and the uses of the
countryside, especially the exploitation of the
local ironstone. The Local History Gallery
illustrates the history of the iron and steel
industry and of the 'industrial island' of
Scunthorpe, as well as the agricultural history of
the town's rural surroundings. The Archaeology
Gallery has collections relating to the earlier
occupation of the area from prehistoric to post-
medieval times. There are also Jacobean,
Georgian and Victorian period rooms and a
reconstruction of an ironworker's cottage.
 The Art Gallery presents temporary
exhibitions from the main collections, together
with works by local artists and craftsmen.

Reconstructed ironworker's cottage,
now part of the south front of Scunthorpe
Museum and Art Gallery.

Seaford

Seaford Museum of Local History

Martello Tower No. 74, Esplanade, Seaford,
*   East Sussex BN25 1JH*   ☎ *0323 893976*
Apr–Sept, Sun & Bank Holiday 11–1,
*   2.30–4.30. Oct–Mar, Sun & Bank Holiday*
*   11–3.*
⬢ ☎ *0323 899333*
Ⓔ ⬀ ⬗

The Martello Tower which houses the Museum
dates from 1805–10 and is the most westerly in
the South-East coastal chain built as a first line
of defence against Napoleon's expected
invasion. In 1979 it was restored as nearly as
possible to its original condition.

The Seaford Museum contains displays
illustrating the history of the town and includes
municipal badges and seals, material relating to
the parish church, and life-size models of the
Town Crier and the last Seaford shepherd.
There are special exhibits relating to
shipwrecks; Seaford during the First and Second
World Wars; needlework and sewing machines.
There are also collections of early office
equipment, domestic appliances and home
entertainment; and a series of tableaux featuring
Church Street School, a war-time kitchen, a
terrace house scullery, an Edwardian 'general
store' and photographer's shop, and other
subjects.

The Museum makes its own video tapes to
illustrate local history themes, which are
available for group visits by prior arrangement.

Selborne

The Oates Memorial Library and Museum and the Gilbert White Museum

The Wakes, Selborne, nr Alton, Hampshire
*   GU34 3JH*   ☎ *042050 275*
Mar–Oct, Tues–Sun 12–5.30 (last admission 5).
*   Open Bank Holiday Mon.*
⬢ *Dr J. E. Chatfield, Curator*
Ⓔ ⬗ ⬀

Selborne is on the B3006, four miles from
Alton. 'The Wakes' dates from the early 16th
century, but it has been altered and enlarged
several times since then. It was the home of the
Rev. Gilbert White, the naturalist, until his
death in 1793 and his book, *The Natural History*
of Selborne, was written here.

The ground floor now contains two rooms
furnished in the style of the 18th century with
displays relating to Gilbert White and to the
natural history and antiquities of Selborne.
Money to save 'The Wakes' and to preserve it as
a museum was provided by Robert Washington
Oates, in memory of two members of his family,
Frank Oates, the 19th-century African explorer,
and Captain Lawrence Oates, who was a
member of Scott's Antarctic expedition, and
who walked out to his death in the snow. The
Museum on the first floor illustrates their lives
and achievements.

The Romany Folklore Museum and Workshop

Selborne, nr Alton, Hampshire GU34 3JW
*   ☎ 042050 486*
Easter–Oct, daily 10.30–5.30
⬢ *Peter Ingram*
Ⓔ ⬗ ⬀

The workshops, which have been altered very
little for 60 years, comprise a complete wagon-
builder's yard, with a smith, joiner's shop,
wheelwright's shop and paintshop. The business
now concentrates on the restoration of all types
of gypsy caravan. A permanent collection of
living vans is on show and visitors can also see
other vehicles undergoing restoration in the
workshop. There are also displays illustrating
the early history, language, music, dress and
crafts of the gypsies. The Museum offers
frequent changes of exhibit.

Selkirk

Bowhill

nr Selkirk TD7 5ET   ☎ *0750 20732*
Mon–Sat 11.30–5; Sun 2–6. Last admission to
*   house 45 mins before closing.*
⬢ *The House Manager*
Ⓔ ⬛ ⬗ ⬀ ♿ HHA

Bowhill, the home of the Duke of Buccleuch
and Queensberry, was built in the 18th century
and remodelled in the 19th. There are fine
collections of tapestries, silver and porcelain,
and of British and French furniture. The
paintings include works by Canaletto, Claude,
Gainsborough, Reynolds, Ruysdael and
Leonardo da Vinci. There is a special exhibition
of 16th and 17th-century English portrait
miniatures.

Among the other attractions at Bowhill are a
restored Victorian kitchen and memorabilia of
the Duke of Monmouth, Sir Walter Scott and
Queen Victoria.

Halliwell's House Museum

Halliwell's Close, Market Place, Selkirk TD7 4AE
*   ☎ 0750 20096/20054*
Apr–Oct, Mon–Sat 10–5; Sun 2–5.
*   Nov–Dec 24, Mon–Fri 2–4.30.*
⬢ *Ettrick and Lauderdale Museum Service,*
*   Municipal Buildings, High Street, Selkirk*
Ⓔ ⬗ ⬀

Halliwell's House, a late 18th-century listed
building, was completely restored in 1982–3
and opened as a museum in the following year.
The ground floor displays relate to the building
and to its past uses, especially its connection
with the ironmongery trade. The Museum's
nationally important collection of ironmongery
is displayed in a reconstruction of an early 20th-
century ironmonger's shop.

Upstairs, the displays concentrate on the
history of Selkirk and show how, from being an
important Royal Burgh, Selkirk declined into a
small market town, before developing into a
major textile centre in the 19th century.

Sevenoaks

Knole

Sevenoaks, Kent TN15 0RP   ☎ *0732 450608*
Easter–Oct, Wed–Sat & Bank Holiday Mon 11–5;
Sun 2–5. Last admission 4.
🄺 *The Administrator*
Ⓔ ⬤ 🏠 [NT]

Knole is at the Tonbridge end of Sevenoaks, on
the A21. It is first referred to in 1291, but little
is known about it until 1456, when it was sold to
Thomas Bourchier, Archbishop of Canterbury,
who transformed the medieval manor house into
a palace. In 1538 Henry VIII compelled
Archbishop Cranmer to give Knole to him and
in 1566 Queen Elizabeth gave the house to her
cousin, Thomas Sackville, who greatly
extended it. It remained in the Sackville family
for 10 generations and passed into the keeping
of the National Trust in 1946. The buildings
cover four acres.

Knole has one of the finest collections of
17th-century furniture in the world – many of
the chairs are still upholstered in the original
material – and there are also important
collections of tapestries, carpets and silver. The
King's Room has silver furniture and silver and
gold embroidery. There are many portraits of
the families of the Earls and Dukes of Dorset and
the Barons Sackville, and among the other
pictures are works by Hoppner, Reynolds and
Gainsborough.

Sewerby

Sewerby Hall Art Gallery and Museum

Sewerby Park, Bridlington, East Yorkshire
YO15 1EA
Good Fri–Spring Bank Holiday, Sun–Fri
10–12.30, 1.30–6; Sat 1.30–6. Spring Bank
Holiday–last Sun in Sept, Sun–Fri, 10–6;
Sat 1.30–6.
🄺 *Director of Tourism and Leisure Services,*
East Yorkshire Borough Council, Bridlington
YO15 3JH   ☎ *0262 678255*
Ⓔ ⬤ 📖 🏠

Sewerby is on the northern outskirts of
Bridlington. During the summer, it can be
reached by the Sewerby Trains, which run along
the cliff top from Bridlington. The Museum is
accommodated in the 1714–20 mansion, owned
until 1934 by the Greame family. The pictures
now displayed here include 19th-century marine
paintings by Henry Redmore of Hull and a series
of early 19th-century local watercolours,
including views of Sewerby and its grounds. The
Museum contains displays of archaeological
material from excavations in the area, farm
implements, vintage motorcycles, horse-drawn
vehicles, military uniforms with local
associations, fossils from the nearby chalk cliffs
and the various sea-birds and waders found in
the area.

The Amy Johnson Room contains trophies,
awards and mementoes belonging to the famous
pioneer airwoman of the 1930s, who was born in
Hull and who formally opened Sewerby Hall
and Park in 1936.

Shackerstone

Shackerstone Railway Museum

Shackerstone Station, Shackerstone, Nuneaton,
Warwickshire
☎ *0827 880754*
Sat, Sun 12.30–6. Other times by appt.
🄺 *The Curator*
Ⓔ ⬤ 📖 🏠 ♿

Shackerstone Station was built in 1873. The
Museum occupies the former First Class waiting
room and the stationmaster's office. The large
collection of railway items includes signalbox
equipment, station signs, timetables from 1857
and dining-car crockery. Eighteen paraffin
lamps are regularly lit, out of more than 100 on
show. There is also a collection of railway
posters issued during the Second World War.

A steam-hauled light railway service operates
from Shackerstone Station to Market Bosworth
on Sundays and Bank Holidays from Easter until
the end of September.

Shaftesbury

The Local History Museum

Gold Hill, Shaftesbury, Dorset SP7 4JW
☎ *0747 2157*
Easter–Sept, Mon–Sat 11–5; Sun 2.30–5.
Other times by appt.
🄺 *Hon. Curator*
Ⓔ ✏ 🏠

**One of the rooms of Shaftesbury's Local
History Museum.**

The Museum is owned and run by the Shaftesbury and District Historical Society. Its five rooms contain collections illustrating life in Shaftesbury and the rural area surrounding it during the past 200 years, together with archaeological finds from local excavations. Among the wide range of exhibits are a number of ingenious mousetraps, agricultural tools and domestic equipment made by the late Mr Freddie Miles, blacksmith, of Melbury Abbas; Dorset buttons; tradesmen's paper bags; sheep and cow bells; horse harness and decorations; maps and pictures of old Shaftesbury; and school slates and spelling cards.

The most remarkable object in the Museum is probably the Shaftesbury Byzant, which was decorated with money and jewels and used in an ancient ceremony for the right to draw water from the springs at Enmore Green.

Shaftesbury Abbey Ruins and Museum

Park Walk, Shaftesbury, Dorset SP7 8JR
☎ *0747 2910*
Good Fri–Oct, daily 10.30–5.30
🏛 *Nicky Ladkin, Curator*
🗉 ⏸ 🚗

The Museum contains objects found during excavations of the church of the Benedictine nunnery founded by Alfred the Great. The exhibits include medieval floor tiles and carved stones. There are also models of the church and of the town as they were before the Dissolution.

Shallowford

Izaak Walton Cottage

Worston Lane, Shallowford, Stone, Staffordshire
ST15 0PA   ☎ *0785 760278*
Mid Mar–late Oct, Mon, Tues, Fri–Sun
12.30–5.30. Late Oct–mid Mar, Sat, Sun
12.30–4.30. Parties by appt. Closed
Dec 24–Jan 1.
🏛 *John Barnes*
🗉 ⏸ 🍽 🚗

The 17th-century half-timbered cottage, half a mile south of Norton Bridge railway station, was once owned by the author of *The Compleat Angler*. It contains displays illustrating Walton's life and the history of angling and of the cottage. The garden contains plants and herbs cultivated in the 17th century.

Shardlow

'Canal Story' Exhibition

Plus Pleasures Marine; Clock Warehouse,
London Road, Shardlow, Derbyshire DE7 2GL
☎ *0332 792844*
Apr–Oct, Mon–Fri 9–5; Sat 9.30–5; Sun 10–5.
Nov–Mar, Sat, Sun 10–4.
🏛 *The Manager*
🗉 ⏸ 🍽 🚗

The Warehouse, on the Trent and Mersey Canal, dates from 1780. It was known as the Clock Warehouse because of the clock on its pediment. Shardlow was a busy transhipment port on the Canal, where cargoes were transferred from barges to narrow boats. The exhibition in the Warehouse illustrates, with the help of models, photographs, objects and an audio-visual presentation, life at the port and the history and importance of the canals.

Shebbear

Alscott Farm Museum

Shebbear, North Devon   ☎ *040928 206*
Easter–Sept, 12–dusk
🏛 *Mrs J. Jenkinson*
🗉 ⏸ 🚗 ♿

Alscott is a working farm. Its Museum illustrates the agricultural past of North Devon. There is a large collection of tractors and agricultural implements, together with dairying and household equipment. Visitors can also see a scale model of an Edwardian travelling fair and a display of circus posters.

Sheffield

Abbeydale Industrial Hamlet

Abbeydale Road South, Sheffield S7 2QW
☎ *0742 367731*
Mon–Sat 10–5; Sun 11–5. Closed Dec 24–26.
🏛 *The Secretary*
🗉 ⏸ 🍽 🚗

Abbeydale is five miles south-west of Sheffield, on the A621 Bakewell road. It consists of an 18th to 19th-century water-powered scythe works, restored to full operational condition, and shows all the processes involved, from making the steel in the crucible steel furnace to forging, grinding and finishing the blades in the workshops surrounding the courtyard. Every aspect of the work is represented, including packing, storing and preparing for market, the clerical work involved (in the Counting House), the living conditions of the workmen (the Workman's Cottage) and of the Manager or site foreman (the Manager's House).

Bishop's House

Meersbrook Park, Norton Lees Lane, Sheffield
S8 9BE   ☎ *0742 557701*
Wed–Sat 10–5; Sun 11–5. Open Bank Holiday
Mon.
🏛 *The Curator*
🗉 ⏸ 🚗

Bishop's House is signposted from Woodseats on the A61 Sheffield to Chesterfield road. It is a 16th-century timber-framed farmhouse with 17th-century improvements, including early Jacobean decorative plasterwork. Two rooms are furnished in the style of a prosperous 17th-century yeoman's home. There are displays and models illustrating the construction of the house and exhibition rooms showing aspects of life in Sheffield in Tudor and Stuart times.

Graves Art Gallery

Surrey Street, Sheffield S1 1XZ
    ☎ 0742 734781
Mon–Sat 10–8; Sun 2–5. Closed Dec 24–26.
🕱 *Art Education Officer*
Ⓕ ⬥ ⬛ ⬥ ⬥ ☐

The principal collections in the Gallery are of
20th-century British paintings and
watercolours. Other sections are devoted to
Chinese ivories, to 16th to 19th-century
European paintings and to non-European fine
art and applied art.

Kelham Island Industrial Museum

Kelham Island, off Alma Street, Sheffield S3 8RY
    ☎ 0742 22106
*Wed–Sat 10–5; Sun 11–5. Open 10–5 Easter
    Mon, May Day Bank Holiday, & Spring and
    Late Summer Bank Holiday Mon.*
🕱 *Assistant Keeper, Extension Services*
Ⓔ ⬥ ⬛ ⬥ ⬥

The Museum building was formerly a generating
station which provided power for the City's
trams. The displays tell the story of Sheffield's
industrial development and of the wide range of
its products. The machines on show include the
12,000hp River Don steam engine and the
150hp Crossley gas engine, both of which can
be seen working. Much attention is given to the
living conditions of Sheffield's workers and two
of the self-employed craftsmen on whom the
cutlery trade depended, the Little Mesters, work
full-time in specialist workshops within the
Museum. Visitors are able to watch the
processes involved and talk to the experts about
their work.

Mappin Art Gallery

Weston Park, Sheffield S10 2TP   ☎ 0742 26281
*Jan–May & Sept–Dec, Mon–Sat 10–5.
    June–Aug, Mon–Sat 10–8; Sun 2–5.
    Closed Dec 25, 26.*
🕱 *The Keeper*
Ⓔ ⬥ ⬛ ⬥ ⬥ ☐

The Gallery occupies an 1887 neo-classical
building. Its main strength is in 18th to 20th-
century British art, but there are also collections
of 20th-century European and American works.
The exhibits are regularly changed and draw
also on the collections of the Graves Art
Gallery.

Ruskin Gallery

101 Norfolk Street, Sheffield S1 2JE
    ☎ 0742 734781
Mon–Fri 10–7.30; Sat 10–5. Closed Dec 24–26.
🕱 *The Keeper*
Ⓕ ⬥

The Gallery was opened in 1985 in a listed
building in the centre of the city, which had
previously been a wine shop. Considerable
alterations were required in order to make it
suitable for its new purpose and the opportunity
was taken to commission work by leading
contemporary craftsmen – iron window grilles

and a staircase and balustrade by Giuseppe
Lund, and two slabs of Westmorland slate,
carved by David Kindersley for the entrance
hall.
    The collection, previously exhibited
elsewhere in Sheffield, belongs to the Guild of
St George, founded by John Ruskin in the
1870s. One of the most successful aspects of the
Guild's work was its museum, established in
Sheffield in 1875 for the liberal education of the
artisans of Sheffield. It was broad in its
conception and included minerals, selected
especially for their colours, watercolours, a
library, illuminated manuscripts, plaster casts of
architectural details, photographs, paintings
and prints. It has now been redisplayed in a way
which shows how it developed naturally from
Ruskin's philosophy and which makes it easier
to experience its overall impact.

Sheffield City Museum

Weston Park, Sheffield S10 2TP   ☎ 0742 27226
*Jan–May & Sept–Dec, Mon–Sat 10–5; Sun 11–5.
    June–Aug, Mon–Sat 10–8; Sun 11–5.
    Closed Dec 24–26.*
🕱 *Keeper of Extension Services*
Ⓕ ⬥ ⬥

The Museum building has a neo-classical
façade, with low-relief friezes illustrating the
industries and arts of Sheffield. The displays
relate to the natural history and history of the
city and the surrounding area. Gallery I contains
the collections of Old Sheffield Plate, Sheffield
silver and ceramics, including Don, Pinxton
and other local products. Gallery II has the
Bateman Collection of archaeological material
from Yorkshire and the Peak District, together
with Etruscan, Greek and Egyptian antiquities
and artefacts from Africa, Asia and the Pacific.
The Museum coin displays are also here.
    Gallery III tells the story of the earth, and

1921 Richardson tourer outside the Kelham
Island Industrial Museum, Sheffield.

Gallery IV is devoted to birds and mammals. The celebrated collection of Sheffield cutlery is in Gallery V, and in the main corridor one can see collections of clocks, sundials, watches, medals and guns. Paintings of old Sheffield are displayed in the large lecture room.

Shepherd Wheel

Whiteley Woods, off Hangingwater Road, Sheffield
Wed–Sat 10–12.30, 1.30–5; Sun 11–12.30,
1.30–5. Closes at 4 in winter. Closed
Dec 24–26.
🏛 *The Secretary, Abbeydale Industrial Hamlet,*
Abbeydale Road South, Sheffield S7 2QW
☎ 0742 36773
F 🐾

Shepherd Wheel is about two and a half miles south-west from the centre of Sheffield. The nearest main road is the A625. The Wheel dates from at least as far back as 1584, although much alteration and rebuilding was carried out during the 18th century. It consists of two cutlery grinding workshops, powered by a single 18-foot overshot waterwheel, and is the only completely restored and fully operational site of its kind. In it can be seen the range of equipment, tools and machinery necessary for the production of the finely ground blades which gave Sheffield its reputation for cutlery manufacture from the 16th century onwards.

Shefford

Chicksands Priory

RAF Chicksands, Shefford, Bedfordshire
SG17 5PR   ☎ 0462 812571 extn 226
Apr–Oct, 1st & 3rd Sun in month, 2–5. Guided
tours only. Parties at other times by appt.
🏛 *RAF Commander*
F *Donations welcome* 🍴 ♿ 🅿 🚻 🚌

There are entrances to RAF Chicksands, now occupied by the United States Air Force, on the A507 and the A600. The basis of the house is the only surviving Gilbertine Priory in Britain, built in the 13th and 15th centuries. Additions were made in 1740, 1813 and 1857 and the Priory, in its present form, provides an exceptionally good opportunity to study building materials and methods of construction over a long period.

Among the especially interesting features are 14th and 16th-century stained glass, Chinese wallpaper (c. 1740) and lodestone plaques and statuary.

Sherborne

Sherborne Castle

Sherborne, Dorset   ☎ 0935 813182
Easter Sat–Sept, Thurs, Sat, Sun & Bank
Holiday Mon 2–6 (last admission 5.30)
🏛 *Sherborne Castle Estates, Cheap Street,*
Sherborne DT9 3PY
£ 🍴 🖼 🚻 HHA

There are two Sherborne Castles. The old castle was leased to Sir Walter Raleigh by Queen Elizabeth, but Raleigh found it unsatisfactory and began another building, on the far side of the lake, in 1594. This came into the possession of the Digby family, the present owners, in 1617, when wings were added to Raleigh's 'Lodge'. It was partially redesigned internally in 1860.

There is an important collection of Japanese and Chinese porcelain. The Chinese items date back to the 15th century, with notable pieces from the Transitional Period of 1640–1660 and K'ang Hsi of 1622–1722. The furniture and paintings, too, are noteworthy. Gainsborough, Lely, Van Dyck and Angelica Kauffmann are among the artists represented. There are game larders, an ice-house and a Gothic dairy, and in the park one can see the grotto visited by Alexander Pope and Raleigh's Seat, on which, according to legend, Raleigh was sitting when his servant poured water over him in order to extinguish his pipe.

The Castle's 20 acres of lawns and pleasure grounds were designed by Capability Brown, around a 50-acre lake, which has recently been restored to its pristine condition.

Sherborne Museum

Abbey Gate House, Sherborne, Dorset DT9 3BP
☎ 0935 812252
Tues and Sat 10.30–12.30, 2.30–4. Apr–Oct,
also Sun 2.30–4.
🏛 *Capt. T. Ash, Hon. Curator*
£ 🐾 🚌

The Gate House was formerly the home of the Verger of the Abbey. It now contains a museum devoted to the history and natural environment of Sherborne, with exhibits relating to geology, ecology, agriculture, archaeology, handicrafts and social themes. There are special displays on the Abbey, founded in 705, the Sherborne Missal (1400) and the 18th-century local silk industry. Other items in the Museum are a Victorian dolls' house, a model of the first Norman castle and prints of the present Castle.

Sheffield penny token, 1812.
Sheffield City Museum.

Worldwide Butterflies and Lullingstone Silk Farm

Compton House, nr Sherborne, Dorset DT9 4QN
☎ *0935 74608*
Apr–Oct, daily 10–5
 The Secretary
£ ♿ ⚑ ☕

Compton House is on the A30, midway between Sherborne and Yeovil. It is a Tudor mansion, considerably altered and extended in the 1830s, a further wing being added at the end of the century. The success of the Worldwide Butterfly enterprise, established in the grounds in the 1970s, allowed the house, then in a decrepit condition, to be fully restored. Part of it is now occupied again by the Goodden family, which lived at Compton House from 1736 until 1976, and other rooms provide ideal accommodation for the Gooddens' celebrated collection of butterflies, other sections of which live in the Jungle and Palm House, which has

Purple Emperor. Sherborne, Worldwide Butterflies and Lullingstone Silk Farm.

been built on the site of the old conservatory. The emphasis is on living butterflies, but there are also worldwide collections of mounted butterflies and moths, grouped by geographical region and by family, which are used for Compton's extensive educational work.

Lullingstone Silk Farm, formerly in Kent, which has provided silk Royal dresses and robes since 1936, and which is also open to the public, became part of the Worldwide Butterflies enterprise in 1977.

Sheringham

The North Norfolk Railway

The Station, Sheringham, Norfolk NR26 8RA
☎ *0263 822045*
Easter–Sept, daily 10–5
 The Commercial Manager
£ ♿ ⚑ ☕

The North Norfolk Railway is a re-creation of a typical rural branch line, with a track running for five miles between Sheringham and Kelling

Camp Halt. Steam trains operate on Sundays during the season, on extra days as the season progresses, and with a daily service during August. The trains use rolling stock, locomotives and signalling equipment which date from the late 19th and early 20th centuries. The two stations, at Sheringham (1887) and Weybourne (1901) are both original.

The Museum contains a collection of railway relics, and visitors can also see locomotives and coaches being restored.

Shildon

Timothy Hackworth Museum

Soho Cottages, Shildon, Co. Durham DL4 1LX
☎ *0388 772036*
Apr–Sept, Wed–Sun & Bank Holiday, 10–12, 1–6. Other times by appt.
 Mr A. Pearce, Recreation Officer
£ 🍴 ⚑ ☕

Timothy Hackworth (1786–1850), the great locomotive designer, had a contract for running the Stockton and Darlington Railway and built locomotives for British and foreign railways at his works at New Shildon. Soho House, where he lived, has been restored, together with the Paint Shop at the Works, as a memorial to him. One part of the house has been furnished as it would have been in his lifetime, the other contains an exhibition illustrating his life and times. There are displays relating to pioneering railway engineers and inventions, and coalmining, together with the wildlife of the area.

A full-size replica of his famous locomotive, *Sans Pareil*, can be seen in the Paint Shop.

Shipton-by-Beningbrough

Beningbrough Hall

Shipton-by-Beningbrough, York, North Yorkshire YO6 1DD　　　　☎ *0904 470666*
Mar 29–Oct, Tues–Thurs, Sat, Sun 12–6; Bank Holiday Mon. Last admission 5.30. Closed Good Fri.
 The Administrator
£ ♿ ⚑ ☕ ♿ NT

Beningbrough, eight miles north-west of York and now a National Trust property, was built for the Bourchier family in 1716. It contains fine carving and plasterwork and an impressive cantilevered staircase, together with collections of 17th and 18th-century furniture and English and Continental porcelain. There is a well-equipped Victorian laundry, an exhibition illustrating life below stairs and an audio-visual display which tells the story of the house and the estate.

A collection of over a hundred portraits, of the period 1688–1760, has been lent by the National Portrait Gallery, and is hung in a number of rooms in the house. They include nearly half of Kneller's portraits of members of the celebrated 'Kit-cat' Club, and among the other subjects are G. F. Handel, Alexander Pope, Queen Anne, George I and George II, the 1st Duke of Marlborough, William III and Mary II, Samuel Pepys, Dr Johnson and David Garrick.

Shoreham-by-Sea

Marlipins Museum

High Street, Shoreham-by-Sea, West Sussex
☎ 0273 462994
May–Oct 5, Mon–Sat 10–1, 2–5; Sun 2–5
⊠ Mrs G. M. Koester, Hon. Secretary, 2 Rectory Road, Shoreham-by-Sea BN4 6EA
F ⊘ ⇔

Marlipins is a 12th-century building, which was used in medieval times as a Custom House, bonded warehouse and courthouse. Alterations were carried out in the 13th and 17th centuries. In 1926 it became a museum of the Sussex Archaeological Society and in 1928 it was extensively renovated. The exhibits illustrate the history of Shoreham. Paintings, sketches and watercolours show the town as it was before the great Victorian expansion took place. A collection of early maps and charts provides evidence of the size and characteristics of Shoreham from 1587 until 1817. The story is continued by the Museum's extensive collection of photographs and postcards, exhibited under such headings as Road and Rail Transport, Shoreham Harbour and Shipbuilding. There are also geological and archaeological collections and exhibits of domestic equipment and craftsmen's tools.

The upper room of the Museum is devoted to Shoreham's maritime history, illustrated by means of models of Shoreham-built ships and ships using Shoreham as a port, and marine paintings and prints.

Shorwell

Yafford Mill and Farm Park

Shorwell, nr Newport, Isle of Wight
☎ 0983 740610
Easter–Sept, daily 10–6
⊠ Mrs A. Morton, Westridge Entertainment Ltd, Brading Road, Ryde, Isle of Wight PO33 1QG
£ ⛔ ⬛ ⇔

The Mill is a mile beyond Shorwell, off the B3399 from Newport to Brighstone. Built in the 19th century, it was operational until 1970 and has since been fully restored and is now the only working watermill on the Island. It contains exhibits related to the miller's trade and way of life. A collection of agricultural tools and implements in common use until the 1950s can be seen in the grounds of the Mill and in specially constructed display sheds. A farm park includes rare breeds of animals and waterfowl, and the Yafford seals.

Shrewsbury

Attingham Park

Atcham, nr Shrewsbury SY4 4TP ☎ 074377 203
Apr–Sept, Sat–Wed 2–5.30, Bank Holiday Mon 11.30–5.30. Oct, Sat, Sun 2–5.30.
Last admission at 5 or sunset if earlier.
⊠ The Administrator
£ ⛔ ⬛ ⇔ ⅙ NT

In 1783 Noel Hill, the 1st Baron Berwick, inherited Tern Hall, a house of modest size, built in 1701, and transformed it into the very much larger Attingham Park, with landscaping by Humphry Repton. In the first decade of the 19th century, Nash was commissioned to make alterations to the house and to build a picture gallery, which has cast-iron window-frames made by the Coalbrookdale Company.

The 2nd Lord Berwick's expensive tastes impoverished the estate and many of the contents had to be sold in 1827. His successor bought a great quantity of Italian paintings, sculpture and furniture and refurnished Attingham in splendid style. The fine collection of diplomatic silver made by Paul Storr was brought to the house by Lord Berwick as a normal perquisite on his retirement from the Diplomatic Service.

The 8th Lord Berwick lived at Attingham for 50 years and bequeathed it to the National Trust in 1947.

Timothy Hackworth's home at Shildon, Co. Durham.

Clive House Museum

College Hill, Shrewsbury, Shropshire SY1 1LZ
☎ 0743 54811
Mon 2–5; Tues–Sat 10–1, 2–5. Closed Good Fri & Christmas week.
⊠ Miss V. M. Bellamy, Museums Curator
£ ⊘

The Museum is in an 18th-century house, occupied by Clive of India while he was Mayor of Shrewsbury in 1762. The ground floor contains one of the finest collections of

Caughley and Coalport ware, together with displays of Maw tiles and silver. The first floor houses the Regimental Museum of the Queen's Dragoon Guards, with uniforms, medals, equipment and campaign relics illustrating the history of the Regiment.

Coleham Pumping Station

Longden Coleham, Shrewsbury   ☎ 0743 61196
Mid May–mid Sept, Mon–Sat 2–5
◪ See Clive House Museum
£

The Pumping Station, which dates from 1900, was built to house two Renshaw beam engines, installed to pump sewage. Still in situ, they worked until 1969, when they were superseded by electric pumps.

Radbrook Culinary Museum

Radbrook Centre for Catering and Management
    Studies, Radbrook Road, Shrewsbury
    SY3 9BL   ☎ 0743 52686
Mon–Thurs 9–3; Fri 9–4 during term-time
◪ Mrs J. Turney, Associate Vice-Principal
F ⇔

Radbrook College was established in 1901 to provide training for girls who intended to enter domestic service or to work on farms. Much interesting equipment in use c. 1900 has survived in the workrooms and dairies of the College, and the kitchen and scullery of the original Principal's House have now been converted into a typical kitchen of the Victorian period, with the equipment as it would have been at the time when Radbrook College was first opened. The Museum is associated with another recent College venture, the British Culinary Research Centre.

Rowley's House Museum

Barker Street, Shrewsbury SY1 1QT
    ☎ 0743 61196
Mon–Sat 10–5. Easter–late Sept, also Sun 12–5.
◪ See Clive House Museum
£ ✎

The Museum building is in two parts: Rowley's House, which is timber-framed and dates from the late 16th century, and an adjoining brick and stone mansion, built in 1618. There are displays illustrating the geology, natural history and archaeology of Shropshire, with an interesting collection of material from the Roman city of Viroconium, the modern Wroxeter, including the original Forum inscription. One gallery is devoted to the history of Shrewsbury since the Civil War and among its special exhibits is a reconstruction of a 17th-century bedroom, with a four-poster bed, and a display of costumes.

The Shropshire Regimental Museum

The Castle, Shrewsbury   ☎ 0743 58516
Easter–Oct, daily 10–5. Nov–Easter,
    Mon–Sat 10–5.
◪ G. Archer Parfitt, Regimental Duty Curator
£ ✎ ▮

The Castle, built in 1083, was modernised by Thomas Telford. The Museum displays the Regimental collections of the King's Shropshire Light Infantry, the Shropshire Yeomanry, the Shropshire Royal Horse Artillery and their predecessors. The exhibits include colours and guidons, uniforms, weapons, medals and campaign relics.

Sibsey

Sibsey Trader Windmill

Sibsey, nr Boston, Lincolnshire   ☎ 0205 750036
Mar 28–Sept, Mon–Sat 9.30–6.30; Sun 2–6.30.
    Closed two days a week (enquire locally).
◪ Historic Buildings & Monuments Commission,
    Cambridge   ☎ 0223 358911
£ ⇔ ⌗

Sibsey is five miles north of Boston, off the A16. The brick-built tower mill with six sails was built in 1877. Its machinery is still intact. There is a site exhibition, illustrating the history of Sibsey Windmill and of milling techniques.

Sidmouth

The Vintage Toy and Train Museum

First Floor, Field's Department Store, Market
    Place, Sidmouth EX10 8LU
    ☎ 03955 5124 extn 34
Easter–Oct, Mon–Sat 10–5. Closed Bank
    Holiday.
◪ Mr R. D. N. Salisbury, Forelands, Redwood
    Road, Sidmouth, Devon EX10 9AD
£ ▮ ▬ ⇔

The Museum presents a collection of metal and mechanical toys made between 1925 and 1975,

A Hornby Dublo 1938 GWR train set on show at the Vintage Toy and Train Museum, Sidmouth.

most of the items being pre-1939. Many of the toys are in their original condition, packaged and fresh from the factory, as they would have been displayed on the shelves of toyshops of the past. The Hornby and Meccano products of Meccano Ltd are well represented. They include a collection of French Hornby trains, made at the Meccano factory in Paris between 1930 and 1950.

The displays also contain sets of GWR wooden jigsaw puzzles and a complete series of the original editions of the famous *Just William* books.

Silchester

Calleva Museum

Rectory Grounds, Silchester, Reading, Berkshire
Daily 9–sunset
🖾 *The Hon. Secretary, Sawyers Lands,*
Silchester, Reading RG7 2NG
  ☎ *0734 700632*
🄵

By the time of the Roman conquest of Britain in A.D. 43, *Calleva*, the modern Silchester, was the residence of a British tribal king. The Romans developed the town, which they called *Calleva Atrebatum*, into an administrative centre for the tribal region of the Atrebates, and it continued to grow and flourish between the 1st and 4th centuries, declining after the withdrawal of Roman troops from Britain at the beginning of the 5th century.

The site was extensively excavated in the 19th century and most of the finds are now in Reading Museum. The Museum at Silchester, run by volunteers, provides a general guide to the site. It contains maps, photographs and other material, including some artefacts, illustrating life in *Calleva Atrebatum*.

Singleton

Weald and Downland Open Air Museum

Singleton, nr Chichester, West Sussex PO18 0EU
  ☎ *024363 348*
Apr–Oct, daily 11–5. Nov–Mar, Wed, Sun 11–4.
🖾 *The Director*
🄴 🛏 🖾 🚗 ♿

The Museum consists of a collection of historic buildings from the region which have been

rescued from destruction and re-erected on a 40-acre downland site. It illustrates the development of traditional building from medieval times to the 19th century in the Weald and Downland area of south-east England. The Museum is continually expanding and its present exhibits include timber-framed medieval houses, farm-buildings, a Tudor market hall, a blacksmith's forge, a village school, a 19th-century toll cottage, a charcoal-burner's camp, and a working watermill, producing stone-ground flour. An introductory exhibition explains the materials and constructional techniques employed in old buildings.

Sittingbourne

Dolphin Yard Sailing Barge Museum

Crown Quay Lane, Sittingbourne, Kent
ME10 3SN   ☎ *0795 24132*
Good Fri–mid Oct, Sun & Bank Holiday 11–5
🖾 *Mrs A. M. Harber, 117 Plains Avenue,*
Maidstone, Kent ME15 7AR ☎ *0622 62531*
🄴 🖉 🖾 🍴 🚗

Dolphin Yard is a small shipbuilding complex on the east bank of Milton Creek, where sailing barges were built and repaired. It is the last complete example of its type, and comprises a sail-loft, carpenter's shop, forge – the main supporting timbers of which are sailing barge tillers – a steam chest, and barge repair blocks. The Museum is housed in the sail-loft and forge, and includes models, paintings, photographs, tools and equipment relating to sailing barges.

Sizergh

Sizergh Castle

Sizergh, Cumbria LA8 8AE.   ☎ *0448 60070*
Sun, Mon, Wed, Thurs 2–5.45 (last admission
  5.15). Closed Good Fri.
🖾 *The Administrator*
🄴 🛏 🖾 🚗 Ⓝ🅃

Sizergh Castle is three and a half miles south of Kendal and one mile north of the junction of the A6 and A591. The home of the Strickland family since 1239, it is now a National Trust property. The Castle is particularly celebrated for its Pele Tower and Elizabethan carved overmantels. It contains a number of pieces of Elizabethan furniture and the panelling and ceilings are noteworthy. The Museum contains displays illustrating the history of the Castle and includes family portraits and a number of relics of the Stuart Royal Family.

The garden was laid out in the 18th century. A large rock garden, dating from 1926, contains a fine collection of dwarf conifers and hardy ferns, as well as the more usual plants, providing colour throughout most of the year.

Walderton Cottage, a flint and brick building of the 16th century, re-erected at the Weald and Downland Open Air Museum, Singleton.

Skegness

Church Farm Museum

Church Road South, Skegness, Lincolnshire
☎ 0754 66658
*Easter–Oct, daily 10.30–5.30. Evening parties
by appt.*
◩ *Mr Rodney Cousins, Museum of Lincolnshire
Life, Burton Road, Lincoln LN1 3LY*
☎ 0522 28448
Ⓔ ● 🍴 ♨

The Museum, which is Lincolnshire's only
open-air museum, is in the farmhouse and
outbuildings of Church Farm. The farmhouse is
furnished in traditional style and the
outbuildings contain collections of agricultural
implements and equipment. There is also a
display of domestic utensils. A timber-framed
cottage has been re-erected on the Museum site.
   Craft demonstrations take place on Sunday
afternoons.

Skelton

Hutton-in-the-Forest

Skelton, Penrith, Cumbria CA11 9TH
☎ 08534 500
*May 23–Sept 14, Thurs, Fri, Sun & Bank Holiday
Mon 1–4.30. Last admission 4.*
◩ *Mrs Rita Blake, Administrator*
Ⓔ ● 🍴 ♨

The Fletcher and Fletcher-Vane family has lived
at Hutton-in-the-Forest for the past 300 years. It
was originally a 14th-century Pele Tower, but
additions made during the 17th to 19th
centuries have created an unusual and
interesting house, with an architecture and
contents which reflect its long history. The
collection of furniture, tapestries, paintings and
porcelain dates from 1600 onwards.

Skidby

Skidby Windmill and Museum

Skidby, Cottingham, North Humberside
☎ 0482 840150
May–Sept, Tues–Sat 10.30–4; Sun 1–4.30
◩ *Mrs Woodcock, Beverley Borough Council,
Lairgate, Beverley, North Humberside
HU17 8HL*   ☎ 0482 882255
Ⓔ ⏦ 🍴 ♨

The Mill was erected in 1821 and was worked
commercially by wind power until 1954, when
electrically-driven plant was installed. In 1974
the windmill was completely restored and is now
in full working order. The warehouse, stables
and other outbuildings have been developed as a
museum relating to milling and agriculture,
particularly the growing of corn. There are also
displays showing the different types of windmill
which were built in Britain and the mills still
surviving in East Yorkshire. The accounts and
millwright's records relating to Skidby are also
on view.

Skipton

The Craven Museum

*Town Hall, High Street, Skipton, North Yorkshire
   BD23 1AH*   ☎ 0756 4079
*Apr–Sept, Mon, Wed–Fri 11–5; Sat 10–12, 1–5;
   Sun 2–5. Oct–Mar, Mon, Wed–Fri 2–5;
   Sat 10–12, 1.30–4.30. Closed Dec 25, 26,
   Jan 1 & some other Bank Holidays.*
◩ *The Curator*
Ⓕ

The main collections and displays deal with the
geology, archaeology, agriculture, crafts and
social history of the Craven Dales of north-west
Yorkshire. Among the themes specially featured
are the local leadmining industry, archaeological
material from local caves, Christianity in
Craven, and the 19th-century history of
Skipton.

George Leatt Industrial and Folk Museum

High Corn Mills, Skipton, North Yorkshire
   ☎ 0756 2883
Wed, Sat, Sun 2–6
◩ *George Leatt, The Woods, 2 Wood Grove,
   Skipton*   ☎ 0756 4725
Ⓔ ♨

The Museum, in a fully-restored water-powered
corn mill, occupies a site where milling was
recorded in the 12th century. It contains a
number of items connected with the milling
industry, a blacksmith's shop and a collection
of traps, gigs and carts. The Mill now grinds
wholemeal flour for sale.

Yorkshire Dales Railway Museum

*Embsay Station, nr Skipton, North Yorkshire
   BD23 6AX*   ☎ 0756 4727
*Site open all year. Operating days: Easter–Oct,
   Sun 11–4.30. July–Aug, Tues 11–4.30;
   Sat 1.30–4.30.*
◩ *Publicity Officer*
Ⓕ *ex. train ride* ● 🍴 ♨

The Yorkshire Dales Railway has one of the
largest and best restored collections of industrial
steam locomotives in Britain. There is also a
number of items of passenger and freight rolling
stock. A display of photographs and documents
illustrates the history of the line and of the Trust
which operates it.
   The main building at Embsay Station
attempts to recapture the atmosphere of a
country station in the 1930s. Visitors are offered
a three-mile round trip on trains hauled by
steam locomotives.

Slane

Francis Ledwidge Cottage

Jeanville, Slane, Co. Meath, Ireland
   ☎ 041 24336
Apr–Sept, Mon–Sat 10–12.30, 2–5; Sun 2–6
◩ *Mr John Clarke, Hon. Secretary*
Ⓔ ♨ ♿

The poet, Francis Ledwidge (1887–1917), was killed in Flanders during the First World War. The Community Council at Slane has bought his former home, a labourer's cottage, and furnished it as far as possible as it was in Ledwidge's lifetime. One room is devoted to an exhibition illustrating his life and work, with recordings of some of his poems.

Sleat

The Headship of the Gael Exhibition and Clan Donald Museum of the Isles

Clan Donald Centre, Armadale Castle, Sleat,
    Isle of Skye IV45 8RS   ☎ 04714 227
Easter–May, Oct, Mon–Sat 10–5. June–Sept,
    Mon–Sat 10–5; Sun 1–5.
𝕏 The Director
£ 🍴 ⚑ 🅿 ⟐

The Macdonald family lived in the late 18th and early 19th-century Armadale Castle until 1925. Parts of the Castle then became ruinous and were demolished. In 1984 the Headship of the Gael Exhibition was opened in the restored section of the Castle. It tells the story of 1,300 years of Clan Donald's history and, in particular, of the Lordship of the Isles, when the Gaelic nation flourished under the Clan's leadership.

Sledmere

Sledmere House

Sledmere, Humberside   ☎ 0377 86208
Easter, then every Sun in Apr 1.30–5.30
    May 3–Sept 25, Tues–Thurs, Sat, Sun
    1.30–5.30.
𝕏 Sir Tatton Sykes, Bart
£ 🍴 ⚑ 🅿 HHA

Sledmere House, 16 miles west of Bridlington, on the B1253, dates from 1787 and was designed by Sir Christopher Sykes, with Greco-Roman decorations by Joseph Rose. It was rebuilt after a fire early in the present century and carefully restored to its original appearance. The furniture, porcelain and paintings are mainly of the 18th and early 19th centuries.

Sligo

County Museum and Art Gallery

Stephen Street, Sligo, Co. Sligo, Ireland
    ☎ 071 2212
June–Sept, Tues–Sat 10.30–12.30, 2.30–4.30
𝕏 The Curator
F 🅿

The Museum has collections relating to the archaeology and history of Sligo, to the traditional life of the area, and the contribution of W. B. Yeats and his contemporaries to the Irish literary renaissance. The Art Gallery has paintings by Jack B. Yeats and contemporary Irish artists.

Smallhythe

Ellen Terry Memorial Museum

Smallhythe Place, Smallhythe, Tenterden, Kent
    TN20 7NG   ☎ 05806 2334
Apr–Oct, Mon, Wed, Thurs, Sat, Sun 2–6
    or dusk if earlier (last admission 5.30). Closed
    Good Fri.
𝕏 The Custodian-in-Charge
£ 🅿 NT

Smallhythe is two and a half miles south of Tenterden, on the B2082. The early 16th-century yeoman's house, now the property of the National Trust, was owned by Dame Ellen Terry from 1899 until her death in 1928. It remains much as it was when she lived in it and contains many of her personal possessions and theatrical mementoes, including photographs, paintings and costumes. Her collection of mementoes of Henry Irving, Sarah Siddons, Garrick and other notabilities of the theatre is also on display.

Smallthorne

Ford Green Hall

Ford Green Road, Smallthorne, Stoke-on-Trent,
    Staffordshire ST6 1NG   ☎ 0782 534771
Mon, Wed, Thurs, Sat 10–12.30, 2–5; Sun 2–5
    (last admission 4.15). Closed Christmas week.
𝕏 Mrs P. J. Woolliscroft, Custodian
F 🍴 🅿

The Hall, a 16th-century timber-framed farmhouse with 18th-century brick additions, is on the B5051, two and a half miles north of Hanley. The home of the Ford family since c. 1580, it subsequently had a number of owners and tenants, until it was bought by the City of Stoke-on-Trent in 1946. It is now furnished with items of the type a well-to-do yeoman family would have used from the 1500s onwards.

Soudley

Dean Heritage Museum

Camp Mill, Soudley, Cinderford, Gloucestershire
    GL14 7UG   ☎ 0594 22170
Apr–Oct, daily 10–6. Nov–Mar, daily 10–5.
    Closed Dec 25, 26.
𝕏 Mrs Sue Ashmole
£ 🍴 ⚑ 🅿 ⟐

Soudley is on the B4227 between Cinderford and Blakeney. The three-storeyed watermill (1876) originally ground corn and was subsequently used as a sawmill and for the manufacture of leather board, ending its working life as a scrapyard. It was presented to the newly formed Dean Heritage Trust in 1981 and now houses exhibitions illustrating the history, traditions and natural environment of the Forest of Dean. Special attention is paid to the quarrying, mining, charcoal-burning, iron-working and forestry carried on in the area.

Camp Mill, which used millstones, was a very late example of its type. By 1876, most British flour mills were steam-powered and had new roller equipment. Because of the many subsequent changes in the use of the Mill, little evidence remains above ground of the original milling processes. The most interesting area is the basement, which was infilled and much of the machinery left intact. This is now being excavated and in due course will be opened to the public as a working display.

Southampton

Bargate Guildhall Museum

The Bargate, Above Bar, Southampton
    ☎ 0703 224216
Tues–Fri 10–12, 1–5; Sat 10–12, 1–4; Sun 2–5.
    Closed Good Fri, Dec 25, 26 & Bank Holiday.
◪ *See Tudor House Museum*
Ⓕ ⬙ ⬈ ☐

The Museum, in the medieval North Gate of the town of Southampton, is used for temporary exhibitions, usually on local themes. Each exhibition continues for several months, sometimes for as long as a year. The 1986–7 exhibition is called *What's in Store* and consists of a very mixed display from the Southampton Museum store, presented to show how a Victorian museum might have looked.

God's House Tower Museum

Winkle Street, Town Quay, Southampton,
    ☎ 0703 220007
Tues–Fri 10–12, 2–5; Sat 10–12, 2–4; Sun 2–5.
    Closed Good Fri, Dec 25, 26 & Bank Holiday.
◪ *See Tudor House Museum*
Ⓕ

The Tower was originally a fortress, built in the 15th century to defend the town. The sea lapped its walls until a century ago. Its displays illustrate the development of Southampton from Roman to late medieval times and include material from local excavations.

Southampton Art Gallery

Civic Centre, Southampton SO9 4XF
    ☎ 0703 223855
Tues–Fri 10–5; Sat 10–4; Sun 2–5.
    Closed Dec 25, Jan 1.
◪ *Education Service (extn 2277)*
Ⓕ ⬤ ⬈ ⬧ ☐

The Gallery's present purchasing policy concentrates on contemporary British painting and sculpture. There are also works by the British Surrealists and by members of the Camden Town Group. There is an important collection of 20th-century portraits, especially of significant figures in the art world. The large Old Master collection includes *The Holy Family* by Jordaens and *Lord Vernon* by Gainsborough.

The 19th century in England and France is represented by Turner, John Martin and the Pre-Raphaelites and by the French Impressionists, including Pissarro, Renoir, Monet and Sisley. The displays are enhanced by loans from private collectors, which include paintings and drawings by Boudin, Picasso, Bonnard and Monet.

Southampton Hall of Aviation

Albert Road South, Southampton SO1 1FR
    ☎ 0703 35830
Tues–Sat 10–5; Sun 12–5
◪ *Squadron Leader A. Jones, Director*
Ⓔ ⬤ ⬛ ⬈ ⬧

The collections illustrate the history of aviation in the Solent area, where 26 aircraft companies have operated. They include the Supermarine Aircraft Works, where R. J. Mitchell designed the Spitfire, and the Schneider Trophy winner, SB6. Both of these aircraft are on show, together with Skeeter and Gazelle helicopters and the Sandringham Flying Boat. Other exhibits include photographs, paintings, models and engines.

Southampton Maritime Museum

The Wool House, Town Quay, Southampton
    ☎ 0703 223941
Tues–Fri 10–1, 2–5; Sat 10–1, 2–4; Sun 2–5.
    Closed Good Fri, Dec 25, 26, & Bank Holiday.
◪ *Keeper of Maritime and Aviation History,*
    Tudor House Museum
Ⓕ ⬤ ⬈

The Museum occupies a 14th-century wool warehouse, later used to house French prisoners of war, whose initials can be seen carved in the roof timbers. The collections include ship models and paintings, recalling Southampton in the days of sail, pioneer steamships, steam yachts, paddle steamers and the great liners.

Special exhibits include *Miss Britain III*, the record-breaking powerboat built by Hubert Scott-Paine and the British Power Boat Company at Hythe in 1933, the only surviving oscillating steam engine, from the paddle steamer, *Empress* (1879), and the vertical compound engine from the local ferry, *Venus* (1947). There is also an exhibition devoted to the ill-fated maiden voyage of the *Titanic* from Southampton to New York in 1912.

Medieval French pottery from Southampton on display in God's House Tower Museum.

Tudor House Museum

*Bugle Street, St Michael's Square, Southampton
  SO1 0AD*   ☎ *0703 224216*
*Tues–Fri 10–5; Sat 10–4; Sun 2–5.
  Closed Good Fri, Dec 25, 26 & Bank Holiday.*
N *Keeper of Local and Social History*
F *⊘ ⚲*

The Museum, in a 16th-century timber-framed
building, concentrates on domestic and family
life in the past. The exhibits include kitchen
and laundry equipment, costumes, toys and
dolls.

A Tudor garden adjoining the Museum has
both a knot garden and a 'secret' garden, with
herbs and many old English flowers.

Southend-on-Sea

Central Museum

*Victoria Avenue, Southend-on-Sea, Essex
  SS2 6EX*   ☎ *0702 330214*
*Mon 1–5; Tues–Sat 10–5. Closed Dec 25, 26 &
  Bank Holiday.*
N *Clerical Officer*
E *⊘ ⚲ ♿*

The Museum collections are concerned with the
natural and human history of south-east Essex,
from the Eocene period to the present day.
Some of the more recent material is arranged in
room settings.

There are also displays of live fish and insects
and the only planetarium in south-east England
outside London.

Prittlewell Priory

*Priory Park, Victoria Avenue, Southend-on-Sea,
  Essex*   ☎ *0702 342878*
*Tues–Sat 10–1, 2–5. Closed Dec 25, 26 &
  Bank Holiday.*
N *The Supervisor*
F *⊘ ⚲ ♿*

Prittlewell Priory, Southend, under snow.

The Priory contains features of a medieval
Cluniac Priory, included in an early 19th-
century house. Now a branch of Southend
Museums, it contains a comprehensive
collection of communications equipment, from
early 19th-century printing presses and
pioneering methods of sound reproduction to
radio and television. There are also sections
dealing with the history of the Priory and
medieval monasticism and with local natural
history.

Southchurch Hall

*Southchurch Hall Gardens, Southend-on-Sea,
  Essex*   ☎ *0702 67671*
*Tues–Sat 10–1, 2–5. Closed Dec 25, 26 &
  Bank Holiday.*
N *The Supervisor*
F *⊘ ⚲*

The Hall is a late 13th to 14th-century moated,
timber-framed manor house, with 16th-century
alterations. It is furnished to reflect the
medieval and post-medieval history of the site
and uses both authentic and reproduction
furnishings for the purpose. A separate
exhibition room contains displays illustrating
the history of the house, the manor, the parish
and the de Southchurch family. There are also
exhibits relating to medieval secular life.

South Harting

Uppark

South Harting, Petersfield, Hampshire GU31 5QR
                          ☎ *073085 317/458*
*Apr–Sept, Wed, Thurs, Sun & Bank Holiday
  Mon 2–6 (last admission 5.30)*
N *The Administrator*
E ♿ 🍴 ⚲ ♿ **NT**

Uppark, now a National Trust property, was
built about 1690 by the Earl of Tankerville. It
was sold in 1747 to the very rich Sir Matthew
Fetherstonhaugh, who redecorated most of the
interior. The Georgian wallpapers, curtains and
upholstery fabrics are remarkably well preserved.
There are also tapestries, Italian paintings,
bronzes and Chinese porcelain, family portraits,
Victorian domestic equipment and a splendid
dolls' house made for the wife of Sir Matthew
Fetherstonhaugh, complete with early Georgian
furniture, glass and silver.

South Molton

South Molton Museum

Market Street, South Molton, Devon
                          ☎ *07695 2951*
*Feb–Nov, Mon, Tues, Thurs, Fri 10.30–12.30,
  2–4; Wed, Sat 10–12. Closed Bank Holiday
  and Mon in Feb–Mar, Oct–Nov.*
N *The Curator*
F *⊘ ⚲ □*

The Museum is on the ground floor of South
Molton's 18th-century Town Hall. It contains a

collection of items of everyday use from the 17th century onwards, reflecting both the agricultural setting of the town and the customs, occupations and social and domestic life of the townspeople themselves. The collection of pewter is one of the best in the West Country, and the fire engine (1736) one of the oldest. The massive cider press, made c. 1800, is noteworthy for its hand-cut wooden screw.

The Royal Charters for South Molton, dated 1590 and 1684, are on display and there are many old photographs illustrating life in the district since the mid-19th century. There are monthly art exhibitions, of works provided by the Area Museums Council and by local artists.

Southport

Atkinson Art Gallery

Lord Street, Southport, Merseyside PR8 1DH
    ☎ *0704 33133 extn 129*
Mon–Wed, Fri 10–5; Thurs, Sat 10–1
🞜 *Stephen Forshaw, Keeper of Fine Art*
F 🖉 🖴

The Gallery's collections include Victorian paintings, 18th and 19th-century English watercolours and early 20th-century works by artists associated with the New English Art Club. There are also smaller collections of silver, 18th-century glass and porcelain.

The Botanic Gardens Museum

Churchtown, Southport, Merseyside PR9 7NB
    ☎ *0704 27547*
Apr–Sept, Tues–Sat 10–6; Sun 2–5.
    Oct–Apr, Tues–Sat 10–5; Sun 2–5.
    Closed Good Fri & Fri following Bank Holiday.
    Open Bank Holiday Mon.
🞜 *See Atkinson Art Gallery*
F 🖦 🖴 🖴

The Museum has collections of natural history, local history, Victoriana, toys and dolls. A special exhibit tells the story of the R.N.L.I.'s worst-ever lifeboat disaster which occurred in 1886 and was connected with the wreck of the *Mexico*. There are also items associated with Scarisbrick Hall, a few miles from the Museum, two shrimping carts and a horse-drawn Merryweather fire engine dating from 1893.

The strong point of the natural history section is the Pennington collection of British birds.

South Queensferry

Dalmeny House

South Queensferry, West Lothian EH30 9TQ
    ☎ *031 331 1888*
May–Sept, Sun–Thurs 2–5.30
🞜 *The Administrator*
£ 🖉 🖦 🖴 🖢 HHA

The Napoleon Room of Dalmeny House, South Queensferry.

Dalmeny House is three miles east of South Queensferry, on the B924. Designed by William Wilkins in the Tudor Gothic style, it was built in 1814–17 for the 4th Earl of Rosebery. It contains 18th-century tapestries, French furniture and porcelain from Mentmore, displayed in the drawing room. The Rothschild Room preserves the plans of the architect, Sir Joseph Paxton, for Mentmore and commemorates the union between the Roseberys and the Rothschilds, the 5th Earl of Rosebery having married the only child of Baron Meyer de Rothschild. The Napoleon Room contains family portraits and items associated with the Emperor, collected by the 5th Earl, who was a Napoleon enthusiast.

Hopetoun House

South Queensferry, West Lothian EH30 9SL
    ☎ *031 331 2451*
Easter, then May–mid Sept, daily 11–5.30
🞜 *The Administrator*
£ 🖦 🖦 🖴 🖢 HHA

Hopetoun, 10 miles west of Edinburgh, is the ancestral home of the Hope family. The present head of the family is the 3rd Earl of Linlithgow. The original house was designed for the 1st Earl of Hopetoun by Sir William Bruce, the architect of Holyrood Palace, and was completed in 1703. In 1721 William Adam was engaged to enlarge and remodel the house, the work being carried out by his son John, who was also responsible for the interior decoration of the principal rooms. Much of the original furniture made for these rooms in the 1760s is still to be seen today, together with the family collections of tapestries and paintings. Among the artists represented are Teniers, Canaletto and Wilkie.

The museum at Hopetoun contains porcelain, costumes and documents relating to the family and to Scottish history. A special exhibition, *Horse and Man in Lowland Scotland*, has been arranged in the stables.

The Burry Man, a bizarre figure in Scottish folklore, covered from head to foot in burr thistles, wearing a helmet of roses, and carrying in each hand a staff decked with flowers. South Queensferry Museum.

South Queensferry Museum

Council Chambers, South Queensferry, West
*   Lothian EH30 9HP*   ☎ *031 331 1590*
Apr–Sept, Tues, Thurs 2–6
🅺 *Keeper of Social History, Huntly House*
*   Museum, 142 Canongate, Edinburgh*
*   EH8 8DD*   ☎ *031 225 2424*
🄵 ↩

The Museum tells the story of the former Royal Burgh of South Queensferry, including the methods of crossing of the Forth. Particular emphasis is given to the construction and history of the rail and road bridges. One of the more remarkable exhibits is the Burry Man, a full-size re-creation of the strange person who walks through the streets of the town each year.

Southsea

Cumberland House and Aquarium

Eastern Parade, Southsea, Hampshire PO4 9RF
Daily 10.30–5.30. Closed Dec 24–26.
🅺 *Mr C. Spendlove, City Museum and Art*
*   Gallery, Museum Road, Portsmouth*
*   PO1 2LJ*   ☎ *0705 82726*
🄴 ⬭ ↩

The displays in the Museum illustrate the development of Portsmouth and the Hampshire Basin from about 200 years ago to modern times. There are exhibits explaining the geological basis of the area and the changes in climate and vegetation which have taken place. The fossils include a full-grown Iguanodon. Birds, mammals and insects are shown in re-creations of their natural habitat. There is a freshwater aquarium, together with displays of live animals.

D-Day Museum

Clarence Esplanade, Southsea, Hampshire
*   PO5 3PA*
Daily 10.30–5.30. Closed Dec 24–26.
🅺 *See Cumberland House and Aquarium*
🄴 🄰 ↩ 🄰

The displays in the Museum tell the story of the Normandy landings in 1944. The military equipment and vehicles include field guns, jeeps and a Sherman tank. There are also uniforms worn by the Allied forces taking part in the invasion. The planning and carrying out of the operation is explained by means of models, maps and photographs.

The celebrated Overlord Embroidery, 272 feet long, illustrates the progress of the operation, in much the same way as the Bayeux Tapestry did for the invasion of Britain by William of Normandy in 1066.

Royal Marines Museum

Royal Marines Eastney, Southsea, Hampshire
*   PO4 9PX*   ☎ *0705 822351 extn 6135*
Daily 10–4.30. Closed Jan 1–15.
🅺 *The Director*
🄵 🄰 💷 *May-Sept* ↩ □

The Museum is in the Officers' Mess of the Royal Marines Eastney, a Victorian building of some magnificence. It presents the history of the Royal Marines from the establishment of the Corps in 1664 to the present day. The exhibits include documents, paintings, weapons and campaign relics, supported by a number of audio-visual presentations. The displays in the Medal Room include all 10 Victoria Crosses won by Royal Marines. There is also a Uniform Room and a Band History Room. Naval bands date from the 1760s, but for nearly a century they were composed mainly of civilians. The Museum's exhibit concentrates on the history of the uniformed Royal Marines Band.

A major exhibition on a selected subject is mounted each year, together with one or two smaller exhibitions.

Southsea Castle

Clarence Esplanade, Southsea, Hampshire
*   PO5 3PA*
Daily 10.30–5.30. Closed Dec 24–26.
🅺 *See Cumberland House and Aquarium*
🄴 🄰 ↩

The Castle was built in 1544–5 on the orders of Henry VIII to protect Portsmouth from invasion. There is a display of artillery and, in the keep, an exhibition on the military history of Portsmouth. Other galleries, around the bailey, contain exhibits on local archaeology, on Sir Marc Brunel's machinery for making ships' blocks and on the history of the local police force.

South Shields

Arbeia Roman Fort and Museum

Baring Street, South Shields, Tyne and Wear
    NE33 2BD   ☎ 0632 4561369
May–Sept, Mon–Sat 10–5.30; Sun 2–5.
    Oct–Apr, Mon–Fri 10–4; Sat 10–12.
Ⓜ Roger Miket
Ⓕ ⬭ ⮞ ⭑

The Roman Fort at South Shields is at the
eastern end of the Hadrianic frontier. It was
built in the late 1st or early 2nd centuries to
guard the mouth of the River Tyne and was
enlarged c. 207–8 A.D. Excavations have
revealed the foundations of the headquarters
building, granaries, barracks and fort defences,
including gateways and ditches. A simulation of
a full-size Roman gateway is under construction
on the site of the west gateway. The Museum
contains displays of objects discovered during
excavations at the Fort. Exhibits include tiles,
some stamped with the mark of the 5th Cohort
of Gauls, bricks, bronze door studs and several
kinds of flooring materials. There are also
swords, enamelled belt-mountings, sling-
stones, fragments of armour, lead baggage seals,
tools and surveying instruments. Among the
wide range of household and personal items are
Samian pots and gaming counters, indicating
one of the ways in which Roman soldiers spent
their off-duty hours.

South Shields Museum and Art Gallery

Ocean Road, South Shields, Tyne and Wear
    NE33 2AU   ☎ 0632 568740
Mon–Fri 10–5.30; Sat 10–4.30; Sun 2–5.
    Closed Good Fri, Dec 25, 26, Jan 1.
Ⓜ The Curator
Ⓕ ⬛ ⭑ ☐

The Museum's collections relate to the natural
history, archaeology and history of South
Shields. The maritime section includes displays
on local shipbuilding, for many years an
important industry in the area and a major
source of employment. South Shields is also
identified with the invention of the lifeboat and
the Museum's section devoted to this contains a
model of W. Wouldhave's pioneering lifeboat
(1789).
    The Art Gallery is organised on the basis of
temporary exhibitions.

**Portable medical cabinet of c. 1805.
Southwold Museum.**

Southwold

Southwold Museum

Bartholomew Green, Southwold, Suffolk IP18 6HZ
Spring Bank Holiday–Sept, daily 2.30–4.30.
    Open Easter Mon & May Day Bank Holiday,
    2.30–4.30. Other times by appt.
Ⓜ Hon. Curator   ☎ 0502 722711
Ⓕ ⬭ ⮞

The original Museum building, opened in 1933,
was formerly a pair of late 17th-century
cottages. Extensions were added in the 1950s
and 1960s. The aim of the Museum is to
illustrate the history of the town and the natural
history of the surrounding countryside. There
are collections of archaeological material,
mostly medieval, 19th and early 20th-century
domestic equipment, and prints and
photographs of the district.
    A special section is devoted to the Southwold
Railway, which opened in 1879 and closed 50
years later. There are also pictures and charts
relating to the Battle of Sole Bay, in 1672.

Spalding

Ayscoughfee Hall Museum

Ayscoughfee Hall, Churchgate, Spalding,
    Lincolnshire PE11 2RB
        ☎ 0775 61161 extn 315 (Curator)
Ⓜ Miss Susanna Davis, Curator
Ⓔ ⬭ ⭑ ⮞

Ayscoughfee Hall dates from the 15th century,
but has been much altered since. The Museum
houses the Ashley Maples collection of British
birds and eggs.

Pinchbeck Marsh Drainage Engine

Pinchbeck Marsh, Spalding, Lincolnshire
    PE11 3UW   ☎ 0775 2444
By appointment with Dennis Lawson, Keeper
Ⓜ John Honnor, Welland and Deepings Internal
    Drainage Board, Welland Terrace, Spalding
    PE11 2TD   ☎ 0775 5861
Ⓕ ⮞

The engine, in the original pumphouse
building, is a simple rotative 'A' frame beam
engine made by Butterly and Co. and erected in
1833. It was not superseded until 1952, when it
was the last of its type still running in the Fens.
Only two other examples survive. The
Lancashire boiler and the scoop wheel have
also been preserved.

Pode Hole Land Drainage Museum

Welland and Deepings Internal Drainage Board,
    Pode Hole Depot, Spalding, Lincolnshire
    PE11 3LL   ☎ 0775 3136
Mon–Fri 8–4. Other times by appt. Closed Bank
    Holiday.
Ⓜ See Pinchbeck Marsh Drainage Engine
Ⓕ ⮞

The Museum is in the boilerhouse of the steam pumping station, built in 1826. The engine house and the beam engines were dismantled in 1952. An 1876 Byelaws Board is still on the site. The displays illustrate the history of land drainage over the last 1,000 years, with exhibits which include drain pipes, pumps, gas and oil engines, a dragline excavator and hand tools. The collection of hand tools covers a wide range. Among them are digging tools, turf cutters, weed cutters, fishing spears, plank road equipment and lamps.

Sparkford

Sparkford Motor Museum

Castle Cary Road, Sparkford, Yeovil, Somerset BA22 7LH   ☎ *0963 40804*
Daily 9.30–5.30. Closed Dec 25, 26, Jan 1.
⚔ *The Curator*
🄲 ⬛ ↝

The Museum occupies a former sawmill. The cars in the collection date from 1905 to 1971 and each vehicle is believed to be in some way special. It may be the fastest, the smallest, the rarest of its kind. The 1905 Daimler detachable-top limousine, for example, is unique; the 1965 AC Cobra was the fastest production sports car.

The collection has been created by a Trust, formed to restore and preserve motoring and motorcycling items of historical and cultural interest.

Staffin

Cnoc an T-Sithein Museum

6 Ellishadder, Staffin, Isle of Skye IV51 9JE
June–Oct, Mon–Sat 9–9
⚔ *Dugald Ross*
🄵 ↝ ♿

Staffin is 15 miles north of Portree, the capital of Skye. The Museum is housed in an early 19th-century thatched cottage, a listed building. Its collections relate to the archaeology and history of Skye, from Neolithic times to the present day. The exhibits include Bronze Age arrowheads and Iron Age artefacts, agricultural tools and equipment and a wide range of fossils from the coasts of Skye.

Stafford

Regimental Museum of the 16th/5th The Queen's Royal Lancers and the Staffordshire Yeomanry

Kitchener House, Lammascote Road, Stafford ST16 3TA   ☎ *0785 45840*
Mon–Fri 9.30–1, 2–4.30. Closed Bank Holiday.
⚔ *Major D. J. H. Farquharson*
🄵 ✎ ↝

The 16th The Queen's Lancers Regiment was raised in 1759 and the 5th Royal Irish Lancers in 1689 at Enniskilling as Wynne's Regiment of Enniskilling Dragoons. These two regiments were amalgamated in 1922 and now form one of the Army's Reconnaissance Regiments. The Museum provides an historic record of the Regiment. The items on display include uniforms, paintings, weapons, models, medals and documents. Among the exhibits are the original Charter which raised the 16th Lancers, an Annual Inspection Report of 1770 and a letter sent from India in 1825 by a Trooper of the 16th Lancers.

Stafford Art Gallery

The Green, Stafford ST17 4BJ   ☎ *0785 57303*
Tues–Fri 10–5, Sat 10–4
⚔ *John Rhodes, Arts and Promotion Officer*
🄵 ⬛ ↝ ☐

The Gallery's collections are primarily of topographical prints, watercolours and of works by 18th to 19th-century Staffordshire artists. There is also a craft study collection, used mainly in connection with the Gallery's educational work. This collection comprises a range of contemporary jewellery by British craftsmen, including specially commissioned items.

The programme of temporary exhibitions covers contemporary fine art, photography and crafts, as well as local and social history.

Stalybridge

Astley Cheetham Art Gallery

Trinity Street, Stalybridge, Cheshire SK15 2BN
☎ *061 338 2708*
Mon–Wed, Fri 1–7.30, Sat 9–4
⚔ *Geoff Preece, Museums Officer,*
Tameside Libraries and Arts Department,
Council Offices, Wellington Road,
Ashton-under-Lyne, Lancashire OL6 6DL
☎ *061 344 3438*
🄵 ✐ ↝ ☐

The Gallery displays the Cheetham collection, which ranges from 14th-century Italian gold ground paintings to works by Burne-Jones. There is also an important collection of paintings and drawings by Harry Rutherford, one of the most celebrated painters in the North-West.

Stamford

Burghley House

Stamford, Lincolnshire PE9 3JY   ☎ *0780 52451*
Easter–Oct, daily 11–5
⚔ *Mr J. Culverhouse, Manager*
🄲 ⬛ 💺 ↝

Burghley House, one of the greatest of Elizabethan houses, with 240 rooms, was built between 1546 and 1587 by William Cecil, 1st Lord Burghley, on the site of a medieval monastery, and has been occupied by his descendants ever since. It contains woodcarvings by Grinling Gibbons, silver decorated fireplaces and ceilings painted by Verrio. The furniture is mostly pre-18th century. There are splendid tapestries, a large collection of paintings, mostly 16th and 17th century, and a display of early Japanese and European porcelain. The medieval kitchen is equipped with over 260 copper utensils.

Stamford Brewery Museum

All Saints Street, Stamford, Lincolnshire
    PE9 2PA   ☎ 0780 52186
Apr (or Good Fri if earlier)–Sept, Wed–Sun &
    Bank Holiday 10–4. Closed Tues & Wed in
    Bank Holiday weeks. Evening parties by appt.
⚒ The Curator
Ⓕ ♠ ▣ ↩

The Museum has been created from a small Victorian steam brewery, one of 22 which existed in Stamford in the late 19th century. Though not now suitable for brewing, the steam engine and original plant remain intact. A rare survival, Melbourn Brothers' All Saints Brewery gives a good impression of the 16,798 small breweries which in 1870 existed all over the British Isles and which have now nearly all disappeared, as the brewing industry has become increasingly centralised.

Stamford Museum

Broad Street, Stamford, Lincolnshire PE9 1PJ
    ☎ 0780 55317
May–Sept, Mon–Sat 10–5; Sun 2–5.
Oct–Apr, Tues–Sat 10–12.30, 1.30–5.
Closed Dec 25, 26.
⚒ The Curator
Ⓔ ⬙ ↩

The Museum illustrates the history and archaeology of Stamford. The entrance hall contains a collection of topographical paintings, drawings and prints of the area and adjoining it is a room devoted to the building crafts of Stamford, with an emphasis on the local stones and their uses. There are also displays relating to other industries, the most important being the engineering firm of Blackstone and Co., manufacturers of stationary oil engines.

The upstairs gallery presents archaeological material discovered during excavations in and around Stamford. Of special note is the collection of Stamford pottery, one of the finest and earliest glazed wares to be made in northern Europe since Roman times. The selection on display covers the whole period of manufacture, from c. 850 to 1250.

Among the subjects dealt with by the displays on the post-medieval town are local newspapers from the 18th century onwards, water and rail communications, elections, the local Volunteer Rifle Corps, schools and the Post Office. The most popular exhibit in the Museum is the life-size model of the celebrated fat man, Daniel Lambert, wearing an original suit of his clothes. Lambert weighed 52 stone 11 pounds and died in 1809 at the age of 39.

Stanley

Beamish: North of England Open Air Museum

Beamish Hall, Chester-le-Street, Stanley,
    Co. Durham DH9 0RG   ☎ 0207 231811
Easter–mid Sept, daily 10–6 (last admission 4).
    Mid Sept–Easter, Tues–Sun 10–5 (last
    admission 4). Certain areas may be closed
    in winter.
⚒ The Director
Ⓔ ♠ ▣ ↩ ⅋

The Museum, on a 200-acre site, has been planned to illustrate life in the North-East as it was in the late 19th and early 20th centuries. Beamish has been steadily developing since 1971. A recent feature is the Town Street, comprising houses; the Sun Inn, with stables; a printing works; the Co-operative stores, and a Victorian park with its bandstand. All these buildings have been carefully dismantled, moved from their original sites to the Museum, rebuilt and furnished as they would have been in the 1920s.

Other parts of Beamish include a railway station, with footbridge, signal-box and operational track, a tramway providing services to different points of the site, a row of miners' cottages, pit-head installations and a drift mine, and the Home Farm, which has collections of agricultural implements and equipment and displays showing changes in farming methods over the past 150 years. Around the farm are pigs and poultry, and in the fields a herd of Durham Shorthorn cattle, which are being bred at Beamish, as they rapidly disappear elsewhere.

There is a regular programme of special events and throughout the Museum there are demonstrators who are happy to talk to visitors and to explain what they are doing.

A large new Interpretation Centre, which puts the whole collection into perspective, opened in April 1987.

Stanmer

Stanmer Rural Museum

Stanmer Stores, Stanmer Village, Brighton,
    East Sussex   ☎ 0273 604041
Easter–Oct, Thurs, Sun 2.30–5
⚒ Mrs N. Turner, Hon. Secretary, Deeside,
    Patcham, Brighton
Ⓕ ⬙ ↩

The Museum is within a 5,000-acre conservation area on the South Downs. It is run by the Stanmer Preservation Society, a voluntary body whose aims include the protection of this beautiful and historic part of Sussex and the maintenance of the Church. There are collections of agricultural implements, blacksmiths' and wheelwrights' tools, together with a donkey wheel and a horse gin. The horse gin, at the entrance to the Museum, stands in its own building, dated 1750, the gin itself being a century older.

Starcross

The Brunel Atmospheric Railway

Brunel Pumping House, Starcross, nr Exeter,
Devon EX6 8PR ☎ *0626 890000*
Easter–Oct, daily 10–6 (last admission 5)
▨ *Mrs V. C. Forrester, Administrator*
£ ◇ ▣ ⌖ ♿

The atmospheric system was patented early in the 19th century. Trains using it literally ran on air, by means of a combination of partial vacuum and atmospheric pressure. No locomotive was required, but a continuous iron pipe had to be laid between the rails. The South Devon atmospheric railway was the fourth and longest to be constructed. Designed by Brunel, it ran for 20 miles between Exeter and Newton Abbot in 1847. Seven pumping houses were built along the line. The one at Starcross is the sole survivor. It contains a passenger-carrying working model of an atmospheric railway and an exhibition of drawings and photographs.

Co-operative shops in the Town Street at Beamish, the North of England Open Air Museum, Stanley.

Stevenage

Knebworth House

nr Stevenage, Hertfordshire SG3 6PY
☎ *0438 812661*
May 24–Sept 14, Tues–Sun and Bank Holiday
Mon 12–5 Apr–May 23, also weekends,
Bank Holiday Mon & half-term week 12–5.
Park 11–5.30.
▨ *The Administrator*
£ ♦ ▣ ⌖ [HHA]

Knebworth, the home of the Hon. David Lytton Cobbold, is one mile south of Stevenage, off the A1(M). Three sides of the original Tudor courtyard house were demolished by Elizabeth Bulwer Lytton in 1811. The remaining wing was given a Gothick skin and in the 1840s Sir Edward Bulwer Lytton, the novelist and statesman, entrusted its embellishment and improvement to the architect, Henry Kendall. The house reflects the Lytton family's long period of ownership.

Bulwer Lytton's study, where he entertained his literary friends, has its original furnishings and the State Drawing Room is an outstanding example of High Victorian Gothic decoration, with appropriate furniture and Daniel Maclise's

painting of Caxton, a subject taken from one of Bulwer Lytton's novels. One of the bedrooms is decorated and furnished in Tudor style, the remainder being 18th century.

In a building adjoining the house, there is an exhibition of mementoes of the British Raj, reflecting the fact that the 1st Earl of Lytton was Viceroy of India and the 2nd Earl Acting Viceroy and Governor of Bengal.

Stevenage Museum

St George's Way, Stevenage, Hertfordshire
SG1 1XX ☎ *0438 354292*
Mon–Sat 10–5. Closed Bank Holiday.
▨ *Education Officer*
F ◇ ▣ ⌖ ♿

The Museum occupies the ground floor of a modern and active church, opened in 1960. It collects items illustrating the geology, natural history, archaeology and history of Stevenage. The displays tell the story of Stevenage and reflect the collections. There is a large archive of photographs of the town, taken before, during and after the development of Stevenage as the First New Town.

Stewarton

Stewarton and District Museum

Council Chambers, Avenue Square, Stewarton,
Ayrshire KA3 5AB
☎ *0563 24748 or 0560 84249*
Last Mon evening in each month, 7–9 & 1st Fri of
each month, 2–5. Other times by appt.
▨ *Mr I. H. Macdonald, 17 Grange Terrace,*
Kilmarnock, Ayrshire KA1 2JR
F ⌖

The Museum has displays of Victoriana, militaria and local industries, especially bonnet-making. There are also photographs illustrating the social history of the area and taped interviews with old people, recording their memories of local life in the past.

Steyning

Steyning Museum

91 High Street, Steyning, West Sussex BN4 3RE
Apr–Oct, Tues, Wed, Sat 10.30–12.30,
2.30–4.30; Sun 2.30–4.30. Nov–Mar,
Wed, Sat 10.30–12.30, 2.30–4.30;
Sun 2.30–4.30. Other times by appt.
▨ *The Curator*
F ◇ ⌖

In this small town, 45 of the buildings are listed as being of special historic or architectural importance. The Museum occupies the basement of an attractive 18th-century house. Its displays illustrate the history of Steyning from Saxon times to the present day. The exhibits include photographs, documents and a wide range of objects, including the Borough mace and Constable's staff, both dating from 1685.

Sticklepath

Finch Foundry Museum

Sticklepath, Okehampton, Devon EX20 2NW
☎ *0837 840286*
Daily 11–6
⚑ *The Secretary*
€ ● ↩

Sticklepath is four miles east of Okehampton, on the A30. The 'Foundry' is, in fact, a 19th-century water-powered edge tool factory. Its three waterwheels and machinery are all in working order. The machinery includes a pair of tilt-hammers, a fan or blower for the forges, grindstone, emery-wheel and bandsaw. Visitors can see all these operating.

Two of the Museum galleries contain exhibitions of tools made or used at the Foundry, together with photographs, documents, catalogues and other items illustrating the history of the business. The third gallery is devoted to the history of the industrial use of water-power.

The forge area was once a three-storey woollen mill. Some of the floor beams of this building can still be seen. The present grinding house was originally a grist mill, the thatched roof of which still exists.

Stirling

Regimental Museum of the Argyll and Sutherland Highlanders

The Castle, Stirling FK8 1EH   ☎ 0786 75165
Easter–Sept, Mon–Sat 10–5.30; Sun 11–5.
   Oct, Mon–Fri 10–3.30.
⚑ *The Visitor Centre*
€ *Castle only* ♺ ➤ ↩

Stirling Castle, the Royal Palace of the Stuart Kings, has been the recruiting and mobilisation base of the Argyll and Sutherland Highlanders since 1881. The Museum tells the story of the Regiment from 1794 to the present day, with displays of Regimental silver and colours, portraits, uniforms, medals and campaign relics.

Ruskie Farm and Landscape Museum

Dunaverig, Ruskie, Thornhill by Stirling,
   Stirlingshire FK8 3QW   ☎ 078685 277
By appt
⚑ *Lewis and Sarah Stewart*
€ ↩

The Museum is on the A873 between Thornhill and the Port of Menteith. It is organised as part of a small mixed farm run by the Stewart family and tells the story of the parish of Ruskie from ancient times to the present day, by means of models, photographs, charts, implements and other artefacts.

Stirling Smith Art Gallery and Museum

40 Albert Place, Dumbarton Road, Stirling
   FK8 2RE   ☎ 0786 71917
Wed, Thurs, Fri, Sun 2–5, Sat 10.30–5
⚑ *The Curator*
€ ● ↩ □

The Museum displays show how people lived in this part of Scotland from prehistoric times to the 20th century. They also illustrate the natural environment of the area. The art collection contains oils, watercolours, prints and drawings, mostly by Scottish artists. The programme of temporary exhibitions covers a wide range of themes, including social history, topical issues and arts and crafts.

Stockport

Stockport Memorial Art Gallery

Wellington Road South, Stockport, Greater
   Manchester SK3 8AB   ☎ 061 480 9433
Mon–Fri 11–5; Sat 10–5. Closed Bank Holiday.
⚑ *Mr A. Firth*
Ⓕ □

The Gallery is a memorial to the men of the Cheshire Regiment who lost their lives in the First World War. The permanent collection consists mainly of early 20th-century paintings and watercolours by British artists. There are, in addition, constantly changing exhibitions of fine art, photography and crafts.

Stockport Museum

Vernon Park, Turncroft Lane, Stockport, Greater
   Manchester SK1 4AR   ☎ 061 480 3668
Apr–Sept, Mon–Sat 1–5. Oct–Mar, Mon–Sat
   1–4. Closed Bank Holiday. Parties by appt.
⚑ *Stockport Museums and Art Gallery Service,*
   Woodbank Hall, Stockport SK1 4JR
   ☎ *061 480 2922*
Ⓕ ● ↩

The Museum displays illustrate the history of the Stockport area from prehistoric times to the present day. Special attention is paid to the important local hatting industry, with a reconstruction of a hat-block maker's workshop.

**Medals awarded to Major Kenneth Muir VC.
Stirling, Regimental Museum of the Argyll and
Sutherland Highlanders.**

Stockton-on-Tees

Green Dragon Museum

Green Dragon Yard, Stockton-on-Tees, Cleveland
TS18 1AT   ☎ 0642 674308
Mon Sat 9.30 5. Closed Bank Holiday.
🔯 Schools Officer, Museum Administration,
76 Norton Road, Stockton-on-Tees
TS18 2DE   ☎ 0642 602474
Ⓕ ✍ ♿ ⎇

This is a local history museum, with displays
devoted to the growth of Stockton and covering
the town's social, industrial and administrative
development. The exhibits include ship models
and a large collection of local pottery.

Preston Hall Museum

Yarm Road, Stockton-on-Tees, Cleveland
TS18 3RH   ☎ 0642 781184
Mon–Sat 9.30–5.30; Sun 2–5.30 (last admission
5). Closed Good Fri, Dec 25, 26, Jan 1.
🔯 See Green Dragon Museum
Ⓕ ♿ 🖻 ⎇

The Museum is three and a half miles from the
centre of Stockton, on the A135 Yarm road. It
is in a Grade II listed building, dating from
1825, and considerably enlarged in the
Victorian period. The cast-iron and teak-framed
Winter Garden is especially noteworthy.

The displays are centred on a reconstruction
of a Victorian street, with a wide range of shops,
the forge of the working blacksmith and farrier,
the workshop of a Northumbrian pipe-maker,
and a series of period rooms. There are also good
collections of weapons and armour and exhibits
devoted to woodwork and metalwork, pewter,
toys, costumes and horse-drawn transport.

One of the Museum's most valued possessions
is the painting, *The Diceplayers*, by de la Tour.

**Minton bone figure in the Dresden style.
Stoke-on-Trent, Minton Museum.**

Stoke Bruerne

The Waterways Museum

Stoke Bruerne, Towcester, Northamptonshire
NN12 7SE   ☎ 0604 862229
Easter–mid Oct, daily 10–6. Mid Oct–Easter,
Tues–Sun 10–4. Last admission 30 mins before
closing. Closed Dec 25, 26.
🔯 The Curator
Ⓔ ♿ ⎇

The Museum is on three floors of what was
formerly a grain warehouse. The exhibits
illustrate the way of life of canal boatmen and
their families over a period of two centuries, and
include bonnets and belts, traditional painted
ware, tools, tokens and Measham Ware teapots,
as well as a large collection of prints, plans and
photographs. A special feature of the Museum is
a full-size replica of a canal boat cabin, complete
with kitchen range, brassware and lace curtains.

The entrance to Blisworth Tunnel, the
longest still in service on the waterways system,
is only a short walk from the Museum along the
towpath.

Stoke-on-Trent

Minton Museum

Minton House, London Road, Stoke-on-Trent,
Staffordshire ST4 7QD   ☎ 0782 49171
Mon–Fri 9–12.30, 2–4.30 Closed Pottery
Holidays.
🔯 Joan Jones, Curator
Ⓕ ♿ ✍ ⎇

The Minton Museum is situated within the
Minton factory. It contains chronological
displays of Minton wares from 1793 to the
present day. Special features include the early
tableware, with corresponding pattern books,
and Thomas Minton's original copper-plate
engravings of the celebrated willow pattern.
Also on show are ornamental wares and figures
exhibited at the Great Exhibition of 1851,
together with life-size maiolica-glazed birds and
animals, examples of decoration by the acid-
gold process, introduced by Minton in 1863,
tiles and Art Nouveau.

The outstanding items in the Minton collection are the Pâte-sur-Pâte decorated ornamental ware by Louis Solon, in which layer upon layer of liquid clay was gradually built up to form three-dimensional semi-clad maidens or cherubs on to a tinted parian body in its unfired state. The first firing was critical and would prove whether or not the relief figure had achieved the desired translucent effect.

Sir Henry Doulton Gallery

Royal Doulton Ltd, Nile Street, Burslem, Stoke-on-Trent, Staffordshire ST6 2AJ
☎ *0782 85747*
Mon–Fri 9–12.30, 1.30–4.30. Closed Bank Holiday & Pottery Holidays.
Tours Organiser
F

The exhibits in the Gallery trace the story of the Royal Doulton pottery since its foundation in 1815. They include wares from both the Lambeth and the Burslem factories. Stoneware jugs and vases by well-known designers, such as the Barlows, George Tinworth and Mark Marshall, are also on show, together with the large bone china Raby Vase, the celebrated Danté Vase and a selection of flambé and experimental glazes.

A section of the Gallery is devoted to the Royal Doulton figure collection, which includes a number of rare items, especially 'Boy on a Crocodile' and 'Madame Sylvestre'. Visitors can also see pattern books, letters and other documents from the Company archives, as well as medals awarded to Royal Doulton at international exhibitions held during the 19th and 20th centuries.

Spode Museum

Royal Worcester Spode Ltd, Spode Division, Church Street, Stoke-on-Trent, Staffordshire ST4 1BX ☎ *0782 46011*
Mon–Thurs 9–12.30, 1.30–4.30; Fri 9–12. Closed Bank Holiday & Pottery Holidays.
Mr Robert Copeland
F

The Spode factory, which contains the Museum, was founded in 1770 and still occupies its original site. There are displays of its earliest wares – drabware, caneware, black basalt, jasper, fine white stoneware, pearl and creamwares – and a collection of Spode's celebrated blue printed wares.

The introduction of fine bone china by Spode c. 1800 allowed further technical improvements to be made. In 1842 the factory developed a very fine porcelain known as Parian, from which the drawing-room statuary beloved of the Victorians was made. There is also a display of recent commemorative wares.

Royal Doulton china commemoratives depicting Edward, Prince of Wales (c. 1930), Queen Mary (1911), and HRH Princess Elizabeth (1937). Stoke-on-Trent, The Sir Henry Doulton Gallery.

Stonehaven

Tolbooth Museum

Old Pier, Stonehaven, Kincardineshire
Jun–Sept, Mon, Thurs–Sat 10–12, 2–5; Wed, Sun 2–5.
Museums Curator, Arbuthnot Museum, St Peter Street, Peterhead, Aberdeenshire AB4 6QD ☎ *0779 77778*
F

The Museum is in Stonehaven's former Custom House, an 18th-century listed building. The displays relate to the history of the port, with particular reference to the fishing industry.

Stourton

Stourhead

Stourton, Warminster, Wiltshire BA12 6QH
☎ *074 840 348*
Apr and Oct–Nov, Sat–Wed 2–6 or dusk if earlier. May–Sept, Sat–Thurs 2–6 (last admission 5.30). Other times by appt. Garden: all year round, daily 8–7 or sunset.
The Administrator
£ NT

The house at Stourhead, now owned by the National Trust, was built for Henry Hoare and completed in 1724. Two wings, containing the picture gallery and a library, were added in 1792 and a portico in 1839. The furniture includes some designed for Stourhead by Thomas Chippendale the Younger. Pictures include 18th-century classical landscapes and portraits, and there is also a collection of porcelain. The library carpet is copied from a Roman pavement.

The famous gardens, created by Henry Hoare II, contain classical temples and sculptures, including works by Michael Rysbrack and John Cheere. The 14th-century Bristol Cross was brought from Bristol and re-erected near the village church.

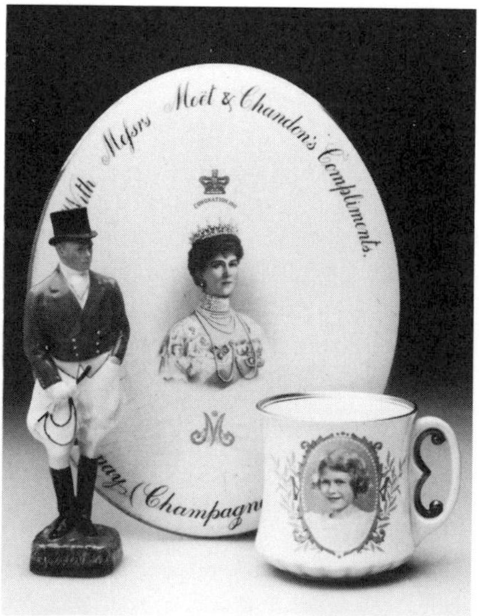

A wind-pump for fen drainage from Eastbridge re-erected at the Museum of East Anglian Life, Stowmarket.

Stowmarket

Museum of East Anglian Life

Abbot's Hall, Stowmarket, Suffolk IP14 1DL
☎ *0449 612229*
Easter–Oct, Mon–Sat 11–5; Sun 12–5
Ⓚ *The Director*
Ⓔ 🏠 💷 ♿ ♿

The Museum is being developed on a 70-acre open-air site, to reflect the agricultural, social and industrial history of the counties of Essex, Cambridgeshire, Norfolk and Suffolk. A number of historic buildings have already been moved to the site. They include a 14th-century farmhouse, an 18th-century timber-framed smithy, a mid 19th-century drainage windmill and an 18th-century watermill.

The largest building at the Museum formed the engineering workshops of Robert Boby Ltd of Bury St Edmunds, and dates from the 1870s. The oldest is the great Abbot's Hall barn, which contains 13th-century roof timbers and is on its original site. The Museum buildings house historic carts and wagons, industrial and domestic displays, craft demonstrations and an exhibition, *The Farming Year*, which illustrates the sequence of tasks which farmers carry out on the land. Among the special exhibits are a pair of steam ploughing engines, dating from 1879, and a general-purpose traction engine of 1912, built by Charles Burrell and Sons of Thetford.

An exhibition, *Travellers and Sporting Men*, is concerned with gypsies, travelling showmen, sporting men with shotguns and poachers with traps. Its exhibits include a small gypsy encampment, a showman's van, part of a fairground site and large horse-drawn game vans, for carrying away the day's bag, which often amounted to several hundred pheasants or partridges.

Strabane

Gray's Printing Press

49 Main Street, Strabane, Co. Tyrone, Northern
*   Ireland BT82 8AU*   ☎ *0504 884094*
Apr–Sept, Mon–Wed, Fri,. Sat 2–6
Ⓚ *The National Trust, Rowallane House,*
*   Saintfield, Ballynahinch, Co. Down,*
*   Northern Ireland BT24 7LH* ☎ *0238 510721*
Ⓔ 🏠 ♿ ⓃⓉ

The print shop at 49 Main Street was in existence in the 18th century and it may have been here that John Dunlap, the printer of the American Declaration of Independence, and James Wilson, the grandfather of President Woodrow Wilson, learned their trade. The range of printing presses on display are survivals from the 18th and 19th centuries, when Strabane was an important publishing centre.

Stradbally

Irish Steam Preservation Society Museum

The Green, Stradbally, Co. Laois, Ireland
By appt
Ⓚ *The Secretary*   ☎ *0502 25136*
Ⓔ ♿

The Museum contains a varied collection of steam-powered equipment, including traction engines, road rollers and threshing machines, all built between 1913 and 1940. Most of the items are on loan from members of the Society.

Straide

Michael Davitt National Memorial Museum

'Land League Place', Straide, Foxford, Co. Mayo,
*   Ireland*
June–Aug, Tues–Sat 10–1, 2–6.30; Sun 2–7
Ⓚ *Mary McHugh, Blanemore, Straide*
Ⓔ ♿ ♿ ♿

Straide is four miles from Foxford, on the Ballina to Castlebar road. The Museum commemorates the Irish patriot, Labour leader, writer and journalist, Michael Davitt (1846–1906), who was born at Straide. Davitt was the founder of the Irish National Land League and the Irish Trade Union Congress and the Founding Patron of the Gaelic Athletic Association. There is an extensive collection of photographs and documents illustrating the many aspects of Davitt's life. Other exhibits are concerned with rural life in Ireland during the second half of the 19th century.

The neo-Classical west front of Castle Ward, Strangford.

Strangford

Castle Ward

Strangford, Co. Down, Northern Ireland
  BT30 7LS   ☎ *039686 204*
Easter–June & Sept–Oct, Sat, Sun 2–6.
  School parties: Mon–Fri 10–5. July–Aug,
  Wed–Mon 12–8. Oct–Mar, by appt only.
▓ *Education Officer*
£ ⚫ 🖳 🚗 ♿ NT

Castle Ward, now a National Trust property, is two miles from the village of Strangford and has splendid views over Strangford Lough. The estate came into the possession of the Ward family in the late 16th century, but the present house was not built until 1770. It was designed by Bernard Ward, who later became Viscount Bangor, and his wife, Anne. The architecture and decorations of the house are a curious compromise between his taste for the classical idiom and hers for the Gothick. In the early 19th century the contents of Castle Ward were dispersed, during the insanity of the 2nd Lord Bangor, so that few of the furnishings, apart from the family portraits, are original to the 18th-century house, although the elaborate and contrasting decorative schemes devised by the Wards have survived almost unchanged.

No servants, except a valet and a lady's maid, slept in the house. The servants' living quarters formed part of the courtyard block, which also contained the stables, bakery and laundry and were connected to the house by means of an underground passage. The laundry has been refurbished, with its separate ironing and airing rooms, ironing boards, flat irons and examples of late 18th-century laundered linen and clothes. The farmyard contains a corn mill and sawmill.

Stranraer

Stranraer Museum

Old Town Hall, George Street, Stranraer,
  Wigtownshire DG9 8ES   ☎ *0776 5088*
Mon–Fri 10–5; Sat 10–1, 2–5. Closed public
  holidays.
▓ *The Curator*
F ⌖ 🚗

The front part of the former Town Hall, which houses the Museum, dates from the 18th century and has an interesting steeple clock. The frequently changing displays illustrate the agriculture and social history of the area and there are also sections devoted to prehistoric archaeology, costumes, fine art and historic photographs, including a number relating to the Gretna Munitions Factory, which operated between 1914 and 1919. A special exhibit relates to the Polar explorer, Sir John Ross, who was a native of Stranraer.

Stratfield Saye

National Dairy Museum

Wellington Country Park, Stratfield Saye,
  Reading RG7 2BT   ☎ *0256 882882*
Mar–Oct, daily 11.30–5. Nov, Sat, Sun
  10–5.30 or dusk if earlier.
▓ *Wellington Office*
£ 🚗 ♿

The Museum illustrates the history of the dairy industry over the past 150 years. Among the themes of the displays are milk transport, the development of the milk churn and the glass bottle, cheese-making, science and the dairy industry, the milk round and milk-processing. There are collections of chocolate moulds and infant feeding bottles, and reconstructions of a Victorian dairy and of a pre-1919 dairy shop window. An audio-visual display presents the main features of the history of the dairy industry in Britain.

Stratfield Saye House and The Wellington Exhibition

Stratfield Saye, Reading RG7 2BT
  ☎ *0256 882882*
Easter Sat–Mon 11.30–5. Apr 1–20, Sat, Sun
  11.30–5. May–Sept 29, Sat–Thurs 11.30–5.
  Wellington Country Park: Mar–Oct, daily
  10–5.30 or dusk. Nov–Feb, Sat, Sun
  10–5.30 or dusk.
▓ *Wellington Office*
£ ⚫ 🖳 🚗 ♿ HHA

After the defeat of Napoleon at Waterloo, the 1st Duke of Wellington was voted £600,000 by a grateful nation to buy himself a suitable house and estate. He chose Stratfield Saye, and his descendants have lived in it ever since. The main part of the house and the stable blocks were built c. 1630. During the 18th century, the red-brick building was covered with stucco and in the 19th century the Iron Duke added a conservatory and two other wings and installed central heating and waterclosets.

The house contains memorabilia of the Duke and relics of his military achievements, family portraits, busts and a magnificent collection of porcelain. Among the special items are paintings of horses, many books from Napoleon's personal library, and an 1837 billiards table. The grave of Copenhagen, the charger ridden by the Duke at Waterloo, is in the grounds.

Part of the stable block and an adjoining barn have been converted to house the Wellington Exhibition, which illustrates the life and times of Arthur, 1st Duke of Wellington. Among the exhibits are mementoes of his long life as a statesman and a soldier, personal possessions and a fine collection of clothes, including the original Wellington boot. There are examples of the stable books, which include records referring to Copenhagen in retirement.

Also on display is the great Funeral Carriage, which weighs 18 tons. It has six wheels and was made of bronze cast from melted down French cannon captured at Waterloo. After the Funeral it spent some years in a shed at Marlborough House, then from 1861 to 1981 it was in the Crypt of St Paul's, before being dismantled and removed to Stratfield Saye.

Stratford-upon-Avon

Anne Hathaway's Cottage

Cottage Lane, Shottery, Stratford-upon-Avon, Warwickshire ☎ *0789 292100*
Apr–Sept, Mon–Sat 9–6; Sun 10–6.
  Oct, Mon–Sat 9–5; Sun 10–5. Nov–March,
  Mon–Sat 9–4.30, Sun 1.30–4.30.
⚑ *See Shakespeare's Birthplace*
£ 🛈 💺 🚻

This thatched, half-timbered cottage was the home of Shakespeare's wife, Anne Hathaway, before her marriage. It was originally a farmhouse, the earliest part of which dates from the 15th century. Most of the present furnishings belonged to the Hathaways, whose descendants lived here until 1892, but other 16th and 17th-century furniture has been added.

Arms and Armour Museum

Poet's Arbour, Sheep Street, Stratford-upon-Avon, Warwickshire CV37 6EF ☎ *0789 293453*
Daily 9.30–5.30. Closed Dec 25.
⚑ *Robin J. Wigington, Curator*
£ 🛈 🚻

The Museum houses a collection of mostly European weapons, armour and accoutrements connected both with sport and with warfare. In forming the collection, quality and original condition have been of primary importance. This is illustrated by the fine flintlock and percussion sporting weapons made for noble families and by the silver-mounted hunting and small swords. The earliest gun dates from c. 1380 and the development of firearms is shown from this time up to the present century. The image of medieval warfare is provided by suits of armour, helmets, polearms and maces, together with bows and arrows and crossbows.

Weapons from India are also represented. They have been chosen mainly for their artistic merits and come from several princely armouries. Of particular interest are the firearms of Tipu Sultan. These silver-mounted guns and pistols form the largest known group of his personal weapons.

Hall's Croft

Old Town, Stratford-upon-Avon, Warwickshire ☎ *0789 292107*
Apr–Sept, Mon–Sat 9–6; Sun 10–6.
  Oct, Mon Sat 9 5; Sun 10–5.
  Nov–Mar, Mon–Sat 9–4.30.
⚑ *See Shakespeare's Birthplace*
£ 🗑 💺

Hall's Croft, a 16th to 17th-century half-timbered house, was the home of Dr John Hall, who married Susanna Shakespeare, the poet's daughter. The rooms are now furnished in the style of a middle-class Elizabethan home, with a garden which attempts to portray something of the formality of Shakespeare's day and at the same time to create the atmosphere of a more homely garden, with familiar trees, flowers and shrubs.

The house contains an exhibition illustrating the theory and practice of medicine in the late 16th and early 17th centuries.

Mary Arden's House

Station Road, Wilmcote, Stratford-upon-Avon, Warwickshire ☎ *0789 293455*
Apr–Sept, Mon–Sat 9–6; Sun 10–6.
  Oct, Mon–Sat 9–5; Sun 10–5.
  Nov–Mar, Mon–Sat 9–4.30.
⚑ *See Shakespeare's Birthplace*
£ 🛈 💺

Mary Arden's House is a mile off the main Stratford to Birmingham road, three and a half miles from Stratford. An early 16th-century farmhouse, it was the home of Shakespeare's mother. Continued occupation by farmers until 1930, when the Shakespeare Birthplace Trust acquired it for conservation, ensured its preservation in substantially its original condition. The rooms contain items of 16th and 17th-century farm furniture, together with domestic utensils of the period.

There is also a Shakespeare Countryside exhibition, which illustrates the traditional rural life and farming methods of the district, with an emphasis on country crafts, which are demonstrated from time to time.

New Place and Nash's House

Chapel Street, Stratford-upon-Avon, Warwickshire ☎ *0789 292325*
Apr–Sept, Mon–Sat 9–6; Sun 10–6.
  Oct, Mon–Sat 9–5; Sun 10–5. Nov–Mar,
  Mon–Sat 9–4.30.
⚑ *See Shakespeare's Birthplace*
£ 🗑

New Place, in which Shakespeare spent his retirement and died in 1616, was one of the largest houses in Elizabethan Stratford. It was demolished in 1759, and its foundations are preserved in a garden setting, approached through the house of Thomas Nash, the first husband of Shakespeare's granddaughter, Elizabeth Hall. Nash's House is now Stratford's local museum and has displays illustrating the archaeology and history of the area.

The converted chapel that now houses the
Stratford-upon-Avon Motor Museum.

Part of the site of New Place contains a
replica of an Elizabethan knot garden, based on
designs shown in contemporary gardening
books. The square-shaped garden is divided by
stone paths into four 'knots' or beds. The Great
Garden, which leads from it, was originally the
orchard and kitchen garden belonging to New
Place.

Royal Shakespeare Company Exhibition

Royal Shakespeare Theatre, Stratford-upon-Avon,
Warwickshire CV37 6BB   ☎ *0789 296655*
Mon–Sat 9–6; Sun 12–5
The Director
£ ● 💺 ➹ □

The RSC at Stratford possesses a large
collection of designs for sets and costumes, and
photographs of productions dating back to the
founding of the Theatre in Stratford over 100
years ago, together with costumes, theatre
properties and paintings spanning nearly two
centuries of Shakespearean performances.

Each year, the Gallery mounts a major
exhibition relating to the current season's plays
and illustrating the changing styles of
production and lighting. The exhibitions are
built up with sound tracks, theatre lighting and
material selected from all the elements of the
Gallery's collections.

Shakespeare's Birthplace

Henley Street, Stratford-upon-Avon, Warwickshire
CV37 6QW   ☎ *0789 204016*
Easter–Sept, Mon–Sat 9–6; Sun 10–6.
Oct, Mon–Sat 10–5, Sun 10–5. Nov–Mar,
Mon–Sat 9–4.30; Sun 1.30–4.30.
Dr Levi Fox, Director
£ ● 💺 ➹

One section of this half-timbered building is the
house in which William Shakespeare was born
and the other forms part of the premises which
his father used for his business as a glover and a
dealer in wool. The rooms of the house are
furnished in the style of the period and in the
former commercial area of the building there is a
museum, with exhibits illustrating the history of
the property and the life, work and times of the
dramatist.

Stratford-upon-Avon Motor Museum

1 Shakespeare Street, Stratford-upon-Avon,
Warwickshire CV37 6RN   ☎ *0789 69413*
Apr–Oct, daily 9.30–6. Nov–Mar, daily 10–4.
Closed Christmas.
Mrs Christine Piper
£ ● ➹

The Museum, housed in a converted Methodist
chapel and Victorian school hall, specialises in
cars of the 1920s and 1930s. Examples of some
of the more distinguished makes and models of
these years are displayed in settings which recapture the atmosphere of a golden age of style
and engineering in the automobile world.

Strathaven

John Hastie Museum

Threestanes Road, Strathaven, Lanarkshire
ML10 6MX
Apr–Sept, Mon–Wed, Fri 2–5; Thurs, 2–4.30;
Sat 2–7
Chief Librarian, Central Library, East Kilbride,
Lanarkshire G74 1LY   ☎ *0357 21257*
F ➹

The Museum concentrates on the history of
Strathaven, with special displays on the
weaving industry, Covenanting and the Radical
Uprising. There is also an interesting collection
of porcelain.

Strathpeffer

Museum of Dolls, Toys and Victoriana

Spa Cottage, The Square, Strathpeffer, Ross-shire
IV14 9DE   ☎ *0997 21549*
Easter–May & Sept–Oct, Mon–Fri 10–12.
June–Aug, Mon–Fri 10–12, 1–3, 8–10.
Other times by appt.
Mrs A. Kellie
£

This privately owned museum occupies a listed
building, which originally belonged to the spa
complex at Strathpeffer, and is the only part of
it still surviving, the Pump Room and Bath
House having been demolished in the 1950s.
The collection of dolls, toys, lace, costumes and
other Victorian items has been formed by Mrs
Kellie and her mother. Mrs Kellie spins daily in
the entrance to the Museum.

Pump Room Exhibition – 'A Spa Exposed'

The Pump Room, Strathpeffer, Ross-shire
IV15 9AS
Mon–Sat 10–12, 2.30–4.30, 7.30–9.30
Mrs M. E. Spark, Spa Pharmacy
£ 🔍 ➹

The exhibition area contains the original tiling,
mosaic floor, taps and other features of the
Pump Room. The history of the Spa between
1890 and 1935 is illustrated by photographs
taken by the local pharmacist, T. Wellwood
Maxwell, during that period. Other exhibits
include prescription books and labels relating to
Mr Maxwell's pharmacy.

Clarks' shoe advertisement, 1914.
Street, The Shoe Museum.

Street

Clarks' shoe advertisement, 1914.
Street, The Shoe Museum.

The Shoe Museum

C. & J. Clark Ltd, Street, Somerset BA16 0YA
☎ 0458 43131
Easter Mon–Oct, Mon–Sat 10–4.45.
  Winter months by appt. Advance booking
  required for parties.
🖾 Secretary to Public Relations Manager
🄵 ♨ ⚲

Cyrus Clark established the family business in
Street in 1825. He took his brother, James, into
partnership in 1833. The Museum is housed in
the oldest part of the factory, dating from 1829,
which was originally used for tanning
sheepskins. The firm made rugs, mops and
chamois leather from sheepskins before
shoemaking began in 1830.

  The exhibits illustrate the development of
shoes and shoemaking, with special reference to
the history of C. & J. Clark Limited. There are
special collections of footwear worn in Britain
during the Roman period and from medieval
times to the present day; shoes from other
countries; Georgian shoe buckles; caricatures
and engravings of shoemakers; costume
illustrations and fashion-plates from the 17th
century onwards; and showcards and other
advertising material.

  Shoemaking machines and hand tools from
the 19th and early 20th centuries form an
important part of the exhibition. A hand-
shoemaker's workshop, at the back of his house,
is on show and the practical ability of earlier
members of the Clark family is illustrated by the
workbench used by John Bright Clark in the
1880s.

Stretton

Stretton Mill

Stretton, nr Farndon, Cheshire
Easter Sat–Sept, Tues–Sun & Bank Holiday Mon
  2 6. Parties all year by appt.
🖾 Mrs M. Warhurst, 162 London Road,
  Northwich, Cheshire CW9 8AB
  ☎ 0606 41331
🄴 ✎ ⚲ ♿

To reach Stretton Mill, one turns off the A534
at Barton, near the junction with the A41. The
water-powered mill was built in the late 16th
century and modified in the 18th and early 19th
centuries. It ceased commercial operations in
1959. In 1975 it was taken over by Cheshire
County Council and restored as a working
museum. Both the Mill and the adjoining stable
block are listed buildings. The stable block
contains a display telling the story of the mill
and its restoration and explaining the milling
process. The machinery can be seen working,
water levels permitting.

Stretton-under-Fosse

Prison Service Museum

HM Prison Service College, Newbold Revel,
  Stretton-under-Fosse, Rugby, Warwickshire
  CV23 0TN
By written appt only
🖾 The Curator
🄴 ⚲

The village of Stretton-under-Fosse is on the
B4114, 12 miles south-west of Lutterworth.
The exhibits, in temporary accommodation
pending a move to a larger, permanent location
at Newbold Revel, illustrate the changes which
have taken place over the last two centuries in
the penal system and in social attitudes to crime
and punishment. Among the items on display
are irons, fetters and gyves discovered behind a
wall at Shrewsbury Prison and a door from cells
visited by the Wesley brothers at Oxford Prison
during the 18th century. Visitors can see
original tools used for oakum picking and the
Governor's entry of Oscar Wilde's application to
be excused from such work at Reading.

Strokestown

St John's Interpretive Centre

Strokestown, Co. Roscommon, Ireland
  ☎ 078 33100/33234/33282
May–Sept, at any reasonable time
🖾 Rev. Francis M. Beirne
🄴 ⚲

This recently established Centre is in an
octagonal church, resembling a medieval
chapter house, which dates from 1820. Its
displays illustrate and interpret the Iron Age
sites in the area, with particular reference to the
royal sites of the Kings of Connaught.

Stromness

Pier Arts Centre

Victoria Street, Stromness, Orkney KW16 3AA
    ☎ *0856 850209*
Jan–June & Sept–Dec, Tues–Sat 10.30–12.30,
    1.30–5. July–Aug, Tues–Sat 10.30–12.30,
    1.30–5; Sun 2–5.
Ⓜ *Erlend Brown, Curator*
Ⓕ ◇ ⚲ □

The Centre's building has been converted from
an 18th-century merchant's house, stores and
offices. The permanent collection contains
20th-century paintings and sculpture. Among
the artists represented are Naum Gabo, Ben
Nicholson, Barbara Hepworth, Patrick Heron
and Eduardo Paolozzi. There is a regular
programme of temporary exhibitions and the
library has a stock of books on modern art, with
particular reference to works in the permanent
collection.

Stromness Museum

52 Alfred Street, Stromness, Orkney KW16 3DF
    ☎ *0856 850025*
Mon–Sat 11–12.30, 1.30–5 (July & Aug open at
    10.30). Closed public holidays & 3 weeks
    Feb/Mar.
Ⓜ *The Curator*
Ⓔ *ex. school parties* ◇ ⚲

The Museum is concerned with the natural and
maritime history of Orkney. The displays cover
whaling, fishing, Orkney and the Hudson's Bay
Company, Scapa Flow and the German Fleet,
and Orkney birds, mammals, fossils, crustacea,
lepidoptera and plants. The Museum has a long
history, having been founded by the Orkney
Natural History Society in 1937.

Stroud

Stroud District Museum

Lansdown, Stroud, Gloucestershire GL5 1BB
    ☎ *04536 3394*
Mon–Sat 10.30–1, 2–5. Closed Bank Holiday and
    District Council Holidays.
Ⓜ *The Curator*
Ⓕ ◇ ⚲

This is primarily a local museum, serving an area
from the outskirts of Gloucester to the southern
border of the County. There is an interesting
collection of Ice Age and Mesozoic fossils,
including dinosaur bones. Visitors can also see a
life-size model of a megalosaurus. The district is
rich in long barrows and from these sites the
Museum has many flint tools of the Neolithic
period. Later material includes a skull fragment
with evidence of an early attempt at brain
surgery, and a group of pagan Roman altars.

The Museum's collections contain many
items connected with local industries, especially
the manufacture of woollen cloth. There are
clocks made in the Stroud area, very early lawnmowers – a Stroud invention – and a rocking
bath.

Styal

Quarry Bank Mill

Styal, Cheshire SK9 4LA   ☎ *0625 527468*
Apr–May, Tues–Sun & Bank Holiday Mon 11–5.
    June–Sept, daily 11–5. Oct–Mar, Tues–Sun
    11–4. Closed Dec 23–25.
Ⓜ *Booking Office*
Ⓔ ⚲ 🏠 ⚲ NT

Founded in 1784, Quarry Bank is the finest
surviving example of a Georgian cotton mill. It
has been preserved and restored by the National
Trust and is leased to the Quarry Bank Mill
Trust, together with the Apprentice House and
the unaltered village of Styal, with cottages,
school, two chapels and a shop built to serve the
millworkers. The buildings, archives and
exhibits at Quarry Bank tell the story of the
origins and growth of the Factory System. The
techniques of textile manufacturing, from
hand processes to mechanisation, are
demonstrated daily by skilled workers. The
section devoted to millworkers illustrates both
the working environment, with a full-scale
working weaving shed and mule spinning room,
and living conditions. An 1850 Fairbairn iron
waterwheel, 24 feet in diameter, has been
restored as a working exhibit.

Sudbury (Derbyshire)

Sudbury Hall Museum of Childhood

Sudbury Hall, Sudbury, Derbyshire DE6 5HT
    ☎ *028378 305*
Apr–Oct, Wed–Sun & Bank Holiday Mon,
    1–5.30 (last admission 5).
Ⓜ *Education Officer*
Ⓔ ⚲ 🏠 ⚲ NT

Sudbury is at the junction of the A50 and A515,
13 miles west of Derby. The Hall, now the
property of the National Trust, was built
between 1659 and 1679 for the Vernon family,
which had owned the estate since 1513. It has
fine decorative plasterwork and carvings by
Grinling Gibbons.

**The Mule Spinning Room at Quarry Bank
Mill, Styal.**

Portrait of John Gainsborough (1711–72) by J. T. Heins. Sudbury, Gainsborough's House.

The Museum, in the 19th-century servants' wing, centres on childhood. Its collections are mainly 19th and 20th century, with a small representation from earlier periods. Its toys, books, games and dolls' houses are displayed in room settings, including an Edwardian nursery and schoolroom, a Victorian parlour, and a poor child's cellar. A section on the child at work emphasises the exploitation of children in the past. There are also holdings of costumes, children's books and educational material. A new gallery, opened in 1986, displays Betty Cadbury's Playthings Past Collection of dolls, toys and games.

The Sudbury Hall Pots Gallery of 20th-century ceramics has an annually selected display and facilities for close study of the collections are provided in the Study Centre.

Sudbury (Suffolk)

Gainsborough's House

46 Gainsborough Street, Sudbury, Suffolk
CO10 6EU   ☎ *0787 72958*
Easter Sat–Sept, Tues–Sat 10–5; Sun & Bank
Holiday Mon 2–5. Oct–Maundy Thurs,
Tues–Sat 10–4; Sun 2–4. Closed Good Fri,
Dec 24–Jan 1.
 The Curator
£ ✐ ✐ □

The birthplace of Thomas Gainsborough is a half-timbered house dating from 1480. It was altered *c.* 1520 and Georgianised in 1723 and *c.* 1790. The exhibition space is equally divided between permanent and temporary exhibitions. The temporary exhibitions are of 18th to 20th-century crafts and fine art. The Gainsborough collection of portraits, landscapes and drawings, based on loans from public and private sources, illustrates the artist's complete career. Works by Heins, Frost, Dupont, Bunbury and other contemporaries of Gainsborough with Suffolk connections are also shown.

Sunderland

Grindon Museum

Grindon Lane, Sunderland, Tyne and Wear
SR4 8HW   ☎ *0783 284042*
Mon, Wed, Fri 9.30–12.30, 1.30–6; Tues
9.30–12.30, 1.30–5; Sat 9.30–12.15,
1.15–4. June–Sept, also Sun 2–5.
Bank Holiday: Mon only.
 See Sunderland Museum and Art Gallery
F ✐

The Museum is just off the A183 Sunderland to Chester-le-Street road, near the Grindon Mill public house. Occupying the first floor of an early 20th-century shipbuilder's house, it reflects the lifestyle of the Edwardian period in Sunderland. Its collections are displayed in period rooms. In the kitchen a woman, surrounded by the day's washing, is preparing the evening meal, while across the corridor is a sitting room, with a pianola ready to be played. Further along the corridor, the lady of the house is laying out clothing and jewellery in a large bedroom, while next door, in the nursery, a child is busy with her toys, games and books.

In addition to the domestic scenes there are also reconstructions of an Edwardian Post Office, a cobbler's workshop, a dentist's surgery and a chemist's shop.

Monkwearmouth Station Museum

North Bridge Street, Sunderland, Tyne and Wear
SR5 1AP   ☎ 0783 77075
Mon–Fri 10–5.30; Sat 10–4.30; Sun 2–5
◪ *P. A. Talbot, Curator*
Ｆ ◪ ◪ ◪

Monkwearmouth Station, on the Newcastle to
Sunderland line, has changed very little since
Victorian times. Its imposing classical façade
and general elegance was a consequence of
George Hudson, the Railway King, being the
Member of Parliament for Sunderland. Porters'
barrows, trunks and a top-hatted passenger at
the ticket window recall travelling before the
First World War. The displays include a section
on George Hudson, and 'Where did the Trams
go?' surveys the development of public street
transport on Tyneside and Wearside between
1900 and 1970. The development of the British
steam locomotive is illustrated by means of
models, plans and photographs and there is an
exhibition of Victorian and Edwardian bicycles.

Sunderland Museum and Art Gallery

Borough Road, Sunderland, Tyne and Wear
SR1 1PP   ☎ 0783 41235
Mon–Fri 10–5.30; Sat 10–4; Sun 2–5. Closed
    Spring Bank Holiday, Dec 25, 26, Jan 1.
◪ *Education Officer*
Ｆ ◪ ◪ ◪ ◪

Although the majority of the exhibits in the
museum relate to Wearside, the natural history
and geology galleries cover a wider area,
extending from the Tyne to the Tees. The
wildlife gallery shows the animals, birds and
plants of the different natural habitats of the
region, while the North-East Before Man
exhibition traces its geological evolution by
means of fossils, rocks and minerals.

The archaeology section illustrates the early
history of man in Wearside. Domestic life from
the 18th century onwards is shown in room
interiors and displays covering community
activities. The physical appearance of the area
is presented in the Changing Face of Wearside
gallery by means of paintings, prints,
photographs and maps. The maritime history
displays feature lighthouse equipment and
models of ships built in Sunderland during the
past 150 years. The town's important glass
industry is illustrated by 18th to 20th-century
products, including bottles, stained glass and
Pyrex ware.

Sutton Cheney

Bosworth Battlefield Visitor Centre

Ambion Hill Farm, Sutton Cheney, nr Market
Bosworth, Leicestershire CV13 0AD
    ☎ 0455 290429
Easter–last Sun in Oct, Mon–Sat 2–5.30, Sun
    & Bank Holiday Mon 1–6. July–Aug, opens
    at 11. Battle Trails: open all year during
    daylight hours.
◪ *Mr J. R. Tinsley, Resident Warden*
Ｅ ◪ ◪ ◪ ◪

The site of the Battle of Bosworth Field (1485)
is bounded by the A5, A444 and B585 roads.
The Visitor Centre complex has been created
from a group of former farm buildings. It
provides a detailed interpretation of the battle,
against a background of contemporary history
and social life. The exhibition includes models
of the Battle, the troops and their homes,
replica weapons and armour.

A film theatre shows films on the battlefield,
the battle and the period. The Battle Trails
around the site have a series of illustrated
information boards. A series of Special Event
Days is organised on the site during the summer
months. These attractions include a re-
enactment of the Battle of Bosworth, a jousting
tournament, hand-to-hand combat, and
demonstrations of the traditional skills of
archery and falconry.

Sutton-on-the-Forest

Sutton Park

Sutton-on-the-Forest, York, North Yorkshire
YO6 1DP   ☎ 0347 810249
Easter weekend, then May 4–Oct 5, Tues and
    Sun, Bank Holiday Mon 1.30–5.30
◪ *Mrs Sheffield*
Ｅ ◪ ◪ HHA

Sutton Park, seven miles north of York, on the
B1363, was built in 1730. The Sheffield family
has been here since 1961. There is 18th-
century furniture, including some Chippendale,
and Victorian furniture; and a special porcelain
room, with pieces from the Meissen, Bow,
Sèvres, Chelsea and Worcester factories. An
18th-century painting of the Thames by the
celebrated topographical artist, Samuel Scott,
was later cut into two sections, in order to fit
appropriate spaces on the walls of the Porcelain
Room.

Swanage

Tithe Barn Museum and Art Centre

Church Hill, Swanage, Dorset   ☎ 0929 424768
Mar 27–Apr 5, daily 10.30–12.30 ex. Sun.
    May 18–Sept 13, daily 10.30–12.30 ex. Sun,
    7.30–9.30.
◪ *Hon. Curator*
Ｅ ◪

The Museum is in a 16th-century barn built of
Purbeck stone. The majority of the exhibits are
directly associated with Swanage and Purbeck.
They include a fine display of fossils, for which
the area is celebrated, and examples of the
various beds of Purbeck stone. There are also
exhibitions of archaeological, architectural and
social history material relating to the district.
The Art Centre shows paintings and sculpture
from the permanent collection.

**Gerald Scarfe exhibition at the Glynn Vivian
Art Gallery and Museum, Swansea.**

Swansea

Glynn Vivian Art Gallery and Museum

Alexandra Road, Swansea SA1 5DZ
☎ *0792 55006/51738*
Mon–Sat 10.30–5.30. Closed Dec 25, 26, Jan 1.
⊠ *Education Officer*
F ▪ ☎ □

The Gallery was purpose-built by Richard Glynn Vivian in 1909 and has since been extended. The permanent collection, based on the Glynn Vivian collection but considerably augmented by gifts and purchases, contains British paintings, drawings and sculpture, 17th-century glass, Tompion clocks, and British and Continental ceramics. The important collection of Swansea china has recently been re-displayed. About 24 temporary exhibitions are arranged each year.

Swansea Maritime and Industrial Museum

Museum Square, Maritime Quarter, Swansea SA1 1SN ☎ *0792 50351/470371*
Daily 10.30 5.30 (last admission 5.15)
⊠ *Gerald Gabb, Education Officer*
F ▪ ☎

The Museum building is an early 20th-century dock warehouse. The maritime section consists of indoor displays and boats moored to a pontoon outside. The floating exhibits are a lightship, steam tug, Bristol Channel pilot cutter and fishing trawler, and the former Mumbles lifeboat, *The William Gammon*. The inside displays illustrate the development of Swansea Docks, cargo handling, navigation and the vessels which used the port of Swansea.

The industrial exhibits refer especially to marine and stationary engines, railway locomotives and local agriculture. There is a working woollen mill, where visitors can watch wool being carded, spun and woven into finished cloth.

Swansea Museum

Victoria Road, Swansea SA1 1SN ☎ *0792 53763*
Tues–Sat 10–4.30
⊠ *Dr M. J.-Isaac, Museum Keeper*
£ ✎ ☎

This is the oldest museum in Wales, founded in 1835. Its collections are concerned mainly with West Glamorgan. The ceramics section is particularly noteworthy, with a large display of Swansea pottery. There is a new exhibition of natural history, arranged in habitat settings. The archaeological displays tell the story of the area over a period of 20,000 years and a chronological exhibition illustrates the history and rehabilitation of the Lower Swansea Valley, once one of the worst areas of industrial dereliction in Britain.

There is a display of Welsh domestic equipment and handicrafts, together with a reconstruction of a 19th-century kitchen.

Graeco-Roman relief of a king's head. Swansea, The Wellcome Museum of Antiquities.

The Wellcome Museum of Antiquities

Department of Classics and Ancient History, University College, Singleton Park, Swansea SA2 8PP   ☎ *0792 205678*
On request, to Porter of the North Arts Building
🅗 *Dr Kate Bosse-Griffiths, Hon. Curator*
Ⓕ 🗘 🖳 🖝

The collection was presented to University College, Swansea, in 1971. It consists of a substantial part of the Egyptian antiquities formerly housed in the Wellcome Museum of the History of Medicine. Other items have been added since 1971.

The 2,000 objects in the collection illustrate 4,000 years of civilisation in the Nile valley, from the prehistoric era, c. 3500 B.C., to the period of Coptic Christianity, c. 500 A.D.

Swindon

Coate Agricultural Museum

Coate Water Country Park, Swindon, Wiltshire SN3 6AA
Easter–Sept, Sun 2–5
🅗 *Mr John Woodward, Museums Curator, 1–4 Euclid Street, Swindon*
Ⓕ 🗘 🖝

The Museum houses a collection of mainly horse-drawn agricultural implements, from the late 19th century to the 1940s. Among the items on display are carts, wagons, ploughs, harrows, rakes and seed drills.

Great Western Railway Museum

Faringdon Road, Swindon, Wiltshire SN1 5BJ
☎ *0793 26161 extn 3131*
Mon–Sat 10–5; Sun 2–5. Closed Good Fri, Dec 25, 26.
🅗 *Mr Tim Bryan, Museum Assistant*
Ⓔ 🗘 🖝

The Museum building, in the historic Railway Village, was originally a model lodging-house for men working at the nearby Great Western works. It subsequently became a Wesleyan Chapel. Its collections illustrate the history of the Great Western Railway and of the leading personalities associated with it, especially Brunel, Churchward and Gooch. Five locomotives are on display, covering practically the whole period of Great Western steam locomotives. Among the wide range of exhibits are early tickets and passes, uniforms and badges, fittings from Queen Victoria's royal saloon, posters, maps and a fine collection of early railway prints by J. C. Bourne and others.

Lydiard Mansion

Lydiard Tregoze, Swindon, Wiltshire SN5 9PA
☎ *0793 770401*
Mon–Sat 10–1, 2–5.30; Sun 2–5.30. Closed Good Fri, Dec 25, 26.
🅗 *The Curator*
Ⓕ 🗘 🖳 🖝

Lydiard Tregoze is five miles west of Swindon, just north of the A420. The Palladian mansion is a remodelling of an earlier house, carried out in 1743 for the 2nd Viscount St John. The state rooms have been carefully restored and many of the contents, including paintings, portraits and Victorian gilded furniture, were originally owned by the St Johns.

The adjoining parish church of Lydiard Tregoze is notable for its 15th-century stained glass, vestiges of 13th-century mural paintings, Jacobean woodwork and 18th-century Italian wrought ironwork. It also has one of the finest groups of church monuments in Britain, especially those of members of the St John family.

Museum and Art Gallery

Bath Road, Swindon, Wiltshire SN1 4BA
☎ *0793 26161 extn 3129*
Mon–Sat 10–6; Sun 2–5. Closed Good Fri, Dec 25, 26.
🅗 *Mr Robert Dickinson, Assistant Curator*
Ⓕ 🗘 🖝 ☐

The Museum is housed in a late Georgian building, with a purpose-built Art Gallery added in 1964. It has collections of Wiltshire geology, archaeology and local and natural history. There are special collections of Roman and British coins and of pot lids and domestic pottery. A room is devoted to the history of the Royal Wiltshire Yeomanry.

The Art Gallery accommodates touring exhibitions and has a permanent collection of works by 20th-century British painters and potters.

Railway Village Museum

34 Faringdon Road, Swindon, Wiltshire SN1 5BJ
☎ *0793 26161 extn 3136*
Mon–Sat 10–1, 2–5; Sun 2–5. Closed Good Fri, Dec 25, 26.
Mr Tim Bryan, Museum Assistant
£

The Railway Village was built in the 1840s by the Great Western Railway to provide housing for its employees. Most of the properties were bought in 1966 by Swindon Borough Council and restored and modernised during the 1970s. One of the cottages, No. 34 Faringdon Road, refurbished inside and out to look as it would have done *c.* 1900, has been preserved as a museum, with furnishings and decorations of the period. No. 34 was built in the 1860s, during the last phase of construction of the Village. These houses were larger, with three bedrooms and two sizeable rooms downstairs. They became known as Foremen's Houses.

Richard Jefferies Museum

Coate, Swindon, Wiltshire SN3 6AA
☎ *0793 26161 extn 3130*
Wed, Sat, Sun 2–5. Closed Dec 25, 26.
See Swindon Museum and Art Gallery
F

The Museum, the 19th-century farmhouse in which the writer, Richard Jefferies, was born, is on the A345 Marlborough to Swindon road, near Coate Water Country Park and overlooks the downland which meant so much to Jefferies. The displays include his personal possessions, manuscripts and first editions and other commemorative material relating to Alfred Williams, the 'Hammerman Poet', who was employed at Swindon Railway Works. There is also an exhibition illustrating the natural history of the area.

T

Tain

Tain and District Museum

Castle Brae, Tain, Easter Ross, Ross-shire IV19 1AJ ☎ *0862 2140*
May–Sept, Mon–Sat 10–12, 2–5
Lesley Jackson, District Museums Curator, 26 High Street, Easter Ross
F

The Museum is in the 19th-century house formerly occupied by the caretaker of St Duthus Memorial Church. The displays relate to the history of the East Ross area, especially the Royal Burgh of Tain.

Tamworth

Tamworth Castle Museum

The Holloway, Tamworth, Staffordshire B79 7LR
☎ *0827 64222 extn 389*
Mon–Thurs, Sat 10–5.30; Sun 2–5.30 (last admission 5). Closed Dec 25.
The Curator
£

Part of the Castle probably dates from the 1180s. Later additions were built within the polygonal shell-keep. They include a medieval banqueting hall and Jacobean state apartments. There are a number of fine fireplaces and an interesting heraldic frieze of the Ferrers family. Most of the furniture belongs to the 17th century, except for that in the banqueting hall, which is 16th century. The local history displays include Saxon pennies from the Tamworth Mint, models of the Saxon fortifications (913 A.D.) and of an early 9th-century watermill.

Heraldic panel in the State Withdrawing Room of Tamworth Castle.

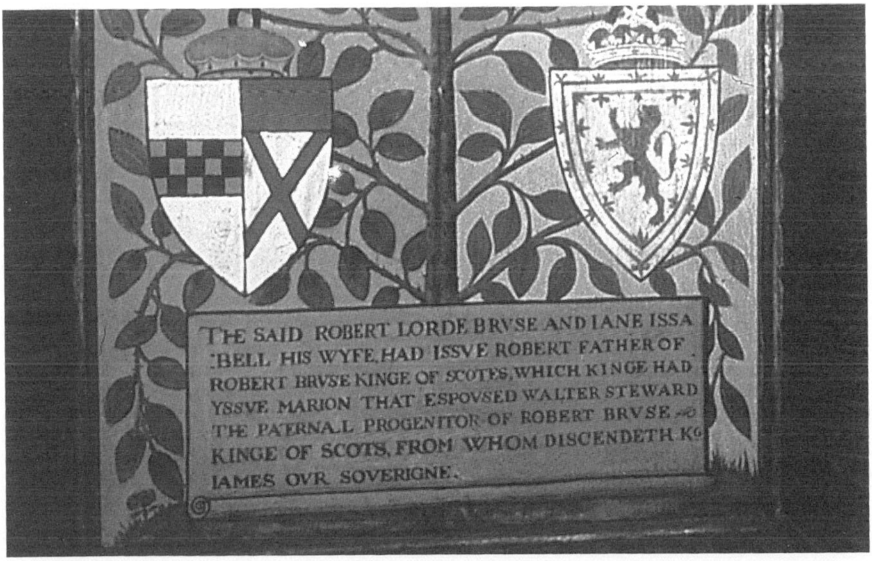

Tangmere

Tangmere Military Aviation Museum

PO Box 50, Tangmere Airfield, Chichester, West
    Sussex PO20 6ER   ☎ 0243 775223
Mar–Oct, daily 11–5.30
🗷 Flt. Lt. B. Hammond, Secretary
£ 🛉 ♿

Tangmere airfield was of great importance
during the Battle of Britain in the Second
World War. The Museum is housed in a former
ground radio workshop, which looks out over
the now abandoned airfield and runways, the
empty hangars and the derelict control tower.
The displays illustrate the history of military
flying from the earliest days to the present time,
with a particular emphasis on the activities of
the RAF at Tangmere from 1916 onwards, and
to the air battles fought over Southern England
from 1939–45, in which fighter stations such as
Tangmere played a crucial role.

Tarbolton

Bachelors' Club

Tarbolton, Ayrshire KA5 5QS   ☎ 0292 541424
Easter–Oct, daily 12–5. Other times by appt.
🗷 Sam May, 7 Croft Street, Tarbolton, Ayrshire
£ ♿ ♿ [NTS]

In this 17th-century thatched house Robert
Burns and some of his friends formed a debating
club in 1780. There are a number of other Burns
links with the building. He attended dancing
classes here, and his initiation into Freemasonry
took place on the premises in 1781. The house
contains period furnishings and exhibits
connected with the poet's seven-year stay in the
parish of Tarbolton.

Tarporley

Beeston Castle

Tarporley, Cheshire
Mar 15–Oct 15, Mon–Sat 9.30–6.30;
    Sun (Apr–Sept) 9.30–6.30.
    Oct 16–Mar 14, Mon–Sat 9.30–4;
    Sun (Oct–Mar), 2–4. Closed May Day
    Bank Holiday, Dec 24–26, Jan 1.
🗷 Historic Buildings & Monuments
    Commission, York   ☎ 0904 22902
£ ♿ ⚏

Beeston Castle, now in the charge of the
Department of the Environment, is three miles
south of Tarporley and west of the A49. It was
built in the early 13th century by Randulph,
Earl of Chester. An exhibition in an extension
to the gatehouse displays material discovered
during excavations and interprets it within the
context of the Castle.

Tattershall

Dogdyke Pumping Station

Bridge Farm, Tattershall, nr Coningsby,
    Lincolnshire LN4 4JG
Easter Sun, then May–Oct, 1st Sun of each month,
    2–5
🗷 The Secretary, Mr J. Parkinson, 124 London
    Road, Long Sutton, Spalding, Lincolnshire
    PE12 9EE   ☎ 0406 362388
£ ♿ ■ ♿

The Pumping Station, a scheduled monument,
is a mile west of Tattershall Castle. It is reached
from the A153 via Bridge Farm. It contains an
1855 beam engine, built by Bradley and Craven,
of Wakefield. The 28-foot diameter scoop wheel
is also original. It is the only known land
drainage pumping station of this type to be
worked by steam. It is demonstrated, subject to
suitable water levels, together with the adjacent
1940 Ruston diesel engine and Gwynnes
centrifugal pump.

The Guardhouse Museum

Tattershall Castle, Tattershall, Lincoln,
    Lincolnshire LN4 4LR   ☎ 0562 42543
Apr–Oct, Mon–Sat 11–6.30; Sun 1–6.30.
    Nov–Mar, Mon–Sat 12–6.30, or dusk if
    earlier; Sun 1–6.30 or dusk.
    Closed Dec 25, 26.
🗷 The Custodian
£ Castle only 🛉 ♿ [NT]

Tattershall Castle was built c. 1440 by Ralph
Cromwell, Treasurer of England, and is now a
National Trust property. It is on the A153,
three and a half miles south-east of Woodhall
Spa. The Museum is on the upper floor of the
15th-century guardhouse. It contains a model of
the Castle as it was at the end of the 17th
century, fossils, axe-heads and other
archaeological material found by residents of
villages in the area, as well as pottery, glass and
metal objects discovered during Lord Curzon's
excavations of the grounds and moats in
1912–14.

**Ralph Cromwell's fortified manor-house
at Tattershall Castle, the home of
The Guardhouse Museum.**

Taunton

Somerset County Museum

Taunton Castle, Taunton, Somerset TA1 4AA
☎ 0823 55504
Mon–Sat 10–5. Open most Bank Holidays.
County Museums Officer
£

Parts of Taunton Castle date from the 12th century. The Museum's collections, built up over the past 135 years, are especially strong in the field of Somerset archaeology. The exhibits include the Low Ham and East Coker Roman mosaics and the finds from Meare Lake village and Ham Hill. A gallery is devoted to the history of the Somerset Light Infantry and other sections of the Museum are concerned with geology, natural history, Nailsea glass and pottery, featuring Donyatt and Elton ware.

The Museum also has important collections of material not directly related to Somerset. Among them are sections devoted to costume, pottery and Chinese ceramics.

Taynuilt

Bonawe Iron Works

Bonawe Furnace, c/o The Hedges, Taynuilt, Argyll
Apr–Sept, Mon–Sat 9.30–7; Sun 2–5
Historic Buildings & Monuments, Edinburgh
☎ 031 5568 400
£

The ironworks at Bonawe was established in 1753 by a Lake District partnership. It operated until 1866. The furnace, which still exists and is in a good state of preservation, was fuelled by charcoal and used Lancashire ore. The company built a village for its workers, including houses, a farm, a school and an inn.

Teignmouth

Teignmouth Museum

29 French Street, Teignmouth, South Devon TQ14 8ST
May–Sept, Tues, Mon–Fri 10–12.30, 2.30–5; Thurs 10–12.30, 2.30–5, 7–9; Sun 2.30–5. Closed winter months, except by appt for school parties.
Mrs M. Weare, 31 Lower Briarley Road, Teignmouth TQ14 8LH ☎ 06267 4084
£

The Museum is concerned mainly with local history. A special feature of the collection is the group of objects from a 16th-century merchant ship, wrecked off Teignmouth 200 yards from the shore, including two bronze Venetian cannons.

Telford

Ironbridge Gorge Museum

The Wharfage, Ironbridge, Telford, Shropshire TF8 7AW ☎ 095245 3522
Mar–Oct, daily 10–6. Nov–Feb, daily 10–5. Closed Dec 25.
Education Officer
£

The Museum complex, based on the industrial monuments of the Ironbridge Gorge, covers an area of six square miles, with six main museum sites. In the 18th century the valley was the most important centre of ironmaking in the world. At Coalbrookdale there is Abraham Darby's original furnace where, in 1709, he pioneered the technique of smelting iron ore with coke. The Museum of Iron, also at Coalbrookdale, illustrates the history of ironmaking and of the Coalbrookdale Company. The Severn Warehouse, built on the banks of the river by the Coalbrookdale Company in the 1840s, has been restored, together with its wharf, and now provides an introduction to the Ironbridge Gorge and its industrial past, with an audio-visual programme and an exhibition.

Further along is the celebrated Iron Bridge and its Tollhouse. Made in 1779, this was the first cast-iron bridge in the world. The town of Ironbridge developed at its northern end in the 1780s. Jackfield in the 1880s had two of the largest decorative tileworks in the world. In the original Cravan Dunnill Works is a museum of decorative wall and floor tiles produced in the area.

Blists Hill is a 50-acre open-air museum, with shops, workshops, ironworks, a candle factory, a coalmine and a printing-shop. The Hay Inclined Plane runs down to the Severn from the Blists Hill site. Also nearby is the Coalport China Works, which has been restored as a museum to illustrate the techniques of china manufacture.

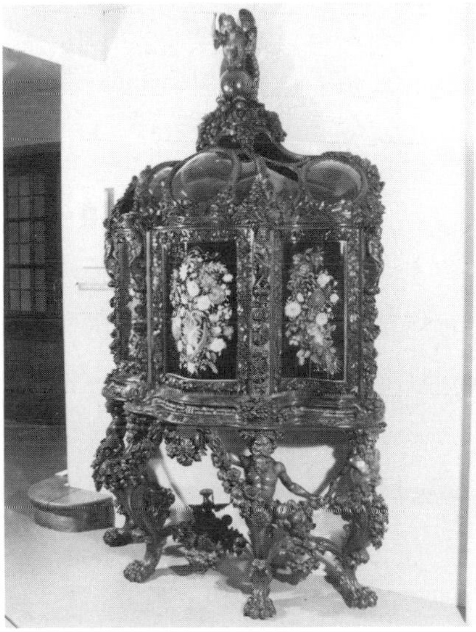

Carved cabinet made in Taunton for The Great Exhibition of 1851. Taunton, Somerset County Museum.

Tenby

Tenby Museum and Picture Gallery

Castle Hill, Tenby, Dyfed SA70 7BP
☎ 0834 2809
Easter–Oct, daily 10–6. Summer, 7–9pm.
Nov–Easter, daily 10–4. Closed Dec 25, 26.
⚱ John Tipton, Curator
ⓔ ex. pre-booked educ. groups ⚲

The Museum, in part of Tenby's medieval castle, was founded in 1878 to preserve a collection of local archaeological finds. It has been administered by honorary curators and officers ever since. The emphasis is on geology, natural history and archaeology of the area, with other collections devoted to local history and militaria. Special sections are devoted to the Pembroke and Tenby Railway, taken over by the Great Western in 1896, to an unsuccessful invasion by French troops, under an American commander, in 1797, and to the Castlemartin Yeomanry,which disobeyed an 1827 order to disband and still survives.

The Maritime Gallery contains many exhibits relating to the long association of the people of Tenby with the sea and the Picture Gallery concentrates on artists and work connected with Tenby. Gwen and Augustus John are among the artists represented.

The Museum has an important collection of photographs and its archives include a large number of documents concerning the ancient Borough of Tenby.

Tenterden

Kent and East Sussex Railway

Tenterden Town Station, Tenterden, Kent
TN30 6HE
☎ 05806 2943 (recorded information)
Easter–Christmas, Sat, Sun & Bank Holiday.
June–July, Wed, Thurs. Aug, daily.
⚱ The Commercial Manager   ☎ 05806 5155
ⓔ ⬤ ▆ ⚲ ♿

This is an Edwardian steam railway, preserved together with its original buildings. There are restored stations, vintage steam locomotives – two are over 100 years old – and 70 items of rolling stock. Passengers are carried over five miles of track.

Tenterden and District Museum

Station Road, Tenterden, Kent TN30 6HN
☎ 05806 3605
Easter–May, Oct, daily 2–5. June–Sept,
Sun–Thurs 10–5; Fri, Sat 10–5.
Nov–Easter, Sat, Sun 2–4.
⚱ The Secretary
ⓔ ⚲ ⚲

The Museum is in a weatherboarded building dating from c. 1850, which was originally a stonemason's and later a builder's workshop, with stabling at one end. The stable section at one time housed the local railway horse-bus, now in the National Railway Museum at York. The displays illustrate the history of Tenterden from Anglo-Saxon times onwards and its incorporation as a limb of the Cinque Ports.

In the first exhibition room are the robes of the Mayor and a Baron of the Cinque Ports, together with the weights and measures of the former Borough and a scale model of the town as it was in the mid 19th century. The second room has exhibits relating to the domestic and business life of Tenterden in the 18th and 19th centuries, to the schools and to the former Borough Police and Fire Brigade. One wall is filled by the Tenterden Tapestry, a 36-foot collage depicting the history of the town, made by pupils of the Junior School in 1974.

The third ground floor room contains the Col. Stephens collection of material relating to the history of light railways, of which the Kent and East Sussex Railway was the first to be constructed under the Light Railways Act of 1896. Upstairs there are agricultural implements, a hop press and examples of local building materials.

Tewkesbury

The John Moore Countryside Museum

41 Church Street, Tewkesbury, Gloucestershire
GL20 5SN   ☎ 0684 297174
Easter–Oct, Tues–Sat & Bank Holiday 10–1,
2–5. Also open some Sun afternoons.
⚱ S. E. Illingworth, Curator
ⓔ ⚲ ⚲ ☐

The Museum is in part of a row of half-timbered cottages, built c. 1450, in the precincts of Tewkesbury Abbey. John Moore was born in Tewkesbury and wrote more than 40 books before his death in 1967. All had countryside settings and themes, and the Museum has aimed at reflecting the author's love of nature. The galleries house countryside collections of the past and present, the displays including The Farming Year, The Willow, Where the Severn and Avon Meet, and Sounds of the Seasons, with recordings of Gloucestershire wildlife. The displays are changed on a seasonal basis.

**The first cast-iron bridge in the world.
Telford, Ironbridge Gorge Museum.**

Robes of a Baron of the Cinque Ports and a Cinque Ports Volunteers' Drum of 1794. Tenterden and District Museum.

The Little Museum

45 Church Street, Tewkesbury, Gloucestershire
    GL20 5SN   **☎** 0684 297174
Easter–Oct, Tues–Sat 10–5
⚑ Mrs Joan Underwood, Curator
F ⚑

The Abbey Lawn Trust was established to buy and restore the row of medieval cottages, originally built as shops, standing in front of Tewkesbury Abbey when the site seemed destined for commercial development. The half-timbered cottages originally consisted of 23 shops, with living accommodation above, built c. 1450. The Little Museum, No. 45 in the row, typifies the original construction and has been simply furnished in oak to suggest the domestic environment of the first occupants.

The restoration project won an award from the British Tourist Authority, as an outstanding enterprise during European Conservation Year (1971).

Tewkesbury Museum

64 Barton Street, Tewkesbury, Gloucestershire
    GL20 5PX
Easter–Oct, daily 10–1, 2–5
⚑ Hon. Secretary
E ⚑

The Museum occupies a fine half-timbered house, which dates from at least the 16th century, possibly earlier. Its collections and displays relate to the history, trades and industries of Tewkesbury. One of the special features is a diorama of the Battle of Tewkesbury in 1471, at which Edward IV defeated the armies of Queen Margaret and Prince Edward of Wales. The Museum also houses the Walker fairground collection.

Thetford

Ancient House Museum

21 White Hart Street, Thetford, Norfolk
    IP24 1AA   **☎** 0842 2599
Mon 10–1, 2–5; Tues–Sat 10–5. Spring Bank
    Holiday–Sept, also Sun 2–5
⚑ Chad Goodwin, Curator
E ⚑ ⚑

The museum is in a listed building, an early Tudor half-timbered house. It contains displays reflecting the history of the town of Thetford and the surrounding Breckland region. Among the subjects especially featured are local industries (one, pumpware, is unique to Thetford), Saxon Thetford, Thomas Paine – born in Thetford in 1737 – and the local flint industry, which has existed since Neolithic times. A replica of the Thetford Treasure is now on display here, the original being in the British Museum.

Euston Hall

nr Thetford, Norfolk IP24 2QP   **☎** 0842 66366
June 4–Sept 24, Thurs 2.30–5.30 (last
    admission 5)
⚑ The Secretary
E ⚑ ⚑ ⚑ [HHA]

Euston Hall, the home of the Duke of Grafton, is three miles south of Thetford, on the A1088. The park and gardens were laid out by John Evelyn and William Kent. The present building is all that remains of a much larger house, built in the 18th century. It is best known for its fine collection of paintings and especially for the outstanding group of 17th-century portraits, which include works by Stubbs, Van Dyck, Kneller and Lely.

Thirsk

Thirsk Museum

16 Kirkgate, Thirsk, North Yorkshire YO7 1PQ
    ☎ 0845 22755
Apr & Oct, Sat–Mon 11–5. May Sept, Mon
    10–5; Tues–Sat 11–5; Sun 2.30–4.30.
⚑ Mrs J. Goldthorp, 28 Kirkgate, Thirsk
    YO7 1PQ
E ⚑ ⚑

The house at 16 Kirkgate was the birthplace of Thomas Lord, the founder of Lord's Cricket Ground. The Museum has displays illustrating local life, history and industry. There are exhibits of cobblers' and blacksmith's tools, veterinary and medical equipment, Victorian clothing, especially underwear, dolls and dolls' furniture, and children's games. Other items on show include archaeological finds from the area, medieval pottery, cameras and cricket mementoes. A further striking feature of the museum is an evocative reconstruction of a Victorian kitchen, fully equipped with utensils of the period.

Thornhill

Drumlanrig Castle

nr Thornhill, Dumfriesshire DG3 4AQ
☎ 0848 30248
Open Easter–late Aug. Check opening times
  locally.
🖎 The Castle Manager
Ⓔ ⬤ ⬛ ⌁

The Castle, four miles north of Thornhill, was
built in 1690 for the Duke of Queensberry, and
is still lived in by the family. The collections
include Verdure tapestries, French furniture,
family portraits, and one of Rembrandt's works,
Old Woman Reading.

Thursford

The Thursford Museum

Thursford, Fakenham, Norfolk NR21 0AS
☎ 032877 477
Mar–Easter & Nov, Sun 2–5. Good Fri–Oct,
  daily 2–5.30.
🖎 Miss Geraldine Rye
Ⓔ ⬤ ⬛ ⌁

The Museum is off the A148, between Holt and
Fakenham. It contains an important collection
of working fairground equipment and large
cinema, dance-hall and fairground organs,
which give performances every day. There are
also a number of showmen's engines and
traction engines and a narrow-gauge steam
railway.

Thurso

Thurso Museum

High Street, Thurso, Caithness KW14 8AG
May–Sept, Mon–Sat 10–12, 2–5
🖎 Mrs G. Angus
Ⓔ ⌕ ⌁

The displays cover the geology, botany and
history of Thurso and Caithness. There are
special exhibits relating to Pictish symbol
stones, and the Caithness flagstone industry.
Domestic equipment is shown in a
reconstruction of a typical croft kitchen.
Among the local celebrities given particular
attention in the Museum are Sir John Sinclair,
of Caithness, who gave the word statistics to the
English language, and Robert Dick, of Thurso, a
Victorian baker, who collected the fossil fish
of Caithness and formed a large herbarium
of plants found in the area.

Tilbury

Thurrock Riverside Museum

Civic Square, Tilbury, Essex   ☎ 03752 79216
Tues–Fri 10–1, 2–5.30; Sat 10–1, 2–5.
  Closed Bank Holiday.
🖎 The Curator
Ⓕ ⌕ ⌁

The Museum's displays reflect the history of
Thurrock's riverside area, from prehistoric times
to the present day. The exhibits include
archaeological material, engravings,
watercolours, paintings, ship models and
maritime relics. A special section of the
Museum is devoted to the history of Tilbury
docks, an important source of employment in
the area during the 19th and 20th centuries.

Tilford

Old Kiln Agricultural Museum

Reeds Road, Tilford, Farnham, Surrey GU10 2DL
☎ 025125 2300
Apr–Sept, Wed–Sun & Bank Holiday 11–6
🖎 Henry Jackson
Ⓔ ⬤ ⌕ ⌁ ♿

The Museum's collections illustrate life in the
district before the coming of the internal
combustion engine. There is a wide range of
hand tools used for all aspects of farm work and
for forestry. The horse-drawn vehicles include a
Surrey wagon from the workshop of the
celebrated George Sturt, of Farnham, and a
timber-wagon. A wheelwright's shop and a
blacksmith's shop have been reconstructed at
the Museum, and among the items illustrating
the local hop-growing industry are stilts used to
enable workers to reach the top wires when
tying up the hops, wicker baskets for measuring
the hops, a hop-press and a hessian hop-pocket.
  The forestry display includes a timber nib – a
horse-drawn vehicle used to tow logs from the
forest – early motorised chain-saws, pit saws,
and machines for de-winging and cleaning seed
before it was sown in the forest nursery.
  Other displays show veterinary and pharmacy
material, Victorian household and nursery
items, and early photographic equipment.

Tintern

Tintern Abbey

Tintern, Gwent   ☎ 02918 251
Mar 15–Oct 15, daily 9.30–6.30.
  Oct 16–Mar 14, Mon–Sat 9.30–4; Sun 2–4.
🖎 The Custodian
Ⓔ ⬤ ⬛ ⌁ ✚

The Cistercian Abbey at Tintern, originally
founded in 1131, was almost completely rebuilt
during the 13th and early 14th centuries. After
the Dissolution in 1536, the lead was stripped
from the roofs and the site became neglected. In
the late 18th century, Tintern Abbey,
beautifully situated in the Wye Valley, became
greatly in favour with the Romantic Movement.
It was the subject of a celebrated poem by
Wordsworth and of paintings by Turner.
  The 'Abbey in a Landscape' exhibition, in a
building next to the new entrance block,
illustrates the history of the Abbey and of the
Cistercian Order and indicates its links with the
late 18th and early 19th-century Romantic
Movement in literature and art.

Tiree

Skerryvore Museum

Hynish, Isle of Tiree, Argyll PA77 6UQ
☎ 08792 691
Daily 9–6
Mr M. Stanfield, 13 Rawlinson Road, Oxford
OX2 6UE ☎ 0865 510424
Ⓕ ♿

The Museum, dedicated to the memory of Alan
Stevenson, the builder of Skerryvore
lighthouse, is in the 150-year-old tower used for
sending messages to the lighthouse before the
days of radio. The displays tell the story of the
building of the lighthouse and include
illustrations of the various stages of
construction.

The adjacent fresh-water flushing harbour
and the pier have been restored by the Museum.

Titchfield

Carron Row Farm Museum

*Segensworth Road, Titchfield, Hampshire
PO15 5DZ* ☎ 0329 43169/45102
*Easter–May & Oct, Wed–Sun 10.30–5.30.
June–Sept, daily 10.30–5.30.*
Mrs Harding or Mrs Ireland
Ⓔ ♦ ▪ ♿

Carron Row Farm once belonged to Titchfield
Abbey and contains the terraced Abbey
fishponds. The Museum is in a 17th-century
barn. The exhibits include agricultural
implements, carts, wagons and tools used by
rural craftsmen. There is also a reconstruction of
a farm kitchen and a working blacksmith's forge.
A special exhibition is devoted to the history of
strawberry growing, important in the district.
Among the items displayed are a horse-drawn
strawberry wagon, used to take baskets of
strawberries to the local railway station.

The Museum also has Titchfield's 1841 horse-
drawn fire-engine, renovated in 1982. It took
10 men each side to pump the water. Volunteer
pumpers received tokens for their work, which
could be exchanged for cash or beer.

Tiverton

Tiverton Museum

St Andrew Street, Tiverton, Devon EX16 6PH
☎ 0884 256295
*Mon–Sat 10.30–4.30. Closed Bank Holiday
& Dec 24–Jan 31. Open to pre-booked parties
only during Jan.*
Hon. Curator
Ⓕ ⌀ ♿

The main Museum building is Tiverton's former
National School, built in 1841. The collections
cover the life and history of Tiverton and mid
Devon from prehistoric to modern times. There
is an Agricultural Hall, with a wide range of
tools and implements once used on local farms,

the Alford Gallery, housing Devon farm wagons
and other horse-drawn vehicles, a reconstructed
smithy from Silverton, and the Authers Gallery,
which displays, among many other items, the
'Tivvy Bumper', a Great Western Railway 0-4-2
tank engine, which ran on the Tiverton
Junction–Tiverton branch line.

The Heathcoat Lace Machine Gallery
features the work of the main local
manufacturer. The exhibits include a lace-
making machine built by John Heathcoat
c. 1820 and in use until 1975, and a display on
the use of Tiverton lace by Royal brides since
Queen Victoria.

A new section deals with domestic baths. A
rare exhibit here is an 18th-century boot bath,
so called from its shape, which allowed the
occupant to be modestly unexposed when a
servant poured in the water.

Toddington

The North Gloucestershire Railway

*The Railway Station, Toddington, Gloucestershire
GL54 5DT*
*Easter–Sept, Steam Open Days 1–5. Enquire
locally for dates.*
Robert F. Hickman, Publicity Manager,
*8 Emerald Close, Tuffley, Gloucestershire
GL4 0RH* ☎ 0452 410568
Ⓔ ⌀ ▪ ♿

What was formerly known as the Dowty Railway
Preservation Society was re-formed in 1985 as
the North Gloucestershire Railway Company.
Based at Toddington Station, the Society has a
large collection of locomotives, carriages and
other exhibits from both standard and narrow
gauge railways.

The standard gauge collection includes an
1881 GWR special saloon and a 1935 GWR
restaurant car, as well as a fully working steam
locomotive, an Avonside 0-4-0 tank, *Cadbury
Bournville No. 1.* The growing narrow gauge
collection includes items from both Britain and
abroad. Visitors to the narrow gauge shed will
see engines in various stages of restoration, as
well as a large collection of wagons. The Society
also has a considerable display of mechanical
signalling equipment, including a Midland
Railway signal-box, *California Crossing,* in
complete operating condition.

1925 'Cadbury Bournville' engine under steam
at the North Gloucestershire Railway,
Toddington.

Tomintoul

Tomintoul Museum

The Square, Tomintoul, Moray AB3 9ET
Easter–May & Oct, Mon–Sat 9–5.30.
  June & Sept, Mon–Sat 9–6; Sun 2–6.
  July–Aug, Mon–Sat 9–7; Sun 11–7.
N *District Curator, Falconer Museum, Tolbooth*
  Street, Forres, Moray IV36 0PH
  ☎ *0309 73701*
F ▢

The Museum illustrates the history and natural
environment of the Tomintoul area. There are
sections on local history, wildlife, climate and
geology and several special exhibits, including a
reconstructed farmhouse kitchen, a blacksmith's
forge and a display devoted to peat cutting.
  The Museum arranges regular temporary
exhibitions on subjects relating to the district.

Tonbridge

The Milne Museum

The Slade, Tonbridge, Kent TN9 1HR
  ☎ *0732 364726*
Tues 2–5. Other times by appt.
N *The Curator*
£ ▮ ⟶

The Museum has been set up by the South-
Eastern Electricity Board in Tonbridge's former
Electricity Works, built in 1902. It houses a
collection of electrical items dating from 1800
to the 1950s. The exhibits range from
transformers, switchgear, cables and joints to
cookers, fires, washing machines and vacuum
cleaners. There is a large collection of small
domestic appliances and a variety of electro-
medical apparatus, as well as sections on home
entertainment, communications and measuring
instruments.

Among the items intended especially for
children are those in the Gordon Gallery, which
has a series of experiments which visitors can
conduct for themselves in order to learn about
basic electrical principles and about the history
of the applications of electricity.

Penshurst Place

Penshurst, Tonbridge, Kent TN11 8DG
  ☎ *0892 870307*
Apr–1st Sun in Oct, Tues–Sun 12.30–6
N *The Comptroller*
£ ▮ ▆ ⟶

Penshurst Place, the birthplace of Sir Philip
Sidney, is five and a half miles west of
Tonbridge on the B2156. The Great Hall dates
from 1338, and additions and alterations were
made to the house during the succeeding
centuries. The more important rooms shown to
the public include the Great Hall, Long
Gallery, Queen Elizabeth Room, and the
tapestry and state dining rooms. There are fine
collections of paintings, tapestries and early
furniture.

Tongwynlais

Castell Coch

Tongwynlais, Cardiff, South Glamorgan
  ☎ *0222 810101*
Mar 15–Oct 15, daily 9.30–6.30.
  Oct 16–Mar 14, Mon–Sat 9.30–4; Sun 2–4.
N *The Custodian*
£ ⟶ ✪

The original castle was built, between 1260 and
1300, of red sandstone. Castell Coch means Red
Castle. During the 1870s the 3rd Marquess of
Bute had the ruins cleared and built a romantic
fairytale castle on the site, with the rooms
lavishly furnished and decorated with scenes
from Greek mythology, Aesop's Fables and
other sources of legend and fantasy.
  Castell Coch now contains an exhibition
describing the 19th-century rebuilding of the
Castle.

Toomevara

Toomevara Folk Museum

Toomevara, Nenagh, Co. Tipperary, Ireland
  ☎ *067 24153*
Key on request
N *Rev. J. A. O'Brien, P.P., Carrig,*
  Ballycommon, Nenagh
£ ⟶ ♿

The large and varied collections of the Museum
relate to the crafts and traditional way of life of
County Tipperary. They are displayed in a
reconstructed domestic setting. The Museum
also serves as a centre for performances of folk
music and popular entertainment.

**Main display area of the Milne Museum,
Tonbridge.**

Topsham

Topsham Museum

Holman House, 25 The Strand, Topsham, Exeter,
  Devon EX3 0AX   ☎ *039287 3244*
Mon, Wed, Sat 2–5
🅼 *Mrs B. Entwistle, 5 Elm Grove Road,*
  Topsham, Exeter
🅔 ⌀ ▬ 🔊

Topsham Museum is run by the Topsham
Museum Society on behalf of Exeter City
Council, which owns the building. Holman
House, which dates from c. 1690, shows rooms
of that period. It is one of a series of Dutch-style
houses built along The Strand at Topsham at a
time when the town was prospering by exporting
Devon-manufactured serge to European ports,
principally Amsterdam and Rotterdam. A
further room contains memorabilia of the
founder of the Museum, Dorothy Holman
(d. 1983), whose 19th-century ancestors were
shipowners and shipbuilders in Topsham.

Local history items are displayed in a former
sail-loft, built behind the house in 1858. Here,
special attention is given to Topsham's trading
days and shipbuilding industry. There are
exhibits of half-models and shipbuilding tools,
and a model of Topsham as it was in 1900. The
displays in the Estuary Room illustrate the
wildlife of the estuary.

Torpoint

Antony House

Torpoint, Cornwall PL11 2QA   ☎ *0752 812191*
Mar 31–Oct, Tues–Thurs & Bank Holiday Mon
  2–6 (last guided tour 5.30)
🅼 *The Administrator*
🅔 ♦ 🔊 [NT]

Antony House came into the possession of the
Carew family in the late 14th century. Early in
the 19th century the estate passed through the
female line to Reginald Pole, a son of Sir John
Pole of Shute. Sir John Carew-Pole gave the
property to the National Trust in 1961 and the
family continues to live in the house.

The furnishings and family possessions
illustrate the history of the Carews and Poles
and their connections with county and national
affairs. Some panelling and items of furniture,
together with a portrait of Richard Carew and a
first edition of his *Survey of Cornwall*, survive
from the original Tudor house. The large
number of Carew and Pole portraits include one
of Sir Alexander Carew, cut out of its frame by
his family when he declared his support for the
Cromwellians and stitched back again after he
recanted and was executed by the
Parliamentarians. The most famous painting in
the house is, however, the Bowyer portrait of
Charles I at his trial.

Torquay

Torquay Museum

529 Babbacombe Road, Torquay, South Devon
  TQ1 1HG   ☎ *0803 23975*
Mon–Fri 10–4.45. Easter–Oct, also Sat.
  Closed Good Fri, Christmas and New Year.
🅼 *B. V. Cooper, Curator*
🅔 ⌀ 🔊

The Torquay Natural History Society was
founded in 1844. For many years it housed its
collections in a series of rented premises, but in
1875 it was able to establish its own purpose-
built museum, which has since been
considerably enlarged. The displays cover the
geology, palaeontology and wildlife of Devon,
paintings, prints and photographs of South
Devon and Torbay, and archaeological finds,
especially from Kent's Caves. There are exhibits
of ethnographical material from Australia, the
Pacific and Africa, time-measurement devices,
pharmaceutical equipment, dolls, Honiton lace,
police mementoes, and Watcombe terracotta.

The Laycock Gallery contains the Society's
holdings of domestic equipment, furniture,
craftsmen's tools and agricultural equipment.
There are also exhibits of cottage ornaments,
Nailsea glass, pewter, club brasses and spring
guns.

Torre Abbey

The King's Drive, Torquay, South Devon
  TQ2 5JX   ☎ *0803 23593*
Apr–Oct, daily 10–5. Nov–Mar, Mon–Fri
  by appt.
🅼 *Mr L. Retallick, Curator*
🅔 ⌀ ▬ 🔊

The Premonstratensian Order at Torre was
established in 1196. In 1598 what remained of
the buildings was converted into living
accommodation by the Ridgeway family and in
1660 the property was bought by the Carys, who
sold it to Torquay Borough Council in 1930.

The collection of paintings now displayed in
the house is particularly strong in works by 19th-

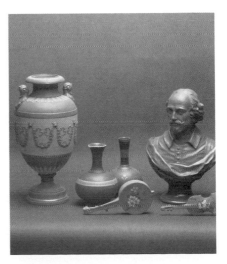

**Characteristic Watcombe terracotta.
Torquay, Torre Abbey.**

century artists, including Burne-Jones, Holman Hunt and John Martin. There are exhibits of marine paintings, silver, pewter, sculpture, ceramics, English drinking glasses and 19th-century Torquay and Watcombe terracotta. The Abbey also contains a number of rooms which have recently been restored and furnished in period style.

By the end of the 16th century, most of the Abbey buildings, including the church, had fallen into ruins. They can, however, still be identified with the help of the guide which is available to visitors.

Torrington

Torrington Museum

Town Hall, Torrington, Devon EX38 8HN
☎ *0805 24324*
*May–Sept, Mon–Fri 10.15–12.45; Sat
    10.15–12.45. Closed Bank Holiday.*
✕ *Mr N. Mantle, Hon. Curator*
🄵 ⬮ ✒

The Museum occupies the main hall of the Town Hall, on the walls of which are portraits of members of the Rolle family and of Philip and Mary, who granted the town its Charter in 1554. The collections are concerned with the history and development of the Anglo-Saxon town of Great Torrington.

Totnes

Devonshire Collection of Period Costume

*Bogan House, 43 High Street, Totnes, Devon
    TQ9 5RY   ☎ 0803 862423*
*Spring Bank Holiday–Oct 1, Mon–Fri 11–5;
    Sun 2–5.*
✕ *Mrs A. Morel, Cobberton Farm, Dartington,
    Totnes TQ9 6DS*
🄴 ⬮ ✒ ▢

The Collection comprises mainly women's and children's clothing from the mid 18th century to the present day, the period from 1800 to 1956 being the best represented. There is a wide range of accessories, a collection of underwear dating from 1840 to 1940, and examples of Liberty clothes and scarves. Men's clothing in the collection consists chiefly of uniforms.

A new exhibition on a particular theme is mounted each summer, usually with 40–45 garments and many accessories.

Totnes Elizabethan Museum

70 Fore Street, Totnes, Devon TQ9 5RU
☎ *0803 863821*
*Apr–Oct, Mon–Fri & Bank Holiday 10.30–1,
    2–5. Also open Sat from late July to Aug.*
✕ *The Custodian*
🄴 ⬮ ✒

The Museum occupies an Elizabethan merchant's home, built *c.* 1575 and considerably altered *c.* 1630. The displays

contain a wide range of local exhibits and include a costume room, dolls' houses and dolls' furniture, craftsmen's tools, and a re-created kitchen and Victorian grocer's shop. The Babbage Room commemorates Charles Babbage, Father of the Computer, who came from a Totnes family, with memorabilia of him and a display telling the story of his inventions.

The displays also devote attention to the cloth-trade, to which Totnes owed much of its prosperity, and to the development of the town's government.

A special section is devoted to John Wills, born in Totnes, who was a member of the ill-fated Burke and Wills expedition in 1860, the first south to north crossing of Australia.

Totnes Motor Museum

Steamer Quay, Totnes, Devon TQ9 5AL
☎ *0803 862777*
Easter–Oct, daily 10–5.30
✕ *The Curator*
🄴 ⬮ ✒

The Museum is in a converted cider warehouse. The collection of vintage, sports and racing cars illustrates 80 years of motoring. The cars are maintained in running order and many of the racing cars still perform on competition circuits. There are also exhibits of instruments, hand-books, engines, motorcycles, bicycles and toy cars.

Trefecca

The Howell Harris Museum

Trefecca, Brecon, Powys LD3 0PP
Mon–Sat 9–5.30. Closed Christmas week.
✕ *Mr Ronwy Rogers, Warden, Coleg Trefeca,
    Trefecca, Brecon   ☎ 0874 711423*
🄵 ⬮ ✒

Trefecca, or Trevecka, is a small village on the Llangorse to Talgarth road, and was the centre of the 18th-century Methodist movement which originated with the Religio-Industrial Settlement established in 1736 by Howell Harris at his home, Trevecka House. Nearby was a seminary set up by the Countess of Huntingdon. The buildings later became a theological college and are now the Lay Training Centre of the Presbyterian Church of Wales.

The Museum is in the vestry of the Howell Harris Memorial Church. The collections illustrate the activities of the Welsh and English Reformers. They include field pulpits, books from the Trevecka press and items illustrating the trades and crafts practised at the Settlement. Also on display are the telescope which Howell Harris's brother, Joseph, brought to Trevecka in 1761, in order to observe the transit of Venus over the Sun, the Electrifying Machine recommended by John Wesley for the treatment of 45 ailments, and the swords and guns which belonged to Howell Harris as a captain of the Brecknock Militia. Harris was anxious to protect Britain against a Catholic invasion during the Seven Years War.

Treffgarne

Nant-y-Coy Mill

Treffgarne, Haverfordwest, Dyfed SA62 5LR
☎ *043787 671/686*
June–Sept, daily 10–5. Other times by appt.
🏛 *Herbert Wilson, Suomi, Treffgarne,*
    Haverfordwest SA62 5PH
£ 🛍 ☕

Treffgarne is on the main A40 Haverfordwest to Fishguard road. The Mill, a listed building, and the adjoining farmhouse and farm buildings date from 1844. The buildings have been restored to their late 19th-century appearance and the house now contains displays of domestic and dairy equipment, craftsmen's tools, old photographs and family histories and account books. China jugs and ornaments are a special feature of the collection.

Tresco

Valhalla: The Tresco Ships' Figurehead Collection

Tresco Tropical Gardens, Tresco, Isles of Scilly
Apr–Oct, daily 10–4
🏛 *National Maritime Museum, Saltash, Cornwall*
    PL12 6TA   ☎ *0579 50830*
£ *Gardens only* 🛍 ☕

Valhalla is part of the National Maritime Museum, and is run as one of its outstations, in conjunction with the Tresco Estate. It contains a large collection of ships' figureheads, together with other decorative ships' carvings from the days of sail and from early steamships. The exhibits come mainly from 19th-century merchant vessels, wrecked around the coasts of Scilly. Skilled woodcarvers were to be found in the shipyards of all the maritime countries and the items displayed at Valhalla form an international museum of the ship-carver's art.

The main wing of the Museum was built in the 1860s by Augustus Smith, Lord Proprietor of the Islands, especially to house the collection. It was decorated with shells to give a submerged grotto effect. This has been retained as far as possible.

Trim

Meath Archaeological and Historical Museum

County Library, Trim, Co. Meath, Ireland
Tues, Thurs 2.30–5, 7–8.30; Wed 10–1, 3–5;
    Fri 10–12.30, 2.30–5; Sat 2–4
🏛 *Hon. Secretary*
£ ☕

The collection of the Meath Archaeological and Historical Society includes a wide range of historical items, especially weapons, together with prehistoric and early Celtic archaeological material found in the area.

Tring

Zoological Museum

Akeman Street, Tring, Hertfordshire HP23 6AP
☎ *044282 4181*
Mon–Sat 10–5; Sun 2–5. Closed Good Fri, May
    Day Bank Holiday, Dec 24–26, Jan 1.
🏛 *Education Department*
£ 🛍 ☕

The Museum was built at the end of the 19th century to house the magnificent zoological collections which had been formed by Lionel Walter, the second Baron Rothschild. The specimens were selected and prepared with exceptional care and illustrate 19th-century taxidermy at its best. They include nearly every kind of large mammal, and an extensive range of birds, reptiles, insects and other invertebrates.

The Museum was bequeathed to the nation in 1938 and is now part of the Natural History Museum in London. The galleries were modernised in 1972, but without changing their basic character and arrangement. Lord Rothschild's study has recently been renovated and restored and contains an exhibition illustrating his life and work.

Troutbeck

Townend

Troutbeck, Windermere, Cumbria LA23 1LB
☎ *0966 32628*
Mar 26–Nov 2, Sun, Tues–Fri 2–6 or dusk if
    earlier. Open Good Fri & Bank Holiday Mon
    2–6. Last admission 5.30.
🏛 *The Administrator*
£ ☕ [NT]

Townend is at the end of the village of Troutbeck, three miles south-east of Ambleside. Built in 1623, it was the home of the Browne family of yeoman farmers until 1944 and, as a National Trust property since then, very little has been changed. Visitors can see the simple oak furniture accumulated over the generations, much of it made by the Brownes themselves, a library which reflects the family's literary tastes, old domestic utensils and 18th-century fabrics woven on local looms.

Giant Galapagos tortoise on display at the Zoological Museum, Tring.

Trowbridge

Trowbridge Museum

Town Hall, Trowbridge, Wiltshire BA14 8EQ
    ☎ *02214 65072*
Tues 9.30–12; Sat 9.30–12.30
𝕏 *Assistant Curator*
F **⚊**

The Museum contains a collection illustrating
the history of Trowbridge and Wiltshire since
the 18th century. The exhibits include portraits
and topographical paintings and prints,
together with household objects, children's toys
and educational games preserved by the Reeves
and Whittaker families of Bratton over the past
200 years, and historical items from the Sir Isaac
Pitman collection, on loan from the University
of Bath and displayed here.

Truro

Cornwall County Museum

The Royal Institution of Cornwall, River Street,
    Truro, Cornwall TR1 2SJ ☎ *0872 72205*
Mon–Sat 9–5. Closed Bank Holiday.
𝕏 *The Curator*
£ **⚋** **⚊**

The Royal Institution of Cornwall was founded
in 1818 and sponsored a museum almost from
the beginning. The Institution has occupied its
present building since 1919 and continues to be
responsible for the Museum, although it now
receives substantial local authority support. The
general emphasis of the collections is on the
archaeology and history of Cornwall. The
Rashleigh collection of Cornish minerals is
internationally famous and so, too, is the De
Pass collection of English and Continental
master-drawings. The fine art collection
includes paintings by the Cornish artists, Henry
Bone and John Opie, and there are also displays
of Japanese ivories and lacquer, scrimshaw,
pewter and English pottery and porcelain.

Tuam

Tuam Mill Museum

Shop Street, Tuam, Co. Galway, Ireland
    ☎ *093 24463*
𝕏 *The Secretary*
£ **⬛** **⚊**

The 19th-century water-powered Bridge Mill at
Tuam was operated for generations by members
of the Farrell family. It was renovated in 1944
and additional storeys added. It was saved from
demolition in the 1970s and a conservation
project, instituted by the Christian Brothers'
School at Tuam, has converted it into a working
museum of milling in Ireland. The displays, in
the former miller's house, include working
models of different types of mill and a selection
of quernstones used locally.

Tullow

Tullow Museum

Bridge Street, Tullow, Co. Carlow, Ireland
    ☎ *0503 51702*
Sun & Bank Holiday, 2–5.30. Other times by appt
    for parties.
𝕏 *The Secretary, Tullowphelim Historical Society,*
    12 St Patrick's Park, Tullow
F **⚋** **⚊**

Tullow Museum, administered by the
Tullowphelim Historical Society, was opened in
1985 in a former Methodist Church. The
displays illustrate the history of the area and
include domestic equipment, agricultural tools
and railway relics. Among the more notable
exhibits are Cardinal Newman's prie dieu and
buttons, dated 1800, from the uniform of the
huntsmen of the Tallow Hunt, the first of its
kind in Ireland.

Tully

The Irish Horse Museum

Irish National Stud, Tully, Co. Kildare, Ireland
    ☎ *045 21251*
Easter–Oct, Mon–Fri 10.30–5; Sat 10.30–5.30;
    Sun 2–5.30
𝕏 *Tourism Supervisor*   ☎ *045 21617*
£ **⬛** **⬛** **⚊**

The Museum is in the grounds of the Irish
National Stud and occupies a building
converted from a groom's house and some old
stallion boxes, in which Tulyar and Royal
Charger, two of the Stud's most famous
stallions, once lived. The displays illustrate the
history of the horse and its uses in Ireland since
prehistoric times. The exhibits include an old
weighing-in chair from the Curragh racecourse,
racing trophies, and the skeleton of the famous
and much-loved steeplechaser, Arkle.

Barge-ware teapot from Polperro, 1798.
Truro, Cornwall County Museum.

Tunbridge Wells

Tunbridge Wells Museum and Art Gallery

Civic Centre, Mount Pleasant, Tunbridge Wells,
    Kent TN1 1RS   ☎ 0892 26121 extn 171
Mon–Fri 10–5.30; Sat 9.30–5. Closed Bank
    Holiday Mon and Tues, and Easter Sat.
⊠ Dr M. A. V. Gill, Curator
Ⓕ ⬙ ⬥ □

Within the general framework of local
archaeology and history, the Museum has
sections devoted to Tunbridge ware, Wealden
ironwork, treen, agricultural implements,
craftsmen's tools and domestic equipment.
There are also collections of costume, dolls and
toys, and specimens illustrating the natural
history of the area.
    The Art Gallery contains the Ashton bequest
of Victorian paintings, prints and drawings, and
collages by Pamela McDowall.

Tunstall

Chatterley Whitfield Mining Museum

Tunstall, Stoke-on-Trent, Staffordshire ST6 8UN
    ☎ 0782 813337
Mar–Sept, daily 10–4. Oct–Feb, Sun–Fri 10–4.
    Last pit tour 3.30.
⊠ Mr P. Gifford
Ⓔ ⬤ ⬛ ⬥ ⬦

Chatterley Whitfield Colliery was worked from
1860 to 1976. A number of the surface
installations have been preserved, including the
lamp-room, canteen, and the steam winding
engine, which raised coal up the 2,000-foot
deep Hesketh shaft. Visitors descend the 700-
foot Winstanley shaft, where they are guided
around the workings by former miners and
shown reconstructed scenes of miners at work,
illustrating the different methods of extraction
used over the past 150 years.

Stationery box of Tunbridge ware by Thomas
Barton, about 1850. Tunbridge Wells Museum
and Art Gallery.

Turriff

Session Cottage

Castle Hill, Turriff, Aberdeenshire
June–Aug, Sat, Sun 2.30–4.30. Other times
    by appt.
⊠ Miss A. E. Cormack, Kemeri, 22 Westfield
    Road, Turriff AB5 7AF   ☎ 0888 63451
Ⓔ

The Museum of the Turriff & District Heritage
Society is housed in an early 18th-century
kitchen and parlour ('but 'n ben'), with a box
bed. The exhibits, donated by local people,
illustrate the traditional life of the district, and
are particularly strong on domestic items.

Turton

Turton Tower

Chapeltown Tower, Turton, nr Bolton, Lancashire
    BL7 0HG   ☎ 0204 852203
Sat–Wed & Bank Holiday 12–5.
    Closed Dec 25, 26, Jan 1.
⊠ The Keeper
Ⓔ ⬙ ⬥

The Tower is one and a half miles north of
Bromley Cross on the B6391 Chapeltown road.
Built in the early 15th century, it had an extra
storey and a porch added before 1600. The
building received a new lease of life when, in
1835, it was bought by James Kay, a Manchester
cotton manufacturer, who extended and
refurbished it. In 1930 it became the property of
a local trust.
    It now contains collections of 17th-century
oak furniture, 17th-century portraits, weapons,
armour and domestic metalwork, displayed in
period settings.

Twickenham

Marble Hill House

Richmond Road, Twickenham, Middlesex
    TW1 2NL   ☎ 01 892 5115
Feb–Oct, Sat–Thurs 10–5. Nov–Jan, Sat–Thurs
    10–4. Closed Dec 24, 25.
⊠ Julius Bryant, Curator
Ⓕ ⬙ ⬛ ⬥ ⬧ ⬢

Marble Hill House was laid out in 1724–9 as a
summer residence for Henrietta Howard,
mistress of George II and later Countess of
Suffolk. The grounds were laid out according to
the advice of Alexander Pope. The house was
later altered and in the 1790s it was occupied for
a short time by another Royal mistress, Mrs
Fitzherbert. In the 19th century it was for many
years the home of General Peel, brother of the
Prime Minister.
    In 1901 a group of local authorities and
preservation societies bought the house and
grounds in order to protect the site from
development. After the Second World War, it
was restored to its original condition by the
Greater London Council and re-opened to the

public in 1966. It is now the responsibility of English Heritage. The furniture includes the Northey Suite, with its original needlework, and there are a number of paintings representative of Lady Suffolk's period, including *Le Lecteur* by Gravelot, a Reynolds portrait, and Richard Wilson's *The Thames at Marble Hill.*

'Le Lecteur' by Hubert Gravelot, about 1745. Twickenham, Marble Hill House.

Museum of the Royal Military School of Music, Kneller Hall

Royal Military School of Music, Kneller Hall, Twickenham, Middlesex TW2 7DU
☎ 01 898 5533
Mon–Fri, by appt only
🖾 *Lt. Col. (Retd) G. E. Evans, Curator*
Ⓔ ◇ ✍

Kneller Hall was formerly the country mansion of Sir Godfrey Kneller (1646–1723), Court painter to Charles II, William III and George I. The collection in the Museum contains instruments, mainly wind instruments, used by military bands since 1780.

Orleans House Gallery

Riverside, Twickenham, Middlesex TW9 3DJ
☎ 01 892 0221
Apr–Sept, Tues–Sat 1–5.30; Sun & Bank Holiday 2–5.30. Oct–Mar, Tues–Sat 1–4.30; Sun & Bank Holiday 2–4.30. Garden: daily–sunset.
🖾 *Assistant Curator*
Ⓕ ◇ ✍

The Octagon at Orleans House, a Grade I listed building, was designed by James Gibb and completed *c*. 1720. It is especially noteworthy for its baroque decoration, and now contains an exhibition of 18th and 19th-century paintings, watercolours and engravings of Richmond and Twickenham.

The Bluebell Railway, Uckfield.

Tywyn

Narrow Gauge Railway Museum

Wharf Station, Tywyn, Gwynedd LL36 9EY
☎ 0654 710472
Easter–Oct opens when morning trains run on the Talyllyn Railway. Other times by appt. Closed Dec 25.
🖾 *General Manager*
Ⓔ ▮ ▆ ✍

The Museum, in a modern industrial-type building, is alongside the platform at Talyllyn Railway Wharf Station, from which a daily service of steam trains operates. The collection includes locomotives, rolling stock and other equipment from narrow gauge railways in Great Britain and Ireland. One gallery is devoted to the Welsh slate industry and its railways and ports. Special features include the development of the permanent way and signalling on narrow gauge railways, with a collection of single line control apparatus displayed in a replica signal-box. Also on show are posters, signs, tickets and timetables, together with nameplates from locomotives long since scrapped.

Uckfield

Bluebell Railway

Sheffield Park Station, nr Uckfield, East Sussex TN22 3QL   ☎ 082572 2370
Jan–Feb, Dec, Sun. Mar–Apr, Nov, Sat, Sun. May, Oct, Wed, Sat, Sun. June–Sept, daily.
🖾 *Traffic Manager*
Ⓔ *Travel ticket only* ▮ ▆ ✍

Sheffield Park Station is on the A275 between East Grinstead and Lewes. The Bluebell Railway was originally part of the line connecting East Grinstead and Lewes, which was opened in

1882 and closed by British Rail in 1958. The Bluebell Railway Preservation Society was formed in the following year and ran its first steam-hauled train in 1960. Since then it has built up an impressive collection of locomotives and rolling stock, with Horsted Keynes Station restored to its Southern Railway condition and Sheffield Park maintained in the Victorian style of the London, Brighton and South Coast Railway. On platform 2 at Sheffield Park there is a museum housing an extensive collection of railway relics and mementoes, most of them relating to lines in the South of England.

Uffculme

Coldharbour Mill

Uffculme, Cullompton, Devon EX15 3EE
☎ 0884 40960/40858
Easter–Oct, Sun–Fri 10.30–5. Oct–Easter
  by appt. Last admission 4.15.
▣ Education Officer
Ⓔ ▪ ▆ ➼

The Mill is two miles from Junction 27 on the M5. During the 18th century the mill on the site was used first as a paper mill and then, after damage from a flood, was rebuilt as a grist mill. In 1797 it was bought by Thomas Fox, a Wellington woollen manufacturer, who needed a new source of water power for the expansion of his business. His new factory, by the side of the mill, continued in production until 1981.

The factory has now been converted into a working museum, with the original machinery. Visitors can watch the whole process of woollen manufacture from fleece to woven cloth or knitting wool. The 18-foot breast-shot waterwheel, used until 1978, can still be seen, as can the 300 horse-power steam engine, which worked from 1910 to 1981 and is still regularly run under steam.

Around the factory yard are a dye-house, dye-plant garden and weaver's workshop, which recall Devon's woollen trade before the coming of mechanisation. A re-created carpenter's shop uses steam power to drive the woodworking machines.

Uffington

Tom Brown School Museum

Broad Street, Uffington, Faringdon, Oxfordshire
  SN7 7RA
Easter Sat–last weekend in Sept, Sat, Sun &
  Bank Holiday 2–5
▣ Mr J. E. Little, The Pantiles, Uffington,
  Faringdon, Oxfordshire SN7 7RY
Ⓔ ex. children ✍ ➼

The Museum is housed in a 17th-century schoolroom, which has the date 1617 over the door. It concentrates especially on the life and work of the author of Tom Brown's Schooldays, Thomas Hughes (1822–96), who was born in Uffington. Much of the material for this exhibition has been made available by members of the Hughes family. Other sections of the

Museum are devoted to the Uffington White Horse, Roman artefacts discovered during the building of new houses in the village, craftsmen's tools, agricultural implements and 17th-century trade tokens. There are also photographs of cottages and village life taken at the turn of the century, mementoes of the First and Second World Wars, and equipment from Uffington signal-box, demolished in 1965.

Ullapool

Lochbroom Museum

Ullapool, Ross-shire   ☎ 0854 2356
Apr–Sept, daily 9–5
▣ Lady Troughton, c/o The Captain's Cabin,
  Ullapool, Ross-shire
Ⓕ ➼

The Museum building was erected in 1760 as the headquarters of The British Society for Extending Fisheries and Improving the Sea-Coasts of this Kingdom. The displays present specimens of local wildlife and rocks, as well as material illustrating the history and traditional culture of the area.

Ulverston

The Laurel and Hardy Museum

4a Upper Brook Street, Ulverston, Cumbria
  LA12 7BQ   ☎ 0229 52292
Mon, Tues, Thurs–Sat 10–4.30
▣ Bill Cubin, Curator
Ⓔ ▪ ➼ ♿ ⬛

The Museum contains the largest collection in the world of material relating to the American comedians, Stan Laurel and Oliver Hardy. In addition to photographs, letters and press cuttings, there are a number of the two men's personal possessions, as well as items which belonged to Laurel's father, Arthur Jefferson.

The Curator provides personal tours of the exhibits and visitors are also able to see some of the 80 Laurel and Hardy films held in the archive. Sound tapes are also available.

Stott Park Bobbin Mill

Finsthwaite, Newby Bridge, Via Ulverston,
  Cumbria LA12 8AX   ☎ 0448 31087
Apr–Sept, Mon–Sat 9.30–6.30; Sun 2–6.30.
  Pre-booked parties during winter months.
▣ Mr J. Dixon
Ⓔ ex. children ✍ ➼

Stott Park is on the road between Newby Bridge and Hawkshead, along the western shore of Windermere. It was built as a bobbin mill in 1835 and was in use until 1971. Now operated as a working museum, it illustrates not only all the processes involved in the manufacture of bobbins, but also the woodland-based economy of the Furness Fells. Bobbin-turning was the one skilled woodland industry it proved possible to mechanise. The steam-driven machinery at the Mill, regularly demonstrated, includes a turbine, steam engine, line shafting and lathes. Visitors are made aware of the cold, dirty, noisy and dangerous working conditions which existed at the Mill before the Factory Acts and the Health and Safety at Work regulations came into force.

Swarthmoor Hall

nr Ulverston, Cumbria　　☎ *0229 53204*
Mar 15–Oct 13, Mon–Wed, Sat 10–12, 2–5.
　Thurs, Sun by appt.
✗ *The Secretary*
F ♿

The Hall, which dates from the early 17th century, now belongs to the Society of Friends. George Fox stayed here at intervals for much of his adult life and there is a balcony from which he used to preach to people assembled in the garden below. It was restored in 1912 and is furnished in 17th-century style, with loan items, gifts and pieces original to the house.

Upminster

Upminster Tithe Barn Agricultural and Folk Museum

Hall Lane, Upminster, Essex RM14 1AU
1st weekend of each month between Apr & Oct,
　1.30–6
✗ *Mr P. M. Butler, Little Silvers, 7 Mendoza*
　Close, Hornchurch, Essex RM11 2RP
　☎ *04024 47535*
F ✍ ♿

The barn, 138 feet long and 40 feet wide, dates from the 15th century. It was renovated and re-thatched during the 1970s. The main collections of the Museum now housed in the barn are of agricultural implements, craftsmen's tools, domestic equipment, locally made bricks and the products of Wedlake's iron foundries at Hornchurch. There is also a display of old photographs of the Upminster area.

Upper Dicker

Michelham Priory

Upper Dicker, nr Hailsham, East Sussex
　BN27 3QS　　☎ *0323 844224*
Mar 25–Oct, daily 11–5.30
✗ *The Administrator*
£ ♨ ☕ ♿ &

Two thirds of the Priory, founded in 1229, were totally destroyed at the time of the Dissolution of the Monasteries in 1536. Later in the century the remaining monastic buildings were repaired and incorporated into two houses which were constructed against them, and the whole 1,000-acre estate then became a working farm. The Child family were tenants from 1791 to 1861 and there is a display of their papers and letters in the Priory. The buildings have been considerably restored and rearranged internally during the present century.

Now the property of the Sussex Archaeological Society, the house contains period furniture, ironwork and domestic fittings, 13th to 20th-century stained glass, tapestries and tapestry cartoons, seals, and the Alice Schuhmann Frank collection of ethnic musical instruments. There is also an embroidery room and a collection of 18th to 20th-century watercolours of Sussex scenes.

The extensive grounds contain a restored and working watermill, producing wholemeal flour, and a wheelwright's and blacksmith's display. The 16th-century barn houses art exhibitions. A number of Sussex wagons and ploughs are on show, and an exhibit telling the story of the Hailsham rope and twine industry.

Upton

British Horological Institute Collection

Upton Hall, Upton, Newark, Nottinghamshire
　NG23 5TE　　☎ *0636 813795/6*
By appt for groups. Also open occasional Exhibition
　Days.
✗ *Mrs B. M. Baker*
£ ✍ ☕ ♿

Upton Hall is on the A612 Nottingham road. Built in 1828 and remodelled and extended later in the century, it is now the property of the British Horological Institute, which uses it as its headquarters and training centre. It contains an extensive collection of historic clocks, watches and horological tools.

Advertisement for Bill Cubin's Laurel and Hardy Museum at Ulverston in the Lake District.

Usk

Gwent Rural Life Museum

*The Malt Barn, New Market Street, Usk, Gwent
    NP5 1AU
Mar & Oct, Mon–Fri 10–12.30, 2–5; Sun 2–5.
    Apr–Sept, Mon–Fri 10–12.30, 2–5; Sat, Sun
    2–5. Nov–Feb, Mon–Fri 10–12.30, 2–5.*
◪ *Mrs S. M. Williams, 14 St Cybi Avenue,
    Llangybi, Usk NP5 1TT*   ☎ *063349 315*
Ⓔ ⌽ ↩

The earliest-known record of the Malt Barn,
which houses the Museum, is 1791, but much of
the structure appears to be older. It was probably
a storehouse for the Maltster's House next door.
The collections reflect the rural past of Gwent,
from about 1850 onwards, and include
agricultural implements and vehicles – there are
fine examples of both the Monmouthshire and
the Glamorgan wagon – craftsmen's tools,
cooking utensils and a wide range of household
items, including two wooden washing
machines.
    This is a private museum, run by the Rural
Crafts Preservation Society on a voluntary basis.

Valentia Island

Valentia Island Museum

Valentia Island, Co. Kerry, Ireland
    ☎ *0667 6132*
June–Sept, daily 2–5. Other times by appt.
◪ *Tessa O'Connor, Hon. Secretary*
Ⓔ ⌽ ↩

The Museum occupies the former National
School building, opened in 1861. Its exhibits
illustrate the history of life in the area. There
are reconstructions of a country kitchen, a
forge, a school room and a shop, and displays
showing settlement patterns, the strategic
significance of Valentia, traditions and customs.
Special attention is given to the development of
Valentia as the European terminal of the
transatlantic cable link in 1858, Valentia
Observatory, the commercial and artistic uses of
Valentia slate and the marine biology of the
district.
    Other items featured are the 18th-century
Erasmus Smith School, the 1933 Italian air
armada and other pioneering air exploits
associated with Valentia, Valentia Wireless
Station (1911), and the sub-tropical gardens of
Glanleam House, the former seat of the Knights
of Kerry.

Ventnor

Museum of Smuggling History

*Botanic Garden, Ventnor, Isle of Wight
    PO38 1UL*   ☎ *0983 853677*
Good Fri–Sept, daily 10–5.30
◪ *The Secretary*
Ⓔ ⓐ ⌽ ⬛ ⌗ ↩

The Museum is one mile west of Ventnor, on
the A3055. Housed in underground vaults, it
shows a wide range of the methods used by
smugglers over a period of 700 years. The
displays cover personalities of the trade,
smuggling episodes and techniques for avoiding
duty and import prohibitions on wool, brandy,
silks, tobacco, tea, gold, watches, drugs and
many other commodities.

Virkie

Jarlshof Museum

Sumburgh Head, Virkie, Shetland Isles
    ☎ *99 60112*
*Apr–Sept, Mon, Thurs–Sat 9.30–7; Wed 9.30–2;
    Sun 2–7. Oct–Mar, Mon, Thurs–Sat 9.30–4;
    Wed 9.30–1; Sun 2–4.*
◪ *The Custodian*
Ⓔ ⌽ ↩ ▦

The area contains the excavated remains of Iron
Age, Bronze Age, Viking and 16th-century
dwellings, illustrating continuous settlement
over a period of nearly 200 years. The Museum
displays stone and bone artefacts found on the
site and dating from 1500 B.C. onwards.

Wakefield

Elizabethan Exhibition Gallery

Brook Street, Wakefield, West Yorkshire
    ☎ *0924 370211 extn 540*
*Mon–Sat 10.30–12.30, 1.30–5. Closed Bank
    holidays and between exhibitions.*
◪ *See Wakefield Art Gallery*
Ⓕ ⌽ ↩ ☐

The main hall of the Gallery was built in the
late 16th century and was the original Free
Grammar School of the City of Wakefield. It
was restored and converted to its present
purpose during the late 1970s and now
accommodates changing exhibitions of art,
crafts, photography, history, archaeology and
science, some organised by Wakefield Museums
and Art Galleries and some brought in from the
Arts Council of Great Britain and other sources.

Nostell Priory

Doncaster Road, Nostell, Wakefield, West
    Yorkshire WF4 1QD   ☎ 0924 863892
Mar–June & Sept–Oct, Sat 12–5; Sun 11–5.
    July–Aug, Mon–Thurs, Sat 12–5; Sun 11–5.
    Parties at other times by appt.
◪ *The Administrator*
Ⓔ 🪑 🍴 🅿 ♿ 🚌 NT

Nostell Priory is six miles south-east of
Wakefield, north of the A638. Now a National
Trust property, it has been the home of the
Winn family since 1654. The present house was
mostly built between 1733 and 1785, the north
wing being completed later by Robert Adam. It
is famous for its Chippendale furniture,
Chippendale having spent his early life nearby
at Otley. An interesting item is the celebrated
Nostell dolls' house, probably Chippendale's
earliest surviving work, which exactly copies the
earlier 18th-century furniture, silver and
decorations previously in the house. There is
also a remarkable long case clock, made in 1717
by the great John Harrison, son of the estate
carpenter at Nostell. The works are almost
entirely of wood and the pendulum rod is the
earliest recorded use of mahogany in England.
    Although this is a National Trust property, its
management and presentation is entirely the
responsibility of Lord St Oswald, who lives here.

Stephen G. Beaumont Museum

Stanley Royd Hospital, Aberford Road, Wakefield,
    West Yorkshire WF1 4DQ   ☎ 0924 375217
Wed 10–1, 1.30–4, by appt
◪ *Unit General Manager*
Ⓕ 🚌

Stanley Royd Hospital is a mile from the centre
of Wakefield, on the A642 Leeds road. The
Museum is in the 1849 extension of the original
1818 Pauper Lunatic Asylum, the sixth in the
country to be built under Wynn's 1808 Act, and
one of the few remaining which are still
operating from the original buildings.
    The collection shows the progress over more
than a century and a half of treatment for the
mentally ill. It contains a scale model of the
1818 building, medical and surgical instruments
associated with treatment, instruments of
restraint and protective measures for staff, as
well as tools and equipment used in tailoring,
brewing and other practical activities in the
Hospital.

Wakefield Art Gallery

Wentworth Terrace, Wakefield, West Yorkshire
    WF1 3QW   ☎ 0924 370211 extn 8031
Mon–Sat 10.30–12.30, 1.30–5. Closed public &
    local government holidays.
◪ *Mrs G. Spencer*
Ⓕ ✏ 🚌

The building, which dates from 1885, was
formerly a vicarage. It has good plasterwork and
fine decorative glass panels on the main
staircase. It became an art gallery in 1934. The
emphasis of the collections is on 20th-century
paintings and sculpture, but Edwardian,
Victorian and earlier artists are well
represented. Special rooms are devoted to
Barbara Hepworth, born and brought up in
Wakefield, and to Henry Moore, a native of
nearby Castleford. The Gallery holds some
outstanding works by both these artists.
    Some of the Barbara Hepworth sculptures are
placed in the garden around the Gallery, where
there are also works by Austin Wright and Kim
Lim.

Wakefield Museum

Wood Street, Wakefield, West Yorkshire
    WF1 3QW   ☎ 0924 370211 extn 7190
Mon–Sat 10.30–12.30, 1.30–5. Closed Bank
    holidays.
◪ *See Wakefield Art Gallery*
Ⓕ ✏ 🚌

The Museum building, which dates from
1820–3, was originally a Music Saloon and
Public Rooms. It later became a Mechanics
Institution. The ground floor displays illustrate
the history of the Wakefield area from
prehistoric times to the present day, and include
finds and models relating to Roman Castleford,
Sandal Castle and the 17th-century potteries at
Wrenthorpe.
    The Waterton Collection consists of exotic
birds and animals collected in South America
and elsewhere by the early 19th-century
traveller and naturalist, Charles Waterton, who
lived close by, at Walton Hall.

Walkerburn

The Scottish Museum of Woollen Textiles

Tweedvale Mills, Walkerburn, Peeblesshire
    EH43 6AH   ☎ 089687 281/283
Mon–Sat 9.30–5. Summer months, also Sun
    12.30–4.30.
◪ *Mr A. Cameron*
Ⓔ 🪑 ♿ 🚌

The Museum was created to show how woollen
manufacturing has developed from its
beginnings as a cottage industry. There is an old
weaver's cottage and weaver's shed, with
appropriate furnishings and equipment, together
with examples of 18th to 20th-century wool and
cloth patterns.

Elmwood reclining figure by Henry Moore,
1936. Wakefield Art Gallery.

Wallasey

Wallasey Museum and Exhibition Centre

Central Library, Earlston Road, Wallasey,
*   Merseyside*   ☎ 051 639 2334
Mon–Fri 10–8; Sat 10–1, 2–5
Ñ *Chief Librarian*
F ☛ □

Wallasey Central Library has within its building
a large display area, where temporary
exhibitions are arranged of items from the
Wallasey Reference Collections, Wallasey Art
Groups, Wallasey Historical Society and from
national bodies. Since the reorganisation of
local government in 1974, the Museum's
permanent collection comes under the authority
of the Williamson Art Gallery and Museum in
Birkenhead.

Wallingford

Wallingford Museum

Flint House, High Street, Wallingford, Oxfordshire
*   OX10 0DB*   ☎ 0491 35065
Mar–Nov, Tues–Fri & Bank Holiday Mon 2–5;
*   Sat 10.30–12.30 and 2–5.*
June–Aug, also Sun 2–5.
Ñ *Mrs J. Dewey*
£ *ex. children* ♡ ☛

Wallingford Museum, in part of a 15th-century
hall-house, concentrates on the history of the
town. Most of the items in the collection date
from the 19th and 20th centuries, but there is
also earlier material, ranging from pagan Saxon
grave goods to Civil War relics. The displays
include a carefully researched model of
Wallingford Castle, the original having been
demolished on the orders of Cromwell and, in
its heyday, one of the strongest and most
important in England.

Three special exhibitions a year are arranged,
one about a village in the area, one specialising
in a particular aspect of Wallingford's history,
and the third on a theme not necessarily related
to local history and sometimes provided by an
individual or an outside group.

Walmer

Walmer Castle

Dover Road, Walmer, Kent   ☎ 0304 364288
Mar 29–Oct 14, Tues–Sun 9.30–6.30.
*   Oct 15–Mar 28, Tues–Sat 9.30–4; Sun 2–4.*
*   Open Bank Holiday Mon. Closed Dec 24–26,*
*   Jan 1 and when the Lord Warden is in*
*   residence.*
Ñ *Historic Buildings & Monuments Commission,*
*   Tunbridge Wells*   ☎ 0892 48166
£ ♡ ☛ EH

Walmer Castle was built on the orders of Henry
VIII. It is in the shape of a Tudor rose and is
celebrated for its gardens. Since the 18th
century, it has been the official home of the
Lords Warden of the Cinque Ports. In their

capacity as Warden, Pitt, Wellington,
Palmerston and Churchill lived here from
time to time and Wellington died in the Castle.
Queen Victoria and Prince Albert were also
among the Castle's temporary residents.

There are a number of fine period pieces
among the furnishings and memorabilia and
personal possessions of the Wardens have been
preserved, including clothing and a camp bed
belonging to Wellington, and Pitt's reading
stool.

Walsall

Jerome K. Jerome Birthplace Museum

Belsize House, Bradford Street, Walsall, West
*   Midlands WS1 1PN*
Tues–Sat 10–5
Ñ *See Walsall Museum and Art Gallery*
F ●

The author of *Three Men in a Boat* was born here
in 1859. The house has been recently renovated
and two rooms arranged as a Jerome museum.
One of these contains displays about the writer's
life and achievements and the other has been
reconstructed as a parlour of the 1850s, to give
the impression of what the interior of a middle-
class Walsall town house of the period looked
like.

Among the Jerome memorabilia on show are
his pens, inkwell, cigarette case and walking
stick.

Maple Brook Pumping Station

Rugeley Road, Burntwood, Walsall, West Midlands
By appt
Ñ *Operations Manager, South Staffordshire*
*   Waterworks Company, Green Lane, Walsall*
*   WS2 7PD*   ☎ 0922 38282
F ☛

The Pumping Station is on the road between
Boney Hall and Chorley in South Staffordshire.
It preserves one of the two original steam
pumps. It is an inverted, triple expansion,
surface condensing rotative pumping engine,
with flywheels at each end. Built by Galloway
Ltd, it was commissioned in 1915 and developed
225 horse-power.

Walsall Museum and Art Gallery

Lichfield Street, Walsall, West Midlands WS1 1TR
*   ☎ 0922 21244 extn 3124/3115*
Mon–Fri 10–6; Sat 10–4.45. Closed Bank
*   Holiday.*
Ñ *Keeper of Local History (Museum) or Keeper*
*   of Fine Art (Art Gallery)*
F ♡ ☛ &

Walsall Art Gallery contains the German-Ryan
Collection, donated by Lady Kathleen Epstein,
the nucleus of which is composed of important
works by her husband, the sculptor, Sir Jacob
Epstein. Among the remainder of the collection
are pieces by Epstein's friends, relations,
colleagues and acquaintances, including

**'Annabel' by Lucian Freud (b.1922).
Walsall Museum and Art Gallery.**

Picasso, Braque, Matthew Smith and Lucien
Freud. Most of the items date from the late 19th
to early 20th century, but there are a number of
earlier works, notably Dürer woodcuts and
Rembrandt drawings.

The Museum uses a selection of its extensive
local history collection to illustrate the origins
and development of Walsall and to show what it
was like to live in the town in the past. There is
good coverage of Walsall's major trades,
saddlery and leatherworking and lorinery
(saddlers' ironmongery) and, at the branch
museum at Willenhall, lock-making.

Waltham Abbey

Epping Forest District Museum

*39–41 Sun Street, Waltham Abbey, Essex
    EN9 1EL*   ☎ 0992 716882
*Fri–Mon 2–5; Tues 12–5. Closed Dec 25, 26,
    Jan 1.*
◪ *Mrs J. Stephens, Assistant Curator*
Ⓕ 🏛 🖼 🚪

The Museum occupies two adjoining timber-
framed buildings, the first dating from 1520 and
the second from 1760. The displays illustrate
the history of the Epping Forest district from
prehistoric times to the 20th century.

Special features of the Museum are the Tudor
herb garden and fine oak panelling, carved
during the reign of Henry VIII and on loan
from the Victoria & Albert Museum. There is a
developing collection of objects, documents,
photographs and pictures relating to the social
history of the area. A selection of these can
always be seen in the Museum.

The Museum organises an annual 'Art in
Essex' exhibition of work by artists living or
working in the county. Items selected from
these exhibitions form the basis of the Museum's
collection of contemporary art.

Wanlockhead

Museum of Scottish Lead Mining

*Goldscaur Row, Wanlockhead, By Biggar,
    Lanarkshire ML12 6UP*   ☎ 06594 387
Easter–Sept, daily 11–4 (last mine tour 3.30)
◪ *Wanlockhead Museum Trust*
Ⓔ 🗒 🚪

Wanlockhead, in the Lowther Hills, is
Scotland's highest village. It is reached from the
A76 via the Mennock Pass, or the A74 via
Abington or Elvanfoot. The Mining Museum
contains relics of 250 years of lead mining in the
area, including machinery, tools and
equipment. There are also displays of maps,
documents, photographs and models, and of
gold, silver and minerals mined locally.
Reconstructions of a miner's kitchen and
miners' library (1756) illustrate social and family
life in the mining community.

The open-air section of the Museum includes
Loch Nell, a drift mine worked from the early
1700s to 1860, the Wanlockhead beam engine,
Pates Knowes, a smelt-mill which operated from
1764 to 1842, and the workshops and forge at
the Bay Mine, where William Symington
assembled his first atmospheric steamboat
engine in 1788.

Wantage

Vale and Downland Museum Centre

*The Old Surgery, Church Street, Wantage,
    Oxfordshire OX12 8BL*   ☎ 02357 66838
*Tues–Sat 10.30–4.30; Sun 2–5.
    Closed Dec 24–26.*
◪ *The Administrator*
Ⓕ 🏛 🖼 🚪 ♿

The core of the Museum building is a 17th-
century house, originally occupied by a cloth
merchant and built in the local blue and red
brick style. An extension has been added to
accommodate museum displays and visitor
services. The displays provide an interpretation
of the landscape and history of the Vale of the
White Horse. Sections are devoted to the
function of Wantage as a market town and to
the industries and trades which serve the rural

**The Long Gallery display at Epping Forest
District Museum, Waltham Abbey.**

population, particular attention being given to milling, malting, wool, tanning and blacksmithing.

Reconstructions of a Downland farmhouse kitchen and dairy give an impression of the once widespread dairying industry of the Vale. The reconstructed Downland barn houses the Museum's collection of agricultural equipment, farm wagons and a locally made threshing machine. Future developments will show what the area is like in the 20th century and trace the effects of wartime activity, the changes in transport and agriculture, new industries and housing.

Wareham

Clouds Hill
Wareham, Dorset BH20 7NQ
Apr–Sept, Wed–Fri, Sun & Bank Holiday Mon 2–5. Oct–Mar, Sun 1–4.
⚑ *National Trust Regional Office, Warminster*
☎ *0747 840224*
[£] [NT]

Clouds Hill, now a National Trust property, was bought by T. E. Lawrence (Lawrence of Arabia) when he rejoined the R.A.F. in 1929. His books are no longer here, but the cottage is otherwise as he left it, with its furniture and fittings intact. It contains photographs taken by Lawrence in the desert in 1916–17 and drawings of him by Eric Kennington and Augustus John.

The cottage is one mile north of Bovington Camp and seven miles west of Wareham.

Wareham Town Museum
East Street, Wareham, Dorset BH20 4NP
☎ *09295 3006*
Good Fri–mid Oct, Mon–Sat 10–1, 2–5
⚑ *The Curator, 12 East Street, Wareham*
☎ *09295 2771*
[F] [◌] [♿]

The Museum's principal displays are concerned with the natural history of the area and with the history of Wareham since Roman times. There are special exhibits relating to the 1762 Fire of Wareham and to coins minted in the town. T. E. Lawrence, who lived near Wareham, is commemorated by a collection of photographs illustrating his life and achievements.

Warley

Avery Historical Museum
W. & T. Avery Ltd, Foundry Lane, Smethwick, Warley, West Midlands B66 2LP
☎ *021 558 1112*
Wed, Thurs 9–3.30, by appt only
⚑ *The Curator*
[F] [♿]

The Museum contains collections illustrating the history of weighing, housed in a building of the Soho Foundry, which has associations with Boulton, Watt and Murdock. There are

examples of the basic types of weights and weighing devices and an archive of documents on the development of weighing techniques.

Warminster

The Dewey Museum
The Library, Three Horse Shoes Mall, Warminster, Wiltshire BA12 9BT **☎** *0985 216022*
Mon 2–5; Tues 10–5; Thurs, Fri 10–8; Sat 9–4. Closed Bank Holiday.
⚑ *Hon. Curator, Mr R. J. Field, Trinity Cottage, 16 Vicarage Street, Warminster BA12 8JE*
[£] [♿]

The Museum collections reflect mainly the social history of Warminster and the surrounding area. There are, in addition, exhibits which illustrate the geology of the area.

Longleat House
Warminster, Wiltshire BA12 7NN **☎** *09853 551*
Easter–Oct, daily 10–6. Nov–Easter, daily 10–4. Closed Dec 25.
⚑ *Caroline Stansbie, Bookings Secretary*
[£] [🍴] [🅿] [♿] [HHA]

Longleat House, the home of the Thynne family for over 400 years, is midway between Frome and Warminster on the A362. It was built over a long period, between 1547 and the early 1580s, and the exterior has remained largely unchanged since then, although it has been considerably altered internally, both by the 2nd Marquess of Bath between 1806 and 1818 and later in the century by the 4th Marquess.

The ornate Drawing Room of Longleat House, Warminster.

There is a notable library of over 30,000 volumes, and fine collections of English and French furniture, Brussels, French and Flemish tapestries, clocks and porcelain, together with Italian, Dutch, English and Flemish paintings and a large number of family portraits. The Dress Corridor displays dresses and robes worn by the Marquesses and Marchionesses of Bath

on important occasions, including every
Coronation since that of George IV. The family
State Coach, displayed at the foot of the Grand
Staircase, dates from *c*. 1750 and was last used at
the Coronation of Queen Elizabeth II. The
elaborate Family Tree, from 1215 to the present
day, hangs in the Entrance Hall.

Weapons Museum

School of Infantry, Warminster, Wiltshire
*   BA12 0DJ   ☎ 0985 214000 extn 2487*
Mon–Fri 10.30–12.30, 2–4, by appt. Sat, Sun &
*   public holidays, parties only, by appt.*
⋈ *The Curator*
F ✐ ⚲

The Museum is on the Imber road out of
Warminster. It has an interesting history. In
1853 the School of Musketry was set up at
Hythe in Kent, in order to instruct the British
Army in the scientific use of the rifle, which was
coming into general use in place of the
inaccurate smoothbore musket. All new
weapons were sent to the School to be tested,
and these, together with many gifts from staff
and students, quickly formed the nucleus of a
weapons museum, which over the years has
grown into what is almost certainly the finest
international collection in Britain of infantry
firearms, dating from the 17th century to the
present day, and ranging from small pocket
pistols to heavy anti-tank weapons. The
Museum was transferred to Warminster in 1969.

Warnham

Warnham War Museum

Durfold Hill, Warnham, nr Horsham, West Sussex
*   RH12 3RZ   ☎ 0403 65607/65179*
Easter–Oct, daily 10–6. Nov–Easter, daily 10–4.
*   Closed Dec 25.*
⋈ *The Curator*
E ♟ ☕ ⚲

The Museum possesses and displays a large
collection of vehicles, uniforms, badges and
equipment relating to the First World War. The
exhibits are given cohesion and added
significance by means of background sounds,
music, commentary and recordings of speeches.

Warrington

The South Lancashire Regiment Museum

Peninsula Barracks, O'Leary Street, Warrington,
*   Cheshire WA2 7BR   ☎ 0925 33563*
Mon–Fri 10–3. Closed Bank Holiday.
⋈ *Lt. Col. (Retd) E. G. Bostock*
E ⚲

The Museum's displays illustrate the history of
the Regiment since 1717. There are collections
of uniforms, weapons, campaign medals and
awards, Regimental colours, trophies,
manuscript records, photographs and paintings,
together with memorabilia of individual
members of the Regiment.

'Still Life' by Jan van Os.
Warrington Museum and Art Gallery.

Warrington Museum and Art Gallery

Bold Street, Warrington, Cheshire WA1 1JG
*   ☎ 0925 30550*
Mon–Fri 10–5.30; Sat 10–5. Closed Bank
*   Holiday.*
⋈ *Education Officer*
F ⚲

The Museum's principal collections are of
natural history, geology, local history – with a
large photographic archive – coins and medals,
antiquities, including a Roman actor's mask,
ethnology and firearms. The Art Gallery has
mainly 19th-century paintings, watercolours
and prints, the most interesting being by local
artists of national and international repute, such
as Sir Luke Fides and Hamlet Winstanley. The
decorative arts section includes exhibits of local
glass and 18th and 19th-century ceramics.

Warwick

The Guildhall

Lord Leycester Hospital, High Street, Warwick
*   CV34 4BH   ☎ 0926 491422*
Easter–Sept, Mon–Sat 10–5.30. Oct–Easter,
*   Mon–Sat 10–4. Closed Good Fri, Dec 25.*
⋈ *The Master*
E ✐ ☕ ⚲

The Lord Leycester Hospital is a complex of
14th and 15th-century halls and residences. In
1571 Robert Dudley, Earl of Leicester, founded
a home for retired soldiers and their wives,
known as Brethren. The Guildhall was built at
the end of the 14th century and has been
restored to its original appearance. It contains a
collection of swords and militaria and of objects
relating to the history of the Hospital. Some of
the exhibits have been given by the Brethren as
mementoes of campaigns in which they took part.

Royal Warwickshire Regimental Museum

St John's House, Warwick CV34 4NF
☎ *0926 491653*
Tues–Sat 10–12.30, 1.30–5.30. May–Sept,
  also Sun 2.30–5.
⚔ *The Curator*
Ⓕ ⬿ ⌂

The Museum is housed on the first floor of a
building which dates from *c.* 1546. It contains a
comprehensive display of uniforms from the
18th century onwards, medals, including a
number from the Peninsular War and the Sudan
War, weapons, saddlery, Regimental colours,
trophies and other campaign relics, paintings,
photographs and documents. There is also a
collection of memorabilia of Field Marshal
Viscount Montgomery.

There is a wide-ranging collection of
archives concerning the history and personnel
of the Royal Warwickshire Regiment.

St John's Museum

St John's House, Warwick CV34 4NF
☎ *0926 493431 extn 2132*
Tues–Sat 10–5.30. May–Sept, also Sun 2.30–5.
  Closed Dec 25, 26, Jan 1.
⚔ *Mr P. Clarke*
Ⓕ ⬿ ⌂

St John's House, which dates from the mid-
16th century, contains the social history
collections of the Warwickshire Museum. The
displays are designed to be particularly suitable
for school groups and include reconstructions of
a Victorian classroom, parlour and kitchen.
There is a particular notable costume collection,
although lack of space prevents more than
occasional displays of items from it.

Warwick Castle

Warwick CV34 4QU   ☎ *0926 495421*
Mar–Oct, daily 10–5.30. Nov–Feb, daily
  10–4.30. Closed Dec 25.
⚔ *Mr J. M. Westwood*
Ⓔ ⬛ ▦ ⌂ HHA

The original Warwick Castle was built soon
after the Norman Conquest. It was considerably
extended and elaborately refurbished in the
17th and 18th centuries. The Beauchamps,
Earls of Warwick, lived here until 1449, when
the line died out, and afterwards it was in the
possession of the Greville family until 1978,
when it was sold to Madame Tussaud's. The
former private apartments, restored in 1871
after a disastrous fire, now contain a re-creation,
with lifelike figures, of 'A Royal Weekend Party
– 1898'. The State Rooms and Great Hall
contain fine collections of weapons and armour,
furniture, paintings and memorabilia of
historical personalities, including Queen
Elizabeth I, Queen Anne, Bonnie Prince
Charlie, Oliver Cromwell and Marie
Antoinette.

Two rooms contain medieval instruments of
torture and in the 14th-century Gatehouse there
is an exhibition recalling the lives and
achievements of the Beauchamps.

Warwick Doll Museum

Oken's House, Castle Street, Warwick
☎ *0926 495546/491600*
Mar–Nov, daily 10.30–5. Dec–Feb, Sat, Sun
  10.30–5
⚔ *Peggy A. Nesbitt*
Ⓔ ⬿ ⌂

Oken's House was the home of a Tudor mercer
and merchant, Thomas Oken. Bequeathed to
the town by a 16th-century benefactor, it now
contains the collections of mainly 18th and
19th-century dolls, dolls' houses, prams, toys,
automata, puzzles, children's books and
miniatures formed by Joy Robinson and
subsequently cared for and developed by her
sister, Peggy Nesbitt. The items on show are
mainly English, but a number of other countries
are also represented, including France, Japan
and Germany.

Warwickshire Museum

Market Place, Warwick CV34 4SA
☎ *0926 493431 extn 2500*
Mon–Sat 10–5.30. May–Sept, also Sun 2.30–5.
  Closed Dec 25, 26, Jan 1.
⚔ *See St John's Museum*
Ⓕ ⬛ ⌂

The Museum is in the town's 17th-century
Market Hall. Its collection reflects the
archaeology, history and natural history of
Warwickshire. It is particularly strong on
geology. Among the displays are a giant
plesiosaurus fossil and the celebrated Sheldon
tapestry map of Warwickshire, made *c.* 1650.
The Biology Gallery includes a Warwickshire
Information Centre, with books and maps for
enthusiasts to browse through and consult.

**A Victorian soirée re-created in the Drawing
Room of Warwick Castle.**

Warwickshire Yeomanry Museum

The Court House, Jury Street, Warwick
CV34 4EW   ☎ *0926 492212*
Good Fri–Oct, Fri–Sun and Bank Holiday 10–1,
2–4. Open Bank Holiday.
🖾 *Major R. Neal, 18 Newfield Avenue,*
Kenilworth, Warwickshire CV8 2AU
☎ *0926 55252*
Ⓕ ✎

The Museum presents the history of the
Yeomanry from 1794 to 1968. The displays
include uniforms, swords, firearms, pictures and
paintings relating to the Regiment, together
with a wide range of campaign relics.

Washington Village

Washington 'F' Pit Industrial Museum

Albany Way, Albany, Washington Village, Tyne
and Wear NE37 1BJ   ☎ *091 4167640*
Apr–Oct, Mon–Fri 10–5.30; Sat 10–1, 2–4.30;
Sun 2–5
🖾 *Mr Norman Tomalin, Museum of Science and*
Engineering, West Blandford Street,
Newcastle-upon-Tyne NE1 4JA
☎ *091 2326789*
Ⓕ ✐

The Museum consists of the winding-engine
house of the former Washington Colliery 'F' Pit,
with its winding-drum and steam engine. Other
subsidiary exhibits are grouped around the
engine house. There is a film showing the
operation of the colliery and the engine in their
working days.

Washington Old Hall

The Avenue, Washington Village, Tyne and Wear
NE38 7LE   ☎ *091 4166879*
Apr and Oct, Wed, Sat, Sun 11–5. May–Sept,
Sat–Thurs 11–5.
🖾 *Mrs P. Embleton*
Ⓔ ⬛ ✐ 〔NT〕

Washington is five miles west of Sunderland and
two miles from the A1. The village now forms
part of Washington New Town. The original
12th-century manor house, from which George
Washington's family took their name, was
partially demolished in 1613 and the present
house was constructed on its foundations. In the
1950s it was restored as an Anglo-American
enterprise and given to the National Trust in
1957. Part of the top floor is now used as a
community centre and the ground floor and a
bedroom have been furnished by the Trust in
the style of a typical 17th and early 18th-century
manor house.

Watchet

Watchet Market House Museum

Market Street, Watchet, Somerset TA23 0AN
☎ *0984 31209*
Easter weekend, then mid May–Sept, daily
10.30–12.30, 2.30–4.30. July–Aug, also
7–9pm.
🖾 *Mr M. V. Sully, 7 Periton Court, Parkhouse*
Road, Minehead, Somerset TA24 8AE
☎ *0643 7132*
Ⓔ ✎ ✐ ☐

The Market House was built *c.* 1820. The
Museum presents the history of this small Bristol
Channel port from prehistoric times to the
present day, a section of the display being
changed each year. There is a good collection of
local fossils and Stone Age implements and a
display on the Saxon Mint and settlement. The
history of the harbour, which is still involved in
international trade, is illustrated by means of
model ships, paintings and photographs. The
important iron-ore mining in the Brendon Hills
and the railway which conveyed the ore to
Watchet harbour are recalled by maps,
photographs and models. Among the exhibits of
special interest are a 17th-century ship's lantern
and a locally made pendulum clock.

Waterford

Brother Rice Museum

Mount Sion, Barrack Street, Waterford,
Co. Waterford, Ireland   ☎ *051 74390*
Daily on request, 9–12.30, 2.30–5.30
🖾 *The Curator*
Ⓕ ✎ ✐

The Museum building dates from 1802 and is
furnished in period style. The purpose of the
Museum is to promote a knowledge of and
devotion to the Waterford merchant, Edmund
Ignatius Rice (1762–1844), founder of the
Presentation Brothers and the Christian
Brothers, two congregations of laymen
dedicated to the education of young people
throughout the world. The displays in the

**Watchet Museum, Somerset, prominently
situated on Market Street.**

Museum illustrate the life and work of Brother Rice and include the room in which he died.

The Rice Trail, organised by the Museum, provides a guide to the places in Waterford which were of significance in Brother Rice's life.

Reginald's Tower

City Hall, The Mall, Waterford, Co. Waterford, Ireland   ☎ *051 73501 extn 408*
Apr–Oct, Mon–Fri 10–12.30; Sat 10–12.30
🗷 *The Caretaker*
Ⓔ *ex. children* 🗇 🛪

The circular building known as Reginald's Tower was erected by the Viking Governor of Waterford, Reginald McIvor, in 1003 A.D. It has played a significant part in the history of Waterford ever since, as a fortress, mint, prison, military stores depot and lock-up. Now used as a museum, its exhibits include the Waterford Charters, items from the City archives and regalia, and the *Liber Antiquissimus*, an oak-bound folio volume containing Acts and Ordinances of the Corporation from 1365 to 1649, together with other municipal documents.

The Charter Roll of Richard II is one of the Museum's most treasured possessions. Dating from the end of the 14th century, it is the only document of its age and type known to be in existence in connection with Ireland. The illustrations and drawings which accompany the text are a most valuable documentation of the period.

There is also a display illustrating Waterford's maritime history and a section devoted to the Young Ireland leader, Thomas Francis Meagher, who was condemned to death in 1848, but escaped to America, where he fought at Fort Sumter and Fredericksburg and became Governor of Montana.

Waterford City Art Gallery

O'Connell Street, Waterford, Co. Waterford, Ireland   ☎ *051 3501*
Mon, Wed, Fri 2–5.30, 7–9; Tues, Sat 11–1, 2 5.30
🗷 *The Director*
Ⓔ 🗇 🛪

The Gallery is in an 18th-century house, which also accommodates Waterford Library. The permanent collection of paintings and sculpture contains mainly works by 20th-century Irish artists. There is also a portrait bust of Vaughan Williams by Epstein and a number of landscape paintings and items of sculpture by local artists.

Watford

Watford Museum

194 High Street, Watford, Hertfordshire WD1 2HG   ☎ *0923 32297*
Mon–Sat 10–5. Closed Dec 25, 26, Jan 1.
🗷 *The Curator*
Ⓔ 🗇 🛪 ᘒ ▢

The Museum occupies a former brewer's house, built in 1775. The collections cover the history of the Watford area, from the earliest times to the present day. There is a special emphasis on local industries, particularly brewing and printing. The art collection is concerned mainly with the works of local artists, including Sir Hubert Herkomer and his students.

Temporary exhibitions are an important feature of the Museum's work. Twelve are organised each year, on a wide range of subjects, including the activities of local firms and societies.

Wednesbury

Wednesbury Art Gallery and Museum

Holyhead Road, Wednesbury, West Midlands WS10 7DF   ☎ *021 556 0683*
Mon–Fri, 10–5; Sat 10–1
🗷 *Mr Martin Senior*
Ⓕ 🗇 🛪

The Museum is concerned mainly with the history of the Wednesbury area. The Art Gallery contains 19th-century paintings, drawings and watercolours and good collections of ivories, Indian silver and Ruskin pottery.

Weem

Castle Menzies

Weem, by Aberfeldy, Perthshire   ☎ *0886 20982*
Apr–Sept, Mon–Sat 10.30–5, Sun 2–5.
   Other months, by appt only.
🗷 *Mr Charles H. Corbett, Warden, Warden's Cottage, Castle Menzies*
Ⓔ ▮ 🛪

The Castle, seat of the chiefs of Clan Menzies, is a notable example of a 16th-century Z-plan tower house, with angle turrets, crow-stepped gables and early Renaissance carved dormers. It has been restored by the Clan Menzies and displays a collection illustrating the history of the Clan and its local associations. Among the exhibits is a bronze reproduction of the plaster death-mask of the Young Pretender, Prince Charles Edward Stuart.

Welbeck

Creswell Crags Visitor Centre

off Crags Road, Welbeck, Worksop, Nottinghamshire S80 3LH   ☎ *0909 720378*
Feb–Oct, Tues–Sun & Bank Holiday 10–4.30. Nov–Jan, Sun 10.30–4.30.
🗷 *Dr R. D. S. Jenkinson*
Ⓕ ▮ 🛪 ᘒ

The collections and displays in the Centre concentrate on the Palaeolithic archaeology and Pleistocene geology of Creswell Crags and its surrounding area.

The Centre is set in a country park, with special educational facilities.

Wellingborough

Hinwick House

Hinwick, nr Wellingborough, Northamptonshire
☎ 09334 53624
Easter, May Day Bank Holiday, Spring & Summer
Bank Holiday, Wed from June–Aug 2–5.
Other times by appt. Parties accepted
throughout the year.
🗓 Mr R. M. Orlebar
£ ⚘

Hinwick House, built in the reign of Queen
Anne, is six miles south-east of
Wellingborough. It has collections of lace,
tapestries, needlework, porcelain and 17th-
century paintings, including works by Van
Dyck, Kneller and Lely. A permanent
exhibition, 'A Century of Fashion', displays
clothes from 1840 to 1940.

Wells

Wells Museum

8 Cathedral Green, Wells, Somerset BA5 2UE
☎ 0749 73477
Easter–Sept, daily 11–5. Oct–Easter, daily
2–4.30. Closed Dec 24–26, Jan 1.
🗓 The Curator
£ ✐

The Museum's most important collections are of
local geology and archaeology. They include
material from the original excavations at
Wookey Hole. There are also many old
photographs of Wells, dating from 1870 to
1950, a large collection of samplers, and items
from Wells Cathedral. A reconstruction of a
Somerset kitchen contains a display of 19th-
century domestic equipment.

Wells-next-the-Sea

Holkham Hall

nr Wells-next-the-Sea, Norfolk NR23 1AB
☎ 0328 710227
May 29–Sept, Sun, Mon, Thurs 1.30–5.
July–Aug, also Wed 1.30–5. Spring &
Summer Bank Holiday Mon, 11.30–5.
🗓 The Administrator
£ ⚓ 🖼 ⚘ HHA

Holkham Hall is two miles west of Wells-next-
the-Sea, on the A149. Built between 1743 and
1762, it has been the home of the Coke family
and the Earls of Leicester for nearly 250 years. It
contains a fine collection of Greek and Roman
statues, 18th and 19th-century tapestries, 18th-
century furniture made for the house, and
notable paintings, including works by Rubens,
Van Dyck, Claude and Poussin. The Old
Kitchen has a large collection of copper and

**William Kent's palatial marble entrance hall
at Holkham Hall, Wells-next-the-Sea,
completed in 1762.**

pewter ware. In the restored stables is the
Holkham collection of Victorian and Edwardian
agricultural tools and implements, steam
engines, tractors, domestic equipment and
craftsmen's tools.

The Holkham Pottery, started in 1951 by
Elizabeth, Countess of Leicester, is in 19th-
century buildings between the Hall and the
stable block. Pottery-making demonstrations
take place on Monday to Friday afternoons
during the season.

Welshpool

Powis Castle

Welshpool, Powys SY21 8RF   ☎ 0938 4336
Easter–June, Sept–Oct, Wed–Sun 12–5.
July–Aug, Tues–Sun 11–6.
🗓 The Administrator
£ ⚓ 🖼 ⚘ ♿ NT

Powis Castle, with its famous gardens, is one
mile south of Welshpool on the A483
Welshpool to Newtown road. Built in the 13th
century, it was remodelled during the 16th, late
17th and late 19th centuries to meet the
changing requirements of the Herbert famiy,
who have lived here since 1587. The Castle is
now a National Trust property. It contains fine
furniture, paintings and tapestries from a variety
of periods. The Blue Drawing Room has,
amongst other pieces, a pair of 18th-century
French commodes. In the Oak Drawing Room is
Bellotto's View of Verona, while the State
Bedroom contains 18th-century silver gesso
furniture. There is an Elizabethan Long Gallery,
with its original oak flooring and painted
wainscot, a Charles II State Bedroom and a
late 17th-century Grand Staircase, with murals
painted and signed by Lancroon. Other items
include the 15th-century sword of the Lord of
the Marches, 16th-century Limoges enamels,
and a 16th-century Italian marble-inlay table.

Among the series of family portraits are works
by Kneller, Gainsborough, Reynolds and
Romney. The Castle includes the Clive
Museum, which displays the collection of
Indian treasures started by Clive of India and
continued by his son, Edward, 2nd Lord Clive
and 1st Earl of Powis.

Powysland Museum

Salop Road, Welshpool, Powys SY21 7EG
☎ 0938 4759
*Mon–Fri, 11–1, 2–5; Sat 2–4.30. Closed Wed
    during winter months & Bank Holiday.*
▨ *Melissa Daniels, Curator*
Ⓕ ⌔ ➔

Formed by the Powysland Club, one of the first
antiquarian societies in Wales, the Museum was
opened to the public in 1874. The collection
still includes a few exotic items contributed
during that period. Today the emphasis is on the
local history of East Montgomeryshire, with
interesting archaeological material, including
finds from recent excavations.

Welwyn

Welwyn Roman Bath House

*Dicket Mead, Welwyn Bypass, Welwyn,
    Hertfordshire AL6 9HT   ☎ 07072 71362
Sun & Bank Holiday 2–5 or dusk if earlier.
    Groups by appt at other times.*
▨ *Christine Johnstone, Curator*
Ⓔ *ex. children* ⌔ ➔

The Bath House dates from *c.* 250 A.D. It is
protected by a corrugated steel vault, since it
now lies under the new A1(M) motorway. The
existing walls provide a detailed plan of the
Roman building. Much of the hypocaust
remains, together with a complete furnace arch
and the hot and cold baths. Graphic displays
alongside the ruins include photographs of the
excavation and of the construction of the
protective steel vault. A model shows how the
Bath House probably looked when it was in use.

Objects from the nearby Roman cemetery are
also on show. They include good examples of
Samian ware and a face urn of unusual type.

Wendron

Poldark Mine

*Poldark Mining Ltd, Wendron, nr Helston,
    Cornwall TR13 0ER   ☎ 03265 73173
Apr–Oct, daily 10–6*
▨ *Mr P. G. Young*
Ⓔ ♿ ⬛

Poldark Mine is the renamed Wheal Roots
Mine, where tin was being mined in the early
18th century. Three levels of the mine are open
to the public and in some of the chambers there
are museum displays. The exhibits include
working steam engines, mining ephemera,
domestic and trade items and mineral
specimens. Other steam engines, including two
Cornish beam engines, two compound beam
engines and a Peckett locomotive, are displayed
in the museum grounds, near the Mine.

West Bretton

Yorkshire Sculpture Park

*Bretton Hall College of Higher Education, West
    Bretton, Wakefield, West Yorkshire WF4 4LG
    ☎ 092485 302 (information only) or
    ☎ 092485 579
Easter–Sept, daily 10–6. Oct–Easter, daily 10–4.
    Closed Dec 25, Jan 1.*
▨ *The Administrator*
Ⓕ ⌔ ➔ ☐

Opened in 1977, this is the first sculpture park
in Britain. It is situated in 260 acres of
landscaped grounds, ranging from rolling
parkland to intimate formal gardens. The Park
defines its aim as 'attempting to bridge the gulf
between the public and contemporary sculpture
and to provide support and stimulus for the
development of sculpture'. In addition to
mounting temporary exhibitions and showing
pieces from the permanent collection, the Park
organises guided tours and workshop sessions for
schools, colleges and the general public.

West Clandon

Clandon Park

*West Clandon, nr Guildford, Surrey GU4 7RQ
    ☎ 0483 222482
Apr–mid Oct, Tues–Thurs, Sat, Sun 2–6. Open
    Bank Holiday 11–6, closed Tues following.*
▨ *The Administrator*
Ⓔ ♨ ⬛ ♿ ➔ ⚓ Ⓝⓣ

Clandon Park, now a National Trust property,
is three miles east of Guildford, on the A247. It
was built in the 1730s by the 2nd Lord Onslow,
to replace his Elizabethan family home on the
site, and designed by the Venetian architect,
Giacomo Leoni. There are fine marble
chimneypieces by Rysbrack and plasterwork by
the Italian stuccoers, Artari and Bagutti. Some
of the original furnishings and Onslow famiy
pictures remain, but much of what is now to be
seen in the house is the late Mrs David Gubbay's
celebrated collection of furniture, porcelain,
jade, textiles and carpets, which was
bequeathed to Clandon. The kitchens give a
fascinating glimpse of life below stairs. Also on
display are exhibits relating to the Queen's
Royal Surrey Regiment.

**'Family of Man' by Barbara Hepworth, 1970.
West Bretton, Yorkshire Sculpture Park.**

Westcliff-on-Sea

Beecroft Art Gallery

Station Road, Westcliff-on-Sea, Essex
☎ *0702 347418*
Mon–Thurs 9.30–1, 2–5.30; Fri 9.30–1, 2–5.
Closed Bank Holiday. Enquire locally for occasional Sat opening.
⚑ *Mrs C. Leming, Keeper of Art*
F ✎ ⚑ ✦ □

The Gallery was created by Walter G. Beecroft of Leigh-on-Sea and was opened in 1953. It contains 16th to 20th-century paintings and 18th and 19th-century watercolours, including works by John Warwick Smith, David Cox and John Varley. A local topographical collection, donated by Sydney Thorpe Smith, consists of maps, prints, drawings and paintings.

There is a varied temporary exhibition programme, including the Open Exhibition, which each summer presents works by amateur and professional artists living within the county of Essex.

Westerham

Chartwell

Westerham, Kent TN16 1PS   ☎ 0732 866368
Mar 1–6, Nov, Wed, Sat, Sun 11–4.
Mar 29–Oct, Tues–Thurs 12–5; Sat, Sun & Bank Holiday Mon 11–5. Tues morning reserved for pre-booked parties only. Closed Good Fri & Tues following Bank Holiday. reserved for pre-booked parties only. Garden & Studio open Mar 29–Oct at same times as house.
⚑ *The Administrator*
£ 🏠 ⚑ NT

Chartwell, the home of Sir Winston Churchill from 1924 until his death in 1965, and now a National Trust property, is two miles south of Westerham. The library, drawing room, dining room and study, preserved as they were in his lifetime, evoke the whole career of the Prime Minister. Two rooms are arranged as a museum, in order to display some of the mementoes acquired in the course of a long lifetime.

The studio, at the bottom of the garden, contains a collection of his paintings, together with brushes and paints and an unfinished canvas on an easel.

Quebec House

Westerham, Kent TN16 1TD   ☎ 0732 62206
Mar 1–23, Sun 2–6. Mar 28–Oct, Mon–Wed, Fri, Sun & Bank Holiday Mon 2–6 (last admission 5.30). Parties by appt.
⚑ *The Custodian*
£ ✦ NT

Quebec House, which dates from the 17th century, was the childhood home of General Wolfe. It has been in the possession of the National Trust since 1918. Two of the staircases are hung with engravings by artists who were with Wolfe during his campaigns in Canada.

Elsewhere in the house there are topographical paintings and drawings, mainly of Quebec and the St Lawrence. There are also maps, letters and personal items relating to Wolfe, his family and the Marquis de Montcalm, who commanded the French troops at the Battle of Quebec.

Squerryes Court

Westerham, Kent TN16 1SJ
☎ *0959 62345*
Mar, Sun 2–6. Apr–Sept, Wed, Sat, Sun 2–6.
⚑ *The Curator*
£ ✎ ✦ HHA

Squerryes Court is half a mile west of Westerham, just off the A25. Built in 1681, it was bought in the early 18th century by John Warde, whose descendants still own the house. Most of the pictures were collected by John Warde's eldest son and include a number by Dutch artists, among them Van Dyck's *St Sebastian and Philip II of Spain*, on which Van Dyck and Rubens worked jointly. There are also many portraits of the family by, among others, Stubbs, Opie and Devis. The furniture is mostly 18th century and there are also Soho tapestries and a collection of porcelain.

The terraced gardens of Chartwell, Sir Winston Churchill's home near Westerham in Kent.

Wester Ross

Eilean Donan Castle

Wester Ross, Ross and Cromarty   ☎ 059985 202
Apr–Sept, daily 10–12.30, 2–6
⚑ *Mr J. D. H. MacRae*
£ ⚑ ✦

The Castle was built in 1220 by Alexander II as a defence against the Danes. It eventually became the property of the Mackenzies, who became Earls of Seaforth. In 1719, when it was held by Spanish Jacobite soldiers, it was destroyed by gunfire from a British warship and remained a ruin for 200 years, until it was rebuilt by Col. MacRae, who descended in the direct line from the last Constable of the Castle. It now contains a display of Jacobite relics, most of which have links with the Clan Mackenzie.

West Hoathly

Priest House Museum

West Hoathly, East Grinstead, West Sussex
    RH19 4PP   ☎ 0342 810479
Apr–Oct, Mon–Sat 11–5.30; Sun 2–5.30
🗷 Resident Custodian
£ 🖉 🚶

Priest House is a timbered yeoman's house. It has fine timber and plasterwork and a stone tile roof. The displays illustrate village life in the 18th and 19th centuries. There is a particularly interesting collection of needlework.

West Mersea

Mersea Museum

High Street, West Mersea, Colchester, Essex
    CO5 8QD
May 12–Sept 13, daily & Bank Holiday 2–5
🗷 Mr R. L. Burrows, Curator
£ 🖉 🚶 ☐

The Museum's largest collection is of items of everyday use in the area from the late 18th to the 20th century. The local history section includes photographs of people at work and in their homes from the 1850s onwards. The maritime history of Mersea is illustrated by exhibits of fishing equipment and boat gear. There are also displays of the natural history of the district.

In order to maintain public interest and to allow as many items from the collection to be shown as possible, the exhibits are changed annually.

The half-timbered Priest House Museum at West Hoathly.

Weston Rhyn

Tyn-y-Rhos Hall Museum

Tyn-y-Rhos Hall, Weston Rhyn, nr Oswestry,
    Shropshire   ☎ 0691 777898
May–Sept, Wed, Thurs, Sat, Sun 2.30–6
🗷 The Chevalier M. Thompson-Butler-Lloyd
£ 🖴 🚶

Tyn-y-Rhos is two and a half miles from the village of Weston Rhyn. The 17th-century house contains a fine oak staircase, carved oak fireplaces and early Delft and Liverpool tiles. The collections include paintings, needlework, shell-work, porcelain, glass, prints and books.

Weston-super-Mare

Woodspring Museum

Burlington Street, Weston-super-Mare, Avon
    BS23 1PR   ☎ 0934 21028
Mar–Oct, Mon–Sat & Bank Holiday 10–5.
    Nov–Feb, Mon–Sat 10–1, 2–5.
🗷 Curator
F 🖴 🖴

The Museum building was formerly the workshops and stores of the Weston-super-Mare Gaslight Company. The collections and displays cover the natural history, archaeology and industries of Woodspring and the immediate surrounding area. The importance of the leisure industry is emphasised in the seaside holiday gallery, an interesting feature of which is a range of period amusement machines, all in working order. There are reconstructions of a Victorian chemist's shop, a dairy and an Edwardian dentist's surgery, and a large collection of cameras and photographic equipment, from box Brownies to spy cameras.

The natural history of the locality is presented by means of an indoor nature trail. There is a display of Mendip minerals, together with the history of lead and calamine mining on Mendip from Roman times onwards.

Weston-under-Lizard

Weston Park

Weston-under-Lizard, nr Shifnal, Shropshire
TF11 8LE   ☎ 095276 207/385
Easter weekend, then late Apr–late May, Sat, Sun
& Bank Holiday 1–5. Late May–late July,
Tues–Thurs, Sat, Sun 1–5. Late July–Aug,
daily 1–5. Sept, Sat, Sun 1–5.
Park open 11–7.
🅺 Christine Lakeland, Administrator
£ 🕯 💺 ♤ ☙ ♿

Weston Park, the seat of the Earls of Bradford
for the past 20 years, lies east of the junction of
the A5 and A41. Built in 1671, in the classical
style, it was designed by the mistress of the
house. Her own annotated copies of Palladio's
Book of Architecture survive in the Library.
The furnishings include 18th-century French
and English furniture, Aubusson and Gobelins
tapestries, paintings by, among others, Holbein,
Van Dyck, Reynolds, Gainsborough and Stubbs,
together with a good collection of porcelain
and glass.

There is a separate Museum of Country
Bygones, with exhibits of farm implements and
craftsmen's tools, all from the Weston estate.

Westonzoyland

Westonzoyland Pumping Station

Hoopers Lane, Westonzoyland, Bridgwater,
Somerset
May–Oct, 1st Sun in month & Bank Holiday,
in steam 2–5. Last weekend in June, narrow-
gauge railway display, 11–5.
🅺 Mrs Mary Miles, Rose Cottage, Lower
Durston, Taunton, Somerset TA3 5AH
☎ 0823 412713
£ ⬗ 💺 ♤

The Pumping Station is one and a half miles
south-west of the village of Westonzoyland, off
the A372 on a side road to Burrowbridge. The
first steam pumping station in Somerset was
built at Westonzoyland in 1830, to pump the
water out of the drainage ditch or rhyne, into
the River Parrett. The original beam engine and
scoop wheel were found to be inadequate and
were replaced in 1861 by the existing Easton
and Amos steam-driven drainage machine,
which worked until 1951, when a new diesel-
driven pumping station was installed alongside
the old one.

The steam pumping station and its equipment
are now maintained by a Trust, which has added
other items to the collection. These include
steam and oil engines, boilers, vintage workshop
equipment and a narrow-gauge contractor's
railway, with its locomotives and rolling stock.
Power for the maintenance workshop comes
from a Crossley engine which until 1984
worked at Durleigh Reservoir, Bridgwater.

**The buildings of Westonzoyland
pumping station.**

Westport

Westport House

Westport, Co. Mayo, Ireland
☎ 098 25430/25141
May 11–30 & Sept 1–14, daily 2–5.
June–Aug, daily 10.30–6.
🅺 The Secretary
£ 🕯 💺 ♤ ♿

Westport House, the home of the Marquess of
Sligo and his ancestors since 1730, is one and a
half miles west of Westport, on the coast road to
Louisburgh, and was completed in 1778 by
James Watt. Many of the ceilings, cornices and
fireplaces are excellent examples of his style and
the dining-room, with doors of mahogany from
the family estates in Jamaica, is perhaps the
finest remaining example of his work.

There are many family portraits, landscapes
painted in the locality and collections of English
and Irish silver and Waterford glass. The large
library includes old Irish books and manuscripts.

One of the family's most treasured possessions
is the flag of the Mayo Legion, brought to
Ireland by General Humbert when he invaded
the country in 1798. It has been in Westport
House, once occupied by his troops, ever since.

West Wycombe

West Wycombe Park

West Wycombe, Buckinghamshire HP14 3AJ
☎ 0494 24411
House & Grounds: June, Mon–Fri 2–6.
July–Aug, Sun–Fri 2–6. Last admission 5.30.
Grounds only: Easter, Spring & May Day
Bank Holiday Sun & Mon 2–6.
🅺 The Administrator
£ ♤ [NT]

The nucleus of West Wycombe Park was built
c. 1698 by Francis Dashwood, who was created a
baronet in 1707. His son, the famous Sir
Francis, founder of the Dilettanti Society and
the less reputable Knights of St Francis of
Wycombe, enlarged and improved the house

and created the remarkable garden and park, which were embellished with a great variety of temples and architectural items. The house contains painted ceilings, fine 18th-century English and French furniture, and Flemish tapestries. There are also interesting paintings, mainly landscapes and family portraits.

In 1943 the 10th Baronet, Sir John Dashwood, gave West Wycombe Park to the National Trust. His son, Sir Francis, continues to live in the house.

Wexford

Wexford Maritime Museum

The Quay, Wexford, Co. Wexford, Ireland
May–Sept, daily 10–8
Ⓜ *The Curator*
Ⓔ 🔊

The Museum is housed in a former lightship, the *Guillemot*, moored alongside the quay, near the Bull Ring. The exhibits are from a number of countries, with a particular emphasis on Irish maritime history, and include a large number of ship models.

Weybridge

Weybridge Museum

Church Street, Weybridge, Surrey KT13 8DE
   ☎ 0932 43573
Mon–Fri 2–5; Sat 10–1, 2–5. Aug only, Mon–Sat 10–1, 2–5. Closed Bank Holiday.
Ⓜ *Mrs A. Landsell, Curator*
Ⓕ 🔊 🔊 ☐

The Museum's displays illustrate the natural history, archaeology and social history of the Borough of Elmbridge. There is a large collection of Surrey costumes and an important archive of Elmbridge photographs. This material is used in both permanent and temporary exhibitions in the Museum and around the Borough.

Weymouth

Museum of Local History

Westham Road, Weymouth, Dorset DT4 8NF
   ☎ 0305 774246
Ⓜ *The Curator*
Ⓔ *ex. children* 🔊 🔊

The Museum has a good collection of paintings, prints and photographs illustrating the history of the town and the surrounding area. There is also a photographic display of warships associated with Weymouth and Portland and the 1837 Weymouth cyclorama, presenting a sailor's view of the coastline from Portland Bill to Lulworth Cove. Other exhibits include the treasure chest left behind by Philip I of Spain, when he and his wife visited Portland in 1506, and the wooden bathing machine reputedly used by George III, during a visit to Weymouth in 1789.

Tudor House

3 Trinity Street, Weymouth, Dorset DT4 8TW
   ☎ 0305 789742
June–Sept, Wed 11–4.30. Other times by appt.
Ⓜ *The Trustees*
Ⓔ 🔊

Tudor House is a restored sea captain's harbourside residence, furnished in the style of the early 17th century and presenting a picture of the domestic life of the period. There are exhibits of domestic equipment and travelling chests.

Whalsay

Hanseatic Booth or The Pier House

Symbister, Whalsay, Shetland ZE2 9AA
Mon–Sat 9–1, 2–5; Sun 2–4
Ⓜ *James A. Sanderson, Secretary*
   ☎ 0595 3535 extn 315
Ⓔ *ex. children* 🔊

The island of Whalsay is reached by ferry from Laxo on the Shetland mainland. In the 16th century, merchants from the Hanseatic trading ports of Hamburg, Bremen and Lubeck set up trading posts or 'booths' all over Shetland. The Bremen booth is used as a dwelling house. The Hamburg booth, a listed building, has been restored and is now used as a museum. It contains displays telling the story of the Hanseatic trade, with examples of the goods which were bought and sold, especially beach-dried fish, which was the Shetland's principal product. The wheel hoist is an interesting technical feature of the building.

Whitby

Whitby Museum

Pannett Park, Whitby, North Yorkshire YO21 1RE
   ☎ 0947 602908
May–Sept, Mon–Sat 9.30–5.30; Sun 2–5.
   Oct–Apr, Mon, Tues, Thurs 10.30–1;
   Wed, Sat 10.30–4; Sun 2–4.
   Closed Dec 24–26, Jan 1.
Ⓜ *Hon. Keeper*
Ⓔ 🔊 🔊

Model of HM Barque *Endeavour*.
Whitby Museum.

Whitby Museum, founded in 1823, is still run by Whitby Literary and Philosophical Society and the curatorial work is still looked after entirely by volunteers. It has important geological and palaeontological collections, including ichthyosaurs and plesiosaurs, type ammonites and belemnites. One section is devoted to Captain James Cook, his Whitby training in seamanship and his Whitby-built ships, and to the Scoresbys, the Whitby whaling captains, and their exploration and scientific work in the Arctic. Other displays are of ship models and items relating to the local shipbuilding industry.

Local archaeology, from the earliest times to the Middle Ages, figures prominently in the Museum. Other exhibits show local fauna and flora, militaria, local history and industry, samplers, dresses, dolls, and coins and medals. The collection of Whitby jet carvings is of exceptional quality. There is a good range of ethnographical items, brought back from Africa, Asia and Oceania by Whitby seafarers. The paintings on display in the Museum are mainly of ships, local scenes and Whitby worthies.

Whitehaven

Whitehaven Museum

Market Place, Whitehaven, Cumbria CA28 7JG
    ☎ *0946 3111 extn 307*
Mon, Tues, Thurs–Sat 10–5
🅧 *The Curator*
Ⓕ ✐ ⚓ ▢

Whitehaven Museum runs between 12 and 20 temporary exhibitions each year. In addition, the permanent displays feature coal and iron mining, shipbuilding, pottery, thread-making and grain milling. There are also exhibits of local geology and archaeology and of ship models.

A recent acquisition is the Beilby Royal Goblet. Enamelled by William Beilby Jr, it shows a picture of a ship and the inscription, 'Success to the African Trade of Whitehaven'. On the reverse side are the Royal Arms of George III. Other items of special interest include the Mathias Reed's *Birdseye View of Whitehaven*, painted in 1738, the Cranke portrait of the How family, and the ship's bell of the *Love* of Whitehaven.

Wick

Wick Heritage Centre

Bank Row, Wick, Caithness KW1 5EY
June–Sept, Tues–Sat 10–12.30, 2–5
🅧 *The Secretary*
Ⓔ ✐

The Centre contains a wide range of exhibits illustrating life in Caithness in the 19th and early 20th centuries. There are reconstructions of a bedroom, scullery, kitchen and parlour *c.* 1900, and of a local cooperage and harbour scene. Other displays show costumes, a 19th-century photographic studio and the rise and fall of the Wick herring industry, 1840–1940. The Centre has an extensive collection of photographs showing Caithness in the late 19th and early 20th centuries.

Widnes

Halton Chemical Industry Museum

Gossage Building, Mersey Road, Widnes, Cheshire
    WA8 0DG   ☎ *051 424 2061*
Mon–Fri 10.30–4.30. Also open at same times
    2nd Sat of each month. Other times by appt
    for parties.
🅧 *Education Officer*
Ⓕ ✐ ⚓ ♿

The Gossage Building, a listed Grade II building, was originally erected in 1860 as an office and laboratory block for John Hutchinson, whose chemical works stood on adjoining land. It is an excellent early example of the use of iron beams in construction. Subsequently the soap manufacturer, William Gossage, took over this building and today it is called after him.

The Museum traces the development of the chemical industry on Merseyside from 1800 to the present day and covers both the technical development of the industry and the urban growth and social change that it brought about. A specialised collection of chemical plant and equipment is being formed. The items on display will range from wooden storage vessels to what is now a fairly rare industrial survival, an early process control computer.

Bleach packer at the Leblanc alkali works, late 19th century. Historic photograph in the Halton Chemical Industry Museum, Widnes.

Wigan

Wigan Pier

Wigan, Lancashire WN3 4EU   ☎ *0942 323666*
Daily 10–5. Closed Dec 25, 26.
🏠 *The Piermaster*
£ 🏛 💺 🚗 ♿

The Museum complex known as Wigan Pier
comprises the Heritage Centre, in a late 19th-
century canal warehouse, and Trencherfield
Mill, a 1907 cotton-spinning mill. The
exhibition in the Heritage Centre, 'The Way
We Were', illustrates social and industrial life
in the Wigan area as it was in 1900. There are
reconstructions of a schoolroom and of a
coalminer's cottage and other settings. Actors
give regular performances in the schoolroom,
with members of the public playing the part of
children in the class, and also conduct
impromptu sessions based on other exhibits.
The displays in Trencherfield Mill include
what is now the world's largest working steam-
powered mill engine and demonstrations of
textile and rope-making machinery.

Wigtown

Wigtown Museum

Wigtown, Wigtownshire
    ☎ *0776 5088 (Stranraer Museum)*
May–Sept, Mon, Wed, Fri 2–4
🏠 *The Curator, Stranraer Museum, Old Town
    Hall, George Street, Stranraer DG9 8ES*
F 🖊 🚗 □

The Museum is in the Victorian building
formerly occupied by Wigtownshire County
Council. Its frequently changing exhibitions,
illustrating the social history of the town and
the county, are drawn from the collections of
the Wigtown District Museum Service, which is
based at Stranraer.

Willenhall

Willenhall Museum

*Willenhall Library, Walsall Street, Willenhall,
    West Midlands*
*Mon, Tues, Thurs, Fri 9.30–6; Sat 9.30–12.30,
    2–4.30. Closed Bank Holiday.*
🏠 *See Walsall Museum and Art Gallery*
£ 🚗

This is the local history museum for Willenhall.
The displays illustrate the development of the
town, with special emphasis on Willenhall as
the main centre of the British lock trade and the
home of many familiar names in the industry,
such as Union, Yale, Century, Era and Squire.
The Museum traces the history of the industry
from its craft origins and includes many fine
specimens of the locksmith's art and a detailed
model of a traditional locksmith's workshop.
The story is brought up-to-date with displays of
modern exhibition locks.

Willingham

Willingham (West Fen) Pumping Station

Earith Road, Willingham, Cambridgeshire
    ☎ *0223 860895*
🏠 *Mr K. S. G. Hinde, Denny House, High
    Steet, Waterbeach, Cambridgeshire*
F 🚗

The pumping station contains a 34 h.p. Ruston
1936 diesel engine, driving a centrifugal pump.
There is also a Gwynnes 10 h.p. vertical steam
engine dating from 1829, together with a
museum devoted to the work of fen drainage.

Wilmington

Wilmington Priory

Wilmington, Polegate, East Sussex BN26 5SW
    ☎ *0323 870537*
Mid Mar–mid Oct, Mon, Wed–Sat 11–5; Sun 2–5
🏠 *Resident Custodian*
£ 🖊 🚗

The site, owned by the Sussex Archaeological
Society, contains substantial remains of a 13th-
century Benedictine Priory, together with an
18th-century farmhouse. The principal
buildings house a museum of old agricultural
implements and equipment.
South of the Priory, and also the property of
the Society, is the celebrated hill figure of the
Long Man of Wilmington.

Wilton

Wilton House

Wilton, Salisbury, Wiltshire SP2 0BJ
    ☎ *0722 743115*
*Easter–Oct 12, Tues–Sat & Bank Holiday 11–6;
    Sun 1–6 (last admission 5.15)*
🏠 *The Administrator*
£ 🏛 💺 🚗 ♿ [HHA]

Wilton House, the home of the Earl of
Pembroke, has been the seat of the Herbert
family since the Dissolution, when Henry VIII
granted them the Abbey and its lands.
Architecturally, it is particularly celebrated for
the south front, which shows the influence of
Inigo Jones, and for the eight magnificent 17th-
century state apartments, especially Inigo
Jones's Double Cube Room, with its *trompe
l'oeil* ceiling and its panelling, designed to take a
collection of Van Dyck portraits of varying sizes.
The furniture includes pieces designed by
Chippendale, Kent and Boulle, and there are
notable paintings, including works by Brueghel,
Rubens, Rembrandt, Van Dyck and Reynolds,
and a set of 55 gouaches of scenes in the Spanish
Riding School in Vienna. A collection of Greek
and Roman sculpture is arranged in the Upper
Cloister.
Among other exhibits is the Pembroke Palace
dolls' house, made in 1907 and designed by Sir
Nevile Wilkinson, son-in-law of Sydney, 14th
Earl of Pembroke, and an important part of the

lives of the family's children since then. It contains miniature copies of some of the paintings in Wilton House. There is also a display of 7,000 model soldiers and, in part of the 14th-century Abbey building, a model railway which runs through a landscape recalling that which surrounds Wilton.

Wimborne Minster

Priest's House Museum

23 High Street, Wimborne Minster, Dorset BH21 1HR
Easter Mon–Sept, Mon–Sat 10.30–12.30, 2–4.30. Dec 27–Jan 15, Mon–Sat 10.30–12.30, 2–4.30.
Mrs E. A. Curry, 43 Julians Road, Wimborne, BH21 1EF ☎ 0202 886604
E Summer only

This mid 16th-century house is the only survivor of four which belonged to the Collegiate College of Wimborne. The present façade was added in the early 1700s, when the old house was restored. There are displays of geology, palaeontology and archaeology, the last related mainly to sites on which members of the Museum Association have been actively engaged – a Bronze Age urn field, a Roman military site, two Romano-British settlements and the site of a deserted medieval village. Other exhibits illustrate the domestic and social history of Wimborne in the 18th to 20th centuries.

The Museum Annexe was formerly a tinsmith's store and workshop, used for re-tinning cooking utensils and other light general blacksmithing work. It contains the tinsmith's forge and an extensive collection of agricultural and craftsmen's tools and domestic equipment.

Special exhibitions on such themes as local trades, household equipment, items of medical interest and toys are arranged each year.

The frontage and garden of the Priest's House Museum, Wimborne Minster.

Wincanton

Wincanton Museum

32 High Street, Wincanton, Somerset BA9 9JF
May–Sept, Sat 10–4
Mr H. C. Rodd, 21 Churchfields, Wincanton BA9 9AJ
F

The Museum is in a late 18th-century three-storeyed cottage. The displays reflect the more recent history of this old market town and include photographs, posters and a wide range of objects dating from the early 19th century onwards.

Winchcombe

Hailes Abbey

Winchcombe, Gloucestershire ☎ 0242 602398
Mar 29–Oct 14, daily 9.30–6.30. Oct 15–Mar 28, Mon–Sat 9.30–4; Sun 2–4. Closed Dec 24–26, Jan 1.
NT Representative
E NT

Hailes Abbey, a Cistercian house, was founded in 1246. The site museum contains a collection of medieval sculpture, tiles and other architectural fragments found in the ruins of the Abbey.

Old Town Hall Museum

Winchcombe, Gloucestershire ☎ 0242 602925
Mar–Oct, Mon–Sat 10–5
Mr H. Simms, Controller
E

Winchcombe Town Hall is an early Victorian building, though part of its foundations date from the Roman period. The main Museum, in the former Court Room, houses the Simms Collection of police equipment, uniforms, badges and relics from all over the world. In the adjoining Judges' Room there are displays of material illustrating the social, domestic and industrial history of Winchcombe and the surrounding area.

Sudeley Castle

Winchcombe, Gloucestershire ☎ 0242 602308
Apr–Oct, daily including Bank Holiday 12–5. Grounds 11–5.30.
The Administrator
E

Sudeley Castle is six miles north-east of Cheltenham on the A46. It was in the possession of Ralph Boteler from 1398 to 1469 and then passed to Richard of Gloucester, later Richard III, and afterwards to Admiral Seymour, who married Henry VIII's ex-wife, Catherine Parr, who died at Sudeley in 1548 and was buried in the chapel. The Castle was partly destroyed by the Parliamentarians during the Civil War and remained a ruin until 1837, when it was bought by the Dent brothers, the glovers, who restored the chapel and part of the house.

The contents include a collection of lace, paintings by Rubens, Van Dyck, Constable and Turner and a 16th-century Sheldon tapestry. Emma Dent's collection of autographs of eminent persons is shown in the morning room and, in a Victorian corridor on the site of the former Great Hall, there is an exhibition on the history of falconry. The medieval Dungeon Tower houses the Kay Desmonde collection of toys and dolls.

Winchelsea

Winchelsea Museum

High Street, Winchelsea, East Sussex
Mid May–Sept, Mon–Sat 10.30–12.30,
2.30–5.30; Sun 2.30–5.30
🏛 *The Curator*
C ✏

The Museum is in a room of the 18th-century Court Hall. It contains collections illustrating the history of Winchelsea and the Cinque Ports. The exhibits include pictures, maps and models, as well as medieval and more recent objects discovered on sites in the town.

Winchester

Guildhall Gallery

Broadway, Winchester, Hampshire
☎ *0962 52874*
Apr–Sept, Tues–Sat 10–5; Sun, Mon 2–5.
Oct–Mar, closed Mon.
🏛 *Miss E. R. Lewis, Curator*
F ✏ □

The Gallery has a changing programme of exhibitions, crafts and sculpture. The city's own collection of topography is exhibited from time to time.

Royal Army Pay Corps Museum

Corps Headquarters, Worthy Down, Winchester,
Hampshire SO21 2RG
☎ *0962 880880 extn 2427*
Mon–Fri 10–12, 2–4. Closed Bank Holiday.
🏛 *The Regimental Secretary*
F

The Museum is five miles north of Winchester on the A34. The displays, illustrating the history of the Corps since its formation in 1878, include uniforms, badges and medals, together with old office machines and documents relating to the Corps and its predecessors.

Royal Green Jackets Museum

Peninsula Barracks, Romsey Road, Winchester,
Hampshire SO23 8TS
☎ *0962 63846*
Apr–Sept, Mon–Fri 10–12.30, 2–4.30;
Sat 2.30–4.30. Oct–Mar, Mon–Fri
10.30–12.30, 2–4.
🏛 *The Curator*
F ✏

Sudeley Castle, Winchcombe, the burial place of Catherine Parr.

The Museum is devoted to the history of the three regiments which were amalgamated to form the Royal Green Jackets in 1966 – the Oxfordshire and Buckinghamshire Light Infantry, The King's Royal Rifle Corps and The Rifle Brigade. The Oxfordshire and Buckinghamshire Light Infantry relics include memorabilia of General Sir John Moore, killed at Corunna, and include his sword and the sashes used to lower his body into the grave.

The King's Royal Rifle Corps was originally raised in North America in 1755 as the 62nd or Royal American Regiment. It historical items include a flag from the German cruiser, *Prinz Eugen*, a 600-year-old Japanese sword surrendered in 1945, and one of the Regiment's own drums, which was lost in the retreat from Greece in 1941 but reappeared in Vienna 11 years later.

The Rifle Brigade mementoes include relics of the Crimean War and a uniform and waistcoat of the Duke of Wellington, who was Colonel-in-Chief of the Regiment from 1820 until his death in 1852.

The Royal Hampshire Regiment Museum and Memorial Garden

Serle's House, Southgate Street, Winchester,
Hampshire SO23 9EG **☎** *0962 63658*
Mon–Fri 10–12.30, 2–4. Closed Bank Holiday.
🏛 *The Curator*
F ✏

Serle's House dates from *c.* 1732. The approach to the museum is through a Memorial Garden, opened in 1952, to commemorate the members of the Regiment who have fallen in battle. The Museum illustrates the history of The Royal Hampshire Regiment and of the Regiments which were combined to form it in 1881 – the 37th (1702) and the 67th (1758). The displays include uniforms, medals, weapons, decorations, orders, Colours, documents and photographs.

The Royal Hussars Museum

Southgate Street, Winchester, Hampshire
*   SO23 9EF*   ☎ *0962 63751*
Easter Mon–Oct, daily 10–4
⚑ *The Regimental Secretary, The Royal Hussars,*
*   Lower Barracks, Winchester SO23 9EF*
⊡ ✐

The Museum tells the story of the Regiment
from the raising of the 10th and 11th Hussars
(originally Light Dragoons) in 1715, through
amalgamation in 1969 to form The Royal
Hussars and up to the present day. The
collections include armoured vehicles,
uniforms, equipment, medals, photographs and
campaign relics. The displays contain many
details of the personal experiences of members
of the Regiment, including Trooper Fowler,
who spent three years in a French farmhouse
cupboard during the First World War.

The Treasury, Winchester College

Winchester, Hampshire SO23 9NA
*   ☎ 0962 64242*
Thurs, Sat, Sun 2–4. Other times by appt.
*   Closed Easter & Christmas periods.*
⚑ *The Curator*
⊞ ✐ ☐

The Treasury is situated in the former Beer
Cellar of the College, a fine vaulted room, with
carved heads below the capitals. The Museum
was set up in 1982 to display the Duberly
Collection of Chinese Porcelain, which ranges
from the T'ang period to the 18th century, but
houses, in addition, displays, changed three
times a year, to show items from other College
collections, including Greek vases, books,
archive material and scientific instruments.

Westgate Museum

High Street, Winchester, Hampshire
*   ☎ 0962 68166 extn 2269*
Apr–Sept, Mon–Sat 10–5; Sun 2–5.
*   Oct–Mar, Tues–Sat 10–5; Sun 2–4.*
⚑ *Miss E. R. Lewis, Curator*
⊡ ✐

The Museum is housed in the City's medieval
West Gate, which dates mainly from the 14th
century. There is a 16th-century painted
ceiling, which was originally in Winchester

Hussar officers' uniforms.
Winchester, The Royal Hussars Museum.

College, and the items on display include
weapons and armour and a number of the official
weights and measures once used in Winchester.

Winchester Cathedral Treasury

Winchester Cathedral, Hampshire
*   ☎ 0962 53137*
May–Sept, Mon–Sat 11–5; Sun 2.30–4.30
⚑ *The Curator, The Cathedral Office,*
*   5 The Close, Winchester SO23 9LS*
⊡ ▮ ✐

Winchester Cathedral, founded in 1079 and
extended and remodelled in the 13th to 15th
centuries, is the longest medieval building in
the world. The displays in the Treasury are of
ornaments and liturgical objects from churches
in the County of Hampshire, ranging in date
from the mid 13th century to the present day.
    Illustrated lectures on the collections are
given to physically handicapped people who are
unable to gain access to the Treasury.

Winchester City Museum

The Square, Winchester, Hampshire
*   ☎ 0962 840222*
Apr–Sept, Mon–Sat 10–5; Sun 2–5.
*   Oct–Mar, Tues–Sat 10–5; Sun 2–4.*
⚑ *Miss E. R. Lewis, Curator*
⊞ ✐

The Museum's displays reflect the archaeology
and history of Winchester, where excavations
have produced a rich collection of Roman,
Anglo-Saxon and medieval material. Among
the exhibits are Anglo-Saxon jewellery and
metalwork, including a reliquary, a late Anglo-
Saxon wall painting, Anglo-Saxon and
Romanesque sculpture, and Roman glass,
metalwork and ceramics from the Lankhills
cemetery.
    The historical collections include
reconstructions of an Edwardian bathroom and
of a chemist's and a tobacconist's shop formerly
in the High Street.

Cat of Chinese K'ang Hsi porcelain, late 17th
century. The Treasury, Winchester College.

Windsor

Berkshire Yeomanry Museum

Territorial Army Centre, Bolton, Road, Windsor,
Berkshire SL4 3JG   ☎ 0753 860600
⚐ *J. G. Handley*
F ✎

The Museum's collections illustrate the history of the Berkshire Yeomanry from 1795 to the present day. They include uniforms, medals, equipment, campaign relics and memorabilia of notable members of the Regiment, as well as documents, pictures and photographs.

Dorney Court

Dorney, nr Windsor, Berkshire   ☎ 06286 4638
Good Fri–Easter Mon, then Apr–12–Oct 13,
Sun & Bank Holiday Mon 2–5.30.
June 2–Sept 30, also Mon, Tues 2–5.30.
⚐ *Mr and Mrs Peregrine Palmer*
E ✿ ▣ ✎ & **HHA**

Dorney Court is two and a half miles west of Eton on the B3026. Built in the late 15th century, it has been the home of the Palmer family since 1600. There is 17th and 18th-century furniture and a collection of paintings in the same period, together with many portraits, especially in the Great Hall. It is said that the first pineapple in Europe was grown here and afterwards presented to Charles II.

Household Cavalry Museum

Combermere Barracks, Windsor, Berkshire
SL4 3DN   ☎ 0753 868222
Mon–Fri 9.30–1, 2–4.30. Also Sun from
May 12 Sept 1, 10 1, 2 4. Closed Bank &
Public Holidays.
⚐ *The Curator*
F ⊘ ✎

The Barracks adjoins the King Edward VII Hospital on the B3022 to Bracknell. The displays illustrate the history of the Regiments of Household Cavalry, dating back to 1660, and include Regimental Standards, firearms, swords, uniforms and equipment, together with prints and watercolours.

Royal Borough Collection

Windsor and Eton Central Station, Windsor,
Berkshire SL4 1PJ   ☎ 0753 857837
Daily 9.30–5.30. Closed Dec 25.
⚐ *Mr P. Haylings*
E ✿ ✎ &

The Royal Borough Collection, formerly displayed in the Guildhall, is an exhibition of Victoriana. The items on display are either owned by the Royal Borough of Windsor and Maidenhead or on permanent loan, and are housed within Madame Tussaud's Royalty and Empire enterprise.

The exhibits illustrate the strong connections between Windsor and the Royal Family, living conditions in Victorian Windsor, which was notorious for its poverty and slums during the earlier years of the Queen's reign, local shops and trades, and the social activities of the town.

Royalty and Empire Exhibition

Windsor and Eton Central Station, Windsor,
Berkshire SL4 1PJ   ☎ 0753 857837
Daily 9.30–5.30. Closed Dec 25.
⚐ *Mr Geoff Messenger*
E ✿ ✎ &

Windsor and Eton was a railway station of exceptional grandeur, in order to meet the requirements of Queen Victoria, her Court and her guests. The buildings, including the Royal Waiting Room, have been restored and refurbished and now house Madame Tussaud's Royalty and Empire exhibition, which re-creates the celebrations of Queen Victoria's Diamond Jubilee in June 1897. A full-size replica of the Royal Train stands at the platform and Queen Victoria awaits her guests in the Royal Waiting Room. On the covered parade ground in front of the station, 70 Coldstream Guards form the Guard of Honour.

In a 250-seat theatre, the audio-visual presentation, 'Sixty Glorious Years', includes speaking representations of Queen Victoria and some of her more illustrious subjects.

Windsor Castle

Windsor, Berkshire   ☎ 07535 68286
Castle Precincts: Mar 31–Apr & Sept–Oct 26,
daily 10–5.15. May–Aug, daily 10–7.15.
Oct 27–Mar, daily 10–4.15.
State Apartments: Jan 3–Mar 9 & Oct 28–
Dec 7, Mon–Sat 10.30–3. May 4–June 2 &
June 29–Oct 26, Mon–Sat 10.30–5;
Sun 1.30–5.
Queen Mary's Dolls' House, Exhibition of
Drawings & Royal Mews Exhibition open
Jan 3–Mar, Oct 27–Dec 21 & Dec 27–31,
Mon–Sat 10.30–3. Mar 31–Apr, Mon–Sat
10.30–5. May 4–June 16 & June 18–Oct 25,
Mon–Sat 10.30–5; Sun 1.30–5.
The Castle is always subject to closure,
sometimes at short notice.
⚐ *The Superintendent*
E ✿

The earliest surviving parts of Windsor Castle date from the reign of Henry II, although the Castle had been a Royal residence since 1110. Extensive building operations were carried out by Edward III, founder of the Order of the Garter, and Elizabeth I. St George's Chapel dates from the late 15th and early 16th centuries. Extensive refurbishment and renovation took place during the reigns of Charles II and George IV.

The State Apartments contain important collections of furniture, tapestries, paintings, Royal portraits and English porcelain, with the Minton and Royal Worcester factories especially well represented. Among the many items of historical interest on display are the French bullet which killed Admiral Lord Nelson and a chair made from the wood of an elm which stood in the British line at Waterloo.

Visitors can see Queen Mary's dolls' house, a large elaborate miniature palace, designed by Sir Edwin Lutyens and given to Queen Mary in 1923. There is also a collection of miniature furniture and furnishings, dolls and other toys.

The Exhibition of Drawings includes many items from the Royal Collection, with some fine examples by Holbein. The Royal Mews Exhibition contains carriages and presents received by Her Majesty the Queen.

St George's Chapel (1475–1511) is a fine example of the late medieval perpendicular style.

Wing

Ascott

Wing, nr Leighton Buzzard, Bedfordshire
    LU7 0PS   ☎ 029 668242
House & Garden: July 22–Sept 21, Tues–Sun
    2–6. Also Bank Holiday Mon, Aug 25 (closed
    Tues 26) 2–6. Garden only: Apr–July 17 &
    Sept 18 & 25, every Thurs & last Sun in each
    month 2–6. Last admission 5.30.
🅈 *The Administrator*
Ⓔ ♿ NT

Ascott is half a mile east of Wing and two miles south of Leighton Buzzard. A 19th-century house, it was bought by Leopold de Rothschild in 1874 and is interesting chiefly for its great collection of works of art, especially paintings, porcelain and French furniture. The paintings include works by Andrea del Sarto, Tiepolo and Lorenzo Lotto, but the main strength of the collection is in examples of the 17th-century Dutch School. Among the English artists represented are Gainsborough, Turner, Reynolds, Romney and Stubbs. The porcelain is mainly Chinese and reflects the taste of Leopold de Rothschild's son, Anthony, who gave Ascott to the National Trust in 1949.

Wisbech

Peckover House

North Brink, Wisbech, Cambridgeshire PE13 1JR
    ☎ 0945 583463
Mar 29–Apr & Oct 1–12, Sat, Sun & Bank
    Holiday 2–5.30. May 1–Sept, Sat–Wed
    2–5.30.
🅈 *The Custodian*
Ⓔ 🚻 ♿ NT

Peckover House was built in 1722 and at the end of the 18th century it was bought by a local banker, Jonathan Peckover. In 1948 it was presented to the National Trust, without any of its contents, by the last of the family. It has fine wood and plaster decorations, fireplaces and overmantels. The staircase and landing are particularly notable.

The house is now furnished with good 18th-century furniture, pictures and porcelain from elsewhere, giving an impression of how the house may have looked soon after it was built. A collection of Cornwallis family portraits is also shown here.

The 18th-century stable block has a fine display of harness. The Victorian garden is full of interesting and rare plants and trees, and in

the conservatory there are fruiting orange trees, reputed to be over 300 years old.

Wisbech and Fenland Museum

Museum Square, Wisbech, Cambridgeshire
    PE13 1ES   ☎ 0945 583817
Apr–Sept, Tues–Sat 10–5. Oct–Mar, Tues–Sat
    10–4. Closed Easter, Dec 25, 26 & Bank
    Holiday.
🅈 *Curator and Librarian*
Ⓕ ⌨ ♿ ☐

The Museum was founded in 1835 and moved into the present building, which was designed for the purpose, in 1847. Visitors can still see many of the original display cases and other features. The first collections concentrated on natural history and archaeology, and these are displayed in the main hall. As a result of the Townshend Bequest in 1868, the Museum received a considerable addition to its library, as well as English and European ceramics, sketchbooks, fossils, shells, objets d'art and many manuscripts.

Other collections are in the fields of costume, ethnology, social history and local history. The Temporary Exhibition Gallery features works by local artists, craftsmen, photographers and schoolchildren.

Woburn

Woburn Abbey

Woburn, Bedfordshire MK43 0TP ☎ 052 525666
Jan–Mar, Sat, Sun 11–4.45. Mar–Nov, daily
    11–5.45. Closed Nov 2–Dec except for
    pre-booked parties.
🅈 *D. W. Garrod, Administrator*
Ⓔ 🍴 🚌 ♿ HHA

Woburn Abbey, with its 3,000-acre deer park, has been the home of first the Earls and then the Dukes of Bedford since 1547. It was largely rebuilt in the 17th and 18th centuries. The house has notable 18th-century French and English furniture and one of the country's great art collections. Among the artists whose paintings are displayed here are Gainsborough, Reynolds, Van Dyck, Rembrandt, Frans Hals, Claude and Poussin. The Canaletto Room, used as a dining room, contains 210 views of Venice commissioned by the 4th Duke from Canaletto. What has been known since the 1970s as the Racing Room displays contemporary paintings and photographs of some of the horses owned by the family, together with the Ascot Gold Cup of 1842.

The Flying Duchess Room commemorates Mary, wife of the 11th Duke, and her many interests, especially flying. In a number of rooms there are family portraits, silver and French, German and English porcelain. The Crypt contains important displays of Meissen, Wedgwood, Chelsea, Davenport, Sèvres and Japanese porcelain, and in the Blue Drawing Room there are sets of enamelled miniatures by Henry Bone, copies of family portraits elsewhere in the house. The Long Gallery has a fine collection of 15th to 17th-century portraits, the most celebrated of which is the Armada portrait of Queen Elizabeth I.

The annual famous Hoburn Sheepshearing is commemorated by an 1804 painting by George Garrard showing the 6th Duke inspecting a piece of his own merino cloth.

The Armada portrait of Queen Elizabeth I by George Gower, now in the Long Gallery at Woburn Abbey.

Wolferton

Wolferton Station Museum

Wolferton, Sandringham Estate, King's Lynn, Norfolk PE31 6HA   ☎ *0485 40674*
Apr–Sept, Mon–Fri 11–1, 2–6; Sun 2–6
◪ *Eric Walker*
£ ▮ ♿

The mock-Tudor station building at Wolferton was designed by the Great Eastern Railway's architect, W. N. Ashbee, to meet the requirements of the Royal Family and their guests when visiting Sandringham. The interior is panelled throughout in oak, with decorative ceilings and all the windows in leaded opaque lights, to prevent the public looking through.

Between 1898 and its closure in 1965, all the kings and queens of Europe passed through its doors. Preserved as it was in its heyday, it now forms part of the home of its present owner. The Equerries' Corridor contains relics of the golden years of steam travel. The Centre Hall displays personal letters, photographs and documents connected with various sovereigns who used it. Queen Alexandra's Room has Queen Victoria's travelling bed, together with some of her clothes and memorabilia of Alexandra and her children.

There is a collection of furniture and other items from Royal trains, and among the exhibits of particular interest are the personal lavatories of the King and Queen, complete with their unique fittings which have been restored to full working order.

Wollaston

Wollaston Museum

102–104 High Street, Wollaston, Wellingborough, Northamptonshire NN9 7QQ
Mar 31–Sept, Sun 2.30–4.30. Other times by appt.
◪ *Mr D. H. Peckham, 7 Red Hill Crescent, Wollaston, Wellingborough NN9 7SX*
ꊰ

The Museum illustrates local life in the 19th and early 20th centuries. There are special exhibits of boot and shoe-making, and old farming implements, as well as archaeological finds from the area and paintings by local artists.

Wolverhampton

Aerospace Museum

Royal Air Force, Cosford, Wolverhampton, West Midlands WV7 3EX   ☎ *090722 4872*
Apr–Oct, daily 10–4. Nov–Mar, Mon–Fri 10–4. Closed 3 weeks over Christmas/New Year.
◪ *Mr John Francis, Administrator*
£ ▮ ▦ ♿ ᵹ

Cosford is on the A41 between Wolverhampton and Newport. The Museum is housed in wartime hangars, on a still active airfield, and contains one of the largest aviation collections in the United Kingdom, with over 60 aircraft on display, together with missiles, engines, uniforms and mementoes. Among the exhibits are some of Britain's largest military and civil aircraft, including the Victor and Vulcan bombers, the Hastings, the York, the Bristol Freighter, the last airworthy Britannia and other airliners used by British Airways. The Trident is accessible to the public.

Visitors to a temporary exhibition at Wolverhampton Art Gallery, 1985.

Bantock House Museum

Bantock Park, Merridale Road, Wolverhampton,
    West Midlands WV3 9LQ   ☎ 0902 24548
Mon–Fri 10–7; Sat 10–6, Sun & Bank Holiday
    2–5. Closed Good Fri, Easter Sun,
    Dec 24–27, Jan 1.
🏛 See Wolverhampton Art Gallery and Museum
F ✍ ⚘

The Museum building is an 18th-century
farmhouse, with considerable 19th-century
alterations and additions. The displays are of
local history and the decorative arts. There are
important collections of English painted
enamels and West Midlands japanning,
together with exhibits of Wedgwood jasper
ware, early Staffordshire pottery and 18th to
20th-century dolls.

Wightwick Manor

Wightwick, Wolverhampton, West Midlands
    WV6 8EE   ☎ 0902 761108
Mar–Jan, Thurs, Sat, Bank Holiday Mon &
    preceding Sun, 2.30–5.30. Closed Dec 25,
    26, Jan 1, 2.
🏛 Mr M. G. Smith, Curator
£ ✍ ⚘ NT

In 1887 Samuel Theodore Mander, a
Wolverhampton manufacturer, commissioned a
new house at Wightwick. For the furniture and
decorations, he turned to the firm of Morris and
Company and to other craftsmen influenced by
the ideas of Ruskin and the Pre-Raphaelites. It
is the survival of so much of their work at
Wightwick which makes the house of such
unusual interest and importance. All aspects of
Morris's work are represented – wallpapers,
embroidery, silk and wool textiles, carpets, tiles
and several volumes from the Kelmscott Press.
The firm also supplied material by W. A. S.
Benson and tiles by William de Morgan.
Designs by Morris are displayed, as he intended,
alongside Jacobean furniture, Chinese porcelain
and Persian rugs.

    The work of other artists allied to the Pre-
Raphaelite Brotherhood is represented at
Wightwick and there are also paintings by
several of the founder members, notably Dante
Gabriel Rossetti, Holman Hunt and J. E.
Millais. The acquisitions of the late Sir Geoffrey
and Lady Mander, who gave the property to the
National Trust in 1937, add to the interest of
the house. Lady Mander, an authority on the
Pre-Raphaelites, still lives at Wightwick.

Victorian dolls in the Bantock House
Museum, Wolverhampton.

Wolverhampton Art Gallery and Museum

Lichfield Street, Wolverhampton, West Midlands
    WV1 1DU   ☎ 0902 24549
Mon–Sat 10–6. Closed Bank Holiday.
🏛 The Curator
F ♿ 🖼 ⚘ &

The fine art collection comprises 18th to 20th
century paintings, prints, drawings and
sculpture, mainly British. Among the earlier
artists represented are Gainsborough, Wilson,
Zoffany, Fuseli, Turner, Sandby, Cox and
Landseer, with special sections devoted to
Edward Bird and the Cranbrook Colony,
including F. D. Hardy. The Modern collection
includes Pop Art by British and American
artists. The earlier 20th-century part of the
collection is still being developed, with recent
acquisitions of paintings by Spencer, Paul Nash,
Wadsworth, Hillier, Grant and Armstrong.

    There is also a good collection of Oriental
applied art, including weapons, ivories,
ceramics and woodcarvings, originating from
China, Japan and the Indian sub-continent.

Wolverton

Stacey Hill Museum

Stacey Hill Farm, Southern Way, Wolverton,
    Milton Keynes, Buckinghamshire
    ☎ 0908 316222
May–Sept, 1st & 3rd Sun in month, 2–5. 3rd
    weekend in May, June, July, Sept, Sat, Sun
    11–5, for demonstrations/events. Other times
    by appt.
🏛 Pamela Diamond, Curator
£ ♿ 🖼 ⚘

The house and farm buildings at Stacey Hill
have remained almost exactly as they were when
they were built in 1860. The Museum now
installed in them illustrates life in North
Buckinghamshire in the 19th and early 20th
centuries. The working displays feature a
blacksmith's shop, wheelwright's shop, printing
shop, stationary engines, and farm tractors and

The Great Parlour of Wightwick Manor,
Wolverhampton.

machinery. The craft demonstrations include thatching, woodcarving and beekeeping.

Among the large number of static exhibits are reconstructions of a dairy, Victorian parlour and kitchen; a fire-engine, a tram, farm carts and agricultural implements. There is also a section devoted to old telephone, radio and photographic equipment.

Wolvesnewton

The Model Farm Folk Museum and Craft Centre

Wolvesnewton, Chepstow, Gwent NP6 6NZ
  ☎ *02915 231*
Easter week–June, Sat–Mon 11–6. June–Sept, daily 11–6. Oct–Nov, Sun 2–5.30.
  ⚑ *Margaret Moreton*

The Museum lies off the B4235 Usk to Chepstow road, on a turning from Llangwm village. The farm buildings, which include a cruciform barn, were constructed in the late 18th century for the Duke of Bedford. The exhibits illustrate all aspects of daily life from the reign of Queen Victoria onwards and include horse-drawn vehicles, agricultural implements, furniture, toys and household equipment. In the Mill Gallery there are craft displays and workshops and changing exhibitions of photography and paintings.

Wonersh

British Red Cross Museum

Barnett Hill, Wonersh, Guildford, Surrey
  GU5 0RF   ☎ *0483 898595*
By appt only
  ⚑ *Mrs M. Poulter*
Ⓔ ▪ ⏎

The Museum has been established to preserve and display material relating to the International Red Cross Movement and particularly the British Red Cross Society. Among the items on display are uniforms, medals and badges and other items of equipment.

Woodbridge

Woodbridge Museum

Market Hill, Woodbridge, Suffolk IP12 4LP
Apr–Oct, Thurs–Sat & Bank Holiday Mon 11–4
  ⚑ *Hon. Curator*
Ⓔ *ex. children* 🔍 ⏎

The Museum, financed and staffed by volunteers, occupies the ground floor of an early 19th-century house. Its collections cover the geology, natural history and history of the Woodbridge area. Among the local personalities

represented in the collections are Edward Fitzgerald, the poet, Isaac Johnson, the surveyor and mapmaker, and Thomas Churchyard, the painter.

The site of the Anglo-Saxon ship burial at Sutton Hoo lies just across the River Deben and a section of the Museum is devoted to telling the story of the excavations and the finds, including up-to-date information on present work at the site.

Woodstock

Blenheim Palace

Woodstock, Oxfordshire OX7 1PX
  ☎ *0993 811325*
Mid Mar–Oct, daily 11–6 (last admission 5)
  ⚑ *Schools Liaison Officer*
Ⓔ ▪ ▣ ⏎ ♿ HHA

The architect of Blenheim was Sir John Vanbrugh, who began work on it in 1705. The baroque palace was designed to glorify John Churchill, 1st Duke of Marlborough, and to celebrate his victory over the French at the Battle of Blenheim in 1704. It continues to be the residence of the Dukes of Marlborough. The 2,000-acre park surrounding the house was landscaped by Capability Brown.

Within the Palace there are extensive collections of sculpture, paintings, tapestries, furniture and Oriental and European porcelain. The Long Library, 183 feet in length, contains over 10,000 volumes. Blenheim was the birthplace of Sir Winston Churchill and the exhibit commemorating him includes letters, books, photographs and personal possessions.

The Long Library at Blenheim Palace, Woodstock.

Oxfordshire County Museum

Fletcher's House, Woodstock, Oxfordshire
OX7 1SP   ☎ 0993 811456
May–Sept, Mon–Fri 10–5; Sat 10–6; Sun 2–6.
Oct–Apr, Tues–Fri 10–4; Sat 10–5; Sun 2–5.
Closed Good Fri, Dec 25, 26.
Ⓧ *Administrative Assistant (Education)*
Ⓕ 🏠 ⛟

Fletcher's House is a 17th-century building,
extended and given a new façade in the 18th
century. The permanent displays present the
archaeology and history of Oxfordshire from the
earliest times to the present day. The emphasis
is on structures in the landscape, ranging from
ancient earthworks to more modern buildings,
and on objects which illustrate human activity
in the past. The Museum's policy has been to
arrange the material chronologically so that
visitors can obtain a clear picture of the way in
which the area included within the County has
developed from the point of view of human
settlement, and at the same time gain an
understanding of the geology and topography of
the region.

Wookey Hole

Wookey Hole Caves and Mill

Wookey Hole, Wells, Somerset BA5 1BB
☎ 0749 72243
Apr–Sept, daily 9.30–5.30. Oct–Mar, daily
10.30–4.30. Closed for 1 week before
Christmas.
Ⓧ *Penny King*
Ⓔ 🏠 ⛟ 🚗

The attractions at Wookey Hole fall into two
parts, those in the famous caves, and those in the
buildings of the Victorian paper-mills. The
whole complex now belongs to Madame Tussaud's,
who have carried out extensive restoration work
and opened up more of the caves to visitors since
they bought the property in 1973.

The caves are spectacular. Archaeologists
have found abundant and interesting evidence
of both Iron Age and Palaeolithic habitation in
them, together with great quantities of the
bones of prehistoric animals, brought into the
caves by hyenas.

The old mill buildings are now used for
museum purposes. In one of them visitors can
now see hand-made paper-making in action
once again. Some of the paper is sold in the
Museum and an increasing amount is finding a
commercial market. Another building contains
Lady Bangor's famous collection of fairground
equipment. The old drying-lofts are now used to
store the plaster moulds in which the parts of
Madame Tussaud's wax figures have been cast.
There is also a reference collection of famous
heads, those of Winston Churchill, Henry VIII
and Jackie Onassis being among them, and a
number of special accessories, such as Ringo
Starr's hat and the shoes belonging to Dr Crippen.

A re-creation of an Edwardian pier forms the
setting for a working collection of penny
amusement machines.

Woolpit

Woolpit Bygones Museum

The Institute, Woolpit, Suffolk
Easter–last weekend in Sept, Sat, Sun 2–5
Ⓧ *Mr John Wiley, Walnut Tree Cottage, Green*
    Road, Woolpit IP30 9RF   ☎ 0359 40822
Ⓕ 🏠 ⛟ ☐

Woolpit is midway between Bury St Edmunds
and Stowmarket, close to the A45. The
Museum contains a varied collection of items
from the village and its immediate surroundings,
recalling events, characters, crafts and
livelihoods of the past. The displays are changed
annually. A special exhibit is devoted to the
400-year history of the Woolpit brickmaking
industry, with photographs, brickmaking
equipment and examples of locally made bricks.

At a nearby farm, the Museum has its
'Farming in a Suffolk Village' section,
containing implements and equipment from the
days of horse power up to the introduction of the
tractor. These items are all in working condition
and are demonstrated on advertised weekends.

Worcester

The Dyson Perrins Museum

Severn Street, Worcester WR1 2NE
    ☎ 0905 23221
Mon–Fri 9.30–5; Sat 10–1, 2–5.
    Closed Dec 25, 26.
Ⓧ *Tours Operator*
Ⓕ 🏠 ⛟ 🚗 ♿

The Museum is housed in a former Victorian
school and contains the world's largest
collection of Royal Worcester porcelain. The
exhibits include the Wigornia Creamboat,
which dates from 1751 and was the first piece
made by the Company, and the giant vase made
for the Chicago Exhibition in 1893. There are
also items from a number of the services made
for British and Continental monarchs and many
examples of the decorative porcelain produced
over the past 235 years.

Tours of the modern factory give visitors an
opportunity to see how Royal Worcester is made.

Tudor House Museum

Friar Street, Worcester WR1 2NA
    ☎ 0905 20904
Mon–Wed, Fri,. Sat 10.30–5. Closed Good Fri,
    Dec 25, 26, Jan 1.
Ⓧ *See Worcester City Museum and Art Gallery*
Ⓕ 🔖 🚗

The Museum is in a late 15th-century half-
timbered house. The displays, which are
constantly changed, illustrate the social history
of Worcester and the surrounding area. The
emphasis is on open displays and on room
settings. Among the exhibits which can usually
be seen are those concerned with dolls and toys,
agricultural history and 'Worcester at War,
1939–45', together with reconstructions of
kitchens of the Victorian period and the 1930s.

Worcester City Museum and Art Gallery

Foregate Street, Worcester WR1 1OT
☎ *0905 25371*
Mon–Wed, Fri 9.30–6; Sat 9.30–5.
Closed Good Fri, Dec 25, 26, Jan 1.
◪ *The Curator*
Ⓕ ⬗ □

The Museum's exhibits illustrate the geology
and natural history of Worcester and the Severn
Valley and its history since the time of the
Romans. There is a costume section and a
reconstruction of a 19th-century chemist's shop.
The exhibitions in the Art Gallery are changed
monthly and include material from both local
and national collections.
   The Museum also houses the collections of
the Worcestershire Regiment and the
Worcestershire Yeomanry Cavalry.

Workington

Helena Thompson Museum

Park End Road, Workington, Cumbria CA14 4DE
☎ *0900 62598*
Mon–Sat 11–3
◪ *Janet Baker, Curator*
Ⓕ ⬕ □

The Museum is in a mid 18th-century building,
which was formerly the residence of the Steward
of the Curwen Estates, centred on Workington
Hall, now a ruin. During the past few years the
Museum has been undergoing a somewhat
leisurely programme of improvement, which has
so far dealt only with the deterioration of the
building. The displays on the ground floor
include 18th to early 20th-century costumes and
accessories, furniture, glass, ceramics, silver and
plate. A growing collection of local historical
material will eventually be displayed on the
upper floor.
   Temporary exhibitions are arranged in a
converted stable block adjoining the Museum.

Worksop

Worksop Museum

*Worksop Public Library and Museum, Memorial
   Avenue, Worksop, Nottinghamshire S80 2BP*
Mon–Wed, Fri 10–5; Thurs, Sat 10–1
◪ *Mr M. J. Dolby, Bassetlaw District Council,
   Amcott House, Grove Street, Retford,
   Nottinghamshire DN22 6JU*
 ☎ *0777 706741 extn 257*
Ⓕ ⬕ ♿

The Museum occupies part of the 1938 museum
and library building provided under the
Carnegie scheme. The displays, recently
redeveloped as part of the Bassetlaw District
Museum Service, illustrate the social and
industrial history of the Worksop area.

Worsbrough

Worsbrough Mill Museum

Worsbrough, Barnsley, South Yorkshire S70 5LJ
☎ *0226 203961*
*Wed–Sun 10–6 or dusk if earlier. Closed May Day
   Bank Holiday, Dec 25, 26, Jan 1.*
◪ *The Curator*
Ⓔ *ex. school groups* ⬕ ♿

There are two mills at Worsbrough, one a 17th-
century watermill and the other a 19th-century
mill, powered by a 1911 oil engine. Both are in
full operational order and provide an
exceptional opportunity to study milling
techniques and machinery of the traditional
type. The mills produce stone-ground
wholemeal flour, which is sold at the Museum
shop.

Worthing

Worthing Museum and Art Gallery

Chapel Road, Worthing, West Sussex BN4 3FN
☎ *0903 39999 extn 121*
*Apr–Sept, Mon–Sat 10–6. Oct–Mar, Mon–Sat
   10–5. Closed Good Fri, Dec 25, 26, Jan 1.*
◪ *The Curator*
Ⓕ ⬕ ♿

The Museum's collections are wide-ranging, but
with an emphasis on local themes. There is good
coverage of local archaeology and social history,
an excellent costume section and paintings and
watercolours of the 19th and 20th centuries, as
well as interesting collections of English glass
and ceramics.
   A recent programme of modernisation has
given the Museum a fresh, appealing
appearance. Particularly noteworthy now are
the Costume Gallery, the Downland section
and the new Archaeology Gallery, which
displays the fine Anglo-Saxon glass and
jewellery from Highdown Hill. The newly
refurbished Art Gallery is one of the most
attractive in the South-East.

**'Bianca' by William Holman Hunt, 1869.
Worthing Museum and Art Gallery.**

The engine-house at Bersham Industrial Heritage Centre, Wrexham.

Wrexham

Bersham Industrial Heritage Centre

Bersham, Wrexham, Clwyd LL14 4HT
☎ 0978 261529
Easter–Oct, Tues–Sat & Bank Holiday Mon
    10–12.30, 1.30–4; Sun 2–4. Nov–Easter,
    Tues–Fri 10–12.30, 1.30–4; Sat 12.30–3.30.
⚑ The Curator
Ⓕ ✎ ⚓ &

The Centre is two miles west of Wrexham, opposite the junction of the B5098 and the B5099. It was established in 1983 to interpret the history of local industries, on the site of the celebrated 18th-century Bersham ironworks. It was here that John 'Iron Mad' Wilkinson made cannons which were used in the American War of Independence, and developed a method of boring cylinders which made the Boulton and Watt steam engine a practical possibility. There is a special exhibition, with an authentically reconstructed forge, on the Davies Brothers, the gatesmiths who made the famous Chirk Castle gates.

The Centre is situated on the eight-mile Bersham to Clywedog Industrial Trail.

Erddig Park

Wrexham, Clwyd LL13 0YT   ☎ 0978 355314
Apr 17–Oct 18, Sat–Thurs 12–5
    (last admission 4)
⚑ The Administrator
Ⓔ ● ⬛ ◔ ⚓ [NT]

Erddig is two miles south of Wrexham on the A483 Oswestry road. Built in the 1680s, it was enlarged early in the 18th century. John Meller, a London lawyer, bought the property in 1715 and equipped it with tapestries, silver, Oriental porcelain and furniture by the best London makers. Mr Meller was childless and left the property to a nephew, Simon Yorke. In 1973 the last of the Yorke family gave Erddig to the National Trust.

Most of the 18th-century contents have survived and both the house and the garden retain their original character. There is a

remarkable series of portraits, which record the likenesses of the Yorkes' servants from the late 18th century onwards. The service and estate buildings have also been preserved and visitors can see them now much as they were in Erddig's heyday. They include the bakehouse, kitchen, blacksmith's shop, sawpit and wet and dry kitchens.

Geological Museum of North Wales

Bwlchgwyn Quarry, nr Wrexham, Clwyd
    LL11 5UY   ☎ 0978 757573
June–Sept, Mon–Fri 9.30–4.30; Sat, Sun 11–5.
    Oct–May, Mon–Fri 9.30–4.30. Closed Good
    Fri, Easter Mon, Dec 25, 26, Jan 1.
⚑ Jim Ryan, Manager
Ⓔ ✎ ⚓

The Quarry containing the Museum is alongside the A525 Wrexham to Ruthin road, at the western end of the village of Bwlchgwyn. Housed in a purpose-built structure, with a viewing tower, it contains an exchange collection of rocks and minerals from all over the world. There are outside displays of old industrial equipment, together with a stone garden.

Wroxeter

Wroxeter Roman City (Viroconium)

Wroxeter, Shrewsbury, Shropshire SY5 6PH
    ☎ 074375 330
Mar 15–Oct 15, Mon–Sat 9.30–6.30;
    Sun 2–6.30. Oct 16–Mar 14, Mon–Sat
    9.30–4; Sun 2–4. Closed May Day Bank
    Holiday, Dec 24–26, Jan 1.
⚑ The Custodian
Ⓔ ● ⚓ ⚏

Wroxeter, the Roman Viroconium, is seven miles south-east of Shrewsbury, on the B4380 to Ironbridge. There is a museum of objects found during the excavation of the site of the former legionary base, the fourth largest town in Roman Britain. The exhibits include bottles, vases, brooches, keys, coins and bracelets, and an inscribed stone bearing a dedication to the Emperor Hadrian, originally set up in A.D. 130 over the entrance to the Forum.

Wye

Wye College Agricultural Museum

Wye College, Wye, Ashford, Kent TN25 5AH
    ☎ 0233 812401
May–July & Sept, Wed 2–5. Aug, Wed,
    Sat 2–5. Parties at other times by appt.
⚑ Hon. Curator
Ⓕ ⚓

The Museum is in the village of Brook, two miles south of Wye. The collections are housed in a well-preserved late 14th-century barn, and in an early 19th-century oast house of unusual design. The exhibits in the barn cover most farming activities of the days when the horse was the main form of power and range from wagons, carts, ploughs and seed drills to dairy equipment and harvesting machines. The oast house displays tools and implements used in hop-growing, together with a wide variety of agricultural and craftsmen's hand tools.

Wylam

Wylam Railway Museum

Falcon Centre, Falcon Terrace, Wylam, Northumberland NE41 8EE ☎ *06614 2174*
Tues, Thurs 2–5, 5.30–7.30; Sat 9–12. Closed for 1–2 weeks during July or Aug.
Mr P. R. B. Brooks, 20 Bluebell Close, Wylam NE41 8EU ☎ *06614 3520*
F

The village of Wylam is on the Tyne, 11 miles west of Newcastle. The Museum, in the former village school, overlooks the Tyne Riverside Country Park, which contains the mid 18th-century Wylam Waggonway, on which the historic locomotives, *Puffing Billy* and *Wylam Dilly* ran. George Stephenson's birthplace, a National Trust property, is by the side of the Waggonway, half a mile from the Museum.

The Museum displays illustrate the importance of Wylam in the history of railway development and the work of local personalities who achieved international fame. The exhibits include photographs, documents and railway relics, especially from the Tyne Valley area and the North-East in general.

Y

Yanworth

Chedworth Roman Villa

Yanworth, Cheltenham, Gloucestershire GL54 3LJ ☎ *024289 256*
May–Oct, Tues–Sun 11–6. Feb & Nov–Dec 15, Tues–Sun 11–4.
The Administrator
£ NT

The Villa site is three miles north-west of Fossebridge off the A429 Cirencester to Northleach road. It is approached by means of the Yanworth to Withington road.

Chedworth is the most completely exposed Romano-British villa in the West of England, and is now owned by the National Trust. The original structure dates from the 2nd century A.D. and there was extensive development until the late 4th century. The Villa was excavated in 1864, after a workman from Northleach had reported seeing 'large grey (Roman) snails crawling across the path'. The Earl of Eldon decided to preserve the remains – including the mosaics – and a half-timbered hunting lodge, in the Villa courtyard, has been converted into a museum to display objects discovered in the course of the excavations.

Yelverton

Buckland Abbey

nr Buckland Monachorum, Yelverton, Devon
Easter–Sept, Mon–Sat 11–6; Sun 2–6. Oct–Easter, Wed, Sat, Sun 2–5. Last admission 30 mins before closing.
The Secretary, City Museum and Art Gallery, Drake Circus, Plymouth PL4 8AJ ☎ *0752 668000 extn 4878*
£

Buckland Abbey, a Cistercian foundation, was the property of the Drake family from soon after the Dissolution of the Monasteries until 1948. Three floors were inserted into the Abbey church to form the present house. Since 1951 it has been managed by Plymouth City Museums as the Drake, Naval and West Country Folk Museum. The displays include model ships, church silver, oak and mahogany furniture, and relics of Sir Francis Drake. The medieval tithe barn contains a collection of horse-drawn vehicles.

Yeovil

Priest House Country Life Museum

Brympton d'Evercy, Yeovil, Somerset BA22 8TD ☎ *093586 2528*
May–Sept, Sat–Wed 2–6
Brympton Estate Office
£ HHA

Brympton d'Evercy lies just west of Yeovil, off either the A30 or the A3088. Between 1220 and today the estate has been owned first by the d'Evercys, then by the Sydenhams and lastly by the Fanes. The house has been enlarged and altered at intervals since the 15th century. The 15th-century Priest House contains an exhibition of equipment for coopering and for wine and cider-making. There is also a collection of old domestic appliances.

Wyndham Museum

Hendford Manor Hall, Yeovil, Somerset ☎ *0935 75171 extn 302*
Mon–Sat 12–5. Closed Bank Holiday.
The Curator
F

Hendford Manor Hall is the 18th-century coach house of the Manor. The Museum displays illustrate the history and archaeology of Yeovil and its immediate neighbourhood from prehistoric to modern times. Among the special features are the Yeovil gloving industry and finds, including mosaics, from Roman sites in Yeovil, Lufton and Ilchester. There is also a good collection of firearms and a 17th-century carved wooden panel, formerly at the Angel Inn.

Fairey Gannet fitted with Advanced Early Warning Radome. Yeovilton, Fleet Air Arm Museum.

A jeweller in Viking York offering silver and bronze brooches, pins and rings for sale. Part of the life-size re-creation of Viking Coppergate to be seen at the Jorvik Viking Centre.

building to itself, as the centrepiece of a specially constructed exhibition hall, which traces the development of Concorde from the early project studies to the present airline operations.

York

Bar Convent Museum

Blossom Street, York YO2 2AH   ☎ 0904 29359
Daily 10–5. Closed Dec 25, 26.
◗ *Sister M. Gregory*
£ ⬛ ▬ ♿ ⚙

The 18th-century building in which the Museum is housed contains an interesting chapel of the period. The theme of the displays is the history of Christianity in the North of England and of the Bar Convent in particular. Among the exhibits are early vestments, church silver, portraits of early members of the Convent community, and religious books of the 16th, 17th and 18th centuries.

Yeovilton

Fleet Air Arm Museum

*Royal Naval Air Station, Yeovilton, Somerset
    BA22 8HT*   ☎ 0935 840565
*Mar–Oct, daily 10–5.30. Nov–Feb, daily
    10–4.30. Closed Dec 24, 25.*
◗ *P.A. to Director*
£ ⬛ ▬ ♿ ⚙

The Museum was opened in 1964 to commemorate the 50th anniversary of the formation of the Royal Naval Air Service, the predecessor of today's Fleet Air Arm. Over 50 historic aircraft illustrate the history of Naval flying from 1903 to the present day. In addition to the aircraft, there are a number of special displays, together with paintings, photographs, weapons, medals and uniforms, and large collections of model aircraft and model ships.

A section of the Museum is devoted to the part played by the Royal Navy and the Fleet Air Arm in the campaign to retake the Falkland Islands and other features include the Warneford Exhibition, which is concerned with the career of Flight Sub-Lieutenant Rex Warneford, the first Naval Air Pilot to be awarded a Victoria Cross, and a display which tells the life-story of Admiral of the Fleet Earl Mountbatten.

Concorde 002, the British-built prototype of the Anglo-French supersonic aircraft, has a

Fairfax House Museum

Castlegate, York YO1 1RN   ☎ 0904 55543
*Mar–Jan 1, Mon–Thurs, Sat 11–5; Sun 1.30–5
    (last admission 4.30). Closed Jan 2–Feb.*
◗ *The Director*
£ ⬛ ♿

Designed by John Carr of York, Fairfax House was completed in 1755–6. It contains stucco work, carving and wrought ironwork of exceptional quality. In 1760 it was bought by the 9th and last Viscount Fairfax, who remodelled it internally at considerable expense. After years of neglect and misuse, it was in a very poor condition until it was fully restored in the 1980s by the York Civic Trust, which provided it with a magnificent collection of 18th-century furniture, paintings, porcelain and clocks, given to the Trust by Noel Terry, who was for 25 years the Trust's Honorary Treasurer.

Jorvik Viking Centre

Coppergate, York, North Yorkshire YO1 1NT
            ☎ 0904 643211
*Apr–Oct, daily 9–7. Nov–Mar, daily 9–5.30.
    Closed Dec 25.*
◗ *Rosalind Bowden, Tourism Officer*
£ ⬛ ♿ ⚙

The Centre is on the site of the Viking settlement discovered by archaeologists at

Coppergate. Visitors are taken by electrically operated train through a reconstruction of a Viking street, with a recorded commentary on the early history of the city, and on living and working conditions in Viking York. The Skipper Gallery contains examples of the wide range of objects found during the excavations and shows techniques employed by the archaeologists.

National Railway Museum

Leeman Road, York YO2 4XJ ☎ *0904 21261*
Mon–Sat 10–6; Sun 2.30–6. Closed Good Fri,
Dec 24–26, Jan 1 and May Day Holiday.
⊠ *Education Department*
£ 🏛 📷 🍴 ⚅

The Museum occupies a former steam locomotive maintenance depot and operates as part of the Science Museum. It was created to tell the story of railways and railway engineering in Britain. Its large collections include locomotives, rolling stock, signalling equipment, sections of rail used at different periods, and uniforms. There are also working models, posters, paintings, photographs, drawings, films and a wide range of smaller railway relics.

Regimental Museum of the 4th/7th Royal Dragoon Guards and the Prince of Wales's Own Regiment of Yorkshire

3A Tower Street, York YO1 1SB ☎ *0904 642038*
Mon–Sat 9.30–4.30 (last admission 4).
Closed Bank Holiday.
⊠ *The Curator*
£ ♻ 🍴 ⚅

The Museum's displays illustrate the history of the two Regiments from the time they were raised in 1685. The exhibits include pictures, weapons, uniforms, photographs and relics of the campaigns in which the Regiments have participated. The Museum also displays the collections of the East Yorkshire Regiment, formerly housed at Beverley.

Treasurer's House

Chapter House Street, York YO1 2JD
☎ *0904 24247*
Apr–Oct, daily 10.30–5.30. Closed Good Fri.
⊠ *The Administrator*
£ 📷 NT

Treasurers of York Minster lived in a house on this site from 1100 until the reign of Henry VIII, when the office was abolished. The main part of the house was rebuilt in 1620 and various changes were made between then and the end of the 19th century. In 1896 it was bought and restored by Frank Green, who lived in it until his death in 1930, when it was given to the National Trust. The bequest included an exceptionally fine collection of 17th and 18th-century furniture, china, pottery and glass. The items on display include a set of Indian ivory chairs which were brought back by Warren Hastings, and a dressing table which belonged to Louis XVI.

York Castle Museum

York YO1 1RY ☎ *0904 53611*
Apr–Oct, Mon–Sat 9.30–6.30; Sun 10–6.30.
Nov–Mar, Mon–Sat 9.30–5; Sun 10–5.
Last admission one hour before closing time.
Closed Dec 25, 26, Jan 1.
⊠ *The Director*
£ 🏛 📷 🍴 ⚅

The Museum is in two 18th-century prisons, built on the site of York Castle. There are displays of armour, weapons, especially swords, musical instruments, toys and dolls. The collection of costumes and accessories is one of the best in Britain. Kirkgate is a reconstruction of a York street, with its courts and alleys, and contains a number of old shop fronts and other buildings from York and elsewhere in Yorkshire, rescued from destruction during the 1930s. Horse-drawn vehicles, including the Sheriff of

Queen Victoria's state railway carriage. York, The National Railway Museum.

York's State Coach, are to be seen in Half Moon Court, the Museum's Edwardian street scene.

Some of the debtors' cells, which formed the late 18th-century prison, have been converted into reconstructions of the workshops of a comb-maker, wheelwright, clay pipe-maker, brush-maker, blacksmith and printer. One of the former cells is arranged as a visiting cell, with late 18th-century fixtures brought from Northallerton Gaol. The former condemned cell, in which, according to tradition, Dick Turpin, the highwayman, was imprisoned before his execution, has also been preserved in its original form.

The 'Every Home Should Have One' gallery contains a large collection of domestic equipment and electrical appliances, including radio and television sets.

York City Art Gallery

Exhibition Square, York YO1 2EW
   ☎ 0904 23839
Mon–Sat 10–5; Sun 2.30–5.
   Closed Dec 25, 26, Jan 1.
🖾 *The Curator*
£ ■

The Gallery's collections consist of European and British paintings from the 14th century to the present day; watercolours and prints, mainly of Yorkshire subjects, works by Yorkshire artists, especially William Etty, whose sketchbooks are also preserved and exhibited here; and modern stoneware pottery.

York Racing Museum

York Racecourse, The Knavesmire, York YO2 1EX
Open on race days, otherwise by appt only
🖾 *The Curator*
F ■ ⚓

York Racecourse is on the A64 York to Leeds road. The Museum is on the fifth floor of the Grandstand. Its collection comprises a wide range of objects connected with the history of racing, including memorabilia of racing personalities.

Yorkshire Museum

Museum Gardens, York, North Yorkshire
   YO1 2DR   ☎ 0904 629745
Mon–Sat 10–5; Sun 1–5.
   Closed Dec 25, 26, Jan 1.
🖾 *The Curator*
£ ■ ⚓

The Museum building was designed in the Doric style by William Wilkins, the architect of the National Gallery in London. There are exceptionally rich collections of Roman, Anglo-Saxon, Viking and medieval antiquities, including Viking weapons and everyday objects from Coppergate and other sites in York. The Museum also has Roman mosaics and a fine display of Yorkshire pottery. The Roman Life Gallery uses archaeological evidence to present a picture of Roman civilisation in Britain, with a special emphasis on York (*Eburacum*), the most important place in the North of England during the Roman period.

Drum captured during the Battle of Dettingen. York, Regimental Museum of the Royal Dragoon Guards.

Youghal

Clock Tower Museum

2 North Main Street, Youghal, Co. Cork, Ireland
   ☎ 024 92390
June–Aug, daily 11–7. Other times by appt.
🖾 *Mrs Alice Walsh, Youghal Failte Ltd,*
   Market Square, Youghal, Co. Cork
£ ⚓

The Clock Tower, built in 1776, straddles the main street of Youghal. The exhibits are mainly items which belonged to the former Youghal Corporation and include the mace, seals, official weights and measures, and the original charters of the town, granted by Elizabeth I and James I.

Z

Zennor

Wayside Museum

Zennor, St Ives, Cornwall TR26 3DA
   ☎ 0736 796945
Easter–Oct, daily 10–sunset
🖾 *R. G. or B. A. Williamson, Curators*
£ ■ ■ ⚓

The Museum is housed in the ground floor rooms of a former miller's house, in the mill and several outbuildings, and in the garden. The house contains domestic equipment and utensils and early 19th-century furnishings. The mill building, with its original machinery, also has a blacksmith's shop, with a forge and various items of ironwork made and used in Zennor.

Adjoining the mill is a wheelwright's shop, where visitors can see a hay wagon, together with the tools that were used in its construction. Another building contains a large collection of tin mining and quarrying tools and fishing equipment, while outside there are several mine trucks and trams.

Museums new to this edition

Aberystwyth

Aberystwyth Arts Centre

*University College of Wales, Penglais, Aberystwyth
    Dyfed, SY23 3DE* ☎ *0970 624278*
*Arts Centre: Mon–Sat 10–5 & during evening
    performances. Closed for a month from the end
    of May (dates vary). Catherine Lewis Gallery:
    Mon– Fri 9.30–5, also Sats in term–time.*
Ⓝ *Polly Mason* ☎ *0970 623339*
Ⓕ ⌷ ☕ ⑂ ☐ ⇶

The Arts Centre contains a concert hall,
theatre, main gallery area, foyer gallery,
photographic gallery, ceramics gallery and café.
There is a continuous programme of exhibitions
throughout the year. The College has a large
ceramics collection, begun in the 1920s, with
fine examples of early studio pottery and English
and Welsh slipware, together with works by
contemporary ceramicists. The Catherine Lewis
Gallery and Print Room, in the Hugh Owen
Library, displays 15th-20th century graphic art,
contemporary prints and British and Italian
photography.

Ashton-under-Lyme

Museum of the Manchesters

*Ashton Town Hall, The Market Place, Ashton-
    under-Lyme OL6 6DL* ☎ *061 344 3078*
Mon–Sat 10–4.
Ⓝ *Geoff Preece* ☎ *061 343 1414*
Ⓕ ⌷ ⑂

This is a new kind of regimental museum,
presenting the history of the Manchester
Regiment in the context of the local community
on which it was based. The military section
begins with the 63rd and 96th regiments,
amalgamated in 1881 to form the Manchester
Regiment, with its headquarters in Ashton-
under-Lyme, and describes its history until it
amalgamated with the King's Regiment
(Liverpool) in 1958. The social history displays
show the unrest which followed the Napoleonic
Wars and examine the social background of
soldiering in the 19th and 20th centuries.

Portland Basin Industrial Heritage Centre

*1 Portland Place, Portland Street South, Ashton-
    under-Lyme OL6 7SY* ☎ *061 308 3374*
Tues–Sat 10–5; Sun 1–5.
Ⓝ *Graham Boxer*
Ⓕ ⌷ ⑂ ⇶

The building housing the Heritage Centre was
formerly a 3-storey warehouse constructed by
the Ashton Canal Company in 1834 at the
junction of three canals to deal with the traffic
to the growing number of cotton mills. In 1972
everything but the ground floor of the
warehouse was destroyed by fire and what
remained was then reconstructed as a museum of
the social and industrial history of Tameside.
There are seven sections – Pre-Industrial
Tameside; Industrialisation; Class and
Community; Radicals and Reformers; Religion;
Local Government; and Tameside Today.

Basildon

National Motorboat Museum

*Wat Tyler Country Park, Pitsea, Basildon, Essex
    SS16 4UW* ☎ *0268 550077*
*Apr–Sept, Mon–Fri 10–4; Sat, Sun 11–5.
    Oct–Mar, daily 10–4.*
Ⓝ *Mr C. Thornton*
Ⓕ ⌷ ☕ ⑂ ⇶

The Museum, the first in the world to be
devoted to restoring and exhibiting historic
motorboats, is on Vange Creek, near Pitsea.
The building was once a transport warehouse
and is in the grounds of Wat Tyler Country
Park. The collection includes boats dating from
1910 to 1980. The most famous exhibit is 'Miss
England', built for Sir Henry Segrave. Powered
by a 925 hp aero-engine, she was capable of 90
mph and, in 1929, just beat Gar Wood's 'Miss
America'. The Museum also has Sir Malcolm
Campbell's hydroplane, 'Bluebird', which broke
the world water-speed record in 1937.

Bath

The Canal Study Centre

Office: 12 Larkhall Terrace, Bath BA1 6RZ
    ☎ *0225 337636*
*April–Oct, Sun 11–6 plus special events. Weekdays
    by appt. Telephone to check location.*
Ⓝ *Tom Wilson*
Ⓕ ⌷

Until 1976, the canal narrow-boat, 'Bodmin',
built in 1936, was still carrying coal on the
Grand Union Canal. Now restored and based at
Bath, she serves as an operational base for the
Canal Study Centre, created to allow members

of the public to learn about the history of the Kennet & Avon Canal and about the techniques of operating a barge of this type. The cabin tells the story of the boatman's way of life and the hold contains a comprehensive exhibition, with computer simulations, video displays and practical activities. Separate groups investigate the wildlife of the canal. During the year, the Centre operates at a number of different sites along the Canal between Bath and Bradford-on-Avon.

Museum of English Naive Art

The Countess of Huntingdon Chapel, The
*   Vineyards, Bath BA1 5NA*   ☎ *0225 446020*
Good Fri–Oct 31, Mon–Sat 10.30–5; Sun 2–6.
Ⓚ *Susie Chambers*
Ⓔ ⬤

The Museum is accommodated in a building dating from 1842 which was designed as a school, founded by the religious sect established by Selina, Countess of Huntingdon. The items on display were created by non-academic artists who worked in England between 1750 and 1900 and whose work was simple and unsophisticated – paintings, shop-signs, weather-vanes, samplers, country furniture and pottery.

Sally Lunn's House Museum

4 North Parade Passage, Bath BA1 1NX
*   ☎ 0225 61634*
Mon–Sat 10–1. Closed Dec 24–27.
Ⓚ *Mrs Angela Overton*
Ⓔ *(ex children)* ⬤ 🍴

The Sally Lunn bun is a Bath speciality. Its creator, a Huguenot refugee, is believed to have come to Bath in 1680 to work for a baker in a kitchen which occupied the same site as a Roman house and a kitchen belonging to the medieval Abbey. The present wooden-framed Tudor building was erected c.1480. The Sally Lunn bun is still baked here today.

Excavations have revealed evidence of both the Roman and medieval occupation of the site. In the museum cellars, visitors can see the foundations of the Roman and medieval houses, together with the remains of the hypocaust, tessera from the floor mosaics, painted plaster and roof tiles. Parts of the medieval kitchen, including a faggot oven, have also survived and there are a Georgian cooking range and old baking utensils.

Battle

Buckleys Museum of Shops

90 High Street, Battle, nr Hastings, East Sussex
*   TN33 0AQ*   ☎ *04246 4269*
Apr–Dec, daily 10–5.30 (dusk in winter);
*   Jan–Mar, open Sat, Sun & school holidays.*
Ⓚ *Mrs Annette Buckley*
Ⓔ ⬤

90 High Street is a medieval hall house, built in 1410 for Richard Curteys, the Treasurer of

Battle Abbey. Its original features include the crown post and close studding, and it is now used partly as a museum of social history. The exhibits include advertising material and the contents of old shops.

Beddgelert

Sygun Copper Mine

Beddgelert, Caernarfon, Gwynedd LL55 4NE
*   ☎ 0766 86595*
Mar–Sept, Mon–Sat from 10 (last tour 5.15; Sat
*   4); Sun from 11 (last tour 5.15). Oct, daily*
*   from 11 (last tour 4.15; Sat 4). Open most*
*   weekends Nov–Feb. Other times by appt.*
Ⓚ *Sandra Amies*
Ⓔ ⬤ 🍴 ♿

There is a tradition of Roman working at Sygun, but production in modern times is not recorded before 1825. Copper continued to be extracted here until the early years of the present century. Sygun is now a museum, with underground tours and a video presentation about the mine and its restoration. Visitors can see objects found during excavation work, together with photographs and models which show equipment and working techniques.

Bradford-on-Avon

The Croker Collection

Pound Lane, Bradford-on-Avon, Wiltshire
*   BA15 1LF*   ☎ *02216 4783*
Apr–Oct, daily 10–6.
Ⓚ *Ron Croker*
Ⓔ ⬤ ♿ ♿

The Croker Collection contains a wide range of farm tools, vehicles and machinery, including carts, waggons and stationary engines. Many of the items are arranged in settings which recall their use – the kitchen, the dairy, gamekeeping, carting, hedging and ditching, sowing, reaping, shepherding, the animal doctor, processing the crop, the blacksmith. The collection is displayed in Bradford's early-14th-century Tithe Barn. Stone-built and 167 ft long, it is now the property of English Heritage.

Bridport

Bridport Museum and Art Gallery

South Street, Bridport, Dorset DT6 3NR
☎ *0308 22116*
Mon–Sat 10.30–1. June–Sept, also Mon, Tues, Wed, Fri, 2.30–4.30.
The Curator
£

The Museum, an early-16th-century building, illustrates the history of the town and surrounding area, with special exhibits devoted to the traditional local trades of rope-making and net-making and to the geology, natural history and archaeology of the region. There is also the Keech collection of agricultural implements, and Dr Donald Omand's celebrated collection of dolls in historical and national costumes, many presented to Dr Omand by circus people from all over the world.

Bristol

The Exploratory

Bristol Old Station, Temple Gate, Bristol BS1 6QQ
☎ *0272 252008*
Tues–Sat & Bank Holidays, 11–5.
Kate Tiffin
£

The Exploratory Hands-on Science Centre has now found what it hopes will be its permanent home in Brunel's original Drawing Offices and Engine Shed at his Old Station at Temple Meads. Its aim is to stimulate and develop the curiosity of people of all ages in the world around them. The interactive exhibits have all been designed and built in the Exploratory workshop. Visitors are encouraged to find out for themselves about light and colour, electricity and magnetism, pulleys and pendulums, structures of bridges, bubbles and other natural phenomena.

Broadstairs

Bleak House Museum

Fort Road, Broadstairs, Kent ☎ *0843 62224*
Mar–Nov, daily 10–5 (check times in advance)
L. A. Longhi, Curator
£

Charles Dickens had a great affection for Broadstairs and lived at Bleak House, then called Fort House, during the summer and autumn months for many years. He wrote most of *David Copperfield* here and entertained his friends in the house which inspired the title of *Bleak House*. The house has since been considerably enlarged but the whole of the building which he occupied still stands and visitors can enter his study, bedroom and dining room. The Museum contains a number of Dickens' letters, items of furniture and other personal effects, as well as first editions of his works.

Dickens House Museum

2 Victoria Parade, Broadstairs ☎ *0843 62853*
Easter–Oct, daily 2.30–5.30
Joyce Smith
£

Charles Dickens paid frequent visits to Broadstairs, worked there a great deal and came to know a number of local people, some of whom became the basis for characters in his novels. One such person was Mary Pearson Strong, the owner of what is now Dickens House, who was the original of Betsey Trotwood, David Copperfield's aunt. The house subsequently became the centre of Dickensian activities in Broadstairs. It now contains exhibitions relating to 19th-century Broadstairs and to Dickens, including a number of the novelist's personal possessions.

Canterbury

Ethnic Doll and Toy Museum

Cogan House, 53 St Peter Street, Canterbury CT1 2BE ☎ *0227 472986*
Daily, including Bank Holidays, 9–5.30.
Lloyd Pickering
£

Cogan House, probably the oldest in Canterbury, is known to have existed as a hospital in 1163. The collections, recently moved to Canterbury, consist of dolls, dolls' houses, miniature rooms, shops and houses from all over the world. A special section is devoted to bridal dolls.

Chard

Hill's Plumbing Museum

D. R. Hill Ltd, Victoria Works, Victoria Avenue, Chard, Somerset TA20 1HE
☎ *04606 3567*
Mon–Fri 8.30–5. Closed Bank Holidays.
David Hill
F

David Hill began collecting historic items relating to his trade when he was an apprentice.

The collection illustrates developments in a trade that changes rapidly in its materials and methods. It includes blow-lamps, taps, ball-cocks, and parts of central heating systems. Other displays show the damage which can be caused to plumbing by frost and by amateur installation.

Colchester

Tymperleys Clock Museum

Trinity Street, Colchester, Essex, CO1 1JN
    ☎ *0206 712492*
Apr–Sept, Tues–Sat 10–1, 2–5. Oct, Tues–Fri
    10–1, 2–5; Sat 10–1, 2–4.
◊ *Miss Herbert* ☎ *0206 712481*
Ⓔ ♦

In 1927 Bernard Mason began collecting clocks by Colchester makers. The collection eventually contained 216 clocks and 12 watches. After his death, it was left to the town and is now displayed in a house he bought in 1956. Medieval in origin, the house had been added to and subsequently Georgianised. Mason restored it, to form a somewhat idealised version of an early-16th-century house. Old timber was available from houses which were being demolished at that time. When the work was completed Bernard Mason named the house Tymperleys, after the home of William Gilbert, the Elizabethan scientist, which had once stood opposite.

Daventry

Daventry Museum

Moot Hall, St John's Square, Daventry,
    Northamptonshire. Correspondence to:
    Daventry District Council, Civic Offices,
    Lodge Road, Daventry   ☎ *0327 300277*
Apr–Sept, Mon–Sat 10–4. Oct–Mar, Tues–Sat
    10–3.30.
◊ *The Curator*
Ⓕ ♦ ☐ ⚘

The Moot Hall is a listed Georgian building. It served as Daventry's meeting place and courthouse from 1806 until 1870 and then as the local Council offices between 1870 and 1974. Now converted into a museum, with a branch at Daventry Country Park, it is concerned with the history, archaeology and natural history of the area. Among the exhibits is a section of the BBC's Daventry transmitter, which operated in the 1930s.

Dorchester

Tutankhamun: The Exhibition

High West Street, Dorchester, Dorset DT1 1UW
    ☎ *0305 69571*
Daily 9.30–5.30. Closed Dec 24–26.
◊ *Tim Batty*
Ⓔ ♦

The Tutankhamun Exhibition recreates the magnificence of the Egyptian king's tomb and recaptures the atmosphere of its discovery by Lord Carnarvon and Howard Carter in 1922. Care has been taken to obtain exact replicas of the tomb itself and of objects contained in it, including the celebrated Golden Mask.

Dover

All The Queen's Men

Dover Castle, Dover, Kent CT16 1HU
    ☎ *0304 201628*
Good Fri–Sept, daily 10–6. Oct–Maundy Thurs,
    daily 10–4. Closed Dec 24–26, Jan 1.
◊ *The Curator*
Ⓔ ♦ 💺 ⚘ 〔EH〕

This is the Regimental Museum of the Queen's Regiment, formed in 1966 from the County Regiments of Surrey, Kent, Sussex and Middlesex, which were themselves the product of earlier amalgamations. The Museum covers 400 years of British military history and its displays illustrate overseas service in seven wars of the 18th century, seven of the 19th and two of the 20th.

Dublin

The Irish Jewish Museum

Walworth Road, South Circular Road, Dublin 8,
    Ireland   ☎ *01 760737*
May–Sept, Tues, Thurs, Sun 11–3.30. Oct–Apr,
    Sun 10.30–2.30. Other times by appt.
◊ *Mrs J. Lynn* ☎ *01 974252*
Ⓕ ♦ ⚘

The Museum, in a former Synagogue, contains displays relating to all aspects of the cultural, commercial and social life of the Jewish people in Ireland, with exhibits illustrating the full cycle of the Jewish year. The Synagogue, dating from the early part of the present century, has been restored and comprises part of the Museum. In another room the scene at the Sabbath table in a Jewish household in Dublin has been re-created.

Dundee

Royal Research Ship, 'Discovery'

Victoria Dock, Dundee
Apr, May, Sept, Mon–Fri 1–5; Sat, Sun & Public
    Holidays, 11–5. June–Aug, daily 10–5.
◊ *Education Officer* ☎ *0382 201175*
Ⓔ ♦ 💺 ⚘

In 1901 the National Antarctic Expedition Committee commissioned a ship to be specially built for exploration in the Antarctic. She was built of wood at the yard of the Dundee Shipbuilders' Company and was used during Captain Scott's expedition of 1901–4. Afterwards, she served as a stores ship for the Hudson Bay Company, carrying arms and ammunition to Russia during the First World War, and in 1923–4 as a research ship once again. Between 1936 and 1939 she was used for training Sea Scouts, and following this, moored on the Thames Embankment, she became a drill ship of the Royal Naval Volunteer Reserve.

In 1979 she was restored by the Maritime Trust, and became part of its Historic Ship Collection at St Katharine's Dock. In 1985 she returned to Dundee where, not far from where she was built, she was restored to the 1924 Vospers refit specification, for which full working drawings exist. 'Discovery' is now open to the public again, under the management of Dundee Heritage Trust.

Earls Barton

Earls Barton Museum

West Street, Earls Barton, Northamptonshire Correspondence to: 5 Saxon Rise, Earls Barton, Northamptonshire   ☎ *0604 810349 Mar–Sept, Sat, Sun & Bank Holidays 2.30–5. Oct–Christmas, Sat, Sun 2–4 or at other times for groups, by appt.*
⊠ *Mrs J. Palmer, Chairman*
£ ♿

The Museum is in the former Men's Reading Room of Earls Barton Baptist Chapel. The displays illustrate the social and industrial history of the parish of Earls Barton. The exhibits include equipment for handmade bobbin lace, with examples of the colourful locally-made bobbins, made to a unique design. One room recreates the working environment of a boot and shoe industry outworker c.1920.

East Bergholt

Bridge Cottage

Flatford, East Bergholt, Colchester, Essex CO7 6OL.   ☎ *0206 298260/298865 April 1 or Easter (if earlier), May, Sept, Oct, Wed–Sun 11–5.30. June–Aug, daily 11–5.30.*
⊠ *Olive Hazell*
F ♿ ☕ ✦ NT

Golding Constable, John Constable's father, was a prosperous merchant who owned Dedham Mill in Essex and Flatford Mill in Suffolk. A number of Constable's more important subjects were close to the mill at Flatford, and in the nearby Bridge Cottage the National Trust has arranged an exhibition illustrating the artist's life and work.

Eastleigh

The Eastleigh Museum

The Citadel, 25 The High Street, Eastleigh, Hampshire SO5 5LF   ☎ *0703 643026 Tues–Fri 10–5; Sat 10–4.*
⊠ *Dr Bowie, Curator*
F ♿ ♿

The Museum occupies a former Salvation Army Hall, which has a moulded portrait of General Booth on an outer wall. There are permanent collections of objects relating to the Eastleigh area. Two new exhibitions are opened every six weeks. Among the subjects covered in this way have been the railway and railway works at Eastleigh, local brickworks, Hampshire sheep farming and the sewing done by Eastleigh schoolchildren in the 1920s.

East Molesey

Embroiderers' Guild Collection

Apartment 41, Hampton Court Palace, East Molesey, Surrey KT8 9AU   ☎ *01 943 1229 Mon–Fri 10.30–4, by appt.*
⊠ *Lynn Szygenda*
£ ♿ ☕ ✦

Situated within the Guild's premises in Hampton Court Palace, the Collection comprises examples of embroidery selected both for historic interest and for technical expertise. The Embroiderers' Guild exists to encourage work of the highest quality and the Collection is intended to provide inspiration for present-day practitioners.

Elvington

Yorkshire Air Museum and Allied Air Forces Memorial

Elvington, York YO4 5AU   ☎ *0904 85595 Apr–Sept, Tues–Thurs 11–4; Sat 2–5; Sun & Bank Holiday Mon 11–4.*
⊠ *Administrative Assistant*
£ ♿ ☕ ♿ ✦

This 1939–45 Bomber Station has been restored to its wartime appearance. The Control Tower has been completely refitted, the Telex Room and Signals Office are in working order, and the refurbished and re-equipped Radio Room is sometimes manned by members of the RAF Amateur Radio Society. The Museum contains replicas, original wartime aircraft and aero-engines, and model aircraft.

Exeter

Rougemont House Museum of Costume and Lace

Castle Street, Exeter. Correspondence to Royal Albert Memorial Museum, Queen Street, Exeter EX4 3RX   ☎ *0392 265858 Mon–Sat 10–5.30. Open Bank Holidays & Suns in summer. No admission charge Fri.*
⊠ *Education Officer*
£ ♿ ☕ ♿ ▢

Rougemont House is a Regency building in the grounds of Exeter Castle. It has outstanding collections of costume and lace, which together with furniture, paintings and decorative objects are displayed in period rooms to illustrate changing fashion from the 1740s to the 1960s. There are regular demonstrations of lace-making and new exhibitions are arranged every year.

Galashiels

Galashiels Museum

Peter Anderson Woollen Mill, Huddersfield Street,
    Galashiels, TD1 3BA   ☎ 0896 2091
Mon–Sat 9–5. June–Sept, also Sun 1–5.
ℵ Jim Renwick
F ♿ 🅿 ↩

The Museum is within the Peter Anderson mill
complex. It presents the history of Galashiels,
emphasising its close involvement with the
woollen trade. A restored water turbine drives a
loom within the Museum. Tours through the
modern mill show visitors all aspects of
production, from spinning to the finished
article.

Glasgow

The Heatherbank Museum of Social Work

163 Mugdock Road, Milngavie, Glasgow
    G62 8MD   ☎ 041 956 2687
Tues, Thurs, Sun 2–5. Other times by appt.
ℵ Rosemary Harvey
F ♿ ↩

'Heatherbank', is a listed house dating from
c.1844. The displays illustrate different forms of
social work over the years, together with aspects
of the life of the people for whom such
assistance was required. The Museum includes a
reconstruction of a street in a Glasgow slum.
Window displays show a variety of aspects of
care for the poor, such as a poorhouse, a model
lodging house and a ticketed house, in which
the number of inhabitants was strictly regulated.
Visitors can recapture the past with the help of a
wide range of documents, pictures and objects,
and the recorded memories of a poorhouse
nurse.

Gloucester

National Waterways Museum at Gloucester

Llanthony Warehouse, Gloucester Docks,
    Gloucester GL1 2EH   ☎ 0452 307009
Summer: daily 10–6. Winter: Tues–Sun 10–5.
ℵ Marilyn McDougall
£ ♿ 🅿 ♿ ↩

Part of the Museum is housed in the 7-storey
Llanthony Warehouse, a listed dockside
building of 1873. The Museum has been created
to tell the story of Britain's canals and of the
people who worked on them. There are sections
devoted to the construction of the canals, to
boatbuilding, to the operation of the barges, to
the living conditions of those on board, and to
the cargoes carried. There is a replica of a canal
maintenance yard, where visitors can watch
craftsmen demonstrating their skills in the
workshops. There is also an engine house and a
stable, with Shire horses. Throughout the
Museum, the exhibits are supplemented by
working models, sound recordings and archive
film.

Outside, in the former canal docks, is a
growing collection of vessels once used on
inland waterways. These include a steam-
dredger, which operates at weekends.

Great Grimsby

Iron Age Settlement Project

Weelsby Avenue, Grimsby
    ☎ 0472 242000 extn 1385
Apr 11–Nov 3, Tues–Fri 10–4.
ℵ Mrs J. S. Tierney, Welholme Galleries,
    Welholme Road, Grimsby DN32 9LP
F ↩

This educational project, financed and
administered by Great Grimsby Borough
Council, is based on the in situ reconstruction
of an Iron Age settlement and consists of a
defended enclosure, within which are two
roundhouses and a granary.

Great Torrington

Dartington Crystal Glass Centre

Dartington Crystal, Great Torrington, North
    Devon EX38 7AN   ☎ 0805 22321
Mon–Fri 9–5. During summer, also Sat, Sun
    10–4.30. Closed for 2 weeks at Christmas
ℵ Stuart Ackland
£ ♿ 🅿 ↩

The Museum, attached to a modern glassworks,
illustrates the history of glassware from 1650
onwards, including 21 years of Dartington
designs. There is a working replica of an 18th-
century glass cone, in which a glassmaker
demonstrates his skills. Further technical and
design aspects of glassmaking can be seen in the
Centre's video theatre.

Halesworth

Halesworth and District Museum

The Almshouses, Steeple End, Halesworth, Suffolk
1st Sun in May, then Wed, Sun 2–5 until end Sept.
ℵ M. Fordham, Secretary ☎ 09867 3030
F

The Museum occupies part of a terrace of 15th-century almshouses, altered and partly rebuilt c.1680 in a Dutch style. At one time 12 widows lived rent-free here, each with her own room, a considerable luxury. The displays illustrate the Halesworth area in all its aspects – geology, archaeology, social history, industry and agriculture. A particularly interesting part of the collection consists of flints and pottery from the route of the Halesworth relief road, revealing six periods of occupation on the same site, from Mesolithic to early Medieval.

Hastings

Shipwreck Heritage Centre

Rock-a-Nore Road, Hastings, East Sussex TN34 3DW   ☎ *0424 43/452*
Late May – mid-Sept, daily 11–5.
🖾 *Peter Marsden, Director*
E 🛍 🚗

The Museum is in Hastings Old Town, an area which has been recently rehabilitated. The sea and the fishermen's quarter are close by. The aim was to save the surviving evidence of old wrecks and to tell the story of wrecks along this part of the coast. Visitors can see a video presentation of how a medieval ship went down, watch on radar shipping passing down the Channel and look at a wide range of objects discovered in wrecks.

Hatfield

Mill Green Museum and Mill

Mill Green, Hatfield, Hertfordshire AL9 5PD   ☎ *07072 71362*
Tues–Fri 10–5; Sat, Sun, Bank Holidays 2–5. Milling takes place Tues, Wed and Sun pm.
🖾 *Sue Kirby, Curator*
F 🛍 ☐ 🚗

This water-mill was rebuilt in 1762 on a site occupied by a mill since Domesday. It was in regular use until 1911, when competition from larger mills forced its closure. The last miller emigrated to Australia. A full restoration was carried out between 1979 and 1986 and flour is now milled again here in the traditional way.

The mill house is used as a museum of local history with permanent displays and a regular programme of temporary exhibitions. On most summer weekends there are special craft displays and demonstrations.

Hednesford

Valley Heritage Centre

Valley Road, Hednesford, Staffordshire, WS12 5QX   ☎ *05438 77666/79115*
May–Sept, Wed–Sun 11–6.30. Oct–Apr, Thurs–Sun 11–4. Group visits any weekday by appt.
🖾 *Susan Jeanes, Curator*
F 🖳 ⅃ 🚗

The Centre is on the site of a former colliery. It contains a museum reflecting the social and industrial history of the area. There are reconstructions of local shops, an Events Area and a group of Craft Workshops, where visitors can watch craftsmen at work and buy their products.

Holmfirth

Holmfirth Postcard Museum

Huddersfield Road, Holmfirth, Huddersfield, West Yorkshire HD7 1JH   ☎ *0484 682231*
Mon–Sat 10–5; Sun 1–5.
🖾 *Roger Penny* ☎ *0484 513808*
F 🛍 &

The Museum is part of the library complex in the centre of Holmfirth and tells the story of the local firm of Bamforth & Company, manufacturers of lantern slides, silent movies and postcards, including the famous 'fat lady' comic cards. The Holmfirth Flood of 1852, in which 81 people drowned, is also documented.

Hunsbury

Northamptonshire Ironstone Railway Museum

Hunsbury, Northampton
Correspondence to: 9 High Street, Hallaton, Leicestershire   ☎ *0858 89 216*
Sun 11–5. Other times by appt. Evening party bookings welcome. Closed Christmas period.
🖾 *A. Clayton, Chairman*
E 🛍 🖳 🚗

The Museum is on the site of a former ironstone railway serving the now-closed Hunsbury Hill quarries. Part of the old track-bed remains. The exhibits include locomotives and rolling stock, together with tools and equipment relating to the Northamptonshire ironstone and ironmaking industries. There is an introductory display, and a number of interpretive models.

Launceston

Lawrence House Museum

9 Castle Street, Launceston, Cornwall PL15 8BA
Easter – mid-Oct, Mon–Fri 2.30–4.30.
🖾 *E. J. Dart* ☎ *0566 2640*
F NT

Lawrence House, close to the Norman keep of Launceston Castle, was built in 1753 for Humphrey Lawrence, a local lawyer, who was four times Mayor of Launceston and political adviser to the Duke of Northumberland. Its last owner gave it to the National Trust in 1964. It now houses the Mayor's Parlour and the town's museum.

The collections include the celebrated Feudal Dues, which date from the 13th century and were last presented to Prince Charles, Duke of Cornwall, in 1973. Among the other exhibits are a collection of watercolours of local river bridges, a Victorian Polyphon and a 1743 town map on vellum.

Steam engines at the Long Shop Museum, Leiston.

Leiston

The Long Shop Museum

Main Street, Leiston, Suffolk IP16 4ES
        ☎ 0728 832189
Apr–Sept, daily 10–4.
🖾 A. J. Errington, Museum Manager
Ⓔ 🏛 ♿

The firm of Richard Garrett was established at Leiston in 1778. In the 19th century it made steam engines, threshing machines and agricultural implements. In the 1920s and 1930s it added tractors, machine-tools and a range of electrically powered vehicles to its products. In 1932 it was taken over by Beyer Peacock and during the Second World War it produced shells and naval guns. After further changes of ownership, it finally closed in 1980.

The Museum buildings are grouped around the Long Shop, built in 1853 for the flow-line production of portable steam engines. 100 ft long and one of the 19th century's most impressive industrial structures, it is now a listed building. It contains a range of Garrett products and exhibits illustrating the history of the firm.

Lincoln

National Cycle Museum

Brayford Wharf North, Lincoln LN1 1YW
        ☎ 0522 545091
Daily 10–5. Closed Dec 25 – Jan 1.
🖾 Mr K. Stanbridge
Ⓔ 🏛

The Museum illustrates the development of the cycle from its beginnings. The collections begin with the early-19th-century Hobby Horse and continue to the Ordinary, or Penny Farthing, the solid-tyred Safety, and the pneumatic-tyred Diamond and hoop frame models which appeared at the turn of the century.

The variations which were popular for a while include the Rotary Tricycle, the Dublin, the Otto, the Dursely Pedersen, the Chopper, the Moulton and many others. There are also collections of racing and touring cycles, fun bikes, cycles and tricycles used to carry goods and others designed specially for the disabled. Signs, lamps and other accessories are also included.

Liverpool

The Tate Gallery, Liverpool

Albert Dock, Liverpool L8 4BB   ☎ 051 709 3223
Tues–Sun & Bank Holidays, 11–7.
🖾 Emmanuel Onwuemene
Ⓕ 🏛 🖼 ♿ ☐ ☕

The Gallery is housed in part of the Albert Dock complex, the largest group of Grade I listed buildings in the United Kingdom, designed by Jesse Hartley and opened in 1846. The works to be seen represent the national collection of modern art in the North of England. The permanent collection is housed at the Tate Gallery in London from which the items on display here are drawn.

London

Bank of England Museum

Threadneedle Street, London EC2R 8AH
        ☎ 01 601 4387
Good Fri – Sept, Mon–Sat 10–6; Sun 2–6.
    Oct–Maundy Thurs, Mon–Fri 10–6.
⊖ Bank
🖾 Sandra Lea
Ⓕ 🏛 ♿

The Museum is situated within the Bank itself. It illustrates the history of the Bank from its foundation by Royal Charter in 1694 to its position today as Britain's central bank.

Visitors enter through the Bank Stock Office, which houses a display on the architectural history of the Bank's premises. Three rooms then deal with the Bank's early years and the chronological history of the Bank is completed in the Rotunda. The route then leads back to the Bank Stock Office through an exhibition called The Bank Today. The up-to-date equipment shown here includes interactive videos and an operational dealing desk.

Florence Nightingale Museum

2 Lambeth Palace Road, London SE1 7EW
        ☎ 01 620 0374
Tues–Sun 10–4
⊖ Waterloo
🖾 Kate Prinsley
Ⓔ 🏛 ♿

The Museum is in a new building on the site of St Thomas's Hospital, the home of Britain's first school of nursing. It contains important material relating to the career of Florence Nightingale and to the Nursing School at St

Thomas's. Included are Florence Nightingale's medicine chest, childhood books and items of her clothing. Period settings are used and there is a reconstruction of one of the wards at Scutari in the Crimea.

The Guards Museum

Wellington Barracks, Birdcage Walk, London SW1E 6HQ   ☎ *01 930 4466 extn 3271 Sat–Thurs 10–4. Closed Dec 25–26.*
⊖ *St James's Park*
Ⓧ *The Curator*
Ⓔ ♠

The exhibits are drawn from the five regiments of the Brigade of Guards – the Grenadier, Coldstream, Scots, Irish and Welsh – and tell their story over more than 300 years. With the help of weapons, uniforms, colours, trophies and personal possessions of the Guardsmen, many famous battles are commemorated. The Battle of Waterloo is specially featured, as is the campaign in the Crimea, when 13 Guardsmen were awarded the Victoria Cross.

Modern warfare is represented by campaigns of the Second World War and by the Scots Guards' battle at Tumbledown in the Falklands. The many skills of Guardsmen are illustrated by the exploits of the Guards Armoured Division, the founding of the SAS and the Guards Independent Parachute Company.

Hackney Museum

Central Hall, Mare Street, London E8 1HE
     ☎ *01 986 6914*
Tues–Fri 10–12.30, 1.30–5; Sat 1.30–5.
⊖ *Bethnal Green*
Ⓧ *Christine Johnstone, Curator*
Ⓕ ♠ &

The Central Hall was built in 1910 as a Methodist hall. The Museum is in the part formerly used by the Sunday School. The emphasis is on the social history of the many nationalities which make up the present population of Hackney and range from child care material from Hackney Hospital to a 12-ft high model of the goddess Sita, from the Hindu festival, Diwali. Most of the items in the collection have been contributed by Hackney people as gifts.

Museum of the Moving Image

South Bank, Waterloo, London SE1 8XT
     ☎ *01 928 3535*
Tues–Sat 10–8; Sun 10–6.
⊖ *Waterloo*
Ⓧ *Ms M. O'Brien*
Ⓔ ♠ ⬛ & ☐

The Museum illustrates the history of moving images from early Chinese shadow theatre to the latest film and television technology. There are 72 laser players for video, allowing images to be shown continuously throughout the exhibition areas. The collections range from early optical toys, such as the Zoetrope, to costumes from modern science fiction films. Among the exhibits are Charlie Chaplin's hat and cane,

Fred Astaire's tail coat, and the IBA collection of period television sets.

The Museum possesses the world's first four-screen unit. The screens for rear, flat, Perlux and 3-D projection are mounted on a travelling gantry, allowing the perfect projection of different film image ratios and light intensities. Many of the exhibits can be operated by visitors themselves, an activity which is encouraged by the Museum's eight actor-guides.

National Hearing Aid Museum

Royal Throat, Nose and Ear Hospital, Grays Inn Road, London WC1X 1DA ☎ *01 837 8855 Mon–Fri, by appt.*
⊖ *King's Cross*
Ⓧ *Miss Peggy Chalmers*
Ⓕ

Financed and administered by the British Society of Audiology, the Museum displays a collection of hearing aids and test equipment, some historic, some in use more recently. Among the items of special interest is the first cochlea implant device to be fitted in the United Kingdom.

The Operating Theatre Museum and Herb Garret

9A St Thomas' Street, Southwark, London SE1 Mon, Wed, Fri 12.30–4. Closed Public Holidays.
⊖ *London Bridge*
Ⓧ *Michael Tambini* ☎ *01 407 7600 extn 2739*
Ⓔ ♠

In 1821 St Thomas's moved its operating theatre for women patients to the attic of what used to be the Parish Church of St Thomas and is now the Chapter House of Southwark Cathedral. In 1862 the theatre ceased to be used and was sealed off. Discovered by chance after the Second World War and since fully restored with the addition of contemporary equipment and instruments, it now gives a good impression of conditions during the first half of the 19th century, when many patients understandably preferred death to surgery.

Ragged School Museum

46–48 Copperfield Road, Bow, London E3 4RR
     ☎ *01 232 2941*
Daily 10–5
⊖ *Mile End*
Ⓧ *The Curator*
Ⓕ ♠ ⬛

In 1877 Dr Barnardo rented three warehouses on the Regent's Canal and installed his Ragged School in them. For more than thirty years it provided free schooling and hot breakfasts and dinners for the children of some of the poorest families in the East End. These are now the only surviving buildings associated with Dr Barnardo in the area where he started his work for destitute children. They have been bought by the Ragged School Museum Trust to house a museum which tells the story of the area and its people and illustrates the contribution of Dr Barnardo and others working for young people in London.

Saatchi Collection

98A Boundary Road, London NW8 0RH
   ☎ 01 624 8299
Fri, Sat 12–6. Check times in advance.
⊖ Swiss Cottage/St Johns Wood
Ⓚ Janice Blackburn
Ⓕ

The Museum contains the collection of
contemporary art formed by Doris and Charles
Saatchi. This was started in 1970 with works of
Minimal Art. This remains the core of the
collection, which concentrates on a relatively
small number of artists, whose work is shown on
a rotating basis in a renovated and converted
paint warehouse.

The Salvation Army International Heritage Centre

117–121 Judd Street, King's Cross, London
   WC1H 9NN   ☎ 01 387 1656 extn 256
Mon–Fri 9.30–3.30, Sat 9.30–12.30.
⊖ King's Cross
Ⓚ Major J. Fairbank, Director
Ⓕ ♦ ⬛

The Salvation Army, originally known as the
Christian Mission, was founded by William
Booth in the East End of London in 1865.
It acquired its present name in 1878 and since
then it has become established in 89 countries.
The Heritage Centre contains a permanent
exhibition telling the story of the origins and
development of the Army worldwide.

Theatre Museum

Russell Street, London WC2E 7PA
   ☎ 01 836 7891
Tues–Sun 11–7.
⊖ Covent Garden
Ⓚ Mike Power, General Manager
Ⓔ ♦ ⬛ ♿ ☐

The Theatre Museum, in the former Flower
Market at Covent Garden, is a branch of the
Victoria and Albert Museum. It illustrates major
developments, events and personalities in all
the performing arts. The story is told with the
help of stage models, costumes, pottery, prints,
drawings, puppets, props and memorabilia.
There are also galleries for temporary
exhibitions, named in honour of Sir John
Gielgud and Sir Henry Irving. Paintings are
displayed in the Lower Foyer.
   Among the Museum's particular treasures are
the Spirit of Gaiety, a gilded angel rescued from
the top of the Gaiety Theatre; the elephant-
decorated boxes from the Palace Theatre,
Glasgow; and the Duke of York's Theatre box
office, from which entrance tickets to the
Museum are sold.

Wandsworth Museum

Disraeli Road, Putney, London SW15 2DR
   ☎ 01 871 7074
Mon–Wed, Fri, Sat 1–5. Closed Bank Holidays.
⊖ East Putney
Ⓚ The Curator
Ⓕ ♦

The Museum presents the history of everyday
life in the area that now forms the London
Borough of Wandsworth. It is housed in Putney
Library, an attractive stone and red brick
building, constructed in 1899. By means of old
maps, paintings and photographs, visitors are
shown the local landscape as it once was, with
the homes of rich and poor, and the farms,
factories, windmills and watermills, streets and
quiet countryside of what is now an almost
completely urbanised area. A portrait gallery of
local worthies helps to add a more personal
aspect to the changes which have taken place
and to life in the past.

Malton

Eden Camp

Old Malton, Malton, North Yorkshire
   YO17 0SD   ☎ 0653 697777
Feb 14 – Dec 23, daily 10–5.
Ⓔ ♦ ⬛ ♿ ⚲

Between 1939 and 1948 Eden Camp accommodated Italian and German prisoners of war.
Bought for conversion into a food factory, it has
now been transformed by the same owner into a
museum and theme park illustrating the history
of the Second World War. The displays and
tableaux use a wide range of original objects,
from ration coupons to airmen's escape-route
maps, to recall civilian and military life during
the war years. The original huts, built by Italian
prisoners in 1942, serve as the museum
buildings, and the barbed wire and guard towers
help to recreate the wartime atmosphere.

Manchester

The Pankhurst Centre

60–62 Nelson Street, Chorlton-on-Medlock,
   Manchester M13 9NQ   ☎ 061 273 5673
Mon–Fri 10–3, Sat 2–5 by telephone appt.
Ⓚ Rachelle Warburton
Ⓕ ♦ ⬛ ♿

62 Nelson Street was the home of Emmeline
Pankhurst. On 10th October 1903, the
Women's Social and Political Union was
founded here and the house can therefore claim
to be the birthplace of the suffragette
movement. No. 60 and No. 62 Nelson Street
have been restored by the Pankhurst Trust and
now house exhibitions related to the history of
British women's struggle to win the vote.
The Pankhurst Parlour reconstructs part of the
home of Mrs Pankhurst and her daughters.

Margate

Margate Old Town Hall Local History Museum

Market Place, Margate, Kent   ☎ 0483 225511
May–Sept, Tues–Sat 10–1, 2–4.
Ⓚ Mr C. Wilson, Thanet District Council,
   Margate CT9 1XZ
Ⓔ ♦ ♿

In its time, the Town Hall has served as Margate's police station and court house, as well as being the municipal centre. The Court Room and police station are now museum exhibits in their own right. The main theme of the museum is the history of Margate in the 18th and 19th centuries, although other areas of Thanet are covered. The displays show how what was originally a small fishing village developed into a famous seaside resort.

Melrose

Melrose Motor Museum

Annay Road, Melrose, Roxburghshire TD6 9LW
☎ *08968 22624*
Mid-May – mid-Oct, daily 10.30–5.30.
🕴 *Mr Dale* ☎ *0835 22356*
£ ● ➤

This important collection of veteran and vintage cars, motorcycles and cycles covers the period from 1914 to 1960. Most of them were seen in large numbers on the road during the 1920s and 1930s. All are in running condition and are taken out on the road from time to time. There are also large collections of road signs, posters, petrol cans, tools and motoring accessories.

Mickley

Cherryburn

Mickley, Stocksfield, Northumberland NE43 7DB
☎ *0661 843276*
Tues–Sun 10–5.
🕴 *Keith Benbow, Warden*
£ ● ➤ ♿ ➤

The engraver and naturalist, Thomas Bewick, was born in the cottage at Cherryburn, overlooking the Tyne valley, in 1753. He was

The Bewick Museum at Cherryburn Cottage, Mickley.

apprenticed to an engraver in Newcastle and later set up his own business in this city. The larger house at Cherryburn was built by the family of Bewick's brother, William. The whole complex now forms the Bewick Museum, with an exhibition of his work and a printing house where demonstrations are given to show how books were printed in Bewick's time, using his wood engravings. The farmyard is stocked with animals and poultry representative of the breeds which were here during Thomas Bewick's childhood.

Minster

Agricultural and Rural Life Museum

Minster Abbey, Minster, Ramsgate, Kent
☎ *0843 823271*
Easter – 2nd week Oct, Mon–Sat 10–4.
🕴 *Phil Sackett* ☎ *0843 225511*
£ ● ➤

The Museum is within the grounds of Minster Abbey, which was founded in AD 670. The exhibits include farm equipment and material relating to rural crafts. There are also herb and marsh gardens and a bird conservation and breeding scheme operates on the site, the birds then being released into the wild.

Monaghan

The Heritage Centre at St Louis Convent

St Louis Convent, Monaghan, Co. Monaghan, Ireland   ☎ *04/ 83529/81411*
Mon, Tues, Thurs, Fri 10–12, 2–5, Sat, Sun 2–5.
🕴 *Sister M. de Lourdes, Curator*
£ ♿

The St Louis Institute was founded in 1842 by Father Louis Bautain at Juilly, in France. Soon afterwards, the first St Louis Sisters began their teaching work and a group of them arrived at Monaghan in 1859, where they were able to buy the Old Brewery as their headquarters, much of the money being contributed by Charles Bianconi, proprietor of Bianconi's Travelling Cars, the first public transport system in Ireland. The original buildings were subsequently considerably extended.
The Heritage Centre tells the story of the Institute and pays particular attention to the work at Monaghan and elsewhere in Ireland.

Morpeth

Morpeth Chantry Bagpipe Museum

Bridge Street, Morpeth, Northumberland, NE61 1PJ   ☎ *0670 519466*
Jan–Feb, Mon–Sat 10–4. Mar–Dec, Mon–Sat 9.30–5.30. Open Bank Holidays.
🕴 *Anne Moore, Curator*
£ ● ♿

The Chantry was built in the 13th century to serve both as a religious building and a Grammar

School. It was later used as a mineral water factory and a ladies' lavatory. In 1965 Morpeth Antiquarian Society began using part as a museum and subsequently the ground floor was occupied by the Northumbrian Craft Centre and the local Tourist Information Office, while the Bagpipe Museum was installed upstairs.

The collection includes Northumbrian small-pipes, Scottish bagpipes, Border half-long bagpipes, Irish Union pipes and many types of foreign bagpipe, as well as replica models of historical instruments.

Newent

The Shambles

20 Church Street, Newent, Gloucestershire
*   GL18 1PP*   ☎ *0531 822144*
Tues–Sun, 10–6 or dusk if earlier.
🕅 *Mrs H. Chapman*
£ 🛈 🖼 ♿

Until 1864 the buildings now occupied by the Museum were used as private dwellings. They then became successively a coach-yard, a slaughterhouse and butcher's shop and the premises of a cycle and motor agent. In 1988 they were opened as a museum of Victorian life, to house a large collection of furniture and other objects, displayed in room and shop settings. There are also a dairy and a stockman's room, with a variety of medicines and equipment for treating animals.

Owermoigne

Mill House Working Cider Museum

Owermoigne, Dorchester, Dorset, DT2 8HZ
*   ☎ 0305 85220*
Daily 9–1, 2–5. Closed Dec 25–28.
🕅 *D. J. Whatmoor*
F 🛈 🐾

In the Museum, the making of traditional farmhouse cider is shown alongside examples of the wood screw presses of the 18th century and the iron presses and mills made after the Industrial Revolution. This equipment can be seen in use from mid-October to December. At other times of the year, a video presentation shows the processes.

Pembroke

Castle Hill Museum: The Museum of the Home

7 Westgate Hill, Pembroke, Dyfed SA71 4LB
*   ☎ 0646 681200*
Easter–Oct, Sun–Wed, Fri 10.30–5.30.
🕅 *Judy Stimson*
£ 🛈

The exhibits illustrate the equipment used for a wide range of domestic activities over a period of 350 years. More than 2,000 items are on display, covering Cooking and the Hearth; Laundry and Ironing; Cleaning; Lighting;

Eating and Drinking; Nursery and Sickroom; Sewing and Home Crafts; Smoking and Snuff Taking; Reading and Writing; Fashion Accessories; Games and Toys; Dairy Equipment: Garden and Country Life; Love Tokens and Souvenirs.

There are many oddities on display, and in designing the Museum, the owners have attempted a return to the richness and excitement of the old Cabinet of Curiosities, which formed the basis of so many museums in the past.

Portsmouth

HMS Warrior 1860

Victory Gate, HM Naval Base, Portsmouth,
*   Hampshire PO1 3QX*   ☎ *0705 291379*
Mar–Oct, daily 10.30–5.30. Nov–Feb, 10.30–5.
🕅 *Miss Jane Skinner, Visitor Services Manager*
£ 🛈 🖼

HMS 'Warrior' was Britain's first iron-hulled warship. Launched in 1860, she was at that time the fastest, strongest and best-armed battleship in the world. After ten years she was outdated, without ever having taken part in any action, and spent the next hundred years as a depot ship, storage hulk and floating workshop for the RN Torpedo School and finally as an oil fuel hulk. In 1979 she was rescued from being broken up for scrap and towed to Hartlepool to be restored to her former glory. Attention to detail extends to the reconstruction of her formidable fire-power, with 110-pounder Armstrong guns, the furnishings of the captain's and officers' cabins, the furnaces, which needed 66 men to stoke them, and the Penn twin-cylinder steam engine.

HMS Warrior, Portsmouth.

Port Talbot

Margam Country Park

*Margam, Port Talbot, West Glamorgan
SA13 2TJ*   ☎ 0639 881635
*Easter–Sept, daily 10–7 (last admission 4). Oct–
Mar, Wed–Sun 10–5 (last admission 3).*
🖾 *Park Director*
Ⓔ 🛈 💷 ♿ ☎

The Park has been established in the grounds of
Margam Castle, a 19th-century mansion in the
Gothic style. Nearby is an 18th-century
orangery and the ruins of a 12th-century
Cistercian abbey. There is a collection of 30
contemporary sculptures, placed at different
points in the Park, and an exhibition illustrating
the history of Margam.

Ramsgate

Maritime Museum Complex

*Clock House, Pier Yard, Royal Harbour,
Ramsgate, Kent CT11 8LS* ☎ 0843 587765
*Apr–Sept, Mon–Fri 11–4; Sat, Sun 2–5. Oct–
Mar, Mon–Fri 11–3.30.*
🖾 *Mrs D. M Chamberlain*
Ⓔ 🛈

The Museum is housed in an early-19th-century
Clock House, in front of which is Smeaton's Dry
Dock, which was opened in 1791 and used for
80 years, before falling into disrepair. It was
converted into an ice-house in 1893 and
restored to its former appearance in the early
1980s. The dock now contains a 1946 steam-tug
which spent most of its working life moving
liners; a 1912 motor yacht, 'Sundowner', which
took part in the Dunkirk evacuation in 1940;
and an 1899 fishing smack, 'Vanessa'.

RAF Manston Spitfire and Hurricane
Memorial Building

RAF Manston, Ramsgate, Kent CT12 5BS
☎ 0843 823351
Apr–Sept, daily 10–5. Oct–Mar, daily 10.30–4.
🖾 *Public Relations Officer*
Ⓕ 🛈 ☎

Manston was one of the most important Second
World War forward fighter stations. The
museum contains wall displays and a large
collection of objects relating to RAF Manston
and the 1939–45 War. There are also a Spitfire
and a Hurricane of the same vintage, both
restored to their original condition.

Ribchester

Ribchester Museum of Childhood

Church Street, Ribchester, Lancashire PR3 3YE
☎ 025484 520
Tues–Sun & Bank Holiday Mon 11–5
🖾 *David Wild*
Ⓔ 🛈 💷 ☎

The displays of toys and dolls in the Museum

cover tinplate toys, soft toys, farm animals,
model trains, national costume dolls, games and
walking dolls. The collection also incudes 54
Victorian and Edwardian dolls' houses, a
working model replica of an Edwardian
fairground, a flea circus, two model circus rings,
and a collection of General Tom Thumb
memorabilia.

Rugby

HM Prison Service Museum

*Newbold Revel, Rugby, Warwickshire CV23 0TH
By written appt.*
🖾 *The Curator*
Ⓕ ☎

The exhibits in the Museum illustrate the
changes which have taken place over the last
two centuries in the penal system and in social
attitudes to crime and punishment. Among the
items on display are irons, fetters and gyves and
a door from cells visited by the Wesley brothers
at Oxford Prison. Visitors can see original tools
used for oakum picking and the Governor's
entry of Oscar Wilde's application to be excused
from such work at Reading.

The James Gilbert Rugby Football Museum

*5 St Matthews Street, Rugby, Warwickshire
CV21 3BY*   ☎ 0788 536500
Mon–Fri 10–5; Sat 10–1, 2–5.
🖾 *Mrs J. J. Chance Harris*
Ⓕ 🛈

The essential feature of Rugby football, catching
the ball and running with it, is believed to have
begun at Rugby School in 1823. The Museum
tells the story of the development of the game
from that time onwards. It has been established
in the shop in which several generations of the
Gilbert family made footballs and gained a high
reputation for their products.
   The business was started by William Gilbert
(1799–1877), a boot and shoe maker to Rugby
School. In 1851 he had two footballs on display
at the Great Exhibition. One of these is the
oldest exhibit in the Museum. James Gilbert
(1885–1969) was the last member of the family
to run the business.

Saffron Walden

The Fry Art Gallery

*Bridge End Gardens, Castle Street, Saffron
    Walden, Essex CB10 1BD*
Easter Sun – last Sun in Oct, Sat, Sun 2.45–5.30.
◪ *The Curator*
F ▲

The Gallery, opened in 1857, was originally
designed to house the collection of Francis
Gibson, a member of the local family which
founded Barclays Bank. The building passed by
descent to the Fry family, who have leased it to
the Fry Art Gallery Society, which was formed
in 1985. The Gallery also houses the L. G. Fry
Collection. Fry (1860–1933) was Gibson's
grandson and a landscape painter of repute.
Works by him are exhibited here. There are
others by Francis Gibson, Roger Fry and
Anthony Fry, together with a collection of
works brought together during the lifetime of
many of the artists, including Edward Bawden,
Michael Rothenstein and Eric Ravilious, who
flourished in and around Great Bardfield more
recently.

St Asaph

The National Portrait Gallery at Bodelwyddan
    Castle

Bodelwyddan Castle, nr St Asaph, Clwyd
    LL18 5YA   ☎ 0745 584060
Seasonal opening times: telephone for details.
◪ *Publicity Officer*
E ▲ ⬛ ♠

The Castle is a 19th-century remodelling of a
15th-century house, which has recently been
restored to its Victorian glory, part of it now
being used to display items from the National
Portrait Gallery's collection of Victorian
portraits.

The Ladies Drawing Room is hung with
portraits of notable Victorian women, such as

The Sculpture Gallery, Bodelwyddan Castle.

Florence Nightingale and Frances Trollope. The
Watts Hall of Fame is devoted to his series of
portraits of leading public figures, including
Lord Salisbury, Robert Browning, and Rossetti.
There are also important works by Holman
Hunt, Sir Thomas Lawrence, Landseer and
Sargent. One of the upstairs rooms contains
Victorian photographs and the Bedroom
displays engravings. The Billiard Room is hung
with portraits of sporting figures and cartoons
from *Vanity Fair*.

The exhibition in the Sculpture Gallery and
Drawing Room includes busts by the North
Wales sculptor, John Gibson.

St Davids

Lleithyr Farm Museum

Nr Whitesands Bay, St Davids, Dyfed
    SA62 6PR   ☎ 0437 720245
May–Oct, Tues-Sun 9.30–5.
◪ *Robert James*
E ▲ ⬛ ♠

The Museum, in the surroundings of a farm,
shows a collection of yesterday's farm and
domestic equipment. These include
implements, carts, dairy utensils, hand tools and
tractors. There are also displays of farm animals.
Historical and technical information is
presented in the Museum's video theatre.

St Helier

Elizabeth Castle

St Helier, Jersey, Channel Islands
        ☎ 0534 23971
Late Mar–Oct, daily 9.30–5.30.
◪ *Doug Ford* ☎ 0534 63333
E ▲ ⬛

This Elizabethan citadel, with its slightly later
(1608) Governor's House, an interesting
example of Jersey vernacular architecture,
contains displays illustrating the military history
of the Castle between 1550 and 1945, the story
of the Jersey militia, and the German
occupation during the Second World War.

Sandhurst

Nature in Art: The International Centre for
    Wildlife Art

Wallsworth Hall, Tewkesbury Road, Sandhurst,
        Gloucester GL2 9PA   ☎ 0452 731422
Tues–Sun & Bank Holidays 10–5.
◪ *Mr Simon H. Trapnell*
E ▲ ⬛ ♿ ☐ ♠

The collections are displayed in a Georgian
country mansion dating from the 1740s, which
has recently been extensively restored. They
form the first museum anywhere in the world
which brings together works of all periods and of
the highest international standard depicting
nature in any medium. They include sculptures,

Painting by J.C. Harrison, in the Nature in Art collection, Sandhurst.

shown both in the building and in the grounds, tapestries, ceramics, glass engravings, prints, Japanese *netsuke* and Chinese painted bottles. There are both changing displays of items from the permanent collection and also temporary exhibitions which complement or highlight particular aspects of the collections.

Sandy Bay

Country Life at Sandy Bay

Sandy Bay, Exmouth, Devon EX8 5BU
    ☎ 0395 274533
Good Fri – Oct 1, daily from 10 am.
◪ *Mr N. Vicary*
Ⓔ 🏛 💂 🍴 ⅏ ⚓

The Exhibition is in the Deer Park, with historic agricultural and domestic equipment ranging in date from 1750 to 1950, as well as vintage cars, fire and steam engines. There is also a furnished Victorian keeper's cottage and farmyard animals.

Shipley

The World and Sooty

Windhill Manor, Leeds Road, Shipley, West
    Yorkshire BD18 1BP   ☎ 0274 531122
Daily 10–5.30.
◪ *Nicola Rawson*
Ⓔ 🏛 💂 ⅏ ⚓

The Sooty children's television programme began in 1952 and has run ever since, first with Harry Corbett and then with his son, Matthew. Centred around a teddy bear with black ears, these shows depended a great deal on the model-maker, Bill Garrett, and on ingenious electrical and sound effects. 'The World and Sooty' illustrates the development of the programmes with original sets, photographs and film.

Stansted

Mountfitchet Castle and Norman Village

Mountfitchet Castle, Stansted, Essex
    CM24 8SP   ☎ 0279 813237
Mid–Mar – mid–Nov, daily 10–5.
◪ *A. Goldsmith*
Ⓔ 🏛 💂 ⚓

This is a reconstruction of a Norman wooden motte and bailey castle and a village associated with it, on their original site. The Duke of Boulogne, a cousin of William the Conqueror, built his castle here soon after the Norman Conquest in 1066. In 1215 it was attacked and razed to the ground as an act of revenge against Richard de Mountfitchet, one of the 25 barons responsible for forcing King John to sign the Magna Carta. The site of the Castle then lay forgotten and overgrown until its reconstruction today, enabling visitors to experience life as it was here in the 11th century.

Stratford-upon-Avon

The Teddy Bear Museum

19 Greenhill Street, Stratford-upon-Avon,
    Warwickshire CV37 0LF   ☎ 0789 293160
Daily 9.30–6. Closed Dec 25.
◪ *Mrs Sylvia Coote*
Ⓔ 🏛

This Elizabethan farmhouse now contains a major international collection of teddy bears. The first 'Teddy's bear', named after Teddy Roosevelt, the President of the United States, was made in 1902 and there are items almost as old as that in the Stratford collection.

The wide range of bears includes a number which formerly belonged to members of the British Royal Family and other celebrities. Special displays are devoted to Mary Tourtel's *Daily Express* strip, 'Rupert Bear', to Paddington bear, Sooty and other well-publicised bear notabilities. William Shakesbear was specially created for the Museum by the House of Nisbet. The Library has an extensive collection of printed material relating to teddy bears.

Sunderland

St Peter's Visitor Centre

St Peter's Vicarage, St Peter's Way, Sunderland,
    Tyne and Wear SR6 0DY   ☎ 091 567 3726
Easter–Oct, Mon–Sat 11–1, 2–5.
◪ *Martin Turner*
Ⓕ 🏛 💂 ⚓

St Peter's Church was built in 674 AD by the monk, St Benedict Biscop, as part of a monastery. The Venerable Bede began his life as a monk here. In 1083 the monastery became a Cell of Durham and it was finally suppressed by Henry VIII in 1545. The porch of the 674 AD church survives, but most of the rest of the building is more modern.

The exhibition in the Visitor Centre tells the story of the church and the monastery. It contains, among other items, a comprehensive collection of grave covers, dating from the 7th to the 19th centuries.

Swannington

Swannington Open-Air Museum

Swannington, Leicestershire   ☎ *0530 222330*
Accessible at any time
⊠ *Swannington Heritage Trust, 123 Main Street,*
*   Swannington, Leicester LE6 4QL*
F

Swannington is an old coalmining village and a
Trust has been established to acquire, preserve
and interpret the remains of the industry. The
sites include Swannington Windmill, an area
containing ancient bell pits, the 18th-century
Califat Mine, Coleorton horse-drawn tramway,
Calcutta Colliery, and Swannington rope-
hauled incline.

Teffont Magna

Wessex Shire Park

Teffont Magna, Salisbury, Wiltshire SP3 4QY
*   ☎ 0722 76393*
Apr–Sept, daily 10–7, Oct, Nov, Mar, daily 10–4.
⊠ *John Webb*
£ ⌂ ⬛ ☘ ☕

The Park area includes a prehistoric enclosure,
Wick Ball Camp. The Display hall contains
exhibits illustrating the development of farming
from Iron Age times onwards. Crops are grown
on a four-year rotation system, with working
horses used. Traditional breeds of farm animal
are also kept in the Park.

Thornbury

Thornbury and District Heritage Trust
Museum

4 Chapel Street, Thornbury, Avon
Wed, Fri 1–4; Sat 10–4. Closed Bank Holidays.
⊠ *Paul Wildgoose, 67 High Street, Thornbury*
*   BS12 2RW*   ☎ *0454 415438*
F

The Museum's collections cover the crafts and
trades of the district. There are exhibits relating
to Severn fishing, to the work of the blacksmith
and to farming, with a special emphasis on
cheese and buttermaking.

Thursford

The Thursford Collection

Thursford, Fakenham, Norfolk NR21 0AS
*   ☎ 037877 477*
Mar 24–27, daily 11–5. Mar 28–Apr 19, daily
*   2–5. Apr 30–May 1, daily 11–5. May 2–27,*
*   daily 2–5. May 28–Sept 3, daily 11–5. Sept*
*   4–Oct 1, daily 1–5. Oct 2–29, daily 2–5.*
⊠ *Geraldine Rye*
£ ⌂ ⬛ ⟐ ☕

The Collection illustrates the fair and circus
business. There are examples of steam-driven
road engines, and of the more specialised and

ornate type, known as showmen's engines,
which hauled fairground and circus equipment
from site to site and also drove generators
providing power and lighting. Another category
of exhibit consists of fairground organs, which
added atmosphere and excitement to the
travelling showman's business.

Tonbridge

Penshurst Place Toy Museum

Penshurst, Tonbridge, Kent TN11 8DG
*   ☎ 0892 870307*
Apr–Sept, Tues–Sun 1–5.
⊠ *The Administrator*
£ ⬛ ☕

The Museum is in the former carpenter's shop of
Penshurst Place, which has a celebrated hall
built in 1338, so providing an additional
attraction for visitors. The collection consists of
toys and dolls' houses, some of considerable
historical interest.

Totnes

The British Photographic Museum

Bowden House, Totnes, South Devon TQ9 7PW
*   ☎ 0803 863664*
Easter Sun–late Oct, Sun–Thurs 11–5.30.
⊠ *Christopher Petersen*
£ ⌂ ⬛ ⟐ ☕

The Museum specialises in still and moving-
picture photographic equipment of the period
1875 to 1960. There are many rare items,
especially British cameras which were produced
in only small numbers. There are reconstructions of a Victorian photographer's
studio and of an Edwardian darkroom.

Turton

Turton Tower Museum

Tower Drive, Chapeltown Road, Turton, Bolton,
*   BL7 0QG*   ☎ *0204 852203*
Mar, Apr, Oct, Sat–Wed 2–5. May–Sept,
*   Mon–Fri 10–12, 1–5; Sat, Sun 1–5. Nov,*
*   Feb, Sun 2–5. Closed Dec–Jan.*
⊠ *The Keeper*
£ ⌂ ⬛ ☕

The earliest part of Turton Tower dates from the
15th century. Its most famous owner,
Humphrey Chetham (1580–1653), was a
Manchester textile merchant and moneylender.
In 1835 the property was bought by James Kay, a
local cotton manufacturer. He enlarged the
house and restored it to his own taste. The last
owner presented it to Turton Urban District
Council and its drawing-room became the
Council Chamber. When the nearby Bradshaw
Hall was demolished in 1948, its owner gave
most of its furniture to the Tower. It is now
administered as a museum by Lancashire County
Council.

The principal collections are of Lancashire-made oak furniture, paintings, arms and armour, and of items relating to the history of the area.

Wakefield

Yorkshire Mining Museum

Caphouse Colliery, New Road, Overton,
Wakefield WF4 4RH   ☎ 0924 848806
Daily 10–5.
🗷 *Mr W. Ferris*
E 🕮 🛄 🕭 🕭

Caphouse Colliery produced coal from 1790 until 1985. Its wooden headstock, the last to survive in Yorkshire, and its stone engine house both date from 1876. The original twin-cylinder steam winding engine has survived and the main shaft, sunk in 1795, may be the oldest usable shaft in Europe. The other buildings show the pit's gradual modernisation, and nearby are bell-pits illustrating the earliest days of coal extraction. A horse-gin shows how coal and men were brought up and down the shaft before the arrival of steam-engines.

There is a tour of the underground workings, with exhibits showing technical developments during the life of the colliery. The museum also has a reference library and a photographic collection relating to Yorkshire coalmining.

Walsall

Walsall Leather Centre Museum

56–57 Wisemore, Walsall WS2 8EQ
    ☎ 0922 721153
Apr–Oct, Tues–Sat 10–5; Sun 12–5. Nov–Mar,
Tues–Sat 10–4; Sun 12–4.
🗷 *S. Randle*
F 🕮 🛄 🕭 🕭

Since the mid 19th century, Walsall has been important for its production of saddlery and leather goods. The Leather Centre was opened in 1988 in a Victorian leather factory to show the skills on which traditional English leatherwork has depended, with regular demonstrations (in workshops restored to their appearance c. 1920) of the manufacture of saddles, bridles, handbags and other leather goods. A section deals with the local tanning and currying industries. The historical displays present a range of leather products, both from Britain and from other countries.

Welwyn

Welwyn Roman Baths

By-Pass, Welwyn, Hertfordshire.
Correspondence to Mill Green Museum & Mill,
Hatfield AL9 5PD   ☎ 07072 71362
Sun & Bank Holidays 2–5 or dusk if earlier.
July–Aug, also Sat 2–5.
🗷 *Jane Bircher*
E 🕮 🕭

The Baths, originally attached to living accommodation, date from the 3rd century AD. They lay on the route of the A1(M) motorway and were saved by being protected by a steel vault, the new road passing directly over them. Visitors can see the layout of the baths and furnace room, together with the remains of the hypocaust heating system. Also on show are related archaeological finds from the Welwyn area and an explanatory exhibition on Roman baths and the history of the site.

Wellingborough

Irchester Narrow Gauge Railway Museum

Irchester Country Park, Wellingborough,
Northamptonshire
Correspondence to: 5 Merchant Lane, Cranfield,
Bedfordshire, MK43 0DA   ☎ 0234 750469
Sun 11–dusk. Apr–Oct, demonstrations on 1st Sun
in month. Groups by appt. at other times.
🗷 *Mr R. Kingston, Secretary*
F 🕮 🛄 🕭

The Museum is located within Irchester Country Park, which is centred around a former ironstone quarry, with a spectacular quarry face over 100 ft high. The collection consists of narrow-gauge locomotives and rolling stock, with interpretive displays relating to the industrial use of narrow-gauge railways in Northamptonshire and neighbouring counties. Among the exhibits is a metre-gauge steam locomotive, once used in an ironstone quarry.

Wellingborough Heritage Centre

Croyland Hall, Wellingborough,
   Northamptonshire   ☎ 0933 76838
Mon–Sat 10.30–4.30
F 🏠 🚊

Croyland Hall was originally a building
associated with the Abbey of Crowland (sic) in
the Fens. The Museum, financed and
administered by Wellingborough Civic Society,
contains displays illustrating the social and
industrial history of the area.

Westbury

The Woodland Heritage Museum

The Woodland Park, Brokerswood, nr Westbury,
   Wiltshire BA13 4EH   ☎ 0373 823880
Apr–Oct, Mon–Fri 9–4; Sat 2–6; Sun 10–6.
   Nov–Mar, Mon–Fri 9–4; Sun 2–4.30.
🗷 *Mrs H. Sonnet*
£ 🏠 🚊 🚗

The Park, in which the Museum is situated,
contains 80 acres of broad leaf woodland which
is still operated commercially. The Museum
functions as an interpretation centre, where
visitors are encouraged to learn about the aims
and methods of woodland conservation. The
displays include a wildlife diorama, a bird wall
and exhibits on forestry, natural history and
conservation.

Weston-super-Mare

The International Helicopter Museum

The Airport, Locking Moor Road, Weston-super-
   Mare, Avon BS22 8PP   ☎ 0934 635227
Mar–Nov, daily 10–6.
🗷 *Elfan ap Rees* ☎ 0934 822524
£ 🏠 🚊 ♿ 🚗

This is the only museum in Britain entirely
devoted to helicopters. The collection is
exhibited both indoors and outdoors, in an
airfield environment. Supporting displays
explain the uses and functioning of helicopters.
There is a number of rare items, among them a
Bristol Belvedere, Cierva C–30A, Fairey
Rotodyne, Saro Skeeter and Westland
Widgeon.

Willenhall

The Lock Museum

55 New Road, Willenhall, West Midlands
   WV13 2DA   ☎ 0902 634542
Mon–Sat 10–5. Closed Dec 24–Jan 2.
🗷 *J. Whistance*
£ 🏠 🚗

The Museum building once belonged to a
Willenhall locksmith, who had his workshop at
the rear of the house. Visitors to the Museum
can see how a locksmith and his family lived at
the turn of the century and watch padlocks
being made in the traditional way, with belt-
driven machines. There are displays of locks and
keys made in Willenhall and drapery items from
the small shop run by the last locksmith's two
sisters in a small downstairs room.

Winchester

Winchester Cathedral Triforium Gallery

Cathedral Office, 5 The Close, Winchester,
   Hampshire SO23 9LS   ☎ 0962 53137
Times vary: check locally
🗷 *John Hardacre*
£ 🏠

The Gallery in the South Triforium of
Winchester Cathedral displays artistic and
archaeological material from the Cathedral.
The medieval stone sculpture dates from the
12th to the 16th centuries. There is also
polychrome wooden sculpture, together with
archaeological and other finds. Among the
outstanding items is the figure sculpture
(1480–90) from the Great Screen, which has
been described as 'without parallel in Europe',
and the marriage chair (1554) of Mary Tudor.

Wollaston

Wollaston Museum

High Street, Wollaston, Wellingborough,
   Northamptonshire
Correspondence to: The Wollaston
   Society, 19 Hookhams Path, Wollaston,
   Wellingborough, Northamptonshire
Apr–Sept, Sun 2–4
🗷 *Miss I. Walker, Secretary*
£

The exhibits in the Museum illustrate the social
and industrial history of the village. Among the
items on display is the only surviving example of
a Northamptonshire hand-worked wool-
weaving loom, dating from c.1820. It is a relic
of what was the county's principal industry
before the arrival of boot and shoe
manufacturing.

Index of museum names

Index of subjects

Index of Museums associated with individuals